Criminal and Civil Investigation Handbook

Joseph J. Grau, Ph.D. Editor in Chief

Department of Criminal Justice
and Security Administration
College of Management, Long Island University
C. W. Post Campus, Brookville, N.Y.

with assistance from

Ben Jacobson
Investigative Consultant
Peregrine International

Second Edition

McGraw-Hill, Inc.

New York San Francisco Washington, D.C. Auckland Bogotá
Caracas Lisbon London Madrid Mexico City Milan
Montreal New Delhi San Juan Singapore
Sydney Tokyo Toronto

To
Johanna M. Grau
—a friend, an inspiration, and my wife,
who, through generous contribution of her
special talents and time, significantly
assisted in production of this
second edition.

Library of Congress Cataloging-in-Publication Data

Criminal and civil investigation handbook / Joseph J. Grau with
   assistance from Ben Jacobson : Forewords by James A. O'Connor and
   Albert R. Roberts.—2nd ed.
      p.   cm.
   Includes bibliographical references and index.
   ISBN 0-07-024156-2
   1. Criminal investigation—Addresses, essays, lectures   I. Grau,
Joseph J.   II. Jacobson, Ben.
HV8073.C694   1993
363.2´5—dc20   92-37289
                                                         CIP

ISBN   0-07-024156-2

1 2 3 4 5 6 7 8 9 0   DOC/DOC   9 9 8 7 6 5 4 3

The sponsoring editor for this book was Karen Hansen, the editing supervisor
was Fred Dahl, and the production supervisor was Suzanne W. Babeuf. It was
set in Palatino by McGraw-Hill's Professional Book Group composition unit.

Printed and bound by R. R. Donnelley & Sons Company.

Contents

Part 1. Introduction to Investigation

Part 2. Legal Considerations

Part 3. Public Police at the Crime Scene

Part 6. Business-Oriented Crimes

Part 7. Insurance Investigations and Loss Prevention

Subject Index and Case Citation Index follow Chapter 63

Contributors

American Insurance Association   Property Claims Service, New York

Lisa Arning, B.A., M.B.A.   President, Corporate Loss Control, New York

Lou E. Ballard, B.A.   Director of Freshman English, Southeastern Louisiana University, Louisiana

Charles J. Bock, Jr.   Vice President, Fraud Prevention and Investigation Department, Chemical Bank Corporation, New York

Edward P. Bracken, L.L.B.   Chief, Education and Training, Suffolk County District Attorney's Office, New York

Hon. Lawrence J. Bracken, B.A., L.L.B.   Associate Justice, Appellate Division, State of New York

Thomas T. Cacavas, B.A., M.A.   Adjunct Professor, C. W. Post Campus, Long Island University; Special Agent (ret.), Federal Bureau of Investigation

Robert Charland, B.A., M.A.   Manager of Security (on leave), Rochester Gas and Electric Corporation; former Major, New York State Police

Neil B. Checkman, B.A., J.D.   Member of the Bar, State of New York, Law Firm of Neil B. Checkman; former Special Assistant Attorney General, Office of the Special Prosecutor for Medicaid Fraud Control, New York State

Joseph P. Cicale, B.A., M.A., C.P.C.U.   Formerly Branch Manager, Northbrook Property and Casualty Insurance Company; Assistant Professor, College of Insurance, Property and Liability Division; past President, Casualty Claims Managers Council, New York

Richard J. Condon, B.A., M.A.   Former Director of Investigations, Office of Special Prosecutor, New York State

Kimberly A. Cordray Assistant Corporate Director of Investigations, Coordinator of Undercover Investigations, Abraham & Straus Department Stores, New York

L. H. Coven, B.A., M.A. President, Bradley Intelligence Group, New York

Gerard J. Cushing, B.A. Genealogist and probate researcher, President, Gerard Cushing, Inc., Kissimee, Florida; member of Westchester County (N.Y.) Genealogical Society, New York, Genealogical and Biological Society, Society of Genealogists, London

Harold S. Daynard, B.A., L.L.B. President, Daynard and Van Thumen Co., Inc., General Adjusters, New York; former President, New York Association of Independent Insurance Adjusters; former President, New York Property Insurance Claims Association

Donald P. Delaney, B.A., M.A. Senior Investigator, New York State Police, Troop L, Major Case Squad Supervisor, Lecturer at the Federal Law Enforcement Training Center, Glynco, Ga.

Fortunato J. De Luca, B.A., M.P.A. Detective Sergeant, Supervisor, Bronx Sex Crimes Squad, New York City Police Department

Dominick Di Maio, B.S., M.D., F.C.A.P. Former Chief Medical Examiner, City of New York; Consultant to the Office of Chief Medical Examiner, City of New York

Timothy Dowd, B.A., M.A. Detective Sergeant, formerly assigned Intelligence Supervisor, Office of Chief of Organized Crime Control, New York City Police Department

Joel K. Dranove, Esq., J.D. Law Offices of Joel K. Dranove, New York City; former Water Pollution Chemist, New York State Department of Health; admitted to practice before the U.S. Court of Appeals for Federal Circuit and Second Circuit; registered patent attorney

Robin Stone Einbinder, Esq., A.B., J.D. Associate, Jones, Hirsch, Connors & Bull, Esq., New York City, specializing in insurance defense and environmental coverage litigation; instructor, Hofstra University Law School; former prosecuting attorney in New York State Education Department, Office of Professional Discipline, Staff Attorney, U.S. Office of the Special Counsel

Michael S. Emanuelo, B.S. Lecturer, Organized Crime; Detective (ret.), New York City Police Department, Manhattan District Attorney's Office

Andre Evans, B.A., J.D. Attorney, Law Firm of Evans, Williams & Levinson; former Commonwealth's Attorney, Virginia Beach, Va.; President, Virginia Association of Commonwealth Attorneys; Chairman, Virginia Commonwealth's Attorneys Services and Training Council; Attorney, U.S. Army, Judge Advocate General's Corps

Federal Bureau of Investigation Terrorist Research and Analytical Center, Counterterrorism Section, Criminal Investigative Division, Washington, D.C.

Edward J. Flanagan, M.B.A., M.P.A. Executive, Prudential-Bache Securities; former Detective-Instructor, New York City Police Academy

James J. Fyfe, Ph.D. Professor, Temple University, Department of Criminal Justice; Consultant, Police Foundation; former Director, Executive Development Program, New York City Police Department

Vernon J. Geberth, B.B.A., M.P.S.   Graduate, Federal Bureau of Investigation, National Academy; Series Editor, Practical Aspects of Criminal and Forensic Investigations, Elsevier Publishers, New York; lecturer, consultant; Lt. Commander (ret.), New York City Police Department

Joseph J. Grau, Ph.D.   Professor, Director of Security Administration Program, Department of Criminal Justice and Security Administration, College of Management. C. W. Post Campus, Long Island University, New York

Sean A. Grennan, Ph.D.   Associate Professor, Department of Criminal Justice and Security Administration, College of Management, C. W. Post Campus, Long Island University, New York

Lewis A. Halpern, B.A., J.D.   Executive Assistant District Attorney, Special Inspector at the Narcotics Court, New York County, N.Y.

James A. Haran, Ph.D., C.S.W.   Assistant Professor, Department of Criminal Justice and Security Administration, C. W. Post Campus, Long Island University; former Chief, U.S. Probation Officers, U.S. District Court, Brooklyn, N.Y.

John F. Haskins   Lieutenant, Intelligence Officer, Bureau of Environmental Conservation Investigations, Division of Law Enforcement Intelligence Officers, New York State Department of Environmental Conservation

Lawrence M. Haut, B.A., M.P.S.   Former Supervisor, Special Agent, U.S. Department of Labor, Office of the Inspector General, Chicago

Tula Hawkins-Lacy, M.S.W.   Deputy Director, Satterwhite Academy of Child Welfare Training (including Child Protective Services), Human Resources Administration, Child Welfare Administration, City of New York

James J. Horan, B.A., M.S., M.P.A.   Forensic Science Faculty, John Jay College of Criminal Justice, New York; Captain (ret.), Commanding Officer, Crime Laboratory, New York City Police Department

Henry Ilian, D.S.W.   Director of Research and Evaluation, Satterwhite Academy for Child Welfare Training, New York City

Ben Jacobson, B.S., M.P.S.   President, Peregrine International, Inc., Detective (ret.), New York City Police Department; Intelligence Investigative Coordinator, Organized Crime Control Bureau; former Investigator (Special Assignment), U.S. Justice Department, Drug Enforcement Administration; former Investigator, Detective Division, Manhattan Hotel/Burglary Unit, New York City Police Department

Jeffrey H. Kay, B.A., J.D.   Deputy Chief, Organized Crime Division, U.S. Department of Justice, Southern District of Florida; former Assistant U.S. Attorney, Southern District of Florida

John G. Kennedy, B.A., M.P.S., J.D.   Lieutenant, Nassau County Police Department, Legal Bureau-Forfeiture Section, New York

Moorhead Kennedy, Esq., Ph.D., J.D.   President, Moorhead Kennedy Associates, Inc., Executive Director, Moorhead Kennedy Institute of the American Forum for Global Education; former hostage in Iran (1979–1981); former U.S. Foreign Service Officer (Medal of Valor)

Claude E. King, B.A., M.P.S.   Special Agent, Federal Bureau of Investigation, Pilot and Aviation Coordinator, Newark, N.J.

Frank E. Klecak, B.A., M.P.S. Chief of Detectives (ret.), Nassau County (New York) Police Department; Adjunct Professor, Nassau Community College

Martin L. Landa, B.A., M.P.S., J.D. Attorney, Law Firm of Tarangelo & Totura; Sergeant (ret.), New York City Police Department, Police Academy, Law Department Chairman

Gerard La Salle, B.A., M.P.S. Special Agent, U.S. Department of Justice, Office of Inspector General (New York); former Criminal Investigator, U.S. Immigration and Naturalization Service, Washington, D.C.

Robert C. Levie, B.A., M.A. Professor, Southeastern Louisiana State University; former member New Orleans Police Force

Linda Little, B.S. Inspector, Office of U.S. Inspector General, U.S. Department of Health and Human Services

George F. Maher, B.A., M.P.S. Chief of Operations, Nassau County (New York) Police Department; former Chief of Detectives and Chief of Headquarters

Joseph F. Maher, B.A., L.L.D. Office of the Inspector General, U.S. Department of Health and Human Services, Washington, D.C.

John F. Markey, B.A., M.P.S., Ph.D. Supervisory Special Agent, U.S. Customs Service; former Special Agent, Financial Investigations Division, U.S. Customs, Miami, Florida; Adjunct Professor, Mercy College, New York

Donald L. Mason, B.A., M.A. Fine Arts and Industrial Security Consultant; Senior Art Crimes Investigator (ret.), Federal Bureau of Investigation, New Jersey

Leonard Miller, B.A., M.P.S. Detective (ret.), Nassau County (New York) Police Department, Vice Squad; Nassau County District Attorney's Office

Bob O'Brien, B.A. Reporter, WNEW-TV News, New York

Lester L. Patt, B.A., M.P.S. Lieutenant (ret.), Commanding Officer, Fifth Narcotics District, New York City Police Department

Raymond M. Pierce, B.A., M.A. Detective New York City Police Department, Detective Bureau, Criminal Assessment and Profiling Unit; former Investigator of Homicide and Major Cases; Graduate of Federal Bureau of Investigation National Academy, Police Fellowship in Criminal Personality Profiling, National Center for Analysis of Violent Crime (1985)

Stanley Pinsley Investigator, WNEW-TV News, New York reporter, *Village Voice*

Frank S. Polestino, J.D. Professor, School of Law, St. John's University, New York

Rochester Police Department Rochester, N.Y.

Albert R. Roberts, D.S.W. Professor and Director, Administration of Justice, Rutgers, the State University of New Jersey, New Brunswick, N.J.

Robert S. Rubine, Esq., B.A., J.D. Law Office of Stein, Rubine & Stein; former Senior Trial Attorney, Legal Aid Society, New York

Wayne, Saey, B.A., M.P.S. Chief of Detectives, Nassau County Police Department; former Inspector, Commanding Officer, Third Precinct, Hostage Negotiating Team Leader, New York City Police Department

Michael P. Seniuk, M.A., L.L.B., M.S.W., J.D. Chairman, Nassau County Conditional Release Commission, New York; Criminal Justice Consultant to the Nassau County Executive; former County Sheriff; former Associate Counsel, New York State Liquor Authority

Anne R. Sowinski, B.A., M.P.S. Graduate of Federal Bureau of Investigation National Academy (161st Session), Detective, New York City Police Department, Detective Bureau, Hostage Negotiation Team; former investigator of Sex Crimes, Child Abuse and Crimes against Senior Citizens

Robert Stoll, B.B.A. Vice President and Deputy Auditor (ret.). Chemical Bank Corporation, New York

James R. Sutton Director, Office of Security Program, University of Illinois at Chicago; former Vice President, Security Plans and Programs, Chase Manhattan Bank, N.A.; Special Agent (ret.), Federal Bureau of Investigation, the California Department of Justice, Bureau of Narcotics Enforcement

Damon T. Taylor, B.A., M.P.S. Special Agent, Federal Bureau of Investigation, New York Office; former Congressional Staff Investigator, U.S. House of Representatives, Committee on Appropriations

Arthur E. Torrington, B.A., M.P.S., C.C.L.C., C.I.I. Chairman/CEO Westport Management Group, Ltd.; President, Executive Security and Intelligence Services; former senior claims representative, Insurance Company of America; special agent, U.S. Army Intelligence.

Thomas F. Walsh, B.A., J.D. Special Agent, Federal Bureau of Investigation, Legal Advisor, New York Office

Isaac Yeffet President, Yeffet Security Consultants, Inc.; former Director, Security Division (Worldwide) El Al Israel Airlines, Ltd.; conducted airport security surveys for *Life Magazine* and the National Broadcasting Company

David E. Zeldin, B.S., M.P.S. President, Asset Protection Corporation; President, Associated Licensed Detectives of New York State; former chairman, Long Island Chapter, American Society for Industrial Security; Adjunct Professor, Long Island University, New York

Foreword

Editor in chief, Dr. Joseph J. Grau has compiled a comprehensive, up-to-date, and in-depth revised edition of the *Criminal and Civil Investigation Handbook*. Dr. Grau selected some of the most experienced and internationally recognized authorities on civil and criminal investigations to prepare original chapters on their specialty fields of investigation, law, forensic sciences, among many other subjects. The wealth of material in this timely second edition is truly encyclopedic in scope. The 63 chapters are clearly written and offer important discussions on techniques, legal considerations, information sources, and technological advances.

During the past decade, major advances in technology have taken place, such as control and computer telecommunications, remote sensing, databank and network-related security, scientific identification of toxic waste disposal sites, and private security and antiterrorist technological innovations. Corporate executives, industrial security directors, attorneys, prosecutors, and criminal and civil investigators are continuously confronted with change. This is the first authoritative handbook to document the critical changes in this field. At long last Dr. Grau has developed a comprehensive and practical guidebook that will prove to be indispensable to all attorneys and law enforcement personnel involved in civil and criminal investigations. More specifically, practitioners faced with investigative issues during environmental inquiries can readily turn to the chapters on environmental investigative considerations for guidance. Insurance company investigators and investigators for the respective state attorney general's office can glean the latest information on probing unmeritorious claims and medicaid fraud from the chapters on insurance investigations. There are a number of excellent chapters on information gathering, forensic investigations, corporate and computer crime investigations, fraud control in banking and health care, and terrorism investigations and hostage negotiations.

Society is continually confronted with critical changes that pose a threat to the life and public safety of its citizens. These threats occur in corporate America, state and local governmental agencies, insurance companies, and the financial services industry. Specifically, these very serious threats to public safety include toxic waste disposal and dumping, date rape on college campuses, terrorism and hostage taking, computer crimes and telecommunications fraud, and credit card fraud. All these vital issues are thoroughly examined in this huge compendium of professional investigative procedures. This comprehensive collection of 63 chapters provides practitioners with all the sources necessary to guide them through legal and procedural applications during formal and informal investigations. This primary reference fills a significant gap in the professional literature. I predict that this masterfully assembled volume will become a classic in the near future.

This 1000-page sourcebook is unique. It is the first handbook to meet the professional needs of practitioners while offering guidance to upper-level undergraduate and graduate students of investigation. Dr. Grau's outstanding book is a valuable resource and a substantial contribution to knowledge building for educators, attorneys, business executives, security directors, law enforcement administrators, prosecutors, forensic scientists, and librarians. Dr. Grau's thoroughness, diligence, care for detail, and meticulous editorial skills are apparent in the results of this significant publication. This "magnum opus" should be purchased by every police agency, prosecutor's office, insurance fraud investigation unit, law office library, as well as college libraries with criminal justice and business administration collections.

ALBERT R. ROBERTS, D.S.W.
Professor and Director
Administration of Justice Program
School of Social Work
Rutgers University
New Brunswick, N.J.

Foreword

Editor in Chief Dr. Joseph Grau, in this expanded, updated second edition of the *Criminal and Civil Investigation Handbook*, has made another impressive and significant contribution to the literature in the field of investigation. Again, he brings together the experience, expertise, and insights of numerous highly respected skilled working practitioners in one volume.

The handbook is an absolute must for the reference shelves not only of civil and criminal investigators but also of educators, trainers, journalists, lawyers, and even laymen interested in gaining insight into the methods, procedures, and techniques of systematically collecting information.

As in the first edition, dozens of experts describe and illustrate the methods that they have found successful in conducting a wide variety of complex, challenging investigations. Dr. Grau again has done a truly admirable job in selecting and compiling an encyclopedic work on investigation.

Today's investigators, if they are to be successful, must master varied and diverse areas of knowledge. They must be facile in utilizing information from accounting, behavioral sciences, business, computer science, engineering, environmental science, finance, forensic science, law, mathematics, medicine, the pure sciences, statistics, and numerous other disciplines. The knowledge explosion and rapid technological change have made being an investigator today a far more demanding pursuit than it once was. It is an art, a craft, and a science. Investigators must maintain their mastery of the basics: the collection and preservation of evidence, interviewing, interrogation, note taking, developing sources of information, and law. But they must also be able to conduct investigations that are largely phenomena of the last two decades, such as telecommunications fraud, computer crime, credit card fraud, money laundering, and the like.

The wide diversity of investigative challenges to not only traditional police investigators but also to investigators in banking, business, educational institutions, insurance companies, and the regulatory and other government agencies make a collection of this breadth and scope urgently needed.

Often compilations with an extensive number of contributors are disjointed and lack coherence and continuity. Yet this does not happen in the handbook because Dr. Grau not only skillfully selected seasoned, professional contributors but he organized the 63 chapters of subject matter logically and meaningfully into nine coherent parts.

There is something for everybody in this reference book from experienced professional investigators to preservice college students, from public law enforcement officers to private security practitioners. Numerous textbooks have been written on the various aspects of investigations, and most promise a comprehensive view of the field but fail to live up to the promise. The handbook succeeds in this respect. It is the most comprehensive book on investigations that I have seen.

Because of its comprehensive scope and its high quality, I believe it will be widely used in colleges and universities, in training academies, and by the police, private security, law firms and other agencies that conduct civil and criminal investigations.

JAMES A. O'CONNOR, PH.D., C.P.P.
Deputy Director of Training,
Federal Bureau of Investigation (retired),
Associate Professor and Director of Administration of Justice
Northern Virginia Community College, Woodbridge, Virginia
Academic Advisor to the American Society for Industrial Security
and member of the Law Enforcement Liaison Council

Preface

This second edition has been updated to meet the needs of professional investigators, educators and trainers, and even nonprofessional persons interested in learning the how's and why's of information gathering. As in the first edition, more than 60 experts explain, describe, and illustrate procedures and techniques, tested by experience and used successfully in their professional endeavors.

What Is New?

One-third of the book consists of new chapters, five have been completely rewritten, and several significantly updated. Eighteen additional professionals, qualified by experience and training in specific fields, explain investigative approaches and techniques that they have found both effective and successful.

There are new, complete, authoritative, easy-to-read chapters, detailing investigation as it applies to:

Information data bases.

Computer crime.

Telecommunications fraud.

Civil and criminal environmental wrongdoing.

Scientific research fraud.

Campus security.

Undercover probes and sting operations in the private sector from the user and provider points of view.

Terrorism assessment and defensive techniques by the former director of security for El Al Airlines Worldwide.

Psychological profiling of the captor by a former hostage in Iran.

Child abuse investigations by child protective services.

Police use of deadly physical force.

Money laundering.

The team approach in hostage negotiations.

Furthermore, complete revisions with new information are provided in the areas of art theft, forgery and credit cards, and the medical examiner at the homicide scene. The treatment of several other areas of investigation have been updated, such as forensics, bank fraud, the organization of police units, immigration and naturalization, to mention a few.

Changes are evident in the expanded business-oriented crime section and the addition of a separate part focusing on terrorism and hostage taking.

All this information is indispensable for effectively conducting complex, controversial investigations in an intensely sophisticated, legalistic, electronic world. Armed with ready access to computerized information, top and middle management business personnel may be in an advantageous position to prevent and control assets loss. Travelers, as well as persons threatened by having their privacy invaded, can learn defensive and offensive strategies and countermoves.

This edition identifies new scams and effective countermeasures, such as those related to cellular phones. It alerts business personnel to potential dangers, many of which did not exist at the time of the first writing because the implementing technology was not available. Furthermore, new legislation, especially environmental, and its impact on investigations required extensive treatment.

Social Changes Initiated This Revision

The cybernetic revolution—with its concomitant electronic sensing devices and remote control, computer-assisted, and internal computer wrongdoing—has made crime commission easy. Simply by pushing a button, the young and old, weak and strong, brilliant and less intelligent, male and female can engage in theft and fraud. Telecommunications widened the arena to anywhere—the home, the office, the car, and even outer space—to any time, day or night, and, as noted, to anyone.

How Can This Book Be Used?

First, since this book is a compilation of authoritative, reference/source information, neatly compressed in one volume, it gives the possessor quick access to a wide range of topics.

Second, the broad, multidisciplinary, comprehensive presentation fosters cross-fertilization of thoughtful, creative, innovative thinking about new investigative approaches. Each chapter is self-contained and therefore can be digested in one reading.

Third, providing not only the expertise, but also the rationale behind guidelines improves job performance. People usually want to know the reason for a directive.

Fourth, along the same lines, the better informed person is more likely to make the correct decision.

Fifth, the researcher can use the facts, suggestions, instances, and cases in generating hypotheses as well as in constructing a rationale for investigations. Since each chapter is written by an expert from personal experience in an area of specialization, the educator/researcher/graduate student has the "nuts and bolts" for developing and testing propositions.

Sixth, the training director may use it for scenario playing and the illustration of basic principles.

Seventh, the chapter on data base intelligence examines the methods of data systems linkages and computerized profiling useful in corporate investigations.

Eighth, this is a handy reference for developing defensive environmental policies and avoiding potential litigation.

In general, reference works are rarely read from cover to cover for enjoyment or professional mind stretching; and, although portions of this handbook provide stimulating reading and suggest answers to emerging problems, its major purpose is to supply easy, quick answers for front line decision making. The style is concise; legal and technical terminology, as well as job and street jargon, are limited to sections in which such language is necessary for accuracy and familiarity.

As with any source book, however, follow-up conferences and further research may be required. For example, the extensive legal section furnishes guides for action based on the U.S. Supreme Court decisions and the U.S. Code, but familiarity with local statutes relative to specific case details and discussions with a knowledgeable attorney are recommended. Although the legal considerations were up-to-date at the time of manuscript preparation, statutory changes and new court rulings inevitably occur. Therefore, in using this handbook, one must be as constantly alert to recent developments as one would be in consulting any reference source.

Procedures vary by jurisdiction. Nevertheless, all investigations follow basic principles. Although each detective may have a distinctive style, all proceed in a similar manner. Each case is unique; however, all contain discernible common features. Were this not so, standard procedures would not exist. What works best for one individual may not be effective for another, but knowing the successful techniques of others with extensive investigative expertise helps. Useful insights can be obtained from operational job reports, based on experience in areas where a tremendous volume and diversity of crime affords the greatest opportunities to investigate. It was therefore the intent of the contributors to offer their suggestions, not to dictate; to present positive, practical approaches, not to prescribe the "right" way.

Who May Use This Handbook to Best Advantage?

The *Criminal and Civil Investigation Handbook* was compiled for use by professional personnel working in the following types of occupational organizations and related interest groups:

1. Corporate leaders in upper and middle management.
2. Private security, loss control, and fraud prevention.
3. Lawyers and investigative units in law offices.
4. Professors, educators, and researchers.
5. Public police and fire departments.
6. Federal, state, and local government agencies.
7. Inspectors, supervisors, investigators employed by regulatory agencies in the executive, legislative, and judicial branches of government.
8. Labor and management groups.
9. Protectors of civil rights and liberties.
10. Self-policing units of the professions, industry, and business.
11. Insurance institutions.
12. Libraries and research centers

The foregoing comments are offered in the hope that they will best serve those for whom this handbook has been compiled.

JOSEPH J. GRAU, PH.D.

PART 1

Introduction to Investigation

1

Investigation, Technology, and the Changing Crime Scene

Damon T. Taylor

Tremendous technological advances in recent years have transformed not only our environmental surroundings but also the attitudes and relationships governing our behavior. Correspondingly, a portion of the world's population is consumed with the prospect that our potential, as thus far envisioned, has no limit and science with its technological artifacts is capable of uniquely charting our destiny. It is a time when traditional beliefs and norms seem on the verge of uselessness.

In this changing world the investigation of crime has proved to be a dynamic process. It seeks to develop and maintain a quality of life, protect social and physical environments, safeguard producers and consumers, and, to some extent, even preserve global sanity. A far cry from earlier and less complicated eras, today the investigation of crime has expanded to nearly every aspect of daily living—in fact, it has become an integral part of contemporary life.

Criminal investigation is no longer merely a localized law enforcement tool used to control street thugs who commit the violent crimes of robbery, rape, and murder. Instead, it has become a process for achieving justice that is available to all facets of the population—reaching into the board rooms of corporations and the offices of public officials, uncovering illegal business practices and government improprieties, and exposing consumer fraud and embezzlement in the business world.

Technology, as utilized in the investigative process, has improved the capabilities of investigation and is thought by many to be the hallmark of modern civilization. Technology has increased the range, redefined the role players, and challenged the adaptive potential of the investigative process. With each succeeding generation, the nature of crimes and methods of committing them have become more sophisticated—and so have the nature and methods of investigation. These methods include the use of intrusive devices and increased mobilization, communication, and mechanization—heretofore manual operations.

Although such methods have improved investigative capabilities and are more readily available to law-abiding citizens, unfortunately such technology is available for use by violators of the law as well. For example, the psyches of *both* victim and offender can be probed through psycholinguistics, hypnosis, and polygraph examinations. The privacy of individuals and organizations can be interdicted by electronic interception devices. The criminal element both uses and, to some extent, can be outmaneuvered by some of the more advanced space-age air and sea transportation equipment. Furthermore, *both* investigator and perpetrator can coordinate and accelerate mobilization time through advanced communication innovations. Even darkness, the traditional camouflage of the criminal, can now be neutralized through night-vision and photographic equipment. The list of technological advances continues to increase with each passing year; the examples cited above obviously represent only a fraction of the advanced techniques available to both investigator and perpetrator.

Not only have opportunities for the successful commission of crimes and their investigation increased, but also technological advances have transformed, almost completely, the context and areas within which crimes can and do occur. For instance, telecommunications have now transformed information gathering into a global affair. Before, the crime scene encompassed a particular neighborhood, house, business, or factory; today it encompasses the world. Today, modern transportation and electronic funds transfer have made it possible for crime and criminal proceeds to move easily from city to city, from state to state, from country to country, and from hemisphere to hemisphere around the globe. No area is remote enough and no population isolated enough to withstand the advances of technology and investigation. At the same time as the crime scene has extended over the entire world, the players have been placed under greater scrutiny through use of telescopic, microscopic, and electronic surveillance. Furthermore, an information explosion has resulted in an unparalleled public intimacy in which so much is known about so many other persons. To the extent that crime has become a world problem and investigation an indispensable segment of the solution, all peoples of the world have been brought together more closely.

It is evident that role players in the new and ever-changing crime scene must be redefined in terms of technologically produced environmental changes. For example, credential certification must be redesigned within the context of emergent social development. Traditionally, local and federal law enforcement agencies restricted their efforts to combatting "street" crimes. Today, however, the new pressures of corporate, white-collar, and consumer crimes have caused law enforcement to redirect and expand its efforts. As more and more criminals appear in business suits, added knowledge is required concerning accounting credentials, complex business concepts and procedures, and computer and electronics systems analysis. The use of modern technology requires discipline, restraint, education, and, sometimes, judicial investigative supervision.

Certainly, the development of sophisticated technology has presented a challenge to the adaptive potential of the law enforcement community. To meet the challenge and to provide possible solutions, two schools of thought and action have come into focus; namely, revisionism and fundamentalism. The revisionist position sharply deviates from established concepts and urges new directions. In some instances, this means casting aside valid methods and techniques in favor of more novel and sometimes less appropriate approaches. Since the position may imply an attack on orthodox criminological traditions, employment of technological equipment is regarded by some individuals as a status symbol—and a license, as it were, to conduct an investigative operation.

On the other hand, fundamentalists are concerned that the use of sophisticated gadgetry may become an end in itself. Use of technological support systems as a means to an end should be qualified by time-honored concepts of sound practical and legal decision making, expertise, and common sense. Although the modern crime scene requires a great deal of advanced expertise, fundamentalists believe that the motivations and vulnerabilities of human beings are timeless and immutable. Advocates of the position rely on the tenacity, experience, and intuition of veteran investigators, who cannot be effectively replaced by any technological invention, regardless of its nature. It has been pointed out by fundamentalists that the choice to use techniques such as electronic interception devices requires considerable forethought. Such tools do not solve crimes; but, rather, problems are solved through interpersonal contacts. Dispute over the use of technological devices can itself cause problems. For example, the departmental importance of a case may rest upon whether or not the investigators have established sufficient plausible cause to employ, with judicial supervision, wire-tapping equipment. Its use may be considered a stamp of approval and a status symbol for the operation, whereas a simpler approach might achieve the same or better results.

There is considerable practicality in both the revisionist and fundamentalist schools of thought, and they should not, therefore, be considered opposed to each other. Instead, present practices must be understood in terms of both fundamentalism and a gradually emerging revisionism. With this attitude in mind, the following guidelines are offered.

To begin with, the multitudinous facets of modern criminal activity must be simplified and reduced to the basic denominators pertinent to an investigation. In other words, the veneer must be stripped away from the victim, the spectrum of suspects, and the methods used to implement the crime. Often an investigator is overwhelmed and intimidated by the complexity of a large industrial or financial corporation's work environment, thus affording the perpetrator (such as an embezzler) an even greater potential for concealment than actual visual impediments might provide. Such a situation could lead the investigator to ask, "Where do I begin?" Here in the great "corporate vastness" it is particularly important to seek a "bottom line" relative to discovering the methods used and the potential suspects. The instruments of crime may be more technically complex than ever before in history, but their theoretical operations still are reducible to a basic level. In other words, computer fraud is still fraud; computerized electronic banking procedures still maintain debits and credits; terrorists still use traditional methods such as bombing, assassination, and extortion.

Although the indiscretions and abuses of celebrities, politicians, and public officials most assuredly should be dealt with by the criminal justice system when they involve a breach of law, nonetheless, the essential priority given such cases must remain consistent with the *overall* legislative mandate of the organization and a *balanced* approach to crime in general. Flaws in past operations should not be blown out of proportion and negate long-established basic principles.

Conventional law enforcement is currently engaged in the business of repackaging and selling itself in an effort to regain its reputation—a reputation lost, in part, because of past ill-advised activities. The mass media have become its principal instrument (and target) for a sales pitch. This is understandable. Newspapers, magazines, television, and various other electronic audio-visual communicational forms are indeed significant in their roles as socializing and value-changing agents. Formerly, the exchange between media and law enforcement took on an adversary connotation; present circumstances, however, suggest a partnership. Nonetheless, investigation must not be relegated to merely providing theater material for media consumers. Such a possibility exists. The media are profit-oriented corporations which are greatly dependent on newsmakers; and law enforcement needs an image maker.

The emerging future may seem to present formidable, if not insurmountable, obstacles for successful investigation by law enforcement. The transparency of investigative operations, the potential civil and physical vulnerability of law officers, the increased expertise necessary to function effectively within legislative mandates—all these factors have changed the context within which investigation can function effectively.

In recent years, public pressure to safeguard the privacy and civil rights of citizens has increased. Law enforcement has attempted to compensate for the resultant decrease of information by increasing its educational and technical expertise. As a result, there is greater reliance on technical equipment than on interpersonal contacts. Current legislative mandates relative to privacy and civil rights have, to some extent, dampened investigative desire—a situation that is based on the risk of civil litigation as a possible aftermath of traditional investigative procedures. As a result, a more academic approach has emerged, and investigators are opting for greater preparation and forethought before conducting even the most routine interview. An extremely real sense of vulnerability pervades the law enforcement community at present. For instance, legislation, such as the Freedom of Information Act, Privacy Act, and "sunshine laws," has negated any idea that law enforcement operations are privileged and beyond scrutiny. Traditional investigative techniques, such as the use of informants, are now often challenged by the loss of confidentiality. Such developments have further pressed the quest for innovative approaches.

Because few agencies have been spared a public airing and criticism of their internal "laundry," law enforcement operations have necessarily become more transparent. Operational decisions made by field commanders are subject to a virtual avalanche of potential critics. In fact, some departments, both federal and local, have suffered public embarrassment—the results of successful civil suits filed against them for activity viewed (in hindsight) as negligent. As law enforcement is increasingly coerced into operating in a fishbowl and as more and more candor is expected (and gained) by the public, the more exposed investigative operations must become. Although such a situation provides an unvarnished portrait of law enforcement, it also benefits the criminal and the potential law violator who know "what's going on" at all times. In other words, although the public has been afforded a new and realistic view of investigation, so, too, has the criminal element—to its benefit.

The mystique that once surrounded investigative agencies has all but vanished, and with it has gone whatever deterrent effect it may have had vis-à-vis criminal activity. In light of the current openness, law violators are far better able to determine the priorities and effectiveness of their adversaries. Criminals can now petition and receive many documents relative to past investigations in which they were principal targets. Furthermore, increased computer and data processing capabilities have decreased the retrieval time for gathering such information. As a result, the public has acquired a greater potential for oversight, and criminally inclined individuals have gained greater access to information to protect their devious conduct.

Investigators in law enforcement must learn to utilize technological advances, but they must temper their adoption of such methods with common sense. There is no reason to assume that *all* criminals strive for sophistication or that *all* significant crimes occur in the board rooms and computer sections of large corporations. Surrounded by gadgets, the investigator runs the risk of believing that operations cannot be successful without them; or worse, that their use bears the seal of approval as being the most advanced, sophisticated, and hence successful, approach.

Despite the advanced technology of the twentieth century, one fact remains: many elements in our society live in physical fear for their lives, for violence in any age is seldom subtle or truly sophisticated. The bottom line must continue to read: Crime in any form possesses the ability to traumatize a population; and although the eventual effectiveness and significance of technology is yet to be defined, still it must remain dependent, at least in part, on its equally important and significant counterpart—the human side of investigation.

2
Principles of Investigation

Frank E. Klecak

Investigation is the medium through which facts necessary for successful criminal prosecution or civil litigation are discovered, identified (in terms of their relationship to an offensive act), gathered, preserved, and subsequently prepared as evidence in anticipation of a legal proceeding.

The investigation of an offensive act is analogous to completing a jigsaw puzzle. In the latter, the individual has all the pieces and must simply, by trial and error, sort through them to locate the interlocking pieces. In the former, the parameters are sometimes less well defined in that all of the pieces, although there, may not be quite as obvious. The cover of the puzzle box may depict the finished product, but this is not always the case for the investigator, who may have to develop that product by the tedious endeavor of identifying, eliminating, and subsequently placing the pieces into their respective niches, thus completing the puzzle.

In attempting to identify specific principles of investigation, one is likely to find a myriad of related factors. Perhaps the most pragmatic approach is to categorize the subject matter to make it more comprehensible.

First, one must identify the purpose of a law enforcement or investigative agency and the conditions that influence a criminal investigation.

Public law enforcement agencies are given the responsibility of safeguarding society's members and their property. They are also charged with maintaining a climate that permits a peaceful, safe, and productive social existence. Private investigators, and security personnel performing similar functions in the business world, establish their concepts and plans of action in close alignment with the thoughts and motivations of their public-sector counterparts.

The protection of life and property, the prevention of crime, the enforcement of our laws and the preservation of the peace cannot always be accomplished by mere law enforcement presence. Often, in-depth follow-up investigation is required.

The investigator's role is assumed when there is need to establish that an offensive act has occurred, or after the fact, when there is need to gather evidence to prove the responsibility of the offender. The investigator then identifies and assists in the apprehension and prosecution of law offenders. The entrance of the investigator into the matter is normally initiated when the routine patrol functions do not or cannot achieve their original purpose.

In public law enforcement, detective units composed of criminal investigators perform, basically, in a reactive posture as opposed to the proactive climate of routine patrol. Crime prevention is a basic function of the uniformed force. The investigator usually reacts after the patrol officer has initiated a preliminary investigation and established that there is reason to believe a criminal act has been committed. In other words, a crime is perpetrated before the expertise of the investigator becomes an important ingredient of the investigatory effort. Positive resolution of this unlawful act is achieved by the apprehension and successful prosecution of the guilty party or parties. This is not to say that the investigator's entrance is always after the fact, since prior entrance is a possibility when information has been developed that a criminal act will be attempted.

Certain basic guidelines should exist within any criminal investigative unit, regardless of the number of personnel or the particular types of crime involved. In terms of investigation, specific crimes have their own motivations and techniques. Certainly, all will concede that violent criminal acts must be afforded the priority that they deserve. All investigations, whether criminal or civil, have the possibility of being successfully concluded and, to that end, the investigator must be prepared in order to perform in the most capable manner. The investigation must proceed according to basic principles and procedures.

The following elements form the foundation upon which criminal and civil investigation should be based:

Preliminary investigation: The investigator's first personal contact with the crime and its location.

Informational development: Gathering and processing essential data upon which the investigation and subsequent prosecution will be based.

Knowledge of human factors: An investigator's study and perception of human qualities and thought processes, which can help to advance the case investigation.

Case assignment priority: Priority accorded those case investigations that deserve immediate follow-up efforts.

Case supervision: The prerogative of the supervisor to assign cases independently and then continue to monitor the investigator's endeavors.

Selection of the investigator: Choosing the right person for the job to be performed.

Knowledge of rules of evidence: The investigator's knowledge and application of the rules of evidence, which will help bring about a positive outcome of the investigation.

FOUNDATION FOR INVESTIGATION

A crime scene investigator usually has but one opportunity to make a possibly crucial discovery, and that occurs at the time of the investigator's initial response to the scene. These initial observations and conclusions are of paramount importance. The possibility of a successful conclusion to a case originates at the inception of the investigator's efforts. The fact that the scene of the offense can never be reproduced in its original state dictates that concerted effort must be made by the investigator to carefully handle the circumstances in which the investigation is initiated. Lack of conscientious and determined efforts to establish all possible evidence and testimony at this location can hinder the investigation and, obviously, the eventual criminal prosecution.

Circumstances under which police custodial interrogations of prospective defendants and suspects are performed, as well as the police methods of searching for and seizing evidentiary materials have been significantly affected by legal implications. Determinations by the U.S. Supreme Court in the 1960s required that police priority be given to the use of legally obtained evidence.

Therefore, the crime scene, that is, the location at which an offense was committed, became an even more important element of the crime. The solution of a criminal act became affected by specific legal requirements for discovery, gathering, identification, and eventual court presentation of evidence uncovered by the crime scene investigator.

Because of the aforementioned decisions, it became evident that important consideration had to be given to the initial recognition and proper handling of crime scene evidence. Closely connected with this search process is the preservation of the scene and its fruits by the first officer to arrive.

At a crime scene the patrol officer must give immediate attention to caring for persons in need of medical assistance and promptly notifying the proper medical authorities. Next, witnesses, if present, must be recognized and maintained for future interviews by the investigator. Prospective defendants present must be detained or arrested without jeopardizing their rights. Appropriate actions, which will permit any oral or documented evidence received from a witness to stand the test for court admissibility, must be taken. All possible evidentiary matter must be preserved and not allowed to be "contaminated" by improper handling.

The investigator must follow an orderly structured procedure in order to develop the details required to further case preparation. A mechanical routine can be followed but it must be realized that all investigations are peculiar to their own environment. Establishment of vital facets of evidence begins at the crime scene. One must be cognizant that the answers to the questions *what, where, when, why, who,* and *how,* were all to be found at this location in the recent past. Both the opportunity and the motivation necessary for the completion of the criminal act probably arose within close proximity to the scene. An in-depth crime scene search helps to develop specifics that will contribute to learning these answers.

INFORMATIONAL DEVELOPMENT

One cannot succeed in any vocation without first searching for informational data and then applying it to problem solving. Basic knowledge must be reinforced with alertness to the facts at issue. This reinforcement would ordinarily come from information developed at the crime scene. Nothing is certain, and the attitude that every case must be concluded successfully (with an arrest and conviction) is ill-advised. However, intelligent and efficient gathering of information is rudimentary for achieving the desired goal of crime solution.

Identification of motive and alleged offender alone is not sufficient to further the criminal justice system's requirements for prosecution. The development of a case skeleton (the basic crime elements and suspicions), although sufficient for probable cause, is inadequate for the eventual court presentation and desired verdict. The meat and sinew of the crime case, composed of "hard" and conclusive evidence coupled with admissions and confessions, cannot be understated. Linking the essential crime elements to the suspected person is imperative for furthering a proper investigation.

Information can come from a myriad of sources. Without overlooking the various means of gathering information from public and municipal agencies, institutions, and so forth, investigators must concentrate their initial fact seeking on the crime scene with its related witnesses and evidence. Even an innocuous comment cannot be overlooked, as every bit or piece of information may possibly link itself to something more obvious as the investigation proceeds. With this thought in mind, written documentation of all facets of witness knowledge should be obtained for eventual future evaluation and possible connection with the crime. Photographic evidence will also serve its purpose in reestablishing crime scene conditions for both the investigator and a prospective jury.

Occasionally, information is developed that precludes a particular suspect's involvement in the case under investigation. When this happens, the investigator has to be concerned with "clearing" the subject. Crime investigation is not a one-way street; although priority must be given to gathering information toward a solution, one cannot disregard data that will exonerate the accused or the suspect.

KNOWLEDGE OF HUMAN FACTORS

Crime that has been committed by one human being against another human being must be pursued to a positive conclusion by still another human being. Despite breakthroughs in science and technology, knowledge of human factors continues to be paramount in criminal investigation. One must bear in mind that the investigator, witnesses, complainants, suspects, and defendants are all part of a social and cultural system.

Although the techniques of the behavioral sciences have not been mastered to the degree of those of the exact sciences, the human factor must be considered in behavioral terms as a part of the investigation.

Since man first walked this earth, crime has existed. To combat deviant behavior, society has developed rules according to which controls are established. These controls provide for peaceful and compatible existence. Unfortunately, rules are broken by those who persist in pursuing unlawful methods for whatever motivation. However, in so doing, criminals usually leave behind something on which trained investigators can focus their skills. Fingerprints, footprints, tireprints, toolmarks, implements, broken glass, and paint scrapings, as well as personal identification by voice and/or physical characteristics described by eyewitnesses are some forms of evidentiary material investigators use to assemble the solution to the jigsaw puzzle.

The evidence and documentation having been gathered, the persistent and curious investigator's knowledge and expertise must now be applied to determining patterns and methods of operation. It must be realized that no two crimes are identical, although they may appear similar. The tools for deduction must not be dulled by a lack of awareness of what goes on in the mind of the offender. These tools must be constantly accompanied by an awareness generated in the investigator through observations, interpretations, and conclusions relative to the human element involved.

The basic facts of the crime are normally self-evident; however, the investigator cannot rely exclusively on these observations and findings but must supplement them by obtaining human reactions from complainant and witnesses. Witnesses are not only persons actually present at the scene, but also those who may have been in a position to observe some portion of or even the entire crime, perhaps without having been aware of what was occurring. Again, human suspicions and imagination can be of primary interest to the investigator, who cannot discount anything that is offered by the public.

The offender moves about in devious ways; therefore the investigator must develop judgments that will contribute to a positive solution. In cases under investigation nothing can be left unanswered, and even the most insignificant lead must be pursued to its end. Frequently, the methods of detection are not unusual, but rather entail a dedicated effort in investigating, interrogating, and eliminating suspects.

The personality of the investigator cannot be overlooked in discussing the human factor. Dedication to a sometimes unrewarding occupation is a major job requirement. Considerations of time and personal social hardships cannot interfere with devotion to the accomplishment of the assigned task. Again, the primary function of the investigator is to solve the crime.

Knowledge of human factors is an important resource for the investigator. The ability to recognize strengths as well as weaknesses in the suspect will contribute greatly to the eventual resolution of a case. Solving a crime can be a complex and tedious experiment in the "science" of human entanglements. Motivations are influenced by numerous wants and desires. Greed, jealousy, revenge, hatred, personal wants, sexual desire, and a feeling of "so, what the hell" are but a few forms of stimulation to perform an offensive act. The penetration of the investigator into this maze of human emotions and stimuli can result in an ulcer at one extreme or a most rewarding experience at the other.

CASE ASSIGNMENT PRIORITY

Generally, the selection of cases for investigative priority should be based on the clues that are uncovered in the preliminary investigation. Certainly, cases of major concern, such as homicide, violent sex offenses, robbery, kidnapping, and so on should be exempted from this priority ranking. They routinely must receive the utmost police effort from the first notification of occurrence. Burglary, larceny, auto theft, vandalism, and other categories of crimes that are not likely to be witnessed by a complainant may receive less concentrated effort, unless significant reason for further investigation is developed by the preliminary investigation. Thus, effort and time can be concentrated on solving those offenses that offer the most probability of solution. Investigators may be assigned according to their particular areas of expertise in order to ensure the most professional follow-up. This approach is not to be considered selective enforcement; rather, it realistically focuses the investigators' efforts in the direction of the most probable accomplishment and, at the same time, utilizes available resources most efficiently.

For proper investigatory effort to be exerted in the right direction, the necessary mechanics must be instituted at the very inception of the crime report. A civilian complaint, in the majority of instances, becomes official with the preparation of the case report by a member of the patrol force. The report format must be preconstructed to include pertinent identifying information relating to the victim and the criminal act, as well as a section that reflects what is known as "factors of solvability." The patrol officer who performs the preliminary investigation is responsible for a complete and accurate compilation of the solvability information that will assist in the next step, the preliminary investigatory effort; for example, information that relates to witnesses, suspicious vehicles, stolen property identification through serial numbers, and evidence found at the scene that could relate to the perpetrator (wallet, footprints, tireprints, fingerprints). Of course, possible suspects known to the complainant, mode of operation, and pertinent results of a neighborhood canvas cannot be disregarded.

These factors, each assigned a weighted value based on prior research, offer the case assignment officer an opportunity to decide the priorities for the various case reports received. It must be reemphasized that particular criminal acts such as felonious homicide, sex offenses, robbery, violent assaults, and kidnapping cannot be included in this case assignment priority concept, as they should normally receive investigatory precedence. Such offenses as larceny, burglary, vandalism, and leaving the scene of an accident, however, lend themselves to a system of weighted values.

Reports that do not contain factors of sufficient weight may receive less immediate follow-up investigation than others bearing higher-weight scores. When these criteria of solvability exist, it is conceivable that a crime report need not be given immediate investigative effort, but can even be placed in a "no-follow-up" file. Reports receiving the necessary weight tally will be investigated immediately. When new factors emerge that reestablish the "no-follow-up" case in a more soluble category, an investigation can be initiated. The principle here is to concentrate efforts where case resolution is more probable.

Solvability factors, linked with proper report dissemination, can offer a more exact basis for determining cases for further investigation.

CASE SUPERVISION

Once the initial investigation is completed—usually on the first day—and it appears that continued investigation is necessary, proper supervision becomes an absolute necessity. The supervisor who made the original case assignment is now in a position to continue to monitor the investigator's endeavors.

When an intensive, concerted effort is required, more than one investigator can be assigned to the same case. The case supervisory officer can then allocate personnel in the area where they are most needed. When necessary, specialized units can be summoned into the investigation to add numbers as well as their particular talents. In such instances, there must be careful coordination of the various units and personnel involved and an orderly and structured procedure must be followed.

The review of supplemental progress reports, statements, neighborhood canvas results, areas of concentration, index-file results of lead sheets, and laboratory analysis reports should be grounds for a supervisor's evaluation of the potential for successful case conclusion.

The relationship between the crime investigator and the prosecutor can also be enhanced by close case scrutiny at the supervisory level. Many investigations require a long time to dovetail all the relevant facts into a proper case presentation. When activity reports are prepared and submitted daily, the supervisor should be able to present a well-rounded picture of the case structure as well as to identify both strengths and weaknesses to the prosecutor for the purpose of establishing the next investigatory steps to be taken. Certain evidentiary areas may need to be firmed up so that a proper trial presentation can be made by the prosecutor, whose input, as the one who will actually be presenting the case before the courts, can be invaluable at this stage of the investigation.

When sufficient incriminating evidence exists for obtaining an arrest warrant or a presentation before a grand jury, reliance on the prosecutor for proper guidance is imperative.

The investigator's primary task is to gather facts. The proper supervision of this accumulation of evidential data and its subsequent presentation in court cannot be just a presumption but must be a reality.

SELECTION OF THE INVESTIGATOR

The right person must be chosen for the job. Public law enforcement personnel assigned to a detective division emerge from the ranks of the patrol officers. Selections for this role should not be haphazard. A popular principle is that this type of assignment should be made through various testing devices, including interviews. Textbook detectives often fall short of the personal requirements necessary to combat the sophistication of the criminal. Regardless of the method of selection, there are certain requisites for the composition of the team performing criminal investigations.

Exceptional perceptiveness is a personality trait necessary for a criminal investigator. A strong sense of confidence coupled with a vivid imagination helps the investigator develop a hypothesis relevant to the circumstances surrounding the offense and the offender's deviant thinking. Awareness of the *who, what, when, where, why,* and *how* questions in regard to a particular act that has been committed enhances the detective's ability to establish a plan of action. An investigator should have the ability to mentally take the role of the offender, thereby recreating the subject's thoughts, motives, and movements.

The mechanics of these suggestions can be illustrated with a homicide investigation case.

Facts: A human body has been discovered in a large field overgrown with vegetation. There are no occupied residences within one-quarter of a mile in any direction. Observation of the body reveals the deceased to be wearing only undergarments. It is obvious to the investigator that a severe head wound is the likely cause of death. A preliminary search of the area does not produce a possible weapon or any means of victim identification. Given these conditions, the criminal investigator must now proceed to establish particular facts.

Who: Identification of the victim most probably would reveal his or her residence, relatives, friends, occupation, station in life and community, possible enemies, and motive (if a crime has been committed). When they exist, fingerprints, footprints, tattoo markings, healed fractures, dental charts, and missing persons reports are some means for identification. (A mutilated body is more of a problem in that the absence of fingerprints, footprints, and so on further complicates determination of the individual's identity.) Once identification is accomplished, the movements of the victim can, up to a point, be determined by retracing activities engaged in prior to death.

What: Once the body is identified, can the investigator determine what actually happened, what was the cause of death? The medical examiner or coroner, in association with the investigator, plays a significant role in arriving at this conclusion. Medical, toxicological, and microscopic testing provides expert opinion on the cause of death and the type of weapon used. These facts then must be linked to the suspected offender.

When: The condition of the body and its temperature could reveal the approximate time of death. Lividity and rigor mortis are factors that must be taken into consideration in determining how much time has lapsed between the death and the discovery of the body. Stomach contents could also suggest when the victim last ate before death, since digestion requires a definite time for completion.

Where: Was the body delivered to the discovery area after death, or was the crime committed where the body was found? The amount of blood found at the scene could be instrumental in making this judgment. The condition of vegetation might reveal that the body was dragged from a vehicle and then "dumped" at the point of discovery. If it appears that the individual was killed somewhere else, then the retracing of movements could develop the answer to this question.

Why: Once the deceased has been identified and the background reconstructed, the investigator can move toward determining the homicide motive. When motive is established, it is quite possible that particular persons can be connected to the deceased by determining why they had such a motive. Financial reward, jealousy, a "hit," anger, family disagreement are but a few of the reasons for homicide.

How: As mentioned under the category, *what,* medical expertise can determine the cause of death, but the criminal investigator must discover the actions that led to that death. Case development is imperative in searching for the actions that preceded commission of the offense and the reasons for such behavior.

I have listed the mechanics of a homicide investigation in a very general way. If answers can be obtained for all the questions and supporting connecting evidence gathered, then the investigator's primary goal—namely, a conclusion—has been accomplished. A criminal investigator who is inquisitive (a "digger") and allows nothing to be left unanswered can arrive at a solution. Efforts guided by imagination and perception are most likely to be rewarded.

A *personnel evaluation* system can also be instituted whereby a member's work performance is constantly reviewed. In this way, the supervisors of criminal investigations can determine those who are capable of productive investigations. Constant review of the investigator's performance and potential is a requisite for efficient and effective investigation management. Obviously, those who do not reveal acceptable standards can be returned to other assignments.

Crime solution also requires certain *social talents* on the part of the investigator. Certainly, the successful investigator has an aptitude for dealing with the public. The resulting rapport will be helpful in eliciting sufficient and useful investigative leads. This is not a characteristic possessed by all, but a distinct almost inbred skill of particular individuals, which can be nurtured by persistence and fortitude, training and experience.

APPLICATION OF THE RULES OF EVIDENCE

Once the more in-depth investigation has been initiated, the investigator cannot proceed aimlessly but must be guided by a basic working knowledge of the rules of evidence. The offender may be apprehended, but without a conviction or guilty plea, case closeout has been only partially accomplished. Every effort should be made to "nail down" the investigation. If there is no positive verdict, due to inadequate or unreasonable evidence accumulation and preparation, the case, as well as the work performance of the investigator, may be considered tainted. Investigators must remember that an arrest simply for the sake of making it, without following prescribed constitutional requirements for evidence gathering, is nonproductive.

The mere arrest of a suspect is but a small fragment of the entire process of bringing the suspect into the criminal justice system. Other responsibilities remain for the investigator, one of which is to identify admissible court evidence. Once this identification has been accomplished, the particular evidentiary items must be linked with the elements of the crime and must link the subject with the offensive act. Many investigations that appeared to be solid on the surface have, unfortunately, been devastated upon presentation at trial. Although the prosecutor is accountable for the interpretation and presentation of evidence, the justification for the original assemblage of the indicting proof is the responsibility of the crime investigator.

Justification pertains not only to the reliability of the evidence but also to the means by which it came into the possession of the investigator. The fact that an arrest has been made and substantial incriminating data gathered is not sufficient if the method of obtaining the data was contrary to the laws of admissibility.

The very fact that there are no established statutes governing evidence is, in itself, an impediment to the investigator, who is influenced by court decisions and interpretations specifying the manner in which investigatory efforts must be exercised. The evidence gatherer must take these decisions and interpretations into consideration and remember that the way evidence is obtained must be acceptable to the presiding justice. Evidence that could conceivably have been admissible in a prior criminal case, according to the interpretation and decision rendered by the presiding magistrate, might not be acceptable to the justice before whom the present case is pending. The investigator must be fully aware that the acceptance of this evidence and its subsequent admissibility in a court of law are dependent on the manner in which it was obtained, preserved, and identified.

Finally, the investigator must contend with the fact that the particular investigation might be making evidentiary-rules history because it is subject to review by higher courts. What is done could lead to a future decision that will affect not only that case but those with similar circumstances throughout the criminal justice system.

In summary, seven basic elements useful to criminal investigators have been offered and reviewed. Their inclusion in investigations, whether public or private, can contribute to a more refined effort and a positive conclusion to a criminal investigation.

The human faculty of deduction can, oftentimes, be clouded by efforts in too many directions. Concentration within the aforementioned seven basic areas could lead to more definitive findings and the accurate fitting together of the various pieces of the puzzle.

Time and space limit the depth of explanation of each of the areas cited; however, while the parameters (legal, economic, social, and so on) within which an investigator must function are in certain instances well defined, other areas may be limited only by imagination and degree of commitment.

Every criminal act has the possibility of being solved. This must be uppermost in the mind of the investigator. The use of these elements of investigation will contribute to success.

3

The Organization and Facilities of an Investigative Unit within a Law Enforcement Agency

Frank E. Klecak

A public police agency's organization and facilities must be aligned so that they successfully accomplish its overall objectives. This requires a well-coordinated structure wherein there are provisions for the components to function in harmony. Unfortunately, many law enforcement agencies are limited in both personnel and equipment, which hampers their ability to cope with the various and diversified techniques of criminal investigation. These restrictions result in a dependence on federal, state, and county agencies that have the resources to assist in furthering their investigative efforts.

The proper agency crime-control strategies and eventual investigative techniques are dictated by available resources. Recognition must be given to the fact that law enforcement agencies do possess unique individual characteristics. These distinguishing features are determined by departmental size, budget, geography, and objectives, to name but a few.

Criminal investigative policy setting and the formulation of plans to positively pursue the chosen policy must be decided rationally. Ideally, every reported criminal act should be investigated to its utmost.

The problem must be diagnosed and then the most promising methods of solution put into practice. Various options must also be researched for eventual insertion into the plan if and when alternatives are necessary to further the investigation. Practical judgments play a large part in the final choice of procedure.

A department's decision to pursue general (centralized) as opposed to specialized (decentralized) criminal investigative procedures can be influenced by the means available to deal with the situation effectively. Their personnel complement determines the investigatory methods that the particular agency must use. The majority of this country's police departments are in the small- to middle-range category. Centralization is most affordable for smaller agencies.

In accordance with the generalization concept, the investigators perform in an overall manner that includes the preliminary investigation, evidence gathering, interviewing and interrogating, eliminating suspects, apprehending wrongdoers, and the eventual court case preparation and presentation. Their responsibility begins at the inception of the crime report and continues until the case investigation is eventually concluded in a court presentation. There are instances when a uniformed member performs the dual functions of patrol and investigation, investigating all types of offenses, not limited to particular crime classifications. The degree of case success depends on the individual investigator's skills and means of accomplishment.

The assumption must be made that within these agencies, the total caseload is lighter than in larger urban departments. Accordingly, investigators have a better opportunity to perform their required functions, because they are not inundated with investigations. Also, they have a closer relationship with all incoming crime reports. This affinity can influence their interactions with the various subject matters that come under their investigative "eyes."

In larger departments, specialization can be more readily incorporated into crime investigation. A substantial personnel complement permits the concentration of effort in particular crime-related fields. In this manner, the more serious crimes of homicide, robbery, rape, burglary, and so on, can receive individual attention by investigators expert in specific areas.

Smaller departments may develop specialists in certain areas where conditions call for a determined investigative plan. However, as mentioned earlier, larger outside agencies are usually available to assist in the more technical and complex investigations.

In the specialization mode, investigators trained in the particular crime-investigation field are used. Special training and guidance are offered to equip the specialists with the tools necessary to further their particular crime-field efforts. These investigators normally possess certain skills and expertise that will promote accomplishment of positive results within their crime category. They are cognizant of similar crimes that have occurred in the past and can therefore make comparisons and possibly connect former suspects or defendants to recently committed offenses. They constitute a pool of experts to draw upon. Thus, preliminary investigators can receive additional investigatory assistance and/or be relieved of particular investigations, so their efforts can be concentrated on other investigative functions.

Usually these specialists maintain a liaison with similar units attached to other agencies. In this way, efforts can be coordinated across jurisdictional boundaries.

Also, a more comprehensive record-keeping system can be maintained under special-unit conditions. Constant updating of specific crime-related data can be the basis of more thoroughgoing methods of investigation.

Table 3.1 Average Number of Full-Time Law Enforcement Officers by Size of City

Population size (number of cities used)	Average number of officers in cities	Average number of officers per 1000 inhabitants
100,000 to 249,999 (121 cities)	267	1.8
50,000 to 99,999 (308 cities)	116	1.7
25,000 to 49,999 (659 cities)	58	1.7
10,000 to 24,999 (1629 cities)	27	1.7
Under 10,000 (6570 cities)	8	2.2

SOURCE: *Source Book of Criminal Justice Statistics, 1989,* United States Department of Justice, Table 1.40.

A law enforcement agency must therefore weigh its priorities when determining its optimum effort in crime investigation. There are no specific criteria for the deployment of crime investigators. Each concerned agency must initiate a plan within its particular limitations.

As previously noted, a department's most valuable resource is manpower. The lack of this commodity constricts the manner in which the agency can perform criminal investigations.

Table 3.1 indicates that many agencies are not endowed with sufficient full-time officers to perform in-depth investigations by specialized units.

The following prototype suggests what a large law enforcement agency's detective division organizational structure could contain. An estimated projection of approximately 500 personnel is necessary to adequately staff it.

The following format was conceived and is operational for a division with primary responsibility for criminal investigation beyond the preliminary stage.

ADMINISTRATION AND SUPERVISION

The chief of detectives is in immediate command of the detective division and, as the titular head, is responsible for establishing priorities and the means by which these objectives will be effectively and efficiently accomplished. The chief of detectives is subordinate to the law enforcement agency executive officer and must be guided by the overall goals promulgated by the departmental administrative staff of which the chief is a member.

Officers of the rank of captain and above, assigned to the office of chief of detectives, assist in the administration and supervision of the detective division. These officers participate in the capacity of deputies to the chief and/or as commanding officers of the various subdivisions established within the division.

Each squad (unit) in the detective division has a commanding officer who is responsible for the proper and efficient operation of the unit. Some squads also have a deputy squad commander and possibly additional supervisory officers, depending on the number of personnel assigned and the type of duty performed.

DETECTIVE UNITS: THEIR DUTIES, EQUIPMENT, AND AVAILABLE SERVICES

Generally, the preliminary investigation of a crime or occurrence is conducted by the uniformed force. The detective division has the responsibility for continuing the investigation beyond the preliminary stage. Composition of the various assigned units will depend on the extent of centralization or decentralization, determined by factors of population, geography, personnel strength of the division, budget, crime rates, types of crime experienced, and objectives. [The detective division includes a combination of units conceived for both specialization and preliminary investigation.]

OFFICE OF CHIEF OF DETECTIVES

This office is particularly charged with and responsible for the administration and supervision of the detective division. It is staffed by the chief of detectives, the chief's deputies, and supervisory officers detailed as commanding officers of the various principal subdivisions of this division.

PRECINCT DETECTIVE SQUADS

The number of precinct detective squads will depend on the size of the department and the number of precincts (zones) into which it is subdivided. These squads can be organized in independent divisions, entitled North/South, East/West, or whatever geographic or numerical/alpha designation is considered appropriate.

Precinct detectives are the "front-line troops" of the detective division. One squad is assigned to and works from each of the various precinct station houses. Because of their front-line status, their personnel resources should not be diminished when and if a financial crisis affects the hiring practices of the agency. Precinct detective squads must be able to function effectively even if the more selective special units have to be curtailed in personnel.

These squads conduct the initial investigation of most crimes and occurrences referred to the detective division for investigation.

Cases of a specialized, complex, or technical nature, are, in turn, referred to detectives of organized crime squads, special squads, major offense squads, and/or the technical service bureau. The precinct squad detective originally responsible for the "squeal" (investigation) can be temporarily assigned to the concerned special unit, in accordance with the conditions and priorities of the investigation.

Detectives assigned to organized crime squads, special squads, major offense squads, and technical service bureau, generally investigate one type of crime or groups of related crimes or occurrences; however, when the need arises, personnel assigned to these units can be assigned anywhere within the detective division.

ORGANIZED CRIME SQUADS

Included in this category are the rackets squad, the vice squad, and the narcotics squad. They are responsible for specialized crime investigation and are grouped for specific emphasis on the investigation of organized crime.

The Rackets Squad. An investigative and enforcement unit, the rackets squad can operate in association with the district attorney's/prosecutor's office. Functions of this unit occasionally overlap with those of the unit responsible for gathering criminal intelligence. The rackets squad serves in the following capacities:

1. It conducts investigations of organized-crime activities, with particular emphasis on labor racketeering, hijacking, loan sharking (other than gambling), untaxed cigarettes, union strikes, and picketing.
2. It provides investigative personnel to the district attorney's complaint bureau and the grand jury as required.
3. It assists the district attorney's commercial frauds bureau and official corruption bureau with investigative personnel and expertise in the investigative field when necessary.
4. It compiles and stores, and disseminates when necessary, pertinent intelligence information concerning the activities of members of organized crime.
5. It conducts selected surveillances of major organized-crime figures.
6. It conducts investigations into any criminal activity (excluding vice or narcotics) reported to a precinct when the suspect is an organized-crime figure. Vice or narcotics activity would be reported to the respective squads.

The Vice Squad. An investigative and enforcement unit, the vice squad can operate in association with the district attorney's/prosecutor's office for investigation and undercover operations regarding vice and gambling. These investigations can stem from vice reports submitted by members of the police department and other law enforcement agencies, as well as civilian or anonymous complaints, which may encompass prostitution, obscenity, pornography, gambling, loan sharking (where related to gambling activity), and other organized-crime activities.

The Narcotics Squad. Charged with enforcement of laws pertaining to controlled substances, the narcotics squad investigates reports and established cases related to the unlawful use, possession, and sale of narcotic drugs, hallucinogens, depressants, stimulants, and the various forms of cannabis. In addition, it performs intelligence-gathering, patrol, surveillance, and undercover activities, and includes an Rx unit that investigates violation of the public health law. The latter focuses on stolen, forged, and falsely uttered prescriptions, and monitors the dispensing of controlled substances by those licensed to do so.

The squad maintains a very close and active liaison with federal, state, and other narcotics agencies in its intelligence and enforcement roles, participates in drug identification training for educators, and acts as an advisor to state and local medical agencies. It also has a close relationship with drug rehabilitation agencies.

The narcotics squad maintains a suspect file—an alphabetical listing of all known or suspected users or dealers in dangerous drugs—and provides an analysis service, supervising the police commissioner's program whereby parents, teachers, and other concerned persons may anonymously turn in suspect substances to be analyzed for narcotic content.

SPECIAL SQUADS

This group of squads is responsible for specialized crime investigation and supportive services to other units of the detective division.

The Automobile Squad. Assisting precinct detective squads and the uniformed force in the investigation of lost, stolen, recovered, and found automobiles, this squad concentrates its activities on organized professional auto theft rings dealing in cars and parts, maintains surveillance of areas where there are heavy losses, and inspects used car lots and premises of junk dealers for stolen items. It also maintains a very close and active liaison with federal and state agencies, the national Auto Theft Bureau, and the International Association of Automobile Theft Investigators in its intelligence and enforcement role.

The automobile squad keeps on hand the following files, references, items, and special equipment: (1) Automobile "Mug" Book (photos of autos from 1959 to the present); (2) Price Book (official used-car valuation book for 1966 models to the present); (3) Known Auto Thieves file (all known car thieves indexed alphabetically, including photos, if available); (4) Out-of-state motor vehicle department telephone listings; and (5) Tools for unlocking car doors—slam hammers, keys, and other devices.

The Forgery Squad. This squad is responsible for conducting investigations into forgeries, grand larcenies, and frauds against banking institutions and cases involving fraudulent checks. It maintains liaison with major credit card companies, banking institutions, clearinghouses, and protective associations. It keeps a master file on all forgers, forgery suspects, and fraudulent check violators. This file also contains a description of all lost or stolen checks, credit cards, and other commercial instruments from information received daily through police and private sources.

The Fugitive Squad. This squad receives, records, retains, and is responsible for the execution of warrants dealing with petty offenses, probation violations, DWI (driving while intoxicated) misdemeanor violations, and parole violations. It enforces fugitive warrants and assists other detective squads in the arraignment and processing of fugitives wanted for crimes in other states. The fugitive squad also keeps a numerical listing of warrants forwarded to precinct squads and other detective units as well as maintaining a liaison with the warrant section, and records bureau.

The Property Recovery Squad. It conducts investigations at pawn shops, secondhand dealers, jewelers, and so on to recover property reported lost or stolen. It forwards reports to precinct detective squads, the burglary squad and the bureau of special operations regarding property sold to pawn shops and secondhand dealers, together with the names and addresses of the persons who sold these goods. If these persons have prior criminal records, it is noted on the reports.

The squad maintains daily liaison with adjacent police departments in regard to property recovery, as well as keeping a central file on all property lost, stolen, or found within the municipal jurisdiction—indexed by type of property, serial numbers, or other identifying data—and an alphabetical file of all persons doing business with pawn shops or secondhand dealers within the municipal jurisdiction.

The Bomb Squad. This squad enforces all laws relative to the field of explosives, dangerous substances, dangerous articles, gases, and radioactive materials and is responsible for the defusing of bombs and explosive devices and for rendering harmless dangerous substances, dangerous articles, gases, and radioactive materials. It is also responsible for the safeguarding and storage of volatile evidence and giving court testimony in regard to this evidence.

The bomb squad investigates the following: (1) technical aspects of explosions, bombs, and explosives, and so on; (2) all injuries resulting from explosions of bombs, devices, substances, articles, or gases, and from radiation; (3) applicants for permits to display fireworks, to conduct commercial blasting, and for pyrotechnic and rocket displays; (4) ammunition and powder sales; (5) firearms problems with dealers and gunsmiths; (6) federal violations in regard to firearms; (7) pistol and rifle ranges and their safety and construction; and (8) firearms turned in at headquarters or shipped to local terminals of Federal Express, United Parcel Service, or other common carriers.

The squad maintains a liaison with the following agencies: (1) Bureau of Alcohol, Tobacco and Firearms—firearms and explosions; (2) Federal Bureau of Investigation (FBI)—explosions and statistics regarding bomb threats; (3) FBI Bomb Data Program—bombs, explosions, and bomb technical data relative to the field of explosives; (4) International Association of Bomb Technicians and Investigators—exchange of pertinent information throughout the free world.

It is responsible for the coordination of escorts and control of radioactive-materials flow into and through the local jurisdiction. For this purpose, the bomb squad maintains liaison with the Nuclear Regulatory Commission, civil defense agencies, state health department radiation control and local health department radiation control.

This command maintains and operates special equipment relative to its responsibility in the field of explosives. This equipment includes: (1) portable X-ray machines capable of fluoroscopy and polaroid X-ray pictures through objects of up to 1-inch-thick steel; (2) cryogenic (supercold) equipment that permits the freezing of bombs and their internal components; (3) a bomb equipment truck that carries special equipment relating to explosives; and (4) a tractor and trailer that carries a special bomb-transport vessel. The squad participates in training, instruction, and assistance to outside public and private agencies in the explosives field as well as in bomb-threat security problems.

The Main Office. This office is manned 24 hours a day, 7 days a week, and serves as a reception, information, and coordination center for the entire detective division and as the keeper of various supplies and equipment, including a tape-lettering machine for making identification tags; polaroid camera and film; binoculars; gasoline credit and auto rental cards, leg irons and waist-restraining chains; handcuffs for mass-arrest situations; shotguns and machine guns and ammunition for both; tear gas gun with shells, gas grenades and smoke grenades; gas masks and bullet-proof vests; computer warrant terminal; motor-vehicle computer terminal; detective division radio; refrigerator for storing perishable evidence; night-vision device for night surveillance and hostage situations; evidence lockers; disaster and mass-arrest kits; microfilm reader; telephone punch cards for emergency mobilization of detective division personnel; monitored telephone for special investigations; inquiry capability into court defendant tracking system.

The main office is also the repository for the following reference material: (1) *Coles Directory*—cross-referenced directory of listed telephone numbers and addresses in the local jurisdiction; (2) *McKinney's Books of State Statutes*; (3) procedure books for emergency mobilization; (4) detective division orders from 1952 to present; (5) commissioner's orders from 1946 to present; (6) miscellaneous local and national maps; (7) master roster of detective division personnel; (8) general information directory of phone numbers and liaison procedures regarding district attorney, Legal Aid Society, and relevant government agencies; and (9) *United States Identification Manual.*

MAJOR-OFFENSE SQUADS

The squads in this category are responsible for the investigation of major crimes and are grouped accordingly.

The Arson Squad. In cooperation with the fire marshall's office, this squad investigates incendiary fires, fires of undetermined origin, and false alarms. It maintains the following files: (1) *location file*—all reported fires are filed under fire district location; (2) *date and time file*—all reported fires are filed according to date and time of occurrence; (3) *owner-occupant file*—owners or occupants of all premises that have reported a fire loss are filed under both the business names and the names of the persons involved; and (4) *suspect file*—all persons causing or suspected of causing a fire to occur, are filed by name.

The Burglary Squad. This squad assists precinct detective squads in the investigation of major burglaries or a concentration of burglaries in a given area. It also maintains liaison with and coordinates burglary investigations between precinct detective squads and other law enforcement agencies. It is responsible for the follow-up investigation of all burglaries involving safes and maintains surveillance of known or suspected burglars, conducting day and night patrols in high-frequency locations. The squad conducts security surveys of public buildings and advises of preventive techniques to safeguard against burglaries. It also gives lectures for citizens groups as part of a burglary prevention program.

The burglary squad maintains the following files and equipment: (1) *suspect file*—lists known or suspected burglars alphabetically, with photos attached when available; (2) *suspect file by village of residence*—lists known or suspected burglars by village of residence, alphabetically; (3) *burglary file*—lists all burglaries occurring in the local jurisdiction during the current year, classified as business or residential and filed chronologically by village of occurrence; and (4) *lock-picking devices*—for use by members of the squad only, as these implements require special manipulative skills.

The Homicide Squad. This squad investigates deaths, or serious injury likely to result in death, in the following categories: (1) criminal violence or assault; (2) accidents in which criminal negligence may be involved; (3) vehicle, railroad, airplane, and boat accidents; (4) suicides; (5) drownings; (6) sudden death, or death occurring under any suspicious or unusual circumstances; (7) all deaths during confinement in jail or in detention cells.

It maintains a liaison with the medical examiner's/coroner's office and the homicide bureau of the district attorney's office as well as keeping a complete homicide index file, alphabetically arranged by last name of decedent and year of death, on all deaths occurring in local jurisdiction that are investigated by the police department.

The Robbery Squad. This unit assists precinct detective squads in the investigation of robberies. It also maintains liaison with and coordinates investigations between precinct squads and other law enforcement agencies and keeps surveillance on known or suspected robbers and conducts patrols and stakeouts in high-frequency locations.

It maintains the following files and services: (1) suspect file—alphabetical listing (cross-indexed with photographs, when available) of all perpetrators of robberies in local jurisdiction, or perpetrators of robberies anywhere if their residence is in local jurisdiction; (2) robbery location file—lists all robberies committed in local jurisdiction, broken down by type (gas station, bank, and so on), precinct of occurrence, race and number of perpetrators, weapons displayed or used, and oddities; (3) bank file—contains photographs of exteriors of banks in local jurisdiction with internal-security details and names and addresses of managers or security officers.

The Special-Investigations Squad. This unit is assigned to and responsible for special or extraordinary investigations. In addition, it conducts previsit investigations and security planning; and provides security for local appearances of governmental and other dignitaries, as well as policing any planned large-scale public gathering within the local jurisdiction, to ensure the safety of life and property.

It maintains the following files: (1) *known subversives/extremists file*—cross-referenced and indexed both alphabetically by last names of individuals and by names of the groups, if any, to which the individuals belong; (2) *motorcycle groups file*; and (3) *aerial photograph file*—aerial photographs depicting various locations throughout the local jurisdiction in which large-scale public gatherings have occurred or are likely to occur, for planning security arrangements.

The squad also includes a sex-crimes unit. This unit assists in investigations of all sex crimes and is responsible for interviewing female victims. All sex-crime reports are received from precinct detective squads daily. Information is taken from these reports to provide an overall picture of sex-crime occurrences within the local jurisdiction. This unit also gives lectures, by request, on "Defensive Tactics for Women" and "Sex Crimes (Warning to Women)."

It maintains the following files: (1) sex offender file—photographs of known sex offenders; (2) information file on sex offenders and their modus operandi; and (3) confidence game file on confidence-games offenders and their modus operandi.

TECHNICAL SERVICE BUREAU

The units of this bureau are responsible for the more technical and scientific aspects of crime investigation. Many departments do not have sworn members who possess the talent and expertise to perform highly technical functions. Therefore, within this area lateral entry occurs and civilian employees are often used.

The Crime Scene Search Unit. Responsibility is for processing crime scenes for physical evidence. Crime scene personnel are not expert in any one field, but are knowledgeable in many. Their functioning can be enhanced by sufficient information about the crime they are investigating. Therefore, it is necessary that the detective investigation officers be aware of their role and cooperate by informing them adequately on the incident. Its basic operation is on a "first-call, first-service" basis. Certain exceptions must exist to this priority, however, including homicide, bank robbery, and violent sex offenses.

The crime scene search unit is responsible for the following services: (1) conducting all crime scene and aerial crime scene photography; (2) searching for, photographing, and lifting latent fingerprints; (3) recovering bullets, fragments, and casings; (4) casting footprints, tire marks, and toolmarks; (5) recovering paint scrapings; (6) swabbing for gunpowder residue; (7) testing for and recovering blood evidence; (8) recovering flammables; (9) measuring and sketching the crime scene; (10) marking evidence and transporting it to the latent fingerprint unit and scientific investigation bureau; (11) using a metal detector to recover hidden articles; (12) sweeping scenes with an "evidence" vacuum cleaner; (13) gathering hair and fiber samples; (14) taking fingernail scrapings of suspects and victims; (15) photographing and sketching scenes of fatal auto accidents; (16) fingerprinting and photographing arrested persons confined to hospitals; (17) fingerprinting and photographing deceased persons at medical examiner/coroner morgue; and (18) collecting evidence from postbombing situations.

Latent Fingerprint Unit. Latent fingerprint evidence that is discovered at the scene of a crime by either the investigating officer or the crime-scene search unit personnel will eventually come into the possession of this unit for the purpose of further developing and then evaluating this evidential matter by both conventional and chemical methods.

This unit supplies the following services and facilities: (1) facility for photographing evidence and all types of latent prints; (2) identification of the person responsible for the latent prints discovered at the scene, an operation including "elimination" prints of the complainant, members of complainant's family, visitors, and so on, who might have had legitimate access to the crime scene (normally a manual operation but, when budget allows, can be computerized for a more thorough search and discovery); (3) obtaining classifiable fingerprints of deceased persons who bear no immediate means of identification, including fingerprints obtained from tissue damaged or in early stages of decomposition; (4) identification of palmprints and footprints; (5) processing motor vehicles for latent prints; (6) supplying fingerprint powders and lifts to all precinct, organized-crime, special, and major-offense squads; and (7) developing latent prints on human skin.

Photography Unit. The photography unit maintains and operates the photography laboratory. Its primary functions are to process all departmental negatives and to make copies and/or enlargements as required. Photographic assignments consist of taking and supplying publicity, aerial and other evidence (jewelry, weapons, and so on) photographs; developing a departmental color slide program; and preparing photo brochures and exhibits.

It is responsible for: (1) inspecting, maintaining, and repairing departmental photo equipment; (2) ordering all photographic supplies for the department; (3) operating the identification camera for the departmental identification photo file; (4) photocopying sketches, departmental flyers and forms, documents, and photographs; (5) maintaining a negative file of crime scene and prisoner photos by identification number; and (6) preparing composite drawings of suspects or perpetrators.

Scientific Investigation Bureau (Laboratory). This bureau consists of six sections: (1) biology, (2) criminalistics, (3) document examination, (4) firearms, (5) controlled substances analysis, and (6) toxicology. Each is responsible for a particular technical investigative function.

The biology section's responsibilities are continually being expanded due to new and innovative technology advancements within this field.

A unique, and probably the eventual major breakthrough in personal identification is being developed in the field of serology. This technique is DNA analysis of blood and body fluids. DNA profiling is a powerful scientific tool used to identify the source of biological evidence by matching it with samples from a victim or suspect. The best sources of DNA are blood and seminal fluid but muscle tissue, hair roots, bone, and dental pulp can also be used. Saliva, urine, and tears are not normally useful.

This genetic means of identification provides the best evidence in cases of sexual assaults. Mixtures of vaginal and seminal fluids can almost routinely be separated using this technology.

Additional responsibilities include: (1) blood identification by major blood group typing; (2) identification of minor blood groups; (3) isoenzyme identification by electrophoretic methods for the purpose of further analysis of blood types; (4) bloodstain pattern examination to determine origin and direction of blood spatters; (5) spermatozoa identification; (6) differentiation of seminal and vaginal fluids; (7) major grouping (ABO) of same; (8) salivary amylase examination for saliva identification; (9) major grouping (ABO) of body fluids; (10) differentiation of hair species (human, animal, or synthetics); (11) race identification by hair samples; (12) comparison of evidence hair with known standards; and (13) examination of crime scenes and preservation of evidence in certain cases.

The criminalistics section provides chemical analysis in the following areas: (1) examination of flammables in arson cases for identification and flash-point determination, (2) blood-alcohol analysis for DWI; (3) examination of alcoholic beverages; (4) examination and identification of poisons; (5) gunpowder and gunshot residues; (6) paint scrapings; (7) metals; and (8) sneak thief detection powders and other substances.

The section has the following responsibilities relative to physical evidence: (1) identification of glass fragments and determination of direction of fracture; (2) fiber identification; and (3) identification and comparison of foot, heel, and tire impressions.

The document examination section examines documents to: (1) determine age; (2) restore charred or water-damaged papers; (3) identify paper; (4) identify writing material; (5) restore erasures, eradications, obliterations, or alterations; and (6) make handwriting and handprinting comparisons. The documents section has the two following additional responsibilities: (1) Polygraph—uses a Stoelting desk model "Deceptograph" and a Stoelting "Arthur IV" polygraph to determine truth and deception as an investigative aid and not as evidence in court. Oral or written statements made during or after a polygraph examination are, however, admissible as evidence in court. Written consent of the person to be tested must be obtained before a polygraph examination is conducted. Juveniles must have permission or consent from a parent or legal guardian. (2) Voice Identification—uses a Base Ten Systems Voice Scan Spectrograph, Model LGK-100, for an investigative recording of speakers' voices by the voiceprint technique.

The firearms section is responsible for: (1) identifying firearms and their working condition; (2) determining possible source of case or identifying type of firearm it came from; (3) chemical testing for gunshot residue—neutron activation analyses (NAA); (4) restoring obliterated serial numbers; (5) comparing toolmark impressions with recovered tools; (6) identifying pick marks on lock cylinders; (7) test patterns to determine distance firearm was held from victim at time of discharge; (8) assisting in recovery of firearms evidence at crime scenes; (9) liaison with firearms manufacturers and dealers in regard to the sale and history of particular weapons; and (10) liaison with other law enforcement agencies in major crimes involving firearms.

The controlled substances analysis section performs quantitative and qualitative analyses of controlled substances and, in the Anonymous Analysis Program, tests samples of substances submitted anonymously by schools and concerned parents for controlled substance content.

The toxicology section is responsible for urine and blood alcohol analysis relating to the suspected operation of a motor vehicle while under the influence of a controlled substance and/or alcohol.

DETECTIVE DIVISION
SUMMARY

It is evident that numerous investigative functions are performed by the various units within a law enforcement agency. It is, therefore, imperative that there be cooperative coordination of the efforts of all the units involved in each criminal investigation to bring it to a successful conclusion.

4

Traditional Public Police

James J. Fyfe

American police are a peculiar institution indeed. They are unique in the country because they are entrusted with greater powers—the authority to arrest and to use force—than any other group. They are also unique among police because they are so decentralized. Police in all other Western countries are either formally coordinated or directed by the national government, but almost all American police report directly only to state or local governments. At this writing, England, for example, has but 43 police departments, all of which receive direction (and a large part of their funding) from that country's Home Office. In the United States, local police are independent of the national government, and it is doubtful that anyone even knows how many police agencies there are. In 1967, the blue-ribbon President's Commission of Law Enforcement and the Administration of Justice was unable to make a more definite statement than the estimate that there are *approximately* 40,000 separate police agencies in this country.

If determining the number of American police agencies is challenging, defining their job is equally difficult. Most of those who have studied American police argue that "law enforcement" is not an adequate description of the police role. To bolster this argument, they point out that police spend most of their time involved in nonenforcement activities and that police overlook as many violations of law as they enforce. Recent definitions of the police, therefore, describe them as "order maintainers," as "social workers," as "community managers," as "street corner politicians," as "a means for enforcing the status quo," and as "a mechanism for the distribution of situationally justified force in society." While some of these definitions reflect differences that are more ideological than real, it is obvious that few students of the police regard them as "law enforcement officers." But that should not be surprising to those familiar with the history of American police: It is doubtful that the police have ever really been law enforcement officers.

THE POLICE: EVOLUTION AND HISTORY

Except for the degree to which they are fragmented, American police are generally modeled after those in England. In that country, police departments were organized in the early nineteenth century as a result of concern over *riots* rather than *crime*. The establishment of police departments was a traumatic experience in England; because crime control there had traditionally been a function of the citizenry and because paid police were generally considered a threat to zealously guarded civil liberties. In the end, however, English police departments were established to serve as a less drastic and less symbolically oppressive alternative to military control of riots. Because an earlier small, paid, semipublic police force in London (the "Bow Street Runners") had been very successful in recovering stolen property, police were also given some carefully limited crime control powers.

Early police departments in both England and the United States were, and remain, generally based on military models of organization. In addition to the benefits of military structure (in terms of fixed authority and command structure) during periods of civil disorder, the military model was perceived as offering the best protection against abuse of police authority. This is so because the military organizational model is characterized by civilian control. Just as the military are directed by and accountable to a civilian president (or monarch), the police are directed by and accountable to a civilian mayor, governor, or other executive.

Like most designs originated for one purpose and adopted for another, the military model has not been an unqualified success among the police. Many argue that the present role of the police—however it is defined—has little to do with the original police mandate to suppress riots. They argue that the military model allows for little discretion among those on the front line and is appropriate during riots but very inappropriate for the day-to-day work of the modern police officer. The military model, in other words, works well during war and riots where the job is "theirs not to reason why, theirs but to do and die"; but it does little to assist patrol officers or investigators in the decisions they most often face.

Furthermore, the concept of civilian control has been a troubling one for much of American police history. Many police view attempts at civilian control as political pressure or as City Hall interference in a job that "should be done by professionals." Some government executives apparently agree: in many American jurisdictions, mayors have washed their hands of the operations of their police after having been elected to office by promising a "strong, independent police force." While such a relationship is usually a reaction to prior political abuses, it also misses the point. The police are *supposed* to be controlled by and accountable to the electorate. Since police organization is based on the military model, it is no more acceptable for a mayor to allow a strong, independent chief a free hand in determining police policies than it would be for a president to wash his hands of the military and to leave national defense policies in the hands of strong, independent generals.

THE POLICE: POWERS AND LIMITATIONS

Safeguards on police powers are a necessity because those powers are so broad. The power to arrest and to detain allows police to deprive citizens of liberty, the power to search and to seize allows police to deprive citizens of property, and the power to use force allows police to deprive citizens of life. Such broad authority can be permitted to run unchecked only in a totalitarian society.

In addition to direct control exerted by civilian executives, checks on American police involve both the legislative and judicial branches of government. The legislature defines and limits police powers by enacting written, or statute, laws. The courts define and limit police powers by applying statute law to specific cases, by determining whether police actions fall within acceptable boundaries, and by providing a means of redress to citizens who feel that they have been wronged by police.

Statute Law and The Police

The Constitution. The fundamental American written law, of course, is the U.S. Constitution. This document reflects the founding fathers' concern with civil liberties. Most generally, it leaves most government operations (including policing) in the hands of state and local governments, where, it was felt, they would be most responsive to the wishes of the citizenry. The colonists had revolted because of what they viewed as the excesses of a remote government; consequently, they provided in the Constitution that the federal government would have only those powers granted to it by the states.

On a more specific level, the Constitution contains several provisions that deal directly with powers now exercised by the police. The Fourth Amendment, for example, requires that a warrant be obtained from a magistrate before the person or property of a citizen is "searched or seized" (arrested). This provision, however, was written at a time when paid police departments were nonexistent and has since been broadened considerably to accommodate the practicalities of American policing: as we shall see, court interpretations of the constitutionality, or reasonableness of given searches and seizures have since created many exceptions to the warrant requirement. On the other hand, we shall see that police crime-control efforts have also been limited in many ways since the Constitution was signed. The restrictions of the Fourth Amendment and the rest of the Bill of Rights were written to apply only to the *federal* government and, except for the citizens' right to seek redress through civil suit, no means were provided to penalize officials who violated them. It was not until much later that the courts ruled that illegally seized evidence would be inadmissible in criminal trials and the Fourteenth Amendment applied the Bill of Rights to state and local policing as well as to federal law enforcement.

State Constitutions and Laws. As just noted, the U.S. Constitution grants the states the right to establish their own constitutions and to pass laws defining criminal conduct and the powers of their police and courts. As a result, there is some variation in criminal law in this country and, until federal courts became involved in the administration of justice by state and local governments, there was comparatively little uniformity in police powers and procedures across the states.

The Courts and the Police

The courts control police conduct in several ways. First, and most obvious, local *trial courts* judge the legitimacy of police actions in all cases brought before them. Second, these same courts may initiate criminal prosecutions against police officers who have committed criminal offenses in the course of their duties. Third, *civil courts* may entertain suits against police departments or individual officers alleged to have committed wrongs under color of their law enforcement powers. Fourth, *appeals courts* may subject police actions to the test of constitutional reasonableness and may enunciate principles that limit the manner in which police may attempt to enforce the laws in the future (for example, the *Miranda* decision).

Limits on the Courts. Before discussing the real effects of the courts on police activities, a consideration of the degree to which the courts are limited in controlling the police is appropriate. The major limitation is the fact that courts may not take action unless police abuses are officially called to their attention. Trial courts, for example, can do little to control police misconduct that does not result in arrest. The actions of a police officer who brutalizes and illegally searches a narcotics addict cannot be reviewed by a trial court unless the addict is arrested. Even if an arrest is effected, it is most likely that the circumstances of the arrest will not come to court attention. Instead, it is probable that the addict's attorney will advise a plea of guilty to whatever charge is lodged, on the grounds that the court is more likely to believe the sworn testimony of the officer than that of the addict. Furthermore, because very few criminal convictions are appealed, it is rare for alleged police abuses to come to the attention of appeals courts. Also, because courts are reluctant to severely penalize police for being too zealous in doing their jobs, they are not likely to initiate a criminal case against the police or to recommend that an arrestee (who is likely to be less than a pillar of the community) sue the officer.

Even if a trial court judge does refer a suspected criminal violation by a police officer to the prosecutor, it is unlikely that much will come of it. Prosecutors enjoy wide discretion, limited only by their perception of the "interests of justice." In addition, the success of prosecutors is largely dependent on the quality of their relationship with the police (who bring them cases and often serve as prosecutors' investigators). Therefore, prosecutors may well decide that jeopardizing that relationship by prosecuting an individual officer for an excess in the line of duty is not in the interests of justice. That such a sentiment exists among prosecutors is suggested by the rarity of criminal cases brought against police for line-of-duty actions. Since 1921, for example, it has been a misdemeanor for federal officers to take part in illegal searches and seizures. Since that time, many federal criminal cases have been dismissed on the grounds that evidence was obtained in illegal searches, but prosecutions against the officers involved are unheard of.

Even in cases serious enough to convince the prosecutor that the interests of justice demand that criminal charges be brought against police, convictions are very unlikely. It has been pointed out that police officers are professional witnesses, and that those whose rights police are most likely to abuse in a criminal manner are, in fact, somewhat shady characters. The prosecutor's problem in a case of an unjustifiable shooting by an on-duty police officer, for example, boils down to convincing the jury that the officer (who passed an intensive screening before joining the police, whose life has been risked for the public, who usually has a family and responsibilities, who has character witnesses, and who is neat and well-spoken) is guilty beyond a reasonable doubt of criminally shooting the accuser (who usually has a record of involvement with the law and who is usually unemployed, unattached, and shifty eyed). Obviously, juries are reluctant to convict officers in such cases.

For the same reason, juries are not likely to decide civil actions brought against police in favor of plaintiffs. Nothing prevents such suits, which are often based on section 1983 of the U.S. Code, which states:

> Every person who, under color of any statute, ordinance, regulation, custom, or usage, of any state or territory, subjects or causes to be subjected, any citizen of the United States or other person within the jurisdiction thereof to the deprivation of any rights, privileges or immunities secured by the Constitution and laws, shall be liable to the party injured in an action at law, suit in equity, or other proper proceedings for redress.

As the Supreme Court has noted, however, the citizen's chances of winning a substantial award from police as a result of a suit filed under section 1983 are "worthless and futile." This is so because, in addition to the reasons cited above, officers (and their departments) are not liable under section 1983 if they have acted in good faith and with probable cause while committing acts alleged by citizens to have violated their rights.

It is not often, therefore, that individual officers are sued as a result of their professional activities. Moreover, even when such cases against police are successful, it is rare that officers themselves are liable for damages. Most jurisdictions provide attorneys and assume liability for officers sued as a result of actions that did not violate internal departmental regulations.

On the other hand, while the actual number of suits against government for police actions remains small, such actions are increasing. For many years, many of the actions brought against police departments (rather than individual officers) sought injunctions against the continuation of illegal practices (for example, indiscriminate searches, harassment) encouraged by police policy makers. More recently, however, damages have been sought from police departments alleged to have failed to control the actions of officers. More specifically, there has recently been an increase in suits against police departments that have failed to dismiss or to remove from field duty those officers with histories of questionable violence, instability, or alcoholism. It is at present likely that a department employing an officer known to have such a background, who has shot someone under questionable circumstances, will be sued for permitting the officer to retain a weapon and enforcement powers. The logic of such actions, of course, is that they will encourage police departments to better police themselves.

Appeals Courts and Case Law. While suits against police departments are increasing, it is probable that the major court check on police authority is the power of appeals courts to make *case law*.

It was noted earlier that American police are based on an English model. So, too, are American courts, which early in colonial history based decisions on the precedents of English *common law*. This common law is a set of legal principles derived from the unwritten decisions of English magistrates. These principles guided the courts in deciding cases brought before them, and involved many presumptions (for example, "The accused is presumed innocent until proven guilty"; "A man's home is his castle") incorporated into the Bill of Rights. American courts continue to operate on the basis of such precedents, which currently include the decisions of appeals courts, called "case law." These opinions are now written and usually include lengthy explanations of the reasoning behind decisions. Thus, although case law changes with court opinions and interpretations, it serves to introduce consistency into judicial decisions.

Many of the principles enunciated in appeals court decisions alter and define police power within their jurisdiction. Even though the Supreme Court has national jurisdiction, for many years it (and other federal appeals courts) followed a hands-off policy where the administration of state and local justice were concerned. This policy remained operative even after the passage of the Fourteenth Amendment, which applied "due process" guarantees to state and local criminal cases. In *Weeks v. United States*, 232 U.S. 383, 58 L.ED. 652, 34 S. Ct. 341 (1914), for example, the Supreme Court decided that "evidence illegally seized by *federal* law enforcement officers is to be excluded from *federal* prosecutions [emphasis added]." Left to individual state appeals courts, therefore, was the question of whether the same rule applied to police in their jurisdictions. Until the Supreme Court's 1961 decision that the "exclusionary rule" was also applicable to state and local criminal trials (*Mapp v. Ohio*, 367 U.S. 643, 6 L.ED. 2d 1081, 81 S. Ct. 1684), illegally seized evidence was admissible in the trial courts of many states.

The Supreme Court as a Control on State and Local Police. The Supreme Court's progression from *Weeks* to *Mapp* provides a good example of the philosophy of federal appeals courts regarding law enforcement practices. The operation of the hands-off policy illustrated by the *Weeks* decision slowly changed to the courts' more recent general assumption that "police will do anything unless we prohibit it." Federal appeals courts became involved in the administration of state and local justice only after observing practices that they felt "shocked the consciences" and "outraged the sensibilities of reasonable men."

The *Weeks* decision was grounded in the Supreme Court's belief that the only effective way to encourage federal police to refrain from illegal searches was to remove their incentive to do so by excluding illegally obtained evidence from trials. What the Court apparently did not anticipate, however, was that federal law enforcement officers would find and exploit a loophole in the wording of their decision: "Evidence illegally seized by *federal* officers is inadmissible ... [emphasis added]." Shortly after *Weeks*, federal officers began introducing into criminal trials evidence illegally seized by *state* and *local* officers at the encouragement of federal officers. While many courts thought this practice (called the "Silver Platter Doctrine") was imaginative police work, they also regarded it as a violation of the spirit of the *Weeks* decision. In 1960, therefore, the Supreme Court ruled in the case of *Eilkins v. United States*, 364 U.S. 206 that *all* illegally seized evidence is inadmissible in federal courts. In 1961, it applied the same rule to all state and local trials.

The progress of Supreme Court decisions involving police interrogations is also enlightening. First, these decisions provide an excellent example of the Court's move away from the philosophy of "hands off." Second, this series of decisions moves from *proscription*—the Court telling the police what they *cannot* do if they wish to introduce the results of interrogations into criminal trials—to *prescription*—the court telling the police in very specific terms what they *must* do if they wish to introduce the results of interrogations into trials. Third, although many regard court controls in this area as a handcuff on police effectiveness, the fact is that recent Supreme Court decisions involving interrogation affect only a minuscule number of police cases.

The 1936 case of *Brown v. Mississippi*, 297 U.S. 278, began the Supreme Court's review of interrogations by state and local police. The case involved a man arrested and charged after having confessed a murder to the police. His attorneys, however, felt strongly that the manner in which police had obtained the confession "shocked the conscience," and appealed Brown's conviction up through the U.S. Supreme Court. After finding that Brown had been held by the police in a field, where he was beaten, threatened, hanged by the neck from a tree, and released for a couple of days before again undergoing the same inducement to confess, the Supreme Court agreed, and reversed Brown's conviction. It was not until 1936, therefore, that the Supreme Court held admissions and confessions obtained by *torture* to be inadmissible in state courts.

During the years following the *Brown* decision, the Supreme Court placed more limits on local police interrogations. In 1940, it ruled that a confession obtained after five days of prolonged police interrogation and other "nonviolent deprivations" was the result of a coercive inquisition and should not be admitted. In 1961, it broadened the definition of coercion to include police behavior "such as to overbear [the suspect's] will to resist to bring about confessions not freely determined." In 1963, the Court ruled in *Gideon v. Wainwright*, 372 U.S. 335, that all criminal defendants were entitled to legal counsel at their trials. In 1964, the Court held that this right would be meaningless if defendants had already confessed to the police before they came to trial. They ruled, therefore, that a police interrogation of a suspect in custody was a "critical stage" of the case against the suspect, who therefore could not be denied permission to confer with an attorney at that point. The Court decided, in *Miranda v. Arizona*, 384 U.S. 436, 16 L.ED. 2d 694, 86 S. Ct. 1602 (1966), that police must advise *all* suspects of their rights to silence and counsel before attempting custodial interrogation. This decision also required police to inform suspects without attorneys that the police would provide them with counsel before questioning.

The *Miranda* decision is widely perceived as detrimental to effective investigation. What is interesting, however, is that federal investigative agencies have quietly labored under similar restraints since 1897, as a result of the Supreme Court's decision in the case of *Bram v. United States*, 168 U.S. 352. Furthermore, *Miranda* does not exclude statements "blurted out" by suspects before police have had a reasonable opportunity to advise them of their rights. Neither does it exclude statements made by persons not in custody, or physical or testimonial evidence obtained independent of questioning.

If, for example, there are witnesses to a murder and police arrest the suspect, seize the weapon, find other physical evidence, and subsequently obtain a confession without advising the suspect of his or her rights, the only evidence that will be excluded from court is the confession and any evidence derived from it. Since it is not unconstitutional to be caught red-handed, the prosecutor should still succeed in obtaining a conviction based on physical evidence and eyewitness testimony, independent of the confession.

Most generally, therefore, *Miranda* is an important factor only in cases in which the primary evidence is statements made by the suspect *after* being taken into custody. Since most arrestees are caught red-handed and since few of those who are not would make any statement to the police with or without counsel or advice to be quiet, it affects very few cases: What suspect confesses to the police when they have no incriminating evidence? Even in the case of Miranda himself, the decision did not result in an outright *dismissal* of the charges against him: Miranda's confession was excluded, and he was retried and convicted on the basis of other evidence in the case.

It should also be noted that from the Supreme Court's perspective, what is most important in any of its landmark decisions is not the guilt or innocence of a particular defendant. The Court selects from among the many cases it is requested to review those that present the opportunity to enunciate important legal principles. When the Court first became involved in local police interrogations by deciding *Brown,* it did so not out of any particular interest in Mr. Brown personally, but in order to put police on notice that it considered torture to be an unconscionable and unconstitutional investigative technique.

The power of the Supreme Court and other appeals courts to make case law, however, is subject to structural limitations. As noted earlier, courts cannot act unless an issue is officially called to their attention. There are, for example, unsettled legal issues that members of the Supreme Court are undoubtedly anxious to address, but they cannot unless an appropriate case reaches them. There also exists the problem of lower court interpretation of high court decisions. The Supreme Court exercises no direct supervisory authority over lower courts, so that little action can be taken against judges who interpret case law in a manner not intended by higher courts. Indeed, the higher courts usually cannot even act on specific cases unless lower court decisions are appealed.

Appeals Courts and Broadened Police Powers. At this point, a balance should be struck by noting that courts have also broadened the powers of the police considerably. Over the years, the courts have permitted several exceptions to the arrest and search warrant requirements of the Constitution. The arrest powers of police are at present broader than those of ordinary citizens, which was not true when the Constitution was drafted and police as we know them did not exist. At present, police may generally arrest for felonies on the basis of *probable cause* (sufficient evidence to lead a "reasonable" person to believe that a felony was committed by the suspect). Misdemeanor arrests usually require that police have actually witnessed the crime. In both cases, however, warrants are no longer an absolute prerequisite to arrest and are, in fact, only rarely used as a basis for arrest.

Exceptions to the warranted search requirement are many. The courts recognized comparatively early that if police are expected to make on-the-spot arrests, they must also be permitted to search arrestees. The most frequent exception to the warranted search requirement, therefore, involves *searches incident to arrest.* The justifications for these searches include only the officer's right to self-protection against assault with a hidden weapon, the need to prevent escape, and the seizure of weapons or other evidence related to the crime. The courts have limited police in this area by ruling that these searches must be made as close in time to the arrest as possible. Thus, the search of a handcuffed prisoner in a police station several hours after arrest cannot be justified as a means of protecting the officer involved. The courts have also ruled that the justification for searches incident to arrest varies with the nature of the offense. Without extenuating circumstances, searches of traffic violators, for example, cannot be justified on the grounds that traffic violators are dangerous or likely to escape or that police may reasonably expect to find other evidence related to the original offense during a search.

Police are also permitted to search without warrants in *emergency situations.* In these cases, they must demonstrate in court that probable cause existed and that delaying the search in order to obtain a warrant would have created danger to life or property, or would have allowed the suspects to escape or to destroy evidence sought by police.

More detailed discussions of emergency searches and of other exceptions to the warrant requirement (for example, consent searches, searches made after "hot pursuit," automobile searches, searches of abandoned property, searches made in open fields, "inventory" searches) may be found in other chapters of this volume. For the present, however, suffice it to say that appeals courts have been reasonably well attuned to the realities of policing. They have, as in the case of the "stop, question, and frisk" decisions discussed later in this volume, increased police powers where appropriate. Conversely, they have also limited police powers where they have detected operational practices that "shock the consciences of reasonable men."

Legislative and Judicial Controls on the Police: A Summary

Although the police are an agency of the executive branch of government, it has been pointed out in this chapter that both legislative and judicial bodies exercise some control over their activities. In a government of checks and balances, this is as it should be; but most legislative and judicial attempts to control the police are very broad and are subject to varying interpretations. An appropriate example of the limits of these external controls on police is provided by the most awesome police power: The authority of the police to use deadly force, which at present almost always involves the use of police firearms.

Deadly Force. This power is derived from the English common law, which authorized the use of deadly force in "defense of life" and in order to apprehend persons committing or fleeing from felonies. In many states the "fleeing-felon" rule has been further narrowed by statute, so that the use of police firearms is limited only to defense-of-life situations and to some specific violent felonies (for example, murder, rape, aggravated assault, arson, burglary).

At first, these limits might seem rather precise and reasonable. Obviously, few reasonable persons would quarrel with the defense-of-life rule, but many do find fault with even limited fleeing-felon justifications for police use of deadly force. Most specifically, they argue that the fleeing-felon rule is overbroad, obsolete, and inconsistent with the philosophies that at present guide most of the operations of American criminal justice.

Their arguments are based on changes that have occurred since the fleeing-felon rule was incorporated into the common law. Centuries ago, they note, the fleeing-felon rule may have been defensible because *all* felonies were capital crimes. We have long since ceased executing all felons, however. Indeed, in recent years very few of those convicted of even the most heinous crimes have been executed. This precipitous drop in executions has not been accidental; the state's power to execute has been challenged and carefully reviewed at every level of government. The death penalty has been treated as an irreversible sentence, which requires that all decisions be carefully made and reviewed and that defendants be executed only after they have received every benefit of due process of law. On the other hand, police in many states are permitted to make hasty decisions "at three o'clock in the morning, in the rain" to take the lives of first-time offenders *suspected* of such felonies as burglaries of unoccupied commercial buildings and auto larceny. If apprehended and convicted, it is argued, many of these individuals would receive very minor sentences; certainly, none would be executed.

Furthermore, critics note, centuries ago the fleeing-felon rule may have been necessary to protect the lives of the unarmed citizens whose duty it was to apprehend fugitives who knew they would be executed if brought to court and convicted. In those days, therefore, there was considerable overlap between the defense-of-life and fleeing-felon rules. Just as we have long ago ceased executing all felons, however, we have long ago ceased requiring unarmed citizens to apprehend felons by engaging in hand-to-hand combat if necessary. The risk to the armed and trained police officer pursuing an unarmed auto thief is generally considerably less than it was to the unarmed and untrained citizen attempting to bring to trial a suspect to whom arrest and conviction were literally matters of life and death.

One who agrees with the critics might reasonably ask why legislatures do not exert more control over the police by enacting laws that limit the use of deadly force to defense-of-life situations. Probably, the major reason lies in the nature of legislatures: Legislators get and keep their jobs only if they win elections. It requires true courage on the part of a legislator to introduce a bill that limits police powers. Doing so exposes the legislator to charges of being "soft on crime" and trying to "handcuff the police." Just as the legislator who introduces a gay rights bill is likely to become the subject of innuendoes and emotional charges during a reelection campaign, the legislator who has "shown more interest in the rights of the criminal than in the rights of society" is likely to be attacked by "law-and-order" candidates.

Even when more restrictive legislation is enacted, it is likely to prove to be unenforceable. The only way in which violations of such legislation can be acted upon is to bring them to court. As we have already seen, however, the police agency is far more likely than the individual officer to suffer as a result of court action. The officer is not likely to be criminally prosecuted nor, if prosecuted, to be convicted, nor even to be held personally liable for the actions in question. Instead, the department is likely to assume liability both for the officer's actions and, if applicable, for failing to have acted upon prior indications of instability.

What all this means, therefore, is that the exclusionary rule remains the major nonexecutive control on the conduct of individual police officers. It also means that police agencies are well-advised to protect themselves against civil liability by closely supervising their officers and by making certain that unstable officers or those with problems are dismissed, removed from field assignments, or otherwise discouraged from violating citizens' rights. Finally, it means that individual police officers would do well to become acquainted with internal checks on their conduct.

Internal Controls on Police

Such administrative checks generally operate independently of civil or criminal actions brought against officers. They consist of internal regulations or guidelines to direct police activity (for example, deadly force regulations more restrictive than state law), means of collecting information regarding possible violations of regulations (for example, supervisory reports, internal affairs units, civilian complaint procedures), and means of enforcing the regulations (for example, internal disciplinary procedures).

Many police agencies have, for instance, promulgated guidelines that prohibit officers from shooting in some situations (for example, at unarmed fleeing suspects) in which it is permitted by law. They are then free to try officers for violations of these regulations, even though the officers have not been criminally charged or have been acquitted of criminal charges resulting from the shooting. Administrative findings of guilt in such cases may also release agencies from liability under section 1983. Many police officers, however, erroneously regard such proceedings as violations of the "double jeopardy" principle.

A Hypothetical Case. The double jeopardy issue may be clarified by the following case.

Detective Jones is employed by a large city police agency in a state where the law allows police to shoot in defense of life or to apprehend fleeing violent felons. The regulations of his employer, however, are far narrower. Jones has been very "active" throughout his police career: he has made many arrests and has had his share of troubles with headquarters. In 1972, he shot a man who had no prior involvement with the police. Jones stated that the man had acted suspiciously and had "pulled a gun" when Jones and his partner approached. The man denied this, pointing out that his alleged gun had not been found. He claimed that Jones and his partner had quickly approached him without identifying themselves, and that he, fearing he was about to be mugged, turned and ran, at which point Jones simultaneously fired and told him to stop. The weapons and attempted murder charges against the man were dismissed, and the prosecutor did not proceed with a case against Jones. The police department reprimanded Jones for his actions.

Eight months later, Jones was accused of beating a handcuffed prisoner in the back of a police station. He was again reprimanded and transferred to another unit, where he quickly distinguished himself by making many arrests. In early 1974, Jones was accused of breaking a prisoner's finger in a police car. These charges were dismissed by the department. Later that year, Jones reported sick with his own broken fingers, an injury he stated had occurred while struggling with a suspect. The suspect claimed Jones had punched and choked him in a police station. While Jones was on sick report, he shot a man in a tavern. Jones stated that the man had been drunk and disorderly and that when Jones had ordered him to be quiet, the man had pulled a knife on him. The man denied this. He complained that Jones had been drunk, had never identified himself as a police officer, and had picked a fight with him. The man claimed that when it became obvious that he was getting the better of Jones, Jones pulled his gun and fired. The man, who had been arrested previously, pleaded guilty to a misdemeanor assault charge. Jones was disciplined for drinking while on sick report.

After Jones returned to duty, he was involved in several spectacular arrests. He was also the subject of several complaints regarding unnecessary use of force and "verbal abuse of citizens," and was injured several times while scuffling with suspects. His supervisors staunchly defended him, arguing that Jones was the best and most highly decorated detective in the unit and that he was "a *real* cop, and not a social worker."

In 1979, Jones stopped two "suspicious men in an automobile." He stated that as he approached the car on foot, its driver "accelerated right at me" while holding a gun in his right hand. Jones drew and fired, killing the driver. A bullet ricocheted and critically wounded the passenger, who had stepped out of the car when Jones first stopped them. An uproar developed when it was learned that the driver's gun was not recovered. Moreover, investigation showed that he was a paraplegic Vietnam war veteran who drove his car with hand controls. His family argued that he had never been in any trouble with police and that he could not have driven the car and pointed a gun at the same time, since driving required both his hands. This story was supported by the wounded passenger, who stated that his companion had merely reached for his driver's license in the car's glove compartment, when Jones, who "appeared high on something," suddenly started shooting.

Under intense pressure from the press and from community and veterans' representatives, the prosecutor charged Jones with murder. Jones's attorney skillfully argued his case, pointing out that the wounded passenger was "not exactly an unbiased witness." The lawyer also showed that the passenger and other witnesses, who stated that they had not seen the car move before Jones fired, had not been in ideal positions to see the actions of the driver. Furthermore, his cross-examination of witnesses revealed that the street on which the incident occurred was dimly lit, that one witness who normally wore glasses was without them at the time of the shooting, and that another was the brother-in-law of a drug addict once arrested by Jones. He strongly suggested that this last witness may have been responsible for the disappearance of the gun from the scene. He also produced testimony that the deceased had been a highly decorated Green Beret who had seen much violence in Vietnam, and who, regrettably, had been under regular physical and mental therapy since suffering the wound that crippled him.

Jones was acquitted by the jury, who found that a reasonable doubt as to his guilt did exist. He was charged by his department with several violations of the regulations: shooting an unarmed suspect, shooting at an automobile, shooting under circumstances dangerous to people not involved (the passenger), and using unauthorized high-powered ammunition. Jones's attorney argued that the departmental trial was "a sham, an example of kangaroo-court double jeopardy and the failure of the department to back up its men." Jones was found guilty of the departmental charges against him and was dismissed from the department.

The family of the deceased then brought a "wrongful death" civil action against Jones and the department. They also charged in a separate suit that the department had been negligent in failing to identify Jones as "a clearly unstable and violence-prone individual who should not have been permitted to walk the streets of the city carrying in his holster the power of life or death." The U.S. Department of Justice also noted that it was considering charging Jones with criminal violation of the decedent's civil rights.

The question of double jeopardy raised by Jones's departmental trial may be best answered thus: Double jeopardy is a principle designed to protect an individual from more than one *criminal* prosecution by the same jurisdiction for the same act. A departmental trial—like any other *administrative* proceeding—is not a criminal trial. It does not involve exposing the accused to the risk of a criminal conviction or imprisonment. Conversely, it is a recognized means by which administrators may preserve the "good order" or their organizations. Such administrative proceedings are not legally required to adhere to the strict evidentiary requirements of criminal proceedings.

In criminal trials, the defendant's basic rights as a citizen are paramount. Jones enjoyed due process in criminal court: the prosecutor was limited in the degree to which he could use Jones's prior record of violence in evidence, Jones could not be compelled to testify, and Jones was presumed innocent until the jury should find him guilty beyond a reasonable doubt—which it did not.

Administrative trials differ in several ways. They are not adversary proceedings, but fact-finding inquiries. Their basic purpose is to find the *truth*, so that action can be taken to fulfill the administrator's mandate to protect the public interest. In cases such as that of Jones, the public interest is best defined as the right to be free of unstable police officers, and the "truth," is whether or not the accused *did commit* the violation charged, not whether or not legal guilt exists beyond a reasonable doubt. Jones has rights as a citizen, and these work to his benefit in a criminal trial. There is, however, no constitutional right to be a police officer: the primary right at stake in police department trials is the public's constitutional right to be free from fear of its own police. Obviously, therefore, the safeguards used in criminal trials have no place here. In order to find Jones guilty as charged, the department's hearing officer had only to determine that *a preponderance of the evidence* indicated his guilt. A preponderance may be defined as 51 percent or more of the evidence—which, by design, obviously leaves room for reasonable doubt. To determine whether that preponderance exists, judges or presiding officers may require the accused to testify (failing to do so often resulting in dismissal), may inquire in depth into the background of the accused, and may accept into evidence statements made in the absence of *Miranda*-related advice and counsel. Thus officers acquitted of criminal charges are often found guilty (by a less stringent evidentiary standard) of departmental violations resulting from the same acts.

The question of double jeopardy in such cases is therefore usually only a smoke screen raised by the accused and attorneys for the accused, who do know better.

The logic behind the civil actions resulting from the shooting has been addressed earlier in this chapter and needs little clarification. The threatened Justice Department criminal action against Jones does, however. It, too, may appear to involve questions of double jeopardy. But the courts have held double jeopardy to bar only "successive prosecutions for the *same* act by the *same* jurisdiction [emphasis added]." The Supreme Court has noted that "if the States are free to prosecute criminal acts violating their laws, and the resultant state prosecutions bar federal prosecutions based on the same acts, federal law enforcement must necessarily be hindered." This observation is especially valid given the federal law (section 241 of the U.S. Code) under which Jones is likely to be prosecuted. This statute makes it a felony "to conspire to injure, oppress, threaten, or intimidate any citizen in the free exercise or enjoyment of any right or privilege secured to him by the Constitution or the laws of the United States." The law was enacted shortly after the Civil War, specifically to provide a means of trying individuals when state prosecutors were reluctant or less than vigorous in their attempts to do so.

CONCLUSIONS

This chapter has, it is hoped, shed some light on the origins, evolution, and limits of American police power. It has tried to demonstrate that police are an executive agency, and that legislatures and courts affect state and local police comparatively slightly. Indeed, even in the extreme case of Detective Jones, statute law and court proceedings were invoked only after it had become apparent that internal controls were not functioning where he was concerned.

It can be reasonably stated, therefore, that external authorities such as the courts and legislatures are generally a "last resort" check on police operations. Members of both bodies do, in fact, generally view themselves in that light and frequently encourage police chiefs to put their own houses in order to reduce the need for external influences on the police. Legislatures do this by serving as advocates for citizens who are dissatisfied with the police, by conducting public hearings on police operations, and by passing laws. The judiciary does so by reviewing police tactics during trials, by incorporating limits on the police into case law, and by serving as a forum before which police can be held criminally or civilly liable for their actions.

Despite these legislative and judicial actions, in the final analysis, police are most directly controlled by the executive. It is the executive—the mayor or the mayor's designate, the police chief—to whom police officers are most accountable. It is also the executive, rather than the individual police officer, who is most likely to be held accountable by the courts and legislature for the failure of officers to observe the limits of their powers. It is imperative, therefore, that police executives clearly define and firmly enforce those limits. It is also imperative that individual officers know and closely observe those limits.

5

Regulatory Agencies

Joseph F. Maher

INTRODUCTION

The United States has a mixed economy in which the public and the private sectors interact in many ways. The public sector purchases over 20 percent of total output and the federal government collects one-third of personal income taxes. Government also influences the economy through monetary policy and by regulating the private sector. Thus, the government affects the functioning of markets by buying and selling goods and services, altering private incentives, determining the availability of credit, and directly intervening in firms' activities.

Direct government intervention in the workings of the private sector developed along two paths simultaneously. On the one hand, the government attempts to enhance competition among firms through federal laws designed to eliminate restraint of trade. This type of legislation dates from the Sherman Antitrust Act of 1890. On the other hand, the federal government directly regulates certain activities, thus substituting government decision making for the normal workings of the marketplace. The first independent regulatory agency, the Interstate Commerce Commission (ICC), was created in 1887. Today government regulation has expanded to the point where virtually every industry and household is affected in some way. An example can be seen in the effect of pollution-control and safety equipment on gasoline consumption and the price of automobiles.

Definition of Regulation

Discussion about government regulatory activities is often muddled by a lack of common understanding of what constitutes regulation. A narrow definition—

including only the control of economic variables such as market entry and price—would exclude the substantial regulatory effort in the health and safety area. The Congressional Budget Office faced this problem in 1976 while preparing a staff paper and resolved it with a useful definition. This definition includes as regulation those activities which (1) affect the operating business environment of broad sectors of private enterprise, including market entry and exit; rate, price, and profit structures; and competition; (2) affect specific commodities, products, or services through permit, certification, or licensing requirements; (3) involve the development, administration, and enforcement of national standards, violations of which could result in civil or criminal penalties, or which result in the types of effect just described.

Scope of Regulation

Interest in regulatory activities is based on several factors. First, there is a natural antagonism toward government regulations in a society which for generations has praised a market system. Second, the increased scope of government regulation now directly affects many citizens, often in ways viewed as unsatisfactory. Third, the public has been made increasingly aware of the costs of regulation.

The increased scope of federal regulation is illustrated by the growth of regulatory agencies and their activities. Since 1970, many regulatory agencies have been established; these include the Environmental Protection Agency (EPA) in 1970, the Occupational Safety and Health Administration (OSHA) in 1970, the Consumer Products Safety Commission (CPSC) in 1972, and the Federal Energy Administration (FEA) in 1974. Unlike most of the older regulatory bodies, these agencies directly and visibly affect many individual citizens.

The concern over government regulation covers a wide spectrum of issues, ranging from the purposes of regulation through its results. Questions have been raised regarding the continued appropriateness of some regulatory objectives, the ability of regulation to achieve its stated goals, the imposition of substantial economic costs on society, the effect of regulation on the distribution of income, the best administrative structure for regulation, and the feasibility range of regulatory reform alternatives.

A discussion of regulation must, of necessity, include the economist's justification for regulation as well as the social, political, and other reasons for regulation.

The economist's justification is based on the concept of market failure. A market failure exists when a naturally occurring flaw interferes with the workings of market forces. Regulation is adopted to correct this flaw. Examples of market failure and its consequences include:

- Natural monopoly, resulting in high prices, reduced output, and excess profits.

- Interdependencies in natural resource extraction, resulting in inefficient use of resources and inequitable sharing of costs.

- Inadequate information in the marketplace, resulting in poor decisions and wasted resources.

- Destructive competition, resulting in chronically sick firms unable to satisfy consumer demand.

When regulation is used to achieve social, political, or other objectives, it is the policy tool of choice. For example, regulation has been used to alter the distribution of income, enhance national security, allocate scarce resources, provide uneconomical service to small communities, and advance macroeconomic policy objectives such as price stability.

The Organization of Petroleum Exporting Countries (OPEC) is an international cartel created by the leading crude oil exporters so that they can jointly price petroleum as if they were a single monopolist. OPEC's price and output activities are examples of a monopoly in action. A monopolist's price and output decisions are subject to the law of demand, which states that price and quantity are inversely related. Not even a monopolist can independently determine both the price charged and the quantity sold. A higher price can be commanded only if the quantity offered for sale is reduced; this fact explains OPEC's activities. OPEC took advantage of a tight world petroleum market in 1973 to transform marginal cutbacks in production into a fourfold increase in the world price of crude oil. The new high price was artificially maintained during slackened demand in 1975 by carefully restraining production. Major OPEC members, such as Saudi Arabia and Kuwait, reduced their production to levels as much as one-third below capacity.

Government intervention may also be justified if interdependencies result from the exploitation of a natural resource.

Interdependencies exist when one producer's activities affect a second producer's access to a natural resource. Efficient utilization of the resource may be possible only with government regulation. For example, the electromagnetic spectrum suitable for radio and television broadcasting is quite limited. Early unregulated use of the airwaves resulted in a disruptive overlapping of signals. Effective use of this scarce resource requires a careful assignment of wavelengths, broadcast power, and the geographic areas served. The Federal Communications Commission (FCC) has been criticized for the way in which it distributes broadcast licenses, but the need for regulation is not generally disputed.

The development of crude petroleum fields is a second case of production interdependencies requiring government regulation. The total quantity of oil that can be recovered from a field is a function of the number of wells in the field and the rate at which the oil is pumped. Too many wells in a single field and excessively rapid pumping will lower the field pressure and reduce the quantity of recoverable oil. Large oil fields are often covered by many separate leases and worked by more than one firm. Early unregulated pumping was an economic version of the game of musical chairs. Oil that one firm was slow to extract was recovered by its competitors. Hence, all firms had a private incentive to overpump and damage the oil fields. Regulation was required to oversee the efficient recovery of this resource.

Use of Regulation and Social Policy Objectives

The government can often achieve a particular policy objective with any one of several different program options. Congress can change the tax laws, vote to spend public funds, pass laws to encourage specific behavior, or decide to regulate a particular activity or industry. Each program alternative may successfully achieve the desired policy objective; the programs themselves, however, might differ in administrative ease, popularity, cost to the government and public, and the extent of unintended consequences.

For example, providing air service to small communities might be desired although it is uneconomical. This service could be provided in a number of ways. Subsidies might be given by the federal government to the private airlines that provide the desired service. The subsidies might come out of the federal government's general tax revenues or be generated by a special tax. A quasi-public corporation might be set up to provide the service.

Alternatively, the industry might be regulated. Such regulation could limit entry into the industry and require that each airline allowed to operate serve a combination of profitable and unprofitable routes. The extra profits from the best routes could be used to subsidize service that otherwise would not be provided.

Several broad social policy objectives that have led to the adoption of regulation are:

- Concern over the distribution of income.
- Considerations of equity or fair play.
- Protection of those deemed worthy of special protection; for example, small businesses and family farms.
- Provisions of service to small communities; for example, airline and surface freight service.
- Allocation of scarce resources.
- Protection of consumers from specific price increases; for example, for natural gas and petroleum distillates.
- Considerations of macroeconomic policy; for example, overall price stability.

The decision to use regulation instead of the taxing and spending powers of the federal government to achieve some objectives is a matter of political choice. Moreover, such a decision is subject only to the judgments of the decision makers. The regulation, however, can and must be analyzed for its usefulness as a policy tool. The questions to ask are:

- What objectives are specified?
- Are the objectives in concert with the current conception of the public purpose?
- Does the regulation achieve the objectives?
- What are the unintended consequences?
- What are the total costs of using regulation to achieve these objectives?
- Who bears the cost of the regulation?
- What alternative mechanisms can achieve the objective?
- Are any of these alternatives less costly (more efficient) ways of reaching the objectives?

The foregoing type of critical analysis is important because regulation can prove a difficult to use, if not unwieldy, policy instrument. Regulation, for any number of reasons, may not produce the desired result. Additionally, even if successful, the undertaking can be very costly for the economy as a whole, if not for the government specifically.

Let us take, for example, the promotion of residential construction, which is a popular social goal. To achieve this goal, home construction is encouraged in several ways, including the regulation of a class of financial intermediaries— namely, the savings and loan associations—designed to provide mortgage funds. The asset portfolios of savings and loan associations consist predominantly of long-term residential mortgages. These institutions, however, do not necessarily ensure an adequate supply of loanable funds to the housing market. The nature of their assets prevents them from substantially increasing in the short run their income and the interest rate they pay depositors. Consequently, periods of rising interest rates have resulted in a severe shortage of mortgage money, which, in turn, adversely affects the housing industry. As funds leave the savings and loan associations in search of higher interest rates, new mortgage money is not available, home sales lag because of a lack of financing, and new construction declines.

THE PROGRAM AND FRAMEWORK OF INVESTIGATION

The Regulatory Agencies

The *regulatory agencies* are those independent regulatory commissions and agencies *outside* the executive department of government. They have authority to set rates, issue permits, require disclosure of information, set safety requirements, or approve hiring and promotion practices. They are as follows:

Board of Governors of the Federal Reserve System. This board regulates state-chartered banks that are members of the Federal Reserve System and has jurisdiction over bank holding companies. It sets monetary and credit policy; examines accounts and books of Federal Reserve and member banks, fixes rates of interest for discounting of paper, regulates Federal Reserve notes, and generally supervises functions of banks in the System; determines reserve requirements for, and limitations on, rates of interest that may be paid by member banks; approves foreign branches of member banks and regulates their activities; and supervises bank holding companies.

Civil Aeronautics Board. This board regulates routes, fares, rates, practices, reports, and accounts of air carriers. It administers subsidy programs; issues operating authority certificates to air carriers engaging in interstate, overseas, and foreign air transportation; and investigates and suspends rates and fares in adjudged unfair, unreasonable, or discriminatory interstate, overseas, and foreign transportation.

Commission on Civil Rights. This commission submits findings and recommendations to the President and to the Congress on the causes of discrimination and means for eliminating it through legislation. It holds public hearings and subpoenas witnesses to investigate written allegations that citizens are being denied the right to vote and appraises laws and policies with respect to denials of equal protection under the Constitution.

Commodity Futures Trading Commission. This commission regulates futures trading of agricultural and other commodities and investigates and prevents price manipulation, market corners, dissemination of false or misleading information, and mishandling of traders' margin money and equity. It fixes limits on the amounts of trading that may be done or positions that may be held by any person under contracts of commodities sale for future delivery, regulates the manner in which the buying and selling orders for commodities are executed, and regulates leverage contracts for gold and silver.

Consumer Product Safety Commission. This commission establishes mandatory product safety standards and bans the sale of products that do not comply. It prohibits introduction of misbranded or banned hazardous substances into interstate commerce, conducts examinations and investigations, and reviews record of interstate shipment and prescribes necessary regulations.

Energy Research and Development Administration. This administration regulates energy development activities, which include utilization of energy for medical, biological, health, and agricultural purposes. It investigates and enforces safety provisions on developmental facilities.

Environmental Protection Agency. This agency develops environmental quality standards, investigates and approves state abatement plans, and rules on the acceptability of environmental impact statements. It establishes ambient air quality standards; and establishes effluent limitations, water quality standards for navigable waters, and federal standards of performance for marine sanitation devices.

Equal Employment Opportunity Commission. This commission investigates and rules on charges of unlawful discriminatory employment practices based on race, color, religion, sex, or national origin. It investigates and rules on unlawful employment practices and initiates civil actions when its own procedures fail.

Farm Credit Administration. This administration supervises, regulates, and investigates activities of credit disbursement through the Farm Credit System. It charters, supervises, and regulates federal land banks, federal intermediate credit banks, and production credit associations.

Federal Communications Commission. This commission regulates interstate and foreign communications by radio, television, wire, cable, and satellite. It investigates and issues certificates of public convenience and necessity for the addition or extension of lines of communication; it investigates and inquires into the business management of all carriers subject to the Federal Communications Act.

Federal Deposit Insurance Corporation. This corporation insures deposits of eligible banks and supervises certain insured banks. It regulates, investigates, and supervises insured state banks that are not members of the Federal Reserve System.

Federal Energy Administration. This administration formulates a comprehensive energy plan, regulates price and allocation of certain petroleum products under emergency energy laws, and determines through investigation energy conservation measures for consumer products other than automobiles. It investigates, analyzes, and projects production and demand and levels of energy reserves; analyzes various conservation measures; and develops complex energy plans.

Federal Home Loan Bank Board: Federal Savings and Loan Insurance Corporation. This agency charters, and regulates through investigations, federal home loan banks and federal savings and loan institutions. It insures savings and loan deposits through a subsidiary.

Federal Maritime Commission. This commission administers shipping statutes that require regulation of the domestic offshore and international waterborne commerce of the United States. It licenses ocean freight forwarders, investigates and certifies the financial responsibility of passenger vessel operators and vessels carrying oil and hazardous substances, regulates rates and charges of common carriers by water in intercoastal commerce, and certifies the financial responsibility of vessel operators to meet liabilities for death or injury of passengers or other persons.

Federal Power Commission. This commission regulates hydroelectric projects, interstate transmission and wholesale price of electric power, and interstate transportation and sale of natural gas; investigates and analyzes rates and routes of natural gas pipelines; and issues certificates of convenience and necessity.

Federal Trade Commission. Through investigation, this commission prevents persons, partnerships, or corporations from using unfair methods of competition and unfair or deceptive acts or practices in commerce. It prevents and eliminates restraints on trade in all commercial transactions.

Interstate Commerce Commission. This commission regulates and investigates complaints concerning railroads, trucking companies, bus lines, domestic water carriers, freight forwarders, and transportation brokers.

National Credit Union Administration. This administration charters, insures, and regulates federal credit unions. It insures savings in all federal credit unions and in state-chartered credit unions that apply for and qualify for insurance.

National Labor Relations Board. This board regulates labor practices of unions and employers through its judicial decisions. It hears cases, issues rules and regulations relating to unfair labor practices, determines appropriate collective bargaining units, conducts hearings, makes investigations, issues complaints, conducts secret ballots for employees to rescind the authority of the bargaining unit, and prevents any person from engaging in unfair labor practices affecting commerce.

National Mediation Board. This board mediates labor-management disputes in the railroad and airline industries. It investigates representation disputes; conducts elections and certifies the designated representative of the employees to the carrier; appoints neutral referees and arbitrators; and administratively oversees the National Railroad Adjustment Board.

National Transportation Safety Board. This board investigates accidents in all modes of transportation and makes recommendations to federal and state agencies.

Nuclear Regulatory Commission. This commission regulates energy activities and establishes standards governing use of nuclear materials to protect health and the environment.

Occupational Safety and Health Review Commission. This commission develops and enforces worker safety and health regulations. It enforces standards by inspection and investigation of workplaces, issuance of citations, and assessment of penalties.

Securities and Exchange Commission. This commission requires financial disclosure by publicly held companies. It regulates and investigates practices of stock exchanges, brokers, and dealers; regulates certain practices of investment companies, investment advisers, and public utility companies; and prescribes regulations to prevent manipulation of security prices.

U.S. Civil Service Commission. This commission enforces civil rights provisions of laws providing for equal rights and opportunities in federal employment. It develops affirmative action plans, reviews national and regional equal employment opportunity plans, prescribes administrative procedures for the consideration of discrimination complaints, issues regulations prohibiting unfair employment practices in federal agencies, and investigates complaints.

U.S. Postal Service. This service establishes mail classifications and size and weight limitations for letter mail and prescribes postal rates and fees.

Regulatory Bureaus within the Executive Branch of Government

In addition to the above agencies and commissions, there are bureaus and bureau offices having regulatory responsibility *within* the executive departments. These include the following:

Federal Grain Inspection Service, U.S. Department of Agriculture

National Oceanic and Atmospheric Administration, U.S. Department of Commerce

Army Corps of Engineers, Department of Defense

Public Health Service, U.S. Department of Health and Human Services (formerly Health, Education, and Welfare)

Office of Consumer Affairs, U.S. Department of Housing and Urban Development

U.S. Fish and Wildlife Service, U.S. Department of the Interior

Civil Rights Division, U.S. Department of Justice

Employment Standards Administration, U.S. Department of Labor

Bureau of Consular Affairs, Passport Office, Visa Office, U.S. Department of State

Coast Guard, U.S. Department of Transportation

Bureau of Alcohol, Tobacco and Firearms, U.S. Department of the Treasury

Federal Supply Service, General Services Administration

THE STAFF MANAGEMENT AND DECISION-MAKING PROCESS

An issue frequently raised in the context of organizational evaluation of regulatory agencies is the effective use and control of staff resources. The efficient development of standards and regulations, scheduling and processing of cases, and avoidance or elimination of backlogs are important components of effective and fair regulation. Frequently, they are functions of the agency's organization.

The management of the regulatory agencies has never been without its critics and detractors. In 1937, a committee on administrative management (the Brownlow Committee), appointed by President Roosevelt, published a report that stressed the lack of coordination among regulatory agencies and between these agencies and other government branches.

The main thrust of the Brownlow Committee Report was that policy and administration could be coordinated in several regulatory fields only if the units were responsible to a Cabinet head and ultimately to the President. *The Executive Reorganization Bill of 1938*, which contained many of the recommendations of the Brownlow Committee, was defeated in Congress, due, in part, to concern that it would give too much power to the President.

1949—Report of the First Hoover Commission. In chronological sequence, the *Report of the First Hoover Commission (1947–1949)* was an important regulatory reform study. Unlike the Brownlow Committee, the Hoover Commission concluded that the regulatory commissions had a rightful place in the political system but found that they had generally failed to perform up to expectations. The Commission's recommendations tended toward concern with the organizational structure and administrative processes of commissions.

1955—Report of the Second Hoover Commission. The *Report of the Second Hoover Commission (1953–1955)* continued the emphasis on internal commission procedural operations, structure, and management. It supported the concept of an integrated legal staff under a general counsel; improving the internal procedures; and separating, where possible, the judicial and executive functions of administrative agencies. It also sought to increase the independence of hearing examiners.

1960—Redford Report and Landis Report. During 1960, two reports that addressed themselves, in a more limited way, to the special operational and coordinational problems posed by independent regulatory commissions were published. They suggested coordinating mechanisms to ensure a greater degree of accountability to the executive branch. The first of these, the *Redford Report*, prepared for the President's Advisory Committee on Government Organization in 1960, suggested statutory changes to allow policy direction from the President. The second report, a *Report on Regulatory Agencies to the President-Elect* (the *Landis Report*) proposed that the administrative powers of heads of commissions be enhanced and staff positions be made more attractive by delegating authority.

1971—Ash Council Report. The President's Advisory Council on Executive Organization (the *Ash Council*, 1971) found regulatory commissions to be essentially ineffective and unable to respond well and in a timely fashion to economic, technological, and social changes. These weaknesses the Council attributed primarily to independence from presidential authority, collegial organization, the judicial cast of agency activities, and the misalignment of certain functional responsibilities.

1970s—Congressional Studies of Regulatory Agencies. Two recent and comprehensive congressional studies of regulatory agencies have been performed by the Subcommittee on Oversight and Investigations of the House Committee on Interstate and Foreign Commerce (*Moss Report*) and by the Senate Committee on Governmental Affairs (*Ribicoff Report*). Both studies concerned the problems attending the regulatory process and the need for regulatory reform.

In contrast to some of the earlier proposals for sweeping reorganization of the regulatory process, the *Moss Report* (1976) concluded that regulatory reform can be accomplished only if approached agency by agency and program by program, not with any across-the-board solution. The report identified certain common failings in the agencies studied. These included excessive attention to the special interests of regulated industries and underrepresentation of the broad public interest, lack of accountability to elected public representatives, unnecessary delays and cumbersome procedures, and weaknesses in the process of selecting regulators (commissioners) of high quality.

The six-volume *Ribicoff Report* (1977–1978), entitled *Study on Federal Regulation*, represents an extremely comprehensive effort to study federal regulation, to assess the impact of regulatory programs, and to express the need for change. Among other things, the study examined the regulatory appointments process, congressional oversight of regulatory agencies, public participation in the regulatory process, the problem of delay in regulatory administration, and questions of regulatory organization and coordination. Rather than reflecting the executive branch perspective evident in the earlier Brownlow, Landis, and Ash reports, both the Moss and Ribicoff studies reflected the congressional perspective. As a result, they were more concerned with maintaining the independence of the regulatory agencies from the executive branch than with the problems of coordination facing the President.

Fiscal Year 1979 Zero-Based Regulatory Studies. The FCC has approved certain zero-based regulatory studies as part of its million-dollar policy-research funding program for the fiscal year 1979. Included is a study of the economics of TV advertising and programming directed toward children.

The FCC has also approved a study to determine the means of measuring the effectiveness of field operations activities. The study will analyze the field operations bureau's information-gathering function; furthermore, it proposes an improved structure to make it more useful for measuring effectiveness in field enforcement activities and for assisting management in determining where and to what extent field enforcement resources should be expanded.

WORK PERFORMED BY THE GENERAL ACCOUNTING OFFICE (GAO) ON FEDERAL REGULATORY ACTIVITIES

The GAO, under the Controller General of the United States, investigates on behalf of the legislative branch of government those allegations and situations deleterious to interests carried out by the executive branch of government. There follow a few examples of the results of GAO investigation in the responsible executive branch.

U.S. Department of Health and Human Services (formerly HEW)-Federal Fire Safety Requirements Do Not Insure Life Safety in Nursing Home Fires (HEW, MWD-76-136, 3 June 1976). Two Chicago nursing home fires killed 31 people during early 1976. GAO was asked to investigate reasons for the severity of the fires and to suggest possible actions to avoid similar situations.

As the investigative arm of Congress, GAO reported that experts said automatic sprinkler systems would have extinguished the fires and saved lives. GAO recommended that the Congress enact legislation requiring all nursing homes to be fully protected with automatic sprinkler systems.

Federal Efforts to Protect the Public from Cancer-Causing Chemicals Are Not Very Effective (MWD-75-59, 16 June 1976). Federal efforts to protect the public from cancer-causing chemicals have not been very successful. Although federal agencies (including the Department of Labor and the former HEW, the Environmental Protection Agency, and the Consumer Product Safety Commission) generally have enough authority to regulate the chemicals, they have encountered scientific problems in relating the results of animal safety tests to humans.

The Director of the National Cancer Institute is responsible for the overall direction of federal efforts and should establish a federal policy on cancer-causing chemicals, or carcinogens, with the cooperation, advice, and support of other federal agencies. The policy should address the scientific issues that have hampered effective public protection from carcinogens.

Department of Commerce—Problems Found in the Financial Disclosure System for Department of Commerce Employees (FPCD-76-55, 10 August 1976). The close relationship between the Department of Commerce and the nation's business community calls for Department vigilance to provide an effective financial disclosure system for its employees.

GAO reported weaknesses in the Department's system, including the need to:

- Improve procedures for collecting, processing, and controlling financial disclosure statements.
- Develop criteria and systematic procedures to review statements.
- Improve procedures for timely follow-up on financial interests.
- Enforce and expand its criteria for identifying persons who should file financial disclosure statements.

Departments of Labor, Agriculture, and Interior; Veterans Administration; and Departments of Air Force, Army, Navy, Defense Supply Agency, Department of Defense—Hazardous Working Conditions in Seven Federal Agencies (HRD-76-144, 4 August 1976). Seven federal agencies, employing more than half of the federal civilian employees, do not have adequate procedures for identifying and correcting hazardous working conditions. The heads of federal agencies and the Secretary of Labor should work together to make safety and health programs for federal agencies effective, as required by the Occupational Safety and Health Act. Congress should amend the Act to bring federal agencies under the inspection authority of the Department of Labor to supplement and strengthen agency inspections.

OSHA and Department of Labor—Better Data on Severity and Causes of Worker Safety and Health Problems Should Be Obtained from Workplaces (HRD-76-118). The Department of Labor needs specific details on causes and potential causes of death and serious disabling injury or illness. This report describes the type of data the Department has compiled and analyzed. It includes recommendations for (1) improving the program for obtaining injury and illness data and (2) setting up a program to obtain data from employers on employee exposure to and effects from toxic chemicals and other health hazards.

THE REGULATORY PROCESS

Studies of regulatory agencies have criticized the administrative procedures and processes that must be followed (such as FCC rules and regulations) in order to obtain a licensing authority or permit for operation. Unnecessary delays and cumbersome practices have resulted in stultifying competition and in frustrating the private sector.

It has been suggested by congressional oversight committees that the particular federal regulatory agency should present a description of how the working level of the agency has designed and is implementing its program. The working level of the agency generally will consist of professional personnel employed in the headquarters offices of the agency.

Although the program-design presentation will, of course, vary from agency to agency, it should include the following information:

1. The parts of the agency involved in implementation and a summary of their implementation progress.

2. The individual who is to manage and who is accountable for the implementation and monitoring of the program.

3. A *summary* of the regulations, guidelines, procedures, and direct program activities or processes that the agency has chosen to use in setting up a specific program.

In a series of hearings on the Rural Development Act, Senator Richard Clark initiated the preparation of an implementation flow chart designed with a separate line for each of the major provisions of the Rural Development Act; in addition, there are boxes to the right of each provision in which the steps taken toward implementation of the provision were entered.

To carry out logical investigations and to receive pertinent data, the following pitfalls must be avoided:

- Becoming buried in uninterpretable data.

- Receiving assorted noncomparable, highly technical agency-evaluation reports that do not bear on the questions for which answers are sought.

- Receiving no information at all.

By using some conceptual tools and a possible oversight framework, the search for information can be accomplished. The steps outlined above in program-design presentation should prove helpful.

REFERENCES

Cohen, Richard E. "Out of the Closet, Into Debate—Regulatory Reform Is Here to Stay." *National Journal,* 22 May 1976.

Congressional Budget Office. *The Number of Federal Employees Engaged in Regulatory Activities.* Subcommittee print of the Subcommittee on Oversight and Investigations of the Committee on Interstate and Foreign Commerce, House of Representatives, August 1976.

Smith, Robert S. *The Occupational Safety and Health Act, Its Goals and Its Achievement.* Washington, The American Enterprises Institute for Public Policy Research, 1976.

U.S., Congress. *Government Regulatory Activity: Justification Processes, Impacts, and Alternatives.* Report by the Comptroller General of the United States, June 1977.

U.S., Congress. *Finding Out How Programs Are Working; Suggestions for Congressional Oversight.* Report by the Comptroller General of the United States, November 1977.

U.S., Congress. *Federal Regulatory Programs and Activities.* Report by the Comptroller General of the United States, March 1978.

U.S., Congress. *Organizing the Federal Communications Commission for Greater Management and Regulatory Effectiveness.* Report by the Comptroller General of the United States, July 1979.

U.S., Congress, Senate. *Resolution 307 Concerning "Assessments of Manageability" of Agency Functions,* 94th Cong., 1975.

Waverman, Leonard. "The Regulation of Intercity Telecommunications," in *Promoting Competition in Regulated Markets,* edited by A. Phillips. Washington, The Brookings Institute, 1975.

6

Scope of Insurance Investigation

Arthur E. Torrington

THE NATURE AND FUNCTION OF INSURANCE

At present the United States is home for over 3000 property and liability insurance companies underwriting more than $219 billion in premium volume. Also, according to the Insurance Information Institute in New York, American insurers, including life and health insurance companies, provide almost 1.4 million jobs and have combined assets of over $527 billion. Through mutual, stock, reciprocal, and government-owned insurance companies, a wide range of insurance coverages are provided to all segments of our society, from the rural farm owner to the urban apartment dweller and from small individual-interest businesses to giant publicly owned multinational conglomerates.

In fulfilling its primary function of providing *financial security through asset protection*, insurance can be seen as a principal factor in the maintenance of individual economic independence as well as a stimulus for social and technological development. Indeed, it is not at all difficult to imagine how threatening our social and economic environment would be without some secured form of indemnification in the event of a serious loss. Furthermore, beyond the natural desire on the part of the insurer to perpetuate profit, insurance has no purpose without the potential for the payment of losses.

If loss prevention techniques could eliminate all risk, meaning chance of loss, there would be no hazards such as earthquakes, fires, windstorms, or burglaries to insure against, thus making the service unnecessary. However, given the incalculability of natural and social forces, not all sources of loss potential can be identified with certainty. Even though loss experience may easily lend itself to classification and quantitative analysis as well as certain levels of predictability based on large numbers of homogeneous risks, expectations do not always lead to realization. No matter how sophisticated the statistical and analytic approach is for estimating the number, size, and type of losses, the fact remains that time and time again sudden tornadoes, unforeseen earthquakes, and erratic hurricanes have proved beyond doubt that in nature there are no absolutes of predictability. Similarly, human beings have never been able to completely cope with the perplexities of human error or create a perfect defense against losses consciously inflicted by their fellows. Therefore, in discussing some of the forms of insurance currently available, it must be remembered that insurance is responsive in nature and is designed to provide asset protection in direct relation to a specific loss potential, with each form of insurance being classified by the type of risk it is intended to protect.

Property insurance generally refers to what is known as "first-party" insurance, wherein the insurer, at the time of claim, indemnifies policyholders for damages sustained to their own property or for the consequential monetary injury suffered as a result of a loss. Included in the property class is Fire and Allied Lines Insurance, which not only covers actual fires, hail, and windstorm; riot and civil commotion; vandalism and malicious mischief; water damage; sprinkler leakage; earthquakes; and even collision but can also be designed to protect against a resulting loss of income on commercial property. Other property forms provide protection through Increased Cost of Construction Insurance, Farm and Crop Insurance, Automobile Physical Damage Insurance, and Business Interruption Insurance, as well as the property coverage sections of Homeowners, Farmowners, and Commercial Package policies.

Historically speaking, *Marine* and *Inland Marine Insurance* have generally been regarded as the earliest kinds of insurance to be offered on a widespread basis. Each of these forms was originally designed to protect property in transit on the high seas or on land, respectively. Today, however, while Ocean Marine Insurance is still used principally as protection against hull and cargo losses, Inland Marine policies are now available to cover not only goods in transit in other than ocean vessels, but also valuable personal property that is easily transportable, such as jewelry, furs, and fine arts. Other areas of protection afforded by outgrowths of the Inland Marine form are such things as communications systems, bailee coverages, and bridges and tunnels, as well as mail services and armored car operations, to name but a few.

Liability insurance differs conceptually from the property forms of coverage in that it is designed primarily to protect policyholders against financial losses arising out of their legal liability to others as a result of bodily injury, death, or property damage. Generally, such liability can be incurred in two ways: it can be imposed by law as a result of one's own negligent acts, covered under the *Law of Torts*, or it can be assumed through contractual obligation, which is subject to interpretation under the *Law of Contracts*. Liability insurance affords what is known as "third-party" coverage and, unlike property insurance, normally pays claims *on behalf* of the insured rather than indemnifying or reimbursing the insured after the damage has been paid for.

Some of the more common forms of liability insurance are Workers' Compensation and Employers' Liability; Professional Liability Insurance, such as medical or legal malpractice; and errors and omissions protection for accountants, real estate agents, and architects. Family and Commercial

Automobile Liability Insurance; Umbrella and Excess Liability Insurance; as well as Title, Plate Glass, and Credit Insurance are also widely issued forms.

Indeed, the list of coverage classifications and the types of insurance policies available to protect against virtually any property or liability loss exposure is almost endless. More importantly, however, as suggested earlier, insurance, because of its ability to provide security through asset protection, has been a driving force in the development of modern finance and technology. Without adequate insurance to protect existing business facilities and operations, the availability of risk capital for new ventures would be severely restricted. For example, credit insurance affords lending institutions the security needed to provide funds for such things as home and industrial expansion loans. Furthermore, insurance serves the social good by providing financial protection to the insuring public at the time of greatest need—following catastrophe, illness, or accident. While these are but a few of the functions of insurance, they characterize the nature and effect of this vital economic facility in our society.

THE CLAIMS ADJUSTER

Once a claim has been presented, the insurer's claims representative must not only *investigate* the facts surrounding the loss but also *determine the extent of damage* and either *negotiate a settlement* or equitably *adjust the loss* to its correct value. Throughout this discussion we will refer to all those engaged in this postloss process as *claims adjusters*.

In actuality, normally four kinds of representatives are employed in the claims process: (1) company staff adjusters, (2) independent adjusters, (3) insurance agents, and (4) public adjusters.

1. Often, when a company finds that it is developing a sufficient number of claims within a given territory, it will hire one or more *staff adjusters*. Among the advantages of employing full-time adjusters are more accurate expense predictability and claims control, particularly in the management of protracted third-party claims. Not only is the cost and benefit package of the staff adjuster more calculable than that of the independent representative but the company can train an individual as an employee in its particular claims handling procedures and philosophy, thereby providing policyholders with more continuity in the processing and disposition of their claims. Over a period of time, this method of loss adjustment also allows the company to develop its own staff of specialists to supervise the claims activities of other field or independent adjusters.

2. At present, the use of *independent adjusters* is one of the most widespread methods of adjusting claims throughout the world in both the property loss and liability claims areas. Ranging in size from one-person shops all the way up to large international organizations, the independent is often the only type of adjuster available to a small insurer. Nonetheless, by using independent adjusters, any insurer can immediately gain a worldwide claims handling capability. In addition to the fact that the range of specialists available to the insurer through the use of independent adjusters is truly impressive, the scope of their services often goes beyond merely adjusting claims. Many independents offer adjunct services such as inspection work, appraisals, dwelling valuations, auditing, and loss control.

Domestically, one of the largest directories of independent adjusting firms is published by The National Association of Independent Insurance Adjusters, which lists hundreds of member companies nationwide. At the same time, several large nonmember independents also publish their own directories listing their national and international facilities.

While the expense of using independents may be substantial if it is done on a continual basis, in areas where only a limited number of claims is anticipated, the costs of individual claim investigations are offset by the savings over having an often idle staff adjuster in the territory. However, since most insurers prefer to maintain tight control over their claims, they seldom provide the independent adjuster with complete authority to settle claims without first seeking their agreement on the issues of liability involved and the amount of proposed settlement.

3. There are situations in which some insurers will allow their local *insurance agents* to settle claims, but normally that settlement authority is strictly limited as to type and amount. In other words, in order to provide policyholders with timely claims payments, particularly in the case of rural-area property losses, and to increase the marketability of their product for local agents, the insurer will allow the agent to settle first-party losses of less than a few hundred dollars. This practice has the effect of enhancing the relationship between the insured and the agent and, as a result, between the agent and the insurer as well. In general, however, this method of loss adjustment is not used in the handling of liability claims. The company's potential exposure to suit from improperly handled third-party claims far outweighs any cost or time advantages that might be realized from this approach.

4. Unlike the claims representatives mentioned above, *public adjusters* do not represent the interests of the insurance companies. Instead, these firms offer their services to the general public and are prepared to act on behalf of the insured in the presentation and negotiation of first-party claims settlements with the company. Many states, however, require that public adjusters, as agents of the insured, be investigated, examined, and licensed by the insurance department, secretary of state, or some other licensing authority. Furthermore, any presentation of a fraudulent claim by a public adjuster is held to be the same as one presented by the insured and vice versa, for in the eyes of the law, these parties are normally seen as being one and the same.

The claims adjuster, of whatever particular status, is indispensable to the insurance process, in that some of the most difficult problems an insurance company must face in the conduct of its operations result from the investigation and adjustment of claims. In addition to the difficulties that may routinely be encountered in the processing of common domestic property and liability claims, insurers are often presented with the adjustment of more problematic losses, such as those relating to international trade; aviation; aerospace; or pollution resulting from chemical seepage, nuclear waste disposal, or oil spills from drilling rigs located far offshore. Of course, reaching an equitable adjustment of such losses can be both complex and time consuming. More importantly, the range of knowledge required by the claims adjuster in order to carry out this kind of detailed assignment is as sweeping as the range of the losses themselves.

Therefore, in order to fully understand the nature of claims investigation and adjustment, it is important to consider not only the role of the claims adjusters in that process but also to examine their qualifications and attitudes, the types of work they must be capable of performing, and some of the difficulties with which they may be faced.

Qualifications and Training

It should be remembered that only at the time of loss do insurance buyers truly realize the potential of the product they have purchased; it is at that same moment that the insurance claims adjuster becomes the key link between the company and the policyholder. Therefore, most insurers exercise extreme care in the selection of their claims adjusters.

As in any other profession, a substantial educational background is, of course, prerequisite. Not only must the adjuster be able to demonstrate the quality of past educational performance but should also be capable of taking on new learning situations, since the amount of technical knowledge required of a claims adjuster is quite extensive.

Bearing witness to this is the fact that in every state in the United States, insurance operations are overseen by some form of state-appointed regulatory authority that has the obligation to protect the interests of the insuring public and the power to take prescribed courses of action against any insurer who violates the tenets of legal or ethical conduct. Because of this, it is incumbent on the insurer to make certain that the terms and conditions of state-approved policy forms are not violated by a company representative during the adjustment process. Therefore, in addition to a rigorous in-field training program, the claims adjuster is normally required to participate in a series of intensive in-house or institutional courses covering not only investigative techniques, such as interviewing, securing signed statements, use of police and other informational records, and report writing but also insurance law, torts, contracts, agency law, common law, bailments, damages, and—most important of all—policy provisions and interpretations.

On hand to assist in this educational process are such facilities as the College of Insurance, a division of the Insurance Society of New York, which offers a wide range of insurance- and claims-related courses; the Insurance Institute of America, which grants an Associate in Claims designation; and the American Institute for Property and Liability Underwriters—all these organizations being directly supported by the property-liability insurance industry. In addition, many private and public schools, colleges, and universities nationwide have initiated both credit and noncredit programs in claims management.

Job Performance Requirements

While many insurers try to specialize their claimspeople, at least to some extent, so that they can accumulate detailed knowledge in a specific field, there are a number of multiperil forms being written today that cover a variety of property *and* liability exposures. Therefore, losses are not always severable and must be adjusted with a multicoverage approach. A number of other insurers attempt to assign their adjusters by territory—giving one person total control over *any* claim arising within that area or using their field personnel as the only company representatives in specified regions. As a result, in many instances the claims adjuster truly becomes a jack-of-all-trades but, at the same time, is expected to perform as a master of all as well.

These *full-service representatives* are not only responsible for claims handling but will also be called on to conduct pre-underwriting inspections and evaluations, to investigate potential employees of the company, and to maintain liaison with local agents and brokers. The investigation of potential insureds for fire, fidelity bond, automobile, and even life insurance, as well as loss prevention consulting, risk management, inspection engineering, and auditing of the insured's ledgers and payroll books for the purpose of collecting premiums of the company may also be an assigned duty of the claims adjuster.

Insofar as *property loss adjustments* are concerned, the truly professional adjuster should be able to represent the company in a broad spectrum of claims situations. For example, in the handling and disposition of a large mercantile fire loss, the claims adjuster not only must work with fire and police officials to determine the exact (or what is often called "proximate") cause of loss, but is also required to have an informed knowledge of building values and replacement costs, including construction materials, contractors' costs, structural design, and contents valuations. If other insurers are also involved in the loss, the adjusters' activities must be coordinated with theirs, and the calculation of co-insurance formulas must be understood.

In unusual situations, such as when a fire stems from suspicious origins and arson can ultimately be proved, the claims adjuster should be knowledgeable about both the criminal and the civil processes. In such cases, it will be necessary to monitor the criminal action while at the same time gathering the evidence needed to deny the claim to the policyholder if there is substantial reason to believe that the insured may be linked to the crime.

Finally, in both property and liability claims, *salvage* and *subrogation* must be considered integral parts of the loss adjustment process. If the company is entitled to take salvage after the adjustment of a loss, it is often the adjuster's responsibility to obtain bids on that salvage and to dispose of the property in a manner that will realize the greatest dollar recovery for the insurance company. This is particularly critical since reimbursements effected through salvage can be a key element in the maintenance of both rate stability and company profit. Similarly, if it is found, in the course of investigating a claim, that a third party may have been partly or fully responsible for the loss, it is the obligation of the adjuster to notify the company's legal department so they can institute a subrogation or cross-claim action for recovery of damages against the malfeasor. This benefits not only the insurance company but the insured as well, if the policy includes an applicable deductible.

In the case of *liability claims adjusting*, the active knowledge required by the adjuster must be as extensive as that required in the disposition of property losses. However, in addition to having the skill to properly assess the extent of property damage sustained the liability claims adjuster must truly shine in the ability to deal with people. Unfortunately, it is extremely difficult, if not impossible, to train someone in the area of interpersonal relationships. Indeed, the talent for successfully dealing with people is either an inherent personal ability or a skill that must be developed over a long period through in-field experience and maturation. Nevertheless, in the course of an investigation, the liability claims adjuster will have to exhibit not only sound judgment in assessing damages but also patience, courtesy, and sympathy toward the insured; the witnesses; and, especially, the claimants.

Hindrances to Job Performance

It is an inherent aspect of liability insurance claims that investigations must often be conducted months or even years after the date of an occurrence, because statutes of limitation existing in the various states set forth the periods of time within which an injured party has the right to bring a claim action. Normally these periods run from two to three years but in some circumstances extensions may be afforded by the statutes or the courts. Also, in the case of infants the statute of limitations may commence on their twenty-first birthdays, thus delaying the first notice of claim for up to 24 years in some states. In other instances, the statute period may not begin until the date the injury is first discovered. This problem may come into play in cancer cases, for example, when individuals discover they are afflicted with the disease and can establish a direct link between the illness and the taking of a specific medication many years before.

As a result of the long delay encountered in receiving many liability claims, the claims adjuster will have to dig deep into the investigation of the facts, will develop the ability to locate the people involved who have long since moved or retired, and—most important of all—will be required to draw logical deductions from the stale piecemeal information that is still available.

In attempting to reconstruct the facts surrounding accidents or in determining the value of either property or liability losses, it is important to note that adjusters do not live in a vacuum. No matter how experienced they may be or how well-rounded their education, practical adjusters must be able to recognize their own limitations. Hence, in the investigation and adjustment of a severe property loss, an adjuster may have to secure the services of a contractor, architect, jeweler, interior decorator, salvager, accountant, or other specialist in order to determine proper values. Similarly, in the course of investigating liability claims, the adjuster is regularly required to seek assistance and cooperation from other professionals, such as police officers, district attorneys, court clerks, Underwriters Laboratory specialists, expert medical or engineering witnesses, and attorneys as well as local, state, and federal regulatory agencies, such as the Federal Aeronautics Administration, Federal Trade Commission, or Securities and Exchange Commission.

PRINCIPLES AND PRACTICE OF CLAIMS ADJUSTMENT

In carrying out almost any claims investigation, there are certain fundamental points that must be established. Most important of all, the claims adjuster will have to ascertain whether or not the loss resulted from a peril covered under the policy and occurred during the period the policy was in force and that the insured, in the case of first-party claims, had an insurable interest.

After these preliminary facts have been established, the next logical step is to investigate the circumstances surrounding the loss or accident to further determine if coverage should be afforded, if the claim being made is meritorious, and the extent of the company's liability in the loss. Finally, as mentioned earlier, it is the adjuster's obligation to investigate the possibility of subrogation against other parties, the salvage potential of damaged items, and the extent to which other available insurance coverages may be applicable to the loss.

In most cases, particularly where staff adjusters are used, the insurer's claims representative is provided with sufficient authority to act with considerable latitude in conducting an investigation and disposing of the claim. Furthermore, even though every state has its own special statutory provisions that outline the authority under which an insurer and its representatives may function, the freedom to investigate the subject of an insurance claim to whatever extent necessary is relatively unrestricted. This lack of restriction includes the privilege of examining the insured's business records; inspecting all public records of state or local authorities with regard to the insured; and, when necessary, conducting surveillance or making inquiries into the character, background, or activities of any claimant. Of course, one must be careful to avoid any illegal invasion of privacy or possible harassment.

The granting of this investigative latitude stems from the fact that the proper investigation of claims and equitable adjustment of losses serve the public interest in several ways. First, in-depth claims investigations are the only true defense an insurer has available *to guard against fraudulent or nonmeritorious claims*, which could cost the insuring public millions of dollars each year in premium increases. Second, they will assist the insurer in determining the true extent of injuries or damages, thus enabling the company to properly evaluate the claim and *equitably compensate* the injured parties.

Investigating Nonmeritorious Claims

It should be noted that insurance rates are based on the sharing of risk among the policyholders, and they are determined by both the frequency and the severity of claims that have occurred or are likely to occur. These factors go into making up the company's loss experience and help in determining the rates that will be applied to specific classes of risks underwritten by an insurer, as well as in applying for rate increases before the various state insurance departments.

To preclude the possibility of the loss experience being distorted by the payment of undeserving claims, the adjuster must constantly be on guard against the possible presentation of a nonmeritorious claim by either a policyholder or a third-party claimant. The first indication of a suspicious situation is, of course, the presentation of a claim that is not covered by the policy. This may be interpretive, however, and can often stem from the insured's misunderstanding of the policy provisions. But even here, in order to determine if coverage applies, an in-depth investigation may be necessary. During that inquiry the adjuster must take great care not to make statements or perform actions that would constitute a *waiver* or *estoppel* for either the company or the insured. In other words, until liability or coverage can be determined, the adjuster must guard against the danger of waiving the rights of either party by expressed or implied agreement to coverage. For if at a later time it is discovered that no coverage should be afforded, the company may be estopped or prevented from denying the claim.

Another instance in which claims without merit may arise is where a moral hazard exists. This type of exposure is often difficult to determine at the time a policy is underwritten; however, it may be made evident to the adjuster during the course of investigation by the way an insured's premises are maintained, business is conducted or records are kept or by how the insured seeks to negotiate the adjustment of the claim. Such insureds are often prone to attempt bribery or make threats against the adjuster. In other cases, it may take an astute and experienced adjuster to determine if a claim is being exaggerated by an insured for the purpose of "building" the claim or merely because the insured lacks the knowledge or competence to understand how the valuation of the loss has been arrived at.

The moral hazard is a particularly key element in the investigation of arson claims, for if, as mentioned previously, a direct link can be established between the commission of such a crime and the insured, the insurance carrier is within its rights to deny coverage. However, it should be noted that the denial of a policyholder's claim is the most serious step an insurer can take in the claims-handling process. In case after case, if there is any reasonable doubt about the legitimacy of that denial of coverage, the courts have ruled in favor of the policyholder against the insurer. The potential danger of such an error on the part of an insurance carrier is compounded by the fact that the insurer may be held liable for the payment of punitive or exemplary damage awards levied against it by the courts. The purpose of this kind of award is so punish or make an example of the insurer that it will, in the future, comply with proper standards of conduct in the handling of similar claims.

Quite obviously, judgments like these are intended to discourage insurance companies from acting in bad faith or in a negligent or irresponsible manner or from failing to give proper consideration to the interests of the insured.

As a result, if a claims investigation is conducted by an unscrupulous representative who contrives to change the story of a witness, tampers with evidence, or fails to act prudently in observing the rights of the parties involved, the company, under law, may have to assume the responsibility for the adjuster's actions and pay the damages thereby incurred.

In regard to the *denial and defense of third-party claims,* most courts have taken a somewhat different view of the rights and obligations of an insurer. Ethical conduct and good faith on the part of the company's representative is still a requirement for testing the validity of the denial of a claim, but such a denial may stem from the interpretation of the facts of the incident in regard to whether or not the insured was actually liable, the extent of that liability, or the true worth of the damages claimed. While it is always the duty of a liability insurer to negotiate the settlement of claims in good faith, part of that duty is also to protect the policyholder's interests by weighing the facts of the incident and determining the extent of the insured's obligation or liability for damages.

Sometimes, although not very often, outright fraud may be discovered during the course of investigating a third-party claim. In such cases the adjuster will normally consult with the company's legal department, which, in turn, may present the facts of the case to the district attorney's office for prosecution. More often than not, however, if there is substantial reason to believe that the claimant is attempting to defraud the company, a judicious presentation of the developed facts surrounding that suspicion may be made to the claimant or the claimant's attorney. Frequently, the result of this action is a sudden withdrawal of the claim.

Standing by to assist the claims adjuster and insurance company in the investigation of fraudulent or questionable claims, are a number of organizations that specialize in gathering pertinent information in this area. For example, the Insurance Crime Prevention Institute assists liability insurers in conducting investigations of potentially fraudulent claims, while the Metropolitan Chicago Loss Bureau helps to conduct property claims adjustments and arson investigations. In addition, some groups are designed to help coordinate the efforts of insurance companies to prevent crimes that have a direct effect on loss experience. Two of these organizations are the National Auto Theft Bureau and the National Crime Prevention Association.

Finally, territorial and centralized *index bureaus* have become prime factors in the detection of possible fraudulent claims. In essence, insurers subscribing to these services submit details of each liability loss, including the claimant's name, date of birth, residence, type of injury, physician, attorney, and other pertinent data. These facts are stored and cross-referenced so that, within a relatively short time, the bureau returns to the insurer's claims department a complete copy of all other indexed reports on file relating to the same claimant.

Occasionally, such research reveals that the same individual has a long list of prior claims against other insurers, frequently for the same injuries. While such information may not be sufficient ground for the denial of a claim, it may prove to be a valuable tool and a driving force for further investigation into the merits of a claim.

Equitable Claims Adjustments: Guidelines for Proper Behavior

In addition to each state having its own regulatory agency to monitor the equitable adjustment of claims and courts to enforce the rules of law, a number of self-imposed regulations and controls are promulgated by the insurance industry itself. For example, at a meeting of the Conference Committee on Adjusters in Chicago in 1939, the American Bar Association, American Mutual Alliance, Association of Casualty and Surety Companies, International Claims Association, and the National Association of Independent Insurers adopted a *Statement of Principles on Respective Rights and Duties of Lawyers, Insurance Companies and Adjusters Relating to the Business of Adjusting Insurance Claims.*

In that statement, the industry and the Bar Association established certain limitations on practice that adjusters must adhere to. It was recognized, of course, that a claim in contract between the insurer and policyholder or beneficiary entitles the two parties to directly conduct negotiations leading to a settlement of any meritorious claim. Similarly, in cases of third-party claims presented in torts against policyholders, insurers' representatives have a right to investigate the facts of accidents, to interview witnesses, appraise damages, and make determinations regarding the liability of the policyholders in relation to the occurrences. However, while adjusters may reach settlements with claimants based on the results of their investigations, they may not advise claimants of their rights under law. Furthermore, insurance companies must keep policyholders informed of the course and progress of such investigations and negotiations so that they may retain personal counsel if desired or if they feel, in the case of suit actions, that they may become personally liable for the payment of damages beyond the limits of their insurance coverages.

Most important of all is the fact that adjusters, no matter how skilled, are prohibited from engaging in the practice of law. Moreover, they may neither deal directly with any claimant or policyholder who is represented by counsel, nor advise any claimant not to seek the assistance of legal counsel. Adjusters are also prohibited from drawing up any kind of legal documents but must merely fill in the blanks on releases and proofs of loss already drafted by counsel.

Finally, the *Statement on Rights and Duties* specifies that all representatives of companies involved in the investigation, adjustment, or settlement of any claims must conduct themselves in an ethical manner.

Another statement of practice generally accepted throughout the insurance industry is the *Guiding Principles for Overlapping Insurance Coverages* as adopted by the Association of Casualty and Surety Companies, the Inland Marine Underwriters Association, the National Automobile Underwriters Association, the National Board of Fire Underwriters, the National Bureau of Casualty Underwriters and the Surety Association of America. In essence, these *Guiding Principles* are designed to prevent disputes with regard to the adjustment and apportionment of losses because of overlapping coverages. The effect of such an agreement is to provide systematic loss adjustment for the insured and eliminate the need for costly litigation or arbitration between coinsurers.

CONCLUSION

Claims adjusters hold a unique position in the insurance process. As suggested earlier, without loss potential there is no need for insurance. At the same time, as long as that loss potential exists, insurers must have the facility to discharge their duties under the terms of the insurance contract. Hence, adjusters are an indispensable part of the insurance industry. For the policyholder, it is the adjuster who gives meaning to the contract of insurance. For the company, the adjusters represent its interests to the insuring public, and their actions will be seen as a direct reflection of the company's attitudes and responsiveness with regard to the disposition of its claim payment obligations.

PART 2

Legal Considerations

7

Stop and Frisk

Martin L. Landa

Revised by
Frank S. Polestino

A law enforcement officer, whether in uniform or civilian clothes, is often faced with street encounters where suspicious circumstances require the officer to take some action. If facts and circumstances are such that the officer has probable cause, the suspect can be placed under arrest. But, as a practical matter, many street encounters are not so "cut and dried." An officer will often feel a need to investigate the activities of a person when insufficient facts are possessed to warrant an arrest. To the practitioner in the field, stopping and questioning suspicious persons is a frequent means of preventing crime and investigating suspected criminal activity. Because of the frequency of its use, and its value in assisting law enforcement officers to investigate criminal conduct, it is extremely important that the investigator have a working knowledge of the legal requirements that must be met. If the street encounter results in the arrest of the suspect, the on-the-street actions become crucial at the trial. If the investigator acted within the established constitutional guidelines, the evidence obtained will be admitted into court. However, if the investigator failed to act as prescribed, such evidence will be excluded, regardless of the apparent guilt of the defendant.

The purpose of this chapter is to clarify those procedural requirements applicable to the questioning of suspicious persons, hereafter referred to as "the stop, question, and frisk" procedure. Throughout the chapter the reader will notice various case citations. These citations refer to the topic discussed immediately before and are included as a source of reference.

FOURTH AMENDMENT APPLICABILITY

The starting point in a discussion of the legal requirements for the temporary detention of suspicious persons is the Fourth Amendment to the U.S. Constitution, which states:

> The right of the people to be secure in their persons, houses, papers and effects against unreasonable searches and seizures shall not be violated, and no warrant shall issue, but upon probable cause, supported by oath or affirmation, and particularly describing the place to be searched and the persons or things to be seized.

The problem of balancing this right of privacy [see *Katz v. United States*, 389 U.S. 347 (1967)] with the police responsibility to investigate suspicious circumstances in the prevention and detection of crime, was addressed by the Supreme Court in 1968. The Court held that:

> Where a police officer observes unusual conduct which leads him reasonably to conclude, in light of his experience, that criminal activity may be afoot and that the persons with whom he is dealing may be armed and presently dangerous; where in the course of investigating this behavior he identifies himself as a policeman and makes reasonable inquiries, and where nothing in the initial stages of the encounter serves to dispel his reasonable fear of his own or another's safety, he is entitled, for the protection of himself and others in the area, to conduct a carefully limited search of the outer clothing of such persons in an attempt to discover weapons which might be used to assault him. [*Terry v. Ohio*, 392 U.S. 1 (1968)]

While the stopping of citizens in the course of an investigation is not a recently developed police technique, *Terry* indicated that this tactic does, in fact, fall within the purview of the Fourth Amendment.

First, *Terry* made it clear that accosting an individual under circumstances where the suspect is not free to walk away constitutes a limited "seizure" of that person under the Fourth Amendment. Second, the frisk, even though not a full-blown search, "is a serious intrusion upon the sanctity of the person" and is to be considered a search under the Fourth Amendment.

The Court went on to recognize, however, that because this stop is more limited in scope than an arrest and the frisk is less intrusive than a full-blown search, these actions are to be judged by the Fourth Amendment general prohibition against unreasonable searches and seizures rather than by the warrant-clause requirement of probable cause.

STREET ENCOUNTERS— DEGREES OF INTRUSION

Terry indicated that when police encounters with citizens reach the level of a "search or seizure," the Fourth Amendment applies. At the same time the Court realized that "not all personal intercourse between policemen and citizens involves `seizures' of persons." Law enforcement officers interact daily with members of the community. These encounters are not necessarily initiated to investigate criminal activity. The police officer has many roles in addition to law enforcement, including "the protection of constitutional rights; the maintenance of order, the control of pedestrian and vehicular traffic; the mediation of domestic and other noncriminal conflicts; and the supplying of emergency help and assistance." [*People v. DeBour*, 40 N.Y. 2d 210 (1976)]

The police officer should keep in mind that, to a degree, a community's attitude toward the police is influenced most by the actions of individual officers on the street. The techniques used during these encounters have a potential for becoming a source of friction between police and minority groups.

These street encounters will usually fall within four degrees of intrusion, which could be characterized as follows:

Voluntary Conversation, Not Necessarily Crime-Related

The minimal intrusion of approaching an individual to seek information is permissible when there is some articulable reason for that interference—not necessarily indicative of criminality. This type of occurrence is sometimes referred to as a *contact*. [*United States v. Mandenhall*, 446 U.S. 544, 553 (1980)]

Example. An officer on patrol late at night observes someone who appears to be walking erratically. The person could be drunk, sick, or the victim of a crime. The officer can investigate, although the person cannot be ordered to halt, be detained involuntarily, or frisked. Similarly, an officer can make inquiries of persons passing by in order to find the parent of a lost child.

Inquiry Regarding Possible Criminal Conduct

The common-law right to inquire upon a founded suspicion that criminal activity is afoot permits the officer to interfere with the citizen to the extent necessary to seek explanatory information, but short of a forcible seizure [*DeBour* at p. 223]. The following examples indicate the types of circumstances that would warrant a forcible stop.

Example 1. During early morning hours two uniformed officers were investigating another crime in an area of apartment houses when they observed a man running. Seeing two other men nearby, the two police officers thought that the man running might be a victim of a crime and called to him. The man stopped, looked at the uniformed officers, and then began running again. The officers pursued and caught him, and then questioned him. The court held that there was reasonable suspicion of criminal activity afoot justifying the two police officers in detaining and questioning this man [*People v. Jones*, 69 N.Y. 2d 853 (1987)].

Example 2. Police officers observed a man running into a busy intersection, frantically waving his arms and jumping in front of vehicles to stop either a passing car or taxicab. The officers further saw the man looking back toward the area he had come from while attempting to stop vehicles. Thus, the police had reason to suspect that the man was either a victim or perpetrator of a recently committed crime and were justified in detaining and questioning him in a nonforcible manner [*People v. Hutchinson*, 47 N.Y. 2d 823 (1979)].

Forcible Stop/Minimal Detention to Investigate Possible Criminal Activity

When an officer has reasonable suspicion that an individual is about to commit, is committing, or has committed a crime, a forcible stop and limited detention are justified. In addition, the officer who reasonably suspects danger of physical injury may frisk such a person. The two examples that follow may be helpful in understanding the type of facts that would warrant a forcible stop.

Example 1. A detective with many years of experience saw two individuals repeatedly walking past a store and looking through the window. To the ordinary citizen, this behavior might not be particularly suspicious; however, to the trained and experienced officer, it would create a reasonable suspicion that the men were "casing" the store for the commission of a robbery (*Terry*).

Example 2. Late at night two police officers received a radio transmission reporting a suspicious male on a fire escape ladder of a multiple dwelling. When the police arrived at the scene, they observed a male walking down a dark alley toward the rear of another building adjacent to the one reported. The police went down the alley after the man and observed him attempting to pull himself up onto a fire escape. When the officers inquired as to what the man was doing, he responded, "Nothing." This was sufficient to establish reasonable suspicion that the man was about to commit a burglary [*People v. Perry*, 71 N.Y. 2d 871 (1988) affirming 133 AD 2d 380 (N.Y. App. Div. 2d Dept, (1987)].

REASONABLE SUSPICION— BASIS FOR THE STOP AND/OR FRISK

In order to justify both a stop and a frisk, the officer must be able to point to specific articulable facts that would warrant these intrusions.

> [I]n justifying the particular intrusion the police officer must be able to point to specific and articulable facts which, taken together with rational inferences from those facts, reasonably warrant that intrusion....Anything less would invite intrusions upon constitutionally guaranteed rights based on nothing more substantial than inarticulate hunches, a result this Court has consistently refused to sanction. (*Terry*)

Terry points out that different government interests are involved in conducting the stop and in performing the frisk. The government interest that permits a temporary detention of a citizen is that of "effective crime prevention and detection." On the other hand, there is a more immediate government interest, the protection of the officer and others in the area, involved in authorizing the frisk.

Because of these different interests involved, the officer must be able to enunciate specific facts to justify the stop, independent of those facts used to justify the frisk. The reasonableness of each must stand on its own merits. It is important to realize that while a reasonable stop is a predicate for a reasonable frisk, a frisk does not necessarily follow every reasonable stop.

In judging the reasonableness of the stop, the officer must be able to point to specific and articulable facts that meet the standard of reasonable suspicion. The term "reasonable suspicion" does not have a precise definition. It is more than a hunch or gut reaction on the part of the investigator, but less than the facts required to establish probable cause to make an arrest. Reasonable suspicion has been defined as "the quantum of knowledge sufficient to induce an ordinarily prudent and cautious man under the circumstances to believe criminal activity is at hand" [*People v. Cantor*, 36 N.Y.2d 106 (1975)]. It should be emphasized that the inferences which may be drawn are based on the officer's experience. What may appear as innocent, innocuous conduct to the general public may be looked at quite differently by an experienced police officer.

The following are some factors that alone or in combination may be sufficient to establish reasonable suspicion for a stop. These facts are compiled principally from the case law of various jurisdictions.

The Suspect's Appearance. Does the suspect fit the general description of a person wanted for a known offense, have a suspicious gait or manner, appear to be suffering from a recent injury or to be under the influence of alcohol or drugs, or have strange or unsuitable attire for the particular season or the time of day or night?

The Suspect's Actions. Is the suspect fleeing from an actual or suspected crime scene or otherwise behaving in a suspicious or peculiar manner tending to indicate possible criminal activity? If so, what is the behavior? Does the suspect make evasive or furtive movements? If so, what are they? Be prepared to describe them in court. Were incriminating statements or conversations overheard?

Prior Knowledge About the Suspect. Does the suspect have an arrest record and, if so, any convictions? Even if not previously arrested, is the suspect known to have committed serious offenses in the past? If so, were these offenses or those responsible for previous arrests similar to the one of which the individual is now suspected?

Demeanor During Questioning. If the suspect responded to questions, were the answers evasive, suspicious, or incriminating? Was excessive nervousness shown during questioning?

Area of the Stop. Is the suspect in the vicinity of the scene of the crime shortly after its commission? Is the area otherwise known as a high-crime area? If so, have there been numerous crimes of the same nature as the one for which the person is under suspicion?

Time of Day. Is the officer's observation made at a peculiar hour? Is it unusual for people to be in the area at that time of the day or night? Is it a time of day when a particular type of crime is most likely to occur?

Police Training and Experience. Does the conduct observed by the officer resemble the modus operandi usual for the type of offense suspected? Does the officer possess a high degree of expertise regarding the type of criminal activity under investigation, such as narcotics or gambling?

Profile. Does the suspect meet an established profile of a person engaged in the offense suspected, such as a drug courier profile? [See *United States v. Sokolow*, 490 U.S. 1 (1989).]

Disclosed or Undisclosed Informants. If the source of the information is other than the officer's own observation, what type of person supplied the information, a disclosed or undisclosed informant? Was that person a criminal informant or a victim of a crime? Is the reliability of the informant known? Was the informant's information corroborated or strengthened in some manner? [See *Adams v. Williams*, 407 U.S. 143 (1971).]

Anonymous Informant. An anonymous type may serve as the basis for reasonable suspicion; however, caution must be exercised in utilizing this information. An anonymous tip that merely relates information of a condition or conditions existing at the time the tip was communicated, when that information is available to any citizen, is not sufficient. For example, a tip indicating that a particularly described person is at a particular location and in possession of cocaine is not sufficient. To be sufficient, the tip must be such as to predict future behavior which, in turn, must be independently verified by the officer. For instance, a tip indicating a person will leave a certain location, get into a described car, and drive in a most direct route to a certain location to deliver cocaine will suffice if the officer observes the targeted person and that person behaves as the tip predicted [*Alabama v. White*, 110 5 Ct 2412 (1990)].

Police Purpose. Was the officer investigating a specific crime or specific type of criminal activity? How serious is the suspected criminal activity? Might innocent people be endangered if investigative action is not taken at once?

The inferences drawn from these factors must create a belief that criminal activity may be afoot and that the suspect is connected with it. Notwithstanding the reasonableness of the stop, the officer must, in addition, articulate a reasonable apprehension of danger to justify the need for the frisk. *Terry* points out:

> The officer need not be absolutely certain that the individual is armed; the issue is whether a reasonably prudent man in the circumstances would be warranted in the belief that his safety or that of others was in danger....And in determining whether the officer acted reasonably in such circumstances, due weight must be given, not to his inchoate and unparticularized suspicion or "hunch," but to the specific reasonable inferences which he is entitled to draw from the facts in light of his experience. (See section entitled "The Frisk" for a discussion of the factors to consider in establishing reasonable suspicion for a frisk.)

Importance of Written Record. It should be apparent that the "thread" that upholds the reasonableness of the stop and/or frisk is those facts and circumstances that aroused the officer's suspicions at the outset. At the earliest opportunity, notes should be made of the suspect's behavior and any other condition that formed the basis for the stop and/or frisk. At the suppression hearing, or in the event that the case should reach the trial stage, the officer's suspicions will have to be justified. The officer's testimony should paint a picture of the scene using words that clearly indicate to the court the reasonableness of the actions. Details which at face value appear insignificant should not be omitted. Often, it is these very details or observations that crystallize in the court's mind the reasonableness of the action by the officer. The court will not be interested in "gut reactions," but will want to know specific facts and the inferences that were drawn from them. It is for these reasons that notes should be taken of the facts and circumstances as soon as it is practical, while these facts and impressions are still fresh in the officer's mind. As a general rule, if the reasons for the stop cannot be verbalized, the stop will, in all likelihood, be difficult to justify.

THE STOP

What is a stop? A *stop* refers to a situation in which an individual is temporarily detained or his or her freedom of movement is restricted under circumstances in which the investigator does not possess sufficient facts to justify an arrest.

A stop is conducted to investigate circumstances which the officer reasonably suspects indicate that criminal activity is imminent, is in progress, or has already occurred. If this objective can be attained without endangering the officer or the public or losing the suspect, the investigation should be conducted by less intrusive means, such as those discussed previously.

What Is Not a Stop?

For a stop to have occurred, there must be either some application of force, even if extremely slight, or a show of authority to which a subject yields. A show of authority without any application of physical force, to which a subject does not yield, is not a stop. For example, an officer approaches a subject and declares, "Police! Stop!" The subject does not stop but flees. This is not a stop [*California v. Hodari D.*, 111 5 Ct 1547 (1991)].

Who Can Stop? As indicated previously, the stopping of individuals to investigate suspicious circumstances has been characterized as a seizure of a person, and therefore is governed by the Fourth Amendment. The Fourth Amendment's prohibition against unreasonable searches and seizures is applicable only to public officers (that is, police officers) or those acting under such officers' authority or guidance. Therefore, the fruits of a frisk or search by a private security guard or investigators such as those employed by large department stores are for the most part not governed by these guidelines.

Location of the Stop. The majority of the situations in which stops take place occur on the street. However, officers can also conduct stops in any other locations where they are lawfully present. This includes, but is not limited to, hallways and stairways of multiple dwellings and office buildings, depots, stations, beaches, and parks. These locations would also generally include any place with the consent of a person legally empowered to give consent, places where circumstances require immediate action to protect life or property, or any place where the officer is present to effect an arrest or execute a court order such as a search warrant [*Michigan v. Summer*, 452 U.S. 692 (1981)].

The stop could also be extended to persons in automobiles. However, in order to make the initial stop, the officer must be able to articulate reasons to justify this intrusion [*Delaware v. Prouse*, 440 U.S. 648 (March 1979)]. Basically, this requirement is not different from that for the forcible stopping of an individual on the street. In either case, you must be able to state the reasons to justify your reasonable suspicion [*People v. Sobotker*, 43 N.Y. 2d 559 (1978)].

Factors to Justify the Stopping of a Vehicle. Some of the factors to be considered in determining whether to stop a vehicle are as follows:

- The vehicle fits the description of a vehicle used in a past robbery or other crime.
- The vehicle has been stolen or fits the description of a stolen vehicle.
- The occupants fit the description of persons wanted in connection with a past crime.
- The driver is under age.
- The driver appears to be under the influence of an intoxicant or narcotic.
- The driver appears to be unfamiliar with the vehicle.
- The driver is making erratic maneuvers, such as weaving across lanes.
- The vehicle concerned has a damaged or missing trunk or doorlocks, broken vent windows, and so on.
- The vehicle is a rental and is damaged. (Rental autos are not normally leased in a damaged condition.)
- A tow truck is towing a late model vehicle without apparent damage.
- The inspection sticker and registration plates on the vehicle are from different states.
- The inspection sticker has expired.
- The license plates are poorly secured to the car (tied with wire, cord, and so on).
- Cardboard or expired license plates are on the vehicle.

While the police officer does have a legal right to stop automobiles, based on reasonable suspicion, the arbitrary stopping of "an automobile and detaining the driver in order to check his driver's license and the registration of the automobile are unreasonable under the Fourth Amendment [*Prouse*]." The use of roadblocks or checkpoints for questioning all on-coming vehicles [*Michigan Dept. of State Police v. Sitz*, 110 S. Ct. 2481 (1990)] or every third vehicle [*People v. Scott*, 63 N.Y. 2d 518 (1984)] are options that must be uniform, systematic, and conducted in a nonarbitrary manner.

PROCEDURAL
REQUIREMENTS

Up to this point we have discussed those facts and circumstances that would warrant the stop and detention of an individual to investigate possible criminal activity. The material that follows clarifies the procedural requirements that must be met in carrying out the stop or stop and frisk of the person under investigation.

Identification. Investigators should identify themselves to individuals stopped. In addition, the officer should state the purpose for the stop, unless the circumstances are such that it is obvious. The identification of the officer would help alleviate the potential problem of persons mistakenly believing they are being accosted as potential victims of a crime and may also facilitate the gathering of information. The necessity of identifying oneself when in uniform seems moot and is not required in some jurisdictions (New York, for example).

Degree of Force Authorized. It would be ideal if all suspects voluntarily submitted to being stopped. As a practical matter, this is not always the case. It is neither realistic nor tactically sound to walk abreast of the suspect asking various questions. While the officer should attempt to use the least coercive means (verbal request or an order) to effect a stop and/or temporary detention, it is permissible to use physical force to keep the individual at the scene [*Terry* at p. 19, Ftnte 16]. Indeed, grabbing, holding, and blocking are all permissible forms of physical force [*Kolender v. Lawson*, 461 U.S. 352, 364 (1983)].

Use of Weapons for Protection. If the officer's safety is in question, then the display of a weapon [*People v. Chestnut*, 51 N.Y. 2d 14 (1980)] or the handcuffing of a suspect [*People v. Allen*, 73 N.Y. 2d 378 (1989)] may be appropriate.

In considering safety aspects of the stop, certain circumstances must be taken into consideration, such as:

What crime is the officer investigating?

Does this type of crime normally involve weapons?

Is this stop being conducted during the daylight hours or at night?

These factors, individually or in combination, may warrant the display of a weapon. Again, it should be emphasized that the purpose of using a weapon under these circumstances is for personal protection and not to detain the individual.

If the display of a weapon or the handcuffing of a suspect is not warranted by the circumstances, then such conduct may elevate the encounter into a full-blown arrest [*People v. Allen*, 73 N.Y. 2d, 378, 380 (1989)].

Frisk of Personal Property. If a suspect who is stopped is carrying a handbag, dufflebag, or similar type of container, a *Terry* search would permit an opening of such a container to ascertain if there is a weapon in it [*United States v. Johnson*, 637F 2d 532 (8th Cir. 1980); *United States v. Walker*, 576F 2d 253 (9th Cir. 1978); *United States v. Vigo*, 487F 2d 295 (2d Cir. 1973); *United States v. Morales*, 549F Supp. 217 (5 D. N.Y. 1982); *People v. Davis*, 64 N.Y. 2d 1143 (1985); *People v. Moore*, 32 N.Y. 2d 67 (1973)].

However, since a *Terry* search should be no greater than the circumstances require, it might be more appropriate to remove the container from the suspect before the questioning phase and place it out of the suspect's reach. When the questioning is concluded and if the suspect is free to leave, the container should be returned to him/her unopened [*People v. Torres*, 74 N.Y. 2d 224 (1989); *People v. Tucker*, 44 N.Y. 2d 941 (1978). If, however, the suspect is arrested, the container may then be searched [*New York v. Belton*, 453 U.S. 454 (1981)].

Ordering a Motorist Out of a Vehicle after a Lawful Stop. The stopping of a vehicle and its occupants poses an added risk to the officer. A significant number of police shooting incidents occur when an officer approaches a suspect seated in a vehicle. The Supreme Court has indicated that once a motor vehicle has been lawfully detained, the officer may order the driver out of the car for the officer's personal protection. This face-to-face contact may prevent a motorist from making any sudden moves for weapons and, at the same time, may negate the necessity of having the officer stand on the roadway side of the vehicle during the encounter [*Commonwealth of Pennsylvania v. Harry Mimms*, 434 U.S. 106 (1977)]. While the Court has deemed the ordering of the motorist out of the vehicle a minimal intrusion on the individual's liberty, the question of what can be done if the driver refuses to comply has not yet been addressed.

It has also been held that ordering a passenger out of a vehicle for the officer's personal protection is authorized too [*People v. Robinson*, 74 N.Y. 2d 773 (1989)].

THE QUESTIONING PHASE

Since the initial stop is based on reasonable suspicion of criminal conduct, it is appropriate to ask questions to clear up or substantiate the suspicions. The questions to be asked should focus on the individual's name and address and an explanation of suspicious presence and/or conduct.

Significance of Individual's Refusal to Answer. The right to ask questions does not compel the suspect to answer. Most people resent being stopped by a law enforcement official. There are many explanations for this, which, in light of the detained individual's experiences, may be reasonable. The fact that the suspect refuses to answer questions cannot, in itself, be used as a basis for a subsequent arrest. However, this refusal may be the basis for continued observation. A person has a constitutional right to refrain from self-incrimination [Fifth Amendment]. The failure to respond to an inquiry may not be considered as a factor in establishing probable cause for an arrest [*People v. Howard*, 50 N.Y. 2d 583, 591 (1980)]. However, false or evasive answers along with other factors that formed the basis for the initial stop may very well be the predicate for an arrest [*People v. Brady*, 16 N.Y. 2d 186, 189 (1965)].

REQUEST FOR IDENTIFICATION

In addition to asking questions, the investigator may properly request identification [*Kolender v. Lawson*, 461 U.S. 352, 356 (Ftnte 5) (1983)].

The refusal to identify oneself may be one of several factors to be considered in establishing probable cause for an arrest [*People v. Spivey*, 41 N.Y. 2d 1014, 1016 (1979)].

Applicability of the *Miranda* Warnings

Does the *Miranda* rule apply? The Supreme Court, in *Miranda v. Arizona*, 384 U.S. 436 (1966), indicated that a warning of rights must be given and a waiver of those rights obtained prior to police questioning in those circumstances where a person is "in custody or otherwise deprived of his freedom of action in any significant way." However, the Court specifically stated that "general on-the-scene questioning as to facts surrounding a crime or the general questioning of citizens in the fact-finding process is not affected by our holding." Indeed, the Supreme Court, in *Pennsylvania v. Bruder*, 488 U.S. 9 (1988), held that *Miranda* warnings need not be given during a traffic stop that was a seizure, since said stops are typically brief and commonly occur in the public view. By an analogy of reasoning, if a stop-and-frisk detention is brief and occurs in public view without a display of weapons, then *Miranda* warnings need not be given.

The following elements are relevant in determining if *Miranda* warnings should be given during a stop-and-frisk detention:

Time of day.

Location of the detention.

Duration of the questioning.

Type of crime being investigated.

Type of suspect (age, mental or physical condition, and intelligence).

Number of officers present.

Manner of questioning (intimidating or bullying the suspect).

Display of weapons.

Amount of force used to stop the suspect or cause the suspect to remain at the scene.

It has been held that questioning after a frisk in a stop-and-frisk detention without doing anything more is not custodial interrogation requiring *Miranda* warnings [*People v. Morales*, 65 N.Y. 2d 997 (1985)].

In any event, an officer encountering a volatile situation in a stop-and-frisk detention, regardless of the circumstances of the detention, may ask one or more questions to clarify a volatile situation. Thus, such questions as, "Is the shoulder bag yours?" [*People v. Johnson*, 59 N.Y. 2d 1014 (1983)], "*What is going on here?*" [*People v. Greer*, 42 N.Y. 2d 170 (1977)], and "What are you doing here?" [*People v. Huffman*, 41 N.Y. 2d 29 (1976)] are proper questions without *Miranda* warnings.

Finally, if an officer in a stop-and-frisk detention, regardless of the circumstances of the detention, is confronted by a situation presenting a danger to the public safety, such as ascertaining the location of a weapon in a public place, he may query, "Where is the gun?" [*New York v. Quarles*, 467 U.S. 649 (1984)].

Where Conducted

The questioning of a suspicious person should be conducted at the scene of the stop. Indeed, involuntary removal of a suspect to a police facility for questioning would be deemed an arrest, which would require probable cause and not reasonable suspicion [*Dunaway v. New York*, 442 U.S. 200 (1979)].

However, the involuntary transportation of a suspect to the crime scene is within the permissible bounds of a stop-and-frisk detention [*People v. Hicks*, 68 N.Y. 2d 234 (1986)].

If the suspect is not being transported to the crime scene, then extenuating practical concerns may warrant the involuntary movement of the suspect. It would not be feasible to attempt to question a suspect in the face of a hostile crowd or to frisk a suspect in an area with limited visibility if there is adequate light one block away. It would also appear reasonable to move a suspect to an area that limits the danger to the officer and innocent persons in the area [*People v. Allen*, 73 N.Y. 2d 378, 379–380 (1989)].

Duration of Detention for the Purpose of Questioning

How long can an individual be detained for questioning? There is no hard and fast rule of law in this regard. It appears that a suspect may be detained for a reasonable length of time in order to adequately resolve the suspicious or ambiguous circumstances. If the individual is detained for longer than is necessary to clear up the situation, an unreasonable amount of time has been taken.

Under normal circumstances 20 to 40 minutes is a good yardstick [*United States v. Sharpe*, 470 U.S. 675 (1985)]. If extenuating circumstances are present, this period can be extended [*United States v. Montoya De Hernandez*, 473 U.S. 531 (1985). Suspected alimentary canal smuggler detained 16 hours]. However, if the suspicious circumstances are cleared up in minutes, further detention is illegal [*People v. Milaski*, 62 N.Y. 2d 147 (1984)].

THE FRISK

The stop, question, and frisk law, on its face, appears to be a three-part procedure, used whenever a stop is made. A discussion of the frisk phase of a street encounter might be more easily understood if the title were more appropriately rephrased as the "stop; question; and, *if necessary*, frisk procedure."

What Is a Frisk?

The *frisk* is the patting down of the exterior garments of an individual. The procedure is designed solely as a protection for the police officer and others in the area during street encounters. The frisk, therefore, must be confined to a search reasonably designed to discover guns, knives, clubs, or other hidden instruments that could be used to assault an officer. As discussed earlier, this intrusion, while limited in scope, has been deemed to be a search under the Fourth Amendment. Therefore, to pass constitutional scrutiny, the frisk must meet the test of reasonableness.

A frisk will be considered reasonable only when it is conducted under those circumstances in which the officer's safety or the safety of others in the area can reasonably be thought to be in danger because the individual stopped may be armed with a weapon. The frisk can be justified only from a safety standpoint and cannot be used for the primary purpose of acquiring contraband for purposes of arrest [*People v. Stroller*, 42 N.Y. 2d 1052 (1977)]. An addict who is stopped based on a reasonable suspicion of mere drug possession cannot be frisked for the drugs prior to an arrest [*Sibron v. New York*, 392 U.S. 40 (1968)]. However, it should be pointed out that if there is reasonable suspicion that the person stopped is a major drug trafficker, there is reason to suspect that person is armed [*United States v. Morales*, 549F Supp. 217, 221 (S.D.N.Y. 1982)].

For a frisk to be considered reasonable, certain criteria must be met. First, the stop must be lawful. If the stop fails to pass the test of reasonableness, the frisk will never be lawful. If the officer did not have grounds to stop the suspect, the fact that during the course of the questioning there was reason to suspect that the individual was armed will not help. Evidence obtained under such circumstances would be excluded by the court.

Second, there must be a reasonable suspicion that the officer's safety or the safety of others may be in danger. It need not be shown that it was *probable* that the person was armed but only that there was reason for fear for the officer's safety or that of others in the area. The officer need show only that there was a substantial possibility that the individual possessed some article that could be used to cause injury. This belief can be based on various factors that alone or in combination may be sufficient to justify a frisk.

Factors That May Justify a Frisk

The person's appearance: Clothing bulging in a manner suggesting the presence of an object capable of inflicting injury [*People v. Perry*, 71 N.Y. 2d 871 (1988); *People v. Prochilo*, 41 N.Y. 2d 759 (1977)].

The person's actions: Threatening actions, such as placing a hand in a pocket and failing to remove the hand when ordered to do so by the officer [*People v. Samuels*, 50 N.Y. 2d 1035 (1980)].

Type of crime: One that is commonly associated with the use of a weapon, such as robbery or homicide [*Terry* case; *People v. Mack*, 26 N.Y. 2d 311, 258 N.E. 2d 703 (1970)].

Third-party information: Information received by the officer from a reliable informant or other citizen which led to the belief that the suspect was armed [*Adams v. Williams*, 407 U.S. 143 (1972)].

Prior knowledge: The officer's knowledge that the person has a police record for weapons offenses or for assaults on police officers or others or a reputation for carrying weapons or for violent behavior [*United States v. Harris*, 403 U.S. 573 (1971)].

Location: An area known for criminal activity (a high-crime area) or sufficiently isolated that the officer is unlikely to receive aid if attacked.

Time of day: The confrontation taking place at night; darkness contributing to the likelihood that the officer will be attacked.

Companions: The officer has detained a number of people at the same time, a frisk of a companion of the suspect revealed a weapon. The officer has assistance immediately available to handle the number of persons stopped.

Procedural Requirements

The frisk is limited to a "pat down" of the exterior garments of an individual. The officer can feel those areas of the outer garments where a weapon may be hidden if the stop is in connection with a suspected crime of violence (robbery, burglary, assault). However, if the suspicion for the frisk is based on a bulge or some other factor that "just isn't right," the patting down should be restricted to the area that gave rise to this suspicion. If a bulge that appears to be the outline of a pistol in a person's jacket pocket is observed, that area may be patted down [*People v. Prochilo*, 41 N.Y. 2d 759 (1977)]. If the suspicions are dispelled, the other pockets or any other part of the suspect cannot automatically be frisked based solely on the initial bulge [*People v. Stewart*, 41 N.Y. 2d (1976)]. The frisk of each area must be based on some articulable suspicion that leads the officer to believe that there may be a weapon there. Upon feeling what is believed to be a weapon, the investigator may intensify the search to determine the nature of the object [*United States v. Lopez*, 328F Supp. 1077 (ED N.Y. 1971); *People v. Perry*, 71 N.Y. 871 (1988)].

Frisk Inside Outer Clothing. In most street encounters the frisk is limited to patting down the outer garments (*Terry*). However, if the officer cannot adequately frisk the outer garment to ascertain if there is a weapon because, for example, the person is wearing heavy outer clothing, such as a winter overcoat, the officer may then reach under such outer garment to pat the inner clothing [*State v. Vasquez*, 167 Ariz. 352 (1991)]. This extension of the frisk would not include intrusion into the inner pockets of an individual whose clothing is of a type normally worn inside a building, such as a jacket or sweater. The sport jacket and other clothes of this type would not impede the efficiency of the frisk.

If, however, there is information as to the location of a weapon, such as in a pocket or in a waistband, the officer may reach into that area and seize the weapon [*Adams v. Williams*, 407 U.S. 143 (1972) (waistband); *People v. Taggart*, 20 N.Y. 2d 335 (1967) (pocket)].

Frisk of Personal Property. There are times when the individual stopped in the course of a field investigation is carrying packages or other personal objects, such as a purse or briefcase. Since the goal of the frisk is the protection of the officer and others in the area, these items can be subject to a limited search for weapons [*People v. Brooks*, 65 N.Y. 2d 1021 (1985). See also the prior section, "Frisk of Personal Property."]

Automobiles and Their Occupants. Most limited searches of vehicles and their occupants are conducted incidental to the arrest of the driver or other occupants. However, in situations not amounting to probable cause for an arrest, a limited frisk of suspects would still be justified if the officer reasonably suspects that occupants are armed. In the case of *Mimms*, cited earlier, the officer ordered the driver out of the vehicle and observed a bulge, resembling a weapon, in the suspect's waistband. The Court concluded that patting down the area where the officer suspected the weapon to be and its subsequent removal were justified, based on the officer's concern for his safety.

A limited search may also extend to that part of the vehicle that had been accessible to the suspect if the officer suspects that the area contains an article or instrument that can be used as a weapon [*Michigan v. Long*, 463 U.S. 1032 (1983)].

It should be noted that some jurisdictions (New York in particular) reject a limited search of a vehicle if the suspect is outside the vehicle and no longer has access to the interior [*People v. Torres*, 74 N.Y. 2d 224 (1989)].

Companions. If a person stopped or arrested is in the company of others, the frisk of the companions would still be justified if the officer reasonably suspects that the individuals are armed.

Frisking Before Questioning. In the introduction to the frisk aspect of an investigative detention, it was suggested that this procedure should be called the "stop, question, and, if necessary, frisk" law [*People v. Perry*, 71 N.Y. 2d 871 (1988)]. However, situations will arise that make adherence to this format unrealistic. For example, suppose that a reliable informant gives an officer information to the effect that a person parked in a nearby vehicle has a gun in the waistband. To approach and begin to question the suspect before ascertaining that the person does, in fact, have a weapon, would, from a tactical point of view, be unrealistic. Under these circumstances, the officer would be justified in reaching into the specific area of the person where a weapon is suspected, without first patting down that individual.

> The purpose of [this] limited search is not to discover evidence of crime, but to allow the officer to pursue his investigation without fear of violence...so long as the officer is entitled to make a forcible stop, and has reason to believe that a suspect is armed and dangerous, he may conduct a weapons search limited in scope to his protection. [*Adams*]

Admissibility of Evidence Obtained

If the frisk based on reasonable suspicion uncovers an illegal weapon, the suspect will be arrested, and the evidence seized may be admissible in court. Why the words "may be"? For the evidence to be admissible, *Terry* indicated that certain criteria must be met:

The stop must be lawful (based on reasonable suspicion).

The frisk must have been based on the officer's reasonable suspicion that the person was armed and dangerous.

The officer must identify himself or herself.

The officer must make reasonable inquiries (except if impractical).

The officer's concern for his or her safety (and that of others in the area) is not dispelled.

Not all frisks, no matter how well intended, result in the discovery of a weapon. Suppose a bulge that appears to be a weapon is observed in a suspect's pocket. The officer conducts a lawful frisk that reveals a hard object, possibly a gun. However, a search of the pocket does not reveal any weapon. Instead, a substantial amount of narcotics is discovered. The narcotics may be seized and used as evidence [*Michigan v. Long*, 463 U.S. 1032 (1983)].

Such a seizure is justified under the plain view exception to a search warrant requirement [*Horton v. California*, 110 S. Ct. 2301 (1990)]. If the seizure involves property other than a weapon, there must be probable cause to believe that the property is evidence of a crime [*Arizona v. Hicks*, 480 U.S. 321 (1987)].

The investigator must be cognizant of the facts and circumstances that gave rise to the frisk, particularly when seizing evidence other than weapons. The investigator's testimony regarding the purpose of the frisk will be closely examined. Remember, the sole justification for a frisk is to determine the presence of weapons. The frisk cannot be used as a pretext to search for evidence other than weapons. The officer's discovery of two decks of heroin under the belief that the bulge was the outline of a razor blade is frequently looked at by the courts with skepticism. Further, merely feeling a hard object without identifying the object as possibly a weapon would not justify intrusion into a pocket where, for example, narcotics are discovered [*People v. Sanchez*, 38 N.Y. 2d 72, 74–75 (1975)].

On the other hand, if the officer feels a large hard object, reasonably suspects it is a weapon, and seizes it, but discovers that, in fact, it was stolen jewelry, the evidence will be admissible [*People v. Perry*, 71 N.Y. 2d 871 (1988)].

CONCLUSION

The investigator bears a heavy responsibility to the public for conduct consistent with the rules of law as interpreted by the courts. It must be remembered that this law was designed to strike a balance between safeguarding civil liberties and the day-to-day functioning of law enforcement officers. As in most aspects of police activity, the guiding word is "reasonableness." An officer who, by the test of reasonableness, is justified in making the stop or, by the test of reasonableness, is justified in frisking the individual for personal safety (or the safety of others) may do so.

The preceding section is intended to serve primarily as a guide for the investigator. Some of the references cited are not Supreme Court cases and, therefore, are not binding in all jurisdictions. The federal, state, and local decisions cited are applicable only in those areas covered by their respective jurisdictions. Therefore, it is recommended that the investigator refer to the case law in his or her respective jurisdiction for further qualification and/or elaboration of the topics discussed.

8

Search and Seizure

Jeffrey H. Kay

Revised by

Frank S. Polestino

This chapter gives a broad overview of the law of search and seizure. This area of the law is continually changing because U.S. Supreme Court decisions keep modifying the requirements and circumstances for reasonable searches. A full discussion of the law of search and seizure would easily fill an entire book. Here, I shall highlight important court decisions, rules of criminal procedure, and the way they affect the law enforcement officer. The Fourth Amendment of the U.S. Constitution emanates from our colonial times when the British authorities were entering homes or commercial establishments at will and conducting searches. Those searches were deemed unreasonable by the colonists as an invasion of their privacy and the right to be secure in their homes. Following the Revolutionary War and the Constitutional Convention, the framers of our Constitution agreed on the following language for the Fourth Amendment:

> The right of the people to be secure in their persons, houses, papers and effects, against unreasonable searches and seizures, shall not be violated, and no warrants shall issue, but upon probable cause supported by oath or affirmation, and particularly describing the place to be searched, and the persons or things to be seized.

Since that time our courts have held that individuals have an expectation of privacy against unreasonable searches and seizures under the Fourth Amendment. As the amendment reads, it requires law enforcement to secure a search warrant to overcome this concept of the individual's expectation of privacy. However, within the body of law on search and seizure, our courts have carved out exceptions to the requirement that all searches and seizures must be made pursuant to a search warrant.

When we talk about the privacy that an individual expects to have in his daily life, we must first turn to the Supreme Court decision in *Katz v. United States* [389 U.S. 347 (1961)]. Briefly, the facts in that case were that a defendant had been making telephone calls from a telephone booth for the purpose of wagering and betting and that federal agents placed an eavesdropping device on the outside of the booth to enable them to overhear the conversations. The Supreme Court found that although the listening device did not penetrate into the telephone booth, there was an intrusion into the privacy that the caller expected in placing a call from that telephone booth. Thus, the fact that the listening device was on the outside of the telephone booth was not significant, as the defendant had an expected right of privacy in making calls from the telephone booth. The Supreme Court held that the search was unconstitutional, because the agents did not obtain a search warrant.

The importance of *Katz* is not the use of electronic surveillance but the expectation-of-privacy issue created by the Court. The expectation-of-privacy concept is firmly entrenched in law involving the Fourth Amendment [*California v. Ciraolo*, 476 U.S. 207 (1986)]. Therefore, in situations where persons could normally have a reasonable expectation of privacy in their lives, they have the right to feel free from unreasonable search or seizure.

PROBABLE CAUSE FOR SEARCH WARRANT

The Fourth Amendment of the U.S. Constitution protects citizens from unreasonable searches, but states that warrants can be issued upon probable cause supported by oath or affirmation describing the place to be searched and the persons or things to be seized. A search warrant is usually sworn out before a judicial official, either a U.S. magistrate in the federal system or a state court judge. Upon a showing of probable cause to believe that the grounds listed in the search warrant exist, the judge will issue the warrant to be served on the place or property to be searched. (See Fig. 8.1.)

The words "probable cause" have been defined in several cases, most notably *Brinegar v. United States* [338 U.S 160, 175–76 (1949)], wherein the Supreme Court found it to be a reasonable ground for belief—less than evidence that would justify conviction, but more than bare suspicion. Probable cause pertains to circumstances in which a person of reasonable caution would believe an offense has been or is being committed.

This concept of probable cause has various formulations, such as only the probability and not a prima facie showing of criminal activity is the standard of probable cause [*Spinelli v. United States*, 393 U.S. 410, 419 (1969)], or behavior that is equally susceptible of innocent as well as of culpable interpretation will not constitute probable cause [*People v. De Bour*, 40 N.Y. 2d 210, 216 (1976)].

The affidavit is usually prepared by the law enforcement officer who is trying to obtain the search warrant. The affidavit's purpose is to state the probable cause, or the grounds of the officer's belief, that the objects being searched for are located on the premises. In the affidavit the officer can report personal observations, the results of an investigation or hearsay provided by a disclosed, undisclosed, or anonymous informant. If the officer is relying on hearsay, it must appear from the totality of circumstances that the informant's information is reliable [*Illinois v. Gates*, 462 U.S. 213 (1983)]. The affidavit is reviewed by the magistrate as a neutral party [*Coolidge v. New Hampshire*, 403 U.S. 443, 449–450 (1971); see also *LO-JI Sales v. New York*, 442 U.S. 319 (1979)]. (For a full treatment of this subject, see Chap. 9, "Arrest and Procedure.")

Upon finding that probable cause exists based on the affidavit, the magistrate or judge will then issue the warrant. In assessing probable cause, the information provided in the affidavit must be current and not stale [*Sgro v. United States*, 287 U.S. 206 (1932)]. For instance, if the data in the affidavit was five months old,

Form A. O. 93 (Rev. Apr. 1973)   Search Warrant

United States District Court

FOR THE

DISTRICT OF NEW YORK

UNITED STATES OF AMERICA

vs.

Ⓑ PREMISES KNOWN AS: ONE STORY GARAGE LOCATED AT▲COFFEE STREET, BROOKLYN, NEW YORK ∗ STREET NUMBER NEEDED

SEARCH WARRANT

Docket No.

Case No.

To ANY SPECIAL AGENTS OF THE U.S. CUSTOMS AND THE FEDERAL BUREAU OF INVESTIGATION

Affidavit(s) having been made before me by

that he has reason to believe that { on the person of ̶X̶ ̶X̶X̶X̶X̶X̶X̶X̶X̶X̶X̶X̶ on the premises known as }

Ⓑ PREMISES KNOWN AS A ONE STORY GARAGE LOCATED AT∗COFFEE STREET, NEW YORK.

in the   District of NEW YORK

there is now being concealed certain property, namely

here describe property

Ⓐ Ⓒ APPROXIMATELY 3,500 STOLEN MENS SUITS VALUED AT APPROXIMATELY $140,000 AND STOLEN COFFEE BAGS IN VIOLATION OF TITLE 18, UNITED STATES CODE, SECTIONS 549 AND 659.

and as I am satisfied that there is probable cause to believe that the property so described is being concealed on the person or premises above described and that grounds for application for issuance of the search warrant exist as stated in the supporting affidavit(s).

Ⓓ *You are hereby commanded* to search within a period of _____ (not to exceed 10 days) the person or place named for the property specified, serving this warrant and making the search { in the daytime (6:00 a.m. to 10:00 p.m.) X̶ ̶a̶t̶ ̶a̶n̶y̶ ̶t̶i̶m̶e̶ ̶i̶n̶ ̶t̶h̶e̶ ̶d̶a̶y̶ ̶o̶r̶ ̶n̶i̶g̶h̶t̶ ̶X̶ } and if the property be found there to seize it, leaving a copy of this warrant and receipt for the property taken, and prepare a written inventory of the property seized and promptly return this warrant and bring the property before _____ as required by law.

Federal Judge or magistrate

Dated this   day of   , 19

_____
Judge (Federal or State Court of Record) or Federal Magistrate.

*The Federal Rules of Criminal Procedure provide: "The warrant shall be served in the daytime, unless the issuing authority, by appropriate provision in the warrant, and for reasonable cause shown, authorizes its execution at times other than daytime." (Rule 41(c)). A statement of grounds for reasonable cause should be made in the affidavit(s) if a search is to be authorized "at any time day or night" pursuant to Rule 41(c).

Figure 8.1 Search warrant.

RETURN

I received the attached search warrant   , 19   , and have executed it as follows:

On   , 19   at   o'clock   M, I searched the person or premises de-
(E) scribed in the warrant and

I left a copy of the warrant with _
                                                            name of person searched or owner or "at the place of search"

together with a receipt for the items seized.

The following is an inventory of property taken pursuant to the warrant:

This inventory was made in the presence of

                                and

I swear that this Inventory is a true and detailed account of all the property taken by me on the warrant.

_ _

Subscribed and sworn to and returned before me this   day of   , 19   .

_ ,
                                                            Federal Magistrate

Figure 8.1 Search warrant (*Continued*).

and this is no showing for a continuing course of illegal conduct, then the information is stale and not the proper basis for a finding of probable cause [*United States v. Paul*, 692 F. Supp. 186 (S.D. N.Y. 1988)].

In reviewing an affidavit based on an informant's information, the magistrate must look for evidence of the reliability of such information depending on the totality of circumstances. An example of such a showing is based on the affidavit in *Massachusetts v. Upton* [466 U.S. 727 (1984)]. The affidavit slightly revised reads as follows:

> At noon on September 11, 1980, I assisted in the execution of a search warrant for a motel room reserved for one Richard Roe at the Snug Harbor Motel. The search produced several items of identification, including credit cards belonging to two persons whose home had recently been burglarized. Other items taken in the burglaries, such as jewelry, silver and gold, were not found at the motel.
>
> At 3:30 P.M. on the same day, I received a call from an unidentified female who told me that there was a motor home full of stolen stuff parked behind #5 Jefferson Avenue, the home of John Doe and his mother. She stated that the stolen items included jewelry, silver and gold.
>
> She further said that John Doe was going to move the motor home any time now because of the fact that Richard Roe's motel room was raided and that John (Doe) had purchased these stolen items from Richard Roe.
>
> This unidentified female stated that she had seen the stolen items but refused to identify herself because "He'll kill me," referring to John Doe. I then told this unidentified female that I knew who she was, giving her the name Mary Smith, whom I had met on May 16, 1980, at John Doe's repair shop off Summer St. in Anytown. She was identified to me by John Doe as being his girlfriend, Mary Smith. The unidentified female admitted that she was the girl that I had named, stating that she was surprised that I knew who she was. She then told me that she'd broken up with John Doe and wanted to burn him. She also told me that she wouldn't give her address and phone number but that she would contact me in the future, if need be.
>
> After the phone call I went to John Doe's home at #5 Jefferson Ave. and verified that there was a motor home parked on the property.

Annexed to the affidavit were the police reports on the two prior burglaries, along with lists of the stolen property.

This was held to be a sufficient showing of the informant's disclosures based on a totality of circumstances approach.

If the informant is anonymous, then substantial information based on investigation by the officer should be included in the affidavit [*Illinois v. Gates*, 462 U.S. 213 (1983)]. [For a discussion of an anonymous informant as the basis of reasonable suspicion, see *Alabama v. White* [110 S. Ct. 2412 (1990).]

Some jurisdictions, such as New York, reject the totality of circumstances approach and require that, to be deemed reliable, an informant's information must pass the two-pronged veracity and basis of knowledge test, that is, the informant is credible and speaking from personal knowledge [*People v. Griminger*, 71 N.Y. 2d 635 (1988)]. An example of an affidavit that sets forth a sufficient showing for this test is entered under Fig. 8.2.

As part of the affidavit and search warrant, it must be alleged that a crime has been committed. See Fig. 8.1, Letter A; Fig. 8.2, Letter A [*United States v. Averrell*, 296 F. Supp. 1004 (E.D. N.Y., 1969)].

The search warrant should describe in detail, as well as possible, the premises to be searched and things to be seized [*Maryland v. Garrison*, 480 U.S. 79 (1987)].

UNITED STATES DISTRICT COURT
EASTERN DISTRICT OF NEW YORK

----------------------------- X

UNITED STATES OF AMERICA

    - against -

(B) PREMISES KNOWN AS: ONE STORY
GARAGE LOCATED AT COFFEE STREET,
BROOKLYN, NEW YORK

----------------------------- X

EASTERN DISTRICT OF NEW YORK, SS:

AFFIDAVIT FOR A
SEARCH WARRANT

T. 18, U.S.C. §§549 and 659

John Doe being duly sworn, deposes and says that he is a Special Agent of the U.S. Customs Service and *MARY JONES* being duly sworn, deposes and says that he is a Special Agent of the Federal Bureau of Investigation, both duly appointed according to law and acting as such.

(A)   Upon information and belief, your deponents have reason to believe that within the above described premises within the Eastern District of New York, there is now being concealed approximately 3,500 stolen mens suits valued at approximately $140,000 and stolen coffee bags in violation of Title 18, United States Code Sections 546, 659.

    The source of your deponents' information and the grounds for their belief are:

    1. An examination of the records of the U.S. Customs Service at Port Newark, Newark, New Jersey revealed that approximately 3,500 mens suits arrived at the Port Newark on April 4, 1978, from Romania, destined to Secaucus, New Jersey, said goods moving in foreign commerce. The aforesaid records also reveal that these suits were released through U.S. Customs at the Port of Newark on April 12, 1978. The examination of the records was made by the deponent. Special Agent *John Doe*

Figure 8.2 Affidavit.

- 2 -

2. The President of Air Freight Co., advised your deponent that the suits were picked up by an Air Freight truck on April 13, 1978 and transported to Building 80 at John F. Kennedy International Airport, Queens, New York, where the tractor trailer containing the suits was then stored.

3. On April 17, 1978, Air Freight Co. reported to the U.S. Customs Service and the Federal Bureau of Investigation at John F. Kennedy International Airport, Queens, New York, that the trailer stored on April 13, 1978 at Building 80 at the airport had been stolen.

① 4. Information received by your deponent Special Agent MARY JONES from U.S. Customs Patrol Officer SAM SMITH on April 17, and April 19, 1978 that an informant, who has furnished reliable information in the past to Patrol Officer SMITH which has led to the recovery of a quantity of stolen cameras, and stolen paint cans, and who has provided information in the past which has led to the conviction of four individuals, furnished the following information to Officer SMITH that the informant observed within the last week inside the premises of a garage located at COFFEE STREET, BROOKLYN, NEW YORK approximately 3500 mens suits marked made in Romania, each contained in a separate plastic bag on a hanger and with red tags on the sleeves, all matching the description of the suits received from the Customs Inspector who examined the suits upon Customs release at Port Newark, New Jersey.

① 5. Information received by your deponent Special Agent MARY JONES on April 17, 1978 from a second informant who has furnished reliable information in the past that has led to the recovery of $2,000,000.00 in stolen merchandise and who has provided information which has led to the conviction of five persons, that the informant had been told Coffee Street, Brooklyn, New York was a drop for stolen merchandise and the building currently contained stolen mens suits and stolen coffee beans.

Figure 8.2 Affidavit (*Continued*).

- 3 -

6. Investigation by your deponent Special Agent
MARY JONES and other agents of the Federal Bureau of
Investigation on April 18, 1978, during a surveillance of
Coffee Street, Brooklyn, New York determined that a Ryder Rent
A Truck was observed leaving the premises of 55 Coffee Street,
Brooklyn, New York and was followed to the vicinity of **6**th Avenue
and **13**th Street in Brooklyn, New York where the truck was abandoned
by the driver who was observed leaving the area by foot. Subsequent surveillance of this Ryder truck on the evening of April
18, 1978 by your deponent and other agents of the Federal Bureau
of Investigation determined the truck had been broken into and
coffee bags containing coffee beans were observed lying on the
street and inside the truck.

7. Investigation by your deponent Special Agent **JONES**
determined that from the markings on these coffee bags
and the bags found in the truck, said bags were part of a shipment
of coffee reported stolen to the Federal Bureau of Investigation
on April 17, 1978 by **ABC** Trucking Inc.

8. Interviews with an official of **ABC** Trucking Inc.,
by your deponent Special Agent **JONES** , revealed that on
April 15, 1978 two **ABC** Trucking Inc. trucks containing 250
bags of coffee beans destined to the Tetley Corporation in New
Jersey, were stolen from 219 41st Street, Brooklyn, New York.

WHEREFORE, your deponent respectfully requests that a
search warrant be issued authorizing your deponents or any other
Special Agents of the U.S. Customs Service and Federal Bureau of
Investigation to search the PREMISES OF **COFFEE STREET, BROOKLYN,**

Figure 8.2 Affidavit (*Continued*).

- 4 -

NEW YORK, to seize the above described 3500 mens suits and coffee bags which constitute evidence and fruits of the aforesaid crime.

_____

Sworn to before me this
____ day of April 19

United States Magistrate
       District of New York

A TRUE COPY

U.S.M. _____ .D.N.Y.

Figure 8.2 Affidavit (_Continued_).

For instance, a search warrant for an entire high-rise apartment building would not be valid if there were no probable cause to search every apartment [*United States v. Votteller*, 544 F 2d 1355 (6th Cir., 1976)].

A search warrant for a particular apartment should be detailed as follows:

> Premises known as Apartment 4C, Northwest corner of the 7th floor of the building located at 1410 Rahway Avenue, Hicksville, New York.

Other examples are, "Approximately 1000 stolen Polish Lot brand men's suits" and "Approximately 50 stolen Nikon cameras."

The warrant should not be vague or general, but must particularize what is to be seized as well as possible. [See *Marron v. United States*, 275 U.S. 192 (1927), and *United States v. Gardner*, 537 F 2d 861 (6th Cir. 1976).] In the latter case, the information only warranted a search for a .38-caliber pistol; the search warrant, however, authorized search and seizure of all ammunition and firearms and thus was too broad.

The word *premises* does not mean only buildings or lots, but can mean a suitcase, briefcase, car, truck, box, or refrigerator. In addition, the item or subject matter expected to be seized must be described in the warrant. (See Fig. 8.1, Letter C.)

Naturally, if while a search warrant is being executed, property indicative of criminality comes into plain view, which is not specified in the warrant, such property may be seized [*United States v. YU*, 755 F Supp. 578 (S.D. N.Y. 1991)]. This plain-view concept will be discussed in detail later in this chapter.

EXECUTING THE WARRANT

Before serving (for example) a search warrant on a home, depending on state law, officers may have to advise the judge whether they expect to serve the warrant during daylight hours or at night, and, if at night, they must justify the necessity of serving the warrant then. [See Fig. 8.1, Letter D; *People v. Rose*, 31 N.Y. 2d 1036, 1039 (dissenting opinion) showing probable cause that the property sought will be removed or destroyed if not seized forthwith and cannot be executed during daylight hours.] Furthermore, if the officers believe that they have to enter the premises without announcing their authority ("no-knock"), the courts will allow such action upon showing that a "no-knock" entry was necessary to avoid danger to the law enforcement officers, or that there was reason to believe the material being sought might easily and quickly be concealed, removed, or destroyed [*People v. Israel*, 161 AD 2d 730 (N.Y. App. Div., 2nd Dept., 1990)].

Pursuant to Federal Law 18 U.S.C., 3109, federal law enforcement officers may break open any outer or inner door, any window of a house, or anything therein to execute a warrant if, after notice of the purpose and authority, they are refused admission. For instance, with respect to forced entry, if officers executing a search warrant for narcotics announce their purpose and authority and then hear someone moving about and the flushing of a toilet, the officers would be justified in breaking into the premises [*United States v. Halliman*, 923 F. 2d 873, 876 (D.C. Cir., 1991); *People v. ILWAIN*, 28 AD 2d 711 (N.Y. App. Div., 2nd Dept., 1967)].

Noncompliance with the notice requirement will be excused if there is an objectively reasonable belief that there is imminent danger of bodily harm to the officer or persons in the premises or of destruction of critical evidence [*Rivera v. United States*, 928 F 2d 592, 606 (2nd Cir., 1991)].

Some states have passed legislation allowing the court to issue search warrants authorizing entry without prior announcement—"no-knock" search warrants. Some states allow such action when a presentation has been made to the magistrate for the need to immediately enter the premises without knocking or announcing the officers' presence. The usual reasons are those mentioned before— destruction of evidence or danger to the officers. Unfortunately, abuses by law enforcement officers in several states in the use of no-knock warrants have caused the state legislature to repeal or restrict these types of warrants. Officers should check their own jurisdictions' rules as to the use of no-knock warrants.

A search conducted pursuant to a warrant must be reasonably related to the nature of the property sought [*Harris v. United States*, 331 U.S. 145, 152 (1947)]. For example, a search warrant had been issued for a search and seizure of stolen tires and wheels. This would not authorize a search of drawers in a bureau or any other space that would be too small to store the tires and wheels. Thus, if the officers do, in fact, open bureau drawers during such a search and discover property indicative of criminality, that property will be suppressed [*United States v. Chadwell*, 427 F. Supp. 692 (D. Del., 1977)]. However, if while searching areas in which the tires and wheels could reasonably be stored, the officers do find, for instance, an illegally possessed weapon, then the weapon may be lawfully seized (*Chadwell*).

When the warrant is sworn out, the magistrate issuing the warrant will put a limit on the number of days the officer has to execute it. The warrant must be executed by the officer during that time for the search to be valid [*Sgro v. United States*, 287 U.S. 206 (1932)]. If for some reason the warrant is not executed during this time, it will be necessary either to obtain a new warrant or to amend the affidavit to update the probable cause for the issuing judicial officer (*Sgro*).

Time limits may vary by jurisdiction and should be checked by the officer. Normal periods run from a direction to execute forthwith up to 10 days, depending on each case's circumstances [*United States v. Dunning*, 425 F 2d 836 (2nd Cir., 1969)]. However, even if a warrant commands a forthwith execution, it will not be invalidated if executed days later but within a 10-day period, if the probable cause has not dissipated and there is a valid reason to delay the execution [*United States v. Wilson*, 491 F 2d 724 (6th Cir., 1973); *United States v. Dunning*, 425 F 2d 836 (2nd Cir., 1970)].

While the better practice is for the officers executing a search warrant to have the warrant in hand at the time of the execution, the failure to have physical possession of the warrant is not fatal to an ensuing search [*United States v. Woodring*, 444 F 2d 749 (9th Cir., 1971); *People v. Mahoney*, 58 N.Y. 2d 475 (1983)]. This is especially so if the warrant authorizes a no-knock entry [*Mahoney*] or if no demand for the warrant is made and there is no resistance to the search [*Woodring*].

Following the issuance and execution of the search warrant, the officer is required to make a return on the search warrant to the judicial officer or court from whom the warrant was obtained. (See Fig. 8.1, Letter E.) Usually, all this means to the officer is filling in on the warrant the date and hour it was served, where served, and a list or inventory of the items seized. It is good policy to leave a copy of the search warrant and inventory at the place searched. The affidavit to the search warrant does not have to be left at the premises.

The failure to comply with these procedures is not of constitutional significance and does not operate to void a valid search, since the derelictions occur after the execution of the warrant and are ministerial in nature [*Cady v. Dombrowski*, 413 U.S. 433, 449 (1973); *United States v. Moore*, 452 F 2d 569, 572–573 (6th Cir., 1971); *People v. Rose*, 52 Misc 2d 648 (N.Y. District Court, Nassau County, 1967)].

In instances in which citizens' Fourth Amendment rights have been violated by law enforcement officers, such action can open the officers to civil suits and/or criminal prosecution. Pursuant to Chapter 13, 18 U.S.C. 241–246, the rights of all citizens are protected from those who would deprive them of their constitutional rights while acting in a law enforcement capacity. Thus, an officer who knowingly falsifies an affidavit to a search warrant or creates a fictitious informant for the purpose of obtaining a search warrant could possibly face a civil suit by the defendant, as well as criminal indictment under the civil rights laws. A warrant obtained to harass a defendant or to subject that person to embarrassment is not only improper, but can lead to serious civil and criminal prosecutions against the officer. Additionally, the officer swearing out the affidavit is placed under oath. False statements knowingly made by the officer to the judge not only subjects the officer to possible criminal prosecution, but at the same time does a disservice to the credibility of other officers who appear before that magistrate or judge.

Another problem officers often face in the execution of a search warrant concerns the search of individuals found in the premises to be searched, or those exiting or coming to said premises. Clearly, a search warrant that authorizes the search of particular premises and a particular person, if that person is found in said premises, authorizes a search of the named person found in premises [*Ybarra v. Illinois*, 444 U.S. 85 (1979); *People v. Marshall*, 13 N.Y. 2d 28 (1963)].

Furthermore, the search of said person may also be authorized as he/she is approaching or entering the premises where the officers are initiating the execution of the warrant or are in fact executing it. Such search would also be permissible if the person had just exited the premises, but was still within the immediate vicinity. These last searches are authorized only, however, if the circumstances are such that it would reasonably be expected that the property sought in the search warrant may be concealed on said individual's person [*People v. Sanin*, 60 N.Y. 2d 575 (1983); *People v. Easterbrook*, 35 N.Y. 2d 913 (1974); *People v. Green*, 33 N.Y. 2d 496, 499 (1974)].

On the other hand, if there is no showing that the particular person named in the search warrant could reasonably be expected to have the property sought concealed on his/her person, then such a search as just mentioned would not be authorized [*People v. Green*, 33 N.Y. 2d 496, 499 (1974); *People v. Smith*, 21 N.Y. 2d 698 (1967)].

If the particular person named in the warrant is found blocks away from the described premises, a search of such person is not authorized, unless the officer has a search warrant permitting the search of said individual wherever found [*People v. Green*, 33 N.Y. 2d 496 (1974)].

More of a problem is presented with search warrants that authorize the search of any persons who may be found in the premises to be searched pursuant to the said warrant. Such warrants are oftentimes used for the search of premises utilized for drug trafficking or illegal gambling, and the names of persons who may be present cannot with due diligence be ascertained. A search warrant to search any person present in particular premises can only be based on a showing of probable cause to believe the premises are confined to on-going illegal activity, and every person within the orbit of the search may be expected to have the property sought concealed on his/her person [*People v. Nieves*, 36 N.Y. 2d 396 (1975)].

Thus, a search warrant for the search of an apartment used exclusively for drug trafficking, which authorized the search of any persons found therein or thereat, was proper, since the criminal activity was of such nature and the premises so limited that there was probable cause to believe that anyone present was a party to the on-going criminal activity [*People v. Easterbrook*, 43 AD 2d 719, 720 (N.Y. App. Div. 2nd Dept., 1973) affd. 35 N.Y. 2d 913 (1974)].

On the other hand, a search warrant for the search of a restaurant open to the public, in which there may be a number of people present, such as patrons, having no connection with the on-going criminal activity, such as an illegal gambling bank, which authorized the search of any person found in said premises, would be invalid [*People v. Nieves*, 36 N.Y. 2d 396 (1975)].

There may be situations in which, while a search warrant is being executed, the officers encounter persons present on the premises who are not specifically named in the search warrant, and there is no authorization to search anyone found therein or thereat. In such circumstances, if the officers executing the warrant have a reasonable suspicion that said persons may be armed and thus pose a threat, the officers may frisk those persons for weapons [*People v. Smith*, 78 N.Y. 2d 897 (1991)]. However, if there is no reasonable suspicion that said persons are armed, then a frisk is not permitted [*Ybarra v. Illinois*, 444 U.S. 85, 92–94 (1979)].

Finally, *Michigan v. Summers* [452 U.S. 692 (1981)] presents a variation of this problem. In *Summers* a search warrant was issued authorizing the search of a certain home of narcotics; there was no permission for the search of any person in the warrant. Officers who approached the house to execute the search warrant observed the occupant of the home leaving the premises; the officers detained the occupant and proceeded with the search. Upon discovering and seizing the sought narcotics, the occupant was arrested and searched, and heroin was found on his person. The heroin so found was not suppressed. The Supreme Court reasoned that the search warrant, founded on probable cause, implicitly carried with it the limited authority to detain the occupant of the premises, while a proper search was conducted; and because it was lawful to detain the occupant until evidence establishing probable cause to arrest him was found, his arrest and the search incident thereto were constitutionally permissible.

THE GOOD FAITH RELIANCE ON A WARRANT EXCEPTION

Evidence obtained as a result of a search made in good faith reliance on a search warrant issued by a neutral, detached magistrate will ordinarily not result in the suppression of such evidence, even though the search warrant may have been improperly issued because of lack of probable cause or some procedural error [*United States v. Leon*, 468 U.S. 897 (1984)]. (For a full discussion of the good faith exception see Chap. 9, "Arrest and Procedure, The Good-Faith Reliance on a Warrant Exception.")

There is a caveat. Some jurisdictions, and in particular New York, reject the good faith warrant exception [*People v. Bigelow*, 66 N.Y. 2d 417 (1985)]. Officers should check the law of their jurisdictions as to whether or not the good faith warrant exception is applicable.

SEARCH INCIDENT TO ARREST

One of the exceptions to the search warrant requirement is when a lawful arrest has been made. In this case, the law enforcement officer may legally search the person arrested and the area within arm's reach of the arrested individual [*New York v. Belton*, 453 U.S. 454, 457 (1981)]. The purpose of searching the arrested individual is not only to secure any weapons or items that the subject may be carrying and that might be usable as a means for escape, but also to attempt to find any contraband, fruits of the crime, instruments used in the crime, and/or evidence that could link the subject to the substantive event [telephone books, receipts, tickets, counterfeit money, and so on (*Belton*)].

It is essential to note that, if the arrest is illegal, any fruits found on the individual by the officer subsequent to that arrest will not be allowed into evidence. An illegal arrest cannot be made good by the fact that contraband was found on the subject following the illegal arrest [*Henry v. United States*, 361 U.S. 98, 104 (1959); *United States v. Di Re*, 332 U.S. 581, 595 (1948); *Byars v. United States*, 273 U.S. 28, 29 (1927)].

How far can the arresting officer go in the search incident to arrest? If a subject is arrested in the kitchen while eating breakfast, it is doubtful a search of the subject's bedroom would be legal without a search warrant [*United States v. Mangeri*, 451 F Supp. 73 (S.D. N.Y. 1978); *People v. Knapp*, 52 N.Y. 2d 689 (1981)]. This is so, since, as stated in *Belton*, only a search of the area within the arrested individual's immediate control is justified.

The arresting officers going into a premises are allowed to make a "protective sweep" of the residence. The courts have taken this to mean that the officers going into a premises to make an arrest have the authority to "sweep," that is, to look in the rest of the apartment for other accomplices, armed perpetrators, or other persons on the premises to protect themselves and secure the area. They must have reason to believe such persons are on the premises. How far a protective sweep would be allowed by the courts appears to go back to the reasonableness test. Opening closets and looking into other rooms and under beds would be permissible. Looking into the defendant's desk drawers or dresser drawers would be unreasonable [*Maryland v. Buie*, 110 S. Ct. 1093 (1990)].

The home of a person arrested on a public street cannot later be searched legally without a warrant, since it would not be a search related to the arrest [*Vale v. Louisiana*, 399 U.S. 30 (1970)].

When an individual is arrested, the search can extend not only to the person and the "grab" area, but to any closed container that the individual possesses, such as a briefcase or suitcase (*Belton*). (For a more detailed treatment of a search incident to an arrest see Chap. 9, Arrest and Procedure.)

MOTOR VEHICLE WARRANTLESS SEARCHES

Motor vehicle searches continue to be a problem area for law enforcement officers. Initially, the Supreme Court decided, in *Carroll v. United States* [267 U.S. 132 (1925)], that the mobility of the vehicle would present circumstances in which the officer would not have the necessary time to obtain a search warrant and, upon a showing of probable cause, a stop of a vehicle and subsequent search thereof without a warrant would be legal. This is what has become to be called the *automobile exception*.

Subsequently, it was held that if there was probable cause to believe a vehicle contained property indicative of criminality, it could be searched after it was taken to a police station [*Chambers v. Maroney*, 399 U.S. 42 (1970)]. Indeed, even though a vehicle is impounded and immobilized, a search pursuant to the automobile exception can be conducted and such search may take place immediately or anytime from eight hours to three days after the vehicle has been immobilized [*United States v. Johns*, 469 U.S. 478 (1985); *Florida v. Meyers*, 466 U.S. 380 (1984)].

Furthermore, the automobile exception has been extended to mobile homes, where such vehicles are readily mobile and are situated in such a place as to objectively indicate they are being used for transportation [*California v. Carney*, 471 U.S. 386 (1985)]. Mobile homes on blocks or connected to utilities and thus not readily mobile would not be subject to the exception.

There is some indication that the automobile exception is limited to situations in which there is probable cause to believe that the vehicle contains contraband fruits of a crime or instrumentalities of a crime [*United States v. Ross*, 456 U.S. 798 (1982), contraband; *Chambers v. Maroney*, 399 U.S. 42 (1970), fruits and instrumentalities of a crime].

It would appear that probable cause to believe a vehicle contains mere evidence of a crime, such as a bloodstain, would make the automobile exception inapplicable [*Coolidge v. New Hampshire*, 403 U.S. 443 (1971); cf. *People v. Brosnan*, 32 N.Y. 2d 254 (1973), automobile exception applicable if there is probable cause to believe vehicle contained mere evidence of a crime, such as bloodstains].

It may also be that the automobile exception would not apply if the search of the vehicle required a warrantless and illegal trespass into private premises to accomplish the search [*Horton v. California*, 110 S. Ct. 2301, 2308 (1990); *Cardwell v. Lewis*, 417 U.S. 583, 593 (1974); *Coolidge v. New Hampshire*, 403 U.S. 443, 447–448 (1971), concurring opinion per *Harlan, J.*].

The extent of a search pursuant to the automobile exception has been set forth in *California v. Acevedo* [111 S. Ct. 1982 (1991)]. Pursuant to *Acevedo*, if there is probable cause to believe that property indicative of criminality is located in a vehicle, but the information does not specify exactly where in the vehicle that property may be located, then the entire vehicle may be searched and all closed containers therein may be opened. However, if there is specific information that a certain container in the vehicle, such as a specific box, contains property indicative of criminality, then an officer may search the vehicle for that box and upon discovering it, he or she may open it. The specific information, as mentioned, is not probable cause to search the entire vehicle.

The search of a vehicle without a search warrant may also be authorized under the inventory search exception. If there is a standardized or routine police procedure to impound a vehicle for violation of traffic regulations, such as parking ordinances [*South Dakota v. Opperman*, 428 U.S. 364 (1976)] or after a person driving a vehicle has been arrested [*Michigan v. Thomas*, 458 U.S. 259 (1982)], then an inventory search of the vehicle would be permissible.

The purpose of the inventory search is to protect the property of the owner of the vehicle, to protect the police from subsequent claims of lost or stolen property, and also to protect the police from dangerous instrumentalities [*South Dakota v. Opperman*, 428 U.S. 364 (1976)]. Thus, the standardized or routine procedures must be so designed and limited as to ensure that the search is conducted for the above purpose [*Colorado v. Bertine*, 479 U.S. 367, 375 (1987)].

An inventory search may not be used as a purposeful and general means of discovering evidence of crime [*Colorado v. Bertine*, 479 U.S. 367, 376 (1987), concurring opinion].

The inventory search must be reasonably related to its purpose of securing and protecting vehicles and their contents. Hence, in addition to visual inspection of the interior of the vehicle, closed containers, such as a glove compartment, a console, the trunk, or packages in the vehicle, which may contain property of value or dangerous instruments, may be opened [*Colorado v. Bertine*, 479 U.S. 367 (1987)]. Nevertheless, the opening of closed containers is authorized only if it is part of the standardized or routine procedure [*Florida v. Wells*, 110 S. Ct. 1632 (1990)].

More intrusive searches, such as dismantling a vehicle in whole or part, would not be permissible, since it is unlikely that property of value or dangerous instruments would be so secretly stored as to require such a search [*United States v. Edwards*, 577 F 2d 883, 893 (5th Cir., 1978)].

An officer may be afforded some discretion as to whether to impound a vehicle after an arrest [*Colorado v. Bertino*, 479 U.S. 367 (1987)] or whether to open any or all closed containers in the vehicle [*Florida v. Wells*, 110 S. Ct. 1632 (1990)]. But such discretion must be exercised according to some standard criteria and on the the basis of something other than a suspicion that evidence of criminal activity may be found [*Colorado v. Bertine*, 479 U.S. 367, 375 (1987)]. The standardized criteria must so regulate the exercise of discretion as to prevent an individual officer from turning the search into a purposeful and general means of discovering evidence of crime [*Florida v. Wells*, 110 S. Ct. 1632, 1635 (1990)].

In short, the policy or practice governing inventory searches should be designed to produce an inventory [*Florida v. Wells*, 110 S. Ct. 1632, 1635 (1990)].

Although the standardized routine inventory procedures need not be in writing, it would appear that such a method is preferred [*Florida v. Wells*, 110 S. Ct. 1632 (1990); *People v. Thomas*, 171 AD 2d 945 (N.Y. App. Div. 3rd Dept., 1971), unwritten policy sufficient]. In addition, if the search is to be deemed an inventory search, a complete inventory report should be prepared, including a survey of the vehicle's exterior and interior for any damage to locate valuables for storage and should cover an itemized list of the things discovered, both in the vehicle's interior and any closed containers in the vehicle [*South Dakota v. Opperman*, 428 U.S. 364, 382 footnote 10, concurring opinion (1976)].

WARRANTLESS SEARCH OF PREMISES

The warrantless search of premises may be justified under certain established exceptions to the warrant requirement. Some of these exceptions are as follows:

1. *Emergency:* A law enforcement officer may enter premises to assist persons in distress or to preserve property. For example a burning building clearly presents an emergency of sufficient proportions to render a warrantless entry reasonable [*Michigan v. Tyler*, 436 U.S. 499, 509 (1978)]. A warrantless entry into premises would also be reasonable where police officers heard screams emanating from a room in a rooming house or where police officers entered premises to aid an unconscious or dying person [*United States v. Barone*, 330 F 2d 543, 545 (2nd Cir., 1964) cert. denied 377 U.S. 1004 (1964); *People v. Rivera*, 171 AD 2d 560 (N.Y. App. Div. 1st Dept., 1991), screams and sounds of scuffling coming from an apartment in multidwelling].

Other examples of emergencies include entering premises on the belief that a child, who was kidnapped at gunpoint, was present in the premises [*People v. Diaz*, 170 AD 2d 618 (N.Y. App. Div. 2nd Dept., 1991)] or making an entry after observing in certain premises a person lying on the floor bleeding profusely, but still alive [*People v. Rivera*, 170 AD 2d 625, 626 (N.Y. App. Div. 2nd Dept., 1991)].

Once a permissible warrantless entry has been made, the officer may seize any evidence that is in plain view [*Michigan v. Tyler*, 346 U.S. 499, 509 (1978)]. The plain-view concept will be discussed in detail later in this chapter.

2. *Crime scene:* Closely related to the emergency exception is the crime scene exception. When a constitutionally protected area becomes the scene of a crime, law enforcement officers may make a warrantless entry and conduct a preliminary search and inspection, whose scope and duration are reasonably related to the exigencies of the situation, and any evidence that is in plain view may be seized [*People v. Cohen*, 87 AD 2d 77, 82–83 (N.Y. App. Div. 2nd Dept., 1982) affd. 58 N.Y. 2d 844 (1983)]. For instance, an officer who comes upon the scene of a homicide may make a prompt warrantless search of the area to see if there are other victims or if a killer is still on the premises [*Thompson v. Louisiana*, 469 U.S. 17, 21 (1984); *Mincey v. Arizona*, 437 U.S. 385, 392–393 (1978)].

However, once a preliminary investigation has come to an end, no further searches for evidence may be conducted on the premises without consent or a warrant.

3. *Exigency:* If truly exigent circumstances exist, no warrant is required to enter premises to search and seize evidence [*United States v. Karo*, 468 U.S. 705, 717–718 (1984); *Segura v. United States*, 468 U.S. 796 (1984); *United States v. MacDonald*, 916 F 2d 766 (2nd Cir., 1990)]. Such exigent circumstances exist when urgent events make it impractical or impossible to obtain a warrant in sufficient time to preserve evidence threatened with removal or destruction [*People v. Knapp*, 52 N.Y. 2d 689, 696 (1981)].

The fact that evidence is of the type that can be easily removed or destroyed is not a sufficient showing of urgent events [*Vale v. Louisiana*, 399 U.S. 30, 34–35 (1970)]. There must be a showing of objective facts that it is likely the evidence will be removed or destroyed within the time frame involved. For example, when a reliable informant indicated that illegal guns were being stored in a certain retail establishment and that the said guns would be gone within less than two hours (the time estimated to obtain a warrant), urgent events were shown permitting a warrantless entry into the premises to seize the guns [*People v. Vaccaro*, 39 N.Y. 2d 468 (1976)].

It should be noted that it has been held, if law enforcement officers otherwise act in a lawful manner they may make a warrantless entry into premises under the exigency exception, even though said officers' conduct created the exigent circumstances as defined above [*United States v. MacDonald*, 916 F 2d 766 (1990)].

Exigency may also exist if there is probable cause to believe that premises contain, for example, an explosive device that may go off and cause a public disaster [*United States v. Perez*, 440 F. Supp. 272, 287–288 (ND Ohio, 1977) affd. 571 F 2d 584 (6th Cir., 1978), cert. denied 435 U.S. 998 (1978)].

4. *Hot pursuit:* If law enforcement officers are in hot pursuit of an individual, the officers may enter premises that the said individual has gone into, without a warrant, and look for him/her in the premises by exploring closets and other areas where the person may be hidden. In addition, until the individual has been apprehended, the officers may also check other places, such as drawers and the like, where a gun or other weapon may be located which the afore-

said individual may reach and thereby threaten the safety of the officers [*Warden v. Hayden*, 387 U.S. 294 (1967)].

PLAIN-VIEW DOCTRINE

The *plain-view doctrine* relies on the presumption that the law enforcement officer has a right to be in a place where evidence or contraband is seen in an area open to plain viewing [*Horton v. California*, 110 S. Ct. 2301, 2308 (1990)]. An illustration would be when an officer is in hot pursuit of an individual fleeing from arrest, pursues him/her into private premises, and, while so engaged, espies an illegal weapon. The officer is legally on the premises and may seize the weapon [*Warden v. Hayden*, 387 U.S. 294 (1967)].

Another instance would be where an officer stops a vehicle for a traffic infraction and, while preparing a traffic citation, sees lug nuts which the officer had probable cause to believe were stolen property. Here the seizure without a warrant would be legally justified [*Colorado v. Bannister*, 449 U.S. 1 (1980)].

Still another example would be a situation in which an officer has a search warrant to search a given area for specified objects and comes across some other article of incriminating character [*Horton v. California*, 110 S. Ct. 2301, 2307 (1990)].

There is a caveat: There must be probable cause to believe that the article is of an incriminating character, such as contraband, fruits of a crime, instrumentalities of a crime, or mere evidence of a crime [*Arizona v. Hicks*, 480 U.S. 321 (1987)].

If the article is legally accessible to the officer, then the officer may immediately seize it without obtaining a warrant [*Horton v. California*, 110 S. Ct. 2301, 2308 (1990)]. But if the article is in constitutionally protected premises and there is a need to enter said premises to seize the article, then, absent exigency, a warrant would be required to seize the article [*Horton v. California*, 110 S. Ct. 2301, 2308 (1990)]. For instance, an officer is walking by on a public sidewalk and through an open window in a person's residence observes contraband [*United States v. Taborda*, 635 F. 2d 131, 139 (2nd Cir., 1980)]. This observation would fall under the plain-view exception. However, absent exigent circumstances or a search warrant, an officer may not enter the premises and seize the contraband [*People v. Spinelli*, 35 N.Y. 2d 77 (1974); see also *Florida v. Riley*, 488 U.S. 445 (1989)]. Parenthetically, it should be noted that it was believed that a plain-view observation had to be inadvertent: for example, if officers were executing a search warrant for narcotics in premises noted for large-scale drug trafficking, it could be expected that guns would also be present. Thus, if in executing the warrant, officers came upon guns, the discovery would not be inadvertent and hence plain view would not apply.

The inadvertent aspect of the plain-view exception has been eliminated by the Supreme Court [*Horton v. California*, 110 S. Ct. 2301 (1990)]. Of course, if an officer illegally enters a person's home and there observes an article indicative of criminality, the plain-view exception would not apply, since the officer is not properly where he or she is to make the observation. (See, e.g., *Mapp v. Ohio*, 367 U.S. 643 (1961).]

Along the same lines, if an officer must use an enhancing device, such as a telescope to observe an article in a constitutionally protected area, which observation would have been impossible to the unaided eye, such an observation is not a plain-view observation [*United States v. Taborda*, 635 F 2d 131 (2nd Cir., 1980)].

CONSENT SEARCH

Situations will arise during the course of an investigation when the investigator believes that an individual may consent to a search of the premises. In these instances, it is incumbent on the officer to secure proper consent from the party. A consent search does not need a search warrant; however, the officer should advise the party of the right not to have a search of the premises made. A person who consents to a search waives the Fourth Amendment right to be free from search without a warrant. The voluntariness of a search is a question to be decided by the court [*Schneckloth v. Bustamonte*, 421 U.S. 218 (1973)]. For a search to be valid, it must be shown from the "totality of the circumstances" of the particular case that the consent was voluntary. The consenting party, according to the *Bustamonte* decision, need not be advised of the right to refuse consent, but it is a factor to be considered in determining voluntariness. Since the prosecution in this type of case will have the burden of proving that consent was, in fact, freely and voluntarily given, many federal agencies and police departments have instituted the use of a Consent-to-Search Form that advises individuals of their constitutional rights and requires them to sign the form waiving their rights. Obviously, a signed Consent-to-Search Form which demonstrates knowledge of the right to refuse will go a long way to prove voluntariness. If coercion, duress, or fraud is used to obtain consent, the search will be deemed involuntary and illegal [*People v. Gonzalez*, 39 N.Y. 2d 122, 127–128 (1976)].

Consent may be verbal or may be implied from word, gestures, or conduct [*United States v. Buettner-Janusch*, 646 F. 2d 759, 764 (2nd Cir., 1981), cert. denied 454 U.S. 830, (1981)]. Certainly, a statement, such as "You have my permission to search" would be sufficient [*United States v. Buettner-Janusch*, 646 F. 2d 759, 764 (2nd Cir., 1981), cert. denied 454 U.S. 830 (1981)]. Some examples of conduct or gestures from which consent may be implied are as follows:

A person handing an officer the keys to his/her car after the officer's request to search the car is consent to search the car [*People v. Aponte*, 124 AD 2d 489 (N.Y. App. Div. 1st Dept., 1986)].

A person giving an officer the keys to his/her apartment and telling him how to operate the lock is consent to enter the apartment [*People v. Updike*, 125 AD 2d 735 (N.Y. App. Div. 3rd Dept., 1986)].

A person opening the door to an officer's knock and stepping back from the open door upon the officer's request to enter is consent to enter [*People v. Taylor*, 111 AD 2d 520 (N.Y. App. Div. 3rd Dept., 1985)].

In such cases, however, the officer should have, if possible, a second witness to the consent, since the burden is on the officer to establish the consent and that it was voluntary.

With regard to voluntary consent, the courts will scrutinize the circumstances weighing the:

Age, education, and intelligence of the person consenting.

Whether the person is in custody.

Events prior to the request, such as resistance or evasive or uncooperative conduct.

Indicia of restraint, for example, handcuffing.

Background of the person consenting, such as prior experience with the law or no such experience [*United States v. Sanchez*, 499 F. Supp. 622, 623–624 (ED N.Y., 1986) affd. 647 F 2d 163 (2nd Cir., 1981); *People v. Gonzalez*, 39 N.Y. 2d 122 (1976)].

An illustration of an invalid consent search occurred when an uneducated elderly widow allowed law enforcement officers to search when they told her they had a valid search warrant which, in fact, they did not have [*Bumper v. North Carolina*, 391 U.S. 543 (1968)].

Nevertheless, if an officer seeking consent indicates that if consent is not given a search warrant would be obtained to conduct the search, and consent is then given, said consent would not be invalid, if the officer really had probable cause to obtain a search warrant [*United States v. Calvente*, 722 F. 2d 1019, 1023–1024 (2nd Cir., 1983) cert. denied 471 U.S. 1021 (1985)]. On the other hand, if the officer did not have probable cause to obtain a search warrant, then the consent so given would be invalid [*United States v. Anderson*, 752 F. Supp. 565, 568 (ED N.Y., 1990) affd. 929 F. 2d 96 (2nd Cir., 1991)].

It should also be noted that if, in seeking consent from a person, an officer makes the assertion that a search warrant could validly be obtained, and then couples the assertion with threats, such as "when the search warrant is obtained and executed and the contraband is found in the person's home, everyone therein, including his wife, would be arrested, and that would result in having the authorities take custody of his infant child," the consent could be deemed coerced and invalid [*People v. Lott*, 71 AD 2d 926 (N.Y. App. Div. 2nd Dept., 1979)].

The fact that a person giving consent is under arrest or otherwise detained would not per se invalidate said consent, if it is otherwise voluntarily given [*United States v. Watson*, 423 U.S. 411, 424–425 (1976); *United States v. Ellis*, 461 F. 2d 962, 968 (2nd Cir., 1972), cert. denied 409 U.S. 866 (1972); *People v. Gonzalez*, 39 N.Y. 2d 122, 129 (1976)].

However, if the arrest or detention is illegal, then the consent given while in illegal custody, voluntary or not, is deemed invalid [*Florida v. Royer*, 460 U.S. 491, 497 (1983); *People v. Henley*, 53 N.Y. 2d 403 (1981)].

If the taint of the illegality is dissipated by attenuation, then the consent, if otherwise voluntary, would be valid [*Florida v. Royer*, 460 U.S. 491, 497 (1983)].

A determination of whether the taint of illegality is dissipated would demand the weighing of several factors. These factors, which were set forth in *People v. Borges* [69 N.Y. 2d 1031 (1987)], are as follows:

1. The temporal proximity of the illegal arrest or detention and the consent.

2. The presence or absence of intervening circumstances.

3. Whether the purpose underlying the illegality was to obtain the consent or the fruits of the search.

4. Whether the consent was volunteered or requested.

5. Whether the person consenting was aware he could decline to consent.

6. The purpose and flagrancy of the illegality.

Examples of attenuation under this test are set forth in Chap. 9, "Arrest and Procedure—Constitutional Ramifications of Arrest and Seizure."

A case of interest concerning the giving of consent during an encounter between a person and law enforcement officers is *Florida v. Bostwick* [111 S. Ct. 2382 (1991)]. In *Bostwick*, law enforcement officers, in an effort to interdict drug trafficking, regularly boarded buses in interstate travel and approached passengers, either randomly or because of a vague feeling that a passenger may be engaged in criminal activity, and requested consent to search such passenger's luggage. The Supreme Court in *Bostwick* held that when two officers, visually displaying their badges and wearing bright green raid jackets bearing insignias of their status, with one holding a gun in a recognizable weapons pouch, approached passengers seated in the bus, with one officer standing near the passenger's seat, partially blocking the narrow aisle leading to the bus exit, and when the officers then identify themselves as narcotics officers and request consent to search the passenger's luggage, this was not a seizure of the passenger, and the consent given, if voluntary, would have been valid.

The scope or extent of a search pursuant to consent is as follows: If, for example, an officer makes a request to search the premises or a vehicle, and the consent is given in general terms, such as "Okay," "Go ahead," "Alright," then the officers may search the entire area involved and open all unlocked closed containers found therein [*Florida v. Jimeno*, 111 S. Ct. 1801 (1991)]. However, if the consent given explicitly limits the scope of the search, then property indicative of criminality found by an officer who exceeds the scope of the limited consent will be suppressed [*United States v. Stricland*, 902 F. 2d 937 (11th Cir., 1990)]. For instance, a boat owner consented to an officer making a visual inspection of a boat's deck, but the officer opened a bench compartment and thus exceeded the scope of the consent given. Therefore, the marijuana observed therein and seized was suppressed [*United States v. Nasworthy*, 710 F. Supp. 1353 (SD Fla., 1989); see also *United States v. Towns*, 913 F. 2d 434 (7th Cir., 1990), consent to enter an apartment was not consent to search the apartment].

Furthermore, consent once given may be revoked by the person originally giving it, and when this occurs, the search must stop [*United States v. Bily*, 406 F. Supp. 726, 728–729 (DC Pa., 1975)]. Evidence found prior to the revocation, however, would be admissible [*Jones v. Berry*, 722 F. 2d 443, 449 (9th Cir., 1983)].

When more than one person occupies premises, possesses property, such as a vehicle or house, or uses other property, such as a duffel bag, then any party with rights in said property may consent to a search of said property. Thus, where spouses, paramours, coinhabitants, such as roommates, occupy a residence or room, either spouse, paramour, or coinhabitant may consent to a search of said residence or room [*United States v. Matlock*, 415 U.S. 164 (1974), paramour; *United States v. Robinson*, 479 F. 2d 300, 302–303 (7th Cir., 1973), paramour; *Roberts v. United States*, 332 F. 2d 892, 896–897 (8th Cir., 1964), cert. denied 380 U.S. 980 (1965), wife; *People v. Carter*, 30 N.Y. 2d 279 (1972), wife; *United States v. De Parias*, 805 F. 2d 1447 (11th Cir., 1986), cert. denied 482 U.S. 916 (1987), roommate)]. When more than one person shares authority over a vehicle, anyone of those persons may consent to a search of it [*People v. Smith*, 54 N.Y. 2d 954 (1981)]. If two persons are sharing the use of a duffel bag, either party may consent to a search thereof [*Frazier v. Cupp*, 394 U.S. 731, 740 (1969)].

A parent, generally, can consent to a search of an infant child's room [*United States v. Miller*, 722 F. Supp. 1, 4 (WD N.Y., 1989); *People v. Rocco*, 107 AD 2d 816 (N.Y. App. Div. 2nd Dept., 1985)].

There is a caveat. Some jurisdictions limit the parents' right to consent to a search of a minor child's effects [*Fare v. Scott William K.*, 24 Cal 3d 395 (1978), cert. denied 444 U.S. 973 (1979), parent consenting to search of 17-year-old son's toolbox, located in son's room, invalid].

In view of the split in authority, officers should check the law in their jurisdictions concerning parental consent before conducting a search.

It should also be noted that if an adult child who is married is residing in his/her parents' home and occupying a bedroom therein, which is specifically set aside for said adult child, then other family members residing therein are without authority to consent to a search of said bedroom [*People v. Petrie*, 89 AD 910 (N.Y. App. Div. 2nd Dept., 1982)].

Persons who may be occupying premises for a limited purpose, such as babysitters, do not have the requisite joint control, which would allow said persons to consent to a search of said premises [*People v. Litwin*, 44 AD 2d 492 (N.Y. App. Div. 2nd Dept., 1974)].

Landlords, too, generally lack the requisite authority to consent to the search of premises rented to tenants [*People v. Ponto*, 103 AD 2d 573 (N.Y. App. Div. 2nd Dept., 1984)]. However, there are exceptions. For example, if a person took in a boarder, who shared a bedroom with that person's 10-year-old son, said person retains a sufficient degree of authority and control to give consent to a search of the bedroom [*People v. Wood*, 31 N.Y. 2d 975 (1973)].

Furthermore, the landlord of a boarding house has sufficient authority and control to consent to a search of common areas in said boardinghouse, such as hallways and common bathrooms [*People v. Snow*, 128 AD 564 (N.Y. App. Div. 2nd Dept., 1987)]. In circumstances where a person is legally occupying a hotel or motel room, the operator of the hotel or motel may not validly consent to a search of said room [*Stone v. California*, 376 U.S. 483 (1964)]. However, if the rental period for said room has expired, then the hotel or motel operator may consent to a search of said room, even if the person continues to occupy it or has left property there [*United States v. Akin*, 562 F 2d 459, 464 (7th Cir., 1977), cert. denied 435 U.S. 933 (1978); *People v. Lerhinan*, 90 AD 2d 74, 78 (N.Y. App. Div. 2nd Dept., 1982)].

The scope or extent of a search pursuant to a third party's consent is an area of concern. Generally, the third party's consent to search would permit the search not only of the premises in which the third party has authority and control, but also of areas in those premises to which the third party has ready access, such as:

Closets in the premises [*United States v. Richardson*, 562 F. 2d 476, 479 (7th Cir., 1977), cert. denied 434 U.S. 1072 (1978)].

Boxes found in the premises [*United States v. Robinson*, 479 F. 2d 300, 302–303 (7th Cir., 1973)].

Bags found in the premises [*United States v. Matlock*, 415 U.S. 164 (1974)].

On the other hand, if there is a closed container on the premises, and the third party does not have ready access thereto, such as a locked trunk which obviously belongs to another occupant [*United States v. Block*, 590 F. 2d 535 (4th Cir., 1978)] or the closed container obviously holds the personal effects of the other occupant [*People v. Gonzalez*, 50 Misc. 2d 508 (N.Y. App. Term 2nd Dept., 1966)], then the third party's consent to a search thereof would be invalid. According to the weight of authority, if more than one person has authority and control over premises or other property, and one of those persons, over the objection of the others, consents to a search, such search pursuant to said consent is valid [*Charles v. Odum*, 664 F. Supp. 747, 751–752 (S.D. N.Y., 1987); *People v. Cosme* 48 N.Y. 2d 286 (1979)].

There is authority to the contrary [*Lucero v. Donovan*, 354 F. 2d 16 (9th Cir., 1968)]. Therefore, officers should check the law in their jurisdictions concerning the matter.

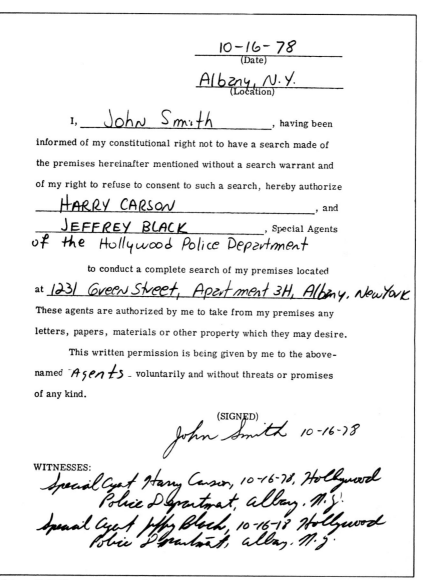

Figure 8.3 Consent to search form.

Finally, there is a good-faith aspect to consent. If officers objectively and reasonably believe that a person giving consent has authority to consent, said consent is valid, even if it turns out the person does not indeed have such authority [*Illinois v. Rodriguez*, 110 S. Ct. 2793 (1990); *People v. Adams*, 53 N.Y. 2d 1 (1981)]. For instance, officers go to an apartment and are admitted by a person, who indicates that he is the roommate of the other individual living there, and the person appears to have joint access to the premises. If that person consents to a search of the common areas of the apartment, said consent will be valid even if the consenting person is not, in fact, the roommate and did not have authority to consent [*People v. Mack*, 107 AD 2d 1023 (N.Y. App. Div. 4th Dept., 1985)].

PROSPECTIVE SEARCH WARRANTS

Anticipatory search warrants—that is, warrants issued before the necessary events have occurred that would allow a constitutional search of premises—are valid so long as certain conditions are met [*United States v. Garcia*, 882 F. 2d 699, 702–704 (2nd Cir., 1989) cert. denied 110 S. Ct. 348 (1990)]. Basically, the conditions are that there be probable cause to believe that the property sought by the anticipatory search warrant is on a sure course to its destination so that said property will be at the designated place when the warrant is executed [*United States v. Garcia*, 882 F. 2d 699, 702 (2nd Cir., 1989), cert. denied 110 S. Ct. 348 (1989)].

The affidavits supporting an application for an anticipatory search warrant must show not only that there is a belief that a delivery of the property sought is going to occur, but also what this belief is based on, how reliable the sources of this belief are, and what part, if any, government agents will play in the delivery. The neutral, detached magistrate must then scrutinize whether there is probable cause to believe that the delivery will be made and whether there is probable cause to believe that the property sought will be located on the premises, when the search takes place. If the warrant is issued, the magistrate should protect against premature execution by listing in the warrant conditions governing execution which are explicit, clear, and narrowly drawn so as to avoid misunderstanding or manipulation by the officers executing the warrant [*United States v. Garcia*, 882 F. 2d 699, 703–704 (2nd Cir., 1989), cert. denied 110 S. Ct. 348 (1990)].

Anticipatory warrants are ordinarily used in situations where narcotics are mailed or there is to be a controlled delivery to a specific location. For instance, a package is mailed in Thailand to a city in the United States. U.S. Customs inspectors, in routinely examining incoming packages, opened the package and discovered heroin. The package was resealed and sent on to the U.S. Post Office. Based on this information, an anticipatory search warrant was issued for the search of the premises to which the package was to be delivered, and the warrant was executed after the package was delivered [*United States v. Lowe*, 575 F. 2d 1193 (6th Cir., 1978)].

Another example is as follows: Two individuals arrived in the United States from Panama and were searched by United States Customs inspectors. The search revealed that each was carrying a quantity of cocaine. Drug Enforcement agents were called in, and the two individuals agreed to cooperate and make a controlled delivery of the cocaine. An anticipatory search warrant was applied for and issued to search the premises to which the cocaine was delivered. The execution of the warrant was contingent upon delivery to the premises of the cocaine by the two individuals. The warrant was properly executed, and the ensuing seizure of the cocaine was held legal [*United States v. Garcia*, 882 F. 2d 705 (2nd Cir., 1989) cert. denied 110 S. Ct. 348 (1990)].

Before trying to obtain an anticipatory search warrant, an officer should fully review the facts in the case with a prosecutor to determine if the case requires such action.

SEARCH BY PRIVATE INDIVIDUAL OR STORE SECURITY PERSONNEL

The Supreme Court, in *Burdeau v. McDowell* [156 U.S. 465 (1921)], held that the Fourth Amendment is a limitation on the government and that evidence secured by a private illegal search does not have to be excluded from a criminal trial. Indeed, if private persons make an illegal search, the fruits of such search may be used in a subsequent open trial [*United States v. Jacobson*, 466 U.S. 109 (1984); *People v. Adler*, 50 N.Y. 2d 730 (1980)].

Problems arise, however, when law enforcement agents request or induce a private person to conduct a search or when a private person requests an officer to conduct a search. Any affirmative participation by an officer in a so-called "private person's search" renders said search subject to Fourth Amendment limitations [*Lustig v. United States*, 338 U.S. 74, 79 (1949); *People v. Adams*, 53 N.Y. 2d 1, 7 (1981)]. Thus, where such an officer requests or induces a private person to conduct a search [*United States v. Klopfenstine*, 673 F. Supp. 356 (W.D. Mo., 1987); *People v. Brown*, 34 AD 2d 108 (N.Y. App. Div. 3rd Dept., 1970)], the private person becomes an agent of the officer, and anything the officer could not constitutionally do, the private person cannot do [*Corngold v. United States*, 367 F. 2d 1 (9th Cir., 1966); *People v. Esposito*, 37 N.Y. 2d 156, 160 (1975)].

By the same token, if a private citizen requests an officer to search, the officer is limited by the Fourth Amendment [*People v. Adams*, 53 N.Y. 2d 1, 7 (1981)].

There is authority, however, if private investigators or private police are regularly engaged in the function of law enforcement, they can be deemed to be performing a public function and are therefore subject to the Fourth Amendment. [See, e.g., *People v. Zelinski*, 24 Cal. 3d 357 (1979); *People v. Stormer*, 136 Misc. 2d 184 (N.Y. County Court, Warren County, 1987), citing *Marsh v. Alabama*, 326 U.S. 501 (1946).] For instance, in *Stormer*, a private security force employed by a hotel located on an island had informed the local law enforcement agency that patrols on the island were unnecessary and that said agency's presence on the island would only be required upon special request. Hence, the private security force was deemed to be performing a public function and was subject to the Fourth Amendment.

Illegal arrests or searches by private citizens can lead to civil suits for damages.

In many states, legislatures to combat shoplifting have passed statutes allowing merchants to detain persons reasonably suspected of shoplifting for a reasonable time to pursue an investigation of the matter. [See, e.g., New York General Business Law, Section 218.] Nevertheless, such detentions are circumscribed by the enabling statutes. Private security personnel should check the law in their jurisdictions to determine if such a statute exists and the limits placed on the detentions that are permitted.

CONCLUSION

The law of search and seizure, as it exists today, places law enforcement officers in a very responsible position. Officers are faced by rules of criminal procedure and case law that they must follow to ensure that the actions they take pursuant to a search warrant or under a warrantless-search exception are valid. An error in judgment or a serious miscue could lead to the suppression of any evidence seized. Officers walk a thin line. They protect citizens, yet face the criminal element whose rights they must respect at the same time.

An illegal search results in tainted and inadmissible evidence and does not assist in the prosecution. If there is any doubt by an officer as to the advisability of a search warrant, the officer should discuss the case or situation with the prosecutor's office. The best course of conduct for the officer is to *always* try to obtain a search warrant. It protects the rights of the individual whose privacy is about to be intruded upon and protects the officer from charges of illegal search, harassment, abuse of authority, and possibly a personal civil suit.

This section has tried to set out the main areas and problems in search and seizure. The cases cited were but a sample. It is most important that state and local officers ascertain any different state or local rules applicable in their own jurisdictions.

Checklist for Search Warrant

1. Full description of object or premises to be searched.

2. Full address or location of objects or premises to be searched.

3. Full description of property or thing being searched for.

4. Description of how the law has been violated.

5. Affidavit for search warrant that meets the standard of probable cause, prepared by the officer who has requisite knowledge of case.

6. Officer who has statutory authority to execute the warrant.

7. If information from an informant is the basis of probable cause:
    a. *Totality of circumstances test*: All relevant information, including informant's information, officer's or fellow officer's own independent investigation or observations.
    b. *Two-prong test*: Facts establishing credibility of the informant and that the information is from personal knowledge.

8. Information in the affidavit is current and not stale.

9
Arrest and Procedure

Frank S. Polestino*

In the area of criminal investigation, investigators will have to evaluate the fruits of their observations and make determinations with regard to the arrests of persons being investigated. Once a police officer formally approaches a person, certain legal consequences follow. This chapter explains legal considerations involved in this encounter and explores some of the constitutional ramifications of the ever-continuing conflict between the right of the officer to arrest and the right of the individual to privacy. It outlines, in general, certain procedural guidelines that are usually followed in an arrest, while recognizing that jurisdictional variations occur.

ARREST AND SEIZURE DEFINED

An arrest by a police officer, as distinguished from an arrest by a private citizen, is governed by the Fourth Amendment, which states:

> The right of people to be secure in their persons...against unreasonable searches and seizures, shall not be violated, and no warrants shall issue, but upon probable cause...[Fourth Amendment of the U.S. Constitution]

It is to be noted that the Fourth Amendment speaks of seizures, not of arrests. An *arrest*, while being defined differently from jurisdiction to jurisdiction, is essentially the taking-into-custody of a person for the purposes of charging him or her with a crime. "Seizure" is a far broader term than "arrest." A *seizure* of a person occurs whenever an individual is physically or constructively detained by virtue of a significant interruption of his or her liberty of movement as a result of police action. Then that individual has been seized within the meaning of the Fourth Amendment [*Terry v. Ohio*, 392 U.S. 1 (1969); *People v. Cantor*, 36 N.Y. 2d 106 (1976)].

For seizure to have occurred, there must either be some application of force, even if it is extremely slight, or a show of authority to which a subject yields; a

---

*Based on Robert S. Rubine's chapter in the first edition.

show of authority without any application of physical force, to which the individual does not yield, is not a seizure [*California v. Hodari D.*, 111 S. Ct. 1547 (1991)].

Prior to the landmark decision of *Terry v. Ohio* [392 U.S. 1, 88 S. Ct. 1868, 20 L. Ed. 2d 880 (1969)], all seizures were governed by the requirement that before an individual's freedom of movement could be restrained, there had to be probable cause that an offense had been or was being committed by the person to be arrested.

With the advent of *Terry*, the Supreme Court for the first time acknowledged an exception to the requirement that the Fourth Amendment seizures must be based on probable cause. A police officer who is thus confronted with facts that give rise to a reasonable suspicion that a person is committing, has committed, or is about to commit either a felony or a misdemeanor may demand that person's name, address and an explanation of suspicious conduct. Additional facts that cause the officer to reasonably believe a person is armed and dangerous will allow a limited search, or frisk, of that person.

In contrast to a seizure, a traditional arrest has a view of not only restraining a person but taking the arrestee to the station house, command post, or other headquarters of the arresting authority to begin processing for an alleged crime. This must be supported by probable cause.

It is very important for the investigator to comprehend the distinction between a stop and frisk authorized in *Terry v. Ohio* and a traditional arrest. The stop and frisk is a limited intrusion, which is narrowly defined and governed by a test of reasonableness. The traditional arrest, however, involves a greater interference with individual privacy and must be supported by probable cause. A seizure that exceeds the authority of *Terry v. Ohio*, even though not a traditional arrest, will require probable cause.[1] It is, therefore, evident that investigators must understand that not every seizure of a person is an arrest. They must be aware of the legal consequences of their decisions to make arrests especially when their actions are not sanctioned by arrest warrants. If the investigator has good reason to stop and inquire of a person's conduct, the detention must be brief and a decision to arrest or allow the person to go free must be made. If the intent is to interfere with a person's freedom to the extent that the person is taken to the police station for some purpose, it will, most likely, be construed as an arrest. It matters very little whether or not the arrestee is formally charged, since many arrests do not result in prosecution for a crime. If the arrest is not made with probable cause, there will be constitutional ramifications if the conduct of the investigator is challenged by the defendant in a court of law.

CONSTITUTIONAL RAMIFICATIONS OF ARREST AND SEIZURE

Prior to the landmark case of *Mapp v. Ohio* [367 U.S. 643, 6 L.Ed. 2d 1081, S. Ct. 1684 (1961)],[2] state police action was not subject to the *Exclusionary Rule*.[3] The Exclusionary Rule stated that police who violated the dictates of the Fourth Amendment would not be allowed to use the evidence derived from that violation in a court of law. The Supreme Court in *Mapp v. Ohio* took the Exclusionary Rule, which had been enforced against the federal police since the rule was first enunciated in *Weeks v. United States* [232 U.S. 383, 58 L.Ed. 652, 34 S. Ct. 341 (1914)], and applied it to the states by virtue of the due process clause of the Fourteenth Amendment.

Applying the Exclusionary Rule to the law of arrest and seizure, it is axiomatic that results in the direct discovery of property indicative of criminality will be suppressed as a violation of the Fourth Amendment [*Delaware v. Prouse,* 440 U.S. 648 (1979); *People v. Cantor,* 36 N.Y. 2d, 106 (1976); *People v. Ingle,* 36 N.Y. 2d, 413 (1975)]. If, however, as an indirect result of an illegal arrest evidence is obtained, that evidence may be suppressed as the "fruit of the poison tree" [*Michigan v. Tucker,* 417 U.S. 433 (1974)]. In the case of *Wong Sun v. United States* [371 U.S. 471 (1963)], the arrest of one "Toy" was held to be unconstitutional because of the lack of probable cause. A confession was subsequently made and resulted in the defendant's conviction. The Supreme Court held the confession inadmissible, because it was the direct result of the illegal arrest. It was, as the Court stated, "the fruit of the poisonous tree" [*Silverthorne Lumber Co. v. United States,* 251 U.S. 385 (1920); *Nardone v. United States,* 308 U.S. 338 (1939)]. In the same case, another defendant, Wong Sun, had also been arrested illegally; however, he voluntarily returned to police headquarters to make a statement. The Court held that the connection between the arrest and the statement had become so attenuated as to dissipate the taint. The question of what will dissipate the taint of an illegal seizure or arrest was highlighted in the case of *Brown v. Illinois* [442 U.S. 590 (1975)], wherein the defendant, after being arrested without probable cause, gave a full confession, but only after receiving his Miranda rights [*Miranda v. Arizona,* 384 U.S. 436, 16 L.Ed. 694 86 S. Ct. 1602 (1966)]. The argument was made that the giving of *Miranda* warnings served to break the causal connection between the illegal arrest and giving of the statement. The Supreme Court, however, refusing to adopt a per se rule, held that not only must the prosecutor allow that the statement meet the Fifth Amendment voluntariness standard but "that the causal connection between the statement and the illegal arrest be broken sufficiently to purge the primary taint of the illegal arrest in light of the distinct policies and interests of the Fourth Amendment" [*Brown v. Illinois,* 442 U.S. 590, at 601]. The Court, in the *Brown v. Illinois* decision, identified several factors to be considered in determining whether a confession is to be purged of the illegal arrest:

1. The temporal proximity of the arrest and the confession.

2. The presence of intervening circumstances and, particularly, the purpose and flagrancy of the official misconduct [*Brown v. Illinois,* 442 U.S. 590, at 603, 604].

In *Taylor v. Alabama* [457 U.S. 687 (1982)], the defendant was arrested without probable cause and taken to a police station. While in custody, he was allowed to visit with his girlfriend and a male companion. Thereafter, he was given *Miranda* warnings, and he waived his rights. As a result of custodial interrogation he confessed some six hours after his arrest.

The Supreme Court held that the passage of six hours between the arrest and the confession was not significant; that the brief visit with his girlfriend and male companion was not deemed a sufficient attenuation to break the connection between the illegal arrest and the confession; and, finally, the facts that the defendant's arrest was based on an uncorroborated informant's tip and that the defendant was taken to the police station for interrogation in the hope that something would turn up constituted flagrant violation of the defendant's rights, particularly since he was taken into custody for the purpose of interrogation.

The Court concluded that the defendant's confession was the fruit of his illegal arrest and suppressed it.

In contrast, in *People v. Martinez* [37 N.Y. 2d 662 (1975)], a defendant's admissions obtained after an illegal arrest were deemed admissible, inasmuch as there was sufficient attenuation to break the connection between the illegal arrest and the confession. The defendant in *Martinez* was illegally stopped for a license and registration check, and a gun was discovered, which led to the defendant's arrest. The defendant was taken to a police station, where a detective spotted him. The detective had information from people in the street that the defendant was involved in a homicide the detective was investigating. About one hour after his arrest the defendant was taken to an interrogation room and given his *Miranda* warnings. He waived his rights and, during the interrogation, made admissions.

The Court, applying the test established in *Brown v. Illinois*, found that the police conduct in arresting the defendant was not flagrantly illegal; that the purpose of the arrest was not to interrogate the defendant as to the homicide; that the information from the people in the street was an intervening circumstance; and that there was an appreciable time lapse between the illegal arrest and the admission. The Court concluded that the taint of the illegal arrest was attenuated.

An arrest may also result in the suppression of fingerprints taken from a suspect unconstitutionally detained. It matters little whether the police label the seizure an investigatory detention or an accusatory arrest.[4] Likewise, if a person is identified as the perpetrator of a crime after an unconstitutional arrest, that identification might also be suppressed.[5] The distinction between whether or not there is an arrest is extremely crucial when considering the voluntariness of a confession. In the landmark case of *Miranda v. Arizona*, the Court held that persons in custody to be interrogated must first be informed of their rights if any statement is to be considered voluntary [*Miranda v. Arizona*, 384 U.S. 436 (1966)].

If a person is not in custody when interrogated, a confession made without *Miranda* warnings will not be invalidated [*Oregon v. Mathiason*, 429 U.S. 492 (1977)]. Therefore, the police investigator who approaches a suspected individual under the *Terry* stop-and-frisk approach does not have to give Miranda warnings when only asking a person for an explanation of suspicious conduct. [See, e.g., *Pennsylvania v. Bruder*, 488 U.S. 9 (1988); *New York v. Quarles*, 467 U.S. 649 (1984); *People v. Morales*, 65 N.Y. 2d 997 (1985).]

It should also be noted that if evidence is obtained as a result of an illegal arrest, it may be admissible under the inevitable-discovery doctrine. The substance of this doctrine is that evidence seized illegally would inevitably have been discovered by legal means [*Nix v. Williams*, 467 U.S. 431 (1984)]. *Nix v. Williams* is illustrative of the doctrine. In *Nix* a defendant in an interrogation, which was conducted in violation of the defendant's right to counsel, revealed the location of the body of a homicide victim. Thus, the location of the body was illegally obtained; however, at the time the body was found, a search party was in the process of looking for it and would have inevitably discovered it by legal means.

Closely related to the inevitable discovery doctrine is the independent source doctrine [*Murray v. United States*, 467 U.S. 533 (1988)]. Similarly, the gist of this doctrine is that, if information concerning certain evidence is obtained illegally, but that evidence is in fact discovered and seized by legal means independently of the illegal conduct, the evidence is admissible.

The following hypothetical case will illustrate this doctrine: A defendant is illegally arrested, and during an interrogation following *Miranda* warnings and a waiver of rights, the defendant reveals the location of a gun used in a murder; however, the police independently of the illegal admission locate the gun by legal means. Hence, the gun would be admissible.

When a lawful custodial arrest has been made, with or without a warrant, a contemporaneous incident of that arrest may include the search of the person of the arrestee and a search of the grab area surrounding the arrestee with the attended power to open all closed containers uncovered as a result of such search [*New York v. Belton*, 453 U.S. 454 (1981)].

There is a temporal limitation on the search of the grab area. Such search must be made while the parties are still at the arrest site.[6] However, the search of the person of the arrestee and closed containers found on the arrestee may be made at any time while the arrestee remains in custody as a result of the arrest [*United States v. Edwards*, 415 U.S. 800 (1974); *People v. Natal*, 75 N.Y. 2d 379 (1990)].

If an arrest is validly made in a private place, then in addition to a search of the person of the arrestee and the grab area, the police may engage in a protective sweep of the premises and look into spaces immediately adjoining the place of arrest, which may be harboring an individual who could launch an attack on those on the arrest scene, provided there are reasonable grounds to believe that a person posing a danger is present in the areas swept [*Maryland v. Buie*, 110 S. Ct. 1093 (1990)].

It should be noted that, if a custodial arrest is validly made for merely a traffic infraction, then the power to search is limited to a search of the person of an arrestee, and there is no power to search the grab area [*United States v. Robinson*, 414 U.S. 218 (1975)].

Finally, it needs to be pointed out that, if there has been a valid custodial arrest with or without a warrant for general criminality or for traffic offenses, the police at the police station may search the person of an arrestee and any container or article in the arrestee's possession as part of an established and routine inventory procedure [*Illinois v. Lafayette*, 462 U.S. 640 (1983)].

It is interesting to note that an illegal arrest does not prevent the prosecution and conviction of the person so arrested.[7] However, where an illegal arrest is effected by conduct that is extremely reprehensible and unconscionable involving acts such as torture, brutality, or unconscionable entrapment, some courts have barred the prosecution and conviction of the person arrested on due process grounds [*United States v. Toscanino*, 500 F 2d 267 (2d Cir. 1974); *People v. Isaacson*, 44 N.Y. 2d 511 (1978)].

Nevertheless, a number of courts have rejected the due process argument in connection with illegal arrests to bar the prosecution and conviction of the person so arrested [*Matta-Ballestros v. Henman*, 896 F 2d 255 (7th Cir.), cert. denied 112 S. Ct. 169 (1990); *United States v. Darby*, 744 F 2d 1508 (11th Cir.), cert. denied 471 U.S. 1100 (1985); *United States v. Winter*, 509 F 2d 975 (5 Cir.), cert. denied 423 U.S. 825 (1975)].

REQUIREMENT OF A WARRANT OF ARREST

If there is probable cause, there is no requirement for a warrant to arrest a person in a public place, even though there is sufficient time and opportunity to obtain a warrant before making the arrest [*United States v. Watson*, 423 U.S. 411 (1976)].

However, the arrest of a person in that individual's dwelling without a warrant, absent exigency or consent to enter the premises, is illegal [*Payton v. New York*, 445 U.S. 573 (1980)].

Clearly, if the person to be arrested voluntarily consents to the police entry, or if someone else freely agrees to it who may have joint dominion and control over said premises, such as a wife, live-in companion, parent, or sibling, then the warrantless arrest in the premises is valid [*United States v. Briley*, 726 F 2d 1301 (8th Cir., 1984); *United States v. Pinham*, 725 F 2d 450 (8th Cir., 1984)].

More problematic are situations where the consent is obtained by means of deceit. It has been stated that consent acquired by use of fictitious names or misrepresentations concerning the nature of the police purpose in gaining entry to premises would render any consent to such entry involuntary [*United States v. Briley*, 726 F 2d 1301 (8th Cir., 1984); *United States v. Turpin*, 707 F 2d 332 (8th Cir., 1983); *United States v. Ruiz-Altschiller*, 694 F 2d 1104 (8th Cir.), cert. denied 462 U.S. 1134 (1983)]. However, if the deceit involves an undercover police officer who obtains consent to enter a suspect's home by concealing his/her true identity for the purported purpose of conducting illegal business, then the consent to so enter is valid [*United States v. Briley*, 726 F 2d 1301 (8th Cir., 1984)].

On the other hand, it has been held that the use of any deceit by police to obtain consent would not destroy the voluntariness of the consent, unless the police made it falsely appear that the consent to enter was essential for safety or other good public policy considerations, such as falsely stating that consent to enter was necessary to investigate a nonexistent gas leak [*People v. Abrams*, 95 AD 2d 155 (App. Div. 2d Dept., 1983)].

What constitutes exigent circumstances is somewhat more complex. Initially it should be noted that the application of the exigent-circumstances exception to the warrant requirement for an arrest in a dwelling is rarely, if ever, sanctioned when there is probable cause to believe that only a minor offense has been committed, such as a traffic infraction [*Welsh v. Wisconsin*, 466 U.S. 740 (1984)]. In many cases a determination as to whether exigency exists if made by considering the following factors [*Dorman v. United States*, 435 F 2d 385 (D.C. Cir., 1970)]:

1. The gravity of the crime involved. Crimes of violence are particularly weighty.

2. A person believes that the individual to be arrested is armed.

3. A clear showing of probable cause somewhat beyond the minimum showing of probable cause for a warrant.

4. A strong reason to believe that the person to be arrested is in the premises being entered.

5. A likelihood that the person to be arrested will flee if not swiftly apprehended.

6. The entry, though not consented to, is made peaceably. But forcible entry may in some instances be justified to avert imminent destruction of evidence, danger of police officer, etc.

7. The time the entry is made, whether day or night.

The most weighty factor, however, is that the person to be arrested will flee if not swiftly apprehended, and there is no time or opportunity to obtain a warrant [*People v. Burr*, 70 N.Y. 2d 354 (1987)].

In some cases exigency may be more simply established. For example, the hot pursuit of a fleeing felon, who has just committed a serious crime, would justify intrusion into the felon's home to effect a warrantless arrest [*Welsh v. Wisconsin*, 466 U.S. 740 (1984); see also *Warden v. Hayden*, 387 U.S. 294 (1967)].

Also presenting exigency is a situation where the person to be arrested is in his/her home, and there are other individuals in the house, such as victims or hostages, and there is reason to believe that said persons would be harmed by the one to be arrested [*People v. Henderson*, 107 AD 2d 469 (N.Y.)App. Div. 4th Dept., 1985)].

A situation somewhat analogous to the exigency situation is the case where a warrantless arrest is initiated in a public place, but the person to be arrested flees into his/her home. In this situation, if the police pursue the person into the home and effect the arrest, there is no *Payton* violation [*United States v. Santana*, 427 U.S. 38 (1976)].

It should be noted that *Payton* is not deemed to be violated if the police, without crossing the threshold of the home of the person to be arrested, direct that person to come out of the house onto a public street without threatening the use of force, the person complies, and the police then effect a warrantless arrest [*People v. Minley*, 68 N.Y. 2d 956 (1986)].

In the same vein, the police may wait until the person to be arrested leaves the home and comes onto a public street and then make a warrantless arrest without offending against *Payton* [*Steagald v. United States*, 451 U.S. 204 (1981)].

The warrantless arrest of a person in the home of a third party would not involve a *Payton* violation, if the person so arrested did not have a reasonable expectation of privacy in said premise [*Steagald v. United States*, 451 U.S. 204 (1981); *People v. Rivers*, 115 AD 2d 570 (N.Y. App. Div. 2d Dept., 1985)].

There is a caveat: If, during the course of said arrest, property indicative of criminality is discovered implicating the third party, said evidence is subject to suppression [*Steagald v. United States*, 451 U.S. 204 (1981); *United States v. Underwood*, 717 F 2d 482 (9th Cir., 1983)].

It would appear that the better course to follow in such situations is to obtain a search warrant to enter the third party's home to arrest the person who is sought. In this way, if evidence is discovered implicating the third party, it will not be suppressed [*Steagald v. United States*, 451 U.S. 204 (1981)].

Finally, whether the *Payton* warrant requirement extends beyond the interior of the dwelling of the persons to be arrested has not clearly been established. It has been held that warrantless arrest at the threshold of a dwelling [*United States v. Santana*, 427 U.S. 38 (1976)], in a common hallway of a multidwelling [*People v. Johnson*, 114 Misc. 2d 578 (Sup. Ct. N.Y. County)], in a warehouse [*United States v. Ponce*, 488 F. Supp. 226 (S.D. N.Y. 1980)], or in a fenced but open backyard of a commercial premise [*United States v. Reed*, 733 F 2d 492 (8th Cir., 1984)] would not involve a *Payton* violation.

However, a warrantless arrest in a hotel or motel room [*United States v. Forker*, 928 F 2d 365 (11th Cir., 1991)], in a hallway of a rooming house [*People v. Lott*, 102 AD 2d 506 (N.Y. App. Div. 4th Dept., 1984)], or in a closed office in a warehouse [*United States v. Driver*, 776 F 2d 807 (9th Cir., 1985)] would involve a *Payton* violation.

With respect to the backyard of a private home, the cases are split as to whether *Payton* would apply to a warrantless arrest made there [*United States v. Karagozian*, 715 F. Supp. 1160 (D. Conn., 1989); *Keyes v. City of Albany*, 694 F. Supp. 1147 (N.D. N.Y., 1984), Payton applies; *People v. Jones*, 150 AD 2d 496 (N.Y. App. Div. 2d Dept., 1989), Payton does not apply].

THE CONSEQUENCES OF A *PAYTON* VIOLATION

If there has been a warrantless arrest in a dwelling in violation of *Payton*, anything incriminating gathered because of the arrest in the dwelling will be suppressed. This should include anything found on the person arrested, in the grab area, or as a result of a protective sweep, as well as any statements that the arrested person may make while in custody in the dwelling.

However, anything obtained outside the dwelling, such as admissions or confessions at the police station, an identification or fingerprints would be admissible.[8]

THE GOOD-FAITH RELIANCE ON A WARRANT EXCEPTION

Evidence obtained as a consequence of an arrest made in good-faith reliance on a warrant issued by a neutral, detached magistrate will ordinarily not result in the suppression of such evidence, even though the warrant may have been improperly handed out because of lack of probable cause or a procedural error.[9]

The good-faith reliance on a warrant exception is not applicable if [*United States v. Leon*, 468 U.S. 897 (1984)]:

1. The warrant is based on knowing or recklessly false information.
2. The issuing magistrate did not perform a neutral and detached function, but merely served as a rubber stamp for the police.
3. The issuing magistrate demonstrated a lack of neutrality by acting as an adjunct law enforcement officer.
4. The probable cause determination is not made on substantial data, but rather on bare bone conclusory assertions.
5. The warrant is obviously defective in form.

If any of these five exceptions is present, then the ensuing arrest may be deemed illegal, and any evidence gathered as a result of such arrest will be subject to suppression.

THE REQUIREMENT OF PROBABLE CAUSE

Any discussion involving the constitutional rights of the accused or the propriety of police conduct will necessarily require an understanding of that exceedingly difficult concept "probable cause." It has been defined as existing when the facts and circumstances within an officer's knowledge, and of which the officer had reasonable trustworthy information, are sufficient in themselves to warrant a person of reasonable caution having the belief that an offense has been, or is being, committed [*Beck v. Ohio*, 379 U.S. 89, 91 (1964)].

Only the probability, and not a prima facie showing of criminal activity, is the standard of probable cause [*Spinelli v. United States*, 393 U.S. 410, 419 (1969)].

It must be recalled that the Fourth Amendment states that "no warrant shall issue, but upon probable cause." An officer who acts on the authority of an arrest warrant has the benefit of having probable cause determined by a neutral magistrate. This judicial endorsement of probable cause will give the enforcement official the full authority to arrest. This can be crucial in any given case because of the good-faith reliance on a warrant exception previously discussed.[10]

Since the actions of police officers acting without a warrant cannot be less demanding than those actions based on a warrant, probable cause is always required. If the police act without a warrant, they must make the initial probable cause determination themselves. The police action in this respect will be subject to review by a judge on a motion to suppress any evidence taken as a result of the arrest.

In assessing probable cause, the police may not depend on the fruit of a search made after an arrest [*United States v. Di Re*, 332 U.S. 581, 595 (1948); *People v. Loria*, 10 N.Y. 2d 368, 373 (1961)] or on acting in good faith on a hunch or unparticularized suspicion [*Terry v. Ohio*, 392 U.S. 1, 27 (1968)]. The police may, however, rely on all the senses, such as sight, hearing, or smell, to gain probable cause [*Beck v. Ohio*, 397 U.S. 89, 94 (1964); *People v. Goldberg*, 19 N.Y. 2d 460, 465 (1967)]. Thus, the police officer who lawfully approaches a vehicle and smells the odor of marijuana will have probable cause to arrest the driver [*People v. Chestnut*, 36 N.Y. 2d 971 (1975)].

If a police officer observes in plain view from a position he has a right to be in [*Horton v. California*, 110 S. Ct. 2301 (1990); *Arizona v. Hicks*, 480 U.S. 321 (1987)] property indicative of criminality, such as an illegal weapon, he or she may seize the weapon and arrest the person possessing it [*People v. Lemmons*, 40 N.Y. 2d 505, 509 (1976)]. Another illustration is that the police officer who hears the making of an illegal bet would also have probable cause to arrest [*People v. Goldberg*, 19 N.Y. 2d 460 (1967)].

In many situations probable cause is gained by combining several certain enumerated factors that make it appear at least more probable than not that a crime has or is taking place [*People v. Carrasguillo*, 54 N.Y. 2d 248, 254 (1981)]. The facts are as follows:

1. A crime or crimes have been committed in the area involved; for example, the area is noted for drug trafficking [*People v. McRay*, 51 N.Y. 2d. 594 (1980)], a number of burglaries have occurred there [*People v. Brady*, 16 N.Y. 2d 186 (1965)], or a bank robbery has just taken place in the area [*People v. Mitchell*, 75 AD 2d 626 (N.Y. App. Div. 2d Dept., 1980)].

2. Police knowledge of the reputation of the person being observed, such as being a drug pusher or burglar, or of the reputation of a companion of that person [*People v. Brown*, 24 N.Y. 2d 421, 422 (1969); *People v. Brady*, 16 N.Y. 2d 186, 189 (1965)].

3. Unusual activity or conduct, such as carrying a cash register or jumping from a second-story window [*People v. Rosemond*, 26 N.Y. 2d 101, 104–105 (1970); *People v. Whitaker*, 168 AD 2d 656 (N.Y. App. Div. 2d Dept., 1990)].

4. Police expertise, such as recognizing that heroin is usually packaged in clear, transparent envelopes [*People v. McRay*, 51 N.Y. 2d 594 (1980)].

5. A person's flight from the police [*People v. Kreichman*, 37 N.Y. 2d 693, 699 (1975)].

6. A person giving false or evasive answers to police inquiry [*People v. Brady*, 16 N.Y. 2d 186 (1965); *People v. Holt*, 121 AD 2d 469 (N.Y. App. Div. 2d Dept., 1986)].

7. Repetition of conduct, such as a number of people approaching the person observed over a period of time and handing that person money in bill form, and that person making a written notation, would be probable cause to believe the person is a bookie [*People v. Valentine*, 17 N.Y. 2d 128 (1966); see also *People v. Pepe*, 32 N.Y. 2d 707 (1973)].

8. Prior information, such as a tip that a robbery is going to take place, that a drug deal is to be made, or that person has a gun [*People v. Hanlon*, 36 N.Y. 2d 549, 558 (1975)].

9. Manner of dress, such as wet clothing or no shoes [*People v. Holt*, 121 AD 2d 469 (N.Y. App. Div. 2d Dept., 1980); *People v. Maize*, 32 AD 2d 1031 (N.Y. App. Div. 2d Dept., 1969)].

10. The time, whether day or night [*People v. Clark*, 45 N.Y. 2d 432 (1978); *People v. Mitchell*, 75 AD 2d 625 (N.Y. App. Div. 2d Dept., 1980)].

11. The area of the street or the place where the observations are made, such as observing someone on a fire escape or at the entrance to a closed retail store [*People v. Perry*, 71 N.Y. 2d 871 (1988); *People v. Clark*, 45 N.Y. 2d 432 (1978)].

12. The gait of the person observed, such as running or walking rapidly [*People v. Gee*, 143 AD 2d 1039, N.Y. App. Div. 2d Dept., 1988); *People v. Lopez*, 94 AD 2d 627 N.Y. App. Div. 1st Dept., 1983)].

13. Furtive behavior, for instance, looking around to ascertain if the person is being watched or hurriedly hiding an object [*People v. Lopez*, 94 AD 2d 627 N.Y. App. Div., 1st Dept., 1983)]; *People v. Barnes*, 149 AD 2d 359 (N.Y. App. Div. 1st Dept., 1989)]. Illustrations of the combining of factors for probable cause are as follows:

   a. A police officer saw a person coming out of a hotel where a series of burglaries had recently taken place (factor 1, the crimes occurred recently). Some months previously, the person had been stopped on one of the upper floors of the hotel and was found to have keys to five different rooms (factor 2, police expertise—possession of keys associated with hotel burglaries; and factor 3, reputation of the person observed). The police officer observed the person repeatedly taking little boxes out of his pocket and looking at the contents (factor 4, unusual activity; and factor 5, police expertise—little boxes usually contain jewelry, a favorite target in hotel burglaries). When stopped, the person denied his name was Brady, which the police knew, and that he had just come out of the hotel (factor 5, false or evasive answers). This combination of factors amounted to probable cause [*People v. Brady*, 16 N.Y. 2d 186 (1965)].

   b. A police officer, an expert in drug trafficking, observed in an area noted for such activity (factor 1, crime area) two men walking together on a public street. The men stopped in front of a schoolyard and began looking up and down the street (factor 2, furtive behavior). One of the men then passed a stack of whitish, transparent envelopes to the other man who put them into his pocket (factor 3, police expertise—whitish transparent envelopes are a telltale indicator of heroin). This combination of factors was also probable cause [*People v. McRay*, 51 N.Y. 2d 594 (1980)].

Probable cause, however, does not necessarily require that a police officer observe the conduct. Often the officer will obtain information from a disclosed, undisclosed, or anonymous informant. For the informant's tip to be the basis of probable cause, it must appear from a totality of circumstances that the information concerning criminality is reliable [*Illinois v. Gates*, 462 U.S. 213 (1983)].

Exactly what totality of circumstances will establish reliability has not been extensively explored by the courts; however, the following cases give examples: *Illinois v. Gates* [462 U.S. 213 (1983)], *Massachusetts v. Upton* [466 U.S. 727 (1984)], *United States v. Harris* [403 U.S. 573 (1971)].[11]

Some jurisdictions (for example, New York) reject the totality of circumstances approach and require that an undisclosed informant's information to be deemed reliable must pass a two-prong veracity and basis of knowledge test, that is, the informant is credible and is speaking from personal knowledge [*People v. Grimminger*, 71 N.Y. 2d 635 (1988)].

ARREST BY WARRANT

While it is recognized that procedures for making an arrest may vary from jurisdiction to jurisdiction, the following guidelines are applicable in most jurisdictions. It is strongly advised that investigators consult the statutes in their jurisdictions for exact local procedure for making arrests with and without a warrant.

A *warrant of arrest* is a process issued by a criminal court directing the police officer to arrest a suspect designated in an accusatory instrument filed with such court for purpose of arraignment.

There are three types of arrest warrants, each serving a different purpose.

1. *Warrant of arrest* is one issued by a local *criminal* court for a suspect in a criminal action who *has not been arraigned.*

2. *Superior court warrant of arrest* is one issued by a superior court after an indictment is filed with it by the grand jury to secure the attendance of the indicted individual for arraignment under the grand jury indictment.

3. *Bench warrant* is one issued by the court to secure custody of a defendant who, after being arraigned, fails to appear in court.

The warrant must be subscribed by the issuing judge and must state the following: name of issuing court, date of issuance, name and title of offense charged, name of defendant (if name is unknown, any name or description may be used by which the defendant can be identified with reasonable certainty), the police officer or officers to whom the warrant is addressed, and a direction to such police officer to arrest the defendant and bring him or her before the issuing court.

Warrants of arrest are issued when a criminal action has been commenced in a criminal court by the filing of a verified accusatory instrument (other than a simplified traffic information). The warrant is one that is issued by the criminal court for a defendant in a criminal action *who has not yet been arraigned.* If the accusatory instrument is sufficient *on its face*, then a warrant will be issued for the defendant's arrest.

The court has further authority to refuse to issue a warrant of arrest, even though the accusatory instrument is sufficient on its face, until it has satisfied itself by inquiry or examination of witnesses that there is *reasonable cause to believe* that the defendant committed the offense charged. The court, during such inquiry, may examine under oath or otherwise any available person whom it believes may possess knowledge concerning the charge.

The court may issue a summons in lieu of a warrant of arrest if it is satisfied that the defendant will respond thereto.

A warrant of arrest may be issued only by the criminal court with which the accusatory instrument has been filed, and it may be made returnable in the issuing court only.

The warrant of arrest may be addressed to any police officer or classification of police officer whose *geographical* area of employment embraces *either* the place where the offense was charged or allegedly committed *or* the site of the court that issued the warrant.

Warrants of arrest when issued by district courts, superior courts, or superior court judges sitting in a local criminal court can be executed anywhere in the state.

Upon issuance by the court, the warrant of arrest may be executed by any police officer to whom it is addressed or any other police officers delegated to execute it pursuant to circumstances specified.

A warrant of arrest may be executed on any day of the week and any hour of the day or night.

With the exception of requiring that the information upon which a warrant is issued be sworn to, a violation of any statute needing the preceding procedures will not necessarily result in suppression of evidence as a consequence of the ensuing arrest. Nor will a violation of state law inevitably lead to a suppression of evidence under the Fourth Amendment [*California v. Greenwood*, 486 U.S. 35, 43 (1988)]. Suppression will follow only when the state statute violated existed to implement a constitutional guarantee [*People v. Silverstein*, 74

N.Y. 2d 768, 773 (dissenting opinion) (1989); *People v. Sampron*, 73 N.Y. 2d 908 (1989)]. Thus, what court issues a warrant, who executes a warrant, or where the warrant is executed is not a matter covered by the Fourth Amendment. Therefore, a violation of a statute dealing with those points will not result in suppression.

However, the Fourth Amendment requires that no warrants shall issue but upon probable cause, supported by oath or affirmation. The failure to have such oath or affirmation in a warrant application will result in suppression [*People v. Sullivan*, 56 N.Y. 2d 378, 384 (1982)], if the good-faith warrant exception is not applicable in the jurisdiction.

There is a caveat for failure to comply with a state statute controlling warrant arrests. Even though the state law did not exist to implement a constitutional guarantee, thus precluding suppression for a violation of the statute, such violation may be the basis for a civil suit for damages.

The arresting officer must inform the defendant that an arrest warrant for the designated offense has been issued. The warrant must be shown to the defendant upon request, if it is in the police officer's possession. It should be noted that the warrant need not be in the police officer's possession and, if it is not, it must be shown to the defendant upon request as soon after the arrest as possible. This procedure must be followed, unless physical resistance, flight, or other factors may render such normal procedure impractical.

To effect an arrest under warrant, a police officer may use such physical force as is justified by the particular statute or the jurisdiction. The use of excessive physical force or the inappropriate use of such may render the arrest illegal and could result in suppression of evidence [*People v. Stevenson*, 31 N.Y. 2d 108, 112 (1972); *Hinton v. City of New York*, 13 AD 2d 475 (App. Div. 1st Dept., 1961)].

In attempting to capture a fleeing felon, deadly physical force (the use of a firearm) is not permitted, unless it is necessary to defend oneself or another from what is reasonably believed to be the use, or imminent use, of deadly physical force [*Tennessee v. Garner*, 471 U.S. 1 (1985)].

If the arrest is made in a public place, then informing the person to be arrested that the arrest is being made pursuant to a warrant for the designated offense is merely a technical violation of the law that would not require suppression of evidence seized as a result of such arrest [*United States ex rel Eidenmuller v. Fay*, 240 F Supp. 591 (D.C. N.Y., 1965), cert. denied 384 U.S. 964 (1966)].

Nevertheless, giving notice that an arrest warrant has been issued for the designated offense before entering private premises may be crucial. Thus, the police knocking on a door and demanding entry without indication that the basis for the demand was an arrest warrant, and the occupant refusing entry resulting in the police making a forced entry, renders the arrest illegal with the consequence that the evidence gathered by reason of the arrest will be suppressed [*People v. Frank*, 35 N.Y. 2d 874 (1974); see opinion on 43 AD 2d 691 at pp. 692–694 (N.Y. App. Div. 2d Dept., 1973)].

There are, however, circumstances in which a police officer may make an unannounced or no-called, no-knock entry into the premises. If there is reasonable cause to believe that the giving of notice will (1) result in the person to be arrested escaping or attempting to escape, (2) endanger the life or safety of the police or another person, (3) result in the destruction, damaging, or secreting of material evidence, then the police may make a no-knock entry using force if necessary [*Ker v. California*, 374 U.S. 23 (1963)].

ARREST AND PROCEDURE
WITHOUT WARRANT

A person may be arrested without warrant if he or she has committed or is believed to have committed an offense and its at liberty within the state, although no criminal action has yet been commenced in any criminal court.

The right to arrest a person without a warrant is generally limited by statute. The provisions for such warrantless arrest are that police officers may arrest a person for any offense when they have *reasonable cause to believe* that the offense was committed in their presence or for a crime when they have *reasonable cause to believe* the person has committed the crime, whether or not in their presence. Police officers may arrest a person for such a crime, whether or not committed within the geographical area of their employment, and they may make such arrest within the state, regardless of the site of the commission of the crime. Police officers may, if necessary, even pursue the person outside the state and may arrest him or her in any state with laws containing equivalent provisions [*People v. Walls*, 35 N.Y. 2d 419 (1974)].

In many instances, the authority of the officer to arrest will depend on whether the offense is a *misdemeanor* or a *felony*. Generally, a felony can be defined as any offense for which the punishment could possibly be imprisonment for 1 year or more. Those offenses that do not require imprisonment in a state prison are considered misdemeanors or violations. The rule is, generally, that enforcement officers may make arrests without warrants for misdemeanors only when the misdemeanors are committed in their presence. This means that a misdemeanor is actually taking place in the officer's presence and the officer knows it is taking place. The rule with regard to felonies is more liberal when it comes to the law enforcement officer's authority to make an arrest. As stated earlier in this chapter, an officer who has probable cause to believe that a felony has been committed and that the person to be arrested is committing or has committed the felony may make a warrantless public arrest.

An arrest without a warrant may be made at any hour of the day or night.

As discussed under "Arrest By Warrant," a violation of any statute dealing with arrest and procedures will not result in suppression, since who makes an arrest, for what offense the arrest is made, or where the arrest is made are not matters covered by the Fourth Amendment.

Again, the caveat is that the failure to comply with state laws involving procedures for an arrest without a warrant may result in a civil suit for damages!

The statute concerning the giving of notice as to the purpose for the arrest in a public or private place, the use of force and no-knock entries (discussed under "Arrest by Warrant") are applicable to arrests made without a warrant.

After an arrest, the person apprehended must be arraigned in a court as soon as practicable [*County of Riverside v. McLaughlin*, 111 S. Ct. 1661 (1991); arraignment must be within 48 hours, unless for good cause shown].

NOTES

[1]*Dunaway v. New York*, 442 U.S. 200 (1979). Defendant was taken to police headquarters and interrogated. He was not told he was under arrest nor was he booked. *Davis v. Mississippi*, 394 U.S. 721 (1969). Defendant was held for investigation without probable cause and was fingerprinted. Court suppressed fingerprints, ignoring the label "investigative detention."

[2]*Mapp v. Ohio*, 367 U.S. 643 (1961). Supreme Court held that any evidence obtained by searches and seizures in violation of the Fourth Amendment of the Constitution should be inadmissible in a state court by the application of the due process clause of the Fourteenth Amendment.

[3]*Wolf v. Colorado*, 338 U.S. 25 (1949). The court refused to impose the Exclusionary Rule as a mandatory method of enforcement to deter violations of the Fourth Amendment and left the states free to adopt or not to adopt the Exclusionary Rule.

[4]*Hayes v. Florida*, 470 U.S. 811 (1985). The Court in *Hayes*, however, indicated that, if a defendant is detained on reasonable suspicion in the field and fingerprints are taken there, the fingerprint evidence would be admissible.

[5]*United States v. Crews*, 445 U.S. 463 (1980). The Court in *Crews*, however, held that an in-court identification would be admissible if said identification is untainted by the out-of-court identification made after the illegal arrest.

[6]*New York v. Belton*, 453 U.S. 454 (1981). There is a caveat: Some jurisdictions, and New York in particular, will permit the opening of closed containers found in the grab area only if the person arrested is not neutralized and is in a position to reach and open the closed container to hide or destroy evidence or procure a weapon [*People v. Gokey*, 60 N.Y. 2d 309 (1983)].

[7]*Gerstein v. Pugh*, 420 U.S. 103, 119 (1974). The principle involved is the *Ker-Frisbie* doctrine [*United States v. Pelaez*, 930 F 2d 520 (6th Cir. 1991)].

[8]*New York v. Harris*, 110 S. Ct. 1640 (1990). However, at least one jurisdiction (New York) would suppress all evidence gathered, whether in the dwelling or elsewhere, as a result of a *Payton* violation, unless the taint of the illegality is dissipated by attenuation under the standards set forth in *Brown v. Illinois* (422 U.S. 590) heretofore discussed [*People v. Harris*, 77 N.Y. 2d 439 (1991)].

[9]*United States v. Leon*, 468 U.S. 897 (1984). At least one jurisdiction has rejected the good faith warrant exception (*People v. Bigelow*, 66 N.Y. 2d 417 (1985)].

[10]In those jurisdictions rejecting the good faith warrant exception, a warrant may also be crucial, since in a marginal case an arrest with a warrant would be sustained, whereas if the arrest had been made without a warrant it would fail [*United States v. Ventresca*, 380 U.S. 102, 106 (1965)].

[11]With respect to anonymous information and reasonable suspicion, see *Alabama v. White* [110 S. Ct. 2412 (1990)].

10

Confessions, *Miranda* Rights, and Waivers

Frank S. Polestino*

This chapter is intended to point out what officers must do or refrain from do-ing if they intend to have statements of guilt obtained by them admitted into ev-idence at criminal trials. It will not be a historical development of the law of con-fessions, which can be found in other competent publications,[1] but it will treat developments in the area of confessions under *Miranda*, which officers will need to be aware of to better conduct their interviewing suspects.

The terms "confessions," "admissions," and "statements" will be used inter-changeably in this chapter, because courts have moved toward a single rule for this type of evidence and also because, from a federal constitutional point of view, the difference is meaningless.

Because of space considerations, the treatment of the topic is not all-encom-passing, but it highlights significant areas. The decisions cited are the prevail-ing positions on the specific questions. If another position is cited, a notation will be made of that fact.

INTRODUCTION

The *Miranda* Decision

In *Miranda v. Arizona* [384 U.S. 436 (1966)], the Supreme Court held that, when an individual is taken into custody or otherwise deprived of freedom of action in a significant way, and is to be questioned for evidence of guilt, certain proce-dural safeguards must be afforded to protect the individual's Fifth Amendment privilege against compulsory self-incrimination. The procedural safeguards

*Based on Thomas F. Walsh's chapter in the first edition.

consist of the familiar fourfold advice of rights coupled with voluntary waiver of those rights. Individuals must be advised (1) of their right to remain silent, (2) that anything they say may be used against them in court, (3) of their right to the presence of an attorney before and during questioning, (4) of their right to an appointed attorney for those who cannot afford one, prior to questioning. Following the warnings and before questioning, a knowing and intelligent waiver must be obtained. Without proof of the warnings and waiver, any incriminating statement thereafter obtained is inadmissible to establish guilt.

The concern of the Supreme Court for the rights of a subject in custody arose from its fear not that an accused might confess under such circumstances, but that the confession might be motivated or forced by the "compulsion inherent in custodial surroundings." The key word which appears frequently in the *Miranda* opinion is "compulsion." The Court thought that the police-dominated atmosphere in which most custodial interrogation occurs is alone a significant threat to the free determination of an accused to cooperate. Accordingly, the Court sought to lessen the pressure of the isolated setting of the police station by demanding that accused persons be informed that they possess certain fundamental protections which they may choose to exercise. In the absence of an arrangement affording rights to the accused, or a valid waiver of those protections, police cannot pursue the questioning. If they do and a statement is obtained, it cannot be admitted into evidence to prove the person's guilt.

The Court went on, by way of clarification, to define custodial interrogation as "questioning initiated by law enforcement officers after a person has been taken into custody or otherwise deprived of his freedom of action in any significant way (384 U.S. 436 at 444).

The Court has described the *Miranda* warnings as a prophylactic rule employed to protect Fifth Amendment rights against the compulsion inherent in custodial surroundings. The exclusion of statements made in the absence of the warnings serves to deter police officers from taking incriminating statements without first informing persons of their Fifth Amendment rights. The Court removes the incentive for police officers to disregard these procedural safeguards in obtaining confessions by not allowing the confessions to be admitted into evidence on the issue of guilt.

The problems in this area of confessions can be reduced to four: (1) whether custody was imposed; (2) whether interrogation took place; (3) whether adequate warnings were given by the law enforcement officer; and (4) whether a valid waiver of rights was obtained.

The final section in our discussion will deal with miscellaneous *Miranda* issues that have been addressed by the courts.

CUSTODY OR "OTHERWISE DEPRIVED OF HIS FREEDOM"

General Rule

The *Miranda* warnings must be given by any law enforcement officer who interrogates (guilt-seeking interview) any person who has been taken into custody or otherwise deprived of freedom of action in any significant way. Note that three factors must coexist in order for *Miranda* to become operative: (1) custody, (2) interrogation (guilt-seeking type), and (3) conducted by the police. The key words at this point of our discussion are "custody or otherwise deprived," and a proper understanding of these terms is critical to the correct application of the *Miranda* rule.

Defining "Custody" for *Miranda* Purposes

Custody is perhaps the most difficult concept to emerge from *Miranda*. But despite the sometimes confusing approaches to *Miranda* custody, certain valid conclusions can be drawn.

First, a formal arrest clearly meets the *Miranda* definition of custody. Any interrogation begun thereafter requires prior warnings and waiver [*United States v. Rubies*, 612 F. 2d 397, 404 (9th Cir., 1980), cert. denied 446 U.S. 940 (1980)].

Second, absent a formal arrest, courts may still make a finding of custody or significant deprivation of freedom. Several standards have been developed to determine if custody has been imposed. There is the subjective approach, depending on the state of mind of either the officer or the individual subjected to interrogation. The first subjective approach depends on the intention of the officer, to wit, the officer intended to take the individual into custody without regard whether said intention was communicated to the individual. This test is only applied by some courts [I La Fave & Israel, *Criminal Procedure*, Chap. 6, Section 6.6 (c), pp. 491–492 (1984); *United States v. Gibson*, 392 F. 2d 373 (4th Cir., 1968)].

The second subjective approach focuses upon the state of mind of the individual being subjected to interrogation, to wit, said individual believed he or she was in custody. This test too is only applied by some courts [I La Fave & Israel, *Criminal Procedure*, Chap. 6, Interrogation and Confessions, Section 6.6 (c), p. 491 (1984); *People v. Ceccone*, 260 Cal. App. 2d 886 (1968)].

There is also the focus approach, that is, where an investigation has centered on the individual being subjected to interrogation. This approach was expressly rejected by the Supreme Court in *Beckwith v. United States* [425 U.S. 341 (1976)].

Finally, there is the objective approach, to wit, whether a reasonable person would under the circumstances believe himself or herself to be in custody. This test is sometimes stated in somewhat different terms; for example, whether a reasonable man *innocent of any crime* would under the circumstances believe himself to be in custody [*People v. Centano*, 76 N.Y. 2d 58.37 (1990); *People v. Yukl*, 25 N.Y. 2d 585 (1969)].

Most courts have adopted the objective approach to determine whether or not there is custody [I La Fave & Israel, *Criminal Procedure*, Chap. 6, Section 6.6 (c), p. 492 (1984); *United States v. Hall*, 421 F. 2d 540, 544 (2nd Cir., 1969), cert. denied 397 U.S. 990 (1970)]. Under the objective approach, a conclusion as to whether a situation is custodial for *Miranda* purposes involves a consideration of the totality of circumstances in a particular case, which would lead to a determination of whether a reasonable man would believe himself to be in custody [*United States v. Beraun-Panez*, 812 F. 2d 578, 580 (9th Cir., 1987) mod. on other grounds 830 F. 2d 129 (9th Cir., 1987); *United States v. Hall*, 421 F. 2d 540, 545 (2nd Cir., 1969), cert. denied 397 U.S. 990 (1970)].

Factors relevant to an objective custody determination are as follows:

1. *Place of questioning* (such as a police station, jail or prison, place of employment, hospital or residence): The place of interrogation is not determinative, but is highly significant. Interrogation at a police station may be noncusto-

dial [*Oregon v. Mathiason*, 429 U.S. 492 (1977)], while an interrogation at a residence may be custodial [*Orozco v. Texas*, 394 U.S. 324 (1969)]. However, interrogation at a police station is more likely to be deemed custodial [see *State v. Saunders*, 102 Ariz. 565 (1969)] than an interrogation at a residence [*United States v. AGY*, 394 F. 2d 94 (6th Cir., 1967)].

2. *Persons present:* Again, although not determinative, a number of police officers present during an interrogation tends to show a custodial situation [*Moore v. Ballone*, 658 F. 2d 218, 226 (4th Cir., 1981)], whereas presence of a relative at an interrogation tends to show a noncustodial situation [*Archer v. United States*, 393 F. 2d 124 (5th Cir., 1968), spouse present].

3. *Person initiating encounter with the officer or voluntarily coming to officer.* Suppose a person initiates an encounter with an officer which results in questioning. This circumstance supports a conclusion that the encounter is noncustodial [*Yount v. Patton*, 710 F. 2d 956, 961–962 (3rd Cir., 1983), rev. on other grounds 467 U.S. 1025 (1984); *People v. Centano*, 76 N.Y. 2d 837 (1990)]. Furthermore, a person voluntarily accompanying an officer to an interrogation site [*California v. Beheler*, 463 U.S. 1121, 1122 (1983); *People v. Mertens*, 97 AD 2d 595 (N.Y. App. Div., 3rd Dept., 1983)] or voluntarily appearing there at an officer's request [*Oregon v. Mathiason*, 429 U.S. 492, 493, 495 (1977)] suggests circumstances indicative of noncustody.

4. *Restraint or lack of restraint:* Drawing a gun on a person to be interrogated [*People v. Shivers*, 21 N.Y. 2d 118, 122 (1967)], handcuffing said person [*United States v. Averell*, 296 F. Supp. 1064 (S.D. N.Y., 1969)], frisking that person [*United States v. Thomas*, 396 F. 2d 310 (2nd Cir., 1968)], and putting hands on the person and leading the person to police car [*State v. Saunders*, 102 Ariz. 565 (1967)] are all strong indications of custody. On the other hand, advising a person to be interrogated that said person is not under arrest [*United States v. SEMKIW*, 712 F. 2d 897, 892–893 (3rd Cir., 1983)] and not restricting the person from leaving the interrogation site are indicative of noncustody [*United States v. Burke*, 700 F. 2d 70 (2nd Cir., 1983), cert. denied 464 U.S. 816 (1983)].

5. *Isolation or holding incommunicado:* Isolating a person subject to questioning in an area remote from his/her home or holding that person incommunicado all tend to show a custodial setting [*United States v. Wauneka*, 770 F. 2d 1434 (9th Cir., 1983); *Moore v. Ballone*, 568 F. 2d 218, 227 (4th Cir., 1981)].

6. *Length of questioning:* An interrogation lasting five hours is an indication of custody [*Moore v. Ballone*, 658 F. 2d 218, 225 (4th Cir., 1981)]. However, a brief questioning of no more than three to four minutes tends to show a noncustodial situation [*People v. Rodney P.*, 21 N.Y. 2d 1, 2 (1967)].

7. *The time of day or night when questioning occurs:* An interrogation occurring during late night or early morning hours is indicative of custody [*Orozco v. Texas*, 394 U.S. 324 (1969); cf. *People v. Yukl*, 25 N.Y. 2d 585 (1969), questioning of person in early morning hours right after a crime is reported is noncustodial].

8. *Form and intensity of questioning:* Intense and persistent interrogation of a person by an officer with suggestions in the questioning that the officer had evidence of the person's guilt and that the person in response to questioning was lying are all indications of a custodial interrogation [*United States v. BEKOWIES*, 432 F. 2d 8, 13 (9th Cir., 1970); *People v. Boyer*, 48 Cal. 3d 247 (1989)].

Furthermore, relay questioning by a number of officers tends to show custody [*People v. Tanner*, 31 AD 2d 148, 150 (N.Y. App. Div., 1st Dept., 1968)].

9. *The person questioned is not arrested after interrogation:* The fact that a person is not arrested after an interrogation is a very strong indication that the encounter was noncustodial [*California v. Beheler*, 463 U.S. 1121 (1983); *Oregon v. Mathiason*, 429 U.S. 492 (1977)].

Places of Interrogation

Person's Residence. Ordinarily, an interrogation in a person's home will be found to be noncustodial [*Beckwith v. United States*, 425 U.S. 341 (1976); *United States v. AGY*, 394 F. 2d (6th Cir., 1967)]. However, there may be situations in which the interrogation is deemed custodial.

In *Orozco v. Texas* [394 U.S. 324 (1969)], four officers proceeded to a boarding house at 4:00 A.M., where the person to be questioned lived. The officers went to the person's bedroom, surrounded the bed in which he was sleeping, woke him, and proceeded to question him. They asked his name, whether he had been at a bar where a murder occurred earlier that night, whether he owned a gun, and where it was. The person's response led to a pistol, which was later determined to be the murder weapon. No *Miranda* warnings were given to the person. The compelling factors leading to a conclusion that the questioning was custodial were the time at which the interrogation occurred, the waking of the sleeping person, and the fact that four officers surrounded the bed.

Station House. An interrogation that takes place at a police station is likely to be deemed custodial [31 ALR 3rd 565 Annot. Custodial Interrogation—*Miranda* Rule, Section 15 (a) p. 629; *Miranda v. Arizona*, 384 U.S. 436 (1966); *United States v. Woods*, 720 F. 2d 1022, 1031 (9th Cir., 1983); *State v. Saunders*, 102 Ariz. 565 (1967), questioning occurred in police car]. However, that the questioning occurred at a police station is not conclusive on the question of custody [*Oregon v. Mathiason*, 429 U.S. 492 (1977)]. Significant factors in determining whether a station house interrogation is noncustodial, so that no *Miranda* warnings are required, are as follows:

1. Suspect comes to the station house voluntarily [*California v. Beheler*, 463 U.S. 1121 (1983); *Yount v. Patton*, 710 F. 2d 956, 961–962 (3rd Cir., 1983); *People v. Centano*, 76 N.Y. 2d 837 (1990)].

2. There is no restriction on suspect's freedom to depart [*Yount v. Patton*, 710 F. 2d 956, 962 (3rd Cir., 1983) rev. on other grounds 467 U.S. 1025 (1984); *United States v. Burke*, 700 F. 2d 70, 84 (2nd Cir., 1983), cert. denied 464 U.S. 816 (1983)].

3. Suspect is advised that he or she is not under arrest or in custody [*California v. Beheler*, 463 U.S. 1121, 1122 (1983); *United States v. SEMKIW*, 712 F. 2d 891, 892 (3rd Cir., 1983)].

4. Period of time suspect is at the station house is brief [*California v. Beheler*, 463 U.S. 1121, 1122 (1983), person at station house only 30 minutes tends to show noncustody; cf. *Moore v. Ballone*, 658 F. 2d 218, 227 (4th Cir., 1981), person at station house for five hours tends to show custody].

5. Suspect departs after being interviewed [*California v. Beheler*, 463 U.S. 1121, 1122 (1983)].

6. There is no physical contact between interrogator and suspect [*United States v. Jones*, 630 F. 2d 613, 616 (8th Cir., 1980); cf. *State v. Saunders*, 102 Ariz. 565 (1967), that officer places hand on person and leads that person to a police car are circumstances tending to show custody].

7. There is no deception about the purpose of the investigation [*United States v. Serlin*, 707 F. 2d 953, 956–957 (7th Cir., 1983); *United States v. Cohen*, 317 F. Supp. 1049, 1050–1051 (D. Neb., 1970), aff. 448 F. 2d 654 (8th Cir., 1971), cert. denied 405 U.S. 926 (1972); cf. *Oregon v. Mathiason*, 429 U.S. 492 (1977), deception is not a factor to consider in whether an interrogation is custodial].

8. There is an offer to return suspect home after interview [cf. *United States v. Wauneka*, 770 F. 2d 1434, 1439 (9th Cir., 1985), a person had no means of transportation from station house and was not offered an opportunity to leave were factors in finding custody].

9. There is no frisk, search, or handcuffing of suspect [*United States v. Thomas*, 396 F. 2d 310 (2nd Cir., 1968), a frisk tends to show custody; *United States v. Averell*, 296 F. Supp. 1064 (S.D. N.Y., 1969), handcuffing tends to show custody].

10. Suspect is not transported in law enforcement vehicle [*McDowell v. Solem*, 447 N.W. 2d 646 (S.D., 1989)].

11. Suspect is not kept in constant company of law enforcement officers [*United States v. Longbehn*, 850 F. 2d 450, 452 (8th Cir., 1988), continuously being chaperoned by five officers is an indication of custody; *South Dakota v. Long*, 465 F. 2d 65, 69–70 (8th Cir., 1972), continuously being with two or three officers is an indication of custody].

12. Investigators engage in an uninterrupted interrogation in an isolated place [cf. *United States v. Beraun-Panez*, 812 F. 2d 578, 580 (9th Cir., 1987), mod. on other grounds 830 F. 2d 127 (9th Cir., 1987), questioning in remote rural area; *Moore v. Ballone*, 658 F. 2d 218, 225, 227 (4th Cir., 1981), continuous questioning for one hour in a station house some ten miles from person's home, and person had no ready means to return home shows custody].

Of the foregoing, no single factor will determine custody for *Miranda* purposes. Rather, the court will look at the totality of the circumstances under which the interrogation takes place to determine if custody was in effect from the point of view of whether reasonable, innocent persons would think they were in custody under the circumstances.

Jail or Prison. A person interrogated in jail is "in custody" for purposes of *Miranda*, and warnings must be given.

Persons who are incarcerated when interrogated for evidence of their own guilt are in custody for *Miranda* purposes. This is irrespective of the nature of the crimes for which they are being held. This applies even if the agency doing the interrogation is not the law enforcement agency that incarcerated the person [*Mathis v. United States*, 391 U.S. 1503 (1968)].

However, if an undercover law enforcement agent, posing as an inmate, elicits a confession or admission from a fellow inmate in a jail or prison, no Miranda warnings are required [*Illinois v. Perkins*, 110 S. Ct. 2394 (1990)].

Place of Business or Employment. The vast majority of cases hold that, without extraordinary circumstances, interrogations at a place of business or employment are noncustodial.[2] One's place of business or employment is not enveloped by the same compulsive air of, say, a jail, prison or station house.

Nevertheless, a place of business or employment can be converted to a custodial setting (that is, inherently coercive) by the officer's manner of approach, the number of officers present, what is said, how long the questioning lasts, whether the person is free to leave, and so on [*United States v. Beraun-Panez*, 812 F. 2d 578 (9th Cir., 1987) mod. on other grounds 830 F. 2d 127 (9th Cir., 1987); *United States v. Mahar*, 801 F. 2d 1477 (6th Cir., 1986); *United States v. Robinson*, 650 F. 2d 84 (5th Cir., 1981); *United States v. Nash*, 563 F. 2d 166 (5th Cir., 1977); *United States v. Castellano*, 488 F. 2d 65 (5th Cir., 1974)].

Hospital. Ordinarily questioning that takes place while a person is confined in a hospital bed will not be deemed to be custodial for *Miranda* purposes [*Johnson v. State*, 252 Ark. 1113 (1972); *People v. Romano*, 139 Ill. App. 3rd 999 (1985); *People v. Phinney*, 22 N.Y. 2d 288 (1968); *People v. David*, 143 AD 2d 1031 (N.Y. App. Div., 2nd Dept., 1988)]. However, a custodial situation for *Miranda* purposes was presented in which a person was in a hospital bed, physically incapable of moving, and officers resorted to relay questioning by different officers for about one hour until one officer gained the person's confidence and a confession [*People v. Tanner*, 31 AD 2d 148 (N.Y. App. Div., 1st Dept., 1968); see also *Robinson v. State*, 45 Ala. App. 675 (1969); *Commonwealth v. D'Nicuola*, 448 Pa. 54 (1972)].

Telephone Questioning or Questioning Through a Locked Door. A telephone interrogation [*Jervis v. Hall*, 622 F. 2d 19, 23 (1st Cir., 1980); *United States v. Fiorillo*, 376 F. 2d 180 (2nd Cir., 1967)] or questioning conducted by an officer when a person is behind a locked door in his/her home [*People v. Merchant*, 260 Cal. App. 2d 875 (1968)] is not custodial for *Miranda* purposes, since there is no possibility of immediate physical restraint with its attendant compulsion.

Street Detention Questioning and on-the-Scene Questioning. In *Pennsylvania v. Bruder* [488 U.S. 9 (1989)], it was held that *Miranda* warnings need not be given during a traffic stop which, indeed, was a seizure, since said stops are typically brief and commonly occur in the public view.

By an analogy of reasoning, if a stop-and-frisk detention is brief and occurs in public view without a display of a weapon, then *Miranda* warnings need not be given [*People v. Morales*, 65 N.Y. 2d 997 (1985)].

Furthermore, if an officer in a stop-and-frisk detention, regardless of the circumstances of the detention, such as displaying a weapon, is confronted by a situation presenting a danger to public safety (to wit, a gun being located in a place readily accessible to any number of people) may, without giving *Miranda* warnings, inquire as follows: "Where is the gun?" [See *New York v. Quarles*, 467 U.S. 649 (1984).] General on-the-scene questioning about the facts surrounding a crime or other general questioning of citizens in the fact-finding process does not constitute custody for *Miranda* purposes [*Miranda v. Arizona*, 384 U.S. 436 (1966)].

If an officer comes upon a volatile situation that might involve criminality, asking one or more questions to clarify the situation without giving *Miranda* warnings is permissible. Examples of such questions are, "What's going on here?" [*People v. Green*, 42 N.Y. 2d, 170 (1977)] or "What are you doing here? [*People v. Huffman*, 41 N.Y. 2d 29 (1976)].

For a full discussion of the need for *Miranda* warnings in such situations, see Chap. 7, "Stop and Frisk."

PERSONS CONDUCTING AN INTERROGATION

Questioning by Security Guards or Private Police

The Fifth Amendment privilege against self-incrimination does not require the giving of constitutional warnings by private citizens or private security personnel who take a suspect into custody.

In the *Miranda* decision, the Court said that by custodial interrogation it meant questioning initiated by law enforcement officers. This decision discusses the relationship of the Fifth Amendment privilege to police interrogation. It is during this custodial interrogation that the privilege against self-incrimination is jeopardized. The cases hold that private persons, after making an arrest, have no duty to warn suspects of their *Miranda* rights prior to obtaining any statement from them [*United States v. Antonelli*, 434 F. 2d 335 (2nd Cir., 1970)].

The decisions equate private security guard or private police with private person; therefore, despite the custody and interrogation, *Miranda* warnings are not required, because the private guard is not a law enforcement officer [*People v. Ray*, 65 N.Y. 2d 282 (1985)].

However, if private security guards or private police officers are acting as agents of law enforcement in conducting an interrogation of a person, then *Miranda* would apply [*People v. Jones*, 47 N.Y. 2d 528 (1979)].

Moreover, there is authority to the effect that, if private security guards or private police are regularly engaged in the function of law enforcement, they can be deemed to be performing a public function and would then be controlled by *Miranda*.[3]

Parole and Probation Officers

A parole or probation officer, who interrogates a charge in the course of performing his/her duties as parole or probation officer, is not acting as a law enforcement officer within the spirit or meaning of *Miranda*. As a consequence, the officer need not give the charge *Miranda* warnings prior to questioning.

If the parolee or probationer makes an admission or confession concerning criminal behavior or parole or probation violation during such questioning, such admission or confession would be admissible in a proceeding to revoke the parolee's or probationer's parole or probation [*People v. Rodney W.*, 24 N.Y. 2d 732 (1969)].

A problem, however, is presented if an admission or a confession made during such questioning is sought to be introduced into evidence at a criminal proceeding outside of the parole or probation systems.

In *Minnesota v. Murphy* [465 U.S. 420 (1984)], it was held that a probationer's confession to his probation officer, made during a probation interview in which he was not given *Miranda* warnings, indicating that he had committed a certain rape and murder, was admissible in the probationer's subsequent criminal trial for such crimes.

Nevertheless, some jurisdictions (New York, for example) reject *Murphy* and hold that an admission or confession made by a parolee or probationer during an interrogation conducted by a parole or probation officer may not be used in a criminal proceeding outside of the parole or probation systems, unless there has been compliance with *Miranda* [*People v. English*, 73 N.Y. 2d 20 (1989); *People v. Parker*, 57 N.Y. 2d 815 (1982) affirming 82 AD 2d 661 (N.Y. 2nd Dept., 1982); *People v. Quickenton*, 129 Misc. 2d 607 (N.Y. County Court, Albany County, 1985)].

In view of the split in authority, the law in the jurisdiction involved should be checked to ascertain which approach is followed.

Interrogation by a Law Enforcement Officer

Miranda described "interrogation" as questioning initiated by law enforcement officers for the purpose of obtaining a confession or incriminating evidence.

This section will discuss the problems investigators have in this area of interrogation as to whether *Miranda* applies. It will be discussed from the point of view of whether interrogation exists and, if so, if it was by a law enforcement officer.

VOLUNTEERED OR SPONTANEOUS STATEMENTS

Volunteered or spontaneous statements of any kind are not barred by the Fifth Amendment, and their admissibility is not affected by the *Miranda* decision [*Arizona v. Mauro*, 481 U.S. 520, 529 (1987)]. A simple illustration is the person who enters or telephones a station house and reports having committed a crime [*Miranda v. Arizona*, 384 U.S. 436, 478 (1966)].

There is no bar to an officer listening to a volunteered or spontaneous incriminating statement, nor does the officer have to take affirmative steps to stop a person from making such a statement [*People v. Krom*, 61 N.Y. 2d 187 (1984); *People v. Rivers*, 56 N.Y. 2d 476, 479 (1982)] interrupt the person and inform the person of his/her rights [*United States v. Godfrey*, 409 F. 2d 1338 (10th Cir., 1969)].

Examples of volunteered or spontaneous statements are:

1. A prearrest spontaneous statement in apartment in response to being informed by police of rape charges [*Bosley v. United States*, 426 F. 2d 1257 (D.C. Cir., 1970)].

2. Postarrest spontaneous statement in police vehicle en route to station, no prodding or encouragement [*United States v. Godfrey*, 407 F. 2d 1338 (10th Cir., 1969); *Cannestraci v. Smith*, 470 F. Supp. 586, 590–591 (S.D. N.Y., 1979); *People v. Kaye*, 25 N.Y. 2d 139 (1969)].

3. Postindictment unsolicited remark by defendant to FBI agents [*State v. Mitchell*, 491 S.W. 2d 292 (MO. 1973); see also *Kuhlman v. Wilson*, 477 U.S. 436, 459 (1986); *United States v. Moore*, 917 F. 2d 215, 223–224 (6th Cir., 1990), cert. denied 111 S. Ct. 1590 (1991)].

4. Postarrest inculpatory statement made to a fellow prisoner, overheard by an officer [*People v. Stewart*, 160 AD 2d 966 (N.Y. App. Div., 2nd Dept., 1990); see also *United States v. Harris*, 460 F. 2d 1041 (5th Cir., 1972), cert. denied 409 U.S. 877 (1972)].

What Is Interrogation?

Miranda warnings are not required in a volunteered or spontaneous statement situation because the proscribed conduct, that is, compulsive interrogation, is not present. Accordingly, when a person makes an admission or a confession that is volunteered or spontaneous and not the result of a systematic questioning, there is no interrogation and hence no *Miranda* problem.

It is critical, then, to ascertain the meaning of interrogation under *Miranda*. In *Rhode Island v. Innis* [446 U.S. 291 (1980)], interrogation for *Miranda* purposes was defined. In *Innis*, the defendant was arrested without a warrant for murder by a police officer, who advised him of his *Miranda* rights. Shortly thereafter another officer arrived at the scene and likewise advised the defendant of his rights. No waiver was obtained by either officer, nor was the defendant interrogated. A police captain then appeared and warned the defendant a third time of his rights. The defendant stated that he wanted an attorney, at which point the captain arranged to have him placed in a police wagon for transportation to police headquarters. Three officers assigned to the vehicle were ordered not to question or coerce the defendant in any way.

En route to the station, two of the officers became engaged in a conversation which suggested that the murder weapon, a shotgun, was still missing. Moreover, the gun was said to be in an area near a school for handicapped children, with the attendant possibility that children might find it and cause injury to themselves The defendant, who clearly was able to hear the conversation, asked the police to return to the scene of the arrest so he could lead them to the hidden shotgun. At no time were direct questions asked of the defendant. The group arrived at the place of arrest, where the police captain again advised the defendant of his *Miranda* rights. He was asked if he understood his rights. He acknowledged that he did and stated he wanted to lead the police to the weapon, which he did. The weapon was later used against him at his trial on the murder charge. The defendant was convicted.

The question in *Innis* was whether the conduct of the officers (which resulted in the defendant leading them to the weapon) was, in fact, interrogation. The Court proceeded to define interrogation as "either express questioning or its functional equivalent" [*Innis*, at pp. 300–301].

The functional equivalent, the Court went on to explain, was "before the words or actions on the part of the police that they should know are reasonably likely to elicit an incriminating response from the suspect" [*Innis*, at p. 301]. The functional equivalent aspect of the definition of interrogation, according to the Court, focuses primarily on the perceptions of the suspect, rather than on the intent of the police [*Innis*, at p. 301].

Applying this definition in *Innis*, the Court concluded that there was no interrogation within the meaning of *Miranda*. There was neither express questioning of the suspect nor its functional equivalent. As to express questioning, the Court noted that the actions of the officers amounted to nothing more than a dialogue to which no response was invited. Moreover, since it could not be said that the officers should have known their conversation was reasonably likely to elicit an incriminating response, the functional equivalent of interrogation was not present.

In arriving at this conclusion, the Court, emphasizing the perceptions of the suspect, pointed out that the record did not suggest that the defendant was particularly susceptible to an appeal to his conscience, nor was he unusually disoriented or upset at the time of his arrest. Finally, the Court observed that the conversation of the officers consisted of a few off-hand remarks rather than a lengthy harangue and the officers' comments were not particularly evocative.

Thereafter, in *Arizona v. Mauro* [481 U.S. 520 (1987)], the *Innis* approach was reaffirmed. In *Mauro* the defendant was arrested without a warrant for killing his son. The defendant was taken to a police station and advised of his *Miranda* rights, whereupon the defendant told the police that he did not wish to make any statements without having a lawyer present, and police questioning ceased. Thereafter the defendant's wife, who was at the police station, asked if she could speak to the defendant. The officer, of whom the request was made, was reluctant to allow the meeting. Finally, the meeting was permitted; however, the officer told both the defendant and his wife that they could speak together only if he were present in the room to observe and hear what was going on. The officer brought the wife to a room where the defendant was, sat at a desk in the room, and placed a tape recorder in plain sight on the desk. The defendant and his wife engaged in a conversation which the officer recorded.

The defendant was then tried for murder in the killing of his son. At the trial, the tape-recorded conversation was put into evidence. The question in *Mauro* was whether the police conduct leading up to and resulting in the tape recording was the functional equivalent of questioning.

The Court, focusing on the defendant's perspective of the situation, concluded that the police conduct was not the functional equivalent of questioning, since it was improbable that the defendant, being told that his wife would be allowed to speak to him, would feel that he was being coerced to incriminate himself in any way. The court also pointed out that, although the police indicated they were aware the defendant would possibly incriminate himself while talking to his wife, police do not interrogate a person simply by hoping he will confess.

In its decision in *Mauro*, the Court set forth examples of what would be the functional equivalent of questioning. The Court indicated that, in an interrogation environment, police conduct that would be deemed the functional equivalent of questioning would include the use by police of a line-up, in which a coached witness would pick a suspect as the perpetrator of the crime involved, or a coached witness would pick a suspect as the perpetrator of a fictitious crime, or an officer employs a psychological ploy, such as minimizing the moral seriousness of the crime with which a suspect is charged and casting blame for the crime on the victim or society [*Mauro* at p. 526].

It should be emphasized that a determination of the functional equivalent of questioning is, at least, problematic. The analysis leading to such a determination is extremely fact sensitive. Consequently, in roughly analogous situations different results may follow because of particular facts present in one situation and not in the other. An example is *People v. Grimaldi* [52 N.Y. 2d 611 (1981)]. In that case the defendant, while in a jail cell, was provided with a telephone to call his father. The officer providing the telephone to the defendant stood about 15 feet from the cell outside of the defendant's view. Furthermore, the officer never informed the defendant that he would be within a short distance of the cell during the telephone call. The incriminating statements the defendant made to his father during the telephone conversation were deemed the product of the functional equivalent of questioning and suppressed. This case, although roughly analogous to *Mauro*, reached a different conclusion based on the fact that the defendant was not aware of the officer's presence during the telephone conversation with his father.

Further examples of apparently conflicting results are as follows:

1. A discussion by officers in a defendant's presence about the likelihood that the investigation would involve his family was held, in *United States v. Thilman* [678 F. 2d 1331 (9th Cir., 1982)], not to be the functional equivalent of questioning, whereas it was held, in *People v. Carmine A.* [53 N.Y. 2d 816 (1981)], to be the functional equivalent of questioning.

2. Confronting the defendant with evidence against him was held in *People v. Ferro* [63 N.Y. 316 (1984)] to be the functional equivalent of questioning, but

in *Ray v. Duckworth* [881 F. 2d 512, 518 (7th Cir., 1989)] and in *United States v. Boston* [508 F. 2d 1171 (2nd Cir., 1974)], it was not held to be the functional equivalent of interrogation.

Another interesting contrast in cases involves *People v. Lynes* [49 N.Y. 2d 286 (1980)] and *People v. Lanahan* [55 N.Y. 2d 711 (1981)]. In *Lynes* the defendant was arraigned on a certain criminal charge. During the arraignment the judge informed the defendant that a warrant of arrest had been issued for him on an unrelated charge. While the defendant was leaving the courtroom in the custody of a police officer, the defendant inquired of the officer, "What is this warrant about?" The officer, who had not administered *Miranda* warnings, responded, "You should know they are looking for you." The officer had no knowledge of or connection with the charge for which the warrant had been issued. The defendant then made incriminating admissions.

The Court in *Lynes* held that the officer's conduct was not the functional equivalent of questioning.

In *Lanahan* the defendant was arrested for a robbery. At the time of this arrest, the defendant asked what robbery it was that he was being charged with. The officer arresting him indicated that an explanation concerning the robbery would be given to him at the police station. At the police station, the defendant was given a very detailed description of the robbery, whereupon the defendant responded, "I did it."

The Court in *Lanahan* held that, since the officer's response was removed in space and time from the defendant's question, and the response went beyond a mere identification of the robbery to the giving of a detailed description of the criminal transaction, including complete particularity both as to the participants and the manner of its achievement, the response was the functional equivalent of questioning, and the defendant's incriminating statement elicited thereby was suppressed.

As can be seen, what is the functional equivalent of interrogation requires a case-by-case analysis. Thus, an officer should take great care in such situations to ensure that conduct does not fall within the definition of the functional equivalent of questioning.

ADEQUACY OF WARNINGS

Adequate warnings and a valid waiver of rights are the means whereby Fifth Amendment protections are accorded an accused in custody who is about to be interrogated. Having considered the conditions that prompt the need for warnings (custody and interrogation), it is necessary next to discuss what constitutes "adequate warnings." Because the *Miranda* decision is so explicit, relatively few legal problems have been generated by the warnings requirement. Miranda points out that, prior to any custodial interrogation, accused persons must be warned that (1) they have the right to remain silent, (2) anything they say can and will be used against them in a court of law, (3) they have the right to the presence of an attorney, and (4) if they cannot afford an attorney, one will be appointed prior to any questioning if they desire.

TIME TO GIVE WARNINGS

There is no need to give *Miranda* warnings when a person is arrested or otherwise taken into custody [*Washington Mobilization Committee v. Cullinane*, 566 F.

2d 107, 123 (D.C. Cir., 1977)]; however, to be effective, *Miranda* warnings must be given immediately preceding custodial interrogation [*People v. Chapple*, 38 N.Y. 2d 112, 115 (1975)].

When *Miranda* warnings are given only after a period of continuous custodial interrogation, the warnings have no force or effect [*Miranda v. Arizona* (*Westover v. United States*), 384 U.S. 436, 496–497 (1966)]. But if there is a definite, pronounced break in the custodial interrogation so that the subject of the questioning may be said to have returned, in effect, to the station, and the subject was not under the influence of custodial questioning, then the giving of *Miranda* warnings thereafter and before the resumption of questioning will be deemed effective [*Oregon v. Elstad*, 470 U.S. 298 (1985); *People v. Chapple*, 38 N.Y. 2d 112, 115 (1975)]. Furthermore, if there has been extensive noncustodial interrogation, the giving of *Miranda* warnings just prior to commencing custodial interrogation will be deemed effective [*People v. Yukl*, 25 N.Y. 2d 585 (1969)].

Warnings After a Break Between Interrogation Sessions

Ordinarily, where *Miranda* warnings are given in a timely fashion and a waiver is obtained, an officer who is interrogating a person may cease the questioning and take a break and need not administer *Miranda* warnings again before a resumption of the interrogation. This is so if the break lasts no more than several hours [*Ballard v. Johnson*, 821 F. 2d 568 (11th Cir., 1987); *United States v. Osterburg*, 423 F. 2d 704 (9th Cir., 1970)]; however, if the break is weeks, then new *Miranda* warnings are required [I La Fave & Israel, *Criminal Procedure*, Chap. 6, "Interrogation and Confessions," Section 6.8 (b), p. 520 (1984)].

Unnecessary Repetition of *Miranda* Warnings

The unnecessary repetition of *Miranda* warnings may be deemed a type of subtle coercion condemned by *Miranda* [*United States v. Hernandez*, 574 F. 2d 1362, 1368 (5th Cir., 1978)].

SUBSTANCE OF WARNINGS AND PARAPHRASING

Miranda warnings are not some mystical formula that must be recited from the words in the *Miranda* decision [*California v. Prysock*, 453 U.S. 355 (1981)]. An officer may give the warnings in a clear understandable way, in words that a person subjected to interrogation may comprehend. All that is required is that the *Miranda* rights be fully conveyed [*California v. Prysock*, 453 U.S. 355 (1981)].

Rather than indicating that a person "has a right to remain silent," an officer may indicate that the person "need not make any statement" [*United States v. Lamia*, 429 F. 2d 373 (2nd Cir., 1970)]. Moreover, an officer may indicate, any statement made "can" [*United States v. Kershner*, 432 F. 2d 1066 (5th Cir., 1970)] or "might" [*United States v. Johnson*, 426 F. 2d 1112 (7th Cir., 1970)] be used against the person rather than an incantation that "any statement can and will be used against" the person.

Also informing a person of the "right to have a lawyer present prior to and during interrogation" and also of the "right to have a lawyer appointed at no cost if...[the person] could not afford one" were sufficient to convey the "right to have a lawyer appointed if...[the person] could not afford one prior to and during interrogation" [*California v. Prysock*, 453 U.S. 355 (1981)].

Finally, advising a person (1) of the "right to talk to a lawyer for advice before we ask you any questions, and to have him with you during questioning," and (2) that "we [the officers] have no way of giving you a lawyer, but one will be appointed for you, if you wish, if and when you go to court" was sufficient to convey the "right to have a lawyer appointed if...[the person] could not afford one prior to and during interrogation" [*Duckworth v. Eagan*, 492 U.A. 195 (1989)].

It should be emphasized, however, that an officer should avoid paraphrasing the *Miranda* warnings, since modifying the language of the warnings may result in losing the meaning of the protections in translation. For example, an officer indicating that any statement made may be used "for or against you" is not sufficient conveyance of the meaning of the *Miranda* protection afforded by the warning "that any statement can and will be used against you" [*Commonwealth v. Singleton*, 439 Pa. 185 (1970)]. Another example would be advising a person "he could consult an attorney prior to any questions." This, too, would not be deemed to be the equivalent of the advice that the person had the "right to have an attorney present during the interrogation" [*United States v. Fox*, 403 F. 2d 97, 100 (2nd Cir., 1968)].

ADVISEMENT OF CHARGES THAT WILL BE THE SUBJECT OF THE INTERROGATION

A person who is in custody and is to be interrogated need not be informed of the crimes that will be the subject matter of the interrogation. In *Colorado v. Spring* [479 U.S. 564 (1987)], the defendant was arrested for interstate transportation of stolen firearms. The defendant was given *Miranda* warnings and waived his rights. During the interrogation he was asked questions concerning the firearms crime; however, the defendant was then queried about a murder, and he made an incriminating statement. It was held, in *Spring*, that the officers interrogating the defendant were not required to advise him he would be questioned concerning the murder, and thereupon the Court refused to suppress his incriminating statement made with regard thereto.

ADVISEMENT OF FULL LEGAL CONSEQUENCES OF STATEMENTS

A person subject to custodial interrogation need *not* to be informed of the full legal consequences of any statement made [*Oregon v. Elstad*, 470 U.S. 298, 316 (1985)]. For example, a person subjected to custodial interrogation makes a statement he believes to be exculpatory but, because of the doctrine of accomplice liability, the statement is in fact inculpatory. The failure of the interrogating officer to explain the accomplice liability doctrine does not require that the statement be suppressed [*Commonwealth v. Cunningham*, 405 Mass. 646 (1989)].

EXPLANATION OF *MIRANDA* WARNINGS

An officer initially administering *Miranda* warnings is not required to elaborate on or otherwise explain the significance of the warnings [*United States v. ISOM*, 588 F. 2d 858, 862 (2nd Cir., 1978)]; however, questions by the person being subjected to interrogation may require an officer to provide some explanation of the warnings [*California v. Prysock*, 453 U.S. 355, 357 (1981)].

Caution should be exercised by the officer in providing the explanation so as to avoid creating a confusing and misleading situation as to the *Miranda* rights involved [*United States v. Garcia*, 431 F. 2d 134 (9th Cir., 1970)]. For example, in *United States v. Anderson* [752 F. Supp. 565 (E.D. N.Y., 1990)], a person being subjected to interrogation was properly warned of the right to the presence of an attorney during questioning; however, the officer conducting the interrogation further warned that it was in the best interest of the person to cooperate and that if the person requested an attorney he would forfeit the opportunity to reap the benefits of such cooperation.

The Court in *Anderson* held that the additional warnings undermined the original *Miranda* warning concerning the presence of the attorney during questioning and rendered it inadequate.

If an officer is dealing with a person unlettered or unlearned in language, the officer may decide to explain the *Miranda* warnings initially so as to give meaningful advice [*Coyote v. United States*, 380 F. 2nd 305 (10th Cir., 1967), cert. denied 389 U.S. 992 (1967)]. This is permissible [*Klinger v. United States*, 409 F. 2d 299 (8th Cir., 1969)]. Nevertheless, such explanation as heretofore indicated should not be so confusing or misleading as to undermine the effectiveness of the *Miranda* warnings.

Omissions

The failure of an officer to give the full, four-point *Miranda* warnings will fatally taint an admission or confession obtained during custodial interrogation [*United States v. Bland*, 908 F. 2d 471 (9th Cir., 1990); *People v. Hutchinson*, 59 N.Y. 2d 923 (1983)]. Furthermore, no amount of circumstantial evidence that a person being subjected to custodial interrogation may have been aware of his/her *Miranda* rights, will suffice to stand in the stead of the actual and explicit giving of *Miranda* warnings [*Miranda v. Arizona*, 384 U.S. 436, 471–472 (1966)]. Nor does the fact that a person being subjected to custodial interrogation is a police officer [*United States v. Longbehn*, 850 F. 2d 450, 453 (8th Cir., 1988)] or, for that matter, a lawyer [I La Fave & Israel, *Criminal Procedure*, Chap. 6, "Interrogation and Confessions," Section 6.8 (a), p. 518 (1984)] permit dispensing with the explicit giving of *Miranda* warnings.

In *Miranda* the following footnote appears:

> While a warning that the indigent may have counsel appointed need not be given to the person who is known to have an attorney or is known to have ample funds to secure one, the expedient of giving a warning is too simple and the rights involved too important to engage in ex post facto inquiries into financial ability when there is any doubt at all on that score. [*Miranda v. Arizona*, 384 U.S. 436, 473, footnote 43 (1966)]

This footnote has led some courts to hold that, if it is not shown that the person subjected to custodial interrogation was indigent at the time of the same, the failure to give the warning will not be fatal to any ensuing admission or confession [*People v. Post*, 23 N.Y. 2d 157 (1968)]. The prevailing view, however, is that a failure to inform a person of the right to an appointed counsel is fatal, regardless of the question of said person's indigency [*United States v. Espinosa-Orlando*, 704 F. 2d 507, 514 (11th Cir., 1983)].

It is recommended that, prior to custodial interrogation, officers give the warning concerning the right to appointed counsel, since, as indicated in *Miranda*, it is simple to give the warning, and the right involved is too important to engage in after-the-fact inquiries as to whether the person had an attorney or could otherwise afford to retain one.

Oftentimes, in administering *Miranda* warnings an officer will advise a person of the right to stop the questioning at any time. This last warning, however, is not one of the enumerated *Miranda* warnings and a failure to advise a person in this regard is not fatal to any subsequent admission or confession [*Gandia v. Hoke*, 648 F. Supp. 1425, 1432 (E.D. N.Y., 1986) affd. 819 F. 2d 1129 (2nd Cir., 1987), cert. denied 484 U.S. 843 (1987); *United States v. Alba*, 732 F. Supp. 306, 309–310 (D. Conn., 1990)].

Failure to Inform a Person Being Subjected to Custodial Interrogation of Efforts of an Attorney to Reach Said Person

An officer is not required as part of the enunciating *Miranda* rights to a person being subjected to custodial interrogation to inform that person of an attorney's efforts to reach him/her [*Moran v. Burbine*, 475 U.S. 412, 425–426 (1986)].

Administering the Warnings

In administering *Miranda* warnings, an officer should not mechanically recite them [*People v. Jenkins*, 56 AD 2d 265, 272 (N.Y. App. Div., 1st Dept., 1982), appeal dismissed 516 N.Y. 2d 737 (1982)]. This is so because a mechanical recitation will not show that the officer administering the warnings is prepared to recognize a person's rights if that person chooses to exercise his or her rights [*Miranda v. Arizona*, 384 U.S. 436, 468 (1966)].

If a person being subjected to custodial interrogation does not understand English, *Miranda* warnings given in English will be ineffective [*United States v. Restrepo-Cruz*, 547 F. Supp. 1048, 1062 (S.D. N.Y., 1982)]. In such case, the warnings must be given in a language the person can understand [*United States v. Munoz*, 748 F. Supp. 167 (S.D. N.Y., 1990)]. This can be done by having an interpreter translate the warnings into a language the person understands [*People v. Jordan*, 110 AD 2d 855 (N.Y. App. Div., 2nd Dept., 1985); see also *United States v. ABOW-SADIA*, 785 F. 2d, 1, 10 (1st Cir., 1986), cert. denied 477 U.S. 908 (1986)], or an officer may do so if the officer is conversant in that language [*United States v. Munoz*, 748 F. Supp. 167 (S.D. N.Y.,. 1990)]. In addition, an officer may provide a written translation of the *Miranda* warnings, and this would be sufficient as long as it is shown that the person did read the warnings and acknowledged he or she understood them [*People v. Sirno*, 76 N.Y. 2d 967 (1990)].

Ordinarily, *Miranda* warnings will be administered orally. Nevertheless, a person being subject to custodial interrogation may be given a writing embodying the *Miranda* warnings [*United States v. Bailey*, 468 F. 2d 652, 660 (5th Cir., 1972)], and this will suffice as the giving of *Miranda* warnings if it is shown that the person could and did read the rights and acknowledged he or she understood them [*United States v. Sledge*, 546 F. 2d 1120, 1122 (4th Cir., 1977), cert. denied 430 U.S. 910 (1977)]. Of course, if a person cannot read, then such a method of administering *Miranda* warnings would be ineffective [*People v. Valle*, 121 Misc. 2d 621, 628–629 (N.Y. County Court, Nassau County, 1983)].

Proof of Warnings

If an admission or confession resulting from custodial interrogation is to be admitted at a criminal trial, the prosecutor must show by a preponderance of the evidence that *Miranda* warnings were administered prior to questioning [*People v. Jenkins*, 85 AD 2d 265, 276 (N.Y. App. Div., 1st Dept., 1982), appeal dismissed 56 N.Y. 2d 737 (1982); see also *Colorado v. Connelly*, 479 U.S. 157 (1987)].

An officer in a *Miranda* situation should be aware of this burden and gather evidence to meet the burden. Such evidence can include an electronic transcription of the giving of *Miranda* warnings [*California v. Prysock*, 453 U.S. 355 (1981)] or a written acknowledgement by a person being subjected to custodial interrogation of the advisement of the warnings [*Duckworth v. Eagan*, 492 U.S. 195 (1989)]; however, a record of the giving of *Miranda* warnings, such as a written acknowledgement is not required [*United States v. Turner*, 926 F. 2d 883, 888 (9th Cir., 1991)]. The fact of the giving of the warnings can be established by the testimony of an officer that the officer read the *Miranda* warnings from a so-called *Miranda* card [*United States v. ISOM*, 588 F. 2d 858, 862 (2nd Cir., 1978); see also *North Carolina v. Butler*, 441 U.S. 369, 370–371 (1979)] or recited them from memory [*United States v. Ricks*, 817 F. 2d 692, 697 (11th Cir., 1987)] to a person subjected to custodial interrogation.

The more prudent approach for an officer, of course, would be either to electronically record the giving of the *Miranda* warnings or to obtain a written acknowledgement of the advisement of the warnings. An example of a written acknowledgement is set forth in the appendix at the end of this chapter.

WAIVER OF *MIRANDA* RIGHTS

An officer who has properly administered full *Miranda* warnings has accomplished only half of what is necessary to assure the admissibility of statements taken thereafter. It is also essential that there be a knowing and voluntary waiver of *Miranda* rights. Before an admission or confession obtained as a result of custodial interrogation will be admissible at a criminal trial, it must be established by the prosecutor by a preponderance of the evidence that the person making the admission or confession waived his or her *Miranda* rights [*Colorado v. Connelly*, 479 U.S. 157 (1987)].

A waiver may be established by showing under a totality of circumstances approach that, indeed, *Miranda* rights were waived [*Moran v. Burbine*, 475 U.S. 412, 421 (1986); *Fare v. Michael C.*, 442 U.S. 707, 724–725 (1979)]. Whether there really was a waiver requires a two-pronged analysis, which was set forth in *Moran*. The first prong requires that the waiver be *knowing*, that is, there must be an awareness both of the nature of the rights being abandoned and the consequences of the decision to abandon them. The second requires that the waiver be *voluntary*, that is, the waiver is the product of a free and deliberate choice and not the product of intimidation, coercion, or deception.

Knowing Waiver

As hereto indicated, the knowing aspect of waiver requires an awareness both of the rights being abandoned and the consequence of the decision to abandon them.

Awareness of the rights being abandoned is ordinarily established by a showing that full *Miranda* warnings were given. Warnings which omit a substantial right, such as the right to have an attorney during questioning, however, fail to establish the awareness of the rights being abandoned for purposes of a knowing waiver [*United States v. Bland*, 908 F. 2d 471 (9th Cir., 1990)]. Also administering warnings in a language not understood by a person being subjected to custodial interrogation would fail to prove the aforementioned awareness of rights [*People v. Williams*, 62 N.Y. 2d 285, 289 (1984)].

By an analogy of reasoning, administering *Miranda* warnings to a person who is so intoxicated[4] or so mentally deficient [*Cooper v. Griffin*, 455 F. 2d 1142, 1144–1145 (5th Cir., 1972); *People v. Posey*, 74 Misc. 2d 149 (N.Y. County Court, Erie County, 1973)] as not to possess enough cognitive capacity to comprehend the language would also fail to establish the requisite awareness of rights. Nevertheless, it should be noted that intoxication or mental deficiency does not alone establish a lack of cognitive capacity to comprehend the language of *Miranda* warnings. An officer encountering such a situation should explore and note the circumstances involved.

With respect to intoxication and mental deficiency, some circumstances that would establish that a person has sufficient cognitive capacity to comprehend *Miranda* warnings include:

- *Intoxication*, the ability to walk regularly without staggering [*United States v. Mathews*, 431 F. Supp. 70 (W.D. Okla., 1976)], the ability to talk clearly and coherently [*United States v. Waxman*, 572 F. Supp. 1136 (E.D. Pa., 1983)], the ability to write [*Chunn v. State*, 339 So. 2d 1100 (Ala. App., 1976)], as well as the lack of drowsiness [*United States v. Ganter*, 436 F. 2d 364, 372 (7th Cir., 1970)] or disorientation [*United States v. Oaxaca*, 569 F. 2d 518, 522–523 (9th Cir., 1978)].

- *Mental deficiency*, steady employment [*State v. Conner*, 241 N.W. 2d 447 (Iowa, 1976)], supporting a wife and child [*State v. Fetters*, 202 N.W. 2d 84 (Iowa, 1972)], 8 or 10 years of schooling [*Hancock v. State*, 299 So. 2d 188 (Miss., 1974)], ability to read and write [*People v. Hoyer*, 140 AD 2d 853 (N.Y. App. Div., 3rd Dept., 1988)], had a driver's license and could operate a motor vehicle [*Fryer v. State*, 325 N.W. 2d 400 (Iowa, 1982)], honorable service in the armed forces [*People v. Lux*, 34 AD 2d 662 (N.Y. App. Div., 2nd Dept., 1970) affd. 29 N.Y. 2d 848 (1971)], and prior experience with law enforcement [*State v. Conner*, 241 NW 2d 447 (Iowa, 1976)] or familiarity with the criminal justice system [*People v. Collazo*, 98 Misc. 2d 58, 61, 62 (N.Y. Supreme Court, Bronx County, 1978)].

It should be noted that, if an officer is confronted with a person who obviously has some mental deficiencies, then the administering of *Miranda* warnings should not be restricted to reading the warning from a card; rather they should be given in more detail and in simpler language to ensure that the person understands the warnings [*People v. Williams*, 62 N.Y. 2d 285, 288, 289 (1984)]. This is one of the few times that the explanation or a paraphrasing of *Miranda* warnings is the recommended approach in administering them. A suggestion for such warnings is contained in the appendix.

The more problematic aspect of a knowing waiver concerns the awareness of the consequences of the decision to abandon the *Miranda* rights. Awareness of the consequences of the decision does not mean an awareness of the full legal consequences of the decision [*Connecticut v. Barrett*, 479 U.S. 523, 530 (1987)]. Rather what is intended is that a person has a mental capacity beyond surface knowledge or cognition of the meaning of the words of the warnings; the person must be able to appreciate the meaning of the words. For example, a person may understand that the right to remain silent may mean that he does not have to talk generally, but not appreciate the fact that he does not have to answer questions. Another example would be that a person may comprehend the words that she has the right to have an attorney present during questioning, but has no idea of the function of an attorney in protecting her [*People v. Posey*, 74 Misc. 2d 149 (N.Y. County Court, Erie County, 1973)]. Thus, the focus of determining awareness of the consequences of the decision to abandon *Miranda* rights is on whether or not a person appreciates the meaning of the *Miranda* warnings.

Harris v. Riddle [551 F. 2d 936 (4th Cir., 1977), cert. denied 434 U.S. 849 (1977)] presents an example of this distinction. In that case, a 17-year-old youth with a dull normal intelligence was suspected of being involved in an armed robbery which resulted in the shooting and killing of an individual. The youth was given his *Miranda* warnings, waived his rights, and thereafter orally confessed to his role in the robbery, but denied that he fired the fatal shot. The youth was thereafter indicted for felony murder. At a hearing to suppress the youth's oral confession, a psychiatrist was produced to testify on the youth's behalf. The psychiatrist testified in substance that the youth had the mental capacity to know and appreciate that he was giving up his right to remain silent and his right to have an attorney present during questioning, but that the youth was not aware of how his statement would be used against him or what charges it would support. The psychiatrist opined that the primary source of the youth's confusion with respect to the last mentioned matter was his ignorance of the felony murder doctrine. The psychiatrist, however, admitted that the youth's limited understanding of the consequences of talking—ignorance of the felony murder doctrine—would be shared by many people, even those with superior intelligence.

The Court in *Harris*, exploring the reasons for the youth's waiver of his *Miranda* rights, indicated in substance that the waiver may not have been based on a lack of mental capacity to knowing waive, but rather because he misunderstood the elements of felony murder and thought that proof that he personally fired the fatal shot was required to convict him of such crime, or simply because he believed an oral confession was inadmissible in court.

The Court in *Harris*, however, held that a waiver of *Miranda* rights is no less knowing because a person misconceives the inculpatory thrust of the fact admitted or because he erroneously thought an oral statement could not be used against him. The Court indicated that *Miranda* did not require that only a person familiar with the substance of criminal law and the rules of evidence could waive *Miranda* rights, since that would obligate an officer, as part of the *Miranda* advisements, to give an explanation of such law and rules which, it was noted, the average interrogating officer is not capable of. The Court in *Harris* held that the youth did know and appreciate his *Miranda* warnings and hence validly waived his rights.

Thus, awareness of the consequences of the decision to abandon *Miranda* rights means nothing more than an appreciation—that is, something more than mere surface knowledge of the meaning of the words—of the concepts of the right to remain silent, the right to have an attorney present during questioning [*Harris v. Riddle*, 551 F. 2d 936, 939 (4th Cir., 1977), cert. denied 434 U.S. 849 (1977)], and that anything said could be used as evidence [*Colorado v. Spring*, 479 U.S. 564, 574 (1987)]. It has also been held that awareness of the consequences of the decision to abandon *Miranda* rights is not diminished because a person is unaware of the accomplice liability doctrine and believes the statement he is giving is exculpatory [*Commonwealth v. Cunningham*, 405 Mass. 646 (1989)] or because the person mistakenly believed he had a valid case of self-defense [*Alfaro v. State*, 478 NE 2d 670 (Ind., 1985)]. The fact that a person's decision to waive *Miranda* rights may in retrospect appear to be unwise, foolish [*Harris v. Riddle*, 551 F. 2d 936, 939 (4th Cir., 1977), cert. denied 434 U.S. 849 (1977)], or illogical [*Colorado v. Barrett*, 479 U.S. 523, 530 (1987)] is not a factor in determining whether a waiver is knowing, since such a decision may have been based on a misapprehension of the law and/or facts, not on a lack of understanding of the *Miranda* concepts.

Ordinarily, awareness of the consequences of the decision to abandon *Miranda* rights is established by showing that the person involved is of average or above-average intelligence or has a high school or college education, is a mature, capable adult, or functions in society by operating a business or having served honorably in the armed forces or, finally, has had prior experience in the criminal justice system.[5]

The fact that a person being subjected to custodial interrogation is a juvenile [*Fare v. Michael C.*, 442 U.S. 707 (1979); *People v. Windell*, 64 N.Y. 2d 826 (1985)], mentally deficient [*People v. Williams*, 62 N.Y. 2d 285 (1984)], or mentally ill [*People v. Boutot*, 89 AD 2d 1027 (N.Y. App. Div., 3rd Dept., 1982)] would not bar a finding that a person was aware of the consequences of the decision to abandon *Miranda* rights.

However, there are cases that hold that such conditions may deprive a person of the requisite cognitive capacity to appreciate the consequences of the decision to waive *Miranda* rights.[6]

Care should be taken by an officer in situations where the person being subjected to custodial interrogation is mentally deficient or mentally ill. An officer encountering such a situation should explore and note the circumstances involved, such as steady employment of the person, the ability to read and write, years of education, the familiarity with the criminal justice systems, coherent speech, lack of disorientation.[7] All of these tend to show the requisite cognitive capacity to waive *Miranda* warnings. If the person being subjected to custodial interrogation is a juvenile, precaution must also be taken as already indicated.

Among the factors that will be considered in determining a juvenile's cognitive capacity concerning the consequences of waiving *Miranda* rights are age, experience, education, background, and intelligence [*Fare v. Michael C.*, 442 U.S. 707, 725 (1979)]. It would also be wise when dealing with a juvenile to administer simplified *Miranda* warnings [*Matter of Julian B.*, 125 AD 2d 666, 668, 670 (N.Y. App. Div., 2nd Dept., 1986)]. A suggested sample for the giving of such warnings in obtaining a waiver of rights is contained in the appendix.

It should be noted that in some jurisdictions (New York, for example) the custodial interrogation of a juvenile under the age of 16 years may occur only in certain designated facilities, and no waiver may be obtained, unless *Miranda* warnings are given not only to the juvenile, but also to one of the juvenile's parents or, if there is no parent involved, to the person legally responsible for the care of the juvenile. If this is the case, a warning is also required to be given to the juvenile [*N.Y. Family Court Act*, Section 305.2 (4b, 7)]. An example of such additional warning is contained in the appendix.

Officers should check the law in their jurisdiction to determine if special procedures must be followed in the custodial questioning of juveniles.

Voluntary Waiver

The waiver of *Miranda* rights, in addition to being knowing, must also be voluntary [*Miller v. Dugger*, 838 F. 2d 1530, 1537–1538 (11th Cir., 1988)]. The relinquishment of *Miranda* rights must be voluntary in the sense that the relinquishment is the product of free choice, rather than governmental intimidation, coercion, or deception [*Moran v. Burbine*, 475 U.S. 412, 421 (1986)].

The focus of any inquiry on whether a waiver is voluntary is the presence or absence of overreaching by officers of the government [*Colorado v. Connelly*, 479 U.S. 157, 170 (1986)]. What is overreaching by officers of the government is informed by the longstanding involuntary confession jurisprudence [*Colorado v. Connelly*, 479 U.S. 157, 169–170 (1986); *Miller v. Dugger*, 838 F. 2d 1530, 1538 (11th Cir., 1988)]. Such overreaching has been found where a person being subjected to custodial interrogation has been whipped [*Brown v. Mississippi*, 297 U.S. 278 (1936)], slapped [*Haynes v. Washington*, 373 U.S. 503 (1963)], deprived of food [*Brooks v. Florida*, 389 U.S. 413 (1967)], deprived of water [*Payne v. Arkansas*, 356 U.S. 560 (1958)], not permitted to sleep [*Reck v. Pate*, 367 U.S. 433 (1961)], or threatened with physical violence [*Beecher v. Alabama*, 389 U.S. 35 (1967), officer threatened to kill person subjected to interrogation; *Ward v. Texas*, 316 U.S. 547 (1942), person being subjected to interrogation threatened with mob violence].

Improper threats also include a statement to a woman being subjected to interrogation that, if she did not cooperate, her children would be taken from her [*Lynum v. Illinois*, 372 U.S. 528 (1963)] and a statement to a man being subjected to interrogation that if he did not cooperate, the woman he lived with would be arrested [*People v. Helstrom*, 50 AD 2d 685 (N.Y. App. Div., 3rd Dept., 1975) affd. 40 N.Y. 2d 914 (1976)].

Improper deception takes a number of forms: A false promise that, if a person being subjected to questioning made a statement, the person would not be arrested [*People v. Hilliard*, 117 AD 2d 969 (N.Y. App. Div., 4th Dept., 1986)] or prosecuted [*United States ex rel Caserino v. Denno*, 259 F. Supp. 784 (S.D. N.Y., 1966)]. Another example is falsely indicating that the waiver of *Miranda* rights would not hurt the person being subjected to interrogation [*United States v. Beale*, 921 F. 2d 1412, 1415 (11th Cir., 1991)], or that anything that this person said could not be used against him or her [*People v. Cosby*, 104 AD 2d 1000, 1002 (N.Y. App. Div., 2nd Dept., 1984)]. Both render the waiver involuntary. Another deception that would be deemed improper includes an officer, a friend of the person being subjected to interrogation, falsely indicating to the person he would lose his job if the person did not confess [*Spano v. New York*, 360 U.S. 315 (1959)]. Still another improper deception is a police psychiatrist, posing as a general practitioner, pretending to treat a person in custody for a sinus condition, creating the impression of a physician and patient confidential relationship, and then inducing a confession [*Leyra v. New York*, 347 U.S. 556 (1954)].

However, it should be noted that all deceptions are not improper. For instance, falsely indicating that an accomplice confessed [*Frazier v. Cupp*, 394 U.S. 731 (1969)], that an accomplice confessed and implicated the person being subjected to interrogation [*People v. Boone*, 22 N.Y. 2d 476, 483 (1968)], that the victim of a fatal assault did not die, but survived and would identify the person being subjected to interrogation [*People v. McQueen*, 18 N.Y. 2d 337, 346 (1966)], or falsely indicating evidence of that person's guilt was available [*People v. Burnett*, 99 AD 2d 786 (N.Y. App. Div., 2nd Dept., 1984)] have all been held not to be improper deception.

Any determination of voluntariness of a waiver must take into account the personal characteristics of the person being subjected to custodial interrogation. These characteristics could include such things as:

- Mental deficiencies [*People v. Williams*, 62 N.Y. 2d 285 (1984)]

- Youth [*Fare v. Michael C.*, 442 U.S. 707 (1979)]

- Intoxication [*People v. Enright*, 122 AD 2d 443 (N.Y. App. Div., 3rd Dept., 1986)]

- Psychosis [*Colorado v. Connelly*, 479 U.S. 157 (1986)]

- Pain [*United States v. Yunes*, 859 F. 2d 953, 961–962 (D.C. Cir., 1988)]

- Stupor [*People v. Holloway*, 131 Ill. App. 3d 290 (1985)]

- Fear [*United States v. Pono*, 746 F. Supp. 220 (D. Maine, 1990)]

- Emotional instability [*People v. Stroman*, 118 AD 2d 1006, 1007 (N.Y. App. Div., 3rd Dept., 1986)]

- Prolonged drug or alcohol abuse [*United States v. Rohrback*, 813 F. 2d 142, 144 (8th Cir., 1987), cert. denied 482 U.S. 909 (1987)]

- Drug withdrawal [*McCarthy v. Bronson*, 683 F. Supp. 880, 886 (D. Conn., 1988)]

However, these characteristics standing alone are insufficient to establish involuntariness. In addition, there must be some governmental overreaching, such as intimidation, coercion, or deception [*United States v. Rohrback*, 813 F. 2d 142, 144 (8th Cir., 1987), cert. denied 482 U.S. 909 (1987)]. Thus, in *Colorado v. Connelly* [479 U.S. 157 (1986)], it was held, just because the defendant, a psychotic, was being subjected to custodial interrogation and suffered a hallucination that God's voice commanded him to confess, his waiver of *Miranda* rights was not rendered involuntary, absent some overreaching by officers of the government.

Nevertheless, when a person being subject to custodial interrogation is especially susceptible to coercion because of any of the previously mentioned characteristics, and the officer conducting the interrogation seeks to exploit the weakness, then conduct that might in normal circumstances not be considered coercive will be deemed so now. For instance, a four-hour interrogation of a person who is incapacitated and sedated in an intensive care unit has been held to be coercive [*Mincey v. Arizona*, 437 U.S. 385 (1978)].

Proof of Knowing and Voluntary Waiver. A knowing and voluntary waiver of *Miranda* rights must be established by a preponderance of evidence [*Colorado v. Connelly*, 479 U.S. 157, 168 (1986)].

Express Waiver. An express written or oral waiver of *Miranda* rights, although not conclusive, is proof of the validity of such waiver [*North Carolina v. Butler*, 441 U.S. 369, 373 (1979); *United States v. Hack*, 782 F. 2d 862, 866 (10th Cir., 1986), cert. denied 476 U.S. 1184 (1986)]. However, because an express written waiver is more concrete evidence, it is preferable [*United States v. D'Antoni*, 856 F. 2d 975, 980 (7th Cir., 1988), interrogating officer well advised to obtain an express written waiver]. For an example of such express written waiver, see the appendix.

Yet the most effective evidence of waiver would be to electronically record the waiver and the ensuring statement. This would allow for a determination as to whether the person subjected to interrogation answered questions calmly, fully, and forthrightly, and whether the interrogating officer put questions calmly with no overbearing tone of voice [*United States ex rel Argo v. Platt*, 684 F. Supp. 1450, 1452 (N.D. Illinois, 1988)]. All this tends to establish voluntariness.

Implied Waiver. A valid waiver will not be implied simply from the silence of a person being subjected to custodial interrogation after *Miranda* warnings are given or simply from the fact that a confession was eventually obtained [*Miranda v. Arizona*, 384 U.S. 436, 475 (1966)]. However, an express statement that a person being subjected to custodial interrogation is willing to make a statement and does not want an attorney, followed closely by a statement, could constitute a valid waiver [*Miranda v. Arizona*, 384 U.S. 436, 475 (1966)].

A valid waiver may also be inferred from other words and actions of a person being subjected to custodial interrogation. *North Carolina v. Butler* [441 U.S. 369 (1979)] is an example of what may be such an implied waiver. The facts are as follows: The defendant and another had robbed a gas station in Goldsboro, North Carolina, in December of 1976, shooting and paralyzing the station attendant. The defendant was arrested in the Bronx, New York, on the basis of a fugitive warrant by Special Agent David C. Martinez of the New Rochelle Office of the FBI. Agent Martinez testified that he had fully advised the defendant of his *Miranda* rights at the time of the arrest. The defendant was transported to the New Rochelle Office of the FBI and again given his *Miranda* rights as listed on the Bureau's Advice of Rights form. The defendant stated he understood his rights. He was told that he did not have to speak or sign the form. The defendant stated that he would talk to the agents but would not sign the form. Agent Martinez testified that the defendant said nothing when advised of his right to the assistance of counsel. At no time did the defendant attempt to terminate the agent's questioning. During the interview, the defendant made inculpatory statements. The defendant was convicted, and the issue on appeal was whether a specific oral waiver was required or a waiver could be inferred by the court.

The Supreme Court in substance held that the silence of a person being subjected to custodial interrogation, coupled with that person's understanding of his rights and a course of conduct indicating waiver, would be sufficient to establish an implied waiver [*North Carolina v. Butler*, 441 U.S. 369, 373 (1979)]. A course of conduct indicating waiver would include answering questions or making a statement [*People v. Sirno*, 76 N.Y. 2d 967, 968 (1990)].

Thus, an implied waiver may be found in situations in which a person being subjected to custodial interrogation expressly states that he or she understands the *Miranda* rights [*United States v. St. Kitts*, 742 F. Supp. 1218, 1222 (W.D. N.Y., 1990); see also *Gorman v. Franzen*, 760 F. 2d 786 (7th Cir., 1985)], or it is clear from the record that he or she understands the rights [*People v. Sirno*, 76 N.Y. 2d 967 (1990)] together with the answering of questions or the making of a statement.

A clear understanding of *Miranda* rights may be found where a person being subjected to custodial interrogation responds affirmatively in writing or orally as to whether he or she understands each of the *Miranda* rights given prior to questioning [*People v. Sirno*, 76 N.Y. 2d 967 (1990)].

Some courts have found that the fact that a person being subjected to custodial interrogation is familiar with the criminal justice system may be significant in finding an implied waiver [*Gorman v. Franzen*, 760 F. 2d 786 (7th Cir., 1985); *People v. Davis*, 55 N.Y. 2d 731, 733 (1981)].

Revocation of Waiver

It is clear that a person being subjected to custodial interrogation may revoke a waiver once given. The mere fact that a person being subjected to custodial interrogation may have initially waived *Miranda* rights does not deprive the person of the opportunity to thereafter invoke those rights [*Miranda v. Arizona*, 384 U.S. 436, 445, 473–474 (1966); *Martin v. Wainwright*, 770 F. 2d 918, 922–924 (11th Cir., 1985) mod. on other grounds 781 F. 2d 185 (11th Cir., 1986), cert. denied 479 U.S. 909 (1986)].

Invocation of the Right to Remain Silent

No problem is presented in a situation where the invocation of the right to remain silent is clear, such as, "I don't wish to answer questions" [*Bradley v. Meachum*, 918 F. 2d 338, 342 (2nd Cir., 1990)] or "I don't want to talk" [*People v. Kinnard*, 62 N.Y. 2d 910 (1984)]. However, no special words or actions are necessary if it is obvious that the right to remain silent is being invoked [*Bradley v. Meachum*, 918 F. 2d 338, 342 (2nd Cir., 1990)]. For example, indicating that, "I have nothing else to say" [*Christopher v. Florida*, 824 F. 2d 836 (11th Cir., 1987)] or responding to a query as to what happened with a "No" and attempting to turn off a tape recorder [*State v. Cauthern*, 778 S.W. 2d 39 (Tenn., 1989)] have been deemed to be an invocation of the right.

On the other hand, a statement, "When will you let me go home?" [*Moore v. Dugger*, 856 F. 2d 129 (11th Cir., 1988)] has not been deemed an invocation of the right. Other examples of words and actions not invoking the right to remain silent include a refusal to answer a single question while giving an exculpatory story [*United States v. Goldman*, 563 F. 2d 501, 503–504 (1st Cir., 1977)], occasional silence during questioning [*United States v. Lorenzo*, 570 F. 2d 294, 298 (9th Cir., 1978)], an indication from a person being subjected to custodial interrogation that the person had provided all the information he or she possessed [*United States v. D'Antoni*, 856 F. 2d 975, 981 (7th Cir., 1988)], or a statement, "Ain't got nothing to tell you" [*People v. Allen*, 147 AD 2d 967 (N.Y. App. Div., 4th Dept., 1989)].

Furthermore, a refusal to sign a written waiver form does not establish the invocation of the right to remain silent [*Jones v. Dugger*, 928 F. 2d 1020, 1027 (11th Cir., 1991)] if the person being subjected to custodial interrogation otherwise clearly indicates a willingness to talk about the crime that is the subject of the questioning [*North Carolina v. Butler*, 441 U.S. 369 (1979)].

More problematic are situations in which the words or actions are equivocal as to whether the right to remain silent is invoked. For example, a statement in a custodial interrogation setting by a person being subjected to questioning to the effect, "Can't we wait until tomorrow?" was held to be an equivocal indication of the desire to remain silent [*Martin v. Wainwright*, 770 F. 2d 918, 923 (11th Cir., 1985) mod. on other grounds 781 F. 2d 185 (11th Cir., 1985), cert. denied 479 U.S. 909 (1986)].

An equivocal invocation of the right to remain silent suffices to cut off further questioning under *Miranda* [*United States v. D'Antoni*, 856 F. 2d 975, 980 (7th Cir., 1988)]. However, an interrogating officer is permitted further questions to clarify whether the person being subjected to interrogation was indeed attempting to invoke the right to remain silent [*United States v. D'Antoni*, 856 F. 2d 975, 980 (7th Cir., 1988)].

It should be emphasized that, if an interrogating officer is confronted with what might be deemed an equivocal indication of the right to remain silent, but proceeds with the questioning without clarifying whether the person was indeed trying to invoke the right to remain silent, any ensuing confession, admission, or statement will be suppressed [*Martin v. Wainwright*, 770 F. 2d 918, 924

(11th Cir., 1985) mod. on other grounds 781 F 2d 185 (11th Cir., 1985), cert. denied 479 U.S. 909 (1986)]. This is a serious problem, since what words or actions are indeed equivocal requests have been treated differently by various courts. For instance, the statement just quoted—"Can't we wait until tomorrow?" was treated by one court as an equivocal indication of the desire to remain silent. Nevertheless, another court indicated that such a statement was clearly not an invocation of the right to remain silent [*United States v. Thierman*, 678 F. 2d 1331 (9th Cir., 1982)].

Further slight variations in the wording of statements have led courts to find a clear indication of the invocation of the right to remain silent or a clear indication that such right was not revoked. For example, "I have nothing else to tell you" held a clear invocation of the right to remain silent. In contrast, "Ain't got nothing to tell" held clearly not an invocation to that right.

It is therefore recommended that if an interrogating officer has any doubt as to whether words or actions may be an attempt to invoke the right to remain silent, he or she should ask clarifying questions to ensure that the person being subjected to custodial interrogation is not seeking to invoke the right to remain silent before proceeding with further questioning [*Martin v. Wainwright*, 770 F. 2d 918, 924 (11th Cir., 1985) mod. on other grounds 781 F. 2d 185 (11th Cir., 1985) 479 U.S. 909 (1986)].

The Consequences of the Invocation of the Right to Remain Silent

If a person being subjected to custodial interrogation invokes the right to remain silent, then all questioning must immediately cease [*Stumes v. Solem*, 752 F. 2d 317, 321 (8th Cir., 1985)]. However, the invocation of the right does not bar a subsequent interrogation [*Michigan v. Mosley*, 423 U.S. 96 (1975)]. Efforts to initiate a second interrogation will be acceptable if:

1. The original interrogation was promptly terminated.

2. There was passage of a significant period of time.

3. The second interrogation is restricted to a crime that was not the subject of the first interrogation [*Jackson v. Wyrick*, 730 F. 2d 1177, 1179 (8th Cir., 1984), cert. denied 469 U.S. 849 (1984)].

It has been held that two hours is the passage of a significant period of time [*Michigan v. Mosley*, 423 U.S. 96, 104 (1975)]. Although when the person being subjected to custodial interrogation initiates a further discussion, 45 minutes has been deemed as sufficient passage of time [*People v. Kinnard*, 98 AD 2d 845, 846 (N.Y. App. Div., 3rd Dept., 1983)].

It has been held that, if it is clear that no effort was made to wear down the resistance of the person being subjected to custodial interrogation who invoked the right to remain silent, and indeed if that right was scrupulously honored, then the second interrogation may concern the same crime as was invoked in the first interrogation. However, it is recommended that an interrogating officer wait a minimum of two hours and also limit the second questioning to a crime that was not the subject of the first interrogation [*Jackson v. Wyrick*, 730 F. 2d 1177, 1179–1180 (8th Cir., 1984), cert. denied 469 U.S. 849 (1984)].

Invocation of the Right to an Attorney

Clearly, an assertion by a person being subjected to custodial interrogation that he "wanted a lawyer before answering questions" [*Arizona v. Roberson*, 486 U.S. 675, 678 (1988)] is an invocation of the right to an attorney. Furthermore, when a person being subjected to custodial interrogation reacts to the admonition concerning the right to have an attorney during questioning with the statement, "Uh, yeah, I'd like to do that" [*Smith v. Illinois*, 469 U.S. 91, 93 (1984)] that person is certainly invoking this right. Also the request by a person after having been given *Miranda* warnings, "May I have Legal Aid," is an unmistakable invocation of the right [*People v. Woodward*, 64 AD 2d 517, 518 (N.Y. App. Div., 1st Dept. 1978)]. The response of "No" by a person being subjected to custodial interrogation to an inquiring interrogation officer as to the willingness to answer questions without an attorney is an unequivocal assertion of the right [*People v. Carmine A.*, 53 N.Y. 2d 816, 818 (1981)].

Edwards v. Arizona [451 U.S. 477 (1981)] presents another example of the invocation of the right. In *Edwards* the defendant indicated during custodial interrogation that he wanted to make a deal before giving a statement. The interrogation officer responded that he would make no deal, whereupon the defendant replied, "I want an attorney before making a deal." At that point, the interrogation ceased. The next day another officer began to reinterrogate the defendant, and the defendant made a statement.

The Court in *Edwards* observed that the defendant wanted an attorney before making a deal and that his part of the deal would have been his statement. Therefore, the Court reasoned, to allow the defendant to make a statement without an attorney would deny him the right to an attorney for the very purpose for which it was invoked. The Court concluded that the defendant's statement, "I want an attorney before making a deal" was a clearcut assertion of the right to an attorney.

It should be pointed out that, if a person being subjected to custodial interrogation initially unequivocally requests an attorney, any postrequest statements by that person may not be used to cast doubt on the clarity of the initial request.

Smith v. Illinois [469 U.S. 91 (1984)] illustrates this last proposition. In *Smith* an interrogating officer was administering *Miranda* warnings, and at one point the officer told the person being subjected to questioning that he was entitled to have an attorney present during interrogation, to which that person responded in substance, "I'd like to do that." The officer, instead of immediately terminating any further attempt at questioning, continued to administer the *Miranda* warnings, and after the recitation of the warnings the person stated in substance, "I'll talk to you."

The Court in *Smith* held that the initial invocation of the right to an attorney controlled the situation, and at that point the interrogation should have ceased. Therefore, reasoned the Court, the subsequent statement, "I'll talk to you" was improperly elicited and could not be properly used to cast doubt retroactively on the initial request for an attorney.

On the other hand, there are words that clearly are not an invocation of the right to an attorney. For example, a request to contact one's probation officer before answering questions is not a request for an attorney [*Fare v. Michael C.*, 442 U.S. 707 (1979)]. Nor is a request to contact one's family such an invocation [*People v. Fuschino*, 59 N.Y. 2d 91, 100 (1983)]. Moreover, a person being subjected to custodial interrogation, who expresses a willingness to talk to an interrogating officer, but indicates a refusal to make a written statement without an attorney present, is not deemed to be invoking the right to an attorney in connection with any ensuing oral statement [*Connecticut v. Barrett*, 479 U.S. 523 (1987)].

Situations are also presented where a person being subjected to custodial interrogation makes an equivocal statement concerning the desire for an attorney. Examples of equivocal statements include asking an interrogating officer, "What do you think about whether I should get a lawyer?" [*Towne v. Dugger*, 899 F. 2d 1104 (11th Cir., 1990)] or an assertion, such as, "Maybe I should talk to an attorney" [*State v. Campbell*, 367 N.W. 2d 454 (Minn., 1985), held the statement not an invocation of the right to an attorney; *People v. Esposito*, 68 N.Y. 2d 961 (1986), held the statement was an invocation of the right to an attorney].

These last present a problem. Some jurisdictions hold that there is an invocation of the right to an attorney upon any reference to an attorney, however equivocal. Other jurisdictions require a threshold standard of clarity before the right can be deemed to be invoked. Still other jurisdictions have adopted a third approach: If a person makes an equivocal statement that arguably can be construed as a request for an attorney, then interrogation must cease, except for questions designed to clarify whether indeed a request for an attorney was made [*Smith v. Illinois*, 469 U.S. 91, 95–96 footnote 3 (1984)].

The Supreme Court of the United States has not resolved this conflict [*Connecticut v. Barrett*, 479 U.S. 523, 529 footnote 3 (1987); *Smith v. Illinois*, 469 U.S. 91, 95–96 (1984)]. Thus, the statement, "Maybe I should get a lawyer" in a jurisdiction that deems the right invoked on any reference to attorney, however equivocal, would be deemed an invocation of the right [*People v. Munoz*, 83 Cal. App. 3d 993 (4th Dist., 1978)].

In a threshold of clarity jurisdiction, the statement would not be considered an invocation of the right [*People v. Krueger*, 82 Ill. 2d 305 (1980), cert. denied 451 U.S. 1019 (1981)].

In a jurisdiction taking the third approach mentioned above, if the clarifying questions reveal that the statement, "Maybe I should get a lawyer" was indeed a request for an attorney, then all interrogation must cease. If the clarification shows that the statement was not a request for an attorney, then the interrogation may continue [*United States v. Fouche*, 776 F. 2d 1398, 1404–1405 (9th Cir., 1985)]. If no clarifying questions are asked, then the statement is deemed an invocation of the right to an attorney, and any subsequent statement will be suppressed [*Towne v. Dugger*, 899 F. 2d 1104 (11th Cir., 1990); *Thompson v. Wainwright*, 601 F. 2d 768 (5th Cir., 1979)]. It appears that more jurisdictions are adopting the third approach [83 ALR 4th 443 Annot. Assertion of Right to Counsel].

Moreover, if a person's statement referring to an attorney is deemed an invocation of the right to an attorney, then any ensuing statement, confession, or admission will be suppressed.

It is therefore recommended that, if an interrogating officer, regardless of the jurisdiction, has any doubt as to whether a person is invoking the right to an attorney, he or she should ask clarifying questions to ensure that the person is not seeking to invoke the right to an attorney before proceeding with any further interrogation [*United States v. Fouche*, 776 F. 2d 1398, 1404–1405 (9th Cir., 1985)].

The Consequences of the Invocation of the Right to an Attorney

A person being subjected to custodial interrogation, who invokes the right to an attorney, is not subject to further questioning until an attorney has been made available, unless that person initiates further communication exchanges or conversations with an interrogating officer [*Edwards v. Arizona*, 451 U.S. 477, 484–485 (1981)]. This bar extends to a contemplated reinterrogation by the same officers who were conducting the original interrogation, but who wish to question the person concerning an offense that was not the subject of the original questioning; it also extends to officers of a different law enforcement authority, who seek to interrogate the person concerning the same offense that was the subject of the original interrogation or concerning a different offense [*Arizona v. Roberson*, 486 U.S. 675, 687–688 (1988)]. For example, if an officer initiates an interrogation concerning a murder, and the person invokes the right to an attorney, the officer may not reinterrogate that person about a burglary. Furthermore, if an officer from a completely different law enforcement seeks to question that person about the murder or the burglary, that too would be barred.

The initiation of a further communication exchange or conversation, which permits further interrogation under *Edwards* is illustrated in *Oregon v. Bradshaw* [462 U.S. 1039 (1983)]. In *Bradshaw* the defendant invoked his right to an attorney during an interrogation concerning a homicide. At that point the interrogation ceased. The defendant was then transferred to a jail. On the way to the jail the defendant asked the interrogating officer, "Well, what is going to happen to me now?" The officer cautioned the defendant that he did not have to speak to him, and the defendant responded he understood. Then the officer and defendant discussed where the defendant was being taken and the offense for which he would be charged. The suggestion was made by the officer that the defendant take a polygraph test. The defendant agreed and was then readvised of his *Miranda* rights, which he waived in writing. After the test, the polygraph examiner told the defendant that he was lying, whereupon the defendant confessed.

The Court in *Bradshaw* held that the defendant's statement, "What is going to happen to me now?" was the initiation of further conversation contemplated in *Edwards* and that the ensuing confession was not a violation of *Edwards*.

Finally, after the person has invoked the right to an attorney, interrogation must of course cease, and reinterrogation may not proceed without an attorney being present, whether or not the person consulted with an attorney.

In *Minnick v. Mississippi* [111 S. Ct. 486 (1990)] the defendant was interrogated by federal law enforcement officers concerning a murder and invoked his right to an attorney. The interrogation then ended. Thereafter, the defendant consulted with his appointed counsel two or three times. The defendant was then questioned by a county deputy sheriff, advised of his *Miranda* rights, which he allegedly waived; thereafter, the defendant confessed.

The Court in *Minnick* held that the defendant could not be reinterrogated without his attorney present and suppressed the confession.

Cat Out of the Bag

In *Oregon v. Elstad* [470 U.S. 298 (1985)], the "cat out of the bag" concept was rejected in the *Miranda* context. In *Elstad* a confession was obtained from the defendant in violation of *Miranda*. About an hour later *Miranda* warnings were given, and the defendant waived his right and thereafter confessed again.

The Court held that the first confession, of course, must be suppressed because of the *Miranda* violation, but that otherwise the confession was uncoerced. Therefore, the second confession would not be suppressed, absent a showing that interrogating officers exploited the unwarned confession to pressure the defendant into waiving his right to remain silent and confessing again.

Miranda and Physical Evidence

Miranda warnings need only be given when nontestimonial evidence is sought. Thus, a video tape of a person performing a sobriety test, including answering questions concerning his name, address, height, weight, eye color, date of birth, current age, and dialogue leading up to his refusal to take a breathalyzer test, which also reflected the slurred nature of his speech, was held to be admissible at a trial, even though the person was not given *Miranda* warnings prior to initiating the sobriety test [*Pennsylvania v. Munoz*, 110 S. Ct. 2638 (1990)].

Other examples of nontestimonial evidence not requiring *Miranda* warnings include a handwriting exemplar [*Gilbert v. California*, 388 U.S. 263 (1967)], voice exemplar [*United States v. Dionisio*, 410 U.S. 1 (1973)], or appearing in a lineup and repeating a phrase for the benefit of an eyewitness [*United States v. Wade*, 388 U.S. 218 (1967)].

Fruits of the Poisonous Tree

Evidence obtained by exploitation of a primary illegality is regularly excluded under traditional taint analysis as the "fruit of the poisonous tree" [*United States v. Morales*, 788 F. 2d 883, 885 (2nd Cir., 1986)]. But whether this concept is to be applied where the primary illegality is a *Miranda* violation is an open question [*Patterson v. United States*, 485 U.S. 922 dissenting opinion (1988); *Oregon v. Elstad*, 470 U.S. 298, 347 footnote 29, dissenting opinion (1985)].

The following hypothetical situation illustrates the problem. A person is being subjected to custodial interrogation in connection with a murder involving a shooting. The interrogation officer, however, fails to properly administer *Miranda* warnings. During the questioning, the officer inquires as to the location of the murder weapon. The person reveals the location of the weapon and admits to owning it. The weapon is then seized, and a ballistics test establishes that it was indeed the murder weapon. The admission to the ownership of the weapon, of course, would be suppressed. Nevertheless, the question is whether or not the weapon and the ballistics test are also to be suppressed [See, e.g., *Orozco v. Texas*, 394 U.S. 324, 325–326 (1969)].

Federal and state courts are divided on the issue. Some would suppress the weapon and ballistics test, while others would not. For a rather comprehensive compilation of federal and state cases on each side of the issue, see *Patterson v. United States* [485 U.S. 922 (1985), dissenting opinion] and *Oregon v. Elstad* [470 U.S. 298, 347 footnote 29 (1985), dissenting opinion].

In connection with this issue, it is imperative for interrogating officers to check the law of their jurisdiction.

Interrogation

ADVICE OF RIGHTS

YOUR RIGHTS

Place_____

Date_____

Time_____

1. Before we ask you any questions, you must understand your rights.
2. You have the right to remain silent.
3. Anything you say can be used against you in court.
4. You have the right to talk to a lawyer for advice before we ask you any questions and to have a lawyer with you during questioning.
5. If you cannot afford a lawyer, one will be appointed for you before any questioning if you wish.
6. If you decide to answer questions now without a lawyer present, you will still have the right to stop answering at any time. You also have the right to stop answering at any time until you talk to a lawyer.

WAIVER OF RIGHTS

I have read this statement of my rights and I understand what my rights are. I am willing to make a statement and answer questions. I do not want a lawyer at this time. I understand and know what I am doing. No promises or threats have been made to me and no pressure or coercion of any kind has been used against me.

Signed_____

Witness:_____

Witness:_____

Time:_____

SIMPLIFIED ADVICE OF RIGHTS*

YOUR RIGHTS

Place_____

Date_____

Time_____

1. You have the right to remain silent. That means, you don't have to say anything. Do you understand that? Any questions?

2. You can refuse to answer any and all questions at any time. That means you don't have to answer any questions now, or if you choose to answer questions now, and then change your mind, you can refuse to answer any more questions. If you decide now or at anytime to refuse to answer any questions, just tell me and I have to stop asking questions. Do you understand? Any questions?

3. Anything you say can and will be used against you in a court of law. That means what you say or write can be used to prove what you may have done. Do you understand that? Any questions?

4. You have the right to talk to a lawyer and have the lawyer present with you while you are being questioned. That means that a lawyer can be with you at all times, and the lawyer may tell you what the lawyer wants you to do or say. Do you understand that? Any questions?

5. You have the right to have a lawyer present now. If you tell me you want a lawyer now, I cannot ask you any questions and I must wait until you have a lawyer before I can question you. If you choose to answer questions now

---

*This Simplified Advice of Rights is based on[2] suggested simplified warning contained in *Matter of Julian B.* [125 AD 2d 666, 671-672 (N.Y. App. Div., 2d Dept., 1986)].

without a lawyer present and then change your mind and decide you want a lawyer present, just tell me and I have to stop asking questions and wait until you have a lawyer present. Do you understand that? Any questions?

6. If you want a lawyer, and you cannot afford to have a lawyer, one will be appointed to represent you during questioning. That means the cost of having a lawyer will be paid by someone else if you cannot pay for it. Do you understand that? Any questions?

WAIVER OF RIGHTS

I have read my rights as listed above. I understand each of them. I have been asked if I have any questions, and I do not have any. I am, right now, willing to give a statement and answer questions and give up my right to have a lawyer present. No promises or threats have been made to me to make me give up my rights. I understand I may change my mind at any time and say I want my rights if I choose.

Signed_____

Witness_____ Date and Time_____

Witness_____ Date and Time_____

ADDENDUM
FOR USE IF A JUVENILE IS INVOLVED

7. Without one of your parents' or your guardian's agreement, you cannot give up your right to remain silent or to have a lawyer with you during questioning. Do you understand that? Any questions?

Signature of Juvenile_____

Witness, Parent or Guardian_____ Date and Time_____

Witness_____ Date and Time_____

NOTES

[1]See, generally, I La Fave & Israel, *Criminal Procedure*, Chap. 6, "Interrogation and Confessions," Sections 6.1–6.10 (1984).

[2]See, e.g., *United States v. Ross* [719 F. 2d 615 (2nd Cir., 1983)]; *United States v. Jameson-McKamer Pharmaceuticals Inc.* [651 F. 2d 532, 542 (8th Cir., 1981), cert. denied 455 U.S. 1016 (1982)]; *United States v. Mapp* [561 F. 2d 685, 688 (7th Cir., 1977)]; *United States v. Sicilia*, 475 F. 2d 308 (7th Cir., 1973), cert. denied 414 U.S. 865 (1973)]; *United States v. Gallagher* [430 F. 2d 1222 (7th Cir., 1970)]; *United States v. White* [417 F. 2d 89 (2nd Cir., 1969), cert. denied 397 U.S. 912 (1970)]; *United States v. Main Street Distributors, Inc.* [741 F. Supp. 353, 359 (E.D. N.Y., 1990)]; *United States v. Berlin* [707 F. Supp. 832 (E.D. VA, 1989)].

[3]See, e.g., *People v. Elliott* [131 Misc. 2d 611 (N.Y. Supreme Court, Queens County, 1986)]; see also Chap. 10, "Search and Seizure, Search by Private Individual or Store Security Personnel."

[4]*People v. Washington* [121 Misc. 2d 451, 452–453 (N.Y. Supreme Court, Kings County, 1985)]; see also *People v. Schimpert* [19 N.Y. 2d 300, 305 (1967) cert. denied 389 U.S. 874 (1967)] and 25 ALR 4th 419 Annot. Confessions—Effect of Alcohol and Drugs, Section 2 (a), pp. 424–425; a person may be so intoxicated as to be unconscious of the meaning of words.

[5]*United States v. Cahill* [920 F. 2d 421, 427 (7th Cir., 1990), cert. denied 111 S. Ct. 2058 (1991)], prior experience in criminal justice system; *United States v. Black-Bear* [878 F. 2d 213, 214 (8th Cir., 1989)], a high school graduate with above-average intelligence; *United States v. Wilson* [787 F. 2d 375 (8th Cir., 1986), cert. denied 479 U.S. 857 (1986)], mentally competent adult, high school education, served honorably 22 years in armed services; *United States v. Marchildon* [519 F. 2d 337, 344 (8th Cir., 1975), 47-year-old college graduate; *United States v. Gazzara* [587 F. Supp. 311 (S.D. N.Y., 1984)], owner of business, intelligent and mature; see also *Crooker v. California*, 357 U.S. 433, 435 (1958), a pre-*Miranda* case dealing with voluntariness of a confession indicating that the fact that the defendant was a college graduate with one year of law school, who took criminal law, was to be considered on the question of voluntariness of his confession.

[6]*Miller v. Dugger* [838 F. 2d 1530, 1539 (11th Cir., 1988)], mental illness may bar knowing waiver; *Cooper v. Griffin* [455 F. 2d 1142, 1145 (5th Cir., 1972)], mental deficiency barred knowing waiver; *Matter of Julian B.* [125 AD 2d 666 (N.Y. App. Div., 1986)]; *Matter of Chad L.* [131 Misc. 2d 965, 970 (N.Y. Family Court, Kings County, 1986)], tender age barred knowing waiver.

[7]These factors were discussed in connection with the cognitive capacity to comprehend *Miranda* warnings under the subdivision dealing with Mental Deficiencies and Intoxication in comprehending *Miranda* warnings and would apply here.

11
Investigative Grand Jury

Hon. Lawrence J. Bracken

Edward P. Bracken

HISTORICAL PERSPECTIVE

The establishing of a grand jury system may be traced to the year 1166 and its initial use at the Assizes of Clarendon. Its origins are not found in the Anglo-Saxon common-law experience but, rather, in the inquest feature of Norman law, first introduced into England by virtue of the Norman conquest. The function of the grand jury system as so instituted was to serve as an instrument of monarchical power, and it was originally designed as one method of centralizing and strengthening the English monarchy.

In or about the middle of the fourteenth century, secrecy was introduced into these proceedings—a precursor to the concept of secrecy in grand jury proceedings. The grand jury system was introduced into this country by the English colonists and was eventually adopted as part of our constitutional and statutory law. Today it is maintained by all the states, although its powers and functions are limited in a number of jurisdictions.

Traditionally, it has been regarded as an institutional bulwark intended to protect the individual from the oppressive conduct of any governmental authority. It is designed to serve as a legal barrier between accuser and accused, regardless of the status of the latter, and to determine whether a charge being brought has a solid foundation in reason or is in fact dictated by virtue of intimidation or by malice or personal ill-will [*Wood v. Georgia*, 370 U.S. 375, 390, 82 S. Ct. 1364, 8 L. Ed. 2d 569 (1962)].

In addition to the constitutional mandate providing for indictment by a grand jury with respect to any capital or other infamous crime, many state constitutions further provide that grand juries have the power to inquire into the willful misconduct in office of public officers and to return indictments and/or direct the filing of informations in connection with all such inquiries. (See, for example, New York State Constitution, Art. I, §6; *California Criminal Procedure*, §§914.1, 917, 923.)

NATURE AND FUNCTION

Grand juries are juries of varying numbers of citizens and generally require a quorum and affirmative vote of a majority and are impaneled by a court. In essence, the grand jury is an arm of the court and not of the prosecution. Its basic function is to determine whether the evidence presented to it is sufficient to allow for further proceedings. Historically, then, the grand jury is an inquisitorial arm of the court, whose function is investigative and not prosecutorial; it is charged with the duty of conducting its own investigation into all crimes within its jurisdiction and, as an investigatory body, it is concerned with determining whether or not a crime has been committed and, if so, who committed the crime. Additionally, in many jurisdictions it is charged with the further duty of exploring whether or not there has been misconduct, malfeasance, or neglect by public officials and is empowered to direct criminal prosecution if warranted or to report its findings if criminal prosecution is not warranted. A grand jury has the widest possible latitude in the exercise of its powers and, in the absence of a clear legislative or statutory intent, may not be curtailed. (See, for example, New York State Constitution, Art. I, §6; *People v. Stern*, 3 N.Y. 2d 658 (1958); see also *California Criminal Procedure*, §914.1, *Ex parte Peart*, 5 Ca. 2d 469.)

SCOPE

Ordinarily, the average grand jury, both federal and state, concerns itself with those cases introduced into the criminal justice process through a summary arrest or by the filing or lodging of a criminal complaint or information, which is followed generally by some type of hearing or finding of probable cause. In these instances, a grand jury, in the vast majority of cases, is involved in merely approving the prior finding of reasonable cause and serves no other function. Our discussion is not concerned with this form of grand jury but with investigative grand juries, which take an active role in the overall investigation and the subsequent indictment or report. In essence, the investigative grand jury is a law enforcement tool whose power to investigate persons and documents serves as the focal point for criminal investigation and testimonial compulsion.

Because of its wide investigatory range, a grand jury may concern itself with an investigation based merely upon suspicion [*Mason & Co. v. Heinz*, 50 A.D. 2d 13 (1975)]. On its own motion it may pursue an investigation solely on the basis of personal knowledge of grand jurors comprising the panel or as a follow-up to rumors and tips circulated to it [*Nigrone v. Murtagh*, 46 A.D. 2d 343, appeal dism'd, 30 N.Y. 2d 664, aff'd 36 N.Y. 2d 421 (1974); *Monroe v. Garrett*, 17 Ca. 3d 280].

This power, of course, is subject to judicial review and control. Also, the secrecy of grand jury proceedings is designed to prevent injury to reputation from roving investigations [*Manning v. Valente*, 272 App. Div. 358, aff'd 297 N.Y. 681 (1947)].

It is no secret that there has been a substantial increase in the number of grand jury investigations throughout this country; the grand jury is widely used as an investigative tool. An investigative grand jury usually concerns itself with bribery, public corruption, organized crime, and white collar and other business crimes, wherein the complaint is not police-originated but is usually made to the prosecutor. The power of such a grand jury, of course, lies in its ability to issue not only subpoenas to secure testimony but also subpoenas duces tecum used to secure books, records, and other documents for examination as a basis for further proceedings. Inherent in this power are the power to punish for contempt in the face of a willful failure to either testify or produce and the right to cite for perjury in the face of false or willfully evasive testimony.

It is in this context, therefore, that the following discussion is presented.

ROLE OF THE PROSECUTOR

The prosecutor is, by statutory definition in most instances, the legal advisor to the grand jury and is charged with the duty of submitting to it evidence of crimes and of advising it of the various crimes which he or she believes the evidence justifies investigating. Therefore, while theoretically the grand jury is considered to be essentially autonomous and an arm of the court that impaneled it, in practical terms the grand jurors rely on the advice of the prosecutor and in many cases are amenable to and accept such advice in connection with a particular matter. In this regard, the relationship between the prosecutor and investigator assumes considerable importance, since it is incumbent on the prosecutor to advise the investigator of the basic elements of the particular crimes which will be necessary to sustain the charges under investigation. Conversely, the investigator must have a good working knowledge of the substantive criminal law and should actively inquire of the prosecutor about any substantive criminal law elements involved, should there be any questions.

The preliminary investigation conducted by the investigator for and on behalf of the prosecutor will, in most instances, serve as the basis for the issuance of grand jury subpoenas and subpoenas duces tecum. (Cf. *California Criminal Procedure*, §939.2, which authorizes district attorneys or their investigators to sign and issue subpoenas requiring the attendance of a witness before a grand jury.) This investigation should be as comprehensive as possible so as to enable the prosecutor to justify the issuance of such subpoenas in the face of a motion to quash being brought by a potential suspect or an accused.

In addition, since it is the prosecutor who ordinarily charts the course of evidence presentation to the grand jury, an investigator for the prosecutor should be fully conversant with the method of serving subpoenas, should have the ability to determine the location of prospective witnesses and documents, and should be able to answer any questions concerning such mechanical processes that might be asked by the prosecutor.

GRAND JURY SECRECY

Historically, grand jury proceedings have been secret, and both federal and most state statutes provide for such secrecy [*Federal Rules of Criminal Procedure* 6(e); *New York CPL*, §190.25(4)]. Such a rule, of course, is not absolute on either the federal or the state level, since there must be limited disclosure in order to enable those upon whom the secrecy is enjoined to lawfully discharge their duties. (Cf. *California Criminal Procedure*, §939.1, providing for a court order directing a grand jury to conduct its investigation in a session or sessions open to the public when the subject matter of the investigation affects the general public welfare.) There is also, of course, the *right of disclosure*, when such disclosure is made in connection with a judicial proceeding [*Federal Rules of Criminal Procedure*, 6(e); *New York CPL*, §210.30(3)(4)]. While it is possible that the minutes of a grand jury proceeding may be available to an outside party, such relief is rarely granted in view of the strong policy of grand jury secrecy. Ordinarily, inspection of grand jury minutes has been limited to public officers or official bodies charged with the duty of criminal investigation who can demonstrate that the examination of a particular grand jury's minutes would be in the public interest. The one significant exception is that when grand jury minutes are to be used to investigate alleged official misconduct not tantamount to criminal misconduct, they may be released to interested parties. The other notable exception is that the grand jury testimony of a trial witness may be used for impeachment, and when a witness so impeached by his or her grand jury testimony on trial, who is subsequently indicted for perjury allegedly committed at the trial, has a right, as a defendant, to examine that grand jury testimony. It should be noted, however, that in all those instances where there was such a release of grand jury minutes, whether to law enforcement agencies or others, either secrecy of the proceeding was no longer necessary or, if secrecy was still relevant, the public need for disclosure overrode the policy of grand jury secrecy. By recent statutory amendments, certain jurisdictions now allow the delivery of the minutes of the grand jury to defendant and counsel [*New York CPL*, §210.30(3); *California Criminal Procedure*, §939.1].

It should be noted that *witnesses before grand juries* are not bound by the secrecy sanctions that pertain to the grand jurors themselves or to those public officials who are privy to the proceedings [*Federal Rules of Criminal Procedure*, 6(e); *New York CPL*, §190.25(4)]. Thus, all grand jury witnesses have the right to disclose what transpired while they were before the grand jury. As part of the investigative process, therefore, it should be determined in advance whether or not the testimony of such witnesses should be subject to public disclosure before action is taken by the grand jury, and the various witnesses, be they defense or prosecution, should be instructed with respect to disclosure. It should also be noted that there appears to be no violation of grand jury secrecy in a defense counsel's debriefing of witnesses as they leave a jury room; thus, it is improper for a prosecutor to advise witnesses that while they are free to discuss their testimony with anyone, they are to report back to the grand jury if they were interrogated regarding any questions put to them by the grand jury [*In Re Grand Jury*, 321 F. Supp. 238 (1970)].

The question of disclosure, therefore, should be carefully considered by both prosecutors and defense counsel, as well as by investigators for both, to determine the efficacy of disclosure or nondisclosure in each particular case. (Cf. *California Penal Code*, §938.1, which mandates that the transcript of grand jury proceedings after an indictment is returned be open to the public 10 days after its delivery to the defendant or the defendant's attorney, to whom it must be delivered within 10 days after return of the indictment.)

As previously noted, a grand jury may issue subpoenas on its own initiative or in conjunction with the prosecutor without prior court approval. Its power of subpoena, however, is not unlimited, and if it is abused, or if compliance with a subpoena would be unreasonable or oppressive, then the subpoena may be quashed or modified pursuant to a motion addressed to the trial court. [See *Federal Rules of Criminal Procedure*, Rule 17(c); *New York CPL*, §§190.50, 610.10 *et seq.*] In a proceeding to quash, or modify, a subpoena duces tecum, the court has the right to litigate the question of the relevance of the materials sought to be produced, and if the subpoena is burdensome, a court may either quash or modify. It should be noted, however, that relevancy and materiality in this context have a broader meaning than they would with respect to the use of the subpoenaed material as evidence in a trial and must be interpreted in relation to the grand jury's function. When, however, subpoenas duces tecum are overbroad and amount to fishing expeditions, they are subject to being quashed as violations of the right to be free from unreasonable search and seizure.

There are many grounds for making application to vacate a subpoena. Among these grounds are defective form of the subpoena, improper service, irrelevance of requested testimony or privilege with respect to such testimony, or an unreasonably broad demand for the production of papers or records. With respect to privileged testimony, an investigator should keep in mind the privilege attaching to physician-patient, confessor-penitent, or attorney-client relationships, which in many instances involve confidential communications protected by statute. It should also be noted that a subpoena duces tecum may not be employed for the purpose of merely procuring evidence or as a substitute for a search warrant. [*Mancusi v. DeForte*, 392 U.S. 364, 88 S. Ct. 2120, 20 L. Ed. 2d 1154 (1968)]. While this issue of subpoenas and their use for procuring testimony will be discussed in connection with evidentiary and constitutional safeguards later in this section, suffice it to say that any circumstances allowing for an intelligent estimate of relevance is sufficient to support the mandate of a subpoena; but when it becomes too broad or oppressive, it is subject to being vacated.

EVIDENTIARY CONSIDERATIONS— GENERAL DISCUSSION

Generally, the question of rules of evidence to be applied in any grand jury proceeding will be primarily the consideration of the prosecutor; but it behooves any investigator, for the prosecution or the defense, to know fully the basis upon which evidence may be introduced in the grand jury and what constitutes legally sufficient evidence to justify any criminal charge resulting from an investigation.

In most jurisdictions, the general rules of evidence applying to testimony and the introduction of evidence at trial are basically the same as the rules of evidence to be applied before the grand jury, although there may be certain exceptions. Knowledge of the standards of evidence to be applied, as well as of the quantum of proof, is essential for investigators preparing cases for presentation and ultimate resolution. As an example, while certain jurisdictions (the federal jurisdiction, for instance) may allow hearsay evidence to be presented, in other jurisdictions such evidence is deemed irrelevant and incompetent to support any or all of the criminal elements necessary to sustain an indictment (see, e.g., *New York CPL*, §190.30; see also *California Criminal Procedure*, §939.6). When evidence used as one of the links in sustaining a legally sufficient case before a grand jury is considered incompetent, the indictment resulting therefrom is clearly invalid. Investigators should be cognizant of the pitfalls in this basic issue of what evidence is clearly competent; that is, what evidence may be used before the grand jury, in contrast to evidence that may be deemed irrelevant and/or incompetent, thereby vitiating any efforts to secure an indictment!

It should be understood also that ruling on the admissibility of evidence and/or the competence of witnesses before a grand jury is not a judicial matter but is primarily one for consideration and determination by the prosecutor who, as the legal advisor to the grand jury, governs the course of conduct with respect to evidence and witnesses. The investigator, working for either prosecutor or defendant, should be cognizant, therefore, of what evidence would be material and competent in the grand jury proceeding and what evidence would fail to meet this standard and would be subject to further attack on the motion to dismiss the indictment.

EVIDENTIARY CONSIDERATIONS CONCERNING CONSTITUTIONAL RIGHTS

In this sophisticated age, there is no question that witnesses and/or potential defendants appearing before the grand jury may invoke certain constitutional rights. The invocation of the Fifth Amendment privilege against self-incrimination is a widely adopted procedure or tactic, although rights under the First, Fourth, Sixth, and Ninth Amendments to the U.S. Constitution may also be invoked by witnesses. In fact the refusal to answer questions solely on Fifth Amendment grounds has resulted in this invocation being deemed a waiver of the defendant's rights under the Fourth Amendment with respect to a contempt prosecution later undertaken [*People v. DeSalvo*, 32 N.Y. 2d 12, 343 N.Y.S. 2d 65 (1973)]. There is no doubt, therefore, that the rights asserted by a witness during a grand jury proceeding may assume considerable significance in later proceedings.

Under the First Amendment, a witness may refuse to answer any questions in a grand jury proceeding if the investigation constitutes a fishing expedition or is unauthorized either by statute or by special legislation or involves an intrusion into protected First Amendment areas, such as the witness's political or religious beliefs or other constitutionally protected associations [*Gibson v. Florida Legislative Committee*, 372 U.S. 539, 83 S. Ct. 889, 9 L. Ed. 2d 939 (1963); *N.A.A.C.P. v. Button*, 371 U.S. 415, 83 S. Ct. 328, 9 L. Ed. 2d 405 (1963)].

The invocation of the Fourth Amendment right is addressed to unlawful searches and seizures of the witness's works or records or to questions asked of the witness before the grand jury that were derived from the illegal use of electronic surveillance or from other unlawfully acquired evidence.

Individual guarantees under the Sixth Amendment primarily concern the right of citizens to counsel throughout the grand jury proceeding, a right granted in some jurisdictions by statute, while invoking the Ninth Amendment generally involves all other rights that must be asserted by the witness in a particular instance, such as the right to privacy.

An investigator must be thoroughly familiar with the right of a witness to invoke privilege against self-incrimination. Fifth Amendment protection applies not only to testimonial compulsion, which would link the witness to the commission of a crime, but also to subjection of the witness to any penalty or forfeiture as a result of such testimony. Therefore, witnesses who are not subject to any direct criminal liability may still invoke the privilege if their testimony might subject them to some other form of forfeiture. In addition, no penalty may be exacted against witnesses who assert their privilege against self-incrimination, because this would be punishing persons for freely exercising their constitutional right. [See, e.g., *Spevack v. Klein*, 385 U.S. 511, 87 S. Ct. 625, 17 L. Ed. 2d 574 (1967); *Garrity v. New Jersey*, 385 U.S. 493, 87 S. Ct. 616, 17 L. Ed. 2d 562 (1967); *Gardner v. Broderick*, 392 U.S. 273, 88 S. Ct. 1913, 20 L. Ed. 2d 1082 (1968); *Lefkowitz v. Turley*, 414 U.S. 70, 94 S. Ct. 316, 38 L. Ed. 2d 274 (1973), all cases in which the individuals involved were subjected to discipline following their invocation of or refusal to waive their privilege against self-incrimination during the course of an investigation.]

That the answer sought would subject the witness to a criminal sanction or other penalty or forfeiture is a determination usually left to the witness, although in certain rare instances exceptions have been made and courts have required, *in camera*, the basis of the invocation of the privilege against self-incrimination. It should be clearly understood, however, that this privilege protects witnesses solely from the compulsion of oral testimony or the production of certain documents. It does not apply to nontestimonial items such as handwriting exemplars, voice exemplars, or blood samples. [See *Gilbert v. California*, 388 U.S. 263, 87 S. Ct. 1951, 18 L. Ed. 2d 1178 (1967); *U.S. v. Dionisio*, 410 U.S. 1, 93 S. Ct. 764, 35 L. Ed. 2d 67 (1973); *Schmerber v. California*, 384 U.S. 757, 86 S. Ct. 1826, 16 L. Ed. 2d 908 (1966).] Nor is the privilege violated by requiring a corporate officer to produce the books and records of the corporation for grand jury perusal. It is violated, however, by compelling a corporate officer to divulge the location of corporate books and records [*Curcio v. United States*, 354 U.S. 118, 77 S. Ct. 1145, 1 L. Ed. 2d 1225 (1957)]. It also may not protect against the divulging of partnership papers held by one partner in a representative capacity for other partners [*Bellis v. United States*, 417 U.S. 85, 94 S. Ct. 2179, 40 L. Ed. 2d 678 (1974)]. In addition, the privilege is not violated by the use in a criminal proceeding of answers given by an officer of a corporation to interrogatories elicited in a civil case [*United States v. Kordel*, 397 U.S. 1, 90 S. Ct. 763, 25 L. Ed. 2d 1 (1970)].

The privilege also does not bar the production of an individual's records entrusted to an accountant for the preparation of tax returns [*Couch v. United States*, 409 U.S. 322, 93 S. Ct. 611, 34 L. Ed. 2d 548 (1973)]. And if a taxpayer has obtained tax returns from an accountant and delivered them to an attorney for legal advice, the compulsion by subpoena addressed to the attorney to produce these documents does not constitute a violation of the Fifth Amendment privilege, because the subpoena is not addressed to the taxpayer. In this regard, it should also be noted that the communications received in this way do not constitute confidential communication between attorney and client, since they are, in fact, the work product of a third party, that is, the accountant [*Fisher v. United States*, 425 U.S. 391, 96 S. Ct. 1569, 46 L. Ed. 2d 39 (1976)].

While there is no question that the seizure of private business records pursuant to subpoena may constitute a violation of the privilege against self-incrimination, seizure of such records pursuant to valid search warrant does not so violate the privilege [*Andresen v. Maryland*, 427 U.S. 463, 96 S. Ct. 2739, 49 L. Ed. 2d 627 (1976)].

Finally, since in many instances the subject matter of a grand jury's investigation involves bank records, it should be understood that there is no reasonable expectation of privacy with respect to bank records or checks or other negotiable instruments for what is revealed to others in such records, and there is no violation of the Fourth Amendment right in their disclosure [*United States v. Miller*, 425 U.S. 435, 96 S. Ct. 1619, 48 L. Ed. 2d 71 (1976)].

With respect to electronic surveillance, the use of illegal wire taps or eavesdropping may vitiate the grand jury proceeding, and the formulating of questions based on information obtained through illegal electronic surveillance directed against the witness may constitute a violation of the witness's Fourth Amendment rights [*In Re Grand Jury Proceedings (1971)*, 450 F. 2d 199, aff'd 408 U.S. 41, 92 S. Ct. 4357, 32 L. Ed. 2d 179].

It should be realized, however, that obtaining pen registers, which record only telephone numbers dialed, does not require a search warrant and does not violate Fourth Amendment guarantees [*Smith v. Maryland*, 442 U.S. 735, 99 S. Ct. 2577, 61 L. Ed. 2d 220 (1979); *United States v. N.Y. Telephone Co.*, 434 U.S. 149, 98 S. Ct. 364, 54 L. Ed. 2d 376 (1977)].

IMMUNITY AND THE COMPELLING OF TESTIMONY

Various federal and state statutes provide for compelling witnesses to testify or otherwise to furnish information in exchange for a grant of immunity from criminal prosecution or from the use of the compelled testimony. See, for example, 18 U.S.C., §6002; *New York CPL*, §§50.00, 50.20. Such compelling of testimony by the grant of immunity from prosecution does not violate any Fifth Amendment guarantee provided that the scope of the immunity granted to the witness is coextensive with the scope of the Fifth Amendment privilege against self-incrimination [*Kastigar v. United States*, 406 U.S. 411, 92 S. Ct. 1653, 32 L. Ed. 2d 212, reh. denied 408 U.S. 931 (1972); *Murphy v. Waterfront Commission of New York*, 378 U.S. 52, 84 S. Ct. 1594, 12 L. Ed. 2d 678 (1964)].

At the outset it should be realized that there exist two basic constitutional immunities: (1) *transactional immunity*, that is, complete immunity from any criminal prosecution on account of any transaction, matter, or thing about which the witness has testified; and (2) *use and derivative use immunity*, that is, immunity from the use in any criminal case of the testimony compelled from the witness or any evidence reasonably derived therefrom [*Kastigar v. United States*; *Ullmann v. United States*, 350 U.S. 422, 76 S. Ct. 497, 100 L. Ed. 2d 511, reh. denied 351 U.S. 928, 76 S. Ct. 777, 100 L. Ed. 2d 1415 (1956)]. The investigator should know, however, that in those instances when an immunity statute merely provides that certain testimony compelled from witnesses will not be used against them in criminal proceedings, such a grant of immunity is not constitutionally adequate to justify the compelling of such testimony [*Counselman v. Hitchcock*, 14 U.S. 547, 12 S. Ct. 195, 35 L. Ed. 2d 1110 (1892)]. Any use of an immunity statute, therefore, must not only grant immunity as to testimony but also as to any evidence which reasonably can be derived therefrom.

Once a grand jury has granted immunity coextensive with the privilege against self-incrimination under the Fifth Amendment, the witness must answer any questions addressed to him by the grand jury or prosecutor in the grand jury or risk the penalty for contempt.

Any grant of immunity, to be constitutionally adequate, must also extend to criminal proceedings in other jurisdictions, federal or state [*Murphy v. Waterfront Commission*; see also *Gardner v. Broderick*, 392 U.S. 273, 88 S. Ct. 1913, 20 L. Ed. 2d 1082 (1968)].

In considering the use of the testimony of a particular witness before an investigative grand jury, therefore, the prosecutor's initial determination whether or not that witness's testimony is essential or vital to the prosecution and whether granting immunity to the witness will vitiate the aims of the investigation by allowing a significant figure therein to escape prosecution. The investigator's role, therefore, is vital in determining the nature of the testimony sought from the witness and the witness's involvement in the matter being investigated.

Once it has been determined that the witness's testimony is necessary and that the prosecution will not be compromised by granting immunity, then immunity should be extended in the most explicit terms and the witness fully advised of the extent of the immunity being granted and what particular transactions it applies to. Once made fully aware of the scope of immunity, the witness must testify or risk criminal contempt charges. In most jurisdictions witnesses will be represented by counsel, and it is the more prudent course, after having extended the grant of immunity, to allow witnesses to confer with counsel for assistance in determining the extent of their rights with respect to the testimony sought from them.

It should be clear to both defense and prosecution that an immunity statute in no way protects from prosecution for offenses not yet committed, including perjury or contempt that may be involved in giving compelled testimony in return for a grant of immunity [*Glickstein v. United States,* 222 U.S. 139, 32 S. Ct. 71, 56 L. Ed. 2d 128 (1911)]. Furthermore, the fact that a witness may be subjected to certain civil disabilities or liabilities as a result of testifying pursuant to a grant of immunity or may be risking personal disgrace or the probability of violent reprisals by those testified against does not make the grant of immunity inadequate [*Ullmann v. United States; Smith v. United States,* 337 U.S. 137, 69 S. Ct. 1000, 93 L. Ed. 2d 1264 (1949); *Piemonte v. U.S.,* 367 U.S. 556, 81 S. Ct. 1720, 6 L. Ed. 2d 1028 (1961)].

The witness may be more concerned about protection from reprisal than about immunity from prosecution. It then behooves the witness, through his or her attorney, to determine whether circumstances exist that would justify an attempt to assure that the witness receives the maximum protection from reprisal afforded by the jurisdiction in question. See, for example, *Title V, Organized Crime Control Act of 1970 (Public Law 452).* In advising such a witness whether to comply and testify pursuant to a grant of immunity or to refuse to testify and thereby risk a charge of contempt, there should be a careful evaluation of the likelihood of the immunity being held constitutionally adequate and an adjudication of contempt being upheld [*Kastigar*].

Subsequent to testimony under a grant of immunity, there may be violations of this immunity by criminal prosecution against a witness or by the use of certain evidence derived from such testimony. In this case, the witness should raise the issue of the prior grant of immunity as a defense to such prosecution as promptly as possible; so that it cannot be deemed that the witness has waived the right to reply on the grant of immunity. See, for example, *Burrell v. Montana* [194 U.S. 572, 24 S. Ct. 787, 48 L. Ed. 2d 1122 (1901)], where it was demonstrated that if the witness has been compelled previously to give testimony under a grant of immunity, the prosecutor must not only negate the fact that there may be the taint of privileged testimony, but also must establish that all the evidence proposed to use against the witness was derived from a legitimate source, wholly independent from the compelled testimony.

There may be instances also when a witness will give evasive answers to the questions of the grand jury. Giving evasive answers is equivalent to giving no answers at all and, therefore, is contemptuous. The failure to answer questions truthfully, if the questions are relevant and material to the grand jury investigation, of course constitutes perjury.

CONCLUSION

The foregoing discussion has demonstrated that the investigative grand jury serves a legitimate purpose; that is, investigating certain criminal activity when other law enforcement measures are not effective. Any abuses of the grand jury's extensive discretionary authority must be condemned and its actions subjected to assiduous control, particularly where there is a contravention of the historic function of the grand jury to keep citizens free from public accusation or opprobrium until probable cause has been established resulting in indictment.

With this important caveat in mind, the investigative grand jury should continue to serve an important function in the resolution of criminal activity, provided it is subject to appropriate legal controls in its investigative activity.

12

The Investigator in Court

Andre Evans

PREPARATION OF THE CASE FOR TRIAL

Pretrial preparation by the investigator has two phases. The first begins with the incident itself. A crime has taken place; a collision has occurred. The job of the investigator is to see what happened, who caused it, and why. Once that has been determined, the emphasis shifts from fact-gathering to preservation of evidence and preparation for trial. Investigators should realize that the latter is as important as the former, and that once the "thrill of the chase" is over, their responsibilities are not completed. The work of the investigator has not ended until the case is presented in court. The sufficiency of the evidence and its presentation is the yardstick by which the investigation will ultimately be judged.

Investigation for the Courtroom

The investigatory phase of case preparation starts at the scene of the crime or with the happening of the incident to be investigated. Investigators should be thorough, bearing in mind that someday they will be called upon to testify to the facts and their observations, and should make proper notations, since memory does not improve with time. The success or failure of the case in court may well depend on the investigator's ability to explain the facts, the actions taken, and the results thereof. A professional investigator is held to a higher standard than is the average witness. There is no excuse for giving approximations of details that should be known accurately.

Presentation of the case in the courtroom is the end result of the investigative process. Both a good investigation and the preparation of the case for the courtroom require action at the scene to locate witnesses and preserve evidence. The duty of the investigator is to gather facts, not to draw conclusions that later events or a turn of circumstance in the courtroom may prove wrong. Not to take photographs because a condition or situation is so obvious is to run the risk of having to do so later when circumstances have changed, or not to be able to do so at all, with disastrous results in the courtroom.

Curiosity is an essential piece of intellectual equipment, but its satisfaction in the investigator's own mind without obtaining substantiating details is a waste of time. Getting the essential facts without getting witnesses or other sources or proof is of little or no value. Added effort expended in the initial investigation is well worth its time and expense. Finding witnesses or getting corroborating evidence shortly before trial, or even during trial, is far more expensive and time-consuming that doing so while the investigation is in progress. The lack of such material may result in compromise of the case prior to trial, or inability to go to trial at all. Additional time spent during the investigation will more than justify itself in the long run.

The investigator begins with the attitude that the case will someday go to trial. Investigators with experience in the courtroom learn to anticipate trial requirements. From case to case, the issues will vary with the evidence available. In one case the determining issue may be the cause of the collision, or possibly the cause of death. In another, the issue may be the identity of the victim or the assailant. In reviewing the report that the investigator has prepared and submitted, the attorney identifies areas of weakness and then asks the investigator to remedy any defects or omissions in the investigation. The attorney tries to anticipate discovery motions and bills of particulars prior to trial and to negate possible claims or defenses at trial. A trained investigator will act in anticipation of these requirements.

Processing the scene of the crime or incident is the first duty of the investigator. Physical dimensions and other data are important, not only for the investigation but at trial; and the investigator should be able to reproduce the scene in photographs, floor plans, and sketches. Physical size and dimension, as well as details of weather, visibility, and other climatic conditions existing at the time should be recorded and preserved for future use and testimony.

Physical evidence is preserved primarily by photographs. When necessary, the object itself is preserved and maintained in the same condition as when the incident occurred. To have the object in better or worse condition than it was at the relevant time is to render it useless at trial.

Oral evidence, statements of witnesses, cannot be preserved like physical evidence. The investigator must first know the applicable rules of law and procedure that apply in the jurisdiction concerning the taking and use of statements of witnesses. The purpose of obtaining such information is twofold. The investigator is interested in obtaining evidence that can be used in court under the rules of evidence and also in obtaining information which, though it may be inadmissible in court, will be fruitful in leading to other avenues of investigation, will corroborate the investigator's case, or will contradict that of the opposing party.

After the investigation has been conducted, the report becomes the principal source of information. Often, it is the basis on which the disposition of a case is decided—whether the accused should be prosecuted or the plaintiff go to trial— or it may mean the successful defense of a lawsuit.

An investigation without a report is of little or no value. A good report is a communication of information set forth in an accurate, concise, clear, and complete manner, serving as a record of a given incident. It is a record of what is seen, heard, read, done, or considered. Reports are a necessary part of the investigator's job. When the report is not complete, the investigator has to be contacted, witnesses reinterviewed, and supplemental reports made. Reports from investigators are the material on which attorneys depend to build their cases, as they accept the burden of proof. If the report is inaccurate or incomplete, the results may well be disastrous.

To be complete, a report must be concise, clear and accurate. It will not be if an oral explanation is required in addition to what has already been included. A report must include the elements of the case and give the information about it that any interested person would want to know. Finally, the contents of the report must be able to be proved.

It has been written that, substantially, all reports are answers to the questions: when, who, where, what, how, and sometimes why.[1] The application of these questions may be clarified as follows:

When? When did the incident occur? What was the time of day, the day of the week, the month? When was this matter discovered? In brief, any information that has to do with the fixing of time may properly be given under the answer to the question "When?" and given in such detail as the purpose of the report demands.

Who? Who were the persons concerned? Who was the principal person involved in the case? The *who* may be the complainant in a felony or misdemeanor, the victim of an accident, or the suspect or offender. The *who* is the principal or title of the case. Information concerning this person, including friends, associates, habits, everything that can be learned about the individual, should be obtained. *Who* will vary somewhat in accordance with the nature of the report. For example, a dog, the property of John Doe, 250 Adams Street, is run over and killed. The principal purpose of making such a report is to have the dead dog removed from the public highway. Therefore, only the information absolutely necessary should be included on a complaint or incident report. But suppose that Doe is involved in a felonious hit-and-run accident or some other serious crime and has not been arrested. Now it becomes necessary that as much information concerning Doe, his friends, his associates, and his habits, as it is possible to secure be obtained in order to locate him.

Where? Where did the incident occur? Note the correct address, name of street, and type of building (house, apartment, store, service station, and so on). Where in the building did it occur—bedroom, hallway, front office? Any information that has to do with the location of places, persons, or objects connected with the matter under investigation should be given under the question "Where?" If it occurred outside, give the exact location. Pinpoint the exact spot where the offense took place. Use stationary objects when taking measurements (for example, 12 feet west of the curb). The correct description of the *where* will aid in further investigation and presentation of evidence and testimony.

What? What is the crime? What happened? Describe in as much detail as necessary for the purpose of the report. In the case of a person found on the street injured, the *what* would be the circumstances leading to the injury. Exactly what took place? This, too, will vary according to the purpose of the report. The investigator should be able to give such information as the actions of the suspects; what evidence was obtained; what knowledge, skill, or strength was needed to commit the crime; what was reported; what did occur; what was done with the evidence; what further action is needed; and what the witnesses know about it.

How? *How* was the event accomplished? Under this heading should be included all the information obtainable that will tend to show exactly how the occurrence took place. Answers should be sought to such questions as: How was the crime committed? How did the suspect get to the scene? How were the tools obtained and used?

Why? In addition to the above questions, reporting officers also seek answers to the question "Why?" The *why* covers the motive involved in the complaint. Motives are usually nothing more than deductions. However, the *why* should not be overlooked. The investigator should consider such things as: Why did so much time elapse before the crime was reported? Why were the witnesses so anxious to point out the guilty party? Why are the witnesses reluctant to talk? Why did the suspect commit a particular violation against a particular person, market, messenger, or premises? In cases of burglary, robbery, or larceny, for example, generally the *why* is answered by the crime itself, as it is presumed that the suspect committed the crime to gain possession. However, it is frequently worth considering why a suspect chose one particular victim, premises, market, and so on, over some other. In traffic cases there is seldom a motive. In homicide cases the motive may take a considerable amount of work to develop, and it may not be possible for the reporting officer to bring it out at the time of the report. Nevertheless, the *why* is still there and has to be considered by the investigator.

The above six questions (when, who, where, what, how, and why) can be used to the investigator's advantage in conducting inquiries of witnesses. They should be part of the wording of the inquiries. Such questioning forces the person being questioned to think more. For example, "What do you think?" "How did it happen?" "Why did you do it?" "Where were you during the incident?" Questions prefaced by these words (when, who, where, what, how, and why) call for definite information and will often result in positive answers.

Answers to these questions will constitute the elements of the case and give the information that any interested person will want to know. The investigator who keeps these questions fixed in mind, devoting attention to securing satisfactory and accurate answers to them, will certainly produce acceptable reports.

Pretrial Preparation

When it becomes known that the case is going to court, the investigation results, including all memorandums, reports, and data concerning the occurrence, as well as the entire case folder, should be reviewed by the investigator. This review should not be limited to the part that the investigator played, since knowledge about the participation of others will be expected. Special attention should be given, however, to the part of the investigation conducted by the investigator, who should be familiar with location, names, addresses, and other details without referring to notes—thus appearing prepared and confident on the witness stand. If possible, the scene should be visited again and recollection refreshed with regard to distances, measurements, and the like.

Trial preparation should include a pretrial conference between the investigator and the trial attorney. Prior to the conference, the investigator should prepare to testify based on logical questions that will probably be asked. The scope of the investigation should be familiar, as well as any part of the evidence-handling procedure that the investigator participated in. While a good report requires no oral explanation, such a meeting will enable the trial counsel to review with the investigator the specifics of the case. The attorney is then better able to pose meaningful questions to the witness in court. The existence of such a pretrial conference should readily be admitted on the stand, since such conferences are an acknowledged part of careful pretrial preparation.

As a result of the pretrial conference, the trial lawyer may request the investigator to conduct experiments or to determine that certain physical facts are, indeed, correct. For the investigator to have driven the distance at a certain speed, or observed the foliage at that time of year, will be not only admissible but convincing to the jury.

As trial nears, the trial attorney will become aware of witnesses for the opposing side, either through "discovery" procedures or examination of subpoena lists. An essential part of pretrial preparation is to determine the identity of opposition witnesses; the probable nature of their testimony; and their strengths and weaknesses, including any criminal record. When time and resources permit, investigators may also be called upon to determine the identity, personal circumstances, and other data about prospective jurors that will enable the trial attorney to best select a jury to fairly evaluate the case.

Skillful investigators will be thoroughly familiar with the case and prepared to present it in a forceful and convincing manner when testifying, using their experience and knowledge as witnesses to best advantage. By being prepared, they can avoid errors and contradictions which may not only leave them flustered, but damage their credibility before judges or juries.

COURTROOM PROCEDURES

The Nature of a Trial

Under our American system of justice, a trial is the process we use for discovering truth and making decisions. The trial is considered an adversary proceeding wherein one side "fights" the other. Opposing parties with conflicting interests face each other in the courtroom, rather than in trial by ordeal or by mutual combat. The modern trial is thus regarded as a more acceptable substitute for ancient modes of determining justice. With much at stake, it is assumed that the competition between contestants and the arguments of differing sides will advance every important consideration. Since individual litigants are unskilled as fighters and lack knowledge of the rules of the contest, they hire those with the requisite skills and knowledge: Lawyers represent the parties in the courtroom. Indeed, in criminal trials the Supreme Court of the United States has held in *Gideon v. Wainwright* [372 U.S. 335 (1963)] that the assistance of counsel is required, since the "noble ideal" in which every defendant stands equal before the law "cannot be realized if the poor man charged with crime has to face his accusers without a lawyer to assist him." Therefore, if a criminal defendant cannot afford an attorney, the government will provide one at no expense.

The parties, whether individuals, corporations, or agencies of government, are referred to in legal terms by designations that depend on the kind of case. In a criminal trial, the party with the burden of going forward with proof is the government referred to as the "United States," the "People," the "State," or a similar reference, depending on the practice in that jurisdiction. The accused in a criminal trial is known as the *defendant*. In a civil trial, that is, one involving money damages, property interests, or individual rights, the moving party is known as the *plaintiff*, and the defending party is, again, the *defendant*. In some types of cases, the terms used may be *complainant* and *respondent*, instead of plaintiff and defendant.

In a struggle between two contestants, by whatever name they are called, someone must decide who won. Unlike an athletic event or a card game, where the winner is the one making the most points, the outcome of a lawsuit depends on the evaluation of many intangibles, most of them subtle and subject to a difference of opinion. Exercise of this judgment is obviously an important task.

The determination of the question of ultimate importance to the litigants is made by a judge or jury. The role of the jury is to listen to witnesses; consider their testimony and other evidence; and to decide, based upon the facts, who is right or wrong, who is telling the truth. The job of the judge is to interpret the law applicable to the case and then to advise the jury so that they can reach a verdict based on legal principles. Although generally each side of a criminal or civil case has the right to request a trial by jury, comparatively few do. Most cases are decided by a judge alone, functioning as both judge and jury.

The amount of proof it takes—the "number of points" required—to win varies with the nature of the case. In a criminal case, the defendant is presumed to be innocent; and the government's lawyer, the prosecutor (usually referred to as the *district attorney*), must prove that the defendant is guilty "beyond a reasonable doubt." In a civil proceeding, the plaintiff's case must be established by a "preponderance of the evidence."

The object of a trial is to proceed in an orderly fashion to decide the issue in question. The parties are even as the contest begins. However, maintenance of the status quo will not lead to a determination of the rights of the parties. The rules of a trial therefore require the party who initiated the contest to proceed first. That party is said to have the *burden of proof*.

The amount of evidence required to prove a case cannot be explained in precise terms, but the basic concept can be illustrated by referring to the traditional image of the scales of justice, which at the outset are evenly balanced, 50:50. In a civil case, the burden on the plaintiff is to establish his or her case by a preponderance of the evidence, to tip the scales even ever so slightly. Naturally, the more that can be proved, the clearer and more convincing will be the case. However, in legal theory, if the scales tipped only 51:49 in the plaintiff's favor, it would mean a victory.

In a criminal case, in which the defendant may be fined or imprisoned, there is much more at stake. The Government must meet the *beyond-a-reasonable-doubt test*. Just a slight tipping of the scales in favor of the prosecution will not be sufficient. On the other hand, the State does not have the burden of proving its case 100:0, or beyond *all* doubt. Rather it must establish the case beyond a reasonable doubt—a doubt with a *reason*. Whether this be 60:40, 75:25, 90:10, or more or less, is a matter that is decided by the judge or jury trying the case. Conscience must be satisfied that the correct decision has been made, one that is fair to the accused and to the public interest and safety.

Trial Procedure

Once the contestants are identified and the required amount of proof known, it is necessary to proceed in an orderly fashion to the final decision of the legal battle. As we have seen, the party that initiated the proceeding has the burden of proof and must go forward with a presentation of evidence.

The procedure is similar in both civil and criminal cases. Once the plaintiff has made a claim and the defendant has denied it, or the accused has pled "not guilty" to a crime charged by the prosecution, the trial begins. The judge, jury, individual litigants, lawyers, witnesses, and various court officials gather at the appointed time and courtroom. After establishing that the parties are ready to proceed, the judge will have the clerk swear all witnesses, who will then usually be excluded from the courtroom so as to not hear one another testify. The plaintiff's lawyer or the district attorney will make an opening statement. This is the moving party's opportunity to tell the judge or jury what they intend to prove to meet the burden of proof and win the case. Thus, the *trier of fact*, whether judge or jury, is given a preview of the case—an idea of what to expect, without which the case would be confusing. The defendants will then have a similar opportunity to explain their case, either before the presentation of evidence begins or before they start their part of the case. The preliminaries having been accomplished, the State or the plaintiff begins to present the evidence to establish its case.

Evidence is said to be either "direct" or "circumstantial." Testimony of witnesses, documents, or such tangible items as photographs or a murder weapon, are considered *direct evidence*. Contrary to popular misconception, circumstantial evidence is not only admissible in court but is sometimes the only evidence available. *Circumstantial evidence* consists of proof of a fact or series of facts that establish by logical inference a matter in issue. For example, it has snowed during the night and you see one set of footprints in the snow leading to your front door. When you open the door, you see there your morning newspaper. You "know" the carrier has been there, although you did not see the delivery. The trier of facts will view inferential evidence with caution, but will give it the weight to which it is entitled.

Witness testimony is the standard method of presenting evidence. To prove the plaintiff's case a logical series of witnesses are called to the stand. Asking questions by the attorney who called the witness is known as *direct examination*. Inquiries must be made in a form that do not suggest the answer: otherwise, the opposing party will object to the question as "leading." The plaintiff's attorney indicates when questioning is finished, and the defense attorney then has an opportunity to *cross-examine* the witness.

The purpose of cross-examination is to test the memory, recall, and recitation of the facts by the witness. Cross-examination is optional with the attorney, and a skillful trial advocate will use it only if something can be gained. Having decided to cross-examine, the attorney has wide latitude as to the form of the questions. Questions may be asked that would not be allowed on direct examination. Following the defense attorney's cross-examination of the witness, the plaintiff's attorney has an opportunity to ask more questions designed to buttress the plaintiff's testimony and repair any damage done. It is within the discretion of the trial judge to allow each attorney to take turns asking more questions, each series of which are to be limited to the scope of the answers last given. When this procedure has been completed, the witness is excused from the stand and leaves the courtroom unless granted permission by the judge to stay.

By using a series of witnesses, documents, photographs, and so on, the nature and order of which will vary with the case, the attorney who has the burden of proof will attempt to prove his or her case. Whether the judge will allow particular testimony or other evidence depends on well-established legal principles known as the *rules of evidence*. Upon feeling that the obligation of proof has been met, the lawyer will "rest" his or her case. Opposing counsel then will usually ask the judge to dismiss the case for insufficient evidence. This tactic is rarely successful, however, because the plaintiff usually has met at least the minimum requirements of a case.

After the plaintiff or the State has completed its case, the defendant has the opportunity to present evidence. The party that does not have the burden of proof is not required to present any evidence but usually does so, as otherwise the case may be lost. In the presentation of the defendant's case, witnesses are called, tangible evidence is presented, and so on, in a manner similar to that used by the plaintiff. The defense attorney conducts the direct examination of defense witnesses and the plaintiff's attorney has an opportunity to cross-examine. The defendant thus proceeds until the opposing evidence appears to have been overcome or surpassed. After the defense rests, the plaintiff may offer evidence in rebuttal. With permission of the court, each side can continue taking turns rebutting the other with additional evidence. In practice, judges are usually reluctant to allow this to continue very long. Each rebuttal is strictly limited to countering the one before it.

When both sides have completed their cases, the defendant usually will make another motion to dismiss the plaintiff's case, based now on all the evidence—that of both the plaintiff and the defense. If it is a jury trial, motions such as this, as well as those to exclude particular evidence, will be made outside the presence of the jury. The attorney making a motion has the obligation to give reasons and to cite supporting law. The opposing attorney will have a similar opportunity before the judge rules on the issue.

When all motions have been completed, the attorneys have a chance to present final argument. If it is a jury trial, the judge will receive from the attorneys suggested statements of law applicable to the case. These jury "instructions," after review for legal sufficiency, will be read to the jury before or after arguments of counsel, depending on procedure in that court. The lawyer for the party with the burden of proof will argue first, pointing out the highlights of that party's case by referring to the evidence presented and the law in support thereof, and will attempt to persuade the judge or jury to decide in his or her favor. Following the presentation by the plaintiff, the defense attorney has a like opportunity. The plaintiff, having the burden of proof, may then have the right to close the arguments by rebutting that just presented.

Following arguments of counsel and the judge's recitation of the applicable principles of law, the jury will retire to the jury room to reach its verdict. Once this is done, the bailiff will be so informed and the court will reconvene, at which time the decision will be announced. The trial is now complete, and the witnesses and jury are excused. The defendant in a criminal trial, or either party in a civil trial, may make motions to set a verdict aside, based on that party's view of the evidence adduced at the trial and the law applicable to it. Finally, there may be a petition of appeal to a higher court.

Courtroom procedures vary somewhat from place to place, but it is important that the investigator have a working knowledge of how a trial progresses.

Suggestions for Witnesses

Most persons have a natural reluctance to speak to a group. Nervousness as a witness in the courtroom is normal, but there are things that can be done to avoid it. The more familiar one is with courtroom procedure and the rules of evidence, the better witness one will be. A witness who is prepared emotionally can to a large degree control the way his or her testimony is perceived and weighed. Remembering that the impression made on the jury is important to the case, the witness should be friendly and calm with an appearance of helpfulness.

Demeanor on the Stand. The jury's first impression of you occurs when you walk into the courtroom and take the oath. Your actions, as well as your attire, should make it apparent to judge and jury that you consider testifying an important duty. Approach the witness stand in a deliberate and unhurried manner. Do not glare at the defendant or opposing party, or act arrogant or overconfident. The jury is forming its initial impression of you, and it is difficult to change a negative first impression. Your appearance as you accept the oath is critical. All eyes in the courtroom are upon you. Stand erect and give the impression that you take the oath seriously and that, in light of it, your testimony will be truthful and conscientious. At the conclusion of the oath, say, "I do," in a clear and unmistakable manner.

When you have taken the oath, be seated in the witness chair in a comfortable but alert manner. You should have a full view of the judge, jury, and attorneys. Wait patiently for the proceedings to begin, and do not make sounds or movements that will be distracting. Your first opportunity to speak is when you are asked your name and, if customary in that court, your address. Unless otherwise directed, you may choose to give your office address. You should answer clearly and firmly, realizing that what you say and how you say it will have an important impact on the outcome of the case.

Avoid nervous mannerisms when testifying. Constant rearranging of clothing, crossing and uncrossing of arms or legs, clearing the throat, putting your hands to your face, or constant repetition of meaningless phrases such as "you know" detract from your testimony and affect the weight it is given. By avoiding such mannerisms and not appearing to be nervous, you will lessen the possibility that the judge or jury thinks you are afraid, or are not telling the truth or the whole truth.

Do tell the whole truth. You are sworn to do so. Every relevant fact should be readily admitted, even if it is not to the advantage of your side of the case. Do not stop to figure out whether your answer will help or hurt. Just answer the question to the best of your ability. To try to color or shade testimony to help your side only invites trouble. By so doing, you give the appearance of taking sides and lose credibility. Sticking to the truth is the best defense against cross-examination. No matter how skillful, a lawyer will be unable to trip you up if you stick to the truth.

Use normal language; do not attempt to use a vocabulary or jargon that is unfamiliar to you or to the jury. In normal conversation, no one would ever "exit the vehicle" but would simply "get out of the car." Obscenities or slang should not be used unless they are an indispensable part of your testimony and are made vital and material by the questions asked in these proceedings.

No matter how many times you have testified in court previously, this is the first time that this jury has had the opportunity to hear you speak. Answer politely and courteously, in a conversational tone, and loudly enough so that all the parties, the judge, and the most distant juror can hear what you have to say. Nothing is more disconcerting than to have a witness who refuses to speak loud enough to be heard. By speaking in a tone of voice that is barely audible, you give the impression that you are not certain of what you are saying. Jurors must ultimately decide the value of what you are saying, and they have the right to hear you say it.

When questions are being asked of you, listen carefully. If you do not understand a question, ask to have it repeated; but it is best to pay attention and avoid having the question repeated. Repetition is annoying to your listeners. Nevertheless, if you do not understand the question, ask that it be explained. You should not try to answer a question that you do not comprehend. This is not only confusing to the judge and jury, but invites contradiction on cross-examination.

Avoid an unnaturally long delay to a simple question if you know the answer, but do not give a snap answer without thinking. Answer all questions directly, but at your own pace. Think before answering, and do not allow the questioner, especially the cross-examiner, to rush you into "shooting from the hip." A pause before answering is beneficial in a variety of ways. It allows you an opportunity to think about the question and thereby better understand it. It also gives the appearance of a believable, well thought-out answer. Moreover, when you are being cross-examined, there will be time for your attorney to object to an improper question.

If you respond slowly enough to consider your thoughts before speaking, your testimony is enhanced. Speaking hurriedly can result in the misunderstanding of testimony because words were slurred, answers were improperly phrased, or the question was misinterpreted. Before replying, wait until you are sure that the question has been completed. Answering before the question is completed may be perceived as eagerness to help your side of the case or, on cross-examination, an attempt to avoid a difficult question. Adopt a deliberate pace, but avoid speaking so slowly as to cause your listeners to doubt your testimony. Body gestures with hands or nods of the head must be avoided, since the court reporter or recording device cannot record them.

Some witnesses think they should have an answer to every question that they are asked. If you do not know the answer, say so. No witness knows all the facts, and it will be to your credit to be candid rather than to try to have an answer for everything. To say, "I don't know" or "I don't remember" is sometimes the only proper and truthful answer. A witness should never guess at the answer to a question. If you do attempt to guess, you are offering uncertain information as legitimate. Guessing may also be taken to indicate bias or inadequacies in your testimony.

Not knowing the answer to a question should not be overdone. If you do not know, say so, and do not make up an answer. However, you should be positive about important details that you would naturally remember. It is the little details that a person would *not* normally remember that you can understandably admit have escaped your recollection. Give positive and definite answers when it is at all possible to do so, and avoid having to answer a series of questions by replying that you do not know. Sometimes a question calls for a yes or no answer. Frequently, however, a question cannot be answered by a simple yes or no, in which case you should so state and before answering, request an opportunity to explain your answer.

If you do not want to answer a question, do not ask the judge whether you must answer it. This is perceived as an appeal for help from the court. If it is an improper question or one that you should not have to answer, the question will be objected to by the attorney who called you to the stand.

When it is understandable that you would not remember a detail (for example, a license number), it is permissible to refer to your notes to refresh your recollection. On such occasions, you should ask the court if you may be allowed to consult your notes, report, memorandums, and so on. Once permitted, refresh your recollection, then put down the notes and continue relating the information. While notes are valuable, it should be remembered that once referred to by the witness, they can be examined by opposing counsel and may even be admitted into evidence. Carefully review with the attorney who will call you as a witness the information contained in the notes, after having discussed with him or her the necessity of referring to them. The attorney may decide that they had best be left outside the courtroom.

Questions should be answered directly and briefly without rambling or long-winded explanations. Do not attempt to elaborate on or dramatize your answer. Nor should you be so anxious to tell your story that you attempt to tell it all in response to the first question. Volunteering information not asked for can be damaging to your case. Respond to each question appropriately and expect the examiner to develop your testimony with a series of logical questions and your answers. Even if you know that the attorney who has called you to the stand is leaving out an important bit of information, it is dangerous to attempt to supply an unresponsive answer. Information not asked for is almost certain to be objected to, and you may suffer the embarrassment of having the court instruct the jury to disregard your answer. Such an occurrence can be damaging to your entire testimony.

In testifying, you should stick to the facts, to information about which you have personal knowledge. Rarely is it permissible for you to state in court what someone told you. Unless you are an expert witness and so recognized by the court, you may not testify as to conclusions or opinions, and should therefore avoid qualifying your testimony by such phrases as, "I think," "I believe," or "In my opinion." What you *think* is not important. What you *know* is. The court and jury are interested only in the facts within your knowledge, so avoid giving your own opinions and conclusions unless you are specifically asked for them.

If you make a mistake while testifying, recognize it as soon as possible, preferably before anyone else does. The simple statement that you have made a mistake and would like to correct it is far better than having your entire testimony discredited later. If you have not recognized your mistake but it becomes apparent, perhaps during cross-examination, admit it. It is better to acknowledge an error than to adamantly maintain a position that is plainly wrong and thereby discredit your entire testimony.

Some things and phenomena are not subject to exact measurement. The judge and jury will understand that by being inexact when describing them, you are being honest and not purposely vague. Do not allow yourself to be trapped into making estimates or approximations on things such as distance, speed, and time unless you have actually measured them.

Avoid conclusory statements such as, "That's the last thing that happened" or "That is all he said." Recitation of testimony on the witness stand is rarely, if ever, that encompassing and on further questioning, you may remember something that has not been recalled earlier.

Objections by one lawyer to the questions of another are not the concern of the witness. It is the duty of the judge to decide whether or not you should answer the question. Do not answer until the judge has ruled on the objection; and when there is such an interruption, stop the moment an objection is made. Objections made by counsel can be distracting to a witness without a working knowledge of the rules of evidence. By understanding the rules of the proceedings and by taking time to observe trials, you will learn how to reply without inviting an objection. When an objection is made, you should wait until the matter is ruled on and you are instructed by the judge to continue. If you continue talking or blurt out the answer to a question that has been objected to, it appears that you are trying to circumvent the rules, and your conduct becomes suspect to the jury. You might also cause a mistrial. By being careful and thoughtful in your testimony, you appear to be a knowledgeable player who abides by the rules of the game.

Trials are serious business. Avoid laughing and talking about the case or anything else in the presence of the jury or other witnesses, or anywhere in the area where you may be observed. Even though you are discussing an entirely different matter, your demeanor may be misunderstood.

Cross-Examination. After having experienced cross-examination, many witnesses might well agree with an expert on the law of evidence who writes, "It may be that in more than one sense it [cross-examination] takes the place in our system which torture occupied in the medieval system..."[2] Of cross-examination, Wigmore hastens to add, "Nevertheless, it is beyond any doubt the greatest legal engine ever designed for the discovery of truth." This "wonderful power" may be more fully appreciated after considering this explanation in an early case.[3]

> The power of cross-examination is the most efficacious test which the law has devised for the discovery of truth. Without it (oral) examinations...would be very unsafe: The ingenious witness, or still more ingenious examiner in chief, might easily evade the truth and at the same time avoid the pains of perjury. The right to be confronted with the witness, and to sift the truth out of a mingled mass of ignorance, prejudice, passion and interest, in which it is often hid, is among the very strongest bulwarks of justice. By means of it the situation of the witness with respect to the parties and to the subject of litigation; his interest, his motives, his inclinations and prejudices; his means of obtaining a correct and certain knowledge of the facts to which he bears testimony; the manner in which he has used some of those means; his powers of discernment, memory and description; are all fully investigated and ascertained, and submitted to the consideration of the jury.

Whether or not you as a witness agree with this statement of legal principle, there are ways to make cross-examination less "torturous." You should relax and take each question as it comes. Do not argue, but remain calm and polite, regardless of the attorney's tactics. Telling the truth and remaining pleasant and courteous will assure your credibility. Answer these questions as you would any others. Information honestly given cannot cause trouble. Only when you contradict yourself can your testimony be shown as unworthy of belief. Your courtesy will require courtesy in return or reveal the cross-examiner's tactics as being unfair to you and therefore resented by the jury. You should testify deliberately on cross-examination, rather than hurriedly, so that your attorney can offer an objection, should one be necessary. If there is no objection, answer the question. Do not substitute your own idea of what you think the rules of evidence should be. Courtroom strategy sometimes dictates that an attorney not object to questions, even if they are clearly improper.

When it seems advantageous, the cross-examiner may ask, "Have you talked to anybody about this case?" The answer to that question will undoubtedly be yes, and that should be your response. If you say that you have not, everyone knows that is incorrect, because attorneys routinely discuss facts of the case with witnesses prior to trial. There is no harm in saying that you have discussed the facts with whomever you have talked to in preparation for your court appearance.

Avoid the appearance of being cocky and overconfident, and, therefore, disrespectful. Control of your emotions will make you appear confident and prepared. A lawyer who can make you angry will probably cause you to exaggerate and appear less than objective in your testimony. You should be impartial but not to the point of being indifferent. Do not appear to have bias or feelings about the case. This invites damage to your credibility, and the jury may disregard your testimony in whole or in part. While it is difficult to work long and hard on

Table 12.1 Common Tactics of Cross-Examination

Counsel's tactic	Example	Purpose	Officer's response
Rapid-fire questions	One question after another with little time to answer.	To confuse the witness; an attempt to force inconsistent answers.	Take time to consider the question; be deliberate in answering; ask to have the question repeated, remain calm.
Condescending counsel	Benevolent approach, over-sympathetic in questions to the point of ridicule.	To give the impression that the witness is inept, lacks confidence, or may not be reliable.	Give firm, decisive answers; ask for the question to be repeated if improperly phrased.
Friendly counsel	Very courteous, polite; questions tend to take witness into counsel's confidence.	To lull the witness into a false sense of security so that answers in favor of the defense will be given.	Stay alert; bear in mind that purpose of defense is to discredit or diminish the effect of your testimony.
Badgering, belligerent	Counsel stares witness right in the face; shouts, "That *is so*, isn't it, officer?"	To make the witness angry enough to lose sense of logic and calmness. Generally, rapid questions will also be included in this approach.	Stay calm; speak in a deliberate voice, giving prosecutor time to make appropriate objections.
Mispronouncing officer's name; using wrong rank	Officer's name is Jansen, counsel calls him Johnson.	To draw the witness's attention to the error in pronunciation rather than to the question asked so that the witness will make inadvertent errors in testimony.	Ignore the mispronunciation and concentrate on the question counsel is asking.
Restrictive question	"Did you discuss this case with anyone?"	A no answer will place the officer in a position of denying having had pretrial conferences. A yes answer would be used to imply that the officer has been told how to testify.	"I have discussed the case with the prosecuting attorney and other officers working on the case. No one has told me how to testify."
Suggestive question (tends to be a leading question allowable on cross-examination)	"Was the color of the car blue?"	To suggest an answer to the question in an attempt to confuse or to lead the witness.	Concentrate carefully on the facts; disregard the suggestion; answer the question.

Table 12.1 Common Tactics of Cross-Examination (*Continued*)

Counsel's tactic	Example	Purpose	Officer's response
Demanding a yes or no answer to a question that needs explanation.	"Did you strike the defendant with your club?"	To prevent all pertinent and mitigating details from being considered by the jury.	Explain the answer to the question; if stopped by the counsel demanding a yes or no answer, pause until the court instructs you to answer in your own words.
Reversing witness's words	Witness answers, "The accident occurred 27 feet from the intersection." Counsel says, "You say the accident occurred 72 feet from the intersection?"	To confuse the witness and demonstrate the witness's lack of confidence.	Listen intently whenever counsel repeats something you have said. Correct any errors.
Repetitious questions	The same question asked several times slightly rephrased.	To obtain inconsistent or conflicting answers from the witness.	Listen carefully to the question and state, "I have just answered that question."
Conflicting answers	"But, Officer Smith, Detective Brown just said...," and so on.	To show inconsistency in the investigation. This tactic is normally used on measurements, times, etc.	Remain calm. Conflicting statements have a tendency to make a witness extremely nervous. Be guarded in your answers on measurements, times, etc. Unless you have exact knowledge, use the term "approximately." Refer to your notes.
Staring	After the witness has answered, counsel just stares as though there were more to come.	To have a long pause that one normally feels must be filled thus saying more than necessary. To provoke the witness into offering more than the question called for.	Wait for the next question.

SOURCE: International Association of Chiefs of Police, Inc., adopted for use in this section with permission.

a case and not become emotionally involved in it, you should not allow personal feelings to influence your testimony or demeanor on the stand. To do so will color your testimony and damage your presentation. For more information as how best to handle specific types of cross-examination techniques, see Table 12.1.

When your testimony has been completed and you are asked to come down from the witness stand, do so with an expression of confidence but not a smile. Be businesslike and unhurried, but do not act triumphant or overconfident; nor should you appear downcast or defeated if things did not go as well as you would have liked. Remember, this is the last chance that the judge or jury will have to gauge you and your testimony; they should be left with the impression that you are a knowledgeable and trustworthy witness who has told the truth.

NOTES

[1]John J. Horgan, *Criminal Investigation*, 2d ed. (New York: McGraw-Hill, 1979), Chap. 9.

[2]John H. Wigmore, *Evidence*, 3d ed. (New York: Little, Brown, 1940), S1367, Vol. 5, p. 29.

[3]Administrators of *McCleskey v. Leadbetter* [1 Georgia 551 (1846)].

13
Process Service

Michael P. Seniuk

When the first American settlers came to this country, they brought with them many of the legal institutions and systems of the country from which they emigrated. The initial settlements, since they were English in background, adopted much of the English system, with certain modifications. One of the systems that was continued was the function of the sheriff. In England, the monarch normally appointed a representative to a shire, known as "the reeve," whose duty it was to represent the king in all civil and criminal matters.

Although the present sheriff's duties encompass both civil and criminal law enforcement, it is essential to understand the probably more complex civil aspect of the sheriff's duties.

In the field of civil law, the sheriff's duties involve the discovery and seizure of property, the arrest of individuals, and service and enforcement of a great variety of mandates, orders, and decrees of the civil courts. These duties affect the rights and privileges of others at every turn and involve problems and questions of law to a high degree. More often than not, these problems and questions must be handled at the time they occur. The legal aspect of the sheriff's duties is emphasized by a unique personal liability, not only for the sheriff's own acts and omissions, but also for those of any deputies or employees in the sheriff's office. This personal liability is found woven throughout the tapestry of most state constitutions.

The purpose of process service is to notify a defendant that legal proceedings are instituted. Failure to do this properly, either through an illegal act or by omission of a required act, may seriously impair or prejudice an individual's rights.

The sheriff's civil responsibilities in this matter have increased dramatically with the Family Court Acts. Family courts, which were initially established as courts of reconciliation and with an interest in the welfare of children, have changed over the years to become quasi-criminal in function. It is imperative that anyone serving in the field of investigation be aware of the civil process, including those mandates of the family court. Since, however, family court procedures vary considerably from jurisdiction to jurisdiction within the 50 states, specialized process service relative to local situations is not treated here. Rather, the following outline reflects the usual procedures for executing civil process in general and represents a combination of basic principles and sound practical experience.

LEGAL REQUIREMENTS BY TYPES OF SERVICE

The Natural Person

A *natural person*—one other than a partnership, corporate officer, and so on—can be served with a summons by one of the following methods, of which the first that should be attempted is delivery to the person to be served.

The second is delivery to a person of suitable age and discretion at the actual place of business, residence, or usual place of abode of the person to be served and mailing a copy of the summons to the person to be served at the last known residence. (If a copy is not mailed, the service will be invalid.) *Suitable age and discretion* means a person who is able to understand the nature and purpose of the delivery of the summons to him or her. For example, it would be proper service to deliver the summons to a defendant's 20-year-old son but improper to deliver it to a 5-year-old son. Also, it would be improper to serve a defendant's mentally incapacitated 35-year-old brother.

The third method (if service by the first two methods cannot be made with "due diligence") is affixing the summons to the door of either the actual place of business, home, or usual place of abode within the state of the person to be served and mailing the summons to that person at his or her last known residence. This form of service is commonly called *nail and mail* and should be employed with caution. First, without a court order to do so, you cannot nail and mail a summons in a matrimonial action (divorce, separation, and so on). Further, *due diligence* has generally been held to mean that you have made every reasonable attempt to personally deliver the summons to the defendant; in other words, that you have made more than one or two attempts at various times during the day and evening. *Affixing to the door* means exactly that. *Do not* put the summons in an envelope and then attach the envelope to the door. Any procedure other than prominently displaying the summons on the door will probably invalidate the service. Likewise, putting the summons in a mail receptacle would constitute a bad service. Before resorting to this method of service, it is recommended that you discuss it with the person who gave the summons to you for service. If the person suggests that you proceed, this directive should be put in a letter of instructions to you. Since they will be required in your proof of service, keep very accurate notes of your attempts at service. (The proof will be discussed in more detail later.) Nail and mail service will be invalid if you fail to mail a copy to the defendant at his or her *last known residence*. If either the second or third methods are used, you must mail the summons to the defendant at the last known residence, which may not necessarily be the same address to which you delivered the summons.

Fourth, a court may direct the manner in which a summons is to be served. If you receive such an order, read it over very carefully to make sure that you comply with every provision it contains. Again, if you fail to carry out any provision of the order, the service will be invalid.

Fifth, a natural person, partnership, or corporation may designate a person as agent for service. To be considered valid, this designation must be filed with the county clerk of the county in which the parties reside or do business. Generally, this type of service is not made unless instructed by the person who delivered the summons for service. Furthermore, this type of service cannot be used for matrimonial actions.

Infants

An *infant* is a natural person who is less than 18 years of age. Service on an infant is made by serving within the state a parent, guardian, or any person having legal custody of the infant. If the infant is married, an *adult* spouse with whom the infant lives must also be served; if none of these are within the state, a person with whom the infant resides or his or her employer is served. An infant 14 years of age or older must also be served within the state. When the service concerns an infant, you will usually receive specific instructions from the person requesting the service.

Incompetents

A person declared incompetent is served by serving the incompetent *and* the committee appointed to manage the individual's affairs; the court, however, may dispense with service on the incompetent. Once again, usually you will receive specific instructions on this type of service from the person delivering the summons to you.

Partnerships

Service is made on a partnership by serving *any* partner; however, caution must be used. Service on a manager of a store who is not a partner in the partnership owning the store would be invalid.

Corporations

Service on a corporation is made by serving an officer, director, managing or general agent, cashier or assistant cashier, or any other agent authorized by appointment or by law to receive service. Good service can be made, for example, on the president, treasurer, or claims manager. Service on an office secretary or security guard who is not authorized by appointment to receive service is a common mistake.

Service on the State

Service is made on the State by serving the attorney general or any assistant attorney general. You may, however, receive a summons with instructions to serve a specific state official. In this case, you would, of course, serve the person you have been instructed to serve.

Governmental Subdivisions

Service on governmental subdivisions is made by delivering the summons as follows:

City: To the mayor, comptroller, treasurer, counsel, or clerk or, if the city lacks such officers, to an officer performing a corresponding function under another name. There may be exceptions; for example, on the City of New York, it would be to the corporation counsel or to any person designated by the corporation counsel to receive process in a writing filed in the office of the Clerk of New York County.

County: To the chairman or clerk of the board of supervisors, clerk, attorney, or treasurer.

Town: To the supervisor or clerk.

Village: To the mayor, clerk, or any trustee.

Park, sewage, or other district: To the clerk, any trustee, or any member of the board.

School district: To a school official as defined in the Education Law.

Some of the officers listed above may be known by equivalent titles. For example, the board of supervisors may be known as the "board of representatives" or the "county legislature" in your county. Make certain that you serve the appropriate officer and not an office clerk.

Other Types of Service

Although the other types of special service are too numerous to list in their entirety, the following will serve as examples: service of out-of-state papers, service on a court, and service on a secretary of state. In all such cases, the instructions given by the person requesting the service should be followed to the letter. Additional types of service commonly used include:

Citations. Issued by the surrogate's court, citations are similar to summonses except that personal delivery is required unless some other manner of service is directed by the court. Citations must be served at least 10 days prior to the hearing date specified in the citations. Only the court can dispense with this requirement.

Show Cause Orders. Since they usually require a specific manner of service to be made within a relatively short period, every show cause order should be read very carefully before serving. It is not uncommon for this type of process to require service within 24 hours of its issuance to be valid.

Subpoena. Here are three details to watch for when serving a subpoena: (1) A subpoena is usually directed to a witness, and the witness is not usually the defendant. (2) You are frequently directed to tender a fee to the witness when making service. (3) Subpoenas must be served before the time set for appearance. Obviously, if you do not serve the subpoena on the witness sometime prior to the time set for the appearance, the service is useless.

PRACTICAL MEANS TO ACHIEVE THE LEGAL REQUIREMENTS

All the elements of service must be complete before the statute of limitations expires for valid service. For example, you have a summons for service and the statute of limitations for that summons expires at midnight tonight. You have delivered a copy of the summons to a person of suitable age and discretion, but you have not mailed a copy. The mailing must be made before midnight. Usually you will not have the faintest idea when the statute expires, so make your service promptly. If the plaintiff or the plaintiff's attorney tells you that a statute is about to expire, you would be well-advised to give the process your immediate attention. If the plaintiff *withdraws the process,* as sometimes happens, ask that it be done in writing.

Proof of Service

You have made your service, and now you must provide the plaintiff with a means to prove to the court that you made a proper service.

Proof of Service of a Summons

Generally: Proof of service shall specify the papers served; the person who was served; and the date, time, address or (in the event there is no address) place, and manner of service; and set forth facts showing that the service was made by an authorized person and in an authorized manner.

Description: Proof of service shall contain a description of the person served. If service on the natural person is made by personal delivery or to a person of suitable age and discretion or to an agent for service, the proof shall also include a description of the person delivery was made to. Such description shall include—but not be limited to—sex, color of skin, hair color, approximate age, approximate weight and height, and other identifying features. If the nail and mail method was used, the proof must contain a record of the dates, times, and addresses of attempted personal delivery. Until recently, a description was required only of a natural person served. Now, however, all persons served with a summons, including corporate officers, must be described.

Other Proofs. Many times plaintiffs or their attorneys will supply you with their own certificates or affidavits. Matrimonial actions, out-of-state papers, and many other types of service require special proof forms; if, therefore, the plaintiff supplies you with a form, it is generally good practice to use it rather than your own form.

Time Limits Relating to Proofs. It is essential that proofs of service be executed as quickly as possible. For example, if service is made on a natural person by delivery to a person of suitable age and discretion or by nail and mail, the proof must be filed by the plaintiff within 20 days of the date of service.

Making the Service

As noted earlier, the purpose of process service is to notify a defendant that legal proceedings are instituted. The following key points are suggested as practical guidelines for performing this all-important function.

Locating Person to Be Served. Presumably you have been provided with an address for service and possibly a letter of instructions. If you are lucky, you have also been provided with a brief description of the person to be served. Proceed to the address and make the service. If you cannot locate the person, make inquiry in the neighborhood to find the individual's whereabouts. If the person has moved to another location in your county, proceed to the new address. Limit inquiries when attempting to locate a person. Common sense would dictate, first, that you probably have other papers that deserve equal attention and, second, that you are not looking for an escaped felon. More specifically, do not invite the whole neighborhood to a glimpse of someone's private affairs. Use discretion!

Identifying the Person to Be Served. There seems to be no way to compel persons to identify themselves. An identification by a neighbor or coworker is usually safe, but remember that service on natural persons, members of their households, or their agents requires that you record a description of the person served. When serving a corporation or government body, it is important to make sure you are serving an authorized person. A description of such officers or agents is also necessary here. If you are not sure you have the proper person for service, it is good practice to seek further advice from the plaintiff before proceeding.

Persons Privileged from Service. Some classes of people are legally immune from service. This, however, is not generally a matter for you to determine. In most cases, you should proceed with the service, since the person claiming immunity has legal means available to prove that immunity. Again, discretion is advised.

Gaining Entrance to Premises. Your entrance into any premises must be peaceful. If the entrance door is locked, you would be ill-advised to break in; however, if you are invited into a premises, you might reasonably enter to find the individual you are seeking. If you gain peaceful entrance and subsequently are ordered off the premises after searching for that person, you should leave at once. Remember, you are not acting under authority of a search warrant and therefore could be guilty of trespass. Use discretion!

The Service. Usually, a true copy of the process is delivered to the person to be served. It is not necessary to touch the person to be served with the process. If the individual refuses to accept service, leave a copy in such a manner that it can readily be reached. Do not forget to comply with any special instructions given to you.

Substituted Service on the Natural Person. In this situation, you may be confronted with a variety of interesting problems to solve. Following are some typical examples: You have a summons to serve on a person who resides in a 12-story apartment complex. The front entrance is locked. You cannot affix a copy of the summons to the entrance door for a nail and mail service. Therefore, you must gain entrance to the building and attach the summons to the door of the individual's apartment. Fearing that someone will remove the summons from the apartment door, frequently a conscientious process server decides to slip the summons under the door. Do not be that discreet! The law clearly states that you must affix the summons to the door. Any other procedure is bad service.

In serving a person of suitable age and discretion on behalf of a natural person, you must serve a member of the defendant's household, not the security guard or the tenant in the neighboring apartment. The law states that the residence of the person is to be served and not someone else's residence.

Pitfalls to Avoid in Making the Service

- Do not make the service on Sunday. In most jurisdictions, service of process on Sunday is void. Service on Saturday on a person who observes that day as the Sabbath is a crime, but only if the service was made "maliciously," that is, with a knowledge of such observance.

- Do not state anything about a certificate or affidavit of service that is not true.

- Do not conceal process in any way or for any reason. Do not conceal a summons in an envelope when delivering it, even if you do so to avoid embarrassment. (If you must, avoid embarrassment by standing close enough to the defendant to avoid anyone seeing what you are doing.)

- Do not use trickery or deceit to effect service. You should be resourceful, but do not represent the process to be something that it is not.

- Do not give legal advice to anyone whom you are serving. This is a matter for attorneys. In other words, do not advise on the specifics of responding to a summons, even if you know. You should, of course, tell the individual what the process is that you are serving.

- Do not take back the process after making service.

- Do not use unreasonable force in effecting service. Protect yourself from assault if a defendant takes unwarranted steps against you, but do not restrain anyone physically merely to make a service.

A SHERIFF'S CIVIL ARREST IN PROCESS SERVICE

A civil arrest is made pursuant to a written order signed by a judge of competent jurisdiction in a civil action or proceeding. The sheriff makes arrests pursuant to the orders of the supreme court, the family court, the surrogate's court, the county court, and the district courts of his county. He or she may also be called upon to make arrests pursuant to orders or warrants of courts of criminal jurisdiction.

Definition of Arrest

To make an arrest, there must be an intent to arrest under a real or apparent authority by a seizure or detention of the person. The defendant should understand that he or she is being arrested. The following elements must be present. The deputy must acquire control of the person to be arrested. The usual method of control is the touching or seizure of the body of the subject. There must be restraint. However, the manual touching of the defendant is not necessary when the defendant, recognizing the authority of the deputy, submits to custody.

At the time of arrest, the deputy should have in possession the original arrest process, or a certified copy if the original was filed with the court, and should serve a certified copy of the arrest order on the defendant.

The Civil Arrest Process

Civil arrests may be made under the following arrest processes: (1) order of arrest, (2) commitment for contempt, (3) attachment against the person, and (4) warrant of arrest.

Order of Arrest. As a provisional remedy, order of arrest may be granted at the discretion of the court without notice; before or after service of summons; and at any time before judgment or, in some instances, after judgment. It should specify the amount of bail, be endorsed with the name and address of the plaintiff's attorney, and be directed to the sheriff of any county wherein the defendant may be located. The order should command that the defendant be arrested and kept in custody by the sheriff and brought before the court in the county where arrest was made for a hearing within the time specified in the order, not exceeding 48 hours, exclusive of Sundays and public holidays, from the time of arrest. Here, local qualifications may apply. For example, the defendant may have to be produced in the county of arrest.

Commitment for Contempt. Under this process, the person arrested must be confined to the jail until the fine fixed in the order is paid or the act required by the court performed. Orders should be read carefully. In some cases, the defendant must pay a fine *and* perform the act required by the order.

Attachment against the Person. Attachments against the person may be bailable or nonbailable. The most common attachment is bailable and is issued for the purpose of having the sheriff produce the defendant in court to show cause why he or she should not be adjudged guilty of contempt or failure to obey a subpoena or order in the enforcement proceedings, for instance (either as a defendant or as a witness), or for failure to obey an injunction.

Bailable Attachment. One method of processing a bailable attachment is to have it submitted to the court by the plaintiff's attorney with the date and place of appearance noted thereon. This method permits the court to control the process.

There is also a nonbailable attachment that may be issued to the sheriff to require the arrest and production of a person who has refused or neglected to obey a writ of habeas corpus. Upon satisfactory proof that a person is wrongfully detained and will be removed from the state or suffer injury, a court authorized to issue such a writ may issue an attachment requiring the immediate production of the detained person before the court.

Preparation for the Arrest. Most of the many difficulties involved in making a civil arrest are caused by lack of preparation and carelessness. Each process must be executed in accordance with the directions it contains. When an arrest process is received, the deputy should read it carefully and then determine what is required of the deputy and what is required of the defendant or other person to be arrested. The process may direct the arrested person to pay a fine or to perform an act, or it may permit the individual to post bail. If questions arise regarding legal matters, the deputy should confer with a superior officer.

Identification. Before attempting to execute the process, the deputy should obtain as much information as possible from plaintiff's attorney; that is, a detailed description of the person, a recent photo if possible, the defendant's place of business or occupation, and so on.

Unattended Children. If the defendant is a woman, the deputy should ascertain if she has young children who cannot be left unattended. If this is the case and the process is a bailable attachment, postpone the arrest until a plan can be worked out with plaintiff's attorney. If the arrest process is a contempt order and the attorney insists on its execution despite the absence of anyone with whom the children may be left, you must get in touch with higher authorities, including the department of social services, to make arrangements for having them take charge of the children.

Assistance. Except in emergencies, a deputy should not attempt to make an arrest without a partner. First, resistance may be encountered or a second person may be needed to guard an exit from the premises. Second, a partner's presence may deter an attempt at resistance or escape. Finally, should a dispute arise as to whether an arrest was or should have been made, or should there be a complaint regarding the manner in which it was made, the testimony of the partner will prove most helpful.

In our experience, the policy of having a representative of the plaintiff accompany the deputy is of dubious value. In most cases, it tends to create an atmosphere of hostility and tension and does not make the deputy's task any easier. If, however, the fine or bail is unusually large and there is danger that the defendant may attempt to flee the jurisdiction, then accompaniment by a representative may be helpful. Furthermore, in a difficult case, the representative may prove helpful in establishing the fact that the defendant is not available.

Time and Place. To aid in determining the best time to make an arrest, the deputy should become familiar with the defendant's habits and hours of employment.

If there is a choice between a home arrest and a place-of-business or outside-the-home arrest, the place of business is preferable for the following reasons: first, the deputy will not encounter the problem of gaining peaceful entry; and, second, there will be present no spouse, child, or other relative to excite the defendant. The next best place for arrest is on the street outside the home.

If the arrest must be made at the defendant's home, the best time is early in the morning, since most individuals have a set time to go to work.

Wherever arrest is to be made, make sure all exits are covered.

Direct Approach. A direct approach is best. If the defendant is not at home and a spouse or other relative asks the purpose of the visit, the deputy sheriff should not hesitate to identify himself or herself as a deputy sheriff with an arrest process. How to dispose of the process is the obligation (and worry) of the defendant and the defendant's family.

When approaching the person believed to be the defendant, the deputy should address the individual by the name appearing in the process. If the response is positive, identification and an announcement of possession of an order for the person's arrest should be made by the deputy. When the deputy is sure of being in the presence of the correct individual, the person then should be taken into custody and given a copy of the arrest papers.

If the alleged defendant denies being the person named in the process, the deputy should require proof of identity. If the individual refuses, the deputy must try to learn the person's true identity. Obviously, refusal to show identification constitutes a suspicious circumstance. If the individual otherwise fits a deputy's description, inquiry is made of neighbors, and so on, and there appears to be no doubt concerning the person's identity, the arrest can be made. If, however, there is the slightest doubt, the deputy should back off and attempt to obtain further proof.

Saturdays and Sundays. Except for a writ of habeas corpus or an injunction if the court issuing it so directs, civil process may not be served or executed on a Sunday. A civil arrest may not be made on a Sunday. Furthermore, any person who keeps Saturday as the Sabbath may not be arrested on a Saturday; hence, it is not good practice to arrest an Orthodox or observing Jew after sundown on Friday.

Arrest in Courthouse. Unless the permission of the presiding judge is obtained first, an arrest should never be made in a courtroom. An arrest should not be made in another part of the courthouse unless there is no other location where the process can be executed and unless the arrest can be made without interrupting or disturbing the proceedings of the court.

Arrest on Federal Property. Although extreme caution must be used, in general, an arrest process may be executed on federal property. An inquiry, however, must be made to determine if the federal property in question comes under state jurisdiction so that civil and criminal process may be executed therein. For example, the state has not reserved jurisdiction over lands owned by the United Nations. Local officers may enter the United Nations headquarters district to perform official duties or to serve legal process only with the consent of and under conditions approved by the Secretary General.

Privilege from Arrest. Certain classes of people are privileged from arrest by specific state, federal, and local enactments. A deputy is most likely to encounter the following categories:

- *Witness and parties:* A person duly subpoenaed as a witness or a litigant duly ordered to attend for the purpose of being examined is exempt from arrest. This privilege must be claimed by the individual, whether a witness or a litigant, who must sign an affidavit to having been legally subpoenaed or ordered to attend. The affidavit must specify the court or officer, place of attendance, and cause in which the person was subpoenaed or ordered. Should a situation of this type occur, it is advisable to check with a superior officer.

  A nonresident witness or civil litigant who voluntarily comes into the jurisdiction for the sole purpose of participating in a lawsuit or other court proceeding is exempt not only from arrest but also from the service of any process.

- *Diplomats:* Ambassadors or public ministers of any foreign state, received as such by the President, are exempt from arrest, as are members of their families and their domestic servants.

- *Legislators:* Members of Congress are exempt while going to, attending, or returning from session. Members of the state legislature are exempt while attending sessions and for 14 days before or after each session.

- *Military:* Members of the armed forces in active service are exempt.

- *Police officers and firefighters:* Members of the police and fire departments, while on actual duty, are exempt. They may be arrested either before beginning or after completing their usual tour of duty. Hence, a volunteer firefighter would be exempt while answering an alarm, during the emergency, and until dismissed by a superior officer after the emergency.

Defendants in Criminal Cases. A resident defendant in a criminal proceeding is not exempt from civil arrest either coming from or going to court; also not exempt is a nonresident defendant in a criminal proceeding who is brought in by compulsion of law or who is extradited.

Difference in Defendant's Name. A difference in the name of the suspected defendant from the name appearing in the process is a warning that the purported defendant may be the wrong individual. If the first or last name is different from that in the process, do not make the arrest. If the first name is fictitious, the process may not be executed unless the person is sufficiently described in the process so as to be positively identified. A fictitious name without proper description of the defendant makes the process void.

Claim of Illness. If there is a claim of serious illness, the deputy should not make the arrest immediately. When satisfied that the defendant is too ill to be removed, the deputy should communicate with the defendant's doctor and the plaintiff's attorney. If, in the doctor's opinion, the defendant is too ill to be removed, the deputy can apply to the court for instructions through a supervisor.

Performance of an Act. When a commitment requires the defendant to perform an act and to pay a fine and the individual offers to do both at the time of arrest, the deputy may safely take the fine. Whether the defendant may be released upon performance of the act depends on the nature of the act. If the act to be performed is simple, the plaintiff's attorney can be called upon to supervise the performance of the act and to state in writing that it has been performed. As is more often the case, if the process requires a more complicated act, such as an accounting by the defendant in either the supreme or the surrogate's court, the defendant should be released only by order of the court.

Authority of Attorney. The attorney has a right to withdraw any arrest process before it is executed. The plaintiff can discharge the attorney at any time and may give the sheriff written directions to release the defendant. In this event, do not release the prisoner without an order of the court unless both the plaintiff and the attorney consent in writing. The plaintiff's signature must be notarized.

Defendant's Address. A deputy may not break into a defendant's home, so may not chase the defendant into the home and subsequently break in to make the arrest. If, on the other hand, the arrest has already been made and the defendant escapes, then the deputy may chase the defendant into the home and break down all barriers necessary to effect a recapture. It is best not to break into a third person's home except to recapture a person who has escaped unless (1) you are certain that the defendant is inside, and (2) your proper demand for peaceful admission is refused after you make known your authority and purpose.

Interference. Willful resistance or interference with a deputy who is executing an arrest process or otherwise attempting to discharge an official duty constitutes a misdemeanor and renders the offender subject to arrest, as does the taking of levied personal property from a deputy's possession or willfully injuring or destroying it. Additionally, any resistance that results in the actual assault of the deputy is deemed a felony. These drastic provisions, however, should be reserved for use in only the most extreme cases; moreover, a deputy should exercise patience and forbearance even in the face of great provocation.

Use of Force. The deputy may use such force as is reasonably required by the circumstances. Although a deputy need not take a beating from anyone, nonetheless, only such force may be used as is commensurate with the resistance encountered.

Opportunity to Raise Bail. In an arrest order, the deputy must give the defendant a reasonable opportunity to raise bail or fine. A defendant whose affairs cannot be settled in a short time may make payment or raise bail while in jail.

CONCLUSION

Process service is a highly specialized function that requires a thorough understanding of the principles and practices used, combined with sound practical experience. An attempt to answer every question that might be encountered would, of course, be unrealistic; nonetheless, it is hoped that the foregoing guide will prove helpful. Most important, the deputy must not violate public trust and confidence by knowingly prejudicing any individual's rights. Be fair and impartial. Make your services promptly and in a legal, professional manner. Execute your proofs of service promptly. Remember that you play an integral part in the administration of justice.

14

Civil and Criminal Environmental Investigations

Robin Stone Einbinder, Esq.

Joel K. Dranove, Esq.

During the past decade, Americans have become increasingly aware of the environment and of the importance of maintaining the delicate balance of nature within the biosphere. The "greening" of America has manifested itself in many forms, from activist Greenpeace demonstrations to Star Trek "Save-the-Whale" movie plots and celebrations of "Earth Day," from the introduction of biodegradable containers to the return of the home-delivered glass milk bottle.[1] Whether expressing concern for the quality of the air we breathe and the purity of our rivers and lakes, demanding a ban on fluorocarbon aerosol cans to protect the ozone layer in the stratosphere, or agitating for active enforcement of legislation designed to remediate soils and groundwaters already contaminated with hazardous chemicals and wastes, Americans in the 1990s are aware of their dependency on the environment. They are demanding radical changes to preserve and protect natural resources for ourselves and for future generations. Haunted by the specter of Love Canal, New York and Times Beach, Missouri,[2] the environmental agenda has reemerged as a major issue not only for federal, state, and local governments, but for industry as well.

This chapter briefly discusses the industrial pollution of America's natural resources, and the enactment of federal legislation designed to regulate future handling of hazardous waste as well as to identify, clean up, and remediate sites previously contaminated by hazardous wastes. The chapter describes the scope of the strict liability scheme of this legislation[3] and its potential impact on any entity directly or indirectly involved in the generation, transport, or disposal of

The views expressed herein are the authors' and do not necessarily represent those of their firm or their clients.

hazardous wastes. The chapter concludes with a discussion of civil and criminal environmental investigations, and considerations that should be addressed in responding to governmental enforcement activities.

THE INDUSTRIAL POLLUTION OF AMERICA

Although industry is not solely responsible for the widespread pollution existing in the United States, in many instances, corporate ignorance, apathy, and efforts to maximize profits have in combination resulted in widespread environmental contamination. During the 1940s and 1950s, in the absence of environmental regulation and public awareness of the potential threat of hazardous waste contamination, many companies routinely disposed of their hazardous wastes by dumping them on the grounds of their facilities or into nearby rivers and lakes. For example, in the early 1950s, a small company was established in southern New Jersey to manufacture arsenic-based pesticides. The company routinely stored its arsenic waste salts in open piles on its property. Although the company later dug concrete pits in which to store these wastes, the amount of waste salts frequently exceeded the capacity of the pits. By 1985, not only were the soils at the plant site highly contaminated with arsenic, but the contamination had also leached into the groundwaters underlying the site, and had spread into the Blackwater Branch of the Maurice River, the Maurice River itself, and Union Lake, an impoundment on the river several miles downstream. The United States Environmental Protection Agency (EPA) eventually added the company's site to the National Priorities List (NPL) of Superfund sites, and has commenced legal action to force the company to pay the estimated multimillion-dollar clean-up costs.[4]

After scientists became aware of the dangers posed by improper disposal of or exposure to hazardous wastes,[5] many companies or individuals involved in generating or handling hazardous waste deliberately chose not to comply with environmentally sound or legislatively mandated disposal practices, in order to increase corporate profits by saving on expensive disposal or processing fees. In one notorious case, a major manufacturer of chemical products and phenoxy herbicides, including Agent Orange, operated a chemical plant in Newark, New Jersey, which abutted the Passaic River. According to the findings of a New Jersey Superior Court judge, the company intentionally discharged all of its waste chemical effluents into the Passaic River from 1951 to 1956, notwithstanding that such discharges had been forbidden by specific statutory enactments since at least 1931. Moreover, although the company had purportedly tied its plant into the Passaic Valley Sewerage District, which was intent on enforcing the no-discharge laws, the company managed to continue its illegal discharges into the river through the use of a by-pass system permitting direct discharges from the main plant building, as well as an alarm system to warn employees to cease such discharges when Passaic Valley inspectors were on the premises. In addition, from 1951 through 1969, constant spills onto the floors and ground surfaces of the plant building drained mostly into the river. The court found that from 1951 through 1969, as part of a consistent, deliberate company policy, the plant regularly discharged into the Passaic River 2,4,5-T-acid, dioxin, DDT, caustic soda, DDT, sulfuric acid, TCP, muriatic acid, and monochlorobenzene, all of which are on the federal government's list of hazardous substances.[6]

Similar environmental "horror stories" abound. In March 1982, New York State Senator Ralph J. Marino, then Chairman of the New York Senate Select

Committee on Crime, published a report entitled *Hazardous Waste Landfill Dumping: The Consequences of Non-Enforcement of Environmental Conservation Law in New York State,* based on material compiled from documents obtained in part from the New York State Department of Environmental Conservation (DEC). The Marino report described the alleged machinations of Russell W. Mahler, owner and president of several fuel oil companies, and it castigated the DEC for failing to investigate properly and to enforce laws protecting the environment. According to the Marino report, in 1976, one of Mahler's companies, Northeast Fuel Oil Service of Syracuse, Inc., was caught discharging hazardous waste from a tank farm in Syracuse, New York into the Syracuse sanitary sewer system, which leads into Lake Onondaga. Due to alleged DEC inefficiency, the subsequent corporate owners of the tank farm, Anchor Oil Company and Hudson Oil Company, both of which companies were headed by Mahler, purportedly continued discharging large quantities of oil into the sewers. A state investigation ultimately revealed that all the storage tanks at the tank farm had "drain down valves," and that the city sewer system had been used illegally for years as a means of disposing of hazardous wastes. The report also alleged that Mahler's companies transported and dumped hazardous wastes in College Point Lagoon in Queens, New York, and down a borehole in Pittston, Pennsylvania, as well as spilled or buried millions of gallons of hazardous wastes in Long Island City, New York, and at various New York City municipal landfills.[7]

Incidents such as these enraged the public, and have propelled both federal and state governments to enact legislation to prevent future contamination and to impose liability on those responsible for the widespread pollution that already exists. Today, even small businesses are not immune to the constraints of regulatory oversight, and most industries have willingly joined the environmental bandwagon. Indeed, in contrast to the seemingly callous disregard for environmental consequences demonstrated by commercial manufacturers less than 40 years ago, industry today is generally highly sensitive to public concerns about widespread pollution, and is anxious to improve its corporate image and to promote itself as environmentally sensitive. Many companies openly tout their recycled, energy-efficient, or nonhazardous products, and are quick to publicize their adherence to "politically correct" principles governing protection of the environment.[8] Several corporations, reluctant to demonstrate a firm commitment to environmental protection, have begun to face stockholder resolutions, orchestrated by various coalitions of environmentally concerned groups and specifically designed to force corporations not only to comply with statutory or regulatory enactments, but also to join in emerging international policies to clean up and to protect the environment for future generations.[9] While these measures and developments potentially bode well for the prevention of future contamination, they do not alleviate the overwhelming problem of the existing—and spreading—contamination of our natural resources.

THE ENACTMENT OF ENVIRONMENTAL LEGISLATION

Since the early 1970s, Congress has enacted several varied laws to protect, preserve, or better the environment. Many states have also enacted environmental protection statutes and regulations to prosecute or fine alleged polluters, using federal statutes and regulations as a model.[10] Among the many federal environmental statutes are the:

- *Clean Air Act* [42 U.S.C. §7401 *et seq.*], which provides for air pollution prevention and control, established air quality and emissions limitations, and authorized measures to protect the ozone layer.

- *Clean Water Act*[11] [33 U.S.C. §1251 *et seq.*], which was enacted to "restore and maintain the chemical, physical and biological integrity of the Nation's waters," by providing funds for research and related programs and grants for construction of treatment works, and establishing standards for effluent emissions and for the enforcement of same.[12]

- *Marine Protection, Research and Sanctuaries Act of 1972 (Ocean Dumping Act)* [33 U.S.C. §1401 *et seq.*], enacted to regulate the transportation and dumping of material into ocean waters, and to identify and conserve marine areas and resources.

- *National Environmental Policy Act* [42 U.S.C. §4321 *et seq.*], which established the Council on Environmental Quality, and promotes efforts to prevent or eliminate damage to the environment and biosphere and to enrich our understanding of ecological systems and of the national natural resources.

- *Safe Drinking Water Act* [42 U.S.C. §300f *et seq.*], which established national drinking water regulations, and provides for the protection of underground sources of drinking water.

- *Resource Conservation and Recovery Act (Solid Waste Disposal Act, or RCRA)* [42 U.S.C. §6901 *et seq.*], which was enacted to promote the protection of health and the environment, and to conserve valuable energy and material resources, by promoting solid waste management plans, including resource recovery and conservation systems, and by regulating underground storage tanks, hazardous waste dumping and management. *RCRA* classified wastes, established a manifest system to identify and track wastes, and instituted record-keeping and reporting requirements for facilities handling hazardous wastes.[13]

The most well-known federal environmental statute, however, is probably the *Comprehensive Environmental Resource, Compensation and Liability Act of 1980 (CERCLA)*, more commonly called the *Superfund Act.*[14] CERCLA was enacted in December 1980 in response to the public outcry about the severe environmental and public health effects posed by improper disposal of hazardous materials: *See generally United States v. Maryland Bank & Trust Co.*, 632 F. Supp. 573, 576 (D. Md. 1986). In enacting CERCLA, Congress sought to implement a global strategy to contain, clean up, remove, and deal with this country's hazardous waste problems, by creating a federal "Superfund" of monies to remediate hazardous waste sites. The Act authorizes the EPA to list the nation's worst toxic waste sites, identify "potentially responsible parties" (PRPs), and sue the PRPs for any necessary clean-up costs. The policy underlying CERCLA is "to place the ultimate responsibility for cleaning up hazardous waste on those responsible for problems caused by the disposal of chemical poison." *See United States v. Fleet Factors Corp.*, 901 F.2d 1550 (11th Cir. 1990), citing *Florida Power & Light Co. v. Allis Chalmers Corp.*, 893 F.2d 1313, 1316 (11th Cir. 1990); *see also United States v. Aceto Agricultural Chems. Corp.*, 872 F.2d 1373 (8th Cir. 1989), and *Dedham Water Co. v. Cumberland Farms Dairy*, 805 F.2d 1074 (1st Cir. 1986). In particular, CERCLA authorizes the government to commence enforcement actions against PRPs under a strict liability scheme that imposes joint and several liability without regard to the PRP's actual knowledge of the contamination.

At present, the United States EPA is actively investigating hundreds of sites throughout this country,[15] in many cases aided by or working in conjunction with state and local environmental protection departments, including municipal or county health departments, in bringing enforcement actions. To establish a *prima facie* case in a cost recovery action brought under *CERCLA*, the government need only prove that the site at issue is a hazardous waste facility, a release or threat of release of any hazardous substance from the site has occurred, and the United States has incurred response costs. *See United States v. Conservation Chem. Co.*, 619 F. Supp. 162 (D. Mo. 1985).[16]

Under *CERCLA*, PRPs may include past and present owners[17] or operators of hazardous waste sites,[18] those who arranged for or generated the wastes at the site,[19] and those who transported the wastes.[20] The definition of *person* under *CERCLA* and similar state laws includes individuals, corporate entities, and local governments; as a consequence, many different "persons," including corporate officers, have found themselves potentially liable for significant clean-up costs incurred in responding to conditions at a hazardous waste site.[21] These costs may include such expenses as (a) preinvestigation studies of environmental conditions; (b) the costs of a remedial investigation performed by an environmental engineering firm acceptable to the federal and/or state agencies involved in overseeing the clean-up; (c) the development of a feasibility study setting forth various remedial alternatives for the site, with an attendant cost/benefit analysis; (d) preparation of a request for proposals by environmental engineering firms for a remedial design to implement the remedy selected by the federal and/or state oversight agency and published in a Record of Decision issued by the agency(ies); (e) the development of the remedial design; and (f) the implementation of the design itself, including the purchase or rental of necessary equipment, pipes, etc., the operation of the remedial mechanisms, with attendant monitoring of progress, and the disposal of wastes removed from the site.[22]

The sheer number of hazardous waste sites at which a PRP may be implicated, coupled with *CERCLA*'s broad definition of the PRP, has resulted in a plethora of third-party, fourth-party, and even fifth-party lawsuits aimed at finding other PRPs to share the frequently heavy financial burden attendant in remediating a Superfund hazardous waste site. Not surprisingly, while the addition of more parties to the lawsuit does offer a potentially larger pool of PRPs from which to pay the ultimate clean-up costs, the transaction costs incurred in expanding and coordinating the litigation, as well as the often precarious financial status of many of the PRPs, sometimes appear to outweigh the benefits derived therefrom. At some sites, such as landfills that operated for nearly a half-century, the list of PRPs that sent waste to the site may include businesses that are no longer in existence or individuals who are no longer alive.[23]

Municipalities that sent *municipal solid waste* (MSW) to landfills have been named as PRPs at several sites,[24] and the courts have thus far refused to exempt the municipalities from potential joint and several liability under *CERCLA*, causing tremendous fiscal stress on municipalities already overburdened by budgetary constraints. In response, the municipalities have strongly lobbied Congress to carve an exemption in *CERCLA* for MSW. In 1991, Senator Frank Lautenberg (D-N.J.) introduced legislation that would vest exclusive authority in the EPA to bring contribution actions against municipalities, and would restrict such actions to those limited circumstances where the EPA finds that a municipality acted similarly to an industrial polluter by contributing hazardous wastes to a site. Industry representatives oppose special treatment for municipalities, and argue that Congress should instead revise *CERCLA* to eliminate all alleged inequities, including those purportedly faced by corporations.

Large corporate PRPs, beset by claimed liability at numerous *CERCLA* sites, have recently adopted a new strategy to minimize their share of Superfund costs. After agreeing to settle Superfund claims with the federal and/or state environmental oversight agencies, these corporate PRPs commence new actions for contribution and indemnification against those parties, previously identified by the oversight agencies, which have refused to participate in the proposed settlement as well as against any other party that is arguably liable under *CERCLA's* broad definition of "responsible" person, even if the latter had not previously been named as a PRP in the governmental action. This strategy naturally induces reluctant, named PRPs to participate in the proposed global settlement, since the costs of defending against a subsequent action for contribution and indemnification are almost invariably greater. But the approach also has potentially devastating effects on the previously unidentified PRPs, particularly where they are small local businesses with limited financial resources. In one well-publicized case, after agreeing to commence a $9 million clean-up of a landfill, two large corporations, Special Metals Corp. and Chesebrough-Pond's USA Co., commenced an action for contribution and indemnification against hundreds of towns, school districts, and small business owners in the Utica, New York region that may have contributed *de minimis* amounts of waste to the landfill. These small businesses are frequently unable to pay either the relatively modest settlement demands made by the plaintiff corporate generators or the attorneys' fees required to defend against the actions.[25] Critics of this strategy allege that corporations are trying to make *CERCLA* so ineffective that Congress will be forced to overhaul, if not eliminate, the statute.

NAMED AS A PRP—IT COULD HAPPEN TO YOU!

Not surprisingly, the strict liability standard utilized to ensure the clean-up of environmentally impaired property encompasses more than the intentional polluter. Those who have unintentionally contributed to the pollution at a site, as well as those who owned, purchased, or leased property without any actual knowledge of pollution damages at the site, have been held liable under CERCLA for the cleanup costs incurred at the site. No longer is the intentional, deliberate polluter, that disposed of its wastes carelessly or illegally, solely at risk. Today, any company involved in the manufacture, generation, transport, or disposal of hazardous wastes, whether a major chemical manufacturer or oil refinery, a small dry-cleaning establishment, a municipality operating a garbage dump or landfill, or a bank that has foreclosed on a loan and assumed control over the operations of a hazardous waste disposal company, may be potentially at risk for Superfund-type liability and a civil enforcement action.[26] The following hypothetical case is offered to illustrate this point.

> About 60 years ago, during the early 1930s, Smallville, U.S.A., a small but growing municipality, discovered that the cost of shipping its municipal waste to a landfill outside the city limits had grown prohibitive. Wishing to avoid raising unwelcome property taxes, the Mayor and City Council decided to buy a vacant piece of property on the northern edge of the city, and

to operate its own municipal landfill at that location. The property was outside the prime residential areas of the City, and had been owned for several years by the Kent family. The Grease & Tar Oil Refinery was situated adjacent to the site, and a major interstate highway ran nearby, on which city garbage trucks could haul the municipal wastes to the site.

Clark Kent, the patriarch of the Kent family and a scion of the Smallville community, had purchased the site from Dumpitall Chemical Company, which used to operate a small plant there. Dumpitall primarily used several small, unlined, man-made lagoons on the site to dispose of its chemical wastes. Prior to offering the property for sale, Dumpitall had filled in the lagoons with dirt from the area, and planted various foliage. Kent never knew that chemicals wastes had been stored in the lagoons, though he often mused about why the foliage had died, and why his normally successful "green thumb" seemed to have no impact on planting efforts in that part of the property.

To increase city revenues and offset the costs of operating the landfill, Smallville offered to collect municipal wastes not only from the adjoining community of Yourtown, but also offered to dispose of wastes from nearby companies and industries, including Leathergoods, Inc., one of the major local tanners, whose leather and suede store and fine products contributed greatly to Smallville's tourist trade.

Unbeknownst to either Jimmy O. Kent, the last surviving member of the Kent family and the current owner of the property, or the City of Smallville, several underground fuel tanks at the Grease & Tar Oil Refinery had been leaking for years, and a plume of oil had escaped from the refinery property onto the Kent family's property. The plume was slowly leaching through the soils into the groundwaters at the site, which fed the Pristine Clean Aquifer, the major source of drinking water for Smallville and Yourtown. Also, at the time of the sale, Jimmy O. Kent was not aware that for several years, the A-1 Chemical Company, which owned property in the next county, had surreptitiously sent its employees to empty and store steel drums on a remote portion of the Kent property. These drums contained hazardous waste products. Frequently, A-1's employees spilled some of the chemicals onto the ground in their rush to complete the job and return to their homes. One of A-1's prime transporters, Joe Sleaze, also transported hazardous wastes in his off-hours from Acme Chemical Company and several other chemical companies outside the region, and buried the drummed wastes in the property. Acme and the other companies believed that Sleaze had hauled the wastes to a landfill in the next state, and had Certificates of Disposal provided by Sleaze, in which Sleaze certified that he had hauled the wastes to a specified disposal location.

By the mid-1960s, the Smallville landfill was doing a booming business. The city's population had more than quadrupled since the 1930s, after Smallville actively recruited major industries to the area, and promised them diminished rates for use of the landfill. Many of these companies' employees, anxious to avoid a lengthy commute, purchased homes in Lois Lanes, a planned development not far from the Smallville Landfill, whose construction was heavily financed by the Greater Bank of Smallville. Several small businesses also relocated to Lois Lanes, including Superclean, a dry-cleaning establishment run by an elderly couple, John and Mary Cleansmith, who had no children. The Cleansmiths were enticed to Lois Lanes by the potential for expanding their business opportunities and the proximity of the landfill.

In the mid-1980s, *The Daily Planet*, Smallville's local newspaper, ran a series of controversial articles concerning the health risks posed by the proximity of the landfill to the development, after several children in the development were born with previously undetected birth defects, five women were diagnosed with breast cancer, and three landfill workers died of rare forms of cancer. The articles prompted investigation by the state's environmental protection agency and by federal officials, whose tests revealed that the soils and groundwater throughout the development were highly contaminated with dangerous levels of volatile organic chemicals and hydrocarbon compounds, posing a threat of cancer or gene mutation. Further investigations revealed the leaching fuel oil plume emanating from the Grease & Tar Oil Refinery, and uncovered the barrels of drummed waste illegally buried on the property, most of which had been leaking for years. Grease & Tar promptly notified its insurer, Premium Insurance Company, which immediately became involved in remediation activities at the landfill, and managed remediation efforts including the installation of monitoring wells, recovery wells, and a soil venting system.

Because the groundwater contamination posed a particular threat to the Smallville drinking water supply, residents of the entire area were ordered not to drink the water, but to use only bottled water for all of their cooking, cleaning, and bathing needs. Lois Lanes residents were evacuated; the developers of the project defaulted on their financing agreements, and the Greater Bank of Smallville assumed day-to-day control over the operations at Lois Lanes.

Federal, state, and local investigators have issued a press release, in which they promise to begin clean-up operations as soon as practicable. They also indicated that a list of PRPs will be forthcoming in the near future.

Which persons or companies should be named as PRPs? And once named, how should these individuals and/or companies respond to the government, if at all, or participate in the remediation process?

Under *CERCLA* or state laws modeled on that legislation, potential PRPs could include the City of Smallville, Jimmy O. Kent, and Dumpitall Chemical Company, as owners or operators of the site;[27] Grease & Tar Oil Refinery, A-1 Chemical, Acme Chemical, and the other companies whose wastes had been illegally transported to the site by Joe Sleaze, as well as Leathergoods, Inc. and Superclean, could each be named as generators of hazardous waste.[28] Joe Sleaze, and any other person, company or entity that transported wastes to the site, including Smallville, whose municipal trucks hauled garbage and wastes, are also likely PRPs. Greater Bank and Premium Insurance Company could also be named as PRPs due to their close involvement in remediation activities at the site.[29]

RESPONDING TO A PRP NOTICE

Generators and transporters of waste typically learn of their possible involvement in a *CERCLA*-type case upon receipt of either a request for information or a more formal PRP letter issued by the state or federal government.[30] Assume that your company, Squeaky Clean (Squeaky), has been identified as a PRP and has received a letter from the EPA informing Squeaky that wastes generated from its main processing plant were shipped to a location that is now a Superfund site. In a typical letter, the EPA will advise that it has determined that there has been a release, or that there is a threatened release of hazardous contaminants at the site, and that the EPA has identified Squeaky as a PRP in connection with the site. The EPA is prepared to commence remedial activities, and wishes to know if Squeaky will participate in funding a remedial investigation and/or feasibility study (RI/FS) at the site. The EPA is hosting a meeting of PRPs, and invites Squeaky to attend to learn more about the site, the government's proposed action, and a timetable for remediation and negotiation. How should Squeaky respond to such a notification?

Internal Investigations

Generally speaking, Squeaky will be more successful ultimately if it initiates its own preliminary, internal investigation as quickly as possible. Such an investigation may help demonstrate, for example, that the wastes that the EPA has identified as having been generated by Squeaky Clean or as having been shipped to the site were not hazardous within the applicable statutory definitions, or it may reflect that the amount of waste shipped to the site was extremely small. To support such assertions, Squeaky must be prepared to provide full documentation of the nature and quantity of the wastes shipped to a site, and of the manufacturing processes implicated in generating the wastes. Since the release of such information may reveal proprietary information or trade secrets, consultation with Squeaky's counsel is important at an early stage of the investigative process. While the use of counsel to coordinate Squeaky's response to any governmental requests for information may seem obvious, the services of counsel should not mistakenly be considered a luxury. On the contrary, since Squeaky's internal records may be officially sought during the course of investigations or any subsequent litigation, all responsive activities must be coordinated so as to take advantage of attorney-client and work-product privileges, as well as to protect confidential information and trade secrets. Note, however, that the EPA will probably be rather unsympathetic to an argument that the amount of waste shipped to the site was minor, since under CERCLA, each PRP is jointly and severally liable for the entire clean-up.[31] Nevertheless, the EPA does typically enter into specific settlements with so-called *de minimis parties,* that is, parties whose allocated share of the total waste at the site is less than a specified amount, such as 1 percent of the total allocated volume of waste at the site. Therefore, highlighting a PRP's potentially *de minimis* role at the site could be beneficial in that it at least focuses the EPA on a possible *de minimis* component to any settlement.

Given the potentially high costs involved in defending a CERCLA claim, Squeaky should, as a matter of course upon receipt of the PRP letter, assign its general counsel the responsibility for responding to the EPA and the state or municipal agencies, as well as for overseeing any internal investigation if questions exist as to whether Squeaky's wastes were hazardous or whether the wastes were shipped to the site in question. Squeaky's investigation must focus on identifying the other generators that shipped wastes to the site, as well as the nature and volume of its own and others' waste materials, and whether any of these materials, particularly Squeaky's wastes, were recycled, reclaimed, destroyed, or transshipped, which would have reduced the volume of wastes potentially implicated at the site.[32]

To learn more about Squeaky's involvement with the site, the investigator should interview those employees familiar with Squeaky Clean's disposal operations, and should obtain information regarding, *inter alia*, the handling of Squeaky Clean's wastes, the preparation and documentation of manifests, the selection of ultimate waste disposal sites, the process of obtaining required governmental permits or approval, the selection of waste transporters, and contractual agreements regarding transportation and disposal (i.e., authorized disposal sites or approved disposal technologies).[33] Inasmuch as the Superfund response costs tend to be quite high, the investigator should also contact Squeaky's insurance and risk management personnel, to learn more about Squeaky's insurance coverage, if any, as an additional insured under policies issued to the transporters or disposal facilities, possible indemnification agreements with the transporters or disposal facilities, and whether Squeaky ever conducted visits to the disposal site, or required certifications from the transporter or facility that the wastes were disposed of in accordance with the contractual provisions.[34] Caution must be exercised, however, in making written memoranda of these investigations, since, as already indicated, such information may be discoverable.

As in any other litigation, learning as much as possible about the background of the claim or the action is of prime importance. Accordingly, Squeaky should also interview neighbors near the site for information about site operations. Neighbors may have an unusual depth of information about the kind of wastes transported to the site, or whether any after-hours dumping allegedly occurred.[35] Information should also be obtained about the ownership and operational history of the site, as well as about any known incidents at the site (fires, explosions, leaks, etc.) that may have contributed to a release of hazardous wastes,[36] or events, such as an unusual number of dead wildlife at or near a site, which may provide anecdotal evidence that a discharge of hazardous wastes was manifest or should have been manifest at an earlier time.

Government Informational Meetings

Generally, by the time the EPA has sent out PRP notification letters, the government has already conducted at least an initial investigation into some of the background issues involving the site. Thus, to the extent that the government offers Squeaky an opportunity to attend an informational meeting, Squeaky should definitely attend, both to meet other potentially responsible parties and to learn as much about the site as possible, including current conditions at the site and any proposed remedy. The EPA or state agency may also be able to provide valuable information about the nature of the hazardous wastes at the site and about the extent of contamination and the alleged threat posed by such contamination.[37]

PRP Defense Groups

Inasmuch as a Superfund site typically implicates many PRPs, Squeaky may wish to consider the benefits of forming or joining a multiparty defense group to defend or to negotiate with the government.[38] PRP defense groups are generally funded by assessments from their membership, paid either on a pro rata or per capita basis, depending on the information available regarding each member's allocated share of waste at the site. Typically, each group is divided into "tiers" reflecting the party's allocated share of waste and its concomitant estimated potential liability; thus, the entities that contributed more waste to the site are generally expected to pay a heavier share of the settlement costs and are typically assessed a proportionately heavier share of the defense costs as well. PRP defense groups usually operate by forming several committees to handle different aspects of the defense or settlement negotiations, including a trial management committee, executive or oversight committee, technical committee, negotiation or settlement committee, etc., whose members may or may not be paid for their services, depending on agreements reached among the membership of the entire group.

The technical subcommittee selects investigators and technical consultants to review the government's assessment of necessary remediation, and to offer counterproposals, and will contract for an environmental engineering firm to perform the remedial investigation and feasibility study if the PRP group decides to undertake it. The EPA's analysis of the contamination at the site and the threat posed by the contamination must be critically evaluated. Thus, if the EPA installed monitoring or sampling wells, well logs must be reviewed to determine if they were adequately constructed or properly situated, and to ascertain whether the sampling methodology was appropriate and representative. Technical consultants should also evaluate the EPA's chain-of-custody procedures in regard to the delivery of samples from the wells to the laboratories for analysis, and should also review laboratory procedures and chemical analyses of the samples, as well as the competency and qualifications of the EPA testing facility itself. The engineering consultants retained by the PRP defense group should include an expert in groundwater hydrogeology, to:

- Evaluate groundwater conditions at the site.

- Classify aquifers.

- Determine such matters as the rates and horizontal and vertical directions of groundwater flow, the depth, extent, and levels of any contamination, and the rate of contamination and any possible dilution of such contamination.

If the site is closely situated to a population, and/or if the EPA has alleged that the hazardous wastes pose a particular threat to the population, then the technical committee may also wish to consider retaining a toxicologist or risk-assessment expert to evaluate the potential adverse effects on the population from exposure to the contaminants at the site, including, *inter alia*, possible carcinogenic, mutagenic, teratologic, or toxic effects.

The trial management committee usually hires investigators to learn more about the site's ownership and operational history and to identify other PRPs that could be named in any litigation. It also coordinates a joint defense if the state or federal government initiates litigation against the PRPs in connection with the forced remediation of the site. The negotiation or settlement committees may be independent committees, or a subcommittee of the trial management committee, established to explore settlement options, including any *de minimis* component, and to determine the nature and extent of claims by the EPA, by state or municipal agencies, and by other federal agencies if federal natural resources have potentially been compromised at the site.[39] The trial management committee also usually determines whether additional administrative, legal, or other tasks should be delegated to individual committee members to handle or assigned to outside counsel.

In deciding whether to join a PRP group, Squeaky should consider that if it or its counsel has never been implicated in a Superfund cleanup, it may benefit greatly from the experience and expertise of other PRPs that have previously been involved in defending against a *CERCLA* claim. Also, by banding together, PRPs may be able to minimize greatly the expenses that they might otherwise have to underwrite as a single defendant in the *CERCLA* recovery action. Participation in a common defense group is particularly attractive when large companies with ample financial and/or legal resources have been designated "major players" in the litigation, by virtue of having contributed a significant share of the wastes to the site. As such, these PRPs are more likely to play a greater role in the defense of the action, and to contribute both a significant share of common defense costs as well as their counsel's time and expertise to resolving the matter. These companies may also have technical expertise in-house that can be made available to assist the PRP group in understanding or evaluating their remedial and settlement options.

Finally, another factor to consider in deciding whether to join a PRP group, in addition to the EPA's potential unwillingness to negotiate with separate parties and its preference for negotiating with a PRP group, is that a PRP group that has successfully negotiated a potential settlement of a Superfund claim will typically try to require nonmember PRPs that wish to take advantage of the settlement proposal to become a member of the group, by making back-payments of its proportionate share of assessments for such items as the common defense costs, remedial investigation and feasibility study environmental costs, etc.[40]

Assuming that Squeaky has joined a PRP defense group, and that its committees have agreed to settle the government's claims, finalizing and achieving that settlement still generally make for a painfully long process, in part because of the governmentally mandated steps to selection and implementation of a site remedy. Estimates for site clean-up rarely, if ever, match the actual cleanup costs; most often, actual costs exceed these estimates. Because PRPs have different views on allocation of waste, verifying the amounts of waste attributed to each would-be settling party, and developing an acceptable formula to allocate each PRP member's proportionate share of waste at the site, are often arduous tasks, notwithstanding the development of computerized databases and other similar litigation support systems. Furthermore, as indicated, even when a settlement is negotiated, some PRPs may be deceased, insolvent, or out of business, while others may lack insurance coverage or have minimal assets that can be attached; under these circumstances, the remaining settling parties must pay their allocated share of any shortfall, without much hope of contribution in a cost-recovery action. As well, the remediation process itself tends to be slow, achieved, if at all, during a number of years. Finally, the EPA and other implicated state or federal agencies will generally not provide every PRP with a full and complete release from liability at the site. Indeed, in some instances, the EPA cannot provide such releases, since legislation mandates a statutory reopener under certain circumstances.

Given the broad interpretations of the potential categories of PRPs, and the strict liability scheme enacted by Congress and followed by various states, virtually any company having a connection to chemicals or hazardous waste products could find itself named as a PRP. Certainly, the risks of being named a PRP may be minimized by practicing, to the extent possible, good prevention, through strong, effective risk management, including regular review and coordination among departments involved in waste disposal operations, contracting, and insurance procurement. Once named as a PRP, however, early investigation, coordination with other PRPs, and cooperation with the federal or state oversight agencies will best minimize a party's ultimate costs for civil liability in connection with the site.

THE RATIONALE FOR CRIMINAL ENVIRONMENTAL PROSECUTIONS

The strict liability policy implicit in civil environmental enforcement actions is intended to deter polluters, encourage compliance with statutory and regulatory guidelines, and obtain funds for the remediation and restoration of polluted environs to their natural state. In addition to actions for response costs, federal and state authorities may also seek other civil sanctions against alleged violators, including fines[41] and injunctive relief. Unfortunately, because civil sanctions have not proved to be an effective deterrent against all potential polluters, prosecutors have been compelled to increase substantially the criminal prosecution of those persons or businesses responsible for a host of unsound environmental practices, including improper record-keeping or reporting, or inadequate waste storage, treatment, transport, or disposal practices. Today, prosecutors carefully scrutinize business decisions, generally undertaken to save company funds, which impact on environmental concerns, including decisions involving such matters as the installation of pollution control devices, the selection of disposal sites or transporters, the method of record-keeping or reporting, and policies for the monitoring of routine discharges of hazardous wastes.

The following sections briefly describe the major federal laws defining environmental crimes, the acts most often prosecuted, the "persons" likely to be subject to prosecution, the factors considered by the U.S. Department of Justice in determining whether to prosecute for environmental offenses, and the range of possible sentences for wrongdoers convicted of violating federal environmental laws.[42]

Federal Statutes Defining Environmental "Crimes"

Numerous federal environmental statutes contain provisions defining criminal penalties for environmental offenses.[43] For example, Sec. 309(c)(3) of the *Clean Water Act* provides that a defendant may be convicted of the crime of "knowing endangerment" if he has violated any one of several sections of the Act and knew at the time of the violation that, in so doing, he had placed another person in "imminent danger" of death or bodily injury. A conviction of "knowing endangerment" may subject a person to "a fine of not more than $250,000 or imprisonment of not more than 15 years, or both." If the "person" so convicted is an organization, then the maximum fine for a conviction may be quadrupled to not more than $1 million.

RCRA contains similar prohibitions against offenses that are knowingly committed. For example, *RCRA* prohibits, *inter alia, knowingly* transporting or causing to be transported any hazardous substance to a facility that does not have a permit, or *knowingly* treating, storing, or disposing of any hazardous wastes either without a permit, or in *knowing* violation of any material condition of a permit. This statute also proscribes conduct such as *knowingly* handling in any manner, including transporting, any hazardous wastes not properly identified as hazardous wastes. A first-time offense under *RCRA* may be punished by a fine of not more than $50,000 for each day of violation, or imprisonment not to exceed two years, or both. The prescribed jail sentence is more severe if the offense involves transporting or treating wastes without or in violation of a permit. Criminal conduct may also occur under *RCRA* when a permit omits information or makes any false material statement in any application, manifest, label, report, or other document filed, maintained, or used for purposes of compliance with EPA or state rules.[44]

Many of the statutes cited earlier in this chapter also define criminal violations or authorize criminal penalties for environmental violations. *See*, e.g., Secs. 103(b) and (c) of *CERCLA* [42 U.S.C. §§9603(b), (c)], Secs. 325(b) and (d) of the

Emergency Planning and Community Right to Know Act [42 U.S.C. §§11045(b), (d)], Sec. 14(b) of the *Federal Insecticide, Fungicide and Rodenticide Act* [7 U.S.C. §136(b)], Sec. 105(b) of the *Marine Protection, Research and Sanctuaries Act* [33 U.S.C. §1415(b)], Sec. 1423(b) of the *Safe Drinking Water Act* [42 U.S.C. §300h-2(b)], and Sec. 16(b) of TSCA [15 U.S.C. §2615(b)].

In addition to knowing criminal acts, various environmental laws define certain negligent—that is, unknowing—acts as criminal. For example, Sec. 113(c)(4) of the *Clean Air Act* [42 U.S.C. §7413(c)(4)] states that any person who "negligently releases" into the ambient air any hazardous air pollutant shall be punished by a fine or imprisonment or both. Similarly, Sec. 309(c)(1) of the *Clean Water Act* [33 U.S.C. §1319(c)(1)] defines certain negligent acts as criminal violations, and provides in part that any person who has negligently violated any permit condition or limitation, or has negligently introduced into a sewer system or a publicly owned treatment works any pollutant or hazardous substance that the individual knew or reasonably should have known could cause personal injury, shall be punishable by a fine or imprisonment or both. Thus, even when the actor did not intend to cause a particular pollution result, he may under some statutes be deemed criminally liable for the consequences of any negligent actions.

Congress recently responded to the need to provide rigorous and thorough enforcement of existing federal and state environmental laws by enacting the *Pollution Prosecution Act of 1991*. The purpose of the Act is to focus federal, state, and local law enforcement authorities upon environmental polluters, and to provide for greater investigation and coordination among agencies. The Act directs the Administrator of the EPA to increase the number of EPA criminal investigators and support staff assigned to the EPA's Office of Criminal Investigations from at least 72, for the 12-month period ending September 30, 1992, to at least 200 employees by no later than October 1, 1995. The statute also provides for the creation of a National Training Institute, as part of the EPA's Office of Enforcement, which will train federal, state, and local lawyers, inspectors, civil and criminal investigators, and technical experts in the enforcement of this country's environmental laws.[45]

The Most Frequently Prosecuted Acts

According to the 1991 edition of the *Summary of Criminal Prosecutions*, published by the EPA's Office of Enforcement, the most frequently charged criminal offenses are violations of the *Clean Air Act, Clean Water Act, CERCLA,* and *RCRA*. A review of each federal prosecution disposed of in fiscal year 1990, as reported by the EPA, discloses that typical charges brought against defendants include:

- Making false statements regarding hazardous wastes.

- Storing, treating, and disposing of hazardous wastes without a permit, in violation of *RCRA*.

- Emitting an air pollutant, in violation of the *Clean Air Act*.

- Failing to notify of a release of a reportable quantity of a hazardous substance, in violation of *CERCLA*.

- Negligently discharging pollutants into a navigable federal waterway without a permit, in violation of the *Clean Water Act*.

Criminal indictments have also frequently accused corporations, corporate officers, owners and operators of hazardous waste facilities, and/or individuals of conspiracy, making false statements, and mail fraud.

"Persons" Who Can Be Prosecuted

As a policy, our courts have broadly construed statutes defining criminal responsibility in matters concerning the public health and welfare. Major environmental laws define *persons* subject to criminal prosecution to include an individual, trust, firm, joint stock company, corporation (including a government corporation), partnership, association, state, municipality, commission, political subdivision of a state, or any interstate body. *See, e.g.,* Sec. 1004(15) of *RCRA* [42 U.S.C. §6903(15)], Sec. 302(e) of the *Clean Air Act* [42 U.S.C. §7602(e)], Sec. 502(5) of the *Clean Water Act* [33 U.S.C. §1362(5)], and Sec. 101(21) of *CERCLA* [42 U.S.C. §9601(21)]. Consequently, corporate officers, supervisors, and employees may be prosecuted for known violations caused either by their own acts[46] or by acts they authorized,[47] overlooked, ignored, condoned, or only suspected. Corporations and corporate officers have also been held criminally responsible for the acts and omissions of their employees, regardless of whether the company or officer had actual knowledge of the acts or omissions.[48]

Corporate Employee Liability for "Knowing Acts." A crucial concern of officers, supervisors, or employees is whether they may be held criminally responsible for corporate violations. In simplest terms, any person who has "knowingly" acted in violation of the law may be held liable for the corporation's violation. For example, in *United States v. Hayes Int'l Corp.* [786 F.2d 1499, 1503 (11th Cir. 1986)], the Eleventh Circuit Court of Appeals construed the degree of knowledge necessary for a conviction under *RCRA*, 42 U.S.C. §6928(d)(1), the section prohibiting the unlawful transportation of hazardous waste. Both the corporation and one of its employees responsible for the disposal of hazardous wastes were convicted of having knowingly transported hazardous wastes to a facility that did not have a permit. The corporation's liability was derived solely from the actions of its employee. The court held that "it is completely fair and reasonable to charge those who choose to operate in [certain regulated areas] with knowledge of the [applicable] regulatory provisions." Since *RCRA* does not make knowledge of the illegality of the act (unlawful disposal of hazardous wastes) an element of the prescribed offense, the defendants did not prevail at trial based on arguments that they had no knowledge that the corporation's wastes were hazardous within the meaning of federal environmental regulations, and that they were ignorant of requirements that the disposal facility required a permit. Similarly, in *United States v. Johnson & Towers, Inc.* [741 F.2d 662, 670 (3d Cir. 1984), cert. denied, 469 U.S. 1208 (1985)], the Third Circuit Court of Appeals found that the criminal penalty provision of *RCRA* covers employees as well as owners and operators of a facility who knowingly treat, store, or dispose of any hazardous waste; employees, however, may be subjected to criminal prosecution only if they knew or should have known that the facility did not comply with statutory provisions requiring a permit from the EPA for waste disposal. The court further held that knowledge of the permit requirement may be inferred by a jury as to "those individuals who hold the requisite responsible positions with the corporate defendant." These decisions provide an implicit warning to corporate management that a "head in the sand" approach to environmental compliance will not necessarily avoid criminal liability for knowing acts. Corporate officers operating in highly regulated areas, such as the manufacture, transport, or disposal of hazardous wastes, are charged with knowledge of all applicable regulatory provisions, and can and will be held criminally liable for failing to ensure that their corporate alter-ego meets or complies with pertinent environmental standards.

Corporate Liability for Authorized Acts.   A corporation may be held liable for criminal conduct authorized by its directors or officers, or authorized at another policy-making level of the organization. As long as the criminal acts are directly related to the performance of the duties that the officer or agent has broad authority to perform, the corporate principal may be held liable for the criminal act and may be deemed to have "authorized" the act. See United States v. Armour, 168 F.2d 342, 344 (3d Cir. 1948). In addition, a corporation may be liable where it is deemed to have ratified prior criminal conduct. Thus, even when corporate employees acted outside the scope of their employment and apparent authority, a corporation may be found criminally liable where subsequent actions or inaction by the corporation are deemed to constitute ratification or adoption of the employee's illegal conduct. See Continental Banking Co. v. United States [281 F.2d 137, 149 (6th Cir. 1960)]; supervisors' knowledge and failure to halt depot managers' practice of contacting competitors could be inferred by jury to constitute adoption or ratification of practice.

Vicarious Liability for Unauthorized Acts

Agents and Employees.   Early decisions addressing the issue of vicarious corporate liability did not impose liability on corporations when the crime as defined required a culpable mental state, since corporations were deemed not to be able to possess the requisite intent. See K. Brickey, "Corporate Criminal Liability: A Primer for Corporate Counsel," 40 *Business Lawyer* 131 (1984) (hereinafter "Brickey") §2.03(2)(c). This rule is no longer followed, and corporations can now be found liable both for strict liability crimes as well as for crimes requiring a culpable mental state, including specific intent crimes. For a corporation to be liable for crimes involving a mental element, however, a corporate agent must act with the specific intent to benefit the corporation. See United States v. LaBar, 521 F. Supp. 203, 213 (M.D. Pa. 1981), aff'd., 688 F.2d 826 (3d Cir.), cert. denied, 103 S. Ct. 260 (1982).

Generally, a corporation may be held vicariously liable for the *unauthorized* criminal acts of its agents if such acts were committed during the course of employment and in connection with the performance of some employment-related activity. A corporation may be held liable for its agent's acts, even when such acts were not within the agent's corporate powers as strictly construed, if the agent has undertaken to perform these acts for the corporation, using corporate powers actually authorized. Under such circumstances, the lack of written authority under seal or vote of the corporation does not negate the implied or vicarious agency, nor does it invalidate the agent's acts within the scope of his employment. See New York Cent. & Hudson River R. Co. v. United States, 212 U.S. 481, 493–94 (1909); United States v. American Radiator & Standard Sanitary Corp., 433 F.2d 174 (3d Cir. 1970); United States v. Hilton Hotels Corp., 467 F.2d 1000 (9th Cir. 1972), cert. denied, 409 U.S. 1125 (1973).

A corporation's vicarious liability for its employee's acts is not affected by the status of the employee in the corporate structure. The standard for liability is "the function" delegated to the corporate officer or agent, and the latter's "power to engage the corporation in a criminal transaction." See CIT Corp. v. United States, 150 F.2d 85, 89 (9th Cir. 1945). Accordingly, the conduct of even "low-level" employees, such as salespeople, clerical workers, or truck drivers, has been deemed sufficient to hold a corporation criminally liable for the employee's acts.[49] Moreover, a corporation may be liable even if its employee acted contrary to corporate policy. *See United States v. Hilton Hotels Corp.* [467 F.2d 1000 (9th Cir. 1972), cert. denied, 409 U.S. 1125 (1973)], in which a corporation was found liable of violations of the *Sherman Act* based on acts of its purchasing agent, even though the agent acted contrary to hotel policy and in violation of instructions. Corporate owners and managers are supposed to expend their maximum efforts to prevent violations of law; accordingly, a corporation may not avoid the consequences of a violation "by issuing general instructions without undertaking to enforce those instructions by means commensurate with the obvious risks" [Id. at 1007].[50] Additionally, under the doctrine of *collective knowledge,* the knowledge required for the intent and commission of a criminal act need not be imputed to the corporation from a single individual, but may be established by imputing to the corporation the aggregate or "collective knowledge" of its employees or agents as a group. *See, e.g., United States v. Sawyer Transp., Inc.,* 337 F. Supp. 29 (D. Minn. 1971), aff'd., 463 F.2d 175 (8th Cir. 1972).[51]

Subsidiaries or Divisions. A corporation may also be found liable for the criminal acts of its subsidiaries or divisions. Liability of a corporate parent is determined by the same standards that govern liability for the acts of corporate employees [*United States v. Wilshire Oil Co.,* 427 F.2d 969 (10th Cir.), cert. denied, 400 U.S. 829 (1970); *United States v. Ira S. Bushey & Sons, Inc.,* 363 F. Supp. 110 (D. Vt.), aff'd., 487 F.2d 1393 (2d Cir. 1973), cert. denied, 417 U.S. 976 (1974); *United States v. Johns-Manville Corp.,* 231 F. Supp. 690 (E.D. Pa. 1963)]. A corporate parent may in particular be held liable for its subsidiary's misconduct where the parent could have detected the illegal practices and prevented their continuation. *See United States v. Wilshire Oil Co.* [427 F.2d 969 (10th Cir. 1970)] (the corporate parent had ample opportunity to detect and reject illegal antitrust scheme implemented by a division prior to acquisition by corporate parent, since the scheme continued for several years after acquisition).

Acquittal or Nonprosecution of Actor. Since a corporation can act only through an individual agent, the latter's acts must be vicariously asserted against the corporation in order to impose any criminal liability against the corporate entity. [*See generally* Brickey, §2:02(3)–2:03(2)(b).] The individual employee need not be prosecuted, however, in order to prosecute the corporation for the wrongful acts of that employee [*United States v. General Motors Corp.,* 121 F.2d 376, 411 (7th Cir.), cert. denied, 314 U.S. 618 (1941); *United States v. Hilton Hotels Corp.,* 467 F.2d 1000, 1008 (9th Cir. 1972)]. A guilty verdict against a corporation may be upheld even when a jury has acquitted the allegedly responsible employee, and such acquittal is logically inconsistent with a finding of guilt against the corporation. Additionally, to prosecute a corporation, a prosecutor is generally not required to prove that a specific employee acted illegally, but rather only that some employee or agent of the corporation has committed the alleged violation. *See United States v. American Stevedore, Inc.* [310 F.2d 47 (2d Cir. 1962), cert. denied, 371 U.S. 969 (1963)].

Prosecutorial Considerations. On July 1, 1991, the U.S. Department of Justice published environmental prosecutorial guidelines, entitled *Factors in Decisions on Criminal Prosecutions for Environmental Violations in the Context of Significant Voluntary Compliance or Disclosure Efforts by the Violator.* The guidelines advise local prosecutors of those activities by an alleged polluter that should be considered most relevant to a decision about whether to prosecute. Prosecutorial considerations include (1) the voluntary, timely, and complete disclosure of an environmental event; (2) the degree and timeliness of cooperation by the entity or person, including identifying and providing responsible persons and complete results of corporate investigations, and (3) the existence and scope of a regular and comprehensive environmental compliance program. The publication provides examples of environmental events, describes different types of corporate disclosure, cooperation, and compliance, and discusses how each factor may impact on the decision to prosecute. These guidelines suggest that the more comprehensive, continual, and updated a company's environmental compliance program is, the more consideration the prosecutor will give to a remedy other than criminal prosecution.

In particular, the guidelines accord great weight to the nature and extent of ongoing corporate environmental compliance audits. These audits are highly regarded by various federal agencies. Indeed, as early as July 1986, the EPA issued an "Environmental Auditing Policy Statement," which in effect officially encouraged the use of environmental audits by regulated businesses to help achieve and maintain compliance with environmental laws and regulations, and to identify and correct unregulated environmental hazards. The EPA also officially encouraged individual states to adopt their own policies to advance the use of environmental auditing on a consistent nationwide basis.

Environmental audits review all possible discharge, release, and transporter activities and policies in light of federal, state, and local laws, to achieve, if possible, full compliance with all applicable laws. Such audits can help ensure that exposure to environmental risks is controlled. Admittedly, written audits, including potentially damaging findings, could be disclosed in a criminal or administrative enforcement action. Nevertheless, the risk of disclosure should not ordinarily deter a company from conducting routine audits. On the contrary, to reduce the risk of disclosure of audit results, the company should prepare and communicate audit materials and information pursuant to instructions from an attorney, in order to afford the audit the benefits of attorney-client privilege.[52]

This privilege is not all-encompassing, however. Any nonconfidential disclosure during or after the environmental audit may cause the attorney-client privilege to be lost. The privilege, in any event, cannot protect the actual underlying facts. An attorney's work product, such as documents reflecting mental impressions, conclusions, opinions, or legal theories, prepared in anticipation of litigation, may have a qualified "privilege" under the attorney work-product doctrine. Audit reports not protected by the attorney-client privilege can be used as evidence against the corporation.[53]

Sentencing Guidelines. The United States Sentencing Commission, an agency in the judicial branch of the federal government, is charged by Congress with establishing sentencing policies and practices for the federal criminal justice system, to ensure that sanctions provide just punishment, adequate deterrence, and incentives for preventing, detecting and reporting criminal conduct. The Commission has formulated detailed guidelines prescribing appropriate sentences for offenders convicted of federal crimes. Environmental offenses covered by the guidelines—that is, "knowing endangerment" or mishandling of hazardous substances—are broadly described. These guidelines became effective November 1, 1991, and at present no record exists of reported sentences under the new guidelines. The guidelines generally instruct a sentencing court to order an organization to pay both restitution (to remediate the damage) and a fine (to deter future wrongdoing). A court may also place an organization on probation for up to five years. The prescribed methods for calculating punishments vary under the guidelines and can be complex in application. Jail sentences of more than five years are even suggested for certain first offenders. Accordingly, companies or individuals facing potential criminal environmental liability should therefore obtain competent, experienced counsel, knowledgeable about not only the plethora of environmental enactments, but also the sentencing guidelines that will dictate the exercise and flexibility of prosecutorial discretion.

NOTES

[1]Preservation and remediation of the environment are not limited to the United States, but rather are part of a growing global concern. International efforts to preserve Antarctica and to prevent the further decimation of the ozone layer are well-known. Americans are less aware, however, of environmental efforts within other countries. Interestingly, with the collapse of the Soviet Union, worldwide attention has again focused on potential problems of environmental pollution in the Soviet Union. *See*, e.g., *New York Times*, Nov. 24, 1991 at A1, "For Black Sea, Slow Choking by Pollutants," discussing extensive marine pollution in the Black Sea and the concomitant physical and economic destruction of the sturgeon, mackerel, anchovy, and other commercial fishery industries.

[2]The citizens of these two communities were forced to evacuate when dangerously high levels of contaminants, including dioxin, the active ingredient in Agent Orange, and other potentially cancer-causing toxic wastes, were discovered to have been buried or indiscriminately disposed of on or around their properties. At Love Canal, New York, near Buffalo, the 1978 discovery of massive leaks of toxic wastes forced 240 families to abandon their homes. Ironically, in or about September 1991, the EPA indicated that it will reevaluate dioxin and its classification as one of the deadliest toxic wastes.

[3]Similar statutes imposing strict liability on environmental polluters have been enacted by various states.

[4]*See*, e.g., *In the Matter of Vineland Chemical Company, Inc.* [Dkt. No. A-2724-89T3 (New Jersey App. Div., Aug. 15, 1990)], a decision by the intermediate court of appeal for the State of New Jersey, describing Vineland Chemical Company's waste disposal operations and the resulting contamination of its site and of the surrounding environment.

[5]Hazardous wastes typically include such compounds as benzene, toluene, and xylene, as well as hydrocarbons. These products have been shown to cause cancer, and have been linked to birth defects.

[6]*See generally Diamond Shamrock Chemicals Co. v. Aetna Casualty & Surety Co., et al.* [Dkt. No. C-3939-84 (N.J. Super., Ch. Div., Morris Cty., Apr. 12, 1989)].

[7]In another egregious incident, millions of gallons of toxic wastes were illegally dumped at a residential site in Lackawanna County, Pennsylvania. According to an EPA description of NPL sites, the "Keyser Avenue Borehole" or "Lavelle Borehole" is located on a residential property in Scranton, Pennsylvania. The borehole, approximately two feet in diameter and 110 feet deep, was originally used in conjunction with coal mining operations. A mine pool lies approximately 152 feet beneath the bottom of the borehole, and other pools, which together hold approximately 10 million gallons of water, are in the area. In 1984, the Pennsylvania Court of Common Pleas convicted William Lavelle of having dumped 3.5 million gallons of liquid wastes, from 1976 through 1979, down the borehole via a floor drain in a commercial garage rented by Lavelle. Samplings in 1984–1985 of the air and sludge at the bottom of the borehole revealed the presence of benzene, chlorobenzene, chloroform, ethylbenzene, and other hazardous chemical compounds. The hazardous waste that was discharged directly into the mine pools threatens groundwater, including private wells within three miles of the site used for drinking water by approximately 1400 persons.

[8]For example, in the wake of the massive 1989 oil spill from the tanker *Exxon Valdes* off the pristine waters of Prince William Sound, Alaska, several companies banded together to formulate the ten-point Valdes Principles. These principles ask subscribing companies to agree to (1) protect the biosphere, by minimizing or eliminating the release of any pollutant that may cause "environmental damage to the air, water or earth and its inhabitants" by safeguarding habitats in rivers, lakes, wetlands, coastal zones and oceans, and by minimizing

the signatories' contribution to the depletion of the ozone layer, acid rain, or smog; (2) make "sustainable use of renewable natural resources, such as water, soils and forests...[and to] conserve nonrenewable natural resources through efficient use and careful planning"; (3) minimize the creation of waste, especially hazardous wastes, recycle wherever possible, and dispose of wastes properly; (4) use environmentally safe and sustainable energy sources to meet corporate needs, by investment in improved energy efficiency and conservation; (5) reduce environmental, health, and safety risks to employees and communities in which the signatories operate, by employing safe technologies and operating procedures and being prepared for emergencies; (6) market safe products and services, that minimize adverse environmental impact, and inform consumers of any adverse impact; (7) take responsibility for harm caused to the environment by their actions, and make every effort to restore the environment fully and to compensate adversely affected persons; (8) disclose to employees and the public incidents related to the signatories' operations that cause environmental harm or pose health or safety risks, and not take action against any "whistleblower" that reveals any adverse condition or incident that endangered the environment or public health or safety; (9) commit management resources to implement these principles, including funding an executive position responsible for environmental affairs, and appointing to the Board of Directors at least one individual familiar with and able to address environmental concerns; and (10) conduct and publicize an annual self-evaluation of the signatories' progress in implementing these principles and complying with all applicable laws and regulations throughout the signatories' world-wide operations. Sadly, but not surprisingly, although these principles were endorsed by several major companies, by "Earth Day 1990," fewer than 20 corporations had signed the principles.

[9]*See*, e.g., *Washington Post* (December 18, 1990 at D1), discussing the introduction of environmentally geared corporate resolutions targeting, in particular, the oil, gas, chemicals, and utilities industries.

[10]State governments, as well as private parties seeking redress for pollution-related damages, may also sue those parties allegedly responsible for the pollution or environmentally related harm under various common law causes of action, including trespass (unlawful interference with possession of property), nuisance (unreasonable interference with use or enjoyment of property), negligence (breach of a recognized duty of care which proximately causes damage to the plaintiff), and strict liability for dangerous or ultrahazardous activities. *See*, e.g., *Suffolk County Water Auth. v. Union Carbide Corp.* [No. 90-14163 (N.Y. Sup.,Ct., May 2, 1991)] (action for nuisance and trespass in connection with groundwater contamination allegedly caused by application of pesticide manufactured by defendants); *New Jersey v. Ventron Corp.* [182 N.J. Super. 210 (App. Div. 1981), aff'd. as modified, 94 N.J. 473 (1983)] (affirming finding of strict liability against Ventron, under common law principles of, *inter alia*, public nuisance and participation in abnormally dangerous activity, in connection with Ventron's having caused extensive mercury contamination of a creek); *Borland v. Sanders Lead Co.* [369 So. 2d 523 (Ala. 1979)] (action for trespass in regard to emissions from lead smelting process that caused sulfoxide gases and lead particulates to enter onto plaintiff's land); *see also Department of Transp. v. P.S.C. Resources* [175 N.J. Super. 447, 419 A.2d 1151 (N.J. Super. , Law Div. 1980)] (successor corporation, which had purchased all of predecessor corporation's assets and continued same operation and waste disposal process alleged to be source of pollution, held strictly liable for prior property owner's dumping of toxic wastes at site and onto adjacent property).

In addition to claims by private parties for damage to their property, many individual plaintiffs seek redress for, *inter alia*, alleged bodily injury caused by exposure to toxic and/or potentially cancer-causing chemicals, emotional distress, costs of long-term medical monitoring, potentially latent illnesses, etc. Multiparty personal injury claims and class action suits in connection with alleged damages at large Superfund sites are not uncommon.

[11]The *Federal Water Pollution Control Act* [P.L. 92-500 (October 18, 1972)] was amended by, *inter alia*, the *Clean Water Act of 1977*, and is commonly known as the *Clean Water Act*.

[12]This act, which does not authorize any private cause of action, provides for strict, joint, and several liability for clean-up costs, but is not applicable to groundwater.

[13]*See also* the *Toxic Substances Control Act* (TSCA) [15 U.S.C. §2601 *et seq*.], providing for the testing and/or regulation of toxic substances, including asbestos, PCB, and dioxin;

and the *Federal Insecticide, Fungicide and Rodenticide Act* [7 U.S.C. §136 *et seq.*], providing for the registration, regulation, and restricted use of pesticides.

[14]*See also* the *Superfund Amendments and Reauthorization Act of 1986* (SARA) [P.L. 99-499, Oct. 17, 1986].

[15]As of February 1991, the number of so-called "Superfund" sites on the federal NPL, that is, the list of hazardous waste sites deemed in need of federal remediation efforts, had mushroomed to nearly 1200. *See* Fig. 14.1. Many of these sites are on federal properties; indeed, the federal government is one of the most egregious polluters in the country. The Senate and House recently passed legislation clarifying the authority of the EPA and states to impose civil fines against federal agencies for failing to comply with federal clean-up requirements. Federal agencies have claimed that they are immune from clean-up requirements and exempt from fines; courts have split on the issue.

[16]Thus, the United States need not prove that the site represents an imminent and substantial endangerment to the public.

[17]*CERCLA* holds the "owner" of a facility liable for the costs of cleaning up hazardous substances released at the facility [42 U.S.C. §§9607(a)(1), (2)]. An "owner" of a site includes a part owner of a "facility," which is itself defined as a "building or structure...where a hazardous substance has been deposited, stored, disposed of, or placed, or otherwise come to be located" [*Id.* §9601(9)]. The definition of "owner" is broadly construed, and persons have been deemed to be "owners" under the statute even if they had no personal connection to the wastes or polluting discharges that allegedly caused the environmental harm. *See, e.g., United States v. Argent Corp.*, No. CIV-83-0523BB, 21 ERC 1345 (D.N.M. May 4, 1984) (property owner who leased property to third party and had no connection to business operated thereon held to be owner subject to *CERCLA* liability). The definition specifically excludes, however, "a person who, without participating in the management of a...facility, holds indicia of ownership primarily to protect his security interest in the...facility" [42 U.S.C. §9601(20)(A)]. *Compare In re Bergsoe Metal Corp.* [910 F.2d 668 (9th Cir. 1990)], with *United States v. Fleet Factors Corp.* [901 F.2d 1550 (11th Cir. 1990)]. In *Bergsoe*, the port authority, which held deed to property on which a lead recycling plant was situated, as part of a transaction whose sole purpose was to provide financing for the plant, was not an "owner" liable for the cost of environmental clean-up under *CERCLA* where the port authority did not participate in the actual management of the plant. In *Fleet Factors*, the court held that the secured creditor of a bankrupt cloth printing facility may be liable under *CERCLA* [42 U.S.C. §9607(a)(2)], even though it was not the actual operator of the facility, by virtue of its participation in the financial management of the facility to a degree indicating its capacity to influence the facility's treatment of hazardous wastes.

[18]An *operator* is defined as one who has "overall" responsibility for the operation of a facility. *See also New York v. Shore Realty Corp.* [759 F.2d 1032 (2d Cir. 1985)] (present property owner who purchased site contaminated by prior owners or operators held subject to *CERCLA* liability, and stockholder and officer of corporate owner liable as an "operator" under *CERCLA)*. Both owners and operators are required to have a permit, and to comply with strict guidelines regarding, *inter alia*, the nature and types of wastes accepted, the method and nature of storage, treatment and disposal, and any closure of the facility, and they must be able to meet specified financial responsibility requirements.

[19]Each generator is required, *inter alia*, to have its own identification number, to produce a manifest for all wastes shipped offsite, to comply with EPA (and state) packaging and labeling requirements, and to maintain its manifests and records to provide a paper trail of the movement of its wastes.

[20]A transporter is defined as one who accepts hazardous waste for transportation "offsite" along a public right-of-way. Transporters must comply with federal hazardous waste manifest rules as well as with U.S. Department of Transportation rules governing the transport of hazardous materials, and must clean up spills incurred during the course of transportation.

[21]*See, e.g., Wisconsin v. Rollfink* [No. 89-1908 (Wis., September 19, 1991)], discussed in *Toxics Law Reporter* (BNA, October 2, 1991) at 555 (Wisconsin Supreme Court refused to re-

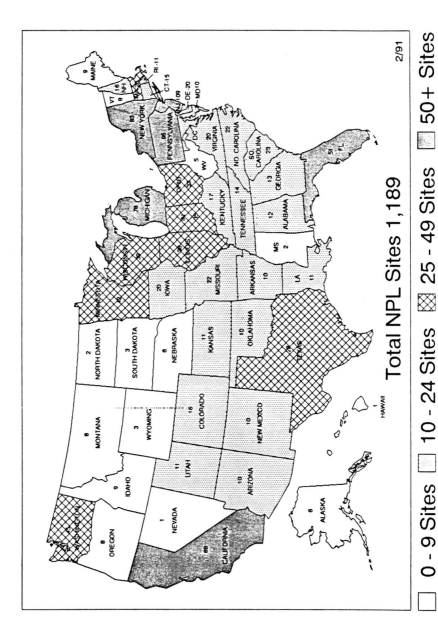

Total NPL Sites 1,189

☐ 0 - 9 Sites   ☐ 10 - 24 Sites   ▨ 25 - 49 Sites   ▦ 50+ Sites

Figure 14.1. National priority list sites.

consider its decision that a corporate operating officer was personally liable for forfeitures or penalties assessed against a corporation for violating state's hazardous waste law, even though no personal participation alleged in unlawful acts); *Department of Environmental Protection v. Engineered Precision Casting Co.* [OAL Dkt. No. EWR 1693-90 (slip op., July 3, 1991)] (administrative ruling that two officers and shareholders of corporation could be held personally liable for civil penalties for violations of New Jersey Water Pollution Control Act); *Mobay v. Allied Signal Corp.* [761 F. Supp. 345 (D.N.J. 1991)] (parent corporation liable under CERCLA for acts of former wholly owned subsidiary); *New York v. Shore Realty Corp.* [759 F.2d 1032 (2d Cir. 1985)] (stockholder and officer of corporation liable as "operator" under CERCLA. See generally 129 *N.J. Law Journal* 398 (October 10, 1991), discussing clean-up liability of corporate officers).

[22]This list does not include such additional transactional expenses as the costs of retaining legal counsel as well as personnel to investigate, oversee, or monitor the remediation, or such incidental costs as expenses incurred in obtaining electrical power or water to operate equipment or conduct tests.

[23]Even when a corporate PRP is still in existence, it may lack the financial resources or insurance coverage to pay its allocated share of clean-up costs.

[24]*See*, e.g., the cities of Johnstown and Gloversville, in upstate New York, are defendants in pending Superfund actions arising in connection with pollution emanating from landfills operated for many years by these municipalities. New Castle County in Delaware faces similar liability. Fifty municipalities have been sued in federal court in Camden, New Jersey in connection with the GEMS Superfund litigation, arising from the operation of a municipal landfill in Gloucester Township, New Jersey. Twenty-four Connecticut communities have been sued in an environmental action in federal court in Hartford.

[25]*See The Wall Street Journal* ("Pollution Ploy—Big Corporations Hit by Superfund Cases Find Way to Share Bill," April 2, 1991). The article reported that among those sued by the two corporations was Doreen Merlino, the owner of a two-table takeout restaurant selling pizza and spicy chicken wings. In naming Merlino as a defendant, the corporate plaintiffs did not even know exactly what kind of hazardous waste Merlino may have sent to the landfill; rather, their attorney "surmised" that the restaurant's waste "might have included empty cleanser or insecticide cans or some other item containing traces of toxins." The corporations sued for $3000, but were willing to accept $1500 if she settled quickly. Unable to afford defense counsel fees, Merlino cut her employees' hours and stopped paying herself, in order to raise the $1500, even though she believed she was not liable of having contributed hazardous waste to the site.

[26]Companies also face potential liability under available common law theories. *See*, e.g., T. Mayer, "Clean-up Cost Liabilities Flowing from Product Sales," *New York Law Journal* (December 17, 1991), describing a May 2, 1991, decision by the New York Supreme Court, a trial court, denying motions by defendants Union Carbide Corp. and Rhone-Poulenc Ag Company to dismiss claims of trespass and nuisance brought by plaintiff landowner Suffolk County Water Authority. The Authority claims that the defendants are liable for extensive groundwater contamination caused by the application of aldicarb, a pesticide manufactured by the defendants and used by Suffolk County potato farmers.

[27]*See generally New Jersey Dep't. of Envtl. Protection v. Arky's Auto Sales* [774 N.J. Super. 700 (App. Div. 1988)] (affirming judgment against Arky's under *New Jersey Water Pollution Control Act* and *New Jersey Spill Act*, finding Arky's liable for contamination of soils on property it had purchased in 1971 and had leased to "Richards" who in turn had permitted "Daldone," apparently without Arky's knowledge or consent, to bring steel drums containing hazardous wastes to the property; during the course of emptying or storing the drums, some drums were ruptured, or hazardous chemicals were spilled onto the site, and the contamination was not discovered until after a chemical fire broke out at the site in or about 1973); *Center Realty v. Petroleum and Chem. Technology, Inc.* [No. W-011751-89 (bench op.) (N.J. Super. Ct., Law Div., Middlesex Co., April 8, 1991)] (discussing, *inter alia*, claims for cleanup made against plaintiff, the owner of Raritan Center, a series of commercial buildings, in connection with the discharge by vandals of pollutants abandoned in Building No. 455 of the Center by defendant Petroleum and Chemical Technology, Inc.,

a former lessee of the property); *New Castle County v. Hartford Accident & Indem. Co.* [685 F. Supp. 1321 (D. Del. 1988)] (describing background of County's liability for environmental contamination resulting from leachate emanating from municipal landfills the county owned and operated); and *Powers Chemco, Inc. v. Federal Ins. Co.* [74 N.Y. 2d 910, 549 N.Y.S. 2d 650 (1989)] (New York Court of Appeals affirmed ruling for insurer, finding pollution exclusion in liability policy issued to Powers Chemco precluded coverage for sudden and accidental pollution-related liability, notwithstanding that insured had not been the polluter and had merely inherited the pollution problem from a prior land owner).

[28]*See generally Central Quality Servs. Corp. d/b/a Traverse Overall Supply Co. v. Insurance Co. of N. Am.* [Civ. No. 87-CV-74473-DT, mem. op. (E.D. Mich., Sept. 6, 1989)] (discussing, *inter alia,* the initiation of claims for pollution clean-up costs by the EPA, pursuant to *CERCLA,* against the plaintiffs in connection with Central Quality Services' discharge of dry-cleaning solvents and chemicals into the environment at its plant); *Beckman Instruments, Inc. v. International Ins. Co.* [No. CV 85-8382 MRP, mem. op. (C.D. Cal. Jan. 27, 1988)] (discussing, *inter alia,* the alleged liability of plaintiff manufacturer for contamination of groundwater and residential wells caused when toxic industrial wastes, dumped into solar ponds on the plaintiff's plant grounds, leaked into the groundwater); *New Jersey v. Ventron Corp.* [182 N.J. Super. 210 (App. Div. 1981), aff'd. as modified, 94 N.J. 473 (1983)] (affirming finding of strict liability against Ventron, under common law principles of, *inter alia,* public nuisance and participation in abnormally dangerous activity, in connection with extensive mercury contamination of a creek). The *Ventron* contamination has spawned substantial litigation. Ventron purchased the assets of Wood Ridge Chemical Company in 1968, and continued the mercury processing plant operations begun by F. W. Berk & Co., Inc. From 1929 to 1960, Berk had dumped untreated waste materials onto its property and allowed mercury-laden effluent to drain on and over the land through open drainage ditches. Subsequent investigation revealed that mercury pollution had seeped into the creek from land saturated by an estimated 268 tons of toxic waste, which accumulated during 50 years of unchecked processing operations. *See also Long Island Newsday* (August 13, 1991, at A-7), which described testimony by a former employee of Northville Industries, a fuel company, that Northville had been aware that its gasoline storage tanks were leaking from its tank farm in Setauket, Long Island. In 1988, Northville announced that approximately one million gallons of petroleum product had escaped from the tank farm, and had spread in an underground plume beneath 550 homes in an adjacent community. Northville was sued by homeowners for property damage, and was also investigated for possible criminal violations in connection with the leak.

[29]*CERCLA* does provide a "security interest exemption" which excludes from the definition of "owner and operator" a person "who, without participating in the management of a vessel or facility, holds indicia of ownership primarily to protect his security interest" [42 U.S.C. §9601(20)(A)]. In several recent decisions, lenders have found themselves potentially liable as an owner or operator of a Superfund site. *See, e.g., United States v. Mirabile* [15 ELR 20994 (E.D. Pa. 1985)] (bank loan officer's frequent visit to site, coupled with his insistence on certain manufacturing and personnel changes, may make bank liable as operator under *CERCLA*); *United States v. Maryland Bank & Trust Co.* [632 F. Supp. 573 (D. Md. 1986)] (denying bank's summary judgment motion to be relieved of liability for clean-up, where bank, which foreclosed on property, then purchased the site at foreclosure sale; court found that bank had purchased property to protect its overall investment in property, rather than to protect its security interest); *United States v. Fleet Factors Corp.* [901 F.2d 1550 (11th Cir. 1990)] (in federal action under *CERCLA* seeking to obtain response costs for cleanup of hazardous chemicals and asbestos at facility from sole shareholders of bankrupt cloth printing facility and from creditor with security interest in the facility and its equipment, inventories, and fixtures, court denied secured creditor's motion for summary judgment, and indicated that creditor may be liable under *CERCLA* section imposing liability on owners and operators of facility, even though it was not an actual operator, by virtue of creditor's having participated in financial management of facility to a degree indicating a capacity to influence facility's treatment of hazardous

waste). *Cf. In re Bergsoe Metal Corp.* [910 F.2d 668 (9th Cir. 1990)] (port authority, which held deed to property on which lead recycling plant was situated, held not to be an "owner" liable for cost of environmental cleanup under *CERCLA* where port authority did not participate in actual management of plant); *see generally* "RTC [Resolution Trust Corporation] Allowed Environmental Tests," *New York Law Journal* (December 18, 1991), indicating that the Resolution Trust Corporation (RTC), acting as receiver for a failed Long Island, New York bank, had obtained permission to conduct environmental tests at five properties before deciding whether to take title to them in a $3.9-million mortgage foreclosure, in order to avoid the risk of potential harm the RTC could face based on recent legal developments increasing the risk that a secured lender may be held liable for the costs of environmental clean-ups of mortgaged property. At least one insurance company that assumed an active role in the remediation of a hazardous waste site has been implicated in a state cost-recovery action. *See also Phoenix v. Garbage Serv. Co.* [33 ERC 1655 (D. Ariz. 1991)] (bank potentially liable as owner of landfill in its capacity as trustee or executor); Kass and Gerard, "Minimizing Lender Liability," *New York Law Journal* (December 27, 1991).

According to a report in *Mealey's Litigation Reports—Insurance* (November 19, 1991), the Washington Department of Ecology has named Federated Mutual Insurance Company as a "potentially liable party" under the state's *Model Toxics Control Act* because Federal allegedly undertook to manage remedial efforts at a site, after the discovery of petroleum releases from underground tanks. In addition to indemnifying its insured, an oil company, in connection with the releases, Federal allegedly controlled such remediation activities as the installation of monitoring wells or recovery wells, and the installation of a remedial soil venting system.

[30]Sometimes, of course, a party first learns that it is a potential PRP upon receipt of a subpoena for documents to be used in a grand jury investigation.

[31]The imposition of joint and several liability may often have a disparate impact on PRPs. In some instances, a corporation with ample financial resources that contributed a relatively small amount of waste to a particular Superfund site has been forced to bear more than its fair share of the allocated costs of clean-up, where other PRPs with greater allocations were insolvent or otherwise unable to pay their proportionate remediation costs.

[32]If Squeaky were an owner or operator of a hazardous waste site, or a transporter of wastes to the site, its initial investigation should still focus on identifying all generators that sent wastes to the site, the types of wastes, the volume of wastes shipped to the site, and whether any such wastes were recycled, reclaimed, transshipped, etc.

[33]Again, because written records are potentially discoverable, the investigator should take care not to create any new records, or to provide written documentation during the investigatory stage.

[34]Obviously, Squeaky should also review its own liability insurance policies, and, if there is coverage in connection with the purported liability, should notify its insurance carriers as quickly as possible of the EPA and/or state claims. Note, however, that the mere existence of insurance policies purchased by Squeaky or naming Squeaky as an additional insured does not mean that coverage is or will be available to respond to the governmental and/or private party claims against Squeaky.

The investigation by Squeaky's counsel should ultimately prove useful in preparing Squeaky's responses to interrogatories and document demands promulgated during the course of any litigation subsequently commenced in connection with the contamination or proposed clean-up of the site.

[35]Neighbors of landfills and other hazardous waste disposal facilities are generally quite willing to discuss the discomfort they experienced from their close proximity to the landfill or facility, including such annoyances as rats, fires, or continual stench. Neighbors may also provide information about complaints to state or local oversight agencies that were ignored, thereby developing possible evidence that deliberate or negligent governmental inaction contributed to the conditions at the site.

[36]The advent of Superfund-type enforcement actions has not only given rise to a plethora of environmental consulting firms, specializing in such matters as site investiga-

tions, remedial design systems, litigation support, risk assessment, and regulatory compliance assistance, but has also spawned a new industry—companies that specialize in developing a history of a site's ownership and operations. Environmental consulting firms now employ persons in a variety of professions, including, for example, hydrogeologists, soil scientists, risk assessment toxicologists, groundwater modelers, environmental engineers, chemical engineers, and civil engineers, all readily available to respond to a PRP's request for information about a site.

[37]The EPA obtains this kind of information by taking samplings from drums, tanks, surface impoundments, soil, groundwater, and the air, and by studying the hydrogeology of the site.

[38]In some instances, the EPA has actually indicated that it will not negotiate with individual PRPs, but only with representatives of PRP committees.

[39]Where federal natural resources have been threatened or injured by polluting discharges at a site, any settlement seeking releases for natural resources damages may require negotiation with and authority from the United States Department of Justice and the United States Department of the Interior, as well as other federal agencies.

[40]Other factors to consider in deciding whether to join a PRP defense group are the solvency of other PRPs, the amount of waste contributed to the site by private parties rather than governmental entities, and the nature of the wastes at the site, and whether one type of waste contributed by one or more parties, such as PCBs or dioxin, is mandating a particular type of clean-up.

[41]In 1991, the EPA stepped up its efforts to collect fines from alleged polluters. For example, the EPA sought fines of more than $2 million from six New Jersey companies allegedly involved in fur processing or the transportation and disposal of sawdust laden with solvent produced by the fur makers. The solvents are potential carcinogens, and the EPA sought the fines because the sawdust had allegedly been disposed of at unapproved sites.

[42]A discussion of individual state environmental crimes is beyond the scope of this chapter. Note, however, that many states deliberately track or model their own environmental laws on the federal statutes described *infra*, in order to ensure that the states are eligible to receive federal funds for environmental law enforcement.

[43]The state of mind of an accused is frequently addressed in criminal statutes as one of the required elements of a crime that must be proven beyond a reasonable doubt. For example, a generic definition of burglary may be to knowingly enter a premises with the intent to commit a crime therein. To convict an accused burglar, a prosecutor would be required to prove that the defendant had entered the burglarized premises, and that the defendant possessed the *mens rea*, that is, the specific criminal intent to commit a crime therein. Criminal laws intended to punish polluters frequently do not require that the actor intended to commit an environmental crime, but rather only that the defendant acted knowingly, that is, he committed the criminal act and was aware of doing so.

[44]Congress enacted *RCRA* in 1976 as a "cradle-to-grave" regulatory scheme for toxic materials, to protect the nation against the dangers of improper disposal of hazardous wastes. As originally enacted, knowing disposal (but not treatment or storage) of hazardous waste without a permit constituted a misdemeanor. Amendments passed in 1978 and 1980 expanded the criminal provision to cover treatment and storage of hazardous wastes, and increased the criminal penalties from a misdemeanor to a felony [*United States v. Johnson & Towers, Inc.*, 741 F.2d 662, 666–67 (3d Cir. 1984)].

[45]To ensure that the Act is broadly enforced on a national basis, Congress has authorized the appropriation of $110 million for the EPA Office of Criminal Investigations.

[46]The corporate employee or agent may face individual liability if he commits an offense, even though acting at the time of the violation for the corporation as an employee or agent. Indeed, it is no defense to individual criminal liability for the employee or agent to claim that he was acting not for himself but for the corporation. *See United States v. North Am. Van Lines, Inc.* [202 F. Supp. 639 (D.D.C. 1962)], *United States v. Amrep Corp.* [560 F.2d 539 (2d Cir. 1977), cert. denied, 434 U.S. 1015 (1978)].

[47]For federal rules regarding accessorial liability, see 18 U.S.C. §§2(a), (b).

[48]Federal statutes do not define corporate criminal liability per se; accordingly, in evaluating the liability of a corporation itself for environmental violations, courts are guided by the general principles of corporate liability that have developed primarily in case law.

[49]The following cases, collected by and cited in the Brickey article, demonstrate that the conduct of low-level employees may affect corporate liability. *See, e.g., United States v. George F. Fish, Inc.,* 154 F.2d 798 (2d Cir.), cert. denied, 328 U.S. 869 (1946); *Zito v. United States,* 64 F.2d 772 (7th Cir. 1933); *United States v. Wilson,* 59 F.2d 97 (W.D. Wash. 1932), (salesmen); *Riss & Co. v. United States,* 262 F.2d 245 (8th Cir. 1958) (rating clerk); *United States v. Harry L. Young & Sons,* 464 F.2d 1295 (10th Cir. 1972); *Texas-Oklahoma Express, Inc. v. United States,* 429 F.2d 100 (10th Cir. 1970); *Steere Tank Lines, Inc. v. United States,* 149 F. Supp. 814 (D. Md. 1957) (truck drivers); *United States v. Illinois Cent. R.R.,* 303 U.S. 239 (1938) (manual laborers); and *United States v. Dye Constr. Co.,* 510 F.2d 78 (10th Cir. 1975) (laborers).

[50]There is a theory of liability under which corporate officers may be held criminally liable for failing to ensure that the corporation meets or complies with certain regulatory standards. Thus far, this principle has been upheld in prosecutions under the United States *Food, Drug, and Cosmetics Act. See United States v. Park* [421 U.S. 658 (1975)] and *United States v. Dotterweich* [320 U.S. 277 (1943)], upholding convictions of high corporate officers for criminal violations in which they did not directly participate, under the theory that those who have the power to prevent violations of regulatory standards or who have the responsibility to detect and correct such violations may be held personally, criminally responsible for failing to ensure that their subordinates meet applicable regulatory standards. One possible defense available to a corporate officer facing alleged "supervisory liability" is impossibility, that is, establishing that the officer exercised extraordinary care but was nevertheless unable to prevent violations of the regulation or statute. *See generally United States v. Gel Spice Co., Inc.* [773 F.2d 427 (2d Cir. 1985)] (criminal violation of federal *Food, Drug, and Cosmetic Act); United States v. New England Grocers Co.* [488 F. Supp. 230 (D. Mass. 1980)].

[51]The doctrine of collective knowledge is most often, if not exclusively, applied in prosecutions under the Interstate Commerce Act.

[52]Note that while an in-house attorney on an audit team may be deemed not to have acted as an attorney, but rather as an officer or business advisor. *See* Fed. R. Evid. 501, an attorney conducting an audit may engage environmental engineers and consultants, and communicate with these persons on a confidential-to-attorney basis.

[53]Audit reports could be demanded by a party as part of routine discovery in civil litigation, and would probably have to be produced.

PART 3

Public Police at the Crime Scene

15
Preliminary Investigations Manual

Rochester Police Department

OBJECTIVES OF A PRELIMINARY INVESTIGATION

The preliminary or initial investigation is the police agency's first response to a report that a crime has occurred. As in every investigative effort, the primary objective of the preliminary investigation is to determine who committed the crime and to apprehend the criminal. The preliminary investigator collects evidence that solidly supports the occurrence of a crime, the identification of the person responsible for the crime, and the arrest and subsequent conviction of the criminal.

These objectives seem simple; yet they are vital. Unfortunately, they are often completely forgotten by preliminary investigators. All too often, preliminary investigators see their role as no more than that of mechanical report takers, when, in fact, the report is the vehicle for conveying the results of the preliminary investigation. Police officers should remember that they are the preliminary investigators, and that their work at this early stage will uncover the majority of usable information about the case.

The framework of the preliminary investigation is based on the following major tasks:

1. Verification that an offense actually occurred.

SOURCE: Reprinted with special permission from James F. Hastings, Chief of Police, Rochester Police Department, New York.

2. Identification of the victim, the place of the crime, and the time the crime occurred.

3. Identification of solvability factors.

4. Communication of the circumstances of the crime.

5. Identification of those investigative tasks completed and those yet to be done.

Completion of these actions is the total objective of the preliminary investigation and will guide the activities of the initial investigator during his work. Although there is no definitive order of priority by which these tasks must be done, the best investigative strategy dictates that the officer should first determine whether a crime occurred.

VERIFICATION OF OCCURRENCE

To verify the occurrence of a crime, the preliminary investigator must do four things:

1. Respond to the scene.

2. Document that a crime has actually happened.

3. Determine when the crime occurred.

4. Identify and assist the victim.

Responding to the Call

The preliminary investigation begins at the time the investigator receives the call to respond to the scene of the crime. As soon as the call is received, the investigator should mentally prepare for arrival at the scene ready to begin asking questions. Factors appropriate to the type of crime committed should be considered. In many types of crime, robbery for example, the preliminary investigator, while traveling to the area of the crime, should look for suspicious people or automobiles speeding away from the scene.

It is good practice for the preliminary investigator, immediately upon arrival, to make a quick visual survey of the scene to determine who is present, the location of objects, and what seems to have occurred. This visual picture may be very important later when the investigator tries to determine exactly who was present at the crime scene, and who the witnesses may be.

The first priority is to determine if anyone is injured. However, even if a person is injured, and while first aid is being secured, the preliminary investigator must be aware of the immediate surroundings and the people present, since eventually the priority will turn toward criminal apprehension.

One of the most important sources of information about the crime is witnesses—witnesses who may watch the investigator arrive, and then leave. Measures must be taken to ensure that such parties remain at the scene until they have been interviewed.

Document Occurrence of Crime

Crime occurrence is relatively simple to loosely document. But the preliminary investigator must record the occurrence to the varying degrees and limitations of criminal law. Therefore, it is best to discover what has occurred and, after other facets of the investigation are completed, define the crime exactly, for example, the degree of the offense.

Here are three determination hints to follow:

1. Thought should be given to whether the lapse in time between the offense and the notification to the police seems normal or questionable.

2. The investigator should be on the lookout for discrepancies in the victim's statement or between statements given by victim and witness(es).

3. Physical evidence should support the crime facts related by victim.

Identify and Assist the Victim

Another important initial task of the preliminary investigator is victim identification. Often, the victim has the most useful information about the incident and who was responsible for it. The victim usually is the complainant and will usually be the first person the officer interviews.

When victims are excited, the officers must first try to calm them enough to allow them to tell their story accurately. Officers should properly identify themselves, then try to establish rapport with each victim. Before asking specific and detailed questions, a general description of what happened should be obtained. This permits the victim to calm down and provides the preliminary investigator with an understanding of the overall sequence of events. The investigator should play a supportive role for the victim by remaining calm, sympathetic, and understanding.

The officer should remain neutral and not offer moral or social criticisms. Victims of crime sometimes suffer long-term reactions of guilt and anxiety if they are not dealt with carefully. If they are questioned about why something happened, victims may feel such questions imply the crime was their fault. The officer, then, must be careful to avoid questions such as, "Why didn't you lock your windows?" or "Why were you carrying so much money?" since such questions may seem improperly punitive and judgmental. If the victim is pregnant and not married, the investigator must not let any personal feelings about unwed mothers enter into the interview. In other words, the preliminary investigator must take care not to set standards of morality for the victim. Personal comments in such situations can cause a victim to refuse to cooperate further in the interview. Eventually, the victim may refuse to file a report of the crime or to prosecute if the criminal is apprehended. Preliminary investigators must remember their purpose is to obtain information concerning the crime and not do anything that will lessen their credibility or impair their ability to obtain the needed information. They are in the unique position of rendering psychological first aid to victims. The sympathy, sensitivity, competence, and confidence they display can be very important in building the required rapport between investigator and victim.

When a degree of rapport has been established, the investigator should begin asking questions about the specifics of the crime. It is important that the interview be kept moving, always toward obtaining useful information. This is sometimes difficult because people often ramble once they have the sympathetic ear of the investigating officer. Comments such as, "That's interesting. Now, to get back to that suspicious man...," can be useful in dealing with the problem.

IDENTIFICATION OF SOLVABILITY FACTORS

A *solvability factor* is information about a crime that can provide the basis for determining who committed it. Or, simply, a solvability factor is a lead, a clue, to who the criminal is.

Not all crimes can be solved, no matter how much investigative effort is put forth. There are so many crimes each day that many police agencies find themselves hard-pressed to provide minimal investigative effort for all reported crimes. As a result of this resource-utilization pressure, the number of crimes solved diminishes, because few crimes receive sufficient investigative resources to produce a result unless, of course, an on-scene arrest is made.

Police resources are limited. Therefore, it makes sense that the effectiveness of police investigations will be increased only if resources are allocated to those occurrences that have a chance of solution. To direct resources to crimes that have little chance of solution is both wasteful and generally unproductive. Solvability factors are so important because they can provide a valid guide to the allocation of scarce resources.

Without a solvability factor, the chances of crime solution are small. When the solvability factor is present, there is a reasonable chance for a solution. Solvability factors have been selected through extensive research into what information results in crime clearances. This research found that at least 1 of 12 leads was present in each of the solved cases reviewed. If none of these 12 leads was present, the crime was not solved.

Throughout the investigation process, we search for leads upon which further investigative efforts can be based. And since only some leads may later become useful, preliminary investigators should concentrate their efforts on finding those leads, or solvability factors. This is the objective of the preliminary investigation.

Twelve Solvability Factors

1. Witnesses to the crime
2. Knowledge of a suspect's name
3. Knowledge of where a suspect can be located
4. Description of a suspect
5. Identification of a suspect
6. Property with identifiable characteristics, marks, or numbers, so it can be traced
7. A significant modus operandi (MO)
8. Significant physical evidence
9. Description that identifies the automobile used by the suspect
10. Positive results from a crime scene evidence search
11. Belief that a crime may be solved with publicity and/or reasonable additional investigative effort
12. Opportunity for but one person to have committed the crime

The preliminary investigator's job is to determine which, if any, of these solvability factors exist. Effective investigative strategy dictates that the investigator consider each factor separately and thoroughly to see if evidence points to its existence.

A measure of success in a preliminary investigation is the identification and description of solvability factors. Adequate effort has been expended by the investigator when every possible avenue for identification of the solvability factors has been explored. At the conclusion of the preliminary investigation, the investigator must believe there is little chance that an unidentified solvability factor exists.

Since crimes are unlikely to be solved unless solvability factors have been identified, it should be clear why the preliminary investigator's work is so important. If preliminary investigative work is competently done and reported, and success in case solution is deemed possible, a police agency can assign follow-up investigators. To avoid duplication of effort, the preliminary investigator must convince the follow-up investigator that all leads or solvability factors have been explored. If the follow-up investigator is not convinced, much of the preliminary investigator's work will be duplicated, thus delaying follow-up investigation efforts directed toward areas with the highest payoff in terms of investigative success.

Utilization of Individual Solvability Factors

Every solvability factor has an identifiable relationship to crime solution. For example, when witnesses are identified, information about the perpetrators of the crime is usually available. When an unusual MO is found, the crime can often be linked with similar crimes, thus permitting merging of investigative information and efforts.

In working to identify solvability factors, the preliminary investigator must keep in mind why that solvability factor is important (its objective), the strategies that might be adopted in deciding whether it exists, and the actions that the investigator should take for identifying solvability factors.

Effective investigators know these solvability factor objectives, strategies, procedures, and measures of accomplishment so well that they apply them automatically to each case.

In the following sections, each solvability factor is explored in the context of these important standards.

IDENTIFICATION OF WITNESSES

Objectives. Witnesses are usually the most important source of information about a crime. The preliminary investigator thoroughly searches the area surrounding the crime to identify persons who may have seen the crime occur, or who may have seen or heard something directly or *indirectly* related to the crime.

This solvability factor is important not only in itself, but also because it is the basis for several others. Suspect information and information about vehicles involved in the crime, for example, are usually obtained from witnesses.

To find witnesses, the investigator must ask those present, *"Who else may have seen what happened?"* If identified, these persons then become potential witnesses.

The investigator seeks those present when the crime occurred, those who may have been in the area when the crime occurred, and those who can identify others who may also have been witnesses.

Strategies. There are two general places where witnesses may be found. The most obvious place is the scene of the crime. Many of the on-scene witnesses will still be at the scene when the investigator arrives, but, often, some will have left. It is, therefore, very important for the investigator to get to the scene of the crime quickly. Another logical source of witnesses is the area immediately surrounding the crime scene. One of the first tasks of the investigator is to determine what would be logical places for the witnesses to have been when the crime occurred or where they might have gone since the crime occurred. Success often depends on the number of contacts the investigator makes in this task through perseverance and ingenuity.

In seeking persons who may know something about the crime, the investigator should consider the broad range of persons who normally are in a given area regularly, such as mail carriers, telephone installers, gas meter readers, landlords, and delivery persons.

In asking for leads to other witnesses, the investigator must be careful to phrase questions in a manner that will encourage information, rather than narrowing the potential for information by asking limiting questions.

Procedures. To find witnesses, the investigator should start in the immediate area of the crime and determine where witnesses may be located.

The first witness discovered may possibly have all the facts; but a second or third witness will be very important when the case eventually goes to court. So, it is important to find all the witnesses possible in the investigation.

Often, the victim is the best witness. But even if the victim is a witness to the crime, the investigator always should seek additional witnesses, since it is always advisable to obtain corroborating evidence. Because crimes are usually emotional events and people's emotions often color their perceptions or memory of the crime, it is advisable never to rely solely on one source of information.

One effective way to identify witnesses is for the investigator to go to the exact scene of the crime and look around carefully to determine the best viewpoints for observation.

As part of the preliminary investigation of a burglary, for example, the investigator should recreate the crime through examination of the premises and determine the points of entry and exit from the scene. The investigator should then record what can be observed from each point. If the view takes in other occupied dwellings or buildings, the investigator may be able to locate additional valuable witnesses from those buildings.

As investigators identify locations of witnesses, they should approach each person in a positive way, aware that the person will have a natural curiosity regarding what has happened. Indeed, it should be no secret that a crime has occurred. Investigators should be willing to explain to any interested person that a crime has occurred and where it happened. They then may explain that they are trying to identify anyone who may have seen something concerning the crime.

Often, the persons questioned will not have information about the crime but may know of someone who has. In these instances, it is important to leave them cards with the preliminary investigator's name and the appropriate police department phone number on it so they will be able to provide information that later becomes available. They may have seen or heard something related to the crime but be unaware (at the moment of questioning) of its importance, because of their detachment from the event. The investigator should also make note of the contact on the preliminary investigation report so that a follow-up investigator may make a later contact.

Persons interviewed may also know of persons who could have been involved in the crime. While such information is almost rumor, it can be useful in providing an important sense of direction for other aspects of the preliminary investigation.

Indicated Actions. The investigator should get witnesses' names, addresses, and telephone numbers. To assist follow-up investigators, the preliminary investigator should record who were contacted as witnesses and what these witnesses saw, heard, or know about the crime. It is also important for the investigator to indicate clearly where other witnesses have been sought without success to avoid duplication by the follow-up investigator.

The quality of this data will largely determine the extent to which supervisors and follow-up investigators will rely on the preliminary investigator's report. All such information should be clearly communicated to the follow-up investigator.

Measures of Success. The investigating officer's task will have been completed if all witnesses have been located or actively sought. The test to measure the success of witness identification is in the following questions:

1. Have all persons present during the crime's occurrence been identified and questioned?

2. Have locations with a plain view of the crime scene or its access and egress been thoroughly searched for witnesses?

3. Have serious attempts been made to identify others who may have been in the vicinity of the crime at the time it occurred?

Crime Scene Search. A search for witnesses, however, is not a complete crime scene search.

The necessity for a thorough crime scene search to develop "best" and/or corroborating evidence is becoming more important every day as confessions, admissions, and search warrants are becoming fragile evidence in court. The nature of the crime will, of course, determine the amount of time that should be spent on a crime scene search. Consequently, a search at a petit larceny scene will not warrant the same thoroughness as a search at a major armed robbery or homicide scene.

As in the search for witnesses, the officer should immediately try to locate the points of entry and exit used by the suspect. Photographs should be taken of felony crime scenes and fingerprints dusted for at the point of entry and exit, at the location of the crime, and in any other locations that could be integral parts of the crime scene.

The investigator should search the area for evidence that might be associated with the offense, including the implements used; stolen property that possibly has been dropped, hidden, or abandoned; the suspect's personal effects; and footprints.

There is much in the way of evidence that may be found at or around the scene which by itself seems insignificant and will not identify the perpetrator, but which may be of critical value in determining the overall crime picture. The identification of this type of evidence and its itemization for future use will in many instances identify a suspect and when added to other information may subsequently lead to a conviction. Items such as footprints in snow, mud, or dust may indicate not only the size of the feet but also a path of escape to be searched for witnesses. A crumpled pack of cigarettes may not identify the burglar, but it might later be an important piece of evidence if it is the suspect's brand of cigarettes. Cigarettes with a trace of lipstick left in a house would certainly reduce the number of suspects being sought. Similarly, a single fingerprint may not immediately identify the suspect; but once we have a suspect, the fingerprint is evidence of presence at the crime scene.

Valuable indicators are often available at the scene for the diligent officer to recognize. A stopped electric clock may tell the time the suspect was in the house, if other electrical appliances were stolen and the clock's connection was disturbed; or the size of the point of entry may indicate the size of the suspect. An officer must be very thorough and use extreme care in observations at a crime scene, for the evidence is sometimes so obvious that it may be overlooked in the hurry to accomplish all that is required.

Once again, the victim can be of great assistance to the officer, for it is only the victim or another member of the family who really knows whether items such as a piece of clothing, a flashlight, or a tool belongs in the house of the victim or is an item that was used by the suspect.

In addition to searching the crime scene, the investigator must make accurate records at the scene. The evidence obtained here may subsequently be used in court. In many major crimes, the record will be made by the evidence technician. But in some instances, when the crime scene does not warrant a technician or one is not available, the investigator will be required to accomplish this task.

The need for an accurate sketch cannot be overemphasized. Many cases are lost on technicalities, as defense attorneys struggle to find any loophole. Recently, a case was lost in the grand jury when an officer recorded that the weapon was in the back seat. In his testimony, he corrected himself and said that it was in the front seat. The officer had effected a good arrest; a weapon was found in the car. And yet, through a slight error, a loophole, the suspect beat the case.

It is important to keep in mind that nothing at a crime scene should be left to memory. The great volume of work confronting police departments today and the lengthy delay before a case goes to court mandates that all information regarding investigations be accurately written.

PROPERTY IDENTIFICATION

Stolen property can also be a witness—a silent witness—to commission of a crime and the suspect's identity. The collection and proper recording of complete property descriptions may later prove to be the most critical aspect of the preliminary investigation.

Lacking exact descriptive information (serial number, color, size, markings, damage, and so on), suspected stolen property cannot be definitively linked to a crime scene for suspect prosecution or to an owner for its return. Search warrants for the recovery of stolen property and arrest of the possessor cannot be obtained if exact property descriptions are not available. Insurance frauds may also later come to light when, for example, an individual reports the loss of an expensive color television when an antiquated black and white set was actually taken.

As the Rochester Police Department moves from a manual stolen property file into a computerized property inventory system, our ability to capture and easily retrieve stolen property data will substantially increase. But, that ability can be realized only if property identification information is sought and recorded by our preliminary investigators.

Property descriptions should be considered as much more than make, model, and serial number. Damage to items (for example, scratches, dents, missing parts, repair tags) further pinpoints identification. A freehand drawing of an unusual item (silver pattern, jewelry, object d'art, and so on) may later help other officers identify the item's origin.

Certain questions may help jog a victim's memory, such as:

1. Are there any dents, scratches, marks, or pieces missing?

2. Has it been repaired?

3. Do you still have the bill of sale that may list the serial number? Or, an owner's manual that may picture it?

4. Do you have a photograph that shows the item?

5. Would anybody else in the family be able to identify it or better describe it?

6. Has your property been marked with any personal identification number? If so, what was the number and where was it marked?

The investigator should be certain when recording stolen property to include credit cards, and check cashing or guarantee cards and to record the issuers and the account numbers of the cards. A charge card number can be obtained from the person's last billing from the company (Sears, Mastercard, and so on). Victims should be reminded to report any missing credit cards immediately as being stolen. Checkbooks should be inspected to see if any checks are missing, especially from the back of the book.

In interviewing the family, no one should be excluded because of age, especially a young person, who is usually very observant and quite possibly can give additional information on the description of property.

When leaving a business card, the investigator should remind the victim to call the department with additional property description information. Quite possibly, other members of the family who are not present at the time of the investigation will have knowledge of serial numbers or additional identifying features that will assist in the investigation.

The information that the preliminary investigator *actively seeks* rather than passively accepts will beneficially affect the final outcome of the investigation.

IDENTIFYING SUSPECTS

Objectives. The object of identifying suspects is to determine the identity of and to locate the criminal.

Strategies. Most suspects are identified by people who observed the crime scene before, during, or immediately after the crime's commission. The identification of witnesses is aimed at providing a valid source for suspect information.

Through this solvability factor, the investigator should gather from witnesses and victims information that will be useful in locating the suspect.

When interviewing witnesses and victims, the preliminary investigator should indicate on the initial report whether future identification can be made and by whom. This information gives the follow-up investigator a projection of who can make an identification if a suspect is apprehended. This kind of reporting helps to eliminate duplication of efforts on the part of the follow-up investigator and saves valuable time.

Several methods for eliciting information from witnesses and victims are:

1. Detailed physical description.
2. Line-up identifications.
3. Photographic identifications.
4. Composite descriptions.
5. Police artist's sketches.
6. Look-alike identification.
7. Modus operandi identification.

It is the job of the investigator to select one or more of these techniques to develop and clarify whatever suspect information exists. The method selected should be the one the investigator believes will best refresh the memory of or assist the victim or witness in describing what was seen.

Procedures. Once witnesses, victims, and other persons with knowledge of the crime have been identified, the investigator must decide which of the following methods is most appropriate for obtaining specific suspect identification data.

1. If the victim or witness knows the name of the suspect, the investigation can proceed along routine and direct channels.

2. If the victim or witness knows where a suspect can be found, even though the name of the suspect is unknown, there is a good chance that the suspect can be located through a follow-up investigation.

3. If the witness/victim saw a suspect but can only give a description, a more detailed effort at exact identification is required.

When only a description is available, any combination of the following may be used.

Detailed Description

1. The witness or victim, with help from the investigator, can usually provide a detailed physical description. However, the investigator must not be suggestive. Witnesses are often too willing to adopt suggestions innocently provided by an overeager investigator. The disciplined and competent investigator will therefore ask clarifying questions only.

When compiling a physical description, it is advantageous for the investigator to ask the victim or witness about distinctive features of the criminal. These are features that would cause a witness or victim to remember the criminal.

As the witness or victim is providing a description, the investigator should keep interruptions to a minimum to obtain the complete perception of the victim or witness before narrowing down information. In questioning witnesses or victims about suspects, the investigator should provide gauging assistance without being suggestive, as mentioned above.

The investigator should not ask, "Were there three men?" or "Was the man very big?" but should phrase the question to let the victim determine the answers; for example, "How many were there?" and "How tall was he?" If the witness cannot visualize height or weight measurements, the investigator should ask the witness to relate the measurements to the investigator's size.

2. Line-up identifications are helpful once a suspect has been identified and located. In those situations where a line-up is used, the investigator must take care to protect the suspect's and witness's rights. Based on the Wade Decision, an attorney for the suspect may be present at the line-up. The investigator arranging the line-up must ensure that others in the line-up generally resemble the suspect.

3. Photographs, usually from police "mug" files, can help the investigator by assisting the witness or victim in suspect identifications. When having witnesses view mug shots, the investigator must confirm that the person selected by the witness has a real likeness to the description originally given.

When photos are used, they should resemble the suspect. Seven photos are adequate. A record of the ID number of each photo should be made and become part of the case file. When a photo is selected, the witness should initial it and mark time and date. The wise investigator always cross-checks mug file selections with MO data obtained from the crime investigation.

When using mug shots the investigator should have "photo albums" available for victim or witness viewing. These albums are products of investigators working a particular sector of the city. They are collections of photos of persons recently arrested for Part I offenses or of those suspected of being active in crime and currently "on the streets" and who frequent or operate in that particular area. It also contains photos of those persons wanted by detectives in the sector for other crimes. These albums can be easily purged and updated. They are portable and can be available to any investigator at a moment's notice. It is more productive to construct the album as a conglomerate and not as categories according to MO or physical description. People currently active in crime, recidivists, and drug abusers known to frequent the sector are best included.

4. When no photos are available, or when they do not produce a suspect, the police artist may be used to construct either a composite or a free-drawing likeness of the suspect, based on the witness's observations.

5. The MO data is another way of providing a suspect pool for witness consideration. Once a pattern of criminal activity is established, the known criminals using that method of operation become suspects, and their photos can be shown to the victim or witnesses. MO data within a neighborhood is often known by the uniformed officers and the investigators in that area.

When witnesses or victims are not available, the investigator must proceed without their help. Intensive work will be required to place suspects at the scene of the crime at the time it occurred. However, even when a suspect is named or selected from photos, the investigator must work toward placing the suspect at the scene, since this later will become a part of the prosecution.

If specific suspect data is not available, witnesses should be asked if they can think of anyone who may have committed the offense. In some cases, a witness or victim has knowledge of someone who may have had reason to commit the crime. Information gathered under the solvability factor of a definite limited opportunity for but one person to commit the crime may be useful, as may a vehicle license number that leads to a suspect. In other words, data leading to suspects can come from many sources.

Indicated Actions. If a description or name of a suspect is found, it should be broadcast immediately so that other units can be on the lookout for that suspect.

Witnesses who have identified a suspect should be told to contact the police if they see the suspect again.

Suspect information should be detailed as soon as possible so that descriptions put out will be of best assistance in finding the suspect. This information must also be clearly communicated to the follow-up investigator and to those officers coming on duty on the next shift so that they may continue the search effectively.

Measures of Success. A solvability factor has been identified if there is any information provided that may lead to the apprehension of a suspect. If descriptive information is so general as to fit a multitude of persons, a solvability factor does not exist.

The following questions can help the investigator decide whether a valid solvability factor exists:

1. If a person is named, is the name descriptive enough or complete enough that the person can be identified?

2. If a description is provided, is it narrow enough to fit a limited number of people?

3. If the location of the suspect is provided, is the information specific enough that follow-up investigation can lead to that suspect?

Affirmative answers to these questions indicate that the investigation has yielded the necessary information for continued investigative effort.

SUSPECT VEHICLE IDENTIFICATION

Objectives. When a vehicle is used in a crime, it may provide a means of identifying a suspect. Since vehicles are so much a part of daily life, the criminal who has exercised caution to assure anonymity in other aspects of the crime may still fail to consider that using a vehicle can lead to identification.

Many people can accurately and completely identify automobiles, trucks, motorcycles, and bicycles. Some people, when they are suspicious of a vehicle, will note identifying data. When this information is obtained by police shortly after the commission of the crime, the potential for apprehension of the suspect is very good. Frequently, suspects are found still in possession of evidence linking them to the crime.

Strategy. It is essential that the investigator avoid limiting consideration of vehicle identification to automobiles and trucks. In some cases, bicycles, motorcycles, and even snowmobiles and boats have been used to commit crimes.

Vehicle identification may be obtained in a number of ways: from witnesses; from physical evidence found at the crime scene; from police reports of accidents, traffic violations, stolen vehicles, and so on; and from a combination of these sources.

When witness information or physical evidence shows that a vehicle was present in the commission of a crime, it becomes a factor in the investigation. Such would be the case when a rape or robbery occurred in a suspect's vehicle. The investigator may assume a vehicle was present in a crime when the nature or location of the crime suggests that probability. The theft of a heavy safe, or a crime occurring in a remote area are examples of this type of situation.

Even if it is not used in the criminal act, an automobile may have been used for the criminal's transportation.

Procedures. When the victim and/or witness knows that a vehicle was used in a crime, the investigator can proceed to obtain straightforward descriptions. The following procedures are recommended:

1. The witnesses should be separated from one another. This assures that the description obtained from one witness does not influence that provided by another.

2. The type of vehicle (automobile, bicycle, motorcycle, and so on) should be identified.

3. When possible, the registration plate number and state of issue should be obtained. A partial number can be of value as a computer printout can give a list of names. For example, "I know it was a Chevy with ABC as the letters." The 999 possibilities can be reduced to those that are Chevrolets, leaving only a few to be investigated.

4. The year, make, model, and body style of vehicle should be determined. The vehicle identification book can also aid in putting together the pieces until a complete vehicle description is obtained; for example, "I know there were four round lights on the rear of the car" or "The rear bumper had a fancy shape." Rear lights and custom bumpers are easily identifiable by dealers.

5. The color or colors should be determined.

6. Distinctive markings (signs, decals, bumper stickers, damage, and so on) that would help pinpoint the vehicle should be identified.

7. The description should be verified by comparing it with those provided by the witnesses, or by testing the ability of the witness to provide the identification.

When obtaining suspect vehicle description and a definite model and make, the investigator should determine how the witness knows that information. For example, "I used to have a Chevy just like it. That's how I know," or "I'm a foreign car buff, and I know that the car was a Toyota G.T."

The witness can be taken to a used car lot to help identify the exact make and model of the vehicle. If the manufacturer is known but the particular model is not, the investigator and witness can go to a particular dealer and make use of their vehicle identification.

The best available description of the suspect vehicle must be accurately communicated to the follow-up investigator so a search can be made for it. Since a vehicle is so often an important link to a suspect, it is also very important that descriptions of suspect vehicles be detailed and concise.

Measures of Success. A solvability factor has been identified if *sufficient information* has been provided about a suspect vehicle so that there is a reasonable chance it can be identified as the suspect's vehicle if it is seen again.

The following questions can help the investigator determine whether a valid solvability factor exists:

1. If a vehicle was involved, is the description of the vehicle sufficiently limiting so that the vehicle could be identified if it were found or seen again?

2. If a specific vehicle description is known, will it fit only a limited number of vehicles?

If these questions are answered in the affirmative, a solvability factor has been identified and continued investigative effort is worthwhile.

IDENTIFYING MODUS OPERANDI

Objectives. The modus operandi is important because it can establish a pattern of activities among a series of criminal acts, thus permitting the investigator to use information from one crime for another investigation. In this sense, the MO is a trademark of a specific suspect or group of suspects, who may be identified by it. This solvability factor has two objectives:

1. To link this crime with others, thus opening up additional useful investigative information.
2. To identify a suspect.

If a weapon was used, a complete description should be obtained. Some offenders may be identified this way, while others are identified by the type of clothing they wear when they commit crimes.

The victim or witnesses should be asked such questions as "Did you follow him to the street when he exited?" "If so, did you observe any vehicles leaving the scene?" "Did you hear any squealing of tires or engine starting?"

Strategies. The investigator must determine how the criminal worked. He may do this by mentally taking the criminal's place and reproducing the crime from its beginning to its end, based on any evidence of the criminal's thinking. The investigator should consider what the criminal's perception of the victim was, how the criminal selected this victim, and how time factors entered into the criminal act.

Determining a modus operandi can be done best after establishing the basic facts about when the crime occurred, who the criminal was, and the sequence of events.

Procedures. When the basic facts about the crime are established, the investigator should try to identify patterns in the criminal's behavior that are clearly unusual for that type of crime; for example, the investigator should consider:

1. How the entry was made in a burglary.
2. What was taken and what was not taken.
3. How the victim was approached in a robbery or crime of violence.
4. What time the crime occurred and why that particular time was selected.

Through questions such as the following, the investigator seeks those elements of the crime that set it apart from other crimes of that type. Again, the objective is to identify what is distinctive.

1. What were the actions of the suspect prior to the robbery? Was the suspect observed making a purchase? hanging around prior to the robbery? getting

out of a vehicle before entering the establishment? in the establishment before the robbery? If so, was the suspect alone at the time?

2. Were there accomplices?

3. What words were spoken by the suspect? (For example, "This is a stick-up," or "Give me all your money.")

4. If silent, did the suspect use gestures or a note?

5. Did the suspect appear calm or excited?

6. Did the suspect reach for the money? If so, with which hand? Did the suspect instruct you to reach for the money?

7. Did the suspect know money was kept under the change tray? Did the suspect lift the tray, or instruct you to? Did you hand over the money?

8. Was the suspect aware of the place where money was kept in the store?

9. Did the suspect ask questions that indicated no prior knowledge of you or your premises? For example, "Where do you keep your money?" or "What's in the back room?"

All human beings—lawbreakers included—are creatures of habit and go about their business by routine; some suspects' MOs are as easily identifiable by experienced investigators as calling cards.

Indicated Action. There are two primary communication needs when this solvability factor is found. First, the investigator should initiate a "wanted" broadcast or include in a wanted broadcast identification of special equipment used to commit the crime or any unusual items that were taken. The information should be given in a format that will make sense to officers receiving it.

Second, the investigator must clearly identify the particulars of the indicated MO so that other investigators will be able to see immediately the link between this crime and other crimes they are investigating. Descriptions of MO should include sufficient particulars. The message to other investigators is, "What knowledge similar to this do you have?"

Measures of Success. A solvability factor has been identified if the investigator has indicated that there is something unusual about this crime that would associate it with other such crimes.

The following questions, if answered positively, indicate that a modus operandi has, in fact, been identified.

1. Is the identified method of operation sufficiently distinct so that not every crime of this type would include this factor?

2. If another crime of this type had been present, could the investigator assume that both crimes were committed by the same person?

To be sure that all potential modus operandi identification efforts have been made, the investigator should feel confident that every possible indicator of unusual activity or method has been considered. If they have been, then this solvability factor has been properly considered.

IDENTIFICATION OF SIGNIFICANT REASON TO BELIEVE THE CRIME MAY BE SOLVED WITH REASONABLE ADDITIONAL INVESTIGATION

Objectives. In some cases, the investigator may be unable to identify any single solvability factor. For a number of reasons, however, even if a case appears unsolvable, it should not be relegated to the office "file" status without additional action; for example, a witness who had not been located at the time of the preliminary investigation might be available later. Publicity about the crime may generate additional information, which may then provide one or more solvability factor.

Consequently, it is essential that the preliminary investigator exercise discretion to keep open cases which, although no solvability factors are present, may warrant additional investigation. In such cases, the discretionary privilege itself becomes a solvability factor.

Strategies. Proper identification of this solvability factor requires the ability to analyze and evaluate a broad range of circumstances that appear at first to be unrelated to the case. For example, does the nature of the crime, the victim, or the MO imply an impact on the community that may produce a reaction helpful to investigative efforts? In short, will the new media feature the case, and if so, will it produce some public reaction that will make investigative effort practical? Can the reaction be expected to produce helpful information?

The investigator must review the available information in terms of the several other factors that may provide a relationship, proceeding from the specific circumstances of this crime to considerations of its environment. For example, knowledge that a blue, later model car containing the suspect fled the scene at high speed is not a good solvability factor. Knowledge that a blue, later model vehicle was involved in a hit-and-run accident while speeding in the area shortly after the commission of the crime, may be related. The witnesses to the hit-and-run accident may become valuable witnesses in court even though they have no actual knowledge of the crime. Similarly, recovery after the accident of a blue, late-model vehicle that was reported stolen and that was damaged after its theft, would certainly warrant extension of the crime scene search to include the vehicle.

The suggestions about schedules of delivery and service persons, mail deliveries, and so on, in the above section about witnesses, may be useful in considering strategies for identification. This is probably one of the most elusive of the solvability factors.

Another consideration here is the effect on future investigations of a decision to discontinue efforts on this investigation. The investigator may see that the victim or another interested party is not satisfied with the investigation. It will then be wise to gauge that person's response. If it is likely that this response will be a demand for a detailed explanation of why the case will not be investigated further, an explanation probably will be required. It will reassure the victim that the case will be reopened when any solvability factors are discovered. The victim should be informed, however, that investigative resources and energies will be directed to cases where criminal apprehension appears more promising.

Based on the presence or the lack of solvability factors, the investigating officer is the person best equipped to make the decision to suspend the case or recommend follow-up investigation.

Procedure. A careful review of the solvability factors is now required. If all other information is insufficient to constitute a solvability factor, the degree to which it is insufficient must be considered.

If completion of the first step has produced no solvability factor, the preliminary investigator must decide if the *sum total of bits and pieces of information,* each insufficient to constitute a solvability factor, produces a basis upon which further investigation might reasonably be justified. At this stage, consideration is limited to the immediate circumstances of the case.

The first application of external factors involves considering this investigation in the light of knowledge of other factors. If this crime is one of a series of like offenses, the data gained in its preliminary investigation may provide a viable lead when combined with data gained from other crimes in the series.

The next consideration is the impact of this crime on the neighborhood when the crime occurred. Speeding vehicles, the sound of gunshots, or loitering suspects, as the case may be, may have made an impression on neighbors or persons passing through the neighborhood. These persons are probably not available to the preliminary investigator, and they will not be able to relate their observations of the crime until they are located and made aware that a crime has been committed.

If the knowledge of the crime spreads through the neighborhood, additional information from the neighborhood may be forthcoming. If the news media features reports of the crime, then additional information also may be generated from the community. Judgment here presupposes that investigators know the workings of the local news media, the mood of the neighborhood they serve, and the policies of their department.

The next step in this solvability factor is the application of the investigator's knowledge of general criminal conduct to this specific case. Perhaps some aspects of the crime indicate probable future action by the suspect. A suspect who is injured during the commission of the crime, for example, may need medical treatment. A criminal who has stolen credit cards, checks, or other noncash negotiables will need to convert them to cash or, in the case of addict crime, to drugs. The investigative implication is limited to surveillance of places or persons likely to provide the required service or commodity.

The final consideration is that of the dissatisfaction of the victim or other interested party. If the preliminary investigator has done a thorough and complete job and conveyed this accomplishment, satisfaction should result. Careful explanation of what has been learned and its value to the investigation will generally satisfy those concerned, when communication with the preliminary investigator has been established. The investigator should inform the victim that the case is not a promising one for solution, if the investigative efforts have reflected the genuine interest and concern of the investigator. One the other hand, if the investigator has not won confidence of the victim, the victim may be dissatisfied. When victim dissatisfaction becomes intense enough to require further investigator contact with the victim, the preliminary investigator should recommend follow-up investigation even when the case shows no promise.

An occasional recommendation of this type need not indicate poor performance by the preliminary investigator, since some people will not be satisfied under any circumstances.

Indicated Action. Communication is the key to the successful utilization of this or of any solvability factor. Vague hunches are seldom worthy of additional investigation. They are also difficult to communicate. If the preliminary investigator can effectively communicate the reasons why the case should be followed up, then it is probably a worthwhile investment of further investigative efforts.

Measures of Success. The preliminary investigator has successfully identified this solvability factor when:

1. Other solvability factors were not clearly established.

2. The relationships have been logically linked.

3. Conclusions are factually supported.

4. Communication has been effectively accomplished.

When these four conditions exist, the solvability factor has been properly identified and continued investigation is probably justified.

COMMUNICATION AND DECISION MAKING

If the case is not closed immediately by arrest, the work of the preliminary investigator concludes when a decision is made to continue or halt the investigation. It is at this stage that investigators must ensure that their work is as complete as time and circumstances will permit, and is properly documented.

Further efforts by the police agency will depend upon this documentation and upon the quality of the preliminary investigator's work. As we have seen, the primary tasks in the preliminary investigation are to: (1) identify solvability factors, (2) determine whether there is a chance for the crime to be solved, and (3) ensure that information obtained is of sufficient quality to be valuable in future court action. All these tasks must be properly documented and recorded.

At the end of the preliminary investigation, the investigator should decide whether sufficient leads have been developed to make solution of the crime possible. This decision is based on whether solvability factors have been identified. If solvability factors are present, it is probable that future investigative effort may solve the case. Research has shown that if solvability factors are not present, there is little chance, if any, that additional investigative effort will solve the case.

For the preliminary investigator, the implications of this decision are obvious. If the initial investigation has been thorough, then the decision to terminate or continue investigative efforts will be based on valid data, and the collection of material for the later court presentation will have begun. However, if a proper preliminary investigation has not been conducted, a faulty decision may well be made or later court action may be unsuccessful.

Therefore, before the decision to terminate or continue is made, it is imperative that the investigator feel sure that the maximum possible effort has been made to identify solvability factors. The investigator should feel confident that all potential witnesses have been sought, that a crime scene search has been conducted in all cases where it is appropriate, and that no reasonable investigative effort has been avoided. At this stage, a decision for further investigative effort can be made, provided that the investigator believes a follow-up investigator will not duplicate work already done.

The decision whether to allocate additional resources is fairly simple. Basically, the question to be asked is whether further investigation will probably result in the clearance of the crime and/or the apprehension of the criminals. Research has shown that when one or more solvability factors are present, there is a good chance that further follow-up of those identified solvability factors may lead to a criminal apprehension. So in most instances, when solvability factors are identified, additional investigative effort is warranted. If no solvability factors have been found after a thorough preliminary investigation, the police agency is best advised to file the case without the commitment of additional resources. This is the decision whether to follow up or file. It can be made only when the preliminary investigator has made every effort possible to follow each lead as far as time will permit.

The success of every investigation then is totally dependent on the quality of work done by the preliminary investigator.

16

Investigation of the Police Use of Deadly Physical Force

Sean A. Grennan

Of all the powers conferred on law enforcement in the United States, the use of force, particularly deadly physical force, is the most fateful and momentous. It gives one human being the right to seriously injure or even kill another. Yet it is a necessary component of the primary police function, which after all consists of preventing and/or stopping the threatened or actual act of violence against those who cannot properly defend themselves. Frequently, the use of deadly force involves a difficult, split-second decision with many unknown factors for the officer. The sufficiently trained officer, however, will avoid discharging a firearm at a fleeing vehicle, an escaping juvenile or felon, or into crowds, as warning shots or while running. The officer will remember that there are a number of nonlethal methods of apprehension, and that the use of deadly force should be limited to circumstances involving the immediate threat of a serious physical injury or death to citizen or police officer.

Until recently most law enforcement agencies in the United States had little or no guidelines in this matter. Moreover, media coverage of deadly force cases was often biased and presented an officer's action in a distorted manner. Is it any wonder, then, that there has been a substantial increase in complaints and civil suits since the mid-1970s?

Certainly, all shooting incidents involving a police officer should be investigated immediately. Misuse of a firearm is a grave offense because it may result in the serious injury or death of an innocent person. Furthermore, the improper application of deadly force creates a negative image of law enforcement within the community. This is especially true when lethal force is applied to minority groups. Indeed, anybody is justified in questioning the appropriateness of an action, and the issue must be dealt with properly. The last thing most people want is trigger-happy police, populated by "Dirty Harry" types. Eroding the public's confidence in this important institution benefits no one but the criminal element.

DEVELOPMENT OF GUIDELINES

Three major policies have helped shape the deadly force guidelines laid down by law enforcement agencies throughout the United States today:

1. The common law's *fleeing-felon rule*, which is the least restrictive of the three. This code considers it legal for police officers to use deadly force when it becomes reasonably necessary to prevent an impending felony or to apprehend a noxious criminal who is struggling or running from a lawful arrest.

2. In the modified common law's *forcible-felon rule*, the use of deadly force is limited to violent or forcible transgressions that threaten a person's life or security. Unlike the fleeing felon rule, it may not be applied when the felony committed is not a threat to public safety (that is, gambling, prostitution, drugs, etc.). Although this dictum is more specific than the earlier one, it keeps most of the common law's ordinances and changes nothing with regard to the appropriateness of deadly force in self-defense.

3. The model penal law's *defense-of-life-only rule* is a very specific statute that instructs an officer to use deadly force only when reasonably sure that the individual he/she is dealing with is a violent felon, who presents an imminent threat of causing either serious physical injury or death to the officer or a citizen.

Today most urban police agencies in large cities, such as New York, Los Angeles, or Chicago, have very strict guidelines that go beyond any state laws.

Supreme Court Decision and the Use of Deadly Force

A major policy change, which has enormously affected law enforcement in the United States and the enactment of tougher ordinances, was the 1985 Supreme Court decision in *Tennessee v. Garner*. A uniformed police officer responded to a burglary call. Upon walking to the rear of a certain house, he observed 15-year-old Edward Garner attempting to escape over a fence in the backyard of the premise that had just been robbed. The officer, who was "reasonably certain" that Garner was unarmed, nevertheless fired a shot that struck the youth in the head, killing him instantly. At the time of this incident, Tennessee had a fleeing-felon rule that permitted the use of deadly force to prevent the getaway of such a criminal.

The case was brought before the Supreme Court of the United States, which found the Tennessee statute unconstitutional. Further, the Court determined such force was absolutely unnecessary, since the escaping suspect did not pose an immediate threat to the officer or any other nonparticipant in the crime. Conversely, the decision in the *Garner* case indicated that, had the offender presented a risk of inflicting serious injury or death on the officer or on an innocent citizen, or had there been the threatened or actual use of a weapon during the commission of the crime, the application of deadly physical force would have been justified and even necessary to impede the suspect's escape. It was also suggested by the Court that some type of warning be given prior to the shooting, such as "Stop, I am a police officer!" or "Stop, police!" These Supreme Court guidelines are the equivalent of the procedures set forth in the model penal code's defense-of-life-only rule.

Thus, the Supreme Court informed the law enforcement community that a suspect who does not pose any type of imminent danger may not be apprehended through the use of deadly physical force. Since the *Garner* decision, the majority of state legislatures have followed suit and adopted similar guidelines; however, the directives of most law enforcement agencies on the proper use of deadly force go beyond these state regulations and are considerably more restrictive. Such changes were appropriate and long overdue, considering that today's police agencies are attempting to achieve professional status.

Media Intervention

As previously stated, the handling of most deadly force cases by the law enforcement community itself is usually not presented accurately to the public. Whether there are open or closed hearings, most police agencies give all the viable data to the media, but in its attempt to sensationalize a news item, the media often distort the information or reveal facts selectively. Hence a misconstrued version is fed to the public—a twisted view of what has actually transpired during a police/citizen confrontation! The problem with such biased and misleading reporting is that there is hardly ever any acknowledgment of error by the press or TV networks. This can cause considerable public unrest and damage to police credibility within the community and contribute to the destabilization of society. On the positive side, the media coverage has indirectly influenced the development of guidelines for the proper use of deadly physical force.

INVESTIGATION OF THE USE OF DEADLY FORCE

Due to the seriousness of its nature, a shooting incident involving a police officer should be investigated immediately by the affected law enforcement agency. After all, the misuse of a firearm is a serious offense that can maim, kill, and erode public confidence in its police. Almost always, it is a violation of the agency's procedures, which since the *Garner* decision mandates officers' use of deadly force only in the defense of life; and in most cases, it is a transgression of state laws. Specifically, the sworn officer should discharge a firearm only when all other available alternatives have failed, and the use of deadly force is absolutely necessary to prevent death or a serious injury. Therefore, if an investigation shows that an officer displayed or improperly shot his weapon, he or she ought to be prosecuted and punished.

One fundamental problem facing the police is the actual investigation of such complaints because these shootings are probed by members of the same law enforcement agency in which the accused functioned. People who have had contact with the accused officer can therefore be considered subjective, if not biased. This, in turn, may create community distrust.

Hence, every effort must be made to conduct the investigation fairly and evenhandedly, equitably and professionally to reassure the participants, the public, and the members of the agency. The results of this inquiry must indicate to the community, as well as to the police, that there will always be a strict enforcement of all the guidelines related to this matter. An extensive and unprejudiced examination will provide the department and the prosecutor's office with reliable documentation to either impeach the accused or establish his or her innocence. A diligent probe will also demonstrate the agency's proficiency in adequately regulating itself.

Investigators need to develop uniformity while collecting the details. In addition, all members of the unit should become acquainted with the circumstances surrounding the case because their assistance may be needed, or this incident may help to improve their skills in handling similar probes in the future.

As with any investigation, time is of the essence. The inquiry should be conducted immediately by a highly trained and sufficiently staffed group of supervisors and experienced police investigators who have been engaged in the instruction of all members of the department in the proper use of deadly force. Their primary function is to probe all shooting incidents involving members of their agency—no matter whether they concern an officer firing at or being shot at by a suspect. Furthermore, the individual placed in charge of the investigation must be, at least, one rank higher than the highest ranking officer implicated in each shooting incident. This will alleviate any future problems that may arise when compelling another officer to perform a certain function, such as answering a question or obeying an order.

Crime Scene Responsibilities

Once notified of a police shooting, the investigative unit must respond quickly. Upon arrival at the location, they need to verify that the whole area of the incident has been properly sealed off and protected to prevent contamination of the site and its evidence. (The isolation of the entire scene, as well as any spot that may contain evidence, should already be accomplished by the first officer to reach it. He is also the person who notifies the essential supervisors and specialized investigative unit.) Officers must restrict the public's movements. No unauthorized people—citizen or police—can be allowed to penetrate the scene. Once the investigators arrive, they will designate who is to be permitted to enter the sealed-off area. They will list any person's name who may be helpful in the probe. It should be mandatory for anyone going in and leaving the crime scene to sign in and out of a police log book.

The first supervisor on the location of a police shooting plays a very important part because there is always the possibility that he or she may have to manage the whole investigation (such as shooting cases where no injury exists, accidental discharges by officers, etc.). The first supervisor must:

a. Contact the investigators and, upon their arrival, at the site assess the scene with them.

b. Set up and maintain perimeter security.

c. Identify all officers involved in the shooting and obtain written statements from them, in addition to oral ones.

d. Secure the weapons of the shooters, and give them to the investigators upon their arrival.

e. Remove shooters from the scene and advise them not to make any statements to unauthorized people.

f. Locate and identify witnesses.

g. Submit a written report to the investigators on their preliminary probe of the area.

When the investigators are assured that the location is properly secured, they conduct a rigorous search of the site. Every spot is thoroughly examined. This inspection includes all places where the flight of a fired projectile or its remnants could have come to an end. A complete going-over must be done, inside and outside, of all buildings where the incident took place. Whenever it is necessary, there should be a full examination of all the vehicles within and around the area of crime. Once every nook and cranny has been searched and all the detectable evidence located, marked, and photographed, the rest of the scene should be accurately sketched and filmed. The uncovered evidence needs to be properly handled, marked, and forwarded to the appropriate authority (the police lab, whether federal, state, or municipal) for testing.

Members of the assigned investigative unit should examine all guns that have been fired and make notes on the type of weapon, model, serial number, ammunition used, proof of recent shooting (that is, powder flaring around the cylinder, muzzle, or chamber), and the number of expended or live rounds remaining in the firing chamber or clip. A search of the scene is necessary for casings that were ejected from the firearm(s). All weapons need to be handled cautiously, and the investigator should be wearing plastic gloves when holding any gun recovered at the shooting site. The retrieved weapon(s), like all other items that might contain evidence, are to be placed in a sealable container for protection against contamination. This is essential to assure lab technicians that the slightest shreds of evidence originally on the weapon are still there for analysis.

If the investigator deems it necessary during the questioning of the subject, a drug or alcohol test should be administered as quickly as possible. An officer's condition at the time of the occurrence could become a point of controversy at a later date. Therefore, documentation as to whether the officer acted under the influence of any intoxicant during the shooting may be critical. A blood or urine test will clear up any question of his or her condition.

Interviewing Procedures

Of the utmost importance is that all officers and citizens who participated in the incident, as well as civilian witnesses to it, be properly identified and then informed that they will be interviewed shortly—the sooner the better. They should be separated and transported to the location where they will be questioned. The immediate interview is very critical because the witnesses may change their depiction of the incident once they have had a chance to discuss their perceptions with others.

Investigators have to obtain a written report at once from all police officers who fired their weapons during the episode. The subjects must be told that they will be questioned soon (usually within two hours) after returning to headquarters and that they ought to have a lawyer or union representative present. It would also be helpful to warn them of the possible outcome of the preliminary interview (such as administrative leave, suspension, assignment change, arrest, vindication, etc.). The initial inquiry is to be conducted by the investigator in charge in the presence of another supervisor who should, preferably, have little or no involvement in the probe. At this point, the examiner must avoid any implication that the officer(s) acted improperly. If later on during the interview it is ascertained that the subject(s) committed a crime, the questioning should continue. In addition, the state prosecutor has to be notified who will decide on the type of action to be taken against the officer(s) and whether proceedings should start right away or after grand jury hearings.

In most situations of this type, the prosecutor usually elects to collect as much evidence as possible before presenting the case to the grand jury. After all, a good prosecutor proceeds cautiously and deliberately, gathering all possible material available to prove a person's innocence or guilt beyond reasonable doubt. Furthermore, most communities in the United States still hold their police officers in high esteem, and thus it would be an injustice to them and society to rush the case before a judge and jury without a meticulous examination of all aspects of the incident.

A member of the investigative unit will answer all questions concerning the uncovered facts, regardless of the circumstances. A report should be made and forwarded by the commanding officer of this unit to the proper authorities within the department. All the evidence and statements must be thoroughly evaluated before conducting any further interviews with the first officer at the scene and/or suspects.

Investigative Review

Once all the phases of the probe have been completed, it is up to the commanding officer of the specialized police shooting unit to analyze all the material gathered by the investigators. To properly evaluate the incident and the suspect(s), he/she should also have all their departmental records available (such as prior firearms discharges, work records, civilian complaints, commendations, etc.). His or her responsibility is to make recommendations on the action to be taken against the shooter(s). All the documents are to be forwarded to the police chief, who will determine how to process the case (such as police trial room, state prosecuting attorney, vindications, suspensions, etc.). The chief may also decide to refer the proceeding to the firearms review board, especially when there is no clear-cut criminal violation by the officer(s). The investigative team will make their presentation to this committee, which should meet whenever necessary. It must have the power to review all the evidence prior to the hearings and be capable of issuing a subpoena or summons mandating that essential witnesses testify before this panel, whose purpose is to propose the appropriate action taken for or against the shooter(s). We must remember, a board is usually composed of police officers, and its functions are:

- Review all incidents in which police officers have discharged a firearm—intentionally or accidentally—and the investigative team has completed its probe.

- Go over every case in which a police officer shot or was fired upon by another person.

- Conduct hearings on officer compliance with departmental shooting procedures (for example, did he or she exhaust available alternatives before firing a weapon?).

- Submit its conclusions to the police chief with recommendations.

- Propose change in policy, procedures, and/or training.

- Maintain and compile statistics on firearm discharges.

The firearms review board should be able to make one of the following propositions to the chief with regard to the shooter.

1. *Within policy:* The officer acted within departmental guidelines on the firearms discharge.

2. *In policy:* Substandard performance within guidelines and poor judgment; no attempt to use possible alternatives to the application of deadly force.

3. *Out of policy:* Not within guidelines, but no violation of state law related to the use of deadly force.

4. *Accidental, no negligence.*

5. *Accidental, negligence involved.*

Accidental shooting by police officers usually results in an injury to the accused or another officer rather than a citizen. In the majority of these cases the shootings take place at home or in the locker rooms. The problem that accidental shootings present to the police agency are clearly shown in the New York City Police Department's firearm discharge numbers over a six-year period (1984 to 1989). These figures reveal that 15.5 percent (365 of 2353 shootings reported) were accidental. Any officer can use the accidental shooting explanation and get away with it, unless the police agency can clearly substantiate that the firing was intentional. It is quite possible that through the use of a specialized and highly trained investigative team, a police agency could eliminate a sizable portion of these accidental shootings.

Recommendation 1 should lead to the exoneration of the police officer, while in recommendations 2 and 3 the subject ought to be retrained and, when applicable, appropriately penalized for violating department policy. Recommendation 4 requires proper reeducation if the officer has no prior accidentals, but recommendation 5 calls for some type of disciplinary action, especially if the officer has a record of previous accidental shootings. The chief should review both the investigation and the recommendations, and decide what appropriate action ought to be taken to exonerate or discipline the shooter. Punishment resulting from negligence in weapons use must remain consistent so that no favoritism is shown to any one officer or group of officers within a police agency.

CONCLUSIONS

As we approach the twenty-first century, it is time for all police agencies to have similar guidelines relating to the use of deadly force. These procedures should be as restrictive as necessary to prevent officers from inappropriately using their firearms. Some statistics point out why: During the late 1960s and early 1970s, when directives were few and flexible, New York City police officers averaged approximately 800 to 1000 shooting incidents a year. In August 1972 stricter ordinances on the use of deadly force were adopted; since that time the average year brings anywhere from 330 to 450 shooting occurrences. A 50 to 60 percent reduction in these incidents reflects on the success of tougher regulations. It is hoped that some time in the near future a type of nonlethal weapon will be invented that will help police agencies avoid the use of deadly force altogether. Certainly, the issuance of high-powered semiautomatic weapons to law enforcement seems to contradict this purpose and may present future problems for police executives, despite strict ordinances. Just consider the number of clips and rounds these weapons can pump out in a short period of time! Personally, during my 21 years on the force carrying a .38 caliber revolver I felt adequately protected, even during the two incidents when I was beset by armed assailants.

Suggestions for the Reduction of Officer Use of Deadly Force

Police officers, as members of the law enforcement community, are sworn to protect life and property, to prevent crime and arrest criminals, and to be continually aware of the importance of a human being's life. In many tragic incidents throughout the history of policing, officers, acting within the spectrum of their legitimate authority, discharged a firearm and killed or injured an innocent person.

The 1985 Supreme Court decision in the *Tennessee v. Garner* case has established policy regarding the use of deadly force in the apprehension of fleeing felons, and this decision should have convinced police agencies everywhere in this country to adopt strict guidelines relating to this matter. Most agencies have indeed introduced tough ordinances; however, in some parts of this country much progress needs to be made. Following are some suggestions which, in my opinion, should be inaugurated uniformly:

1. Use only the minimum amount of force that is consistent with the accomplishment of the mission.
2. A firearm is a defensive weapon. It should not be used to apprehend a suspect.
3. An officer must apply every alternative option before resorting to the use of a firearm.
4. Deadly force will not be used to effect the apprehension of a fleeing felon, unless the officer has probable cause to believe that
   a. Deadly force was used or threatened by the suspect.
   b. Or the culprit caused serious physical injury to another person.
   c. Or the suspect is armed with deadly weapon.
5. The use of deadly force must be prohibited, unless all of the following factors are present:
   a. The officer must have probable cause based on the knowledge of the crime committed and the circumstances surrounding this crime.
   b. And the officer must have probable cause to believe that the fleeing felon presents an immediate threat of serious physical injury or death to the officer.
   c. Or the officer must have probable cause to believe that failure to apprehend the fleeing felon would create the danger of a serious physical injury or death to another person.
   d. And there are no other rational means readily available to the officer at this time of apprehending this felon.
6. Deadly force will not be used to prevent or terminate a felony, unless the officer is reasonably sure that there is no other alternative to prevent a person from being seriously injured or killed.
7. An officer can use deadly physical force only when absolutely necessary to prevent another person killing or maiming the officer or anybody else.
8. The firing of warning shots is prohibited.
9. An officer will not use a firearm to summon assistance, unless a person's life is endangered.
10. A firearm will not be discharged at or from a moving vehicle, unless persons in other vehicles are using deadly force against the officer or another person.
11. Shooting animals is forbidden, unless there is no other alternative method of controlling the animal.
12. Remember that deadly physical force can only be used as a last resort.

17
Homicide Investigation

Vernon J. Geberth

Homicide investigation is one of the most significant investigations that a police officer or criminal investigator confronts. Because of its subject matter—death by violence or unnatural causes—what has occurred can be determined only after a careful, intelligent examination of the crime scene, a professional forensic autopsy, and an evaluation of the various bits and pieces gathered by the criminal investigator.

The latter facts may be in the form of trace evidence found at the scene, statements taken from suspects or persons within the vicinity of the crime, direct eyewitness accounts, other informational sources and records checks, or autopsy results from the medical examination.

The homicide detective, to be successful, must:

- Have an eye for details and the ability to recognize and evaluate evidence.

- Have above-average intelligence to absorb the innumerable details that arise during the case.

- Most importantly, be able to develop a talent for effectively interviewing and interrogating many different types of people and personalities with whom he or she comes into contact.

The ingredients of an effective homicide investigation are teamwork, documentation, preservation, flexibility, and common sense.

This is true despite the remarkable scientific advances that have been made since the first edition of this book. Computerized law enforcement data base systems, which include NCIC, VI-CAP, RISS, and other intelligence networks, provide state-of-the-art electronic technology for the criminal investigator. LETN and other satellite and cable networks provide the law enforcement community with contemporary issues and the techniques for effective crime fighting strategies. The scientific community has developed forensic techniques that put criminal investigation on the cutting edge of science. DNA technology promises to be the future of forensic law enforcement operations.

These advanced technologies, however, will never replace the human element or the time-proven, traditional methodologies used by homicide detectives. The practical homicide investigation techniques stressed in this chapter are therefore absolutely essential for effective inquiry into sudden and violent death.

As we approach the twenty-first century with advanced forensics and technological changes available to the law enforcement community, there is an important prerequisite. The investigation of homicide and the initial actions by the police at the homicide crime scene will eventually determine whether or not the crime is ever solved or the guilty person is brought to justice.

THE BASICS OF A HOMICIDE INVESTIGATION

Homicide. *Homicide* is the killing of one human being by another. According to law, it may be criminal or noncriminal depending on the legal circumstances. Before a determination can be made, there must be a thorough inquiry into the death of the deceased by the criminal investigator, the medical examiner, and the district attorney's office. These professional practitioners act independently and as colleagues in arriving at the cause of death and its surrounding facts. It is imperative that the criminal investigator have extensive background in scientific investigative techniques as well as knowledge of the law as it applies to homicide.

In most instances, the investigator initiates the formal investigation and has the duty and responsibility of formulating an unbiased presentation of facts to the appropriate authority. Final determination of "criminal" or "noncriminal" is decided by a grand jury in states where this procedure exists. Nevertheless, the criminal investigator may very well be the determining factor in whether or not there is a successful and scrupulous inquiry into facts surrounding the demise of the deceased.

The Crime Scene.   Homicide investigation begins when the body is first found. This location is referred to as the *crime scene.* There may be two or more crime scenes attached to the original location of the body. Additional crime scenes may include where the body was moved from, where the actual assault leading to death took place, where any physical or trace evidence connected with the crime was discovered, and the vehicle used to transport the body to where it was eventually found.

Responding police officers must be aware of this multiple crime scene possibility. During the initial receipt of information by the police concerning a possible homicide, the officer or person receiving this communication should attempt to ascertain exactly where the incident or situation requiring police investigation is located and additional locations for possible coverage.

The term "crime scene," as it appears in this text, means the location where the body was first discovered. Here, the preliminary homicide investigation begins, and it is appropriately called the *primary crime scene.*

The Person Receiving First Notification of a Possible Homicide.   A police department's first notification of an actual or suspected homicide, or an incident that may develop into one, is usually received by telephone. This first call may be simply a request for assistance for an injured person, a call stating that there were shots fired, or a screaming man or woman. It does not always provide sufficient data for the receiving officer to assess the true nature and extent of the incident. However, under circumstances where the information received suggests the possibility of a homicide, the person receiving the information should:

1. Obtain and record the following information:
   a. The exact time the call was received.
   b. The exact location(s) of occurrence.
   c. Whether or not the perpetrator(s) or suspicious persons or vehicles just left the scene. Try to get descriptive information and direction of travel for immediate transmission of alarms and/or notifications to other radio motor patrol units.
   d. The location of the one calling the police; if that person will remain; and, if not, where the person can be contacted.
   e. The name, address, and telephone number of the person reporting the incident.
2. Request the caller's assistance. If the person making the report seems to be of suitable age and discretion (is calm, and so on), request assistance in safeguarding the location of occurrence. This request should be put in specific terms so that no one is admitted except law enforcement or medical people and nothing is disturbed.
3. Dispatch officers to the scene.
   a. The dispatcher should be aware of the many initial officer duties and provide sufficient personnel to handle the situation according to the data obtained from the reporting person.
   b. Make appropriate notifications to supervisors.
4. Be aware that in many cases the person making the call to the police is actually the perpetrator, but may not say so. (This applies particularly to switchboard operators.) If the caller indicates having just killed someone, the necessary information should be obtained in an ordinary, detached manner; radio cars dispatched; and then the operator should attempt to keep the caller on the line in the hope that the call will still be in progress when the officers arrive. These responding officers can verify the call with the switchboard, thereby preparing the basis for a later courtroom presentation. Even if this cannot be accomplished, the operator should be alert to any identifying characteristics of the caller for later voice identification.

In any case, the first person receiving the notification should, as soon as possible, record in writing the word-for-word content of the call. The individual who first reported the incident may later become a suspect, whose exact words become critical to the case.

Most departments today, especially in major cities, record all incoming calls as a matter of procedure. In departments that either cannot afford this type of operation or do not wish to record calls, the opportunity still exists to invest in an inexpensive tape recorder with telephone pickup. This equipment can be activated manually by the switchboard operator to record incoming calls relating to homicides or serious assaults.

Recording the initial call, especially if it is made by the perpetrator, can be invaluable later. In one case, the common-law husband of the deceased called the police to report that he had found his wife wandering around the street in a beaten, dazed state. This call was received through our central 911 system and automatically taped before the "job" was given to an assigned unit. Upon our arrival at the scene and a preliminary examination of the body, it was soon apparent that the husband was our suspect. In fact, he had already changed his story about finding his wife outside and was thoroughly enmeshed in a much more involved "fairy tale," now claiming that his wife must be the victim of a burglary and that he had found her in this beaten condition when he arrived home. Steadfastly, he denied that he had beaten her and continued to embellish his story in an attempt to explain the inconsistencies that we pointed out. However, when I requested the communications division to rerun his original taped call, there was our suspect, telling a completely different story *on tape.* After hearing his own fairy tale, he changed his mind and gave a full confession.

Response to the Homicide Crime Scene. This includes: (1) the actions that should be taken by police officers who first receive a report of a possible homicide, (2) the actions that should be taken by these officers on arrival at the homicide crime scene, and (3) the preliminary investigation that should be initiated.

Many texts on investigation use the acronym, PRELIMINARY, as a guide to assist the first officer arriving at a crime scene.

P	Proceed to the scene promptly and safely.
R	Render assistance to the injured.
E	Effect the arrest of the suspect.
L	Locate and identify witnesses.
I	Interview.
M	Maintain the crime scene and protect evidence.
I	Interrogate the suspect (make sure he or she has been advised).
N	Note conditions, event, and remarks.
A	Arrange for collection of evidence (or collect it).
R	Report the incident fully and accurately.
Y	Yield responsibility to the follow-up investigator.

The First Officer. At the scene of a homicide, the first officer responding is immediately confronted with a multitude of problems that must be quickly analyzed so that the necessary steps can be taken in accordance with proper priorities. Quickness, however, does not imply haste. The first officer must be deliberate and controlled. When the assignment-information received by radio or telephone suggests an incident that is or may become a homicide, the officer approaching the given location must become scene conscious; that is, be alert to important details that are transient and subject to chemical change.

Modifications may occur through dissipation or by the movement of persons on or arriving at the scene. In general, these include but are not limited to:

- The condition of doors and windows (whether closed or ajar, locked or unlocked).

- Evidence that may be obliterated or damaged on the approach to the central scene, such as tire marks on the roadway, stains, fibers, shell casing on the floor, and so on.

- Odors, such as perfume, gunpowder, gas, marijuana, cigar, or cigarette smoke.
- Whether lights are on or off.
- Original position of furniture or articles that must be moved to render first aid or determine death, and so on.

In almost all instances, the first officer to arrive at any homicide crime scene is the uniformed patrol officer. That officer is rarely a witness to the actual homicide, usually arriving a short time after in response to a radio transmission or emergency call made by a citizen who has either witnessed the crime or stumbled upon the scene. There is no doubt in my mind that the initial actions taken by this officer may determine whether or not there will be a successful homicide investigation. All officers responding to and arriving at the homicide crime scene have a responsibility to preserve and refrain from disturbing it in any manner, whether by walking through or by touching certain items. Certainly, curiosity to get a better look does not justify disturbing the setting.

Upon arrival at the homicide crime scene, the first officer could be confronted with either of the following extreme situations: (1) Someone, calm and composed, might direct the officer to a body that manifests obvious, conclusive signs of death in a location that is easily secured and/or safeguarded; or (2) the scene might be filled with people milling about, shouting and/or weeping; the perpetrators might still be at the scene or just escaping therefrom; the victim might still be alive and in need of immediate medical assistance; and the scene itself might be a public or quasi-public place which is difficult to safeguard.

First Officer Duties. Whatever the situation, the first officer has three primary concerns: (1) determining whether the victim is alive or dead and implementing necessary action; (2) apprehending the perpetrator, if still present, or making appropriate notifications, if escaping or escaped; and (3) safeguarding the scene and detaining witnesses.

Each case requires a different response pattern, but the major guiding principle is protection of life. This includes the possibility of saving the victim and self-protection. Wherever there is any doubt as to death, the officer should presume life and proceed accordingly.

The Signs of Death. The first officer should be aware of the following signs of death:

1. *Breath stoppage:* This is best determined by observation of the upper abdomen, just below the point where the lowest rib meets the breast bone. Any up and down motion here, however slight, indicates breath and hence life. If no motion is seen here, breathing may have stopped or may be too shallow for observation. Death, however, must not be presumed from the cessation of breathing alone.

2. *Cessation of pulse:* In most cases, the heart continues to beat anywhere from a few seconds to a few minutes after cessation of breathing. Pulse can be detected by placing the tips of the fingers on the undersurface of the radial bone at the base of the thumb and firmly pressing inward. The absence of pulse, coupled with the cessation of breathing, suggests a high probability of death.

3. *Eye reflexes:* During life, the pupils of the eyes are round and equal in size; the eyeball is extremely sensitive. At death, the muscles that control the

pupils relax, causing loss of symmetrical appearance. They may differ in size. The eyelids become flabby in death and if they are opened by someone, remain open. Finally, whereas in life touching the eyeball causes some reactive movement of the eyeball or eyelid, no such reaction occurs in death. The absence of eye reflexes, coupled with the cessation of pulse and breath are conclusive signs of death.

In addition, there are other convincing signs including rigor mortis, lividity, and putrefaction. These will be treated in greater detail later in this chapter.

First Notification Received in Person.   It is very important that the first officer responding to the homicide crime scene note the time of the call and/or any initial information that stimulated the original investigation—especially if informed of the crime by a passerby or witness. Even while responding to the scene and while exiting from the patrol vehicle, the officer should remain observant and alert to unusual activity or actions.

If the first notification is *received in person* by an officer on patrol, the person reporting should be returned to the scene by the officer and detained for the investigators. Valuable information is often irretrievably lost because the person who reported the information is allowed to wander off in the confusion at the scene or was not returned to the scene in the first instance. If, for any reason, the officer cannot detain this person, at least sufficient identification should be obtained so that an interview at a later date by the follow-up investigator is possible.

FIRST OFFICER—INITIATING THE HOMICIDE INVESTIGATION

This section focuses on the initial steps to be taken by the first officer who is confronted with the homicide crime scene. Although the formal investigation will be conducted by the detectives or criminal investigator, the first officer is responsible for initiating the investigation. The following procedures are recommended for officers who initiate the homicide investigation:

1. Attempt to determine the entire area of the crime scene, including paths of entry and exit as well as areas that may contain evidence.

2. Isolate the area and seek assistance, if necessary. Notify superiors, investigating officers, and specialized units.

3. Refrain from entering the scene and/or disturbing, touching, or using any items found therein. (*Never use the crime scene itself as a command post or the telephone as a communications center.*)

4. Exclude all unauthorized persons from entering the crime scene until the arrival of the crime scene technicians. The detective supervisor and the assigned detective are allowed entry to the scene for evaluation. Other unavoidable exceptions may include the medical examiner or a doctor. *If there will be some unavoidable entry into the scene, establish a pathway in and out, to avoid unnecessary disturbance.*

5. Keep a chronological log containing the names, shield numbers, commands, titles, and offices of the police officers, ambulance personnel, and other officials and the names and addresses of any civilians entering the scene.

Often, such a basic step as item three is completely forgotten in the confusion of the homicide crime scene. For instance, many times, after a homicide in an apartment, the telephone is used for communications and one of the rooms as an office. Valuable trace evidence can be lost as a result of such carelessness. To avoid this situation:

1. Secure the entire area or apartment and mark it "off limits."

2. Establish the temporary command in an adjoining apartment or completely outside the crime scene.

3. Have responding units report to the command center rather than to the crime scene.

4. Have someone familiar with the case, preferably a detective superior, brief these additional officers and make assignments from the command center.

5. The first officer, however, should remain at the crime scene in order to brief the detective and detective superior who will direct the homicide investigation.

Communicating with the Command.   In communicating with the station house, the officer should *not*, unless absolutely necessary, use a telephone at the scene. Establish a temporary command outside the crime scene, preferably where there can be access to two phones—one for incoming and another for outgoing calls. In the early stages of the investigation, there is need for rapid communication between various centers.

The Changing Sequence of Command.   All officers should be aware of the changing command sequence at homicide crime scenes. The first officer on the scene is in command until a uniformed officer of higher rank or an investigator arrives. The ranking uniformed officer continues to command the activities at the crime scene until a superior or an investigator arrives. On arrival at the scene, the investigator will assume command and be responsible for the activities carried on from that point until superseded by an investigator of superior rank. Department regulations should provide for such shifts of command so as to avoid conflict and maintain the investigation.

Patrol Officer's Response Action.   The police officer responding to or confronted by the homicide crime scene should prepare to take five basic steps upon arrival. If they are executed carefully, the officer will have initiated a professional and proper investigation.

For most officers, the homicide crime scene is not an everyday situation. Usually, police activities are either fast-paced emergencies requiring automatic reaction, or the routine handling of called-for services. Officers in the homicide crime situation find themselves somewhere between these extremes and must, therefore, force themselves to *adapt* to the situation. I offer the acronym, ADAPT, as a basic five-step method of approach:

A   Arrest the perpetrator if possible.

D   Detail and identify witnesses and/or suspects at the scene for follow-up investigators.

A   Assess the crime scene.

P   Protect the crime scene.

T   Take notes.

First Officer Duties: General

The first officer is sometimes faced with hysterical or violent persons at the crime scene, who may include the perpetrator or hostile family members and friends of the deceased. Under such circumstances, it would be foolhardy *not* to pick up any weapons, thus preventing the possibility of someone using them against the officer or others. Life protection certainly takes precedence over the general rule: Do not pick up or disturb anything at the scene. For example, one crime scene looked like a shootout at the O.K. Corral. There were two bodies and a number of guns strewn about. The first officers had picked up the guns to prevent any further problems, particularly since the scene was in a South Bronx social club and common sense dictates removing the weapons so as not to increase the body count. Even so, the officers should remain "scene conscious," disturbing only what is necessary and carefully noting the location and condition of any items before they are moved or changed.

In some extreme cases, it may even be necessary to move the body. A militant or radical group gathering, rumor circulating, or an incident capable of triggering a large-scale civil disturbance may require such action. In these cases, the officers should make every effort, in moving the body, to keep it in the position in which it was found, that is, without breaking such rigor as may exist or moving the extremities, which may be in a flexed position. Here, too, the officers should realize that changing the position of the body can cause new blood to flow and/or alter the direction of existing flows, which, if unobserved and unreported, can give a false picture to the pathologist and the detective attempting to reconstruct events.

The Dying Declaration. If the victim is still alive, the officer must be alert to the possibility of obtaining a dying declaration while waiting for the ambulance or while en route to or at the hospital. Officers should be knowledgeable in the requirements of a valid dying declaration and periodically review them. Briefly, the conditions are that the subject:

1. Is the victim of homicide (upon death).

2. Is *in extremis* (and later dies).

3. Is otherwise competent and rational.

4. Believes that death is imminent.

5. Has no hope of recovering from injuries.

Victim Removed to Hospital. Upon arrival of the ambulance the officer should guide the intern and/or ambulance attendants to and through the central scene via a preselected route so that they do not destroy evidence. Whatever they touch or move must be observed by the officers on the scene and reported to the investigators when they arrive. An officer should ride in the rear of the ambulance with the victim and remain with the victim at the hospital without interfering in any way with required medical treatment. If the prognosis indicates that death is likely, the officer's constant presence is required to record any statement the victim may make or important facts disclosed.

At the hospital, the officer should attempt to have the victim's clothing removed intact. If cutting is necessary, it should *not* be done through holes, cuts, or tears caused by bullets, knives, or other instruments. To facilitate this procedure, it is recommended that hospital emergency room personnel be contacted in advance to secure their cooperation.

Victim Pronounced Dead on Arrival (DOA) at Hospital. If the victim is pronounced dead at the hospital, the officer should obtain the necessary information and immediately communicate with the detective supervisor at the scene and the desk officer at the station house; then, he or she should be guided by further instructions received.

Officer's Duty at Hospital. At the first opportunity, an officer at the hospital should communicate with the investigators on the scene in order to keep them apprised of the developments at the hospital and to receive information necessary for intelligent talk with the victim, should consciousness be regained.

Death Confirmed at the Scene. If the first officer arriving at the scene is confronted with a body manifesting conclusive signs of death, the body should not be disturbed. Sometimes inexperienced officers feel a need to do something, particularly in the presence of family or friends. This may impel them to cut down a hanging body or otherwise disturb it even in the face of rigor mortis, lividity, and incipient putrefaction. In other instances, officers feel that they should immediately search the decedent for quick identification or to get all the information for their report to the desk officer. The body *should not be searched* until all other necessary procedures have been completed and the medical examiner has finished the on-the-scene examination. I would suggest that the search and inventory be conducted in the presence of a supervising officer and a member of the family or civilian in order to minimize a later charge of theft from the body. An officer who does cut down a hanging body because there are no conclusive signs of death must be careful to leave the knot and to observe its position when suspended.

Handling Witnesses at the Scene. All witnesses present at the scene upon the officer's arrival *must be detained* for the investigators. The officer should also be alert to the possibility that one of the witnesses or persons who "discovered" the body may, in fact, be the perpetrator. A suspect who is taken into custody at the scene should be removed to the station house as soon as additional assistance arrives, or as soon as practical, to protect the scene. This avoids creating additional trace impressions by unnecessary movement about the scene.

Witnesses and/or suspects should be kept separate from one another. When this is impossible at the onset, no discussion should be permitted concerning the incident, either within the hearing of or between such persons. At the same time, the officer must be alert to any circumstances or declaration that may be admissible under the *res gestae* rule. As soon as circumstances allow and the number of officers present permit, the witnesses should be moved outside the crime scene area or, at the very least, away from it. Ordinarily, witnesses should not be moved to the station house until the investigators arrive. This gives them an opportunity to obtain the basic details necessary for expediting an intelligent crime scene search.

The first officer should report all conversations with the witnesses to the investigators when they arrive and note them carefully and promptly.

At times, the person who discovered the body, the witnesses, or perhaps members of the immediate family at the scene are so distraught that some well-meaning person (even a doctor present to pronounce death) suggests that they take or be given a sedative. Officers present should attempt to delay this medication until the investigators arrive. Often, sedated persons cannot be spoken to for several hours or until the next day. This could become critical where the sedated individual emerges as a possible perpetrator. Such a situation requires tact and discretion.

Additional Officers at the Scene.   As other officers arrive, they must be careful to conduct themselves in an appropriate manner. Too often, officers who have not seen each other for a while meet at crime scenes and drift into irrelevant conversation while waiting for the morgue wagon. Sometimes, this banter produces snickers or outright laughter that can be heard by members of the family or friends of the victim. The image of the officers, the department, and police may be ruined in the eyes of that family, the neighborhood, or even the entire community. This is one of the reasons that officers, especially additional reinforcements arriving at homicide scenes, should be directed to report to the command center located outside the general area of the crime scene. Here they can await assignments, be supervised, and converse without being overheard by persons at the central scene.

News Media Personnel at the Scene.   If newspaper or television personnel arrive on the scene, they should not be permitted access or given information at this time. First officers can tactfully explain that all information about the case will come from the chief investigator or detective supervisor in charge at the scene. It can be explained that it would be unfair to make information available piecemeal because all members would not have equal access. Rather, information will be given uniformly as soon as possible. This approach must be taken by *all* members of the department, whether at the scene, the hospital, the morgue, the station house, or on patrol.

Documentation of Events by First Officer.   The first officer and, indeed, all officers taking part in the investigation must be *time-conscious*. As soon as circumstances permit, the officer must record the time of dispatch, the time of arrival on the scene, the time assistance was requested, and so on. Time may become an important factor in terms of the suspect's alibi. In any case, accurate recording of times makes for a more precise investigation, a more professional report, and a favorable impression during later testimony in court.

The first officer and other officers who arrive on the scene before the investigators should realize that they will have to recount all their activities at the scene to the investigators when they arrive and before any crime scene search or handling of items. The investigators must be fully aware of everything that these first officers or anyone else touched, moved, or altered in any way. Officers must not smoke, flush toilets, run tap water, use the bathroom, or do anything else at or near the crime scene, unless absolutely necessary.

As soon as the first officers have performed their immediate duties and responsibilities, they should take advantage of lulls or waiting time to promptly record times, details, conversations, and names and addresses of witnesses or persons known to have been on the scene.

When the investigators arrive, the officers should immediately fill them in, out of the hearing of the family or witnesses or others, on what has transpired up to that point. The investigators assume responsibility at the time they enter the investigation and for the subsequent conduct of the investigation.

CONDUCTING THE HOMICIDE INVESTIGATION

This section focuses on the work of the investigator and detective supervisor for a proper, professional homicide investigation. Such an investigation is probably one of the most exacting tasks. It begins with the initial notification that a homicide has occurred.

Initial Receipt of Information. The response of a detective supervisor and a homicide detective must be methodical and procedural. To avoid overlooking the obvious, the most basic details should be recorded. It is a recommended procedure that the homicide detective "open" a new steno pad or notebook for exclusive use in each homicide investigation. The first entry should record the following:

- Date and exact time of receiving information
- Method of information transmission
- Name and other data identifying the person giving the information
- Complete details of the information

Many times, from a false sense of urgency and/or a desire to take immediate action, the investigator gets caught up in the excitement or confusion permeating the homicide crime scene and consequently, may lose that "cool, calm and detached" projection necessary to assume control and initiate professional investigation. A good thing to keep in mind is this: The deceased is not going anywhere. More importantly, the patrol officers are already taking preliminary action.

Teamwork Approach. Not only are the detective and detective supervisor faced with a crime of the utmost gravity, but also one fraught with a complexity of possible motives and methods and a variety of physical evidence. Professional teamwork is the essence of successful homicide investigation—teamwork that begins with the very first officer on the scene.

The detective supervisor and the homicide investigators must set the tone for this teamwork approach that is so vital for success. They become coordinators of several different units and people who are charged with responsibility for inquiry into death. Included at the homicide crime scene are:

- Patrol service or uniform division.
- Detective division.
- Medical examiner.
- Crime scene technicians.
- District attorney.
- Other homicide detectives who assist at the scene.

Preliminary Interview of the First Officer. The inquiry into death starts with effective protection of the crime scene. The detective must be certain that nothing has been removed from or added to it since the arrival of the responding police, ascertaining that the scene is intact by going directly to the first officer. A preliminary interview with this officer can provide the detective and detective supervisor with an up-to-date appraisal of the crime scene as well as an assessment of what transpired since the discovery of the body. It is advisable to keep first officers at the scene to answer questions about the appearance of certain objects present when they arrived and to report observations they may have made upon their arrival concerning persons who were in the area or who expressed some interest in the activities of the police.

For example, in one case the police were notified by the fire department that there was a body on fire in the basement of a South Bronx tenement. Two uniformed officers in the vicinity responded immediately and arrived as firemen were still extinguishing the fire. The fire officer in charge informed them that an individual had been quite helpful upon their arrival and had directed them through the unlit basement to the source of the fire. Taking note that denizens of the area were less than civic-minded, these two police officers detained the "good citizen" pending my arrival and that of other Seventh Homicide Zone detectives. They told us about his actions and had detained him as a witness. Needless to say, it was not long before we were able to reconstruct what had occurred. The suspect had been staying with the deceased in a rear basement apartment. They were both from Jamaica and belonged to the Rastifarian sect, a Jamaican subculture some of whose members deal in marijuana and engage in other illegal activities. The suspect and the victim had apparently fallen out over business. As a result, the suspect shot and killed the deceased with a .22 caliber revolver. Why he did not take off, I shall never know; instead, he stayed with the cadaver all night. The next day, he purchased kerosene at the corner hardware store, dragged the body to the front of the basement, poured the liquid over the deceased, and ignited it. However, he did not expect the initial burst of flame and smoke and was therefore faced with the problem of keeping down the flames. Spotting the smoke emanating from the basement, the people on the first floor called the fire department. A fire company returning to its station from a previous alarm in the area responded, arriving in less than a minute. The suspect, finding himself trapped with the body and the fire, decided to play the part of a good citizen. Because the two police officers did not "buy his act," they detained him. The subsequent gathering of evidence and talking to people in the area provided sufficient evidence to charge the suspect with murder. Because the police officers took the initiative and detained this individual, a successful homicide investigation resulted. The case would have become a real mystery if the first officers had not been alert, because neither the deceased nor the suspect were known to the department, neither had a criminal record with the New York City Police Department, neither was known by neighbors, both were from Jamaica, and there was no tenant of record for the basement apartment. Instead, this case was solved.

Direction of the Investigation at the Scene.   The homicide detective or investigator will enter the investigation at different levels depending upon the circumstances and the investigator's time of arrival. All pertinent information must be obtained from the first officer while out of the hearing of witnesses, press, and public. If the victim has not been pronounced dead by the physician or ambulance attendant, the detective should confirm the fact of death. The responsibility now devolves upon the first investigator to see that the necessary duties of the first officer have been accomplished. Furthermore, arrival of the detective supervisor or chief investigator means that either will assume responsibility for conducting the homicide investigation and will replace the initial investigator as the ranking officer in charge of the case.

The detective supervisor should beware of getting into a fixed routine whereby an exact course is followed. Experience and format are invaluable, but they can be hindrances if they do not allow for new possibilities. Each case is distinct and unique; each requires a fresh approach.

Duties of the Detective Supervisor on Arrival at the Scene

1. Give priority to the removal of the suspect and/or witnesses to the station house, if not already accomplished. The witnesses should be interviewed briefly by the detective before removal.

2. Ascertain that there is an investigator present and that the crime scene is amply protected.

3. Confer with the ranking uniformed officer at the scene and interview the first officer so that proper instructions can be given to responding investigators.

4. If the suspect has fled the scene, ascertain exactly what alarms have been transmitted, if any, and the exact information contained therein. Upon verification and new information, *retransmit*.

5. If a suitable communications center or command post has not been established by the patrol officers, take immediate steps to arrange one, as discussed previously, and notify the station house, hospital, communications division, and so on, of the telephone numbers.

6. Have an assignment sheet prepared to indicate the assignments as given, including identification of the officers, the car numbers, and locations of the assignment.

7. Designate an officer to keep a running timetable of events at the scene, including arrivals and departures. When the scene is released, the timetable should be turned over to the chief investigator.

8. If the victim has been removed to the hospital, ensure that proper action is being taken there regarding any dying declarations, clothing, evidence, and so on. It is advisable to assign a detective to contact the hospital and assist in these procedures.

9. Provide for information dissemination to all units charged with the investigation. In the ideal situation, all investigators will be on top of every aspect of the case, thus relating to their own assigned functions more intelligently and thereby contributing to the overall effort. This is especially true for those officers assigned to conduct canvasses.

10. On occasion, too many officers respond to the homicide crime scene. The detective supervisor should not hesitate to direct a return of these officers to their posts if, in fact, they cannot contribute to safeguarding the scene, assisting in the canvass, or transportation.

Action upon Arrival at the Scene

Upon arrival, the investigator should stop and observe the area as a whole, noting everything before entering the actual crime scene for a detailed examination. Actually, only the homicide detective and detective supervisor should enter the homicide crime scene and, even then, only make their preliminary observations.

Photographing the scene upon arrival is a valuable procedure, either with a camera maintained in the homicide squad office for use at crime scenes or with a camera carried in your pocket and ready for use at any time. A camera with a built-in or flip flash device is preferable because of its convenience and simplicity. A photo taken at this point is a priceless recording for showing the court exactly how the crime scene appeared initially to the detective.

Although the police photographer takes many pictures of the homicide crime scene that will be submitted as evidence in the later prosecution, this preliminary picture, taken before the arrival of additional personnel, usually proves to be quite valuable when attempting to recall the initial crime scene.

Crime Scene Photographs. Photography is important because it is a permanent record; it provides visible evidence to recreate the original event; it enables the detective to recall significant details and review particular aspects of the scene.

The body and entire scene should be photographed and sketched. At this stage of the investigation, it is impossible to determine all the factors that will become important; therefore, photos must be taken of the entire home, apartment, office, building, or structure. Outdoor locations should include the central crime scene and the surrounding area. All small items that are recognized as actual or potential evidence require close-up shots. Do not add chalk marks or other indicators to the scene before a long shot and detailed picture have been taken. Objections can be made to the introduction of a photo into evidence for a trial because the scene has been altered and the photo is an inaccurate representation of the scene as it was upon discovery of the crime. If such chalk marks or markers are needed to pinpoint the location of a small item, photos should first be taken without the markers and then additional photos made with them. As each photo is taken, an accurate record must be made of the time, exact location, detail being photographed, compass direction, focus distance, and identity of the photographer. After the film is developed, this information should be placed on the back of the appropriate photo or recorded on a separate form. In case the crime scene search uncovers additional items or details that need to be photographed, the detective supervisor or chief investigator should hold the photographer at the scene. Also, it is important to eliminate persons or items, including police equipment, that do not belong in the scene.

The following photographs are required in homicide investigations:

1. The front entrance to the building.

2. The entrance to the apartment or room in which the deceased was discovered.

3. Two full body views (one from each side); if the body has been moved, the original body location will be photographed.

4. Two photographs relating the body location area to its general surroundings from opposite and/or diagonal directions.

5. Possible entrance and/or escape routes of the perpetrator(s) to and from the crime scene.

6. Areas where force was used for entry or exit.

7. Area photograph of evidence *in situ* and a close-up photograph of the specific evidence.

8. Plastic bags or sheetings, when they are the apparent cause of death.

9. Identification photographs of the deceased, which are normally taken at the morgue.

The Crime Scene Sketch. No matter how many homicides one has investigated, no one can know for sure just what witness, suspect, feature, or piece of physical or "trace" evidence will assume the greatest importance in the case. It is for this reason that we resort to photography and copious note taking. The notebook or steno pad is of utmost importance for the accumulation of vast amounts of information, some of which may seem inconsequential at the time it is taken but often proves to be crucial later.

The crime scene sketch, unlike a two-dimensional photo, allows for measurement and distance factors not readily apparent in a photo. A rough sketch can be made in the investigator's notebook indicating distances. It need not be a "Rembrandt."

A good crime scene sketch is a simple line drawing indicating the position of the body in relation to fixed and/or significant objects. The position of doors, windows, and staircases should be indicated as well as the position of furniture, blood, weapons, stains, and any other significant trace evidence. Such items should be noted by number and reference made to each in the investigator's notebook (see Fig. 17.1). Later, this rough sketch can be redrawn to scale for

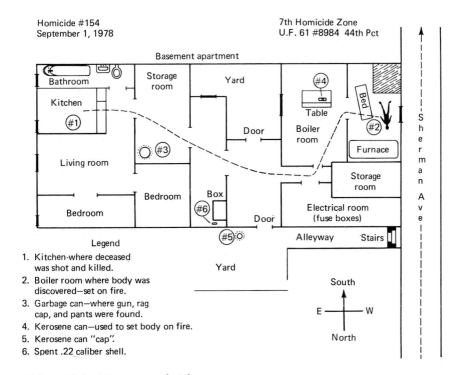

Figure 17.1 Crime scene sketch.

court presentation. It should, therefore, contain a legend explaining the numbers and symbols used, identification numbers assigned to the case, and a reference to compass direction.

Identity of the Deceased.   To prove a charge of homicide, it must be established that a named or described person is in fact *dead*. This verification of death is usually made by a physician.

Identifying the victim is a critical investigative step for two reasons: First, the identification provides a starting point for further inquiry. Who were the friends, family, or business associates of the deceased? Where the "hangouts" were and what the habits of the victim were can be very important information when conducting the canvass. It usually results in additional information. Second, the identification can also be the basis for determining whether the life of the deceased may have been threatened or whether the deceased was connected with a criminal enterprise. The clothes or possessions of the deceased usually supply information about identity. This identification, however, is only tentative, pending an official identification of the body by a relative or friend.

If the body is a "dump job," that is, badly mutilated, identification will be harder to obtain. Fingerprinting is usually the best method in these cases and reveals, quite rapidly, whether or not the deceased was "known to the department." Photographs can be taken at the morgue for later use by detectives in canvassing and identification.

The medical examiner can usually approximate age and body conditions during the autopsy. Analyzing teeth and dental work is an excellent method of establishing positive identification and determining age when there are no dental records. This particular procedure is usually performed by the forensic dentist attached to the medical examiner's office. However, for the initial stages of investigation at the homicide crime scene, informational materials and clothing of the deceased will be the most immediate evidence for determining identity.

The Canvass.   As additional investigators become available, officers should be assigned to canvass the immediate and surrounding area, including the routes along the approach to and/or escape from the crime scene. Canvassers should obtain the names and addresses of all persons spoken to, whether or not they provide any information. Similarly, when no one is at home or there is no answer at a given location, a note should be made so as to facilitate a call-back later on.

A canvass is simply a door-to-door inquiry or the stopping of persons on the street by detectives in an attempt to ascertain whether or not anyone at a particular location saw anything or can supply information relative to a specific crime. It is an important investigative tool and a vital part of the preliminary investigation. The detective supervisor should assign a sufficient number of investigators to conduct a preliminary canvass, while the assigned homicide detective can remain with the crime scene. As the detectives conduct the canvass, their primary purpose is to locate possible witnesses or persons who may have valuable information, eliminate unnecessary information, and keep notes of the locations where there was no response or negative results. In this phase of the case, we are interested merely in locating possible witnesses, not conducting in-depth interviews.

The assigned homicide detective or immediate partner should conduct the actual formal interviews of anyone located by the canvassers. In this way, both will be aware of all the developments in the case and better able to put this information into proper perspective.

At the homicide scene, there is a vast amount of information generated in a very short period. For this reason, everyone involved in a homicide investigation needs a notebook. To properly canvass a location, each apartment, place, and person should be recorded for later official reports and recanvass as the case may warrant. People should not be arbitrarily assigned to do a canvass because one is supposed to be done.

Usually, there are numerous personnel—sometimes more than can be used effectively. A common error committed by some supervisors is the indiscriminate assignment of personnel to do a canvass. *This can do more harm than good.* Experience shows that those who have a personal interest in a case are most effective in canvassing. This is not to say that a number of investigators should not be "shotgunned" into an initial canvass, but the personnel selected should be either good at this investigative technique or have an interest in the particular investigation. The extra people can be used for other necessary jobs.

Many homicides have been solved because a determined group of canvassers uncovered some vital bits of information, including the location of an eyewitness to the crime and sometimes even a motive behind it. Such canvassers do not just go through the motions but take time to effectively elicit information from persons. This information would never surface during a sloppy, perfunctory type of canvass.

Correctly done, a canvass is an invaluable investigative technique that can provide:

- An eyewitness to the crime.
- Information about the circumstances of the crime.
- An approximate time of occurrence or estimate of time of death.
- Information about the deceased, such as identity, habits, and friends.
- A motive.

Preliminary Medical Examination at the Scene

The body should not be moved before an examination by the medical examiner. It is important to keep in mind that the physical aspects of the cadaver will never be exactly the same after the body has been moved. Upon arrival at the scene, the chief investigator should immediately confirm the signs of death or that a pronouncement has been made.

The medical examiner should be immediately brought up to date by the chief investigator or detective supervisor concerning all developments in the case. The teamwork aspect of homicide investigation cannot be overemphasized. The medical examiner provides the cause, manner, and mode of death; advice concerning medical aspects; and information derived from the post-mortem examination and toxicological analyses. The chief investigator should seek the advice and counsel of the medical examiner. Such conferences and exchanges of information often result in modification of the investigator's approach to a case or a particular aspect thereof.

Doctors who specialize in forensic medicine have an interest in homicide crime scenes. Many times they can be helpful in reconstructing the scene and formulating the sequence of events. Their inquiry is directed toward the circumstances that led to death, the manner in which the death occurred, and the condition of the body consistent with the cause of death. In actuality, the medical examiner and the homicide detective act as a team. Each should be aware of the other's capabilities and duties. By working together and exchanging information, these two practitioners arrive at a final determination of what actually occurred.

Estimating the Time of Death. Time is most important in a murder case. It may very well be the factor that convicts a murderer, breaks an alibi, or eliminates a suspect. A good homicide investigator wants to know the working time frame in establishing an investigative foundation for further inquiry.

Although the detective supervisor and the homicide detective are not expected to have the knowledge of a forensic pathologist, they would certainly do well to have some basic understanding of post-mortem changes that occur in the human body and the effect of time and atmosphere on blood pools or stains. Such knowledge will enable them to make intelligent observations at the scene. So that it may be related to the medical examiner exactly, I have found it a good practice to take notes of the deceased's appearance and blood immediately. In New York City, the medical examiner usually responds within a reasonable time. If, however, there is a delay or a release of the body without a preliminary scene examination, the investigator's observations may become very important for establishing the approximate time of death.

There are four basic gauges used to approximate the time of death. Since it is impossible to fix the exact time, we refer to an *estimate* of time. The technique is not an exact science. It is dependent on a number of variables that affect post-mortem changes.

Dying is a process, and estimating the time of death depends on changes that occur during that process. Death can be said to occur in stages and a good medical examiner will want to see the scene before attempting to make any determination about the time of death; even then, it is only an estimate.

Time-of-death determination is based on:

1. *Body heat:* The human body gives off heat until it is the same temperature as the environment. This is affected by clothing, body build, age, and the surface on which the body lies. By placing your hand on a protected portion of the body, usually under the arms, you can make a rough determination of time: warm—the body has been dead a few hours; cold and clammy—under ordinary circumstances and conditions, the body has been dead 18 to 24 hours. The medical examiner usually uses a thermometer placed into the body to establish these conditions.

2. *Rigor mortis:* This condition is the poorest gauge because of the many variables involved: Obese people do not always develop rigor, thin people quickly do; a fight or body shock usually accelerates it; heat speeds it, whereas cold maintains it. Contrary to popular belief, rigor mortis starts at the same time throughout the entire body. It is present within 8 to 12 hours. (See Fig. 17.2.)

3. *Livor mortis (lividity):* In this condition, the blood in the body settles to the lowest point of the body as a result of gravity. It begins about 30 minutes after death and takes 8 hours to "fix." Upon completion of the process (12 hours), the blood changes in appearance from bright to dark red. The intensity of color gives you the time factor. Also, it can reveal emphatically whether or not the body has been moved. This is the most reliable factor.

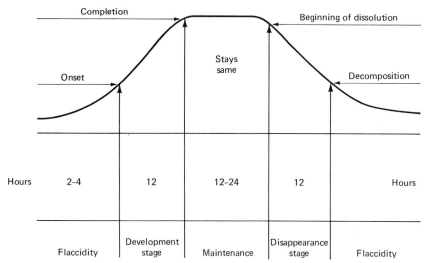

| Hours | 2-4 | 12 | 12-24 | 12 | Hours |

| | Flaccidity | Development stage | Maintenance | Disappearance stage | Flaccidity |

Figure 17.2 Rigor mortis flow.

4. *Stomach contents:* The contents of the stomach indicate when the person ate last. It takes two to three hours for digestion to occur. The autopsy can identify and measure these contents.

The Homicide Crime Scene Search.   The detective supervisor should formulate the search objectives and organize the crime scene search.

Before any search is made, the forensic technician or detective should *dust* the crime scene in an attempt to lift latent prints that can be used to place the criminal at the scene. In addition, special attention should be given to any weapons or objects that were apparently handled by the suspect as well as door handles, telephone, windows, light switches, glasses, and so on.

Search of the crime scene is the most important part of the homicide investigation. Crimes of violence, such as homicide, usually involve a struggle, a break, use of weapons, physical force, or some type of contact between the perpetrator and the deceased. Therefore, there is a good possibility that trace evidence will be found and recovered.

In most cases, it is good procedure to bag the hands of the deceased in order to preserve any trace evidence that may be found under the fingernails during the autopsy. A paper bag is preferable to plastic, especially if there is any blood on the hands of the deceased. Plastic tends to accelerate putrefaction.

All visible details should be observed and described before altering anything; locations of stains, weapons, and so on should be noted.

Immediately upon completion of the examination by the medical examiner at the scene, the body can be moved and a systematic search begun from the point where the body was found and then outward until the entire room or location has been covered. The area under the body must be carefully examined, bearing in mind that extensive bleeding may create pooling that conceals bullets, cartridge cases, or other small items of evidence. If any such items are discovered, they should be photographed in the position in which they were found before being collected and marked. While this procedure is particularly important in cases of death apparently from gunshot wounds, it should be followed as a matter of routine in all cases. Where the body has been lying on soft earth, bullets may be embedded in the soil.

All murders are distinctively different and unique. There is, however, one solid base on which to build the case. That base is the factual determination obtained from a study of the crime scene. Any physical act will usually leave a trace. The moment a murder is committed, whether it is a long-range premeditated act or a spur-of-the-moment impulsive gesture, the killer must go places, handle objects, and move things—either on purpose or by accident. Trace evidence may be left in the form of clothing, shoe impressions, fingerprints, blood stains, overturned furniture, disturbed articles in general, and even toolmarks. Not only the effect of the crime on the scene is considered, but also the manner in which something within the scene may have imparted traces to the criminal.

The homicide detective is responsible for gathering these bits and pieces of trace and physical evidence for proper delivery to the laboratory and, later, for interpreting the lab results and bringing them together with the other information developed during the investigation. Thus, all the knowledge obtained from the homicide investigation becomes a total picture or set of facts that does what the deceased cannot do—"points the finger" at the murderer.

The ability to recognize and discover evidence at the homicide crime scene is a prerequisite of successful search. The expertise of the homicide detective and the chief investigator, acquired by training and experience, will probably determine what trace evidence is found.

In the ideal situation, only one officer makes the actual search and gathering of evidence. Other homicide officers follow up in locating materials, but they do not handle the evidence. Instead, another officer who spots something of significance can alert the searching officer, who will actually take it into custody or "handle" it. This procedure shortens the *chain of custody* and makes the recording of evidence more uniform and professional.

In addition to recording information in a notebook or steno pad, a reference should be made on the crime scene sketch to indicate where each piece was located and whence it was removed. Special attention should be given to objects that may have caused death, newly damaged areas, or items apparently missing from their original location.

An effective procedure is to have someone thoroughly familiar with the scene go over the whole place with the investigator—bit by bit—identifying the usual positions of furniture and objects and recognizing any foreign material now found there. It is in this search phase that one can see the need for closer cooperation between police officers and forensic scientists. It is imperative that the officers doing the search have a good working knowledge of how to handle physical evidence.

Investigation of homicide crime scenes involves the most intricate and time-consuming procedures in order not to destroy valuable trace evidence left by the criminal. In New York City, the crime scene unit has specially trained personnel available for searches of important crime scenes. Together with the homicide detective and under the direction of the detective supervisor, they are valuable in properly and effectively securing physical evidence. The products of the crime-scene search for informational sources such as papers, personal effects, and address books, which may aid in the investigation, are taken by the homicide detective for later perusal and disposition.

The patrol force of uniformed division is responsible for the administrative search and safekeeping of any valuables and/or the property of the deceased. These items are vouchered and safeguarded in the precinct of record for later disposition to the property clerk's office or the family of the deceased.

Finally, during the crime scene search, the investigators should be alert to the usefulness of snapshots of the deceased, taken in life, and should collect them for (1) use in canvass—they identify the victim for persons to be interviewed— and (2) use in questioning friends or associates of the victim. If such photos are not available at the scene, they should be obtained from the family, yearbooks, or friends. These photos should be a good likeness of the deceased just prior to death, so as not to mislead persons who view them.

Collection of Evidence.   The proper collection and disposition of trace or physical evidence from the homicide crime scene is of utmost importance to the investigation and final court presentation.

1. Each item should be described exactly and completely, with the corresponding case numbers affixed, with the date and time.

2. Each item should be packaged in a separate, clean, and proper size container to prevent cross-contamination and/or damage.

3. Each package should be sealed to retain evidence and prevent unauthorized handling.

4. Each piece should be marked with original location and position, and this information should be in the investigator's notebook.

5. Each piece should be marked distinctively by the searching officer to identify the officer finding it.

6. Each piece of evidence should show proper disposition, namely, police department laboratory, property clerk, FBI laboratory.

7. Proper records should be kept regarding the evidence and chain of custody. These records reflect any movement of the evidence from point of origin to final disposition.

Identification and final disposition of evidence is paramount to the proper judicial presentation in which certain issues will arise. To reiterate, the introduction of physical evidence in a trial requires that: (1) the article be properly identified, (2) continuity of the *chain of custody* be proved, and (3) the evidence be material and relevant. These facts must be considered by the detective supervisor and homicide detective while at the homicide crime scene. With proper search and collection techniques at this stage of the investigation, the investigator will avoid problems later when the case enters the adversary proceedings of the courtroom.

Interview of Witnesses.   When the work at the homicide crime scene is completed, the attention of the detective assigned should be directed to interviewing possible witnesses and persons having information relative to the investigation.

Although the homicide crime scene offers an abundance of informational evidentiary material, the vital question of the identity of the perpetrator usually will be answered through intelligent interviewing of witnesses. The questioning of possible witnesses at the crime scene should begin as soon as possible. The best procedure is to designate homicide detectives responsible for taking informal preliminary statements immediately upon arrival, while the case detective goes over the crime scene and establishes some basic information. This procedure ensures obtaining a candid statement before any deterioration of memory due to time lapse or desire not to get involved. Usually, a person who tells a detective a particular story, will not suddenly change it when making a formal statement. This preliminary statement can be taken and the witnesses requested to accompany the investigator to the office or homicide squad. In this way, the case officer has immediate information available at the crime scene and the presence of the witnesses for later formal statement before they wander away or change their minds in the confusion and hustle-bustle at the scene. The proper place for formal interviews is the homicide office, where there are rooms and equipment conducive to obtaining a formal recorded statement. (See Fig. 17.3.)

The formal statement and evaluation of each witness should be made by the detective assigned and the chief investigator. Needless to say, the original officer taking the preliminary statement confers with the case officer before, during, and after, so that no point is misunderstood or overlooked. This phase becomes crucial when dealing with persons who do not speak English and require an interpreter. The interviewer should make sure that the interpreter is phrasing the question properly, so that there is no confusion or misunderstanding of the meaning of the question and that the exact response is recorded (not the interpreter's assumption of what the interviewee meant). If possible, an officer who speaks the language should conduct the interview with the case officer. Together they can formulate the questions and evaluate the responses.

Obviously, the eyewitness to the fatal act is the most valuable witness to consider in the interview. Other witnesses, however, may have important information that places the suspect at the homicide crime scene, supplies the motive for the crime, or gives personal information about the suspect. This is a strong reason for getting the witnesses from the scene to the homicide office.

It is equally important to separate witnesses from each other. Many times, after conferring with one another, witnesses change their stories—not from a desire to mislead the police, but from a very basic factor in human behavior; namely, they do not want to make a mistake about a thing they saw or know to have happened. Sometimes they compromise with each other to find solace in agreement. In other words, one or more persons in a group may force their dominant personalities on the group. Some witnesses, not wanting to offend the stronger personalities or to seem stupid by having seen something no one else saw, may hide this fact or simply forget to tell it to the police.

In some instances, especially when dealing with criminals or persons sympathetic to the criminal enterprise, there may be a conscious effort to mislead and thwart any type of police inquiry into the crime. The detective should realize these possibilities when questioning prospective witnesses and must be more than thorough and patient in this investigative function—attempting to get the witnesses to relax and to talk about themselves and encouraging them to tell the story in their own words. When dealing with the criminal sympathizer or "bad-guy" type, questioning will have to be more authoritative. In that way, the detective can determine very often the weaknesses or fears of the interviewee. Usually persons of this type are not anxious for police to probe into their lifestyle and so may be willing to cooperate, either for a price or just to "get the cops off my back." The police may be lucky enough to have something on them, such as lesser crimes that can be traded off for information on the homicide. In any

NAME _____ ADDRESS _____

M ____ F ____ RACE _____ D.O.B. _____ AGE ____ TEL # _____

HEIGHT _____ WEIGHT _____ BUILD _____ COMPLEXION _____

WELFARE # _____ SOCIAL SECURITY NUMBER _____

DRIVER'S LICENSE # _____ AUTO DRIVEN & REGISTRATION # _____

WIFE OR HUSBANDS NAME _____ ADDRESS _____

WELFARE # _____ SOCIAL SECURITY # _____

D.O.B. _____ AGE _____ SOCIAL STATUS _____

GIRLFRIEND OR BOYFRIEND'S NAME _____ TEL # _____

LAST KNOWN ADDRESS _____ AGE ____ D.O.B. _____

WELFARE # _____ SOCIAL SECURITY # _____

NUMBER OF CHILDREN _____ NAMES AND AGES _____

SCHOOL ATTENDING _____

ADDRESS _____

MOTHER'S MAIDEN NAME (OR FAMILY NAME) _____

ADDRESS _____ TEL # _____

BUSINESS ADDRESS _____ TEL # _____

AREA FREQUENTS _____ PLACE OF BIRTH _____

MISCELLANEOUS INFORMATION _____

_____

WITNESS KNOWS PERPETRATOR PERSONALLY? _____ (YES/NO) HOW? _____

DID WITNESS ID PERPETRATOR _____ (YES/NO) HOW? _____

CASE # _____ OFFICER ASSIGNED _____ HOMICIDE # _____

DATE OF INTERVIEW _____ INTERVIEWING OFFICER _____

Figure 17.3 Witness interview form.

case, dealing with such persons is always frustrating and fraught with danger. One never knows for sure which side of the fence they are on, or their motivation or when they will turn on the investigator. The best defense is proper documentation of their activities and conferences with superiors. In certain instances, where part of the deal concerns "court consideration" or lack of prosecution in return for testimony against a suspect, the office of the district attorney must be consulted.

Effective interviewing is an art that requires constant improvement. It is also a very time-consuming procedure. Frequently, however, it is worth every minute spent, especially for the final analysis of information discovered. It is often a good idea for detectives to work in pairs on a particular case. Both can perform the necessary duties and thereby divide the enormous workload generated. Further, there is provision for continuing the investigation should one of the officers be unavailable for any reason. Homicide supervisors or chief investigators should also be aware of each witness and the interview results so that they can make proper investigative assignments and provide for the effective follow-up of any new leads or vital information.

Release of the Body.   The body should not be moved until after the arrival of the medical examiner and prosecutor (if responding) since an opportunity to view the body in its original position is very helpful to these officials in carrying out their responsibilities. Sometimes, after all necessary photos have been taken, diagrams made, and details noted, a question arises as to when the body can and should be moved. This decision is critical. Since its consequences are irrevocable, removal should be undertaken only after consideration of several factors:

1. If the medical examiner is not going to conduct an immediate autopsy and the body will be lying in the morgue until the following day, there should be no rush to remove it, particularly in cases of apparent homicide where there exist no witnesses, no named perpetrator, and no arrests. Furthermore, there should be no hurry to remove the body if it is not in a public place and the location can be easily secured. The reason is that information may be developed during the canvass or while talking to witnesses at the station house that requires additional photos or other police procedure with respect to the body.

2. If an immediate autopsy is to be conducted by the medical examiner, the removal should be directed only after conferring with the canvass investigators and interviewing teams at the station house to determine whether there is any new information requiring additional investigative use of the body before removal.

3. If the body is in a public place, the medical examiner's examination completed, and the crime scene work accomplished, then the detective supervisor can release the body, usually after checking with the detectives at the station house and officers doing the canvass.

4. If the body is in a public place and the medical examiner is not responding, the chief investigator will authorize the removal after the crime scene work has been completed.

5. As previously discussed, in situations involving violent crowds or public disorders, and so on, the body may have to be removed immediately.

Release of the Scene.   The decision to release the scene should be carefully considered. Obviously, the problem with releasing the scene prematurely is that soon information may be developed that would have required different photos or the collection of or search for other items. The scene should never be released before the initial canvass has been completed, all the known witnesses interviewed, or the suspect in custody questioned fully. In some cases, it may be necessary to secure the scene and post a guard, pending interview of witnesses who cannot be located immediately. In other instances, the scene must be held until completion of the autopsy. This may not always be practical, but it is a recommended procedure in the event that additional examinations or searches are necessary as a result of information obtained during the autopsy. If the autopsy is conducted while the investigators are still at the scene, any additional information required can be immediately communicated back to the chief investigator at the scene. In any event, autopsy findings should be made available to the homicide investigators as soon as possible so that they may be guided in their investigation and in formulating their questions to the witnesses.

Before releasing the scene, the chief investigator should bear in mind that any good defense attorney will visit the crime scene at the first opportunity and from this inspection will be able to gauge the nature, character, and extent of the investigation at the scene. The attorney will be alert to details that may have been overlooked; to areas that have been dusted or not dusted; to the shape, pattern, and location of blood and other stains; to flash bulbs and film packs; and perhaps other debris that the investigators have carelessly strewn about and left at the scene. During police activities at the scene, the chief investigator should see that all waste materials from the lab work and photography are deposited in one container in a location that will not interfere with other activities; such a container should be removed before the scene is released. The detective supervisor or the chief investigator would do well to check over the whole crime scene from the point of view of the defense attorney before releasing it. In addition, before abandoning the crime scene and securing it against reentry, it should be made sure that any police equipment, including portable radios, has been removed. Radios seem to have a way of causing embarrassment to officers, especially when they must break back into the recently secured crime scene to retrieve them!

The Autopsy

A detective or investigator, fully apprised of all developments of the case, should be present at the autopsy. If the pathologist performing the autopsy has not been at the scene, the investigator can provide a detailed account of all that has transpired, thus assuring that the autopsy will cover every necessary phase. The pathologist will have the benefit of all available information so as to proceed intelligently.

If the pathologist is not familiar with the requirements of a police investigation and/or prosecution, the investigator may have to explain the necessity for certain procedures and see that they are carried out as follows:

1. Photos must be taken of the body before and after cleaning off blood and dirt, so as to show detail of death wounds (include a scale for dimension of wounds).

2. In gunshot cases, before removing blood or sponging the skin, the wound should be carefully examined to determine whether or not there are evidences of powder or metal particles. If such exist, they should be photographed. When the gunshot wounds might involve powder residues, the victim's clothing should be carefully removed without shaking and with a minimum of handling to avoid dislodging minute particles of powder or metal that may adhere to the clothing.

3. Nothing is to be thrown away. Clothing, when removed, should be tagged with pertinent information.

4. In all cases the body should be x-rayed. Before commencement of the autopsy, body surfaces should be carefully examined for possible bloody fingerprints of the perpetrator.

5. Fingernail scrapings should be taken from all victims (in gunshot cases, appropriate residue test, then fingerprints, then palmprints).
6. The autopsy must be complete so as to rule out contributing causes. What is *not* found is just as important as what *is* found.
7. Blood and hair samples should be taken from all victims.

Today, most pathologists are familiar with and knowledgeable about the legal requirements in autopsies. This, however, may not be so in all jurisdictions, and the investigator would do well to know the reasons for and the necessity of the above procedures. I have found that both the medical examiner and the investigator can benefit from this mutual understanding of each other's duties and responsibility.

Identification.   The legal identification of the body is one of the requirements in the chain of evidence that is vital to the case. There are two identifications: the *police identification of the body* (see Fig.17.4) is made by the first officer or member of a law enforcement agency having jurisdiction to the medical examiner who will do the autopsy; the *personal identification* (see Fig.17.5) is the one made by a member of the family. These identifications are made on official forms, sworn to in the presence of witnesses, with the date and time affixed, and signed by the person making the identification. The police identification is made to the medical examiner, while the personal identification can be made to an authorized representative of the medical examiner.

The Protocol.   *Protocol* is the official recording of the autopsy by the medical examiner. It reflects the entire examination, both negative and positive, and gives the official cause of death. The protocol, also referred to as the *autopsy report* in some jurisdictions, contains the following information: clothing—description; external examination; central nervous system—head and brain; internal examination—cardiovascular system, heart, aorta, pulmonary system, lungs, gastrointestinal system, stomach, small and large intestine, appendix, liver, gall bladder, pancreas, kidneys, endocrine system, thyroid, adrenals, skeletal system; anatomical findings; toxicological findings.

At the end of this protocol, the medical examiner reports the official diagnosis of the cause of death and, if homicidal, indicates this on the protocol. The value of this diagnosis and protocol from an investigator's point of view is for determining whether the facts developed and evidence gathered during the homicide investigation are consistent with the cause of death as determined by the medical examiner.

DOCUMENTATION REQUIRED
IN HOMICIDE
INVESTIGATIONS

Official Reports

The *official police report* is the vehicle used by criminal investigators to document the findings of their investigative actions. It is the principal source used by the courts, the defense, the district attorney's office, and the police department to evaluate the thoroughness of investigations and the ability of the reporting detectives. A thorough field investigation, accompanied by an accurate and read-

OFFICE OF THE CHIEF MEDICAL EXAMINER
CITY OF NEW YORK

POLICE IDENTIFICATION OF BODY

STATE OF NEW YORK
CITY AND COUNTY OF NEW YORK,
BOROUGH OF _____

Police Officer _____ Shield # _____ Command _____

1. That he was the officer who first saw the body of deceased:

Name of deceased	M. E. case no.
Place of death	Date of death

2. PLACE OF OCCURRENCE (State exact location)
               Time and Date

THAT HE OBTAINED THE FOLLOWING INFORMATION AS TO CIRCUMSTANCES
OF THE OCCURRENCE

THAT HE IDENTIFIED THE BODY OF THE DECEASED AT THE OFFICE OF THE
CHIEF MEDICAL EXAMINER, IN THE PRESENCE OF OR TO:

DRS. _____

_____

Sworn to before me this _____

    day of _____ 19 _____

Time _____

_____
Signature of Officer

Figure 17.4 Police identification form.

able report, are the elements of professionalism and success. A good report starts with an intelligent, organized approach to the investigation. The opening of a new steno pad for each homicide case, to be used exclusively in that case, and the immediate recording of the receipt of information that initiates the homicide investigation are examples of a good beginning. There are three basic steps involved in official reporting: (1) collecting the information, (2) collating the information and organizing the notes, and (3) writing the report.

Collecting the Information. A good report requires a good field investiga-

---

OFFICE OF THE CHIEF MEDICAL EXAMINER
OF THE CITY OF NEW YORK

IDENTIFICATION OF BODY

STATE OF NEW YORK
CITY AND COUNTY OF NEW YORK,
BOROUGH OF

_____ age _____ residing at
(NAME OF PERSON MAKING ID)

_____ in the _____
(ADDRESS)   (COUNTY)

being duly sworn, deposes and says: That he is a _____
(RELATIONSHIP)

of the person whose body was found at _____ date _____
(LOCATION)

and subsequently sent to the office of the ME; that deponent has seen

body of said deceased, and has every reason to believe that the body now

recorded at the office of the Chief Medical Examiner as

_____ is _____
(NAME OF BODY RECORDED)   (NAME OF DECEASED)

who was last seen or heard from by deponent on _____
(DATE)

Deponent therefore prays that _____(HIS/HER)_____ identification of said
deceased person be accepted by the Chief Medical Examiner of the
City of New York.

PEDIGREE

AGE _____ SEX _____ COLOR _____

MARITAL STATUS _____

OCCUPATION _____

RESIDENCE _____

Sworn to before me this _____

day of _____ 19 ____

_____
(SIGNATURE OF RELATIVE MAKING ID)

Identified to: _____ Death Cert. issued by _____ Date _____

Figure 17.5 Relative identification form.

tion. No amount of rhetoric or literary expertise can disguise the fact that an investigator has failed to conduct a thorough investigation. However, even a good investigation may look haphazard if the report is not properly prepared or written. The investigator should:

- Gather and record as much information as possible while conducting the investigation; for example, time of initial report, who reported the death, condition of the body when the investigator arrived, who was present, and so on.

- Record the facts in a clear and logical order. (The notes are subject to subpoena during trial, so the investigator should be able to read and interpret them at a later date.)

- When collecting the information, make clear distinction between hearsay, opinions, and facts.

- Keep the notes on file with the case folder. If the investigator is transferred or otherwise unavailable, the detective who is assigned to the case will be aware of investigative efforts already made.

Collating the Information and Organizing the Notes

- Completely review the information obtained during the investigation. This includes any information that was obtained by other investigators at the scene, such as interviews, names, and canvass results. The value of this procedure is twofold: (1) it enables the investigator to prepare a better report, and (2) it highlights what future steps may be required in the investigation.

- Decide which factors of information are appropriate and necessary, since all the information that is gathered during the investigation cannot possibly be put in the report. The official report must be a *complete* and *true* account of what has transpired, whether favorable or not to the suspect, victim, or witness. The investigator should attempt to include all the facts necessary to present a candid account to the reader.

- Organize the material in a logical order so that it can be understood by anyone who reads it.

- Include all investigative steps that were taken, with their results—*positive* or *negative.*

Sometimes it helps to compose a rough draft on scrap paper first. This procedure will give an idea of how the finished report will look and read.

Writing the Report.   If you have collected and organized your material as discussed, then the actual writing of the report is relatively simple:

- The information must be *accurate* and *complete.*

- The language should be *clear* and *concise.*

- The entire report should be *as brief as possible* yet still contain the necessary information.

Below is an example of an official report referred to as a *response report.*

COMPLAINT: Homicide   METHOD: Shotgun   DATE: 2/21/78

VICTIM: Mary Smith F/B 18   HOMICIDE: 32/78

SUBJECT: Response to the Scene

1. On the above date at 2205 hours, the undersigned officer was informed by Police Officer Doe, 4th Pct. that there was a homicide at 637 Jefferson Place, 4th floor landing.

2. Detective Sergeant Jones and Detective Scroop of the Homicide Detail responded and arrived at 2215 hours.

3. The deceased identified as MARY SMITH F/B 18 yrs. address 1392 Main Street, Apt. 6D, Tele #998——— was lying face up on the 4th floor landing, dressed in a brown coat, blue sweater, blue shirt, gray pants, rust colored boots, and a blue kerchief on her head. It appeared that she was shot in the right chest area.

4. Attendant Browne #1721 County General Hospital, Ambulance #237, pronounced the victim DOA at 2230 hours.

5. The deceased's cousin, Sarah smith, 1679 Franklin Avenue, Apt. 3B, Tele #783——— present and identified the body.

The structure and process of homicide report writing is flexible and usually varies with the length of the investigation and the number of investigators involved. For example, if the perpetrator has been arrested on the scene or shortly after the commission of the crime or the discovery of the body, the assigned detective will be able to assemble all the facts from notes and type them into a unified, complete, and well-structured report. This can usually be accomplished shortly after the initial chaos characteristic at homicide crime scenes subsides. In these cases, the report itself serves primarily as a record of the details of the crime, the subsequent investigation, and the apprehension. Usually such rapidly cleared cases present no major problems; the investigator must, however, be careful not to leave out any significant factors or to treat the report too lightly.

On the other hand, in a large-scale, continuing investigation involving a relatively large number of investigators, reports must be filed daily to expedite the indexing of the vast amount of information being gathered, thereby making the information available to the various investigators when needed.

In the latter type of investigation, usually there is a mass of reports prepared by any number of different individuals, some of whom may be brought in from different units. This creates a problem in terms of format, structure, and readability of the whole report when finally put together. At some future time, the prosecutor and possibly another investigator assigned to the case will have to decipher these reports (which are, in effect, the reports of numerous separate investigations representing distinct phases of the entire case) and be able to relate them to the whole.

To clarify these voluminous reports and provide uniformity, the report filed for each new facet of an investigation should begin with an assignment paragraph which clearly sets forth:

1. The date and time of the assignment.
2. The rank, name, badge number (if any), and the command of the person who made the assignment.

3. Full details concerning the source and nature of the lead, if any.

4. The objective of the investigation, if it arises in the normal course of investigative routine or from the particular needs of this investigation.

Without these explanatory "pegs," a long report can possibly degenerate into a meaningless mass of disjointed interviews.

When the final report is correlated, it should be arranged with the main portion of the investigation appearing first, followed by a grouping of reports on the results of neighborhood canvassing, grouping of leads checked under appropriate subtitles, and so on. The final report, whether long or short, should begin with a résumé, or summary, of the case. This will enable the reader to relate the details to the overall picture while going through the case.

In a large-scale investigation, the first day is generally taken up with a lot of investigative requirements, which invariably precludes any typing or formal reports, except for a brief official report to headquarters. At this stage, investigators should take copious notes, while orally keeping the chief investigator filled in concerning developments.

This flow of information should be a two-way communication so the investigator can better evaluate any information received. The chief investigator at this phase should appoint a recorder so that any assignments given out can be listed with the names and commands of the investigator, thus avoiding duplication of effort and fixing responsibility for any given report. Such a procedure will also enable the investigator to review what has been accomplished and plan for additional activities. If, by the end of the second day, an arrest has not been effected or the perpetrators identified and the department is committing a large number of investigators to the case, formal typed reports should be required and filed at the conclusion of each investigator's tour. This requires a sufficient number of typewriters, supplies, and space to accommodate the number of persons involved. Also, confusion is reduced when the newly assigned investigators, along with the regular investigators from the command assignment, are thoroughly briefed and instructed about what is required of them.

Indexing the Homicide Investigation. As the volume of daily reports grows, the amount of information contained therein becomes unmanageable unless an indexing procedure is instituted and maintained. Index cards should be prepared for all names of persons that arise in an investigation, locations or premises mentioned, vehicles and/or license plate numbers, and any other categories that may be required in a particular investigation. An investigator should be assigned to type and file the various index cards according to the following procedure: Daily reports from the investigator will be prepared in duplicate, the original forwarded according to departmental requirements, and the duplicate given to the index officer after review and signature by the chief investigator. The officer who prepares the report will underline in *red* on the *case folder* copies of the report all names, addresses, vehicles and/or plate numbers, phone numbers, and any other such information that the chief investigator decides is necessary. The case folder copies of the reports are filed chronologically and numbered consecutively, with the *Response Report* as number 1.

The *index officer* then prepares an index card for each name, address, and so on. The name cards will be filed alphabetically by last name. If only a first name or nickname appears, it will be filed according to that single name. Name cards will be cross-referenced to location cards, vehicle cards, and so on where applicable, and vice versa. Each card will list the *case number*, a brief summary of the information, and a reference to the original report by listing the *consecutive number* from the *case folder copy*. Below is an example of such an index card.

JONES, HOWARD A.   HOMICIDE: #73/78

1368 Central Avenue

Apt. 3D   REPORT #37

Name found in wallet of deceased.

A quick glance at the index card indicates that the name Howard Jones was in the deceased's wallet. As other information comes in relative to Jones, it can be added to the card with a reference to the original report. If further information is required, the investigator can refer back to the report by number. The location cards can be filed according to any plan, for example, alphabetically by name of street, then in house-number order for that particular street; numbered streets in numerical order, subdivided by house numbers. Where deemed necessary, subdivisions can be prepared for different towns, communities, boroughs, or counties. The vehicle cards can be filed alphabetically by make, year, and so on. The license plates can be filed alphabetically or numerically.

Before preparing an index card for any red-lined name, location, and so on, the index officer will first consult the existing files to determine whether any such name, and so on, has previously appeared. If a card already exists, it should be brought to the attention of the chief investigator and other investigators concerned. The index officer then adds the new information to the existing card, with the number of the corresponding report from the case folder. This system of calling "hits" to the attention of the investigators minimizes the possibility of important information being lost or delayed in a mass of uncatalogued information.

The index officer, especially one who becomes meticulously aware of each phase of the case, can be a valuable aid in the investigation. This officer should attend all conferences and freely contribute to all discussion of the case. As the case begins to run its course, a point will be reached where there is little new typing and filing. The index officer should, however, remain with the investigation as long as it remains active or until it is cleared. The officer can be used to fill in on teams when a partner may be sick or in court and can be assigned to investigations that can be handled by one person part-time, using the remaining time to attend to the typing and filing and to clipping and filing all newspaper articles about the case. Such clippings may come in handy later when questions arise concerning what information was made public (for example, when evaluating the validity of a confession or an anonymous tip). Sometimes a person or persons, for some unknown reason, will confess to a crime. They will implicate themselves and refer to information that makes them primary suspects. Later, the investigator may learn that the confession was not only false but was based on some newspaper report.

The Investigative Conference. The daily investigative conference is, without a doubt, the most important phase of any well-run investigation. The conference is directed by the chief investigator who calls each investigator or team, in turn, to relate their particular assignment and results. The chief investigator and other teams are in this way made aware of each other's progress in the case and, as a result, can make meaningful suggestions or contributions to the investigation. Everyone is kept abreast of any new developments; and the chief investigator, using these oral summaries, notes suggestions offered by the teams' unassigned "lead sheets," and list of "things to do," will be better able to plan the next day's work for the various detectives.

At these conferences, investigators should be encouraged to speak freely and to make any and all suggestions that they feel merit consideration. The chief investigator should bear in mind that the other investigators, working and living with a case day to day, begin to develop a "feel" for the case that sometimes engenders excellent ideas and fresh approaches. The final decisions, however, rest with the chief investigator. Granting the limitations of space, time, manpower, and money, successful homicide investigation demands that nothing be considered too much trouble and no detail too minor.

18

Role of the Medical Examiner in Homicide Investigations

Dominick J. DiMaio, M.D.

LAW AND POLICIES

The rights, duties, obligations, and procedures of the medical examiner are delineated by law as specified by governmental and administrative regulations.

As in most jurisdictions in the United States, in New York City, the medical examiner has the duty of investigating every case of homicide or suspected homicide. The *New York City Charter and Administrative Code* [Chap. 39, Chief Medical Examiner, 878 Powers and Duties] states: "The Chief Medical Examiner shall have such powers and perform such duties as may be provided by law in respect to the bodies of persons dying from criminal violence."

Upon any such death, the officer in charge of the station house in the police precinct in which such person died must immediately notify the Office of Chief Medical Examiner of the known facts concerning the time, place, manner, and circumstances of the death. Following this notification, it is the duty of the medical examiner or representative to proceed immediately to the scene of the crime and to take complete charge of the dead body, its surroundings, and any weapon or object useful in establishing the cause of death. The representative of the medical examiner's office must investigate fully the essential facts concerning the circumstances of the death—taking names and addresses of all available witnesses. Before leaving the premises, he or she must reduce all facts to writing and file this data in his or her office. In addition, the representative is responsible for taking possession of any portable objects which may be useful in establishing the cause of death.

At the crime scene, the representative is met by the detective of the homicide squad who is in charge of the investigation. The detective will make the representative aware of all known facts relating to the circumstances under which the body was found, such as whether the body or evidence has been disturbed, and which areas to avoid when approaching the body.

Protection of the Crime Scene

The first officer on the scene is responsible for securing the scene from unauthorized intrusion by persons not directly involved in the investigation, including curiosity seekers and souvenir hunters that frequently haunt crime scenes. Upon arrival, it is the duty of the officer in charge and other members of his investigative team to rope off the crime scene and post "Crime Area" signs. Only a trained investigative team can properly safeguard the evidence at the crime scene and thereby prevent contamination, damage, loss, or needless movement of physical evidence. If any piece of evidence is moved or altered by a member of the investigative team, this information should be made known to all other members of the team, such as police personnel, forensic scientists, and the medical examiner investigator. Only members of the forensic or investigative team are permitted to enter or leave the "Crime Area." The order in which they enter the scene and carry out their particular investigation is determined by the officer in charge and/or the representative of the medical examiner's office. Through the efforts of a trained investigative team, there should be little or no unnecessary disturbance to the scene of death.

Forensic Team

The forensic team is concerned with the recognition, identification, collection, preservation, and proper safeguarding of all evidence found at the scene of death. A vital part of any investigation is the complete cooperation among the various investigative teams. It is especially important for the forensic scientists to be in constant communication with the representative of the medical examiner's office and district attorneys.

Photographing the Crime Scene

Members of the crime scene unit are trained in forensic photography. Regardless of who arrives on the scene first, nothing must be moved or disturbed until the entire scene of death is photographed from all angles. Although the admissibility of photographs of any sort rests with the judge, it has become fairly well established that photographs, including color, are admissible provided: (1) what they depict is relevant to the issues in the case; (2) they have been shown to be true and accurate representations; and (3) their probative value is not outweighed by gruesomeness or inflammatory character. According to law, "The predicate for introduction of a photograph requires proof of its accuracy as a correct representation of the subject at a given time, in addition to its material relevance to a disputed issue."

During the photographic procedure, all equipment and persons not part of the original undisturbed crime scene must be removed from the scene of death. No additional objects or persons should be included; otherwise the investigator cannot testify in court that the photographs accurately depict the original undisturbed crime area, including the persons and evidence observed.

The following types of photographs are usually taken:

- Exteriors depicting the crime area and, when necessary the surrounding areas.
- Interiors showing the location and position of the body in relation to its surroundings.
- Close-ups of the exterior or interior scenes as requested by a superior officer or medical examiner investigator.
- Close-ups of the body to show fatal wounds and the lethal weapon when present and adjacent to the body.
- Close-ups of all evidentiary material that is visible after the body is removed, such as trace evidence, weapons, and other evidentiary material.
- Blood stains, to show their color, size, shape, locations, and distribution.
- Views of trace evidence, weapons, and other important evidence prior to removal from the scene.
- When necessary, latent fingerprints or footprints.

In addition, the representative of the medical examiner's office may ask for photographs that may serve as evidence. Also, the crime scene photographer is responsible for photographing arson scenes and vehicular accidents.

Just prior to examination of the undisturbed body and its surroundings, the medical examiner investigator takes his or her own color photographs—as many as are necessary to include all the details of the scene of death, the location, and the position of the body and its relation to the scene and/or its surroundings; blood stains, weapons, arrangement of the furniture and other household articles, signs of a struggle, and any other unusual findings.

Whether or not the photographs are admissible in court as evidence, they are routinely used by the medical examiner who has performed the autopsy to refresh his or her memory prior to testifying in court. Further, should anyone question the accuracy or completeness of the medical report, the photographs will dispute the allegations. Lastly, they prove valuable in teaching medical students, police officers, district attorneys, and others how to investigate violent deaths.

Sketching the Crime Scene

In addition to the notes made during the search of the exterior and interior scenes of the crime area, the medical investigator and police officers frequently make sketches of the crime scene. These sketches are used in the preparation of medical and investigative reports and are useful in refreshing one's memory prior to testifying in court.

Chain of Custody—Chain of Evidence

If physical evidence is to be legally acceptable and admissible in court, the investigator, forensic scientist, and medical examiner or investigator, must document and certify:

1. Where (the exact location), when (date and time), and how the evidence was collected at the scene and how each item was identified (name of deceased, place of occurrence, date and time, case number and signature of person collecting the evidence).

2. They must prove that the integrity of evidence was continuously maintained. By this is meant that the continuity of possession must have been

maintained intact from the time the evidence was collected; that it must be known to have been in proper custody continuously; and that, whenever the evidence was transported or transferred for analysis, it was associated with specific detailed descriptive receipts.

Physical Evidence and Trace Material Collection

When the crime scene photographers have completed photographing the crime scene, the medical examiner or representative and/or the homicide detective(s) locate and collect the various items of evidence to be examined, photographed, and recorded in the sketches and/or notes made at the scene. Such items cannot be removed from the crime scene without permission from the officer in charge, the forensic scientist, or the medical examiner's representative conducting the search at the scene. Prior to its removal from the crime scene, each piece of evidence must also be examined for trace evidence, such as blood, hair, fibers, or other bits of evidence that can only be discovered in a thorough and meticulous examination by an experienced forensic scientist. Dusting for fingerprints should not be undertaken until the search for trace evidence has been completed.

Certain pieces of evidence are processed first, for example, those immediately adjacent to the deceased, those that may interfere with a proper search of the premises, and those that are subjected to weather conditions that could damage, alter, or contaminate the evidence or destroy its evidentiary value.

The forensic team is responsible for the examination and collection of evidence found at the crime scene, including trace evidence and lethal weapons, knives, guns, blunt instruments, bullets, cartridge cases, and the like. These items are delivered to the various specialized crime laboratory divisions for examination and/or analyses.

To prevent contamination and changes induced by weather conditions, blood, seminal, urinary, vomit, or fecal stains and other samples of body fluid should be collected during the initial stage of the search for evidence. All specimens (evidence) should be individually packaged and sealed in dry, clean, labeled containers. Some investigators use 1 percent sodium fluoride as a preservative when they collect liquid blood at the scene. This should not be done if DNA typing is to be performed on the blood. Rather, if liquid blood is to be collected for such purposes, it should be placed in a test tube containing EDTA. All specimens should be refrigerated to preserve them. It is imperative that standards accompany the unknown stains. The unstained surface material—that is, cloth, flooring, tile, etc. found near the unknown stain—should also be submitted to the laboratory (in a separate container), to provide a test comparison with the unknown stain. This comparison will rule out a false positive test; for example, the positive test for blood could be due not to the unknown stain but rather to the material containing the stain.

PHASES OF PRELIMINARY WORK AT THE SCENE

After photography is complete and the crime scene unit has removed all evidence that might be lost, damaged, contaminated, or altered during examination of the body, the medical examiner or representative begins an examination of the body and its surroundings. During the examination, the investigator should avoid touching any objects that might alter or disturb the scene. The first officer on the scene is asked to identify the deceased, to state the time he or she arrived and found the deceased, and to give his or her name, shield number, and precinct. The medical examiner's investigator gathers the following routine information from the officer: name of the person who found the body; whether or not the body was moved from its original position after it was found; whether or not the body has been disturbed in any way. The investigator will incorporate this information with a recording of the undisturbed scene. Recorded notes should also contain time the investigator was notified, the date and time of arrival at the scene, the location, the weather conditions, and the temperature of the room in which the deceased was found, the names of all officers and persons on the scene, and a sketch of the crime scene.

According to the *Administrative Code* (Sec. 878-1.0):

> Any person who without written order from a Medical Examiner shall willfully touch, remove or disturb the body of any such person, or willfully touch, remove or disturb the clothing or any article upon or near such body, shall be guilty of misdemeanor.

However, there are exceptions—as there are to any rule. In one particular case the wife was the first to arrive at the scene. She had loosened the gag over her husband's mouth and had removed the handkerchief impacted in the oropharynx (throat). The gag and handkerchief were submitted to the serological laboratory for analysis, and blood groups determined from the saliva and blood stains found on the gag and handkerchief were similar to those of the deceased. During the trial, the following hypothetical question was addressed to the medical examiner:

> Assuming a gag over the mouth of the deceased was loosened and a handkerchief impacted in his mouth was removed, and assuming further that the blood groups on the gag and handkerchief were similar to those of the deceased and that the cause of death was mechanical asphyxia, Doctor, do you have an opinion as to the cause of death?

The Doctor's answer was that death was caused by asphyxia due to gagging. The wife, believing her husband was alive, removed the gags without malice.

In other cases, if the victim is believed to be still alive, attempts at resuscitation are made, disturbing not only the original position of the body but also the clothing. During resuscitation, unsuspected injuries may be inflicted upon the body, including contusions of the chest or upper abdomen, fractures of the ribs or sternum, lacerations of the liver, spleen, and other organs. If the reasons for such injuries are not made known by the ambulance attendant, police officer, firefighter, or doctor, the medical examiner may attribute them to the perpetrator.

The first police officer at the scene is ordered to appear at the county morgue the next day to identify the deceased and clothing to the medical examiner who will perform the autopsy and to at least one or more medical examiners who are witnessing the autopsy. The presence of one or more medical examiners at the identification procedure and autopsy is necessary so that, if the medical examiner performing the autopsy is unable to testify in court, any of the other medical examiners present are qualified to do so. The police identification is vital in establishing evidence that the autopsied body and the one seen at the homicide scene are one and the same—a required link in the chain of evidence.

In examination of the entire body, the medical investigator carefully notes and records the following data:

■ Position of the body.

- Its exact location in relation to its surroundings.
- Appearance of the clothing.
- Presence and distribution of any injuries and relationship they bear to various portions of the clothing.
- Absence or presence of postmortem lividity—its location, color, and distribution.
- Cooling of the body—its extent and distribution.
- Absence or presence of rigor mortis—its extent and distribution.
- Absence or presence of blood.

Hair, fibers, powder residue, or other trace evidence, which may become dislodged or lost during the body's removal to the morgue, should be individually packaged and sealed in clean, dry, labeled containers. To preserve the presence of hair, fibers, powder residue, or other trace evidence found on the hands, the hands should be placed immediately in ordinary paper bags and sealed, thus preventing a loss of essential and vital trace evidence. Plastic bags should not be used because moving the body to and from areas with different temperatures may cause condensation on the hands inside the bags with subsequent loss of trace evidence.

Probable Time of Death

Next, the medical examiner's investigator formulates an estimate of the probable time of death based on:

- The cooling rate of the body.
- The onset, distribution, and disappearance of rigor mortis.
- The time of appearance, distribution, and fixation of postmortem lividity or putrefactive changes, their color and distribution.
- The various other factors that influence these postmortem changes.

The detectives are then immediately informed of the probable time of death. That this estimate is based on probabilities and therefore open to question and subject to limitation is stressed. The estimated time of death, however, answers questions frequently asked by detectives: Is it possible for the murder to have occurred at such a place, at a known time, and on a given date? Is it possible for the eyewitness to have seen the deceased alive at a set time? Is the eyewitness deliberately lying or merely mistaken? Thus the estimated time of death is useful to detectives in their investigation to confirm, deny, or discredit information supplied by eyewitnesses, to check alibis offered by the perpetrator, or to trace the last movements of the victim.

In one case, the estimated time of death was advantageously used by a detective to refute a perpetrator's statement that the victim was alive when he, the perpetrator, last saw her. The deliberate falsification of the time of death soon became obvious. The perpetrator, a young man, told of having left at 7 A.M. to go to a picnic with his friends. He recounted how he had told his brother that their mother was asleep and was not to be disturbed. When he returned from the picnic that night, he informed the police that he had found his mother dead in bed. The medical examiner visiting the scene found that the mother had met with a violent death. The detectives wanted to know if the postmortem changes were compatible with the death having occurred prior to the young man leaving to go to the picnic. The answer was yes. After extensive questioning, the young man confessed to killing his mother at 7 A.M. and then leaving for the picnic.

In another case, a husband and wife were in a next-door apartment drinking with another female companion when a quarrel broke out between the couple. When they returned to their apartment that night, the husband strangled his wife with a towel after she allegedly attacked him with a knife. He left the apartment. When he returned to the apartment the next day, he called the police, feigning innocence. He confessed only after the medical examiner insisted that she had been strangled and that her death had occurred the night before.

During a trial for criminal abortion in which the medical examiner was asked to estimate the time of death, the question had arisen as to whether or not the young woman had died during the procedure of Lysol-induced abortion. Although no one had spoken to her, the defense contended that she was carried out alive. The medical examiner stated that the microscopic examination of the uterus showed necrosis of the endometrium and superficial myometrium due to the corrosive Lysol and that there was no evidence of inflammatory response. Therefore, in his opinion, the woman died during the procedure.

Postmortem Lividity. Postmortem lividity is normally visible within one-half to two hours after death, and it continues to increase in intensity while the body is cooling and the blood retains some liquidity. It is found on the dependent portions of the body, that is, the side of the body in contact with the surface on which the body rests. It is absent in the portions of the body constricted by clothing or in those that bear the weight of the resting body. Once the blood begins to hemolyze, lividity sets permanently; at this time, pressure on postmortem lividity stains will not blanch those areas of the skin. Hemolysis begins when the body begins to decompose.

Postmortem lividity is of practical value in determining the position of the body at the time of death and can be a useful tool if there is any question about movement of the body after death. If a body is found in a position that is not consistent with the pattern of discoloration, it can be assumed that the body was shifted after death.

In a recent New York case, which yielded evidence that the body's position was changed after death, the sole witness, the decedent's husband, stated that he found his wife face down in bed. Examination at the scene revealed the presence of dorsal lividity and the absence of ventral lividity, which was not compatible with the husband's statement. This inconsistency regarding the position in which the body was originally found necessitated further police inquiry into the circumstances of death. Ultimately the husband confessed to smothering his wife with a pillow.

Rigor Mortis. Due to the variable conditions that may influence the onset and duration of rigor mortis, it is generally impossible to state with any degree of certainty the definitive sequence of onset and duration of rigor mortis. Several generalizations, however, may be used as guidelines.

Onset in voluntary muscles is readily perceived within two to four hours after death. It usually occurs in the eyelids within two hours and, more frequently, in the muscles of the lower jaw within three hours. It will spread over the entire body within six to 12 hours after death. From beginning to end, the average duration is from 24 to 72 hours.

Unless forcibly broken, rigor mortis recedes spontaneously in the same order it appears, never to return. The medical examiner's investigator responding to a homicide, not infrequently, will lift a lower or upper extremity of the body that is in full rigor, thereby lifting the body as a solid mass. However, should the stiffened knee or elbow be forcibly extended or flexed, the forcible stretching of the muscles will destroy the rigor mortis permanently and the ensuing flaccidity will remain permanently. This frequently occurs when the medical examiner's investigator moves or undresses the rigid body to examine stab or bullet wounds, or during the transportation of the body from the scene to the morgue. A morgue attendant can testify to this condition when he lifts bodies onto morgue tables or breaks the rigidity of flexed upper arms prior to postmortem examination.

Thus, at a homicide scene, should the medical examiner investigator find a body in full rigor mortis, except for one flaccid extremity, he should bear in mind that a police officer or ambulance attendant may have forcibly flexed the extremity during examination or resuscitative attempts.

Cadaveric Spasm. In violent sudden deaths associated with extreme emotional tension, the muscles in active contraction just prior to death undergo instantaneous muscle rigidity. This is known as *cadaveric spasm.* Frequently only a small group of muscles is affected, usually those of the hand. However, the phenomenon may involve the musculature of the entire extremity or that of the whole body and, as a consequence, the precise position or attitude of the deceased's extremity or whole body is retained at the time of death.

At the moment of death, any object held in the decedent's hand during the development of cadaveric spasm will remain firmly grasped, and considerable force is required to extract it—far more force than is needed to break down ordinary rigor mortis—a condition tantamount to prove that the object held was in the deceased's hand at the time of death. In all violent deaths, therefore, the importance of examining the hands for weapons, hairs, portions of clothing, or other objects cannot be overemphasized.

When examining a body at the scene, the relationship it bears to its surroundings or to the surface upon which it lies must be given serious consideration. The position of the body and its immediate surroundings determine the amount of flexion and/or extension the joints will assume, including the ultimate attitude of the body, when rigor sets in. Some years ago, a young female was found dead beneath the stairway in a lobby of an apartment house. The dress and undergarments were above the pubic region with exposure of the genitalia. The entire body was cold and rigid with permanently established postmortem lividity over the posterior portions of the body. The right thigh and leg were in 90-degree flexion, the typical position assumed during sexual intercourse. Cadaveric spasm of the right lower extremity occurred during rape and manual strangulation. Had this body been removed from its natural environment and placed on the street, it would have been easy to determine that the body was moved after rigor mortis had set in. The neck showed evidence of manual strangulation, abrasions, and contusions with petechial hemorrhages of the conjunctival sacs, forehead, and cheeks.

Fluids, Bite Marks, and Other Trace Evidence

In rape cases, it is obligatory that apparent seminal stains should be collected at the scene, placed in a proper container, sealed, and properly labeled. At the morgue a wet mount of vaginal fluid from the posterior vaginal region should be examined for motile sperms.

Visible bite marks should be photographed with a fingerprint camera yielding life-size photographs. They should be swabbed with cotton wool saline moistened swabs; these should be individually stored in sealed test tubes and given to the serologist for blood grouping. To preserve the integrity of bite marks, cover them with clean gauze sponges. Impressions of the bite mark should be made by a forensic odontologist, and the police officer and district attorney should correlate the bite marks with the serological findings. This correlation is potentially damaging evidence with which to confront a suspect, particularly inasmuch as the courts have ruled proper the taking of dental impressions from a defendant. Bite mark comparisons can be offered conclusively to prove the identity of an assailant in a criminal case.

At a postmortem examination, vaginal, oral, and anal swabs are taken for serologic examination. Apparent seminal stains of the body or clothing are also submitted for serologic examination. Pubic hair should be combed for foreign hairs and fibers, and matted seminal-containing pubic hairs should be cut and submitted for serological analysis. The nails should be examined for blood, fibers, hairs, and other trace evidence. Fragments of fingernails found at the crime scene should be collected and preserved for future comparison with broken fingernails of the victim or perpetrator. In a rape case, the hair clutched in the victim's hands may be identified as having come from the victim's own head since, in rape cases or other violent assaults, it is not unusual for the victim to pull out her scalp hair. During a struggle the victim may scratch the assailant's or rapist's skin, pull out strands of hair, shred clothing, or rip off buttons. Therefore, this procedure should be carried out in all cases of rape and homicidal assault.

Cooling of the Body

Accurate measurements of body temperature can be made only through the use of a thermometer. Therefore, no less than two readings, two hours apart, are taken by a thermometer placed in the rectum. It is apparent that no single formula can be used to accurately determine the time of death as derived from observations of the temperature of the corpse. The following formula is frequently used to calculate the time interval since death:

$$\frac{\text{Normal temperature (98.6°F)} - \text{rectal temperature}}{1.5°\text{F per hour}} = \text{Approximate hours since death}$$

Examination of Victim's Hands

A careful examination of the victim's hands should be neither omitted nor minimized. Weapons (gun, knife, or blunt instrument) or articles firmly grasped by the victim at the moment of death (strands of hair, torn fragments of the murderer's clothing, and the like) may prove of extreme importance. In fact, such evidence may be the decisive factor in determining the circumstances and manner of death.

Further, the hands may reveal characteristic particles embedded in the skin. In a recent case, a police officer was shot at close range by an unknown bandit. The bullet recovered from the body contained a link from a watchband, which had adhered to the nose of the bullet. Subsequently, it was proved that it was the missing link of the watchband found at the scene. From this evidence, the medical examiner reasoned that one of the hands of the perpetrator would show powder stains and burns. When the perpetrator was apprehended, this reasoning was confirmed. Flameless atomic absorption spectrophotometry is a reliable and sensitive method for detecting firearm discharge residues on the skin or clothing since it detects the presence of lead, barium, and antimony found in primer composition of most United States and European ammunition. This method of analysis is inexpensive and easy to perform.

After the medical examiner or investigator has concluded the preliminary examination of the deceased's hands at the scene, the hands should be placed in paper bags, which are tied off to protect the hands from contamination or loss of vital evidence during transportation to the morgue.

In one case a medical examiner from another state removed minute pieces of red-stained tissue from beneath the victim's right index fingernail; the police and district attorney wanted to know what was found in these nail scrapings. Well-preserved red blood cells, pieces of skin, and some fibers were discovered. The red blood cells were too few in number to determine blood group, but microscopic examination revealed white portions of skin and an immunoprecipitation test proved the skin to be of human origin. Microscopic stains and study for Barr bodies revealed none were to be found. I concluded that the nail scrapings contained white male skin and recent red blood cell loss. Later it turned out that the perpetrator was a white male who had smothered his wife and two children, and that, on the morning of her death, a fresh scratch mark was apparent on the right side of his neck. I testified in court that the nail scrapings removed from the right index fingernail of the victim were consistent with the scratch would sustained by the husband of the victim.

Examination of Wounds

In homicidal shootings, the number and location of the entrance and exit wounds are reported to the homicide detectives as soon as they are determined by the medical examiner or investigator. The detectives frequently seek the following information: (1) The distance from the body at which the gun was fired; (2) the exact location and nature of the entrance and exit wounds; (3) the direction of fire; (4) the type and caliber of any bullet or bullets recovered at the scene; (5) any evidence of powder residue on the hands.

The victim's clothing is examined for perforations corresponding to the entrance and exit wounds. Such perforations are then examined for charring or powder residue which, if filtered out by the clothing, do not appear on the body. Powder residue on the clothing can be detected by infrared photography, soft x-ray studies, and by Flameless Atomic Absorption spectrophotometry. At the scene, the hands are also examined for powder residue, but the tests are conducted at the morgue and adjacent laboratories. When examining the victim's clothing, the lack of corresponding entrance and exit perforations may be the result of the bullet's passing through folded-over clothing. When stretched, the clothing will show multiple bullet holes but, in reality, only one bullet has penetrated. This must be explained to the detectives, thereby preventing an exhaustive search for a bullet or additional bullets that do not exist.

If a gun is found at the scene, the medical examiner or investigator who recovers a bullet from the body confers with the ballistic detective and immediately determines whether or not the caliber of the bullet matches the caliber of the gun. This enables the ballistic detective to return to the laboratory and make comparison studies on the bullet recovered and those fired from the gun found at the scene. The ballistic detective should examine all weapons found at the scene, and the weapons should be handled with great care so as not to damage fingerprints, blood stains, hairs, fibers, or other trace evidence adhering to the gun. The medical examiner or investigator must be told how many bullets were fired, and this number must correspond to the number of bullets found at the scene and those recovered from the body.

Any entrance wound on the body is a determining factor in indicating the distance from the body at which the gun was held when fired. There are various types of entrance wounds.

Contact Wound.   When firmly applied to the skin and fired, the gun causes a lacerated charred contact wound, including flame burns of the skin and hair due to the rapidly expanding explosive gases. Smudges from carbon deposits appear within the subcutaneous tissue, muscle, and bone. On such occasions, the impact of the muzzle leaves a distinct abraded and contused imprint on the skin. Such features are typical of a contact gunshot wound of the skull. However, a contact gunshot wound of the abdomen will not show a lacerated charred skin. In this case, there is a circular area of charred skin since the rapidly expanding explosive gases are freely dispersed within the abdominal (peritoneal) cavity.

Near Contact Wound.   When the gun is fired immediately adjacent to the skin but not in contact with it, the wound is rounded with inverted abraded edges, surrounded by a zone of scorching, a soot deposit but no powder tattoo.

Intermediate Range Wound.   As the distance between the gun and the skin is increased, the flame burns are lost and tattooing is spread in a wide circle about the bullet wound. The tattooing is caused by burning and unburned powder grains embedded in the skin. In intermediate range (close-up) bullet wounds, the flame, smoke, and powder grains may be deposited on the clothing; then the resulting bullet wound resembles a distant shot.

Distant Wound.   In a distant shot, the flame, smoke, and powder grains of the discharge are absent, since the gun is too far from the body for it to produce these effects. When a bullet penetrates the body perpendicular to the skin, it produces a round wound with abraded margins (collar). When the bullet penetrates the skin at an angle, the direction from which the bullet enters the skin is indicated by an eccentric abrasion and undermining of the skin opposite the abrasion. Depending on its location on the body, the bullet wound of exit varies from a stellate to a slit-like or irregular shape with everted edges.

In a graze wound, a bullet striking the skin at a shallow angle produces a superficial elongated abraded bullet wound. In a tangential wound, the bullet penetrates and lacerates the subcutaneous tissue.

Shotgun Wounds.   Shotgun wounds may be classified as follows:

1. *Contact wounds:* Contact shotgun wounds of the head show extensive destruction of the head and face. Contact wounds of the chest may show muzzle imprints of single or double shotguns.

2. *Loose contact wounds:* The wound is rounded with abraded edges, surrounded by a zone of considerable scorching, soot, and powder residue.

3. *Intermediate range (close-up) wounds:* The wound is round with abraded margins, with powder tattooing of the adjacent skin.

4. *Distant shotgun wounds:* There is no searing, soot, or powder tattooing of the skin. At 3 feet the wound is typically round with slight scalloping of the edges. By 4 feet, a round wound with ragged margins and some satellite pellet holes is present. Beyond 6 feet, the diameter of the entrance wound increases; the main bulk of shots begin to spread out and stray pellets enter the body away from the main wound to produce small round wounds with abraded margins.

Evidence of Away-from-the-Scene Death

On occasion, the deceased has been shot elsewhere and then dumped at the scene of discovery. In such cases, examination of the clothing may be of particular value in concluding that the body was shot elsewhere. In one case, a victim was shot in a bar, dragged outside, and placed on his back on the sidewalk between garbage cans. The shoes showed scuff marks and the soles were dry. The back of the victim's clothing was wet against a wet pavement; whereas the exposed clothing in the front was dry. There had been rain, but by the time the deceased had been dragged out of the bar across wet pavement, the rain had stopped. It was reasonable to conclude, therefore, that the victim had been killed elsewhere and his body dragged to the scene.

Not infrequently a detective asks the medical examiner how to determine whether the victim was killed elsewhere. A thorough and meticulous examination of the clothing, a search for drag marks, and the presence or absence of abrasions on exposed parts of the body are often tell-tale signs.

Scuff marks on the clothing, how the clothing is displaced (such as rolled upward toward the head or downward toward the feet), and the situation and distribution of the abrasions on exposed parts of the body all indicate the position and manner in which the body was dragged. If a perpetrator drags the body face upwards by the feet, the posterior chest being dragged will offer resistance and cause the clothing to roll upwards; there will be abrasions and scuff marks on the back of the head, chest, and flanks. If the body is dragged face down by the feet, the abrasions and scuff marks will occur on the face, anterior chest, and abdomen. The perpetrator who drags the body face upwards by placing his or her arms beneath the victims armpits will cause abrasions and scuff marks on the lower back, buttocks, thighs, calves, and heels. If the body is dragged face down by the armpits, the abrasions and scuff marks will occur on the lower abdomen, external genitalia, thighs, knees, legs, and toes.

Should the body be dragged over an extremely rough surface—such as pavement or street—the rolled clothing and abrasions frequently contain embedded particles of gravel, dirt, grease, oil spillage, and other foreign debris. Samples of such material should be collected, properly identified, and labeled for future identification and comparison with control samples collected from the scene of discovery. The direction of dragging can be detected by the broad ruffling of the skin at the beginning of the abrasions and by the heaped-up tags of skin at the distal end.

Some years ago, a young woman was found dead in the lobby of an apartment house. The tenants who viewed the body emphatically stated she was not a resident there. Subsequently, the medical examiner who examined the body at the scene found scuff marks on the stockings and shoe on the right foot; there were abrasions on both knees. Investigating various approaches to the apartment house, detectives found the missing left shoe at the edge of the curb facing the apartment house entrance. The medical examiner concluded that the body had been transported by car to the apartment house. While the body was being moved from the car, one shoe fell off and therefore was free from scuff marks. The perpetrator then dragged the body face down by the armpits across the pavement into the apartment house lobby and dumped her.

Weapons and Wounds as Evidence

As already stated, cadaveric spasm of the hands sometimes has been the decisive factor in furnishing evidence of the manner and circumstances of death. A weapon remaining firmly clenched in the hand due to the rapid onset of rigor mortis has more than once supplied the necessary objective evidence to confirm, refute, or discredit an eyewitness's statement of the circumstances of death or a perpetrator's confession. Such a spasm cannot be reproduced by the assailant. In an interesting case, the perpetrator confessed that he shot the victim in self-defense. He stated that while he was seated on an armchair adjacent to a sofa, the deceased came at him with a razor and that he kept shooting until the victim collapsed and died when almost on top of him. Examination of the deceased at the scene of death confirmed his confession. The deceased was found, partially slumped over the sofa, a razor tightly clenched in his right hand, facing the armchair on which the perpetrator was seated. In this illustrative case, the uncovered evidence substantiated the confession of the perpetrator.

In a recent case, the retained weapon in the victim's clenched hand due to cadaveric spasm was the undoing of a perpetrator. A middle-aged man walked into a local precinct and confessed to shooting his girlfriend's son following an argument. He stated that the young boy had ordered him out of his mother's house at gunpoint and that he took the gun away from the boy and shot him in self-defense. At the scene of death, the victim was found on his back with his right hand hidden from view beneath the body. This hidden, clenched hand held a knife. The examination of the body at the scene refuted the perpetrator's story and his alibi. In fact, he destroyed his own defense—self-defense.

The recording of knife wounds must include their number, location, size, shape and appearance, direction, and whether they are incised or penetrating stab wounds. For the purpose of comparison to knife wounds found on the body, clothing should be examined for perforations. In addition, the medical examiner or investigator must record the presence or absence of a weapon adjacent to the body; the distribution of blood stains on the clothing and relationship of blood splattering to the body and its surroundings; and defense wounds of the extremities. Fatal knife wounds may occur in hidden places on the body; and when there is little bleeding, such wounds may at first escape notice and are discovered only at autopsy.

Not infrequently, the medical examiner is asked whether or not the knife found at the scene was capable of inflicting the knife wounds found on the body. Any knife whose blade width is the same size or is smaller than the largest wound length is capable of causing the wound or wounds; any knife whose blade width is larger cannot. It is important for the detective to recognize the appearance and characteristic of an *incised wound*, which is a wound produced by any weapon or instrument with a sharp edge that has been pressed and drawn across the surface of the skin, the superficial length being greater than its depth. By contrast a *stab wound* penetrates a body cavity, thereby producing a wound that is greater in depth than in external length.

The knife, blood-stained clothing, and premises must be serologically tested to determine (1) whether or not the stains are blood stains; (2) whether or not they are human blood stains; and (3), when possible, the identity of blood groups (A, B, AB, or O), and other various enzymes and proteins that may be detected in human blood. The victim's blood taken at the autopsy will be used for comparison. With the recent introduction of DNA typing, it is now possible—given that a sufficient amount of well-preserved blood is obtained from a weapon, scene, or garment—to conclusively link it to its source, victim, or assailant.

In assaults with blunt weapons, pattern wounds, characteristic of the weapon used, may be seen on the skin surface at the point of impact. The medical examiner should inform the detectives of the probable nature of the weapon, directing a search for such a weapon at the scene. On the other hand, the homicide detectives may find a blunt weapon at the scene and present it to the medical examiner with the possibility of its having been used to inflict the wound(s) on the body. In one case, a woman with compound fractures of the facial bones was found dead in bed. The forehead showed an unusual "H-shaped" lacerated wound. On investigation, the blood stained base of a lamp was found beneath the bed. The outlines of its construction were the same as those appearing in the peculiar shape of the inflicted wound. This was demonstrated at the autopsy table.

In another case, the victim was beaten to death with a blunt instrument which left a grease-stained pattern wound on the right side of the face. It was composed of parallel abraded and contused wounds, which subsequently were found to correspond to the tread pattern on a car jack. On close examination, hair fragments were found sticking to the car jack; and, on microscopic examination, these fragments displayed physical characteristics similar to those of the decedent's hair. Further, the blood stain samples matched the blood group of the deceased. Had it been necessary, the grease stains on the victim's face and those on the car jack could have been compared by chemical analysis.

All blunt instruments or weapons should be carefully examined for blood stains, hair or fibers, foreign particles of clothing, and other trace evidence, and then compared to those of the deceased. If not used immediately, they should be preserved in properly sealed containers and marked with identification for future comparison.

Wounds Lacking External Evidence

A certain number of homicides lack external evidence of violence. For example, blunt trauma to the head, chest, and abdomen may fail to show external signs of trauma. However, a careful study of the undisturbed body at the scene and a careful investigation of the circumstances surrounding the death will arouse suspicion that the death may be a homicide. The autopsy usually confirms such a suspicion. This is especially true of asphyxial deaths, which may readily escape suspicion and detection if the scenes are not visited.

In smothering, examination at the scene and subsequent autopsy may only reveal evidence of asphyxiation. The suspicion of homicide arises from the investigation of the dead body at the scene and the circumstances surrounding the death, as illustrated by the following case. Neighbors recalled a quarrel between a husband and wife during the night. The next morning, the husband walked out with his child. Later he returned and allegedly found his wife dead in bed, face up. The medical examiner at the scene, however, found that postmortem lividity was located over the front of the body with asphyxial hemorrhages of the eyes, forehead, and cheeks, thereby definitely establishing that the body had been moved after death. When the husband was confronted with the medical evidence, he finally confessed to smothering his wife by pressing her face down into the pillow.

In cases of manual strangulation, the grouped abrasions and contusions of the neck produced by the fingers or nails of the assailant are not always visible at the initial examination. In fact, they may be noticed only hours later at the autopsy table, along with evidence of injury to the larynx (voice box). In mugging, when the assailant approaches the victim from behind using the forearm to compress the victim's neck, there are frequently no visible external marks of violence about the neck.

In strangulation by ligature, if a soft material is used and then loosened after death, the mark(s) of violence about the neck may be absent both at the scene and at the postmortem examination. When the assailant does not come prepared or equipped for the crime, any article of clothing or household article that is close by and readily available at the moment will be used. The ligature may be looped around the neck and knotted, or twisted in tourniquet fashion. The ligature mark is usually horizontal characterized by a groove that encircles the neck at the level of the thyroid cartilage. The ligature groove is most distinct when a firm, rough, and coarse ligature is used. On occasion, a coarse ligature will leave a distinct imprint of its texture on the skin. Due to the struggle that ensues, it is usually abraded and contused with scattered hemorrhages. The groove is most apparent when the body is cold.

The ligature should be photographed in situ. It must not be tampered with at the scene nor disturbed during transportation to the morgue. The ligature may be described at the scene provided it is not disturbed. At the morgue the ligature is rephotographed and removed without soiling or disturbing the knot(s). During its removal, it must be cut opposite the knot(s) and the cut ends secured by adhesive tape which contains an identifying label: name of the deceased, place of death, date and time of death, case number, autopsy number, name of medical examiner, and date autopsy was performed. After removal, the ligature should be examined for blood stains, foreign hairs, and fibers; in the case of clothing used as a ligature, laundry markings, identifying labels, and the like should be noted and recorded.

Sometimes the ligature is removed by the assailant who is attempting to conceal the manner of death. If the ligature has been removed by the police or relatives while attempting to revive the victim, the medical examiner or investigator should compare the ligature with the ligature mark on the body.

The ligature is usually retained in the evidence unit of the medical examiner's office. However, it may be released to the investigating homicide officer after receiving a properly executed receipt. If it is foreign to the household articles or clothing, the homicide detective may study the ligature and knot(s) for comparison with previous ligature strangulation cases or possibly trace the ligature to its owner.

In gaggings or chokings, great emphasis must be placed on the circumstances and examination of the scene, particularly if the gag has been removed and signs of asphyxia are present. For example, an elderly lady was found fully dressed face down in bed with her false teeth on the pillow adjacent to her mouth. Her hands were crossed and tied behind her back; the lower extremities were tied as well. There were no external signs of violence but the apartment had been ransacked. The body was cold and rigid with postmortem lividity anteriorly and green-stained lower abdomen. The detectives were informed that the victim had been dead approximately two to three days and most probably died of asphyxia, manner undetermined. The body had been found at 4:45 P.M., on November 18. Two drug addicts were apprehended and confessed that on

November 16, about 10:00 A.M.; they had bound and gagged the deceased, stuffing a towel in her mouth. They returned the same day between 5 and 6 P.M. and removed the gag. In such a case the gag or article suspected of being the gag should be examined for blood stains, blood groups, lipstick stains, and other stains or foreign items.

In another case, a 15-year-old girl was found dead on the sidewalk. An overdose of narcotics was suspected. Postmortem examination revealed asphyxia due to impaction of a handkerchief within the laryngo-pharynx (throat).

On occasion, homicide detectives are asked to investigate the death of a neglected, starved, or abandoned child. The physical findings are usually obvious. A postmortem examination will reveal the extent of neglect or starvation suffered by the young child and will rule out any natural disease masquerading as neglect. In the case of a "battered baby" death, the medical examiner must report to the detective the repeated injuries inflicted on the child—bruises, abrasions, and burns of all sizes, shapes, and color indicating repeated battering. In virtually all cases, the initial story as to how the injuries occurred will be a lie as parents, relatives, guardians, and other caretakers will attempt to deceive the investigating doctor, nurse, health officer, or social worker. The postmortem examination will reveal old and recent skull and brain injuries, rib fractures, long bone injuries, injuries to the internal organs, and hemorrhages deep within the soft tissues of the body.

AT-THE-SCENE FOLLOW-UP

After the medical examiner or investigator has completed the preliminary examination, the police sergeant, in the presence of witnesses, searches the clothing of the deceased, removing all personal belongings. These personal belongings—social security card, driver's license, credit cards, and the like—usually disclose the name and address of the deceased. A record is made of all valuables and personal belongings, which are then delivered to police headquarters and placed in the custody of the property clerk.

Following these procedures, the medical examiner or investigator arranges for transportation of the body from the scene to the morgue. The individual transporting the body should be cautioned and instructed to exercise care in transporting the body to avoid disturbing or altering the appearance of the body or the clothing. In one case, in order to preserve the facial features of a partially decomposed body, the mortuary caretaker placed a plastic bag over the victim's head. This was not mentioned to the medical examiner, nor was it recorded. As a result, the body was in process of being signed out as asphyxia due to smothering when the true facts were discovered. It is recommended that the body be transported wrapped in a clean white sheet. The purpose is that, if any trace evidence on the body falls off during transport, it will be on the sheet. In addition, the sheet prevents the body from picking up foreign material from the transporting vehicle, which may subsequently be found on the body and mistakenly thought to be trace evidence. Ligatures about the neck, hands, or feet should never be disturbed or cut in order to make transportation of the body easier.

The medical examiner or investigator must write a complete report of the investigation and findings. He or she takes possession of any weapon(s), objects, strands of hair, clothing fibers, blood stains, medicines, chemicals, drugs, and other evidence that may have a bearing on the case or that may furnish a clue in establishing the cause of death. Every item of evidence must be properly marked with name of deceased, place of death, date, circumstances of death, and type of examination requested (that is, serological or toxicological).

THE AUTOPSY

The scene investigative report must be given to the forensic pathologist prior to the performance of the autopsy. The first police officer on the scene should identify the deceased for the medical examiners present at the autopsy. Thereafter, the officer signs a sworn affidavit (Police Identification of Body) stating his or her name, shield number, precinct, the name of the deceased, the circumstances under which the body was found, the day and time of identification, and the medical examiners present. In some cases, the identity of the decedent is definitely established by the relatives or friends who view the body at the morgue in the presence of the same medical examiners. But the prevailing practice is showing a photograph of the deceased for the purpose of identification by the relatives or friends. The witnesses must also sign a sworn affidavit known as Person Identification of Body, stating the name, age, address, and relationship to the deceased. Additional information required is sex, race, marital status, occupation, and the circumstances surrounding the decedent's death, if known.

Following identification, the face of the deceased is photographed by a photographer from the police department as a permanent record of police identification. In cases of alleged police brutality or where an individual is shot by an officer of the law, the victim is completely photographed—full front, back, and sides—and closeup photographs are taken of all bullet wounds, contusions, abrasions, lacerations, and so on. (This procedure was initiated by the writer after a relative of a deceased alleged police brutality.) The photographs constitute a permanent record of the condition of the body prior to postmortem examination and may be viewed by any interested party. In addition, a qualified forensic pathologist representing the family is permitted to witness the autopsy.

In New York City, representatives of the Bureau of Identification of the police department routinely fingerprint every person who dies as a result of violence or is unknown. In cases of unknown persons, the fingerprints are compared with those on file with the City of New York, New York State, and Federal Bureau of Investigation. Fingerprints are valuable not only in establishing the identity of the deceased but are of even greater value for comparison with fingerprints found at the scene of the crime. Not infrequently, latent fingerprints have proved helpful in identifying persons present at the scene, as well as the presence of the perpetrator. In selected cases, the police department uses palm prints to identify the perpetrator.

Examination of Body and Wounds

A thorough autopsy should be performed either by an authorized, specially trained pathologist or by a forensic pathologist acting in an official capacity as medical examiner. Photographs of the body are taken fully clothed and naked. This is followed by x-rays of the body. The body is accurately weighed and its height measured, noting the skeletal, muscular, and nutritional state, sex, color, and age. The external surfaces of the body are then examined very carefully.

The size, shape, appearance, probable duration, and exact location of external wounds from two fixed anatomical sites on the body should be accurately recorded. The wounds are routinely photographed. Diagrams of the location and, when appropriate, appearance of the wounds should be made.

The direction, depth, and length of every penetrating stab wound of organs and tissues should be thoroughly described. On occasion, a broken-off fragment of a knife or ice pick is found deeply embedded in the body. It should be marked for identification and preserved for comparison with the original weapon.

The clothing involved in homicides should be carefully described, making note of the number and distribution of defects corresponding to wounds and blood stains. Clothing should be marked for identification, dried if necessary, sealed in a paper bag, and given to the first police officer whose duty it is to sign a mortuary clothing book. If the victim dies in a hospital, the first police officer takes the clothing removed before death to the medical examiner for examination. It is imperative that, during removal of the clothing from the body, the medical examiner avoid losing any trace evidence present on the clothing.

The appearance of bullet wounds of entrance has been previously described. If requested or if necessary for court testimony, the appearance of intermediate range (close-up) bullet wounds on the body may be compared with test fire patterns performed by the ballistic squad; through such a method, the distance of the gun from the body when fired may be determined.

The direction of the bullet as it penetrates the various body organs and tissues must be described in detail. All bullets or bullet fragments, shotgun pellets, slugs, and wads recovered from the body should be described, marked for identification, and placed in properly labeled envelopes. The envelopes should be labeled with the name of deceased, source of recovery, date of autopsy, medical examiner's name, and case number. The ballistic detective receiving the missiles will give the medical examiner a receipt, which is filed with the autopsy report. This chain of continuity must not be broken, for the medical examiner must certify to it in criminal proceedings.

When recovering bullets from the body, the distinct rifle markings must not be defaced since they are used for comparison with test bullets fired from the assailant's pistol. On occasion, two types of bullets or bullets of different caliber are recovered from the body; this indicates that more than one gun was used to commit the crime.

Not infrequently, hospital reports fail to mention a patient's wounds or accurately describe them. Further, such reports fail to indicate the removal of bullets from the body or the obliteration of wounds by surgical procedures. In addition, details of surgical procedures with consequent complications are often not included.

Investigating Nonvisible Causes of Death

As stated, nonpenetrating blunt injuries to the head and other parts of the body may leave no visible external signs of injury. During a recent robbery, a middle-aged man was assaulted with a stick. The deceased was wearing a hat, and examination of his head failed to reveal external signs of injury. The dorsal aspect of both hands, however, showed contused defense wounds. At autopsy the skull showed multiple comminuted skull fractures with corresponding brain injuries.

A kick or severe blow to the abdomen may cause contusion or laceration of a solid organ, or it may cause contusion of a hollow organ with delayed or immediate rupture, despite the absence of an outward indication of violence to the abdomen.

Recently, resuscitative attempts were made on the body of an alcoholic woman who had a large friable fatty liver. The liver sustained several lacerations with intraperitoneal hemorrhage. Because the hospital neglected to accurately record its attempt at resuscitation, the lacerations were thought to be of traumatic origin. This impression was corrected when the true facts were made known.

At times, a person thrown from a car or falling from a height will show no external signs of injury, but on autopsy the examiner will find multiple fractures and lacerations of the viscera.

In certain violent deaths, the medical examiner may suspect a homicide, yet the autopsy findings are consistent with suicidal or accidental death as well. A ruling of homicide may be made only by careful investigation of the circumstances, a thorough autopsy, and complete toxicological examination. This is especially true in poisonings, bodies recovered from fires, falls from heights, and vehicular deaths.

In New York, since it is not unusual to dispose of a homicide in nearby city waters, all drowning cases are carefully examined for fatal wounds due to stabbing or shooting. Some injuries to the body are caused by the initial jump from a height into the water or by passing motorboats or ships. In cases of death by submersion, the police investigation is sometimes more helpful than the autopsy. For example, in 1958:

> An 11-year-old boy, because of petty grudges, twice lured younger children, a girl of 4 and a boy of 7, onto West Side piers and then pushed them to their deaths in the Hudson River. When he confessed, he explained his grudges. The girl had told tales about him to his mother, and the boy had failed to pay him a promised dime.

The importance of a good investigation in medical examiner cases is shown by the following case: In 1958, six bodies were brought into the Bellevue morgue for examination and possible autopsy. Four came from different hospitals, and two directly from home. The deaths were initially felt to be the result of natural disease. Suspicion was not aroused until the brother of a deceased informed the medical examiner that all six had been present at the same party. In collectively reviewing the reports of the six decedents, the symptoms were diagnostic of methyl alcohol poisoning. The suspicion of poisoning was confirmed by toxicological examinations. This led to an investigation that revealed 27 deaths from methyl alcohol poisoning.

Some years ago, a young man's death was attributed to multiple injuries sustained when he presumably jumped or fell from an apartment window. Later, a man in jail confessed he had been hired to kill the victim, but he was jailed for robbery before he could commit the crime. He mentioned the perpetrator's name, and it was the same man who had identified the deceased as his brother. This individual was now attempting to collect on an accidental insurance policy. Falls from heights may be left undetermined unless there is a witness to the fall or supporting information as to how it actually occurred.

In a rather unusual case, the death of a $1\frac{1}{2}$-year-old mongoloid child was attributed to a fall from an apartment window. The medical examiner, however, was able to scientifically refute the story of accidental fall. The investigation included the height of the window, the height of the boy with his arms outstretched, and a possible toy used to stand on. It turned out that the window's size would have necessitated great effort on the part of the child to squeeze through it. On further police investigation, the father was found to be an alcoholic with many illegitimate children, two of whom he had raped. He had been jailed and released. It was difficult to prove that he had thrown his son out the window. He was jailed, however, for raping another of his illegitimate daughters.

Bodies recovered from fires should always be autopsied, not only to determine the actual cause of death, but also to detect possible homicides committed to fire for the purpose of destroying criminal evidence. The absence of carboxyhemoglobin does not rule out asphyxia due to conflagration. When inhaled, the hot gaseous fumes may cause laryngeal burns and edema (swelling) with asphyxia without a high intake of carbon monoxide. This is especially true in the case of flash fires due to gasoline.

In hit-and-run vehicular homicides, clothing should be carefully examined for tire marks, paint, embedded fragments of glass, automobile parts, etc. This clothing and other items must be marked for identification and given to the first police officer on the scene. When the body is autopsied, the surfaces of the body should be fully examined for tire marks, paint stains, or distinct pattern contusions indicative of an imprint of some portion of the car. Samples of blood and scalp hair should be gathered for blood grouping and future comparison. Any blood, hair, paint, glass, and fragments of clothing found on parts of the vehicle should be compared with the same evidence removed from the victim's body and clothes.

In some homicides, the type of food found in the stomach may be helpful in establishing the composition of the last meal. Although the digestive stage of the meal cannot be used to accurately determine the time of death, in some cases it may eliminate or suggest a suspect. In one case, the Chinese meal found in the victim's stomach led to the identification of the victim and apprehension of the perpetrator.

In cases where there is definite suspicion of poisoning, portions of various organs are submitted for toxicological examination. The toxicologist should be made aware of the circumstances of death, autopsy findings, the diagnosis, and possible poisoning. In all homicidal deaths, examination should be made for the presence or absence of ethyl alcohol, acid, neutral and alkaline drugs, as well as narcotics. The organs should be sealed in clean containers and properly marked for identification with the name of the deceased, the place of death, the date of the autopsy, the organs contained therein, the medical examiner's name, and the case number.

In all homicides, blood is submitted for blood grouping and other specialized analysis. In all suspected homosexual homicides, oral and rectal smears should be taken for detection of sperm, P30, and acid phosphatase analysis.

CONCLUSION

Homicide investigation is an important function of city government. It begins with the discovery of a homicide and the official arrival of the medical examiner or investigator at the scene. The medical examiner or investigator conducts a preliminary examination, which is followed by a thorough autopsy to determine the cause and manner of death. Specimens are submitted for toxicological and serological examinations.

Finally, the results of the investigation, autopsy findings, and toxicological and serological reports are incorporated into a certified report. A copy of this report is then submitted to the Office of the District Attorney. At that point, the homicide investigation of the Office of Chief Medical Examiner is completed.

19

Taking Notes During the Investigation

Robert C. Levie

Lou E. Ballard

The purpose of the investigation is to obtain all the facts in the case. The purpose of the written report is to communicate to other authorities the facts obtained during the investigation. Therefore, the first step in preparation for writing the report is conducting a thorough and proper investigation, including taking complete, accurate notes of all facts and details that can be obtained during the investigation. The following discussion of note-taking is intended particularly for the officer assigned to a car, a post, or a beat—the officer who normally takes a call, who is the first officer on the scene, and who conducts the initial or primary investigation. However, the basic principles and form of note taking are the same for all law enforcement officers.

Taking notes means writing down all information at the time the officer obtains the information, while he is conducting the investigation. Generally, in a police investigation, *essential information* includes the following:

1. A notation of the time the officer received the call or complaint and the means by which it was made.
2. Identification of the investigating officer or officers.

SOURCE: From Robert C. Levie and Lou E. Ballard, *Writing Effective Reports on Police Investigations*, Chap. 3, pp. 27–52. Copyright ©1978 by Holbrook Press, Boston. Reprinted with permission of Allyn and Bacon, Inc.

3. Exact identification of the offense, the location, the time, the methods.

4. Exact identification and description of each item of evidence which the officer observes or obtains.

5. A notation of the marking and disposition of each item of evidence, of other officials notified, of the taking of photographs, of the making of drawings, of the taking of measurements.

6. All facts, with details, which the officer himself obtains.

7. All statements, with details, made by witnesses or other persons who provide information about the offense.

8. Complete identifying information on each person who makes statements or gives information.

9. Complete identification and description of the offender or offenders.

10. Details of the follow-up on each separate lead and of the search for leads.

11. Details of the arrest if an arrest is made.

12. Details of the route by which the offender entered and left.

13. Present location of the offender, if known.

14. Further action indicated.

The facts and details recorded in the notes become the content of the report which the officer writes when he has concluded the investigation, or when he has concluded his particular assignment in the investigation. Under *Details* in the report, the officer writes the relevant facts, in detail, in complete sentences and paragraphs. However, when he is taking notes, writing in complete sentences and paragraphs is impractical because it requires additional time, and it is not necessary. Complete expression in sentences and paragraphs is necessary in the account of the *Details* in the report because the officer must communicate his findings, clearly and completely, to those who review his report. Expression in words and phrases is sufficient in the notes because the officer needs only to record the findings for information and reference. However, the officer must make certain that the information he records in notes will be complete and clear when he reads the notes later or when any other officer reviews them or refers to them.

For example, in taking notes an officer writes the following:

VICTIM: John Doe, WM, age 45
1002 Riverside Drive

Statements
1. Locked front and back doors at about 12:30 P.M., March 15, 1976.[1]
2. Met friend Richard Roe, WM, age 35, 600 Auburn Ave., for lunch at Sweet Shoppe, 120 Main, about 12:45.

Under *Details* in the report, the officer writes this same information in complete sentences in a paragraph:

The Victim, JOHN DOE, WM, age 45, residing at 1002 Riverside Drive, stated that he locked both the front door and the back door of his residence at about 12:30 P.M., March 15, 1976. At about 12:45 he met a friend, RICHARD ROE,

WM, age 35, residing at 600 Auburn Avenue, for lunch at the Sweet Shoppe, located at 120 Main Street.

For the purpose of taking notes, the officer routinely keeps a *Field Notebook* in which he records the information he obtains during investigation. In some cases he may record part of the information on a Field Report Form, with designated spaces for names, addresses, date, time, and so forth. Also, some departments provide a Field Worksheet, with headings for basic information and blank space for additional notes. Whether the officer uses a Field Report Form, a Worksheet, a Notebook, or a combination of these, he must record, in detail, all descriptions, remarks, statements, interviews, observations, official police action, and results obtained through that action. The following discussion focuses on taking notes in the Field Notebook because the notebook is the basic item of equipment for taking notes. The same principles and form for note-taking apply in using a Field Report Form or a Worksheet.

THE FIELD NOTEBOOK

The officer should keep his notebook with him at all times when he is on duty because he must make notes on each call to which he responds. Even when a call produces no results and no case, he must note the complaint or observation, the time he received the call or was assigned to investigate the complaint, the means by which he received the call, and the name of the person who made the complaint or observation. He must also note his response (the time of arrival on the scene and actions taken on the scene), and the fact that no offense was committed. When the officer responds to a call that results in a case, he must record complete notes on the investigation. On each separate case, he begins taking notes with the complaint or observation, his assignment to the case, and his arrival on the scene. He continues taking notes on each step in the investigation until the investigation is terminated, or until his particular part in the investigation is concluded.

PURPOSES

During each particular investigation, the officer must record all the facts and details that he will need in order to write a complete, accurate report: that is, all facts and details that are relevant to the case he is investigating. Therefore, *from the beginning of the investigation* (his arrival on the scene), *the officer should keep in mind the type of case he is investigating* so that he will be certain to record all facts relevant to the particular case. For example, the particulars that he needs to obtain and record on a murder case and those that he needs to obtain and record on a burglary case differ somewhat. According to the type of case, the particular details are different in relation to the offense itself, the type of evidence, the specific evidence, the particular details in statements of persons interviewed, and so forth. It is necessary for the officer to make notes on the particular details relevant to each particular case because *his notes are essential* to him for several purposes.

1. A good set of notes on an investigation contains the complete, accurate details that the officer will need to write his report later.

2. No one can be expected to recall from memory all details obtained during an

investigation. Furthermore, while the officer is conducting the investigation, he needs to concentrate on obtaining all relevant information rather than on trying to memorize details. For these reasons, taking written notes is a practical way both to record all relevant facts and to retain them for further use.

3. Making accurate notes enables the officer to check his information as he is conducting the investigation to make certain that he records exact descriptions of evidence, the figures and measurements, exact details of witnesses' statements, exact details of his own activities in conducting the investigation.

4. Notes taken on each step in the investigation can be a helpful reference in conducting later steps.

5. If the officer is called as a witness in court, an accurate and complete set of notes taken as he conducted the investigation constitutes sound testimony. The prosecutor or the defense attorney may ask to see the notes. If the officer has the original notes and if the notes are accurate, complete, and objective, the attorneys have less reason to question the officer than if he testifies from memory. A good set of original notes carries validity and credibility. Such notes are the best evidence the police officer can give.

6. Accurate and complete notes on each investigation are an official record of the officer's activities: a record that shows exactly what actions the officer took in conducting each investigation, a record that accounts for his performance as an investigating officer.

PROPER FORM

The officer's notes can best serve these purposes if he keeps the notes in a proper form and in a systematic way.

1. He should identify the notebook as his by writing his name and identification in front of the notebook, and either his name or his initials on each page. Pages removed from the notebook (as for filing) will thus be identified with the officer's name or initials.

2. He should make his notes in either blue or black ink because notes made with a pencil will smear and fade. A ballpoint pen is convenient and practical.

3. He should make certain that all notes are legible and that names, addresses, and places are spelled correctly. If the writing or printing is illegible, the officer will be unable to use the information for his report, for reference, or for filing. Similarly, other officials who may refer to the notes will be unable to make use of the information. If names, addresses, or places are misspelled in the notes, they are likely to be misspelled in the report and in any other records to which they may be transferred from the report.

4. He should use only these standard abbreviations that all officers readily understand. For example, he may use *WM*, for *White Male*, or *Feb.* for *February*; *Sgt.* for *Sergeant*, or *Tech.* for *Technician*, followed by the names; *St.* for *Street* in an address. Abbreviations other than such standard ones can result in confusion or even misinterpretation.

5. He should make clear and concise notes. For clarity the information should be correct, exact, detailed, and complete. Details should be recorded under headings for easy reference later (VICTIM, with all information relating to

the victim recorded under this heading). The names of persons should be printed in capital letters so that the names will stand out in the notes (for example, Victim DOE). For conciseness the notes should be written in words and phrases, not in complete sentences and paragraphs.

6. He should make certain that he records all essential information accurately and clearly in the notes. The officer's written report is likely to reflect any inaccuracy, discrepancy, or ambiguity in the notes. Furthermore, inaccurate or ambiguous, or incomplete notes are not trustworthy for reference.

7. He should write the date and his initials beside any change or insertion. For a variety of reasons, the officer may need to add information or to make changes in the notes as the investigation proceeds. For example, if a witness makes additional statements at a later time, these statements should be inserted in the notes on that witness's statements, with the date and time the additional statements were made, along with the officer's initials.

8. He should keep together the pages containing the notes on each separate case. The officer may investigate more than one case during any given shift; he may begin a new investigation before he has concluded one or more investigations already in progress; or he may continue an investigation over a period of days. In taking notes on each separate investigation, he should begin on a new page in his notebook. He should leave a sufficient number of blank pages to complete his notes on any investigation already in progress. Following this procedure in note taking will aid the officer later in writing his report. When he analyzes his findings in preparation for writing his report, he can readily review all notes on the particular case. He can be certain that he does not confuse information obtained on two separate cases. Following this procedure is also useful in filing the notes because all the notes on each separate case will be together and in order, making it easy to use the notes as a reference. Further, it will help the officer when he appears in court because organized notes will help him give acceptable testimony.

These principles of *form* for keeping the notebook are the ideal, which the officer should do his best to realize in keeping his own notebook. *When he is not rushed* in an investigation, he should take the time to make notes in proper form as he obtains the information is. *In a crisis*, when confusion prevails and he is rushed, he must adapt his note-taking to the situation. For example, when the officer arrives on the scene of an armed robbery to find the perpetrator still on the scene with a gun pointed at a half a dozen frightened people, he must deal with the situation first. When he reaches the point of note taking, he will be required to work against such odds as frightened witnesses, several people talking at once, and no reasonable degree of privacy for interviews. In such a situation the officer must rely on his own resources of training, experience, common sense, and sound judgment. He must take the notes primarily for accuracy and completeness of information; he will not have time to think about form. He must try to make the notes sufficiently complete and clear that he himself can read and understand them. Then, as soon as possible, while the information is still fresh in his mind, he should rewrite the notes in proper form.

THE CHECKLIST

The *requirements* for the officer's notebook are *accuracy, completeness, conciseness,* and *clarity*. Accuracy and clarity include writing or printing legibly and spelling all names, addresses, and places correctly. All four requirements depend on conducting a thorough, an accurate, an objective investigation. To make certain that his notes meet all these requirements, the officer should keep in his notebook a *Checklist* of kinds of information that he needs to be certain to obtain and to record during an investigation. This information includes all facts and details necessary to answer the questions WHO? WHAT? WHEN? WHERE? HOW? and sometimes WHY? in relation to the offense and to the investigation. This information will make up the content of the written report and will serve as a source of reference.

For example, to answer the question WHO? in relation to the victim, the officer must record full details, with all identifying information: name, sex, race, age, occupation, address and telephone number (both residence and business), and any other particular identifying information. The officer must record the same kind of information on the perpetrator and any accessory, as well as on each witness or anyone else who makes any statement about the offense or about the persons involved in the offense. The officer must also record the information necessary to answer the question WHO? in relation to all officers who participate in the investigation; for example, who responded to the call, who conducted the investigation, who preserved the scene, who marked each item of evidence, who apprehended the perpetrator, who took custody of the perpetrator, who took custody of the evidence.

In a similar manner, the officer must record all facts and details necessary to answer the other five basic questions:

WHAT? in relation to all details of what happened: what offense was reported; what offense was committed; what police action was taken; what statements were made by the victim, by the witnesses, by the perpetrator; what agencies were notified; what further action is indicated.

WHEN? in relation to the date and time that each action or event occurred: when the offense was discovered, when the offense was committed; when the police arrived, when the witnesses and the victim were contacted, when they were interviewed; when the victim was last seen; when an arrest was made; when the perpetrator was charged.

WHERE? in relation to the exact location of each action and event in the committing of the offense and in the police investigation: where the victim was and where he lives; where the offense was committed and where it was discovered; where the perpetrator was seen and where he was apprehended; where tools and weapons were obtained and where they were discovered; where the witnesses were at the time of the offense and where they were interviewed; where the evidence was obtained, marked, stored; where the perpetrator resides and where he can be found.

HOW? in relation to the manner in which all actions and events occurred: how the offense was discovered, how it was committed, how it was reported; how the victim got to the scene; how the perpetrator got to the scene, how he got the tools and weapons and how he used them, how he got away, or how he was apprehended; how the witnesses happened to be on the scene.

WHY? (if it is possible to obtain this information) in relation to the reasons for all actions and events that occurred: why the offense was committed and why it was reported; why time lapses occurred; why particular tools or weapons were used; why the particular means of entry was used; why the perpetrator injured the victim; why a witness was cooperative or uncooperative; why the victim was moved from the scene.

The following is sample checklist. The officer can use it as a basic list and add questions that arise during his investigations. Or he can use this list as a guide for preparing his own checklist that will meet his particular needs. The checklist should be as nearly complete as possible. It should be set up in a form similar to the one following, a form that will enable the officer to glance at it and determine whether all information relative to the particular investigation he has obtained.

Sample Checklist[2]
The question WHO?

1. In relation to persons connected with the offense:

    WHO is the victim?

    WHO is the perpetrator or subject?

    WHO is an accessory?

    WHO are witnesses?

    WHO made statements or gave information that could be relevant?

    WHO turned over evidence to the police?

2. In relation to officers participating in the investigation:

    WHO responded to the call?

    WHO conducted the investigation?

    WHO preserved the scene?

    WHO conducted the search?

    WHO obtained evidence?

    WHO marked and preserved evidence?

    WHO took custody of the evidence?

    WHO interviewed each witness?

    WHO checked out possible leads?

    WHO notified another officer or agency?

    WHO dusted for fingerprints (or executed any other technical job)?

    WHO reported to the officer from the crime lab (or any other assisting department)?

    WHO identified and who located the perpetrator?

    WHO was unable to identify or to locate the perpetrator (or both)?

    WHO obtained a warrant for arrest?

    WHO made the arrest?

    WHO transported the perpetrator to headquarters?

The question WHAT?

1. In relation to the offense:

   WHAT offense was reported?

   WHAT offense was committed?

   WHAT damages were done?

   WHAT injuries were done?

   WHAT was the condition of the victim? of the subject?

   WHAT statements were made by the victim?

   WHAT statements were made by the witness?

   WHAT statements were made by the subject?

2. In relation to the evidence:

   WHAT evidence was obtained?

   WHAT evidence could not be obtained?

3. In relation to police action:

   WHAT police action was taken?

   WHAT officers were notified?

   WHAT agencies were notified?

   WHAT further action is indicated?

The question WHEN (day, month, date, year, hour)?
1. In relation to the offense:

   WHEN was the offense reported?

   WHEN was the offense discovered?

   WHEN was the offense committed?

2. In relation to persons connected with the offense:

   WHEN was the subject observed at the scene?

   WHEN did the subject leave the scene?

   WHEN did the accessory arrive, leave?

   WHEN did the victim arrive at the scene?

   WHEN did the victim leave (or when was he removed from the scene)?

   WHEN was the victim last seen?

   WHEN did witnesses observe the scene?

   WHEN did witnesses arrive? leave?

3. In relation to police action:

   WHEN did the officer arrive at the scene?

WHEN did the officer contact the victim and take his statement?

WHEN did the officer contact each witness and take his statement?

WHEN did the officer check out other possible sources of information?

WHEN did the officer obtain each item of evidence?

WHEN did the officer notify another officer or agency?

WHEN did assisting officers from other agencies arrive at the scene?

WHEN did the officer receive a report from assisting officers (such as, a report from a technician in the crime laboratory)?

WHEN was the perpetrator definitely identified and located?

WHEN was a warrant obtained?

WHEN was the perpetrator arrested?

WHEN did the officer inform the perpetrator of his rights?

WHEN was the perpetrator charged?

The question WHERE (exact location, address)?
1. In relation to the offense:

    WHERE was the offense committed?

    WHERE was the offense discovered?

    WHERE was the offense reported?

2. In relation to persons connected with the offense:

    WHERE was the victim?

    WHERE does the victim reside?

    WHERE did the victim go (or where was he removed to)?

    WHERE was the subject or perpetrator?

    WHERE does the perpetrator reside?

    WHERE did the perpetrator obtain tools and weapons?

    WHERE were the tools and weapons discovered?

    WHERE was the perpetrator last seen?

    WHERE is the perpetrator at present?

    WHERE were the witnesses?

    WHERE do the witnesses reside?

3. In relation to police action:

    WHERE was the evidence obtained?

    WHERE was the evidence marked?

WHERE was the evidence stored?

WHERE did the officer interview the victim? the witness?

WHERE did the officer apprehend the perpetrator?

WHERE did the officer inform the perpetrator of his rights?

WHERE did the officer take the perpetrator into custody?

WHERE did the perpetrator make his statement?

The question HOW?

1. In relation to the offense:

   HOW was the offense committed?

   HOW were tools and weapons used?

   HOW was the offense discovered?

   HOW was the offense reported?

2. In relation to persons connected with the offense:

   HOW did the victim get to the scene of the offense?

   HOW did the victim get to the scene of discovery?

   HOW did the victim get to the hospital?

   HOW did the perpetrator get to the scene?

   HOW did the perpetrator commit the offense?

   HOW did the perpetrator obtain the tools and weapons used?

   HOW did the perpetrator use the tools and weapons?

   HOW did the perpetrator get away?

   HOW did the witnesses happen to be on the scene?

3. In relation to police action:

   HOW did the officer identify the victim?

   HOW did the officer obtain evidence?

   HOW did the officer identify the perpetrator?

   HOW did the officer locate the perpetrator?

   HOW did the officer apprehend the perpetrator?

The question WHY (if facts are obtainable)?

1. In relation to the offense:

   WHY was the offense committed?

   WHY was the offense reported?

   WHY was there a lapse of time between the committing of the offense and the reporting of the offense? or between the reporting of the offense and the arrival of the officer?

2. In relation to the perpetrator:

WHY did the perpetrator use the particular tools or weapons?

WHY did the perpetrator use the particular means of entry?

WHY did the perpetrator injure the victim?

WHY did the perpetrator use the particular vehicle (stolen or other)?

3. In relation to others involved:

WHY was a witness at the scene?

WHY was a witness eager, or willing, or hesitant to give information?

WHY was the victim moved from the scene?

In this particular form for the checklist, the questions are organized under each basic question: WHO? WHAT? WHEN? HOW? and WHY? Further, under each basic question, specific questions are grouped under subheadings according to the persons involved, the offense, the police action, and so forth. This method of organization enables the officer to locate at a glance the questions he needs to check during any step of the particular investigation. Each officer should organize his checklist according to the plan that he can use most efficiently. The officer should never assume that any checklist includes all questions that he will ever need to answer in any investigation. However, he can prepare and use such a basic checklist and add questions as they arise during the investigations. The officer should be aware that any checklist will contain questions that do not apply in a particular investigation. For example, let us suppose that the officer's notes on a particular investigation show that no arrest was made and why. Under these circumstances, the question "When was the perpetrator arrested?" and all other questions relating to the arrest do not apply. Even though the officer will sometimes need to add some questions or disregard other questions, the basic checklist can be of great help to him as a quick reference to make certain that he records all essential facts and details that do apply in the particular investigation.

The checklist is not a set of questions to be answered one by one. Rather, it is a *reference* to enable the officer to check at a glance to see if he has obtained all essential information from the victim and the witnesses; to see if he has recorded all essential information on the offense, the perpetrator, the weapons and tools used; and so forth. During any particular step in an investigation, the officer is likely to obtain answers to more than one of these questions. For example, in taking the victim's statement, the officer will obtain answers to all the questions about the victim, such as WHO he is, WHERE he resides, WHERE he was at the time the offense was committed, WHY he was there, and so forth. He may also obtain information on the offense, the time, the location, the perpetrator, the tools and weapons. During the investigation the officer obtains information as he finds it, not in the order of an organized set of questions to be answered. However, referring to the checklist can help to ensure that he does not forget to obtain essential information while it is available to him. Also, by keeping a checklist and reviewing it regularly, the officer will form the habit of keeping in mind the types of information that are essential in any particular investigation. Inexperienced officers may rely heavily upon the checklist until they have formed this habit. The experienced officer may use the checklist in much the same way that an experienced speaker uses his notes while making a speech: primarily as a periodic reference, a reminder.

RECORDING DETAILS OF THE SEARCH

To obtain the information necessary to answer all the basic questions, the officer must conduct several different kinds of activities. One such activity is making a thorough search of the scene of the offense. The officer should record in his notes on each separate investigation all details of the search for evidence:

1. The time that the officer begins the search.

2. The names of officers participating in the search and of any other persons present.

3. A description of the area of the search and of the procedure step by step as the officer conducts the search.

4. The weather conditions: fair, raining, daylight, overcast, dark.

5. Identification of any special equipment used in the search.

6. Specific, accurate details on each item of evidence obtained in the search: what the item is, when and where it was found, who found it, and a description of the item; figures on any measurements made; information on the marking and disposition of each item of evidence.

7. Possibly diagrams, graphic illustrations of the facts written in the notes.

RECORDING MODUS OPERANDI DATA

During his investigation on the scene, the officer must also obtain information on the method or methods which the perpetrator used in committing the offense (*modus operandi* information).[3] The officer must record the details of this information in his notes on the investigation of each separate case. Methods of operation differ with different types of cases, with different types of perpetrators, and with particular perpetrators. In some cases, whether or not the perpetrator can be identified depends on the accuracy and completeness of the information which the officer records (and later reports) on the method of operation the perpetrator employed. Information on the method is stored in a *modus operandi file* according to major parts or segments of the perpetrator's method. Therefore, in making notes on this information, the officer needs to record the details according to the main segments of the perpetrator's technique:

1. The type of offense committed.

2. The time the offense was committed (the specific date and time if known; the general period, such as inclusive dates; the general time of day, such as late afternoon or between midnight and dawn).

3. The type of person attacked (a single woman, a preschool-age girl, a gas station attendant).

4. The manner in which the person was attacked (hit on the head from the rear, threatened, beaten) or the means of entry into a building or other property.

5. The tools and weapons or other means used in the attack.

6. The purpose, or intent, or object of the attack (to get money, to get jewelry, to get revenge).

7. The trademark or the peculiarities of the perpetrator (gestures, actions, behavior, attitudes, methods that can help to distinguish him from others, anything unusual about him).

8. The words spoken or written notes employed in connection with the committing of the offense.

9. The complete identification and description of any vehicles used in connection with the offense.

10. The identification and description of any property stolen or other damages done, such as the type of building or other property attacked and the kind of damage done.

11. The identifying information on the perpetrator: name, sex, age, his physical description, occupation, ethnic and geographical origins, education.

If no information can be obtained on a segment of the method of operation, the officer should make a note to that effect. For example, if the officer can find no information on any words spoken or written notes used, the officer should note that there is no evidence of either. Information on the method of operation must be recorded accurately, completely, and clearly because this information is essential for the written report and for the modus operandi file.

RECORDING INTERVIEWS

During his investigation, the officer must record in his notes the information obtained by conducting interviews. An *interview* is a conversation between the investigating officer and another person who may have information relevant to the case. The officer may interview the victim, the witnesses, the complainant, or any other persons who can provide information that may help the officer in obtaining all facts and details that are relevant to the case. (In this discussion, the *witness* is used as an example of the person interviewed.) The officer conducts the interview for the purpose of obtaining and recording in his notes the following types of information:

1. All information that the witness can supply in relation to the offense itself, such as what happened, where it happened, when it happened, how it happened.

2. All the information that the witness can supply about persons who were connected with the offense or who may have been connected, such as who committed the offense, who the victim is, who was present, who saw or heard anything connected with the offense, who may know anything about evidence or motive.

3. Information on the witness, such as where he was, what he was doing at the

time of the offense, and whether there is any relationship between the witness and any person who may have been involved in the offense.

In conducting the interview, the officer should follow a general procedure:

1. In his *approach to the witness*, the officer should practice the ordinary rules of courtesy and diplomacy. It is the officer who must put the witness at ease, and not the other way around, because the officer is the person who is in control of the situation. The officer should be calm, courteous, respectful, confident, efficient, and professional. He should introduce himself, show his identification, and then begin an ordinary conversation with the witness, as he would do with anyone else to whom he introduces himself. Such an introduction and opening conversation can help the witness to relax, to trust the officer, and to begin talking with him. During this opening conversation, the officer should try to "size up" the witness and decide on the best way to bring up the subject of the interview. In order to approach the witness effectively, the officer assuredly needs training and practice in conducting interviews. In addition, he must:

Exercise good manners, sound judgment, and common sense.

Be sensitive to the witness's physical condition, emotional state, and position.

Be able to sense the point in the conversation at which he can introduce the subject of the interview with naturalness and ease, so that the witness will continue talking.

2. In *beginning the interview* itself, it is best for the officer first to allow the witness to tell what he knows without interrupting him to ask questions. When the witness has finished his story, the officer can review the story with the witness, checking it for accuracy and completeness. At this point, the officer should take out his notebook and begin making notes. Before he takes out his notebook, it is advisable to refer casually to this action so that the witness will not become tense or cease to talk at the sight of the notebook. For example, the officer can say something like this: "If you don't mind, I'd like to write down the facts you have told me and check them with you, so I can be sure to get them right." The words "If you don't mind" are polite and courteous; they show the officer's consideration for the witness. The words "so I can be sure to get them right" show the officer's concern with recording exactly and accurately what the witness tells him instead of relying on his own memory.

3. In *recording each interview*, the officer should begin on a new page in his notebook, to avoid confusing information obtained from two different persons and to enable him to remove from his notebook the record of any particular interview to use as testimony in court, or to provide information for other officers, or to organize his notes for writing his report. At the top of the page, the officer should write the following:

Identification of the case.

Time of the interview (Friday, March 2, 1976, 2:30 P.M. to 2:45).

Exact location of the interview.

Complete identifying information on the witness and on any other persons present at the interview.

4. The officer should *begin with factual questions* that will enable him to obtain identifying information on the witness: name, address, telephone number, occupation. He should continue with questions that will enable him to review the witness's story and that will encourage the witness to supply additional details and to clarify any contradictions, discrepancies, or omissions. The officer should make accurate notes of what the witness says, recording all key statements in the exact words the witness uses, as nearly as he can. The officer should ask questions that will enable him to obtain and to record all information the witness can give in answer to the questions WHO? WHAT? WHEN? WHERE? HOW? and WHY? The purpose of the investigation is to obtain and record information. The officer cannot make a valid analysis and determine the relevancy of information until he has completed the investigation so that he can review his findings as a whole. Therefore, it is important to record all information obtained in each interview. Some information may later prove to be irrelevant. However, it is much better to find in the notes information that is not relevant than to realize later that the information that is missing in the notes is relevant after all. When the officer analyzes his findings and organizes them for his report, he can identify irrelevant information and omit it. At that point, however, it may be impossible for him to obtain relevant information that he did not record during the interview.

5. The officer should *not ask two or more questions together.* Rather, he should ask the questions and obtain the answers one at a time. He should ask general questions first, giving the witness an opportunity to elaborate in his own way. Then he should ask specific questions, rechecking essential facts and details for accuracy and consistency. He should phrase questions in such a way that the witness will be encouraged to offer details. If the officer asks questions that can be answered with only a yes or no, he will have difficulty obtaining all the facts and details. He should ask *open questions.* For example, the witness has just stated that he heard three shots around 10:00 P.M. The officer asks, "Did you go outside to find out where the shots came from?" That is a *leading question.* It can give the witness a suggestion as to what he did, or what he thinks he should have done, or what he thinks he should say he did. Suppose the officer asks, "What did you do when you heard the three shots?" That is an open question. It requires that the witness give his own response; the question itself does not suggest (lead him toward) a particular response. In his notes on the interview, the officer should identify the information that the witness states as *fact,* the information that he states as *hearsay,* and the information that reflects *conclusions* drawn by the witness. These distinctions are essential to an adequate police report. If the officer does not make the distinctions in his notes, he may not be able to make them later when writing the report. The officer should record accurately and precisely all *essential information* obtained during the interview, such as time, names, addresses, tools and weapons, words spoken.

6. The officer should listen carefully, showing a genuine *interest in the witness* and his information. He should pay close attention to *how* the witness phrases what he says and to the *manner* in which he tells his story and responds to questions. Does the witness use mainly factual, objective words; or does he use mainly emotional, subjective words? Does his attitude appear to be matter-of-fact? careful? eager? hesitant? anxious? or what? He should not appear impatient or seem to hurry the witness. The officer should encourage the witness to keep talking. If the witness strays from the subject, the officer can gently bring him back by referring to a previous statement made by the witness: "You say you

heard three shots at around 10:00 P.M.?" The officer should note accurately all information that the witness gives, as well as any inconsistencies, contradictions, or omissions. He should ask additional questions, or rephrase questions he has already asked, in an attempt to clarify any such discrepancies.

7. It is best not to erase any information in the notes on the interview. If a witness contradicts or changes a statement which the officer has written into his notes, the notes should show the discrepancy and its clarification. For example, the officer has recorded the witness's statement that the witness heard three shots at approximately 10:00 P.M. Later the witness says that it must have been between 10:30 and 10:45 P.M. because he had just turned off the television set when the news was over at 10:30. The officer can (1) write "Note: the witness stated..." and record the new statement, leaving the original statement intact; or (2) draw a line through the original statement, leaving it readable, and write in the change. He should write his initials beside any change to show that it is an official change that the officer himself made. When he reviews his notes later, the contradiction or the change in the witness's statement may prove to be significant in the case as a whole. Or if a second investigator works on the case, the change can be important in his continuing investigation. If the record of the interview is to be accurate, it must contain all information that the witness gives, including discrepancies and their clarification. Therefore, an erasure constitutes an inaccuracy in the record of the interview.

8. When the officer has heard the witness's story and has reviewed the story, obtained answers to his questions, and clarified any discrepancies, he should obtain background information on the witness; how the witness happened to be on or near the scene; where the witness was when the offense was committed; the relationship, if any, between the witness and any persons involved in the offense.

9. The officer should then make certain that the witness is satisfied with the facts and details as the officer has recorded them. He should express his appreciation for the witness's help and dismiss the witness: "That is all. Thank you very much. I appreciate your help."

If it is feasible, the officer should get the witness to make a *signed statement*. He or she should take the statement in a police office. The statement should be written in the language that the witness uses. Nothing he says should be omitted. When the written statement has been completed, the officer should read it to the witness and make certain that the witness understands exactly what the statement says in each sentence and each detail. If the witness requests any changes in the statement, the officer should make the changes and then reread to the witness the statement as corrected. Both the witness and the officer should initial each change or correction. When the witness is completely satisfied with the statement, the officer should ask the witness to write his initials on each page. Then, both the witness and the officer should write their signatures at the end of the statement. A third person (such as another officer who is present) acting as witness to the signing should add his signature at the end of the statement.

CONTENT AND FORM OF A SET OF NOTES

The complete set of notes on an investigation should include all information relevant to the questions WHO? WHAT? WHEN? WHERE? HOW? and WHY?

The notes should contain details on the search for evidence, the items of evidence obtained, the marking and disposition of the evidence, the method of operation, each separate interview, and all additional information which the officer could obtain.

The following is a sample partial set of notes on a hypothetical case. These notes illustrate the principles of the content and form of the officer's notes discussed in this chapter. The notes are set up to resemble pages of notes in an officer's notebook.

Sample Notes

Officer No Name
  Badge 001
  District 5
  Car 52
Monday, March 15, 1976 2:40 P.M. Residence Burglary
                              120 South St.
                              Reported via police radio

VICTIM: JOHN DOE, WM, age 40, residing 120 South St.
STATEMENT:
Locked both doors, front and back about 12:30, same date. Met friend RICHARD ROE, residing 600 Auburn Ave., for lunch at Sweet Shoppe, 120 Main.
Returned home alone 2:30 P.M. Found front door forced.
Missing: 1 string pearls ($100.00)
             1 lady's white metal Timex wristwatch ($25.00)
             1 GE Toast-R-Oven, Model E-36453, ($30.00)

SEARCH:
1. Fresh small $\frac{1}{2}$ inch pry marks and chipped paint on wooden door and wooden frame near metal lock. Apparently made by small prying object worked between frame and lock to force door open.
2. Bedroom. Lady's wooden jewelry box on top of chest. Lid open. Sectioned tray—empty. Missing pearls and watch placed in tray, first two left-hand sections, about 12:15, same day, by victim before going to lunch. Surprise for wife when she returns home same evening from out-of-town visit with friend.
3. Kitchen. One GE Toast-R-Oven, model E-36453, missing from counter top.
4. Other rooms. Nothing missing or disturbed.

EVIDENCE:
1. Pry marks ($\frac{1}{2}$ inch), wooden door and wooden frame near metal lock.
2. Paint sample from front door next to pry marks. Taken by Officer No Name about 3:00 P.M. Envelope #1.

AGENCIES CONTACTED:
1. 3:15 P.M. notified Crime Lab.
2. 3:30 Tech. Pi Square dusted for fingerprints. None suitable for lifting. Pry marks photographed.
3. Officer No Name gave paint sample, Envelope #1, to Tech. Square.

WITNESS: (*Note to Officer:* Begin on a separate page.)

Residence burglary, 120 South St., March 15, 1976
MRS. JANE X. DOE, housewife
122 South St. 002-7821
Next-door neighbor. March 15, 3:45 P.M. 4:00 P.M. at her residence
STATEMENT:
Washing dishes, kitchen sink about 1:00 P.M., same date. Noticed WM, middle age, tall, wearing green sport shirt, dark green trousers, golfing-type cap, leaving victim's front door. Saw brown paper bag, like grocery bag, in his hands. Saw no suspicious actions. Walked up South St. toward her house. Disappeared from her view. Witness not suspicious. Victim often comes home during lunch hour. Witness assumed he was home and the man was a friend.

In a similar form and manner, the officer continues making notes on each step in the investigation. He makes notes through the last action he takes, including a note on the status of the case at the time he concludes the investigation or his part in it, and of any further action indicated. Recording his findings under headings and putting each main heading on a separate page will help the officer in organizing his notes and in writing his report later.

TYPES OF NOTEBOOKS

A police department may have regulations on the type of notebook the officer is to use. Or the department may issue a particular type of notebook as an item of police equipment. In either case, types, sizes, and formats of notebooks vary with different departments. A notebook of any kind is preferred to loose sheets of paper, even sheets on a clip board, because loose sheets are more likely to be lost or misplaced. Also, a notebook is a more orderly and systematic instrument for taking notes than are loose sheets. A small notebook is practical because the officer can easily carry it in his pocket, keeping it always on his person when he is on duty and bringing it out only when he needs to use it. A small notebook is also practical because the officer can use a separate page for each main heading without leaving wasted blank space on a page; and this system enables him to organize his notes more rapidly. A small bound notebook can serve some of these purposes. However, a *small loose-leaf notebook* has certain practical advantages over the bound notebook.

1. The officer needs to keep together all notes on each separate case. When working on two or more cases simultaneously, he cannot know how many pages he will need for his notes on any one case. If he uses a loose-leaf notebook, he can add pages wherever he needs and still keep together all the notes on each case, with notes on all cases in the same notebook.

2. The officer cannot always collect information in order. If he uses a loose-leaf notebook and puts information under each main heading on a separate page, he can easily rearrange the sequence of the pages in order to group related information together.

3. When he is analyzing and organizing his findings, the officer may need to organize and reorganize his notes as he prepares to write different sections of his report. If he uses a loose-leaf notebook, he can remove the pages, group them in stacks, and then regroup them as he needs to. When he has finished writing his report, he can arrange the set of notes in a systematic order for filing.

4. The officer may need to take to court his notes on a particular case. If he

uses a loose-leaf notebook, he can remove and take to court only those pages that contain information on the particular case. Since the officer's notebook can be entered as evidence, the loose-leaf notebook thus assures that the defense attorney will see only the notes on the case being tried.

THE DAILY ACTIVITY RECORD

All law enforcement officers routinely keep a daily activity record, sometimes called the Police Daily Log or the Daily Diary.[4] This is a permanent record of the officer's activities in the line of duty on each shift. Some departments provide a separate form called a Worksheet or Field Worksheet on which the officer keeps the record of his daily activities. If the officer is not provided with such a worksheet, he keeps his daily activity record in a separate section of this notebook. He begins on a new page for each separate shift.

At the top of the sheet, the officer writes his identification, the identification of his shift, the identification of his vehicle or beat, and the date. He begins the daily activity record with a notation of the hour he comes on duty. As he responds to calls or assignments, he notes the item number, the exact time that he receives the call or assignment, and a summary of his actions in response to it. As in making other notes, the officer writes the account of his daily activities in words and phrases. However, as with all notes, he must make certain that the information is accurate, clear, and legible. The officer does not include all the details that he has noted on the investigation, such as the full details of the search for evidence or the complete record of an interview. Rather, he accounts for his activities, he notes that he searched the scene and lists the main items of evidence that he obtained and marked; or he notes that he conducted an interview with a particular witness and summarizes the main information that he obtained from the witness.

The daily activity record thus shows where the officer was and what he was doing at any given time on a particular shift, information that is sometimes important to the officer for his own protection and accountability. The daily activity record serves as a reference on cases which the officer has investigated or calls to which he has responded. It can serve as a reference for writing reports on his investigations. At the end of each shift, the officer hands in a copy of his daily activity record at the station. The record goes into his supervisor's files for purposes of reference, accountability, and evaluation.

There is no specified method or form for keeping the daily activity record. Any form that is effective for the officer and that is approved by his department is satisfactory. However, a few *basic guidelines* can be helpful:

1. Print the information in ink.
2. Print at the top of each page the officer's name and identification, identification of the shift, identification of the car or post or beat, the date.
3. List activities in order of time, beginning with the hour the officer comes on duty for the shift and concluding with the hour he goes off duty at the end of the shift.
4. Make the entries brief, concise, to the point.
5. Keep a daily activity record for each shift, even if nothing important happens.

6. Include an entry for time spent in the station, out of service: "In the station, writing a report on residence burglary Item #C-2468-1976."
7. Keep a daily activity record for days off and indicate reasons: illness, vacation, leave.

The following is a sample of the kind of information to include in the daily activity record and of a practical form to use.

Sample Daily Activity Record

1st Shift	Officer Nameless
Car 802	6th District
5/5/76	Badge 002
8:00 A.M.	Came on duty.
8:46	Responded to burglary call via police radio reported by JOHN DOE, WM, from his residence 1002 Ward St. Doe said that between 5:00 P.M. May 4, 1976, and 8:15 A.M., May 5, someone forced his front door open and ransacked his kitchen. All cabinet doors open. Contents on counters. Several bottles (8 or 10) liquor missing.
	Search revealed no other items missing.
	Door appeared forced by small prying object [1/2 inch pry marks].
	Photographs taken of scene.
	Fingerprints taken from cabinet doors and sent to Lab for analysis.
	No witnesses located at this time.
10:05	Responded to complaint via police radio called by James X, Principal Wilson Ele. School, 110 N. Pine. Strange man observed loitering near playground area—nicely dressed in dark blue suit, white shirt, blue striped tie. Tall, about 190 lbs., dark hair, med. dark complexion. Cruised area during school's recess and for 1 hr. afterwards. No sign of subject. Broadcast description of subject.
12:00	Called in out of service for lunch.
12:30	Called in, return to service.
2:00	Cruised area around Wilson during afternoon recess. No sign of subject.
2:30	Checked with Lab on fingerprints from burglary, 1002 Ward St. No report at this time.
4:00 P.M.	Went off duty (shift completed).

SUMMARY

The Field Notebook is an essential item of police equipment. It is essential to the officer in recording and retaining all relevant facts and details that he obtains during an investigation; in writing his report later; in providing necessary information for other officials; in testifying in court; in keeping on file a complete record of his activities and of information obtained in each investigation, for purposes of reference and accountability. It can be essential to other officers as a source of information necessary for continuing an investigation or as a cross-reference in checking possible connections between cases. It is essential to the police department for purposes of filing and accountability. It can be essential to the prosecutor or the defense attorney as a source of evidence in court.

If the notebook is to serve these purposes adequately, the notes must be complete, accurate, clear, and legible. The notes must:

- Provide complete answers, in accurate detail, to the basic questions WHO? WHAT? WHEN? WHERE? HOW? and WHY? (when this answer is obtainable).

- Provide complete, accurate, identifying details on all persons, objects, and locations connected in any way with the offense or the investigation.

- Include a record of each interview conducted, complete information on all evidence obtained, and information on the method of operation.

- Be recorded according to a form, such as headings and subheadings, that will enable those who refer to the notebook to find any particular item with ease and speed.

The Field Notebook can be considered an official document. Therefore, the officer should maintain and preserve his notebook with the same care and respect with which he maintains and preserves any other item of police equipment. He should maintain the notebook in a professional manner, according to proper content and form. He should keep it entirely separate from any of his personal belongings. For example, he should not place his notes in a wallet, a card folder, or any other packet or holder that contains money, pictures, addresses, telephone numbers, or other personal items of any kind. Official papers of any kind maintained by an individual are properly kept in a separate holder. For example, a doctor, a lawyer, and a teacher keep a patient's, a client's, and a student's official papers in a separate holder, apart from personal belongings. The officer should keep his notes in a separate notebook for personal reasons as well. For example, an officer testifying in court takes out his wallet, in which he has stored the notes he needs to use. The defense attorney can examine the entire wallet and all its contents, in the presence of the court, because the notes are contained in the wallet. He can also question the officer about any item that he finds in the wallet. Therefore, a professional and practical way to keep official notes on police investigations is to keep the notes between the covers of an official Field Notebook which contains nothing except information obtained or used in the officer's official work. When the officer removes from his notebook the notes on an investigation that has been concluded, he should file these notes in a secure place where only notes on his investigations are filed or in the folder containing the file on the case. If it is the policy of the particular department to file notes in the office of the department, then, of course, the officer complies with this policy.

A proper Field Notebook shows that the officer has conducted a complete and accurate investigation. It assures that the officer is fully prepared to file notes that will be of actual use to the officer and to other authorities for future reference and to the department for purposes of filing and accountability. It assures that the officer is prepared to appear in court with acceptable testimony, should he be called as a witness. It assures that he is prepared with the relevant information necessary to write complete, accurate reports that will communicate objectively the findings of his investigations. For all these reasons, the officer must keep a proper Field Notebook if he is to complete his assignments adequately.

SOME COMMON FLAWS IN POLICE REPORTS

The following section is taken from Appendix *A* of *Writing Effective Reports on Police Investigations.*

Flaws in Content

A. Title Page

1. Inaccurate identification of offense, such as confusing burglary, theft, and robbery; confusing criminal and civil offenses; omitting ATTEMPT if the subject was unsuccessful.
2. Improper order in listing multiple offenses: most serious first, with others in descending order.
3. Failure to report exact location or approximate time of offense.
4. Failure to report weather conditions and lighting.
5. Failure to report inclusive time of handling of the case 2-6-1980, 10:50 P.M.–2-7-80, 3:15 A.M.
6. Failure to record full names and/or exact addresses of victim or of witnesses.
7. Inaccurate or incomplete identification or type of premises.
8. Inaccurate or incomplete identification of weapon and/or use of force.
9. Incomplete identification of subject.
10. Omission of any of the following items on page 2: Synopsis List of Property Stolen, List of Evidence, List of Witnesses, Description of Vehicle, Description of Subject.

B. Narrative

1. Basis for the investigation

   a. Incomplete identification of officers.
   b. Omission of name of complainant.
   c. Omission of time complaint was received.
   d. Omission of means by which complaint was received.
   e. Omission of time of officer's arrival on the scene.

2. Victim and witnesses

   a. Incomplete identifying information on victim or witnesses.
   b. Incomplete identifying information on subject, as supplied by victim or witnesses.
   c. Omission of physician's examination, as in a rape case.
   d. Omission of autopsy on deceased victim.
   e. Incomplete details of interview with victim or witnesses.

3. Search and preservation of crime scene

   a. Incomplete details of the search and evidence obtained.
   b. Failure to report the search by areas, such as room by room in a residence.
   c. Failure to report details of tagging and securing evidence, of disposition of evidence, of entering in Evidence Book.
   d. Omission of entry and exit subject used or of exact means of entry and exit.
   e. Omission of the taking of photographs or the making of sketches.
   f. Omission of dusting for latent fingerprints.
   g. Omission of proper preservation of evidence such as blood stains.

    h. Inadequate details of securing the crime scene.
    i. Omission, or inadequate details, of taking measurements.

4. Communications

    a. Incomplete details on information broadcast.
    b. Omission of exact agencies notified or of names of officers responding.
    c. Omission of time information was broadcast.
    d. Omission of means by which information was broadcast.

5. Written Statements

    a. Failure to report taking written statements.
    b. Omission of essential content of written statements.
    c. Omission of location and time of taking written statements.
    d. Omission of notation on attachment of written statements to the report.

6. Apprehending subject

    a. Omission of preparation and signing of Arrest Warrant and/or Search Warrant.
    b. Omission of some details in preparation of Arrest Warrant or of Search Warrant.
    c. Omission of details of date, time, location or means of apprehending the subject.
    d. Omission of details of reading the subject's rights and/or the subject's response.
    e. Omission of details of the arrest of the subject or of the subject's escape.

7. Booking arrested subject

    a. Omission of location, date, or time of booking.
    b. Omission of name of officer.
    c. Incomplete or inaccurate identification of the offense.

8. Attachments to the report

    a. Omission of any attachment appropriate to the report (properly filled in, witnessed, signed, notarized, according to requirements), such as the following items: Arrest Warrant, Autopsy Report, Crime Lab Reports, Physician's Report, Rights Form, Search Warrant, Sketches, Supplementary Report, Written Statements.

C. Traffic Accident Reports

  1. Incomplete or inexact information on location and time of accident.
  2. Inexact information on condition of vehicles.
  3. Inexact information on positions of vehicles and/or point of contact.
  4. Inexact information on drivers, passengers, or pedestrians involved.
  5. Omission, or inexact reporting, of conditions of the road or street.
  6. Incomplete or inexact reporting of weather conditions.
  7. Incomplete or inexact reporting of time of day and lighting conditions.
  8. Omission of information on traffic signs, street signs, warning signs.
  9. Omission of means of measurement used.
 10. Omission of measurements or reporting of inexact measurements.
 11. Omission of alcohol test on drivers.
 12. Omission of medical or first aid information.
 13. Omission of witnesses' written statements.

Flaws in Written Expression

A. Sentences

   1. Incomplete sentences (fragments).
   2. Incomplete expression of thought.
   3. Lack of clarity in phrasing sentences.
   4. Inexact verbs.
   5. Failure to use logical subjects in sentences.

B. Word Choice

   1. Using subjective rather than objective words, such as *home* for *house* or *residence*.
   2. Using inaccurate words, such as *disturbed* for *disarranged*.
   3. Using incorrect words, such as confusing *there* and *their*.
   4. Using inexact words, such as *ran from the house* for *ran out the back door of the residence and disappeared in an unknown direction*.

C. Correctness

   1. Incorrect forms of pronouns, verbs, adjectives, adverbs.
   2. Incorrect use of singular, plural, and possessive forms.
   3. Incorrect or inadequate basic punctuation.
   4. Incorrect spelling.
   5. Improper use of lower-case and capital letters.
   6. Improper use of abbreviations.

D. Paragraphs

   1. Failure to indicate proper paragraph divisions.
   2. Omissions of paragraph numbers.
   3. Omission of topic sentence stating the main topic of each paragraph.
   4. Improper order of paragraphs or of items of information in paragraphs.
   5. Omission of relevant details or inclusion of irrelevant details in paragraph.

E. Transitions

   1. Omission of transitions between paragraphs.
   2. Omission of transitions within paragraphs.
   3. Use of inaccurate transitions.

NOTES

[1]Some departments use military time designations (16 January 1976, 1800 hours).

[2]Refer also to A. F. Brandstatter and Allen A. Hyman, *Fundamentals of Law Enforcement* (Beverly Hills, Calif.: Glencoe Press, © 1971), pp. 63–65.

[3]Refer also to John J. Horgan, *Criminal Investigation* (New York: McGraw-Hill, © 1974), pp. 41–47.

[4]Refer also to Brandstatter and Hyman, *Fundamentals of Law Enforcement*, pp. 66–69.

PART 4

Gathering Information from Persons

20
Interviewing and Interrogation Techniques

Edward J. Flanagan

The existence of blood, semen, fingerprints, toolmarks, or other physical evidence at a crime scene is extremely important. These items can assist an investigator to eliminate or identify a possible suspect. It is a rare day though, when physical evidence alone is all that one has available to assist in an investigation. In fact, physical evidence amounts to only 5 or 10 percent of what is normally offered in testimony in a judicial setting. Consequently, the remaining 90 to 95 percent concerns itself with conversations—whatever an investigator can glean from discussion with individuals who might have information relevant to the matter at hand.

It is this latter area, the conversations, that will be examined in this chapter, which explains the mechanics of a professionally conducted investigative interview. First, the psychological and physiological forces that affect both the interviewer and the interviewee will be discussed, and later, the different techniques, tactics, and strategies that allow for a productive interview by reducing inhibiting elements and maximizing the flow of valid, accurate information.

DEFINITION OF THE INTERVIEW

What is an interview and how is it used in the investigative process? It can be defined in many ways. Basically, an *interview* is the questioning of individuals who possess information of official interest to the investigation and who are not reluctant to cooperate. In actuality, it is a conversation between two people for the purpose of gathering any data relating to the investigation and substantiating or corroborating physical evidence or other sources.

It is through this questioning session that the investigator may associate meaning to physical evidence that has surfaced. Unless this is done with the proper preparation and a high degree of professionalism, the investigation may remain forever a mystery.

We must differentiate between an interview and an interrogation. The interrogation does not usually involve witnesses, victims, or complainants as the interview does, but rather those individuals who are less cooperative. This generally includes suspects and others who are reluctant to furnish necessary information.

The interview session, because of this definition, requires strategies different from those used in interrogation. We will initially discuss, in this chapter, problems inherent in the investigative interview, and explore possible solutions. Later, we will concern ourselves with those techniques that are germane to the field of interrogation.

THE INTERVIEWER

Successful investigators, by their very nature, possess the ability to obtain accurate facts from various individuals. They do this by developing skill in communication. They cultivate techniques that incorporate a sophisticated knowledge of human relations and the art of sympathetic listening and understanding. Investigators become aware of the sciences of psychology and sociology and their impact on communication. They develop skill in identifying what hinders and what facilitates the productive flow of information. Thus, they can determine which tactic or technique would be most profitably utilized with a particular personality.

Interviewing is an art, and it can be developed. Good interviewers are not born. Medical science, to date, has not discovered the interviewing gene. Instead, this skill is a product of a genuine understanding of human nature, observation of other successful interviewers, and constant practice and self-evaluation of acquired techniques.

Successful interviewers are aware of the interviewee's feelings. They will identify specific attitudes or responses and prescribe the corresponding techniques that should be used in each situation. They keep the subjects talking about the important issues, periodically letting them stray, but always redirecting the conversation back to the important elements. They control the conversation without being unnecessarily authoritarian.

This interviewing process can be referred to as the communication network. It has three component parts: the interviewer; the interviewee, or subject; and the topic to be discussed. If the interview is conducted properly, the interviewer will, to a great degree, control all of these elements. This is done surreptitiously, never allowing the subject to feel controlled or manipulated.

Interviewers' functions are varied. First they must increase or decrease the level of stress, depending on the subject and the information being solicited; second, they should assist individuals to tell the truth; and last, they must be able to decipher the truth from conflicting accounts. To perform these functions properly, investigators must be capable of modifying their behavior so it corresponds to the elements of the crime and the individuals involved. This may require performing roles that run counter to their personalities. For example, if one were assigned to investigate a serious case of child abuse, one's function would be to gather facts in order to reconstruct the events. If, in an interview with the parents, a judgmental attitude were projected, probably little or no cooperation would be received. If, instead, a sympathetic and understanding approach were used, one would more likely encounter cooperation. Consequently, successful interviewers develop the ability to play many roles and wear different masks. They modify their behavior to coincide with the situation, so they can discover the truth. It is important though, that this acting ability appear sincere, because if their real feelings show through, then all cooperation will cease. Interviewers must attempt to put the subjects at ease, evaluate their actions, and choose the most productive role or technique. If they cultivate this skill, they will be able to successfully interview almost anyone in any setting.

TIMING THE INTERVIEW

Usually, the optimum time for an interview is immediately after the criminal event. This will allow the investigator to obtain facts while they are still vivid in the witness's mind. Additionally, the sooner the interview, the more likely that no one will interfere with the subject's ability to recall.

This can be demonstrated by a situation in which a man on his lunch hour witnessed a robbery of a cab. After the thief stole the driver's money, he fired his gun at the driver, missing him. The suspect escaped before the police arrived. The witness was interviewed by the responding officers and appeared cooperative. After the officers received a brief account of the events from the excited witness, they drove him to his office.

At his business, the witness related the story to his supervisor and other employees. What was their reaction? You guessed it—don't get involved! His boss explained that if he lost any work time because of this case, he would not be paid. His friends told him that he was crazy to get involved because "everyone knows that witnesses become victims at court."

Later that evening, our witness went home and recounted the same story to his wife. She, in the presence of their four little children, told him he was "crazy to get involved." First, the guy had a gun, and second, she was too young to be a widow.

It was no wonder that when the police reinterviewed the witness, he had developed a severe case of amnesia.

This situation exemplifies the importance of timing the interview to prevent outside influences on a witness's ability or willingness to cooperate. If the responding officers or investigator assigned had thoroughly questioned the subject immediately after the crime was committed, they probably would have received more cooperation. Thus, it would have become considerably more difficult for the witness to later have recanted his initial account.

In other than emergency situations (immediately after a serious offense) the interviewer must consider the subject and select a period convenient for both. In cases where witnesses are emotionally upset, the investigator must consider briefly delaying questioning.

In police work there are two prevalent theories regarding timing in such cases. The more traditional states that in serious crime situations, it is imperative to immediately interview the witness and get a description. As soon as a brief statement and description is gathered, it should be broadcast to all units. The prompt dissemination of information to other police units will increase the possibility of apprehension.

The other school of thought states that it is counterproductive to immediately question an individual who is emotionally upset. Its theorists believe that there is a direct relationship between memory and stress. As emotion increases, the witness's memory decreases; and as emotions are reduced, memory increases.

The latter concept specifies that the interview of persons who are extremely anxious will be of little value. It suggests that interviewers will receive misinformation rather than accurate facts. I believe this to be true, especially in tragic situations, and recommend that investigators take a few minutes to comfort witnesses and reduce their fears before proceeding with the necessary questioning. Only then will interviewers receive information that will be of value to them and to other police units. Only factual, pertinent information will be beneficial toward apprehension, and it is this that investigators must assemble.

SETTING OR LOCATION OF THE INTERVIEW

The location of investigative interview can add to or detract from subject cooperation. Usually the choice of location can be made by the investigator, but there are other urgent situations when the setting is determined by the events.

Interviews generally take place in one of four locations:

1. The crime scene area.
2. A place chosen by the witness.
3. A neutral setting.
4. The investigator's office.

A crime scene interview is one that takes place immediately after the crime occurs, and in the same area. Usually, the investigator has more control where the interview will take place. It is imperative, though, that the most distraction-free location be chosen and that some time be spent in preparation before commencing the questioning. The impact of the criminal events on the subject must also be considered.

The investigator, in choosing a location for the interview, may ask the subject what area would be convenient. This technique can be used to relax the subject and allow for a more cooperative relationship. Many times the subject will choose to be interviewed at home, and this can be extremely advantageous for the investigator. A situation that I experienced in November 1973 demonstrates this concept. A police officer had just been shot. One of the responding officers noticed a woman looking from her window, which was close to the crime scene. The officer signaled to the woman to come down to the street. After complying with the officer's instructions, the woman stated that she had been sleeping and had not witnessed anything. Later, after the crowd had dispersed, the investigator assigned visited the woman in her apartment and attempted to interview her. Surprisingly, she was very cooperative and assisted the investigators in identifying the suspect. She also apologized for lying to the police officer but stated that her reluctance was due to a fear of suspect retaliation. This situation demonstrates how witnesses can experience anxiety about the police interview and how the location can affect their cooperation.

Sometimes an interviewer wants the questioning session to take place in a neutral location, especially when criminal activities are to be discussed with an informant or someone hesitant to be observed conversing with the police. The individual might be more comfortable, and consequently more cooperative, in a neutral setting.

Investigators might also choose their own offices or some other formal facility where the subject is deprived of the comfort of familiar surroundings, thus giving the psychological advantage to the investigator. This is often necessary with less cooperative or hostile witnesses. In fact, most questioning of suspects takes place at a police location.

The investigator must scrutinize the facts of the case and decide what location would be ideal for encouraging the interviewee to speak freely, considering possible distractions and trying to avoid them. Whether the interview takes place in the witness's home or the interviewer's office, it should be devoid of all distractions. The interview should be kept private—just the interviewer and the interviewee. If at the witness's home, the family members should be politely asked for privacy. If in the interviewer's office, a quiet location should be chosen and associates requested to prevent any interruption. The interviewer should never hesitate to ask another investigator for privacy.

The only exceptions to the principle of using a secluded location are interviews of juveniles or women. In both cases, it is beneficial that someone else be present (preferably another investigator or a parent of a juvenile) to ensure that questioning is conducted in a professional manner.

It is also advantageous for the investigator to consider the subject's schedule when making appointments for interviews. Cooperation will be difficult to gain if an interview is unreasonably scheduled. The interviewer will find that a little consideration will not go unnoticed. Any reasonable requests made by the investigator usually activate a cooperative effort by most witnesses. Investigators should learn to frame their questions so that an unreasonable response by the witness will be difficult. If this technique is developed, most witnesses will be compelled to be cooperative.

INTERVIEWER'S ATTITUDE

A professional investigator is a flexible, insightful individual, who must perceive more than the obvious when speaking with people. If it appears that a victim has just suffered some serious wrong and is extremely upset, the interviewer must endeavor to reduce this anxiety, discussing any fears before attempting to get meaningful information. For example, an investigator who is interviewing a witness of a bank robbery might receive replies to questions about the suspect's identity such as "Officer, I really don't recall—that gun was so big!"

If, during the questioning, the witness continues to mention the gun, the officer should be aware that the subject is venting fear. This may be the only socially acceptable way in which the witness's fear can be indicated to the interviewer. By ignoring these feelings and continuing the questioning, the investigator is inadvertently demonstrating unconcern about the victim's trepidation. A keen interviewee will sense this, and it may be the reason for turning a cooperative session into an antagonistic one.

Investigators must be capable of showing concern when it is necessary and should not be apprehensive about allowing witnesses or victims to see their human side. Many times this view is all an individual needs to confide in an investigator. He or she may feel more comfortable with an interviewer who can demonstrate some sympathetic understanding—one who will allow the venting of feelings and frustrations.

To be capable of "reading" subjects and anticipating their needs in a nonjudgmental manner is an attribute that interviewers must develop. If investigators can focus on the interviewees, analyze their psychological and physical states, develop the appropriate strategies, and question them in a sincere fashion, they will gain the witnesses' confidence and be considerably more successful.

PREPARING FOR THE INTERVIEW

Investigation requires methodical and systematic behavior. Interviewing necessitates proper preparation and the establishment of a functional game plan. The sequence in which individuals who have information relevant to a crime are interviewed is important. Under ideal conditions, subjects should be interviewed in the following order:

1. A victim or complainant.

2. A witness who observed the crime.

3. A witness who did not observe the actual crime but who has important information about anything that either preceded or occurred after the crime.

4. A hostile witness or suspects.

It must be remembered that these are ideal conditions and that this order may not always be possible. In emergency situations, the events may dictate a different order.

The interviewer should prepare for each step in the process. This preparation may be hasty and take only a few minutes, but it is extremely important. One may have time only to mentally review the events and possibly speak to the officers at the scene. Some preparation is always better than none.

If there is ample time to review, the successful interviewer should become familiar with whatever is available regarding the case. This involves the *who*, *what, where, how,* and *why* of the investigation. All relevant information must be identified, and special note made of those facts that are not public knowledge. If some information surfaces that was never released by the police or not public knowledge, the investigator should know that the interviewee is a witness or a suspect.

Next, the interviewer should acquire some background information on the individual to be questioned, considering the subject's relationship to the criminal act, association with the suspect, and any predispositions toward the police. Such knowledge will assist the investigator in questioning the subject.

The investigator must also know the legal components of the criminal act and the options available to the questioner. This will allow the direction of questioning into certain essential areas and the recognition of incriminating statements. It will also assist in evaluating information offered by victims or witnesses. A thorough awareness of the possible constitutional issues involved in the investigation will help the interviewer to plan an approach. After all, the investigator's *raison d'être* is to protect the rights of everyone involved in the case and to guarantee that all information collected is legally admissible.

Last, the adroit interviewer will compose a "game plan" and estimate what information must be acquired. This should be accomplished before the interview. It is done by use of a checklist of specific questions. These inquiries should be open-ended to necessitate narrative responses. For example, the investigator might say, "Can you tell me, in your own words, what you saw when the gunman entered?" rather than a direct question, such as "Did you see the gunman enter?" Obviously, the first question allows for more latitude and requires a more comprehensive answer.

There is considerable controversy about using prepared notes in an interview. Some experts believe it inhibits the interviewer, and others feel it adds to a logical development of the interview. Some suggest that the questions should be committed to memory, thus allowing for continuity without distraction. I believe, from a practical viewpoint, the latter combination is productive, but each investigator must adopt the technique that is compatible with his or her personal style. The important thing is that the investigator has prepared for the interview. Random questioning is seldom successful and its lack of professionalism is telegraphed to the subject of the interview. Without preparation there is no control or direction.

Planning means choosing the best questioning techniques for the situation and the individual involved. It also necessitates developing secondary strategies if the primary one fails. The investigator who takes the time to properly research and plan the interview will be rewarded many times over.

PROMISES TO THE INTERVIEWEE

Sometimes it is necessary in an investigative interview to make a promise to the interviewee. Be sure that whatever is promised can legally be performed. Victims should not be told that they are safe unless commensurate protection will be offered. If an informant interview is being conducted, a subject who is "working off a case" should not be promised something that cannot be delivered. The prosecutor should always be consulted before anything is promised concerning a jail sentence.

The interviewee should be treated fairly, because if promises are made that cannot be fulfilled, the investigator's efficiency (and reputation) in the future will be diminished. Investigators have a reputation in their assigned area. Anything they do that detracts from it will make their function more difficult in the future.

INTRODUCTION AND IDENTIFICATION

The initial stage of the interview is the introduction. Investigators should courteously introduce themselves and show their credentials. When speaking with witnesses, complainants, or victims, it is wise to use an official title and last name. When interviewing a hostile witness or suspect, omit the title. With suspects, police position should not be overemphasized, whereas it is desirable for cooperative individuals to be sure of the investigators' identity and feel safe in their presence. This technique will reduce unwarranted stress and give the investigator time to evaluate the subject.

Whether the interview is to occur in the witness's home or the investigator's office, it is important that the interviewer be cognizant of the psychological effects of physical barriers on the interviewee. Eliminating desks or coffee tables between the interview participants can reduce the formality of the session and relax the subject. Instead of the subject's chair being placed directly in front of the interviewer's desk, it should be placed to the side and the investigator should move closer to the subject. This will reduce the inhibiting effect of the barrier.

Another concern for investigators is the physical distance between themselves and the subjects. It can be used productively to increase or decrease anxiety levels. The investigator's chair can be moved away from the subject to show disapproval or to psychologically challenge a subject's truthfulness. To accent the importance of a particular question, the investigator may move closer to the witness. The distance between the investigator and the interviewee can be regulated to the advantage of the interviewer, who should become aware of the utility of space and body language in an interview.

After identifying himself or herself and choosing the proper physical setting, the interviewer should attempt to "warm up" the witness. Areas not specifically connected with the investigation may be discussed to allow the respondent to relax and feel more comfortable.

During the session, the investigator should consider using a humanistic approach after evaluating the witness and determining if it will be beneficial. With most subjects, the investigator will receive more cooperation with honey than with vinegar. It is important, though, to be aware of the possibility of overusing this approach.

Towards the end of the warm-up period, the investigator should slowly direct the conversation into the area of concern. Before getting to the central issues, the investigator must properly identify the witness, initially getting his or her proper name, address, and telephone number. Later in the questioning, the individual's place of business and any local family ties can be ascertained (surreptitiously, if necessary). If there is a question about the witness's identity, the necessary credentials should be requested.

This is extremely important, because in many cases witnesses move due to fear of retaliation. A large percentage of rape victims also relocate, so that they do not have to experience the embarrassment associated with being victims of sexual assault. The investigator may never detect these fears in the witness during the initial interview but later, when trying to locate the witness or victim, may be informed that the person has moved without a forwarding address. If the suspect in this case has been identified and arrested, the investigator will discover that without a victim's or witness's cooperation, there will be no prosecution. A serious offender might be set free because the investigator did not properly identify the subject of the interview.

It is important that, during the initial few minutes of the interview, the investigator develop rapport with the witness, being flexible and allowing the subject to save face, if necessary. If, for example, a witness chooses to lie (and they do for a variety of reasons), it may be beneficial to allude to additional information that the investigator possesses. An interviewee who knows that the investigator has additional information available may make a correction. If, instead, the witness is confronted and called a liar, any rapport for future questioning will have been destroyed. The investigator must be flexible and allow the witness the opportunity to rethink answers. If this is done in the proper manner, a "confused" witness may suddenly recall exactly what happened.

LISTENING AND NOTE-TAKING SKILLS

One of the most difficult skills that an investigator must develop is the ability to listen attentively to the subject. Confusion, noise, and other distractions interfere with this process.

Listening runs counter to our personalities. For example, take a discussion on a topic with some political significance. While one person is relating his or her feelings, the other probably is developing his or her own thoughts in logical, presentable order instead of listening. As soon as one finishes, the other begins speaking. Quite often both vehemently air their views only to later find that they are in agreement.

This happens every day, in many different settings. We like to hear ourselves talk, and develop incontrovertible arguments, never taking time to listen to others.

Listening takes patience and considerable practice. It cannot be developed overnight. As soon as witnesses start talking about "the gun" in "that shooting," there is usually an overpowering tendency to stop them and ask details about the gun. Once subjects are interrupted their thought processes are forever broken and important elements possibly omitted.

Other distractions that affect the interviewer and interviewee are unusual mannerisms, heavy accents, and emotional reactions (such as extreme fear or crying). They capture the attention of the listener, who focuses on the mannerism (for example, stuttering) rather than what is being said.

In conjunction with this, it is important to mention stereotypes or biases. Everyone develops feelings about different categories of people. The academic community criticizes these prejudices, but they still exist. Most people have them because they are a part of our social and cultural development. Our environment, to a great degree, generates their existence.

In investigative interviewing, it is important to realize that biases exist and that they affect both participants in the interview. Investigators who consciously are aware of their own stereotypical thinking or biases can make strong efforts not to evaluate respondent's information in the light of prejudice. For example, what is the stereotype of fat persons? They are happy and not very intelligent. An investigator who held "these truths to be self-evident" might improperly evaluate responses made by a robust individual. Investigators must become aware of their own feelings and also examine witnesses' reasons for concluding something. If this is practiced consciously, interviewers will be able to attach the proper degree of validity to subjects' statements.

Note taking is the last major tactic to be discussed. It is a distraction to both interviewer and interviewee. The subject follows the eyes of the investigator lowered to the paper and watches the hand move across the paper, while the investigator stops concentrating on what the subject is relating.

To keep note taking to a minimum, the following technique can be used the *initial* time the witness's story is related. This would take place after the warm-up period, when the investigator asks the subject to relate what he witnessed concerning the event. All information can be categorized into two areas:

1. *Trivia:* Unimportant, irrelevant information.

2. *Important Information:* (a) Important programmed information, such as *who, what, when, where, why,* or *how.* (b) Unusual important information, such as unusual temperature at a crime scene, unusual odors, or a gut feeling mentioned in an interview.

Much of a subject's story may be trivia. We must be able to identify this and separate it out. The second category is further subdivided into important programmed information and unusual important information. The former, the programmed information, is information that we are programmed to ask. It is directly related to the captions on a crime report—*who, what, where, when, why,* and *how.*

The unusual important information is just that: something that is important but unusual. It is the unusual items that investigators focus on and return to after the subject finishes telling his or her story. These ideas should be the only items noted during the subject's initial discussion of events. If the investigator can limit the number of notes, the distracting influence note taking has on the subject will be considerably reduced. One or two words should be used to capture an idea, if possible, to reduce the amount of writing.

It is often useful at the beginning of the interview, to allow the interviewee to become part of the decision-making process. It might be explained that the case is somewhat complicated and that the investigator would like to take a few notes. After the explanation, the investigator can ask the witness, "Would you mind if I take some notes?" Most reasonable individuals will feel compelled to say yes. Once the subject agrees to notes being taken, the potential for distraction is considerably reduced. This does not mean that the interviewer should take exhaustive notes; rather they should be kept to a minimum. An interviewer who anticipates a negative answer by the subject to this question must then consider alternatives, for example:

1. Not posing the question but just taking the notes.

2. Eliminating note taking and attempting to commit important points to memory.

3. Having the conversation taped or listened to by an unobservable assistant.

All alternatives has possible drawbacks. The investigator must evaluate the potential witness in light of the situation and decide which technique would be most productive.

The investigator will be required to take more detailed notes during the question-and-answer period of the interview. The note-taking technique described above (unusual important information) is useful during the initial few minutes, when the subject relates the story for the first time. The notes are then referred to by the investigator during the question-and-answer period to formulate meaningful inquiries. This may decrease distractions and allow the interviewee to better relate the events.

COMMON PITFALLS ENCOUNTERED IN INTERVIEWING

Human Factors

Human factors affect both interviewer and interviewee. How the subject perceives the investigator is very important. Depending on the approach used, the investigator can receive total cooperation or experience hostility.

Perception and memory also play an important part in interviews. The validity associated with subjects' comments should be related to their ability to understand what took place at the crime scene, to recollect that information, and to tell it properly to the interviewer.

Mistakes made by witnesses can be due to weakness in one of their senses (seeing, hearing, and so on). They can also be due to the physical position of the witness relative to the criminal act, or the amount of time that passed between the event and the interview. The probability is that if five patrons witness a robbery of a bar, there will be five different accounts. This is because people interpret occurrences through their social development. What one determines as important may be totally different from another's determination. The investigator is required to sift through the witnesses' varied accounts, and piece together the puzzle.

Prejudice heavily affects the witness's interpretation of the events encountered. The investigator must attempt to discover the motivation for a prejudiced observation and analyze the validity of the statement carefully.

Sometimes witnesses are hesitant to speak to the interviewer. This can be caused by many factors. First, the subject may be afraid of getting involved or of the publicity that may be associated with a cooperating effort. Second, it may be inconvenient for a witness to testify in court, consequently he or she may disclaim any knowledge. Third, as mentioned above, there may be a personality conflict between the participants; and last, the witness may have something to lose by cooperating. The suspect may be a friend or a relative of the witness. In most cases this will dampen any cooperative zeal.

Confusion at the crime scene may hinder victims' ability to recall. They may confuse the order of events, placing them in improper sequence. This can lead investigators astray; consequently they must be always alert to this possibility.

The same situation may allow other witnesses to confuse what took place. They may, because of violent or chaotic environment, develop incorrect inferences and pass them on to the investigator as the truth.

Many of these problems can be circumvented only by a comparative analysis of conflicting reports. If there is only one witness or victim, it will be very difficult for the interviewer to get the facts.

Last, status can interfere with communication. This inhibitor can affect either the subject or the investigator. Investigators sometimes experience this when interviewing professional people. Often, because they are trying to make a good impression, they will be more concerned with their speech patterns or projected image than with the content of the interview.

For some witnesses, the perceived status of the interviewer changes their responses. Quite often, someone does not recall the description of the suspect, but rather than admitting this in the interview, will create a fictitious suspect. Other times, an individual may be embarrassed by having become a victim. To compensate for these feelings, a 5-foot 6-inch, 130-pound suspect may be described as two 6-foot 3-inch, 230-pounders. Both these situations are common and difficult to detect. The investigator must always be aware of these potential enigmas and cognizant of possible solutions.

Investigative Problems

Besides the human considerations, investigators experience a few additional problems. First, it is often difficult to obtain citizen cooperation at the crime scene. I have found it useful to discreetly photograph the crowd at the scene, including individuals peering out windows or looking down from roofs. Such pictures will assist investigators in identifying possible witnesses. They can also be used to controvert or motivate a hesitant witness.

The unnecessary use of police jargon causes difficulties too. Most professions develop phrases that are understood only by their members. People in law enforcement also do this. An investigator might feel uncomfortable at a social event when a group of individuals (doctors, lawyers, or bond specialists) converse in their professional tongue. Witnesses and victims also experience the same uneasiness at hearing unfamiliar expressions. It is therefore incumbent on the investigator to properly explain, in language that the subject understands, what is happening.

In keeping with the topic of jargon, we should be aware that people "from the street" also develop their own language. To be capable of identifying and understanding certain phrases can be enormously useful.

Words slip out in conversation that can give the investigator leverage in questioning. For example, if you are speaking to someone who relates, "I was on my way to my program...and it just happened." The mention of the word "program" may alert you to the possibility of the subject being a participant in a methadone program.

You may then nonchalantly examine the person's arms for needle marks or eyes for dilated pupils—all possible signs of drug abuse. If your suspicions prove to be positive and the subject becomes uncooperative, you may allude to your knowledge of his participation in a drug program. If this is properly done, you may gain the psychological advantage and divert the interview into a productive channel.

Interviewers must learn to control their behavior, including modifying or regulating their reactions to correspond to any situation. Investigators should never lose their tempers or criticize the interviewees. They may sometimes act annoyed so long as it is only acting, but once the temper is lost, control is lost. Investigators should also never correct a subject's pronunciation or grammar, because it will result in resentment.

If the witness, or even a suspect, catches the investigator off guard with some unexpected information, the investigator should not register surprise. Any verbal or physical signs of astonishment could show the interviewee that the investigator is only partially informed, which might induce the witness to be less truthful.

Investigators may encounter unusual problems in interviewing senior citizens. Their memory may be failing, their interpretative abilities may have declined, or they may experience considerably more fear than would younger persons. Investigators must be patient and try to allay unwarranted fears. These interviews usually take longer, but, if conducted properly, they can be very productive.

USEFUL TECHNIQUES

Now that some of the problem areas have been identified, a few useful strategies will be discussed. As mentioned before, the attitude and actions of the interviewer usually determine the success or failure of the investigation.

The primary purpose of the investigative interview is to arrive at the truth by motivating the subject to talk about the area of concern. To do this effectively, interviewers must assume a friendly and businesslike attitude. They should develop analytical skills that will assist in identifying the motives and drives of witnesses and any related emotional strains. If any barriers to an effective interview are anticipated, they must immediately be dealt with.

If a victim is emotionally upset due to a violent experience, the investigator must dispose of this problem before attempting to ascertain specific information. It is useful to permit victims or witnesses to explain their fears. The investigator should demonstrate concern for their feelings and allow them to believe that trauma is normally experienced in similar situations. After they vent these anxieties, their minds will be more clear to explain the sequence of events.

The sympathetic understanding that encourages catharsis is useful as long as it is effective. A sympathetic approach toward a witness or victim may induce cooperation. The technique is only useful when the investigator is trying to lower emotional barriers to the truth, and must be tempered to the situation. A witness who starts to wander from the topic should be gently redirected toward the central matter.

Most people have a need to discuss tragic experiences. The investigator can capitalize on this need by offering a sympathetic and understanding ear. This is a good technique with the elderly, who are often not initially motivated to cooperate with the officer because they feel "there is no use." An investigator who can create some reason for them to cooperate may gain access to the requisite information.

I have often observed that a retired woman will call only a specific detective when she has important information. If this detective is not on duty, she will refuse to offer the information to anyone else. Why does this happen? Most often it is because of the sympathetic approach that the woman experienced when dealing with the investigator. The persons spoken with today may be sources of information tomorrow. Individuals who are treated fairly will usually cooperate in the future.

Some people require other motivating techniques. With self-centered individuals who have a need for recognition, it may be useful to flatter their abilities to recollect or their retention capabilities. Actually, this is merely inflating their egos, but some individuals thrive on this, and it can be effective.

Recognition can also be helpful when dealing with people who have specialized knowledge. A sincere demonstration of gratitude for their assistance is always useful. If you leave people with a good taste in their mouths, the door will always be open.

Other people must be induced to cooperate by some sense of justice. It can run the gamut from a general desire to be on "the side of the law" to revenge for some past wrongdoing. The investigator must try to determine how to motivate potential witnesses, what element in the individual's personality will ignite the spark of cooperation. There is usually some reason, however hidden, which, when accented properly, will activate cooperation.

Finally, investigators may capitalize on the status associated with their position. The television networks are often competing for the best detective series. Many depict investigators as supersleuths who can successfully investigate the most complex situation in one hour. A major portion of the network's weekly ratings are based on these stereotyped shows. This can be translated to mean that people are concerned with the investigative function. If used properly, this interest can be transformed into meaningful cooperation.

It is clear that one of the most important talents that an investigator can develop is the ability to analyze and understand people and their behavior. Once needs or weaknesses can be identified, the most productive strategy for the situation can be chosen. It is this talent that separates good interviewers from poor ones and which allows them to successfully solve complex cases.

STRATEGIES

When interviewees are cooperative, it is often useful in the beginning of the interview to ask them to relate the series of events in their own words. They should be allowed to tell the whole story once. If they stop, and the interviewer believes they have additional information, nodding the head or repeating a phrase that they used may stimulate them to continue.

The interview should not be started by asking questions that call for specific answers. Instead, the subject should be allowed to tell the story. It is also not productive to ask questions that require yes or no answers. The answer to the question may be something other than yes or no, and the use of this technique may cause the subject to reply no. This answer may not be a true representation of the facts and could lead the investigator astray.

The specific, more direct questions are useful after the witness's account is completed. Then the witness can assist the investigator to clear up any inconsistencies or identify important nuances through specific responses.

How can the investigator evaluate the validity of the witness's account? One technique is to examine the psychological and physiological state of the subject during two periods and compare them. The investigator should initially analyze the subject during the warm-up period. Does the witness feel comfortable, have good eye-to-eye contact, or act fidgety? Later, during the specific questioning, does the witness demonstrate different behavior? Is considerably more nervousness shown, eye-to-eye contact avoided? This is not to say that the lack of eye-to-eye contact always indicates lying, but that the sudden change in behavior may indicate that the investigator is touching on an uncomfortable area. Now the interviewer can examine the witness and related area of questioning more closely. If it can be determined that questioning about a particular element causes changes in behavior, then the witness's account must be scrutinized for validity.

During investigative interviews, especially with emotional subjects, it is not a good technique to ask leading questions. Someone who is upset or under considerable strain will follow suggestions rather than answer questions independently. Many times an area of an interview is terrifying for the subject to relive. If asked leading questions, witnesses may opt to follow the questioner's reasoning rather than use their own. This, again, may cause the investigator to pursue unproductive avenues, due to unintentional misinformation.

Questions should be kept simple. The witness should not be led or asked two questions in one sentence. This would make unclear which statement corresponds to which question and would only succeed in confusing the witness.

ENDING THE INTERVIEW

When interviewers believe they have received all the information possible, they should terminate the interview. This requires some forethought and planning. An interview that drags on unproductively creates tension and reduces cooperation. At the same time, if the interviewer stops suddenly after the last question, the subject will feel jolted by the lack of continuity.

At this point, it is important that the interviewer correctly understand the subject's account. Many times what individuals say is not what they mean; or what they say is translated by the receiver improperly. To reduce the chance of misinterpretation, interviewers should make certain they have accurate information. This can be done by summarizing what they believe happened. Then witnesses have an opportunity to correct any discrepancies.

After this has been accomplished, interviewers should show their appreciation for the subjects' cooperation and commend them for the valuable service performed. Investigators may choose to emphasize the importance of the information offered and assure subjects that it will be used.

Investigators should be aware that they may receive valuable information after the formal session has ended. As they walk witnesses to the door, they should attempt, in an informal manner, to elicit additional information. Quite often subjects will confide new facts that may be helpful in solving the investigation.

At the conclusion, the interviewer should offer assistance to subjects who need transportation home. It is this concern for witnesses that solidifies cooperation for the future meetings.

EVALUATION OF THE INTERVIEW

There are three important elements that investigators must examine in evaluating the questioning session. They should review the reactions of the interviewee, the information received and their own performances. If any discrepancies surface, they must be compared with other information that the investigators possess. An investigator who honestly believes a different technique could have been used more productively should make note of it for future interviews. It is important for investigators to review their interviews critically and learn from their own mistakes. After examining these areas, they should have some valid insight into the events under scrutiny.

INTERROGATION

Interrogation is the questioning of an uncooperative witness or suspect to ascertain the facts in a particular investigation. It is closely related to the art of interviewing, but sometimes requires a different approach. Where interviewing may require the alignment of the interviewer's personality with the subject, interrogation may call for the opposite. In this section, the proper setting for an interrogation, some problems usually encountered, and a few successful strategies will be discussed. Most often the investigator will question a suspect, so this section will emphasize techniques and their relationships to possible defendants.

Good interrogators, much like interviewers, must have a working knowledge of psychology. To be effective they should know when to stress an area, and when to relax the subject. They cannot lose their tempers or composure, otherwise they will relinquish control. At the same time, they can never resort to the use of physical force or intimidation. Interrogation is actually a battle of wits. Interrogators match their talents and intelligence against the subjects'. If force is used, the opponent has won.

The first and foremost concern of an interrogation is that interviewers inform the subjects of their constitutional rights as delineated in the *Miranda* decision. If the environment is not coercive and the subject voluntarily waives the right to remain silent, and so on, then the interviewer can begin questioning. It would be wise for the reader to consult the appropriate legal chapter upon completion of this section.

It is important today to note that the art of interrogation has definite negative associations in the legal and judicial setting. It is my suggestion that the word "interrogation" never be used in testimony or official reports by the investigator. To emphasize this, I shall limit use of the term in this section and discuss the skill of questioning or interviewing an uncooperative individual as a positive process.

NECESSARY QUALITIES

Because of the nature of the questioning, investigators must be more patient and tactful than in normal interviews. They should also be flexible and adaptable, because, if a subject takes an adverse or uncooperative position, the investigator may be required to use many strategies before arriving at the truth. The interviewer must be perceptive, so personality weaknesses can be identified and utilized productively. A situation may require a kind, sympathetic approach or a discriminating, piercing glance. Every person involved in this type of questioning must believe that, given the correct strategy, a good interviewer can penetrate any façade and locate the necessary information. It is the talent of identifying the suspect's personality and choosing the correct strategy that separates successful investigators from unsuccessful ones.

PLANNING THE INTERROGATION

Investigators should research the case as was explained in the preceding interviewing section. They must also examine records and talk with witnesses or victims before speaking with suspects. The suspect should be the last individual interviewed, except in emergency situations.

It is extremely important that the interviewer make a background search of the suspect before the questioning session begins. Any information, however insignificant, can give investigators the necessary leverage to make suspects believe they know more than they actually do.

Interviewers, in planning their approach, must not be myopic and only concern themselves with acknowledgments of guilt. Instead, they should endeavor to learn all the facts surrounding the investigation—what actually triggered the incident, where the gun is now, and so on. Sometimes a suspect will admit guilt but reconsider the admission when asked about the specifics of the crime.

To effectively anticipate or counteract these possibilities, interviewers should examine what they actually know and what they must learn. Then they should list specific areas of questioning to ensure that the conversation will cover all elements of the investigation. They must be mindful that once the session is complete, it will be extremely difficult to gain additional information that may have been overlooked originally.

Lastly, successful interviewers will formulate tactical plans. They must decide which techniques to use initially and have secondary strategies available, if the primary one is unproductive.

Proper research and planning offer psychological advantages to the investigator and must be utilized if the investigator is to be successful.

SETTING

When speaking with witnesses or victims, the interviewer attempts to choose a location that is convenient for the subject and also conducive to cooperation. When hostile witnesses or suspects are being interviewed, the investigator's own office at the police facility should be used.

A misconception about interrogation is that it should always take place in a formal setting. This is far from true. Many times a suspect will discuss the case with the investigator in an informal atmosphere, and possibly this will be the most productive setting for that individual.

Usually though, the investigator will choose a location that affords maximum privacy. It should not cause distractions to either the interviewer or the interviewee. This means that the walls should be bare, the windows covered, and only essential furniture in the room.

Some successful questioners who subscribe to the need for a psychological advantage place the furniture in specific locations. They believe the suspect should be seated in a straight-backed chair with back to the door while the investigator sits in a more luxurious chair directly in front of the suspect.

Whatever the facility, it should be simple and free from distractions.

USE OF A RECORDER

It is generally advantageous to have equipment available for recording the entire interview. This can be a tremendous aid to the investigator, who can review the session later to clear up uncertainties, and is also useful to disclaim any accusations of threats or violence made by the suspect. And if the subject confesses, then attempts to recant before signing a confession, the recording can be introduced as evidence at trial.

The equipment must be ideally placed, so an assistant can operate it without informing the subject. Usually there is a microphone secreted in the room, and the machine is located in the adjoining office. This will allow the assistant to change tapes, if necessary, without distracting the suspect.

THE INTERVIEW

When investigators finally meet the subjects, they should properly introduce themselves, but without emphasizing official rank—this can be used as a psychological force later, if necessary.

After the formal introduction, suspects should be directed to the questioning location. Before seating them, it is a good practice to ask if they wish to use the bathroom. This will help later when the investigator is trying to identify the cause for nervous behavior; this possibility can be eliminated.

The investigators' initial concern is to attempt to place the subjects at ease. They should be polite but firm, and try to break the ice by first talking about areas not immediately involving the investigation. Interviewees will be nervous, so they should be allowed to speak about anything to reduce this anxiety. When they have calmed down, the conversation should be slowly directed into your area of concern.

If subjects start to cooperate, they must be rewarded by offering a cigarette, a cup of coffee, or an understanding attitude. This will again decrease their emotional upheaval.

During the questioning session, taking notes should initially be avoided, especially if the conversation is being recorded. As in the normal interview situation, note taking will introduce distractions and be inhibiting to the subject. At the conclusion of his or her version, the subject can be questioned on particular points. This is the only time notes should be taken.

During the session, it is useful to listen to everything said with an objective mind and not to jump to conclusions before all the facts are in. The investigator should compare what the subject says to information already possessed, and analyze the account for its truthfulness.

The investigator must also maintain control and composure. If the subject lies, it is unprofessional to get angry and swear. First, the investigator loses control, but more important, the environment may be legally interpreted as intimidating or coercive. If this is true, any evidence gathered will be ruled inadmissible.

The interviewer must be careful of the manner in which the questions are asked. It doesn't matter whether the suspect is a free person appearing in the investigator's office voluntarily or is under arrest. The questioning session must be free of any intimidation or coercion. It is preferable to accent a positive approach in soliciting details.

Any statements gathered during the interview session will be legally reviewed if the suspect is arrested. It is important that the investigator can demonstrate that subjects were advised of their constitutional rights and voluntarily and intelligently waived them before offering statements; otherwise, all statements will be considered inadmissible.

SPECIFIC TECHNIQUES

During interrogation, it is beneficial not to ask narrative questions, especially in the beginning. The investigator should try first to determine where the subject was at the time of the criminal events. If, instead, general questions are asked, the subject may answer by developing an alibi. Once an alibi is offered, it will be extremely difficult to get a recantation. Additionally, the alibi gives the subject a psychological advantage, because now the investigator must disprove the subject's version.

Initially, an investigator may choose to stress the need for a confession. This works with some suspects. Here the interviewer persuades the suspect, by showing the futility of lying, to cooperate and offer a full statement. Other times it is beneficial to be empathetic with the subject and say, "I would have done the same thing." This is very useful in family assaults, where the investigator can appear to identify with the suspect's dilemma and understand his or her behavior.

In using this technique, the interviewer may attempt to make the crime seem less serious or allow the suspect an opportunity to blame someone else. If suspects are allowed to feel that their actions were not so unusual or if they can project their guilt feelings toward someone (another individual was really responsible), it may be easier for them to discuss the issues.

It is important that interviewers choose their words carefully, not using negative terms such as "assault," "kill," or "injure" but translating them into more palatable terms. This makes it easier for subjects to admit playing a role in the events.

If investigators believe a suspect is lying, they should allow an opportunity to correct the story—perhaps by paraphrasing it, comparing it to reality, and alluding to the discrepancies. If allowed to comment, the suspect may recant any lies and relate the truth.

If a variety of techniques has been used and the suspect continues to lie, it is only at this point that he or she can be challenged. The investigator has nothing to lose. This can be done by questioning the suspect's sincerity or attempting to obtain cooperation by bluffing. This course of action can be used only as a last resort, and if it doesn't work, the interviewer will never be able to regain any rapport with the suspect. The investigator must also be aware of the legal environment—no coercion.

If the subject decides to offer a confession, the interviewer should listen attentively without taking notes and, at the end, request that it be written. If this is refused, the investigator may be required to compose a confession based on the subject's rendition. If a few minor but obvious mistakes are included and the suspect allowed the opportunity to correct them, this will demonstrate that the suspect was not forced or coerced into a confession.

When either a confession has been received or a standoff reached, it is time to terminate the interview. If the suspect is to leave, the interview should be ended on a calm, relaxed note. The interviewer should spend a few minutes with a subject who is still upset until composure is regained. In any case, the subject should be thanked in a polite manner. This will keep the door open for any future contacts.

After suspects depart, investigators must set aside ample time to review what transpired, examining what the suspects said and how it was said. Then they should evaluate their own techniques and their usefulness. If investigators sincerely evaluate their interviews in an objective manner, they will benefit from their mistakes, perhaps deciding that one technique excited the subject and mentally substituting another. This assessment will assist investigators in developing future "game plans." They should also identify those strategies that were effective and store them for future use. The investigator who does this will grow and become an excellent questioner.

We have discovered that interviewing is probably the single most important skill an investigator can develop. Is it possible then, that investigators could survive in our sophisticated world without substantial knowledge in this area? Unequivocally, the answer is no! They would suffer from lack of information every day. Investigators' success depends on information, and without being cognizant of the elements of interviewing they will quickly experience failure in their careers.

Briefly, we have found that successful investigators always plan their interviews. They receive the information at hand, decide what their needs are, and then formulate the interview "game plan." During the actual interview or interrogation, they always *listen* to what is being said and the manner in which it is delivered. They are ever alert to inhibiting or distracting influences and ready to circumvent their negative effects. They are aware that sometimes they will be required to play different roles to successfully elicit information but that they must always appear sincere and concerned. They are cognizant that a nonjudgmental, objective approach is the most productive and professional one, while the authoritarian, coercive technique only ends in frustration and polarization of the participants.

If investigators evaluate their interview sessions honestly, and critically examine the effectiveness of their strategies, they will develop a level of expertise that will be extremely beneficial. They should also witness other interview sessions and adopt useful techniques. They must keep abreast of any new developments in this field and study the legal aspects of their function.

21
Information Sources

Joseph J. Grau

Ben Jacobson

In any investigation, knowing where to look for the first, basic piece of information is crucial; and of equal importance is knowing how to find this information easily and quickly. Since obtaining vital data requires familiarity with information sources, this chapter focuses on where to begin the search—where to look for such facts as birth, death, and marriage dates; travel schedules and photographs; licenses and qualifications. Obviously, the requirements for various inquiries may differ, and this creates the need for a variety of source bases. Familiarity with the appropriate access channels can save time, a factor that may prove vital in an investigation.

In many instances throughout the *Handbook*, authors of the individual chapters have provided directions for recovering pieces of information related to specific types of investigations, including finding missing persons, art, or certificates. Furthermore, some readers may already be familiar with the sources and agencies identified. However, the following collation and categorization of sources into a simplified, organized digest may be of additional assistance.

CATEGORIES OF SOURCE INFORMATION

Federal. Post offices, Library of Congress, departmental computer retrieval systems, congressional hearings, various regulatory agencies.

State. Secretary of state, comptroller, livestock inspector's office, industrial relations, natural resources, state gambling commissions, bureau of professional and vocational standards, narcotics enforcement, criminal identification, state liquor authorities, state legislative hearings.

County. Recorder of records, health certificates, civil files, probate index, criminal index, auditors, assessors, tax collectors, surveyors, voter registration, roster of voters, medical examiner.

City. Assessor's office, taxation and finance department, highway and buildings department, fire marshall and sanitary inspectors, personnel department, civil service commission, credit unions, welfare department, education records.

Private Directories. Telephone directories; public utilities; trade directories; medical, legal, and professional listings; scientific; educational; funeral directors; dry cleaners; better business bureaus; real estate agencies; chambers of commerce; and directories in numerous special areas.

Private Corporate. Surveys, personnel, mailing lists, cost analysis, financial transactions and statements, corporate index, manufacturers' index, and so on.

SAMPLE OF AVAILABLE SOURCES

The following selection of available directories and centers is by no means complete and merely represents avenues for further research.

International Level

Data pertaining to the international community can be retrieved from various sources, including the United Nations, libraries, and the following directories.

Bas Directory Bulletin

SOURCE: Overseas Publications Ltd., 45 Sheen Lane, London, SW 148 AB

CONTENTS: Names and addresses of international manufacturers, wholesalers, importers, representatives, suppliers of raw material. The publication is indexed in English and other languages depending on the country.

Association of British Directory Publishers

SOURCE: Imperial House, 17 Kings Way, London, W.C. 2

CONTENTS: Directories of British business enterprises

Jaeger & Waldman International Telex Directory

SOURCE: Universal Media Co., Division, Shamgar Inc., P.O. Box 45, Bethpage, NY 11714

CONTENTS: Six volumes. Contains over 900,000 telex subscribers worldwide, alphabetical by country, classified by products and services and by answerback codes.

Stame and B.V.

SOURCE: International Book Sellers, P.O. Box 505, Hilversum, Holland

CONTENTS: Assorted international manufacturers' and trade directories.

Federal Level

Directories. Key directories at the federal level include the following:
Federal Register—Privacy Act Issuances, Vols. I–IV

> SOURCE: Superintendent of Documents, U.S. Government Printing Office, Washington, D.C. 20402
>
> CONTENTS: Research aids—agencies in compilation, annual publication, tables of dates and pages, table of Privacy Act regulations in the Code of Federal Regulations, systems of codes and rules; lists each department as well as every subdivision in U.S. government, its rules and regulations, and addresses of data sources; more than 3500 pages.

Directories and Lists of Persons and Organizations: A Guide for Handicapped Visitors

> SOURCE: Superintendent of Documents, U.S. Government Printing Office, Washington, D.C. 20402 (Code—SB 114)
>
> CONTENTS: Detailed information concerning accessibility of facilities, services, and interpretive programs in approximately 300 areas of the national park system. Data includes addresses and telephone numbers, average elevations (where pertinent), available first aid and medical services, descriptions of special programs, wheelchair accessibility, and other vital data.

National Informational and Statistics Service, National Criminal Justice Information: Criminal Justice by Regions

> SOURCE: Law Enforcement Assistance Administration, Superintendent of Documents, U.S. Government Printing Office, Washington, D.C. 20402
>
> CONTENTS: Presents an updated listing of criminal justice agencies (individual names and addresses) in cities and states comprising 10 LEAA regions.

Pamphlets. Each of the following specifies the government agency providing the requested document.

> SOURCE: Superintendent of Documents, U.S. Government Printing Office, Washington, D.C. 20402

Where to Write for Vital Records: Births, Deaths, Marriages, and Divorces

U.S. Department of Health and Human Services, National Center for Health Statistics, Hyattsville, Maryland for specific directives 1992 publication (cost $4.50).

Divorce Records—United States

Office of Health and Human Services Publication No. (PHS) 78-1145, revised 1978

Marriage Records—United States

Office of Health and Human Services, Publication No. (PHS) 78-1144

Federal Office of Safety and Health Administration (OSHA) Regional Offices

REGION I: Conn., Maine, Mass., N.H., R.I., Vt.
18 Olive Street, Boston, MA 02110

REGION II: N.Y., N.J., P.R., V.I., C.Z.
151 Broadway (One Astor Plaza), New York, NY 10036

REGION III: Del., D.C., Md., Pa., Va., W. Va .
15220 Gateway Center, 3535 Market Street, Philadelphia, PA, 19104

REGION IV: Ala., Fla., Ga., Ky., Miss., N.C., S.C., Tenn.
1375 Peachtree St., N.E., Atlanta, GA 30309

REGION V: Ill., Ind., Mich., Minn., Ohio, Wis.
300 Wacker Dr., Rm. 1201, Chicago, IL 60606

REGION VI: Ark., La., N. Mex., Okla., Tex.
1512 Commerce St., 7th Floor, Dallas, TX 75201

REGION VII: Iowa, Kans., Mo., Neb.
823 Walnut St., Rm. 300, Kansas City, MO 64106

REGION VIII: Colo., Mont., N.D., S.D., Utah, Wyo.
1961 Stout St., Rm. 15010, Denver, CO 80202

REGION IX: Ariz., Calif., Hawaii, Nev., Guam, American Samoa, Trust Terr. of the Pacific Islands
450 Golden Gate Ave., San Francisco, CA 94102

REGION X: Alaska, Idaho, Oreg., Wash.
506 Second Ave., Seattle, WA 98104

Federal Information Centers. U.S. Civil Service Commissions and the U.S. General Services Administration have been established to simplify and expedite dealings with federal agencies. Centers, located in key cities across the nation, are equipped to answer questions directly or to give referral to the proper agency. A listing of these Federal Information Centers and telephone tielines follows:

ALABAMA

Birmingham 322-8591, toll-free tieline to Atlanta, Ga. Mobile 438-1421, toll-free tieline to New Orleans, La.

ARIZONA

Phoenix (602) 261-3313, Federal Bldg., 2310 N. First Ave., 85025

Tucson 622-1511, toll-free tieline to Phoenix

ARKANSAS

Little Rock 378-6177, toll-free tieline to Memphis, Tenn.

CALIFORNIA

Los Angeles (213) 688-3800, Federal Bldg., 300 N. Los Angeles St., 90012

Sacramento (916) 440-3344, Federal Bldg. and U.S. Courthouse, 650 Capitol Mall, 95814

San Diego (714) 293-6030, Federal Bldg., 800 Front St., Rm. 1S11, 92188

San Francisco (415) 566-6600, Federal Bldg. and U.S. Courthouse, 450 Golden Gate Ave., P.O. Box 36082, 94102

San Jose 275-7422, toll-free tieline to San Francisco

Santa Ana 836-2386, toll-free tieline to Los Angeles

COLORADO

Colorado Springs 471-9491, toll-free tieline to Denver

Denver (303) 837-3602, Federal Bldg., 1961 Stout St., 80294

Pueblo 544-9523, toll-free tieline to Denver

CONNECTICUT

Hartford 527-2617, toll-free tieline to New York, N.Y.

New Haven 624-4720, toll-free tieline to New York, N.Y.

DISTRICT OF COLUMBIA

Washington (202) 755-8660, Seventh and D Sts., S.W., Rm 5716, 20407

FLORIDA

Fort Lauderdale 522-8531, toll-free tieline to Miami

Jacksonville 354-4756, toll-free tieline to St. Petersburg

Miami (305) 350-4155, Federal Bldg., 52 Southwest First Ave., 33130

Orlando 422-1800, toll-free tieline to St. Petersburg

St. Petersburg (813) 893-3495, Wm. C. Cramer, Federal Bldg., 144 First Ave., South, 33701

Tampa 229-7911, toll-free tieline to St. Petersburg

West Palm Beach 833-7566, toll-free tieline to Miami

GEORGIA

Atlanta (404) 221-6891, Federal Bldg., 275 Peachtree St., N.E., 30303

HAWAII

Honolulu (808) 546-8620, Federal Bldg., 300 Ala Moana Blvd., P.O. Box 50091, 96850

ILLINOIS

Chicago (312) 353-4242, Everett McKinley Dirksen Bldg., 219 S. Dearborn St., Rm. 250, 60604

INDIANA

Gary/Hammond 883-4110, toll-free tieline to Indianapolis
Indianapolis (317) 269-7373, Federal Bldg., 575 N. Pennsylvania, 46204

IOWA

Des Moines 284-4448, toll-free tieline to Omaha, Nebr.

KANSAS

Topeka 295-2866, toll-free tieline to Kansas City, Mo.
Wichita 263-6931, toll-free tieline to Kansas City, Mo.

KENTUCKY

Louisville (502) 582-6261, Federal Bldg., 600 Federal Pl., 40202

LOUISIANA

New Orleans (504) 589-6696, U.S. Postal Service Bldg., 701 Loyola Ave., Rm. 1210, 70113

MARYLAND

Baltimore (301) 962-4980, Federal Bldg., 31 Hopkins Plaza, 21201

MASSACHUSETTS

Boston (617) 223-7121, JFK Federal Bldg., Cambridge St., Rm. E-130, 02203

MICHIGAN

Detroit (313) 266-7016, McNamara Federal Bldg., 477 Michigan Ave., Rm. 103, 48226
Grand Rapids 451-2628, toll-free tieline to Detroit

MINNESOTA

Minneapolis (612) 725-2073, Federal Bldg., U.S. Courthouse, 110 S. Fourth St., 55401

MISSOURI

Kansas City (816) 374-2466, Federal Bldg., 601 E. 12 St., 64106

St. Joseph 233-8206, toll-free tieline to Kansas City

St. Louis (314) 425-4106, Federal Bldg., 1520 Market St., 63103

NEBRASKA

Omaha (402) 221-3353, Federal Bldg., U.S. Post Office and Courthouse, 215 N. 17 St., 68102

NEW JERSEY

Newark (201) 645-3600, Federal Bldg., 970 Broad St., 07102

Paterson/Passaic 523-0717, toll-free tieline to Newark

Trenton 396-4400, toll-free tieline to Newark

NEW MEXICO

Albuquerque (505) 766-3091, Federal Bldg. and U.S. Courthouse, 500 Gold Ave., S.W., 87102

Santa Fe 983-7743, toll-free tieline to Albuquerque

NEW YORK

Albany 463-4421, toll-free tieline to New York

Buffalo (716) 846-4010, Federal Bldg., 111 W. Huron St., 14202

New York (212) 264-4464, Federal Bldg., 26 Federal Plaza, Rm. 1-114, 10007

Rochester 546-5075, toll-free tieline to Buffalo

Syracuse 476-8545, toll-free tieline to Buffalo

NORTH CAROLINA

Charlotte 376-3600, toll-free tieline to Atlanta, Ga.

OHIO

Akron 375-5638, toll-free tieline to Cleveland

Cincinnati (513) 684-2801, Federal Bldg., 550 Main St., 45202

Cleveland (216) 522-4040, Federal Bldg., 1240 E. Ninth St., 44199

Columbus 221-1014, toll-free tieline to Cincinnati

Dayton 223-7377, toll-free tieline to Cincinnati

Toledo 241-3223, toll-free tieline to Cleveland

OKLAHOMA

Oklahoma City (405) 231-4868, U.S. Post Office and Courthouse, 201 Northwest 3rd St., 73102

Tulsa 584-4193, toll-free tieline to Oklahoma City

OREGON

Portland (503) 221-2222, Federal Bldg., 1220 S.W. Third Ave., Rm. 109, 97204

PENNSYLVANIA

Allentown/Bethlehem 821-7785, toll-free tieline to Philadelphia
Philadelphia (215) 597-7042, Federal Bldg., 600 Arch St., 19106
Pittsburgh (412) 644-3456, Federal Bldg., 1000 Liberty Ave., 15222
Scranton 346-7081, toll-free tieline to Philadelphia

RHODE ISLAND

Providence 331-5565, toll-free tieline to Boston, Mass.

TENNESSEE

Chattanooga 265-8231, toll-free tieline to Memphis
Memphis (901) 521-3285, Clifford Davis Federal Bldg., 167 N. Main St., 38103
Nashville 242-5056, toll-free tieline to Memphis

TEXAS

Austin 472-5494, toll-free tieline to Houston

Dallas 749-2131, toll-free tieline to Fort Worth

Fort Worth (817) 334-3624, Fritz Garland Lanham, Federal Bldg., 819 Taylor St., 76102

Houston (713) 226-5711, Federal Bldg. and U.S. Courthouse, 515 Rusk Ave., 77208

San Antonio 224-4471, toll-free tieline to Houston

UTAH

Ogden 399-1347, toll-free tieline to Salt Lake City

Salt Lake City (801) 524-5353, Federal Bldg., 125 S. State St., Rm. 1205, 84138

VIRGINIA

Newport News 244-0480, toll-free tieline to Norfolk

Norfolk (804) 441-6723, Stanwick Bldg., 3661 E. Virginia Beach Blvd., Rm. 106, 23502

Richmond 643-4928, toll-free tieline to Norfolk

Roanoke 982-8591, toll-free tieline to Norfolk

WASHINGTON

Seattle (206) 442-0570, Federal Bldg., 915 Second Ave., 98174

Tacoma 383-5230, toll-free tieline to Seattle

WISCONSIN

Milwaukee 271-2273, toll-free tieline to Chicago, Ill.

State Level

Directory of State Agencies—New York State

SOURCE: Secretary of State, 162 Washington Ave., Albany, NY 12231

CONTENTS: Developed to assist local officials and citizens to make effective contact with state agencies, it is designed to serve as a quick and current reference. Most (but not all) agencies having direct contact with the public are included. It is not intended, however, to replace the *Legislative Manual*, which is the comprehensive and official state directory.

Citizen's Guide to State Services

SOURCE: Citizen's Information Service, Office of the Secretary of the Commonwealth, State House, Boston, MA 02133

CONTENTS: Provides telephone information and referral agency assistance to the people of Massachusetts in need of state governmental assistance, thereby making the state government more accessible and understandable. Prepared by Citizen Information Service.

Other state agencies from which data can be obtained include: state comptroller's office, livestock inspector's office, state department of agriculture, department of industrial relations, state liquor authority, California Horse Racing Board, New York State Department of Education, state bureau of criminal identification, to mention but a selected few.

County and City Levels

On local proceedings, information can be gathered from the county government offices which provide data relative to business ownerships, land development, real estate parcels, sales of businesses, and other documented deeds and records. The following directory can be used to discover such information in one New York State county, but other counties throughout the United States can provide comparable editions.

Directory of Vital Statistics

SOURCE: Office of Nassau County Clerk, Nassau County Office Bldg., 240 Old Country Rd., Mineola, NY 11501

CONTENTS: Lists names of town registrars from whom can be obtained data pertaining to birth records, marriage certificates, and death certificates.

Additional data collected by county offices may include naturalization records, health certificates, civil files (for example, liens, damages, divorces, changes of name), probate index, criminal index, county auditor, county tax collector, surveyor, voter's registrar, coroner, public administrator.

Most county and state governments provide listings of services. In addition, the City of New York publishes a directory that identifies every service available to persons in that city. Such publications may be found in other jurisdictions and are available for nominal fees.

The City of New York Official Directory (The "Green Book")

SOURCE: Department of General Services, 52 Chambers St., New York, NY 10010

CONTENTS: City, state, and federal agencies within the City of New York (addresses, telephone numbers, and names of administrators included) and application locations for permits, licenses, and certificates.

The following information is also available from city agencies: maps of real property (city assessor's office); names and addresses of taxpayers (tax collector's office); construction permits, blueprints, and diagrams showing construction details (building inspector's office); birth and death certificates and information on communicable diseases (health department); documents relative to welfare clients, which, in most cases, require a subpoena order of court (welfare department).

Information gathered at a courthouse usually is of public record and is therefore available for examination by the general public. Locating the necessary facts, however, can be confusing, tricky, and time-consuming for the neophyte; and court clerks, therefore, can prove useful friends in the retrieval of court documents because their methods for locating data often cut through the maze of bureaucracy. Other employees also can retrieve such data easily. In either case, however, developing personal relationships with such individuals, which encourage their willingness to be of assistance, will help the investigator's cause immeasurably.

Private Level

Gathering information from the private sector can prove vital to any investigation. Many private directories list corporations that belong to associations, trade groups, and manufacturer's affiliates. Offered for research and data collection, these directories include:

City Directory

SOURCE: R. L. Polk Co., 6400 Monroe Blvd., Box 500, Taylor, MI 48180

CONTENTS: An alphabetical sheet directory lists complete address, apartment number, zip code, telephone number (including possible pay phones), locations under construction, apartment buildings and occupants, widow or divorcee, business operated out of home, office building, showroom, vacancy, nature of business, branch of business firm, renter without telephone, nearest telephone. A resident directory lists householders alphabetically and lists correct full name, occupation and employer, street address and apartment number, student 18 years of age or older, out-of-town resident employed in areas, armed forces member and branch of service, wife's name, corporations designating offices and nature of business, homeowner, retiree, business partnership, husband and wife employed, unmarried and/or unemployed resident, church and name of pastor. Additional directories include numerical telephone and classified business.

Cole's Directory

SOURCE: Cole's Publication, 550 Old Country Road, Hicksville, NY 11801

CONTENTS: *Street Address Directory* lists name of telephone subscriber at each street address, including street location and zip code; *Numerical Telephone Directory* lists name of each telephone subscriber according to telephone number, new business listings, new residential listings; *Office Building Directory* includes names, titles, occupations of tenants in each office building; *City and Newcomer Guide* gives new listings on each street; *Family Income and Buyer Power Guide* lists average wealth ratings on each street; *Census Tract Marketing Guide* is comprised of maps of the entire area, including street guides; *Zip Code Marketing Guide* indicates zip codes for entire area; *Demographic Section* designates trade areas by median age, persons per household, and percentage of owner-occupied households.

Guide to American Directories

SOURCE: B. Klein Publications, Rye, NY

CONTENTS: Guide to major directories of the United States and encompassing all industrial, professional, and mercantile categories.

Assorted Publications

SOURCE: ASLIB Publications, 3 Belgrave Square, London, S.W. IX 8 PL

CONTENTS: Various catalogs, including a European user series, data bases in Europe, information on economics, and user education.

In addition to the above samples of private sector directories, information can be gathered from insurance reporting services, which provide data from agencies in business with or subsidized by insurance companies or underwriters, National Auto Theft Bureau, telephone and mail services, funeral directors, laundry and dry cleaners, jewelers, shipping companies, and employers' personal records.

Depending on the nature of the investigation and the ingenuity of the inquirer, the following sources will be of varying usefulness: doctors, accountants, clergy, hospitals, newspapers, school records, housing projects, street photographers, blueprint and photostat makers, rental and real estate agencies, better business bureaus, and the local chamber of commerce.

Vital information can also be gathered from credit reporting agencies, but it must be noted that under the Fair Credit Reporting Act a court-ordered subpoena must be obtained before distributing the facts. In the state of New York, under this system the reporting agency must inform the creditor of the request within 30 days. A request for extension of this notification can come from the issuing court, but a limit of 60 days is the maximum.

USE OF INFORMATION SOURCES

Basic know-how for gathering data from the foregoing supportive directories and centers can save many hours of investigative time. For approaching a research project, a simple guideline list such as the following is suggested:

- Know the specific topic.

- Use library facilities: card catalogs, federal depository libraries, public affairs information services, and public document indexes.
- Thoroughly research the subject.
- Request assistance from public officials, librarians, and private sources.
- Use private directories (such as *Polk's Directory*) as a cross-reference and/or information index.
- Use government directories, corporate surveys, censuses, and polls.

In every case, effort must be made to establish sources before they are needed. Therefore, the investigator must explore local sources and at the same time strive to develop county, state, federal, and international information banks. By maintaining lists, according to types of data, of available records, directories, public officials, and business personnel that may be of assistance, the researcher can save valuable time during future investigations.

Not only must investigators proceed centrifugally—from within the locality to the international—and with previously prepared sources, but they must also maintain sensitivity to the obvious. Particularly with regard to the enforcement of rules and regulations, the close relationship that exists between law enforcement personnel and city offices may tend to dull the investigator's awareness, which, in turn, can cause an oversight or disregard for vital information. In many instances, the investigator could locate facts in the local courthouse or city hall records, but may fail to look there—due to either oversight or an assumption of simple answers.

The utilities that serve our citizens offer another general information base. Often, however, it is more feasible for a liaison officer rather than an investigator to contact these corporations. This creates less interference with the business's operations, the liaison officer can relay any requested data back to the inquirer, and the use of a telephone company's security department can alleviate confusion and speed up inquiry.

Many sources of information are located in various types of business establishments which maintain ongoing files as their stock-in-trade.

Licensing and regulatory activities are fertile fields for data searches. Government documents and publications offer a wealth of information that can provide the investigator with personal facts, including photographs, a subject's professional background, and past and present employment—information that can lead to other sources. Because they perform primary functions such as licensing and regulatory actions, state agencies should be checked first.

It should be noted that some federal sources of information are not open to state or local law enforcement officials because of legal restrictions; if, however, the investigated subject is taxed, regulated, or licensed by the federal government, then it may be possible to gather such information by legal process. The *Congressional Directory* may also furnish data relative to the proper taxing or regulating authority.

In essence, access to information services is limited only by the investigator's ingenuity in bypassing bureaucracy through personal contacts and the Privacy and Information Acts. Of prime importance to the investigator is the maintenance of a 3 × 5-inch index card system or computerized file under the following headings: (a) type of available information, (b) name and address of organization or record, and (c) name of individual able to supply the requested data. Very important also is familiarity with the *Freedom of Information Act* and the *Privacy Act* (reprinted in part at the end of this chapter) to avoid illegalities and expand investigative efforts.

BUREAUCRATIC BYPASSING

The capability of moving smoothly through the maze of bureaucracy is essential to any investigative procedure; and to do so the investigator must develop a method of gathering data from agencies and corporations that is quick, precise, and productive. In other words, the investigator must be able to manipulate and slip through "the system" with little disruption.

Methods of bureaucratic bypassing must be formulated within the guidelines and limits of constitutional and legal statutes. Therefore, when these procedures are to be used, the investigator in the public sector must consider the legal limits of search and seizure. Furthermore, bypassers must develop individual methods of operation—methods that suit their personalities and capabilities. The same particular processes may not prove useful to all individuals.

There are, of course, various methods of bypassing. When combating the criminal, for example, methods of gathering data can divert from the basic investigative steps. Common methods used to cut through the formal procedure include deception, false stories, and sometimes misrepresentation. The following points should be considered:

- Deception can be used but must remain within the limits of the law.
- The ultimate goal is to gather facts to further the investigation.
- Personal gain should not result from the methods employed.
- Testimony during legal proceedings (when asked) must reveal any methods used during the course of the inquiry.

Since defense attorneys will attempt to present the bypasser as a liar who has possibly violated legal controls, when bypassing is used, all facts should be noted and documented for future legal proceedings. Such documentation offers protection from accusations without suspicion created by the adversary.

To be used effectively, the bypass process must be related with the necessary gathering of facts. In other words, casual acquaintances, friendships, and familiar associations provide an avenue essential to the bypass system. For gathering information, associations must be maintained over periods of weeks, months, and even years, for these associations will provide a necessary shortcut through the maze of formal procedures normally required.

When gathering data from outside the network of associates, the bypasser must attempt the direct approach first. The smile of persuasion and a presentation of the needed facts often helps to enlist the support and cooperation of others. Although this approach generally works, from time to time it does fail. Should this occur, the experienced investigator does not resort to anger or become excited but merely looks for other avenues of information. A polite withdrawal will provide time for decisions and alternatives. A request to converse with the immediate supervisor may prevent the investigator from leaving empty-handed.

In many instances, the inquirer encounters civil servants who feel it is their duty to wield power and to follow procedures with extreme meticulousness. Offering compassion, friendship, and interest in the bureaucrat's problems often breaks the ice; and basic psychological understanding assists the bypasser who is confronted with stubbornness. Warmth and concern for the individual's professional problems usually lead to a relationship that can be utilized in the future.

In gaining information, social acquaintances, dinner dates, and sometimes even flirtation become necessary tools. From time to time, the investigator must cultivate associations through social relationships, because they can lead to willing cooperation by others. Such meetings can also offer solutions to the problems of those giving information as well as of the inquirer. First and foremost, personal feelings must not interfere with obtaining desired data. Rules must be set forth at dinner dates so that emotional relationships will not develop during the course of the inquiry.

To cite a specific instance, a female receptionist was cultivated to supply data outside of formal procedures, and during the investigation she supplied confidential information concerning corporate meetings—information which was conveyed over coffee and at lunch breaks. Although a personal relationship was initiated, it remained professional, never became intimate, and both parties understood the roles they were playing.

The telephone bypass can be used effectively to gather details and can save many hours of travel, time, and research.

When seeking information by telephone, the investigator must present a positive personality. Bypassers should identify themselves in clear, strong voices, and, at times, exaggeration of their positions or rank can be used to advantage. They must then indicate the offices with which they are associated and request the desired data.

In many instances, the telephone short-cut makes it possible to obtain the necessary facts without ever having to leave one's desk. Many telephone contacts require a telephone call-back number. If a call-back is necessary, the investigator must answer confidently and then immediately begin to ask the necessary questions.

From time to time, false identity must be used to gather facts by telephone. There are no legal restrictions on deception so long as it does not violate the statutes of search and seizure. Ethical questions may be raised at legal proceedings, however, in an effort to discredit the investigator.

Written communications are usually time-consuming and provide limited contact with the source. In a lengthy investigation, a letter can be used as an introduction. In most cases, the letter is discarded unless an emergency is implied—usually by a sharp, urgent opening sentence. The importance of the matter and a request for assistance must also be stated clearly and precisely.

After the letter has been sent, a telephone conversation with the proper authority follows, with a reminder of the matter's urgency.

It should be kept in mind that bypassers are successful only if their approach works! Furthermore, attempts at bypassing agencies, corporations, and even one's own municipal administration will lead to questions, comments, and, at times, verbal abuse from coworkers. Bypassing must be formulated to increase productivity and to rid the investigator of many unnecessary administrative policies—policies created over years of accumulated bureaucratic red tape. The successful bypasser is the innovative investigator.

THE FREEDOM OF INFORMATION ACT (FOIA) AND THE PRIVACY ACT

The following information has been obtained from Union Calendar No. 412, House Report No. 95-793, 95th Congress, 1st Session. The U.S. Government Printing Office, Stock No. 052-071-00540-4/Catalog No. X95-1: H. RP. 793.

WHICH ACT TO USE

Investigators who are interested in obtaining documents concerning the general activities of government should make their requests under the *FOIA*. If, on the other hand, individuals are seeking access to government records pertaining solely to themselves, they should make requests under the *Privacy Act*.

Congress intended that the two acts be considered together in processing requests for information. And indeed, many government agencies handle requests under both acts out of the same office. Nevertheless, it is still a good idea to make requests in a way that guarantees the fullest possible disclosure. Therefore, if after reading this guide on how to use the two acts and noting the exemptions from disclosure which both contain, investigators are uncertain which of the acts will afford the best results, they would be wise to make their requests under both the *FOIA* and the *Privacy Act*.

HOW TO REQUEST
GOVERNMENT DOCUMENTS

Information Available Under the *FOIA*

The *FOIA* applies only to documents held by the administrative agencies of the executive branch of the federal government. It does not apply to information maintained by the legislative and judicial branches. The executive branch includes executive departments and offices, military departments, government corporations, government-controlled corporations, and independent regulatory agencies. All records in possession of these entities must be released upon request unless the information falls within one of the nine specific and narrowly drawn categories.[1]

Among other things, the act grants public access to final opinions and orders of agencies, policy statements and interpretations not published in the *Federal Register*,[2] administrative staff manuals, and government records that affect the public. Presidential papers have not been considered government records and have therefore not been required to be disclosed under the act.

There are many government documents that may be of interest to the investigator. For example:

- Reports compiled by the Department of Health and Human Services concerning conditions in federally supported nursing homes.

- Data collected by the Agriculture Department regarding the purity and quality of meat and poultry products and the harmful effects of pesticides.

- Records of regulatory agencies concerning such matters as air-pollution-control programs, the adverse effects of television violence, and the safety records of airlines.

- Test results maintained by departments and agencies concerning the nutritional content of processed foods, the efficacy of drugs, and the safety and efficiency of all makes of automobiles.

- Consumer complaints registered with the Federal Trade Commission regarding interstate moving companies, corporate marketing practices, and faulty products.

All this and more is available under the *FOIA*. The *FOIA* does not obligate federal agencies to do research for investigators. For example, an agency cannot be expected to analyze documents or to collect information it does not have. However, if the information is on record—a document, a tape recording, a computer printout—the act can help the investigator get it.

The only information that may be withheld under the act is that which falls within nine designated categories. These exemptions from disclosure are discussed under the section entitled "Reasons Why Access May Be Denied."

Locating Records

To obtain information, one should first determine which agency is most likely to have it. The *United States Government Manual* lists all federal agencies and describes their functions. In addition, it usually lists their local and regional office addresses and telephone numbers. The *Manual* can be found in most libraries and can be purchased for $23.00 by writing to the Superintendent of Documents, U.S. Government Printing Office, Washington D.C. 20402. The *Congressional Directory* can also be useful since, like the *Manual*, it lists the administrators of the various agencies. This, too, is available in most public libraries and can be purchased from the Government Printing office for $27.00.

Investigators who are unable to obtain copies of the *Manual* and are unsure of the location of records needed should write to the agency they think is most likely to have them. In most cases, if an agency doesn't have a record, it will forward the letter to the appropriate source or suggest whom to write to.

If there is reason to believe that a local or field office of a federal agency has the information being sought, it may also be helpful to contact that office. Most states have local federal offices, which are listed in the telephone books of the major cities. Or the regional federal telephone books listing the agencies operating in each area, along with the names and titles of the policy-level employees, can be used. These books can usually be obtained at cost from the regional offices.

Making a Request

When the investigator has accumulated as much information about the desired record as is conveniently available, a letter should be directed to the head of the agency, whose address can be found in the *Government Manual*, the *Congressional Directory*, or in the list provided in this *Handbook*. Or one can write to the *FOIA* officer of the agency. However, if telephone calls have uncovered the official directly responsible for the record needed, that official should be written to. In any event, it is always a good idea to write "Freedom of Information Request" on the bottom left-hand corner of the envelope.

The records wanted should be identified as accurately as possible. Although it is not required under the *FOIA* that a document be specified by name or title, requests must "reasonably describe" the information sought.[3] The more specific and limited the request, the greater the likelihood that it will be processed expeditiously. This could also result in savings in the cost of searching fees. (See section on fees.)

One of the principal differences between the *FOIA* and previous laws is that the individual seeking information is not required to demonstrate a need or even a reason for wanting it. But, in some instances, the probability of getting the desired information may be enhanced by explaining the reasons for requesting it. Agency officials have the discretionary power to release files even when the law does not require it, and they may be more inclined to disclose information that could be withheld if they understand the uses to which it is to be put.

Fees. The House-Senate conference report on the 1974 amendments to the *FOIA* made it clear that Congress intended that "fees should not be used for the purpose of discouraging requests for information or as obstacles to disclosure of requested information."

Pursuant to the act, each agency is required to publish a uniform schedule of fees covering all the divisions of the agency. These fees may not exceed the actual costs of searching for and copying the requested documents. Moreover, agencies cannot charge for reviewing documents to determine whether all or portions of them should be withheld. Searching fees run around $5 an hour. The average charge for copying is 10 cents a page for standard size copies of 8 × 11 inches and 8 × 14 inches. Many agencies do not charge anything when the aggregate cost is less than $3 or $4.

It may be possible to obtain a waiver or reduction of the fees by stating the reasons for requesting the information, since the act provides that agencies can waive or reduce fees when "furnishing the information can be considered as primarily benefiting the general public." They also have the option of disregarding charges for indigent requesters. Another way to save money on reproduction expenses is to ask to see the documents at the agency rather than having copies made. Most agencies will be glad to make the necessary arrangements for this.

Sample Request Letter. The following general form is suggested:

Agency Head or *FOIA* Officer
Title
Name of Agency
Address of Agency
City, State, ZIP

Re: *Freedom of Information Act* Request
Dear_____:

Under the provisions of the *Freedom of Information Act*, 5 U.S.C. 552, I am requesting access to (identify the records as clearly and specifically as possible).

If there are any fees for searching for or copying the records I have requested, please inform me before you fill the request. (Or:…please supply the records without informing me if the fees do not exceed $_____.)

[Optional] I am requesting this information (state the reason for your request if you think it will assist in obtaining the information).

[Optional] As you know, the act permits you to reduce or waive fees when the release of the information is considered as "primarily benefiting the public." I believe that this request fits that category, and I therefore ask that you waive any fees.

If all or any part of this request is denied, please cite the specific exemption(s) which you think justifies your refusal to release the information, and inform me of the appeal procedures available to me under the law.

I would appreciate your handling this request as quickly as possible, and I look forward to hearing from you within 10 days, as the law stipulates.

Sincerely,
Signature
Name
Address
City, State, ZIP

Requirements for Agency Responses

Federal agencies are required to respond to all requests for information within 10 working days (excluding Saturdays, Sundays, and holidays) after receipt of the request. If the material is needed quickly, a letter can be sent by certified mail and a return receipt requested so the sender will know when the 10 days have run out. If a reply has not been received by the end of that time (allowing for the return mail), a follow-up letter can be written or the agency telephoned to inquire about the delay.

If an agency runs into difficulty in meeting the 10-day time requirement due to "unusual circumstances,"[4] it must inform the requester in writing that an extension—not to exceed 10 more working days—will be required. Moreover, should the request be denied, the agency must give the reasons for the denial and advise whom to appeal to within the agency. It must also give the names and addresses of those responsible for denying the request.

In most cases, agencies will do their best to respond within the designated time periods. However, they sometimes fail to meet the 10-day guidelines due to substantial backlogs of requests. While it is the investigators' right to contest this in court, they should also realize that the government's failure to comply with the prescribed time limits may not of itself constitute a basis for the release of the records.[5]

Reasons Why Access May Be Denied

Government agencies can refuse to disclose information if it falls within one of nine specified categories. However, the legislative history of the act makes it clear that Congress did not intend for agencies to use these exempt categories to justify the automatic withholding of information. Rather, the exemptions are intended to designate those areas in which, under certain circumstances, information may be withheld. It would be a good idea for investigators to familiarize themselves with these general exemptions before making requests so they will know in advance what sort of documents may not be available. It will also help them to understand the reasons agencies give for refusing to release information. The exemptions are usually referred to as (b)(1), (b)(2), and so on, in accordance with their designations in the act.

Exemption (b)(1): Classified Documents Concerning National Defense and Foreign Policy. Exemption (b)(1) relates to documents that are "(A) specifically authorized under criteria established by an Executive order to be kept secret in the interest of national defense or foreign policy and (B) are in fact properly classified pursuant to such Executive order."

This refers to information that is properly classified "Confidential," "Secret," and "Top Secret" under the terms and procedures of the Presidential order establishing the classification system.

The fact that the document requested is classified does not mean, in and of itself, that it will be withheld. Upon receipt of a request, the agency concerned will determine whether the document should continue to be classified. If not, it will be declassified before being released. If the agency decides that the classification should be continued, it will notify the requester accordingly.

The 1974 amendments to the act made it clear that when *FOIA* requests for classified documents are taken to court, the judge has a duty to determine whether such documents are properly classified. Judges are now authorized to examine the documents in question and make their own independent determination as to whether the claims of national security are justified. The mere fact that information is classified will not automatically exempt it from disclosure. The burden is on the government to convince the court that a document is correctly classified and should be withheld.

While this new procedure involves the courts as well as the executive branch in the classification process, it should be pointed out that in most instances the courts have been reluctant to change the classifications imposed by the government.

Exemption (b)(2): Internal Personnel Rules and Practices. Exemption (b)(2) covers matters "related solely to the internal personnel rules and practices of an agency."

For the most part, this exemption has been limited by the courts to mean information such as agency rules concerning the employees' use of parking facilities or the management of cafeterias and internal policies with regard to sick leave, vacations, and the like.

The Supreme Court's ruling in *Rose v. Department of the Air Force*[6] illustrates how the majority of the courts have construed this provision. In that case, an individual sought access to case summaries of Air Force Academy disciplinary proceedings against cadets. The Court held that the information should be released since it did not relate "solely to the internal personnel rules and practices" of the Academy. In the Court's view, information about the treatment of cadets, whose education is publicly financed and who furnish a good portion of the country's future military leadership, had "substantial" potential for public interest outside the government.

Therefore, if documents affect interests outside the agency or deal with practices and procedures that are not strictly internal, they must be released.

Exemption (b)(3): Information Exempt under Other Laws. Exemption (b)(3) protects information "specifically exempted from disclosure by statute (other than section 552b of this title), provided that such statute (*A*) requires that the matters be withheld from the public in such a manner as to leave no discretion on the issue, or (*B*) establishes particular criteria for withholding or refers to particular types of matters to be withheld."

This exemption permits the government to withhold information where other laws clearly require that it be withheld.

The original provision that covered information "specifically exempted from disclosure by statute" was amended in 1976 by language added to the government in the *Sunshine Act* (552b of the *Administrative Procedure Act* as noted above). The 1976 amendment was enacted due to congressional dissatisfaction with the expansive judicial interpretation given to the word "specifically" by the Supreme Court in *FAA v. Robertson*.[7] In that case, the Court ruled that according to the *Federal Aviation Act of 1958*, the FAA Administrator was permitted to withhold certain information unless disclosure was required "in the interest of the public." The 1976 amendment narrowed this exemption by specifying that it be used to withhold from the public only information required to be withheld by a law containing specific criteria for withholding or designating particular types of information to be withheld.

Examples of the types of information that could be withheld under this exemption include patent applications, income tax returns, and records regarding nuclear testing.

Exemption (b)(4): Confidential Business Information. Exemption (b)(4) protects from disclosure "trade secrets, and commercial or financial information obtained from a person and privileged and confidential."

This exemption pertains to information concerning trade secrets and confidential commercial or financial data. The judicial consensus is that it does not apply to general information obtained by the government with the understanding that it will be held in confidence.

Trade secrets data pertains to such things as processes, formulas, manufacturing plans, and chemical compositions.

Commercial and financial information includes corporate sales data, salaries and bonuses of industry personnel, and bids received by corporations in the course of their acquisitions. However, commercial and financial information other than trade secrets can be withheld from disclosure only if it meets certain criteria: It must be privileged and confidential and it must be obtained from a "person" by the government.

The courts have defined "confidential" information as information which if disclosed would be likely to (1) impair the government's ability to obtain similar information in the future or (2) harm the competitive position of the person who supplied it.

Information obtained from a "person" includes data supplied by corporations and partnerships as well as by individual citizens. It does not apply to records generated by the government such as government-prepared documents based on government information.

There have been a number of instances in which corporations that have submitted information to the departments and agencies have later appealed to the courts to issue injunctions against its disclosure to others. These are referred to as "reverse" *FOIA* cases.

Exemption (b)(5): Internal Communications. Exemption (b)(5) applies to "inter-agency or intra-agency memorandums or letters which would not be available by law to a party other than an agency in litigation with the agency."

This exemption was enacted to safeguard the deliberative policy-making processes of government. Congress was concerned that staff assistants and agency personnel might be reluctant to engage in a free exchange of ideas if they knew that all their communications were subject to public disclosure. However, the Supreme Court has drawn a distinction between agency communications prior to the rendering of a decision and communications concerning a decision once it has been made. Memorandums and letters that reflect predecisional attitudes regarding policy alternatives are not required to be disclosed, but communications that relate to decisions already made must be released. In the Court's view, once a policy is adopted, the public has a right to know the basis for that decision.

The Court has also distinguished between purely factual information and information relating to policy making. Factual information must always be disclosed unless it is (1) inextricably intertwined with information concerning a decision-making process or is (2) part of a summary of material of an otherwise public record to be used in the agency's deliberative process.

Exemption (b)(6): Protection of Privacy. Exemption (b)(6) covers "personnel and medical files and similar files, the disclosure of which would constitute a clearly unwarranted invasion of personal privacy."

This exemption relates to records that contain details about the private lives of individuals. It is the only exemption that allows a balancing of interests between disclosure and nondisclosure. The public's right to know must be weighed against the individual's right to privacy. Therefore, when requesting information of a personal nature, it is always a good idea to give a brief explanation of why it is needed unless, of course, it pertains to the requester.

In attempting to determine what constitutes a "clearly unwarranted invasion of personal privacy," the courts have taken two separate approaches. In some cases, they have balanced the potential severity of the privacy invasion against the general public interest to be served. In others, they have considered the intrusion in relation to the needs and interests of the requester.

Exemption (b)(7): Investigatory Files. Exemption (b)(7) exempts from disclosure

investigatory records compiled for law enforcement purposes, but only to the extent that the production of such records would (A) interfere with enforcement proceedings, (B) deprive a person of a right to a fair trial or an impartial adjudication, (C) constitute an unwarranted invasion of personal privacy, (D) disclose the identity of a confidential source and, in the case of a record compiled by a criminal law enforcement authority in the course of a criminal investigation, or by an agency conducting a lawful national security intelligence investigation, confidential information furnished only by the confidential source, (E) disclose investigative techniques and procedures, or (F) endanger the life or physical safety of law enforcement personnel.

The original provision concerning investigatory files was interpreted by the courts to include almost any file which would be labeled "investigatory" in nature. However, the 1974 amendments to the act narrowed the exemption by providing that investigatory records could be withheld only if their release would result in one or more of six specific harms (listed above). The amendments also changed the language of the provision to cover investigatory "records" rather than investigatory "files." The fact that a particular record is an investigatory file does not mean that it is automatically exempt. Each document or part of each document in the file must now be examined to determine whether its disclosure would result in one or more of the six enumerated harms. Moreover, those portions that do not fall within any of these categories must be released.

Exemption (b)(8): Information Concerning Financial Institutions. Exemption (b)(8) exempts from disclosure requirement matters "contained in or related to examination, operating, or condition reports prepared by, on behalf of, or for the use of, an agency responsible for the regulation or supervision of financial institutions."

This includes, for example, investigatory reports of the Federal Reserve Board concerning federal banks, documents prepared by the Securities and Exchange

Commission regarding the New York Stock Exchange, and other similar information.

Exemption (b)(9): Information Concerning Wells. Exemption (b)(9) exempts from disclosure "geological and geophysical information and data, including maps concerning wells."

This was added as a specific exemption because at the time of the act's passage, it was unclear whether this type of information was covered by the trade-secret provision of the act.

Appeal Procedure

If a request for information is denied, a letter of appeal should be sent to the person or office specified in the agency's reply. If for some reason this information is not provided, an appeal should be filed with the head of the agency. A copy of the rejection letter should be included, along with a copy of the original request, and as strong a case as possible made for the right of the requester to know. It is important to clarify the request if the denial indicates some confusion on the part of the agency about what is being sought.

Although it is not necessary, it will strengthen the appeal if court rulings are cited concerning why the agency's use of a particular exemption to withhold information is inappropriate. Depending on the urgency of the need for the information, a lawyer might be consulted to help with this. Furthermore, since the chances of getting the desired information are sometimes enhanced by explaining the reasons for wanting it, the investigator should consider doing this, especially if it was not done in the initial request. If it is planned to pursue the matter in court in the event an appeal is denied, this information might also be included in the letter.

Most agency regulations require that appeals be made within 30 days after notification that a request has been denied. The agency is required to respond to an appeal within 20 working days after receiving it. However, if the initial request was answered within the 10-day period, an extension of up to 10 working days may be granted.

If the agency denies an appeal in whole or in part, it must inform the requester of the right to seek judicial review. If after 20 working days from the time of the agency's receipt of the appeal, a reply has not been received, the case may be taken to court.

Sample Appeal Letter

> Name of Agency Official
> Title
> Name of Agency
> Address of Agency
> City, State, ZIP
>
> Re: *Freedom of Information Act* Appeal
>
> Dear_____:
> This is to appeal the denial of my request for information pursuant to the *Freedom of Information Act*, 5 U.S. 552.

On_____ (date), I received a letter from_____ (individual's name) of your agency denying my request for access to...(description of the information sought). I am enclosing a copy of this denial along with a copy of my original request. I trust that upon examination of these communications you will conclude that the information I am seeking should be disclosed.

As provided for in the Act, I will expect to receive a reply within 20 working days.

[Optional] If you decide not to release the requested information, I plan to take this matter to court.

Sincerely,
Signature
Name
Address
City, State, ZIP

Taking Your Case to Court

If the appeal is rejected and the requester is willing to invest some time and money to get the information, the case can be taken to court. A suit can be filed in the U.S. district court in the district where the requester lives or does business or where the agency records are kept. Or the case can be taken to the U.S. District Court for the District of Columbia.

If the investigator has a strong case, there is a good possibility that the decision to seek judicial review will itself produce results. Unless the agency withholding the information has a well-founded reason for doing so, it may decide to release it rather than go to court. Under a directive issued by the Attorney General in May of 1977, the burden is on the federal agencies to convince the Justice Department that they will win *FOIA* suits before the Department will take their cases.

Plaintiffs under the *FOIA* go into court with the presumption that right is on their side: the burden of proof is on the government to justify withholding information. Whenever there is a doubt about which side is right, the courts are supposed to rule in favor of disclosure. Moreover, pursuant to the 1974 amendments to the act, judges are authorized to examine the contents of contested documents to determine whether all or any part of them can be withheld. The law requires that "reasonably segregable portions" of the exempt records be released: This means nonexempt portions that are intelligible.

The courts are supposed to expedite *FOIA* cases and, whenever possible, consider them ahead of other matters. The act also specifies that court costs and attorney fees be awarded if the plaintiff has "substantially prevailed." In other words, if it is clear that the information should have been released to the plaintiff in the beginning, the government may be required to pay the court costs and attorney's fee. In addition, if the judge finds that agency officials have acted "arbitrarily and capriciously" in withholding information, the Civil Service Commission may initiate proceedings to determine whether disciplinary action is warranted.

An investigator who decides to go to court should consult a lawyer. It would be preferable to find one who has had some experience in federal practice. If private counsel is too expensive, the local legal aid society should be contacted.

HOW TO REQUEST PERSONAL RECORDS

Information Available Under the *Privacy Act*

The *Privacy Act* applies only to personal records maintained by the executive branch of the federal government concerning individual citizens. It does not apply to records held by state and local governments or private organizations. The federal agencies covered by the act include executive departments and offices, military departments, government corporations, government-controlled corporations, and independent regulatory agencies. Subject to specified exceptions, files that are part of a system of records held by these agencies must be made available to the individual subject of the record upon request.[8] A system of records as defined by the *Privacy Act* is a group of records from which information is retrieved by reference to a name or other personal identifier such as a social security number.

The federal government is a vast storehouse of information concerning individual citizens. For example:

- The federal government has a file on anyone who has worked for a federal agency or government contractor or been a member of any branch of the armed services.

- Some agency probably has a record of anyone who has participated in any federally financed project.

- The FBI maintains a record of the arrest of anyone arrested by local, state, or federal authorities whose fingerprints were taken.[9]

- The Department of Agriculture is likely to have information about anyone who has applied for a government farm subsidy.

- The Veteran's Administration has a file on anyone who has received veterans' benefits, such as mortgage or education loans, employment opportunities, or medical services.

- The Department of Health and Human Services has recorded information about anyone who has applied for or received a student loan or grant certified by the government.

- There is a good chance that the Department of Defense has a record of anyone who has applied for or been investigated for a security clearance for any reason.

- The Department of Health and Human Services has a file on anyone who has received medicare or social security benefits.

In addition, federal files on individuals includes such items as:

- Investigatory reports on the Federal Communications Commission concerning whether individuals holding citizens band and/or amateur radio licenses are violating operating rules.

- Records of the Internal Revenue Service listing the names of individuals entitled to undeliverable refund checks.

- Records compiled by the State Department regarding the conduct of American citizens in foreign countries.

This is just a fraction of the information held on individual citizens. In fact, there is a good chance that some federal agency has a file on anyone who has ever engaged in any activity that might be of interest to the federal government.

The only information that may be withheld under the act is that which falls within seven designated categories. These exemptions are discussed under the section entitled "Reasons Why Access May Be Denied."

Locating Records

Persons who think that a particular agency maintains records concerning them should write to the head of that agency or to the *Privacy Act* officer. Agencies are required to inform persons who inquire whether they have files on them.

To make a more thorough search to determine what records other federal departments may have, the compilation of *Privacy Act* notices published annually by the *Federal Register* should be consulted. This multivolume work contains descriptions of all federal record systems: it describes the kinds of data covered by the systems and lists the categories of individuals to whom the information pertains. It also includes the procedures that different agencies follow in helping individuals who request information about their records, and it specifies the agency official to whom to write to find out whether one is the subject of a file.

The compilation is usually available in large reference, law, and university libraries. It can be purchased from the Superintendent of Documents, Government Printing Office, Washington, D.C. 20402. The cost per volume runs from $6 to $12. If one is interested in specific agencies, the Superintendent of Documents can help to identify the particular volume or volumes containing the information wanted. However, this word of caution: At the present time, the compilation is poorly indexed and, as a consequence, difficult to use. Therefore, the work should be examined before being ordered.

While it may be helpful to agency officials if a particular record system which is believed to contain information about a person is specified, it is not necessary to provide this information. Individuals who have a general idea of the records they want should not hesitate to write the agencies which they think maintain these records.

Making a Request

A request can be made in writing, by telephone, or in person. One advantage to writing is that it allows documenting the date and contents of the request and the agency's replies. This could be helpful in the event of future disputes. Copies of all correspondence concerning the request should be kept.

The request should be addressed to the head of the agency that maintains the records wanted or to the agency official specified in the compilation of *Privacy Act* notices. (See section on "Locating Records.") "*Privacy Act* Request" should be written on the bottom left-hand corner of the envelope. Along with the requester's name and permanent address, as much information as possible should always be given about the record being sought.[10] The more specific the inquiry, the faster can a response be expected. If access is wanted to a record concerning one's application for a government loan, for example, the date of the application, the place where the application was filed, the specific use to which the loan was put, and any relevant identifying numbers should be given. Of course, if the *Federal Register*'s compilation of notices has been used to identify a particular record system that might contain the desired information, that system should be cited.

Most agencies require some proof of identity before they will release records. Therefore, when making a request, it is a good idea to provide some identifying data, such as a copy of an official document containing the requester's complete name and address. The request should be signed, since a signature provides a form of identification. It might also help to have the signature notarized. In seeking access to a record that has something to do with a government benefit, it could be helpful to give one's social security number. Some agencies may request additional information such as a document containing a signature and/or photograph, depending on the nature and sensitivity of the material to be released.

Anyone who "knowingly and willfully" requests or receives access to a record about an individual "under false pretenses" is subject to criminal penalties. This means that a person can be prosecuted for deliberately attempting to obtain someone else's record.

Fees. Under the *Privacy Act*, agencies are permitted to charge fees to cover the actual costs of copying records. However, they are not allowed to charge for the time spent in locating records or in preparing them for your inspection. Copying fees are about 10 cents a page for standard size copies of 8 × 14 inches.

As mentioned above, fees for locating files *can* be charged for requests processed under the *Freedom of Information Act*. Therefore, if access is sought to records under the *Privacy Act* which can be withheld under that act but are available under the *FOIA*, searching fees could be charged. However, as noted elsewhere in this guide, the legislative histories of both the *FOIA* and the *Privacy Act* clearly indicate that Congress intended that access to records not be obstructed by costs. Consequently, if an agency's fees are beyond one's means, a reduction or waiver of the charges should be asked for when the request is made.

Sample Request Letter

Agency Head or *Privacy Act* Officer
Title
Agency
Address of Agency
City, State, ZIP

Re: *Privacy Act* Request

Dear_____:
Under the provisions of the *Privacy Act of 1974*, 5 U.S.C. 552a, I hereby request a copy of (or: access to) (describe as accurately and specifically as possible the record or records wanted, and provide all the relevant information you have concerning them).

If there are any fees for copying the records I am requesting, please inform me before you fill the request. (Or:...please supply the records without informing me, if the fees do not exceed $_____.)

If all or any part of this request is denied, please cite the specific exemption(s) which you think justifies your refusal to release the information. Also, please inform me of your agency's appeal procedure.

In order to expedite consideration of my request, I am enclosing a copy of (some document of identification).

Thank you for your prompt attention to this matter.

Sincerely,
Signature
Name
Address
City, State, ZIP

Requirements for Agency Responses

Unlike the *Freedom of Information Act,* which requires agencies to respond within 10 working days after receipt of a request, the *Privacy Act* imposes no time limits for agency responses. However, the guidelines for implementing the act's provisions recommended by the executive branch state that a request for records should be acknowledged within 10 working days of its receipt. Moreover, the acknowledgment should indicate whether or not access will be granted and, if so, when and where. The records themselves should be produced within 30 working days. And if this is not possible, the agency should state the reason and advise the requester when it is anticipated that access will be granted.

Most agencies will do their best to comply with these recommendations. Therefore, it is probably advisable to bear with some reasonable delay before taking further action.

Disclosure of Records

Agencies are required to release records in a form that is "comprehensible." This means that all computer codes and unintelligible notes must be translated into understandable language.

Individuals can examine their records in person or have copies mailed to them, whichever they prefer. If they want to see the records at the agency and for some reason the agency is unable to provide for this, they cannot be charged copying fees if the records are later mailed.

Individuals who view the records in person are entitled to take someone along with them. If this is done, the viewer will probably be asked to sign a statement authorizing the agency to disclose and discuss the record in the other person's presence.

Special rules apply to the release of medical records. In most cases, when persons request to see their own medical records, they are permitted to view the records directly. However, if it appears that the information contained in such a record could have an "adverse effect" on an individual, the agency may give it to someone of that person's choice, such as a family doctor, who would be willing to review its contents and discuss them with the subject.

Reasons Why Access May Be Denied

Under the *Privacy Act,* certain systems of records can be exempted from disclosure. Agencies are required to publish annually in the *Federal Register* the existence and characteristics of all record systems, including those that have been exempted from access. However, records declared exempt are not necessarily beyond reach, since agencies do not always use the exemptions they have claimed. Therefore, one should not hesitate to request any record desired. The burden is on the agency to justify withholding any information.

Individuals who intend to make requests should first familiarize themselves with these exemptions, so they will know in advance what kind of documents may not be available. It will also help them to understand the reasons agencies give for refusing to release information.

General Exemptions. The general exemptions apply only to the Central Intelligence Agency (CIA) and criminal law enforcement agencies. The records held by these agencies can be exempt from more provisions of the act than those maintained by other agencies. However, even the systems of these agencies are subject to many of the act's basic provisions: (1) the existence and characteristics of all record systems must be publicly reported; (2) subject to specified exceptions, no personal records can be disclosed to other agencies or persons without the prior consent of the individual to whom the record pertains; (3) all disclosures must be accurately accounted for; (4) records which are disclosed must be accurate, relevant, up to date, and complete; and (5) no records describing how an individual exercises his first amendment rights can be maintained unless such maintenance is authorized by statute or by the individual to whom it pertains or unless it is relevant to and within the scope of an authorized law enforcement activity.

General exemptions are referred to as (j)(1) and (j)(2) in accordance with their designations in the act.

Exemption (j)(1): Files Maintained by the CIA. Exemption (j)(1) covers records "maintained by the Central Intelligence Agency." This exemption permits the heads of the CIA to exclude certain systems of records within the agency from many of the act's requirements. The provisions from which the systems can be exempted are primarily those permitting individual access. Consequently, in most instances, individuals would not be allowed to inspect and correct records about themselves maintained by this agency. Congress permitted the exemption of these records from access because CIA files often contain highly sensitive information regarding national security. Nevertheless, it should always be borne in mind that agencies are not required to invoke all the exemptions allowed them. Therefore, individuals who really want to see records containing information about themselves that are maintained by this agency should go ahead and make requests.

Exemption (j)(2): Files Maintained by Federal Criminal Law Enforcement Agencies. Exemption (j)(2) covers records

maintained by an agency or component thereof which performs as its principal function any activity pertaining to the enforcement of criminal laws, including police efforts to prevent, control, or reduce crime or to apprehend criminals, and the activities of prosecutors, courts, correctional, probation, pardon, or parole authorities, and which consist of (A) information compiled for the purpose of identifying data and notations of arrests, the nature and disposition of criminal charges, sentencing, confinement, release, and parole and probation status; (B) information compiled for the purpose of a criminal investigation, including reports of informants and investigators, and associated with an identifiable individual; or (C) reports identifiable to an individual compiled at any stage of the process of enforcement of the criminal laws from arrest or indictment through release from supervision.

This exemption would permit the heads of criminal law enforcement agencies such as the FBI, the Drug Enforcement Administration, and the Immigration and Naturalization Service to exclude certain systems of records from many of the act's requirements. As with the CIA, the allowed exemptions are primarily those permitting individual access. However, many agencies do not always use the exemptions available to them. Remember, too, the act explicitly states that records available under the *FOIA* must also be available under the *Privacy Act*. And under the *FOIA*, the CIA and FBI and other federal agencies are required to release all nonexempt portions of their intelligence and investigatory files. Nevertheless, even though Congress intended that *Privacy Act* requests be coordinated with *FOIA* provisions, it is still a good idea to cite both of these acts when seeking information of an intelligence or investigatory nature.

Specific Exemptions. There are seven specific exemptions that apply to all agencies. Under specified circumstances, agency heads are permitted to exclude certain record systems from the access and challenge provisions of the act. However, even exempted systems are subject to many of the act's requirements. In addition to the provisions listed under "General Exemptions" (which apply to all record systems), a record system that falls under any one of the seven specific exemptions (listed below) is subject to the following requirements: (1) information that might be used to deny a person a right, benefit, or privilege must, whenever possible, be collected directly from the individual; (2) individuals asked to supply information must be informed of the authority for collecting it, the purposes to which it will be put, and whether or not the imparting of it is voluntary or mandatory; (3) individuals must be notified when records concerning them are disclosed in accordance with a compulsory legal process, such as a court subpoena; (4) agencies must notify persons or agencies who have previously received information about an individual if any corrections or disputes over the accuracy of the information; and (5) all records must be accurate, relevant, up to date, and complete.[11]

Record systems that fall within the seven exempt categories are also subject to the civil remedies provisions of the act. Therefore, if an agency denies access to a record in an exempt record system or refuses to amend a record in accordance with its subject's request, these actions can be contested in court. Individuals can also bring suit against the agency if denied a right, benefit, or privilege as a result of records that have been improperly maintained. These remedies are not available under the general exemptions.

Specific exemptions are referred to as (k)(1), (k)(2), and so on, in accordance with their designations in the act.

Exemption (k)(1): Classified Documents Concerning National Defense and Foreign Policy. Exemption (k)(1) covers records "subject to the provisions of section 552 (b)(1) of this title."

This refers to the first exemption of the *Freedom of Information Act*, which excepts from disclosure records that "(A) are specifically authorized under criteria established by an Executive order to be kept secret in the interest of national defense or foreign policy and (B) are in fact properly classified pursuant to such Executive order." (For further discussion of the provision, see "Exemption 1: Classified Documents Concerning National Defense and Foreign Policy" under the *FOIA* section.)

Exemption (k)(2): Investigatory Material Compiled for Law Enforcement Purposes. Exemption (k)(2) pertains to

investigatory material compiled for law enforcement purposes, other than material within the scope of subsection (j)(2) of this section: *Provided, however,* that if any individual is denied any right, privilege, or benefit that he would otherwise be entitled by Federal law, or for which he would otherwise be eligible, as a result of the maintenance of such material, such material shall be provided to such individual, except to the extent that the disclosure of such material would reveal the identity of a source who furnished information to the Government under an express promise that the identity of the source would be held in confidence, or, prior to the effective date of this section, under an implied promise that the identity of the source would be held in confidence.

This applies to investigatory materials compiled for law enforcement purposes by agencies whose principal function is other than criminal law enforcement. Included are such items as files maintained by the IRS concerning taxpayers who are delinquent in filing federal tax returns, records compiled by the Customs Bureau on narcotic suspects, investigatory reports of the Federal Deposit Insurance Corporation regarding banking irregularities, and files maintained by the Securities and Exchange Commission on individuals who are being investigated by the agency.

Such files cannot be withheld from an individual, however, if they are used to deny a benefit, right, or privilege to which that individual is entitled by law, unless their disclosure would reveal the identity of a confidential source. It should always be borne in mind that Congress intended that information available under either the *FOIA* or the *Privacy Act* be disclosed. Moreover, since the *FOIA* requires agencies to release all nonexempt portions of a file, some of the information exempted under this provision might be obtained under the *FOIA*. In any event, as mentioned, when seeking information of an investigatory nature, it is a good idea to request it under both acts.

Exemption (k)(3): Secret Service Intelligence Files. Exemption (k)(3) covers records "maintained in connection with providing protective services to the President of the United States or other individuals pursuant to section 3056 of title 18."

This exemption pertains to files held by the Secret Service that are necessary to ensure the safety of the President and other individuals under Secret Service protection.

Exemption (k)(4): Files Used Solely for Statistical Purposes. Exemption (k)(4) applies to records "required by statute to be maintained and used solely as statistical records."

This includes such items as IRS files regarding the income of selected individuals used in computing national income averages, and records on births and deaths maintained by the Department of Health and Human Services for compiling vital statistics.

Exemption (k)(5): Investigatory Materials Used in Making Decisions Concerning Federal Employment, Military Service, Federal Contracts, and Security Clearances. Exemption (k)(5) relates to

investigatory material compiled solely for the purpose of determining suitability, eligibility, or qualifications for Federal civilian employment, military service, Federal contracts, or access to classified information, but only to the extent that the disclosure of such material would reveal the identity of a source who furnished information to the Government under an express promise that the identity of the source would be held in confidence.

This exemption applies only to investigatory records that would reveal the identity of a confidential source. Since it is not customary for agencies to grant pledges of confidentiality in collecting information concerning employment, federal contracts, and security clearance, in most instances these records would be available.

Exemption (k)(6): Testing or Examination Material Used Solely for Employment Purposes. Exemption (k)(6) covers "testing or examination material used solely to determine individual qualifications for appointment or promotion in the Federal service the disclosure of which would compromise the objectivity or fairness of the testing or examination process."

This provision permits agencies to withhold information concerning the testing process that would give an individual an unfair competitive advantage. It applies solely to information that would reveal test qualifications and answers or testing procedures.

Exemption (k)(7): Evaluation Material Used in Making Decisions Regarding Promotions in the Armed Services. Exemption (k)(7) pertains to "evaluation material used to determine potential for promotion in the armed services, but only to the extent that the disclosure of such material would reveal the identity of a source who furnished information to the Government under an express promise that the identity of the source would be held in confidence, or, prior to the effective date of this section, under an implied promise that the identity of the source would be held in confidence."

This exemption is used solely by the armed services. Moreover, due to the nature of military promotion where numerous individuals compete for the same job, it is often necessary to grant pledges of confidentiality in collecting information so that those questioned about potential candidates will feel free to be candid in their assessments. Therefore, efficiency reports and other materials used in making decisions about military promotions may be difficult to get. But, again, when seeking information of an investigatory nature, it is a good idea to request it under both the *Privacy Act* and the *FOIA*.

Appeal Procedure for Denial of Access

Unlike the *FOIA*, the *Privacy Act* provides no standard procedure for appealing denials to release information. However, many agencies have their own regulations governing this. If a request is denied, the agency should inform the applicant of its appeal procedure and to whom to address an appeal. If this information is not provided, a letter should be sent to the head of the agency including a copy of the rejection letter along with a copy of the original request and stating the reason for wanting access.

If an agency withholds all or any part of an individual's record, it must state which *Privacy Act* exemption it is claiming as a justification. It should also tell why it believes the record can be withheld under the *Freedom of Information Act*, since Congress intended that information sought under either the *Privacy Act* or the *FOIA* be released unless it could be withheld under both acts. Therefore, in making an appeal, it is a good idea to cite both the *FOIA* and the *Privacy Act*. Moreover, if one is able to do so, it might also help to explain why the exemptions used to refuse access appear unjustified.

Sample Letter for Appealing Denial of Access

Agency Head or Appeal Officer
Title
Agency

Agency Address
City, State, ZIP

Re: *Privacy Act* Appeal

Dear_____:
On_____ (date), I received a letter from_____ (individual's name) of your agency denying my request for access to (description of the information sought). Enclosed is a copy of this denial along with a copy of my original request. By this letter, I am appealing the denial.

Since Congress intended that information sought under the *Privacy Act of 1974*, 5 U.S.C. 552a, be released unless it could be withheld under both this act and the *Freedom of Information Act*, *FOIA* 5 U.S.C. 552, I hereby request that you also refer to the *FOIA* in consideration of this appeal. [Optional] I am seeking access to these records (state the reasons for the request if it might assist in obtaining the information, and give any arguments that could justify its release).

Thank you for your prompt attention to this matter.

Sincerely,
Signature
Name
Address
City, State, ZIP

Amending Your Records

The *Privacy Act* requires agencies to keep all personal records on individuals accurate, complete, up to date, and relevant. Therefore, if after seeing their records, individuals wish to correct, delete, or add information, they should write to the agency official who released the information to them, giving the reasons for the desired changes as well as any documentary evidence they might have to justify the changes. Some agencies may allow requests for corrections in person or by telephone.

While there should be no trouble in determining whether or not the information contained in a file is accurate, complete, and up to date, it might be somewhat more difficult to ascertain whether it is "relevant" to the agency's purpose. However, if there is doubt about anything found in the records, the information should be challenged and the agency forced to justify its retention in the file. There is one thing in particular to look for: The *Privacy Act* prohibits the maintenance of information concerning how individuals exercise their first amendment rights unless the maintenance is (1) authorized by statute or the individual to whom it pertains, or (2) pertinent to and within the scope of an authorized law enforcement activity. In most instances, one would be on solid ground in challenging any information describing one's religious and political beliefs, activities, and association, unless this information was voluntarily given to the agency. The act requires agencies to acknowledge in writing all requests for amending records within 10 working days of their receipt. In addition, individuals must be notified what action will be taken regarding the requested amendments. Moreover, agencies are directed to complete action on all such requests within 30 working days of their receipt.

If the agency agrees to amend a record, it must notify all past and future recipients of the changes made. However, unless the agency has kept some record of disclosure prior to September 27, 1975—the date the act went into effect—it might not be possible for it to notify all prior recipients.

Sample Letter for Request to Amend Records

Agency Head or Privacy Officer
Title
Agency
Agency Address
City, State, ZIP

Re: *Privacy Act* Request to Amend Records

Dear_____:
By letter dated_____, I requested access to (use same description as in request letter).
In viewing the information forwarded to me, I found that it was (inaccurate)(incomplete)(outdated)(not relevant to the purpose of your agency).
Therefore, pursuant to the *Privacy Act of 1974*, 5 U.S.C. 552a, I hereby request that you amend my record in the following manner: (Describe errors, new information, irrelevance, and so on).
In accordance with the act, I look forward to an acknowledgment of this request within 10 working days of its receipt.
Thank you for your assistance in this matter.

Sincerely,
Signature
Name
Address
City, State, ZIP

Appeal Procedure for Agency Refusal to Amend Records

If an agency refuses to amend an individual's records, it must give reasons for the refusal as well as the appeal procedures available within the agency. It must also tell to whom to address an appeal. Amendment appeals are usually handled by agency heads or a senior official appointed by the agency head.

The appeal letter should include a copy of the original request along with a copy of the agency's denial. It should also include any additional information available to substantiate claims regarding the disputed material.

A decision on an appeal must be rendered within 30 working days from its receipt. In unusual circumstances, such as the need to obtain information from retired records or another agency, an additional 30 days may be granted.

If the agency denies an appeal and still refuses to make the changes requested, one has the right to file a brief statement giving reasons for disputing the record. This statement of disagreement then becomes part of the record and must be forwarded to all past and future recipients of the file. However, as previously noted, unless the agency has kept some record of disclosures prior to September 27, 1975, it might not be possible to notify all past recipients. The agency is also permitted to place in the file a short explanation of its refusal to change the record. This, too, becomes a part of the permanent file and is forwarded along with the subject's statement of disagreement.

If an appeal is denied or if the agency fails to act on it within the specified time, the case can be taken to court.

Sample Letter for Appealing Agency's Refusal to Amend Records

Agency Head or Designated Official
Title
Agency
Agency Address
City, State, ZIP

Re: Privacy Act Appeal

Dear_____:

By letter dated_____ to Mr._____ (official to whom amendment request was addressed), I requested that information held by your agency concerning me be amended. This request was denied, and I am hereby appealing that denial. For your information, I am enclosing a copy of my request letter along with a copy of Mr._____'s reply. (Any additional relevant information should be sent too.)

I trust that upon consideration of my reasons for seeking the desired changes, you will grant my request to amend the disputed material. However, in the event you refuse this request, please advise me of the agency procedures for filing a statement of disagreement. [Optional] I plan to initiate legal action if my appeal is denied.

Thank you for your prompt attention to this matter.

Sincerely,
Signature
Name
Address
City, State, ZIP

Taking Your Case to Court

Under the *Privacy Act,* an agency can be sued for refusing to release an individual's records, for denial of an appeal to amend a record, and for failure to act upon an appeal within the designated time. It can also be sued if an individual is adversely affected by the agency's failure to comply with any of the provisions of the act. For example, a person who is denied a job promotion due to inaccurate, incomplete, outdated, or irrelevant information in a file can contest this action in court.

While the *FOIA* requires individuals to use agency appeal procedures before seeking judicial review, the *Privacy Act* permits individuals to appeal denials of access directly to the courts (although most agencies have their own appeal procedures, which should be used when available). On the other hand, individuals are required by the act to use administrative appeal procedures in contesting agency refusals to amend their records.

A favorable judicial ruling could result in the release or amendment of the records in question. In addition, money damages can be obtained if it is proved that a person has been adversely affected as a result of the agency's intentional and willful disregard of the act's provisions. Court costs and attorney fees might also be awarded.

The act provides criminal penalties for the knowing and willful disclosure of personal records to those not entitled to receive them, for the knowing and willful failure to publish the existence and characteristics of all record systems, and for the knowing and willful attempt to gain access to an individual's records under false pretenses.

A person who decides to go to court can file suit in the federal district court where he or she resides or does business or where the agency records are situated. Or the case can be taken to the U.S. District Court for the District of Columbia. Under the *Privacy Act*, individuals are required to bring suit within two years from the date of the violation being challenged. However, in cases where the agency has materially or willfully misrepresented information, the statute of limitations runs two years from the date the individual discovers the misrepresentation. As with lawsuits brought under the *FOIA*, the burden is on the agency to justify its refusal to release or amend records.

The same advice applies here as with suits filed under the *FOIA*: Anyone who goes to court should consult a lawyer. If one cannot afford private counsel, the legal aid society should be contacted.

Other Rights Provided under the Privacy Act

One of the most important provisions of the *Privacy Act* is the one that requires agencies to obtain individuals' written permission prior to disclosing to other persons or agencies information concerning them, unless such disclosures are specifically authorized under the act. Information can be disclosed without an individual's consent under the following circumstances:

> To employees and officers of the agency maintaining the records who have a need for the information in order to perform their duties, if the information is required to be disclosed under the *FOIA*, for "routine uses," that is, uses compatible with the purpose for which the information was collected.[12]

> To the Census Bureau.

> To the National Archives.

> To a law enforcement agency upon the written request of the agency head.

> To individuals acting in behalf of the health or safety of the subject of the record.

> To Congress.

> To the General Accounting Office.

> Or pursuant to court order.

In all other circumstances, however, the subject of the record must give written consent before an agency can divulge information concerning him or her to others.

Under the act, individuals are also entitled to know to whom information about them has been sent. Agencies must keep an accurate accounting of all disclosures made to other agencies or persons except those required under the *FOIA*. Moreover, this information must be maintained for at least five years or until the record disclosed is destroyed, whichever is longer. With the exception of disclosures requested by law enforcement agencies, a list of all recipients of information concerning a person must be made available upon request. Therefore, persons interested in knowing who has received records about them should write to the *Privacy Act* officer or the head of the agency that maintains the records and request that an accounting of disclosures be sent to them.

Finally, the *Privacy Act* places a moratorium on any new uses of individuals' social security numbers by federal, state, and local government agencies after January 1, 1975.[13] No agency may deny a right, benefit, or privilege to which one is entitled by law because of refusal to disclose one's number, unless the disclosure is specifically authorized by statute or regulation adopted before January 1, 1975, or by a later act of Congress. Moreover, in requesting a social security number, agencies are required to state whether the disclosure is mandatory or voluntary, under what law or regulation the request is authorized, and what uses will be made of the number. It should be borne in mind, however, that this provision applies only to government agencies. It does not apply to the private sector: requests for social security numbers by private organizations are not prohibited by law.

ADDRESSES OF SELECTED GOVERNMENT AGENCIES[14]

ACTION, 806 Connecticut Ave., N.W., Washington, D.C. 20525

Administrative Conference of the United States, Suite 500, 2120 L St., N.W., Washington, D.C. 20037

Agriculture, Department of: Department of Agriculture, Washington, D.C. 20250

Air Force, Department of the: Department of the Air Force, The Pentagon, Washington, D.C. 20330

Alcohol, Drug Abuse, and Mental Health Administration, 5600 Fishers Ln., Rockville, MD 20857

Alcohol, Tobacco and Firearms, Bureau of: Bureau of Alcohol, Tobacco and Firearms, 1200 Pennsylvania Ave., N.W., Washington, D.C. 20226

American Battle Monuments Commission, 40014 Forrestal Bldg., Washington, D.C. 20314

Appalachian Regional Commission, 1666 Connecticut Ave., N.W., Washington, D.C. 20235

Arms Control and Disarmament Agency, U.S.: U.S. Arms Control and Disarmament Agency, 310 21st St., Washington, D.C. 20451

Army, Department of the: Department of the Army, The Pentagon, Washington, D.C. 20314

Census, Bureau of the: Bureau of the Census, Federal Bldg. 3, Washington, D.C. 20233

Central Intelligence Agency, Washington, D.C. 20505

Civil Aeronautics Board, 1825 Connecticut Ave., N.W., Washington, D.C. 20428

Civil Rights Commission, 1121 Vermont Ave., N.W., Washington, D.C. 20425

Civil Service Commission, 1900 E Street, N.W., Washington, D.C. 20415

Coastal Plains Regional Commission, 1725 K Street, N.W., Washington, D.C. 20006

Commerce, Department of: Department of Commerce, Washington, D.C. 20230

Commodity Futures Trading Commission, 2033 K Street, N.W., Washington, D.C. 20581

Community Services Administration, 1200 19th Street, N.W., Washington, D.C. 20506

Comptroller of the Currency, Office of: Office of Comptroller of the Currency, 490 L'Enfant Plaza E., S.W., Washington, D.C. 20219

Consumer Product Safety Commission, 1111 18th Street, N.W., Washington, D.C. 20207

Copyright Office, Library of Congress, Washington, D.C. 20559

Customs Service, United States: U.S. Customs Service, 1301 Constitution Ave., N.W., Washington, D.C. 20229

Defense, Department of: Department of Defense, The Pentagon, Washington, D.C. 20301

Defense Contracts Audits Agency, Cameron Station, Alexandria, VA 22314

Defense Intelligence Agency, RDS-3A, Washington, D.C. 20301

Defense Investigative Service, D0020, Washington, D.C. 20304

Defense Logistics Agency, Cameron Station, Alexandria, VA 22314

Defense Mapping Agency, Naval Observatory, Washington, D.C. 20305

Disease Control, Center for: Center for Disease Control, Atlanta, GA 30333

Economic Development Administration, Department of Commerce, 14th & Constitution Ave., N.W., Washington, D.C. 20230

Education, Office of: Office of Education, 400 Maryland Ave., S.W., Washington, D.C. 20202

Energy, Department of: Department of Energy, U.S. Department of ENERGY, Washington, D.C. 20461

Environmental Protection Agency, 401 M Street, S.W., Washington, D.C. 20460

Environmental Quality, Council on: Council on Environmental Quality, 722 Jackson Pl., N.W., Washington, D.C. 20006

Equal Employment Opportunity Commission, 2401 E Street, N.W., Washington, D.C. 20506

Export-Import Bank of the United States, 811 Vermont Ave., N.W., Washington, D.C. 20571

Farm Credit Administration, 490 L'Enfant Plaza, S.W., Washington, D.C. 20578

Federal Aviation Administration (FAA), 800 Independence Ave., S.W., Washington, D.C. 20591

Federal Bureau of Investigation, 9th and Pennsylvania Ave., N.W., Washington, D.C. 20535

Federal Communications Commission, 1919 M Street, N.W., Washington, D.C. 20554

Federal Deposit Insurance Corporation, 550 17th St., N.W., Washington, D.C. 20429

Federal Election Commission, 1325 K Street, N.W., Washington, D.C. 20463

Federal Highway Administration, 400 7th Street, S.W., Washington, D.C. 20590

Federal Home Loan Bank Board, 320 First St., N.W., Washington, D.C. 20552

Federal Maritime Commission, 1100 L Street, N.W., Washington, D.C. 20573

Federal Mediation and Conciliation Service, 2100 K Street, N.W., Washington, D.C. 20427

Federal Power Commission, 825 North Capitol St., Washington, D.C. 20426

Federal Trade Commission, 6th and Pennsylvania Ave., N.W., Washington, D.C. 20580

Food and Drug Administration, 5600 Fishers Ln., Rockville, MD 20857

Foreign Claims Settlement Commission, 1111 20th Street, N.W., Washington, D.C. 20579

General Accounting Office, 441 G Street, N.W., Washington, D.C. 20548

General Services Administration, 18th and F Streets, N.W., Washington, D.C. 20405

Health Care Financing Administration, 330 C Street, S.W., Washington, D.C. 20201

Health, Education, and Welfare, Department of: U.S. Department of Health, Education, and Welfare, 200 Independence Ave., S.W., Washington, D.C. 20201

Health Resources Administration, 3700 East West Highway, Hyattsville, MD 20782

Health Service Administration, 5600 Fishers Lane, Rockville, MD 20857

Housing and Urban Development, Department of: Department of Housing and Urban Development, Washington, D.C. 20410

Immigration and Naturalization Service, 425 I Street, N.W., Washington, D.C. 20536

Indian Claims Commission, 1730 K Street, N.W., Washington, D.C. 20006

Information Agency, U.S. (USIA): U.S. Information Agency, 1750 Pennsylvania Ave., N.W., Washington, D.C. 20547

Interior, Department of: Department of the Interior, 18th and C Street, N.W., Washington, D.C. 20240

Internal Revenue Service, 1111 Constitution Ave., N.W., Washington, D.C. 20224

International Development (AID), Agency for: Agency for International Development, 21st and Virginia Ave., N.W., Washington, D.C. 20532

International Trade Commission, U.S.: U.S. International Trade Commission, 701 E St., N.W., Washington, D.C. 20436

Interstate Commerce Commission, 12th and Constitution Ave., N.W., Washington, D.C. 20423

Justice, Department of: Department of Justice, Washington, D.C. 20530

Labor, Department of: Department of Labor, Washington, D.C. 20210

Law Enforcement Assistance Administration, 633 Indiana Ave., N.W., Washington, D.C. 20531

Maritime Administration, Washington, D.C. 20230

National Aeronautics and Space Administration (NASA), 400 Maryland Ave., S.W., Washington, D.C. 20546

National Archives and Records Service, Washington, D.C. 20408

National Credit Union Administration, 2025 M Street, N.W., Washington, D.C. 20456

National Endowment for the Arts, 806 15th Street, N.W., Washington, D.C. 20506

National Endowment for the Humanities, 806 15th Street, N.W., Washington, D.C. 20506

National Highway Traffic Safety Administration: National Highway Traffic Administration, 400 7th St., S.W., Washington, D.C. 20590

National Institute of Education, 1200-19th Street, N.W., Washington, D.C. 20208

National Institutes of Health, 9000 Rockville Pike, Rockville, MD 20014

National Labor Relations Board, 1717 Pennsylvania Ave., N.W., Washington, D.C. 20570

National Oceanic and Atmospheric Administration, 6010 Executive Blvd., Rockville, MD 20852

National Railroad Passenger Corporation (AMTRAK), 955 N. L'Enfant Plaza, S.W., Washington, D.C. 20024

National Science Foundation, 1800 G St., N.W., Washington, D.C. 20550

National Security Agency, Fort George Meade, MD 20755

National Security Council, Old Executive Office Bldg., Washington, D.C. 20506

National Transportation Safety Board, 800 Independence Ave., S.W., Washington, D.C. 20594

Navy, Department of the: Department of the Navy, The Pentagon, Washington, D.C. 20350

Nuclear Regulatory Commission, Washington, D.C. 20555

Occupational Safety and Health Review Commission, 1825 K Street, N.W., Washington, D.C. 20006

Office of Management and Budget, Old Executive Office Bldg., Washington, D.C. 20503

Overseas Private Investment Corporation, 1129 20th St., N.W., Washington, D.C. 20527

Postal Service, U.S.: U.S. Postal Service, 475 L'Enfant Plaza, S.W., Washington, D.C. 20260

Prisons, Bureau of: Bureau of Prisons, 320 First Street, N.W., Washington, D.C. 20534

Public Health Service, 200 Independence Ave., S.W., Washington, D.C. 20201

Railroad Retirement Board, 844 N. Rush St., Chicago, IL 60611

Renegotiation Board, 2000 M Street, N.W., Washington, D.C. 20446

Secret Service: U.S. Secret Service, 1800 G Street, N.W., Washington, D.C. 20223

Securities and Exchange Commission, 500 N. Capitol St., Washington, D.C. 20549

Selective Service System, 600 E Street, N.W., Washington, D.C. 20435

Small Business Administration, 1441 L Street, N.W., Washington, D.C. 20416

Social Security Administration, 6401 Security Blvd., Baltimore, MD 21235

State, Department of: Department of State, Washington, D.C. 20520

Tennessee Valley Authority (TVA), 400 Commerce Ave., Knoxville, TN 37902

Transportation, Department of: Department of Transportation, 400 7th Street, S.W., Washington, D.C. 20590

Treasury, Department of: Department of the Treasury, 1500 Pennsylvania Ave., N.W., Washington, D.C. 20220

Urban Mass Transit Administration, 400 7th Street, S.W., Washington, D.C. 20590

Veterans Administration, Vermont Avenue, N.W., Washington, D.C. 20420

NOTES

[1]The *FOIA* can be used by any member of the general public including noncitizens.

[2]The *Federal Register* is a government document issued daily in which government agencies publish their regulations implementing acts of Congress along with other notices of public interest. It also lists Executive orders and Presidential proclamations.

[3]The report of the House Government Operation Committee defines "reasonably describes" by stating that a description "would be sufficient if it enabled a professional employee of the agency who was familiar with the subject area of the request to locate the record with a reasonable amount of effort." (H.R. No. 93-876, 1974, p. 6.)

[4]Under the provisions of the act, "unusual circumstances" involve such things as collecting records from field offices or other establishments, reviewing a voluminous amount of material, and consulting with another agency in order to fill the request.

[5]In July 1976, the U.S. Court of Appeals for the District of Columbia ruled that the time requirements of the *FOIA* are "not mandatory but directory" when certain conditions are met. If an agency can show that it is "deluged" with requests "vastly in excess" of what Congress anticipated, that the resources are "inadequate" to deal with this volume, and that "due diligence" is being exercised in processing the request, time extensions will be permitted [*Open America v. Watergate Special Prosecution Force,* 547 F.2d 605 (D.C. Cir. 1976)].

[6]425 U.S. 352 (1976).

[7]422 U.S. 255 (1975).

[8]Unlike the *FOIA*—which applies to anyone making a request, including foreigners as well as American citizens—the *Privacy Act* applies only to American citizens and aliens lawfully admitted for permanent residence.

[9]If an individual is arrested more than once, he builds up a criminal history, called a rap sheet. Rap sheets chronologically list all fingerprint submissions by local, state, and federal agencies. They also contain the charges lodged against the individual and what disposition is made of the case, if the arresting agency supplies this information. An indi-

vidual can get a copy of his or her rap sheet by forwarding to the Identification Division of the FBI in Washington, D.C., a set of rolled-ink fingerprint impressions along with $5 in the form of a certified check or money order made to the Treasury of the United States.

[10]If a different name was being used at the time the record was compiled, this information should be provided.

[11]This provision differs from the one pertaining to all record systems that requires that records disclosed be accurate, relevant, up to date, and complete. Record systems subject to the seven specific exemptions must at all times be accurate, relevant, up to date, and complete.

[12]All federal agencies must publish annually in the *Federal Register* the "routine uses" of the information they maintain.

[13]This is the only provision in the *Privacy Act* that applies to state and local as well as federal agencies.

[14]"*FOIA* request" should always be written on bottom left-hand corner of your envelope.

22
Informants and the Public Police

Ben Jacobson

The success of the criminal investigator, whether private or public, is determined by the way such an individual gathers information; and information comes from numerous sources, including persons who have been classified as "informants." Generally speaking, informant assistance is the most useful, direct form of information an investigator can obtain, but it takes experience and training to determine its credibility and value.

SOURCES OF INFORMATION

The investigator has many sources of information concerning ongoing inquiries, including (1) concerned and interested citizens, (2) communications media documentation, (3) public documents, and (4) criminal informant cooperation.

In many instances, the information appears to be valuable, but the trained detective must take a moment to observe its usefulness and feasibility. The facts should consistently parallel the other information from varying sources. Many times interested and concerned citizens offer what they believe to be meaningful data. Although much of it is of little value, nevertheless, some information may prove to be effective. Often it is useful but initially inaccurate. It must be translated into reasonable, useful, and valuable data. Concerned citizens should always be reinterviewed—the investigator, meanwhile, keeping in mind the already known facts and the shortcomings of the data being received.

The most reliable information can be gathered from the informant involved in criminal activity or its fringes. Before any meaningful facts can be obtained, however, an alliance between the informant and the inquirer must be reached. Criminal informants are aware of their vulnerability and know that they are caught in a conflict between the enforcer and the criminal subculture on which they inform. Such persons choose to locate themselves between the lines of criminality and society's protectors, the police. By so doing, they pose many hazards to an investigation, including risks to human life, risks to the career and reputation of the contact investigator, and a danger to the positive outcome of the inquiry. Their information is often accurate and, in most instances, can determine the results of the case.

The procedures used to obtain vital facts, the personal relationships developed between the informant and investigator, the socioeconomic pressures, and the guidelines agreed upon—all these factors play an important part in providing a meaningful working relationship. After some time, a trusting alliance begins to develop, offering additional cooperation in other matters.

Knowledge supplied by persons who have overheard conversations through walls, in bars, night clubs, bowling alleys, and so on, has little to offer. Usually such individuals cannot or will not identify persons they claim to know. Hearsay data is useful only in the corroboration of facts from other reliable sources. The hearsay complainant should be used for support information which can be incorporated into furthering the inquiry. Although information concerning any matter should not be ignored, the inquirer must learn to recognize the difference between valuable and useless data. In general, an open mind must be maintained toward all information received from any source, with more importance being placed on some.

In order to ascertain the value of the informant, the investigator must determine the significance of the data which the supplier has to offer. It is important to remember that a person of value to the investigator is one who can:

1. Supply meaningful information toward the *direction* of the inquiry.

2. Provide descriptive data vital to the *furtherance* of the investigation.

3. Offer *direct contact* with the subject of the inquiry.

4. Furnish photographs, personal documents, and layouts of apartments, business establishments, and locations frequented by subjects of the investigation.

The informant need not supply all of the above, but any facet is vital and should be deemed essential.

TYPES OF INFORMANTS: OBSERVER, EAVESDROPPER, PARTICIPATING

Observer Informants. Persons who are considered observers and offer their personal reflections as a means of gathering data are, of course, useful to an investigator. However, the inquirer must remember to take an objective look at the facts. In many instances, observer informants confuse their gathered facts. Although accurate at times, such information should be scrutinized and used as support for direct valuable information. Observers, in general, "read into" the actions of others, thereby supplying their own viewpoints. There is a tendency to miss vital points while becoming engrossed in actions which are irrelevant. Persons who observe are useful for preliminary case buildup and direction for the corroboration of other informant data.

Eavesdropper Informants. Eavesdropper informants, like observer informants, overhear conversations concerning the inquiry. They manage to retain the gathered knowledge in their heads and usually get these facts tangled with other facts and conversations. They become useful when their information is supplied immediately after the "overhear." Both types of operatives usually expand on the data received. Eavesdropper informants can be considered reliable, and the information supplied usually results in a helpful direction. These facts supplement other information or can provide the springboard toward further areas of the inquiry including search warrant applications, additional interviews of knowledgeable persons, surveillance, and, in some instances, support for an ex parte order (electronic court-ordered surveillance). The gathered facts can assure the inquirer about the dependability of other data. Through them rumors, street talk, observations, and innuendoes can now be substantiated.

Participating Informants.   These individuals are actively involved in criminal behavior and can supply the most direct information obtainable. Participating informants usually are caught in the web of criminality and face possible incarceration for their acts. They choose to bargain for considerations when sentencing is imposed. Their reliability and interest provide the inquirer with the best possible data-gathering sources. Such informants know that their necks are on the line if they are caught by the criminal subculture; however, if they do not perform to expectations, incarceration is inevitable. Participating informants usually work with the public police and with the consent of the prosecutor. In some instances, they perform with the knowledge of the court. Their cooperation may be rewarded by minimum sentences or, in some instances, probation.

DEVELOPING AND LOCATING THE INFORMANT

One of the most complicated and necessary responsibilities of an investigator is the development and recruitment of informants, and this endeavor should be accomplished tactfully. Persons who are knowledgeable, but not criminal in habit, must be wooed. Furthermore, the formation of trust must be established before any operational activity begins. The detective can develop a reliable association after many hours of negotiations. Such a project may be pursued over dinner when discussion of personal associations and business problems arise. In other words, sociability sessions are a tool for acquiring recruits.

In cultivating individuals for participation in an operation, the investigator must convince potential recruits of their importance. The meaninglessness of such descriptive terms as "rats," "squealers," or "stool pigeons" should be emphasized and the importance of cooperation as vital and sincerely appreciated should be stressed. The investigator must persist in aligning the prospective informant with a sense of social values and a commitment to aiding the public interest.

Once the need for cooperation has been elaborated and a positive reaction displayed, agreement on rules for the operation is set forth. If there is a negative response, the investigator must leave the door open for the individual to reconsider. When this person returns, the investigator persists and emphasizes the need for the individual's assistance. It may be persuasive to mention the aspects of personal responsibility. In many instances, this method results in a positive reaction.

The psychological games used in developing cooperative persons varies with the type of individual, as each personality responds differently to the various approaches; the outcome, however, rests on the investigator's ability to reach the inner feelings and emotions of the prospective informant and to make the individual responsive to self-interests and also to the needs of the community.

In developing criminal informants, the detective must notify the candidates of the positions in which they will be used and the pitfalls of cooperation. The benefits of cooperation must appear to outweigh the problems; that is, advantages such as court considerations, financial assistance, and community service. In the matter of court considerations, the informant may be "working off a case." Cooperation can result in a lighter criminal sentence. Financial considerations can be employed after positive data is correlated and cooperation proved valuable. The pitfalls may include personal danger to the informants or their families, loss of close friends, family discontent, and, most serious, loss of self-respect (guilt complex).

For the incarcerated offender, a thinking period should be established. Time in a prison cell, local jail, or detention facility may be used in developing a cooperative informant.

When approached for recruitment, prospective incarcerated informants should be offered as much confidentiality as possible. In an effort to conceal their activity, subjects can be removed from detention without the knowledge of other prisoners. This can be done by signing them out following normal procedures. Reasons may include court appearances or questioning for other alleged crimes. Defendants can also be removed under the guise of probation interviews or rearrest procedures. All of these actions are taken with the consent of the individuals, usually following the initial contact and subsequent expression of interest by the persons involved.

From the detention facility, recruits must be brought to a cooperating district attorney's office for interview. Cooperation and agreement can be reached by those responsible for decisions. Upon their return to the detention facility, the inmates need a convincing story to satisfy inquisitive fellow prisoners. It must be conceivable, realistic, and formulated during the interview. To perform their function, informants must be "on the street," that is, released from incarceration. This can be done through the district attorney and with the cooperation of the presiding court of jurisdiction. The release should be formulated in the judge's chambers, with security being mandated for all concerned and with responsibility assumed by the contact investigator to ensure the court that the defendant will reappear at a later date. Upon release from detention, informants have the career and reputation of the contact investigator in their hands. In the event that individuals evade and leave the jurisdiction of the court, the responsibility usually is on the shoulders of the investigator, whose problem it becomes to bring back the informants and to face the court.

Criminal informants whose development has been completed are now the working tools of the detective; and the investigator must elicit as much information as possible and must also constantly remind informants of their commitment to the court and others who have aided in their release. If their actions become criminal, uncontrollable, or negative, the threat of being returned to prison becomes a vital leverage for the control of their behavior. In some instances, the threat of disclosure ("spread the word" approach) usually attains control. While this method may appear cruel or unethical to some, the technique is essential to ensure cooperation. Most informants like to be pampered and treated "a little special" by the investigator. Such a measure may seem degrading to some investigators, but it achieves the working goals by gaining cooperation.

Public police can find informants among the numerous persons who daily pass through the criminal justice system. They can be judged good or poor candidates depending upon the knowledge they possess considering the needs at the time. These individuals can be placed in the active or informational files.

The recruitment of criminal informants leaves public investigators with an overabundance of useful and questionable individuals. They are forced to pick and choose those who can supply immediate results—casting aside borderline informants for future inquiries.

Method of Approach

In locating noncriminal informants, investigators must associate with persons from all walks of life. Countless hours must be spent frequenting restaurants, night spots, bars, disco clubs, and so on, to familiarize them with the inhabitants and the area. This method, however, rarely results in obtaining an informant for current investigations. Investigators need to enlist persons familiar and close to the inquiry; and this is done by the use of deception, concern, or sympathy.

The Deception Approach. This approach uses methods which can be defined as unethical, yet remain legal in practice. To recruit the informant, the detective offers information that appears to support a possible pending criminal charge against the individual. If the information has some credibility, the informant may consider aiding the inquiry in exchange for the disregarding of some facts. With information that appears sound and concrete for criminal prosecution, this is really a "fishing trip" to add to the data already gathered and in the possession of the investigator. Offering photos and documents also creates an atmosphere of suspected criminality and helps obtain cooperation. This method is useful with persons who border on criminality and are aware of the facts being given them.

The Sympathy Approach. This approach is reached by suggesting that the individual's activities may be considered criminal and that cooperation may provide a route away from criminal liability. It should be indicated that when the cooperation is complete, the subject will be exempted from the prosecution faced by others. The investigator must, of course, have some knowledge that the individual is actually involved in criminal activity. All the facts should be offered in a mood of sympathy and concern for the person's family, and there should be constant reminders concerning the prospective informant's personal relationships and responsibilities. In instances where this tactic has worked, the persons were involved in criminality, were not familiar with investigative procedures, and had close family ties. The sympathy approach stimulates informants to question their own thoughts, review their actions, and try to remember the part they played in any criminal acts; while they are in this state, it is possible for the investigator to implant a feeling that other individuals are informing on them.

The Importance of Trust

In the relationship between investigator and informant, the most important quality is trust—which must be mutual. Without trust, a working relationship cannot exist or an inquiry end successfully. Any relationship is a two-way street; each participant is dependent on the other—the life of the informant versus the career of the investigator. Therefore, this trust must be developed in the first stages of interaction and recruitment. Furthermore, the confidence of the informant must be captured through the use of trust and confidentiality. Along with trust, there should be agreement on "no holding back" of information—applicable to both sides. The informant must be provided with knowledge of the direction of and dangers involved in the investigation and given the feeling of being part of the investigative team; but this must be done without revealing the total picture. Such a strategy provides the informants with a psychological understanding of their role and its importance in the inquiry. It creates within them a positive attitude, supportive of their accomplishments, which, in the beginning, all new informants seem to doubt. The question of betrayal lies dormant in their minds. Also, trust must be developed to sustain the ongoing relationship for use during the entire investigation.

In sum, trust must be developed to ensure the formation of a working relationship, increased control over the informant, and increased production of new information.

Criminal investigators should never forget the type of individual with whom they are dealing. In many instances, the trusted informant becomes the adversary and betrayer of the inquirer. Remember that informants will just as easily make deals with suspected individuals as with the law—using both sides to their advantage. I classify such individuals as "double dealers," for they have their cake with one side and their coffee with the other. They live in two worlds—faithful to neither and, in most instances, trusted in both. The investigator never learns about the double dealer until a major incident affects the inquiry. That position is common with informants who feel they can remove competition while they keep the investigation from their doorsteps.

The dangers of double dealing can apply to the informant as well as the contact investigator. This is evidenced in the many deaths that are listed as homicides or suicides but, in fact, are the outcomes for persons associating in both societies. For the investigator, the best protection is to *know the informant* and to give only the least amount of information operationally necessary and no information not relevant to the inquiry. Criminality breeds contempt—not only for society, but for others in the criminal subculture as well. There appears to be little trust among persons who seek gain through informing on others or competitors. In pretended gestures of good will, double dealers sometimes offer the competitor assistance because they want to gather data for personal use.

The double dealer is frequently found among narcotic addicts, gamblers, and alcoholics. These three types of individuals will provide information to anyone whom they can use as a means to support their dependencies. An investigator in contact with such an informant must exercise constant vigilance over the actions and interplay between inquirer and supplier.

Informant Motives

The first step of an inquirer is to establish the motives and usefulness of the informant. Such persons have numerous reasons for becoming involved in such a life-style. At times, the reasons are intriguing and, in many instances, point to a path toward increased criminality. Some use cooperation as an avenue for achieving emotional stability or revealing personal problems. They feel compelled to divulge intimate personal data to the investigator who becomes a father-confessor figure. This desperate need stems from the desire to reach out for help, advice, or friendship. Indeed, some peculiar relationships have evolved from informant-investigator interaction. Once I was asked to be the best man at a trusted informant's wedding. I did not attend but wished him well, and our professional relationship continued for years.

Generally speaking, informant motives can be classified as follows: (1) out from under (trade-off), (2) revenge, (3) greed, (4) jealousy, and (5) monetary considerations (paid informant). Each type reveals a different personality with which the investigator must deal. Keeping in mind the category into which a particular informant falls provides the investigative team forewarnings of potential problems. While a working relationship exists, such problems must be taken into account.

The Out-from-Under Informant. Informants of this type must be considered the most useful and dependable. They are direct routes to a successful inquiry and offer additional information without constant pressure from the detective. Such individuals have a direction and purpose for informing. They are striving to remain free from incarceration and offer their knowledge and contacts as a trade-off for consideration of leniency by the criminal justice system. They reveal direct information and updated facts.

This type of informant can be recruited from persons arrested or facing criminal charges. They can also be recruited from private industry when faced with occupational loss or threat of sanctions resulting from misdeeds. Such persons will make deals to avoid embarrassment within the community and can be cultivated for specific duties, including internal security in the private sector. The direct contact of such an informant can be aimed at others in the industry committing unethical or criminal violations.

The Revenge Informant. This informant by comparison, usually can provide intimate data about subjects and is willing to pursue any route to reach the goal of revenge. However, inability to control the informant who is caught up in personal tangles between the subject and the investigator may hamper the ongoing inquiry. Such individuals tend to supply false data in an attempt to correct a soured relationship. Moreover, by assuming the worse tale will bring the better results, the revenge informant expands upon his or her story, which may give the investigation a false direction. Before using this type of informant, the investigator should attempt to substantiate all information and corroborate all data received. Among the good prospects for revenge informants are spurned lovers, former business partners, gambling victims, loan shark victims, and persons who have suffered losses as a result of others' deeds.

The Greed Informant. This informant should be considered a danger to the investigator and the inquiry. This individual deals in innuendos, hearsay, and half truths, the greed developing in attempts to control business relationships or for personal gain. Usually such informants are detrimental to an inquiry and offer little value to the project.

The Jealous Informant. Like the greed informant, this individual can be detrimental to an ongoing investigation. In most cases, the information is directly attributable to personal involvement. The jealous informant has lost something and, in trying to recapture it by any method, will lead the untrained investigator on a trail of dead ends, false leads, and, in some instances, misdeeds. For example, the informant will attempt to set up the inquirer to retaliate against the proposed target. The uninformed detective can be used as a pawn in unwittingly performing tasks that lead to encounters with attorneys, the courts, or administrative supervisors.

The Paid Informant. Informants in this category are in the game of "information for sale." Their total outlook is related to dollars and cents, and, therefore, each encounter is recorded for monetary considerations. These individuals, considered by some as professional informants, will use any method, resource, or deception to gather facts. In their chosen occupation, they accept responsibility toward their contact investigators and accept their position—even if failure occurs. Professional informants are unique and differ from the rest of the informant community. Their information is considered valuable, and their relationships with the investigator are on a professional basis.

Many paid informants view themselves as deputized agents, responsible only to the contact investigator. Unless tight controls are administered, these individuals can interfere with and obstruct the inquiry and even cause it to fail. This results from overzealous actions, lack of information, or simple slips of the tongue. In many instances, they deal in data that places them on the border of criminality, and they fish for supportive information concerning their own activities from the law enforcer.

A set price for information is decided on in prearranged negotiations, and remuneration should be determined by the value of the data available. There should be a verbal agreement; and as the information begins to flow into the inquiry, periods of payment should be established. Paid informants seek few personal considerations. They usually maintain records of information and, in some instances, record conversations as proof of knowledge. The investigator must be cautious when the informant appears to be running the operation. Such an individual's push or drive and forceful personality can cause problems for the investigation.

In utilizing the above informants, the contact investigator must never make a promise that cannot be kept. In public investigations, an agreement is formulated with the assistance of the prosecutor's office. The individual is expected to perform at a specific level, supplying data in exchange for leniency or payment. "Out-from-under" informants expect deals on all information given, whether trivial or supportive of other data. As the sentencing date approaches, such informants tend to increase their productivity with hope of putting off the final decision. Concerning people who know about their activities, informants under the threat of incarceration have this philosophy: The fewer who know, the better off I am. The system begins to fail, however, when these individuals realize they are avoiding imprisonment by giving up close friends, associates, relatives, or business partners. Such a situation creates a recidivist informant society. If caught in other jurisdictions, they will become informants there and attempt to support their credibility by offering the new investigator the names of other investigators for whom they have worked. By this method they can incorporate their criminal activity in other jurisdictions, thus working off a case, that is, getting "out from under" and expanding their criminality geographically.

Informant Preregistration Conditions

Before an informant is registered, it must be decided whether or not the individual's knowledge can be useful to the investigation. This is accomplished through:

1. *Debriefing.* A complete interview of the prospective informant should be conducted by an experienced intelligence debriefing investigator. Such an interview will substantiate and corroborate information gathered by contact detectives.

2. *History check.* A total background examination should be conducted prior to active cooperation. Listed in this evaluation will be criminal associates, their associates, locations frequented, and family members listed on reports.

3. *Social life-style.* A complete picture of the informant's habits and life-style offers the investigator a decisive understanding of the prospective informant.

The investigation of housing, auto, and types of associates provides a basis for evaluating the usefulness of the individual.

Confidentiality of Informants

There is a great need to preserve from public record and street rumor the identity of informants. The number one factor is the safety of informants and their families. In fact, the importance of the investigation takes a back seat when informants' security is at stake. Furthermore, maintaining their confidentiality will also ensure informants' respect and cooperation. To limit the number of persons coming into contact with the performance and activity of the individual, the investigator must operate on a need-to-know basis. The inquirer has asked for the informant's trust and, in return, has promised to provide anonymity from public view.

In public law enforcement, the identity of the informer should be known to a limited number of persons. In numerous institutions, the delator is expected to testify in open court proceedings as a corroborating witness. This policy is dangerous and wasteful, resulting in a "burn-out" of the informant for future use. Following are examples of methods used to "cover" cooperative informants.

1. Federal authorities, working within the complexity of the Witness Protection Program, uses informants for specific inquiries. These individuals are used for major investigations. They are utilized during trials connected with their previous cooperation. Once this task has been performed, the individual and family are moved from their familiar surroundings and placed in a protective halfway house secured by U.S. marshals. From this location, they are assimilated into a new life-style in another community. Changes of identity, occupation, and official records to support such data provide the new life-style. Because there is sometimes reluctance to relocate from a familiar community to a strange environment, this method creates problems of security. It is common for such individuals to return to their old community and friends and, by so doing, create danger to themselves and others. Once the informant has relinquished the new identity, the Witness Protection Program ceases its commitment of protection.

2. Local law enforcement offers a totally different approach to the safety of cooperating informants. The informants are controlled by specific investigative officers; and accountability for the informants' behavior and its results is left to the contact investigator or supervisor. Prospective informants are debriefed by trained intelligence investigators, the debriefing determining the validity and knowledge of the informants. After a complete background check of the individuals' criminal and personal histories has been made, they are accepted or rejected. Upon acceptance, the informants are registered by the contact investigator. This

registration takes place with the authority of the intelligence command and immediate supervisors. Approval or disapproval is determined by the following factors: (1) *Knowledge:* Does the individual have vital facts or hearsay information? (2) *Criminal history:* Is the subject violent or trustworthy in performing with investigators? Does the subject's criminal history coincide with the knowledge claimed? (3) *Personal history:* Will the subject's personal life interfere with ongoing inquiries? Can it be separated from the activities of an informant? (4) *Causes and reasons for cooperation:* Why does the individual wish to become an informant?

Once approved, informants are given coded serial numbers, which are filed with the intelligence command and recorded by the contact investigator. The detective records all facts supplied, and this data is forwarded to the intelligence command for interpretation and filing. This procedure is followed to establish the informants' credibility and to provide them support in questioned court matters. The foregoing data can be made available through the use of the coded serial number, hence without revealing the identities of individuals. It also provides a screen of protection from corrupt or inefficient and inexperienced persons. Through the use of confidential serial numbers, informants can be used in many situations. The informants are *not* required to testify in court matters and they remain anonymous.

In many instances, the courts, prosecutors, and even police administrators request a face-to-face meeting with an informant as a means of confirming that such an individual exists and that the investigator's credibility is intact. Such a request should be met with as much resistance as possible, since security, trust, and emotional interplay are factors in informant-investigator relations. Informants *do not want* to meet persons with whom they have no agreement. The trust and agreement are established with the contact investigator and, in some instances, with other members of the investigative team. If trust and confidentiality are jeopardized, a feeling of betrayal results. In some cases, a judge, during a criminal trial, will demand the identity of the informant from the detective who is testifying in open court. This situation can develop into a legal question and moral issue. It is my opinion that *identity must remain concealed at all costs—* regardless of fines, administrative sanctions, or even imprisonment for contempt. The informant *must remain anonymous*—and this takes priority over any other issue or legal gimmickry.

In the matter of *McCary v. Illinois*, 386 U.S. 300 (1967), the court ruled in favor of the investigator's refusal to disclose the identity of an informant. This case evolved from the arrest of McCary for possession of narcotics. Upon testimony by the investigator, it was revealed that an informant had supplied information leading to the arrest. The informant had previously supplied the investigator on 15 previous occasions; and this established the credibility of the informant before the court, based on the sworn testimony of the law enforcement officer. The identity of the informant was requested by defense counsel, but the court ruled that the officer's sworn testimony would suffice and held that the identity would not be necessary. In most cases, corroborating evidence and testimony will substantiate the information supplied by the informant.

In the matter of *People v. Tatum*, 319 N.Y.S.2d 266 (1971), the court ruled that corroboration is necessary and if it cannot be established, identification of the informant is necessary to avoid the suppression of evidence. In many instances, it would be advantageous to allow the suppression of evidence rather than the identity of an informant. In important criminal trials, it may be necessary to reveal the identity of the informant, but only after all efforts to avoid this situation have failed. The revelation should be made with as much security as possible, and cooperation of the court and prosecutor in this matter should be offered.

Precautions in maintaining security of informants should prevail—not only for the case at hand, but also out of concern for the informants and their families. Many informants have a tendency to reveal their activities as cooperative informants to close associates, as can be seen in the following instance: An active informant, considered vital to many ongoing investigations, was murdered as the result of personal habits and associations with untrustworthy friends. The informant's lover, while having an affair with another individual, revealed that her lover was working with the police. This was discovered during the homicide investigation of the informant. In this case, the informant allowed his romantic life to enter into his double life as an informant.

Informants should be reminded constantly of the dangers that exist; revealing their identities to close associates, lovers, or business partners will only come back to haunt them. This fact should be impressed on all informants. Only *they* will reveal their identities, *not* the investigator. Furthermore, their confidence in the investigator must be maintained at all times.

Registered and Unregistered Informants

There are two types of informants who deal with the public police: registered and unregistered. In public enforcement, it is necessary to register the informant. This is done to create credibility, reliability, and continuity of data. It can be supportive in court testimony, used for obtaining search warrants, and, in some instances, in requesting ex parte orders (electronic wiretapping orders).

The registered informant is a vital weapon used by an investigator in gathering information and furthering the inquiry. Along with the registered informant, the public police should use an array of unregistered informants. These are individuals who do not qualify for the distinction of registration but who can provide bits and pieces of facts. They can be used to substantiate the registered informant's validity and to provide additional facts to be incorporated into the case. In many instances, unregistered informants are unaware of their activity and act as friends and contributors to the investigator's knowledge. Often their support of police efforts develops along with a personal relationship. Such unwitting informants can come from all walks of life—bartenders, taxi drivers, prostitutes, or even business executives. In general, persons involved on the fringes of the inquiry can be the most supportive toward the investigation. They can supply data from personal knowledge, "overhears," and personal contact; they then reveal such information as good samaritans or concerned citizens. Many of these informants provide their information through the course of normal conversations. Such individuals, however, should not be confused with the interested citizen or witness who steps forward and provides facts and identifications in expectation of being called as a witness in later criminal proceedings. Unregistered informants provide the bulk of the data used to substantiate the quality of the registered informants' data. An informant in the private sector need not be registered but, in the event of court presentation, facts should be documented.

A Policy of Honesty

In dealing with informants, the investigator must maintain a policy of honesty. This consists of informing them that the investigator is in charge and makes the decisions in the inquiry. Mostly, dealing with informants is an adventure of keeping tight controls and maintaining cooperative efforts. The informant must never be given explicit data pertaining to the ongoing inquiry. Operational procedures should be as simple as possible and only used when direct contact with the informant is necessary. The plans, operational goals, and other pertinent information of a prolonged investigation should never be discussed in the presence of the informant. Conversations between investigators should be kept to a minimum, with important facts spoken in private, away from the delator. Overheard conversations can be turned into financial windfalls for informants dealing with both sides (double dealers). Many informants begin to see themselves as part of the investigative team; and investigators sometimes develop the same outlook, thereby losing sight of the informant's role.

Professional conduct should always prevail in the presence of the informant. Except in the performance of official duties, drinking, socializing, dinner parties, and so on should be avoided. Informants gain control of the inquiry when the investigator becomes personal and intimate.

While working the informant, the investigator's reputation, professional ethics, and conduct are constantly "on the line," and many investigators get caught in unethical or criminal acts as a result of informant relations. In some instances, these actions are initiated by informants and usually result in the investigators compromising their official positions and then losing control of the delators. This is common in informant-investigator relations with addicts. Such individuals provide ways for making a quick dollar and thus enlist the inquirer in a "scam." Now caught in the web of criminality, the investigator begins to reverse roles, working for the informant. Such a situation breaks a fundamental rule: Remain in control.

Persons who jump from one law enforcement agency to another, providing their questionable knowledge in exchange for the best possible results from the agencies, are known as bad-risk informants. Such individuals usually give little information to the investigator before jumping over to another law enforcement agency to supply the same data. They will describe their previous performances as informants, naming contact investigators and depicting them as uninterested or inefficient. Such persons are looking for the best deals they can find; in a sense, they are shopping for an investigator. It has been my experience that these individuals will attempt to work with more than one agency at a time and, while providing little of value, will take as much financial funding as is available. They not only become nuisances but also create dissension among the agencies. Eventually they become "known" and can either be blacklisted among cooperating agencies or worked by more than one in joint ventures. If their information is vital, using it is in the interest of the investigative team. Cooperation and planning can be worked out between the competing agencies, each sharing the effort. To provide vital data on useless cooperatives, namely, the "bargain basement informers," blacklisted informants' identities should be circulated among law enforcement agencies.

Entrapment Cases

Entrapment is an ever present danger for the investigator and the inquiry which takes reasonable intelligence to avoid. How can investigators protect themselves and still remain efficient? Entrapment has as its base the provision of the "fruits of the crime," which are offered initially by members or agents of a law enforcement agency who are sworn to officially perform as police agents or informants for the law enforcement community. Following is an example of entrapment:

First, the informant seizes upon an individual who is active in criminal conduct. Then, working in conjunction with a law enforcement agency but *not* on the directions of the investigative team, the informant provides the intended criminal with contraband, which will, in turn, be offered to an undercover police officer. With the police officer unaware of the dealings of the informant, the entrapment takes place, and the informant provides the "fruits of the crime" to complete the act.

Often, this example is observed in narcotic cases in which unscrupulous informants are maneuvering for control of the trade. In most narcotics cases, informants are enlisted from the "out-from-under" category. In the event of entrapment by the informant, the solution, after completion of the inquiry, will be the informant's arrest. This step is taken to ensure legal sanctions and to avoid accusations of a police conspiracy. The importance of *total control* plays an enormous part in avoiding such a problem.

Every investigator would like to work with the ideal informant—a knowledgeable person with few personal problems and willing to conform and respond to investigative direction. This dream rarely comes true. In most cases, the informant is developed from a breed of mistrusted criminal offenders; and the addict informant, in particular, should be subjected to the most stringent controls possible. These controls should include reporting at definite times by telephone or personal meetings. In extreme situations, a curfew should be imposed. Without revealing the informant's activity as an operative, other informants can be used to verify the stability of the working informant.

Informants should never be trusted with or allowed to know the workings of ongoing inquiries. If they become familiar with the operation and targets before completion of the inquiry, the possibility of a "sellout" exists. This sellout takes place for prestige, money, control of illegal operations, or many other favors in exchange for supplying data concerning an investigation.

If the informant is a nonaddict, there will be fewer problems in the supply of facts and cooperation throughout the investigation—but the investigator must beware the pitfalls of overtrusting and the establishment of personal friendships which enable the informant to gather facts relating to the inquiry. There is no uniform basis for cooperation. As in the case of all informants, the investigator should become aware of the personal problems and needs of these individuals. In many situations, their knowledge may be limited and only useful for specific investigations. By contrast, the addict informant associates with criminality, in some instances participating in various acts, with the result that direct data is reported to the investigative team.

Working the Informant

In working the informant, total emphasis should be on remembering that the individual has been employed to supply data necessary for expediting the investigation. The facts supplied should be incorporated with other data from independent sources. The specific approach to and use of informants, of course, depends on the type of case under examination. In insurance matters where there is an expectation of recovering stolen property through information developed from informant cooperation, payment can be offered as a reward. This reward should be agreed upon in advance and supplied when results are favorable.

Caution should be used in the preceding type of case, however. The ploy of "property kidnapping" and the entanglement of the informant in a conspiracy with others frequently develops. The delator, working with both sides, accepts payment for recovery while splitting the profits with associates. In all aspects of the inquiry, the objective remains the same—recovery of the property and dealing with the offenders after the fact.

Working an informant is a complicated and specific science which must be studied and examined thoroughly by the investigator. There should be minimum contact but enough to maintain control of the informant and the inquiry. Contact should be limited to ongoing inquiries. Since informants seem to develop many personal problems when cooperating, accountability for activities and relationship with family members is essential for investigative control. The family need not be informed of the cooperation, but the suggestion of interest and concern offers valid excuses for visits.

Informants expect what is promised; their personalities present a natural interference to the inquiry. Working the informant by using the idea of respectability, in contrast to such labels as "rat" or "stool pigeon" is essential in developing a relationship. The informant should be pampered and constantly lauded for favorable cooperation. Such individuals display varying attitudes, taking on roles as a good actor does on Broadway.

To establish favorable working conditions, the location selected for meetings is as important as the inquiry itself. Location should be consistent with the informant's personality and attire and the type of inquiry. Business executive informants prefer a rendezvous in a restaurant, park, or other area befitting their looks, while the street junkie can be met in a bar, park, or slum location. The selection of the location should be agreed upon with the informant—an area removed from the location of the inquiry yet close enough to avoid a lengthy trip to the "set" or meeting place.

On the Set

The informant's presence at locations to gather data is considered an "on-the-set" operation. The set, occupied by the informant either alone or together with an undercover agent, can be an office building, residence, or any other location in which the inquiry is headed. The contact investigator should be in complete control during all activities. This power or control, however, becomes limited when the operation calls for the informant to operate alone. In such cases, the informant must be advised of the necessity of using tape recordings, photo surveillance, and electronic bugging. Also, the informant must be aware of the hazards involved in this type of operation and the problems that may develop if discovery occurs—such problems as physical harm, threats, or the kidnapping of family members.

The set in corporate crimes often differs from the scenes of traditional crime; it may be the home of a business executive or corrupt official, a computer room, or even behind the teller's cage of a bank. Informants for corporate crimes differ from traditional informants as well. They are usually educated and may offer their knowledge as concerned employees. Their concerns about criminal liability may be used in trade-offs of information for consideration relative to criminal charges or continued employment.

The Tactical Plan

The tactical plan should be based on data supporting the inquiry on the location and diagram of the set. It should provide for "on-set" mobility, and should include an alternative plan in the event complications develop. The location of the inquiry should be well known to both the informant and the investigative team. Before each operation, exits and routes should be preplanned and studied. It is advisable to keep hand-drawn maps of the area along with the tactical plan and folder. Time limits should be determined (but not kept rigid) for clandestine meetings. Visual observations must be attempted, but not at the cost of "burning" the informant or the investigation.

In the event that the informant or undercover officer does not return within the prescribed time, a plan of action must be initiated. This plan should be formulated without the knowledge of the informant. Gradual steps should be taken before an all-out search begins; scouting the area in an attempt to locate the missing operatives should be undertaken by one member of the investigative team first.

An informant who cannot return by the designated time should telephone to assures security and contact. Such a call can be made to a designated telephone number not associated with the law enforcement officers—usually an outside booth number.

Informant Safety

Of primary importance in the tactical plan is a formula for informant safety. To overlook or disregard this could not only cost the case but also the lives of the informant and family members. During the agreement on cooperation, security arrangements should be formulated for each family member coming into contact with the inquiry. To avoid disclosure, the investigator must keep the cooperating person from participating in any act that might require an appearance in court. During the investigative process, this can be accomplished by keeping the informant away from locations while criminal acts are being committed.

A security plan, incorporated with the tactical plan and retained by members of the investigative contact team, contains the following items:

- Listing of known associates of the informant.
- Listing of locations frequented by the informant.
- Registration card with coded serial number.
- Debriefing report, including initial interview.
- Names of persons familiar with the informant's activities, including investigators, prosecutors, and family members.
- Listing of vehicles available to the informant.
- Photos of the informant.

This data affords the investigative team an immediate informational history and, consequently, a course of action for locating informants and securing their safety. In other words, these facts offer immediate assistance in locating an informant during emergencies. During operations, the documents should be kept at the location in a sealed folder. While the informant is not in operation, the folder should be maintained in the intelligence command or other designated security area. Supervisory personnel or contact investigators are responsible for the security of this data.

Security at the Completion of Inquiry

After the inquiry is completed, the element of security should remain as important as it was during the investigation. Informants are responsible for their own silence; but within the law enforcement agency, the investigator's obligation to ensure the safety and confidentiality of the individual continues after completion.

Inactive informant files should be sealed, with all documents labeled in registered coded CI (confidential informant) numbers. In the event of a security breach, an immediate plan for safety should be initiated. At the completion of cooperation, a security plan must be established between the investigator and the informant ensuring a confidential meeting location in the event of security problems. This location should be a distance away from previously frequented locations and suitable for family members.

Investigators must recognize the problems of security and their responsibility to informants in this area. Such a responsibility extends beyond the working relationship; I have known security problems to arise years after active cooperation. Finally, the informant's guarantee of safe and sound existence is the responsibility of the court, the law enforcement agency, the prosecutor, and other officials involved in interactions with the informant.

Interactions of Informants

The interaction of informants with law enforcers, the courts, and prosecutors mandates cooperation among these members of the criminal justice community. The police must inform the prosecutor of offers relative to cooperation. If an informant is "working off a case," the amount of data supplied affects the response from the court when criminal matters are pending.

The informant must rely on the word of the prosecutor to inform the presiding judge, either in private chambers or before the bench, of the pending cooperative offer. In many situations, it is advisable for informants not to apprise the defense counsel, privately or publicly, of their cooperation. This counsel will eventually be informed by the prosecutor in court. I suggest this after having observed numerous occasions in which attorneys revealed to others, either intentionally or through unwitting conversation, the activity of informants.

The decisions of judges depend on their personal viewpoints, the substance of the cases, and the statutory laws with which they are working. A decision may rest on the comparison between the type of crime with which the informant is charged and the type of crimes about which the informant is informing. The court must also take into account the informant's criminal history and family relationships.

The interaction between informants and other criminal offenders is not the problem of the contact investigator. Informants will associate with other criminals. Furthermore, the life-styles of informants are their own choosing and should remain so. It should be stressed, however, that during cooperative activity informants should make every effort to avoid associates other than those required for the performance of their cooperative agreement. While passing time, criminal offenders converse constantly about crime, muggings, swindles, and rip-offs and usually question each other about the game of risk. The interaction between the informant and other criminals remains up to the individual. Nevertheless, it cannot be overemphasized that, during cooperation, an informant's arrest by law enforcement agencies will only make the investigation difficult. Moreover, informants' cooperation may not bring about their release on new charges that are pending.

CONCLUSION

Trust, security, confidentiality, and control are the essential working tools for a proper informant-investigator relationship. Such an atmosphere must be created to ensure a successful investigation and a positive role for the investigator. The knowledgeable detective who is aided by an interested, trusted informant is able to establish a more professional atmosphere and a less complicated inquiry. Although difficult to manage at times, the greater the number of cooperating informants, the better the results—this is generally the rule. Informant activity is essential for the direction of inquiries and for the trained detective's career.

23
Applicant Investigation

Thomas T. Cacavas

PRELIMINARY INVESTIGATIONS

Before considering the factors involved in background investigations, it is essential to know the specific position to be filled. If it is a sensitive one wherein the new employee will have access to classified data, then as complete an investigation as possible is required. However, if the person to be hired will not have access to restricted information and the position is such that it can be filled with no great concern for a thorough background check, some of the factors discussed in this chapter may not apply.

This discussion deals with items involved in a *complete* background investigation. It is intended to show how to proceed, what to look for during the interview that may have direct bearing on the applicant, and the problems often arising during the investigation. Besides financial limitations, the agency may, during its hiring process, encounter other limitations pertaining to specific information sought. These are determined by federal, state, and local laws as well as ordinances which exclude the dissemination of certain data. They vary according to jurisdiction, and the background investigator must know them thoroughly.

Data Sought and Limited Access

1. Birth data.
2. Educational records.
3. Credit records.
4. Medical records.
5. Criminal records.

The hiring agency or company must be aware of the limitations within its own area. For example certain municipalities will not make data public relative to an individual's birth, such as verification of date of birth, parents, and place, even with an authorized release from the applicant (see authorized release below). Verification of birth data is important. For example, pension plans require exact date of birth. If the hiring company or agency has a mandatory retirement limitation, then age verification is vital. In addition, date of birth is essential for identification.

If the position to be filled requires a college graduate with training in a specific field, then it is essential that this be verified. Most institutions of learning will not give such information without presentation of a release form.

Certain state laws consider credit information confidential and forbid its release without specific permission. The same applies to medical records; hospital and doctors' records are regarded as confidential, and forwarding such data is a violation of the confidential patient-doctor relationship.

Several jurisdictions will not provide data of a criminal nature for employment purposes in spite of a "release." The state of New York enacted a law that strictly forbids its police departments from releasing any data for the specific purpose of employment. This restriction is nonexcludable and must be accepted, although a severe limitation. On the positive side, the applicant in his or her application must indicate any convictions, swear to the truth of these statements, and acknowledge that any false assertions are grounds for dismissal. This fact, in most instances, precludes falsification, particularly if the applicant is advised beforehand that *all* statements made in the application must be true and that lying, making any erroneous statements, or an omission is grounds for dismissal. Furthermore, it should be known that the investigator, in speaking to neighbors, may uncover an arrest or conviction.

Release

Reference has been made to the release. It must be emphasized that this is not a cure-all for the problems of the investigator, but a legal instrument whereby certain types of information are made available. It is useful and necessary for pertinent information for a background investigation.

The release allows the investigator, with the applicant's consent, to review birth data; educational records, such as transcripts of scholastic standing; credit records; and medical files, including interviews with a physician. A release might read as follows:

> I (name of applicant) hereby release the depository of records relating to birth, education, employment, credit, and medical records from any liability in disclosing the information in its custody as it relates to me for the purpose of employment with the (name of hiring agency). I authorize the credit institution to furnish its record relating to my credit standing; the educational institution to furnish a copy of my transcript and any disciplinary information in my school records; and hospitals, clinics, or physicians to furnish medical records relating to my health and any care given to me. I absolve any agency which releases the information for the purpose of my employment with the (name of company or agency). This release is valid for 6 months from the date of execution.

> Signed_____

Address_____

Phone Number_____

Witness_____

(Interviewer)   Date_____

Any question arising from the above release can be resolved by contacting me at the above address.

Note: A copy of the release may be left with the person or company making the records available, for inclusion in this individual's files, or placed in the applicant's folder.

Recruitment

As previously mentioned, it is essential to know the position to be filled specifically, or at least generally. Will a person with a college education be required? What specific skills are needed? Are there residency, age, physical, or medical requirements involved? The hiring agency must have a well-established set of standards for its applicants. If the agency requires a college-educated person, recruitment has been narrowed.

The employing agency will find it advantageous to have contacts with educational institutions throughout its area so that the recruiter can attend "career days" sponsored by schools seeking to place their students. Most large colleges have departments such as criminal justice, and students graduating with degrees in this field and a well-developed theory of law enforcement may very well meet the educational requirements of the hiring agency. *Recruitment* of personnel is possibly the least difficult aspect of the hiring process. The *selection* of personnel entails a much more involved program if it is to be done properly.

The interview of the applicant and the background investigation that follows are possibly the most important undertakings of a personnel department responsible for hiring. These functions develop the applicant's background into such a clear picture that the individual making the ultimate decision to hire will have all the data necessary for a proper choice.

The purpose of the background investigation is to ascertain the applicant's qualifications, suitability, and moral character and to answer the question, "Is this applicant the right person for the position?"

It is essential that the applicant complete a questionnaire before any other action is taken for employment. This document must be as inclusive as possible.

Application

The application usually includes the following:

1. *Applicant's name.* Also, any other names used, maiden name, initials, nicknames, and variations of spelling.

2. *Date and place of birth.* This specifies country, state, county, and city.

    As indicated above, some municipalities will not release date and place of birth in spite of the fact that the investigator has a release. One way to circumvent this obstacle is to have the applicant produce a copy of his or her birth record. This copy, to be properly authentic, will have a raised seal imprinted thereon by the issuing court clerk or the department clerk for vital statistics in whose custody such records are.

In the event the applicant is foreign born, an Immigration and Naturalization certificate will have been issued by the Immigration and Naturalization Service. It indicates the applicant's date of birth and country of origin. Usually referred to as the "green card," it is issued to all foreign nationals legally admitted into the United States. If the applicant is a naturalized U.S. citizen, naturalization papers will have been issued by the court located in the jurisdiction of the applicant's residence at the time of naturalization.

Assuming that none of the above verifies the applicant's date and place of birth, another alternative is to note the applicant's birth date on all public records, such as school files, employment records, and driver's license. The applicant's consistent use of the same date of birth is an indicator that this information is accurate. It may be possible to accept sworn affidavits from relatives, neighbors, or references who have known the applicant since birth.

3. *All residences for the past 10 years.* This should include specific dates for residing at addresses and or apartment numbers listed.

4. *All education received.* This includes not only high schools attended but all colleges, technical schools, and any other training received.

5. *All employments, even part-time, after-school jobs.* If the applicant does not want his or her current employer contacted at the time of the investigation, this should be noted on the application. Records of unemployment for a period of two weeks or more should be noted.

6. *Military record.* Applicant should produce a copy of discharge.

7. *References.* Three names with addresses.

8. *Social acquaintances.* Three names with addresses.

9. *Names of all relatives.* Parents, brothers, sisters, and spouses of married brothers and sisters.

10. *Arrests, including charge, date, and disposition. Caution:* Refer to limitations noted above.

11. *Foreign travel.* Including purpose, such as vacation.

12. *Medical history.* (Limitation.)

13. *Credit history.* (Limitation.)

14. *Signature of applicant.* This is accompanied by the notation that all data therein is true and correct to the best of his or her knowledge and that any false statement therein is grounds for future dismissal.

Interview

Once the application has been received and reviewed, the applicant can be scheduled for an interview. The number of interviewing officials present is the hiring agency's decision; however, two or three are advantageous in order to make certain that major questions are answered and that any discrepancies discovered during the interview can be more readily resolved. The first step is to review the application for completeness and legibility. In this way questions can be resolved at the initial stage of the interview, one purpose of which is to ascertain the applicant's attitude with regard to the position being applied for.

In addition, use of an interview checklist is advisable. It may contain the following items:

- *Personal appearance:*

    Poor, careless, unkempt

    No special care, clothing or person

    Neat and of good appearance

    Very careful to appear neat

    Immaculate in attire and appearance

- *Physical characteristics:*

    Obese, sickly, slouchy, unkempt

    Facial marks, not clean-cut

    Physically in good shape

    Clear skin, looks energetic

    Excellent appearance and neat

- *Voice:*

    Irritating, unpleasant

    Poor enunciation, indistinct, hard to hear

    Good tone, pleasant

    Easy to understand, clear

    Strength in voice and extremely pleasant

- *Poise:*

    Ill at ease, embarrassed

    Somewhat ill at ease

    No unusual lack of poise

    Appears entirely at ease

    Completely self-possessed

- *Ability to express self:*

    Shy, hesitant, confused

    Overbearing, thinking scattered

    Ideas get across fairly well

    Logical, clear, convincing

    Excellent ability to express self

- *Self-confidence:*

Timid, shy, hesitant

Overbearing

Assured

Assured, but not aggressive

Assured and shows confidence in ability

- *Education:*

No fundamental training

Fair education

Good education

Good education and seeking to improve

Exceptionally well-educated

- *Intelligence:*

Slow

Dull, offers little

Good listener, grasps ideas well

Alert, asks intelligent questions

Alert, understanding, keen mind

- *Ambition:*

Not in line with position

Wants job, not thinking beyond

Wants job and wants to advance

Has drive and plans for advancement

Motivated for effective, thorough plans for progress

- *Personality:*

Not suited

Questionable

Satisfactory

Very desirable

Outstanding

Each interviewing official can circle one descriptive characteristic in each category that best fits the person. Under each heading a slight variation can be noted in the margin if it is deemed necessary. This is usually done during the course of the interview and makes unnecessary the writing of a lengthy narrative at the conclusion when recall of specific details under each item is more difficult.

During the course of the questioning, the officials can be asking themselves questions such as: "Is this the person we want for the position? Is the applicant showing the proper amount of enthusiasm? Is it a job the applicant seeks or a position with a firm such as ours? Would I want this person working for me?" Naturally these are meant to be not all-inclusive or exact questions, but the type one should have in mind.

The interviewer must be alert to the content of the applicant's response to all questions. The manner of answering certain questions such as, "Have you ever used marijuana?" should be noted. Was the applicant nervous? Did he or she attempt to justify the act by stating that everyone does it? Does the applicant use alcohol to some or any extent? Again the manner of response may be a key to a deeper probing question concerning true feelings relative to the use of pot, alcohol, and hard drugs. Does the applicant differentiate by answering that excessive drinking is a more serious problem than smoking marijuana? If the answer is positive, then the applicant can be asked about his or her feelings about the laws regulating the sale and smoking of marijuana. Are the laws too severe? Would he or she enforce the law against marijuana with the same force as against hard drugs?

During the discussion of former employment, questions can be raised about why the applicant left his or her previous job. Was it because of its routine nature, boredom, or lack of advancement opportunities? In many instances replies to these questions will give an insight into the applicant's aims and ambitions. The interviewer may ascertain that the applicant terminated previous employment in order to advance. This is certainly a plus in the interview. If, on the other hand, the applicant frequently changed jobs because of conflicts with superiors or fellow workers or because working hours were not congenial or assignments too difficult, then a reasonable doubt may be raised: If the applicant was not well adjusted to previous jobs, how will he or she do with our firm? As a general rule, the response from the applicant insofar as sincerity in answering questions, desire to work for the hiring company, and poise during the interview can be deciding factors in the next step of the hiring process.

An appropriate time to tell the applicant of disadvantages of the position is during the interview. If there is a dangerous aspect he or she should be so informed. If the applicant is married, then he spouse must be aware of any dangers also. If appropriate, it should be pointed out that the position is not a "9-to-5" job and might entail overtime with no advance notice. That there is the possibility of rotating shifts and evening and weekend assignments could also be mentioned.

Assuming that all the answers to these questions have proved favorable to the applicant, the next step is to give this person an examination. Its purpose is to ascertain the individual's ability to comprehend written matter within a given period, to show general overall comprehension of English, and to reveal some personality qualities through a stress test and a psychological evaluation. These examinations are available from various independent companies specializing in such testing.

If the examination results are also favorable, the applicant is given a physical examination. This requires the examining physician's certification that the applicant is able to perform arduous duties and is capable of participating in strenuous exercise. It is during this phase of the inquiry that the applicant's notations concerning previous treatment or hospitalization can be brought to the attention of the examining physician so that any physical problems may be resolved. Unfortunately, there have been occasions when an applicant had been hired but, because of some chronic physical problem, later became unsuited for the position. If that happens, then the individual must be assigned to some limited duty or placed on a disability pension.

If the applicant passes the physical examination, the next phase of the hiring process, which is the background investigation, will follow.

BACKGROUND INVESTIGATION

The investigator, with the application, is now prepared to conduct the background investigation, the purpose of which is not only to verify the data in the application but to ascertain all possible information relating to the applicant. There is no rule of precedence as to where the investigation should start. Let us assume the investigator selects as the initial step verification of the applicant's educational qualifications. Recall that the applicant's signed release is required.

Education

Before contacting the pertinent school, the investigator should know that in the majority of cases students' college records are kept by the registrar and a fee is usually required from the applicant before they are made available. As a general rule, the applicant will be billed by the school. For high schools, the guidance counselor who had been assigned to the student would be the logical person to contact. This person, while providing the records, may also have some recollection of the student that the transcript does not show. The counselor's files contain ratings by instructors concerning deportment, absences, latenesses, illnesses, and so on. In addition, these records have the addresses of the student during school attendance. A date of birth will also be shown and can be useful if needed to verify the applicant's statement. The transcript will show the student's academic grades and will verify degrees awarded. Other data, such as professors' personal records, are either with the guidance counselor or, in the case of college students, in the memories of teachers.

In either high school or college, an effort should be made to locate and interview as many of the applicant's instructors as possible. These persons can be asked not only about the student's scholastic ability but also about awards, extracurricular activities, or honors. In many instances, such persons are in a position to evaluate the applicant. They can provide information useful in determining character, such as problems in class; promptness in fulfilling assignments; leadership; and rapport with peers, subordinates, and superiors. Attempting to locate these instructors is time-consuming; therefore, it may be advantageous to ask during the interview for the names of teachers who may recall the applicant.

Employment

Contact should be made with all former employers listed by the applicant. Prior to contacting current employers, it should be noted on the application whether or not the applicant would want the present employer approached at this point of the investigation. If the applicant is not hired, it may have a detrimental effect on relationships with superiors and interfere with the opportunity for future advancement in current employment. The applicant can be informed by the investigating agency that contact will have to be made with the current employer, but that this can be done when an appointment is imminent and all other investigation is favorable for hiring the applicant.

The first step in this line of investigation would be to refer to the telephone directories for the addresses of the previous employers to determine their locations. Much investigative time and expense can be saved in this way, because experience has shown that often companies move to larger quarters or go out of business. While reviewing the application, it is advisable to note the dates listed by the applicant with respect to past employment. However, keep in mind that many companies do not retain records of former employees beyond a specific period, for example, five or six years. In the case of employment dating back several years, it may be expedient to call the employer first to determine the availability of filed data. In some instances, records may have been placed in storage and hence are not readily available.

In the verification of past employment the investigator should take note of the following:

1. Specific dates of employment.

2. Type of work performed.

3. Previous employment noted on application. Applicant may have omitted one position from the application for some reason unknown to the investigator. This will have to be checked later.

4. Reason for termination.

5. Any evaluation by former supervisor.

6. Eligibility for reemployment by this firm.

7. Interviews with previous superiors and any coworkers.

8. Records showing whether the person was on time, chronically late, or absent for long periods due to illness.

9. Work habits. Was a great deal of supervision required? Was responsibility, honesty, and reliability shown? Was he or she considered an asset to the company?

Referring to point 1, the investigator is interested not only in verifying the exact dates of employment but also in determining whether there were any periods of unexplained unemployment. Over 30 days of unemployment may be looked upon with suspicion. Where was the applicant for this length of time? On vacation? In a hospital? In trouble? Why did the application fail to include the reason for the periods of unemployment? Noting the limitation concerning the availability of access to arrest records, it may be advisable to dig further into this area of the investigation.

Residences

In conducting an investigation with neighbors, be certain to impress upon them that the purpose of the interview is for employment. It would not be desirable to leave anyone with the impression that the individual in question is other than an applicant for a position that requires this background check.

The neighbors should be interviewed in order to determine the applicant's reputation in the community where he or she resides or lived previously.

Questions such as the following could be asked: Was he friendly? Did he contribute anything to the neighborhood? Did he get along with other neighbors? Was she dependable and honest? Did they trust her? Would they recommend her for a position of responsibility?

In the event a neighbor furnishes derogatory information regarding the applicant, such statements must be verified through other neighbors or discounted as possibly atypical. A particular neighbor may not be getting along with the applicant. An arbitrary number of three is adequate to complete this phase of the investigation. Derogatory information will require a much more intensive search and more interviews.

References and Associates

The three references and three associates listed by the applicant are not to be considered as "routine." The fact that the applicant listed these individuals as persons who know him or her and who will attest to good character, reputation, and so on, does not exclude their being interviewed thoroughly. Specific questions can be asked of these interviewees in the event a problem arises in any phase of the investigation. They may relate to employment which could not be verified due to the passage of years or the demise of the business or owner.

References can be asked specifically about the applicant's character and reputation. Would they recommend the named person for the position to be filled? References are also good sources of information for any family problems in the applicant's background that may have been uncovered in some other phase of the check.

The applicant's social references are individuals closer to the applicant's age and better able to provide information relative to the person's reputation and peer relationships. Furthermore, social references would know whether the applicant has used marijuana or drinks excessively. Is she trustworthy? Did she keep confidences? Has she any habits relating to drugs? Would they recommend him as being stable and emotionally suited for the position for which he is applying?

When conducting all of the above interviews, whether it be with neighbors, former employers, or references, it is advisable to keep in mind the status and background of the persons interviewed. For example, how long have they known the applicant? Are they prejudiced against the applicant? Here are factors that the interviewer should be alert to when speaking to persons who know the applicant:

1. How long have they known the applicant?

2. Are they acquainted with the applicant's family?

3. Do they hesitate in answering any specific questions? If so, press this matter further.

4. Is their recommendation sincere, "lukewarm," or enthusiastic?

5. Do they appreciate the nature of the inquiry which the investigator is undertaking?

6. Do they offer to assist the investigator by stating that they will answer any question which they can, or do they appear to be very cautious in committing themselves? If they comment that they are not well enough acquainted

with the applicant to answer a specific question, will they furnish the name of anyone who might know him or her better?

No specific list of questions can be set forth in this section, as investigators will develop their own questions arising during the background check, and others will not be necessary because references and associates have answered them.

Credit History

It will be recalled that during the interview, the applicant was asked to sign a release for specific information. Without this release, most companies will not cooperate in making records available. In addition, there may be a fee for searching these records. In some instances the credit agency may not provide information even with the release. This is an unavoidable factor that confronts the investigator in our era of consumer protection.

If the applicant purchased a new car, it may be possible to determine the lien holder from the applicant. If it is a bank, the bank records may contain information available through use of the release. If the applicant has a home mortgage, credit may be verified through the lending institution by use of the release. Thus importance of the release becomes more evident.

Medical Records

Again, the release signed by the applicant is essential to an examination of these records. It should be borne in mind that the examination of medical records is to ascertain any physical problem that could be chronic and hence preclude the applicant's functioning up to the expectations of the hiring agency.

It is presumed that with the information obtained from these records and from the physical examination given the applicant, a determination of the individual's acceptability can be established. Several medical institutions, such as hospitals and clinics, have policies dictating the release of the information relating to a person's medical history. They may want a letter on the stationery of the hiring agency to accompany the release requesting the information, which will then be mailed to the address furnished.

Caution: Requests to the medical center, and so on, for medical records by insurance companies, doctors, and other interested agencies may cause a delay in this phase of the investigation. It is recommended that such requests be made at the outset of the investigation, and by the time the remainder of the investigation is completed, the results of this inquiry will have been received.

Contacts

Several mentions have been made of contacts during this treatment of background investigations. It cannot be overemphasized that the investigator will do a better and more thorough job with the use of contacts. These individuals can shortcut many hours of investigative effort by furnishing pertinent information. For example, through the establishment of personnel department contacts in major companies covered by the investigator, a short telephone call can verify past employment. The needed information can be obtained quickly through the company's records. Likewise, the background investigator can assist contacts when they request information about other individuals. The old adage of one hand washing the other is certainly true in background investigation.

The investigator would be farsighted to keep a card index of cooperative persons. These index cards can be cross-indexed by company and the individuals' names.

Sometimes the contact company prefers a telephone inquiry first, so that the records can be retrieved before the investigator calls on the company personally.

LEGAL CONSTRAINTS

Investigators, whether federal, state, local, or private must be aware of the *Privacy Act* as it relates to obtaining data regarding an applicant. The *Privacy Act of 1974* controls the gathering and dissemination of personnel information by certain federal agencies. Some states have, or are enacting, similar legislation. What does the act ensure?

1. It guarantees the individual's right to determine and to obtain a copy of information obtained about him or her.

2. The individual can contest the accuracy of the information.

3. It requires the hiring agency that has gathered the information to notify the applicant, on request, of the uses it has made of the information.

4. The applicant may refuse to disclose his or her social security number unless it is required by federal statute.

All of the above has a direct bearing on investigators' interviews with regard to background investigations. They must inform the individuals being interviewed, particularly those who might furnish derogatory information, that the *Privacy Act* guarantees that a copy of a person's "dossier" will be made available to him or her for inspection in order to ascertain who might have said something against the person's character, and so on. Again, *this act applies to the federal sector*, and specifically to all executive departments, the military, independent regulatory bodies, and government-controlled corporations such as the Federal Reserve Bank.

Although the *Privacy Act of 1974* applies to the federal government, local jurisdictions are giving consideration to enacting, or already have, similar laws. The hiring agency must be aware of this act; and also of any local statute that may apply in a similar fashion.

For additional information regarding the *Privacy Act*, the investigator is referred to Public Law 93-579, 93d Congress, S. 3418, December 31, 1974.

The *Family Educational Rights and Privacy Act of 1974*, also known as the *Buckley Amendments*, guarantees parents access to the records schools keep on their children; and it places constraints on dissemination of this information to third parties.

This act is one of the reasons that the release of information signed by the applicant is most important. Schools will not release any information without the release, lest they be held in violation of this law.

CONCLUSION

With the *Privacy Act* and the *Freedom of Information Act* serving as certain guidelines to the investigator, bear in mind that agencies may have certain restrictions in dealing with civil liabilities concerning individual lawsuits. As an example, the investigator may report information obtained from an interview which may be erroneous, hearsay, or rumor—and not make an effort to either verify or refute this information. The applicant who has access to his or her investigative report may institute proceedings to purge the unsubstantiated data or may seek redress through the courts. The investigator then must pursue all derogatory information obtained so that the issue can be appropriately resolved. It may be necessary for the investigator to request the person furnishing the derogatory information to give a written statement regarding this information.

The interviewee must indicate the source of the derogatory information. Is it hearsay or first hand? Is there bias or prejudice behind the allegation? At this point the reliability of the the informant must be ascertained.

In general, by being aware of their agency's support, in the event any civil proceedings are instituted against them, investigators are better able to thoroughly conduct the required investigation and properly follow the required procedure for reporting derogatory information.

24

Media Investigations

Bob O'Brien

Stanley Pinsley

The bare-bones equation that is drummed into the head of every journalism student on his or her way to a first story is to find out "who, what, where, when, how, and why." As sophisticated as the media may have become in the past years of the information explosion, the same tenets still guide the most proficient exponents of our craft.

Seasoned reporters may not consciously think of the old maxim as they approach each new assignment or take complex and sometimes baffling investigative work; they do not have to—it has become ingrained in their subconscious. Those six questions, though, provide a guide for any explanation of how the media tackles the often convoluted task of finding out things the public needs to know but others may not wish to have revealed.

Reporters are not police officers, nor can they ever be perceived as such by their sources. For any number of reasons, there are hundreds of people who are willing to talk to reporters but who shy away from direct dealings with law enforcement officials.

This is not to say that publicly disseminated results of such contacts never dovetail into effective cooperation between journalists and law enforcement; they often do. However, journalists jealously guard the separation that exists constitutionally between the fourth estate and government officials.

In many instances, prosecutors have developed successful cases that never would have come to trial had it not been for information elicited by the public media.

WHO AND WHAT—SOURCES AND INSTINCT: A CASE IN POINT

Tuesday morning, November 6, 1973, New York City firefighters struck for the first time in the department's 108-year history.

President of the Uniformed Firefighters Association (U.F.A.), Richard Vizzini, led more than 10,000 firefighters onto the picket line leaving the entire city defenseless against fire or other disasters for six hours.

On October 30, several days prior to the walkout, Vizzini called a news conference to announce that the rank and file had held a referendum on whether or not to authorize the union leadership to call a strike should negotiations with the city fail to produce a contract.

Vizzini said the result of that secret mail ballot was certified by the head of the Honest Ballot Association, George Abrams, and told reporters the result of that vote was "an overwhelming one." He implied the vote was in favor of a strike.

Never during that news conference did Vizzini respond to direct questions about the precise outcome of the vote. When asked repeatedly if the referendum was in favor of a walkout, Vizzini simply responded "I've gotten on overwhelming return—the vote is positive. The referendum that went out stated a total strike of the firefighters of the city. That's very clear in my mind. If there's any deaths in this city, it is not because of the irresponsibility of the firefighters."[1]

Having spoken to dozens of firefighters in companies all across the city, I knew instinctively that most firefighters felt it would be a terrible blow to the dedication and professionalism of the city's firefighters to abandon their firehouses over a labor dispute.

That, combined with Vizzini's hedging on giving a direct answer on the numerical outcome of the vote, convinced me he was lying. The strike came and went on that cold and windy November day but I knew the true story of why it happened was still to be told.

Firemen on the picket lines kept saying they would not have struck except for what they considered to be fact: that the majority of their union brothers had voted to strike. I felt it was imperative to substantiate my impression that this simply was not the case and to discover what really had happened.

WNEW-TV Managing Editor Mark Monsky (now news director of the station) shared my doubts, and together we set out to prove our hypothesis. The question was, how to pin it down.

Together we found a confidential source close to the U.F.A. leadership who confirmed to us that three members of the union executive board had told him the result of the secret ballot was *not* in favor of a strike. The vote was overwhelming all right, but overwhelmingly against a walkout.

The morning after the strike, Monsky and I confronted Honest Ballot Association head Abrams with our information. Together we went to Abrams' office and told him we were convinced Vizzini had lied about the outcome of the vote.

Abrams waffled, immediately making a phone call to his attorney. With Monsky and me at his desk he told his lawyer, "I don't know how they found out; there must have been a leak somewhere." We had our story.

Nonetheless, Abrams' only statement to us for the record was that because of the confidentiality imposed on the Honest Ballot Association by U.F.A. President Vizzini, he was not in a position to confirm or deny any statement about the outcome of the vote.

The only thing remaining to be done before going on the air with the first part of our story was to confront the man who had now become the focus of our investigation, Richard Vizzini. Unlike law enforcement officials, we had no legal way to compel him to reveal what had really happened.

When we confronted Vizzini with our findings on the phone, he told us his union had never released the results of a secret referendum. He maintained, however, that the vote did authorize him to call a strike. He also refused to release the Honest Ballot Association from the bond of confidentiality. He would not even let Abrams tell us if the vote was yes or no.

Vizzini declined our offer of answering the allegations we were about to make against him on the *Ten O'Clock News* that night. Our story informed the city that Vizzini had lied about the secret ballots.

The next morning, Fire Commissioner John O'Hagan briefed Mayor John Lindsay about our exclusive report. On Lindsay's instructions, O'Hagan contacted City Corporation Counsel Norman Redlich to see if the city had a legal interest in the issue.

We called the Manhattan District Attorney's office. Acting District Attorney Alfred Scotti referred us to Assistant District Attorney John Patten, assigned to the DA's Rackets Bureau. I told Patten of our findings and asked him if he planned to investigate the matter. Patten at first seemed unclear about what, if any, laws could have been broken, were the allegations we had brought against Vizzini to prove true.

"How about reckless endangerment of 8 million residents of this city?" I asked. "Pulling the firefighters off the job certainly obstructed governmental administration, if only for six hours; and hiding the true outcome of the ballot could certainly not have been accomplished by one person," I said, "so it would seem to me that you have a possible conspiracy to deal with too."

For the record, the district attorney's office would only make this public statement that day: "As of this time we're not aware that if such action happened there would be a violation of the criminal laws of the state but the DA's office intends to look into that possibility."

Now the synergistic effect of news and law enforcement began. On Friday, November 9, Honest Ballot head Abrams said he *would* reveal the true vote tally if requested to do so by a government agency with authority to compel him to do so.

Over the weekend, for the first time, other news agencies began reporting the story. The following Monday, Manhattan grand jury began its own investigation of the secret ballot. Acting DA Scotti used his subpoena powers to accomplish what we could not—getting the Honest Ballot Association to turn over the results of the strike vote.

Manhattan Supreme Court Justice Jawn Sandifer denied a motion of U.F.A. attorney Richard O'Hara to quash the subpoena after asking O'Hara, "What about the public interest when there's a strike called that possibly endangers the lives of the public?"

Scotti told Judge Sandifer, "As a result of information I received last Thursday [from WNEW-TV (eds.)] that the strike action taken by the U.F.A. had not been authorized by the membership, it becomes important to ascertain the facts to determine if there is a basis for criminal action."

"If there were a misrepresentation in the vote count," Scotti said, "there might be violations of the penal code involving conspiracy, obstructing governmental administration, reckless endangerment, and coercion."

That day, George Abrams testified before the grand jury and disclosed the results of the vote. Two days later, the district attorney subpoenaed the fire union's records on the vote. The DA had expected to find the actual mail ballots, which had been destroyed the day after the strike—which, coincidentally, was the day we broke our story that Vizzini had lied about the vote's outcome.

When he was told about the destruction of the ballots, Honest Ballot Association chief Abrams called it "a mini-Watergate," and added: "We know

White House to Yield 'Tape' Memos

By JEFFREY ANTEVIL

Washington, Nov. 9 (News Bureau)—The White House indicated today that it | indicate the tapes removed in | July were ever ye

Cough Up Fire-Vote Totals, Judge Orders

By MICHAEL PATTERSON

Manhattan Supreme Court Justi... ...citing "the public interest."

Pair Held in Abduction

Two men have been light when the young victim   Police said the girl who

Figure 24-1. Newspaper headline stories for reported crime.

the figures, the district attorney knows the figures, and the U.F.A. knows the figures. All I can really do is laugh. When will they learn?"

Vizzini apparently had learned something, because that same day he renounced the use of the strike as a collective bargaining weapon and promised that his union would "live up to (its) responsibility for providing continuous service to the citizens of New York."

On November 19, Richard Vizzini admitted that he had lied about the true result of the secret ballot, claiming that he was badgered, needled, and prodded *by the press* into saying the vote was in favor of a strike. However, the grand jury held that Vizzini himself was responsible, and on December 6, Vizzini, U.F.A. Financial and Recording Secretary John O'Sullivan, and the union's sergeant at arms Dominick Gentiluomo, were indicted (Indictment No. 6544/1976).

Based on information we had developed, the grand jury collected enough evidence to charge the three men with the crimes of reckless endangerment, attempted coercion, obstructing governmental administration, and conspiracy to commit these crimes—the very recommendation we had made in our original conversation with Assistant District Attorney Patten.

On May 28, 1974, Supreme Court Justice Burton Roberts, in denying a defense motion to dismiss the indictment handed down by the grand jury, wrote "the gravamen of the charges against these defendants, then, is not in striking but rather in causing the City of New York to be deprived of the protection of its firefighters in a way that bears the same relationship to a *bona fide* labor action as kidnapping does to babysitting."

Roberts further wrote, "Indeed, a jury in this case could probably find that the power the defendants exercised to cause the abandonment of this city by its firemen, especially in view of the phony 'mandate' they allegedly utilized, was as real and immediate as pushing a button."

On June 18, Vizzini and his fellow defendants pleaded guilty to reckless endangerment in the second degree, a class A misdemeanor. On July 24, Justice Roberts sentenced each of them to three years probation. There has never since been a strike or serious threat of strike by New York City firemen.

Journalistic instinct and tenacity, combined with precise information provided by our "reliable and confidential" sources created the context within which the synergistic forces of the press and the law enforcement and judicial communities coalesced to protect the people of New York City.

WHERE AND WHEN—
PERCEPTION OF A PROBLEM
AND PROPER TIMING

On April 13, 1975, the Tsung Ngar Club in Lower Manhattan's Chinatown was raided by police officers from the Fifth Precinct and the Public Morals Division. It was one of dozens of illegal gambling dens that had flourished in Chinatown.

It was not as though lawmen were unaware of what had been going on. A confidential federal Drug Enforcement Agency intelligence document (which had never been made public but was available to me) detailed the structure of crime in Chinatown.

The intelligence report made it clear that the two so-called Tongs, On Leong and Hip Sing, which are ostensibly business and merchant associations, actually control not only the legitimate but also the illegitimate economic life of Chinatown. The federal report alleged that the Tongs raked in millions of dollars a year from illegal gambling operations.

Traditionally, the attitude toward Chinatown policies taken by New York's political establishment in City Hall was to listen to those "leaders" who seemed to be in control and revered by the community.

It is a matter of reasoned speculation how many successive City Hall Administrations were actually aware that the "leaders" with whom they dealt were sometimes the top gangsters in the Chinese community.

In July 1974, Captain Edward McCabe took command of the Fifth Precinct, which covers Chinatown and part of Little Italy; he saw that the gangsters and their youthful minions, the Chinese street gangs, had virtual free rein in the community.

McCabe took almost a third of the police officers under his command out of uniform. He told them to patrol the streets and alleyways in plainclothes teams. The men were given orders to spot known gang members before they could cause trouble. If they looked as if they were carrying a weapon—"toss 'em" right on the street where the younger kids who looked up to them (and the older people who feared them) would soon get the idea that the police were going to make their presence in Chinatown meaningful.

Starting late in December 1974, McCabe teamed up with Captain Frank Broderick, who was then in command of the covering Public Morals District, and started going after the gangsters where it hurt the most—in the pocketbook. A series of raids over several months succeeded in virtually shutting down the wide-open and lucrative gambling dens.

It was not going to last long. In May 1975, the Tongs seized upon an incident of alleged police brutality to get rid of Captain McCabe. On May 19, several thousand Chinese demonstrators circled City Hall demanding an end to what they claimed was police brutality and harassment of the Chinese population.

The focal point of the demonstration was the alleged beating of Peter Yew, a 27-year-old Chinese engineer from Brooklyn. The rally's leaders claimed Yew was beaten and dragged into the Fifth Precinct station house after he protested police "mishandling" of a Chinese youth in a crowd that had gathered around the scene of a traffic accident on April 26.

Almost every factory, restaurant, and store in Chinatown was shut down for the City Hall rally. Our sources within the Chinatown community told us that the Tongs passed the word to businesspeople and Chinese garment manufacturers that they must order their workers to attend the march on City Hall.

The protest made a clear demand on the Mayor of New York, Abe Beame: get rid of Captain McCabe. A delegation of six spokespersons for the demonstrators met with Special Mayoral Assistant Joseph Erazo, who later told reporters, "There appears to be a lack of communication between Chinatown and the police department. When you get 2500 to 3000 people demonstrating from the Chinese community, someone should respond, because this is a group that doesn't usually demonstrate this way."

It didn't take long. Eight days later, Captain McCabe came to work and was unceremoniously informed he had been relieved of his command. City Hall had buckled to the pressure created by the Chinese demonstrations. McCabe was transferred to the Twentieth Precinct on Manhattan's Upper West Side. At the same time, the commander of the Public Morals Squad who had helped McCabe shut down Chinatown gambling dens, Captain Frank Broderick, was, in effect, made a traffic cop boss—put in charge of a highway district subunit in the Bronx.

Our sources within the police department told us that McCabe's replacement as Fifth Precinct commander was told by high police brass to "cool out" the tempers within the Chinese community that were grabbing so much public attention. It was to be a "don't make waves" order of business for police in Chinatown.

Within a year, the police "cooling it" had put a chilly grip on the legitimate population of Chinatown. Rival youth gangs, The Ghost Shadows, White Eagles, and Flying Dragons, were shooting it out (often on the streets) in a battle for the again lucrative dominance in the two areas of Chinatown controlled by the Tongs.

In the first nine months of 1976, seven persons were murdered by gang members. Among the victims was Vittoria Kira, a Chinese housewife from Queens, who happened to be eating at the Co Luck restaurant when gun-toting gang toughs entered and opened fire—killing her and wounding six other restaurant customers.

Federal agents told us the even more bloody battle was being fought over money. The gang members were paid by the Tongs to protect gambling operations. Our Chinese sources informed us that even the Tongs were losing control of the gangs. On September 8, 1976—one month after the gangs announced a so-called truce at the behest of the Tongs—a fusillade of 20 shots on Bayard Street left five Chinese youth gang members wounded. The "truce" was over.

Apparently, the prospect of getting caught in the crossfire of a gang war was killing the appetite of the tourists and city folk for Chinese food. Chinese businesses claimed that fully half the customers Chinatown had enjoyed a year before had vanished. They complained that if the gang violence continued, Chinatown would become a "dead city."

We found out that several Chinatown business and political leaders had arranged a meeting with Manhattan District Attorney Robert Morgenthau, to be held in the basement auditorium of the Chinese Consolidated Benevolent Association headquarters on Mott Street.

We went there with our cameras as the Chinese demanded that Morgenthau do something to once again begin a crackdown on the youth gangs. Sensing that the timing was now perfect to expose what we had learned about how and why the situation in Chinatown had deteriorated, we shot film of the deserted streets; restaurants like the On Luck Rice Shop of Pell Street, which were built to serve 100 people at a single sitting, had customers at only one table.

We told the public how Captain McCabe had been booted out of the area for doing just what the Chinese business people were then demanding be done again. We also reported that although many police in Chinatown were still trying to do their job of enforcing the law, there was nonetheless a pervasive feeling among police there that if they became too aggressive in the performance of their duties, they, too, could wind up like Captains McCabe and Broderick—bounced by City Hall.

Our sources in Chinatown said the effect of our report was to encourage the honest community leaders to make noise of their own. City Hall then began hearing about how exasperating it was for a person to run a business in Chinatown and be the constant target of youth gang extortionists. High-ranking police commanders came to us privately and said that the accuracy of the facts revealed in our report had created an impact that rattled through the office of Police Commissioner Michael Codd and echoed on across the Civic Center to City Hall.

Within a few months, a new commander was named to take over the Fifth Precinct. He had a reputation as a tough cop. This time, the new Fifth Precinct commander apparently came in without any prior constraints from the mayor's office that would keep him from doing his job as effectively as possible.

The department's Organized Crime Control Bureau was brought in to coordinate raids on gambling houses, making it too unprofitable for the big money gangsters, who are the invisible part of the Chinatown organized crime network, to continue investing in the gambling dens. Those dens served not only as hubs for gambling, but also as havens for dope transactions and the gangs that would claim the streets of Chinatown as their "turf."

Our investigative reports provided a catalyst that set off a sequence of events within the police department, City Hall, and the Chinese community that helped to turn a very bad situation around. This is not to say there is no crime left in Chinatown, but the cold fear that was killing the community in 1976 has been replaced by a feeling that the legitimate people who live and work there now have a way to fight back.

HOW AND WHY: TECHNIQUES AND CHOICES

As we mentioned at the outset, reporters are not police.

Print and electronic media have certain advantages and definite disadvantages in putting together effective investigations. Reporters do not have to depend on a strict hierarchy of control when working on a story. Unlike a police investigator, a reporter does not have to have absolute clearance before beginning a story.

A reporter can walk by a group of deserted movie houses in Manhattan and wonder why they are derelict and who is responsible. A story, like that of multimillionaire developer Christopher Boomis, is born. From those two empty shells on 96th Street in Manhattan, to the real estate records on those properties, to the incorporation records of other Boomis properties, to his international holdings, to his dealings with the City of New York at Hunts Point Terminal market an investigation grows. At first, there is no evidence of criminal wrongdoing or of civil mischief.

But, the skein of evidence is wound through conversations with Boomis's partners, several of whom had become disenchanted with his operations. The incorporation records yield the name of Luis Alimena, a top Teamster officer, who had somehow become a partner in Boomis's interests. Calls to various politically alert gentlemen suggest that Boomis has considerable political clout. Alimena is also known to have powerful political connections in the city. The skein begins to grow into a web of operations.

More records, this time of political contributions, show Boomis to be one of the heaviest benefactors of Governor Carey, Mayor John Lindsay, and Mayor Abe Beame. *The New York Times* does a puff piece on Boomis in March 1974, calling him a new force in city realty, listing some of the properties he is in the process of developing. More calls are made to determine where Boomis came from and how he had arranged financing for the properties.

Calls are made to the finance group in Massachusetts that was backing Boomis, calls to the bank where Boomis held lines of credit. Laboriously, the reporter builds, piece by piece, a picture of the man, his operations, his partners, his friends, his connections, his achievements, his intentions, his background, his wife's background (she is a partner in several of his companies).

Before a word goes into print and before a picture is shown on television, months of effort go into constructing a detailed sense of who he is, what he is doing, where he expects to operate, what his timetable for actions appears to be, how he manages his burgeoning financial empire, and why he structures his work in a particular way.

Before going public with the story, there is usually a final step, as there was in this case. Law enforcement officials, who have clear jurisdiction, are informed in advance of basic details of the media investigation. In the Boomis situation, Manhattan District Attorney Robert Morgenthau is given a complete rundown and begins his own investigation, using the media work as a basis for a more thorough determination of whether criminal violations have occurred in the awarding of city contracts to Boomis or in the involvement of a union official in his operations.

In this case, Boomis was not convicted of criminal trespass of any kind. But the press revelations of his activities, particularly revolving around the awarding of a multimillion-dollar lease to develop the Hunts Point Terminal, led first to a suspension of the contract and then to a lengthy, if inconclusive, investigation of Boomis by the City Investigations Department. Press coverage of Boomis's activities at the 96th Street site and elsewhere in the city, where he was promising far more than he could deliver and where he had been the recipient of special largesse from the city fathers, led to a freeze on his bank loans and credit. Within six months of the opening of an investigation, based on a reporter's curiosity about two destroyed neighborhood movie houses Christopher Boomis, who had been trumpeted as one of the most powerful new real estate developers in the city of New York, was out of business.

WHYS AND HOWS OF
REPORTERS AND POLICE
OFFICERS

Sometimes a reporter just happens on a story, as in the tale of Christopher Boomis. Sometimes a story happens to a reporter: a tip from an anonymous source, a suggestion from a news director or an editor, an enraged civil servant, a community activist, a bitter politician, a clerk in the courts. In each case the media person looks at the story to see whether it has a unique angle, whether it has been done before, and whether it can be done efficiently and presented effectively.

Unlike law enforcement officials, reporters are usually not directed strictly toward the prospect of criminal conviction, but are looking to enlighten, to amuse, to reflect, to excite and interest their public. So it is not only the direct criminal action that they illuminate. Frequently it is ethical or moral misconduct bordering on criminal behavior. Or it is social injustice that can be remedied only by legislation.

Reporters do not have to operate alone. They can build on what others have done before. They will pick up an investigation done elsewhere but not completed and try to add a new twist and a new dimension to an old story. They will review, reconstruct, and reevaluate earlier investigations in the hope of breaking new ground.

From time to time, media investigators pick a story because of its dramatic implications or because, in the case of television, it will have a particularly striking visual impact. The nature of the story becomes secondary to the way it can be told. There are stories which, because of their complexities, are much more suitable for the print media than for television. In television, a story must be cut to its essential pieces and must be understood clearly by viewers the first time they see it. They cannot go back and look again. In print, a story can be presented with a third and fourth dimension, because the readers can go back again and again to determine what they have been told and how well they understand a story.

Television has a linear time component, that can limit the structure of a story and reduce its analytical context. A story must be told in anywhere from three to five minutes, no matter how involute and complicated. Print media has the luxury of critical details, explanations, histories, analyses pro and con—all of which can make for a kind of report that parallels expert police work.

But television, for its part, has the advantage of a vast audience and immense visual impact. Television, by compressing a story, producing salient points, and interviewing principal participants, can bring a story to life as effectively as direct courtroom confrontations, with even more theatrical conviction.

Police investigations are frequently limited to or begin with individual criminal activities. The media is more frequently involved in generalized social injustices and the explication of grand-scale moral and political disorder—witness Watergate, where at first there may have been no prima facie case of criminal misconduct. From the generalized indictments of the media, specific criminal charges can be and frequently are developed by law enforcement agencies. The media indicts elements in the social fabric of society, law enforcement indicts the individuals responsible for the disorder apparent in those elements.

Reporters cannot employ subpoena powers; they have none. They cannot gain official access to private records. They cannot grant immunity to a witness. They cannot force a suspect into a lineup. They have no powers to arrest. They frequently lack a complete computerized history of prior convictions and prior criminal investigations. These are the provinces and the advantages of law enforcement.

But investigative journalists do have the advantage of special access to sources denied police because individuals fear involvement in the courts or in the processes of legal investigation. They can hear testimony without advising suspected culprits of their rights and without having a lawyer present.

Reporters do not have to prove a case in court. They have the advantage of presenting a partial and even inconclusive brief if they feel it is a useful tool for enlightening the public. And they have the advantage of working with cooperative enforcement officials, to whom they may entrust confidences in return for critical technical assistance. Together, the investigative journalist and the law enforcement official are a potent team. They complement one another when they work together or when either builds an investigation on work done by the other. Unknown to the public, many of the most important stories to hit the media have depended on the quiet background work of the police and many of the most sensational convictions have come through cooperation between law enforcement entities and the media.

In the future, as law enforcement comes to work more closely with media, we can expect even more effective and more sensational results. As each begins to understand and respect the other, both will benefit. And the public will be the final and most important beneficiary of such collective action.

NOTE

[1]Quoted directly from ensuing indictment of Vizzini; John O'Sullivan, U.F.A. Financial and Recording Secretary; and Dominick Gentiluomo, the union's sergeant at arms.

25

Use of the Genealogical Approach in Searching for Missing Persons

Gerard J. Cushing

GETTING STARTED

In trying to locate an individual, whether a missing person whose name is known but whose whereabouts are unknown or a possible ancestor or relative whose name *and* whereabouts are unknown, the procedure is basically the same. *Go from the known to the unknown and from the present to the past.* This involves research into the individual's friends, business associates, places of residence, employers, marriages, children, religious and fraternal affiliations, education, military background, and so on (Fig. 25.1). Keep in mind that names, relationships, dates, places, and events are of the utmost importance. It is a good idea to construct a chart including all the information currently available. Leave blank spaces for information to be acquired from interviews with informants and research from various sources.

RELATIONSHIPS

Basically, the researcher will be interested in the following relationships: (1) *Lineal,* in which one person is the parent or offspring of another (Fig 25.2). In the following example, Gerard J. Cushing is in a lineal relationship because he is the

```
                        Gerard J. Cushing
                       Forensic Genealogist

         122 Broadway, Suite 3          50 Three Sisters Rd.
         Kissimmee, Florida 32741       St. James, L.I.
         (305) 847-6635                 New York  11780
                                        (516) 584-5431

                     GENEALOGICAL QUESTIONNAIRE
                                     RE:_____


Dear Sir:

I am searching for any next of kin that the above may have

had.  If found, they may be entitled to share in an estate.

Would you have information about (his) (her):

Place and date of birth?_____

Place and date of marriage?_____

Place and date of death?_____

Place of burial?_____

Names of children?_____

Father's name?_____

Father's occupation?_____

Mother's maiden name?_____

Date of parent's marriage?_____Place?_____

Date of father's death?_____Place?_____

Date of mother's death?_____Place?_____

Deceased a citizen of U.S.A.?_____

Armed Forces veteran?_____Branch?_____When?_____

Previous addresses?_____When?_____
```

Figure 25.1 Genealogical questionnaire.

son of Cyril J. Cushing; (2) *collateral,* in which a number of persons are related to one another by a common stock (for example, Gerard, Bernard, and Eileen are sister and brothers having the same parents); (3) *consanguine,* in which the parties are related by blood; and (4) *affinal,* in which persons are related through marriage (for example, my sister-in-law, Joanne, and I have an affinal relationship). Interrelationships do occur, and the differentiation becomes important when completing the family chart. There is no problem determining brothers and sisters of whole blood because they share common parents. Brothers and sisters of *half-blood* share only *one* common parent. Therefore, a half brother or a half sister has

Employer?_____

Please complete this form to the best of your ability and

return at your earliest convenience. I appreciate your

cooperation and assistance in this matter and have

enclosed a stamped self-addressed return envelope for your

convenience.

                Very truly yours,

                GERARD J. CUSHING

Figure 25.1 (*Continued*) Genealogical questionnaire.

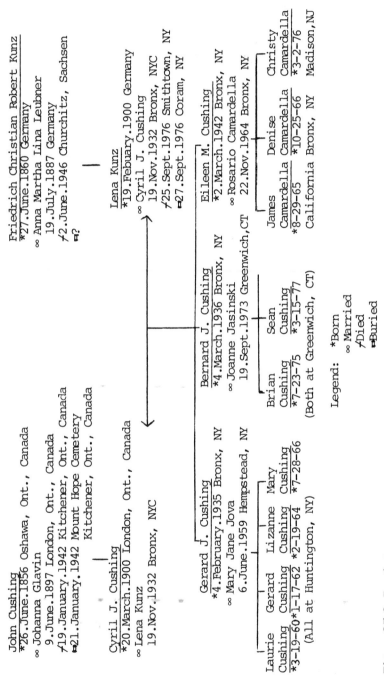

Figure 25.2 Family tree.

Legend: *Born
       ∞ Married
       ✝Died
       ⚰Buried

John Cushing
*26.June.1856 Oshawa, Ont., Canada
∞ Johanna Glavin
9.June.1897 London, Ont., Canada
✝19.January.1942 Kitchener, Ont., Canada
⚰21.January.1942 Mount Hope Cemetery
        Kitchener, Ont., Canada

Cyril J. Cushing
*20.March.1900 London, Ont., Canada
∞ Lena Kunz
19.Nov.1932 Bronx, NYC

Friedrich Christian Robert Kunz
*27.June.1860 Germany
∞ Anna Martha Lina Leubner
19.July.1887 Germany
✝2.June.1946 Churchitz, Sachsen
⚰?

Lena Kunz
*19.Febuary.1900 Germany
∞ Cyril J. Cushing
19.Nov.1932 Bronx, NYC
✝25.Sept.1976 Smithtown, NY
⚰27.Sept.1976 Coram, NY

Gerard J. Cushing
*4.February.1935 Bronx, NY
∞ Mary Jane Jova
6.June.1959 Hempstead, NY

Bernard J. Cushing
*4.March.1936 Bronx, NY
∞ Joanne Jasinski
19.Sept.1973 Greenwich,CT

Eileen M. Cushing
*2.March.1942 Bronx, NY
∞ Rosario Camardella
22.Nov.1964 Bronx, NY

Laurie   Gerard   Lizanne   Mary
Cushing   Cushing   Cushing   Cushing
*3-19-60   *1-17-62   *2-19-64   *7-28-66
(All at Huntington, NY)

Brian   Sean
Cushing   Cushing
*7-23-75   *3-15-77
(Both at Greenwich, CT)

James   Denise   Christy
Camardella   Camardella   Camardella
*8-29-65   *10-25-66   *3-2-76
California   Bronx, NY   Madison,NJ

the same blood as the one common parent. A *stepbrother* or a *stepsister* is not the same as a half brother or half sister. This is only an affinal (legal) relationship established through marriage. A stepchild does not share common natural parents. Stepchildren are not related to one another by blood. However, in some states, children of halfblood are legally entitled to inherit estates to the same degree as children of whole blood who share common parents.

The Germans have a very descriptive term for a cousin once removed, *einmal entfernt*, or "once distant." A child or issue of a first cousin is a first cousin once removed to any other first cousin. However, a first cousin once removed is a second cousin to another first cousin once removed. First cousins share a grandparent as the common progenitor. Second cousins share a great-grandparent as the common progenitor. Third cousins share a great-great-grandparent as the common progenitor, and so on.

RESOURCES

The key to any effective research involves having good resources and knowing where to locate them. Many times, attorneys with whom I have associated on various estate settlements are amazed that I have been able to locate a missing person when they were stymied. The secret to effective genealogical research is knowing the sources and location of information available to the researcher. I have found that an effective genealogical researcher must be a detective, historian, linguist, diplomat, and genealogical specialist and have an inquisitive mind that puts all the facts together. The most reliable information base for a genealogical researcher is called a primary source. Into this category fall all the vital statistics inscribed on birth, marriage, divorce, and death certificates. They are original records recorded on or near the day of the event and are likely to be accurate. Secondary sources are newspaper stories, death and obituary notices, census and probate records, immigration and naturalization files, military and social security records, and so on. One must remember to assess the accuracy of all these records and try to corroborate the information with that from other data banks.

Primary Record Sources

Birth, marriage, divorce, and death records generally give the following information (Fig. 25.3): date and location where the event took place; name of the individual to whom the record pertains; legal residence; names (if known) of the parents of the person to whom the record pertains; the name and address of the person supplying the information; the age and date of birth of the individual identified; and, in the case of death records, the name and address of the funeral director as well as the place of interment. All clues for further information. Especially important would be a letter or trip to the funeral director and the cemetery to uncover whatever information their files contain that is pertinent to the next of kin, relatives, or person responsible for maintaining the family cemetery plot.

Birth, marriage, divorce, and death records are usually maintained on a state or county level. Some incorporated villages also maintain a registrar's office for vital statistics; that is, birth, marriage, divorce, and death records. Copies can usually be obtained for a small fee. The Superintendent of Documents, U.S. Government Printing Office, Washington, DC 20402 has the following publication, which sells for $4.50 cents each:

"Where to Write for Vital Records: Births, Deaths, Marriages, and Divorces," Hyattsville, MD: U.S. Department of Health and Human Services, National Center for Health Statistics, 1992.

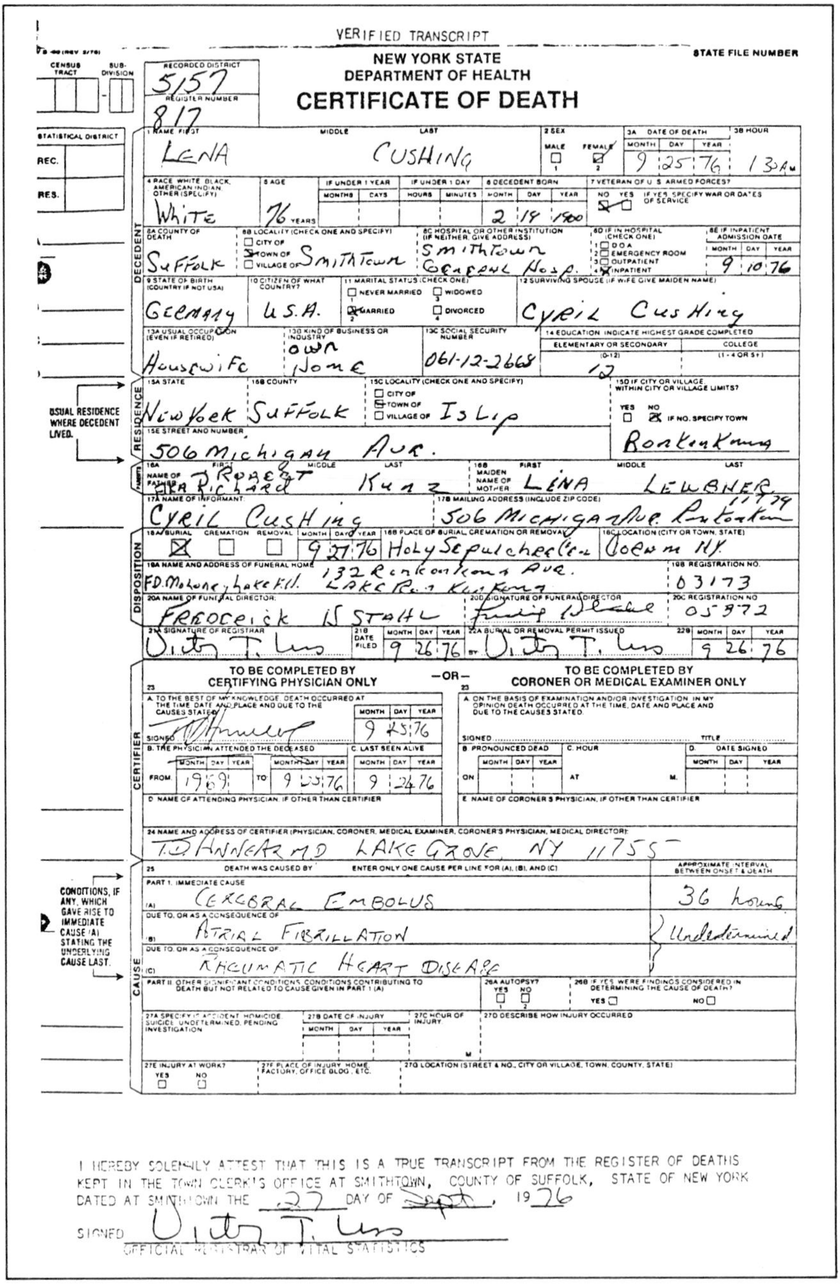

Figure 25.3 Certificate of death.

Secondary Record Resources

Although these records may not be as accurate or precise with respect to genealogical information as the vital statistics records, nevertheless they provide good leads for gathering genealogical facts and should not be overlooked.

The Federal Census. Most recent census schedules are closed to the public because they must be closed for 72 years from the date they were taken. By "closed" I mean they are not available to the general public, since there is a presumption that the individuals therein may still be alive. However, a request can be made for a personal review of a recent census pertaining to oneself, a parent, or a grandparent, using request form BC-600, "Application of Search of Census Records" of the Bureau of the Census, Personal Census Service Branch, Pittsburg, KA 66762 (Fig. 25.4). Census records for 1880 and earlier have been transferred to the National Archives and Records Service, Washington, DC 20408 and are considered public records. The census of 1890 was destroyed in a fire and only limited returns of that census are available. The federal censuses of 1900, 1910, and 1920 have been recently opened for personal inspection only at a branch archive. Microfilm records of the federal census up to 1880 and the federal censuses of 1900, 1910, and 1920 may be studied at any of the branch archives listed below. The microfilm of the federal census up to 1880 *only* may also be ordered through the local library or research institution that has a microfilm reader. The addresses of the branch archives are:

Building 22—MOT Bayonne
Bayonne, NJ 07002
(201) 858-7164

380 Trapelo Road
Waltham, MA 02154
(617) 223-2657

5000 Wissahickon Ave.
Philadelphia, PA 19144
(215) 951-5591

2306 E. Bannister Road
Kansas City, MO 64131
(816) 926-7271

1557 St. Joseph Ave.
East Point, GA
(404) 763-7474

4900 Hampbill Street
P.O. Box 6216
Fort Worth, TX 76115
(817) 334-5515

7358 South Pulaski Road
Chicago, IL 60629
(312) 353-8541

Building 48
Denver Federal Center
Denver, CO 80255
(303) 234-5271

1000 Commodore Drive
San Bruno, CA 94066
(415) 876-9001

6125 Sand Point Way N.E.
Seattle, WA 98115
(206) 442-4502

2400 Avila Road
Laguna Niguel, CA 92677
(714) 831-4242

A federal census enumeration was conducted by the U.S. government in 1990.

The State Census. In addition to the federal census undertaken every 10 years, some states have made their own demographic surveys, including censuses in years between the federal censuses. New York State, in particular, conducted its own enumeration of residents in 1892, 1905, 1915, and 1925. A request should be submitted, with the name of the head of the household and the address for all the years specified, to the clerk of the county, who is the repository of the state census returns. Or a letter can be directed to the Manuscripts and History Section, State Library, Albany, NY 11230.

FORM BC-600
(10-5-76)

U.S. DEPARTMENT OF COMMERCE
BUREAU OF THE CENSUS

FORM APPROVED
O.M.B. NO. 41-R2181

APPLICATION FOR SEARCH OF CENSUS RECORDS

DO NOT USE THIS SPACE

CASE NO.

$ _____ (Fee)

☐ Money Order
☐ Check
☐ Other

PURPOSE FOR WHICH RECORD IS TO BE USED (MUST BE STATED HERE) (See Instruction 1)

▶ RETURN TO: U.S. Department of Commerce, Bureau of the Census, PITTSBURG, KANSAS 66762

FULL NAME OF PERSON WHOSE CENSUS RECORD IS REQUESTED
(Print or type)

| FIRST NAME | MIDDLE NAME | MAIDEN NAME (If any) | PRESENT LAST NAME | NICKNAMES |

DATE OF BIRTH (If unknown — estimate) | PLACE OF BIRTH (City, county, State) | RACE | SEX

FULL NAME OF FATHER (Stepfather, guardian, etc.)

Please give FULL name of husband or wife of person whose record is requested.

FIRST MARRIAGE (Name of husband or wife) | YEAR MARRIED (Approximate)

FULL MAIDEN NAME OF MOTHER (Stepmother, etc.)

SECOND MARRIAGE (Name of husband or wife) | YEAR MARRIED (Approximate)

GIVE PLACE OF RESIDENCE AT EACH DATE LISTED BELOW

CENSUS DATE	NUMBER AND STREET (Very important)	CITY, TOWN, TOWNSHIP (Precinct, beat, etc.)	COUNTY AND STATE	NAME OF PERSON WITH WHOM LIVING (Head of household)	RELATIONSHIP
JUNE 1, 1900 (See Instruction 2)					
APRIL 15, 1910 (See Instruction 3)					
JAN. 1, 1920 (See Instruction 2)					
APRIL 1, 1930 (See Instruction 3)					
APRIL 1, 1940 (See Instruction 3)					
APRIL 1, 1950 (See Instruction 3)					
APRIL 1, 1960 (See Instructions 3 and 9)					
APRIL 1, 1970 (See Instructions 3 and 9)					

• If the census information is to be sent to someone other than the person whose record is requested, give the name and address, including ZIP code, of the other person or agency.

• This authorizes the Bureau of the Census to send the record to: (See Instruction 4)

FEE REQUIRED: See Instructions 5, 6, and 7 on the reverse side.

A check or money order (DO NOT SEND CASH) payable to "Commerce — Census," must be sent with the application. This fee covers the cost of a search of not more than two census years about one person only.

Fee required . . . . $ 8.50

_____ extra copies @ $1.00 each . . $ _____

_____ full schedules @ $2.00 each . $ _____

TOTAL amount enclosed ──▶ $ _____

I certify that information furnished about anyone other than the applicant will not be used to the detriment of such person or persons by me or by anyone else with my permission.

SIGNATURE — Do not print
(Read Instruction 8 carefully before signing)

PRESENT ADDRESS | NUMBER AND STREET

SIGNATURE

CITY | STATE | ZIP CODE

IF SIGNED ABOVE BY MARK (X), TWO WITNESSES MUST SIGN HERE

SIGNATURE

NOTICE — Intentially falsifying this application may result in a fine of $10,000 or five years imprisonment, or both (title 18, U.S. Code, section (001)).

Figure 25.4 Application for search of census records.

Probate Records. Many persons think of court records in terms of criminal documentation, but there are other kinds of court proceedings. Much genealogical information can be derived from wills or administrative proceedings. Such records are usually on deposit at the county level. One exception to this is in the state of Connecticut, where the probate records are maintained by the towns. In general, these records are found in the probate, surrogate, circuit, county, orphans, and superior courts of different states. If real property is located somewhere else, the location may give the researcher a clue to where the owner lived previously and where relatives may subsequently be found. These public records are available to the general public by simply asking the record-room clerk for the "Estate of John Jones" and indicating whether the proceeding is probate or administrative. Sometimes this information can be found in a central file-card index of the court-record room.

Immigration and Naturalization Records. There have been many mass migrations to this country. Records for immigrants entering the port of New York and other Atlantic ports can be obtained from the National Archives, Washington, DC 20408 (Fig. 25.5). A ship's passenger list may reveal an ancestor's name, place of birth, occupation, and approximate dates of travel and other members of the family, the place to which they were traveling, and possibly the name and address of a relative in the United States. Naturalization and immigration papers are a good source of genealogical data. They usually provide the researcher with the approximate date when the ancestor arrived in this country and, most important, the name and location of the town and country from which the person emigrated. One of the most puzzling yet rewarding cases that I ever worked on involved an ancestor who, according to naturalization records in New York Supreme Court (Old Records Room, County Clerk's Office, 31 Chambers St., New York, NY), had emigrated from the village of Masmunster, Germany about the year 1872. Elated at this bit of information, I checked my map of Germany to ascertain the exact location of this small German village, but it did not appear there or on any other available maps. I knew that after World War II, Germany was divided into the Federal Republic, with its capital in Bonn, and the German Democratic Republic, with its capital in East Berlin. At the time of the investigation, therefore, Masmunster did not appear on any of my German maps. Perplexed by the disappearance of this village, I happened to mention my plight to a friendly librarian, who suggested I cross-check with an international geographical gazeteer in the library. Previously, I had sent letters to both German states, only to receive negative replies. Inquiries sent to Lufthansa German Airlines and to the German Tourist Board turned up no new information. However, by digging further, I discovered that Masmunster, a small village on the west bank of the Rhine river, formerly German territory, was now known as Masveaux and located in the French Department of Alsace. Apparently, when the subject of my research left Europe in 1872 he was a German citizen. However, in 1918 the village became French territory until the Germans occupied it in 1939. At the conclusion of World War II, it became French territory again. By writing letters in German and French, I was able to locate two relatives still living in Masveaux who spoke French, German, and Alsatian. They became heirs to a large estate that was pending in the New York Surrogate Court. Preliminary letters to these people, written in French, culminated in my trip to Masveaux, where I located other distributees.

For a copy of the naturalization record, one can apply to the Immigration and Naturalization Service, U.S. Department of Justice, Jacob Javitz Center, 26 Federal Plaza, New York, NY 10278 and request Form G-641. If the record is found, the INS will bill you through an invoice.

UNITED STATES DEPARTMENT OF JUSTICE	Form approved
Immigration and Naturalization Service	OMB No. 043-R0570

**APPLICATION FOR
VERIFICATION OF INFORMATION FROM
IMMIGRATION AND NATURALIZATION SERVICE
RECORDS**

Fee Stamp

TYPE OR PRINT THE NAME AND MAILING ADDRESS OF THE PERSONS TO WHOM
INFORMATION OR COPIES OF RECORD SHOULD BE RETURNED IN THE BOX BELOW:

NAME	
STREET ADDRESS	
CITY, STATE ZIP CODE	

PERSON CONSENTING

NAME AND ADDRESS

SIGNATURE OF PERSON CONSENTING

---

1. CHECK TYPE OF VERIFICATION REQUESTED:	2. STATE PURPOSE FOR WHICH DESIRED	3. NUMBER OF COPIES DESIRED, IF ANY:
☐ AGE OR DATE OF BIRTH		
☐ NATURALIZATION OR CITIZENSHIP	2A. NAMES OF BENEFICIARIES	4. IF INFORMATION IS FOR SOCIAL SECURITY BENEFITS, SHOW SOCIAL SECURITY NUMBER:
☐ GENEALOGICAL INFORMATION		
☐ OTHER (CERTIFICATE OF BIRTH DATA, ETC.)		

DATA FOR IDENTIFICATION OF THE RECORD TO BE VERIFIED

5. FAMILY NAME	GIVEN NAME	MIDDLE NAME	6. ALIEN REGISTRATION NUMBER

7. OTHER NAMES USED, IF ANY	8. NAME USED AT TIME OF ENTRY INTO UNITED STATES

9. PLACE OF BIRTH	10. DATE OF BIRTH	11. PORT ABROAD FROM WHICH LEFT FOR UNITED STATES

12. PORT OF ENTRY INTO UNITED STATES	13. DATE OF ENTRY	14. NAME OF VESSEL OR OTHER MEANS OF ENTRY

GIVE THE FOLLOWING INFORMATION FOR VERIFICATION OF NATURALIZATION OR CERTIFICATE OF CITIZENSHIP

15. NAME ON CERTIFICATE	16. CERTIFICATE NUMBER	17. DATE ISSUED

18. ADDRESS WHEN CERTIFICATE WAS ISSUED	19. NAME AND LOCATION OF NATURALIZATION COURT OR IMMIGRATION OFFICE ISSUING CERTIFICATE OF CITIZENSHIP

| **DO NOT COMPLETE THIS BLOCK —
RESERVED FOR GOVERNMENT USE ONLY**	20. SIGNATURE OF APPLICANT

THE RECORDS OF THE IMMIGRATION AND NATURALIZATION SERVICE REFLECT THE FOLLOWING:
VERIFICATION OF INFORMATION REQUESTED WAS MADE ON THE DATE SHOWN AT RIGHT

DATE:

☐ LAWFUL ADMISSION FOR PERMANENT RESIDENCE ON _____ AT _____
☐ NATURALIZATION INFORMATION AS SHOWN ABOVE IS CORRECT
☐ NATURALIZATION IN (COURT) _____ ON (DATE) _____
   AT (LOCATION) _____
☐ DATE OF BIRTH _____
☐ ARRIVAL RECORD DATED _____ SHOWED SUBJECT'S AGE AT TIME TO BE _____
☐ UNABLE TO IDENTIFY ANY RECORD
☐ COPIES ATTACHED AS REQUESTED   SIGNATURE _____

TITLE _____

PRIVACY ACT		Approved By	DATE
IDENTIFICATION	☐ IDENTITY ESTABLISHED IN PERSON		
(WHEN REQUIRED)	DOCUMENTS ATTACHED ☐ G-652 Affidavit ☐ OTHER (List)		

FORM G-641 (REV. 8 2-78) N

Figure 25.5 Application for verification of information from Immigration and Naturalization Service records.

Military Records. Write to the National Records Center, 9700 Page Boulevard, St. Louis, MO 63132 for information regarding a soldier's name; date of service; date and place of birth; names of father and mother and, if married, wife. Service records less than 75 years old are subject to restrictions. However, you can obtain the genealogical information in them under certain circumstances. Explain your reasons in the originating letter or on Form 180.

**ORDER AND BILLING
FOR COPIES OF
PASSENGER ARRIVAL
RECORDS**

Please follow instructions below.
Submit a separate set of order forms for each passenger arrival.
Do not remove any of the sheets of this 4 part set. You will be
billed $3.00 for each list reproduced. **Do not mail payment with
your order.** This form will be returned to you and serves as your
bill when we fill your order.

*Date received by
National Archives*

**Mail the complete
set of this order to** ▶ Passenger Arrival Records (NNCC), National Archives (GSA), Washington, DC 20408

IDENTIFICATION OF ENTRY

DATE OF ARRIVAL	NAME OF IMMIGRANT OR NAMES OF MEMBERS OF IMMIGRANT FAMILY	AGE	SEX
PORT OF ENTRY			
WHERE NATURALIZED *(IF KNOWN)*			
SHIP NAME *(OR CARRIER LINE)*			
PASSENGER'S COUNTRY OF ORIGIN			

NOTE

The National Archives has customs passenger lists dating back to 1820 with a few as early as 1787. Lists prior to 1820 that are not at
the National Archives may be on file at the port of entry or the State archives in the State where the port is located. The Morton Allan
Directory of European Passenger Steamship Arrivals may be useful in determining the name and arrival date of ships arriving at New
York, 1890—1930, and Philadelphia, Baltimore, and Boston, 1904—1926.
Please fill in as much of the information called for above as possible. We will advise you if the information is inadequate to enable us to
locate the entry you are seeking.
If you wish to hire a researcher to assist you, write to the following organization which will provide you a list: Board for Certification of
Genealogists, 1307 New Hampshire Avenue NW., Washington, DC 20036.

YOUR NAME AND ADDRESS	**DO NOT WRITE BELOW - SPACE IS FOR NATIONAL ARCHIVES TO REPLY TO YOU**

City & State / Number & Street / Name — Type or print legibly PRESS HARD

	THIS IS YOUR BILL	RECORD ENCLOSED ▶	ARRIVAL DATE	PORT	SHIP
			MICROFILM PUBLICATION		make check or money order payable to NATF (NNCC)
			ROLL	PAGE	AMOUNT DUE ▶ $

	WE WERE UNABLE TO COMPLETE YOUR ORDER	RECORD SEARCHED FOR BUT NOT FOUND ▶	RECORDS SEARCHED		
	SEE REVERSE		MICROFILM PUBLICATION	SEARCHER	
			ROLL	PAGE	DATE SEARCHED

☐ A SEARCH WAS NOT MADE FOR THE REASON INDICATED:

☐ 1. Our index to New York passenger arrivals covers the periods 1820—1846 and 1897—1943. We
regret that we cannot undertake a page-by-page search of the lists for the period between 1847
—1896, inclusive.

☐ 2. Masters of vessels departing from U.S. ports were not required to list the names of passengers.
Therefore, we would not have a list for the passenger you have cited.

☐ 3. Our holdings of passenger lists do not include any for Pacific coast ports. The San Francisco
passenger lists were destroyed by fires in 1851 and 1940. The California Historical Society, 2090
Jackson Street, San Francisco, Ca. 94109, has lists of persons who arrived in California, chiefly
1820—69, and indexes to the names on the lists. The lists are not original records but were
prepared from newspapers and other sources.

☐ 4. Overland arrivals into the U.S. from Canada and Mexico are not documented in passenger list
records. Perhaps information can be furnished by the Public Archives, Ottawa, Canada; or the
Archivo General, Palacio Nacional, Mexico City DF, Mexico.

☐ 5. Justice Department restrictions prohibit us from making searches in Immigration and Naturalization records less than 50 years old. We suggest that you direct an inquiry to: District Director,
Immigration and Naturalization Service, New York, NY 10007.

**NUMBER OF BLANK ORDER
FORMS YOU WOULD
LIKE SENT TO YOU** ▶

(zip code)

GENERAL SERVICES ADMINISTRATION   **GSA FORM 7111** (REV. 7-76)

Figure 25.6 Order and billing for copies of passenger-arrival records (front).

Ship's Passenger Lists. At some point in American ancestral development,
a forebear came to this country aboard a ship that entered one of the many ports
along the Atlantic, Gulf, and Pacific coasts. The place to begin this phase of a search
is in the National Archives, Washington, DC 20408. Form GSA 7111 (Fig. 25.6),
which will be sent to you on request, should be submitted. Information about an
ancestor, if found, may contain name and age; sex and occupation; nationality;
and, sometimes, the name and address of a relative whom he or she was visiting

PASSENGER LISTS IN THE NATIONAL ARCHIVES

_____ 1. We found several entries for persons of the same name arriving at the same port during the same period. Additional information, such as age occupation, etc., will help in resolving this problem.

_____ 2. We found the requested information on the passenger index, but we regret that the corresponding passenger list is missing. A copy of the index card is enclosed.

_____ 3. We are unable to locate the passenger list for the ship listed and have found no entry on the passenger index for the requested party at that port.

_____ 4. We examined the passenger list for the requested ship and were unable to find an entry for the requested passenger.

_____ 5. The register of ship arrivals did not show any entry for the ship named.

_____ 6. Our only passenger lists for the cited port do not cover the date that you have requested, and we were unable to find an entry on the index to the lists we have.

_____ 7. You may find some help in the book Irish and Scotch-Irish Ancestral Research by Margaret Dickson Falley (1962). It is a guide to genealogical records and repositories in Ireland and is normally available in larger libraries.

_____ 8. Passports are issued to persons leaving the U.S., not arriving, but early arrivals are frequently documented in passenger lists, which are described in the enclosed leaflet.

_____ 9. The National Archives has custody of Naturalization proceedings for the New England States (1787—1906) and the District of Columbia (1802—1926). For information about citizenship granted elsewhere before September 27, 1906, send inquiries to the clerk of the Federal, State, or other court that issued the naturalization certificate. The Immigration and Naturalization Service, Washington, DC 20536, can furnish information on naturalizations that occurred after September 26, 1906.

_____ 10. It should be noted that the passenger lists in our custody do not represent a complete collection. Some passenger lists of the 19th century were either lost or destroyed by dampness, fire, and other causes before records of this type were deposited in the National Archives.

_____ 11. We found an entry in the Naturalization records for the person in whom you are interested. Since Federal law prohibits reproduction of these records, we have listed the pertinent information below:

Figure 25.6 (_Continued_) Order and billing for copies of passenger-arrival records (back).

in this country. If the name of the immigrant's ship is unknown, consult the _Morton Allen Directory of European Passenger Steamship Arrivals_, 1890 to 1930 at the port of New York and 1904 to 1926 in the ports of New York, Philadelphia, Boston, and Baltimore.[1] The records of the Pacific ports were destroyed in a fire. Usually, this book can be found in any large library.

Passport Applications. Passport applications sometimes provide helpful genealogical information. Apparently, the general public is sometimes confused about the difference between a passport and a visa. An American passport is evidence of American citizenship and is required for reentry after a trip outside the United States. Passports contain a picture of the applicant and are currently valid for five years. Visas are entry permits issued by some foreign nations to allow the passport bearer to enter that country and remain for a specified period. A fee is usually charged for the issuance of a passport and a visa. Visas from foreign nations usually can be obtained by writing to the embassy of that particular country in Washington, DC.

If an ancestor might have traveled and applied for a passport before 1905, information about his or her passport application can be obtained from the National Archives, Washington, DC 20408, by submitting the name, address if known, and the approximate date of application. If the application is found, a nominal fee will be charged for copies. If the individual being sought traveled and applied for a passport after 1906, one can write to the Passport Office, Department of State, Washington, DC 20504, submitting the individual's name and, if known, the date and place of birth and year and place of application. If the application is found, the Passport Office will send a bill after the search has been completed (Fig. 25.7).

Civilian Personnel Records. If the individual being sought works or may have worked as a civilian employee in the federal government, certain information can be obtained which may reveal his or her title, grade, and work station. It will not provide much genealogical data but may help determine where the individual was during a specific time span. Write to the Civilian Personnel Records, GSA, 11 Winnebago Street, St. Louis, MO 63118.

Other Record Resources. These are perhaps not as fruitful as the primary and secondary resources. Yet because they may very well provide useful information and helpful leads that can tie the loose pieces of the puzzle together, do not overlook:

- Telephone books and city directories located in the local library or university library.
- Hospital records.
- Church records.
- Cemetery records.
- A family Bible.
- Banks—savings and commercial.
- Insurance company records.
- School records.
- Police and FBI records.
- Social security records in Baltimore, Maryland.
- Obituary and death notices in local newspapers where the event occurred.
- Real estate brokers.
- Real property records located in the county courthouses.
- Maps (geographical, road, survey, and so on).

DEPARTMENT OF STATE
PASSPORT APPLICATION

(PASSPORT OFFICE USE ONLY)
R D O DP Endorsement ________

A

TO BE COMPLETED BY ALL APPLICANTS

(First name) (Middle name) (Last name)

I, ________________________________

a citizen of the United States, do hereby apply to the Department of State for a passport.

MAIL PASSPORT TO:
IN CARE OF (If applicable): ________
STREET ________
CITY ________ STATE ________ ZIP CODE ________
PHONE NO. Area Code: ____ Home: ________ Business: ________

SEX (M-F)	BIRTHPLACE (City, State or Province, Country)		BIRTH DATE Month Day Year
DEPARTURE DATE	HEIGHT ___ Ft. ___ In.	COLOR OF HAIR	COLOR OF EYES
PERMANENT RESIDENCE (Street address, City, State, ZIP Code)			SOCIAL SECURITY NO. (Not mandatory)

APPLICANT'S EVIDENCE OF CITIZENSHIP
☐ Birth Certificate SR CR City
☐ Certificate of Naturalization or Citizenship
☐ Passport
Bearer's Name:
No.: Filed/Issued:
Place: ☐ Seen & Returned

2" X 2" FROM 1" TO 1-3/8"

FOR DETAILED PHOTOGRAPH REQUIREMENTS, SEE ATTACHED INFORMATION SHEET. ACCEPTANCE AGENT WILL STAPLE PHOTO OF BEARER HERE.

IN THE EVENT OF ACCIDENT OR DEATH NOTIFY (Not mandatory) (Do not give name of person who will accompany you when traveling)
Name in full: Relationship:
Address: Phone No.:

FATHER'S NAME	BIRTHPLACE	BIRTH DATE	U.S. CITIZEN ☐Yes ☐No
MOTHER'S MAIDEN NAME	BIRTHPLACE	BIRTH DATE	U.S. CITIZEN ☐Yes ☐No

☐ I WAS LAST MARRIED ON ________ TO (Wife's/Husband's full legal/maiden name - complete whether married, widowed or divorced)
☐ I WAS NEVER MARRIED

HAVE YOU OR ANYONE INCLUDED IN SECTION B OF THIS APPLICATION BEEN ISSUED OR INCLUDED IN A U.S. PASSPORT? ☐Yes ☐No
IF YES, SUBMIT PASSPORT. IF UNABLE TO SUBMIT MOST RECENT PASSPORT, STATE ITS DISPOSITION: No.: Issue Date:

B

ACCEPTANCE AGENT WILL STAPLE PHOTO OF INCLUSION(S) HERE.

AGENT SHALL NOT IMPRESS SEAL ON ANY PHOTOGRAPHS.

PHOTO REQUIREMENTS FOR PERSON(S) TO BE INCLUDED
See detailed photograph requirements on the attached information sheet.
Photo must be ONLY of person(s) to be included (other than passport bearer). When more than one person is to be included, a group photo of the inclusions is required.

COMPLETE IF CHILDREN OR BROTHERS AND SISTERS UNDER AGE 13, AND/OR WIFE/HUSBAND, ARE TO BE INCLUDED AND SUBMIT PHOTO

WIFE'S/HUSBAND'S FULL LEGAL NAME

BIRTHPLACE (City, State or Province, Country) | BIRTH DATE (Mo., Day, Yr.)

(PASSPORT OFFICE USE ONLY)
WIFE'S/HUSBAND'S EVIDENCE
☐ Seen & Returned

CHILD(REN)'S NAME(S) IN FULL	BIRTHPLACE(S) (City, State or Country)	BIRTH DATE(S) (Mo., Day, Yr.)	CHILD(REN)'S EVIDENCE
			☐ Seen & Returned

I have not (and no other person included in this application has), since acquiring United States citizenship, performed any of the acts listed in section I on the reverse of this application form (unless explanatory statement is attached). I solemnly swear (or affirm) that the statements made on all of the pages of this application are true and the photograph(s) attached is (are) a likeness of me and of those persons to be included in the passport.

________ (SEAL) ________
(To be signed at same time by husband/wife to be included in passport) (To be signed by Applicant in presence of person administering oath)

Subscribed and sworn to (affirmed) before me this ________ day of ________ 19 ____.

Clerk of the ________, Postal Employee/Passport Agent at ________
(Signature of person authorized to accept application)

(PASSPORT OFFICE USE ONLY)

FEE ______ EXEC. ______ POST. ______

FORM 1-78 DSP-11 PLEASE TYPE OR PRINT CLEARLY IN INK (Pencil is not acceptable) (OVER – YOU MUST COMPLETE PAGE 2) FORM APPROVED O.M.B. No. 47–R0061

Figure 25.7 Passport application (back).

The Latter-Day Saints, or Mormons. I would be remiss if I did not include information about the genealogical library maintained by the Church of Jesus Christ of the Latter-Day Saints. The main library, which I have visited, is in Temple Square, Salt Lake City, Utah. Its facilities and genealogical information are available to anyone doing genealogical research. A small handling fee is charged for mail inquiries. Contrary to popular belief, the records pertain not only to those of

FORM DSP-11 1-78

PAGE 2

C

TO BE COMPLETED BY ALL APPLICANTS

OCCUPATION	VISIBLE DISTINGUISHING MARKS	COUNTY OF RESIDENCE (Not mandatory)

D

APPLICANTS MUST COMPLETE FOLLOWING IF MARRIED, WIDOWED OR DIVORCED

WIFE'S/HUSBAND'S BIRTHPLACE	WIFE'S/HUSBAND'S BIRTH DATE	U.S. CITIZEN ☐ Yes ☐ No	☐ MARRIAGE NOT TERMINATED ☐ MARRIAGE TERMINATED BY ☐ DEATH ☐ DIVORCE ON (Date)

E

WOMEN MUST COMPLETE FOLLOWING IF CHILDREN OF A PREVIOUS MARRIAGE ARE INCLUDED OR IF PREVIOUSLY MARRIED BEFORE MARCH 3, 1931

I WAS PREVIOUSLY MARRIED ON	TO (Full legal name)	WHO WAS BORN AT (City, State, Country)
ON (Date of birth)	☐ FORMER HUSBAND WAS U.S. CITIZEN ☐ FORMER HUSBAND WAS NOT U.S. CITIZEN	PREVIOUS MARRIAGE TERMINATED BY ☐ DEATH ☐ DIVORCE ON (Date)

F

COMPLETE IF APPLICANT OR ANY PERSON INCLUDED IN SECTION B WAS NOT BORN IN THE UNITED STATES AND CLAIMS CITIZENSHIP THROUGH PARENT(S)

ENTERED THE U.S. (Month) (Year) ☐ Applicant ☐ Wife ☐ Husband ☐ Child	IF FATHER NATURALIZED:		IF KNOWN, FATHER'S RESIDENCE/ PHYSICAL PRESENCE IN U.S. From (Year) To (Year)
	Date	Certificate No.	
	Before (Name of Court)	Place (City, State)	
RESIDENCE/CONTINUOUS PHYSICAL PRESENCE IN U.S. From(Year) To (Year) ☐ Applicant ☐ Wife ☐ Husband ☐ Child	IF MOTHER NATURALIZED:		IF KNOWN, MOTHER'S RESIDENCE/ PHYSICAL PRESENCE IN U.S. From (Year) To (Year)
	Date	Certificate No.	
	Before (Name of Court)	Place (City, State)	

G

PROPOSED TRAVEL PLANS (For statistical reporting purposes—Not Mandatory)

PURPOSE OF TRIP	MEANS OF TRANSPORTATION Ship Air Other Departure ☐ ☐ ☐	COUNTRIES TO BE VISITED
PROPOSED LENGTH OF STAY	Return ☐ ☐ ☐	
NO. OF PREVIOUS TRIPS ABROAD WITHIN LAST 12 MONTHS	DO YOU EXPECT TO TAKE ANOTHER TRIP ABROAD? ☐ Yes ☐ No IF SO, WITHIN ☐ 1 Year ☐ 2 Years ☐ 5 Years	

H

PRIVACY ACT STATEMENT

The information solicited on this form is authorized by, but not limited to, those statutes codified in Titles 8, 18, and 22, United States Code, and all predecessor statutes whether or not codified, and all regulations issued pursuant to Executive Order 11295 of August 5, 1966. The primary purpose for soliciting the information is to establish citizenship, identity and entitlement to issuance of a United States Passport or related facility, and to properly administer and enforce the laws pertaining thereto.

The information is made available as a routine use on a need-to-know basis to personnel of the Department of State and other government agencies having statutory or other lawful authority to maintain such information in the performance of their official duties; pursuant to a subpoena or court order; and, as set forth in Part 6a, Title 22, Code of Federal Regulations (See Federal Register Volume 40, pages 45755, 45756, 47419 and 47420).

Failure to provide the information requested on this form may result in the denial of a United States Passport, related document or service to the individual seeking such passport, document or service.

NOTE: The disclosure of your Social Security Number or of the identity and location of a person to be notified in the event of death or accident is entirely voluntary. However, failure to provide this information may prevent the Department of State from providing you with timely assistance or protection in the event you should encounter an emergency situation while outside the United States.

I

ACTS OR CONDITIONS

(If any of the below-mentioned acts or conditions have been performed by or apply to the applicant, or to any other person to be included in the passport, the portion which applies should be struck out, and a supplementary explanatory statement under oath (or affirmation) by the person to whom the portion is applicable should be attached and made a part of this application.)

I have not (and no other person included in this application has), since acquiring United States citizenship, been naturalized as a citizen of a foreign state; taken an oath or made an affirmation or other formal declaration of allegiance to a foreign state; entered or served in the armed forces of a foreign state; accepted or performed the duties of any office, post, or employment under the government of a foreign state or political subdivision thereof; made a formal renunciation of nationality either in the United States or before a diplomatic or consular officer of the United States in a foreign state; ever sought or claimed the benefits of the nationality of any foreign state; been convicted by a court or court martial of competent jurisdiction of committing any act of treason against, or attempting by force to overthrow, or bearing arms against, the United States, or conspiring to overthrow, put down or destroy by force, the Government of the United States.

WARNING: False statements made knowingly and willfully in passport applications or in affidavits or other supporting documents submitted therewith are punishable by fine and/or imprisonment under the provisions of 18 USC 1001 and/or 18 USC 1542. Alteration or mutilation of a passport issued pursuant to this application is punishable by fine and/or imprisonment under the provisions of 18 USC 1543. The use of a passport in violation of the restrictions contained therein or of the passport regulations is punishable by fine and/or imprisonment under 18 USC 1544. All statements and documents submitted are subject to verification.

J

(FOR USE OF APPLICATION ACCEPTANCE AGENT ONLY)

APPLICANT'S IDENTIFYING DOCUMENT(S)		IDENTIFYING DOCUMENT(S) OF WIFE/HUSBAND TO BE INCLUDED IN PASSPORT	
☐ Certificate of Natural- ization or Citizenship	No.:	☐ Certificate of Natural- ization or Citizenship	No.:
☐ Passport	Issue Date:	☐ Passport	Issue Date:
☐ Driver's License	Place of Issue:	☐ Driver's License	Place of Issue:
☐ Other (Specify):	Issued in Name of:	☐ Other (Specify):	Issued in Name of:

U.S. GOVERNMENT PRINTING OFFICE 1978—258-410 5236

Figure 25.7 (*Continued*) Passport application (front).

the Mormon faith, but to Catholic, Protestant, Jewish, and civil records form countries all over the world. The Mormons have been busy microfilming records from churches; cemeteries; and city, town, and county offices for many years, and it is said that over 60 million names are contained in their files.

Microfilms and other materials can be borrowed through one of the branch libraries located in 44 states of the United States, Canada, and Mexico. Simply look in the telephone book for the listing, Church of Jesus Christ of the Latter-Day Saints (LDS). If there is no LDS church or branch library nearby, a reference librarian can provide the name and the address of the LDS. One may write directly to the LDS for further information: The Genealogy Department, Church of Jesus Christ of the Latter-Day Saints, 50 East North Temple Street, Salt Lake City, UT 84150.

Genealogical Societies and Organizations

Genealogical Publishing Company, Inc.
111 Water Street
Baltimore, MD 21202

Everton Publishers
P.O. Box 368
Logan, UT 85321

Augustan Society, Inc.
1510 Cravens Avenue
Torrance, CA 90501

New York Genealogical and
Biographical Society
122 East 58 Street
New York, NY 10022

Genealogists Bookshelf
343 East 85 Street
New York, NY 10028

Goodspeed's Bookshop, Inc.
Department 3
18 Beacon Street
Boston, MA 02108

Society of Genealogists
37 Harrington Gardens
London, England SW74JX

CONCLUSION

Genealogy as a pastime and a profession is, indeed, interesting and intriguing. The recent showing of the TV movie *Roots* has made genealogy the third most popular pastime in the United States. Librarians, as well as genealogical and historical societies have been inundated with requests for ancestral information. The success and credibility of any genealogical probe rests on the researcher as well as on the availability and accessibility of records. Various obstacles will be encountered on the road to the goal. However, one will also learn and experience the meanings of people, events and places.

NOTE

[1]Allan, Morton. *Directory of European Passenger Steamship Arrivals* (Baltimore MD: Genealogical Publishing Company, Inc., 1979).

26

U.S. Immigration Service Investigation

Gerard LaSalle

The U.S. Immigration and Naturalization Service (INS) is an agency under the U.S. Department of Justice with a multifaceted mission. It regulates the flow of aliens into this country, processes them for U.S. citizenship, and locates and apprehends those here in violation of the law. It also participates with other law enforcement agencies in the detection and prosecution of organized crime narcotic violators.

This chapter serves a dual purpose. First, it assists local, state, and other federal law enforcement agencies by explaining the immigration process. Second, it provides a ready reference for businesspeople on the requirements of employing aliens in the United States. (An *alien* is a person who is not a citizen of this country.)

To comprehend fully the INS enforcement function, a general overview of the INS and the alien process is necessary.

CATEGORIES OF ALIENS

Immigrants

Immigrants are aliens admitted to the United States who can remain indefinitely, own property, work, and move about without restriction. By and large, they enjoy the same privileges as U.S. citizens, except the right to vote. They must comply with certain registration procedures. These legal aliens may become subject to deportation if they are convicted of serious felony crimes, engage in subversive or immoral activities, or become public charges.

Any alien admitted to this country as a permanent resident is issued an immigrant visa by the Department of State at an office (U.S consulate) outside the United States. The visa is a separate document, which is surrendered to INS at the port of entry and made part of a record relating to the alien. The INS then issues an Alien Registration Receipt Card (Form I-551) as evidence of lawful admission for permanent residence. This card is commonly called a "green card" because it derived the name from its original color. Through the years the tint has changed to blue, and the most recent version is pink (Fig. 26.1).

Basically, legal aliens enter the United States under two broad categories: family sponsorship or employment related. However, the Immigration and Nationality Act (Title 8 United States Code) contains other provisions to obtain permanent residency either through special immigrant categories or as political asylees.

Family Sponsorship. Family-based visas are given to spouses, children (under 21 years), and parents of United States citizens (USCs), as well as to widows and widowers of USCs, provided they were the spouse for at least two years at the time of the citizen's death and were not legally separated. This entire group is usually referred to as the *Immediate Relative* category.

Family-based *preference* classifications are similar to those just mentioned, but contain numerical limitations on the number of entrants to the United States. These visas are provided to unmarried sons and daughters (over 21 years) of USCs, spouses and children of legal permanent residents, unmarried sons and

Alien Registration Receipt Card I-151: Issued by INS prior to June 1978, to lawful permanent resident aliens. There are numerous versions of this card because it was periodically revised. Although this card is no longer issued, it is valid indefinitely. This card is also commonly referred to as a "green card" although most versions were blue.

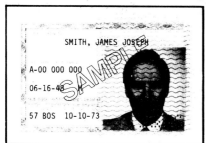 

Alien Registration Receipt Card (Resident Alien Card) I-551: Issued by INS after March 1977, to lawful permanent resident aliens. Although this card is no longer issued, it is valid indefinitely. This card is commonly referred to as a "green card" and is the replacement for the Form I-151. This version is white with a blue logo.

Figure 26.1 Types of alien registration receipt cards.

daughters of legal permanent residents, spouses and children of legal permanent residents (exempt from numerical limitations), married sons and daughters of USCs, and brothers and sisters of USCs.

Employment-Related. Employment-based immigration is divided into five categories:

1. Priority workers:
   a. Aliens with extraordinary ability.
   b. Outstanding professors and researchers.
   c. Certain multinational executives and managers.
2. Members of the professions holding advanced degrees or aliens of exceptional ability.

Alien Registration Receipt Card (Conditional Resident Alien Card) I-551: Issued by INS after January 1987, to conditional permanent resident aliens such as alien spouses of United States citizens or lawful permanent resident aliens. It is similar to the I-551 issued to permanent resident aliens. Although this card is no longer issued, it is valid for two years from the date of admission or adjustment. The expiration date is stated on the back of the card. This version is white with a blue logo.

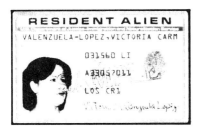 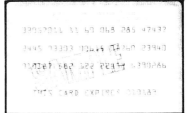

Alien Registration Receipt Card (Resident Alien Card) I-551: Currently issued by INS since 1989 to both conditional and lawful permanent resident aliens. Although it is similar to the previously issued I-551s, this card is valid only for a limited period of time—two years from the date of admission or adjustment for conditional permanent resident aliens and 10 years from issuance for lawful permanent resident aliens. The expiration date is stated on the front of the card. This version is rose-colored with a blue logo.

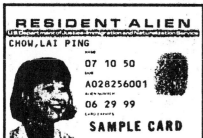 

Figure 26.1 (*Continued*) Types of alien registration receipt cards.

3. Skilled workers, professionals, and other workers.
4. Certain special immigrants:
   a. Returning permanent resident aliens who may have technically abandoned their residence.
   b. Religious workers.
5. Employment creation immigrants: This category requires a capital investment of $1 million and the creation of 10 full-time positions for legal permanent residents or United States citizens. The Attorney General may decide that certain geographical areas call for a lower investment, such as $500,000.

Spouses and children of these classifications will receive derivative permanent residency from the principal petitioner.

Nonimmigrants

Nonimmigrant aliens are admitted temporarily for specific purposes and for definite periods of time. Generally, they must carry an Immigration Form I-94 (Arrival/Departure Record), endorsed to show their immigration status. This form serves as a control document, entry-departure record, identification card, and proof of alien registration. The information appearing in the lower right-hand corner is placed there by the inspecting INS officer and includes the date of entry, a three-letter code signifying the port through which the alien entered, and the date on which the alien's stay expires. Other data may be contained on the back of the form, such as change of status, extension dates, and permission to accept employment. Upon departure from the United States, the I-94 must be surrendered to the transportation company or the Immigration Service as a record of departure. Mexican aliens may enter at a border port with Form I-186 in lieu of Form I-94. This border-crossing card limits their stay to 72 hours and restricts their travel to no more than 25 miles from the border area. The I-94 will bear one of the following letters, indicating how the alien was admitted into the United States.

Designated Letters

A-1	Ambassador, career diplomatic, or consular officer, and members of the immediate family.
A-2	Other foreign government officials or employees and members of their immediate family.
A-3	Attendant, servant, or personal employee of A-1 and A-2 classes and members of their immediate family.
B-1	Temporary visitor for business.
B-2	Temporary visitor for pleasure.
C-1	Alien in immediate and continuous transit through the United States.
TWOV	Aliens in transit to another country through the United States.
D-1	Crewmember (sea or air).
E-1	Treaty trader, spouse, and children.
E-2	Treaty investor, spouse, and children.
F-1	Student (academic). Note that academic students are those pursuing a full-time course of study. They no longer need extensions of stay in the U.S. and are permitted to work 20 hours per week.

F-2	Spouse and child of student.
G-1	Principal resident representative of recognized foreign government, member of international organization, staff, and members of immediate family.
H	Temporary workers or trainees (registered nurses, agricultural workers).
I	Representatives of foreign information media, spouse, and children.
J	Exchange visitor.
K	Fiance or fiancee of a United States citizen.
L	Intracompany transferee (executive, managerial, and specialized personnel continuing employment with an international firm or corporation).
M	Vocational and nonacademic students.
O	Aliens with extraordinary ability or achievements (arts, sciences, business, athletics, or education).
P	Members of entertainment groups and internationally recognized athletes.
Q	Aliens participating in an international cultural exchange program.
R	Religious workers.

Illegal Entrants

Illegal entrants are aliens who illegally enter the United States in such a manner or place as to avoid inspection by an INS officer. They are deportable and are commonly referred to as EWIs (*entry without inspection*).

An alien in an illegal status may present a false or altered identification card or a genuine document belonging to someone else. The first step is to ascertain that the holder is actually the person named on the certificate. Next, check the document issued by the INS to determine the conditions of admission as well as the duration of the stay. Often, after examining these records and briefly questioning the alien, it can be confirmed that he/she is illegally in the United States. The most common violation of temporary admission is unauthorized employment and/or remaining beyond the time allowed.

Aliens who entered surreptitiously will possess no valid papers. However, they may claim legal status or even U.S. citizenship and present some type of fraudulent documentation to substantiate their claims.

Temporary (nonimmigrant) visas are issued by the U.S. Department of State at offices (consulates) in foreign countries. Such a visa is a stamp placed on one of the pages in a passport, which usually is issued in the country of the alien's nationality. The visa does not establish a right to be in, or to remain in, the United States. It merely allows an alien to proceed to a port of entry to apply to the INS for admission. The conditions and period of admission are decided by the Immigration officer at the port of entry after the alien has been interviewed. Form I-94 (Arrival-Departure Record), showing the period of authorized admission, is issued by the Immigration officer and placed in the alien's passport. Extensions of stay are shown on the reverse of the form, which is surrendered at time of departure from the United States. To be valid, the visa must be unexpired when the alien applies at the port of entry. However, the remaining duration of the visa's validity has no bearing on the period of authorized admission granted by the Immigration officer. For example, an alien may be admitted for six months (and perhaps receive one or more extensions of stay), even though the visa had been good for only one day beyond the date on which he or she applied for entry. On the other hand, an alien's admission might be limited to one week, even though at the time of entry the visa may have been valid for four years. Moreover, entry can be refused altogether, notwithstanding possession of a valid unexpired visa.

EMPLOYER SANCTIONS

This section is extremely important for those who employ both aliens and U.S. citizens. It sets forth the requirement for legal compliance as well as providing a hands-on reference in reviewing the necessary documents for employment.

In 1986 the Immigration Reform and Control Act (IRCA) overhauled the entire Immigration and Naturalization Service (INS) process for employers. On November 29, 1990, President Bush signed the *Immigration Act of 1990* (*IMMACT '90*), which significantly altered the 1986 IRCA regarding the employment verification provisions. The employers now became responsible for ensuring that their workers met the statutory requirement for a job in the United States. This prerequisite extended to both the United States citizen and alien wage earners. The law necessitated that employers verify the employment eligibility of anyone hired after November 6, 1986.

Jobs are the greatest magnet attracting persons to enter and overstay in the United States. Since this nation's average weekly wage often equals monthly incomes of other countries, it becomes obvious that, to curtail illegal immigration, control of employment is needed.

To implement this statute, the INS requires employers to complete Form I-9 (Employment Eligibility Verification Form) for all job holders as a means to verify eligibility to work in the United States.

The law demands that employers have their workers complete Form I-9, while the employer must verify the prospective jobholder's identity and eligibility to work by checking certain documents. This form also has to be available for inspection by the INS and the Department of Labor.

The law exempts those hired after November 6, 1986, who are periodic domestic workers, those who are subcontracted or independently contracted to an employer, and those who are self-employed. Domestic help retained on a regular basis require completion of Form I-9.

IRCA also provided for the eventual permanent residency for those aliens who were in an illegal status after January 1, 1982, and those employed as Special Agricultural Workers (SAW). Both are issued employment cards with photographs (Form I-688B) and thereafter a temporary resident alien card (Form I-688) (Fig. 26.2). Eventually, they may apply for permanent residency and after approval is issued an alien registration card (Form I-551). These individuals also need to show work authorization documents for employment.

The form is divided into two sections: one completed by the employer and the other by the employee. The latter provides documents establishing identity and employment eligibility. The INS provides three separate listings of acceptable documentation. The records in list A establish both identity and employment eligibility. Lists B and C provide identity and employment eligibility, respectively. An employee who fails to provide a document from list A must then produce one from list B and one from list C. It is the employer's responsibility to review the documents, which should appear authentic and relate to the worker. An employer may not specify which record(s) an employee must present.

Temporary Resident Card I-688: Issued by INS to aliens granted temporary resident status under the Legalization or Special Agricultural Worker program. It is valid until the expiration date stated on the face of the card or on the sticker(s) placed on the back of the card.

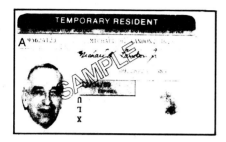

Employment Authorization Card I-688A: Issued by INS to applicants for temporary resident status after their interview for Legalization or Special Agricultural Worker status. It is valid until the expiration date stated on the face of the card or on the sticker(s) placed on the back of the card.

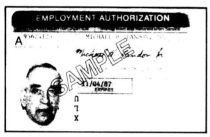

Figure 26.2 Temporary resident alien cards.

List A. Documents that establish both identity and employment eligibility (Fig. 26.3) are:

1. U.S. passport (unexpired or expired).

2. Certificate of U.S. Citizenship (INS Form N-560 or N-561).

3. Certificate of Naturalization (INS Form N-550 or N-570, Fig. 26.4).

4. Unexpired foreign passport with I-551 stamp or attached INS Form I-94 indicating unexpired employment authorization (Fig. 26.5).

5. Alien Registration Receipt Card with photograph (INS Form I-151 or I-551).

6. Unexpired Temporary Resident Card (INS Form I-688).

7. Unexpired Employment Authorization Card (INS Form I-688A).

8. Expired Reentry Permit (INS Form I-327).

9. Unexpired Refugee Travel Document (INS Form I-571, Fig. 26.5).

10. Unexpired Employment Authorization Document issued by the INS, which contains a photograph (INS Form I-688B).

Employment Authorization Card I-688B: Issued by INS to aliens granted temporary employment authorization in the United States. The expiration date is noted on the face of the card.

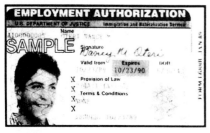

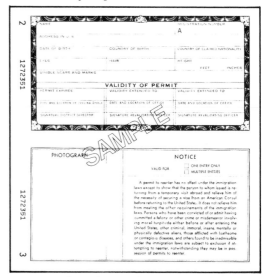

Unexpired Reentry Permit I-327: Issued by INS to lawful permanent resident aliens before they leave the United States for a 1–2 year period.

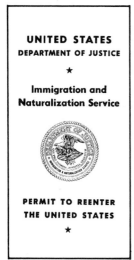

Figure 26.2 (*Continued*) Temporary resident alien cards.

Certificate of Naturalization (N-550 or N-570): Issued by INS to naturalized United States citizens.

Certificate of Naturalization (N-550): Issued by INS to naturalized United States citizens who file for naturalization after October 1, 1991.

Figure 26.3 Document list A: documents that establish both identity and employment eligibility.

United States Passport: Issued by the Department of State to United States citizens and nationals.

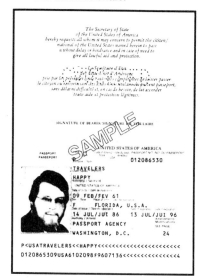

Certificate of United States Citizenship (N-560 or N-561): Issued by INS to individuals who (1) derived citizenship through parental naturalization; (2) acquired citizenship at birth abroad through a United States parent or parents; or (3) acquired citizenship through application by United States citizen adoptive parent(s); and who, pursuant to Section 341 of the Act, have applied for a certificate of citizenship.

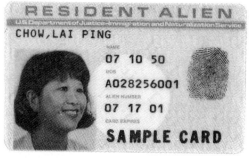

(a)

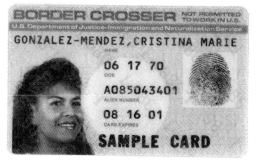

(b)

Figure 26.3 *(Continued)* Document list A: documents that establish both identity and employment eligibility. (*a*) Resident alien card; (*b*) border crosser card.

Certificate of Naturalization (N-550 or N-570): Issued by INS to naturalized United States citizens.

Certificate of Naturalization (N-550): Issued by INS to naturalized United States citizens who file for naturalization after October 1, 1991.

Figure 26.4 Certificates of Naturalization.

 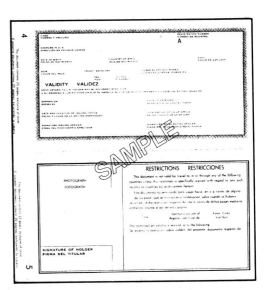

Figure 26.5 *Unexpired Refugee Travel Document I-571:* Issued by INS to aliens who have been granted refugee status. The expiration date is stated on page 4.

List B. Documents that establish identity are:

1. Driver's license or ID card issued by a state or outlying possession of the United States, provided it contains a photograph or information, such as name, date of birth, sex, height, eye color, and address.

2. ID card issued by federal, state, or local government agencies or entities, provided it contains a photograph or information, such as name, date of birth, sex, height, eye color, and address.

3. School ID card with photograph.
4. Voter's registration card.
5. U.S. military card or draft card.
6. Military dependent's ID card.
7. U.S. Coast Guard Merchant Mariner card.
8. Native American tribal document.
9. Driver's license issued by a Canadian government authority.

For persons under age 18 who are unable to present a document from the preceding list:

10. School record or report card.
11. Clinic, doctor, or hospital record.
12. Day care or nursery school record.

List C.   Documents that establish employment eligibility are:

1. U.S. social security card issued by the Social Security Administration (other than a card stating it is not valid for employment).
2. Certification of Birth Abroad issued by the Department of State (Form FS-545 or Form DS-1350, Fig. 26.6).
3. Original or certified copy of a birth certificate issued by a state, county, municipal authority, or outlying possession of the United States bearing an official seal.
4. Native American tribal document.
5. U.S. Citizen ID Card (INS Form I-197).
6. ID Card for use of Resident Citizen in the United States (INS Form I-179, Fig. 26.7).
7. Unexpired employment authorization document issued by the INS (other than those in list A).

FS-545: Issued by U.S. embassies and consulates overseas to United States citizens born abroad.

DS-1350: Issued by the U.S. Department of State to United States citizens born abroad.

Figure 26.6 Certifications of Birth issued by the Department of State.

United States Citizen Identification Card I-197: Issued by INS to U.S. citizens. Although INS no longer issues this card, it is valid indefinitely.

Identification Card for Use of Resident Citizen in the United States I-179: Issued by INS to U.S citizens who are residents of the United States. Although INS no longer issues this card, it is valid indefinitely.

 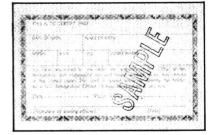

Figure 26.7 Identification cards.

The new law also prohibits discrimination on the basis of national origin or citizenship status, as it relates to hiring and discharging an individual. An employer can avoid discrimination by ensuring that the law is equally applied to all. Requesting documents only from those employees of a particular origin, or from those who appear or sound foreign, violates the law. Basically, employers cannot set different employment verification standards or require different documents for different groups of workers.

Violations and Corresponding Criminal Penalties

If an employer has violated the law with regard to those hired after November 6, 1986, INS may institute regulatory action. INS can impose penalties, and, if an employer does not request a hearing before an administrative judge within 30 days, a disciplinary action may be imposed. Penalties are as follows:

1. *Hiring or continuing to employ unauthorized workers:* Employers found knowingly to hire unauthorized employees or continue to employ them after notification that they are unauthorized may be fined not less than $250 and not more than $2000 for each unauthorized employee. The second violation is not less than $2000 and not more than $5000 for each unauthorized employee. Subsequent violations are to be not less than $3000 and not more than $10,000 for each unauthorized employee.

2. *Failing to comply with record-keeping requirements:* Employers must complete, retain, and present for inspection Form I-9, or face civil penalties of not less than $100 and not more than $1000 for each employee violated. In assessing penalties, INS will consider the size of the company, the good faith efforts to comply, the seriousness of the violation, and whether the violation involved unauthorized employees.

Other penalties apply to those employers who may have required a bond or indemnity as condition of employment and those who knowingly recruit unauthorized workers outside the United States to perform seasonal agricultural labor.

1. *Engaging in a pattern or practice of knowingly hiring or continuing to employ unauthorized workers:* Employers falling into this category face fines up to $3000 per employee and/or six months imprisonment.

2. *Engaging in fraud or false statements or otherwise misusing visas, immigration permits, and identity documents:* Using documents falsely issued to another or false statements or attestations to satisfy employment eligibility can result in imprisonment for up to five years or a fine of $250 and not more than $2000 for each fraudulent document issued, accepted, or created and for each instance of use, acceptance, or creation (first offense). Subsequent offenses are not less than $2000 and not more than $5000 for each offense.

The I-9 is required only for those actually hired and not just applicants. The employer's responsibility as it relates to documents is to ensure that they appear genuine and relate to the individual presenting them. Employers will have an affirmative defense if they had their workers fill out their portion of the I-9, checked to see if the required documents appear genuine, completed the I-9 employer portion, retained the form and made it available to INS or the Department of Labor. A person who is rehired within three years by the same employer need not complete a new I-9, nor is an I-9 required if an employee is promoted or transferred within the company.

An employer may designate someone, such as a personnel officer, to actually complete the I-9 form. Though the law does not require photocopying documents submitted to support eligibility to work, an employer may make copies, but they must be retained with the I-9. The I-9 may be destroyed either one year after termination or three years after the date of original hire, whichever is later. Of course, the I-9 must be retained if the individual is still employed.

To combat the use of fraudulent documents, it is now unlawful to use, possess, obtain, accept, or receive any forged, counterfeit, altered, or falsely made document to satisfy any requirement of the Immigration and Nationality Act. This provision encompasses employer and employee.

The INS and Other Law Enforcement Agencies

Apprehensions along the southern border for the first nine months of fiscal year 1991 numbered 788,419. At this rate the yearly projection was expected to exceed 1.05 million. This did not take into account aliens illegally entering the United States through Canada or those illegally here by overstaying their time of admission or accepting unauthorized employment.

In 1987 United States attorneys throughout the country prosecuted approximately 7500 persons suspected of committing immigration offenses, such as smuggling aliens, using fraudulent documents, and entering the United States without inspection. The average sentence in federal prison was five years. Clearly, criminal aliens are making their presence felt within the criminal justice system. INS has devoted investigative positions and financial resources to participate in the interdiction of narcotic violators at border areas, as well as to the detection and apprehension of violators within the United States. INS recognizes the integral role aliens of all nationalities play in the transportation and distribution of narcotics. Cocaine and heroin are manufactured abroad and, somewhere along the line before final street sale, alien intervention occurs. Consequently, all levels of law enforcement are served well by having a working knowledge of INS regulations. Knowledge on how to determine proper immigration status results in law enforcement officers having an added tool at their disposal. As already indicated, most nonimmigrants should possess Form I-94 (Fig. 26.8). From this form, law enforcement officers can determine on what date an alien becomes illegal. Furthermore, by examining the reverse side they are able to establish whether an alien has received an extension and when the authorized stay expires.

Officers should also bear in mind that an individual may violate status and be deported if he or she accepts unauthorized employment, even though the time of stay granted upon entry to the United States has not expired. Since these individuals come into this country as B-2 visitors for pleasure, employment is prohibited. Officers should be aware that the duration for which they were legally admitted has no bearing on their deportability if they are found to be employed.

Officers can now tell an alien that this information concerning immigration status will be forwarded to INS and a determination made as to deportability. However, they may further advise the alien that through their intercession deportation may be stayed. Depending on the merits of each individual case, the INS, after placing an alien under deportation proceedings, can allow the alien to remain in the United States if he or she is serving a useful purpose for another law enforcement agency.

Accordingly, law enforcement officers, by identifying aliens illegally in the United States, can create an additional advantage for their investigations that may be of vital importance to the successful resolution of their own particular cases, notwithstanding the INS violations.

The officer should also realize that legal questions may arise as to the right of other than INS officers stopping and interrogating individuals for possible immigration violations. Some states have addressed the legality of such stops and issued their own guidelines.

CONCLUSION

We have examined the portions of the Immigration process that affect law enforcement and business. Defining alien classification and status may become an added investigative tool at their disposal. Through alien identification and cooperation with the Immigration Service, police can extend their sphere of influence in combatting crime. Aliens may serve as a useful source of information within a criminal community where police officers, because of cultural or language barriers, have been unable to penetrate.

This chapter also provided employers an overview of changes in the Immigration law that directly affect their businesses. By delineating the legal requirements for employment in the United States, business can ensure that it is in compliance with the law and will avoid possible civil and criminal penalties.

I-20 ID Card Accompanied by a Form I-94: The Form I-94 for F-1 nonimmigrant students must be accompanied by an I-20 Student ID endorsed with employment authorization by the Designated School Official for off-campus employment or curriculum practical training. INS will issue Form I-688B (Employment Authorization Document) to all student (F-1 and M-1) authorized for a postcompletion practical training period.

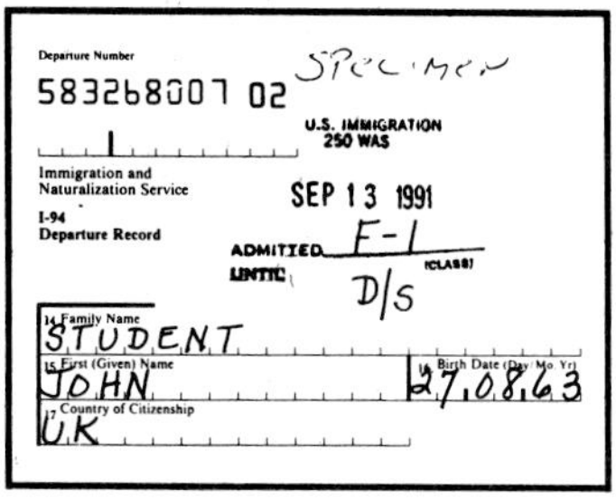
Departure Number
583268007 02 SPECIMEN
U.S. IMMIGRATION
250 WAS
Immigration and Naturalization Service
I-94
Departure Record
SEP 13 1991
ADMITTED F-1
UNTIL (CLASS)
D/S
14 Family Name
STUDENT
15 First (Given) Name
JOHN
16 Birth Date (Day/Mo/Yr)
27.08.63
17 Country of Citizenship
U.K

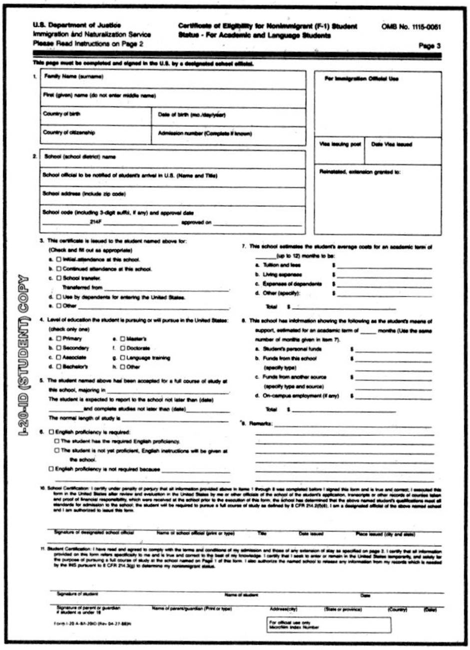
U.S. Department of Justice
Immigration and Naturalization Service
Please Read Instructions on Page 2

Certificate of Eligibility for Nonimmigrant (F-1) Student Status - For Academic and Language Students

OMB No. 1115-0051

Page 3

This page must be completed and signed in the U.S. by a designated school official.

1. Family Name (surname)
First (given) name (do not enter middle name)
Country of birth — Date of birth (mo./day/year)
Country of citizenship — Admission number (Complete if known)

For Immigration Official Use
Visa issuing post — Date Visa issued
Reinstated, extension granted to:

2. School (school district) name
School official to be notified of student's arrival in U.S. (Name and Title)
School address (include zip code)
School code (including 3-digit suffix, if any) and approval date
_____ 214F _____ approved on _____

3. This certificate is issued to the student named above for:
(Check and fill out as appropriate)
a. ☐ Initial attendance at this school.
b. ☐ Continued attendance at this school.
c. ☐ School transfer.
Transferred from _____
d. ☐ Use by dependents for entering the United States.
e. ☐ Other _____

4. Level of education the student is pursuing or will pursue in the United States:
(check only one)
a. ☐ Primary e. ☐ Master's
b. ☐ Secondary f. ☐ Doctorate
c. ☐ Associate g. ☐ Language training
d. ☐ Bachelor's h. ☐ Other

5. The student named above has been accepted for a full course of study at this school, majoring in _____
The student is expected to report to the school not later than (date) _____ and complete studies not later than (date) _____
The normal length of study is _____

6. ☐ English proficiency is required:
☐ The student has the required English proficiency.
☐ The student is not yet proficient, English instructions will be given at the school.
☐ English proficiency is not required because _____

7. This school estimates the student's average costs for an academic term of _____ (up to 12) months to be:
a. Tuition and fees $ _____
b. Living expenses $ _____
c. Expenses of dependents $ _____
d. Other (specify): $ _____
Total $ _____

8. This school has information showing the following as the student's means of support, estimated for an academic term of _____ months (Use the same number of months given in item 7).
a. Student's personal funds $ _____
b. Funds from this school (specify type) $ _____
c. Funds from another source (specify type and source) $ _____
d. On-campus employment (if any) $ _____
Total $ _____

9. Remarks: _____

10. School Certification: I certify under penalty of perjury that all information provided above in items 1 through 8 was completed before I signed this form and is true and correct; I executed this form in the United States after review and evaluation in the United States by me or other officials of the school of the student's application, transcripts or other records of courses taken and proof of financial responsibility, which were received at the school prior to the execution of this form; the school has determined that the above named student's qualifications meet all standards for admission to the school; the student will be required to pursue a full course of study as defined by 8 CFR 214.2(f)(6). I am a designated official of the above named school and I am authorized to issue this form.

Signature of designated school official — Name of school official (print or type) — Title — Date issued — Place issued (city and state)

11. Student Certification: I have read and agreed to comply with the terms and conditions of my admission and those of any extension of stay as specified on page 2. I certify that all information provided on this form refers specifically to me and is true and correct to the best of my knowledge. I certify that I seek to enter or remain in the United States temporarily, and solely for the purpose of pursuing a full course of study at the school named on Page 1 of this form. I also authorize the named school to release any information from my records which is needed by the INS pursuant to 8 CFR 214.3(g) to determine my nonimmigrant status.

Signature of student — Name of student — Date

Signature of parent or guardian if student is under 18 — Name of parent/guardian (Print or type) — Address(city) — (State or province) — (Country) — (Date)

Form I-20 A-B/I-20ID (Rev 04-27-88)N

For official use only
Microfilm Index Number

I-20-ID (STUDENT) COPY

Form I-20 Student ID (Reverse)
Endorsement by Designated School Official for Employment Authorization.

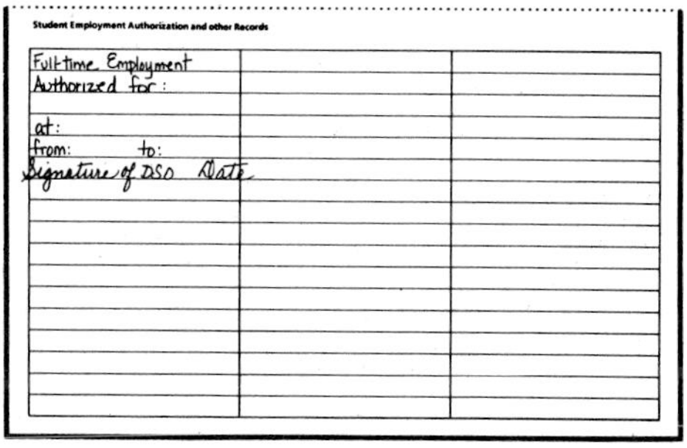
Student Employment Authorization and other Records
Full-time Employment
Authorized for:
at:
from: to:
Signature of DSO Date

Figure 26.8 Other types of identification cards.

PART 5

Operational and Nonoperational Police Units

27

Forensic Investigation

James J. Horan

When the average person and, for that matter, even most investigators think about forensic science, they envision a laboratory technician searching for fingerprints and bloodstains at the scene of a homicide. Television and mystery writers have conditioned the public to think of forensic science in connection with the investigation of homicides and other violent crimes. Although it is true that forensic science can play an important part in these major investigations, some of the most productive work of the forensic scientist is performed in other types of investigation.

This chapter will examine what forensic science is and how it can assist the investigator in all areas of investigation and will also show investigators that they are a vital part of the scientific examination of evidence. It will look at what physical evidence is, its uses, and the general rules for its collection, marking, and packaging for submission to the forensic scientist. Once the general picture has been shown, some possible applications of specific types of evidence and their value to investigators can be suggested. Finally, some suggestions are made on how and where to find a forensic expert to meet the specific needs of an investigator.

What Is Forensic Science?

The word "forensic" as an adjective means legal. So the simplest definition of forensic science would be *any science used in the legal process. Forensic science* has come to mean the study, practice, and application of science to the purposes of the law. As a practical matter, there is not one forensic science, but rather forensic sciences. It has come to be used as a collective description for all the various scientific disciplines which specialize in applying science to answering questions raised in the legal process.

The American Academy of Forensic Sciences illustrates the breadth of the forensic sciences. It is the leading professional society in the field, with a membership including the most prestigious experts in the various areas of this discipline. Although such professionals share a common interest in forensic science, they are divided into sections that reflect special areas of expertise. These sections provide a good overview of the major areas of forensic science today: pathology, toxicology, odontology, physical anthropology, psychiatry, questioned documents, criminalistics, and general. In addition, there is a jurisprudence section consisting of lawyers who specialize in cases involving forensic science. Although most investigators will never have a case that requires the expertise of all the different disciplines, they should be aware that they exist and have some idea of their content. It is knowing where to look for help in an unusual case that makes a good investigator. As a basis for this knowledge, the forensic specializations are briefly described.

Pathology.   Pathology is a specialty in medicine that deals with the diagnosis of diseases. Forensic pathologists are further specialized in that they study the causes of deaths, especially unnatural deaths. Most forensic pathologists are either medical examiners or coroners who work as part of the investigative team. They not only perform autopsies, but work in close conjunction with toxicologists, serologists, and other forensic scientists as well as investigators. Pathologists must conduct complete postmortem examinations during which they consider not only the physical condition of the body but also the circumstances and conditions at the time of death and the victim's past history. The examination is not complete if it focuses only on the most obvious. It must evaluate the toxicologist's report to see if there is a foreign chemical in the body, and if the level of those that are normally present is consistent with the circumstances of the case. The pathologist must also consider that a natural disease could have caused death and that injuries could have resulted from the victim falling.

Forensic Toxicology.   This is the biomedical science that studies the effect of foreign substances introduced into the living body.

The toxicologist assists the pathologist in the postmortem investigation by analyzing organs and tissues for poisons, drugs, alcohol, and other foreign substances. Because of their expertise in the identification of foreign substances in the body, forensic toxicologists are often called on to assist in hospitals and to help doctors in emergency poisoning and drug overdose cases.

Important areas where forensic toxicologists become involved with the legal system are "driving under the influence of alcohol" and drug cases. Not only do they analyze blood samples to determine if the alcohol content falls within the limits set by law but they also help develop analytic techniques to detect new drugs in the blood and the level at which they affect driving.

Odontology.   This is a branch of dentistry which deals with the examination of dental evidence. The odontologist may be called upon to evaluate the extent of injuries to teeth, jaw, and oral tissues. This type of examination is used mainly in civil cases, but, on occasion, it may involve injury cases such as assault.

The forensic odontologist is a specialist in the identification of bodies from the dental records of the individual. This can be extremely important in the case of badly decomposed or burnt bodies. The odontologist is usually part of a disaster team that responds to the scene of mass havoc, such as plane crashes, where there are large numbers of traumatized bodies to be identified. The disaster team is usually made up of fingerprint experts, odontologists, pathologists, and physical anthropologists. All these experts pool their skills in an effort to identify and piece together the bodies at the disaster.

Bite mark identification is another area where the forensic odontologist may be able to provide valuable evidence. For example, in some sex crimes and homicides the perpetrator may bite the victim. Also, there have been cases where the perpetrator had bitten into cheese, candy, or other foods at the crime scene, leaving dental impressions. If the circumstances are right, bite marks can be identified as having been made by the teeth of a specific individual.

Physical Anthropology. This is basically a study of the physical development of man. Most of the physical anthropologist's studies center around skeletal remains, mainly prehistoric. Forensic physical anthropologists are trained to apply the same techniques to modern forensic problems. They may be called on to identify the skeletal remains found in a secluded woods to determine if they are of recent origin or date back hundreds of years. They can also determine the sex, age, race, and physical condition of the skeleton. This information would be critical in a homicide investigation. The information which physical anthropologists can supply would also be valuable in identifying skeletal remains in insurance and missing persons investigations.

Physical anthropologists are a vital part of identification teams at mass disasters. They are able, by the examination of bones, to assist in proper labeling of the individuals and in putting severed parts together with the right body.

Engineering Sciences. The science of engineering has many applications in the forensic area. Engineers investigate why bridges and buildings collapse, why planes crash, and other areas in which engineering interfaces with the law. One area, the use of computer simulations for automobile accidents, has seen a great increase. Using computer models, the engineer is able to reconstruct how an accident happened.

Forensic Psychiatry. A forensic psychiatrist is a medical doctor who has received special training in psychiatry and its application to legal problems. We are all familiar with the use of psychiatry in a defense of insanity in criminal cases and in the examination of defendants to determine if they are competent to stand trial. These are important applications of forensic psychiatry for the administration of justice, but psychiatrists can also aid investigators in other ways.

They can be called upon to give investigators a psychological profile of a perpetrator who has committed unusual and bizarre crimes. Forensic psychiatrists can aid investigators in questioning important witnesses who cannot remember what happened for some psychological reason. By the use of hypnosis or drugs, they can sometimes help witnesses remember what happened.

Questioned Documents. This specialization involves the scientific examination of handwriting, hand printing, typing, ink, paper, or any other means of written or printed communication. The examination could involve determining authorship of a document; identifying forgeries; determining the age of documents; deciphering obliterated, erased, mutilated, or charred documents; or any other questions that may be raised about how, when, or by whom a document was produced.

The examiner of questioned documents should not be confused with the graphologist or graphoanalyst. The document examiner uses scientific techniques to determine the genuineness of handwriting by comparison of details in the known and the questioned writing. The graphologist tries to determine the character and personality of the writer by the general formulation of the letters. Graphology is an art form that has received little acceptance in the scientific community.

Document evidence is one type of evidence the average investigator will have frequent contact with. It will be examined later in this chapter in greater detail.

Criminalistics. This is the branch of forensic science that deals with the recognition, analysis, identification, individualization, and interpretation of physical evidence by the use of the natural sciences. For the most part, the criminalist is the forensic scientist who deals with the evidence submitted to the crime laboratories. Criminalistics has a number of subspecialties: firearms identification, drug chemistry, serology, and trace evidence analysis.

Present-day criminalists are equipped with a variety of modern scientific instruments: gas chromatographs, mass spectrometers, scanning electron microscopes, and so on. These instruments allow them to conduct detailed chemical analyses of microscopic pieces of evidence, which only a few years ago would have been of no value. Today it is possible for criminalists using atomic absorption or plasma emission spectrometry to determine the elemental composition of a speck of paint in parts per billion. The scanning electron microscope allows particles to be examined at a magnification of over 100,000 times.

Some of the evidence the criminalist examines will be discussed in greater detail later in this chapter.

General. The final section of the Academy is called "General." It is composed of forensic experts who do not come under one of the other sections. In most cases they are experts in areas where there are relatively few specialists. Some are forensic photographers, who not only take pictures of evidence but also are able to identify from a negative the camera that was used, or forensic archaeologists, who may be specialists in digging up buried bodies in such a way as to get every trace of evidence and information from the scene. They may even be forensic entomologists who are able to examine bugs and larvae at the scene or in the evidence to reveal information about the time of death or whether the body or evidence may have been moved.

The potential for the scientific community to assist the investigator is limited only by the imagination of each. Many areas of scientific research are detective stories in their own right. Investigators who have scientific or technical problems should seek out the help of forensic scientists. If they cannot help, at least they may be able to direct investigators to experts who can.

Physical Evidence

The items, or "things," that the forensic scientist works with are, for the most part, inanimate objects that answer some question concerning the investigation. In the legal system they are classified as physical evidence.

Physical evidence can be defined as any item or condition that tells when, where, how, or why an event took place or who committed an act. This definition uses the word "event" instead of "crime," because physical evidence could be important not only in criminal investigations but also in civil or other types of investigations. For any investigator, awareness that things associated with the event have a story to tell is basic to investigative technique. The story that evidence tells depends on its nature and condition. Not all physical evidence will identify the perpetrator of the crime, but all evidence can be of value in the hands of a good investigator.

Physical evidence can be used to:

1. Identify the perpetrator.

2. Associate the perpetrator and the scene.

3. Prove an element of the crime.

4. Associate the crime or event with another.

5. Provide the investigator with leads.

Identification of the perpetrator can be accomplished with fingerprints, with handwriting, and in some rare cases by the analysis of blood. In these cases, the expert is able to make a positive identification of a person to the exclusion of all others.

Many examinations of physical evidence are the type that identify an object in the possession of the perpetrator as having been used at the scene of the crime or event in question or objects found on the scene as belonging to the suspect. For example, a firearms identification examination may determine that the bullet found at the scene was fired from a gun in the suspect's possession; or it may be determined that paint from the suspect's car was the same as the paint from the scene of a hit-and-run case, or that glass on the suspect's clothes came from a broken window at the scene.

Many times it is by forensic analysis that an important element of the crime must be proved. Narcotics analysis is the most common example: If the substance in the perpetrator's possession is not one of the drugs or narcotics prohibited under the law, the criminal charge will not be substantiated. Other examples would be proving that a flammable substance was used in an arson case, that semen is present in a rape case, or that the percentage of alcohol present in the blood of a driver exceeds the limits under the DWI law.

The association of one crime or event with another can be accomplished by analysis of physical evidence. This is usually done when the perpetrator employs the same instrument to commit a number of crimes. For example, the same gun may have been used in a series of shootings; the same typewriter to type a number of letters or checks.

Modus operandi files have been recognized for years as an important investigative resource. The use of physical evidence to associate one event with another can be an important adjunct to these files. Open-case bullet files, fraudulent check files, robbery note files, and anonymous letter files have been valuable but their full potential has never been realized. If detailed information about the physical evidence involved in a case were included in computerized modus operandi files, it could be a valuable aid to the investigator.

The final use of physical evidence is when the forensic scientist provides the investigator with information about the evidence that does not in itself prove any point in the case but can be valuable as an investigative lead. If, for example, in the vacuum sweepings from a car used in a crime, the criminalist finds brass particles and one of the suspects works in a brass factory, this could give direction to the investigation. Another example would be the identification of the manufacturer of one of the items used in the crime. By checking with the manufacturer, the investigator may be able to trace it to the perpetrator.

The value of this type of information is demonstrated by a homicide case in which a body was found in a homemade plywood box. The name of the plywood manufacturer was covered with paint. The laboratory was able, using infrared photography, to bring up the name of the manufacturer. With this information, the investigator contacted the manufacturer and received a list of lumberyards in the area that purchased their plywood, then contacted the lumberyards in the area of the homicide and found that a neighbor of the victim had bought the same type of wood at the time of the homicide. The investigator went to the neighbor's house and found another piece of plywood that could be positively matched with that used for the box. The neighbor admitted his part in the crime and was convicted.

The last two uses of physical evidence, associating crimes and providing investigative leads, are probably the most productive and the least employed. Investigators sometimes think that forensic scientists are not doing their job unless they give the name of the person who committed the crime. Not so. Rather, physical evidence and the answers of the forensic scientist should be looked upon as parts of a puzzle. It is up to the investigators to take the pieces given to them and add them to others to solve the case. Rarely can a case be solved by forensic laboratory work alone.

Role of the Investigator

The most important person in any forensic analysis is the investigator who collects and submits the evidence. If this job is not done properly, even the best forensic expert with the most sophisticated scientific instruments cannot hope to uncover the story that the evidence has to tell. Investigators must train themselves to be alert for physical evidence and must know how to preserve it for maximum evidential value. Only in very rare cases will the forensic scientist be called to the scene to collect evidence; and even then, the investigator must protect the scene so that the evidence is not destroyed. He or she should realize that to get the information that the crime laboratory or other forensic laboratory has to offer requires the submission of useful material. Just as the investigator needs information to solve a case, so the forensic scientist must have appropriate material to conduct a proper analysis.

The investigator and the forensic scientist assist each other and have empathy for each other's problems. Probably both have heavy caseloads, poor working conditions, and too many demands on their time, but both have roles to play in the investigation, and they are interdependent. Ideally, there should be rapport between them; however, in large bureaucracies this is not usually the case. Therefore the investigator, as the one who is looking for the information, should make sure that the forensic scientist has the material needed to work with.

In large crime laboratories, procedures are established and forms designed for submission of evidence; but even the best designed forms cannot tell the whole story. The letter requesting laboratory analysis should spell out how each item of evidence is related to the case; give a brief summary of the case, especially any aspects that are related to the evidence; and, finally, specify what questions the investigator would like the laboratory to answer. If the case is unusual or very complex, it would be advisable to personally contact the forensic scientist, who must have a clear picture of the relationship of the evidence to the case in order to do a proper analysis. This will not only permit proper selection of analytical methods but also help in deciding what control samples will be needed from the investigator. Knowledge of the role of evidence in the case also enables the analyst to recognize things the significance of which would go undetected under routine analysis.

GENERAL RULES FOR COLLECTION OF EVIDENCE

There are no hard-and-fast rules about what physical evidence should be collected, or how. Investigators must make these decisions based on the facts of particular cases, using their experience and common sense. There are, however, some general guidelines that must be followed if the evidence is to have any value from a scientific and legal viewpoint.

1. The evidence must be obtained legally.

2. The evidence must be documented.

3. The evidence must be properly marked.

4. The evidence should be separately packaged to avoid contamination and damage.

5. Proper controls and standards must be maintained if the evidence is to be compared.

6. The chain of custody must be maintained.

In the collection of physical evidence, investigators must remember that ultimately the evidence may be used in court and, therefore, must be obtained legally. The recent Supreme Court decisions of *Michigan v. Tyler* and *Mincey v. Arizona*, which held that a warrant is necessary to search even the scene of a homicide if a person other than the victim has any possessory right to the premises or the property, have greatly restricted the warrantless search for physical evidence. Although there are still cases in which investigators can search for evidence without a warrant (for example, emergency, plain view, incident to an arrest, and with consent) they should have a clear understanding of when a search warrant is needed and when it is not. If there is any doubt, a warrant should be obtained.

Documentation of where and how the evidence was obtained is a basic duty of investigators, who must maintain detailed notebooks about the case and the search of the crime scene. Every item collected should be entered in the notes. The date, time, exact location, and circumstance of how each item of evidence was obtained should be included as well as a full description of it. The description must also state how the evidence was marked. The documentation of any major crime scene should contain photographs and sketches showing the overall scene and the location of the evidence collected.

The evidence should be marked in a way that does not destroy its evidential value. If possible, the evidence itself should be marked with the date and case number and the initials of the investigator. If the evidence is a liquid or a very small item, it should be placed in a suitable container that is marked and sealed. Lead seals and other such devices can also be used to identify evidence. The object is to mark the evidence in such a way that the investigator can identify it in court as coming from a particular location at the scene. For this reason, two items of the same type of material should be marked so they can be differentiated. If there is any question about the evidential value of the evidence being destroyed it should be placed in a container and the container marked and sealed.

To properly package evidence sometimes presents a problem. How does one package a wall with writing on it? There are such unusual cases. The best advice is to photograph the evidence and contact the laboratory for advice. But in the average case, where the evidence is portable, each item should be packaged separately to avoid the question later of where the item was at the scene and to eliminate the chance that material from one part of the crime scene was accidentally mixed with that from another area or source. If the item is very small, such as a fiber or a paint chip, it should be wrapped in paper before being placed in an envelope or pill box to prevent loss.

All items should be placed in the containers in such a way as to prevent damage or contamination. The containers should be marked and sealed with the initials of the person collecting the evidence.

To have any meaning, most physical evidence examined by the forensic scientist must be compared with some other item from a known source. If glass is collected at a crime scene, it has little value until it can be compared with glass from a known source, such as the clothing of the suspect. In most cases it is up to the investigator to obtain the standards for comparison. Investigators must make it their business to learn what standards are necessary for comparison and to supply them. If they do not know, they should consult with the experts involved. They should also remember that controls from areas adjacent to stains, paint, and other such evidence should be taken to ensure the accuracy of the tests.

The chain of custody is one subject that is often attacked in court. Investigators must be aware that they should be able to document every person who had custody of the evidence from the time it was found at the scene until it is presented in court. Although most law enforcement agencies have procedures to document the chain of custody, it is still the investigator's duty to make sure they are followed.

Arson Evidence. Arson has become a crime of increasing proportions throughout the United States. The investigation of an arson scene is most difficult, because the damage caused by the fire may obscure most of the scene and make every item suspect. Preferably, the scene should be examined by a trained arson investigator who is knowledgeable about how fire travels and reacts. However, an investigator who is obliged to examine a scene should first look for containers, such as gasoline cans, in which a flammable substance could have been carried; then try to locate the point of origin of the fire. Since heat and fire rise, it is logical to start at the lowest point of the fire, looking for charred wood, rags, and so on. The investigator should be aware of odors, especially those of gasoline, paint thinner, and other flammable substances.

Once evidence that may contain remnants of flammable fluid has been found, the investigator should protect it carefully, since flammables are very volatile and will evaporate in the air in a relatively short time. The evidence must therefore be put into a sealed container as soon as possible. The best containers are clean metal paint cans or glass jars that can be tightly sealed. If nothing else is available, plastic bags could be used in an emergency, provided they are placed one inside another.

The clothing of a homicide victim who has been burned should be submitted to determine if flammable substances were poured on the body.

Biological Evidence

The value of blood and other biological evidence has increased in the past decade. During that same period the problems and dangers of biological evidence have also increased.

Not long ago, the investigator was lucky to be able to determine the ABO group of an individual from a dried bloodstain at the scene of a crime. Today it is not only possible to identify a number of blood group systems but also the enzymes and antibodies present in blood. It is now possible to determine the DNA (deoxyribonucleic acid) profile of an individual from biological material found at the crime scene. This makes this type of evidence potentially some of the most valuable evidence available.

Blood. The investigator should be aware that blood at the crime scene has value not only relative to typing to determine whose blood it is, but also in reconstructing the crime scene.

The value of blood stain patterns should not be overlooked by the investigator. They can provide an opportunity to evaluate statements by suspects or witnesses as to what happened at the scene. The bloody record of the crime can be interpreted by examiners experienced in crime scene reconstruction. They may be able to determine how many blows were struck, the location of the victim, or many other pieces of information. To be able to make any determination, it is necessary that the scene be properly photographed and adequate measurements be taken. The photographs should be close-up and indicate a ruler.

Even without DNA analysis it is possible today to type dry blood stains using a number of different blood grouping systems. In addition, enzymes and antibodies that will individualize blood can be determined. This makes it possible to say in some cases that the chances of the blood coming from a different person are one in many million.

If the blood is on clothing or other textile material, the stain should be air-dried and the entire item submitted. If the stain is on a portable object, it should be submitted to the laboratory without removing the stain. If the stain is on an object that cannot be moved, it should be scraped off with a clean knife. A scraping should also be taken from an adjacent unstained area as a control. If liquid blood is available, it should be collected in a clean test tube or bottle.

Seminal and Other Body Fluids. In addition to the identification of seminal and other body fluid stains, this type of evidence holds the potential for the identification of the blood group. Eighty percent of the population are secretors, who carry their blood group factors in other body fluids. To conduct an examination to identify the blood group of a secretor, it is necessary to take a saliva specimen not only from the suspect but also from the victim if there was any chance of cross-contamination.

Evidence containing seminal and other body fluid stains should be handled in the same way as blood evidence.

DNA. All biological material is composed of cells. DNA is the substance that is found in the chromosomes of the cells and contains the genetic code. This genetic code (or DNA fingerprint) is unique to an individual (except for identical twins).

In the analysis of DNA the scientist first extracts DNA from the biological evidence. The pure DNA is then cut by restriction enzymes at a specific selected location on the DNA. The DNA fragments are then separated by size using a technique known as *electrophoresis*. The separated DNA fragments are transferred to a membrane so that they cannot move. Depending on the technique used, different molecular probes are used to radioactivate the DNA at different locations. The location of the radioactive labeled fragments of DNA can then be read on X-ray plates. The radioactive labeled fragments will appear as lines on the plates. This sample is then compared with other samples from the case that have been treated the same way. Depending on the techniques used, different numbers of lines appear on the X-ray plate for each sample. These lines are something like the universal bar codes used on groceries.

There is little question in the scientific community as to the validity of the theory of DNA identification of blood, semen, and other biological material. The major question today is the reliability and quality control used in the laboratories. Another area of concern is the relevance and reliability of the statistical basis used to interpret the results of analysis. These questions are presently being addressed by the forensic science community.

For investigators at the crime scene, these questions are of little importance. Their main concern should be the collection of all biological evidence in the proper manner to avoid contamination. The types of biological material that have potential value for DNA typing are:

Blood.

Semen.

Tissue.

Bone (marrow).

Hair (root).

Saliva.

Urine.

Tooth (pulp).

The DNA evidence should be collected in the same way as other biological evidence.

Safety. When approaching a crime scene, investigators must think about their personal safety. All personnel at the scene can no longer take a macho attitude toward blood and other biological fluids at the scene. They must protect not only themselves but also their spouses and future children from potential deadly diseases, such as AIDS.

There should be no question that the victims of homicide and other violent crimes are at high risk for AIDS and other diseases transmitted through biological fluid. Many homicides are drug related and, since IV drug users are the highest risk group for AIDS, the chances of infection are very high. It should be the practice of the investigator to routinely consider every homicide, rape, or other violent crime scene as one that is infected. To do less at this time is foolhardy.

The minimum precautionary measures that should be taken by the crime scene investigator are:

1. Wearing disposable coveralls and latex gloves while conducting the search.
2. Wearing a surgical mask and eye protection when handling or scraping blood evidence.
3. Being alert for sharp objects.
4. Not smoking, eating, drinking, putting on makeup, or doing other things that require hand-to-face contact.
5. Not using personal items, such as expensive pens at the crime scene.
6. Using disposable items, where possible, at the crime scene. Equipment and other items that cannot be disposed of should be decontaminated after use.
7. Marking all items collected from the scene "Caution: Possible Biologically Infected Material."
8. After a crime scene search, disposing of the coveralls, gloves, and other material in a proper and approved manner.
9. Washing hands and decontaminating equipment.

Every agency should develop very strict guidelines for the safe processing of crime scenes to ensure the safety of the personnel. It would not be beyond the realm of possibility that crime scene technicians who routinely process many crime scenes should be required to wear "space suits" with self-contained air supplies and other safety equipment.

Drugs and Narcotics. Drugs and narcotics are the largest single type of evidence submitted for analysis to crime laboratories in the United States. Their analysis is primarily concerned with the identification of the contraband substance in arrest cases, when identification is necessary to substantiate the charge in court. In these cases the investigator should submit all the evidence to the laboratory in a properly sealed package to ensure that the chain of custody is maintained.

In addition to such routine analysis, the forensic chemist can, in special cases, do a total analysis of not only the controlled substance but also all the cutting agents used and the percentage of each. This type of analysis has been used by the New York City Police Department Crime Laboratory in heroin cases not only to provide intelligence information that certain cases probably were cut in the same cutting operation but also to provide evidence in conspiracy-to-sell cases.

Explosives. If investigators are involved in cases in which they find explosives or other types of bomb evidence, the best advice that can be given is to call for the bomb experts in the area. Handling this type of evidence and searching the scene where a bomb has exploded, can best be done by those who have the proper training and experience. The potential hazards in the improper handling of explosives cannot be overstated.

Firearms Evidence. The use of firearms in crimes of violence makes firearms evidence an important type of physical evidence. The fact that a firearms identification expert can identify a bullet fired from a particular gun has been recognized since the 1920s, and the firearms identification expert has become an important part of every crime laboratory. The same basic principle, namely, that the weapon transfers microscopic accidental markings to the bullet as it passes down the barrel, can be used to identify cartridge cases, shotgun shells, and toolmarks. All these receive accidental traces transferred from weapons or tools.

For the investigator, the recognition of guns and bullets is relatively easy. It is the collection and marking that can give problems. Bullets and cartridge cases should be marked so as not to destroy the area where the examination will be conducted—land and grooves on bullets and the bases on cartridge cases.

The distance of the gun from the victim when fired can be determined within certain limits. To do this type of test, the forensic scientist needs the clothing of the victim which contains the powder residue and muzzle blast pattern. If available, the actual gun and ammunition used should be submitted to improve the accuracy of the test.

Glass. The value of glass as evidence is not fully realized. Not only can glass from the scene be compared with glass found on the suspect or from the suspect's car but the examination of the broken fragments can determine how the glass was broken.

The best method of collecting glass evidence is to collect every fragment available. This not only allows the pane to be reconstructed but also increases the chances of making a jigsaw match between a piece from the scene and a piece from the suspect. All the fragments should be carefully packaged to prevent further breakage.

Hair and Fibers. Hairs and fibers are the type of evidence that can easily be transferred from the perpetrator to the scene or victim and from the scene or victim to the perpetrator. Although their value is limited in that they cannot positively be identified as having come from a particular source, they can provide circumstantial evidence and valuable investigative information. The forensic microscopist can tell from a single hair not only species (human, dog, cat, and so on) but also if the hair fell naturally or was pulled, if it was dyed, if it was cut, and many other conditions.

To make a comparison, at least 12 full-length hairs should be pulled from various areas of the head. In all cases in which there is any possibility that the hair could have come from persons other than the victim, samples should be taken from them. Specimen hairs should also be taken from other parts of the body, such as the limbs, chest, and pubic area. All samples should be packaged separately indicating the person from whom they were taken and the area of the body they were taken from.

If fiber evidence is to be compared, the suspect garment should be submitted to the laboratory. If the fibers are believed to have come from a rug or another item that is not portable, samples should be taken from various areas of the object.

QUESTIONED DOCUMENTS

There is no instrument used in more crimes than the paper and pen. Documents play a role in almost every type of crime from homicide to bad checks. There does not seem to be any crime in which the investigator may not encounter some kind of document evidence. Mass murderers write letters to the police and press, as in the Son of Sam case and Jack the Ripper. Kidnappers write letters demanding money. Bank robbers use notes to rob banks. In today's society with checks, credit cards, and all types of records, it is almost impossible for criminals not to sign something or use paper in their criminal activities.

In fraud and white-collar crimes, documents are often the only form of physical evidence. The investigator should be alert to the value of all written, typed, or printed material. They all have potential value in the investigation of white-collar crimes, since they may help to prove how the crime was committed and who was involved. When faced with the examination of corporate records, the investigator should consider seeking the help of the document examiner, whose experience and knowledge of documents can help in determining any irregularities in the records. This expert can determine not only how or by whom the records were prepared but also, possibly, the time or sequence in which the records were prepared.

Care and Handling of Document Evidence

Proper handling and preservation of documents that may be used as evidence requires ensuring that they reach the document examiner in the same condition in which they were received. This can be accomplished by placing the documents in clean plastic envelopes or plastic page protectors. Documents should not be folded once they have been opened. Pens, pencils, or other pointed instruments should not be used to point at or underline features on documents. If documents are to be processed for latent fingerprints or indented writing, they should be held lightly between the sides of the fingers or with pieces of paper. (Document examination should be done before fingerprint examination.) Questioned documents should never be left under papers or in envelopes which might be written on, since the indentations will show on the documents.

Investigators should confine the marking of the evidence to blank spaces on the backs of documents, unless judgment or some legal reason dictates that they should not be marked. In that case, initials and other information should be put in the envelopes on slips of paper with the documents. All other marking of the document should be avoided. No one should attempt to bring out indented writing on the document by rubbing it with the side of a lead pencil. This will prevent the use of other techniques.

In all cases the original documents, if available, should be submitted to the document examiner. If the questioned writing is on a wall, body, or other object that cannot be sent to the document laboratory, it should be photographed close up, with a ruler in the picture.

If charred documents are involved, they should not be removed from their container if it is possible to move it. The container must be covered to prevent damage from air and wind and transported to the document examiner. If the charred documents are in a fireplace or other place that cannot be moved, they should be picked up by gently sliding a piece of cardboard under them, then placed in a covered box.

Handwritten Documents

The results obtained in a handwriting examination are dependent on and directly related to the quality of the standard or known writing obtained. The object of handwriting standards is to give the examiner a clear and complete picture of the handwriting of their author.

There are two classes of standard writing. One is spontaneous writing done in the normal course of events, such as letters, records, reports, checks, licenses, applications, and so on. Unless the questioned material is a signature of the same name, documents with only the signature of the suspect will not meet the document examiner's needs for comparable material. The document examiner making a comparison must use the same letters and letter combinations.

The second class of writing is "request writing," in which individuals prepare standards of their writing at the request of an investigator. In obtaining this type of standard, the investigator should endeavor to put the individuals at ease and tell them to write naturally. The circumstances under which the questioned writing was made should be duplicated as nearly as possible. Subjects should not be allowed to see the questioned documents. The questioned writing should be dictated word for word. If asked about arrangement, spelling, or punctuation, the investigator should advise subjects to use their own judgment. A single piece of paper similar to the paper of the questioned writing should be used for each sample. If the questioned writing is a check, a blank check or a piece of paper the size of the check, with lines to match, should be used. If the questioned material is on lined paper, the standards should be taken on the same kind of lined paper. The same type of writing instrument (ballpoint pen, pencil, fiber-tip pen, and so on) should be used. The practice of having individuals write their names a number of times on the same piece of paper is of limited value. It should go without saying that if the questioned material is hand printed, the standards should be hand printed. If the questioned material is script, the standards should be script. Several standards should be taken, removing the previous ones from the view of the writer to prevent copying them, if a disguised writing style is being attempted. It is also a good practice to talk to the writer about something else between standards. This makes it harder to remember what disguise was being used. If there are indications that a person may be trying to disguise his or her writing or that a disguise was used in the questioned material, the individual should also be requested to write with the other hand. When the questioned writing is a signature, at least 12 separate specimens of the signature should be taken. For letters, two or three pages of specimen along with specimens of the envelopes should be obtained. In all cases, but particularly in forgery and anonymous letter cases, standards should also be obtained from the complainant. In forgery cases it is necessary to show that the questioned signature is actually forged and what type of forgery it is. In the letter cases occasionally the complainant is found to be the author of the anonymous letter.

Typed Documents. If the questioned document is typed, the investigator should, if possible, submit the suspect typewriter for examination, without changing any of the settings or using the typewriter. If it is not possible to submit the typewriter, several copies of the complete text of the questioned material should be typed along with several copies of the entire keyboard. In addition to the ribbon impression, at least two impressions of the full keyboard should be taken with a fresh sheet of carbon paper placed on top of the paper and the machine set in the stencil position. This gives a very clear impression of the typeface.

The ribbon from the suspect machine should also be removed and submitted for analysis. Especially in the case of one-time carbon ribbons, it is possible to determine what was typed on the ribbon. If the machine in question is in an office, normal business documents typed on the machine around the time of the questioned document should also be obtained. In addition to signing and dating the specimens, the investigator should indicate the make, model, and serial number of the machine from which the standards were taken.

In other types of document problems—paper comparisons, ink comparisons, erasure cases, and so on—the investigator should submit the original documents and all available comparison material. The investigator should remember that for document examiners to do their job, they need the original documents and adequate comparison standards.

WHERE TO FIND A FORENSIC SCIENTIST

For investigators in law enforcement agencies, the problem of finding forensic experts is not difficult. Local or state crime laboratories can, in most cases, either do the examination that is required or direct investigators to someone who can. The federal law enforcement agencies also maintain laboratories that will, in most cases, do work for local law enforcement agencies. The FBI laboratory is the largest and best-known of these laboratories. It will do cases for law enforcement agencies at no charge. If an investigator has a problem in the medical area, the local medical examiner would be the best source of help and advice.

For private and defense investigators, locating competent forensic experts can be a problem. If they do not know any or have any recommended to them, the local crime laboratory may be able to recommend someone who could do the forensic investigation. The nearest university with a forensic science faculty may also be able to help. The professional societies in the field can provide a list of qualified experts. The American Academy of Forensic Sciences is the largest and has members in the various areas of expertise. There are also a number of societies that deal with only one aspect of forensic science and whose members are some of the best in the field. The American Society of Questioned Document Examiners is the most important group in their area. In firearms identification, the Association of Firearms and Toolmark Examiners is the leading group. For fingerprint experts, the International Association for Identification is the largest professional group.

In an effort to increase professionalization and to provide some means to identify qualified forensic experts, the Forensic Science Foundation undertook a program of evaluating and establishing certification boards in the various areas of forensic science. To date, certification boards have been established in toxicology, physical anthropology, odontology, psychiatry, and questioned documents. Pathologists have been certified for a number of years by a medical board, and the criminalists are still in the process of developing a certification board. Investigators interested in obtaining a directory of diplomates of the different boards should contact the Forensic Science Foundation, PO Box 669, Colorado Springs, CO 80901-0669, 719-656-1100.

28

Criminal Investigative Analysis

Raymond M. Pierce

Formerly known as psychological profiling, criminal investigative analysis has evolved into an effective tool that is used to assist law enforcement in a wide variety of investigations. What began as informal crime pattern identification during the late eighteenth century has been developed into an indirect science by the researchers and investigators of the Federal Bureau of Investigation's National Center for the Analysis of Violent Crime. Located in the FBI's National Academy in Quantico, Virginia, the Center is comprised of two units: the Behavioral Science Instruction and Research Unit and the Behavioral Science Investigative Support Unit. The overall Behavioral Science Unit (BSU) has devoted thousands of hours of research to understanding the criminal mind. From that research they have been able to identify characteristics of offenders based on their behavior before, during, and after committing the crime.

Since the mid-1970s the BSU has been providing these descriptions of offenders to requesting law enforcement agencies from the United States and the free world. Their research has determined that behavior remains consistent. Although cultures, names, and locations change throughout our country and the world, the deviant patterns of criminal behavior tend to remain the same. While there may be a few microcultures that differ, generally people act out violently towards others for similar reasons worldwide. While using the research for the formulation of this list of characteristics is a long, involved process, the criminal personality profile provided to the requesting investigator simply portrays offenders as an acquaintance would describe them.

The purpose of this chapter is not to instruct the reader in the research and methodology used in criminal investigative analysis, but to give investigators a working knowledge of how this process can assist their investigations. A list will also be provided of the types of cases where criminal investigative analysis has been successful, and a detailed guide as to how this assistance can be obtained through the BSU and local law enforcement agencies.

THE CRIMINAL PERSONALITY PROFILE

The criminal personality profile provides the requesting investigator with a general description of the offender. This is not necessarily the same type of description that would be offered by an eyewitness to the crime, but more of a list of personality characteristics that portrays the offender as an acquaintance would. The profile can be particularly helpful to investigators when they have no witnesses to the crime, or when there are too many possible suspects and only one or two people are responsible for the crime. In the first case, the profile will provide a description of a previously unknown offender. In the second case, the profile may help by refocusing the direction of the investigation by assisting the detective to focus on one or two people from a series of possible suspects.

A criminal personality profile does not always provide the same information for similar types of crimes. Because the profile is based on the amount of case information available at the time the investigator requests assistance, the description of the offender will vary in the number of characteristics provided. The criminal personality profile may include:

1. The offender's approximate age.
2. Sex.
3. Race.
4. Marital status/adjustment.
5. Level of scholastic achievement.
6. Rearing environment.
7. Current lifestyle, demeanor, social adjustment, and personality.
8. Description of mental decompensation and/or prior criminal arrest history.
9. Prior knowledge of the victim and offender residency in relation to the crime scene.
10. Possible motive for the crime.

The criminal personality profile is usually requested when all investigative leads have been exhausted and the offender is still unknown. At this point in the investigation criminal investigative analysis can frequently determine what took place at the crime scene, why the crime occurred, and, through a profile, describe the type of individual responsible for the offense.

OFFENDER PERSONALITY ASSESSMENT

When the offender is known, or when there is a strong suspect in a case, another aspect of criminal investigative analysis is employed, namely, offender personality assessment. Since this offender or suspect has been identified, a profile is unnecessary. If the investigator had anything stronger than circumstantial evidence to incriminate the subject, he or she would be arrested. Often, a personality assessment can predict how the offender will respond to various investigative strategies, as well as reinforce or abrogate his or her viability as a suspect. Of particular importance would be the expected response to methods of interview and interrogation. The personality assessment will identify for the investigator the strengths and weaknesses of the subject, and how he or she will react to the stress of an interview.

During World War II, this aspect of criminal investigative analysis was used to evaluate Adolph Hitler. A psychiatrist, William Langer, assisted the Office of Strategic Services with a detailed analysis of Hitler's personality based on the available intelligence information. From this unique diagnosis, Dr. Langer provided valuable information to the OSS about Hitler's dominant personality features and deficiencies. He was also able to successfully predict Hitler's reaction to defeat.

HOW CRIMINAL INVESTIGATIVE ANALYSIS ASSISTS INVESTIGATIONS

Through the use of criminal personality profiles and assessments, criminal investigative analysis provides a threefold service to the requesting law enforcement agency:

1. It reduces the number of most possible suspects through the detailed description provided in the profile.

2. It refocuses the investigation when all leads have been exhausted.

3. By narrowing the number of suspects and the focus of the case, it decreases investigative time.

Interview and Interrogation Assistance

Once a suspect has been identified, assistance is also provided in the actual interview and interrogation process. Ideally, this begins long before the day of the interview, with the investigator completing a simple checklist of information about the subject to be interviewed. This information is analyzed and a detailed interrogation format is developed of the most suitable interview techniques that would apply to the subject. This is commonly based on a thorough personality assessment of the subject and a review of the unique elements of the crime that indicated this subject was responsible for, or at least capable of, committing the crime.

A major factor determining the thoroughness of investigative assistance is time. If the investigator is not under pressure to solve the case immediately, detailed research of the subject's criminal, employment, and social history could prove most useful during a well-planned interview. However, if for various reasons a subject must be interviewed quickly before he or she cuts off all contact with the investigating agency, then less extensive, but not necessarily less effective interviewing techniques will be suggested.

And that is exactly what they are—suggestions. In no way do persons providing the criminal investigative analysis take over the investigation. Their sole purpose is to provide investigative support to the case investigator. No one is more familiar with the case than the investigator, who is free to make the decision about implementing the investigative suggestions. If so, as much support as time and resources permit will be provided to assist the investigator bring about a successful conclusion of the case.

A recent example of interviewing techniques assisting an investigation occurred in an East Coast homicide. A young, mentally handicapped girl was abducted from a quiet residential street corner. A suspect had frequented the area on a bicycle. He had been seen speaking to her shortly before she had disappeared, and there were conflicting reports indicating he might have led her away from the street corner while walking with the bicycle. Quite a bit of time had passed since her disappearance and the recovery of her body, and the investigators had the luxury of not being pressured into making an immediate arrest.

The suspect had disposed of his bicycle, but it had been traced and recovered. Although it proved to be of no forensic value, it was suggested that the bicycle be retained for future use during a staged interview. His military and criminal backgrounds were also researched, and much information was learned that assisted the future interview. He had obtained a high school diploma and taken several college courses while in the service. He had several arrests for child molestation, and while in jail he had taken law courses which assisted him in preparing his own documents for appeal. He also had surgery in a Veteran's Administration Hospital shortly after his first arrest for sexually abusing a child. This surgery removed a tattoo that indicated his preference for children.

When the interview was conducted, the bicycle was strategically placed in the detective squad room, clearly visible from the interview room. Before the interview began he had the opportunity to look at the bicycle for several minutes. Although it was never mentioned during the four-hour interview, the presence of the bicycle certainly increased his level of respect for the investigative abilities of his interviewers, as well as increasing his level of stress. During the interview, questions related to the tattoo and to the surgery to remove it enabled the interviewers to identify nonverbal behavior the subject unconsciously relied on to relieve stress every time he lied about the tattoo. His main movement to relieve stress was to press his right thumb over his left thumb as he lied. As the length of the lie increased, the pressure over his left thumb increased, moving the underlying blood from the upper portion of his hand. This nonverbal cue was noted numerous times during the interview to identify lies in other areas of questioning.

The subject had been questioned about other crimes in the past. When the questions reached a topic he was uncomfortable with, he simply explained that he was an uneducated street person, and he wouldn't know how to answer that question. Armed with the information gathered about the subject's educational background, the interviewers were able to turn his ploy to their advantage. His disclaimer, which may have misled investigators in the past, was used to show the subject that the interviewers knew he was lying about his education. Further, if he would lie about something as nonthreatening as that, why shouldn't they think he was lying about the abduction and murder of the child.

He didn't confess during the interview, but many contradictions and confirmed lies were recorded for use at his trial. He was later convicted of only the kidnapping, but was sentenced to 25 years to life for the crime.

FORMULATION OF SEARCH WARRANT APPLICATIONS

In a case such as the investigation just described, the offender was a long-term pedophile. When dealing with child molestation cases, the investigator's main witness is generally the live victim. Typically, when applying for a search warrant for the suspect's home or area where the assault took place, the investigator will include articles described by the child that were used during the molestation. Photographs taken by the suspect would also be included in the application for the warrant.

Criminal investigative analysis can effectively assist child molestation cases, and a wide variety of other investigations, by increasing the amount and type of evidence to be searched for with the warrant. The investigation is approached form both the forensic and behavioral aspects of the crime. Through a detailed, behaviorally oriented interview of the victim, much information can be learned about the type of pedophile involved in the case. After classifying the pedophile, certain characteristics and sexual preferences of that category of offender can be predicted. These predictions are based on research conducted with incarcerated pedophiles within the United States. However, these preferences appear to be consistent with pedophiles around the world.

By gently asking the victim to describe the adult's behavior, it is possible to return to the scene and identify areas where additional activity would have taken place. Forensic evidence recovered from these areas would tend to enhance courtroom testimony. Understanding not just what the pedophile did, but why he did it can also be crucial to the investigation.

What we may see as a terrible vicious assault against an unsuspecting child is frequently seen by the pedophile as a simple romantic encounter. For just that reason there may be a "courting" period that precedes the actual assault. During that period, which may last hours, days, weeks, or more, the pedophile attempts to con the child over to his way of thinking. To assist the pedophile in this seduction, he generally stocks his home with articles that could be used to lure a child inside and then keep that child interested enough to want to return. The victim should be asked to describe the interior of the pedophile's home. And if that home is a studio apartment of a 40-year-old male living alone, perhaps a judge and jury would like to see all the paraphernalia he had packed into that apartment to ensure he would maintain the interest of the child. Frequently, pedophiles involved in nonviolent seduction of their victims will have full-sized soda machines, pool tables, children's telephones, numerous board games, and computer games that reflect the age group of the pedophile's fixation. A judge may be interested in seeing the pornography that would also be included in the application for the search warrant. It would not be uncommon for a pedophile to have both heterosexually and homosexually oriented pornography to be used in the seduction of a child. After luring a young boy into his apartment with heterosexually oriented photographs, the homosexual literature is eased into the displays. After a period of time, the child becomes indoctrinated and is shown only homosexual material.

Each request for assistance with the formulation of a search warrant will be individually evaluated. That evaluation will consist of a thorough review of all forensic information related to the case, possible reinterviews of witnesses, and a personality assessment of the suspect.

INVESTIGATIVE SUGGESTIONS AND TECHNIQUES

As criminals become more sophisticated, new techniques must be developed to overcome their antisocial behavior. Just as forensic technology has grown with the identification procedures now available in DNA, law enforcement must expand the basic investigative techniques they have relied upon for so long. Criminal investigative analysis can provide investigative suggestions and techniques that are designed to cause an offender to come to the attention of the investigator. When pressured, these suspects will generally surface through errors in judgment or paranoia.

Every investigator has worked on cases where they have been unable to identify the offender or cases where they had a strong possible suspect, but the absence of physical evidence left them unable to make an arrest. Often a simple contradiction or error in judgment by the possible suspect would be enough to confirm the investigator's belief. There are innovative investigative steps that have been proven effective in many of these cases. Some are more elaborate than others and some are just improvements on established procedures.

A recent example involved a serial rapist committing daytime sexual assaults in the business district of a major city. The criminal personality profile in this case indicated that he was the type of serial rapist that would strike every seven to 15 days, and he would continue to attack until he was apprehended. He would follow lone women onto elevators in high rise office buildings and force them off the elevator to secluded stairways before beginning the sexual assault. Of his eight attacks, three had occurred in the same building. All of the incidents, over a three-month period, were within a two-block area in six different buildings.

Because of his preference for the one building, it was suggested that a concentrated effort in that area would be more productive than spreading surveillance teams throughout the two-block strip. On the days he was projected to strike again, an increased uniform foot patrol presence was suggested near every building except the one the rapist had returned to most often. That building was saturated with male and female plainclothes officers. They all had composite sketches of the offender and were familiar with the more vulnerable areas of the building. On the second day of surveillance, the rapist was apprehended shortly after 2 P.M. as he loitered near a first floor newsstand. He later explained that he was waiting for women returning late from lunch.

The alternative investigative suggestion in that case was to construct a temporary facade near the bank of elevators in the same building. By placing prior victims and detectives behind a viewing mirror, it was expected that they would identify the rapist as he entered the building. In this case the assigned investigators felt the sketch of the offender was good enough to identify the offender, and they correctly chose not to use the more elaborate plan. Every case differs, and the investigative suggestions are tailored to the needs of the requesting agency and to the pattern of behavior exhibited by the offender.

While much of the research has been in the area of violent crime, criminal investigative analysis has also been effective in the analysis of nonviolent crime. The application of the investigative process has proven to be particularly beneficial in select cases of homicide, serial rape and sexual assault, child molestations, kidnapping, equivocal and autoerotic death, serial arsons, government corruption, false allegations, threats, and extortions.

Homicide

Continuing research conducted by the BSU has concentrated on the not so new phenomenon of serial murder. A *serial murderer* is generally defined as a person who kills three or more people with extended cooling-off periods between each homicide. The cooling-off period can be weeks, months, or even years. Due to the media attraction to such infamous killers as David Berkowitz, Theodore Bundy, Ottis Toole, and Henry Lee Lucas over the last decade, the attention of the general public and the law enforcement community has been drawn to this topic. In the early 1980s a formal research project was undertaken by the BSU, the most extensive of its kind, to study the behavior of 25 serial murderers and 11 men convicted of one homicide each which was sexual in nature. All 36 men had been sentenced and their opportunities for appeal had been exhausted at the time of the study. This in-depth look into the mind of a murderer first researched their background and then studied, as related to the specific crimes for which they were convicted, their degree of planning, fantasy, rationale, and manner of escape. The invaluable information gained from this study was combined with less formal research conducted over the years by the BSU to form the basis of the different characterizations for homicidal behavior within the process of criminal investigative analysis.

Although serial murder receives the bulk of notoriety in homicide investigation, the majority of requests for criminal investigative analysis in this area are for assistance with unsolved single murder cases. Hundreds of investigators every year are provided criminal personality profiles of unknown offenders as well as the additional investigative services already described. Frequently this investigative assistance gives homicide investigators enough information to support an unsubstantiated "gut feeling" in the case, which may cause them to focus on one subject from a long series of possible suspects. Or the process may provide detailed direction in a case that had been dragging on for an extended period.

Pathologists, pediatricians, and veterinary doctors have been described as an elite group within the medical profession because they work with patients that are unable to describe their symptoms. That uniqueness could be extended to homicide detectives, among criminal investigators, since their complainants are unable to describe their assassins. Criminal investigative analysis often fills that void with investigative assistance and offender descriptions provided in the criminal personality profile.

Because the analytic process keys on the behavior of the offender before, during, and after the crime, homicides that are apparently random in nature leave little "behavioral evidence" to be identified. A random robbery and murder of a convenience store clerk or a drive-by shooting of several people on an urban street corner may indicate drug-related activity, but leave little information for analysis. However, when something extra is done by the offender that is not necessary for the completion of the crime, that is the most suitable type of case for criminal investigative analysis.

An example of behavioral evidence was illustrated in an unsolved killing of a young hospital employee. She and her husband, an intern in the same hospital, lived in an apartment adjacent to the hospital. She was found on her kitchen floor, apparently sexually assaulted, brutally beaten from her forehead to chin, and stabbed to death, several hours after her husband left for work on a weekday morning. After confirming the husband's alibi, the investigation centered on people from the area with prior arrest records. Directly across the street from the victim's apartment was a low income city housing development with thousands of residents.

At the autopsy the next day it was found that the victim wasn't sexually assaulted and she wasn't stabbed to death. She had been strangled to death and stabbed numerous times in the throat sometime after she expired. With the absence of sexual assault, and because there was jewelry and property missing from the apartment, it was now strongly believed that she was the victim of a daytime burglary that went bad, and she was killed when she surprised the burglar. The investigation continued to look at the hundreds of people in the housing development with prior arrest records. After six weeks of nonproductive interviews, the case investigator requested assistance from the BSU.

Within three weeks he was provided with a practical reconstruction of the crime and a criminal personality profile that described a lone offender. It was determined that the facial assault and manual strangulation occurred on the living room rug. When the victim was most probably dead, she was then transported to the kitchen floor where the mild blood splatter and heavy seepage indicated she received the series of stab wounds in her neck. The killer was described as exhibiting a great deal of rage toward the victim, whom he knew very well. Before the killer left, the victim's housecoat was pulled above her waist and the property was removed to stage the crime scene. The proposed motive, not burglary, was that the victim was preventing the offender from obtaining a goal related to work, romance, or money. In part, the criminal personality profile described the killer as an unmarried, white male, over 6 feet tall, and in good physical condition with very good upper body strength. He would have a similar educational and employment background as the victim and her husband. The all important information was provided last: The killer would have been in the victim's apartment numerous times in the past.

The victim and her husband had lived in the apartment for less than a year, and only six people had been guests in their home. Five of the six were family members who didn't fit the description in the profile, and the sixth was a male intern at the hospital. He matched the profile in each category except one. Although he was over 6 feet tall and possessed good upper body strength, he was grossly obese. During the course of the investigation rumors were heard in the hospital hinting that this intern had a homosexual attraction to the victim's husband.

Three days after receiving the information from the BSU the intern described in the profile, a frequent dinner guest at the victim's apartment, was identified as the killer. The obvious behavioral evidence, or actions taken by the offender that weren't necessary for the completion of the crime, in this case was the intense controlled rage displayed by the killer in stabbing the already dead victim repeatedly in her neck. The less obvious, but equally important, behavioral evidence was the killer's conscious decision to move the victim's body from the carpeted living room to the tiled kitchen floor before stabbing her. Both examples of behavioral evidence, combined with the killer's need to stage the crime scene, indicated the offender had a deep hatred of the victim, but he saw no need to ruin his friend's carpeting.

SERIAL RAPE AND SEXUAL ASSAULT

Comparable research has been conducted by the BSU in the area of deviant sexual behavior. In the mid-1980s another project was undertaken to study the background of 41 serial rapists. The *serial rapist* is typically a male who rapes three or more women with cooling-off periods between each assault. By combining earlier research with the analysis of the reported behavior of the rapist during the sexual assault, the BSU has developed a series of categorizations of rapists. From these categorizations they can project typical background and physical characteristics of the various types of rapists through a criminal personality profile. As described in the earlier serial rape case, they can also appraise the rapist's underlying need to act out violently toward women and often provide direction to the requesting agency with a suggested time span between attacks. Providing the approximate time of the next attack, along with an investigative strategy that may contain the rapist to a limited area, can be crucial information particularly when the requesting agency has limited manpower and resources.

Child Molestations—Kidnapping

A research project is under way studying the specific aspects of child molestation and kidnapping that will assist law enforcement in the apprehension of these criminals that prey on defenseless children. The information gained from this study will be compared with less formal research conducted by the BSU throughout the last decade. The results of the new project will be used to enhance the criminal personality profiles of these offenders. By understanding more about how these criminals, violent and nonviolent, think, it should become easier to anticipate their behavior. This should also expand the investigative strategies that have been used since the last 1970s to assist in the identification and apprehension of these offenders.

Equivocal and Autoerotic Death

Equivocal deaths are generally defined as violent deaths in which the manner of death has not been determined after a complete investigation and autopsy. When a person dies, the coroner or medical examiner is required to identify the manner of death as natural causes, homicide, suicide, or accident. If that cannot be determined, the case is returned to the investigator. The manner of death will remain "unknown" until that investigator presents enough information to the medical examiner (ME) to identify the manner of death.

These investigations can drag on for years, causing tremendous anguish and financial stress on family members awaiting a decision that could affect the reputation of the deceased and hundreds of thousands of dollars of insurance benefits. Equivocal death investigations also have the potential to create a great deal of stress for the assigned investigator. Often new investigators are given these cases when they are assigned to a detective squad because the original investigator has retired, leaving the case unsolved.

A similar problem can arise when a coroner or ME declines to make a determination of manner of death in cases that are apparently autoerotic fatalities. This phenomenon occurs when normally cautious practitioners of this abnormal form of sexual self-stimulation make the final error of their lives and accidentally cause their own asphyxiation. Generally, males and females who engage in this typically private activity, use a ligature around their necks to restrict the flow of oxygen and blood to the brain. The limitation of oxygen and blood causes a euphoria that they experience, while sexually stimulating themselves, up to the point of losing consciousness. At this point their slip knot or fail-safe escape device releases the neck restriction, and they regain consciousness. However, when their knot fails to slip, law enforcement becomes involved in this dangerous endeavor.

This type of death also presents a major problem for the deceased's family because, for insurance purposes, autoerotic fatalities are considered accidents. The problem for the investigator usually begins when the family finds the body and decides to cut the person down and remove evidence normally associated with this type of death. Frequently relatives of the deceased, particularly with adolescent victims, would prefer trying to make the scene appear to be that of a suicide rather than deal with the stigma of having a loved one die in a bizarre sexual accident. Whether the scene is altered or the ME fails to determine the manner of death, cases of this type can present a serious obstacle for investigators.

The process employed by the BSU in resolving these cases generally begins with a psychological autopsy of the victim. This is simply an extension of the investigative process begun by the case detective. However, in this aspect of criminal investigative analysis the normal procedure is augmented with a thorough behavioral analysis of the deceased personality, as well as his or her social, medical, academic, and financial history. This information, sometimes going back to the victim's childhood, is evaluated with facts observed at the scene of the death to present an overall picture of the deceased to the coroner. Within that personality overview, a solution to the questionable death is usually found.

Serial Arsons

An extensive automatic arson evaluation system has been in place within the BSU since the early 1980s. Most fires are not related to profit or revenge. The overwhelming numbers of intentionally set fires, single and serial, are called *nuisance fires*. Typically, they are set by vandals in abandoned buildings or vehicles, vacant lots, and trash disposal sites. The ongoing research of arsonists indicates that, with the exception of arson for profit, the majority of these offenders are fulfilling an abnormal need for power, recognition, and sexual gratification. Because of what at times appears to be a compulsion to set these fires, criminal personality profiles generally describe offender characteristics that cause these people to stand out in the general population. This becomes most important in serial arson investigations because this type of arsonist frequently returns to the scene. They receive stimulation and gratification watching the blaze and the efforts of the firefighters attempting to extinguish their "creation." While they think they are blending in with the crowd of spectators, investigative suggestions provided with this type of serial offense often bring the arsonist to the attention of the fire investigators.

Government Corruption Cases

In cases of individual or systematic corruption of government officials, the primary investigative step taken by the BSU, when practical, is the preparation of in-depth personality assessments for each subject believed to be involved in corrupt activities. From this personality assessment and the available case material, detailed investigative steps and interviewing strategies are tailored to each individual. This approach has proven to be most effective with almost every level of government service throughout the country and overseas. However, because the investigators are generally not dealing with hardened criminals, and many of these people may still have something that resembles a conscience, a major portion of the personality assessment is devoted to the subject's response when arrested. In addition to projecting the subject's potential for acting out violently toward others when confronted, serious attention is given to the possibility of suicide. When faced with public disgrace, they may quickly turn to suicide. Therefore, personality assessments, investigative strategies, and interviewing techniques are provided with that potential for violence in mind in these cases.

False Allegations

Much of the early research related to people falsely reporting crimes was conducted by military investigators. They found an increase in the reported incidents of sexual abuse and rape by female military dependents shortly after or shortly before the return of their husbands from an extended assignment. While they were away, their wives had become pregnant or contracted venereal diseases from persons other than their husbands. At the time, it was expected that at least some of the assaults were reported to cover promiscuous activity by the spouse who remained home.

Recently, in the northeast, we have seen false allegations by people who have duped investigators and the media, causing much embarrassment, financial loss to investigative agencies, and racial unrest. In Massachusetts, a man killed his pregnant wife and falsely reported it as murder by a third party, who he said also attempted to murder and rob him in their family car. He later identified an innocent suspect and kept the entire state in unrest for over a month until it was determined his reports were false. Before that incident, a young New York girl falsely reported a kidnapping, multiple rape, and racially biased assault that misled investigators, sympathizers, and the media for months.

The research conducted by the BSU into false allegations of crimes has incorporated the early sexual assault fabrications studied by the military to provide a wide ranging data base for criminal investigative analysis of these false reports. Requesting agencies are provided with detailed incident reports analysis, which (1) support or systematically disprove the allegation, (2) explain the possible underlying motivation for the subject to falsely report an incident or series of crimes, and (3) provide the investigator with interviewing techniques and a step-by-step investigative strategy designed to cause "false allegators" to incriminate themselves or withdraw the complaint.

While the BSU has researched hundreds of false allegations, they are not common occurrences. Often the people making these false reports are mentally disturbed. Because they may be unstable, investigators should be aware that they may resort to suicide if confronted too harshly or are publicly embarrassed. Caution should be used with these individuals and assistance requested from the BSU if one is in doubt as how to handle an allegation thought to be false.

Threat Analysis and Extortion

Written and taped threats and extortion attempts can be analyzed by the BSU, and frequently criminal personality profiles will be provided to describe the sender. Included with the profile will be a detailed assessment of the sender's potential to carry out the threats described in the communication. Extortion attempts will also be evaluated, and investigative strategies offered that may cause the offender to surface through an error in judgment.

In cooperation with the mental health community, the BSU is conducting an extensive study of threatening behavior and threat assessment. While it appears that the general public has only recently become aware of serious threats to political figures and celebrities, the government and the entertainment industries have endured this harassment and violence for many years. During the last decade, mentally disordered persons have repeatedly assaulted and even killed public figures.

In December 1980, Mark David Chapman, a disturbed fan, killed John Lennon on a New York City street. The next year John Hinkley attempted to assassinate

President Reagan in a bizarre plan to attract the attention of actress Jodie Foster. A television actress, Rebecca Schaeffer, was later killed by a mentally disturbed fan. And another actress, Theresa Saldana, survived a life-threatening attack, and Senator John Glenn was less seriously attacked while being interviewed on television by a disturbed self-styled political activist.

This delusional romantic attraction to celebrities was identified by the psychiatric community as erotomania in 1921. Often these people suffer from additional psychiatric conditions, and many are diagnosed or, at least believed to be, schizophrenic. They can be impulsive and violent; therefore, extreme caution should be used when they are identified and approached.

HOW TO OBTAIN ASSISTANCE

Within the National Center for the Analysis of Violent Crime (NCAVC), the Criminal Investigative Analysis Program is administered through the Behavioral Science Investigative Support Unit (800-634-4097). Investigative support is provided to law enforcement agencies through NCAVC Coordinators in every FBI field office. When your agency requires assistance with an investigation, simply contact the nearest FBI field office, and the coordinator will answer any questions you may have and assist you with forwarding the case to the NCAVC for analysis.

As the investigative case load increased over the years, the FBI decided to train local law enforcement and other federal law enforcement investigators to aid in dealing with the overflow of requests for assistance. In 1984 the FBI began awarding Police Fellowships in Criminal Investigative Analysis to law enforcement agencies. The fellowships are devoted to approximately 10 months of intensive training at NCAVC in Quantico, Virginia. The candidates are selected by their agencies and the agencies are chosen based on the number of sworn officers in the department, the population served, the amount of violent crime committed within the jurisdiction, and the agency's willingness to allow their participant to provide investigative assistance to neighboring departments. In 1989 the Fellowship Program was extended to foreign countries, and as of 1992 there were a total of 29 certified Criminal Investigative Analysis augmenting the FBI's program in local and foreign jurisdictions.

By contacting the Criminal Investigative Analysis Program, within the investigative branch of the following agencies, all requesting investigators will be given assistance within the general area of the jurisdiction indicated.

Domestic

California

Los Angeles Police Department
150 N. Los Angeles Street, Room 321
Los Angeles, CA 90012
(213) 485-7579/2531

California Department of Justice
3046 Prospect Park Drive, Suite 1
Rancho Cordova, CA 95670
(916) 631-1607/739-2771

Connecticut

Department of Treasury, Alcohol,
  Tobacco and Firearms
450 Main Street, Room 501
Hartford, CT 06103
(203) 240-3185

Florida

Florida Department of Law
Enforcement
PO Box 1489
Tallahassee, FL 32302
(904) 487-6711

Georgia

Georgia Bureau of Investigation
PO Box 370808
Decatur, GA 30037
(404) 244-2539

Illinois

Illinois State Police
1100 Eastport Plaza Drive
Collinsville, IL 62234
(618) 346-3700

Iowa

Iowa Division of Criminal
Investigation
Wallace State Office Building
Des Moines, IA 50319
(515) 281-5138

Maryland

Baltimore County Police Department
400 Kenilworth Drive
Towson, MD 21204
(301) 887-2137

Massachusetts

Boston Police Department
154 Berkeley Street
Boston, MA 02116
(617) 247-4700

Minnesota

Minnesota Bureau of Criminal
Apprehension
1246 University Avenue
St. Paul, MN 55104
(612) 642-0610

Missouri

Kansas City Police Department
1125 Locust Road
Kansas City, MO 64106
(816) 234-5074

Nebraska

Nebraska State Patrol
PO Box 94907
Lincoln, NE 68509
(402) 471-4545

New Jersey

New Jersey State Police
State Highway 130
Beverly, NJ 08010
(609) 877-2304

New York

New York State Police
Building 22, State Campus
Albany, NY 12226
(518) 485-1004

New York City Police Department
One Police Plaza, Room 1312S
New York, NY 10038
(212) 374-5549/5260

South Carolina

South Carolina Law Enforcement
Division
PO Box 21398
Columbia, SC 29221
(803) 737-4358

Texas

Texas Department of Public Safety
Box 4087
Austin, TX 78773
(512) 465-2200

Virginia

Virginia State Police
PO Box 9108
Richmond, VA 23227
(804) 323-2326

Washington

Seattle Police Department
610 Third Avenue, Room 529
Seattle, WA 98104
(206) 284-5550

Washington, D.C.

U.S. Secret Service
800 G Street, N.W.
Washington, D.C. 20223
(202) 566-6903/535-5731

U.S. Treasury Department
Bureau of Alcohol, Tobacco and
 Firearms
1700 Pennsylvania Avenue, N.W.,
 Room 2209
Washington, D.C. 20226
(202) 566-7395

Foreign Countries

Australia

South Australia Police Department
1 Angas Street
South Australia
08-218-1212

Victoria Police Department
412 St. Kida Road, 11th Floor
Melbourne, Victoria 3004
Australia
03-865-2321

Canada

Ontario Provincial Police
90 Harbour Street
Toronto, Ontario, Canada M7A-2S1
416-965-8105

Royal Canadian Mounted Police
1200 Vanier Parkway
Ottawa, Ontario, Canada K1A-OR2
613-993-2982

The Netherlands

National Criminal Intelligence
 Service
P.O. Box 20304
2500 EH The Hague
The Netherlands
31-70-3769911

29

Eyewitness Identification

George F. Maher

Positive identification of the perpetrator of a crime by a victim or eyewitness is one of the strongest pieces of evidence that can be obtained during a criminal investigation. It is also one of the most challenged and least trustworthy. Because of the inherent danger of human error in observation and interpretation of an event, the courts have required that this kind of evidence be intelligently and carefully obtained. Witnesses and, particularly, victims of crimes are often in a frame of mind that makes them susceptible to suggestion. Police may inadvertently influence the identification, and if this can be determined, the evidence obtained will be suppressed. Good "stand-up" witnesses are extremely important to the prosecution, so care must be taken to preserve the value of their evidence by properly conducting the identification process along accepted legal guidelines.

There are two basic means of postincident identification commonly used by police—the live line-up and the photo file or "rogues' gallery." The line-up is usually a formal identification session at which a witness attempts to identify a suspect from among a group of persons. However, it can also be an informal viewing of a group of persons at a gathering where a suspect is believed to be located. The gathering may or may not have been formed by the police.

There is another "live" procedure that has been questioned in depth by the courts because of its obvious drawbacks. The "show-up" of one suspect alone, viewed by a witness or victim, is the least desirable method of identification. This is mainly because of the suggestiveness of having the witness view the suspect and then being asked, "Is this the one?" However, the show-up has been allowed in cases of immediate "back-to-the-scene" viewing after a crime and also when it is possible for the police to create a fair line-up because of the perpetrator's unique appearance.

The second major method of identification commonly used by law enforcement is the photographic line-up, or rogues' gallery, in which the witness picks out the suspect's photograph from a group of photographs of persons of the same general description. Naturally, an identification of this type should be supported by live identification before a formal court proceeding. If it is not, a serious problem would develop if the appearance of the subject changed drastically between the time of identification and later court appearance, when the witness probably will be called on to identify the perpetrator.

All methods of eyewitness identification are open to challenge by the defense attorney. Whether he or she is successful in suppressing the evidence depends on the circumstances of the identification and the attitude of the witness. But a large measure of the success in the introduction of eyewitness identification evidence depends on fair and proper methods being used by the police in conducting the identification.

THE LINE-UP

The line-up, in most instances, is the safest and fairest way to proceed with an identification, assuming, of course, that it is conducted properly. The line-up is generally used when a subject is taken into custody and the witness is available to make the identification.

There are three main predicates for having a suspect appear in a line-up: (1) the suspect consents to appear in the line-up, (2) following an arrest, and (3) on order of a court. Although in some states where there is no statute authorizing such orders, courts have issued them on a showing of a reasonable belief that the subject will be identified as the person who committed the offense.

Procedure for Conducting a Line-up

Whenever a person is to be viewed in a line-up by the victim, witnesses, or other persons for the purpose of establishing the subject's identify in connection with an offense, the following procedures should be applied:

1. The suspect should be advised that he or she is going to be viewed by others for the purpose of establishing identity insofar as a particular offense or offenses are concerned. *Miranda* warnings are not required.
2. Generally, a defendant arrested without a warrant does not have a right to counsel before being placed in a line-up. However, there is a right to counsel in any of the following circumstances:
   a. The defendant has been indicted, arraigned, or arrested pursuant to an arrest warrant.
   b. An accusatory instrument has been filed (that is, attendance secured by means of a court summons).
   c. There has been an unreasonable delay in arraignment.
   d. It is known by the person preparing the identification procedure that the suspect has an attorney.
   e. An attorney is seeking access to the defendant.
   f. The defendant asks for an attorney.

   In such cases advise suspects that they are entitled to have an attorney present during identification proceedings. If they do not already have an attorney or cannot afford to retain one, an attorney should be made available to them before a viewing for identification.
3. The suspect may waive the presence of an attorney, in which case the subject's consent to be viewed without an attorney present must be expressly given, free from any threats, inducements, or promises.

4. If the suspect is entitled to have an attorney present during the identification proceedings and does not waive that right, the attorney selected or known should be contacted and advised of the time and place of the line-up.
5. The attorney for the suspect should be given a reasonable opportunity to attend the line-up, consistent with the prevailing circumstances, such as the hour of the day or night and the conditions of the victim or witnesses involved. If, after a reasonable time the attorney does not appear, the line-up may begin. (What is "reasonable" depends on the circumstances—time, weather conditions, location of attorney, and so on.)
6. An attorney for the suspect present during the identification proceeding should be permitted to observe the manner in which the line-up is conducted. The attorney is not permitted to talk to any of the witnesses participating in the identification of the suspect but may confer with the client. Any suggestion that the attorney may make to improve the fairness of the line-up procedure should be followed by the officer conducting the line-up if, in the officer's judgment, the suggestions are reasonable and practical. The officers conducting the line-up should ask the attorney for suggestions. The attorney can view the line-up from any position desired as long as there is no unreasonable interference.

All line-ups in the station house or other place of custody must be conducted in the following manner to help ensure fairness:

1. The suspect should be viewed with at least four other persons of the same sex and race, and approximately the same age, height, weight, and manner of dress. The person is permitted to select a position in the group and may change that position at any time during the course of the line-up.

2. There must be no visible indication of which person of the group is in custody for the particular offense.

3. No member of the group may be asked to say or do anything to facilitate identification unless all are asked to do the same thing.

4. No interrogation of any member of the group may occur in the presence of the viewing witness or victim.

5. Special care must be taken so that no member of the group is seen by the witness or victim prior to appearance in the group.

6. Two or more victims or witnesses should not view the same suspect in each other's presence or be permitted to communicate with each other during the viewing procedure. The fact that one or more of them may have made a positive or negative identification may not be revealed to the others. The witnesses or victim may remain unseen or masked when viewing the line-up.

7. If practicable, a color photograph should be taken of the entire group, including the subject, showing their physical appearance at the time and the clothing worn for the identification.

8. The officer conducting the investigation or the viewing should record fully the details of the procedure used, including specific utterances and actions required of the group to facilitate identification, all the responses of the viewing witness or victim, and the time intervals involved. The names and addresses of all participants in the viewing must also be recorded. This includes, in addition to the suspect and the victim or other witnesses, the others in the group with the suspect; the police officers or other officials present; any lawyer, friend, or relative of the suspect; any other persons participating in or witnessing the conduct of the viewing procedure.

9. No person present at or participating in such viewing should do or say anything calculated or likely to influence a witness or victim to make or not to make a particular identification. Specifically, no suggestions, direct or indirect, may be communicated to the witness or victim as to which member of the group is a suspect or who is not a suspect. Nothing may be said to or in the presence of the witness or victim that suggests, in any way, which member or whether any member of the group has been arrested for the offense in question or for any other offense. Personal details relating to any member of the group may not be revealed. A positive or negative identification, if any, must in all cases be the product of the free choice of the identifying witness or victim, based wholly on independent recollection and recognition. It is the responsibility of the officer conducting the proceeding to take all appropriate precautions to ensure this.

10. In cases of two or more perpetrators and/or multiple suspects, it may be necessary to enlarge the line-up. If the size of the line-up becomes unmanageable due to space, it may be more practical to run more than one showing using different persons. Common sense dictates that there should never be more suspects in the line-up than persons of similar description.

Note: The taking of a *color* photograph of a line-up cannot be overstressed. During a trial, six months, or a year after an identification, an attempt to discredit the fairness of a line-up could concentrate on the color of clothing, skin tones, and so on. Questions could be asked such as: "Isn't it true that all persons in the line-up were wearing blue uniform police trousers except the defendant, who was wearing brown? A black-and-white photograph may not be able to prove to a jury that the allegation is not true. The same applies to skin tones and hair color. To offset problems of this type, especially when time dulls the memory of the event, complete and accurate records and photographs must be obtained.

THE SHOW-UP

Many factors are taken into account when deciding which form of identification to use. The show-up is the least desirable method of identification because of the obvious suggestiveness of having the witness view the suspect and be asked, "Is this the one?" There are circumstances, however, in which a show-up can be practical; for instance, in an emergency situation when the victim or witness is in danger of death or is seriously incapacitated and time does not allow use of a line-up.

The most common situation where the show-up is permissible is a "back-to-the-scene" viewing after a crime. Police officers may, under certain circumstances, allow a victim or witness to view a suspect without a line-up. Although this procedure is suggestive, the rationale for permitting it is that when a very short period has elapsed after the crime and the suspect is apprehended nearby, it is desirable to have a witness who had the opportunity to adequately view the perpetrator attempt an identification. If the *wrong* person has been detained, that individual can be released on the spot. This is less of an intrusion than subjecting the subject to a line-up at some future time after memories have faded.

An officer conducting a show-up should use common sense to ensure that the procedure be as fair as possible under the circumstances. Some courts have taken into consideration the difficulty the police have when faced with the problem of a suspect whose appearance is unique. Producing a fair line-up when the suspect is of an ethnic background not common to the area or is bizarre in appearance is sometimes impossible. The impossibility of the task has been recognized by the courts in some states and the "show-up" type identification has been allowed.

THE PHOTOGRAPH LINE-UP, OR "ROGUES' GALLERY"

Photographic identification can be a useful tool and of greatest importance when the suspect is not in custody. It must be stressed that when using this form of identification, the same precautions concerning suggestiveness which apply to a lineup also apply to photographic identification. The suspect's photo should be placed among photos of nonsuspects of the same race, age, general features, and so on. Naturally, the photographs should all be similar; that is, the suspect's photo cannot be in color and all the others in black and white. A record of the photos used should be made so that they can be produced at a later time, if necessary, and the set of photographs kept for future trial use if an identification is made. The witness should initial and date the identified photograph on the back and a statement should be taken describing the identification. The ideal situation is to have witnesses formally view many photographs in a structured environment; that is, a rogues' gallery.

The Nassau County, New York, Talking Rogues' Gallery. The young woman, a victim of a recent sexual assault, sat in a darkened room nervously fingering a small device connected to a slide projector. She continually pushed a button, changing the images of various young men displayed on a large screen. As each life-size image materialized, it spoke to the viewers. Suddenly the woman stopped the systematic changing of slides and stared fixedly at one image as it spoke. "That's him and that's his voice," she screamed to the detective sitting next to her. The detective tried to calm her as she started to cry while staring at the image on the screen.

This incident took place recently at Headquarters of the Nassau County Police Department's Talking Rogues' Gallery installation. The Talking Rogues' Gallery is the end result of a program of continuous improvement in perpetrator identification in the area of crimes against persons.

In 1947, the Nassau County, New York, Police Department pioneered the use of color film in prisoner photography. A system was initiated whereby 5 × 7-inch full-length color prints of each prisoner were filed according to sex, race, age, and height. Sections of this rogues' gallery were shown to witnesses according to the description given to the investigating detective. As years went by, a sizable file was established, and the program was fairly successful in the identification of suspects. However, the file eventually grew to the point of being unmanageable, in spite of constant purging. It was found that witness interest time, an important factor in the rogues' gallery concept, did not lengthen at the same rate as the increase in the time necessary to view the complete file. This situation resulted in a gradual reduction in effectiveness of the system as the file grew in size.

Eventually, the in-house processing of color prints of prisoners was discontinued in favor of the more economical practice of using 35-mm transparencies processed by Kodak. A procedure was established whereby all legally photographable prisoners were filmed full-length, in both black-and-white and 35-mm Kodachrome. The black-and-white film was handled by the department, and the color sent to Kodak for a normal slide/mount processing. On return of the mounted slides, usually in less than a week, they were placed in 80-unit trays and filed in the same descriptive categories that had been established for the color print file.

Victims and witnesses now viewed suspects in the rogues' gallery, projected life-size and in color. The images appeared to be standing in the room with the viewer and, in some cases, vehement and unequivocal identifications were made. The witness was usually encouraged to control the rate at which slides were changed by using the remote control unit of the projector. It was found that the victims took more interest in the identification process if they could become more involved. The rate of image change was found to be a fair indication of witness interest—a fast display of images most often resulted from a "going-through-the-motions" attitude of an apathetic viewer.

The overall result of the projected rogues' gallery was a decrease in witness viewing time and an increase in effectiveness. The descriptive categories were deemed appropriate, but a marked increase in photographable prisoners, due to a change in state law in 1971, necessitated the introduction of a new category, "major crime," into the file to cut down viewing time. For example, witnesses who were the victims of robbery now viewed prior robbery arrests and weapons possession offenders before prisoners charged with lesser crimes. Recidivism in some categories of crime was found to be an important factor; therefore, the most probable suspects were shown when witness interest was at its peak.

In 1973, a demonstration of the 3M Corporation Sound/Slide System was witnessed by members of the department, and the idea of using this type of equipment in the rogues' gallery was formulated. An application for federal funding was initiated, describing the concept of a Talking Rogues' Gallery combined with the use of a sound spectrograph. Voice print analysis had been practiced by the Nassau County Police Department since 1968, and tests indicated that the use of a file of sound/slides of prisoners could be an effective addition to the process. The application for federal funding was approved, and three sound/slide systems and a modern sound spectrograph were purchased.

A procedure was implemented whereby each prisoner arrested for any one of a group of 30 crimes is requested to speak into a microphone—name, address, place of birth, age, date of birth, and height. The crimes selected were those in which witnesses would most likely be talked to by the perpetrator. The prisoner's voice is recorded directly onto a sound/slide frame, using the projector as the recorder. This recording is obtained from the prisoner at the time of fingerprinting and photographing at police headquarters in a room set aside for that purpose. Signs in English and Spanish are posted to help prisoners remember what they are requested to say. Even if they refuse orally to give the information, their speech is considered to be of value. The resulting sound/slide frame is identified and forwarded to the rogues' gallery for eventual correlation with the film slide of the prisoner when it is received from Kodak.

The sound/slide frames are filed in cassettes in the same descriptive categories as maintained in the "Quiet Rogues' Gallery" and shown to all witnesses. The sound portion of the frame is not always used if the witness indicates that the perpetrator did not speak during the confrontation. Because each individual frame contains both voice and photo, there are no misfiling or correlation problems once the combination has been established on the frame.

Also completed at the time of prisoner processing is a physical description coding form for entry of the prisoner's description into the rogues' gallery computer terminal. This form has an almost identical twin, the Witness Interview Form used by the rogues' gallery operator while interviewing the victim or eyewitness.

The resulting information is entered into the terminal, and a computer printout of the location of the slides of the most similar suspects on file is obtained. The elimination of showing many unnecessary photographs resulted in maintaining witness interest, which is conducive to more and better identifications.

The rogues' gallery area is actually a room set aside only for the identification of suspects, both on film and live. In addition to being equipped with a floor-to-ceiling projection screen and loudspeakers behind the screen, the room houses all the slide files. Provision has also been made for live line-ups with variable controlled lighting, one-way viewing glass, and facilities for various angle viewing of suspects. All life line-ups are also photographed in color against a neutral gray background for future court use. The facilities and procedures have been used with great success and have been court tested and approved by both prosecution and defense attorneys. The rogues' gallery finds plenty of use and is in operation around the clock.

The computerized Talking Rogues' Gallery, where a life-size, full-length talking color photograph is shown to witnesses, is believed to be near the ultimate in perpetrator identification. Witness apathy, fright, fatigue, and other factors that usually prohibit or inhibit positive identifications can never be totally overcome, but a modern approach to photo viewing can help considerably. Even though the positive identification of a perpetrator in the rogues' gallery does not stand alone (that is, without further corroboration) as the cause for arrest, it is considered to be a valuable investigative tool and worth the time and money expended.

Since the institution of a computerized Talking Rogues' Gallery, there have been many identifications. There have also been many attempts by defense attorneys to negate the evidence. However, the testimony of the rogues' gallery operator describing how the operation is conducted has always counteracted any defense argument of an unfair identification.

A recent innovation has been added to the eyewitness identification process. A digital image of an arrestee, entered onto an optical disc, now allows each precinct squad and some special squads to call up a high-resolution color photograph of suspects by physical description. The computer in the Rogues' Gallery now feeds a network of terminals, allowing detectives immediate access to the department photo file. Detectives utilizing the system can not only produce an immediate photo of the suspect(s) on a monitor, but also, if necessary, produce a high-resolution print of the main suspect and, if required, additional subjects who fit the same general description for Photo Pack identification.

Whatever method of identification used—live or photo, line-up or show-up—it must be conducted as fairly as possible to maintain its evidentiary value. The weakness of eyewitness identification without strong corroboration must be recognized, and safeguards against suggestiveness during the identification process taken. A fully cooperative, accurate, "stand-up" eyewitness is rare. He or she should not be wasted by sloppy police techniques during the identification process.

30
Intelligence Operations

Ben Jacobson

Timothy M. Dowd

THE CONCEPT OF INTELLIGENCE

Intelligence gathering is a necessary law enforcement tool for countering criminal societies. It can be focused on specific fact gathering or directed toward the total responsibility of law enforcement. In either case, this process of data collection and distribution plays an integral part in formulating enforcement policy and in planning requirements for future action. Although the intelligence community has been raked over the coals on many counts—inefficiency, illegal actions, and failing to properly inform the line officers—such allegations have been proved false and mere conjecture by opponents of the intelligence system.

Through intelligence operations, fact gathering can be formulated into the creation of an informational community which makes use of results obtained from (1) prior investigations, (2) public documents, (3) mass media, (4) internal police information, (5) informant responses, and (6) documented actions of individuals under observation. Such information must be scrutinized, correlated, and disseminated among members of the law enforcement community where it should be employed when needed to assist concerned investigators in decision making.

To help in understanding intelligence objectives and operations, this chapter was based on the experiences of the authors, both of whom participated in organized criminal intelligence gathering for several years. Several factors have altered the thinking behind intelligence gathering over the years. Therefore, it is hoped that this presentation will enable the reader to better select the proper action to be taken in organizing and operating a criminal intelligence agency.

Because of the intelligence operations to which the authors were exposed, aspects of the chapter are slanted toward organized criminal activity. The chapter's purpose, however, is to expose the reader to greater knowledge and experience of the intelligence-gathering mission; and the important consideration is that the organization devise an efficient plan for effectively enforcing criminal statutes and attacking the criminal society.

Although highly specialized intelligence departments and squads have been created to deal with specific areas within the criminal justice field, police intelligence undoubtedly comprises the largest segment of total operations in the field.

The common assumption that police departments have a legitimate right to collect intelligence is based on the fact that the police have a legitimate role in an urban society, that of ensuring a certain degree of social control. To effect this control, police have the absolute right to (1) identify and apprehend criminal offenders, (2) suppress criminal activity, (3) reduce opportunities for crime through patrols or other preventive measures, (4) protect the constitutional guarantees of citizens, and (5) identify potentially serious law enforcement and government problems.

It is commonly assumed that police officers are obligated to take the initiative in ferreting out all criminal behavior; in practice, however, their initiative is highly selective. In fact, some of the terms used in intelligence are foreign to the police world, having evolved from the practice of selectivity.

Selectivity is illustrated in organized crime investigation in which only the major figures are assigned close surveillance and attention. To indicate functions associated with the techniques of gathering police intelligence, administrators use such terms as collect, collate, and analyze—terms that resemble concepts used in stock brokerage. Nonetheless, a detective investigator's duty and responsibility are correlated with these intelligence functions, that is, collection, collation, and analysis of information.

To survive, a detective must be innovative and aggressive in developing sources of information. Once established, these sources are tapped to collect data pertinent to a particular investigation. All facts must be collated in a way that ensures an accurate and logical conclusion. Additionally, a detective must analyze intelligence coming from several sources, including "the street" and formal sources within the law enforcement field itself. Police intelligence is a term used broadly in today's investigative work.

Most detective squads are involved in some type of intelligence gathering. For example, the typical urban police department might include the following specialized detective squads: (1) pickpocket and confidence squad; (2) auto squad; (3) bank squad; (4) safe, loft, and hijack squad; and (5) commercial robbery and burglary squads. To make their jobs easier and improve their case clearance rate, all the specialized squads collect intelligence; and most of them, at minimum, maintain photographic and intelligence files on individuals arrested or suspected of involvement in a specific category, such as vehicle theft, con games, or bank robbery.

Additionally, in a particular metropolitan police force, the senior citizens robbery team maintains intelligence files containing photos and the modus operandi of persons suspected of preying on the elderly.

In most urban police departments at the local precinct level, the precinct detective squad acts as an intelligence-gathering agency for the commanding officer of the precinct. All precinct detective squad members are instructed to use an intelligence summary form to report information supplied by criminals regarding other crimes or criminals. This information is the result of questioning all arrested suspects about their knowledge of other crimes committed by themselves or others.

In some cases, highly sophisticated methods of intelligence are employed. For example, some police departments maintain intelligence data on explosive or incendiary bombings (or attempts) of which organized groups are suspected. This same special data bank is also used to collect and collate intelligence concerning arson. It is particularly important because of the complexity and magnitude of long-range and detailed investigations common to such cases.

In some situations, decentralized intelligence gathering is effective: That is, each operational division is responsible for maintaining its own specialized intelligence, correlated with the goals and functions of the unit. For example, in one major police department, the intelligence unit of the chief of organized crime is totally separate in the organizational structure from the department's central intelligence office. This unit's files contain only information pertaining to narcotics, gambling, loan sharking, pornography, and prostitution.

INTELLIGENCE IN ITS BROADEST SENSE

As pointed out earlier, intelligence in the broadest sense of the word means much more than the concept as used in police intelligence.

The Drug Enforcement Administration (DEA), for instance, specializes in intelligence gathering related to narcotics violators: smugglers, financiers, high-level dealers, and finally kilo distributors. The DEA uses a computer information bank known as Dangerous Drug Intelligence System.

Based on existing federal statutes, the IRS maintains a squad responsible for selecting targets for prosecution for tax law violations. This unit pursues "closed major cases investigated by police departments." Sources of leads for other tax-related cases against major organized crime figures and their close associates are generally supplied by local police organized crime investigating units.

Special agents of the U.S. Treasury employ intelligence to investigate and develop counterfeit charges against criminal violators. Most are members of organized-crime groups which distribute counterfeit U.S. currency. In such cases, organized-crime connections are used to print and distribute large quantities of bogus currency. Treasury agents generally check the possible organized crime affiliation of major suspects in counterfeiting cases as part of routine procedure.

The New York office of the FBI maintains an intelligence squad for the express purpose of developing massive profiles and information on all five of the New York crime families and their associates. Furthermore, the U.S. attorneys for both the Eastern and Southern Districts in New York City have been known to use their investigators as intelligence and organized crime experts.

Also, in conjunction with the New York special prosecutor's office, intelligence agents investigate such specialized areas as organized crime subjects who are either actively engaged in or suspected of bribery and corruption of public servants, members of the New York State Bar Association, or members of the criminal justice system.

In the areas of New York, Brooklyn, and Queens, district attorney's office squads are all actively involved in developing intelligence regarding organized crime figures. Although the detectives assigned to these squads are members of the New York City Police Department, they operate independent of it. Such investigations are usually handled by an assistant district attorney who is not responsible for formally reporting any intelligence gathered as a result of surveillance or wiretaps (except, perhaps, to give periodic briefing summaries to the detective's supervisor). Therefore, because there are no formal requirements for disseminating this intelligence to other law enforcement agencies in the same geographic area, much of this extremely valuable intelligence developed during the course of DA crime probes is virtually lost. Using guidelines suggested by the National District Attorney's Association, an "intelligence sharing" plan might prove effective in standardizing methods of getting intelligence obtained into police intelligence files.

The Law Enforcement Intelligent Unit (LEIU) was initiated in 1956 to exchange data vital to the proper performance of the police intelligence function and now totals a membership of 227 state and local police departments in the United States and Canada. The organization is supported by public funds, including $36,000 from California and $2 million contributed by the LEAA in the past. This intelligence concept was discussed in *Time* magazine of June 25, 1979.

SOURCES OF INTELLIGENCE

In an effective and efficiently operating intelligence system, all sources of information must be considered toward the final objective of an organized compilation of current, reliable, and appropriate data which reveals criminal activity—data concerning either persons or occurrences at specific sites. Such sources are the "life line" of the intelligence community, because they support documentation offered to prove the existence of criminal behavior.

Data can be collected from the public by the patrol officer on the street. The sources must be reviewed continually and updated daily. Without sources of information, intelligence operations would come to a standstill and the scope and sequence of criminal activities could not be examined. Intelligence is not *predicting* crime. Rather, it is *gathering facts* to aid in deploying personnel and planning the direction of selective enforcement. Additionally, intelligence is critical in aiding the suppression of violent street crime, which often demands unusually intense investigative efforts.

The intelligence community must decide where it will gather its data. This decision will determine which contacts to develop, according to the requirements of a thorough informational bank. The intelligence community must rely on data that it receives and subsequently files for future reference. Therefore, such reports go into an incorporated intelligence retrieval system. Sources may include local law enforcement personnel; informants; journalists; libraries; newspapers; periodicals; public interest groups; regional, state, and federal law enforcement agencies; other state agencies; local officials; and the criminal community itself. Each of these sources can supply data which may prove useful not only in future inquiries but also in analyzing the operations of offenders. Without exception, the individual's rights of privacy must be considered; information gathered from informed sources must be kept confidential and any release of such material strictly accounted for.

Although the criminal informant has been deemed the most reliable source of data by many observers, in actuality, data collected from other sources is equally important. Analysis of the information gathered must determine its validity. Unfortunately, ever since the publication of Joseph Valachi's famous tales of organized criminal activity in America, the law enforcement community has tended to consider the informant as the best source of information. Although the criminal informant is useful, and sometimes critical, to an inquiry, the intelligence operation must look to other sources, as well.

Information gathered from ongoing investigations, wiretaps, and search warrant evidence is essential in the classification and analysis of facts concerning the criminal subculture. Two of the best sources of information are personal telephone books and records of transactions between suspected criminals. Such sources become vital in future criminal investigations and may reveal other individuals who have close ties with the offenders. Although the seizure of such data may be illegal (unless under search warrant), an intelligence officer can copy it and return it to the offender.

Other sources may derive from business transactions and/or corporate operations. While some subjects are able to remain anonymous, many must file applications for state licenses and, in many instances, are listed in private business directories and publications of public informational services. Such sources can be valuable for tracing syndicated crime's infiltration into legitimate business. For example, facts can be gathered from county offices where public records document corporate operations and organizations. This will aid in determining the persons in control of specific businesses. In some instances the banking industry can supply information; however, a subpoena is usually required. In this type of action, after 30 days the banking institution or credit reporting institution may inform the individual in question. To avoid this the institution can be requested to delay notification until further notice. In some cases, a court-ordered delay be imposed.

Once information from all possible sources has been gathered, a complete picture of an individual's criminal operation can be constructed and the data can be analyzed. If the analysis is objective, the direction and logistics of the investigation can be planned. Some data may support only an inquiry; some may support a covert operation; while still other data may reveal information that should go directly to a grand jury for indictment proceedings.

Another prime concern of intelligence is updating information. The informational search should be continuous to supply facts which will aid the ongoing inquiries. Updating information is extremely important; otherwise intelligence quickly becomes stale and ineffective.

Certain sources of information are never revealed to the intelligence community; however, these instances usually involve criminal information useful only to local detectives. These investigators develop their own sources of information during the course of an investigation, and such data is often critical to the success of the investigation.

There is an old maxim regarding detective work; namely, that a detective is as good as his or her information—received from a variety of sources. The more contacts developed, the more information obtained. In spite of the progress made in formalizing the intelligence process, the maxim still holds true. Detectives who work in "busy shops" (units with heavy caseloads) are concerned only with closing cases through clearance. To obtain clearance, an investigator must identify the offenders and make an arrest. In some cases, however, "exceptional clearance" is obtained. In such instances, the subject has been identified but, for some legitimate reason, is not arrested. As a result, the intelligence gathered in regard to that individual remains "under the hats" of detectives who are too busy to send the information through the proper channels.

QUESTIONS OF ETHICS IN INTELLIGENCE

The intelligence community received adverse publicity during the 1960s when it came to be seen as "big brother." Social change, the Vietnam war, and the assassination of a president modified conventional intelligence investigative techniques and raised disturbing ethical questions about the role of intelligence—a marked change from the past, when it was viewed as a paper-shuffling operation. Actually, the intelligence officer plays an important role in policy formulation and links police administrators with the enforcement effort.

Some questions to be considered are: Is the purpose of intelligence political, economic, or social? What is its goal? Are its views and objectives on data analysis adequate for establishing that there is a criminal society? In many instances, its operations focus on visible activities in the criminal community; at other times, infiltration merely changes criminal methods or creates new forms of crime. Curtailing one aspect may give rise to others, which signal the need for a new intelligence mission. Briefly, the intelligence community in formulating enforcement policy should take the position that criminals participate in many facets of crime; that counterintelligence may create variations; and that its mission is to search for crime factors, not causes.

The organized criminal intelligence theory that some crimes are organized while others are not is part of a social trend which has encompassed the enforcement intelligence community since the Valachi revelations. Such a theory fails to recognize that organized criminal behavior is a product of a subculture involving people from all walks of life. Intelligence must expose illegal behavior without suggesting that specific ethnic, racial, or sexual variables are correlated with such behavior. La Cosa Nostra exists, but syndicated criminal activities are not limited to persons from any one ethnic group. Who creates organized crime: a criminal element in a specific, formal family structure or the intelligence labeling of data on individuals, businesses, families, and blood relations?

The relationship between the intelligence community and the decentralization of the intelligence function is critical. Decentralization is necessary for proper identification of criminal offenders and for information gathering. If intelligence specialists remain within a centralized office, their body of knowledge and collected data diminishes; their interaction with members of specialized investigative teams and other officials may not lead to valuable input, because they are unable to identify offenders and their operational methods on the basis of daily experience. Moreover, they may be seen by some as outsiders—unable to understand the situation and lacking in expertise. Simply stated, limited day-by-day participation in investigation and restricted outreach can only have a negative effect on the intelligent operation.

The authors recommend that those selected for centralized intelligence units have extensive field experience in specialized squads, thereby reducing the tendency of the outside intelligence command function to be distrusted or seen as intrusive. Such a background would increase the likelihood of free exchange of confidential and significant data essential for gathering a total picture.

CONFIDENTIALITY AND SECURITY

Confidentiality and security go hand in hand in determining the existence and survival of the intelligence operation. Confidentiality must be established to obtain data for analysis and filing within the command; internal safeguards incorporated into operating procedures should guide the selection of trusted staff and the dissemination of information. Many law enforcement management personnel believe that the intelligence function is gathering and processing information for use within *various* commands, but indiscriminate dissemination can cause sensitive information to reach the hands of adversaries. The erroneous idea that all personnel should have vital intelligence data and the lack of integrity controls can only jeopardize criminal investigations.

It has been the authors' experience that such information should be placed in the hands of selected personnel only on a need-to-know basis. Accountability and control are then strengthened. Some lower-echelon officers may consider such a policy a "slap in the face" to their integrity, but it serves to prevent inadvertent comments from being overheard by the wrong people.

If, for example, during a meeting concerning use of narcotics in schools, a community relations police officer informs an interest group that undercover officers are purchasing various contraband from students within a particular school, the undercover operation would have to cease because of safety problems. Although the officer's statement may have been only a slip of the tongue, nonetheless, it could not have occurred had the need-to-know policy been in effect. Briefing the officer on such an operation was not essential for his or her performance as an officer. Problems of confidentiality necessarily revolve around the intelligence investigator, informants, and supervisory personnel. Some individuals are not attuned to intelligence problems and, therefore, sometimes offer information to a community, the press, or other interest groups that should not have been disclosed.

A problem of confidentiality can also develop from the intelligence officer–informant relationship. Disseminating information piecemeal and limiting the scope of the inquiry to fragmented facts can preserve the total intelligence operation from exposure. Fragmenting informant power prevents double dealing or selling information; it allows the intelligence investigator time to gather facts to build up a total picture of the criminal problem while permitting control of confidentiality. If there is a breach, a specific informant or single source can be identified.

The commander or supervisory personnel can use fragmented investigatory procedures as a security measure. It takes the form of a puzzle, with the supervisor receiving pieces from each investigator and placing them in their proper positions. Thus confidentiality remains intact and security is maintained by the need-to-know formula.

Breaches of confidentiality must be thoroughly investigated and standards and procedures implemented to ensure that they do not occur again. Intelligence supervisory personnel are responsible for investigating security leaks and reviewing procedures relative to the affected area. The commanding officer controls the establishment of policy for distribution of confidential and informative reports. However, this policy should be developed in training, specified in policy statements, and implemented. Integrity control is the joint responsibility of all officers within the intelligence command.

Security procedural advice should be gathered by intelligence officers who establish rapport with other agencies within and outside the law enforcement community. Establishment of documentation control and the creation of checklists help to guarantee safe intelligence operations. Security control over files should include:

- Name, ID number, requesting agent's command or office location.

- Call-back telephone number and verification.

- Ledger of requested information and security maintenance records.

- Signed request form verified with ID number.

The secure maintenance of such files is the sole responsibility of one assigned officer, with a supervisor as a backup. Whatever goes into the file as a result of confidential informant debriefing must be strictly controlled.

Responsibilities of the assigned officer should include the following:

- Establishment of an intelligence informant file.

- Maintenance of informant ID file.

- Establishment of security indexing procedures, such as coded numbers for confidential informants (CI).

- Reporting of informant activity to command officer, intelligence unit, and jurisdictional courts requesting it.

- Establishment of liaison with contact officers.

- Maintenance of informant records and history of cooperation.

- Maintenance of security emergency plan procedures.

- Maintenance of related information on the informant's knowledge of particular locations, premises, or persons.

- Determination of active or inactive status of CIs.

Other forms of security pertain to a telephone call system whereby all outgoing calls from within the intelligence command must be recorded on a form when information is released. The telephone and case numbers of the person contacted and the purpose of the call must be noted to maintain accountability—a particularly useful procedure when strategy meetings are held regarding raids. Although the contents of personal conversations need not be recorded, the calls must be documented.

Confidential reporting systems must be developed to limit access to exposed data. The information should be forwarded in sealed envelopes, secured files, and by personal delivery to the command officer who will determine its critical importance. All personnel involved in the transmission process must be instructed on the importance of security and confidentiality of the documents possessed temporarily.

In selecting staff, applicant screening and background checks by trusted personnel are required. This procedure requires many hours, but by revealing such information as drinking habits, gambling problems, or associations with suspected offenders, it can avoid weaknesses which may jeopardize future operations.

Applicant screening should be explicit and directed toward individuals who can engage in intelligence operations without any personal gain. The intelligence function is demanding and, in the law enforcement community, requires the ability to separate oneself from the cops-and-robbers syndrome. This tedious work sometimes leads to minimal results, which may be visible only to the intelligence officer. Hence the profession is not as exciting as popularly presented.

An intelligence communications log will benefit operations and security. Other forms of accountability may include a search log: a ledger of "information-requested" data with the name of inquirer, date of request, time, command, code number or purpose of request, and results and disposition of facts. The name of the transmitting officer and telephone call-back number must also be logged.

Such a system develops an ever-present security blanket covering intelligence output operations and personnel controls.

CRIMINAL TARGETING

Selective targeting is a method which can be used in gathering data about specific persons or areas of crime, such as major organized-crime figures or the Times Square area (under the aegis of the Times Square Enforcement Program). Priorities are established by determining the magnitude of the enforcement problem and the alleged level of the subjects' involvement in criminal enterprise. Personnel, budget, and work hours are overall considerations in assessing targets. The probability of successful prosecution is also considered.

Targeting of criminal offenders, locations, or specific criminal acts must be developed carefully through round-table discussions including the intelligence community and enforcement personnel not directly involved in the intelligence function. It is a method of selective enforcement encompassing all phases of investigative intelligence. The political arena should *never* influence its decision making. In profiling targets, the commander must review the total picture of the crime, the potential target's penetration and vulnerability to attack, informant input, and the potential cooperation of other regulatory and administrative agencies.

In developing the target, the operational direction of the inquiry must comply with procedural guidelines, the legal restrictions of constitutional guarantees, and judicial decisions. It should take the most direct route to the final objective, yet remain flexible to allow for failures and diversionary tactics. Contingency options should be built into the targeted design and implemented in the event that the plan requires modification.

The process of targeting individuals should incorporate a procedural file and methods of observation and detection. The file should include a brief history of the individuals, their criminal background and known associates, family members, vehicles, residences and known frequented places, photos of the individuals, and listings of their suspected criminal activities. Since such information is useful for future inquiries, it should be verified before filing.

Criminal conspirators also can be listed but should be cross-indexed in a master case file for easy identification and review. When the target is an active member of a syndicated criminal group, the process must include suspected associates and their questionable criminal activities.

To establish a targeting procedure, the intelligence commander must enlist the knowledge of field investigators and informants. Consideration should be given to major enforcement problems that have negative effects on communities, such as narcotics-related street conditions which have gotten out of control.

Targeting plans should be implemented through a three-pronged attack:

1. *History research project:* Associates, criminal background, vehicles, locations frequented, addresses, known or suspected activity.

2. *Informant data:* Compiled and verified facts from criminal informants and similar sources.

3. *Field observation reports:* Information gathered from various sources of the law enforcement community.

Once the target selection has been completed, the intelligence investigation begins—with additional gathering of evidence to support a criminal conspiracy. When the inquiry moves to a level at which it can become operational, the intelligence function must terminate and present the facts to the operational investigatory units within either the municipal law enforcement department or other governing agencies. The purpose of intelligence field operations is to update and validate gathered facts and then forward them for investigatory action. Most criminal violators who act alone or in groups maintain liaisons with other offenders. This information is important for the intelligence community in profiling criminal subjects.

Targeting can also be directed toward a specific industry or business suspected of criminal operations. Here, too, verification of data is crucial in planning personnel allocations and budgeting. Business targeting must be kept confidential until a criminal conspiracy can be sustained or additional criminal facts have been gathered for presentation to the prosecuting attorney for action. Often, the criminal activity of business can be determined through the investigative expertise and knowledge of other agencies. For example, the New York Banking Department was able to establish that members of a syndicated crime group were affiliated with certain banking and accounting professionals. Its confirmation of suspected activity and unconfirmed informant data verified that this cooperative criminal activity was skimming off hundreds of thousands of dollars and manipulating the savings of innocent citizens. The targeting must be subtle—using informant information, court-ordered wire-taps, examination of garbage, and other secret intelligence-gathering methods. It may include infiltration by undercover officers. Once uncovered, the criminally involved targeted business must be exposed to investigatory authorities. The minimum intelligence input at this juncture would be an analysis of the background and activities of those involved.

When selecting targets, the rules governing privacy and constitutional rights must be adhered to. A violation would place the intelligence operation in jeopardy and thus provide a smoke screen defense for dismissal of criminal charges at a later date. The operation must follow procedural guidelines and legislative rules to be successful.

Investigative innuendos, suggestiveness, and unverified data must never be included in a final target folder.

INTELLIGENCE OPERATIONS

In the opinion of some individuals, the only function of intelligence is to keep the chief informed. Others assume that staff should be operating secretly and in isolation from all other departmental divisions—an attitude considered to be in the interest of confidentiality and security. Isolation, however, can only lead to stagnation. Any intelligence agency that loses contact with other operating divisions becomes ineffective.

In the authors' opinion, law enforcement agencies could improve intelligence gathering by adopting a more decentralized intelligence concept. Perhaps we should be concerned not only with sophisticated intelligence work but also with street crime, that is, intelligence for detectives assigned to violent, high-crime urban areas. Photo files and information on street names should be made available to all detectives as aids for complaint clearance. An intelligence officer could be assigned to manage these files and detectives encouraged to have victims view photos for offender identification. Techniques such as debriefing and photo surveillance could be supplied by the intelligence unit, together with videotape equipment for viewing known muggers.

COOPERATION AND MISCONCEPTIONS

Lack of trust among agencies involved in intelligence is a true problem. Interagency rivalry often creates animosity among various operational personnel within the law enforcement community.

The so-called intelligence mystique clouds the purpose of intelligence, and it has emerged because many investigators do not know or understand the nature of intelligence work. At times, the feeling develops that intelligence personnel think they are above the rest of the law enforcement community. Such an appraisal can result from the methods by which the agency must operate; namely, reporting directly to the chief of a division or to the commissioner. Thus it has almost total control over its own destiny. While such a practice is sound for the intelligence community, it tends to alienate it from the rest of law enforcement. A lack of operational understanding of the intelligence function and the practice of isolation encourage feelings of alienation and superiority.

The intelligence community faces another problem that revolves around policy and operation. Some persons believe it should investigate only narcotics, loan sharking, and gambling violations; others, opposed to intelligence, feel a new policy for organized crime information is unnecessary. The authors, however, feel the time has come for intelligence to change focus and direction and that it should develop white-collar investigative techniques and recruit those educated in accounting and business procedures.

Organized crime does not operate strictly within a family structure. However, we have observed various "experts" from different intelligence agencies disagreeing about the proper assignment of individuals to specific crime families. More important than the families are the criminals and the associates with whom they conspire. This is not to say that organized families do not exist or that specific individuals of a particular ethnic background do not conspire in criminal activities, but the fact remains that we often accept an informant's word readily without actually corroborating facts.

The discovery of the infamous Appalachia meeting (1957) established the fact that a conspiracy among criminals was controlling the American crime culture. In his book, *The Valachi Papers*, Peter Mas said, "Organized crime is a product and reflection of our national culture." The intelligence community has solidified this concept into a family structure; therefore, it has not focused attention or personnel on the invisible organized criminal; namely, the "white-collar" criminal. Such an individual can siphon billions of dollars and not be traced, or rig the stock market and create frauds against the consumer—and yet the intelligence community fails to recognize these crimes. It has concentrated its efforts in one direction—crime families. Hence it is unprepared to deal with modern criminality.

FLOW OF INTELLIGENCE

Under the guidelines of the *Federal Privacy Act* (1974), the flow of intelligence from local and state law enforcement agencies has become restricted. Intelligence which may be considered speculative concerning the criminal involvement of individuals should not be disseminated outside the command.

Certain categories of information, including the following, may be given to federal agencies: criminal history files, fingerprints, photographs, arrest dispositions, modus operandi, arrest warrant, information arrest reports, and any other public record. However, any other intelligence data should be forwarded to federal agencies only on the condition that a signed promise of confidentiality be obtained by a local police department from the agency receiving such information. The federal agency must then file the intelligence data in a record system, generally exempt under Subsection (552) (A) (j) of the *Privacy Act* or specifically exempt under Subsection (552) (a–k) of the Act.

This signed promise ensures that such information will be protected to the fullest extent allowed under the exemption claimed. Furthermore, the identity of the local source agency will be held confidential. It should be noted that federal agencies are permitted to forward intelligence information to local police departments under a "routine use" provision of the federal *Privacy Act* (1974). "Routine use" means that the manner in which the information is used is compatible with the purpose for which it was collected.

It is important to remember that the nature of police work generates the flow of intelligence and that any hesitancy to exchange intelligence is greatly diminished in most organized-crime–related homicides. In police administration, the fact that priority is given to any homicide guarantees that many persons will be interviewed concerning associates of the deceased. Close relatives sometimes supply valuable information about the victim's criminal associates. Telephone numbers found in the possession of the deceased sometimes provide intelligence data.

The arrest process and complaint reporting systems are also conduits for the flow of intelligence information. Fingerprinting and photographing supplies current data about criminal activity to the criminal records and photo unit of police departments. Debriefing of prisoners and confidential informants will provide intelligence input and updated facts to be forwarded for action. A wiretap on a suspect's telephone will supply direct intelligence. The recording of conversations, follow-up investigations, and surveillance will corroborate the overheard activity. Along with electronic surveillance, the execution of search warrants in narcotic and gambling cases leads to the documentation of the volume of illegally transacted business and the resulting financial profit.

CONCLUSION

Large departments should be divided into decentralized intelligence functions. Each specialty should maintain an intelligence reporting officer responsible for the flow of gathered facts and reporting directly to the commander of the specialty squad. This officer will also forward data to the umbrella intelligence administration unit which, in turn, will filter data to the proper agency, either within or outside the reporting agency.

The results of the centralized intelligence process will be reported to the commissioner and persons with command responsibility, such as the chief of detectives and the chief of patrol. Within this unit, the research and analysis unit is responsible for collecting, analyzing, collating, indexing, and disseminating intelligence which is of value to field and operational personnel. Once distributed, the operational personnel must report the results and any new data received.

31
Aerial Surveillance

Claude E. King

A logical extension of law enforcement's use of technical developments to its advantage has been the increase in the use of aircraft by law enforcement agencies throughout the country to add a third dimension to the human ability to see and observe. The third-dimensional view of a city, or a portion thereof, affords law enforcement officers a vantage point which they are unable to attain from anywhere on the ground.

Helicopters, often used for air patrol duties, are usually thought of as the aircraft used by law enforcement agencies; however, a light airplane is often used with equal effectiveness at a significantly lower cost.

Aviation units have become commonplace in police departments and other law enforcement agencies throughout the country, with numerous state and local authorities conducting surveys and studies on the relative merits of aircraft use. From the studies available for review to date, it appears that aircraft use provides an additional technical capability to be taken advantage of, and for modern investigative personnel to ignore this capability is unrealistic.

Since every law enforcement agency's scope of operations depends on the peculiarities of a given geographic area for which it may be responsible, no two agencies are likely to have identical needs for aircraft use. Each agency must weigh the advantages gained, if any, in using aircraft against the cost of operating it. Obviously, a judgment must eventually be made on what is justified in expenditures versus operational advantages of aircraft use.

PHYSICAL SURVEILLANCE

Before looking at the more expensive and complex uses of aircraft applicable to the major law enforcement agencies, consideration should first be given to the aircraft as a simple observation platform.

Both airplanes and helicopters can be considered as observation platforms allowing a third-dimensional view of the area or subject of interest. Although the helicopter is often thought of as an almost stationary platform from which to make observations, it is most often used as a moving platform, usually circling an area or subject much as an airplane would do.

The less conspicuous and less noisy airplane, when used as an observation platform, also allows the observer to keep surveillance over a point of interest, such as a moving subject, virtually 100 percent of the time, whereas ground vehicles rarely allow continuous observation of a subject without being observed by the subject. Quite frequently, ground surveillance vehicles are forced to risk either being detected by or losing visual contact with the subject, whereas visual contact from aircraft is rarely lost and rarely detected.

Likewise, while occupants of normal ground patrol or surveillance vehicles are restricted to a field of vision incorporating only their immediate area, aircraft observers can quickly scan entire neighborhoods to locate a particular subject's automobile or for observations of groups of persons, looters, fires, and so on.

A growing number of police agencies are using aerial surveillance to target criminal suspects, greatly increasing the success of a physical surveillance. Targets of physical surveillance quite often know or suspect that they are being followed by law enforcement personnel, and therefore, use evasive driving tactics to either lose or expose ground surveillance units. Observers from an aircraft, however, can watch with amusement from their aerial platform while a subject drives the wrong way on one-way streets, drives down dead-end streets, makes U-turns, or otherwise attempts to lose or expose ground units. The experienced aircraft observer can almost always maintain visual contact throughout the "dry-cleaning" efforts of the subject, while transmitting by radio the information needed by ground units to catch up or avoid detection during the surveillance.

The use of aircraft for physical surveillance of a moving subject is more effective and less conspicuous than the traditional method employing a ground surveillance team, usually consisting of several men in several cars. Surveillance aircraft can operate at thousands of feet above the ground, often being more than a mile away from the target, while still allowing direct observation of a moving subject by aircrew members. As proficiency at aerial observations increases, an aircraft with as few as one pilot/observer (but preferably two for safety reasons) can continuously observe a subject's travel for hours at a time without the subject ever seeing the aircraft. Using aircraft not only diminishes the risk that the surveillance effort will be detected by its target, but also greatly increases the probability of success.

Countless physical surveillances using modern aerial observation techniques have been successful, while the success of the same surveillances using a ground team alone would have been highly unlikely. The traditional method of ensuring a higher probability of success by using more and more ground units on the surveillance has been reversed to some extent with the use of aerial surveillance. In most instances, in fact, two ground units (or even a single unit) are sufficient to complete a successful surveillance when they are working with an airborne observation vehicle. Personnel savings are therefore obvious when two airborne and two ground officers can replace a six- or eight-person team attempting ground surveillance alone. This, with the higher success ratio and decreased likelihood of detection, makes air surveillance a preferred method of physical surveillance in a growing number of law enforcement agencies nationwide.

OTHER MISSIONS

The Los Angeles County Sheriff's Department, one of the forerunners in aircraft use in law enforcement, has assigned its aircraft to a variety of duties, with the objectives of (1) improving police response time, (2) demonstrating day and night surveillance methods, (3) increasing patrol observation, (4) increasing officer security, and (5) reducing crime in the project area.

Police radios were installed in helicopters that were used for routine day and night patrol duties in the project area, allowing third-dimensional observation, which was described as giving expansive observational advantages.

Helicopter units were assigned to respond to calls suitable for helicopter patrol response, such as burglary and armed robbery calls, fleeing suspects, and other backup duties. Briefly, it was soon learned that helicopter response to these calls considerably shortened police response time and provided backup for regular ground police units when those units were the first to respond. This was viewed as being especially valuable in high-crime zones and dangerous areas of the city.

Upon targeting high-crime areas for helicopter patrol, it was discovered during the tense Watts riots in 1968 that citizens were much less likely to cause disturbances when confronted with police actions if a helicopter was hovering overhead. The Watts riots required numerous police actions in the riot area, which were interpreted with great hostility by the inhabitants. Prior to helicopter responses, the rate of assaults on police officers was significantly higher than after helicopters began hovering over the scene of a potential confrontation. Helicopter responses, therefore, soon were considered to have had a deterrent effect on antipolice actions during the Watts confrontations.

A Law Enforcement Assistance Administration (LEAA) survey of the use of helicopters for police air mobility indicated that the main emphasis on aircraft use continues to be on traffic surveillance and control, speed-law enforcement, and search-and-rescue activities.

Traffic surveillance, the monitoring of vehicular traffic along key roadways, primarily serves motorists, who can be advised by radio of traffic tie-ups due to disabled automobiles or road conditions which would favor the use of an alternate route. The effect of traffic surveillance, if properly publicized, is to reduce traffic jams and generally improve the orderly flow of vehicular traffic along major roadways.

Speed law enforcement applies aviation patrol vehicles to normal speed enforcement programs, allowing an airborne vehicle to observe and time automotive traffic along the highways to detect speeders. Radio notification from an aircraft to a ground police unit enables ground units to remain unobserved by motorists until the traffic stop.

Search-and-rescue activities expand to the third dimension the visual range of police observation in efforts to locate lost persons, boats, vehicles, or aircraft. Often, police agencies are called to search for people lost in the woods or for boats reported missing or capsized. Obviously, with the speed and third-dimensional view offered by an aircraft, a capsized boat, for example, can be located in minimum time, and a properly equipped helicopter and properly trained crew can hoist survivors from the water. Such a capability of search and rescue, while not producing crime-solving statistics, can save lives, a traditional function of police agencies everywhere.

Dead or dying accident victims are often donors of organs that hospital patients elsewhere may require in order to survive. Helicopters can provide the rapid transportation essential to preserve such organs en route from one hospital to another in a metropolitan area.

Likewise, there are often medical emergencies requiring rapid transportation of blood, serum, or other medical supplies from one location to another.

The versatility of the helicopter as an instrument of rescue has been demonstrated on innumerable occasions in the New York metropolitan area, according to the New York City Police Department (NYCPD) aviation unit. New York City has 568 miles of waterfront comprised of rivers, bays, marshes, and the Atlantic Ocean (off Rockaway Beach and Coney Island). NYCPD performes many rescues of persons from disabled, overturned, or burning boats. Persons trapped on reefs by rising tides have been removed to safety, and persons marooned in inaccessible marshlands have been rescued. When rough water conditions jeopardize the actual landing or hovering of the helicopter in performing a rescue, an electric hoist is often used to lift the victim to safety.

In a recent rescue by the NYCPD aviation unit, the pilot of a helicopter prevented the dinghy loaded with survivors from blowing into the burning yacht from which they had escaped by using the downdraft of the turning blades to blow the dinghy away from the fire.

One unique rescue performed by the NYCPD aviation unit was the removal of an injured workman from the Cathedral of St. John when, due to the nature of his injury, he could not be removed through the stairwell leading to the roof.

The LEAA survey also indicated that other types of police aviation activities are becoming increasingly evident in modern law enforcement agencies.

Air evacuation has been performed by law enforcement agencies in addition to military air units during disasters such as floods or earthquakes. Accident victims have similarly been removed from remote accident sites, often saving their lives by rapid transportation to a medical facility.

Air and water pollution patrols have enabled enforcement agencies to monitor actual and prospective pollution sources. Aircraft are dispatched, for example, by the Environmental Protection Agency whenever harmful oil spills or air contamination sources are suspected, so that photographs and on-the-spot evaluations by inspectors can be made for possible prosecution.

The LEAA study observed that law enforcement aircraft have been used for riot control, especially in urban areas when crowd dispersal was desired. Riot control disperser systems were determined to be effective when helicopter dissemination of tear gas in a riot or prospective riot situation allowed mild concentrations of tear gas to disperse a crowd without undue hazard to participants.

When police operations call for the emplacement of a tactical team on the roof of a building, obstructions such as antennas or chimneys often preclude a helicopter landing on the roof. However, a helicopter can be hovered (flown in a stationary position) over the roof, so that specially trained law enforcement personnel can be lowered by ropes and rappelling.

The concept of rappelling was developed years ago by mountain climbers and was developed by the U.S. Marine Corps and Army in the late 1950s to meet various military needs. Beginning in 1973, special agent instructors at the FBI Academy, Quantico, Virginia, undertook research and experimentation regarding helicopter rappelling.

It was determined during the study that helicopter rappel operations were suitable for police training, giving a police unit the capability of deploying from a hovering helicopter onto a rooftop in times averaging from 12 to 15 seconds. It was observed that special training taking approximately one week was required to enable a police unit to safely use this technique. With further training and practice, the interval between establishing a helicopter in a hover 30 feet over the building and successfully landing rappellers on the roof could be reduced to 3 seconds.

Discussions with members of the Metropolitan Police Department, Washington, D.C., indicate that during the Hanafi Muslim takeover of government buildings in Washington in March 1977, it was contemplated that SWAT (Special Weapons and Tactics) teams from the Metropolitan Police Department could rappel down ropes tied to a hovering helicopter to the roof of the occupied building in an effort to free the hostages held inside. In this instance, the stairwells to the occupied upper floors had been barricaded by the Muslims to preclude attack by the police from the lower levels of the building, so that the only feasible way for police officers to gain access to the area where the hostages were located was from the roof. Obstacles on the roof prevented a helicopter from landing, which would have required SWAT teams to rappel down ropes from the helicopter. The plan was never implemented because the Muslims surrendered before the actual assault. However, the incident demonstrated the value of the unique ability of a helicopter to hover over a prospective landing area. The helicopter's provision of a way for the officers to enter from the roof could have prevented the greater danger in attempting to penetrate a well-defended barricade on the stairwells below the hostages.

Communications relay can be an important assignment for a law enforcement aircraft, which can serve as an airborne antenna. Since police radios have generally line-of-sight transmission capabilities, ground obstacles such as high buildings and high terrain often prevent one ground unit from transmitting to or receiving from another unit. Often, special remote antenna sites are constructed to assist in communications relay. However, even these relay sites are limited to line-of-sight transmit-receive capabilities.

An excellent radio relay asset is some type of aircraft that can relay radio messages from high altitudes to a distant location. The line-of-sight transmitting range of an aircraft is generally 90 miles at an altitude of 8000 feet, assuming average power output is available from law enforcement portable radios.

This is of obvious advantage to a law enforcement agency investigating a fast-moving major case in a remote area. Rapid communications from field officers to headquarters supervisors are often vital to the successful investigation of a case, with an aircraft often being the sole method of relaying such communications by radio.

Additional missions assigned aircraft by Dade County, Florida (covering the Miami metropolitan area), are illumination, surveillance over crowd movements and curfew violators, pursuing fugitives, detecting fire bombings and looting in progress, and assisting in command and control functions.

Searchlights mounted on aircraft, especially the slow-moving or hovering helicopter, can be effective in illuminating an area during hours of darkness, especially areas not served by street lights. Helicopter-mounted searchlights allow law enforcement personnel in the aircraft and on the ground alike to see in dark areas where they would otherwise be limited to the relatively narrow-beam searchlights on police patrol cars. The beam from a helicopter-mounted searchlight is broad enough to illuminate an entire city block, depending on the candlepower of the light itself, and on the altitude of the aircraft.

During periods of civil disturbances, the Dade County aircraft have been assigned to maintain surveillance over crowds, reporting by police radio the movements of a crowd of protesters. The aircraft were similarly used to observe and report curfew violators. Both these missions are especially useful to a law enforcement agency which can take advantage of the overhead view afforded by an aircraft.

Use of the aircraft to pursue fugitives has proved valuable in Dade County, as elsewhere. A fleeing automobile is especially vulnerable to aircraft surveillance even though it may be capable of outrunning police cars in the immediate area. An aircraft crew need only keep the escaping automobile in sight while reporting its travel to ground police units by radio, so that roadblocks may be set up or units ahead of the fleeing vehicle alerted to respond.

Especially important, again during civil disturbances, is an aircraft's ability to easily see a fire bombing or looters. While normal ground patrol vehicles are restricted to a field of vision incorporating only their immediate area, an aircraft crew can quickly scan entire neighborhoods to report fires and observe groups of looters attempting to escape with stolen goods.

A wide-ranging view being especially important during these major disturbances, Dade County has often assigned its aircraft to command and control functions. Either the normal aircraft crew or a passenger who is a ranking official within the agency can make immediate tactical decisions based on what is being observed from the air and can direct action to be taken by appropriate ground units. This same aircraft tactical function has been used by U.S. military forces to enable the commanding officer of a unit to observe from overhead progress being made on the ground, allowing decisions to be made on the spot.

The simplest task performed by a law enforcement agency's aircraft is transportation—moving personnel from one place to another. The movement of key personnel to where they are needed is not the most common use of law enforcement aircraft; however, it is the most readily apparent reason for rural and metropolitan departments alike to have access to aircraft.

A rural county or state agency investigating a major case may often need key personnel quickly in a remote area; only an aircraft can transport them in minimum time.

A more metropolitan area may also find that rapid transportation of high-ranking or key personnel is well worth the expenditure of funds for aviation capabilities, just as many key businesspersons find it commonplace to travel by helicopter to meetings they otherwise would not have time to attend.

Air transportation is the quickest way to deliver evidence critical to the development of leads and clues in a major case to a processing laboratory.

Prisoner and witness transportation is likewise more expeditiously handled by aircraft, with light airplanes being an ideal way to keep prisoners and witnesses more secluded and protected.

HELICOPTERS VERSUS FIXED-WING AIRPLANES

It is important for users of aircraft to match mission requirements with aircraft capabilities. Without analyzing the detailed capabilities of the individual aircraft used by law enforcement agencies, it is appropriate to comment generally on the different characteristics of airplanes and helicopters.

The typical light airplane used in general aviation and in law enforcement needs a runway of some type for takeoffs and landings, with a usual length requirement of about 1000 feet. Most airports have runway lengths well over 2000 feet.

Airplanes can be modified, however, to enable a shorter takeoff and landing run by adding aerodynamic devices to the wings. Aircraft of this type are said to have a STOL (short field takeoff and landing) capability. This capability reduces the required runway by approximately one-third. Nevertheless, all airplanes require a relatively long runway compared to landing area requirements for helicopters.

A helicopter needs an area only large enough to allow clearance for the turning rotor blades—that is, an area only slightly larger than the helicopter itself—for successful takeoffs and landings. Safe helicopter landing areas could easily be no larger than a baseball diamond infield, a parking lot, or a vacant lot. For law enforcement purposes, the ability of a helicopter to land in small areas is an obvious advantage if there is likely to be such a need. The flight characteristics of helicopters also allow them to slow down during flight so that they can, if necessary, hover over a fixed point.

A fixed-wing aircraft, in accordance with fundamental aerodynamic principles, must remain in forward flight in order to stay aloft. When slowed to an airspeed below its stall speed (usually 50 to 60 miles per hour in most light airplanes), the airplane will cease flying and will fall downward in a stall. Thus it is mandatory for the pilot to keep the airplane in forward flight, usually over 60 miles per hour, in order to remain safely aloft.

In most police work there is no need for the aircraft to actually land in a small area to perform its primary role of patrol and surveillance. There are adequate airport facilities near most urban areas to allow relatively quick response from even an airplane on the ground, enabling it to take off and fly to the area of concern, usually in time to perform the required mission.

A fixed-wing airplane often has a greater load-carrying capacity than most light helicopters used for police work, an advantage only when transporting people or equipment. This advantage may be negated, however, when rapid transportation is important, inasmuch as using a helicopter for this purpose often eliminates the need for passengers to drive to an airport.

Of more significant advantage is the greater operating range of airplanes over helicopters. Airplanes are normally able to transport passengers easily over 400 miles without refueling, whereas helicopter range is usually less than 300 miles. And, if increased range or endurance (time the aircraft can remain aloft on one tank of fuel) is considered significant, airplanes can be equipped with extended-range fuel tanks, which add two hours of endurance to a typical light airplane, such as a Cessna-172.

In law enforcement patrol and surveillance, it is often desired that the aircraft employed be as inconspicuous as possible. A significant factor in the relative conspicuousness of an aircraft is the amount of noise it generates. Helicopters are generally noisier than airplanes at the same altitude or when operating at normal surveillance altitudes.

The greatest advantage of the fixed-wing airplane is its comparative operating cost. Being relatively simple, with few moving parts, it requires minimum maintenance, which reduces expenses required to keep it in operating condition. Maintenance of the more complex helicopter requires much more attention than the airplane, a factor which must be paid for by the operating agency, increasing operating costs significantly.

Total operating costs for each type of aircraft were surveyed in 1974 by the California Peace Officer's Association and reduced to an average cost per flight hour. The cost per flight hour on the helicopters surveyed was $27.70 per hour, contrasted to the hourly rate of $7.74 for the airplane. These figures are given for relative cost comparisons only, with more likely costs for operation in the 1990s being considerably more than this amount, depending on the exact model of aircraft. The California report thus concluded that most police assignments could be covered by airplanes as well as or better than by helicopters at a fraction of the cost. The report, however, neglected to mention what specific aircraft were used for the survey, a factor which could easily change the hourly figures and hence the cost evaluation.

In another study completed by the Cornell University Aeronautical Laboratory, the results were not in complete agreement with the California study.

This study evaluated the patrolling capabilities and cost effectiveness of helicopters and STOL airplanes in Dade County, Florida.

The STOL aircraft used was a single-engine, six-seat helio supercourier.

The comparison aircraft was a Bell-47G-2 helicopter. Both aircraft were assigned to fly 10 different types of patrols over the waterfront, vacant land, rooftops, recreational areas, and rural areas, for fire detection, and to search for stolen vehicles.

The advantages that each type of aircraft demonstrated during use in a major disturbance in the Miami area are described as similar to those advantages in the California report. The comparative evaluation showed that helicopters are preferred when missions are no longer than two hours, when the patrol area is compact, and when there is a need for low-altitude operations and hovering.

The airplane was viewed as preferable to a small piston-engine-driven helicopter when the patrol area is large, when missions are longer than two hours, or when the required payload is large.

The direct flight expenses were determined to be lower for the airplane than for the helicopter, although the report concluded that for Dade County's operational commitments, the helicopter appeared to be the more cost-effective of the two.

The cost-effectiveness, which at first appears surprising, was based on more apprehensions and discoveries being attributable to the helicopter, during fewer flight hours, so that its cost per discovery and apprehension was less than for the airplane.

Inasmuch as this conclusion is based on only one airplane and one helicopter, with no information available on the relative experience and background of the aircrews operating each, the findings of the Cornell report cannot be viewed as being entirely valid.

Having had experience in flying both types of aircraft, this author believes that there is a place for each in law enforcement. The versatile and highly mobile helicopter can be invaluable for surveillance in a congested high-building environment, such as Manhattan, New York City, and for use under low-visibility flight conditions suitable only for slow-moving aircraft.

However, for the majority of law enforcement missions, for airborne observation, the less expensive small airplane is equally suitable—and considerably less noisy and obvious as a police surveillance vehicle.

AIR CREW REQUIREMENTS— COORDINATION

For police and investigative personnel to use aircraft effectively for most of the missions mentioned, it is essential to develop a program for adequately training aviation personnel to safely operate the aircraft on law enforcement missions.

Most law enforcement agencies that use aircraft have pilots who are first trained as law enforcement officers and who are also FAA-licensed pilots with considerable flight experience. Although civilian (non–law enforcement) pilots can be hired or chartered for particular flight operations, they are not familiar with the operations, objectives, or methods of the police or investigative agency, so that maximum effectiveness is usually not achieved when using such personnel. Likewise, training civilian pilots for law enforcement missions such as aerial surveillance not only takes time, but also tends to compromise the confidentiality of the techniques employed by police agencies as well as the specifics of particular operations.

Many law enforcement agencies have found it inherently more advantageous to train aircrew members from within their ranks, first as law enforcement personnel, and then to achieve flight proficiency by additional flight training. Flight proficiency comes relatively quickly if the personnel have had prior training and are holders of Commercial Instrument FAA licenses. However, if no one exists with proper credentials or recent experience, it is very expensive to train pilots from the beginning.

A high level of knowledge of FAA air-traffic control procedures is required of law enforcement pilots who operate in major population centers, because of FAA control over the airspace surrounding cities with major airports. In complex metropolitan areas two pilots are necessary (and desirable in other areas as well) as a minimum aircrew. One pilot maintains contact with ground law enforcement units and directs the surveillance while the other concentrates on negotiating appropriate FAA airspace clearances and watching for other air traffic.

Aircrew experience and coordination is absolutely critical if successful surveillance missions are anticipated in major metropolitan areas. For this reason, most major users of law enforcement aircraft require relatively high standards of flight experience from their pilots and also require a minimum FAA license of a commercial and instrument rating in the category of aircraft being used.

Former military pilots are often used by law enforcement agencies to great advantage, since they have previously undergone extensive flight training courses and usually have considerable flight experience as well. Military-trained pilots, whether trained in fixed-wing aircraft or in helicopters (often both), are not only trained to handle an aircraft in normal flight environments, but are conditioned also to fly for some tactical purpose.

Law enforcement pilots need to have the ability to divert their attention from the physical flying of an aircraft to make purposeful observations of ground activity, while simultaneously transmitting by police radio an account of what is being observed. Often, former military pilots are trained to perform similar missions or, at least, to fly and think tactically—flying the aircraft for a purpose other than simple transportation. Former military pilots also have the prerequisites for the FAA commercial instrument pilot license.

LEGAL ASPECTS OF AIR SURVEILLANCE

With the increased use of aircraft by law enforcement personnel, a question has surfaced regarding the constitutionality of aerial surveillance. Some writers have contended that to conduct aerial surveillance of private property may constitute state invasion of the "reasonable expectation of privacy," and thus may constitute a search without a warrant in violation of the Fourth Amendment.

Others have indicated that police use of aircraft does not in and of itself pose a threat to personal privacy; however, when aircraft use coupled with electronic magnifying devices enables law enforcement officers to look into an area enclosed by a fence or foliage, the individual's reasonable expectation of privacy is violated. It is contended that such an act invades the sanctity of a constitutionally protected area, just as an electronic listening device would.

To my knowledge, there has been no court ruling to date which challenges law enforcement's use of aircraft and optical devices. It would seem that viewing criminal activity is no different in principle whether by an officer on the street, a plainclothes officer from a vehicle, or an officer from an aircraft, as long as the activity under observation is in plain view.

As is the case with general law enforcement investigative procedures, air surveillance will continue to be judged as being reasonable and without sinister implications when pursuing a proper police function and if carried out in a reasonable manner.

32
Use of Electronic Surveillance in Narcotics Investigation

Lester L. Patt

Lewis A. Halpern

Electronic surveillance is indispensable in securing evidence against those engaging in organized criminal activity such as gambling, loan sharking, racketeering, and drug trafficking. While this article will focus on the use of electronic surveillance as it relates to the investigation and prosecution of major drug-trafficking organizations, much of what will be discussed is applicable to other areas of criminal investigation as well.

The objectives of narcotics enforcement are to reach the highest possible sources of drug supply and to seize the greatest possible quantity of illicit drugs before they reach the street. These are difficult goals, given the fact that drug

Note: The information contained in this article is based primarily on the authors' experience conducting electronic surveillance according to the eavesdropping laws in New York State, which are modeled after Title III of the *Federal Omnibus Crime Control and Safe Streets Act of 1968*. However, most of the practices and procedures detailed in this article have more general applicability, since the majority of the jurisdictions in the United States that have enacted eavesdropping laws have statutes which, like those of New York, closely parallel Title III. These jurisdictions are Arizona, Massachusetts, Nevada, Colorado, Connecticut, Delaware, Florida, Kansas, Minnesota, New Jersey, Rhode Island, South Dakota, Virginia, Wisconsin, and the District of Columbia. Since judicial interpretations of similar or even identical statutory provisions may vary from one jurisdiction to the next, it is important for the investigator to consult the relevant statutes and court decisions interpreting those statutes before applying to a court for an eavesdropping warrant.

transactions are always consensual. There are no complaining witnesses or victims; there are only sellers and willing buyers. The enforcement officer must therefore initiate cases. The standard technique for doing this is undercover investigation during which an officer assumes another identity for the purpose of gathering evidence or making a "buy" of evidence. The use of informants to obtain leads and to arrange introductions is also standard and essential. Informants may or may not be persons facing criminal charges. If they are not, they may supply information out of motives of revenge or monetary reward. More typically, the informant is under charges and is induced to give information in return for a "break" in the criminal process such as a reduction of these charges.

Because the leaders of high-level narcotics-trafficking organizations normally insulate themselves from overt illegal acts by delegating these acts to subordinates, it is virtually impossible for an informant to introduce an undercover officer to an importer or a high-level distributor. Usually, a good informant can introduce an undercover officer to a middle-level dealer.

Undercover narcotics buys are inexpensive at street level. As undercover officers penetrate the higher levels of the organization, the buys become more difficult and more expensive. They are exposing themselves to more personal danger with every contact they make. Undercover officers in any large city spend thousands of dollars buying from lower- and middle-level narcotics dealers without getting any closer to the top leaders of the organization. The end result of this type of traditional narcotics investigative technique is that many arrests are made of insignificant dealers with only a slight disruption to the higher-ups. The lower- and middle-level dealers are easily replaced and business continues as usual.

Every narcotics investigation technique should have a purpose when planned properly and used effectively toward an investigative goal. The best enforcement method to limit the availability of illicit narcotics is to arrest the high-level distributors and importers. Frequently the only investigative strategy available to make any inroads into organized crime's involvement with narcotics distribution is the use of electronic surveillance coordinated intelligently with undercover buys and the use of productive informants.

Strict constitutional safeguards exist for obtaining eavesdropping warrants. Supreme Court decisions immediately prior to the passage of Public Law 90-351, the *Omnibus Crime Control and Safe Streets Act of 1968,* and the act which actually governs eavesdropping in the United States, reflect decisive steps toward eliminating unauthorized interception of private communications. Although many have attacked the entire rationale upon which the *Omnibus Act* has been structured, most civil libertarians agree that it clearly delineates the circumstances under which authorized interception is permitted and the manner in which such authorization may be obtained. Section 700 of the *New York State Criminal Procedure Law,* which authorizes the interception of communications in this state, is consistent with and follows closely Title III of the *Omnibus Act.* In fact, it is even more stringent.

This chapter discusses the legal steps that must be followed prior to the issuance of an eavesdropping warrant, during execution, and following the expiration of the warrant. It offers the authors' own experiences in utilizing electronic surveillance in narcotics investigations.

The federal statute, Title III: Wiretapping and Electronic Surveillance of Public Law 90-351, the *Omnibus Crime Control and Safe Streets Act,* provides as follows:

1. Prohibits all private wiretapping and all private bugging.

2. Permits private consent recording only when the private recording is not done to commit a tort or crime.

3. Prohibits state and federal law enforcement wiretapping and bugging except when done under court order.

4. Permits state or federal law enforcement recording.

5. Sets up a federal court order system for wiretapping or bugging.

6. Sets standards for optional state court order systems for wiretapping or bugging.

7. Makes unauthorized wiretapping or bugging a federal civil tort.

8. Requires annual reports for federal and state wiretapping and bugging.

9. Sets up a commission to review the operation of the first seven years of the statute in its seventh year.

The statutes that currently apply to wiretapping and eavesdropping are very recent, issuing from 1968 and 1969, and are very respectful of constitutional rights. Many of the court decisions which have been issued interpreting these statutes construe its provisions strictly. Unless the letter of the law is followed, the result may be the suppression by a court of all the conversations seized and recorded pursuant to the eavesdropping warrant.

In New York State, the eavesdropping laws are contained in Article 700 of the *Criminal Procedure Law*. That article is based on and derives its authority from Title III of Public Law 90-351, the *Omnibus Crime Control and Safe Streets Act of 1968*, which is federal legislation regarding how federal wiretapping is to be conducted and which authorizes the 50 states to write their own eavesdropping statutes.

In New York State, a valid eavesdropping warrant must comply with both the federal and state statutes. If there is any difference between the two laws, local district attorneys are bound by the stricter of the two statutes.

By statute an "intercepted communication" is defined as a conversational discussion, whether oral or telephonic, that is intentionally overheard or recorded by instrument, device, or equipment without the consent of any party thereto. That necessarily excludes consent recordings of conversations which an informant or an undercover agent might have in the field using a recorder, miniphone, transmitter, or recordings made by tape recorder attached to a telephone while on is conversing. In addition, it excludes conversations which are overheard without instruments, devices, or equipment; so "overheards" made by police officers listening in on the conversations of others for the purpose of establishing probable cause do not come within the purview of Article 700 of the *Criminal Procedure Law*, and they are all excluded.

If communications that do fall within Article 700 of the *Criminal Procedure Law* are intercepted without proper authority, reports of them are subject to the exclusionary rule; they cannot be used as investigative leads, and the interceptor is subject to criminal penalties, both federal and state.[1]

THE EAVESDROPPING APPLICATION AND COURT ORDER

Definition of Terms

Eavesdropping is a term covering three distinct kinds of activity: (1) wiretapping, (2) mechanical overhearing of a conversation, commonly referred to as "bugging," and (3) accessing an electronic communication.[2] Therefore, a lexicon of key terms is absolutely crucial. Generally, "wiretapping," "bugging," and similar terms are used loosely, without discriminating carefully among their various meanings. Precise definitions, specifying what each of these legal terms technically signifies, follow:

1. *Eavesdropping:* Wiretapping, mechanical overhearing of a conversation, or intercepting or accessing of an electronic communication.
2. *Wiretapping:* Intentional overhearing or recording of an aural telephonic or telegraphic communication by a person other than the sender or receiver, without the consent of either the sender or receiver, by means of any instrument, device, or equipment.
3. *Bugging (mechanical overhearing of a conversation):* Intentional overhearing or recording of a conversation or discussion, without the consent of at least one party thereto, by a person not present, by means of any instrument, device, or equipment.
4. *Video surveillance:* Intentional visual observation by law enforcement of a person by means of a television camera or other electronic device that is part of a television transmitting apparatus, *whether or not such observation is recorded on film or video tape*, without the consent of that person or another person and under circumstances in which such observation in the absence of a video surveillance warrant infringes on such person's reasonable expectation of privacy under the Constitution of this state or the United States.
5. *Electronic communication:* Any transfer of signs, signals, writing, images, sounds, data, or intelligence of any nature transmitted in whole or in part by wire, radio, electromagnetic, photoelectric, or photo-optical system, but does not include:

   a. Any telephonic or telegraphic communication.
   b. Any communication made through tone-only communication devices.
   c. Communication made through a tracking device permitting the tracking of the movement of a person or object.
   d. Any communication that is disseminated by the sender through a method of transmission that is configured so that such communication is readily accessible to the general public.

6. *Consent recording:* Electronic recording of wire, oral, video, or electronic communications with the consent of a participant.

Absent consent, a court order is generally needed to conduct eavesdropping or video surveillance. The only exceptions are for the situations in which video surveillance is conducted under circumstances where the person or persons being surveilled could not reasonably have an expectation of privacy, or where "electronic communications" are readily accessible to the general public.

Recent federal legislation, the *Electronic Communications Privacy Act of 1986*, has clarified the law in a number of areas. For example, during an investigation of a ring of Columbian cocaine distributors several years ago, it was learned that members of the group were communicating with each other about their drug dealings over a "voice beeper." To send a message over the voice beeper, one member of the group would go to a telephone and call a number designated specifically for that purpose. The message spoken into the telephone would simultaneously be recorded and then, shortly thereafter, be broadcast by radio wave on a radio frequency over which the voice beeper company was licensed to transmit by the FCC. This radio transmission would be preceded by a distinctive beep assigned to the group, so they would be alerted that the next radio transmission was coming from one of their members. The beeper instrument held by each member of the groups would then be turned to the "on" position to receive the message. Since any member of the public could lawfully tune a radio scanner to the frequency over which all these beeper messages were transmitted, a warrant would not seem necessary for law enforcement to intercept these transmission. However, at least one court, in interpreting the federal wiretapping statute, ruled that since the communication intercepted was at least in part a "wire communication" a warrant was necessary.

Under the 1986 legislation, it is clear that interception of these communications constitutes "wiretapping" since it involves the transfer of a communication that includes the human voice at some point and the transfer is in part through the use of a communication transmission facility with the aid of a wire. The new law makes it clear that only the interception wire communications containing the human voice at some point, but not the interception of other nonvoice communications constitutes wiretapping. Under federal law, court orders to intercept "electronic communications" have less stringent requirements than wiretap orders, but under state law in some states applications to intercept "electronic communications" must comply with the same requirements as applications for wiretap orders. As always, it's best to check with your local prosecutor to ascertain the law in your jurisdiction.

Is a warrant necessary before you wire for sound a room used by the police department as an "undercover apartment"? The answer is no, so long as the undercover officer is a party to every conversation which takes place inside the apartment and can therefore consent to its recording. A problem exists, however, when more than one target of an investigation is inside the undercover apartment. Should these persons wander to a corner of the room to conduct a private conversation among themselves, out of the hearing of the undercover officer, a warrant is necessary before this conversation can be intercepted and recorded.

Issuance of Warrants

An eavesdropping warrant may be issued by a justice, only on receipt of a sworn written application by a district attorney, with an affidavit containing "probable cause" to believe that evidence of a crime, designated in a specific section of criminal law is being, has been, or will be committed by a *particularly described* individual; and that evidence will be obtained through eavesdropping at the subject facilities and/or premises; and that normal investigative procedures have been tried and have failed, or reasonably appear to be unlikely to succeed if tried, or are too dangerous to employ.[3]

The requirements concerning the exhaustion of other investigative methods is unique to the decision to issue a surveillance order. No similar requirement is a prerequisite for a conventional search warrant.

Probable Cause

The probable cause requirement stems from the Fourth Amendment to the U.S. Constitution of the United States which was written by our founding fathers in response to their distaste for the tyrannical pre-Revolution "general warrant" which permitted search and seizure without demonstration of "probable cause or any requirement of particularity."

The Fourth Amendment is designed to protect every citizen against any search becoming a generalized encroachment on that individual's right of privacy, and it accomplishes this by directing that "no warrants shall issue, but upon probable cause...and particularly describing the place to be searched or things to be seized."

The Fourth Amendment also protects an individual's private conversations.[4] Therefore, both state and federal statutes require that a judge, before issuing an electronic surveillance order, find "probable cause" to believe that "particular" communications will be intercepted.

Apparently reliable facts and circumstances to establish probable cause may be obtained through criminal associates, observations, overheard conversations in public places, coconspirators, and undercover agents.

The requirement concerning probable cause about the offense, person, and place relates basically to the legal sufficiency of the application and supporting affidavit.

In narcotics cases, probable cause for the issuance of eavesdropping warrants is usually based on information from either an undercover officer or a confidential informant. Where there is an ongoing "buy operation," undercover officers are frequently given the subject's telephone number and told to call the subject whenever they wish to set up a narcotics transaction. These conversations between officer and subject frequently provide sufficient probable cause to support a wiretap order for that particular phone. If an undercover officer is present inside the subject's residence and actually observes the subject using the telephone to discuss narcotics with other persons, these observations will provide ample probable cause to support a wiretap on that phone.

If confidential informants are the source of information to be used to provide probable cause, the reliability of the information must be established. This may be done in a number of ways. If the informants on more than one occasion in the past, have provided information which proved to be reliable, this should suffice. Statements of informants which are against their own penal interest are considered more reliable than those which are not. If any of the information provided by informants can be corroborated, this will enhance its reliability. Also, detailed first hand information which is known personally to an informant is inherently more reliable than general information which the informant heard from some else. In a situation where an informant's reliability cannot be established by any of the means previously mentioned, the information may be found to be reliable if the informant testifies under oath before a judge. In these cases, it is not necessary for the informant's true name to be used. A fictitious name or confidential informant number may be used in order to protect the identity of the informant.

Stale Information

Under the Fourth Amendment, probable cause for the issuance of a warrant must be based on recently acquired information, so that the issuing judge can be reasonably certain that the circumstances giving rise to probable cause continue to exist. The same standard applies for surveillance applications.

In response to this constitutional requirement, the Justice Department has adopted a 21-day "freshness" rule. Under this provision, "no more than three weeks may transpire between the date of the last information relating to probable cause in the affidavit and the time the affidavit itself reached the Attorney General's desk for approval."[5]

The New York County District Attorney's office maintains a more stringent requirement than the Justice Department's rule regarding "freshness of information." In our experience in acquiring surveillance orders, investigators would have to update some of their information if it were more than three weeks old. The undercover officer or informant would have to acquire a more recently taped telephone conversation with the subject and would probably need surveillance reports that indicated the subject was living at the same premises and using the same telephone.

A challenge to an eavesdropping warrant alleging it is based on stale information can also be averted if a continuing course of conduct is established in the eavesdropping application. For example, if an informant tells an investigator that the target of the investigation has been selling narcotics out of the same apartment continuously for several years and has been using the same telephone inside that apartment to conduct narcotics transactions during that period, the fact that the informant has not spoken with the target for the past month will not defeat probable cause. This can be particularly important in those situations where targets know that their customer, the informant, has been arrested, suspect cooperation with the police, and refuse to meet or speak with the informant, thus making it impossible to "freshen up" the probable cause.

Designated Crimes

"Designated crime" is a legal term: Only certain crimes are designated crimes and therefore proper subjects for electronic surveillance. Federal law allows the states to make designated crimes any crimes relating to murder, kidnapping, rape, gambling, bribery, narcotics, or any crime punishable by more than one year in prison.

Time Limit

Authorization to eavesdrop is permitted only for the period necessary to obtain the evidence of the specific crime(s) being investigated. This period of authorization can never exceed 30 days. The law permits renewals of the authorization for periods not to exceed 30 days, but eavesdropping may proceed only as long as is necessary to obtain the evidence sought. The court may decide to approve a given warrant for a period of less than 30 days.

For example, during one investigation, when a seller telephoned a connection in the presence of the undercover officer and ordered 2000 bootleg pills (depressants, seconals), the connection refused to meet with any new customers and let the seller handle the business. The judge signed the surveillance order for 10 days. This was not an organized-crime operation, and the time limit imposed did not hinder the success of the investigation.

Usually, conversations among high-level heroin dealers are secretive about time and content. Even when probable cause is very strong but the purpose of the surveillance is to seize contraband, officers may have to wait weeks for a revealing conversation. Thus, authorization for a 30-day period is essential in this type of surveillance.

Applicants for Eavesdropping Warrants

Under Title III, 2516(1), no application for a federal court order to conduct electronic surveillance may be submitted to a judge unless it has been authorized by the attorney general, or any assistant attorney general specifically designated by the attorney general to make such authorization. Section 2516(2) permits state surveillance applications to be submitted by the principal prosecuting attorney of any state or political subdivision thereof. Thus at both the federal and state levels, participation by prosecutorial officials is a prerequisite for submission of an eavesdropping application.[6]

Exhaustion of Normal Investigative Techniques

Although Congress specifically sanctions eavesdropping, it is an *extraordinary* means of investigation. It can only be employed as the last resort. In order to obtain an eavesdropping warrant, it must be shown factually that eavesdropping is the *only* method of investigation that will work, that other means of investigation cannot work, have been tried and have failed, or are too dangerous to employ. It is widely known that the district attorney, in drawing up the eavesdropping order, the application, and affidavits, is going to have to account for "conventional" means of investigation.

Conventional means of investigation include but are not limited to the use of witnesses, informants, and undercover agents, the possibility of "turning" a coconspirator, the use of conventional surveillance, "overheards," searches, seizures, and other documentary evidence. Essentially, what has to be done in writing an eavesdropping order is to account for each one of the conventional means and demonstrate why each does not work—commonly because no leads are available; coconspirators cannot be approached because they might tip off the others; searches and seizures will not produce the important people in, for example, a gambling or a narcotics investigation; there are no documents available; and so on. In New York the order itself must comply with Article 700.30 of the *Criminal Procedure Laws*.

A sample paragraph demonstrating the exhaustion of normal investigative techniques might read as follows:

Normal investigative procedures have been tried during this investigation but have proved unsuccessful in gathering sufficient evidence to identity and successfully prosecute those persons who are supplying "Dopey" Dealer with narcotics.

1. Physical surveillance of Dealer was attempted when he left his apartment after telling our undercover officer he was going to meet his connection to get the drugs. Dealer made four U-turns and drove at an excessive rate of speed through six red lights, at which time he was lost to the surveilling officers.

2. The undercover officer's attempts to get Dealer to introduce him to Dealer's heroin supplier have not been successful. (These attempts should be detailed).

3. There is no confidential informant known to me who knows the identity of Dealer's heroin supplier.

4. Dealer's toll records have been obtained. While these give us a good idea of some of the person's Dealer contacts by telephone, without knowing the content of the conversations, there is no way of knowing which are narcotics related.

5. A search warrant could be obtained for Dealer's apartment, but this would not likely provide any evidence against those persons supplying the drugs to Dealer. Since the goal of this investigation is to gather sufficient evidence not only to successfully prosecute "Dopey" Dealer, but also to gather evidence against those persons supplying him with drugs and to determine the full scope of this conspiracy to distribute drugs, an eavesdropping device is the only investigative technique likely to be successful.

Telephone Company Cooperation

Even though there is probable cause to believe a person is engaged in a designated criminal activity, it must be shown that that person used a telephone to carry on the designated criminal activity; and it must be shown that the person used the particular telephone which is the subject of the order to carry on that criminal activity.

One recent experience with the New York Telephone Company regarded a request for cable and pair information, which enables officers to identify the subject's line from the dozens which may be contained in one cable. In order to get this information, the eavesdropping order must first be physically presented to the telephone company official. Telephone company officials are very much aware that there are drastic penalties, both civil and criminal, if there is a violation of the conditions and responsibilities imposed on the carriers by Title III.

A *leased line* is essentially an extension telephone that can be installed at any location desired by the officers. Such installation can substantially reduce the inconvenience of conducting a tap and the potential for discovery. Some telephone companies furnish leased lines to authorized law enforcement officials so that the wiretap can be monitored at a central police location. Other telephone companies have refused to give leased lines upon receipt of an order, thereby requiring law enforcement officers to establish their own "plants." These plants are frequently difficult to set up; they may have to be located in unhealthy, uncomfortable and dangerous surroundings; and they sometimes must be located so near the phone being intercepted that there is a high risk of discovery. To overcome these obstacles, the federal statute and some state statutes have explicitly required telephone company cooperation when directed by a court order.

In 1975, certain surveillance orders were issued for investigations in ghetto areas, and it would have been virtually impossible to set up a plant without being detected. At this time, the cooperation of the New York Telephone Company was obtained after the difficulties of setting up a plant in these locations was explained to an official.

In 1976, an official of the telephone company was contacted to request a leased line because of a difficult investigative location. This request was in relation to an important heroin-distribution surveillance. The official flatly refused to cooperate in this matter. He indicated that the New York Telephone Company had changed its policy in regard to giving leased lines even in inaccessible locations. The company maintained there was no statute directing them to provide leased lines; thus, they were not free from legal responsibility regarding any liabilities that could occur.

A recent court decision clearly indicated that the telephone company must provide the necessary assistance in these matters so long as it is compensated for its efforts at the prevailing rates. Thus, in any situation where the need for a leased line is anticipated, the surveillance order should contain the appropriate directive to the telephone company.

One recent problem that has emerged relates to cellular telephones. For law enforcement to intercept conversations over a cellular telephone, the cellular phone service provider must make a "port" available. Unfortunately, many of these providers currently have an insufficient number of "ports" available to satisfy the needs of law enforcement. As a result, in some situations court orders authorizing electronic surveillance have been signed, but they cannot be executed.

Particularizing the Telephone. An investigator who knows that a person is committing a crime and is using some telephone to commit that crime cannot tap all the telephones available to that person or to which he or she subscribes. It must be shown that the *particular* telephone named in the application is actually being used to discuss criminal activity, not that the person merely has the ability to use or, even, commonly uses that telephone. There must be a factual basis for probable cause to believe that is the subject *in fact*, using that telephone.

In one recent case, the telephone sought to be tapped was located at the subject's office. The telephone instruments used to conduct the narcotics transactions had the general office number HEROIN 1-3000, plus six extension numbers 3001 to 3006. Whenever a call came into the office for the subject it would be channeled to any one of the open lines. Similarly, whenever the subject placed an outgoing call, he used whichever line was open at the time but always called from the same instrument. In this case it was impossible to particularize the specific telephone line that would be used, so the order authorized interceptions over all seven lines but particularized the specific telephone instrument and authorized interception only of calls made to or from this particular instrument. The telephone technicians were able to set up the equipment so that the recording and monitoring devices would be activated only when this particular telephone instrument was in use.

The Premises Named in the Order. A particular description must be given of the nature and location of the facilities from which or the place where the communications are to be intercepted. That means, in the case of a bug, the particular room or a particular area which is to be bugged must be specified, and that room must be described physically. If an undercover officer or informant does not have access to the place to be bugged, it may be difficult to secure this required information. The easiest method would be to check the building department for the plans of the premises. If this does not work, the investigator must try to enter the premises posing as a telephone company worker, gas meter reader, police officer in uniform, salesperson or other guise to obtain the physical description of the premises to be bugged, while pretending to be on legitimate business.

In regard to telephones, the investigator must describe where the phones are, in whose name they are listed, and during what hours they are to be used. The telephone company will provide the location and the name of the subscriber. Surveillance reports and the undercover officer's or informant's taped conversations will show approximately what hours the subject uses the telephone to transact illicit business. Sometimes the judge will limit surveillance to a specific time of day.

The Subjects of the Order. In a conventional search warrant, it is not necessary to name the individual whose premises are to be searched, because the description of that place imposes an adequate limitation on the scope of the officer's intrusion. A telephone, however, can be used to transmit and receive the conversations of countless numbers of individuals, only a few of whom may live where it is located. Thus, limitation to description solely by identification of the telephone number would provide little protection to the conversational privacy of many, if not most, of the persons who might be overheard by a wiretap.

Particular descriptions must be supplied of those persons who are to be the subjects of the order. Generally speaking, every person known to use those particular telephones to commit the designated crimes specified in the application must be described in order to set forth a proper basis for saying there is probable cause to believe that those persons are using the telephones to commit those crimes.

In cases where there is reason to believe persons other than those whose identity is known to the investigator will be using the particular telephone, authorization should be requested to intercept the criminal conversations of those known persons "and their agents, coconspirators, and accomplices, some of whom are as yet unknown." In these cases the investigator will be permitted to listen to any criminal conversation involving the specific crime named in the warrant, even if neither of the persons participating in these conversations is specifically named in the warrant.

In those cases where there is no evidence to indicate that anyone other than the particular identified subject speaks over the phone to be tapped, the authorization will be limited to the interception of the conversations of the named subject(s) "*with* his agents, coconspirators, and accomplices." The investigator will be permitted, in these instances, to intercept only those conversations to which the named subject is a party and which concern the particular crime named in the warrant.

The Goals of the Investigation

The goals of the investigation, the period of time necessary to achieve those goals, and the factual basis for that objective must be set forth. The investigator must check to see whether or not the persons and premises named in the order were previously subjects of electronic surveillance. This is purely an administrative task; retrieval of this information can be difficult, but the statute requires this information to be set forth in the application.

A check with the intelligence files of local law enforcement agencies or the Unified Intelligence Section of the U.S. Drug Enforcement Agency may disclose the desired information. It is important, however, to make a thorough search and to establish some way of determining whether or not the parties who are subjects of the order previously have been subjects of eavesdropping. If it is found that they have been, the investigator must set forth in a statement of fact the period of surveillance, who signed the orders, what the results were, and any other relevant information. As already indicated, the reasons why conventional means of investigation did not succeed when tried or were too dangerous must also be set forth.

Retrieval and inclusion of this information in the application does not necessarily resolve all the problems created by this provision. If the prior application and order have been determined to be illegal and not in compliance with statutory law, reference to it in the present application provides defense counsel with a ready-made claim that the earlier illegality infected the later application and order. To avoid these difficulties, when reference to the prior application is made solely for informational purposes, the applicant may ask the judge to make an express finding that his or her decision on probable cause is not based on any information obtained from the prior surveillance.

Description of the Conversation to Be Seized

The Fourth Amendment requires that a conventional search warrant describe the place to be searched and the person or thing to be seized. With a conventional warrant, it is usually more difficult to describe the place to be searched than the thing to be seized, which is usually a known, tangible item. With an electronic search, the opposite is true, as the place of the conversation—the place to be searched—is usually known and easily described. The "thing to be seized"—the conversation to be overheard—is, however, often difficult to describe. Future conversations are not tangible. Their content in many instances can be predicted only in terms of general category or type. It is acceptable to describe tangible items by generic terms (for example, narcotics, implements, firearms), and this practice is more frequently employed in electronic searches than in conventional searches.

The order contains a series of clauses, the most important of which is how the "wire" will be delineated, how the conversations that are to be intercepted will be "particularly described." This should be done as carefully as possible. The conversations should be described *in detail*. If illicit narcotics are being investigated the investigator might state that authority is being requested to intercept conversations between A and B involving the purchase of narcotics and their intention to order, receive, or resell narcotics, which, in turn, will lead to conversations between B and C about resale.

Although the American Bar Association's "Project on Minimum Standards for Criminal Justice Standards Relating to Electronic Surveillance" argues that an electronic surveillance is no different from an ordinary search and seizure, there is growing conviction among jurists and legal scholars that the probable cause requirement should be more stringently applied to electronic surveillances, because of the great difficulty, if not outright impossibility, of "particularly describing" conversations which have not as yet taken place.[7]

Opponents argue that since particularly describing a conversation that has not yet taken place is difficult, electronic surveillance poses a great danger. The danger lies in the possibility that it will be used to gather strategic intelligence relating to a suspect's associations, political views, and life-style, rather than to gather tactical information concerning a specific crime. Proponents of electronic surveillance argue that the special advantage of electronic eavesdropping is its value for gathering strategic intelligence about organized crime and thus enabling law enforcement officials to obtain an overall picture of organized crime to aid in prevention.

The federal and state statutes direct electronic eavesdropping toward gathering tactical information by their specification of the crimes for which federal and state governments may issue eavesdropping warrants. These provisions limit the scope and duration of legal surveillance. Conversations cannot be merely irrelevant social chatter; they must be necessary to secure sufficient evidence that a designated crime has been, is being, or is about to be committed by a particularly described individual.

Confidential Information— Disclosure of Informants

When an application is made for an eavesdropping warrant, the true name of the informant or undercover officer involved may be withheld. Normally, they will be referred to in the application as "the undercover police officer" or "the informant" and perhaps by an identifying shield number or confidential informant number. This is done to ensure the safety of the informant or undercover officer and the integrity of the investigation.

In most cases, the identity of the informant need not be disclosed. In some instances, however, once the investigation has been completed and arrests made, a court may order either the disclosure of the name of the informant, or that the informant testify at a hearing or a trial. In certain cases, where the information in the eavesdropping application could only be known by one person—the informant—the informant's true identity will certainly be known to the subject of the warrant once he or she sees the application, even if the informant is not specifically named. For these reasons, investigators should never guarantee informants that they will not have to testify later or that their identities will never be disclosed.

As a general rule, judges rarely require production of the informant as a prerequisite to issuing a surveillance order. Some, however, will do so on a case-by-case basis. The judge may demand either to see the informant or to hear satisfactory reasons why the informant cannot be produced. Efforts to verify the accuracy of the informant's information should be made and should be spelled out in the application. This protects several interests. The prosecutor's case is protected against taint by perjury. The prospective subject of the surveillance does not become a victim of unjustified or ill-founded eavesdropping. The public profits from convictions that cannot be undone.

The Prosecuting Attorney's Office

In the New York County district attorney's office, eavesdropping orders and applications must be approved by members of the Appeals Bureau before they are submitted to the district attorney. An attorney in the Appeals Bureau checks them for legal sufficiency to avoid controversion on appeal or during a hearing. Again, the district attorney must sign the application. Although he or she does not have to appear personally before the judge, the judge must be given the opportunity to question the assistant district attorney who prepared the application and any police officers whose affidavits support the application.

Investigative Techniques for Obtaining an Eavesdropping Order

The court cannot be expected to authorize a wiretap or a bug on someone who will not further the investigation. The target of the electronic surveillance proposed should be someone who will take the investigation up the pyramid of a narcotics-trafficking organization. In narcotics enforcement, the investigator wants to go from the visible level of a distribution system to the higher echelons of an organization. "Working up the ladder" is one of the justifications for using wiretaps and bugs in narcotics enforcement.

Thus, a fundamental and specific responsibility of the investigator in connection with obtaining an eavesdropping warrant to wiretap or bug is to establish clearly and exactly how he or she will be able to "work up the ladder" in the structure of a given narcotics-trafficking organization by using electronic surveillance techniques.

According to law, the investigator must establish that the investigative goals cannot be accomplished by any other means of investigation and that every other investigative technique has been exhausted. Electronic surveillance should be the last form of investigation to be used to accomplish the goals.

Usually, in narcotics enforcement, information about a high-level narcotics-trafficking organization will be received from an informant. The informant will give this information either for financial gain or, if arrested, for a promise of a reduction in sentence by the assistant district attorney. The investigator must verify the information the informant gives to establish reliability. For example, if the information is that an individual is "moving" 7 kilos of heroin a week, the first thing to do is to verify it by checking out everything the informant says about this person.

An individual who is, in fact, moving 7 kilos of heroin a week must have an organization to sell this much heroin on the street. The informant must be able to introduce an undercover officer to make a heroin buy at some level of the organization. If the informant can introduce the officer to the top man for a buy, then a wiretap or a bug is not needed—but this rarely happens. The top person in a high-level heroin organization, who handles the financial arrangements for importing and distributing the heroin, is insulated from performing any illegal acts in regard to the selling of drugs.

Let us assume that the information the informant has given has been established as true; the informant cannot take the investigator to the person at the top but can take him or her to a middle-level dealer who works for that individual. The informant then introduces the undercover officer to the middle-level dealer for the purpose of purchasing heroin. After making one or two heroin buys from the dealer, the undercover officer will be trusted by the dealer and will no longer need to be accompanied by the informant to make a buy because credibility has been established with the dealer.

The next step is for the undercover officer to obtain the dealer's phone number for further narcotics transactions and, every time the dealer is called to tape record the conversations. When *two* taped conversations of the undercover officer discussing narcotics with the middle-level dealer have been acquired, they can be taken to the district attorney so he or she can determine if there is enough probable cause for the issuance of an eavesdropping order.

The next step in the investigation is to show that the dealer talks to the connection over the dealer's own telephone. This "particularizing" of the telephone is a requirement for the issuance of an eavesdropping warrant. To accomplish this aspect of the investigation, the investigator will have to maintain surveillance at the dealer's residence at the time the heroin deal is being set up with the undercover officer over the telephone. For example, after talking to the undercover officer, the dealer calls the connection to find out when the kilo of heroin can be picked up for delivery and then calls the undercover officer back to set up a time and delivery date for the heroin buy. The surveillance officers will document their observations on a report stating the time the dealer was seen entering and leaving the premises. The investigator now has two taped conversations of the dealer setting up the heroin buy with the undercover officer. There is also an observations report during the time of the conversations, establishing that the dealer was at home while setting up the heroin transaction. Both the surveillance report and the tapes will be submitted to the assistant district attorney, whose responsibility it is to check each proposition in the warrant application. He or she will listen to the tapes and read the surveillance reports. The investigator now has the documented evidence showing that the dealer is calling the connection from the dealer's telephone. Probable cause has been established for the issuance of an eavesdropping warrant for the dealer's telephone, on the basis that the goal of the investigation is to reach the dealer's connection. The connection will not want to meet the undercover officer, and can be reached only by a wiretap on the dealer's telephone.

In another situation, for example, if the home telephone of the dealer from whom the undercover officer was buying the heroin was not used to call the connection, there would not be probable cause for a wiretap. Let us assume that after receiving a phone call form the undercover officer, who ordered a kilo of heroin, the dealer left and drove to a predesignated location to meet the connection. In this instance, surveillance of the dealer is extremely important to establish where the meeting will take place and with whom. The surveillance officers will have to be very careful and sophisticated in their tailing of the dealer in order not to be discovered. It is common practice for narcotics dealers to be extremely vigilant for a "tail" when they are going to a "meet location." It is good surveillance procedure to use at least two, and preferably three, cars to tail a subject. If the subject becomes suspicious of the "lead tail" automobile, the surveillance officer should transmit a radio message to another unit to take over the tail. Let us assume, in this instance, that the dealer was tailed by the surveillance team to a restaurant, then was observed entering a back room of the premises with an unknown male. Immediately after this meeting, the dealer called the undercover officer at the officer's apartment from a public phone and said that he just met with his "man" to set up a deal for a kilo of heroin. The undercover officer will always have a tape recorder attached to the telephone to record pertinent conversations. The apartment the undercover officer uses is rented by the police department, and it is used as the officer's base of operations in the undercover work.

Documented surveillance reports and tape-recorded telephone calls made by the dealer to the undercover officer regarding the transaction of a kilo of heroin have now been accumulated. There now may be enough probable cause for the issuance of an order to bug the back room of the restaurant. The investigator will have to present the facts to the assistant district attorney and confer with him or her about every aspect of this investigation. Let us examine the facts: The dealer does not talk to the connection on the telephone, having probably been warned never to use the phone to set up a deal with the connection. Some type of communication must be used to transact the narcotics business. In this case, the dealer went to the back room of the restaurant and arranged to get a kilo of heroin from the connection. The surveillance reports and tape recordings have been presented to the assistant district attorney, who probably will want more evidence than an initial meeting between dealer and connection to prove they are transacting their illicit business in the back room of the restaurant.

The next step is to go ahead with the buy between the undercover officer and the dealer. The dealer will have to meet the connection again and arrange for the delivery of the kilo of heroin. This meeting will give an opportunity for more surveillance of the dealer. There will be additional telephone calls between the dealer and the undercover officer to set up the deal. By this time, probable cause that the dealer and the connection are conversing about narcotics (a kilo of heroin) in the back room of the restaurant will definitely have been established. Now sufficient information has been acquired for the issuance of a court-authorized warrant for a bug that will not be upset in case of a suppression hearing.

Consequently, the bug in the back room may be productive enough to transmit pertinent conversations between the connection and the importer. This is the technique of "working up the ladder" of an organized crime group by using the various investigative techniques at every level of the organization until the highest echelons are reached.

EXECUTING THE EAVESDROPPING WARRANT

Wiretap Instructions and Supervision

Under New York law, an eavesdropping warrant must be executed by a member of the law enforcement agency that is specifically authorized in the warrant to conduct the surveillance. One New York case upheld a warrant directing the district attorney to execute a warrant where the conversations were actually monitored by another law enforcement agency not named in the warrant, under the supervision of the district attorney. It is preferable, however, to specifically name in the warrant the agency or agencies who will actually be intercepting the conversations. Thus, so long as they are named in the warrant, federal agents may monitor conversations intercepted pursuant to a state wiretap when there is a joint federal-state investigation.

There are instructions for the police officer who will actually implement the order in the "wire plant." (A *plant* is a location close to the bug or telephone involved, in which recording devices are placed for the purpose of authorized eavesdropping.) All participating officers must read the order, the application, and the affidavits, since the order refers back to them.

If a conversation refers to the specified criminal activity, it should be intercepted. If the conversation is clearly not criminal, the recorder must be turned off and spot-monitored.

The American Bar Association has made specific suggestions in this area. They suggest that the assistant district attorney go carefully through the logs each day. The investigators, after listening to the conversations, should prepare abstracts and verbatim transcripts of the conversations recorded and give them (and the daily plant reports) to the assistant district attorney the following morning. The assistant district attorney's responsibility is to read them. If there are then any questions about the relevancy of the conversations, the manner of their interception, whether or not there is sufficient evidence to end the electronic surveillance, and so on, the supervising police officer should be consulted *immediately*.

The supervising police officer should meet with the assistant district attorney fairly regularly. The assistant district attorney will want to spot-check the tapes personally and will want a copy of the tapes as they are turned in, to listen to the important conversations, to see if the daily plant reports are being kept properly, and to see if any changes should be made.

Some district attorneys, or even judges, will want to visit the plant to watch the actual interception once or twice; others will not. The reason for such a visit is to be able to take the stand at a hearing involving suppression of evidence and testify that he or she, as assistant district attorney or judge, not only gave the investigator legal instruction, not only read the plant reports, not only heard the tapes, but even physically observed the police officers and was satisfied that they understood what they had been told and were following those instructions in executing the court's warrant.

In addition, the judge who issued the warrant may require periodic progress reports regarding its execution. This generally involves presenting copies of all the plant logs and transcripts to the judge for inspection and making tapes available if the judge wishes to hear them.

The importance of having knowledgeable monitoring officers executing the eavesdropping order cannot be overemphasized. All the work put in to acquire the warrant by the investigators and the district attorney will be a total waste of time and money if the order is upset in court on a suppression hearing because of injudicious monitoring procedures.

Minimization

The requirement of minimization of interception of irrelevant conversations presents investigators with a dilemma. Too much minimizing may keep inculpatory evidence off the tape; too little minimizing, on the other hand, may invade privacy in a way that invites suppression. The dilemma is heightened by the investigator's need to identify voices, grasp the pattern of alleged criminal activity, decipher coded messages, occasionally record foreign language conversations, and listen to portions of seemingly innocent conversations when there is a good possibility that crimes will be discussed in the course of the conversations.

The general standard is that, as stated in *United States v. Tortello*, a court should not admit evidence derived from an electronic surveillance order unless, after reviewing the monitoring log and hearing testimony of the monitoring agents, it is left with the conviction that on the whole the agents have shown high regard for the right of privacy and have done all they reasonably could to to avoid unnecessary intrusion.

In accordance with this standard, a usual instruction for listening to a conversation is to listen at the very beginning to determine who the parties to that conversation are and the subjects of their discussion. If one party to the conversation is the subject of the order and the conversation involves the crime specified, it can be intercepted/recorded. If the conversation is of a noncriminal nature, it cannot be listened to or recorded. Conversations about crimes not covered by the warrant sometimes will be overheard at the outset of a conversation or during a period of spot monitoring. These conversations should be intercepted and the assistant district attorney contacted, in order to amend the warrant to include the new crime.

Spot Monitoring

Pertinent calls can be taped and recorded in their entirety; nonpertinent calls can only be spot-monitored. The investigator must wait a period of time without recording to listening, then may cut back for a few seconds. If nonpertinent conversation continues, the investigator must cut out again. The general rule is to listen for a few seconds every 30 to 60 seconds.

Even in the case of a call involving the subject of the eavesdropping order, the plant agent must establish that the call relates to the crime specified in the order or some other criminal activity which would permit the order to be amended to cover it. In such cases, amendment must be sought; otherwise, the investigator is not authorized to overhear or to record conversations, in spite of the fact that is is his or her responsibility to cut in periodically to reaffirm that the conversations does not switch to the criminal activity specified in the eavesdropping warrant.

Judicious spot monitoring will show that the monitoring agents displayed good faith in trying to accomplish minimization of the subject's conversations.

No Automatic Interceptions

Automatic eavesdropping is absolutely forbidden. To accomplish minimization it is obvious that an investigator must always be present at the plant during the times that communications are being intercepted. Some tape recorders that are used have an automatic switch. Experts will have to testify that this switch was disengaged when the machine was at the plant. Automatic recording and erasures can be detected, and if they are, the credibility of the evidence seized will be destroyed.

Anyone who thinks an automatic plant can be operated today is absolutely wrong, because one cannot demonstrate minimization under such procedure. How could it possibly be proved that only pertinent conversations were listened to?

The proper operation of the plant is absolutely fundamental. Everything rests on that foundation. The credibility and acceptability of the evidence rests on it. It is the groundwork supporting the case. The best information, applications, and affidavits will be thrown out the window if the investigator does not understand that automatic intercepts are outside the law.

Privileged Communications

Investigators may not listen to any conversation that falls under any legal privilege such as the following.

Attorney-Client.   A conversation between a subject and his or her attorney may never knowingly be listened to or recorded unless the district attorney agrees that the attorney in question is a coconspirator. If at any time during the investigation the name and/or phone number of any attorney retained by the subject is learned, this name and number must be posted in a conspicuous place in the plant. Any calls out to that number require that the recorder and monitoring device be turned off. This also applies to any incoming calls from an attorney to the subject.

Parishioner-Clergyman.   All conversations between a parishioner and a clergyman are to be considered privileged. An eavesdropping warrant could not be obtained to listen to a person confessing to a priest in a confessional booth; similarly, investigators must not listen to a subject discussing personal, financial, or *legal* problems with a priest, minister, or rabbi.

Doctor-Patient. Any conversations a patient has with a doctor relating to any aspect of physical, mental, or emotional health is privileged.

Husband-Wife. Any conversation between a husband and wife which relates *in any way* to the marital relationship is privileged. The only exception would be if the subject's spouse acts as a message taker or message deliverer for the subject. Then limited spot monitoring of conversations between them may be maintained.

In all these cases, the following procedure is mandatory: Turn off the machine, stop listening, stop recording, stop seizing, and stop intercepting.

Recording Equipment

Tape recorders for eavesdropping have the ability to either simultaneously audio-monitor conversation that is being recorded or just monitor both sides of the conversation without recording by merely "stopping" the motor or tape-transport mechanism. This monitoring ability while the tape is in a "stopped" position is a major issue at minimization hearings. The law enforcement officer, after turning the motor switch off, must then turn the listening volume to the "low" position so that he or she is unable to hear the conversation. In spot monitoring, which is permitted by law, the officer must turn the motor switch "on" and then the listening volume "up" to hear and record. There is no way of knowing whether or not the listening volume was turned "down" during the nonrecording intervals.

Based on experience in supervising wiretap plants, we are of the opinion that the supervisor sets the monitoring conduct for the officers assigned to the plant. The officers are told that listening to conversations without recording will not be condoned, and that they can be charged with civil or criminal charges for violation of this regulation. We have never found any instance of failure to comply with recording requirements.

Recommendations

Technical experts have recommended the addition of a "double pole, double throw" switch which controls the "off" switch, as well as minor circuit changes which would allow the tape recorder to record whatever is overheard but would not permit audio to be heard when the motor is in the "off" position. Therefore no conversations could be intercepted unless they were also recorded. The cost for modifying each machine is approximately $2 plus labor costs. This simple modification would settle any question of integrity involving officers listening without recording.

The Plant Log—Sample Log Sheet

The plant log can be as important as the tapes themselves. Logs, required by law, must be made available to defense attorneys. Logs are used in court by defense attorneys, prosecutors, judges, and the officers giving testimony; so they should be made with that thought keenly in mind. All entries must be made as accurately as possible and include the call number, time, meter number, and telephone number dialed. A separate sheet (or set of sheets) is kept for each reel used. These sheets should be numbered for each session. The time requested at the top of the sheet is the period of actual monitoring. A duplicate copy is essential.

The log should include as much of the conversation as the officer can write down while monitoring. When a call is of extraordinary importance, that should be noted in the log. When a call cannot be clearly and distinctly overheard due to noise or other conditions, that, too, should be noted in the margin of the log. Entries should also be made regarding any unusual occurrences while monitoring, such as machine malfunctions, visits by supervisors, or reel changes made during conversations. Figures 32.1 and 32.2 are sample plant reports and pertinent conversation reports. ("Pert" refers to pertinent conversations; "NS" to nonsubjects; and "MTO" indicates that the recording machine was turned off.)

Amending the Warrant

During the course of executing an eavesdropping warrant, a situation might arise in which conversations of persons not named in the original order are intercepted, or crimes not specified in the original order are discussed. The law provides that these can be used in subsequent court proceedings. They can also be used as a basis for probable cause for amending the original order to allow for the continued interception of conversations of those persons regarding those crimes during the remaining tenure of the warrant, *if* there is probable cause to believe that those conversations will continue in the future. As soon as a conversation that is outside the specific ones named in the order has been intercepted in conformity with the order, the assistant district attorney must be contacted to amend the order.

Extending the Warrant

Article 700 of the *Criminal Procedure Law* permits eavesdropping only for a period of time *necessary* to obtain the evidence sought. As soon as that evidence is obtained, the execution must terminate immediately. If at the end of the 30-day period (assuming that to be the maximum period set forth in the original order—it may be less), there does not appear to be sufficient evidence, the district attorney has the right to apply for an extension. The procedure for obtaining an extension is the same as for the original, upon the application of the district attorney. The assistant district attorney must set forth in the affidavits and application for the extension the results thus far achieved and/or demonstrate why he or she expects the investigator to achieve the remaining results in the future and why these results could not be achieved up to that particular time.

The application for the extension order must be made to the original justice, who will pass on the extension application unless he or she is actually absent.

The Use of Bugs and Problems Encountered

In our experience, there are many problems to consider if a bug is contemplated for an investigation. A meeting should be arranged of the officers assigned to

Date 1/4/80 Day Friday Reel No. 8423 Plant NO. 11
Telephone Number 638-9062 FROM _____ TO _____
Assigned Officers: Smith SH. #7314 CMD ND TOUR 12x8
　　　　　　　　　Jones SH. #812 CMD ND TOUR 8x4
　　　　　　　　　Doe SH. #976 CMD ND TOUR 4x12

Time	Lines	Inc. Tele.	Monitoring Officers	Report
1.0750	00/8	Incoming	Smith	No Answer
2.1042	08/14	Incoming	Jones	O-Dealer I- Bakery cake will be ready at 12
3.1118	14/121	Incoming	Jones	O-Dealer Is Dealer inter- ested in a kilo of heroin? PERT. I- Johnny
4.1130	121/400	831-7426	Jones	O-Dealer Dealer expects a package PERT. I- Steve
5.1220	400/406	438-7149	Jones	BUSY
6.1223	406/412	438-7149	Jones	BUSY
7.1230	412/517	Incoming	Jones	O-Wife I- Joan　NS　MTO
8.1325	517/600	Incoming	Jones	O-Dealer I- Steve　I'll take an 　　　　　1/8 PERT.
9.1402	600/640	438-7149	Jones	O-Dealer　Business is 　　　　　good I- Al　　Al will take a 　　　　　1/4
10.1602	640/648	Incoming	Doe	O-Wife　re New Year's 　　　　　Party I- Susan
11.1630	648/711	812-1106	Doe	O-Dealer　Dinner reserva- 　　　　　tion for 2 NP I- Restaurant
12.1800	711/940	724-1372	Doe	O-Dealer　Dealer will 　　　　　take kilo I- Johnny　PERT.
13.2240	940/950	Incoming	Doe	O-Wife I- Ida　NS　MTO

Figure 32.1　Daily Plant Report.

32-22 Operational and Nonoperational Police Units

PERTINENT CONVERSATION

Date 1/4/80	Case Number MC 001-80
Time 1800	Plant Number 11
Consecutive Call No. 12	Reel Number 8423
Intercepted by Doe	
Subject in Johnny	Counter No. from 711 TO 940
Subject Out Dealer	Transcribed by Roe
Incoming ( ) Outgoing (X)	Telephone Number 724-1372

SUBJECT

DEALER: Hey Johnny?

JOHNNY: How you doin?

DEALER: OK, listen, I spoke to a few of my people and that kilo we discussed before.

JOHNNY: Yeah?

DEALER: I'll take it for the price we discussed.

JOHNNY: Seventy-five?

DEALER: Right.

Figure 32.2 Pertinent conversation report.

the technical unit to discuss all the difficulties that may be encountered. A bug is basically two things—a transmitter and a power source. The first question to be asked is, How far will the transmitter transmit? The plant will have to be set up near the bug if the range of the transmitter is short. A place from which to observe the subjects entering and exiting the bugged location is required. If there is no place to set up a plant and no secluded area from which to observe the subjects without being detected, the installation of a bug will not be feasible.

Next, the power supply must be considered. Most bugs are placed in rooms that have built-in power sources such as electric lights, outlets, and telephones. Electricity going through these units can be drawn off to keep the bug permanently charged. However, if the place to be bugged has no power source or if the available power cannot be used for any reason, then batteries must be used. No matter how good the batteries are, they will have to be replaced or recharged frequently. To accomplish this the premises must be reentered, which may not be very practicable, especially if the initial entry was effected by a ruse. After all, how many times can a meter reader check a meter or a telephone repairperson repair the telephone without causing the subjects to become suspicious? If lengthy surveillance is likely to be needed to get the incriminating conversation, the use of a battery-operated bug will not be feasible.

The court order will authorize a forced entry or an entry by ruse which is deemed necessary for the installation of the bug. The investigator's prior surveillance of the subjects and the premises should document the difficulties that may be encountered by the installers. All these problems should be discussed and a plan devised of how to overcome each one. Are there guards or guard dogs on the premises? What type of locks are on the door to be opened? Is there an alarm system? During what hours do the people enter and exit from the premises? If there is a guard dog on the premises, a specially trained officer may have to be there to handle the dog when entry is made. The installers may have to pick locks, run wires, drill holes, and then plaster and repaint a wall. They should have a floor plan of the premises to be entered so they can accomplish their installation as quickly as possible without being discovered.

After the bug is installed and transmitting, the investigator will have the problem of minimizing the bug for the subject's pertinent conversation. This is not as easy as a wiretap, when two people are talking over the telephone. If it is not known who is in the location and minimizing must be done by voice identification, the subject's voice should, if possible, be recorded on tape before the court order is obtained. All the plant monitors must listen to the tape recording of the subject's voice so that they can recognize it during transmission.

The observations post is an important aspect of the investigation. If the investigator observes the subject entering the premises at 12 noon and the monitoring officer records the subject discussing a narcotics transaction shortly after entering, the observations and the recording will verify that the subject was in the location and was discussing narcotics.

These are many of the things to consider before applying for a court order for a bug, but if there is probable cause and present investigative techniques are not accomplishing anything, then it may be the only alternative to try in order to achieve the investigative goal.

Cooperation between Investigators and the District Attorney's Office

In our experience in obtaining and investigating eavesdropping orders, we have become aware of the benefits of a close working relationship between the prosecutor and the investigators in an eavesdropping case. It is important for the success of the case to have an experienced prosecutor who can give the investigation the necessary attention from the beginning to end.

The investigator should keep in mind that eavesdropping warrants are obtained through the cooperation of a specific assistant district attorney who must ensure that the warrants are properly executed. The justice of the court who issues an eavesdropping warrant has the right to require the district attorney to submit periodic reports about the progress of the investigation and the manner in which the warrant is being executed.

In every electronic surveillance investigation, there should be a liaison officer assigned to keep the assistant district attorney informed of the daily progress of the case. The liaison officer or coordinator will deliver a copy of all logs, transcripts, and surveillance reports regularly.

The time may come when a search warrant, additional eavesdropping warrants, or some other legal document is needed. It will be necessary to request the district attorney's assistance and cooperation. To cooperate effectively, the district attorney must be informed of the progress of the case daily. The assistant district attorney's phone number should be posted on the plant wall to be called immediately if anything important is happening in the investigation.

POSTEXECUTION PROCEDURES

Custody of Tapes and Warrants

The original tape reels must be sealed immediately at the termination of the eavesdropping warrant. The reels are wrapped with tape and brought before the issuing justice, who signs a sealing order, then stamps the package and signs each tape and puts the date on it. To open an original tape, an order of a supreme court justice is required. After a tape is opened, resealing it requires another order from a justice.

To work with the tape, duplicates should be made of the original reels before sealing, and the original reel should then be sealed and remain sealed until the trial. Defense counsel arranges with the district attorney to have a copy prior to trial.

The importance of this procedure of sealing and reopening tapes cannot be overstressed. Recently, an eavesdropping order was suppressed because an assistant district attorney opened an original tape without getting an order from the judge to do so. In another case, the tapes were not sealed immediately at the end of the eavesdropping order and were ordered suppressed. All the work will be in vain if the procedure is not followed scrupulously.

The statute provides that the application and warrants as well as the original tape recordings may not be destroyed except on order of the justice who issued the warrant, and in any event must be kept for at least 10 years.

Notification of Subjects Prior to Trial

Upon expiration of the order, the assistant district attorney must serve a notice on the parties who were named in the warrant. This must be done within 90 days after termination of the order unless there are exigent circumstances, which means that the investigation is continuing and notification of the parties at this time would interfere with the investigation. If there are exigent circumstances, the assistant district attorney will prepare an affidavit and present it to the judge. The judge will grant an order of postponement of notice for a reasonable time, generally for another 90 days. Although the law mandates only that the persons named in the order be served, notice will also be served on the parties who will be potential defendants, potential grand jury witnesses, or individuals who may be personally affected by the interception.

Disclosure and Use of Eavesdropping Information

Information obtained through court-ordered electronic surveillance can be shared by the law enforcement agency which originally obtained it. Such information may be disclosed to another law enforcement officer or agency to the extent that the disclosure is appropriate to the performance of the official duties of the receiving officer or agency. Thus information obtained from eavesdropping in one jurisdiction may be used as probable cause for an eavesdropping warrant in another jurisdiction, and the tapes themselves may be used as evidence in a jurisdiction other than the one in which the warrant was executed.

WARRANTLESS ELECTRONIC SURVEILLANCE

Electronic Tracking Devices

Electronic tracking devices are used by law enforcement officials primarily to enhance visual surveillance of motor vehicles. They usually take the form of a beeper attached to the bumper of the vehicle they are surveilling. Since these devices do not intercept any conversation, they do not fall within the eavesdropping statutes, either state or federal. The use of beeper tracking devices has been upheld without a court order of any kind.[8] Courts have held that there is no reasonable expectation of privacy while driving along public roads, and analogize these electronic tracking devices to such other surveillance aides as binoculars, searchlights, and tracking dogs.

Pen Registers and Trap and Trace Devices

A *pen register* is an electronic device capable of simultaneously recording the number dialed from a telephone instrument and the line to which it is attached. A *trap and trace device* captures the incoming electronic or other impulses that identify the originating number of an instrument or device from which a wire or electronic communication was transmitted. A court order is necessary to utilize either device, but it is far easier to obtain than an eavesdropping warrant. There is no "probable cause" showing necessary and no requirement that alternative investigative techniques be exhausted. An order authorizing either a pen register or a trap and trace device will issue simply upon a showing of "reasonable suspicion" that a designated crime has been, is being, or is about to be committed, and that the information likely to be obtained is or will be relevant to an ongoing criminal investigation of that designated crime.

For a pen register to be installed, however, the same pair and cable information must be obtained from the telephone company that is necessary for the installation of a wiretap. The New York Telephone Company requires either a grand jury subpoena or a court order before releasing this information. It is important to include in the subpoena or court order a request that the phone company not disclose to the subscriber that a pen register is being installed, where such disclosure might jeopardize the investigation.

Results from Case Histories

In our experience, we have found electronic surveillance to be especially effective in narcotics investigations when properly combined with other investigative techniques.

Two important narcotics investigations that have been directed against major heroin-trafficking organizations and the results obtained will be detailed.

1. *Simmons Organization:* The objective of this major case was to infiltrate and investigate the organization of James "Hank" Simmons, a major black heroin distributor who was servicing the New York City Harlem area and portions of the East Coast. It was estimated that this organization distributed an average of 10 pounds of heroin a week at an estimated sales value of $200,000.

An undercover officer was used at the beginning of this investigation, and he began by making a street buy of $150. During the course of this major case, the undercover officer purchased 6 pounds of heroin from the subjects as he worked up the ladder of the organization. The target of this investigation was Hank Simmons, but the undercover officer could not penetrate the organization high enough to arrange a meeting with him. Simmons was entirely insulated from the lower levels of the organization.

Five successive wiretaps were made in trying to reach the upper levels of this organization. Finally, the undercover officer negotiated a $20,000 heroin buy with a close associate of Hank Simmons. The associate's telephone was tapped when he called Simmons after the buy was concluded to set up a "meet" to give Simmons $16,000 of the $20,000 he had received from the undercover officer for the heroin. This telephone call directly implicated Simmons in the heroin sale to the undercover officer.

From monitoring one of the wiretaps, it was learned that Simmons had a narcotics "factory" where workers cut the heroin for street sales. A search warrant was obtained and executed at this factory; 3 pounds of heroin were seized and the workers were arrested.

Hank Simmons' organization was totally eliminated by the use of undercover buys coordinated with electronic surveillance techniques to reach the upper echelons. Simmons and 10 of his major distributors received substantial jail sentences.

2. *Operation Rainbow:* Operation Rainbow is a perfect example of how a major narcotics investigation should be conducted in working up the ladder of a criminal organization. This major case was established on August 9, 1974. The targets of the operation were the major multikilo heroin dealers in the New York City area.

The investigation was initiated with a $260 street buy made by an undercover officer. During the course of this investigation, the undercover officer spent $100,000 in NYCPD "buy money" to buy heroin from 27 dealers. Throughout this time we were successful enough to secure sufficient probable cause for the issuance of eavesdropping orders to place wiretaps on the targeted subjects' telephones. For example, the undercover officer telephoned one subject, "Ricky Ward," on December 18, 1974, to make arrangements to purchase 500 quarter bags of heroin for $25,000. After the arrangements were negotiated, Ricky Ward called his connection to order enough heroin to be able to supply the undercover officer. The wiretap on Ward's phone succeeded in identifying his connection. The undercover officer was successful in penetrating into the upper levels of the organization, but he could not go any higher than Ricky Ward.

From this point in the investigation, we used the technique of successive wiretaps in working up the ladder. With the employment of seven wiretaps and one bug, we reached four multikilo heroin importers with crime family connections.

More than 30 persons pleaded guilty, before trial, in the prosecution of this case, and all received substantial jail sentences. In October 1979, one of the top heroin dealers in New York City, Julian "Toby" Ross, was convicted after a lengthy trial for conspiracy to distribute more than 20 kilograms of heroin and sentenced to a term of 5 to 15 years in prison. This investigation also provided us with a clear picture of the impact that electronic surveillance evidence has on the defendants when they are presented with the incriminating tapes.

These two investigations are illustrative of a number of important points about criminal organization and the proper use of surveillance techniques. More than criminal prosecutions are needed to stem the tide of drug addiction. Education, jobs, and decent housing are all needed to eliminate the social conditions that breed addiction in the ghetto, where narcotics are a special problem. But narcotics are not confined to areas where such conditions exist.

Any serious attack on narcotics in this country must be made against all levels of buying, selling, and importing these drugs. This attack cannot be successful without the use of intelligent, well-trained police officers combining conventional investigative methods with the latest techniques of electronic surveillance. Since eavesdropping is one of the gravest intrusions into a citizen's personal privacy, however, it must be used intelligently, and only as an investigative tool of last resort. The individual law enforcement officer's sensitivity to the spirit as well as the letter of the law is the best safeguard against losing this invaluable tool of investigation.

NOTES

[1] Section 2520 of Title III also provides for a civil cause of action for any person whose communications are intercepted in violation of the act.

[2] *New York Criminal Procedure Law*, Part 3, Article 700: Eavesdropping Warrants and Practices, commentary by Richard G. Denzer.

[3] *New York City Police Department Investigator's Eavesdropping Handbook*, p. 3.

[4] *Katz v. United States* [389 U.S. 347 (1967)].

[5] *Report of the National Commission for Review of Federal and State Laws Relating to Wiretapping and Electronic Surveillance*, p. 63.

[6] Ibid., p. 45.

[7] *Berger v. New York* [388 U.S. 41, 4809 (1967)].

[8] *People v. Colon* [409 N.Y.S. 2d 617,96 Misc. 2d 659]; *United States v. Hufford* [539 F. 2d 32].

PART 6

Business-Oriented Crimes

33
Corporate Crime: New Investigative Horizons

Ben Jacobson

Community concern over rapidly increasing criminality has brought about an urgent need for changes in the investigative process. Traditionally, the public police has been satisfied with enforcing index crimes; in the meantime, suite and office criminals have been operating effectively as hidden partners in small business operations and in major corporations. Today, the office suite criminal is becoming a prominent threat to economic stability.

Business offenders' direct access to vital data can affect corporations, entire industries, and consumers. Their activities include a wide variety of illegalities, such as embezzlement, environmental violations, adulteration of foods and drugs, larceny, espionage, and extortion. Although their acts may appear similar to index crimes, the subject matter and methods of inquiry are radically different and extremely complex. Hence the public enforcement community, including local and national investigators, prosecutors, and legislators must increasingly become aware of the nature and scope of business crime.

THE NATURE OF
CORPORATE CRIME

Briefly, corporate crime lacks a specific, identifiable crime scene in most instances; the victim is the entire social system, with offenders counting on the ignorance or carelessness of the victim to achieve their own, often disguised, purposes. Victims may be in collusion with offenders or cover up illegal operations, shortages, and shrinkages in legitimate domestic and foreign corporations, labor unions, and government institutions. Proof of violation, often concerning civil or regulative matters rather than criminal, may be extremely difficult to establish; and once discovered, a corporation may not bring charges lest its public image be tarnished.

Types of Corporate Crime

Although the variety of corporate crime seems to be limited only by the imagination of offenders, the offenses include:

- Mergers and consolidations to eliminate small competitors.
- Practices in restraint of trade that are forbidden by the *Sherman Act*.
- Illegal price fixing.
- Rebates and kickbacks.
- Patent and copyright infringements.
- Misrepresentation in advertising.
- Unfair labor practices.
- Financial manipulation of the stock and other obligations of a company.
- Tax evasion.
- Bribery of government officials.
- Creation of occupational hazards for employees and failure to invest in adequate safeguards to prevent sickness, injury, and death resulting from the production and/or manufacture of goods and services.
- Environmental pollution.
- Production of national health hazards.

Treatment of Corporate Crime

Corporate crime is treated differently from street crime in the criminal justice system. Administrative regulations take the place of laws. Administrative inquiry replaces police investigation. Adjudication in criminal courts gives way to administrative hearings before noncriminal tribunals. Violators are usually punished by fines rather than imprisonment. When prison sentences are imposed, they are served in special institutions rather than in ordinary prisons. Skillful professionals counsel corporate offenders on how to violate the law without being punished.

Understanding the Investigation

Methods of investigating technological and business-related crimes are set forth on the following pages to facilitate a modern approach to the corporate crime problem. The search for business criminals is tedious and demanding because of the complexity and variety of their activities. Therefore, a carefully selected staff must be trained in methods and procedures that can help it interact effectively with the business community.

The initial review of business data and organization can be overwhelming. The complexity is often bewildering, specially for those to whom it is unfamiliar territory. This may generate hostility in the untrained and create an investigative block that can result in sloppy work and limited success. The professionally (not necessarily academically) trained and experienced business investigator breaks down complex data into simple, meaningful statements by piercing through the maze of paper and the highly particularized industrial jargon. This task is made easier by acquiring familiarity with specific, intricate instruments and institutions.

For example, if the elements of the offense point to the environment, then the inquiry must focus on environmental laws and the development of associations with experts in that field, including the scientific community. Of course, this approach is common to any investigation, but the elements of these acts may be such that the criminality does not appear until after many years have elapsed. In such cases, one must know how to research documents logged in corporate transactions, the records of licensing agencies, and the morgue files of local newspapers.

Furthermore, the problem can be better understood by assessing the intertwining associations among corporations, individuals, and contracts—both private and public. In this matter, one must attend to the participants' social and economic relations, noting the "insiders" (those directly responsible for such illegalities as dumping toxic wastes or introducing pollutants into a community's drinking water) and the "outsiders" (those responsible for control of possible improper action by others, such as nuclear regulatory agencies).

Sophisticated computer technology has become a part of corporate procedures, thereby creating additional "unknowns" for the investigator. For example, murder by computer in an intensive care unit of any modern hospital is possible; destruction or manipulation of corporate data can intensify the complexity of crime; tampering with international communications can transform a simple act into an international crime problem; persons familiar with computer operations can divert hundreds of thousands of dollars from any large corporation or banking institution.

In general, the business investigator must be familiar with the specifics of an operation, such as accounting procedures, banking practices, computer programming, contract terminology, and research and development in the field. One does not necessarily have to be an expert in these areas but should be able to understand them as they relate to the complexity of business. Armed with this information, the investigator can ask the right questions, that is, those that need to be answered; can reach out to experts in the field for advice;and can obtain documentation required for prosecution. Simply, one should be able to identify (1) current and projected objectives of the industry; (2) prescribed codes of behavior; (3) informational norms and common practices industry-wide; (4) local, state, and federal legislation, especially regulatory, that affects the business activity under consideration.

Interlocking Corporations

The investigator of corporate crime must understand the society of corporations, that is, the interlocking relationships within and among companies and the various aspects and levels of business. A sociological conceptualization of the problem is required, because a relatively small group of decision makers at the highest corporate levels holds and exercises power, experiences a distinctive life-style, and tends to be self-perpetuating. These people and their children may have attended the same exclusive schools. They are real determinants of policy and procedures. Often they are isolated through in-group social contacts from the obvious and formal decision makers.

The analysis of interlocking corporations and their controls requires in-depth research. This includes a survey of ownerships, stock transactions, and methods of acquiring corporations. Dun & Bradstreet reports, Moody's Investors Service, and even individual corporate stock prospectuses provide essential data for understanding stock movements and corporate holdings. The review of past stock reports from newspaper morgues can reveal patterns that can be graphed for better understanding of downturns and upswings. These occur at various levels of complexity, according to whether the enterprise is national, international, or multinational.

Corporations function in a political arena which allows for corruption and official misconduct in the awarding of government contracts. Bidding procedures, policies, and relationships offer insights into the existence of potential irregularities. Political influence in contract awards may be uncovered by probing for campaign contribution patterns and prior associations or family connections. The very size of a corporation enhances its position in the political arena and allows for activity against the public interest. It may happen that a popular, respected corporation gains so positive an image that almost any action it undertakes is legitimized. However, no inference should be drawn that bigness is bad in itself, but rather that corporate expansion, to some extent, dictates organizational arrangements. As the mass increases, it tends to subdivide into smaller and more specialized units. These multiple divisions must then be coordinated to maintain a functioning whole—the bureaucratic business organization.

For the investigator, multidivisions constitute obstacles in data gathering; they present layers of secrecy that protect against probings and inquiries. Through acquisition of corporations, conglomerates merge, enlarge, and seek power. A recent report indicates that soap companies sell food, food corporations sell clothing, and conglomerates sell just about everything. Intentionally or unintentionally, conglomerates control prices through interlockings and manipulations of systems, thereby affecting even international currency. The investigator probing the complex organization of the corporate world is aided by informants, confidential sources, internal memorandums, and hearsay. Although hearsay information is not admissible as concrete evidence in a court of law, it does provide direction for the inquirer. Although wading through voluminous transactions, files, and officially registered records can be tiring and tedious, it can uncover secret internal crimes of individuals and companies. Searching paper transfers of ownership and stock certificates is a research approach that the average fact gatherer rarely touches; for the business investigator, however, it is a basic, crucial avenue.

Corporate *street names* (brokers who hold securities registered in their names instead of the buyers' names), which may never appear in the public telephone directory, do exist in the corporate world. They should be commonplace terms for the investigative team. Institutional investors are frequently hidden through the use of "multiple nominees," which makes government identification and control difficult. Translation of street names requires a copy of nominee lists such as that published and distributed by the American Society of Corporate Secretaries, Rockefeller Plaza, New York, New York.[1]

Use of nominees in ownership reports screens stockholdings of a select few. This coupling practice offers the investigator data that may be necessary in establishing conspiracy and price fixing. It may also answer questions concerning the individual financial stability of those who may appear to be living beyond their means. Tracing assets and corporate affiliations through nominee listings is essential in background and overt investigations. It is vital for moving an investigation forward.

Cooperative Investigations

The investigative process for business-related crimes proceeds through the institutional bureaucratic structure. It requires the cooperation of many local, state, and federal law enforcement agencies outside the business context. Depending on them for enlightenment and assistance is wise. For example, the Environmental Protection Agency or interest groups can provide expertise and necessary information for completing an inquiry which indicates possible environmental crime. Computer abuse may be exposed by electronic data processing professionals, such as systems analysts, programmers, or operational officers. When accounting and business management procedures are beyond the investigator's specific expertise, accountants or professionals from other fields must be utilized. Colleges and universities have a wide variety of consultants who are willing and able to assist. Simply stated, investigators are experienced data gatherers, but they need the cooperation of carefully selected specialists. Think tank sessions are also important for conceptualizing the problem and identifying the approach.

Basically, there are two types of business inquiries: internal and external.

Internal. Informants or concerned employees from middle or upper management and even lower levels can contribute facts that bear directly on internal operations. At least, they can familiarize the investigator with the unique, specialized jargon of each industrial setting. Although gathering such information may appear simple, it is essential for in-depth penetration of operations. By cultivating cooperative industrial experts, the investigator can reduce time spent and have readily available sophisticated references for times when complications arise.

External. Public officials and agency personnel can make the job easier by specifying relevant regulative guidelines. Vital data can be retrieved through the *Freedom of Information Act,* but sometimes developing relations with cooperative employees can effect the same results faster. The assistance of the Securities and Exchange Commission may be required if the inquiry is directed toward stock manipulation or majority control. It can gather pertinent data through its governance of corporate transactions and ownerships. In one instance, information about a real estate transaction between a corporate executive and an individual from syndicated crime led to indications of criminal extortion and business infiltration. Through further assistance from county real estate records, insights into particular internal problems of the company emerged. Note that a specific transaction may not be a crime, but information about it may support other gathered facts.

Libraries are excellent reference sources which are often overlooked, perhaps because they are so obvious. Both public and private libraries contain periodicals, manuals, clippings, and circulars that identify corporate holdings, financial statements, executive listings and transfers, dates of stockholder meetings, executive office locations, and telephone numbers. Here will be found the business section of local and sometimes international newspapers and industrial trade publications.

Legislative Cooperation

Cooperative inquiries also involve the use of the regulations and laws of different municipalities, governments,and agencies. The *Organized Crime Control Act*, Title IX, U.S. Code, 1970, known as the RICO (Racketeer-Influenced and Corrupt Organizations) statute, facilitates and requires cooperation among the various levels of law enforcement. It specifies that violations of state laws can be used to substantiate the "probable cause" necessary for violation of the statute.

This statute provided *all* law enforcement with a tool for penetrating business-related crime by expanding its jurisdiction and interpreting "enterprise" in a way that has significant implications for internal and external business activities. It facilitated law enforcement's reach into formal business proceedings and institutions such as labor unions, government agencies, and syndicated crime organizations.

RICO jurisdiction applies when individuals, through a pattern of *racketeering* or unlawful debt collection, directly or indirectly invest or maintain interest in or participate in an "enterprise" during or in response to activities which affect interstate commerce. *Enterprise* was herein defined as any individual, partnership, cooperation, association, or group of individuals affiliated in fact although not as a legal entity. To constitute a pattern of racketeering, at least two acts are required. One must have occurred after the effective date of the *Organized Crime Control Act* (1970) and the other, the last, must have taken place within 10 years following the commission of a prior act.

By encompassing the investigation of a broad range of index crimes or threats, violent and nonviolent, the statute aims to combat syndicated crime's movement into the legitimate arena. The index crimes of murder, kidnapping, and robbery are covered, along with the business-related crimes of larceny, extortion, interference with commerce, payments to labor unions or organizations, embezzlement, bankruptcy, and fraud, to name but a few.

METHODS OF INQUIRY

In developing an investigative formula for gathering business-related data, the inquirer must remain open and willing to change direction. Whereas the index-oriented criminal investigator can respond in terms of a first "gut" reaction, the business inquirer must evaluate complex, statistical information and organizational charts to determine direction before affirmative action is taken. Note, however, that corporate crime probing usually takes several directions at the same time and may suggest numerous individuals as suspects. Although no one direction may reach the targeted area directly, collectively they provide offshoots that may be useful in developing a total picture of the criminal activity. Months and even years may be involved in retrieving facts lost in record keeping, financial transactions, stock transfers, bank loans, and company mergers. These extended inquiries use modern investigative techniques such as electronic surveillance, visual and photographic identification, auditing procedures, computer auditing operations, research, and interviews. Auditing and analysis of financial transactions are usually main avenues for corporate investigation. The fact that they extend over longer periods of time increases the likelihood that directional change may occur.

In general, victim-offender attitudes and relations, industrywide objectives, formally prescribed and informal codes of behavior, and common practices in relation to legislation pertinent to the industry should be identified. Then data should be collected concerning the particular corporation or business activity. Finally, the case should be analyzed and prepared for presentation.

In more detail, the investigative course of action should include:

- Review of business record information (Dun & Bradstreet, Moody's reports and manuals, McGraw-Hill business reports).
- Research of the industry to increase familiarity with its prescribed and common practices.
- Review of specific organizational charts to identify actual or potential problem areas.
- Interview of chief executives and complaining witnesses.
- Examination of reported or suspected crime problems.
- A feasibility study of the crime problem (what are the past problems and current solutions?).
- Examination of principals to assess their psychological, economic, and political advantages and disadvantages.
- Documentation gathering about affiliates—business, labor, associations, and so on.
- Review of security policies and procedures for tracing funds, through records of deposits to bank accounts, personal checks, corporation records, or stock transactions.
- Identification of known offenders associated with the business.
- Review of management procedures. Look for the unintended consequences of productivity and efficiency programs that may provide a motive for disgruntled or disloyal parties.
- Gathering of documents from regulatory agencies.
- Interview of complainants and suspected offenders.
- Identification of specific crimes. What occurred after the act?

A complete survey such as suggested above must be conducted to identify the weak links and vulnerable points in the organization. For example, past and developing procurement practices may provide the first indicator of illicit activity. Suspected patterns of criminal activity such as extortion, loan sharking, or arson may suggest a move by syndicated crime toward infiltration of a legitimate business. Purchases by foreign investors or proxy ownership may point to laundered money. The purchase of a business may not be a law violation, but identification of the principals and the kinds of transactions may offer insights to potential or existing criminality. These facts can reveal takeover patterns within the industry, expanding control by foreign elements, labor racketeering, price fixing, or political corruption.

Tip-offs of Crime in Progress

Fully utilizing the techniques for discovering and identifying business-related crimes is never easy; therefore, knowing common, basic features and recognizing them in altered forms is essential. With the foregoing in mind, the following tip-offs of crime in progress (originally noted in a U.S. Chamber of Commerce booklet) are offered.

The Fraudulent Association (Dummy Corporation).   In this situation, people are induced to join various types of fraudulent associations through threatened or actual violence; for example, they may be intimidated by threats of labor trouble or actually experience sudden picketing. Representatives from fraudulent associations then offer to resolve the labor problems, sometimes by spreading the word that others in the industry have joined this organization. They exert pressure on companies. An investigator needs such information for determining the infiltration of criminal associations into the legitimate sector.

Bankruptcy Fraud.   This ordinary scam has credit-related problems as a common denominator. Inventory is increased by purchasing merchandise on credit or through loans; then the corporate staff sells off, cashes in, or diverts through other channels. This illicit operation, sometimes called a "bust-out," is screened so that creditors are left unpaid while the company is protected under federal bankruptcy laws. Of course, the creditor has the right to file inventory petitions. Signs of bankruptcy fraud include the following: (1) A company that is supplied comes under new management with little or no publicity, and the identity of the principals is obscured. (2) Goods are ordered by a customer that are not consistent with his or her line or past practices. (3) Orders are increased but cannot be explained in terms of the customer's seasonal business. (4) Financial statements requested from new accounts are unaudited and unverified. (5) The accounts receivable balance climbs, while notes or postdated checks are remitted. (6) Trade references do not check out; for example, the new account's name is very similar to that of a reputable corporation. (7) An above-average number of new orders develops. (8) Bank balances of customers show a persistent decline; perhaps just before the bust-out, large withdrawals are made.

Labor Racketeering.   Wildcat strikes may occur very unexpectedly and become frequent. This may leave management with the task of dealing with "new faces" on short notice. These may be radically different labor union officials who are unfamiliar with past practices. Competitive wages of unionized employees in similar industrial shops may be considerably lower. A change in interunion ties from one trade to another suggests union control by outside forces. Union officer affiliations and associations with known criminals may be a tip-off.

Monopoly and Coercive Competitive Practices.   The "below-the-going-price sale" is a formulation of syndicated crime which provides an opportunity for organized crime to buy into any industry and draw it away from legitimate business. Syndicated business is capable of using illegal practices such as bribery of public officials or threat of force. They may also counterfeit popular items, that is, use similar names and packaging, thereby causing the loss of millions of dollars to the legitimate company.

Illegal Use of Stocks and Bonds.   Stolen securities are useful in many ways: They may be sold to bargain-hungry investors at discount from face value, offered to banks as collateral for loans to finance syndicated businesses, and in many instances rented to businesses for a show of assets when seeking additional business funds from financial institutions or even government agencies. Hence, always check an excessive line of credit or the sale of a business at inflated prices.

Countering Internal Fraud

Management policies should be set and procedures established to include the following areas.

Evaluation of Management Policies. The degree of social involvement between management personnel and other employees should be determined. Management procedures in evaluating security interests, accountability, and organizational charting can be used in formulating an independent antifraud policy.

Auditing Procedures. Essential for discovering inconsistencies and fraudulent practices by individuals, auditing may occur as a formal review of policies and procedures or in actual accounting of control methods. It may be used to uncover accounting frauds, computer improprieties, and inventory control thefts. Auditing may also prevent padding of expense accounts or suggest changes in organization responsibility and reporting procedures.

Using Informants. Internal feedback supplies direct input from line employees. The maintenance of social relationships and the use of cooperative employee activities can provide management with knowledge of internal criminality and serve as a source for gathering facts and projecting exposure potential.

Union Activities. Maintaining cooperative relations with union officials and shop stewards is essential to reduce labor problems. Formal notification to union officials about pending inquiries and allowing their assistance to become a reality may reduce the risk of wildcat or unauthorized strikes. This informing should take place only after some facts have been gathered, substantiated, and preliminary investigation completed. In this way, potential leaks or sellout of information by labor officials to its membership is reduced. Internal control is strengthened by a cooperative dialogue between union and management on internal control.

Evaluation of Structural Design. Such an evaluation offers management, internal security officers, and public investigators knowledge of the layout and building design. It may provide information necessary for exposure of criminal activities, either internal or external. Security scanning cameras, storage, and trash disposal should be carefully examined for any weaknesses in the system.

Review of Receiving and Shipping Procedures. A review of routing and counting procedures can expose undercounting, which may be used to hide products from spot-checkers. Bills of lading, routing slips, and shipping receipts should be reviewed and audited.

Evaluation of Personnel Histories. Such an evaluation helps to determine the weak links in the corporation. Drinking, gambling, and excessive use of narcotics may be a basis for employing selective managerial controls. Personnel who may be living beyond their means should be identified and the fact established. A credit check as well as an active financial questionnaire pertaining to employees should be maintained. The resulting facts should be collated to target potential trouble spots for special supervision. Such measures can reduce the internal crime problem considerably.

The Business of Business Crime

While we hear more and more about corporate crime through the media, court cases and personal experience, the average citizen and even the law enforcer often consider this crime relevant only to large, multinational corporations. In the meantime, small business establishments are suffering large losses that appear to many as "small fish in the big pool" of crime priorities. Small business is vulnerable because of facts that include little or no internal control, close management-employee relations, and owners' inability to recognize that acts are being directed against their establishments.

In actuality, purchasing agents do conspire with vendors in such illicit schemes as double billing or the creation of nonexistent merchandise. The illegal profits are then gathered up and divided. A common practice is the creation of a "shell" company—complete with printed invoices and billing, bank accounts, formal documentation, a legitimate sounding name, and a postal box with address to transmit and validate the scam. The purchasing agent receives the invoice, pays the bill through an approval-of-transmittal form to the accounts department (thereby legitimizing it), then picks up and cashes the check—which makes it a clean, safe process of internal fraud.

The unholy alliance between internal and external criminal forces places the corporation in a vulnerable position which is unusually difficult for law enforcement to penetrate. An internal crime watch formula to reduce exposure and establish a clear antifraud campaign will limit "trusted employee" losses.

Although management does have control over the selection of an employee, the employer's psychological trust in the chosen individual can be a blinding factor which exposes the corporation or small business to criminal behavior. This trust, combined with long-time employment, creates a bonding that may interfere with the employer's objective observations and willingness to admit a judgmental mistake in the selection process. Often the executive prefers to pay the way and keep the employee rather than place restrictions on employment.

Investigative Accountants

The business community's exposure to internal financial loss has created a new position, namely, the investigative accountant. Through education and formal training, these individuals offer law enforcement distinctive tools for combating corporate crime. This new breed of inquirer can significantly determine the purchasing and inventory control practices as well as the financial status of the corporation. Through auditing and monitoring, the accountant supports the internal control function in a way that is seldom found in the public law enforcement community. Usually, investigative accountants practice first in the public sector by engaging in tax reviews or budgetary controls; later they acquire experience and certification to enter the private sector. Some accountants are "law-enforcing" public servants, who disregard financial rewards for community service.

By establishing an audit control program, these inquirers can uncover various financial schemes and frauds, such as illicit kickbacks, bribery, embezzlement, and double billing. Since their expertise is available for ongoing business inquiries, it should be built into the business investigative team, thereby performing a unique function and giving an important picture of businesses' financial status. Review of books, ledgers, checking accounts, and other data is the basis for actual auditing. In the public sector, these documents can be obtained by subpoena, but management may give them to the private business investigative team to uncover internal fraud. Review of such data by the accounting auditor may reveal conspiracies, cover-ups, and ordinary errors. Although most corporations employ accounting firms, investigative accountants may discover facts, either known or unknown to their counterparts, which are routinely overlooked or conveniently omitted to cover errors, frauds, or mismanagement. The task of the accountant has become even more challenging with the emergence of computer technology and electronic funds transfer. Accountants must be familiar with such modern mechanical techniques, because very often they will be working with computer data. Accountants are legally responsible for audits that they submit and sign.

In reviewing records, however, the basic problem is the common practice of maintaining two complete but different sets of books. One is kept for tax purposes and the other, not publicly available, is kept for yearly business comparisons. The inquirer must discover both sets and compare the statistics and information. Most businesses would not admit to this practice, about which IRS officials have expressed concern. Obviously, the use of a double set of books can be a way to hide excessive funds or assets and thereby evade or limit tax payments. It is important to remember that a corporation, unincorporated association, or labor union has no constitutional protections under the self-incrimination, or Fifth Amendment, rule; they are not persons under this statute.

The illicit cash flow business, either over the counter or through the back door, rarely gets logged. Items disappear from shelves and stockrooms and from shipments during the delivery process. Funds lost to a corporation go undiscovered or even overlooked by managers. It causes a considerable drain on a business's economy, which is then passed on to the customer, insurance company, and tax collector, who may accept those losses as legitimate write-offs. Such legitimation, however, creates apathy toward discovering, prosecuting, or exposing internal theft. The accountant, armed with procedural expertise in detecting "mistakes" in business, can offer the corporation an inventory control model, accounting policies, and an internal crime watch that the general law enforcement investigator may not be able to provide.

The corporation must set investigative standards before implementing auditing procedures. These standards must be supported by gathered facts and include avenues for investigative questioning. The internal audit investigator must not only set standards and objectives but also produce a clear picture for review by the other members and executives desiring information about the inquiry. In one instance, an internal account auditor not only discovered numerous cases of embezzlement by board members of a financial institution but also uncovered official governmental corruption. An internal audit, therefore, can achieve its objectives and also show how crimes were kept secret through government improprieties. Auditors can inform the nontechnical investigative team in direct, simple and readily understood language. Their function is highly technical and essential for business-related criminal investigations. Records and documents are the accountant investigator's "tools of the trade," just as notes and diagrams are the homicide detective's.

CONCLUSION: CORPORATE CONFIDENCE

Acknowledgement of internal theft problems, computer crime or exposure and loss due to outside forces is an embarrassment that does not benefit a business operation. Therefore every effort must be made to maintain an untainted corporate image in the eyes of the public, the industry, and the financial community. Business relations can be seriously affected by the mere hint that a corporation is plagued with fraud. Activities that indicate outside control and lack of integrity have negative consequences for business transactions in obtaining financial assistance or in being awarded government contracts. As a result, many large corporations are beginning to develop internal task forces and rap sessions geared toward discussing internal controls. Managers meet directly with executives and subordinates, with everyone having some input significant to the corporation's interests. Each has a stake in preventing internal crime patterns and in preserving his or her own job, yet they all work together in countering the silent criminal.

NOTE

[1]Minitz, Morton, and Jerry S. Cohen, Power Inc. (New York: Viking Press, 1976).

34

Investigating Computer Crime

Donald P. Delaney

Investigating wrongdoing in a button-pushing electronic age presents new challenges to law enforcement. In this and the following chapter, "Investigating Telecommunications Fraud," the ever-increasing types of computer crimes and telecommunication frauds are identified. The modus operandi of the computer-assisted criminal in narcotics, sex crimes, espionage, cracking and phreaking, and other illicit business operations is explained. Indeed, the computer has become as common a tool in the commission of traditional crime as the ledger, cash register, gun, or knife.

A critical challenge, which often confronts the computer investigator, is a lack of adequate comprehension of the computer crime environment. This involves understanding the computer and the way it can be used at any time (day or night), anywhere (at home, in the office, in the car), domestically or internationally, by anybody (weak or strong, young or old, male or female).

Most local and state policing agencies in the United States do not have a dedicated computer crime unit or even one person trained for computer crime investigations. This chapter addresses the resources available for computer investigations and procedures for obtaining and executing a search warrant. The information is also applicable for the investigation of telecommunications fraud.

The need for such information exchange is urgent. Many corporations and individuals have reported being victimized by computer criminals, only to discover that, at best, just a report was taken. The resulting frustration was poignantly illustrated by Cliff Stoll in the *Cuckoo's Egg*.[1] It seems reasonable to assume that the reluctance of some law enforcement agencies to investigate computer crime derives from insufficient understanding of the methods, the time involved, the cost, and the necessity for specialized training in computer crime investigation.

THE COMPUTER CRIME ENVIRONMENT

Computer crime is any violation of law committed by an individual or individuals which, in any part, is accomplished or assisted by use of a computer.

34-1

Computers can be hacked locally by an employee or remotely over a telephone line, or they can be used by traditional criminals to assist in their wrongdoing. The new investigator in this field should have a rudimentary understanding of the relevant terminology.

Definitions

Audit Trail: A record of a computer system's activities from beginning to end.

Bulletin Board System (BBS): A program on a computer system set up to be accessed by others over telephone lines. Users may post messages, and can upload and download software.

CPU: Central processing unit, the microprocessor or brains of the computer.

Cracking: Deciphering copy protection codes, passwords, or personal identification numbers (PINs) to be used in phreaking.

DNR: Dial number recorder. Similar to a pen register in that it records the outgoing numbers dialed from a known telephone, along with the date and time of each outdial.

Download: Transfer programs or files from a remote computer to the user's computer.

Hacking: A wide range of activity, with different meanings to different people. The pioneers of hacking from the fifties and sixties would explain that it refers to the legitimate practice of computer programming skills and may include, without authorization, someone else's system. Writing about the MIT hackers of the late 1950s, Levy indicated that "the most productive people working on 'exploring' Signals and Power called themselves `hackers' with great pride."[2] The more common uses or "hacking" in the press include unlawfully accessing the computer system or another; deleting, altering, or damaging computer data or hardware; or using a computer to decipher codes or personal identification numbers (PINs). Can mean the attempts to break through the security systems of computers for the theft of information or unlawful bank transfers. Also used by some to cover the activities of "phreaking," "cracking," and "crashing."

Hardware: The computer and its physical connections.

Logic Bomb: A set of instructions placed in a computer which, when executed, causes an alteration of computer data.

Modem: A device that connects to the computer, either internally or externally, and facilitates the transfer of information from the computer across telephone lines. The modem change the computerized digital data to analog data for the communications lines. Modems allow computers—and users—to speak to each other.

PBX: Private branch exchange, a computerized switchboard.

PC: Personal computer.

Phreaking: Unlawfully obtaining telephone service. Methods including using tone generators, stolen telephone credit card numbers, call diverter fraud, and PBX fraud. A mix of the words "phone" and "freak."

Salami Slicing: Typically an employee will hide a Trojan Horse in his employer's computer that causes an unnoticed and infinitesimal debiting to occur from a large number of accounts over a period of time, which the employee can then transfer to his or her own account.

Shoulder Surfing: The practice of looking over someone's shoulder when he types access codes or PINs on computer keyboards or telephone keypads. A crude way of stealing access codes, passwords, and PINs.

Software: Generally, computer programs that can be run on a system.

Trojan Horse: A set of instructions to the CPU that appear to have a legitimate function. Used for inserting hidden codes, such as logic bombs, viruses, and salami slicing.

Upload: To send programs or files from the user's computer to another computer.

Victims

Computer crime is unique in that its perpetrators often never see or interact with their victims. Individuals may suffer losses of good credit ratings, privacy, or an increased product or service cost all from an unseen, unknown hacker. With more and more people owning personal computers connected to modems, there is also an increased number of persons suffering loss of computer data, computer material, and recently hardware damage at the hands of malicious individuals.

Corporations and small companies are most frequently computer crime victims. Seventy to 80 percent of all computer crime is committed by the victim's employees. The company's computer can be attacked by a disgruntled current or former worker. On many occasions, the computer criminal is unaware of who the victim is. The losses might be as slight as the copying of a file or as large as millions of dollars of lost revenue due to downtime at the hands of a saboteur.

Universities have been victimized in several ways and their losses vary. Computer systems available for students' purposes are often unlawfully accessed by individuals off campus who use the systems for a myriad of reasons. This drain on the system and the many extra hours of computing time add up to slower computer service.

The Computer Criminal Profile

In profiling any crime or criminal, the investigator is doing more than just stereotyping. The profiling is based on scientific studies conducted over an extended period of time. The profile provides information which may apply for a particular type case. It is only an aid and never 100 percent reliable.

Motivation. The motivation of the computer criminal may be difficult to understand. Henry A. Murray, a psychologist, theorist, and "the central influence in achievement motivation research" based his hypothesis of motivation on the concept of need.[3] Satisfaction of need provides a reduction in tension. Some of Murray's needs (aggression, autonomy, counteraction, deference, dominance, exhibition, order, sentience, and understanding) are evident in motivations admitted to by some of those arrested for computer crime. Naturally, for certain computer crimes, one can infer the rationale; others seem to baffle even experienced investigators. For instance, if a company's computers have been under attack from the outside over a period of time, and files appear to be maliciously deleted, or the systems have been knocked off line, we may be looking for a disgruntled or former employee. This could be a case of corporate sabotage. On the other hand, a novice hacker may be merely looking around and inadvertently doing the damage. There are documented cases for each of these causes.

Some people are motivated to access another's CPU for their own educational advancement or corporate spying. The unscrupulous company, wanting to get ahead fast, may theorize that it is easier to invade the competition's computers for information than to spend the money on research, development, and marketing. In fact, international spying by computer is documented in Cliff Stoll's *Cuckoo's Egg*. Recently, Dutch hackers, caught invading American computers, did so with impunity. This is not illegal in their country.

People may use their computers for personal profit or to benefit accomplices. Software costs money that many are unwilling to spend. To obtain useful software, some belong to electronic bulletin board groups. Occasionally, software is in the "public domain." This means that the manufacturer, who owns the source code for a program, has announced that anyone who wishes may copy the program for free. Everybody then can legally duplicate it from a bulletin board system where it is posted. Some, however, will upload copyrighted software to the BBS for others to download. This gives individuals free access to a program that they would have had to buy otherwise to own it legally. One such criminal arrested had over 1000 stolen proprietary programs. Others use their computers to steal credit card numbers from credit review companies. They do this by dialing into corporate credit data bases from their computers using the victim's account numbers and downloading his or her credit history and credit card number. Then they use the information to make telephone purchases from mail order companies. The losses due to this type of fraud are in the millions of dollars.

In one case, a bank employee accessed the bank's computer and changed the address of a customer to her own. She would then call a co-worker in her bank to report that the customer had lost his credit card and request another to be sent. The unwitting employee would mail out the new credit cards to the criminal's address. As soon as the first employee noticed in the computer that the cards had been sent, she would change the customer's address back to the correct one. Upon receiving the credit cards, the crooked employee would then set out charging purchases over several counties up to the card's maximum. In other cases the bank's computers have been accessed and money was transferred from one account to another, or the balance of an account was increased.

Today's society often finds young persons living in a community where they cannot relate easily to others their age. If a person is frail in a tough neighborhood or just does not get along with his or her peers, he or she may retreat to the safety of the home. To fulfill a need to be social, the person can utilize the computer and modem to interact with others who have similar needs. Often, there is some attempt to be competitive with them in this nonconfrontational milieu. Going back as far as the 1950s, MIT hackers engaged in computer wars to test their abilities. Today some take pride in being the best in stealing telephone credit card numbers (CODES), others in obtaining unauthorized credit information, and still others in being the first to access a UNIX system with a toll-free 800 number, gain root access, and establish a BBS inside. It does wonders for one's low self-esteem to be admired by peers for having the most pirated software available on BBS. Furthermore, one can find many cases of students accessing academic administrative computer files to change grades, courses taken, or even the type of degree achieved.

During the monthly meetings of a computer crackers group in New York City, members were given assignments to perform prior to the next month's gathering. One member was asked to bring in telephone PINs, another credit card numbers, one received the dubious distinction of "dumpster diving," that is, climbing around in a dumpster outside a telephone company office for employee information to be utilized in social engineering (discussed later). Other assignments required hacking "call diverters" and "PBX" codes for free phone service. As one defendant put it, "You've got to perform to belong."

Computer-Assisted Crimes. Although these do not involve unlawfully accessing another's computer, they qualify as computer crimes. The hard drive and disks must still be examined and the evidence documented. The more popular crimes facilitated by computer for record-keeping are:

1. *Narcotics:* One group used a computer log for everything the organization did, right down to recording the miles per gallon of their drug dealers' cars.

2. *Prostitution:* A madam kept track of her girls and Johns with a data bank schedule.

3. *Sexual abuse:* Some pedophiles were found to have kept meticulous records on their hard drive and disks. Search warrants on these types of cases should always include seizure of the CPU, disks, and tapes.

4. *Money laundering:* (The investigator may need an accountant for this one.) A CPA on Long Island was found to have been laundering money for a narcotics distribution network. The damning evidence against him was discovered on his hard drive, along with three years of records on the disk.

5. *Call-sell operations:* Computerized telephone account systems were being used (and have been seized upon execution of search warrants) for recording all outgoing calls made for others with stolen codes or utilizing PBX fraud.

Methodology. Not only do computer criminals often vary in motivation, but they also employ a variety of methods to engage in computer crime.

The PC at Home. A lad pesters his parents until they accede to buy him his own personal computer, monitor, modem, and printer. Once connected to his computer and modem, this dangerous equipment can lay siege to the on-line world. It is not just a few interconnected systems. With the correct information, a beginner can dial into literally thousands of personal, corporate, university, military, and government computers, both domestic and abroad. He can now access a BBS from which he can download pirated software. After consulting with his friends who already have systems, he learns basic commands, and he receives a few stolen codes for free long distance phone service. After all, he needs it, since he does not want Mom and Dad to get high bills or know what he is doing.

Networking and Weaving. If you read *Cuckoo's Egg,* you already know about Milnet, Arpernet, Internet, and other systems. Local telephone companies serve their area and are connected to the long-distance carriers, such as AT&T, SPRINT, MCI, and ALLNET. They connect internationally through ITT; and there are other networks that are either private or government. There are thousands of computers on the nets, which can be accessed by typing in the address of where you wish to go. The stolen user ID and passwords for many systems are posted on public bulletin boards. Going from one system back out to another system is referred to as *weaving* or *looping*. This makes it difficult to locate the originating telephone number.

Dumpster Diving. This dubious activity can involve physically climbing into a dumpster or trash bin, or standing next to it and reaching in, for the purposes of obtaining information that may be useful. It also extends to picking up household trash that has been put out to the curb.

Some companies, police departments, and governmental agencies do not shred enough of the documents they produce before discarding them. Often corporate records contain trade secrets as well as employee and customer account information. The computer print may include user ID and passwords. Police departments frequently shred all the teletype documentation, but may throw out reams of paperwork from office cans containing sensitive, internal, or personal information.

While executing a search warrant at the residence of a computer criminal last year, a gold mine of information was discovered in a notebook. From a dumpster diving jaunt behind a telephone company office, this lad had found the names, phone numbers, addresses, and positions of their technical and executive staff. Also in this find were the pay stubs, which the employees had discarded. The real value of the information is its usefulness in social engineering.

"Garbage" is not only stolen by hackers, crackers, and phreakers, but also by corporate spies and private investigators.

Legal Concerns. If the dumpster is on private property and the interloper is not legally present, he could be subject to arrest for trespass and larceny (should he take something he finds). Clearly, it is legal to pick up garbage that a homeowner or company puts out on the curb. Police do this routinely to gain evidence from suspects' trash.

Social Engineering. This operation refers to the act of deceiving another to provide information that is sensitive and guarded. In a previous example, a criminal gleaned data outside the telephone company office. He then used it to gain passwords, PINs, computerized switch and additional employee information for future social engineering, which may be accomplished in the following fashion: The culprit calls one of the staff members in an office from which he wishes to obtain specific facts. He identifies himself as a co-worker at a branch office and may just chat on and off for several days, referring to other personnel and their positions. After establishing rapport, he explains that he now needs information to which he normally has access but is unable to access today. Those who are good at social engineering are held in high esteem by their peers.

Computer Clubs

Computer clubs, such as the Legion of Doom (LOD), Masters of Disaster (MOD), CHAOS, and PARADOX have each had members arrested for committing computer crimes. With initiates teaching criminal skills to a group, computer crime can grow quickly in a local community. Legitimate computer clubs flourish around the world and in contrast do not ban police from joining.

Electronic Bulletin Boards

Although most bulletin board systems administrators run legal systems, others set them up for a variety of fraud. Software piracy and dissemination is the illegal purpose of many BBSs. The international group called PARADOX pirated more than 1000 pieces of software before its demise. Their need for long distance codes became their Achilles tendon. They were discovered by the phone company when a club member used a sequential number dial-out program (scanning) to crack telephone PIN codes. The phone company recorded the "cracking" activity and provided it to the police. A search warrant was obtained, and the group's source of codes was out of business.

Crashing

The malicious individuals who engage in "crashing" are dangerous. To intentionally knock out a system or network can be costly and even life-threatening. The attacked system may be controlling life support systems in a hospital, a satellite's guidance system, a state's criminal records, or a long distance carrier's switch through which worldwide financial and banking information flows. "Crashing" is often accomplished by means of a "virus," "worm," "logic bomb," or reprogramming.

False Data Entry

An employee with access to the computer may enter or alter data. A good audit trail deters this crime.

Systems Security

Naturally, some computer systems are more easily accessed and vulnerable to criminals than others. The cost and practicality of security for the system should be a concern. In some cases, a system will contain nothing of value to anyone but the owner. As the worth of the information increases, so also must the security of the system. Another consideration is the number of other persons that have potential access. If connected to a modem, will the system be on without real-time monitoring by the system's administrator? Does the system create a good audit trail and is it preserved? Should the system be backed up on a daily basis? What level of security should be provided to protect the backup tapes, and where should they be stored? Should data being handled be encrypted? How complex should passwords be? Have the common default codes been changed? Who will have root access (the ability to access all information in the system)? These concerns should be dealt with prior to purchasing a system. It would be exasperating to install it, set it up, and come on-line only to find that it is vulnerable. You may need a completely different system or expensive alteration.

Some of the most common errors in security, which allow the computer crime to occur, are now discussed.

Default Codes.   Normally, when a system is delivered to its new home, it is equipped with default codes having different levels of access, including root. An individual with root access is empowered to add or delete any data contained therein. Naturally, computer criminals relish gaining root access, for now they can install back doors and Trojan Horses, change or copy passwords and the user ID, alter the time date stamps, and even eliminate the audit trail. Having done this, criminals will be able to reaccess the root after they are discovered and denied root through their previous method.

It seems common sense, then, that the system administrator would immediately change the default passwords, such as "quest" or "root" to something more effective. Long alphanumeric codes (combinations of numbers and letters, such as CZ6L93B) are much more suitable. Of course, they are also harder to remember. Often an employee will write down default codes or their user ID with password, and leave them on their desk or taped to the monitor. A computer criminal in that work area will steal the information to use when accessing the system. Should the criminal commit a crime and it is discovered, the audit trail may point to the wrong person.

User ID/Password. For the computer with multiple users, an identification and password system is used. The *user ID* allows the computer to keep track of who did what while on-line. The password ought to be known only to the user to prevent unauthorized access. Passwords should not be common words associated with the user that might be easily guessed by another. Again, alphanumeric ones work well. Donn B. Parker indicates the following additional considerations:

> The system should force users to change their passwords on a periodic basis, typically sixty days. Passwords should not be visible on the screen to other people nor visible on any printed paper coming from the terminal. Password holders should be periodically indoctrinated about the secrecy of their passwords. Safe password administration is required as should background investigations of those people in high positions of trust who administer passwords. Password lists stored on computers should be encrypted. Using this method, incoming passwords are immediately encrypted and then compared to the encrypted list. If an individual uses an incorrect password three times, he should be disconnected. The system should display a banner message during the log-on process warning unauthorized users and potential intruders about trespassing. The audit trail should include all attempts at logon. Sanctions should be clearly known by password holders and violators should be punished.[4]

Resources for a Computer Crime Investigator

Knowledge of the applicable state and federal computer crime laws is a must. If not previously trained in this area, review the state's criminal law regarding computer tampering, computer trespass, unauthorized access of a computer, and the unlawful duplication of computer-related material! Pay particular attention to definitions, such as "computer," and circumstances, such as notification of authorized use only! For federal law, see Title 18USC 1029 and 1030 and the *Electronic Communications Privacy Act.* Special Agents of the United States Secret Service, who are trained computer crime investigators, are particularly helpful. Other assistance is available from the Federal Bureau of Investigation, U.S. Air Force OSI (Office of Special Investigations), and state police computer crime labs, such as the New York State Police Computer Crime Lab in Albany, New York.

In Glynco, Georgia, training is available for federal, state, and local law enforcement officers at the Federal Law Enforcement training Center's Financial

Fraud Institute. A valuable two-week course there is titled "Criminal Investigations in an Automated Environment."

Helpful seminars are conducted periodically by the U.S. Secret Service, AT&T, and local telephone companies, such as the New York Telephone Company. If this is not already being done in an area, check with local telephone companies for possible assistance and/or training! Their security departments are a good first step.

For a much more comprehensive manual than the space in this chapter allows, see the National Institute of Justice (NIJ) publication, *Computer Crime: Criminal Justice Resource Manual*, 2d ed. (1989), by Donn B. Parker. Other relevant NIJ publications are *Organizing for Computer Crime Investigation and Prosecution* and *Dedicated Computer Crime Units*.[5]

Accounting firms have accredited certified public accountants, trained to conduct computer mainframe audits. Where this is cost-prohibitive, explore the possibility of relying on the system's administrator for assistance!

The HTCIA (High Tech Criminal Investigations Association) is a nationwide organization, composed of law enforcement officers, prosecutors, private investigators, and corporate security officers. This organization provides an excellent source of contacts for assistance and recommendations.

Most large law enforcement agencies have members with computer backgrounds. This may include an AS or BS degree in computer science, experience in programming, running a bulletin board, or just being knowledgeable enough with MS-DOS to operate one's own PC at home. These individuals are a resource that should not be overlooked. Computer education is also proliferating. Various levels of computer science courses are being offered in adult education in high schools and colleges.

Computer conferences sponsored by universities, government, and industry often present panel discussions that include experienced law enforcement officers, civil libertarians, members of the Electronic Frontier Foundation, prosecutors, and the media. A treasure of information for the novice computer crime investigator is generally discussed. The most relevant topics are the First and the Fourth Amendment concerns. The electronic media, E-mail, BBSs, and the seizure and search of hard drives are only a few of the topics. One must also stay informed of local law, federal requirements, and Supreme Court decisions to ensure that enforcement does not violate individual rights.

The computer and software manufacturers are often helpful in providing assistance with information when examining evidence. Furthermore, let them know when you have discovered a crime against their company, such as an individual's selling pirated software or stolen microchips.

Remember, a good investigator should develop and maintain contacts in many areas. The computer crime investigator should consider developing contacts with long distance carrier companies, local telephone companies, media, utility companies, computer publications, universities, credit card investigators, the U.S. Secret Service, the FBI, state and local police agencies, U.S. postal inspectors, and national-level private investigation agencies.

Often an excellent tool for an investigator is an informant. Many of those arrested are willing to provide information for a better deal in court. The computer criminal is most frequently a first-time offender and, if approached properly, will be a source for additional arrests. In Cyberpunk, by Katie Hafner and John Markoff, informant Lenny Decicco ended the criminal career of the infamous Kevin Mitnick, who, among other things, reconfigured a telephone company (telco) switch to route the hotline for missing credit cards to his home, thereby getting a nice list of credit card numbers.[6]

THE INVESTIGATIONS

With a working understanding of what has preceded this portion of the chapter, the investigator is now ready to handle a complaint or report of a computer crime from a victim.

If the complainant is within the investigator's local area, such as the county or city, the investigator should attempt to interview the complainant at the scene of the crime. The interview may take place in the victim's residence regarding his PC being attacked, or in an office building concerning a corporate mainframe. When the call comes in from another state, however, an in-depth interview may be conducted by phone.

During this initial interview, investigators have to determine that, in fact, a crime was committed. They must decide who in the company will be the person signing affidavits, and who is the employee with the most and accurate information regarding the allegation. In addition to a claim of monetary loss, there ought to be an explanation as to how the value of the loss was determined. This must be done accurately and without embellishing. Federal sentencing guidelines specify that larger losses cause longer sentences, and the dollar value of the loss can change the level of the state charge. For example, in New York a larceny of less than $1000 is a misdemeanor. The theft of over $1000 is a felony and results in higher fines and potentially longer sentences.

Always start with a fresh notebook, and record every relevant fact.

A victim, including the telecommunications companies, need not be provided with a subpoena for information. When in the normal course of business a telephone company (telco) discovers an individual engaged in a fraud against it, the company has the right to investigate who is committing the crime, develop evidence against him or her, and provide it to law enforcement. In one case, a long distance carrier reported that it found someone using a sequential dial-out program and attempting to crack telephone PINs. The company activated a DNR (dial number recorder) and observed the criminal scanning, cracking, and using the stolen codes. The telco was also able to determine the subscriber information and conduct a physical line search to ensure that the phone line went into the subscriber's home. All this information was supplied to law enforcement without subpoena.

The investigator must determine how current the data is. If the complaint indicates a computer crime was committed from a remote location more than a couple of weeks ago, the information may be considered "stale," and an application for a search warrant may be denied. If the crime is ongoing, the next step is to collect evidence that would identify the perpetrator, as well as the site at which the crime is being carried out.

Very often complainants do not have all the data necessary for the investigator to conduct the probe. They must provide the complainant with a list of the additional information needed. This frequently includes the method for the determination of loss, how and when the crime was perpetrated and discovered, employee lists (for in-house investigations), and printouts of the audit trails, such as the user log, sign-on log, and the like.

There must be a discussion of the elements of the crime that need to be included in the company's affidavit. If the complainants are not familiar with preparing an affidavit, refer them to their company's legal staff or offer to help.

When the crime involves more than one state, you must consider jurisdiction. If the criminal conduct is originating from a computer terminal in Texas, and this action is damaging or altering data on a system in New York, there are three possible prosecutions. First, if New York investigators are able to determine the identity of the intruder, they may obtain an arrest warrant and extradite the criminal from Texas. Second, the complainant in New York may call police in Texas, supplying them with the documentation and the appropriate affidavits. Police in Texas could then arrest and prosecute the individual. Third, federally, the U.S. Secret Service or FBI could conduct the investigation and have the U.S. Attorney's Office prosecute the case in either state.

Before concluding the interview, make sure that the complainant makes a backup copy of the evidence on the hard drive or tape and preserves the audit trail.

How to Proceed

After the initial interview, investigators must make some decisions: Have they received sufficient information to determine the nature of the crime? Did they get enough evidence to demonstrate who committed the crime, and when and where? This is usually not the case. Typically, after the first interview, investigators have to work to determine the how, when, and who. They must obtain reliable and demonstrable evidence.

When an in-house probe is conducted, it is likely that the evidence will be reviewed on site. This may be done by the trained investigator, the systems administrator, or the EDP (electronic data processing) auditor. If it is suspected that the employee removed evidence to another location, or that the crime has been perpetrated from a remote location, investigators will probably need to obtain a search warrant.

To procure a search warrant, investigators will want to develop evidence that demonstrates where and when the crime was committed. There are several techniques to obtain additional proof. Initially seek to acquire a legally sufficient affidavit from the victim. This should contain all the factual data available. Next, telephone records ought to be obtained. Unless the telco is the victim of the crime, investigators need to procure a subpoena for the local and/or long distance records of the suspect's outgoing phone calls for the period during which the crime was being committed.

If the victim's incoming phone calls are to an 800 or 900 number, investigators can request the lists of telephone numbers that dialed in during the period of the crime from the long distance carrier. This system is ANI (automatic number identification). Should the crime be ongoing, such as an unauthorized incursion into a corporate or military computer, investigators may determine the telephone number from which the call is coming in by having a trap placed on the victim's phone line. A letter of permission from the victim is usually necessary for the trap. In addition, the telco may require the victim to pay a fee for the trap.

Consider real-time monitoring using a serial-line analyzer on the incoming port. This captures the incoming keystrokes, which should be recorded on a disk to be used as evidence.

When the probe has established that a suspect is continuing to use phone lines to commit a crime, a court order for a DNR (dial number recorder) or pen register should be obtained. This will provide the investigator with the telephone numbers being dialed from the suspect's phone.

Whether investigators procured the evidence of the suspect's phone dialing the victim's computer from the trap, DNR, or ANI, each out-dial is time- and date-stamped. Part of the victim's computer's audit trail is the time- and date-stamping of the actions of a user.

The long distance carrier or the telephone company security specialist will then prepare an affidavit which, in plain English, indicates the activity from the suspect's phone to the victim's computer. The affidavit of the system's administrator will explain the crime and state when it occurred. Investigators now match the computer evidence with the telecommunications evidence, and prepare an affidavit for a search warrant for the residence, office, or building where the phone calls originate.

Other Relevant Evidence

Law enforcement cannot arrest the suspect's phone, modem, or computer. Enforcing the law means apprehending the person against whom probable cause has been developed, the one who most likely committed the crime. The purpose of the search warrant is to obtain evidence. While the results of the search warrant will usually provide proof that this was the location from which the crime was carried out, it will not necessarily indicate *who* the culprit is. So the good guys have to do more.

Develop a Target Profile

Very often the type of crime being perpetrated will supply investigators with information about the type of person who commits it, as well as his or her abilities and motives, and determine who has access to "pull it off."

Consider, as a sample period, the statistics of 26 computer crime and eight telecommunications arrests during the 18 months prior to writing this chapter. None of these crimes was committed against the defendant's employer.

Twenty-six defendants were apprehended for a variety of cracker computer crimes, which included computer tampering, unlawful use of a computer, computer trespass, unlawful duplication of computer-related material, grand larceny, and possession of stolen credit cards. Twenty-five of the defendants were arrested during or after search warrants were executed at their residences. Evidence obtained in 24 of 26 searches revealed that the defendant had been involved in multiple crimes with a mix of statutes. This group ranged in age from 14 to 32 years. Nine were under 16 years (the New York State legal age of an adult), and 16 were under 18 years (the federal legal age of an adult). So we can see that most often we can expect the cracker to be a teenager.

By comparison, over the same period, eight other people were arrested for their engagement in call selling schemes. This group ranged in age from 27 to 41, and the average was 33 years and three months. After reviewing many bulletin boards used for and by crackers, it was found that those who post messages using foul language are usually in the 13- to 16-year range. College students use much better grammar in comparison, and most over 21 years of age do not spend much time chatting. They tend to sign on, post or take what they need, and log off. However, there are always exceptions.

Target Authentication

Attempt to identify the computer criminal prior to executing the search warrant! Sources of information regarding the occupants of the suspect residence are surveillance, a U.S. postal employee who delivers mail to the address, local schools, telephone companies, power companies, banks and credit card companies, town clerk's offices, and informants.

In some cases, the prosecutor will need to provide a subpoena to obtain information. Do not despair if you do not identify the cracker prior to execution of the search warrant. As we shall see, you have an outstanding chance of determining the perpetrator during the execution of the search warrant.

Obtaining the Search Warrant

Law enforcement officers' affidavits for a search warrant will include a statement of who they are, as well as their training and expertise. They will recite from the onset of the investigation the allegations, the evidence procured, the reason for a search warrant for the address specified, a description of the building, the violations of law, and the evidence they expect to find during the execution of the search warrant.

If investigators have not previously drafted a computer crime or telecommunications fraud affidavit for a search warrant, they should request assistance from the prosecutor or senior investigator.

When investigators face the judge from whom they wish to obtain the search warrant, they should expect many questions. It has been the author's experience that judges are as interested in Fourth Amendment rights as the investigators. For the judge who is also new to computer crime law, this affidavit may pose a problem. He or she may wish to take several days reviewing the case and speaking to others who are experienced in this area. Prepare for delays; however, you will probably get the search warrant.

An additional consideration is whether or not to ask for a no-knock warrant. This does not exist federally. Where it is available, reflect whether there is an expectation that evidence would be destroyed if investigators do knock. Data can be obliterated in seconds or irretrievably encrypted with a keystroke.

PREPARATION FOR SEARCH WARRANT EXECUTION

Proper planning prevents painfully poor performance. The proper plotting for the search warrant execution may determine the success of the investigation. As with the execution of other criminal search warrants, law enforcement must take into consideration entry equipment, safety, evidence seizure, protection, and, of course, documentation (written or photographed). For computer crime and telecommunications fraud, the planning should also consider some extras:

- A 200-megabyte hard disk with cablelink to back up the system before moving it.

- A telephone company security technician who can assist in identifying equipment used in telecommunications fraud and trace telephone lines.

- A clean DOS boot disk to boot off. This helps to ensure that the hard disk is not erased by a hidden program.

- A double set of numbered labels for matching the corresponding plugs and ports. This facilitates putting the system back together in the lab.

- A compass. This is necessary to locate any magnetic fields in the building that may have been established. The magnetic field around the door could erase evidence from the disks and hard drive as it leaves the building.

- A computer literate person, preferably a law enforcement member. He or she should be able to park the head if necessary and view additional computer systems. This can help to avoid seizing computers that were not used in the commission of the crime.

- A trained law enforcement interviewer. This is very important. We may need admissions to be able to charge someone (and these are often juveniles who will be questioned in the presence of their parents).

- Questionnaires. Each resident ought to be asked pertinent questions. These interviews should be conducted in separate rooms when possible.

- Statement forms for recording confessions or allegations.

- "Consent to Search" forms for other areas not mentioned in the search warrant.

Timing

Timing is everything. Usually, a cracker repeatedly engages in the crime during certain periods of the day, such as before and after school, at night after homework, or immediately after dinner. These patterns should be noted and exploited. On the day you plan to execute the search warrant, have the telephone company monitor the DNR and advise you when the cracker comes on-line. A quick entry then will often find the cracker at the keyboard with evidence on the monitor. Also, try to coordinate this with a time of the day that the fewest number of people are in the house with the suspect. But if the search warrant is going to be executed at a time you do not expect the crime to be in progress, try to execute it at an hour the suspect is in the residence.

EXECUTION

Entry. The author's personal feeling is that not all entries should be made alike. If, in gaining entry to execute a search warrant, we expect to encounter armed suspects with a penchant for shooting at police, we probably would call in the mobile response team (NYSP) or SWAT team. On the other hand, if we think the perpetrator is a 14-year-old computer criminal with no criminal record and with parents who are respected members of the community, we probably should be dressed in suits and ties, ring the bell, and accept an invitation into the home. Somewhere between these extremes, we encounter the unknown suspect of unknown parents living in an apartment building in a rundown neighborhood. If the computer crime is malicious, and he has posted messages on BBSs that will "blow up" the first cop who attempts to arrest him, we may want to hit his place at 5:00 A.M. with a no-knock warrant wearing protective vests. We must be flexible. Our actual experience has been that, in the 24 search warrants executed for computer crime during the 18-month sample period, a forceful entry was needed only once. In fact, even in the case of a forced entry, no evidence was destroyed prior to our securing the scene. No injuries have been incurred.

It is also significant that, when the information is as old as two months since the crime has been committed, in 100 percent of the warrants executed, the computers and evidence were located at the targeted addresses. Therefore, it should be suggested to prosecutors that the evidence is not like drugs or money, which would be expected to disappear in a short period. Computer equipment and evidence ought to be treated like business records. The evidence may remain at the site for a longer time, and the information may indeed not be stale, even if it is three months old.

Obtaining a Confession

The confession or corroborating admissions during the search warrant execution are valuable. Have the appointed interviewer reduce this to writing and have the criminal sign it!

PREPARATION FOR PROSECUTION

Although the evidence seized may be voluminous, every effort should be made to review it as soon as possible. Confer with the prosecutor regarding the evidence that indicates additional crimes committed by the defendant. For a defendant unwilling to plead guilty to a class A misdemeanor, the prosecutor will be armed with the other potential charges, which ought to secure a plea arrangement.

Should the prosecution need to go to a grand jury presentation for the obstinate or second-time offender, a felony plea or trial is appropriate.

During the plea bargaining, a prosecutor should always request that criminals sign over the seized system as the instrument of the crime. If not, take them to trial on a felony! After all, do we give back the gun to the murderer, the knife to the stabber, or the scales to the drug dealer? Law enforcement works hard to solve crimes. We do not need to rearm the computer criminal at the conclusion of the case.

Case in Point

A university systems administrator (SYSOP) discovered a significant increase in its 800 telephone bill to the UNIX computer. After contacting AT&T, the SYSOP received a printout of the phone numbers dialing into the university's computer. He noticed an unusually high percentage of incoming calls from another state and examined the computer. To his surprise, he discovered an unauthorized bulletin board had been installed in the system. The userlog demonstrated the time of the incoming calls and the computer handles (names that the users go by). The SYSOP provided law enforcement investigators in the other state with this audit trail, the AT&T records, and assistance in understanding the data. A review of the audit trail revealed that unknown individuals from specific telephone numbers committed the crimes of computer trespass and computer tampering. After receiving the affidavit from the university, the subscriber information from the telephone company, and the affidavit from AT&T, the investigator prepared an affidavit and secured search warrants for 17 different residents. The sweep resulted in the arrest of 15 individuals.

NOTES

¹Cliff Stoll, *Cuckoo's Egg* (New York: Doubleday, 1989).

²Steven Levy, *Hackers* (New York: Anchor/Doubleday, 1984).

[3]Bernard Weiner, *Theories of Motivation* (New York: A Markham Book/Rand McNally, 1972).

[4]Donn B. Parker, *Computer Crime: Criminal Justice Resource Manual*, 2d ed. (Washington, D.C.: National Institute of Justice).

[5]J. Thomas McEwen, *Dedicated Computer Crime Units* (Washington, D.C.: National Institute of Justice, 1989), Catherine H. Conly, *Organizing for Computer Crime Investigation* (Washington, D.C.: National Institute of Justice, 1989).

[6]Katie Hafner and John Markoff, *Cyberpunks* (New York: Simon & Schuster, 1991).

35

Investigating Telecommunications Fraud

Donald P. Delaney

Telecommunications companies (telcos) have reported $1–$1.5 billion in losses for 1990 due to intentional fraud. As telcos identify the cause of their losses, they often seek law enforcement to conduct investigations and to arrest those responsible.

This chapter examines the reasons for its proliferation, the types of telecommunications fraud, and the methods of investigation. Furthermore, the networking frequently used by those involved in such crimes is described.

REASONS FOR THE INCREASE IN TELECOMMUNICATIONS FRAUD

Profit

Telco criminals profit every time they make a telephone call and do not pay for it, and the telco incurs a loss of revenue. For the call to a country halfway around the world, which may last for 18 hours or more, the losses add up quickly. Individuals who unlawfully access telephone service and then sell it to others at a cut rate realize large profits fast. Imagine that an enterprising person is able to access unlimited, free long distance service. Using this scheme with five telephone lines running from his apartment, he sells telephone service to South America for 18 hours each day. The collection rate is $10 for 20 minutes. The profit is $30 a phone per hour. Five phones, working 18 hours per day, can yield $2700 in revenue each day. On a yearly basis, this equals $985,500. In contrast, the costs are only for basic service for the five phones, the expense of a PC, modem, software programs, and computerized telephone accountants. This totals less than $5000 per year.

What is the risk to sharp entrepreneurs? If arrested, as some have been, they may pay a fine and be back in operation soon after. After all, how many people get excited about the fraud? It is not drugs; it is not a violent crime; and it takes trained, motivated investigators to obtain the search warrants necessary to make a case against those running a call-sell operation. Still other people are making money by stealing codes (telephone credit card numbers, PBX codes, call diverter codes, and other codes that access long distance) and selling them to those who manage the call-sell operation.

Computer Crime

Those who engage in a variety of crimes—such as computer crime, espionage, narcotics importation and distribution, corporate spying, cracking, and software piracy—need to engage in telco fraud for two main reasons:

1. *Anonymity:* Telephone fraud, such as network looping, PBX outdials, cellular fraud, can give the criminal anonymity. Law enforcement and the telephone companies may find it difficult to locate the originating call.

2. *Cost of service:* It is expensive to spend several hours a day on the phone. If hackers had to pay for all their calls, they could easily run up phone bills for over $1000 each month.

Speaking Long Distance

Less expensive long distance service is appealing to many. Calling relatives in a foreign country, parents and friends from college, or family members while away in the military or in jail is often the incentive. There are many who provide this less expensive phone service by means of stolen telephone credit cards, PBX fraud, call diverters, and rechipped cellular phones. Let us examine how the criminal commits these and other types of telecommunications fraud!

TYPES OF TELECOMMUNICATIONS FRAUD

Telephone Credit Cards (TCC)

When people receive a TCC from a telco, consisting of a telephone number plus a PIN (personal identification number), they have obtained another credit card. Each time it is used, a charge is added to the account of the person to whom the card was issued. Having the account numbers of others is potentially very valuable. It provides unlimited, worldwide, free telephone service. How do the criminals obtain the stolen PINs?

1. *Shoulder surfing:* People enter their PINs on the telephone keypads in public each day. Criminals lurk in the area and observe the number being entered by looking over a shoulder or from afar, using binoculars or a telescope. They write down or enter the numbers on a tape recorder. In a busy location, such as

an airline terminal with batteries of phones, a quick thief can steal 20 to 30 telephone credit card numbers each day by shoulder surfing. Others stand near public rotary phones. To use a PIN, the customer needs to tell it to the operator. The PIN thief can record the number as fast as it is given to the operator. These stolen codes are sold to those running call selling operations, hackers, narcotics dealers, and even business people.

2. *Code cracking or scanning:* A common method for stealing another's telephone credit card numbers involves using a computer and a sequential number dial-out program to crack the four-digit PIN that follows the area code and telephone number. When the dial-out program discovers a working PIN and gains access to service, the computer saves the code on a disk and it can be read later. This activity is referred to as *cracking* or *scanning.* Many of those arrested for computer crimes had computer programs for cracking codes. The possession of this type of program could be illegal under federal law—insofar as the criminal has the use of an illegal "access device"—and under New York State law—where it is seen as a burglar's tool (used to facilitate the crime of theft of services).

3. *Social engineering:* There are some who have developed the skill of social engineering or conning codes from others. One method is to call customers listed in the phone book, pose as a telco employee, and ask for verification of only the last four numbers of the telephone credit card number. The con man explains that it is to prevent misbilling. Many customers comply. Of course, the con man already has the first ten digits of the number, which are the area code and telephone number, from the telephone book.

PBX (Private Branch Exchange) Fraud

Like a computerized switchboard, a PBX answers the telephone and offers the caller a variety of options. You might enter the extension of someone you wish to speak to, an extension to hear a prerecorded message, or a code to obtain a dial tone. The outgoing call is then billed to the company who owns the PBX. Companies whose PBX has a two- or three-digit code are extremely vulnerable, even to the novice hacker. Once the PBX out-dial code is discovered by the criminal, fraud through it expands at a trigonometric rate. Companies all over the country are suffering staggering losses due to this fraud. Sometimes a company may notice that their PBX is being abused and manage to change the access codes before the losses go over a few thousand dollars. Typically, however, the company's losses run in the tens and hundreds of thousands of dollars. In a few instances, they have even reached over $1 million.

Many PBXs are accessed through a toll-free 800 number. The long distance carrier provides a list of the telephone numbers that accessed the PBX during the last billing period. In a review of these records from the companies, it becomes apparent that the majority of the fraud emanates from New York City and more than 90 percent from pay telephones.

By the time the victim receives the exorbitant bill, complains to the telephone company, gets a printout of the phone numbers that accessed the PBX, and forwards the information to law enforcement, usually several months have gone by. Because thousands of phone numbers may be furnished, it will most likely take telephone companies a protracted period of time to go through the lists of numbers and determine which calls came from residences. After all, law enforcement will not resolve who made a call from a pay phone in New York City's Port Authority three months earlier. On being told which numbers are residences, law enforcement needs to obtain a subpoena for the subscriber information for the nonpublished telephone numbers. Most residential customers engaged in PBX fraud and call selling operations utilize phones with nonpublished numbers. After convincing the prosecutor that the subpoena is needed, the investigator files it with the telephone company and again waits for information. Upon receipt of the subscriber information, the investigator can then target those residences that were responsible for significant fraud. Since several months have elapsed by now from the point the crime was committed, the investigator will not be able to obtain a search warrant. Therefore, law enforcement may wish to secure a court order for a DNR (dial number recorder) on the targeted suspect's phones. Should the daily DNR demonstrate continuing fraud, a search warrant ought to be acquired. The warrant should be executed after target authentication and while the criminal is on the line, that is, engaged in a fraud.

If the investigation confirms that several phones are being fraudulently used for a call selling operation from one residence, consideration must be given to having an undercover officer buy a long distance call. Once inside, the undercover officer can observe who is running the operation and collecting the money.

It should be obvious by now that PBX fraud enforcement can be difficult. Prevention through education and security is a "must." The person responsible for the system should look for early warning signs, such as rapidly increased use, system slow-down due to excessive use, outgoing calls to foreign countries or unusual areas, and high off-hour utilization.

Boxing

Boxing refers to the use of a variety of electronic devices that enable their users to obtain free phone service from pay phones. The blue box, red box, and silver box are a few. These generate tones to simulate signals or the sounds of coins dropping or touch pulses. The black box uses a device to block the answer signal at the terminating end of a call. Most boxing has been eliminated due to electronic and computer advances made by the telephone companies.

Telco Switches

Telephone companies utilize electronic and digital switches, which are computerized. Hackers and other criminals have unlawfully accessed these computers for a variety of reasons. Some hackers have intentionally attacked switches for the purpose of knocking out phone service for an area. Others have unlawfully accessed the switches to activate telephone numbers and call forward them to 900 numbers. This provides the criminal with expensive 900 number access for the price of a local call.

One individual would obtain stolen Visa and Mastercard credit card numbers. She would access a telco switch late at night and call forward the legitimate cardholder's telephone to her second house phone. Then, by impersonating the cardholder, she would have Western Union wire money to an office for her accomplice to pick up. Western Union would call the legitimate customer for verification of customer authorization, but the customer's number had already been forwarded to the criminal's number. She would then impersonate the card holder, and the money would be transferred. The telco switch would be accessed again and the call forwarding undone. Prior to her arrest, this criminal stole money on many occasions in this manner. Telco lineworkers have switch codes for listening on lines for noise and other testing. Misuse of this information allows criminals to engage in illegal wiretaps.

Call Diverters

Call diverters are usually employed on small business or home phones. This enables its owner to call forward incoming calls to another phone. For example, a plumber wishes to receive calls at his or a customer's home where he is working. A glitch in many of the diverters allows a caller to obtain a dial tone from the diverter. When the criminal dials out at that moment, the plumber will be charged for the call. Just another method for criminals to obtain free telephone service!

Network Looping or Weaving

Tens of thousands of computers are interconnected nationwide and internationally over telephone lines. These interconnections are networks with such names as Internet, Milnet, Arpernet, Telenet, and Tymenet. Many of these linked computers enable the individual dialing in to out-dial to another location. From the next computer one might again out-dial to another computer. If a criminal initiates the first call using a stolen telco credit card or a PBX on an 800 number, and then loops through several network computers, he or she virtually ensures anonymity. Only due to a fluke and an incredible amount of work on the part of Cliff Stoll were the network looping "Hanover Hacker" and friends criminally charged!

Cellular Phone Fraud

"The losses are staggering," says Michael Guidry of Guidry and Associates, a spokesperson for the cellular industry. Mr. Guidry estimates 1990 revenue losses, domestically, at more than $300 million due to cellular fraud.

Only two years earlier this fraud did not exist. It spread nationwide like wildfire for several reasons: It is easy, relatively safe, provides anonymity and mobility, and can generate large profits fast. One defendant suggested that some drug dealers have moved away from selling drugs to cellular call selling operations for greater profit, the lack of enforcement, and, if convicted, no expectation of serving time.

At this point the logical question is what went wrong? For the cellular phone firm to collect revenue, it must be able to identify the customers using the cellular company's service. The system was devised so that the outgoing cellular phone call would send two numbers to the cellular company as identifiers. The company's computers would then compare the two numbers, determine if they are both assigned to one phone, and either allow or deny service. One number transmitted from the cellular phone is the MIN (mobile identification number). This is programmed into the phone by the shop selling the cellular phone for the cellular carrier. The other number transmitted is the ESN (electronic serial number). This number is assigned to the phone by the manufacturer and is electronically stored in the phone's memory. The ESN was expected to remain unchanged in the phone, independent of the number of owners, just as a vehicle identification number (VIN) is not supposed to be changed. The MIN is like the car's license plate which is changed with each new owner. Criminals have been altering VINs for a long time and reselling cars. Now they do the same with the phone's ESN, and "roaming" assists them in evading justice.

So what is roaming? A cellular phone is said to be in a roam status when it is operating outside the issuing company's assigned area. The company of this remote area does not have a record of the ESN and assigned phone number to check. This receiving carrier usually will not be able to determine if the incoming call is legitimate or fraudulent. So it goes through even if the MIN and ESN are fraudulent. When the carrier finds out it was a fraudulent call, it has no one to bill, no suspects, and no exact idea from where the call came.

How did this type of fraud begin? Seeing the opportunity for free phone service, an individual wrote a computer program containing an algorithm that would allow the phone's ESN to be changed. This program is burned into an EPROM (microchip) and inserted into the cellular phone, replacing the original EPROM. The program can do a variety of things. It may tell the phone to send out a different ESN on each out-dial, and it may give the owner the ability to reprogram the phone's ESN from the keypad whenever he or she wants. The program contains a combination of numbers with the minimum amount of information to get by when in a roaming status.

The criminals knew how to use cellular phones that were activated in cell areas other than the one in which they would be operating. The 256E EPROM was programmed with the fraudulent information and then replicated thousands and thousands of times. The fraud began in California in 1988 and reached New York in 1989.

Cellular carriers were totally confused. The "tumbling" ESN phone calls were coming in faster than they could be denied access. During 1990 this fraud exploded so quickly that the Elmhurst, New York, cell site receiver had every port busy within one 24-hour period without one legitimate call going through. In fact, it became common for carriers to have limited ability to bill for calls to certain countries. Thus blocking began. Countries of narcotics importation, such as Columbia, the Dominican Republic, and others have been blocked in high fraud areas of New York City, that is, in a neighborhood of people with predominantly foreign ancestry. When the local cell site lost money due to fraudulent calls to a particular criminal's country of origin, the cellular carrier responded by blocking any outgoing calls to it. This simply became a necessity because the cellular carrier has to pay the long distance carrier for all the calls handed off to land lines. Rightfully so, the long distance carriers expect to be paid. During one month in 1990 Metro One, a cellular company in New Jersey, complained that it suffered a $1.5-million revenue loss because $1 million had to be paid to long distance carriers.

What are the destinations of some of these long distance calls? It has been determined that many of the targeted drug entrepreneurs in the Cali and Medellin cartels are receiving calls from fraudulent cell phones. The bad guys know that law enforcement rarely can locate a specific fraudulent phone. This protects them from police wiretaps.

During 1990 the U.S. Secret Service provided an algorithm to cellular carriers that would prevent the tumbling phones from gaining service. Thousands of phones seemed useless, but only temporarily.

Fraudulent applications began flooding in. Cellular phones were being activated for fictitious or unaware customers. At the end of the second billing period the phones were denied access for nonpayment. Cloning became the criminal's answer. By obtaining a legitimate customer's ESN and MIN, one could reprogram the phone with the customer's ESN and MIN to get service. In fact, a person could reprogram dozens of phones with the legitimate customer's numbers. These numbers could be obtained from the air, using tuned radio receivers, or from the paperwork in the storefronts that activate the cellular phones.

During 1992, blocking reduced a significant portion of the Cellular Phone Company's losses. The resourceful criminals discovered they could still obtain international access by first accessing a PBX RAU and then dialing out. In addition, dialing a 700-conference call line with your cloned phone still obtains interntional long distance service.

Law enforcement responded. Many have been arrested from coast to coast for crimes related to cellular phone fraud. Under federal law, the altered phone is an "illegal access device." State statutes usually forbid possession of devices used to commit fraud, larceny, or theft of services. In New York a person caught owning this phone would be guilty of burglar's tool possession and possession of unlawfully duplicated computer material (the reprogrammed microchip). Selling such fraudulent telephone service or knowingly using the rechipped phones bears the charge of computer tampering, theft of services, falsifying business records, and unauthorized use of a computer.

Electronic equipment used by law enforcement to locate and wiretap fraudulent cellular phones include the IFR 1200, the Harris triggerfish, and swordfish.

Three-Party Billing

"Operator, I'd like to bill this call to my home phone." I am sure that most people have done this one time or another. Usually, the operator will call the "home" to obtain authorization; however, frequently the operator will only check the name used against the subscriber's telephone number. When a phone book is the only check, a thief once again may gain free telephone service.

540 Scam

Most people are aware that dialing a 900 number generates an additional charge on their telephone bill, but few know that this applies to the 540 exchange in New York City. Other exchanges (which vary from area to area) also generate an extra charge. A customer dialing a 540 number must be told during the first ten seconds of the call that there is a charge for the call, the amount of the charge and that the caller has the opportunity to hang up and not be charged. An individual was arrested in New York City during 1990 for abusing his 540 number. His agreement with the New York Telephone Company stipulated that anyone calling his 540 number would be charged $55. A tape recorded message greeted the caller, yet failed to mention the $55 charge for the call. To get individuals to dial his 540 number, the conniver used computers to sequentially dial out blocks of beeper numbers. When the beeper company answered, the computer entered the 540 number. Done late at night, this caught beeper owners off guard. The unsuspecting victim called the number and listened to worthless information about real estate. During a one-month period, more than $90,000 in customer charges were accrued. Fortunately, the check did not go out, the customers' accounts were credited for their $55 phone call, and the thief was arrested.

Voice Mail Boxes

When a person calls into a voice mail system, a code is needed to obtain the recorded messages. One can also record a message for those dialing in. Voice mail box abuse spans the globe. The telco criminal dials into the computer that maintains the voice mail box system. He makes changes in the mail box codes which preclude the box owner from using it, or the boxes are activated and assigned the criminal's code (password). Very often the same individual is engaged in the dissemination of stolen credit card numbers, telco codes, PBX codes, and call diverter numbers.

COCOTS

Customer-owned coin-operated phones (COCOTS) are another means to gain free telephone service. An AT&T representative recently estimated there are 250,000 COCOTS operating in the United States today. These pay phones are very susceptible to fraud. The phone itself usually employs a couple of security measures to prevent free access to unrestricted dialtones. The normal telco pay phones do not have these security measures built in. Instead, the telcos have elaborate computerized security systems that deter the free access to the unrestricted dialtone. There is a wide variety of illegal methods for gaining COCOTS access. Furthermore, an individual who can determine the number of the COCOT can give it to a friend or relative overseas, who can call the COCOT collect at a preordained time and date. The friend in the United States picks up the receiver when the phone rings and agrees to accept the charges.

Due to the large losses, telcos are compelled to fight back with increased security forces and ever greater investments in security research and development. However, the cost of all this telecommunications fraud is passed on to you and me and to everyone who pays for telephone service.

NOTE

[1]Cliff Stoll, *Cuckoo's Egg* (New York: Doubleday, 1989).

36

Money Laundering: An Investigator's Perspective

John F. Markey

The estimated annual dollar volume in drug trafficking exceeds $100 billion in the United States and $300 billion worldwide. To place these figures in perspective, these sums compare with an annual dollar volume in the legitimate pharmaceutical industry in the United States of approximately $43 billion. Proceeds from other forms of illicit activities, such as tax evasion, gambling, prostitution, embezzlement, fraud, and potentially licit activities such as capital flight, are also laundered. Some estimates place the annual total from these sources, which do not include narcotics proceeds, also in the $100 billion arena.

According to a report submitted by the United States General Accounting Office, *Drug Investigations, 1986*, "drug trafficking is the most widespread and lucrative organized crime operation in the United States, accounting for nearly 40 percent of this country's organized crime activity." Updates of both the $100 billion and 40 percent figures, however, only confirm that this analysis, while possibly accurate five years ago, grossly underestimates the financial scope and social threat of the illicit narcotics industry. Not only have the monetary amounts involved in the trafficking, purchase, and profit from the drug trade increased to staggering proportions, but also the traffickers' organizational structures have encompassed and evolved beyond the so-called "traditional" organized crime elements previously known to law enforcement officials. The association of organized crime and terror has far outstripped the familiar *Cosa Nostra*. Groups such as the Jamaican "posses," Asian Triads, Tongs, and Yakuza, to name just a few, often use terror—violence against citizens within their "territories" or against those law enforcement officials who cannot be paid off to look the other way.

The American government has declared a "war on drugs," and the term is aptly applied. Narcotics have long been used to procure power and profits for the "source of supply." But the modernization of communications, travel, and the shipping industries have raised previously geographically limited trafficking and consequent money laundering to an international conglomerate. Southeast Asian organized crime and South American cartels—indeed, any of the power structures supporting the drug lords, and any of the nationally or internationally operating terrorist organizations "employed" by narcotics traffickers—have raised the threat and the monetary profits of the transit and distribution of both narcotics and narcotic proceeds to a global scale.

This chapter focuses on the tools available to law enforcement agents in combating the "weak link" in the narcotics traffickers' chain of criminal activities. First, it identifies the federal statutes relevant to anti-money laundering activities, then discusses the common principles associated with money laundering investigations, and concludes with illustrations of investigative techniques. Offered within this context will be the typology and methodology of the money launderer acting in concert with proactive investigations by police to dismantle the cartels.

FEDERAL STATUTES RELEVANT TO ANTI-MONEY LAUNDERING ACTIVITIES

On October 26, 1970, the President signed the *Bank Records and Foreign Transactions Act*. Titles I and II of that act constitute what is commonly known as the *Bank Secrecy Act*. The Act was an attempt to respond to the growing amount of money laundering in U.S. financial institutions from the proceeds of narcotics transactions. The theory behind the act was simple. The *Bank Secrecy Act* imposed currency reporting requirements on financial institutions and on all persons crossing U.S. borders. The reporting requirements were designed to create a "paper trail" for significant cash transactions in U.S. financial institutions or across U.S. borders. Failure to comply with the act set forth civil penalties, civil forfeitures, and/or criminal sanctions, which in turn facilitated investigations of currency violations by narcotics traffickers.

The primary purpose of the act was to identify the sources, volumes, and movements of United States currency being transported into or out of the country or being deposited in financial institutions. It was designed to aid law enforcement officials in the detection and investigation of criminal, tax, and regulatory violations.

The financial transaction reporting requirements accomplishes a number of objectives. First, it assists in removing some of the anonymity that is essential to persons laundering money in financial institutions in the United States or abroad. These requirements attempt to secure detailed identification of persons conducting the transactions.

- The Currency Transaction Reports (CTRs) filed with and maintained by the U.S. Internal Revenue Service (IRS) require detailed information regarding transactions between individuals or business entities and financial institutions.

- The Currency and Monetary Instrument Reports (CMIRs), filed with and maintained by the U.S. Customs Service, require detailed identification of persons crossing the border (inbound or outbound) with, as of 1992, $10,000 or more in currency or negotiable instruments.

- The Foreign Banking Account Reports, maintained by the IRS, are filed by U.S. citizens who have monetary accounts overseas.

- The Casino Transaction Report requires the filing of deposits or withdrawals of currency in a casino.

- Finally the Treasury Form 8300 requires reports from merchants, particularly in cash-rich businesses.

Since 1985, all of these reports are triggered when the dollar amounts transported, banked, or transacted exceeds $10,000.

Removing the anonymity from large currency transactions creates a much higher probability of law enforcement agencies' detecting currency money launderers. The higher probability of detection discourages money launderers from operating in U.S. financial institutions. It also makes it more hazardous for these launderers to smuggle currency outside the United States for laundering in foreign financial institutions. The result is a greater risk of detection and prosecution of money launderers. To lessen the risk, organized criminals and their associates, such as co-opted attorneys, accountants, and bank officials must expend greater efforts and greater portions of their profits to launder their money. Imposing this cost on money launderers has been one of the most successful aspects of the *Bank Secrecy Act.*

Another important aspect of the act pertains to the dissemination of financial information to other law enforcement entities. Title 31 U.S.C. Section 5319 provides that the Secretary of the Treasury may transfer information from domestic financial transaction reports, export/import reports, and foreign financial agency transaction reports to other agencies for use in criminal, tax, or regulatory investigations or proceedings. Any information disseminated, however, must be received in confidence and can be disclosed only to persons utilizing the information for official purposes relating to the criminal, tax, or regulatory investigations or proceedings for which the information was sought (31 C.F.R. Section 103.43). All state and local agencies seeking *Bank Secrecy Act* information must submit a written request to the Secretary of the Treasury, signed by the head of the agency, requesting access to *Bank Secrecy Act* information for use in an official criminal, tax, or regulatory investigation or proceeding. The relevance of all requests to an official investigation or proceeding must be certified. Also, the specific nature or purpose of the investigation or the violations of federal law, along with a statement containing sufficient identification of the individual or entity named in the request, must be given to permit a valid examination of available files. Each request will be reviewed by the Deputy Assistant Secretary for Enforcement of the Department of the Treasury before disclosure to that agency.

In conjunction with the *Bank Secrecy Act*, the *Organized Crime Control Act* was enacted in 1970. A section of this Act (P.L. 91-542) addressed the need to identify, seize, and forfeit illegally earned money in Title IX, Racketeer Influenced and Corrupt Organizations (RICO). The RICO statute prohibits:

- The use of income derived from a pattern of racketeering in any enterprise that affects interstate or foreign commerce.

- The acquisition or maintenance of any interest or control of any enterprise that affects interstate or foreign commerce.

- Any person employed or associated with an enterprise conducting or participating in racketeering activity through the enterprise.

- Any person conspiring to violate any of the above.

For any willful violation of the RICO statute, civil and criminal penalties may be assessed as well as forfeiture of any interest in the enterprise.

Money laundering under the RICO statute violates provisions of Title 18 U.S.C. 1961-1964. Money derived from racketeering activities such as gambling, bribery, extortion, narcotic violations, and wire and securities fraud fall within the purview of the RICO statute.

In the first few years of the *Bank Secrecy Act*, it was not very successful in its objective to stop illicit activity. This era saw questions about the Act's constitutionality and doubts about the Department of the Treasury's ability to implement the reporting requirements set forth in Title II. The reporting requirements were also not effective because of deficiencies in the regulations, a lack of coordination among various law enforcement agencies responsible for the administration of the Act, and shortcomings in the reporting requirements themselves. As a result, it was not until the late 1970s that government agencies began to enforce the *Bank Secrecy Act*.

Although there were administrative changes made by the law enforcement agencies to remedy some of the problems, the *Comprehensive Crime Control Act of 1984* (Public Law 98-473) was signed into law to correct several of these deficiencies endemic to the *Bank Secrecy Act*. Particularly, this law was amended to apply to persons "attempting" to transport monetary instruments into or out of the United States; U.S. Customs search authority was thereby expanded to include currency cases. Prior to this statutory authority, Customs officers did not routinely search departing travelers for unreported currency. As discussed later in this chapter, this authority also included searching for inbound currency not declared. Overreporting of inbound currency is a scheme utilized by money launderers in the false declaration of fictitiously large amount of currency. In reality, the individual is carrying little or no money. Once in the United States, that individual receives illegally derived proceeds, then deposits it in a U.S. bank account for a wire transfer overseas. Based on the inbound declaration, the individual has been able to "mask" the laundering activity.

In 1985, the *Bank Secrecy Act* was further amended to include Currency Transaction Reports (CTRs) being filed by casinos conducting business in excess of $1 million annually on currency transactions greater than $10,000. This amendment assisted investigatory capabilities by creating an audit trail to impinge on organized crime figures who deposited illegal funds into the coffers of a casino and then wire transferred the deposit in an attempt to disguise the source of the proceeds. A second amendment to the Act required domestic financial institutions to report transactions with foreign financial institutions. Although the identification of a singular or block of wire transfers is difficult in a transfer system handling billions of dollars worth of transactions weekly, this amendment allows for a data base of reviewable records, which acts as a potential investigatory resource.

Two schemes used by launderers to disguise transactions through bank deposits and wire transfers are "smurfing" and bank exempt lists. *Smurfing* is a technique in which several deposits under the $10,000 reporting requirement (CTR) are made by one or several individuals over a period of time and then transferred electronically to an overseas account in an attempt to launder the funds. The *bank exempt lists*, in essence, allow an individual or business entity to avoid filing currency transaction reports based on the number and type of deposits made in a given period of time. For example, revenue produced and deposited daily by entities such as car dealerships, precious metal brokers, or restaurant owners will request exemption from the encumbrance of filing. If agreed to by the banking institution, no Currency Transaction Reports are generated or filed. Without question, access by an individual or entity to these lists should be scrutinized by an investigator engaged in a money laundering inquiry. In 1986, the *Anti-Drug Abuse Act* was signed into law (Public Law 99-570). Pertinent to this discussion is Subtitle H, which sets forth the *Money Laundering Control Act*. This act created a federal violation for the structuring (that is, smurfing) of currency transactions to evade reporting requirements (Title 31 U.S.C. 5324). Second, bank exempt lists were subjected to summons authority by the Secretary of the Treasury and to tighter controls upon financial institutions in granting exemptions. Third, both criminal (Title 18 U.S.C. 982) and civil (Title 18 U.S.C. 981) forfeiture provisions, in relation to money laundering, were added to the investigator's quiver. Fourth, Section 1956 (laundering of monetary instruments) and Section 1957 (engaging in monetary transactions in property derived from specified unlawful activity) were added to Title 31, which for the first time made the laundering of monetary instruments a federal offense. Violations of 1956 and 1957 both qualify as predicate offenses for issuance of a wiretap (18 U.S.C. 2510), International Traffic in Arms Regulations (18 U.S.C. 1952) and RICO (18 U.S.C. 1961).

The success of this evolving legislation on both the investigation and prosecution of currency violations has resulted in the present stratagem by the government of "hitting the target" in the wallet, that is, allowing for, attaching, and forfeiting by the government of all property associated with illicit proceeds.

As stated earlier, in the 1970s, there was limited enforcement of the provisions of the *Bank Secrecy Act*. In the 1980s, as the government and the public became increasingly aware of the threat from narcotics traffickers in the United States and from the money laundering that supported those traffickers, the Departments of Treasury and Justice significantly escalated the enforcement of the Act to include the development of new legislation to shore up loopholes and questions of constitutionality. This resulted in many more financial institutions filing many more reports. As the enforcement of this legislation evolved, so did the activities of the agents working on this type of case, thereby forcing the criminals to react and make mistakes.

COMMON PRINCIPLES ASSOCIATED WITH MONEY LAUNDERING INVESTIGATIONS

Having identified the legislation used by narcotics/financial investigators in prosecuting currency violations, let us discuss the techniques and methodologies used by the investigators to put a money laundering case together.

Throughout the narcotics selling chain, drug trafficking is found to be a cash-and-carry business. The enormous amounts of cash received from drug sales must be stored, transported, and made available for subsequent use. Funds must be maintained by narcotraffickers in forms that are safe, reliable, and accessible. These funds must be hidden from regulatory agencies, law enforcement authorities, other narcotraffickers, and other criminals. This creates a substantial problem for narcotraffickers. The solution most frequently selected is money laundering. In a large narcotics network, laundering profits from drug sales is as much a problem as acquiring and distributing the narcotics.

The definition of money laundering, as used in this chapter, is based on the concept used by the 1988 United Nations Convention Against Illicit Traffic in Narcotic Drugs and Psychotropic Substances, which can be summarized as the *conversion* of illicit cash to another asset, the *concealment* of the true source or ownership of the illegally acquired proceeds, and the *creation* of the perception of the legitimacy of source and ownership.

The wide variety of money laundering schemes researched for this chapter all have in common the elements of conversion, concealment, and the creation of the perception of legitimacy. It must be emphasized that money laundering is a process rather than an act. This process may involve numerous and complex stages. Anyone who has played or watched three card monte, whether on the Coney Island pier or Venice beach, is familiar with the hustle. If police investigators enter the investigation with that analogy in mind, they will have a leg up and not become frustrated by the "shell" created by the money launderers. The laundering activity must be worked deductively through data provided by legislation, credit records, net worth, and mistakes by the launderer.

A review of local, state, and federal police cases reveals that methods of money laundering range from the simple to the sophisticated, and they are limited only by the imagination of the criminal enterprise. Indeed, the vast majority of legitimate business and financial transactions available to our society can be used as laundering vehicles. Further, the apparently divergent sectors of U.S. business and financial communities in the laundering world are not mutually exclusive but critically interconnected. In other words, sectors vulnerable to money laundering will often be used in conjunction with one another in a laundering scheme.

An analysis of several law enforcement investigations has identified the following financial or business entities used by criminal enterprises in their laundering activities:

- *Deposit-taking institutions:* Chartered banks, trust companies, and credit unions are the single most frequently used conveyances available to the launderer.

- *Currency exchange houses:* These offer many services traditionally associated with banking institutions, often serving as an intermediary between the criminal client and the banking institution in obtaining negotiable instruments and wire transfers.

- *The securities industry:* Securities transactions offer the criminal enterprise the opportunity to convert illicit funds into a highly liquid asset while retaining anonymity through such means as nominee accounts.

- *The real estate industry:* A purchase can be used to create a seemingly legitimate source of revenue; schemes may involve manipulating the reported value of property, with the result that inflated purchase prices or profit generating sales "legitimize" the acquisition of illicit profits.

- *The incorporation and operation of companies:* This technique offers criminals a legitimate source of employment, a source of reportable income that can account for a conspicuous display of wealth, and apparent respectability.

- *Gold and precious gems:* Artwork, coins, stamps, and collectibles provide the criminal launderer the conveyance to convert a large quantity of cash into a less conspicuous asset. For example, a million dollars in twenties and fifties, which would fill a suitcase, can easily be converted into a small envelope of cut, precious gems.

- *Miscellaneous laundering vehicles:* The insurance industry, legalized gaming facilities, dealerships (automobile, boat, and plane), professional courier services, and travel agencies are all either financial investment intermediaries or cash businesses capable of the converting, concealing, and creating the perception of legitimacy of illicit proceeds.

- *White-collar professionals:* Stockbrokers, real estate agents, financial advisors, accountants, and lawyers can provide their expertise in both the construction and maintenance of sophisticated laundering operations.

- *Transborder movement of illicit proceeds:* This tool of the money launderer clearly reflects the rise of an international global economy in such areas as Free Trade Agreements, the establishment of international financial business centers, and the internationalization of the banking and securities industries.

Clearly, as this list shows, a wide variety of money laundering schemes and opportunities are employed by narcotraffickers and other criminals. Increasingly imaginative schemes are likely to emerge as law enforcement agencies improve their ability to detect existing schemes. Nonetheless, variations and combinations of three basic elements are used. The launderer must then:

- Deposit cash into financial institutions (legitimate and otherwise) in ways that avoid triggering reports to the Treasury Department or regulatory agencies.

- Establish "front" companies (foreign and domestic) that can be used to hide the source(s) and beneficiary(ies) of cash deposited into financial institutions.

- Smuggle cash out of the United States and into financial institutions in other countries that do not have stringent, fully enforced laws regarding the reporting of financial transactions for subsequent wire transfer to final destinations inside or outside the United States.

Once illicit proceeds have been deposited into a financial institution, they can be moved quickly anywhere in the world by wire transfer. In this way, audit trails are virtually eliminated for at least two reasons. The first is the sheer volume of transactions (an estimated 150,000 legitimate wire transfers move in and out of the United States daily). Monitoring this volume of transactions for potentially illegal activities in a way that does not slow legitimate commerce is not an easy task. The second is that, until recently, the U.S. authorities have not considered establishing reporting requirements for wire transfers that would facilitate audit trails needed for apprehension and convictions. Most wire transactions, particularly those originating outside the United States, are accompanied only by the information needed to identify the originator's account, the beneficiary's account, and the amount of the transaction.

Some of the principles set forth in this section are illustrated by the following case. In a local, federal enforcement "take-down" of a most wanted money launderer, who worked for both the Medellin and Cali drug cartels, Stephen Saccoccia was arrested and charged with money laundering on Thanksgiving weekend 1991. Allegedly, Saccoccia had washed as much as $750 million in the prior five years.

As explained earlier, money laundering operations are intertwined with business entities and processed through stages. In Saccoccia's operation, hundreds of thousands of dollars flowed into dummy shops in Manhattan's jewelry district each day from nationwide drug couriers. The cash was bundled into duffel bags or gold shipment crates and driven by Brinks or Loomis armored trucks to the Saccoccia Coin Co., a storefront in Cranston, Rhode Island, or to a second location in Los Angeles. Thereafter, most of the money was subdivided, deposited in U.S. banks—ranging from Rhode Island's Fleet/Norstar to Bank of America—and then converted into cashier's checks made out to nonexistent businesses. Next, the money was moved electronically to foreign banks and eventually to the Colombian narcotraffickers.

Saccoccia's operating costs charged to these traffickers were 10 percent of the proceeds. When arrested in Geneva, Switzerland, Saccoccia was carrying $500,000 in cash. As a reported precious metals trader, Saccoccia was able to buy and sell hundreds of millions of dollars worth of gold in a year in numerous transactions, show a minimal profit, and produce limited business records that appear legitimate and do not normally raise the suspicion of law enforcement entities.

PROACTIVE ENFORCEMENT: SPECIAL OPERATIONS

The 1980s, the decade of cocaine, began with federal agents working with state and local investigators badly outnumbered and money launderers depositing sacks of cash with impunity. By 1990, law enforcement had followed the money trail to the drug lords' inner sanctum. As a result of effective legislation and intelligence agencies' profiling and targetting organized money, traffickers' operations continue to evolve positively and become more effective.

Across the board, elements enforcing and prosecuting these organizations have found that money laundering involves disguising the origin of dirty money so that it can be used openly to buy goods, properties, and services. Intelligence analysts assigned (posted) to anti-money laundering—task forces such as Operation Greenback in Florida—describe three common steps necessary to properly launder illicit proceeds:

1. *Placement:* This involves placing cash into financial institutions so that it can be turned into a paperless deposit and used conveniently. Money launderers can smuggle the proceeds to foreign countries with little or no reporting requirements. Or they can use businesses in the United States as fronts to explain the cash deposits, or bribe American bankers to ignore U.S. reporting requirements.

2. *Layering:* Money launderers create layers of disguised transactions to stymie narcotics agents. They may transfer the money electronically from the United States to countries with strict bank secrecy rules. They may use shell corporations in foreign countries to maintain the deposits. These corporations are sometimes owned by corporations in other countries. The idea is to create so many layers in so many bank secrecy havens that the proceeds appear impossible to trace.

3. *Integration:* Once the proceeds have gone through enough shells or layers of secrecy, it can be used with little fear of seizure. Narcotics traffickers might send the money back to the United States disguised as a "loan" from a foreign corporation. Or they might pretend to be consultants on a "salary" for a nonexistent business. The proceeds can buy businesses, land, gold, or other valuables. The proceeds, at this stage, can be integrated into the legitimate economy.

Having studied and worked on money laundering investigations, criminal justice experts have identified six landmark narcotics/money laundering investigations. Each scheme utilized the three stages in the laundering process—placement, layering, and integration. However, a synopsis of these operations shows the continuing evolution of criminals attempting to identify weaknesses in the enforcement chain and the investigators' reactions to stymie those attempts.

Operation Pisces

A three-year undercover sting finally pierced the veil of Panamanian bank secrecy. In Pisces, agents simply set up a storefront office and used their law enforcement undercover capabilities to launder money for the traffickers in hopes of identifying the narcotics network. By using money laundering as an investigative tool, the agents figured they could get closer than ever to major cartel associates. From June 1984 to May 1987, agents in Miami, New York, Los Angeles, and San Francisco used seven phony laundering businesses to dismantle two major smuggling rings associated with the Medellin cartel. The agents laundered $124 million, ultimately seized $58 million in cash and 24 airplanes, and arrested 42 individuals.

Operation Cash Web/Expressway

At the time, the FBI's largest money laundering sting came to an end in June 1987 when FBI agents arrested more than 40 people nationwide in an operation that involved seven U.S. cities and the country of Panama. In the three-year sting, agents laundered $200 million for narcotics traffickers, including $40 million previously seized in Miami. They seized only $24 million in cash and assets at the operation's culmination, leading to criticism that the FBI had helped the Medellin cartel more than it hurt it. The investigation did, however, result in the arrest and conviction of numerous high-level cartel money launderers, including Carlos Restrepo.

Operation Man

Narcotics traffickers, in this operation, were identified utilizing attorneys in South Florida to cover up illicit proceeds through the purchase of second nominee investment property. In this case, the narcotics proceeds moved through phony companies in both the Isle of Man and the British Virgin Islands. This 1986 investigation also uncovered smuggling activities among South Florida's power boat racers and their builders.

Operation C-Chase

The repercussions of this undercover "sting" are still being felt in both Congress and the media. On the heels of Operation Pisces, Operation C-Chase offered a completely new look at money laundering. Instead of dealing merely with the money brokers for the Colombian cartel, U.S. Customs agents got inside a major international bank and learned how it used hard-to-trace schemes to move money around the world. Operating a relatively modest storefront money laundering sting, customs agents were approached and guided by officials of the Bank of Credit and Commerce International (BCCI) on the rudiments of safely laundering money through their institution.

During the course of the operation, the agents laundered $32 million for the Medellin cartel utilizing the deceptive tactics taught them by those banking officials. In January 1989, two divisions of the bank pleaded guilty to Title 31 violations (money laundering) and agreed to forfeit $14 million. As a sidelight, C-Chase investigators also uncovered $20 million of Panama's General Manuel Noriega's money in BCCI accounts in Europe. Eight months earlier, Noriega had been indicted in Miami and charged with accepting bribes of $4.6 million to turn his country into a sanctuary for the Medellin cartel. Besides the obvious merits of this investigation, close cooperation between international and U.S. law enforcement in unfolding the complexity of this case is worthy of recognition.

Operation Polar Cap

In March 1989, the U.S. government filed charges against 127 narcotics/money laundering associates in the United States and Colombia. It indicted the entire cartel leadership, although at the time Pablo Escobar and other top bosses of that cartel escaped arrest. It froze $80 million in assets, including a 10-story building in downtown Los Angeles. It seized $6.7 million in cash, $7 million in bank accounts, and $30 million in gold and jewelry at 13 stores in the Los Angeles Jewelry Mart. Prosecutors also indicted Banco de Occidente, a Colombian bank that assisted the launderers. The bank has since pleaded guilty and has paid $5 million in fines and penalties to the U.S. government. Never before had banks not charged with crimes been commanded to return narcotics proceeds wired out of the United States to their overseas branches. Those identified proceeds, $433 million worth, were filed for civilly by the U.S. government from the financial institutions acting as unwitting conduits for the cartel, which included the Bank of New York, Citibank, Bank of Credit and Commerce International, and Republic National Bank.

The "La Mina" or Polar Cap investigation was triggered by a known money launderer bragging to a federal agent that a ring of jewelers in Los Angeles could launder $25 million a month. The laundering scheme was brilliant in its simplicity:

1. Traffickers delivered boxes and bags of cash from drug sales to phony jewelry stores in New York, Houston, and Los Angeles.

2. In Hollywood, Florida, Ronel Refining—a gold refiner—created phony gold bars and arranged bogus sales with a Los Angeles jeweler to create the appearance of a legitimate business transaction.

3. The cash was loaded onto trucks and hauled to a wholesale jewelry business in downtown Los Angeles.

4. The Los Angeles jeweler deposited the money in the bank, using the phony sales to explain the large amount of cash—thereby skirting the Treasury reporting requirement (Currency Transaction Reports).

5. The Los Angeles jeweler then transferred the proceeds by wire to accounts in New York. From New York, the money was transferred again by wire to accounts in Montevideo, Uruguay.

6. In Montevideo, a currency exchanger, fronting for narcotics traffickers, again transferred the money to the accounts of the international cocaine cartel based in Medellin, Colombia.

Operation Bolivar

In the midst of a crackdown against the cartel, Colombian police in the fall of 1989 located the financial records of one of the world's top cocaine traffickers, Jose Gonzalo Rodriquez Gacha. Those records were consequently passed to the DEA for action. In December 1989, the DEA, as a result of its investigation of those records, announced it had frozen $61.5 million in Gacha's assets in Luxembourg, Austria, England, and the United States. On December 15, 1989, in an armed confrontation with Colombian police, Gacha was shot and killed.

INVESTIGATIVE TECHNIQUES

Money is, of course, at the root of all financial crimes. Investigators and prosecutors must know how to uncover hidden transactions, trace illicit funds, find and prove bribes and embezzlements, show secret profits, and so on. This requires a familiarity with the money flow patterns through the business and banking systems and financial records, as well as a knowledge of how the typical illicit scheme operates and how they can be unraveled. All investigators worth their salt know that the most complex and sophisticated cases are based not only on luck but three primary factors: informants, informants, and informants. However, even if investigators have a cooperating source in the Cali cartel, cases can be dismissed that have taken months to put together through a failure to maintain investigative efficacy and proper prosecutorial preparation.

The techniques discussed in this section involve the application of routine investigative procedures—interviews of the target and third parties, public record searches, analysis of basic financial and bank account records, all of which are within the capabilities of virtually all investigators and prosecutors.

Money laundering investigations must incorporate all aspects of traditional police investigative techniques and resources, including:

- Street-level enforcement.
- Undercover operations.
- Surveillance.
- Search warrants.
- Sophisticated intelligence gathering and analysis.
- Informants.
- Criminal, as well as financial, investigative experience.

Case Initiation

The first stage of a money laundering investigation is the case predicate or initiation. The majority of cases are initiated by (1) a "cold hit" (the happenstance discovery of a large amount of currency or negotiable instruments on an individual's person, in luggage, in a vehicle or residence, etc.), (2) ongoing narcotics trafficking or RICO investigation, (3) a referral from an informant, or (4) a referral from a financial institution. Often enough, investigators utilize the "cold hit" seizure to avoid identification of an informant who has triggered the seizure, particularly when the fruits of the crime cannot be allowed "to walk."

Case Development

The next step of a police investigation, initiated by a referral, would be to establish all facts as reported by the suspicious parties. This includes interviewing a representative of the financial institution or informant, and conducting traditional police work to discover as much as possible about the suspect(s) and the suspicious incident.

A distinction should be made early in the investigation between "money hiding" and "money moving" schemes. *Money hiding* schemes are intended merely to conceal the source of existence of illicit proceeds. *Money moving* schemes hide the actual source *and* provide an apparently legitimate source for the funds. Technically, money laundering refers only to the second situation, although the term is often used imprecisely to describe both.

In conducting the investigation it is necessary for the agent to delineate, for prosecutorial purposes, the elemental differences between hiding and laundering. The most common money hiding methods are:

1. The illegally acquired funds may simply be hoarded, spent, or deposited inconspicuously.

2. The illicit funds may be deposited in, or transferred through, financial institutions and the reporting requirements (*Bank Secrecy Act*) evaded by engaging in multiple transactions under the $10,000 reporting limit (smurfing).

3. Fictitious accounts may be established, or deposits made to known accounts in fictitious names, using phony social security or tax identification numbers—a method often used in collusion with dishonest bank employees.

4. The trafficker may open an account under the guise of a business, exempt from the Treasury reporting requirements, such as a restaurant.

5. The launderer may corrupt bank officials into ignoring filing requirements, facilitating the use of fictitious accounts, or falsely certifying a business as an exempt account.

6. The trafficker may smuggle the illicit currency directly out of the country by ocean container, private airplane, body carrier, or other vehicle, again evading the Currency and Monetary Instrument reporting requirement of the *Bank Secrecy Act*.

Investigative Data Bases

With the increased enforcement of money laundering legislation, the U.S. Department of Treasury began compiling a much more comprehensive and extensive data base of currency transactions, profiles, and methodology. This enabled the Treasury to begin utilizing advanced computer technology to conduct network and link analysis studies on the currency reports filed. Federal data bases, such as the Treasury Enforcement Communications System (TECS) and the Financial Crimes Enforcement Network (FinCEN), are relatively new initiatives and accessible by members of the law enforcement community.

In essence, the TECS data base is a composite of information with specifically assigned levels of access. That composite consists of, but is not limited to:

1. The Border Enforcement System, consisting of five major files that contain documented violations and suspect information on persons, vehicles, vessels, aircraft, and businesses. This information is received from multiple sources within the U.S. Customs Service and other participating agencies.

2. The Private Aircraft Inspection Report System, which provides aircraft arrival data, overflight exemptions, and records of intended arrivals. Although this data base is not a suspect or look-out system, it provides significant investigative and intelligence data for law enforcement analysis.

3. The Currency and Monetary Instrument Report (CMIR) system, which catalogues information contained in the required filing of U.S. Customs form 4790 on individuals who transport currency or monetary instruments in excess of $10,000 into or out of the United States.

4. The Currency Transaction Report (CTR) system, providing investigative personnel with information on subjects that are involved with currency transactions in excess of $10,000 in U.S. currency or its foreign equivalent. Financial institutions are required to report these transactions to the Internal Revenue Service on IRS form 4789.

5. The Foreign Bank Account (FBA) system, which provides investigative information on each United States citizen who has a financial interest in, signature, or other authority over a bank account, securities or other financial accounts in a foreign country. Such persons are required to file Treasury Form 90-22.1 on an annual basis.

TECS, as a source of financial information for currency investigations is unparalleled.

The FinCEN, located in Northern Virginia, is a composite of various law enforcement and regulatory agency data bases housed within one building. This center serves as a centralized national clearinghouse and repository for criminal-financial intelligence and expertise. FinCEN is responsible for receiving, storing, analyzing, and disseminating all information collected pursuant to the *Bank Secrecy Act*. Upon receipt of this information, FinCEN can analyze the information contained in the reports and identify financial characteristics of criminal markets. FinCEN also assists in developing law enforcement strategies.

Access to FinCEN-generated information is not limited solely to United States government agencies. At the same time, however, extreme care must be taken to ensure that the information contained in the data base is not misused or improperly or erroneously retained. Upon the written request of a domestic or foreign law enforcement agency, the Secretary of the Treasury can authorize FinCEN to provide information requested about a named subject or organization. Access to this information is predicated, however, on the requirement that the subject or subjects are bona fide targets of an ongoing criminal investigation.

Modus Operandi

Criminal methodology associated with money laundering schemes normally seems to be some form or variation of one of the following three basic schemes.

1. Proceeds moved off-shore surreptitiously or through banking channels may be returned to the owner as a sham loan, acting as an investment or payment for nonexistent goods and services. Documentation to prove the illicit source of the funds and true nature of the transaction are normally beyond the subpoena power of the United States and, if a bank secrecy jurisdiction is involved, unavailable through treaty agreements. Proceeds repatriated by this method not only come back washed, but tax free; if "interest" is paid on the sham loan, they may even provide additional tax deductions.

Most sophisticated traffickers use banks or business fronts in countries with strict bank secrecy laws, such as the Cayman Islands, Luxembourg, and the Isle of Man, and no treaty relationship with the United States. In such cases, there is virtually no way to obtain documentation of off-shore transactions. Jurisdiction may be obtained, however, over a foreign bank that transacts business in the United States and a subpoena served on its local U.S. branch.

2. Real estate or other transactions can be manipulated to hide the use of illicit funds and provide an apparent source of legitimate income. A buyer and seller may agree to convey property worth $2 million for a stated price of $1 million, with the balance paid in illicit funds under the table. When the property is sold, the "profits" provide a source of apparently legitimate income. The same principle can be used to generate false profits in other commercial transactions, particularly between related entities.

As usual, in developing a case in this type of scheme, an inside source is a valuable asset. An independent appraisal or some comparative sales data may establish that real property was sold substantially below market value. Techniques to trace illicit funds and find hidden assets may be employed to find under-the-table payments. These techniques attempt to trace the underlying funds to their source. The investigations generally proceed in reverse order to the acquisition process: back from the asset to the account from which the funds were drawn to the source of deposit to the account, and so on until the ultimate payer is identified.

3. The use of a legitimate business enterprise as a front to conceal and commingle illicit dollars goes back to the 1960s in the Pizza Connection case. Ideally, the business is one that deals primarily in cash, has relatively fixed costs, such as a movie theatre or massage parlor, and is exempt from bank currency reporting requirements. Bars and restaurants, which meet two of the three criteria and also provide a ready location for illicit sales and clandestine meetings, are probably the most common fronts.

Laundering schemes conducted through a front business are best proven through the cooperation of an inside source, such as the business's accountant or tax preparer, or by infiltrating an agent. Indirect methods of proving laundering activity include ratio analyses, sampling, and flowchart techniques.

In the ratio analysis and sampling technique, there may be an overreporting of the revenues of a front business to launder funds, which can result in an imbalance of the normal ratio of costs to sales: Costs will appear unduly low compared to reported revenue. This is why the ideal money laundering operation would have relatively fixed costs against sales. Surveillance of the suspect enterprise may provide additional evidence that revenues are being underreported, by showing low customer traffic, and so on. Surveillance may also permit sampling procedures, a standard audit method in which a count of the number of customers or sales during a given period is used to extrapolate total sales.

A laundering operation may also be revealed by flow chart techniques. Business enterprises used to launder funds generally have common ownership or other connections, usually under the control of the targets. Therefore, corporate and other business filings and records showing the principles in the suspect businesses should be obtained and patterns of ownership noted. Financial and bank records can then be subpoenaed to trace the flow of funds between the enterprises.

Forfeiture and Asset Removal

Unlike other types of investigations, a financial case is not over when the suspect is arrested. The investigation continues incorporating any information surrendered by the suspect. More importantly, however, the investigating officer can now utilize legal powers to freeze and/or seize the suspected proceeds of the crime. The financial analysis, including flowcharts, financial statements, and net worth analysis, is essential at this stage in determining the amount to be forfeited. There are three basic methods by which properties are forfeited: administrative, civil judicial, and criminal judicial. In the administrative forfeiture, notifications of forfeiture are sent to potential owners. If there is no response to that notification, the items are forfeited without court action. If a claimant files a claim and cost bond during an administrative forfeiture, a civil forfeiture proceeding is undertaken, in which the claimant has an opportunity to assert defenses to seek relief. The criminal judicial forfeiture is accomplished in conjunction with the criminal prosecution of the defendant and is part of the court's final judgment.

As a side note, through March 1990 the Department of Justice's forfeiture fund has shared over $354 million in cash and $46 million in tangible property with participating state and local law enforcement agencies. The establishment of separate asset identification and the targeting of proceeds by forfeiture squads have become effective in enhancing the overall goal of taking the war to the wallet and having the criminals pay for investigative resources attempting to put them in jail.

CONCLUSION

As can be clearly seen from this chapter, the detection and investigation of money laundering are constantly evolving. However, this evolution should not be misunderstood in respect to complexity and enhanced techniques on the part of the violators. Like any other criminal activity, violators will seek out the point of least resistance whether, in the case of money laundering, it be body carriers, smurfing, or wire transfers.

Throughout the United States today, particularly in the cities that have been identified as money laundering hubs, such as Los Angeles, New York, and Miami, several successful federal, state, and local financial enforcement task forces are working in close cooperation. These composites have mutually shared benefits, particularly the personnel resources provided by state and local communities for such labor-intensive activities as a Title I (wiretap) or surveillance. The federal agents, however, can provide international and national networks of information such as TECS, the DEA data banks (NADDIS), the El Paso Intelligence Center, or FinCEN. Working in conjunction on a task force allows for that information to be provided by the federal agents to their state and local contemporaries in a much smoother fashion than application through departmental entities.

In closing, the laws and investigative techniques, such as undercover operations, have allowed for ever-increasing seizures and arrests throughout the world. The weakest link in the commerce of narcotics trafficking is money; efforts to attack this vulnerability, then, should be increased to assist in stemming the flow of narcotics throughout the world.

37
Forgery and Credit Card Fraud

John G. Kennedy

In defining and analyzing the various aspects of forgery, we must begin with the basic elements and reflect on each area related to the subject. After an examination of the basic academic term and the establishment of a common definition of this crime, practical investigative techniques and some miscellaneous fraudulent schemes will be discussed. In this way the investigator can better understand the motives of the forger, and will be better able to establish a criminal action against the suspect.

Check forgery is not just the reproduction of the handwriting of a true account holder; it is making or completing an instrument that is acceptable as an authentic document. There is no need to actually duplicate style or handwriting on any item presented for cashing. Obviously, a person accepting a check cannot know if a signature is authentic unless they know the signer.

The actual legal definition of forgery and various related terms are contained in the *Model Penal Code* of the American Law Institute (1962) under the general title of "Theft." However, for purposes of this chapter we will use the following definitions for terms which apply to the crime of forgery:

1. *Written instrument* means any instrument or article containing written or printed matter or its equivalent, used for the purpose of conveying or recording information, or constituting a symbol or evidence of value, right, privilege, or identification which is capable of being used to the advantage or disadvantage of some person (including wills, deeds, credit invoices, drivers' licenses, checks, currency, security, public records, prescriptions, and so on).

2. *Complete written instrument* means one that purports to be a genuine written instrument fully drawn with respect to every essential feature. An endorsement, attestation, acknowledgment, or often similar signature of statement is deemed a complete written instrument in itself.

3. *Incomplete written instrument* means one that contains some matter by way of content or authentication, but that requires additional matter in order to render it a complete written instrument.

4. A person *falsely makes* a written instrument when he or she makes or draws a complete written instrument or an incomplete written instrument in its entirety, which purports to be an authentic creation of its apparent maker or drawer, but which is not such either because the maker or drawer is fictitious or because, if real, the maker did not authorize the making or drawing of the document.

5. To *falsely complete* an instrument, a person transforms an incomplete written instrument into a complete one by adding, inserting, or changing matter, without the authority of anyone entitled to grant it, so that such complete instrument appears or purports to be in all respects an authentic creation or fully authorized creation of and by its ostensible maker or drawer.

6. A person *falsely alters* a written instrument when, without the authority of anyone entitled to grant it, he or she changes a written instrument, whether it be in complete or incomplete form, by means of erasure, obliteration, deletion, insertion of new matter, or in any other manner, so that such instrument in this altered form appears or purports to be in all respects an authentic creation of or fully authorized by its apparent maker or drawer.

7. *Forged instrument* means a written instrument that has been falsely made, completed, or altered.

Forgery defined: A person is guilty of forgery when, with intent to defraud, deceive or injure another, such person falsely makes, completes or alters a written instrument. The term written instrument includes: a deed, will, contract, public record, check, commercial instrument, money, securities, stamps, prescription of a duly licensed physician, etc. In general, forgery statutes refer to the alteration of any document that may evidence, create, transfer, terminate or otherwise affect a legal right, interest, obligation, or status.[1]

CHECK FORGERY

This chapter focuses on five major types of criminal forgery grouped into two areas. The first group includes check forgery and credit card abuse; the second includes forgery of identification, currency, and travelers' checks.

The U.S. Department of Commerce estimates that over 28 billion checks are transacted each year in this country. FBI statistics indicate that a good percentage of these checks are forged, thus completely worthless to those who accept them. This drain from our economy is passed on to the consumer in higher prices for goods and services.

Check forgery, in contrast to crimes such as robbery, assault, and burglary, is distinguished by its low social visibility. Check forgers are individuals who fit within the particular environment that they select to strike. They are the epitome of the white-collar criminal, with pride in their craft and usually nonviolent. Forgers' single most important concern is their supply of checks. Checks are, of course, the main tool of their trade, just as a hammer is to a carpenter. "Good" check forgers want to work with superior-quality material.

The amateur forger generally does not require the complex schemes that professionals use to bewilder and confuse their victims or trackers. The amateur is more concerned with completing the act with as little difficulty as possible and moving on. For this reason, they generally obtain starter checks from financial institutions through a secondary source or with no personal identification at all.

Investigators, whether criminal or civil, must be aware that persons, legitimately or not, can open checking accounts in almost any bank in this country with a minimum preliminary deposit and the absolute minimum of personal identification. They will be assigned checking account numbers and issued a series of starter checks, generally for an initial $25 deposit into a new account. Although the starter checks show an assigned account number, they lack the particular name and address of the account holder. They are issued for the new customer's use while waiting for personalized checks to be prepared. If individuals are legitimate, there is no threat to the community; however, if spurious identification was used in opening the account, we can rest assured that they will be heard from shortly. Amateur forgers are fairly easy to deal with. They are using the crudest of tools, that is, starter checks and usually secondary personal identification such as social security cards, lighting company bills, or other unofficial sources. Generally, they pass checks at supermarkets or department stores, usually for small amounts. When asked to substantiate their identities, they quite often abandon their objectives. Of course, the major defense against this type of operation is insistence on several sources of primary identification during the transaction. Later, this chapter will analyze the various safeguards that can be used by those in private enterprise to insulate against all types of check-passing schemes, but first, the various types of forgery are examined and safeguards discussed in general.

Types of Check Forgers

Most checks that become the subject of criminal investigation are acquired by three separate methods: (1) burglary, (2) posing as a legitimate businessperson, and (3) having them actually printed by an individual using blank check stock and any combination of account titles, banks, and account numbers.

Burglary. Generally, checks obtained during a burglary are taken as an afterthought. Of course, the prime objective of an individual who enters another's premises or business establishment to commit burglary is currency or other valuables that can be converted easily into cash. On occasion, burglars are frustrated because an informed public is likely to safeguard currency and those items of jewelry that have particular sentimental value. Thwarted in the primary goal, the burglar will take almost anything of value to pay for the time invested. Checkbooks belonging to a business or corporation, for some reason, are quite often left unsecured and sometimes in full view. Whether an individual takes checks because they are left unguarded or takes them deliberately is difficult to determine. One thing is certain: Burglars do come into possession of legitimate corporate checks, and those checks in turn are the subject of forgery investigations.

Often the burglar who steals checks also takes the firm's check-imprinting machine to add to the authenticity of the document. Normally, burglars are not in the forgery business. They have little knowledge of banking procedures, and will ordinarily try to sell the stolen checks to an associate for a percentage of the issued amount or to sell the blank checks in bulk. But whether they use the checks themselves or transfer them to someone else, the transaction of checks originally stolen during burglaries accounts for a large percentage of forgery losses each year.

Posing as a Legitimate Businessperson. The second type of individual can best be labeled the "paraprofessional forger." Such persons are truly involved in forgery and have a good working knowledge of the many intricacies of check handling by banking institutions. In addition, they take a great deal of time to plan the entire operation. For example, they use good commercial stock and unquestionable identification, set up a believable background for possessing the check, and actually sell themselves and their product to their victims.

Paraprofessional forgers actually set themselves up in business, or what has every appearance of being a legitimate enterprise. By first renting a small storefront and applying to the local town or county clerk for a certificate of business under an assumed name, they set the stage for securing corporate checks from a local bank. To the general public, they look like any other small business just starting out in a commercial venture.

Of course, the first thing any legitimate merchant must do is establish a financial background and get the cooperation of a local bank. The individual engaging in this type of forgery will look no more suspicious than any genuine businessperson in securing the cooperation of the banking institution. Armed with the certificate of business or incorporation, the person approaches a chosen bank, declares the intention of beginning business, and requests its cooperation. Indeed, the banking officer will most likely not only grant the request but encourage the forger in becoming a member of the local business community.

At this point, the forger need only return to the rented storefront and wait the two or three weeks required for the bank to process the new account request and print the commercial checks. Once these checks arrive, the storefront operation will normally close and the paraprofessional forger, armed with a new printing of commercial checks, will be in the business planned all along, the business of preying on the public.

Printing. The third type of forger can best be categorized as "the true professionals," because they customarily print their own commercial checks. Using blank commercial check stock, they print the account holder's name, the bank from which the check originates, and the required microencoded account identification characters on the check, making the document appear to have been issued by a bank in the normal course of its daily business. They can also reproduce other documents, including many primary sources of identification.

Of the various types of forgers discussed, the professionals not only are aware of various banking policies and procedures, but usually have a good working knowledge of the Federal Reserve Board regulations. They traditionally have backgrounds as professional printers and usually some type of banking training and experience. They are obviously the most difficult forgers to investigate.

They are designated "professional" because their exposure in committing the actual crime is limited to one confrontation with the victim. As with all forgers, there are few or no indications of unusual behavior during the actual transaction. They do not place themselves in jeopardy of being apprehended, the one exception being, of course, when they offer the checks to be cashed.

The chances of being physically identified by the tellers or cashiers with whom they do business are certainly slim. The time for a check to go through the routine banking procedure for actual payment, be refused by the drawee bank, and return to the place it was cashed is normally a week to 10 days. After that period, few employees would remember any details of the transaction.

In contrast, both of the other types of forgers are subject to identification by any number of methods. The paraprofessional must confront many potential witnesses even before securing the check stock: the person from whom the storefront is rented, the town or county clerk's representative, the banking officer who opens the account, and, of course, the teller or clerk with whom the business is finally transacted. The "semiprofessionals," or burglars turned forgers, ordinarily leave some physical evidence of their identity at the scene of the burglary and can be observed during the commission of the crime. In addition, as noted, they are unfamiliar with check forgery, and their novice approach is fairly easy for potential victims to recognize.

An authentic-looking check does not begin and end with securing commercial bank stock. The objective in check forgery is to create a commercial instrument that is pictorially and physically acceptable as a genuine document. Aware that it is easier to sell a check that looks good, forgers ordinarily add their own professional touches to the check. Simply by using a typewriter to insert the date drawn and the name of the payee on the face of the check, the forger begins to create a reasonable facsimile of an authentic document. In addition, using a check-writing machine to indicate the amount of the check and, in some cases, even applying a "certified" stamp to the check face, gives the document the appearance of authenticity.

Once a check has been obtained, the forger must consider how to transact the instrument in order to benefit monetarily. The goal is to use the same check stock within the same area for the longest period of time without being apprehended or forced to seek additional identification. Generally, a check forger can work an area with the same check stock for about 14 days without encountering problems.

Case Examples

Perhaps the best way to understand the mind of the forger is to discuss and analyze some case histories of individual subjects.

In a recent forgery case, the subject opened a series of savings accounts in various branches and local banks. Within three weeks, he had opened 27 separate accounts. Each time he entered a bank, he used the same approach in dealing with the unsuspecting employees.

To begin with, he was young (25 to 28), well dressed, well groomed, and seemed to be fairly well educated. On entering the bank, the subject would approach the platform personnel and indicate that he wanted to open a savings account with a small initial deposit of $25. While completing the application, he would engage the bank employees in a conversation, telling them that he had just found a job with a particular firm, that he got paid a certain amount biweekly, and that he intended to make small deposits on those paydays to please his parents. Of course, the firm's name was by mere coincidence the name of the check stock in his possession. When leaving the bank, he sometimes asked one of the tellers for a date or made some advance toward another employee.

Having successfully set the stage, when he returned to the bank on "payday," he would be immediately recognized as the nice young man who was trying to please his parents by saving a portion of his salary each payday. All he had to do at this point was present his passbook, a deposit ticket in some small amount, and his "paycheck." The teller (the same one he had asked for a date the week before) would react by immediately and without question cashing his check. Multiply this incident by the number of accounts he had opened and the substantial loss that was generated is obvious.

In another case, an individual entered a large jewelry retailing firm. He approached a salesperson and declared that he had just proposed to the girl of his dreams and she had accepted. He wanted an engagement ring and, of course, it had to be the biggest and best in the store. Money was no object, because he was overwhelmingly happy over his betrothal.

The forger identified himself, giving his name and address. After picking out the largest diamond he could find, he requested a bill from the jeweler. He indicated that he would return the following day to pick up the ring and would bring a certified check to pay the bill, which should include the cost of the diamond ring, commission and store fees, and taxes.

In this case, again, the forger built confidence between himself and his intended victim. The jeweler thought he was standing on firm ground because he was told he would receive a certified check, and he was convinced that certified checks are as good as, if not better than, cash. The forger was also relying on the fact that businesses like to turn their investments over quickly.

In studying these typical schemes, we see that in each case salesmanship and confidence are two of the primary attributes which, coupled with an authentic facsimile of a check, make the forger so successful. One is able to develop some insight into how this type of antisocial behavior actually fits into our commercialized society.

Ordinarily, forgeries occur under less elaborate circumstances. Traditionally, forgers want to hit and run, that is, pass as many checks in as little time as possible within an area—and then move on. For that reason, most will rely on the product they have and subject themselves to some type of personal identification procedure.

IDENTIFICATION SOURCES

Forgers usually know what type of questions will be asked and the best kind of identification to produce when transacting a check. For instance, if using corporate checks, they will indicate that they either own or work for the company represented on the check. They will also carry some type of primary identification to further build the illusion of acting in a normal manner during the transaction.

Sources of primary identification are certainly not as abundant or easily available to the general public as other types that are worthless in themselves. With this in mind, check forgers sometimes steal valid drivers' licenses and accompanying personal identification and make checks payable to those particular names. At other times, they buy from various sources identification that has been stolen from the mail or parked automobiles or during the commission of a burglary. The professional forger can also reproduce drivers' licenses in blank form and simply insert the desired name, address, and other personal identification.

Besides drivers' licenses, there are several other means of verifying an individual's true identity. These include automobile registration certificates, major credit cards, and employee identification cards issued by companies, the armed services, and police departments (these should carry a photo and description and signature). Several types of cards and documents are not good identification. Some of them are easily forged and others were never intended to be used as identification. They include social security cards, business cards, insurance cards, bank books, birth certificates, library cards, and so on. When merchants require more than one type of primary identification during a check transaction, they do not automatically ensure against a potential loss; they do, however, diminish their vulnerability.

COMPLAINT NOTIFICATION

On receiving a complaint of forgery, the investigator should immediately obtain and preserve the documents as evidence. It must be protected from handling because it might contain additional evidence of the forger's identity, including latent fingerprints and handwriting standards. The document should be safeguarded for latent fingerprint elimination, even though this possibility is extremely slim. In addition, comparisons are possible in the event that typewriter and check imprinter identification is required.

After the document has been secured, the investigator should question the employee involved in the transaction. The interview must include a complete description of the suspect, the cover story for the suspect's possession of the check, whether the witness actually saw the suspect sign the document, and the type of identification used. This information is immediately recorded for future reference and comparison in similar forgery cases in which the same checks are used.

Of course, in the investigation of forgery, as in all criminal investigations, interviews of complainants and witnesses should be put in writing and made part of this case. Determining who is to be the actual complainant is one of the first critical areas to be discussed. For example, as a general rule, the complainant is the one who has sustained a loss as a direct result of the forgery and, for this reason, need not be the person or company whose name appears on the check.

If a quantity of checks is stolen during the commission of a burglary in one community and is later forged and transacted in another, the actual place of cashing becomes the place of occurrence for the forgery. In addition, the owner of the business that accepts the check will sustain the loss. The actual account holder whose checks were stolen and forged will not generally be held responsible for any loss incurred.

For this reason, when canceled checks are returned by banks and the true account holders discover irregularities, they should return all unauthorized checks to the bank for credit. These checks, will, in turn, be forwarded as chargeable items against those individuals who honored them as genuine documents. Of course, the actual account holder will be required to start any forgery investigation because only the person authorized to sign the checks can subscribe to an affidavit of forgery. Forgery complaints must formally originate with a declaration of an unauthorized signature.

FORGERY STATEMENT

Even in the simplest forgery investigations, statements are required from the account holder (affidavit of forgery), from the complainant (regarding sustaining loss), from the teller or cashier (describing the transaction), and from all persons who witnessed the transaction. All statements must specifically identify the questioned document and indicate that the check was unauthorized and that there was no financial gain by any witness in the transaction.

Statements should begin with the formal identification of the witness, that is, name, age, residence, place of business, occupation, and relationship to the occurrence. The actual document should be identified as follows:

> I have been shown a check by the police/investigator described as follows: Check number 101, dated: January 1, 19XX, drawn on the account of XYZ Associates, 1000 Northern Blvd., City, State, payable to John Q. Public in the amount of $1000.00, signed Joseph Doe as maker.

The witness is asked to initial the document and this action is included in the statement. For example, "I have initialed and dated this check for future identification."

The statement should continue with a brief description of the relationship between the witness and the check. If the witness is the account holder, the statement would indicate the following:

> I have examined the described check and wish to state that I did not author it, nor did I give anyone else permission to issue it. Further, that due to the issuance of this check, I did not directly or indirectly benefit in any way.

In the event the witness is the complainant, the statement should indicate the date, time, and place of acceptance of the check and how much loss was sustained as a result of the transaction. The statement must also completely detail the facts involved in receipt of the forged item and identify the perpetrator by alias as well as by physical description.

INVESTIGATION OF FORGERY

To control and combat forgery in a community or business, a specialized unit trained in the various aspects of forgery and aware of the total impact of this crime has to be established. Studies conducted by the federal government and many state and local agencies indicate that persons involved in forgery develop a style of doing business that dictates not only their methods of operation but even the continued use of names with which they easily identify. Time and time again, forgers use derivatives of names they have used in the past, probably because they develop a sense of security and react more naturally in public using names that are somewhat familiar.

For this reason, most larger operations develop a name file system through which individuals involved in forgery may be identified by the various aliases used during the course of their careers. This type of record keeping can also help correlate active investigations.

The two major areas in forgery investigations are handwriting comparisons and personal or photo pack identification. Most major police departments have facilities for document examination, as do many state police agencies and the FBI laboratory in Washington. In the private sector, numerous document examiners are available; however, their expertise should be carefully validated.

Most document examiners require the original document. In fact, any expert opinion reached by using other than the original certainly deserves to be challenged. Along with the original document, known handwriting standards of suspected individuals should be submitted for comparison. Ideally, when signatures are being obtained for comparison, the individuals should be instructed to write the questioned signature. Of course, this should be accomplished with their complete cooperation and without first showing them the document.

The space available for the required signature must be approximately the same as the area within which the questioned signature is located. Handwriting standards should be taken on single sheets of paper, so that the individual submitting to the test is unable to copy any prior signature. Most document examiners require several known standards before conducting a comparison. It should be realized that the investigator will be unable to sustain a criminal case based on these handwriting standards alone.

In the area of photo or physical identification, the investigator should be guided by the procedure specifically outlined in Chap. 29. It might be noted, however, that forgers are well aware of their nemesis, the camera. Merchants and bankers would be well-advised to install cameras at check cashing areas, not only as a protection but for their obvious deterrent effect.

Those in law enforcement and related fields realize that in spite of the potential risk in accepting checks, merchants, bankers, and the business community in general must extend trust to the public and accept these documents. This type of extension of credit has become a necessity in today's society. It is the duty of law enforcement officials, therefore, to communicate their knowledge and expertise to private industry to control this potential economic drain.

SAFEGUARDS AGAINST FORGERY

Merchants in the community should be made aware that there are many ways to deal successfully and safely with the public and, at the same time, minimize this potential for loss. Some suggestions for lessening opportunities for successful forgery follow:

1. Require identification (more than one piece of primary identification) that is current and unaltered.

2. Require an endorsement in the clerk's presence (even if the item is already endorsed).

3. Make sure the check is not postdated and that it is drawn on an existing bank.

4. Educate employees about the widespread existence of forgery and its potential for loss to the business.

5. Beware of "quick sales," that is, carry-out items (TVs and so on) purchased during the evening or weekend, when banks are normally closed.

6. Beware of large sales using certified checks delivered after cost, tax, commission, and often miscellaneous charges have been calculated in advance.

7. Above all, stress that anyone accepting a check for a purchase or service must know the endorser either personally or through various types of primary identification. The salesperson should be able to honestly state that he or she could locate the customer if the need later were to arise.

8. Establish a clearly stated policy for cashing checks. The policy might include issuing check cashing cards, verifying every check through the bank that issued it, and frequently reviewing company procedure with employees.

9. Make sure the person presenting the check fits the check. For example, young persons would not generally have social security checks issued to them.

10. Checks showing signs of alteration should not be cashed. Watch for misspelled words, smudged words, and eraser marks. On checkwriter-prepared checks, watch for poor letter or numeral spacing.

CREDIT CARDS

The credit card is the most rapidly growing form of commercial exchange in the United States. Credit cards have become a way of life, accepted by both the consumer and the business community, and are a vital part of the nation's economy. To all intents and purposes, we now have a second currency in this country. That currency, in the form of a simple piece of plastic, has grown beyond the wildest dreams of even its most ardent proponents.

In the United States today, about 8000 companies annually issue 500 million credit cards. That is approximately 2.5 credit cards for every man, woman, and child in our country.

Types of Credit Cards

Many types of credit cards are in use today. The best-known group is the travel and entertainment (T&E) cards. They are issued by major corporations such as American Express, Diners Club, and Carte Blanche. These cards are oriented toward a particular segment of the consumer market—the businessperson and the expense account user. These cards are, and always have been, obtained by written application. The cardholder is billed within a one-month cycle, and payment is due immediately.

The next major, and possibly the largest, group in the United States is the oil company cards. These are also oriented toward a particular segment of the market—specifically, motorists. They can be used for gasoline and oil, automotive service, and to a certain degree allied services such as hotels and restaurants.

Another group consists of department store cards (which can be used only at the store or branches of the store issuing them), airline cards, restaurant cards, hotel cards, and many others, all of which are oriented toward a small segment of the total consumer market.

The last major group consists of the bank cards. Originally, banks entered the credit card field through huge mass mailing campaigns, and cards were sent to all current depositors. Any person who maintained a checking account, automobile loan, or savings account received a credit card. Some adverse publicity was generated by this unsolicited mailing of credit cards, and banks soon discovered that people had savings accounts in the names of their dogs, cats, or parrots. News stories relating these incidents became the comic relief of the day.

Liability Restriction. The federal government enacted a law that went into effect February 1, 1970. The *Truth in Lending Act* (Public Law 91-508, Title V, Section 502) provided that no credit card could be issued to a cardholder except as a result of a written application. The maximum liability to cardholders was reduced from $100 to $50. In addition, the credit card issuer had to provide a stamped, addressed envelope for recipients to return the card if they did not want it.

The law further stated that every credit card company must put on the card some method by which the cardholder could be identified, and required that by February 1, 1971, every credit card company in the United States must be in compliance with this provision. A card should have one or more of the following items: (1) a signature panel for the cardholder to sign, (2) a photograph of the cardholder, (3) a thumbprint, or (4) some means of electronic identification.

Criminal Involvement. Criminals who fraudulently use credit cards generally fall into two categories. The first is the organized criminal, that is, a member of any group of people who organize and conspire to defraud a credit card issuer. The second is the occasional thief.

The organized criminal wants a lot of cards with which to make a quick killing. The cards may be acquired in quantity from certain places, such as the plastics manufacturer. Because these plants must be extremely security-conscious and employ a vast array of intrusion protection, burglary is generally out of the question. Recognizing this difficulty, the criminal will try to corrupt the employees through involvement with a loan shark, a bookmaker, or homosexual.

The second source of cards in quantity is the U.S. mails, which must be used to reach the vast majority of cardholders. Many cards are lost while in postal custody, through either internal theft by postal employees or mailbox theft.

Occasional thieves may be persons who operate alone and are trying to use a credit card for the first time. If so, they very soon become proficient when they experience the ease with which merchandise can be obtained.

They may be lone operators who use credit cards for a living. They are not adverse to trying to get cards from the sources previously mentioned, but usually obtain them from prostitutes, those who prey on homosexuals, or pickpockets. The cards could be the proceeds of burglaries, robberies, auto thefts, and other crimes.

Many businesspeople visiting major cities become involved with prostitutes. In the beginning, while the prostitute entertains the client, an accomplice removes his wallet. It was discovered that this was not desirable because the victim raised the alarm almost immediately. This method of obtaining credit cards has been refined to removing only a few credit cards, substituting "burned-out" cards (cards previously stolen and used), and replacing the client's wallet.

As a result, the victim does not know for some time that the credit cards have been stolen. By the time he does find out, there has often been heavy use of the card. An investigator, upon inquiring into the circumstances of a reported loss, often has to cut through a tissue of evasion before ascertaining the actual facts.

LAWS PERTAINING TO CREDIT CARD USE

The American Express Company sponsored a study of credit card fraud by a research team headed by two professors at Columbia Law School. This study proposed a model bill, which has been enacted in 41 states. In 1969, the New York State Legislature enacted changes in both the *Penal Law* and the *General Business Law* in relation to credit cards. Entitled the *Credit Card Crime Act*, this bill amended both laws to specifically define additional credit card crimes and provide for increased penalties. These changes and additions, which have subsequently been amended, were made in both the forgery and larceny sections of the *Penal Law* as follows:

Credit Card Defined. A *credit card* is any credit card, credit plate, charge plate, courtesy card, or other identification card or device issued by a person to another person that may be used to obtain cash advance, a loan, or credit or to purchase or lease property or services on the credit of the issuer or of the holder.[2] Simply, a credit card is a negotiable instrument through which three different parties enter into an agreement for the sale of goods and or services for which the buyer will pay at a later date.[3]

Debit Card Defined. A *debit card* is any card, plate, or other similar device issued by a person to another person that may be used, without a personal identification number, code, or similar identification number, code, or similar identification, to purchase or lease property or services.[4]

Possessing a Stolen Credit Card or Debit Card. A person found in possession of a stolen credit card or debit card can be charged with fourth-degree criminal possession of stolen property, a class E felony. This change recognizes the value of a stolen credit card or debit card as an instrument for the commission of many crimes, in addition to the intrinsic value of the card.[5]

A person who possesses two or more stolen credit cards or debit cards is presumed to know that such credit cards or debit cards were stolen. This section, by adding additional presumptions, was designed to facilitate the prosecution of possessors of stolen property. These presumptions are aimed at the professional criminal who frequently deals in stolen credit cards or debit cards and the property stolen by reason of having been obtained by the use of stolen or forged credit cards or debit cards.[6]

Credit Invoice. A credit invoice is a commercial instrument that does or may evidence, create, transfer, terminate, or otherwise affect a legal right, interest, obligation, or status. It is used to show that a sale or service was completed between two parties, the merchant and the credit cardholder. It represents a promise on the part of the cardholder to repay a third party, namely the card issuer, the amount charged, according to the terms previously agreed upon.

Possessing a Forged Card. A person found in possession of a forged card can be charged with criminal possession of a forged instrument, a class D felony.[7]

A person who possesses two or more forged credit cards or debit cards is presumed to know the cards were forged and intended to defraud.[8]

Possessing an Illegally Obtained Ticket for Air Travel or Any Other Service. If a person is found in possession of a ticket for air travel or other service obtained by use of a stolen or forged credit card, he or she can be charged with criminal possession of stolen property, and the degree of crime would depend on the value of the ticket as established on the face of the ticket or, if no price is stated, the amount charged the general public by the issuer.[9]

A person who possesses three or more air travel tickets obtained through the use of a stolen or forged credit card is presumed to know that the tickets were stolen. All airline tickets purchased with a credit card have clearly imprinted on the face of the ticket the credit card number and the name of the cardholder.[10]

Incidentally, one of the most massive conspiracies involving credit cards is directed toward the procurement and sale of transportation services. The following is a typical case: A credit card is stolen in a Los Angeles hotel room and turned over to a dealer or fence, whose agent immediately takes the card to the airport and procures thousands of dollars worth of tickets from different airlines. Card and tickets are then flown to New York, where another round of ticket buying occurs. Although tickets purchased with credit cards cannot usually be exchanged for cash, they can be exchanged for tickets to other destinations. These tickets are then sold in a bar or other place of public accommodation.

Obtaining a Card by Lying about Credit Information or Identity ("Fraud App.").

A cardholder who lies about his or her credit card information, identity, or both—or puts such false information on a credit card application—to obtain the issuance of a credit card, can be charged with third-degree grand larceny, a class E felony.[11]

Other sections in the penal law with application to the misuse of credit cards are those pertaining to forgery, criminal possession of stolen property, criminal impersonation, varying degrees of larceny, and under certain conditions conspiracy. Those sections outlined in this article constitute the major thrust of the Columbia law study.

Reviewing those sections of law, we find that various presumptions are contained in the credit card statutes. For example, possession of a stolen credit card is a felony. The burden of proof, however, is on the investigator to show that the suspect knows the card was stolen. This is generally difficult in the absence of supportive information or an admission. The law recognizes this difficulty and further states that the possession of two or more credit cards is presumptive evidence that the possessor knows they were stolen.

The problem of the loss of credit cards while in postal custody was mentioned. Should such a card containing a signature be recovered in possession of a suspect, he or she can be charged with criminal possession of a forged instrument as a felony. The law is unusual in that it does not have to be proved that the person in whose possession the card is found actually signed it. The only thing required is to prove that the cardholder, the person for whom the card was intended, did not sign it or authorize anyone else to sign it.

Under the larceny section, the amount of property obtained governs the degree of larceny to be charged. This is similar to the section pertaining to check forgery in that the degree of larceny is dependent on the amount for which the check is issued. However, taking a credit card from another person, or appropriating for one's own use another person's credit card which has been found, is grand larceny (a felony). Clearly, the law recognizes the potential that can be realized through the fraudulent use of the credit card.

CREDIT CARD ABUSE

An estimate, generally accepted within the credit card industry, is that yearly losses due to the fraudulent use of credit cards amounts to over $128 million. This figure has risen 33 percent over the past decade. Methods of using the credit card illegally range from a simple purchase of an item to elaborate schemes involving multiphased purchases and returns for credit. The most common method is for the user to work from a shopping list. The "plastic workers" know which items to purchase since they already have buyers waiting. By supplying $200 wristwatches for $100, they turn a profit for themselves and satisfy their customers, thus ensuring further business.

Another common ploy is for employees of businesses that accept credit cards to use misplaced or stolen ones for their own profit. In restaurants, the method involves charging the customer's bill to a fraudulent card and pocketing the customer's cash. Restaurants also provide an excellent opportunity to swap a stolen card for a customer's card when ringing up a charge, thus providing the thief with a fresh card good for at least several days.

A popular scheme also used in restaurants, service stations, and businesses accepting both credit cards and large amounts of cash is "double banging." The waiter, clerk, or attendant inserts the customer's credit card into the machine for imprinting along with two or more blank credit invoices. Returning the credit card with the invoice for authorized signature, the employee retains the blank invoices for future use. These invoices, in the required amounts, can then be simply substituted in cash sales by an employee, who merely pockets the cash tendered.

Organized credit card thieves employ certain techniques designed to upset and disorient salesclerks. They usually also have a working knowledge of exactly the kind of security measures used by the various credit card companies. They attempt to manipulate the exchange in such a way that salesclerks fail to follow proper security procedures. Cautious plastic workers limit their purchases to keep under the "floor limit" (the maximum amount that can be charged on a credit card without undue attention or investigation). Organized thieves are professionals; so they are always prepared for the unusual. In almost every case, they have identical forged identification with them and will be quick to produce it if asked by sales personnel. Usually this forged identification is an operator's license.

Some professional thieves have developed the capability of altering account numbers on stolen or lost credit cards by placing the lost or stolen card in an embossing machine and striking over certain numbers that readily lend themselves to alteration; for example, changing a 3 to an 8, a 5 to 6, or a 7 to a 9. The result is obvious—the "hot card" is transformed into a brand new source of credit.

A new fraud scheme, which has recently plagued the Northeast, is known as "shave and paste." In this system an embossed authenticator character is shaved off a stolen or lost credit card, and a new character is pasted on the card in its place. The "new" card then used shows no holds against it.

INVESTIGATION

Credit card fraud is considered a white-collar crime inasmuch as no force or violence is used in completing the crime. However, the fact is that in many instances these cards are obtained as the result of crimes of violence. Investigation into their possession or use may possibly lead to the solution of more serious crimes, such as homicide, robbery, rape, or burglary.

Most credit card abuse is detected by the cardholder when the monthly bill is received. This is when the theft or loss of individual credit cards is discovered and when unauthorized charges on card legitimately presented to dishonest clerks for purchases and services are found. The remaining incidents of credit card abuse are uncovered at the time of presentation by alert salespersons who check "hot sheets" or call for authorization; and some stolen credit cards are recovered by police in effecting arrests for unrelated crimes.

The actual investigation of this type of crime centers around the credit invoice and the eventual recovery of the stolen credit card. The investigator should treat the suspect credit invoice as primary evidence. It should be safeguarded for the possibility of future handwriting comparison and presentation in court. The forged credit invoice is prima facie evidence of the commission of the crime.

In general, the forged credit invoice should be treated by the investigator exactly like a forged check. They are both substantially the same type of commercial instrument in that they imply the same type of obligation on the author.

Investigations of credit card abuse are often confusing. For example, the legitimate cardholder who discovers the forged invoice during the regular billing cycle will rarely be the complainant in a criminal case. In fact, in most cases the complainant will be either the company who accepted the credit card for payment or the credit card issuer. The cardholder will, of course, be a witness in the case, required to testify to not having signed the credit invoice nor authorizing another person to sign the cardholder's name on it. A statement or affidavit of forgery must be taken from the cardholder pertaining to each unauthorized credit invoice involved.

The next logical step to be taken is to determine the actual place of occurrence. There is a good possibility that it is not within the investigator's geographical jurisdiction; and in some cases the credit card may have been used in another state or even another country. To determine the exact place of occurrence, all the investigator need do is examine the credit invoice. Generally, two areas are completed on each invoice by machine imprint. One is the merchant's authorized charge imprint, and the other is the imprint made by the inserted credit card. The merchant's imprint includes the firm's name, city, and assigned account number. From this, the place of occurrence can easily be determined.

Continuing the investigation, the salespersonnel and owner of the establishment where the card was tendered should be interviewed. Of course, they must be questioned about possible identification of the individual who presented the credit card, any particular details regarding the sale, the item or service sold, and whether or not the card is on the "hot list" or if sale authorization was obtained. It must be remembered that, as in check forgery cases, the time elapsing between occurrence and eventual discovery is generally a minimum of 30 days. For this reason, it is usually difficult to obtain a reasonable description of the card abuser. However, some salespersons are extremely competent in retaining even the smallest details of past transactions. This potential source of information cannot be overlooked.

In a prosecution, each and every credit invoice fraudulently signed becomes a separate charge of forgery. In addition, individual larceny charges can be made for each total amount charged on each credit invoice.

Discovering a missing credit card being used at a particular location is another way in which credit card abuse is uncovered. Generally, the merchant has determined that the card was reported lost or stolen and has detained the suspect. The responding investigator should interview the store owner and find out the general circumstances. Usually the suspect has made or attempted to make a purchase using a stolen credit card. The investigator should take possession of the credit card and examine it for any alterations or changes. If a sales slip has been signed, it should be impounded, because it is the basis for a forgery complaint.

After talking to the store owner, the investigator should let the suspect's story be told without interruption. Remember that a forger is a con artist and will attempt to convince the investigator that he or she is the actual cardholder, perhaps trying to establish identity with a fraudulent driver's license or with the contents of a stolen wallet. The investigator should determine if the suspect has other credit cards and whether they are in the same name or different names. In many states the possession of two or more cards is presumptive evidence that the suspect knew they were stolen and intends to use them unlawfully.

After talking to the suspect, the investigator should contact the credit card security division by telephone to find out if the credit card was previously reported either lost, stolen, or never received. For instance, if the card is stolen, they will generally know the circumstances and if other personal identification was also stolen. They will also have additional information pertaining to the true cardholder, usually including the first name of the cardholder's spouse, previous home address, phone number, social security number, place of employment, length of time there, salary range, and bank and charge accounts. Supplied with this information, the investigator can further question the suspect. Even with stolen identification, the suspect will not be able to answer these questions.

At the conclusion of this preliminary investigation, the following facts have so far been developed: (1) A merchant alleges that the suspect committed or attempted to commit a crime by using a stolen credit card for the purchase or merchandise at his place of business. (2) A representative of the credit card company says that the card in question has been reported lost, stolen, or never received. (3) A suspect, although possessing some identification, cannot answer questions that the true cardholder would know. At this point, sufficient prima facie evidence has been established to detain the suspect in lieu of a criminal complaint.

Consider at this point the criminal charges that could be placed against the suspect: possession of a stolen credit card, which is a felony; second-degree forgery if a credit invoice was signed; larceny if the merchandise is in the suspect's possession. The degree of larceny would, of course, depend on the value of the property. If the card was stolen from the mails and it bears a signature, the suspect may be additionally charged with criminal possession of a forged instrument.

An investigator can become involved in a credit card situation also when a person is taken into custody for an unrelated crime and found to be in possession of credit cards during a routine search incidental to the arrest. At the earliest moment, the investigator should contact the credit card companies involved and ascertain whether the cards have been reported stolen and under what circumstances.

If the credit card company records indicate that the loss has not been reported, they will immediately contact the cardholder. In many cases, this is the first inkling the cardholder has that the credit card is missing. Many crimes have been solved through in-depth investigation of how suspects acquired the credit cards in their possession. There are many documented cases of homicides being solved, robbery suspects identified, and burglars and muggers apprehended.

CREDIT CARD SAFEGUARDS

The criminal justice system must be prepared to help merchants by keeping them from being victimized by credit card abuse. The credit card industry has made great strides to protect itself within a comparatively short period. Sophisticated operating procedures and enlightened management have made the credit card organization viable. Security has been advanced to the point that there is a free exchange of information among all segments of credit card investigation agencies. The credit card industry has initiated many innovations, including modern technological programs to prevent fraud losses, such as embossed character reading, magnetic tape, embedded codes, printed codes, holograms, and dual dating credit cards. In addition, in the future the industry is looking to issue "smart cards," which will have a miniature computer chip inside each card.

These procedures have not only protected the issuing agency, but also enhanced the integrity of the particular credit card. Using a set of simple procedures, merchants can accept credit cards with confidence in payment for goods and services.

It takes two parties to complete a credit card fraud, an unsuspecting merchant and a credit card thief. A credit card thief can be successful only if someone is careless. The following procedures are suggested to merchants who accept credit cards:

1. Most major credit card companies issue monthly cancellation bulletins. Check the presented credit card against the cards listed in this bulletin. Remember, the listed card numbers have been reported stolen, lost, or never received.

2. Examine the card for any noticeable alterations.

3. Examine the validity date on the card. Is the card valid, or has it expired?

4. Examine the signature panel on the reverse of the credit card. Has it been altered or overwritten?

5. Examine the signature on the card and the signature on the credit invoice. Look for contradictions. Is the name misspelled? Are there differences in handwriting?

6. Be alert for indiscriminate or nonselective buying without regard to size, color, or, more important, cost.

7. Be suspicious of the customer who questions salespersons about the floor limit and who charges just below the limit.

8. Be alert for persons arriving near closing time and causing confusion to upset salespersons.

9. Be suspicious when large tips are given in restaurants.

10. In general, when in doubt or when suspicious, call the credit card company for authorizations. Most major companies maintain 24-hour, toll-free authorization centers; merchants should be urged to take advantage of this service.

COUNTERFEITING (CURRENCY)

The U.S. Secret Service reports that, during the past decade, American counterfeiters have produced over $780 million worth of fake U.S. currency, of which $93 million has been successfully passed to individual merchants and banks. The remaining $687 million was seized prior to circulation.

Probably the one word automatically equated with the subject of counterfeit currency is "plates." The plates used in the printing of bogus currency are generally thought to be the product of some unscrupulous craftsperson whose artistic ability is wrongly directed.

In today's society, automation has been a major thrust for change, which has unfortunately also benefited the counterfeiting business. With sophisticated photo offset presses, modern forgers can reproduce almost any paper that represents a tangible value. During the eighties, office machine copies (OMC) have become very prominent with the increased quality of color copier technology. The nation's currency, stock certificates, stock debentures, travelers' checks, and official identification all have fallen victim to dishonest presspeople. These individuals reproduce and attempt to circulate millions of dollars each year in all types of counterfeit assets.

Legitimate objects that represent value in our commercial dealings—national currency, stock certificates, travelers' checks, and so on—have numerous technical qualities demanded by the true issuing agency. These agencies still employ craftspersons to engrave the printing plates that will be used in the production of their representative products. This fact alone is responsible for one of the major defects that appears on all counterfeits, whatever their origin. Simply, photo offset reproductions do not have the clearly defined lines of the original and lack any third-dimensional quality in the portrait area of the document.

Regulations of the Securities and Exchange Commission for authentic issues further require that the portrait and corporation title be in raised printing. Thus authentic issues can immediately be identified because the photo offset press is incapable of fulfilling this requirement. It is limited to making a photocopy of the original, from which all subsequent duplicates are made. Therefore, the finished items are flat and without any embossed areas.

The most common reproductions continue to be counterfeit currency. One of the major safeguards to protect a business against this potential loss is the installation of a "black-light" identification system near the cash register. This simple, effective, and reasonably priced tool immediately identifies counterfeit currency by an abnormal color reaction when the questioned bill is exposed to the light.

In the absence of this aid, there are several guidelines for detecting counterfeit money. The best method of detecting a counterfeit note is to compare it with a genuine of the same denomination and series, looking for differences, not similarities. If available, a small magnifying glass should be used to look for the red and blue fibers in the paper.

The portrait and oval background comprise one of the main areas that clearly show the definable impressions of a genuine bill. A genuine portrait should appear lifelike and stand out distinctly from the fine screenlike background, while the photomechanical process usually causes dullness in the portrait and extra dark or light shading in the background.

The Treasury seal, as well as the serial numbers, should be clear and distinct. On suspected bills, watch for irregularities in the seals, sawlike points; they are generally uneven, blunt, and broken off.

The "check letter" and face-plate number appear on the lower right corner, just above the denomination numeral. On suspected bills, the merchant should be certain that these items appear clean and that the check letter matches the check letter at the upper left corner. It is important to learn to pick these items out, for they are among the principal recording items to warn businesses of counterfeit money.

The main agency involved in the control of the national currency is the U.S. Secret Service. They have field and resident offices in most major communities in the country, and are fully cooperative with all individuals requesting assistance regarding the identification of questioned currency.

COUNTERFEITING TRAVELER'S CHECKS

Hundreds of millions of traveler's checks are legitimately exchanged every year for goods, services, and cash, representing a large percentage of business transacted, especially in areas catering to tourists. Traveler's checks are more readily accepted by most businesses than personal checks because they represent an authentic face value in the amount shown.

Merchants, because of their lack of experience in accepting traveler's check, are particularly vulnerable to being victimized by passers of forged or stolen checks. Naturally, outside those areas where people are used to dealing with tourists, traveler's checks are not normally part of the daily business transaction. Because of this unfamiliarity, many merchants will unquestioningly accept them in payment for goods or services.

There are two major sources of unauthorized traveler's checks: counterfeiting and theft. The same technology employed in the reproduction of currency is used to counterfeit traveler's checks. The major method for this type of counterfeiting is, once again, the photo offset press.

Generally, the same methods suggested to identify counterfeit currency can be employed to identify bogus traveler's checks. Comparing the presented check with specimens made available by most major traveler's check issuers will generally cut losses to a minimum. The black-light system of identifying counterfeit currency can also be used with traveler's checks. In addition, most major suppliers of traveler's checks offer 24-hour service for authenticating their products.

Stolen traveler's checks can be controlled by instituting a basic acceptance procedure within the business. Most major traveler's check issuers require the buyer to sign the face of the check in the upper left corner at the time of purchase. When the check is used, they require a countersignature on the lower left face of the check. Naturally, the two signatures should be compared by the merchant accepting the check. This basic signature comparison is normally all that is required by the issuing company to assure those accepting the check that it is being cashed by the same person who legitimately purchased it.

Merchants who honor traveler's checks should be acquainted with some tricks passers may use. Some use one hand as a cover while pretending to countersign checks on which the signatures have already been forged, trying to make the merchant think he or she is watching the checks being countersigned. In another instance, the passer lets the merchant see the top check, then blocking the view with this check, fakes signing the remaining items, which have already been fraudulently countersigned. Again, the passer is trying to make the merchant think he or she is watching the countersigning of the checks. The passer then palms the top check and transacts the rest. Naturally, in both instances, all the merchants need do is make sure they actually see the countersigning of each and every check.

Another scheme typical of passers is to resign the stolen checks in the upper left corner with a thick-line felt-tip pen to cover the original signature, then let the merchant watch the countersigning of each check with the same felt-tip pen. When comparing signatures, merchants should make sure there is no indication of an erasure or alteration or another signature under the felt-tip signature in the upper left corner. Whenever in doubt, they should insist on watching a resigning on the back of each item. In addition, following the same suggestions for cashing traveler's checks as for cashing other checks should control this problem.

CONTENDING WITH THE PROBLEM

In dealing with the many intricate and complex problems that arise within the business and financial community, the investigator must be cognizant of the fact that checks, credit cards, currency, and so on are basic to the everyday dealings with the public. In accepting these instruments for a service or product, merchants and their employees should try to adjust their roles during the various phases of transactions.

The merchant has many obligations to meet, including payroll expenses, rent or mortgage payments, bills for merchandise, insurance costs, utilities, and all the unseen expenses of running a business. A customer entering the business can scrutinize the merchandise, complain about service, and in general become so obnoxious that the sale becomes frustrating to the merchant and salespersons. These are the things that must be accepted in business.

However, after the customer has selected the merchandise or service, the obligation imposed by the purchase must be satisfied. At this point, the roles are reversed; the customer is now asking for his or her merchandise to be accepted, and the businessperson truly becomes the customer. It would be fairly safe to predict that, if the safeguards suggested in this section are used, annual forgery losses could be cut in half.

Unfortunately, we are confronted with reality. Successful forgers usually strike during the busiest hours, when there are many people in the place of business, making it almost impossible to use normal safeguards. They may also strike after banking hours, making it impossible to check the authenticity of the account. During these times the forger runs the least risk of being discovered.

There is also another psychological factor involved at the time of any sale, that is, a profit is being made. Businesspeople should not let this promise of profit blind them to obvious faults in checks and currency they accept. There is no profit in accepting a worthless instrument.

NOTES

[1]Section 170.00 Penal Law—N.Y.S.

[2]Section 155.00 Subd. 7 Penal Law—N.Y.S.

[3]General Business Law Section 511.Subd. 1, N.Y.S.

[4]General Business Law Section 511.Subd. 9, N.Y.S.

[5]Section 165.45(2) Penal Law—N.Y.S.

[6]Section 165.55 Penal Law—N.Y.S.

[7]Section 170.25 Penal Law—N.Y.S.

[8]Section 170.27 Penal Law—N.Y.S.

[9]Section 155.20 Penal Law—N.Y.S.

[10]Section 165.55 Penal Law—N.Y.S.

[11]Section 155.05 Subd.2 Penal Law—N.Y.S.

38

Fraud Control
in Banking

Charles J. Bock, Jr.

Robert F. Stoll

In the past 10 to 15 years, American businesses have seen a steady and frightening increase in lost assets due to fraudulent activity. These losses have not only taken a heavy toll in profits but have tarnished company reputations and caused company failures. What is equally alarming is that the theft of these billions of dollars results from the efforts of highly organized and sophisticated groups who know the inner workings of most business activities. Competition between companies, the high volume of business, and lax controls have also greatly aided this criminal activity.

The banking community has experienced steadily increasing frauds as well. Recent problems in the banking industry have caused intense competition among banks. In an environment where mergers, acquisitions, and bank failures are commonplace, customer service has become a number one priority, as banks struggle to attract new customers. This emphasis on customer service has attracted a criminal element that has learned to take advantage of banks across America. In addition, banks are holders of highly liquid assets, making them a target for fraud. High dollar losses have been encountered in connection with deposit accounts, commercial loans, consumer loans, and credit cards. Banks have also had their share of losses due to employee dishonesty. Thus there has been concern on the part of management to institute programs geared to halting this growth. These programs have been implemented in a growing number of banks, along with an expanding role for the investigative function.

Two areas are necessary in the fight to stop, or at least lessen, crimes against business: (1) prevention and (2) internal control and investigation. Prevention,

Modifications and updating of this chapter for the second edition was done by Lisa Arning, President, Corporate Loss Control Company.

of course, is the first step. When it fails, a professional investigation team is needed to find out who did it and why, and then pass on its findings to management. The last is what makes a bank's investigation department different from traditional law enforcement, because industry has the power to make changes in its business environment. Before discussing the investigative role, it is essential to understand prevention, since an investigation will usually start with an examination of the weaknesses or breakdown of prevention controls.

THE PREVENTION MODEL AS AN INVESTIGATIVE TOOL

The development of a sound loss prevention program requires that a great deal of attention be given to the sophistication and general capabilities of the persons who engage in fraudulent activities or white-collar crimes. Such persons often have higher-than-average intelligence and more than a second education, and frequently they come from middle- to upper-income families. Ingratiating at social events and wise to the ways of the business world, they make formidable enemies.

When such individuals become organized into groups, the results can be devastating. During the late 1970s the London press carried a series of articles about a group that had successfully defrauded various financial institutions on the European continent of approximately $500 million. They were so highly organized that those arrested were said to be part of the middle management of the organization. Equipped with the latest printing presses and a carefully selected, highly trained staff, they entered a number of countries in pairs. Each pair carried two sets of forged passports, an assortment of forged and counterfeit checks, corporate and government bonds, letters of credit, letters of introduction, and banking and insurance company references. In several instances, the banks and insurance companies were fictitious. To add credibility to these organizations, they also carried prepared financial statements and stock certificates. This scheme has become increasingly popular, and many American financial institutions have since suffered losses.

Equally sophisticated but less subtle are the efforts of organized crime, which has been highly successful in defrauding the banking and business communities. Through the use of prostitution, gambling, loan sharking, bribery, and drugs, many people inside and outside business organizations have been persuaded to lend their position, influence, and credibility to this criminal element. This has resulted in success in opening fraudulent accounts, obtaining credit, and using services of bank employees to hide or disguise illegal financial transactions.

Against this backdrop, it can be seen that prevention programs should not be treated lightly. These programs must be carefully developed so that the end-product will be easily understood by employees at all levels. Equally important is continuously updating and disseminating information, remaining alert to the current forms of criminality, and knowing the possible problems of staff and customers that could give rise to fraud.

Many publications and services provide a wealth of information in such categories as general business climates, specific industry problems, businesses susceptible to criminal domination or influence, and individuals associated with the criminal element. Many banks have developed an index of such information through computer information systems or manual programs, which is readily available to those seeking this vital knowledge. So that this information can be utilized properly, it is also important that senior management have clearly defined policies and standards for the types of business relationships desirable in meeting corporate objectives.

Theft of Identity

During the 1980s a scheme involving the theft of consumer identities became extremely popular among organized rings of white-collar criminals. This scheme continues to cause significant losses to American banks. Criminals have gained access to personal information, such as a customer's address, employer, date of birth, social security number, salary, mother's maiden name, bank account numbers, and so on, and they have used this information to commit frauds. They have done such things as withdrawing money from accounts belonging to unknown customers; ordering new checks, debit cards, and credit cards using the victim's identity; opening new credit accounts; applying for loans; and taking out insurance policies—all the time pretending to be customers that they are not.

Banks must safeguard all personal customer information, as the information is priceless in the hands of those who know how to misuse it. In addition, procedures must be in place that ensure proper verification of customer identity before access is granted to an account or before credit and loan relationships are established. Since many financial institutions use computer-programmed point-scoring systems to grant credit, consideration should be given to creating electronic verification systems designed to prevent this specific type of fraud.

Account and Credit Fraud

There should be a clearly defined practice for opening accounts or granting credit. "Know your customer" is an adage as appropriate today as when banking first started. In keeping with this advice, it is important to verify information supplied by the customer before the customer is permitted to draw funds, especially when checks deposited are drawn on out-of-area banks. Verification of addresses, phone numbers, and employers is of particular importance. Research has revealed that fictitious addresses and employers are used over and over again to commit frauds. Once a fraud has occurred involving such fictitious information, measures should be taken to ensure that no new accounts are opened using the same address or employer, unless in-depth research has been completed. A simple computer program can help accomplish this review. In the instance of business accounts, a visit should be made to the firm's location to establish the validity of the operation. A review of financial information should give careful consideration to the authenticity of receivables and sales activity. Inventories should be examined, particularly from the standpoint of marketability. Much information can be obtained from specific trade groups and organizations, such as the Better Business Bureau. When a doubt exists, the investigation department should be asked to review the applicant before any account is opened.

Once an account or loan has been established, it is important to periodically review account activity or loan payments for signs of inappropriate behavior. A high volume of in-and-out account transactions and frequent overdrafts could be a clue to fraud. Loan payments made by checks drawn on individuals or companies not known to be part of the borrower's business activity could also indicate fraud.

Check Cashing Fraud. Check cashing practices should also be of great concern. The banking community loses many millions of dollars each year through the cashing of forged or fraudulent checks. The theft and cashing of checks, as well as counterfeiting, have become highly organized. In years gone by most counterfeit checks were manufactured in print shops. The advent of desktop publishers and laser printers has added a whole new dimension to counterfeiting. The laser printer is able to print with MICR (magnetic ink character recognition) encoding, making it difficult for check-processing computers to detect a counterfeit. If MICR ink is not used, it may still be difficult for check-processing systems to detect a counterfeit since many banks have added optical scanners to their processors. If the numbers are recognizable to the optical scanner, there is no need for MICR ink. Prevention is in the hands of the acceptor of the check. Tellers and other employees who process checks should be alert to checks drawn on known customers that do not look exactly "right." The wrong color paper is a common tip-off. In addition, employees should be advised of all customers whose checks have been counterfeited through an internal warning bulletin.

By far the greatest source of blank checks for the criminal is the bank customer. In this instance, established procedures and investigations will not stop the activity. Too many bank depositors regard their blank checks in the same light as any other piece of stationery. Continuous reminders to customers about the importance of safeguarding checks is probably one of the best approaches. Some of the reminders for bank customers follow:

1. Safeguard your checkbooks, statements, and canceled checks.

2. Destroy obsolete blank checkbooks and loose checks.

3. Use only the form of checks approved by your bank.

4. Write checks carefully, to prevent alterations (leave no space where words or figures can be inserted).

Notify bank immediately:

1. If you change your address (to assure safe delivery of checkbooks, statements, and canceled checks).

2. If you do not receive your monthly statement at the usual time (forgers rob mailboxes to get signatures).

3. If your ordered check forms are not received within a reasonable length of time.

4. If you notice any irregularity when you compare your statement and your checkbook record.

5. If any of your blank checks are lost or stolen.

Some banks have conducted check cashing clinics to alert customers to check fraud problems. Local merchants' associations, chambers of commerce, local and federal law enforcement officials, and other citizens' groups have cooperated with bankers in setting up these communitywide projects. This is good community service and shows genuine concern on the part of the bank for the protection of their customers.

Credit Card Fraud. Many bank losses are also attributed to the misuse of credit cards. Thousands of cards are lost or stolen each year, largely because of the careless actions of the cardholder. Here too customer alertness must be constant. However, the merchant is also a cause for concern. The approval of a merchant as a deposit account should be as carefully screened as is the granting of a loan. All the elements of sound credit practice should be enforced. Once approved, the merchant should be instructed about proper procedures, especially those designed to prevent fraud, and should also be made aware of the various types of fraud schemes being used.

Credit card fraud has also become highly organized. Through counterfeiting, the theft of cards from cardholders, postal facilities, airports, and so on, and fraudulent applications, many millions of dollars have been fraudulently obtained through a variety of relatively simple schemes. Speed is a key element for success in these frauds; therefore a business must be alert and quick to react. A carefully planned program, with the proper use of resources such as computers and a knowledge of the types of schemes and patterns of losses, is fundamental. Effective communication is probably the most important ingredient of an early detection system. This system must involve the three major areas of the credit card program: credit, operation, and collection. Each is in a position to detect a variety of potentially fraudulent activities. Defining each area's responsibility and establishing lines of prompt communications between these areas and an investigative unit will do a great deal to reduce loss exposure.

Fraud Prevention Training

It goes without saying, the bank's staff must also be trained in fraud prevention. To be effective, prevention programs geared to staff must be continuous. Meetings, the circulation of warning procedures, and the reinforcement of proper procedures through supervision should be part of this ongoing process. To aid in this program, the investigative unit should be in a position to analyze the deficiencies precipitating losses as well as provide information to lien management about current fraud schemes. It is recommended that staff discussion should be held prior to the Hanukkah-Christmas Season, which is known in most urban areas as the time of increased fraud activity.

On a more formal basis, financial institutions should develop training materials for the education of line management and their staffs regarding significant aspects of external fraud and the potential for loss within their areas of responsibility. Check cashing programs should include information about identification of the check casher. It is generally felt that proper identification should be based on documents that are more difficult to obtain, such as passports of well-known employers, corporate identification cards (preferably with the employee's picture and signature) or an alien registration card with a signature. These documents should be examined for alterations and form. Training materials should include points regarding the instrument being cashed. Methods for identifying forgeries, counterfeiting, alterations and false MICR encoding, and ABA routing symbols are important elements in this review. Popular schemes such as new account frauds, forging official approvals, split deposits (a partial deposit of the instrument being cashed), and kiting should be discussed in detail. The need for cash controls to avoid loss to sneak thieves and the "quick change artist" should be emphasized.

Part of the bank's account opening practices should be alertness to the signs of possible fraud. Why would an individual who lives and works in one part of town want to open an account in another? Why can a prospective customer not offer current bank references or suitable personal identification? Why is an individual who is opening an account for a new business not able to offer information about prior employment or business activity? Many of the fundamentals in opening accounts are matters of common sense, but because they are frequently regarded as simple instructions, they may be overlooked or taken for granted. More than one financial institution has suffered a loss as a result of poor or incomplete reference checks. Once again, no checkbook should be issued before the information on the application has been verified. It is also important to periodically monitor account activity.

To ensure proper account conduct, bank management ought to be thoroughly familiar with the illegal activity known as "laundering." For many years laundering was a means of evading income taxes. In recent years, however, the term has referred to the means by which organized criminal elements carry on or hide illegal narcotic, loan sharking, prostitution, and gambling operations. An unsuspecting bank may open accounts for supposed legitimate businesses and suddenly find large sums of cash, usually in bills of small denomination, being deposited into accounts in amounts that cannot be supported by the stated business purpose. It is not always necessary for the money to be deposited; the clue to illegal activity can also be in the exchange of small-denomination bills for large-denomination bills, using the accounts as the basis for requesting this service. "Exchanging small for large," as it is frequently referred to, can be an essential part of some loan sharking and narcotics operations, since it is not convenient to lend money or purchase narcotics with small denominations. Traveler's checks and personal money orders are often used in these schemes as well. In an attempt to stop such actions, the *Bank Secrecy Act* was adopted. It is important to note at this point that the Act bears criminal penalties of fines and prison terms for noncompliance by a financial institution. Therefore, the bank staff should be familiar with its provisions.

Credit Control and Training. Credit is the backbone of our economy and one of the most important factors in the success or failure of a bank, a great deal of training and control has been provided for the credit function. The banking industry has been highly successful in combating fraud in commercial lending. In large measure, this success is the result of training, controls, and the adoption of sound credit standards. These training programs should continue to emphasize background checks of borrowers, including three- to five-year financial histories, bank references, and general financial conditions within and outside the industry associated with the borrower. In recent years, through specialization, credit officers have become more and more familiar with the businesses of industries to which they lend. They have knowledge of inventories, plant equipment, and accounting practices unique to the specific business. Additionally, time is taken at the outset and over the duration of the loan to visit and observe the company's operation.

INTERNAL CONTROL AND INVESTIGATION

Another major factor in fraud prevention and detection is internal control. This chapter considers internal controls as a primary means of preventing fraud losses and relates this to the bank investigative function.

Organization and Procedures

The growth and diversification of the banking industry today requires that lines of communication among the various levels of management be clear, prompt, and effective. Organizationally, many banks have developed a variety of middle-management levels with fewer line personnel to supervise. This, coupled with clearly defined job descriptions, have greatly aided communication. This, in turn, leads to closer supervision, which helps in detecting internal problems such as defalcation.

In instances of successful fraud, the investigator is able to identify the persons with whom to speak and thus investigate the incident quickly and thoroughly. Timeliness is of great significance to any investigation, and when clearly defined control procedures and levels of accountability exist, there is a greater chance of success in apprehension, recovery, and discovery of what went wrong. The organizational approach also provides for the dissemination of information regarding current fraud schemes. Preparation of operational flow charts provides a visual representation that is useful to those who may be unfamiliar with a procedure.

When completed, charts are analyzed to determine the major areas of responsibility, as well as high-risk and control checkpoints. Once the sensitive areas are identified, procedures can be developed with them in mind. Studies focused on particular fraud schemes as they occur can be helpful in determining the patterns of a scheme and the development of preventive measures. Results of these studies should be retained and used for comparative purposes as new "twists" develop.

Provision should be made for the periodic inspection of the sensitive functions to ensure proper performance. It is also recommended that such internal review be put in written form and that management reports be required on the findings of such reviews. The extent of these reports would obviously depend on the importance of the control or the degree of risk exposure. With respect to major controls or risks, the chart can be an important aid in determining the need for a check-and-balance arrangement, frequently referred to as *dual control*. In its simplest form the physical possession of the asset is entrusted to one individual, while the responsibility to disburse or transfer the asset is entrusted to another.

As investigative tools, clearly defined procedures and flow charts are invaluable, especially when fraud involves a large-scale or complex operation. For the investigation to be successful, it is important for the investigator to have a working knowledge of the operation, the point at which the disappearance occurred, and the people most closely associated with the asset that has been lost. Procedures not only provide a means of defining responsibility but they also set performance standards. Frequently, in a disappearance the investigator is confronted with determining whether the loss was accidental or deliberate. The investigation can be further complicated if persons are not properly trained and responsibilities are not understood. In the absence of training and understanding, it is difficult to assess performance standards. The net effect is an unsolved disappearance and the inability to fix responsibility.

Flow charting and operating procedures are a means of identifying risks and can also be the basis for developing an early fraud detection program. Another approach which can be added is to bring together knowledgeable managers within the institution. The selection should be from all parts of the organization and not just the people associated with the specific function. For example, a credit card program involves a variety of operations, such as purchasing, mailing, check processing, receipts, and handling. Each of these functions exists on a broader scale in other parts of the bank, where the expertise may even be greater than in the credit card area. Since the subject is fraud, the investigation unit should participate.

Each manager, after being given a review of the credit card function, would be asked to contribute fraud schemes from either past experiences or general knowledge. At such sessions, people have been known to express (hypothetically, of course) schemes which they have thought of as a result of being intimately familiar with an operation for a period of years. The next phase is to examine or develop procedures which will prevent the problem and bring together the investigative resources of the bank to coordinate the early warning system.

Personnel Practices. In addition to organizational planning and the establishment of procedures, there are important personnel practices, including uniform standards for screening applicants, that should be thoughtfully developed. In this process, careful consideration should be given to the type of reference checking that will be performed and whether personnel are to be fingerprinted. Such practices are to be the same for full-time, part-time, and contract help. Screening should also extend to consultant services. An in-depth interview is a must for every job applicant. At this initial interview, prospective employees should be impressed with the fact that they are entering into a fiduciary relationship where they will be entrusted with the assets of the bank and its customers. They should be asked about any convictions for unlawful acts, and the need for truthful answers should be stressed. "Convictions" is the appropriate word. The company should be warned against using "arrest," as arrest without a conviction signifies innocence under the law. Conviction need not necessarily disqualify an individual from employment, as long as the crime does not violate the bank's commitment to the Federal Deposit Insurance Corporation (12 U.S.C. 1829), or to its insurance carrier.

Fingerprinting should also be required, although in some states fingerprints may not be taken unless the individual is hired. Although in most cases new employees are subjected to training and careful watching, fingerprinting should still turn up the "bad apples" before they are placed in responsible positions. These procedures should be conducted thoroughly but in an atmosphere of consideration, thus causing only those applicants unsuited for a banking position to rebel. Some businesses have begun to use the services of credit reporting companies for preemployment evaluation. A credit report will verify such things as name, address, social security number, birth date, and employers, as well as reveal any public records of court cases, judgments, bankruptcies, and back taxes.

The importance of a thorough interview cannot be overemphasized. Since a great many former employers are reluctant to disclose information in reference checks, more can be accomplished by an interviewer digging under the surface of an application. Warning signals for employee disqualification include a bad credit record, inordinate indebtedness, and failure to pass a drug screening test. Even with intense screening, however, borderline applicants still may not be turned down if the bank weakly decides to hire them against its better judgment.

Standards of performance set within the bank should be approved by the personnel department. Due to the enactment of civil rights legislation, it is vitally important for an organization to have personnel standards that are fair to all employees. Performance requirements (discussed in greater detail later in the chapter) should also extend to codes of conduct, rules that clearly define management wishes with respect to conflict of interest, the managing of personal finances, and cooperation in investigation matters. These guidelines should be presented to new employees, at all levels, on their first day of employment. It should be pointed out that violations of such codes could be grounds for immediate dismissal. While hiring and performance standards are important prevention tools, they are also important to investigators, since such a program will enable them to make recommendations that will be fair, just, and accepted by management.

Use of Records. Two further aids to the prevention/investigation process, are the proper analysis of losses and the safeguarding of bank records. Reports of losses should state all the circumstances surrounding the problem. Not only will this approach point out potentially weak controls or possible trends but it will have a psychological effect, especially when such reports are to be reviewed by upper levels of management. From an investigative standpoint, these detailed reports will save a great deal of time in establishing the facts of a problem.

When a fraud has been committed, particularly an internal fraud, the records of the bank are vital to a successful investigation. A formal records protection and retention program is as important as the need for operating procedures. All bank records should be identified, and with the aid of the legal and audit departments, time periods should be established for retention. Methods of storage should be set, and if records are determined to be vital, provisions should be made for a formal control system. Adequate locking facilities, fire resistant storage, and the possible need for dual control are some considerations in establishing a proper control system.

Management Auditing: Risk Reduction and Risk Detection. Traditionally, the role of the internal auditor has been to safeguard assets and review the internal controls of the bank through a program of financial audits. This is vital for the prevention of internal dishonesty. The role of the auditor today is as dynamic as the industry itself. Auditors must be aware of the "in's and out's" of such transactions as leveraged buyouts and asset-backed scrutinization. With rapid growth and constantly changing conditions, bank management must confront a wide range of complex problems. The bank auditor, in many cases, is now engaged in a program of management audits, examining not only existing procedures but also the organizational structure to be sure it provides an effective operation with adequate protective controls. The auditor must also determine if there is a proper network of communications within the organization for the dissemination of important information to senior management. In spotting weaknesses in internal controls and in monitoring problem areas, the auditor can be very instrumental in prevention.

Management auditing begins with the auditor becoming fully acquainted with actual operations and operating problems, followed by analysis and appraisal of existing controls to ensure that they minimize risk. With rapidly changing bank programs and reliance on computer technology, the auditor may find it necessary to spend considerable time in several areas prior to an audit in order to become thoroughly familiar with an operation.

As a part of the investigative process, the auditor should work very closely with the investigative unit, establishing the extent of a crime, its prosecution, and any possible recovery. In such matters, each has expertise that can be applied to the resolution of a fraud loss. When a problem is suspected, an audit will uncover a great deal, if not the full extent, of the fraud. This is generally accomplished as a result of the auditor's knowledge of the operation and vulnerable areas. Combining this knowledge with an analysis of fraud trend has led to what has been referred to as a "discovery audit approach," particularly useful for areas of greatest susceptibility to fraudulent attack. Such an audit program has been carried out by pooling the knowledge of audit, investigative, and line management about possible avenues of fraud loss. The results are audit steps to detect fraudulent activity.

BANKING AND INTERNAL FRAUD

Much of this chapter has been devoted to the prevention of fraud losses. By design, this follows the old saying, "An ounce of prevention..." An equally important reason, however, for presenting the material in this fashion is to emphasize the diverse and important role of investigation. Knowledge of procedures, identifying weaknesses and schemes for management, is as much a part of this responsibility as the recovery of assets.

Policies and procedures guarding against external frauds and investigation of these criminal acts are only part of the overall investigative function. Much of the financial investigator's role is devoted to the problem of employee dishonesty.

Employee Dishonesty

In 1990 the FBI completed 13,700 cases pertaining to bank fraud and embezzlement. The losses sustained by the financial institutions who referred these complaints were $1.3 billion. Of these frauds, 55 percent were internal. A glimpse back to 1978 fraud statistics reveals an alarming increase. In 1978 the FBI completed 6000 cases pertaining to bank fraud and embezzlement, resulting in $85 million in losses to financial institutions.

In addition, there are numerous cases of small bank employee thefts that are not investigated or even reported. The types of manipulations that are employed in defalcations are limited only by the ingenuity and innovative capacity of the embezzler. What is clear after an analysis of embezzlement cases is that despite the sound efforts of management and investigators, the general problems of employee dishonesty remain largely unsolved and appear to be growing worse.

Embezzlement in banks has always received much publicity, and it is said that bank employees are subjected to a higher degree of temptation than employees in most other types of business enterprises. The Comptroller of the Currency attributed more than one-third of national bank failures in the late 1800s to criminal acts of certain employees.

Honesty has always been the pillar of the banking system. Dishonesty is contrary to its very concept. Acting as holders for the resources of its depositors and as the clearinghouse through which business transactions are settled, banks and bankers must display the highest degree of integrity. Without this there would undoubtedly be no banks. The notoriety of dishonest employees can erode the foundation of the industry itself.

In most cases of embezzlement the act is committed by a "trusted" employee. Thousands of investigators have heard the supervisor of an employee who had recently admitted to stealing, respond, "Not John Doe, he was one of my best employees." The majority of bank embezzlers do not start their fraudulent activity until they have worked in their positions for an extended period. There are very few cases on record of an employee commencing such escapades during the first year of employment.

Fraud often begins with what the employee deems to be a "temporary loan," which is intended to be paid back within a very short time; but whatever the basis of the initial wrongful act might be, the assumption on the part of the embezzler is that the crime will be relatively easy to accomplish and conceal. Honesty requires a person to resist this temptation under all circumstances. The "test" occurs when there is an urgent need for funds and a person is faced with the opportunity to defraud without fear of detection. If little attempt is made on the part of management to control or minimize defalcations by adopting preventive measures, the temptation may become too great for the employee who needs money. It is clearly unfair to all concerned to allow weak internal accounting controls or poor operating procedures within any organization. Just as an employer in a welding plant must provide protective goggles for the employees to safeguard them against injury, so must employees in a financial environment be protected from harm through adequate systems and internal controls.

Since the degree of profit and success of any institution depends on its management and their goals and ability to gain public support, the primary step in good bank management lies in the formulation of sound business policies. The introduction of good policies and procedures in a bank is the major ingredient for the control of fraud.

Areas of Internal Bank Fraud

Although no two banks are identical, the banking community shares characteristics such as services offered and functions. All members of the financial industry are similarly concerned with internal problems and how they relate to these common areas of operation. As a result, management will often examine past experiences and have knowledge of general industry problems, so that future policies and procedures will be designed to strengthen safeguards against internal frauds.

The following conditions have been known to be susceptible to internal problems in any area of a bank:

- The "one-man shop" or institution, in which an officer has absolute control over an area's operation.
- Weak internal controls and no audit programs.
- A carelessly operated institution, where back office premises are untidy and records are poorly maintained.
- No mandatory vacation policy or career paths for employees.
- Lack of close supervision by the board of directors and/or senior management (especially when rapid growth has occurred).
- Abnormal fluctuations in capital or expense accounts, either in dollar amounts or in relation to other operating accounts.
- Earnings and yields below average, and expenses high in comparison with past operating periods.
- A steady decline in deposits, despite general prosperity in competitor institutions.

Characteristics of Internal Fraud. Studies conducted by the Bank Administration Institute have revealed that bank size is related to internal fraud. It becomes more common as an institution grows. All banks are targets, regardless of whether they have a statewide branching system or just one unit. Many of the frauds reported by banks involve cash or a cash item function. The majority of internal frauds do not involve large sums of money, but those that do often share one or more features. They will:

- Be perpetrated by a supervisor or officer.

- Be concealed for more than one year.

- Involve collusion.

- Entail methods using either fictitious or irregular accounting entries.

The investigation of internal fraud has revealed certain characteristics regarding persons who commonly commit fraud, such as the positions they are most likely to hold within a bank and the types of schemes used. It has also been found that much imagination is used; thus the bank investigator is faced with tremendous diversity.

Fraud is more prevalent among tellers than any other type of bank employee. This is attributable to the position they occupy. Hundreds of thousands of dollars pass through a teller's hands within a period of several days. Accordingly, their duties expose them to one of the "richest" areas in a bank for fraudulent activity. Misappropriation of customer deposits occurs more frequently than any other type of defalcation. Tellers usually commit this type of fraud by choosing the deposits of customers whom they feel will be the least likely to detect the misappropriations. Usually, a teller who feels that concealment is necessary reverts to what is known as "lapping," which is withholding another deposit of an amount equal to or greater than a deposit previously stolen. The teller must continue with this procedure or the fraud will be detected through a customer complaint.

Tellers also resort to "dipping into the till," which is reflected by a series of daily shortages in their proofs of the day's transactions. Their belief is that management will assume a clerical error has occurred rather than a fraudulent act. Sometimes a teller is faced with a large difference at the close of the day's business which cannot be located. These shortages have frequently been traced to another teller from whom cash had been accepted in the form of a teller's cash transfer. Usually the teller from whom the cash was received had removed money from these strapped cash packages and the teller who obtained the currency had not verified the packaged contents, thus experiencing a shortage.

Tellers also steal from their cash position and attempt to offset the resulting shortage by indicating that a check in an amount equal to their theft was cashed as part of their day's activity. They often claim that the check was sent to their transit department but was apparently lost; or, due to the large volume of checks processed by the check-processing area, the check was misplaced. In addition, tellers attempt to forge checks and make withdrawals against customer accounts for the purpose of obtaining funds for their own personal use. Often such transactions will affect dormant accounts, as the possibility of discovery is less than with an active account.

A case was reported in which tellers who had excellent previous work records gained employment at a second bank with the intention of committing a fraud. Shortly after being employed, the tellers sought out several large inactive savings accounts. In order to steal money from these accounts, blank signature cards were obtained and given to accomplices, who signed them in their own handwriting, using the name of the true depositor. The tellers also furnished the accomplices with depositors' account information, such as social security number and spouse's name. On a selected date the tellers replaced the true signature cards with the forged ones. Later, the accomplices entered the bank and made withdrawals. They were able to provide the necessary information about the accounts, and the signatures on the withdrawal slips compared with those on the signature cards. Thus the transactions were approved and payments made. The "insiders" were not used to process these transactions, since it would ruin their work records at the current bank and preclude their future employment at another selected target.

After the fraudulent withdrawals were made, the forged signature cards were replaced by the genuine cards. Several weeks later the "inside persons" resigned with good work records. When the fraudulent withdrawals were detected, management noted that other tellers processed the transactions and contended that these tellers apparently did not compare signatures in accordance with bank policy. The blame was therefore cast on innocent tellers, and there was little or nothing to implicate the parties who committed the fraud.

Lending and Internal Fraud. Bank loan departments are also vulnerable to internal fraud, since thousands of transactions are processed in this area. When loans are granted, either customers are given a check or their accounts are credited, interest and principal payments are collected and posted, rebates are calculated and paid out, various fees are accepted and processed, and stocks or other marketable securities are accepted and held as collateral. In the case of loans, the forgery of a customer's signature is a frequently used method to defraud. However, employees might also tap the bank's "pocketbook" by understating income received in the form of interest payments made on loans or overstating interest rebates for loans paid in advance of maturity. In this manner, the employee would gain from the difference between the true amount of the rebate and the overstated amount. These funds are often taken in the form of a check or deposit to an existing employee checking account.

Other schemes involve bank loan officers who establish credit files and loan notes with all the appearance of legitimate transactions but in reality pertaining to fictitious individuals with nonexistent addresses. These are known as "dummy loans." Officers may do this on their own accord, or they may be receiving a kickback from an outside party who applies for the loans. In a recent issue of *Bank Fraud*, an industry journal, a case was reported that involved a vice president who received kickbacks for $16 million in loans to dubious borrowers. The officer worked for the bank for 21 years and managed to conceal his actions for 14 months. A clever employee can explain the loss sustained when a loan is not repaid as, perhaps, a poor credit decision. Some banks permit the acceptance of notes signed in blank by debtors. These notes are held until needed, usually for the renewal of existing loans. This practice gives an employee the opportunity to defraud, which is usually carried out by increasing the loan amount on the renewal date and diverting the difference between the matured obligation and the raised renewal.

Vulnerability of Assets. Fraud in the safekeeping area of a bank occurs with the misappropriation of securities held for customers and/or the diversion of income from these securities. There have been cases of shortages being revealed when customers requested securities left with the bank for safekeeping. Investigation disclosed that an employee forged a customer's receipt for pickup of the securities.

Fictitious charges to operating expenses is yet another method frequently used to embezzle bank funds. These charges may be small, but over a period of time they can grow into a sizable amount. Overstatement of charges to expense accounts, with cash taken for the difference between the actual amount of the expense and the raised amount, is a common fraud, and overpaying invoices covering expense items and diverting the refund is another method.

The creativity of a dishonest employee is limitless, as the following illustrates.

> A securities clerk in the trust department of a bank was able to steal a large amount of securities by a combination of forgery and changing an address for a trustee account. The clerk, over a long period, studied the habits of the trustees of substantial trusts. After careful consideration, he selected one who was away for long periods. Having mastered the trustee's signature, the clerk went to a fine hotel and registered in the trustee's name. He then submitted a change of address to the trust department, naming the hotel as his residence. The clerk proceeded to embezzle all the securities in the account, carefully forging the signature of the customer on all receipts. When the auditing department mailed its periodic audit confirmation, the address on file for the customer was the hotel, which was given instructions by the clerk to hold his mail, as he would pick it up when he was back in town. The clerk thus received the audit confirmations, which he forged and returned to the bank. He intended to use the stolen securities as collateral for speculation in the market, hoping to be able to return them before the actual trustee discovered they were missing.

Although computer fraud is not discussed in this section, one point that is worthy of mention is the dollar loss that can be sustained in computer fraud within the banking industry. Technology in banking has provided systems that allow employees to access a wealth of customer information, both personal and financial. This information is misused time and time again by employees. Information can be sold to outside parties who perpetrate frauds, or employees themselves can manipulate such things as address and other personal data. It is possible that at a stroke of a finger an address can be changed, thereby rerouting statements and allowing an internal fraud to occur without immediate discovery. In addition, new credit cards and debit cards can be ordered and received by a dishonest employee who takes advantage of systems designed to provide quality customer service. In one instance, the head teller in a savings bank manipulated hundreds of accounts through his teller terminal in the bank's computer system. The individual was prosecuted for embezzling $1.5 million.

Investigations of Internal Fraud in Banks and Bank Documents

The following is a discussion regarding certain aspects of internal fraud investigations which are unique to the banking community.

One of the key elements in a successful investigation, which also minimizes the bank's exposure to additional loss is the immediate reporting of a suspicion of fraud. Management policies should be established which clearly define the steps that line management should and *should not* take when internal fraud is suspected. Taking matters into their own hands or "washing their own laundry" should not be encouraged. Conducting one's own investigations has many drawbacks that are not appreciated until too late. Investigation in banking is hard, tedious, and painstaking work, which is documented by many supporting schedules, notes, and reports. The continued employment or the entire career of the employee suspected of committing a fraudulent act is on the line. The suspicion of fraud should be a closely guarded matter and discussion should be limited to those individuals who have a genuine need to know.

The Investigative Function. The investigation department within a bank must be able to cope with the myriad of cases that occur continually. Therefore its staff must be acquainted with bank procedures and systems, accounting, auditing, trend analysis, flow charting, and laws specific to the banking industry as well as criminal law. The experienced financial investigator must have sound communication skills (both oral and written) and be able to interact with all levels of law enforcement, management, and bank employees. Often a financial investigator will have acquired knowledge of white-collar crime investigations through previous employment in the various federal, state, and local agencies.

The policies for conducting fraud investigations should include coordination of areas within the bank, such as the legal department to provide legal guidance and the personnel department to protect the interest of the employees.

One designated unit of the bank should be responsible for initiating, conducting, and satisfactorily concluding all investigations as well as reporting its progress to interested parties. It should also render final reports to senior management in addition to the appropriate regulatory and law enforcement authorities. These policies and procedures should be set forth in writing and fully discussed within all major areas of the bank. Specific action should not be taken without an agreement between management of the area conducting the investigation, the bank's counsel, and senior management of the affected area. Some investigative actions are:

- Removal of the offending employees from their work areas.
- Discussion with or interview of suspected employees.
- Termination of employees.

Once the area responsible for conducting the investigation is apprised of a suspected fraud and has obtained *all* the available facts, the next step is usually a review of the appropriate related bank records. Although the timing of the employee interview is extremely important and it should be conducted as soon as possible, it should not take place without the compilation of all necessary facts. The approach might change depending on the case; whether, for example, a mysterious disappearance of cash or an apparently fraudulent entry. In the first instance the investigator will be searching for facts and information, while in the latter there is a possibility of evidence and documentation supporting a fraud.

Records as an Investigator's Tool. Bank records are the main documentation that the investigator will have to review; and, where required, the investigator should become familiar with the operating procedures of the area in which the fraud occurred. Most banks have written operating procedures formulated on sound business and internal control practices.

For our purposes, only certain records pertaining to customer transactions will be discussed. Banks are mandated by federal law to retain records of customer transactions for specific periods of time. This assists the investigator in retrieving vital information.

Most banks maintain computer files on all customers so as to easily extract account information. This source of data helps in determining the total banking relationships in existence at a particular institution. Many banks require customers to fill out account applications. Applications should be readily available to the investigator because they are a valuable source of information. Usually, banks also provide their employees with checking accounts in which their salaries are deposited. The investigator should review the account of the suspected employee to ensure that all transactions are in order. This review should go back at least six months prior to the date the incident occurred.

The cashed checks of most banks can be easily recognized. A series of codes or letters will be stamped or validated on the face of each cashed check, which is recorded when it is processed by a teller. The information usually contained on the validating stamp is the bank, branch, and teller identification and the date and time of cashing.

Tracing cashed or deposited checks is facilitated by bank identification symbols. These symbols are called "ABA transit numbers" and were developed by the American Bankers' Association. This numbering code, which allows for the proper routing of a check back to the bank of origin, is listed in the upper right-hand corner of checks. It indicates the city or state of the bank it was drawn against, the name of the bank, and the Federal Reserve Bank District. The key to the ABA code can be obtained through the American Bankers' Association.

The deposit ticket is the main source document for crediting a customer's account. Bank record-keeping systems make it possible to identify a deposit and trace it to its source. While reviewing deposit tickets it should be kept in mind that a deposit recorded as cash could in fact be the partial proceeds of a cashed check. This is referred to as a *split deposit*. Usually the same teller who cashed the check has accepted the deposit from the customer. It can be determined if a cash deposit was "split" by reviewing the teller's cashed checks for an amount greater than the amount deposited. Keep in mind that the back of the check will also have to be examined to assure that it is the item being investigated. The endorsement of the individual who negotiated the check should be present.

Bank signature cards are evidence of the contract between the customer and the bank; therefore, the customer's signature must be on this card. For a corporation, the signature card is accompanied by corporate resolutions of the board of directors, naming the individuals authorized to draw checks against the account. The signature card may also contain other information, such as date and amount of initial deposit, identification of the bank employee who opened the account, the address of the depositor, the social security number or tax identification number of the account, and the assigned account number.

The Investigation

After reviewing all the facts, figures, and supporting documentation, the investigator will use this information to develop the answer to six basic questions: Who? What? When? Where? Why? and How? The facts of the incident should be discussed with the investigator's supervisor to ensure that all investigative steps taken thus far are in line with the "game plan" that was established at the inception of the case. The next step is to obtain background information, if necessary, on the suspect employee through an examination of the personnel file; an employee checking account; or a credit agency report, if thought worthwhile; since this report could indicate a pattern of financial difficulty or heavy indebtedness. It might also be wise, if circumstances warrant, to talk with the employee's supervisor; thus, additional information such as past performance record or any personal problems could be brought to the investigator's attention. If facts are developed showing that the employee appeared to have an abnormally high amount of funds, the source of those funds should be determined.

The Employee Interview. The next step is to speak to the employee. Detailed questions should be planned before the interview. It cannot be stressed enough that the employee should be interviewed and *not* interrogated. A planned list of questions will help the investigator maintain the continuity of the questions to be asked of the subject and will also ensure that main points are covered. Key questions should be carefully positioned, because they might be asked several times to test consistency in answers. Copies or original documents that are to be shown the employee should be arranged in the order they will be presented. The interview itself should be conducted in a conference room or other private office that is away from the employee's work area. In addition to the investigator, a member of the bank's counsel should be present if deemed necessary. Only under special circumstances should the employee's supervisor be allowed to attend the interview.

At present, only law enforcement authorities must inform suspects of their rights (*Miranda*); therefore, the financial investigator does not have to be concerned with this topic. However, a bank with sound business ethics should have a "code of conduct" for all its personnel. In recent years, many corporations have formalized at least broad guidelines of conduct in a "code of ethics." The existence of such codes communicates to the employee senior management's concern for and expectation of ethical conduct. If the bank has such a code of ethics, the employee, at the inception of the interview, should be reminded of certain aspects of the code; for example, full cooperation during the course of any investigation. This introduction will set the stage for the investigator's request for the employee's cooperation and truthfulness.

In the majority of instances, the suspected employee will be a first-time offender; so the interview will most likely be an uncomfortable experience. In order to induce the employee to speak freely and honestly, it is necessary to establish a pleasant rapport. The proper attitude for an investigator is one of courtesy, frankness, and sincerity, combined with *maintaining command of the situation*. The employee should never be allowed to dominate the interview, and the investigator should never be placed on the defense by lack of knowledge. Even strong circumstantial evidence is not justification for jumping to hasty conclusions; do not be accusatory!

As the interview proceeds, the investigator should observe the physical actions of the employee which could be used as a gauge to measure truthfulness (for example, a tendency to repeat questions or overemphasis on minute points). The investigator should always create an impression of having complete knowledge of all facts concerning the suspected fraud, but it is crucial to state only known facts.

During the course of the interview, outline form notes should be taken that are brief but contain pertinent facts and statements. The employee should be advised that any new information that is presented during the interview will have to be verified and that a second interview might be necessary. If, during the interview, there is an oral admission of the crime, the employee should immediately be advised to submit a statement in writing. The statement of admission should contain all relevant facts and should be signed and dated by the employee. It would be wise to have a witness sign the statement also. If the bank seeks restitution, this would be the time to have all legal documentation completed in addition to arranging for a schedule of repayment. Based on either a written or an oral statement of admission, the employee should be advised of immediate termination. Resignation is not in the best interest of the banking community.

If no admission of the suspected fraud is obtained during the interview, the investigator should tell the employee not to return to work until he or she hears from the bank. After the interview, the investigator's supervisors ought to be advised of the facts and results of the interview. Such information should also be passed on to the employee's supervisor.

Investigative Results. The investigator should then prepare a written report of the findings. This report should contain all the key elements of the investigation as well as any procedural violations found which contributed to the loss. Banks are required under certain federal and state laws to report suspicions of employee embezzlement to agencies such as the Federal Deposit Insurance Corporation, state banking departments, and the FBI.

With regard to prosecution of criminal offenders, banks seem to vary in their positions. Some feel that self-protection demands that the victim bank should prosecute without compromise. Others will accept restitution and drop the issue for fear of adverse publicity. Reporting criminal activity and prosecution is needed to stem the rising tide of bank theft. If the FBI cannot investigate and a U.S. Attorney will not prosecute a case due to their increased caseloads, the bank should attempt prosecution at either the state or local level. Some bankers argue that a major goal for the industry is to report crimes perpetrated by employees and to assist however possible in their prosecution. If this is not done, the same individuals could be employed by other financial institutions which have no knowledge of past dishonest acts. It should also be noted that most bank crimes violate federal criminal statutes under Title 18 of the *U.S. Criminal Code*. In general, the FBI is charged with the responsibility for investigating violations of these statutes.

Today, more than ever before, it is necessary for a bank investigation unit and law enforcement authorities to strengthen or establish a close working relationship to combat the effects that white-collar crime has on financial institutions. Law enforcement authorities can be extremely valuable during an investigation. Their expertise in areas such as forensic science and handwriting analysis is important for the investigator to utilize whenever possible.

Qualifications for Financial Investigators

Several of the qualifications necessary for competent financial investigators were mentioned earlier in this chapter. In addition, their position requires the ability to investigate potential losses, which include complex schemes like kiting, self-dealing, income tax evasion, identity theft, SEC violations, and international plots. They must be able to develop systems of recording and correlating information related to investigations, and these systems must be amendable to meaningful analysis, quick retrieval, and dissemination.

Financial investigators should be able to contribute to the development of "awareness programs" for the education and training of line management regarding the potential for fraud losses within their areas of responsibility. They can assist management in the development of prevention strategies and techniques. A sophisticated investigation unit staffed with highly qualified individuals is not the panacea for internal or external fraud in the banking industry; however, it certainly is one of the most positive steps that can be implemented.

The Future of Financial Investigation. Banking is in a continual state of change. Analysts predict that banks will eventually become "financial supermarkets," offering a broad variety of financial services, and may become more active in the securities market. As this evolution takes place, bank systems and procedures will change and white-collar crime will become more and more sophisticated. Those responsible for protecting the bank assets and its reputation must remain aware of the changes, and institute preventive controls in order to stay one step ahead of white-collar crime.

39

Signals of Crime in Progress

Chamber of Commerce of the United States

INDICATORS OF CORRUPT PRACTICES

Tip-offs of bribery, kickbacks, and other payoffs are divided into two categories: (1) those relating to dealings between business and government and (2) those pertaining to transactions among private sector parties.[1] (However, there may be indicators assigned to one category that are also applicable to the other.)

Business-Government

First, in question form, these symptoms can be indicative of potential payoffs in a business-government context:

1. Do respected and well-qualified companies refuse to conduct business with the city or state?
2. Are municipal or state contracts let to a narrow group of firms?
3. Is competitive bidding required? Or contracts above what dollar amount?
4. Are there numerous situations that justify the letting of contracts without competitive bidding? For example, are there frequent "emergency contracts" for which bids are not solicited? Are professional services (architectural, engineering, and so on) purchased on a bid basis or "by invitation"?
5. Have there been disclosures of companies submitting low bids but disqualified for certain unspecified technical reasons?

6. Is double-parking permitted in front of some restaurants or taverns but not in front of others?

7. Do some contractors keep the streets and sidewalks reasonably free from materials, debris, and so on, while others show little concern about such matters?

8. Do architects add a sum to their fees to cover "research" at the city's planning or building department?

9. How much delay does a business encounter when applying for a liquor license, building permit, or remittance in payment for services rendered to the city or state?

10. Are government procedures so complicated that a "middleman" is often required to unravel the mystery and get through to the "right people"?

11. Do public officials have significant interests in firms doing business with the government?

12. Have public officials accepted high posts with companies that have recently secured contracts from agencies formerly employing those officials?

13. Is there an effective antibribery statute that embraces all government personnel—not just department heads?

14. Do large campaign contributions precede/follow favorable government rulings?

15. Are costs of conducting similar business operations in two states markedly different, even after allowance is made for legitimate differentials in labor rates, transportation costs, and so on?

Private Sector

Second, also in question form, are possible warning signals of corrupt practices often associated with transactions among private sector parties.

1. Do employees complain about the quality of supplies they must work with? For example, do clerks and secretaries complain about the quality of typewriter ribbons, paper, and other office supplies? Or do they use the petty cash fund to purchase from outside sources supplies that are available in bulk from the stockroom?

2. Do reputable suppliers seem disinclined to submit bids to, or otherwise deal with, the purchasing department?

3. Despite a policy of rotating suppliers, is there frequent use of the same supplier?

4. Are vacations refused or promotions shunned—for fear that corrupt arrangements will be discovered?

5. Is an employee constantly associating with and being entertained by vendors?

6. Is the standard of living of anyone who can influence company purchases higher than can be explained by wage or salary level or other legitimate sources of income?

7. Are costs of certain materials or services out of line with industry norms for no apparent reason?

8. For any given category of purchases, are the responsibilities related to issuing requests for bids and approving bids all possessed by one individual?

9. Are there vague "extra charges" associated with obtaining a loan from a pension and welfare fund or any other source?

10. Does anyone who can influence the selection of suppliers have a financial interest in or relatives employed by current vendors?

11. Is there a high incidence of order splitting, perhaps calculated to avoid the competitive bidding required for purchases above a certain dollar amount?

12. Does a buyer seem to have a relatively easy time acquiring tickets for hit shows, sports events, and so on?

EARLY SYMPTOMS OF BUSINESS-ORIENTED FRAUD AND OTHER ILLEGALITIES

Symptoms indicative of a possible *advance-fee fraud* include the following:

1. A lending institution advertises the availability of millions of dollars for loans at reasonable rates, even though the economy is in a period of tight money.

2. The lending institution is located offshore or in Europe.

3. The institution's financial statements are unaudited.

4. The name of the institution sounds impressive—too much so.

5. The listed assets of the lender are also incredibly impressive.

6. Names of board members are not familiar.

7. Your banker does not have firsthand knowledge of the lending institution.

8. Loan applications arrive in the mail unsolicited.

The best warning signal of a *Ponzi operation* is the very reason why it succeeds so often: the promised returns are "too good to be true." Among other tip-offs are these:

1. The background and reputation of the person to whom money is entrusted are not documented but can be "verified" only through hearsay.

2. Claims are made of little or no financial risk.

3. Periodic statements indicating substantial profits are not audited.

4. Contrary to original promises, requests to withdraw funds meet resistance.

5. The "financial wizard" handling the funds seems to make a point of creating an aura of personal affluence and claims to be investing money of well-known personalities.

The principal tip-off of a *pyramid sales scheme* is that the emphasis is on the money-making potential of selling lower-level distributorships rather than on the earnings possible from selling the product or service itself. Other indicators of this fraud are:

1. Claims of enormous profits from a relatively small investment.

2. Hard sell techniques to recruit distributors—perhaps involving a series of revival-like meetings characterized by emotional "sermons," money- or success-oriented songs, and persistent attempts to sign up distributors.

3. Numerous ploys to pressure or embarrass individuals into buying a distributionship ("Those of you who want to join, sit down—the rest of you keep standing.")

4. Refusals to take down payments except in cash.

The related area of *franchise fraud* is often associated with one or more of the preceding tip-offs as well as with the following early warning indicators:

1. The franchisor has just started operations and does not have a track record.

2. The franchisor resists giving the names and addresses of franchisees.

3. The name of the franchise is suspiciously similar to that of a well-known operation.

4. The territory to be served by the franchise is not spelled out and profit forecasts are not supported by a market survey.

5. "No experience necessary" is emphasized.

6. Certified profit figures of other franchises are not available.

7. The franchise product or service seems gimmick-oriented or is based on nothing more than a current fad.

Advance symptoms of a *land sales fraud* include the following:

1. The proposed contract would have you waive the cooling-off period provided by law.

2. Salespersons imply that the government has inspected and endorsed the development because it is registered with HUD.

3. A government-required property report is not provided more than 48 hours before you sign or does not contain on the front page this warning in red, half-inch letters—*Purchaser Should Read This Document Before Signing Anything.*

4. Advertising claims are inconsistent with what is contained in the property report.

5. An on-site inspection of the property is discouraged.

6. The developer imputes future success to the current project by emphasizing past accomplishments.

7. Key oral promises are not reflected in the written contract.

Signs of the *counterfeiting of a company's product* include:

1. Quality-related complaints from consumers who live in sections of the nation where the firm does not carry on marketing activities.

2. The theft of packing cartons or labeling equipment. Receipt of complaints about products you do not manufacture but which bear your label or trademark is indicative of someone passing off his products as yours.

Grumbling among the rank and file can reflect concern about *illegal employment of aliens* by other firms. A possible sign of *sweetheart contracts* is that wages of a competitor's unionized workers are conspicuously below those in similar businesses in the region.

DANGER SIGNALS OF CREDIT CARD SCHEMES

The credit **card user** can be alert for these danger signals:

1. The usual monthly bill from the issuer does not arrive (address changed by a defrauder, perhaps).
2. A charge slip included with the monthly bill indicates a total larger than that on the corresponding "customer's copy" slip.
3. A charge slip enclosed with the monthly bill does not correspond with any of the "customer's copy" slips (indicative of double imprinting at the point of sale).
4. The person behind you at the sales counter seems unusually attentive to your credit card transaction (as if to note your card number and name).
5. A renewal card does not arrive several weeks before the expiration date of the current card.
6. Double imprinting by the cashier is observed.
7. A waiter misplaces the card.

And there are plenty of fraud symptoms that credit **card acceptors** can detect:

1. Card has expired or is not yet valid.
2. Alteration of the card is obvious.
3. Card is on the issuer's cancellation notice.
4. Signature on the card and charge slip are significantly different.
5. Customer selects purchases rapidly.
6. Customer's attire is inconsistent with the nature of the purchases or with the type of card being presented (shabbily dressed person presents an "executive card").
7. Card is presented by a youth or a drunk.
8. Cardholder asks to split the purchase between charge slips—possibly in an attempt to forestall an authorization call to the issuer.
9. Cardholder attempts to rush a transaction.
10. Cardholder makes purchases, leaves the store, and returns for more purchases.
11. Cardholder makes multiple purchases—all under the floor limit.
12. Cardholder purchases many of the same items but in different colors, sizes, and so on.
13. Customer does not appear to be the type of person who lives in the section of the city indicated by the address on the card.

Note: Failure to note items 1–4 in the preceding list could make the acceptor liable for any loss resultant from the sale. The acceptor is also liable if he or she fails to call the issuer for authorization of the transaction when the amount of the sale exceeds a predetermined sum.

As for credit card issuers, their suspicions are aroused by such things as unusual activity in an account, spending inconsistent with past patterns, merchandise hand-delivered in a way to circumvent the mail fraud statute, and cardholder complaints about overcharging or extra charges.

TIP-OFFS INDICATIVE OF CHECK FRAUD

The handwriting of the person presenting the check may not be consistent with his or her character and age. In one case, the forger was a tall, athletic-looking man, but his handwriting was small and precise, like a woman's. And he wrote very slowly.

Haphazardly set type for counterfeit checks may contain misspelled company names, towns, and so on; for example, "segurity" instead of "security." Beware of odd spellings for common names.

Oddly shaped numerals may indicate a raised check—as might poor spacing, blots, erasures, or changes in ink color or thickness of lines.

The payee's name as indicated by the endorsement is different from the way it is spelled on the face of the check.

A juvenile presents a check. Or a teenager presents a government pension check (as indicated on the left side of such checks).

The date on the check is old or postdated. Or the check is prepared in pencil.

The person presenting the check is a glib or distracting talker, is overattentive to the people nearby, or tries to rush the transaction because, "I'm late for an appointment."

The customer is unable to provide adequate identification. Or, although the signature on the identification document matches that of the customer, the physical description indicated by the document is at variance with the customer's appearance. Or the document indicates the customer's residence is in a state different from that of the bank on which his personal check is drawn.

Symptoms of possible fraud in connection with *traveler's checks* include the following:

1. Many traveler's checks are cashed at one time, which is not the typical pattern.

2. Traveler's checks have been countersigned in advance.

3. The signature at the top of the check is by felt-tip pen, perhaps used to alter the signature so it can be more easily forged when the check is countersigned.

4. A low-priced item is paid for with a high-denomination check.

5. The person countersigning the checks uses his or her free hand to obstruct the cashier's view of the procedure.

6. After countersigning a book of legitimately acquired traveler's checks, a customer "accidentally" drops them on the floor, pockets them, and produces a second book of checks, which were stolen and leisurely countersigned in advance.

HOW THE PILFERER AND EMBEZZLER CAN HURT YOU

A cashier does not ring up a sale for which the customer has paid the exact amount. A $5 shirt is rung up as a $2 sale. Overring slips cover up a cashier's dipping into the till. Fraudulent cash refunds are made. A cashier gives an unauthorized discount or markdown to a friend. Or this is done by one department manager for another, on a reciprocal basis.

A manager's lawn is mowed by company employees on company time. A secretary uses the copying machine for her husband's at-home business. In-house counsel uses corporate secretarial help in connection with his private practice. A retail buyer also places orders for her side business.

Payments are made to fictitious suppliers or employees. An employee, for a fee, gives a customer an allowance for trumped-up defects. An employee pockets funds obtained from delinquent accounts and tells the company that the debt was uncollectible. A clerk steals from incoming payments and then applies subsequent remittances on other items to cover the amounts stolen (lapping). A disbursements manager forges a company check to his or her own order and destroys the check when returned by the bank. Among many other tactics are:

- Overcharging customers and pocketing the difference.
- Paying suppliers twice and keeping the second check for personal use.
- Pocketing unclaimed wages.
- Increasing the amounts of suppliers' invoices and appropriating the difference or splitting it with the suppliers.
- Making fictitious advances to employees.
- Pilfering merchandise covered by doctored inventory lists.
- Manipulating time cards.
- Kiting checks.
- Overloading expense accounts.
- Carrying employees on the payroll beyond their actual severance date—and pocketing their checks.
- Altering a cash sales ticket after handing the copy to a customer.
- Shipping merchandise to an employee's or relative's home for disposal.
- Secreting tools or products on one's person, in a lunch box, or in a vehicle.
- Substituting valuable materials for scrap being loaded on a truck.
- Throwing pilfered items over the perimeter fence for retrieval later.
- Altering bills of lading to cover up partial off-loading prior to destination.
- Putting incorrect shipping labels on packages that were rewrapped because of damage.
- Declaring incoming shipments short when such is not the case.
- Recording that an outgoing truck had one more carton than it actually carried.
- Removing appliances from cartons of outgoing shipments and substituting bricks.
- Carrying cartons from a shipping dock to a personal car.

EARLY WARNING SIGNALS OF EMBEZZLEMENT AND PILFERAGE

Personal checks or IOUs are placed in petty cash funds. Vague reasons are given for bad debt write-offs. Collections decline as a percentage of what is due. Records are rewritten, allegedly for reasons of neatness. Inventory shortages are noted—perhaps indicative of fraudulent purchases, unrecorded sales, or pilferage.

An accounting clerk refuses to relinquish custody of records during the day and works overtime regularly. Standard usage rates for raw materials are exceeded. A spurt in sales returns is noted—possibly indicative of a concealment of accounts receivable payments.

Books are not kept up to date. Sensitivity to routine questions is abnormally high. Customers complain about errors in their statements. An identical second endorsement is on several payroll checks—a possible clue that employees are dealing with a loan shark, who may ask repayment in the form of merchandise. Gambling or associating with undesirables by an employee is noted.

The pattern of cash receipts is different during the absence of the employee normally handling them. Collectors or creditors ask for a given employee. A clerk is inclined to cover up inefficiencies. Vacations are refused and promotions shunned—perhaps in fear that irregularities will surface.

Company products appear in outlets that have never placed orders. Drivers take too much time to make deliveries. The tool replacement rate is inconsistent with production loads. Containers of desirable parts or merchandise are frequently damaged. An employee purchases the noon meal at the company cafeteria, yet always brings a lunch box to work. Cartons are partially empty in an area where only full containers are supposed to be stored.

An employee goes to his car during working hours, loiters in areas other than his own department, is overeager to show the gate guard his lunch box, approaches the gate too nonchalantly, walks too fast or too slowly, walks too erect or too stooped, carries his arms rigidly, or seems overdressed.

THE INDICATORS OF INSURANCE FRAUD

Tip-offs of false claims include the following:

- The person who "fell" or was in the "accident" expresses a desire for an expeditious settlement and, with apparent thoughtfulness, adds that he or she does not want to put anyone to a great deal of trouble. Besides he or she has an out-of-town appointment and wishes to conclude matters in a simple fashion before leaving. The real objective, of course, is to avoid a thorough investigation.

- The claimant seems to have retained an attorney with exceptional speed.

- Claimant appears extraordinarily knowledgeable about the claim-adjustment process, using the right words and phrases.

- An injured claimant is treated at a hospital operated by his physician.

- The doctor fails to itemize her bill despite requests for this.

- The injured parties are all treated by the same doctor.

- An attorney offers to include an adjustor on his Christmas list or otherwise tries to probe the extent of the adjustor's integrity.
- Attempts at contacting the employer or someone who is claiming lost time at work are repeatedly unsuccessful.
- The signature of the claimant differs significantly on various documents he or she supposedly prepared. This may indicate that a dishonest attorney may be diverting insurance proceeds to his or her own use.
- The claimant uses a lawyer-physician combination that has been implicated in prior suspected frauds.

Regarding victimization by "paper" insurance companies to milk the assets of insurance-company subsidiaries, one tip-off might be the transfer of a blue-chip asset from the subsidiary to the parent company, which replaces it with something of lower quality. Or the parent might purchase real estate and sell it to the subsidiary at a substantial markup, which reflects alleged improvements. Or a cash-rich insurance subsidiary declares a hefty dividend to its shareholders, that is, the parent.

FENCES AND OTHER RECEIVERS—THE DANGER SIGNS

Many of the following tip-offs should be evaluated from two perspectives: (1) the possible intentional or unwitting decision of your company's purchasing agent or buyer to deal with fences (for no other reason, perhaps, than to impress management with his or her skill at obtaining bargain rates); and (2) the possibility that competitors are dealing with fences.

1. Management sets unrealistically high performance standards for buyers and purchasing agents.
2. Salespersons report that customers are buying a competitor's products and selling them at abnormally low prices. Or customers substantially reduce orders yet seem to continue to sell your products at a brisk rate.
3. Salespersons or customers report your product is being sold at abnormal discounts or through unusual outlets.
4. An unusual drop in unit costs for purchases is associated with a switch from one supplier to another, whose address turns out to be an answering service.
5. A neighborhood outlet opens for business and then closes after a few weeks or months.
6. An outlet receives deliveries which appear inconsistent with the nature of the business, such as bulky packages delivered to a coin shop.
7. Goods delivered to a store are unloaded from the back of a car.
8. A retailer seems to have a perpetual sale. Or a store remains in operation after a going-out-of-business sale.
9. Supplies are delivered to your firm in cartons whose labels have been removed by a razor.

10. Someone offers you an incredibly low price in return for cash.

11. Employees are discovered to be operating a side business similar to your own, and you are experiencing a particularly severe pilferage problem.

12. Wholesalers start complaining about losing business to "retailers."

TIP-OFFS OF SECURITIES THEFT AND FRAUD

1. Stock offered as loan collateral is in a street name.

2. Securities are offered for private sale at a substantial discount from currently quoted prices—perhaps the desire to quickly liquidate an estate is given as the reason for the low price.

3. The balance sheet of a previously poor credit risk shows a sudden and substantial increase in securities listed as assets.

4. Financial statements of a firm contain highly questionable entries, such as substantial mining interests, which, according to "some sources," are valued at $X, or $100,000 worth of notes of an obscure company appear in the asset column.

5. No one has seen, or knows anyone who has seen, the premises of the hitherto unfamiliar company you are thinking of dealing with.

6. The proper number of shares is accounted for by an inventory check, but the number of certificates on hand does not correspond with records.

7. The transaction involves a numbered Swiss bank account or a secretive foreign trust.

8. The transaction involves trading through a bulk segregation or omnibus account established here by a foreign financial institution.

9. The insurer, bank, or mutual fund is located offshore.

10. A relatively obscure stock displays an unexplained increase in trading activity.

11. A certificate is characterized by one or more indicators of counterfeit paper:

    - One-color printing; color is muddy.
    - Absence of a human figure.
    - Border lines are broken in a few places or poorly aligned.
    - The colored dots (planchettes) are missing or, if present, can be erased or appear in precisely the same location on several certificates.
    - The three-dimensional look is missing.
    - The corporate name does not have a raised feel.
    - Line work is not clear and distinct, and liens bleed into one another.
    - Certificate numbers are not clear and distinct.
    - Misspellings occur.

12. A credit report on a company does not indicate that the figures cited in the report have been verified or, if so, to what extent.

13. The monthly statement from the broker does not indicate that a security held in street name was "delivered out" to you as requested.

14. The potential borrower who is offering stock as collateral gives a somewhat tortuous explanation of why satisfactory identification documentation cannot be produced.

15. A security is issued by a company whose name is almost, but not quite, identical to a respected firm.

16. The assets of an unfamiliar firm are principally comprised of obscure securities.

WHAT ARE SOME OF THE TIP-OFFS OF COMPUTER-RELATED FRAUD?

This discussion of danger signs of computer-related fraud is restricted to those tip-offs that could conceivably come to the attention of and be recognized by executives with little or no technical background. One expert interviewed for this report stated that an indicator of possible problems was the presence of some or all of the following elements of a vulnerable computer system:

1. The computer generates negotiable instruments or is used to transfer credit, process loans, or obtain credit ratings.

2. Employee relations are poor—perhaps there is a conflict with a union or with a disgruntled computer operator. Dismissed EDP personnel are allowed to remain on the job until their termination date. A computer programmer is overqualified for the job, with the possible result that bottled-up creativity will seek undesirable outlets.

3. Separation of key functions is inadequate, in terms of either responsibility or physical access. (Programmers should not also be computer operators—a likely situation in small businesses with minicomputers.)

4. After-hours EDP operations are loosely supervised. Second and third shifts are typically very informal—programmers are at consoles debugging online, whereas they would never get within a hundred feet of the computer room during the day.

5. Auditors have little, if any, expertise or background in computer operations. (As a result, they may audit "around the computer," not "through" it, and miss weak spots that are being exploited.)

Among the many other indicators that may warrant follow-up investigation are these:

1. Computer reports, or carbons of continuous forms, are in the outside trash bin.

2. EDP auditors were not involved in development of the application programs. Possible result: absence of built-in tests and checks.

3. Your industry is depressed, yet computer-generated data indicate record sales for your firm.

4. Frequent violations are noted of the generally accepted rule that at least two people should be present when EDP equipment is operating.

5. Computer operations, including storage of output data, can be viewed by the general public.

6. System components are near open windows, next to outside walls, or in front of open doors. (Exposure to the telephoto lens, parabolic microphone, or electromagnetic device is thereby increased.)

7. The personnel department subjects candidates for EDP positions to only routine screening. (The chief weakness of computer systems is people.)

8. Data preparation equipment is easily available and loosely controlled.

9. Access to computer facilities is not limited to those with a "need to know."

10. Transactions rejected by the system because they did not pass one or more control points are put aside, ignored, or deliberately overridden.

11. An increase is noted in employee complaints about overwithholding "by the computer" or about inaccuracies in year-end earnings statements.

12. There is a surge in customer complaints about delays in crediting their accounts.

13. Key forms such as purchase orders, invoices, and checks are not numbered sequentially.

14. Continuous-form checks are not stored securely.

15. The bill from the time-sharing service bureau is significantly more than what the customer's computer-time logs seem to justify. Or charges allocated to other departments by a company's computer facility seem out of line. (Indicative of unauthorized use of computer time, perhaps.)

16. Payments are sent to new suppliers, but they are not listed in various directories.

17. Access to the central processor is attempted from a remote terminal whose exclusive user is on vacation.

NOTE

[1]Many of the listed tip-offs are based on the "Questionnaire on Corruption" in *Community Crime Prevention*, a report of the National Advisory Commission on Criminal Justice Standards and Goals (1973). Available from the U.S. Government Printing Office, Stock number 2700-00181.

40

Labor Union Investigation

Lawrence M. Haut

SIGNIFICANT LAWS AND STATUTES

An examination of the primary laws dealing with the investigation and prosecution of corrupt labor union officials and employers indicates that they are primarily federal statutes. Local and state enforcement in this area, although existent, is largely lumped together with the prosecution of crimes such as grand or petty larceny, bribery, and extortion involving general statutes. Frequently, local authorities refer cases involving labor union racketeers to the federal system, since specific laws dealing with the offenses involved are all codified under federal law. These laws cover areas as diverse as embezzlement, false record keeping and filing false reports, kickbacks, extortion, payoffs, bribery, and engaging in racketeering. The following acts and laws contain the significant statutes investigated.

Labor Management Reporting and Disclosure Act (LMRDA)

Also known as the *Landrum-Griffin Act*, this legislation was passed in 1959. It was largely prompted by increased public awareness relative to labor corruption as portrayed in the U.S. Senate's McClellan committee hearings. The law contains

Mr. Haut's views do not necessarily reflect the policies and practices of his employer.

both civil and criminal provisions. It provides standards for fair union elections, stipulates reporting and financial disclosure requirements and provides criminal penalties for fiduciary breaches by union officials and employees.

The criminal statutes included in *LMRDA* are the following:

29 U.S.C. 501c, which states that any person who embezzles, steals, or willfully abstracts to his or her own use or another's, any of the monies, funds, securities, or other assets of a labor organization of which he or she is an officer or by whom he or she is employed can be fined $10,000 or imprisoned for five years or both.

Under the provisions of LMRDA, all labor organizations are required to file an annual financial report with the U.S. Department of Labor (DOL) outlining fiduciary information relative to the monies taken in and expended. 29 U.S.C. 439 describes a fine and/or one year's imprisonment for any person who willfully makes false statements; fails to disclose a material fact; or makes false entry in or willfully conceals, withholds, or destroys any required books, records or report.

One of the most significant sections in LMRDA is 29 U.S.C. 504, which states that any person convicted of any of a list of enumerated offenses including robbery, extortion, burglary, violent assaults, bribery, murder, rape, narcotics violations, arson, and grand larceny, as well as embezzlement and falsifying union records, is barred from serving in any union capacity other than "clerical or custodial" for a five-year period after "such conviction or after the end of such imprisonment. This bar is in addition to any prescribed sentence for the crime. The successful investigation and conviction for a *barrable* offense is a high-priority goal of law enforcement in labor racketeering cases.

Other sections of LMRDA specify misdemeanor penalties for willfully making excessive loans to union officials, depriving members from exercising their union rights through the threat of violence, and unlawfully placing a union in trusteeship.

Welfare and Pension Plans Disclosure Act (WPPDA), 29 U.S.C. 301-309

This act of March 30, 1962, established similar provisions for employee benefit plans (pension, health-welfare, vacation, annuity, and so on) which had been established by *LMRDA* for union general fund monies. Union members' benefits plans frequently rely on employer contributions for their funding. As a condition of the negotiated contract, the amount and rate of contributions is often determined. The plan trustees having fiduciary obligations and responsibility thus always include both union and employer representatives. The provisions of this act are applicable not only to labor union members' benefit plans, but to many different categories of plans as well. However, because a great deal of influence is wielded through the use of the often large assets and funds of union benefit plans, Congress also enacted embezzlement, false reporting, and kickback statutes to deal with these monies, similar to those established earlier for union monies under *LMRDA*. Amid increased public concern about abuses of benefit fund monies, Congress passed a somewhat broader law, effective January 1, 1975, to replace *WPPDA*.

Employee Retirement Income Security Act of 1974 (ERISA)

This act is basically civil. It primarily involves the government filing civil suits against those who breach prescribed fiduciary duties. The new law incorporates the three basic criminal statutes previously enumerated under *WPPDA* and adds another section, analogous to *LMRDA*'s 29 U.S.C., relative to the deprivation of rights through the threat or use of violence. All criminal violations prior to January 1, 1975 are prosecutable under *WPPDA*, while all acts occurring after this date are prosecutable under *ERISA*. Incorporated into *WPPDA* and *ERISA* are the following:

18 U.S.C. 664 states that it is a federal crime for any person, officer, or employee of any labor organization to willfully embezzle, abstract, or convert to his own use the funds, assets, or property of any employee benefit fund. This section is analogous to the 501c embezzlement section in *LMRDA* for union funds.

18 U.S.C. 1027 provides for criminal penalties for falsifying documents, records, or reports which must be filed with DOL relative to employee benefit plans. Like *LMRDA*, which prescribes an annual (LM-2) report for union general funds, *WPPDA* prescribes D-2 annual reports and *ERISA* the 5500 reports. Unlike *LMRDA*, which prescribes a one-year misdemeanor penalty for falsifying records, the penalty for 18 U.S.C. 1027 is a maximum five-year sentence. However, due to an ironic loophole in the law, 18 U.S.C. 1027, a felony, is not a "barrable offense" from unions, but only from welfare and pension funds. This interesting circumstance often leads to paradoxical plea bargaining offers to accept a felony rather than a misdemeanor charge.

18 U.S.C. 1954 prohibits attempts to buy favor or sell influence in connection with the welfare and pension plans subject to *WPPDA* and *ERISA*. It prohibits officers, counsel, agents and employees of the benefit plan, the employer, the employee organization, or any organization which provides benefit services to the plan from soliciting or agreeing to receive certain payments. Similarly, it is illegal for any person to promise, offer, or make the prohibited payments to any of the above. (Payments for legitimate services rendered are the only exception.) This statute is intended to punish both the corrupt employer who pays the kickback and the labor official who accepts or solicits it. The maximum penalty for conviction is three years in prison and/or a fine of up to $10,000.

Labor-Management Relations Act of 1947 (Taft-Hartley Act)

This law was passed by Congress despite widespread opposition by many in organized labor. In addition to prescribing and reiterating restrictions on employers who might attempt to deprive employees of their union rights, it also imposed strong penalties on labor officials and employers engaging in improper financial arrangements. Like other federal labor-management relations laws, it is primarily civil, although it also includes criminal provisions under 29 U.S.C. 186.

29 U.S.C. 186a makes it unlawful for employers to pay, lend, deliver, or agree to deliver any money or thing of value to any of the following:

1. Any representative of their employees.
2. To any union or officer or employee that represents or seeks to represent or would admit their employees to membership.

3. To employees in excess of their normal compensation to cause them to influence other employees in the exercise of their rights to bargain collectively.

4. To any union officers or union employees intending to influence them in their actions as representatives of employees or as officers of a labor union.

29 U.S.C. 186b–d prohibits the demand, request, acceptance, or agreement to accept any of the above payments, except for payments to representatives of employees for legitimate services rendered. This is necessary because in many unions the officials are not full-time union officers and must also hold a job to make their living. The law is not intended to prevent the payment of wages to people who are truly employed while also holding a union office. Payment for judgments, arbitrations, and purchases of property at prevailing rates are also exempted. Other than these, all payments between employer and employee representatives are illegal. These provisions were instituted to deal with bribery and payoffs in labor-management relations.

Hobbs Act (18 U.S.C. 1951)

Passed on July 3, 1946, this act updated provisions initially passed in the original federal antiracketeering statute of 1934 (18 U.S.C. 42). This law deals with interference with interstate commerce by threats or violence. The *Hobbs Act* differs from the previous laws described in this chapter in that it does not deal exclusively with labor-management relations and it is solely criminal in nature, not a mixture of civil and criminal. Although the law was not intended to deal only with labor-related extortion, a review of the legislative hearings indicates that it was a widespread concern. It was not an intent of the act to interfere with labor's legitimate right to strike and picket peacefully.

The Hobbs Act has become increasingly used in dealing with labor racketeering. It is designed to deal with robbery, extortion, and the wrongful taking of the property of another person through threatened or actual force. The element of fear, of either violence or property damage to the victim's business is requisite to the crime. The fear of economic loss is considered to be sufficient to prove extortion under the act. The prescribed sentence for conviction is a fine of up to $10,000 or 20 years in prison. As shown by the severe sentence, congressional intent was to strongly punish this kind of criminality.

Racketeer Influenced and Corrupt Organizations Act (18 U.S.C. 1961-1968)

This antiracketeering statute, known as *RICO*, effective October 15, 1970, sets strict penalties relative to patterns of racketeering activity. It enumerates a group of offenses covered by federal law that constitute racketeering activity. These include bribery, counterfeiting, theft from interstate commerce, embezzlement of labor union and benefit funds monies, extortionate credit transactions, mail and wire frauds, *Hobbs Act* violations, gambling offenses, unlawful welfare-pension fund payments, *Taft-Hartley* offenses, and security frauds. Although *RICO* was not intended to deal only with labor offenses, they constitute a significant portion of the crimes covered. A pattern of racketeering requires at least two acts, one which occurred after the statute's effective date, and the last of which occurred within 10 years after the commission of a prior act. The law calls for severe penalties. Whoever violates any provision can be fined up to $25,000 or imprisoned for up to 20 years. In addition, a powerful civil redress provision directs that those convicted must totally forfeit any and all interest they had in the racketeer-influenced organization with which they were involved.

In addition to the primary laws described relative to enforcement in the labor-management corruption sphere, secondary labor statutes with criminal penalties also exist. Although not as commonly used in combating labor corruption and racketeering, these laws should be briefly noted.

29 U.S.C. 216, *Fair Labor Standards Act* (*Wage and Hour Act*) provides a national minimum wage and restrictions on the employment of minors. Although enforcement is primarily civil, criminal provisions exist for employers who are willfully repeating offenders. The penalties called for are a maximum of a $10,000 fine and six months imprisonment.

29 U.S.C. 162 makes it a misdemeanor to willfully interfere with or impede any agent of the National Labor Relations Board in the performance of his duties.

18 U.S.C. 844 prescribes criminal penalties for the use of explosives when a labor dispute is involved.

18 U.S.C. 1231 imposes felony sanctions on any person convicted of willfully transporting any person to obstruct or interfere with by force or threats (*a*) any peaceful labor picketing or (*b*) an employee's exercise of organizational or collective bargaining rights. This was enacted to deal harshly with employers hiring professional strikebreakers who employ strong-arm methods against employees who are peacefully exercising legitimate rights under the collective bargaining agreement.

Railway Labor Act (RLA)

The *Railway Labor Act* covers employees of interstate transportation carriers not covered by other federal labor laws such as the *National Labor Relations Act, LMRDA,* and *Taft-Hartley.* The *RLA* criminal provisions relate only to the carriers (employers) and prescribe penalties for illegally preventing employees from exercising their lawful union rights. However, employers, employees, and labor organizations covered by the *RLA* are covered by some criminal provisions already described.

In addition to all the laws described, it must be realized that other federal criminal statutes not characteristically associated with labor are utilized in labor-related racketeering investigations. Prosecution of labor subjects under such other statutes as mail and wire fraud, obstruction of justice, perjury, tax violations, and hijacking has taken place fairly frequently. Often this is accomplished within the context of cooperative investigations involving such agencies as the Labor Department, Postal Inspectors, IRS, ATF, and, on some occasions, the FBI.

INVESTIGATION OF LABOR-MANAGEMENT CORRUPTION AND RACKETEERING

Existing federal "delegations of authority" have issued the predominant investigative authority to the U.S. Department of Justice for most federal criminal offenses under Title 18. This includes most of the offenses already described. DOL has also received formal delegations for some *Landrum-Griffin, ERISA,* and *Taft-Hartley* provisions. However, the actual factors determining what agency will investigate a case and which Justice Department office will prosecute are often determined more by practical and political factors than by formal memorandums of understanding.

Investigations in this area can be initiated by various factors. Some cases are opened based on specific allegations of improprieties made by labor union members, other officials, or employers. Other cases are opened with a specific, identifiable "target" union or subjects in mind. These cases may be opened largely based on the sordid reputation of the person or organization involved, as much as on any specific allegation of criminality. Other cases may be opened to placate outside pressure exerted by the media or political power groups. Still other cases may arrive by referral from other law enforcement agencies which lack investigative jurisdiction.

The DOL, the FBI, and, to a lesser extent, the IRS have been the predominant investigators of federal labor racketeering offenses. There have been striking similarities and differences relative to their approaches to this area over the last 10 to 20 years.

Prior to the passage of *LMRDA* in 1959 and *WPPDA* in 1962, DOL rarely, if ever, participated in any criminal investigations. Motivated as much by a philosophical perception of serving labor union officials as by its lack of criminal statutory authority, DOL would rather leave criminal investigation to the FBI. Although the force of Senate hearings, public concern, and FBI ambivalence about these investigations was to force the Department into a more active role, the attitude of many in the highest reaches of the Department's bureaucracy was not going to change. Before 1969, DOL basically conducted field audits and rather limited embezzlement cases based primarily on specific complaints and dubious entries on annual reports it received from labor unions. This thrust was to expand, however, when the Department sent representative investigators to the U.S. Justice Department's Organized Crime Strike Forces which were initially set up in 1968 and 1969. DOL participation in the strike forces, which marshalled the resources of numerous federal investigative agencies, with special grand juries and the U.S. Justice Department to specifically focus on organized crime and racketeering, served to broaden DOL's scope and its commitment toward criminal investigations. Even with this increased contribution, however, only one agency among the many sections of DOL, the Labor Management Services Administration (LMSA), contributed personnel to the strike forces. Also, in some offices, the agents assigned were often susceptible to reassignment and temporary recall for such "high-priority" civil matters as union officer election supervision and enforcing veterans' reemployment rights regulations. DOL also refused to formally classify its strike force agents as criminal investigators, thus preventing them from utilizing investigative tools and protections that were afforded other federal investigators on the strike force.

Within recent years, the issue of DOL commitment to investigating labor corruption and racketeering has gained increased publicity. As a result of a large public and senatorial reaction, DOL removed the program from LMSA and incorporated its labor racketeering and strike force program into a new Office of the Inspector General. Its agents are classified as criminal investigators and, in addition to a full-time fraud section, its strike force contingent is permanently assigned to conduct labor racketeering and labor-management corruption investigations.

In some cities, such as New York, Miami, and Detroit, DOL has had many successful criminal cases involving labor racketeers, in spite of past roadblocks already described. In other cities, the new organization must start from the bottom up building credibility and public confidence in its commitment and integrity.

The record of the FBI in investigating labor corruption and racketeering has also been plagued by inconsistency and ambivalence. The FBI has investigative responsibility for close to 200 statutes. Labor racketeering represents only a small portion of those laws. In addition, the Department of Justice, of which the FBI is a part, only recently categorized labor corruption specifically and white-collar crime in general as among the highest priorities for law enforcement. Prior to this, the FBI generally had little interest in conducting time-consuming technical "paper cases" against oftentimes politically sensitive labor union officials. Its investigative orientation in the labor area was more disposed toward highly visible "street type" offenses such as hijacking and extortion. In some cities where DOL would do little or no criminal work, the FBI had no choice but to accept cases referred to it by these "civil-oriented" offices or irate citizens. Few FBI agents, however, had expertise or much interest in developing labor cases.

During the early 1980's, largely because the Justice Department gave priority to this area, the FBI set up separate labor squads. Although the FBI has traditionally been reluctant to impart information and share the fruits of its victories with DOL and other federal agencies, it has indicated an increased desire to engage in cooperative efforts with many DOL investigators. Whether the FBI and DOL can truly cooperate and establish common, unified long-range investigative goals and efforts remains to be seen.

INVESTIGATIVE TECHNIQUES AND PROCEDURES

Case Initiation

The information and the rationale used to determine what labor racketeering investigations will be conducted emanate from various areas. The following represent the most common reasons for conducting federal labor racketeering probes.

Specific complaints are furnished which identify particular offenses committed by an individual, groups of individuals, or representatives of a labor organization. These complaints are commonly furnished by disgruntled union dissidents, victims of the specific act alleged, ambitious political rivals of the union official being complained against, or frightened secret informants.

Organizations or individuals are targeted for an overall investigation due to their unsavory reputation or intelligence information which identifies them as corrupt and/or linked with organized crime. The information used may have been obtained from such places as local or state enforcement agencies, Crime Commission reports, media exposés, other union officials, prior investigative reports by enforcement agencies, and direct victims of the organized crime persons in the labor movement. The maintenance of intelligence files by law enforcement agencies is an ongoing function of great importance when planning strategy to combat corruption and criminality.

Labor racketeering investigations may be initiated on the basis of referrals from another law enforcement agency that lacks the jurisdiction or expertise to handle the case. Because many citizens frequently do not know which federal agency has responsibility for which laws, such referrals are commonplace.

Investigations may be opened because of strong outside pressure generated by such sources as the media, political bodies, or powerful politicians. This can occur when bureaucratic inertia has prevented earlier action.

In all the above areas, it is necessary to thoroughly screen the validity and reliability of the source providing the information and the accuracy of the information itself. In all major investigations, the necessity of performing preliminary background work cannot be overemphasized. Because most, if not all, enforcement agencies do not have enough personnel to investigate all complaints or to target all known criminals in the area, such screening can save valuable time and resources. Before initiating an active investigation, the following background information should be obtained to ensure that the complaint information received has not already been investigated and/or discounted. The following data should be reviewed:

1. All prior investigative files and references.

2. All known police records and arrest files.

3. All available information about known associates of the potential subjects.

4. A general inquiry to other investigative agencies which also have jurisdiction to investigate the offenses complained of to ascertain if they have any open investigations of the subject or have made any recent investigations. Although interagency rivalries sometimes make this difficult, it should be attempted if at all feasible. An inquiring agent who does not fully trust the other agency can keep the inquiry general or make it through a trusted individual.

Case Investigation

In investigations involving labor organizations and their related benefit fund plans, the required annual reports filed with DOL should be thoroughly analyzed prior to conducting a field examination.

The LM-2 reports reflect information about union general fund monies. These reports, however, are not all-inclusive but are in summary form. They contain schedules of total amount spent or collected per category and include such items as schedules of total receipts and disbursements, assets and liabilities, the names and salaries of union officials, and beginning and end of reporting period cash flow data. These reports do not provide information on each specific financial transaction in which the union was involved. To obtain this data, the union's financial records must be examined. Item 15 of the report requires a yes or no answer to whether or not the union did "discover any loss or shortage of funds or property." A yes answer requires an explanation. Individual schedules for loans receivable and payable, purchase and sale of investments, and fixed assets require the disclosure of more specific information. Although the reports are general, scrutiny of them can provide good preliminary information about a union and its finances. In addition, such specific items as organizing expenses, salaries, other disbursements, allowances, or excessive loans, if out of line with the total union receipts or disproportionate share of union costs, can serve as preliminary warning indicators of possible impropriety. If the cash flow balance does not reconcile, obvious suspicions are aroused.

The EBS 5500 form is the annual benefit fund financial report reflecting information about welfare and pension fund monies. Like the LM-2 for general union monies, this report reflects similar information for plans maintained to provide benefits to union members. It reflects summary information for such items as total receipts and disbursements, loans, and assets and liabilities. Of particular interest should be the schedules reflecting the sale and purchase of investments. Special interest should also be aroused by a fund which reflects inordinately high administrative costs, many loans, or a yes answer to the question asking whether any trustee of the fund engaged in a party-in-interest transaction involving the fund and its assets. A *party-in-interest transaction* occurs when a fund trustee or person servicing the fund had a personal fiduciary relationship with an entity which had business dealings with the union benefit plan. Failure to report such a transaction is a felony under 18 U.S.C. 1027. Note that such a transaction, although leaving one vulnerable to suspicion possibly leading to a kickback investigation, is nevertheless not in itself a criminal violation. Scrutiny of these reports can give the investigator direction as well as shed further light on the validity of complaint-provided information.

Investigative techniques vary, based on such factors as the nature of the complaint received, the purpose and scope of the investigation, and the skills and abilities of the individual conducting the case. Other variables influencing the approaches used in criminal investigations in labor relate to the accessibility and availability of records, whether a grand jury is being used, enforceability of subpoenas, competence and interest of the Justice Department attorney working with the investigation, and the nature and degree of administrative or bureaucratic restraints which may be imposed. Aside from these variables, however, commonly used techniques and steps are followed that have proved effective in federal labor corruption cases.

THE MECHANICS OF CONDUCTING LABOR RACKETEERING AND LABOR-MANAGEMENT CORRUPTION INVESTIGATIONS

The offenses included in this area are varied and multidimensional. There is no one prescribed method of investigation, because of the diversity of activities involved. Therefore, the investigative techniques and procedures described in this article treat two general case types: (1) embezzlement and false records and (2) racketeering activities. The latter include such acts as kickbacks, extortion, payoffs, and conspiracies involving numerous offenses. The two categories are not mutually exclusive, and they share many common elements. For the purposes of this chapter, however, the specific investigative techniques and procedures of the two areas will be outlined and discussed separately.

Embezzlement and False Record Offenses

Such offenses represent the classic "paper chase" cases. Although witness testimony is almost always necessary to document and confirm the entries in the union records, frequently it is the record itself which provides the incriminating evidence. As already mentioned, the majority of labor cases in the past have dealt with embezzlement and falsification of records. Aside from broader statutory authority to examine union records, DOL has traditionally felt more comfortable conducting what is considered white-collar investigations, preferring to leave "street" offenses, including extortions, kickbacks, and racketeering, to other agencies such as the FBI. To some extent, increased involvement with the strike force has changed this policy. Nevertheless, as a rule, embezzlements have been more actively pursued. With the exception of a few cases in which specific complainant information will be either confirmed or rebutted by a quick in-and-out examination, the great majority of labor corruption investigations involve an intensive and exhaustive audit and examination of union and benefit fund financial records. Although tedious and time-consuming, this examination has proved to be the most effective method to ascertain whether criminal offenses have been committed by labor corruption subjects.

The following investigative steps should be taken in conducting examinations of union and benefit fund records.

Taking an Inventory. When first entering the union, the investigator should spend the first few days taking an inventory of all available financial records and all machines, furniture, and equipment in the hall. Among the union records commonly maintained and examined are general union fund and benefit fund records.

1. *General union fund:*

   a. Books and ledgers. The most important book is "Cash Receipts and Cash Disbursement." This reflects, usually on a month-by-month basis, the individual transactions relative to union disbursements (expenditures) and union receipts (income). The disbursements are broken down according to date, check number, payee, and category. The receipts are posted daily in most union books and include income from dues, initiation fees, and interest. Other books maintained are payroll ledgers, general journals, union bylaws, and constitution.

   b. Bank account records, canceled checks, and deposit slips. Scrutiny of the books frequently leads to the bank records. These should be examined to confirm whether or not the totals and amounts posted in the books are accurate. In addition, endorsements on canceled checks and entries on deposit slips should be cross-checked against the union books.

   c. Paid bills, vouchers, expense records. It is necessary to examine these when verifying the legitimacy of disbursements.

   d. General membership and executive board meeting minutes. The transcripts of these meetings must be maintained by the union. Depending on the union constitution and bylaws provisions, certain expenditures must be approved by both the board and membership. The question of whether an expenditure was authorized by the membership is frequently pivotal when determining whether willfulness existed relative to a possible embezzlement. The executive board is comprised of the union officers and a few other elected or appointed members, while the general membership meetings are open to all rank-and-file members.

e. Union membership records include dues and initiation records as well as remittance sheets showing contributions for benefit funds or dues check-off sent to the union.

f. Contracts and collective bargaining agreements negotiated by the union.

g. Files on any subsidiary entities or investments owned by the union.

h. Reports filed by the union with DOL, the IRS, or the state.

2. *Benefit fund records:* In addition to books and ledgers, bank records, paid bills, vouchers, and expense sheets, the following additional records should be present.

a. Investments files and documents. Since much contemporary labor racketeering revolves around the illicit use of the often multimillion-dollar benefit fund monies, the fund loans, investments, and costs should be thoroughly analyzed.

b. Claim files for such areas as medical benefits, pensions, and death benefits should at least be spot-checked to ascertain if recipients were actually eligible to receive the benefit and, if, in reality, they received the money.

c. The plan trust agreement and plan descriptions which outline the provisions and eligibility requirements for the fund should be evaluated.

d. The trustees' meeting minutes must be examined relative to authorization and to provide leads on what transactions seem significant.

Initial Interview. After inventory of the records, an initial interview with the principal officers should be conducted. The purpose of this interview is to establish who performs the everyday duties associated with the financial records. Who signs the checks? Who approves disbursements? Who collects union receipts? Who makes entries in the union book? Who deposits monies in the bank? Who reviews paid bills? Who has credit cards? What responsibilities do the officers and employees have? With whom does the union have contracts? Information about the kind of employees represented by the union and dues information is required. What kind of authorization is needed to approve union financial transactions? During the interview, certain procedural facts should be established for the record. The interviewer should avoid discussing specific transactions or areas in which the officer might be directly suspected of committing a criminal act. Once this occurs, a Fifth Amendment warning might be necessary, and the availability of any information, even procedural, might be lost. Occurring early in the examination, such an immediate polarization may be detrimental to the investigator who is still trying to get a grasp on the union records.

When examining benefit fund records, a similar interview should be conducted with the fund administrator, who is normally hired by the union trustees and approved by union and employer trustees. At the direction of the trustees, the administrator runs the day-to-day affairs of the fund. Actually, in most union benefit fund plans, the union officer trustees are more influential than the employer trustees. The employer trustees are businesspersons who have a contract with the union; they must get along with the union officers. Because the employers contribute money to the plan, Taft-Hartley requires equal representation, but in reality the union officials run the show.

Examination of Documents. After the inventory and initial interview, the examination takes place. The receipts and disbursements should be thoroughly analyzed. After reviewing the ledgers, the investigator should begin to schedule transactions on accounting paper. These investigations hinge on knowing what one is looking at and not always accepting it at face value. The methods and means of embezzlement and the falsification of union records are extensive and widespread. It is possible, however, to uncover the crime through the various records kept and through the availability of many different records which can be cross-checked to verify the transaction in question. For instance, as stated earlier, the bank statements and checks correlated with the ledger, paid bills, and vouchers cross-check the canceled checks; membership dues records can be verified by interviewing individual members; and so on. However, once the scheme is uncovered, it is still necessary to tie up many loose ends. To establish that a union disbursement is an embezzlement, it must be shown that the money was not expended for a legitimate union purpose and that it was not authorized by the union bylaws and constitution. Frequently, it is not a completely cut-and-dried situation. Furthermore, there is no regulation or specific rule to cover every conceivable occurrence. As in almost all law enforcement, the elements of discretion and subjectivity come into play, and, ultimately, the decision will always involve evaluation by attorneys, the grand jury, and other investigative personnel. In most cases, therefore, one's individual opinion is not sufficient. The investigator's actions determine which decisions finally can be made.

Some Modes of Crime and Types of Embezzlement and Record Falsification

1. Excessive salary payments or unauthorized increases. In these cases, it is necessary to show not only the increase but also that the transaction was unauthorized. Interviews must be conducted with those who would be authorized to issue the raise according to the union constitution. Past union precedent should be investigated and past union officials approached.

2. Fictitious expense claims or the collection of duplicate expenses from two different entities. This is a common form of embezzlement in labor. In such a situation, the union official or trustee bills two organizations for the same expenses. The fraudulence of the scheme is enhanced by obtaining testimony that one fund did not know the other was picking up the expenses. Further strengthening the case are situations in which the official claims such expenses as air fare for one trip from each of the funds. The union official's most common defense is that all the money obtained from both funds was used for a legitimate union purpose, even though one fund was not informed that the other was paying. Other related offenses include misuse of union credit cards, claiming reimbursement for personal expenses, and personal use of union assets such as cars.

3. Schemes involving union disbursements. Common ones include submitting false invoices to support cash disbursements; raising the amount of the check after the authorized signature has been obtained; raising canceled checks returned by the bank to agree with false inflated entries, in which case checks are forged or destroyed when returned by the bank; making unentered deposits;

drawing unentered checks and destroying the canceled checks; improper use of blank checks; and withholding and later cashing undelivered checks.

4. Schemes involving union receipts. These include withholding from deposit into the bank such items as bank interest and refunds on overpayments, pocketing dues money or benefit fund contributions, withholding proceeds from rent if the union owns the building, falsifying the receipts ledger by understating total receipts to cover an embezzlement, or delaying (lapping) the posting of monies received to make it appear that all money has been posted when, in reality, past monies were embezzled. In many cases, it is more difficult to prove such receipts embezzlements than it is to prove disbursement crimes, because it is necessary to reconstruct all receipts in many of these cases, especially with such items as dues, to show that specific monies did exist and were not deposited. This often involves many interviews and third-party contacts. In actuality, money is being looked for which union records fail to show exists. Although burdened by the need to prove lack of union benefit and/or authorization in cases of disbursement embezzlement, at least, once discovered, the check or false document is tangible evidence.

As a general rule, disbursement embezzlements are more commonly investigated and prosecuted. If a receipts embezzlement is uncovered, it is usually more difficult to defend.

Once the investigator has successfully pinned down suspicious areas in the union or benefit fund records, scheduled them out, and identified which documents should be entered into evidence, the following steps are normally taken. If a grand jury is used, the conduct of these investigations is greatly facilitated, because corroboration of documents and witnesses by grand jury subpoena is much stronger than attempting to get cooperation through an agency administrative subpoena or by appealing to a citizen's sense of public duty. Because only grand juries have been generally exempt from recently enacted disclosure restrictions and because they are less influenced by administrative or bureaucratic whims and fears, both the investigative and witness potential of a grand jury make investigating complex white-collar crime much easier.

Witness testimony is very important in corroborating or contradicting the validity and credibility of suspicious document entries. Furthermore, such testimony sheds light on such areas as whether an expenditure was legally authorized by the union's other officials or membership and whether the money was spent for a legitimate union purpose. Although the document itself is the evidence of the crime, testimony (other than investigator testimony) dealing with what the document reflects increases the chances of obtaining a conviction.

Once all records and witnesses have been brought into the grand jury and enough evidence has been obtained to justify an indictment by vote of the grand jury, defendants must decide whether to attempt plea bargaining or go to trial in return for consideration in their cases. The government may attempt to induce subjects to cooperate in providing information about higher-level criminals. In labor racketeering cases, frequently it is necessary to work up the ladder by investigating and convicting lesser officials who may then be asked to testify against the more important higher officials. It is the nature of labor racketeering, in many American cities, for the union official to answer to high syndicate or organized crime figures. In some areas, such as Chicago, some of the highest syndicate leaders are themselves labor union leaders. In constructing investigative and prosecutive strategy, these factors always should be weighed.

Racketeering Activities Cases

Racketeering activity refers to corruption and criminality in the context of labor-management relations, as differentiated from embezzlement and falsification of records, which more often involve an individual breach of fiduciary responsibilities. The racketeering area involves deals consummated between corrupt union officials and corrupt employers for the benefit of each other and to the detriment of the workers and employees.

The "sweetheart" contract is the most basic manifestation of this arrangement. In exchange for a payoff, the union official negotiates a favorable contract with the employer. In this mutually advantageous arrangement, the employer's illegal payment to the union official will be large enough to satisfy that official, while the favorable contract may save the employer more than enough money to make the payoff and still come out ahead. The victims are the employees whose wages are substandard or whose benefits are inadequate. Sometimes the offer is made by the employer; in other cases, the union leader makes the approach; in either case, the criminal culpability is shared.

Another common ploy involves the use of "paper locals" to provide an opportunity for mutually advantageous arrangements. Within this context, a large and seemingly legitimate established union attempts to organize and represent the workers in a nonunion shop. The employer reaches an arrangement with a labor racketeer to come in and represent the workers at a more "reasonable" rate. On some occasions, the larger local's officials will "take a walk" for a proper consideration. On other occasions, they might actually control the "paper local" and have orchestrated the situation so that they are able to get a payoff through either vehicle. The "paper locals" are so called because they are unions that exist only on paper. They do nothing or little to benefit the employees and exist solely as a vehicle for extracting payoffs or providing hoodlums with "legitimate" covers.

Perhaps the most damaging and widespread labor corruption exists in the areas of kickbacks and improprieties involving the misuse of lucrative benefit fund monies and assets. Investigations in this area are extremely complex and time-consuming.

Investigations involving racketeering activities can be precipitated by either specific complainant information or a general targeting of the subject persons and the funds with which they may be affiliated.

In cases involving such activities as payoffs, kickbacks, and extortion in which specific information and leads are furnished, there is a much greater chance of success. When only general allegations of impropriety are made, uncovering corruption and racketeering is more difficult. The most common investigative technique used in the development of a labor kickback or payoff case is to focus on employers who are believed to be giving money or items of value to the labor official illegally, and, by so doing, to try to pressure them into making admissions. Few, if any, individuals will be motivated to testify out of a patriotic sense of duty. Since making payoffs often necessitates book juggling, the most common incentive to induce cooperation is proving that such record-related offenses as tax violations, mail frauds, or falsifying records and/or documents have been committed. An employer who feels threatened enough by the consequences of this situation might be inclined to state the real reason for committing these offenses, namely, to cover up payoff or kickback payments.

On the other side of the coin, proving an income tax violation might increase the possibility of tracing payoff or kickback money to a union official. Unlike many paper-chase cases dealing with embezzlements and false records, kickback searches by examining untargeted records do not bring great statistical results. Sometimes a poorly hidden transaction may be noticeable immediately, but that does not happen very often.

Union benefit fund trustees receiving kickbacks and payoffs from loan fund recipients constitutes about the most common racketeering ploy. In exchange for issuing poor-risk loans to persons or companies that cannot secure legitimate bank financing, the fund trustees agree to loan them money. Of course, the trustees seek a personal return for issuing the loan. Many benefit funds for corrupt international and local unions have become repositories and lending institutions to finance organized crime syndicates.

Once again, the most successful investigative procedure is to attempt to work up the ladder, trying to establish an initial criminal culpability, whether for falsifying a record used to issue a loan or mail fraud for sending fictitious and fraudulent information through the mails.

Because this form of racketeering and corruption involves collusive subjects and mutually advantageous conspiratorial schemes, a wedge must be driven between the participants. If one domino can be toppled, the rest may follow.

Sometimes a dissatisfied coconspirator may be induced to cooperate. The element of fear, however, poses a serious problem in developing racketeer-oriented labor cases. Employers who openly defy labor racketeers are jeopardizing not only their businesses but perhaps their lives. Given these factors, the government is not in a strong position to produce a counterweight to spur cooperation. Furthermore, it has been my observation that there is public skepticism about the government's ability to protect and look after the interests of witnesses who testify against racketeers and persons related to organized crime. Such an appraisal is based not only on such specifics as adverse publicity concerning the witness protection program but also on a basic distrust of government and the integrity of its employees and officials by the public.

In attempting to develop payoff, kickback, extortion, and related racketeering offenses, the following subject records should be scrutinized and examined:

1. *Bank account records (personal and business):* Specifically, large deposits and withdrawals; the source of income and destination of expenditures; related loan and credit files reflecting the overall financial assets, obligations, and properties.

2. *Tax records:* Returns, salary payments, and interest and security income, both personal and corporate. Stringent IRS disclosure laws can make obtaining these records a problem.

3. *Contracts and agreements:* Those negotiated among and between subjects and third parties. This should include examination of correspondence files.

4. *Records reflecting ownership and principals of a business:* All possible avenues of funneling money through allied or affiliated corporate or personal entities must be explored, such as Dun & Bradstreet reports, certificates of incorporation, and county clerk records.

5. *Cash receipts and disbursement records:* Sudden large receipts or expenditures of money; a sudden influx of money coupled with a large disbursement.

In cases involving statutes outside of labor law jurisdiction, cooperative liaison between agencies can lead to better enforcement. Sometimes witnesses or subjects for one type of investigation may give information designed to prove their innocence in one area while providing incriminating evidence in another. Such a situation has developed when, for instance, an IRS special agent questioning employers about unsubstantiated expenses is informed that actually the payment was made to a labor official. Such a response, designed to avoid a tax violation charge, is evidence of another possible federal violation. Hence, when such information is received, establishing liaison and using a cooperative approach can have beneficial investigative results.

As in embezzlement and record-keeping cases, the grand jury is important in developing conspiracy cases. Through its ability to subpoena witnesses and records and to grant immunity, the development of these cases is greatly enhanced.

Witness testimony relative to relationships between suspect parties is important. In racketeering offenses, witness testimony is especially necessary to obtain sufficient evidence to justify the grand jury indictment. Frequently, it is necessary to immunize or plea bargain with one conspirator to obtain needed testimony against others.

PART 7

Insurance Investigations and Loss Prevention

41
Health Care Fraud

Neil B. Checkman

One of the largest problems facing state and federally funded programs charged with delivering health care services is provider fraud. Unfortunately, the more ambitious the program is in terms of delivering a wide range of services to the poor and elderly, the easier it is for the unscrupulous to prey upon it. This chapter is designed to highlight the overall problems relating to health care fraud, focusing on the New York City area.

THE MEDICAID MILL

In New York City, the vast majority of health services delivered to Medicaid recipients are provided in a Medicaid clinic. While many of the clinics are merely rented storefronts in low-rent sections of the City, the size and structure of the clinics vary. If a Medicaid clinic has several offices, a common waiting room, and conforms to certain physical specifications, it is called a *shared health facility* and is required to register with the state. This requirement is honored in the breach, due mainly to the fact that, once a clinic is registered as a shared health facility, it is then subject to regulation.

The typical Medicaid clinic has a common waiting room, an administrative area with a receptionist to keep track of the patient charts, and several offices. Some of the offices are for doctors, podiatrists, and dentists, others for technicians such as phlebotimists (blood drawers).

Usually there is a pharmacy next door or within a few storefronts of the clinic.

The clinics are run by an administrator, who may or may not be the owner and who need have no medical qualifications or license whatsoever.

The clinic itself is not enrolled in the Medicaid system, and thus has no formal relationship with the Medicaid system.

In New York State the Medicaid system is administered by the New York State Department of Social Services (DSS). DSS contracts out the claims process to a fiscal agent. As of this writing that fiscal agent is Computer Sciences Corporation. The entire claim and payment process is recorded and stored in the Medicaid Management Information System (MMIS).

Most Medicaid recipients are poor people who cannot afford to pay for their family's medical needs. Some recipients, however, are "professional patients" who spend their days going from clinic to clinic seeing Medicaid doctors as a source of "employment."

For the purposes of illustration I will describe a worst-case scenario. This scenario, though not always as extreme as presented, is all too common throughout the City of New York.

The professional patient arrives early in the morning at a Medicaid clinic or "Medicaid mill." He (or she) enters the clinic and provides his Medicaid card to the receptionist who immediately, through the use of a swipe-card phone device connected to the MMIS system in Albany, determines that our "patient" is eligible for service today. (Each Medicaid card has a unique number that identifies the recipient, and family members are distinguished by suffixes to the master Medicaid number.)

Upon verification of eligibility, our patient is ushered into a back room where, prior to seeing a doctor, he is given an electrocardiogram, spirometry (breath) test, and sonogram. He then has blood drawn for laboratory testing and is directed to see a doctor.

Many of the doctors work at hospital jobs and attend clinics to supplement their incomes. Some bounce from clinic to clinic in various boroughs at varying schedules. The clinic-owner tries to ensure that there are always enough doctors to cover each of their clinics.

Doctors, podiatrists, and dentists are providers of medical services under the Medicaid system.

Upon submitting an application to the Medicaid program, together with proof of proper licensure, they are given a unique provider number, which entitles them to bill for medical services given to eligible Medicaid recipients.

They submit bills to the fiscal agent for payment. The claim system is designed to be "provider-friendly," which means that the system endeavors to pay claims as quickly as possible in order to encourage medical professionals to enter and remain in the system.

The system presumes the honesty of the provider. No proof of actual treatment is required. This provides an open invitation to the unscrupulous. The only requirement for billing is a completed claim form containing the names and Medicaid numbers of the patients, the diagnosis codes and procedure codes of the services, the dollar amount claimed, the dates of service, and the provider's unique identification number. Billing can be on paper claim forms (hard copy) or by magnetic tape submissions. Providers are required to enter into agreements with the Medicaid program, which entitle them to submit magnetic tape claims directly, or through companies that will provide this service for several providers.

Our "patient" has now seen the first doctor of the day and, after being "examined," is then given one or more prescriptions. Our patient takes his "script" next door to a pharmacy where he can get the prescription filled or receive a cash payment in lieu of the items on the prescription form. All too often the pharmacy is little more than an empty room with a counter with a slit, behind which the pharmacist or his employee sits and fills the prescriptions or reaches for the items. The New York State Medicaid system is particularly generous. Aside from prescription drugs, the system provides aspirin, condoms, seat canes, shower massagers, heating pads, bandages of all types, and various forms of durable Medicaid equipment.

Our patient, if he chooses not to sell the items back to the pharmacy (or if the pharmacy will not act that brazenly), can go out on the street and sell the items for whatever the traffic may bear. Sometimes an employee of the pharmacy will station himself outside the pharmacy to purchase back the drugs and equipment at a discount. Our patient, time permitting, can repeat the process at a different clinic later that same day. If our patient uses his own card, there is a race to bill since the system will only pay for a service once on the same service date.

However, it is often the case that our professional patient is in possession of two "live" cards at the same time and thus can be two different people.

Let's backtrack a bit. So far we have seen the recipient giving blood, taking tests, and being examined. We then followed him to a pharmacy. Let us now trace how the Medicaid system has been victimized.

The doctor examining and treating our "patient" commonly spends as little as five minutes with him. He or she may touch the patient with a stethoscope and ask how he is. This accomplished, the doctor inquires as to what the patient needs. The professional patient describes appropriate symptoms, memorized from previous repetition, and requests various expensive drugs and salable items and supplies. The doctor bills the program for an examination and whatever else he or she wishes, limited only by the level of personal greed, or imagination. The more careful doctors make appropriate notations in the patient's chart. The sonogram, EKG, and spirometry tests are all billed by the doctor. The blood samples are sent to a clinical testing laboratory where hundreds of dollars in unnecessary tests for each patient are performed and billed by the laboratory to the Medicaid program.

During an investigation and prosecution in 1988 it was learned that drug addicts were selling their blood every other day in store fronts and apartments throughout the City, and the blood was finding its way, together with test request forms with forged doctor's signatures and the names of real Medicaid recipients, to several area clinical blood-testing laboratories. The names and Medicaid numbers of the recipients were taken from test result forms, which were purchased from clinic employees throughout the City.

The lab billings to the State of New York went from a norm of about $2.5 million per month to over $28 million per month at the height of the scam in 1988. The fraud was uncovered when the addicts started showing at area hospital emergency rooms appearing as if they were attacked by vampires.

It is a common fraud in the system for the clinic administrator to contract with a clinical testing laboratory to provide blood samples to the lab in return for kickbacks based on a percentage of the lab's Medicaid billings. It is in everyone's interest (except the tax-paying public) to order as many tests as possible. The doctors are willing to sign the lab test request forms because they are given rent-free offices, free blood drawers, free equipment, and a percentage of the kickbacks themselves.

Let us turn to our pharmacies. The pharmacy owner, not necessarily the pharmacist, has many opportunities to commit fraud. One can "short" the prescription. This is simply dispensing less than the full amount of pills or items called for on the prescription. The more expensive the medicine, the more profit in "shorting." The entire amount is billed as if dispensed. We have already seen that some pharmacies will buy back the dispensed items or the prescriptions themselves at a discount. Another form of fraud practiced by unscrupulous pharmacy owners, is the "rain check." When the patient gives the script to the pharmacy they are told we're out of this, come back tomorrow. The script is billed as if dispensed, and commonly the patient never returns. Still another scam is the substitution of a low-cost generic drug for the prescribed high-price brand name drug. The pharmacy, of course, bills for the brand name drug. The difference is pure profit. Finally, the pharmacist can create prescriptions out of thin air. Phoned in prescriptions require a written script to follow, but it is common for the doctors to forget to send them. The pharmacy entrepreneur takes advantage of this by creating bogus phoned-in records for renewal prescriptions. One can also alter the number on a prescription form, which permits renewals in excess of what the doctor authorized, and then these "renewals" can be billed on dates when nothing was actually dispensed.

This is nowhere near an exhaustive listing of the frauds commonly encountered in the Medicaid system in New York City. Those who victimize the Medicaid system are limited only by their imagination and the depth of their greed.

DETECTING AND PROSECUTING FRAUD

The methods used in detecting these frauds range from the classic recipient interview to the use of high-tech computer technology.

One method of investigation that has produced positive results over a long period is the team approach. The Office of the Special Prosecutor for Medicaid Fraud Control, the agency charged with medicaid fraud control in New York State, employs a team consisting of an attorney, an investigator, and an auditor-investigator on each investigation.

The auditor-investigator has an accounting background, and develops expertise in the examination of books and records of the providers who are being investigated, as well as the information contained in the files of the Medicaid system. A good auditor-investigator can effectively target a problem, and point the other disciplines in the right direction.

The field investigator, usually a law enforcement veteran, uses his or her experience to conduct field interviews, develop and exploit sources of information, and maintain on-the-scene control of undercover and sting operations.

Finally, the attorney is responsible for coordination of the audit and investigative disciplines and the channeling of efforts into a form that allows for a determination as to whether an abuse is occurring and whether that abuse is criminal or civil in nature. The attorney then guides the overall investigative effort to maximize its potential to produce usable evidence for presentation to a grand jury and for trial.

We live in the age of the computer, and just as people have learned to use the computer to steal, the investigator must learn to utilize the computer to detect and investigate.

TARGETING

Before you can investigate for fraud, you need to know which areas to devote your attention to. This is commonly called *targeting*. The health care fraud investigator can employ several methods of targeting simultaneously. First, there is the random recipient canvass. This is accomplished by periodically sending out listings of paid-for medical services to recipients who are chosen at random. The form used in New York State is called an Explanation of Medical Benefits (EOMB). The recipient who receives an EOMB is encouraged to review it and report to the program whether listed services have not been actually provided. There is no penalty for not responding, but often the recipients fear that they will lose services if they do not respond. While only a small percentage of EOMB forms are returned, it is usually enough to highlight likely areas for further investigation.

The Medicaid system has the details of all paid claims in its history files. The files consist of magnetic tape from which information can be extracted tracing the claim from receipt to payment.

The Department of Social Services employs their own computer programs to extract hard-copy printouts of paid claims in several formats. An investigator can order printouts by provider or by recipient.

Special reports have been created to enable the investigator to determine which trends require a closer look. These reports show quantitative changes in the billing practices of individual providers, provider-types (i.e., doctors, podiatrists, laboratories), or categories of service (sonograms, AZT prescriptions, thyroid tests). "Growth industries" can be spotted and full-scale targeting projects can be designed to cope with these new areas of program abuse.

One example of how this has worked is in the sonogram area. A review of monthly printouts of categories of services indicated that sonogram services over several months were being billed at levels much higher than previously seen.

It was determined that it would be worthwhile to try and discover the reason behind the increased billings. A review of computer printouts revealed that sonogram services were being billed at the rate of five services per patient each and every visit. In addition, the amounts billed seemed to ignore the billing directives in the Medicaid manual. The question posed was, why are so many radiologists suddenly doing so many sonograms and repeating the same billing "misinterpretation"? This review eventually led to an extensive investigation, prosecutions, and a tightening of controls over the provision of sonograms as a diagnostic tool.

It is often useful to examine the monthly billings of the top 10 or 20 individual providers in any single category of service. A comparison of billings from month to month indicates who are the top billers in a "peer group" and raises the inevitable question why?

METHOD OF APPROACH

After the team selects an appropriate target, the investigator is then ready to choose the technique or techniques to be employed in the investigation.

At the onset of the investigation of a provider, you first must evaluate what information one already has. If you have a recipient EMOB stating "I never got this service," you immediately attempt to interview the recipient. The more EOMBs relating to a particular provider, the better the chance to get the flavor of the problem. After a full set of interviews, the provider's profile should be ordered. A provider profile is a computer printout in varying data order of all the services rendered by the provider and billed to the system within a particular period. It can be in service date order, category of service order, alphabetical order, etc. Programs can be designed (or purchased) to put the data into whatever order the investigator requires.

Upon receipt of the provider profile, a workable number of recipients can be chosen (usually 50 to start), their individual service profiles ordered, and letters requesting interviews mailed. It is useful to send out a large number of requests because few people will respond, and fewer still will actually submit to an interview.

Once a problem has been identified, many classic investigative tools can be employed.

"Shoppers" can be sent in, posing as Medicaid recipients, to gather intelligence information. A large body of information can be garnered by a good undercover shopper while sitting around a busy clinic waiting to see a doctor. The shopper can see how the clinic operates, who seems to be in charge, what services are being "pushed," how the doctors conduct their examinations, and then, after the visit, how the pharmacy treats the prescriptions submitted by the shopper. When the shopper billings come back from the program, the investigator can either narrow down the scope of the investigation, expand it to encompass newly discovered areas of abuse, or even switch targets.

Cooperating witnesses are the best source of successful investigations. They tend to allow for daisy chains of sting-type operations, whereby each success spawns another investigation and so on.

A low- or mid-level insider who has been discovered stealing a little, and has been caught through a classic painstaking investigation, can be offered an opportunity to cooperate in return for lenient treatment. It is of course important to weigh the benefits to the investigation against the public policy of punishing those caught victimizing the system in making the decision on who can be or should be "turned."

The insider, who is caught cheating but who is willing to cooperate, allows the investigator to gain rare access to the criminal enterprise. The more criminally involved the cooperators are, the more areas of concern they can assist you with.

In a well-designed cooperator-assisted investigation, an investigator will be able to capture and preserve evidence of criminal acts on video and audio tape for use in the grand jury and on trial, and, in addition, will be able to recruit a second generation of cooperators.

INFORMATION CONTROL

At this point it is useful to remember that, in the area of health care fraud investigations, you will encounter vast amounts of evidence and information. Investigators who cannot manage their information effectively will drown in the paper, and ultimately the investigation will suffer.

Systems must be developed to receive, collate, and store information as it comes in, so as to render it easily accessible for later retrieval and use. The better the system is at the beginning, the easier the job is at the end.

The system can be a paper report system or a computer data entry system. The dollar resources of the investigative agency often determines the method to be employed.

Whatever the form the system takes, the goal remains the same. The information must be preserved, evidence must be safeguarded, chains of custody must be carefully preserved, and the information and evidence must be retrievable.

It is important that techniques of cross-indexing be developed. An investigator should be able to run a name of a person or a business entity, and be able to access all previous references to that person or entity. This requires that information be accurately inputted into the system, as soon as practicable. Backlogs severely undermine the usefulness of the system. In setting up any such indexing and retrieval system, proper staffing is a must.

It is in this area that computer technology can play its most useful role. Dollars initially spent in setting up such a system will save money in the long run. The returns to the investigative agency will be increased efficiency and better results.

CONCLUSION

The health care fraud problem is limited only by the imagination and inventiveness of the abuser. Those who would seek to stop the hemorrhaging will need to be as imaginative and inventive as those who they wish to deter. Those who prey upon the Medicaid program undermine the legitimate attempts of government to deliver health care to the poor and the elderly. They must be shown that the risk of being caught is great, before the waste of taxpayer money can be abated.

Real deterrence can be achieved only by increasing the probability of detection and punishment. If a good investigative system is in place and if good people are employed, positive results should follow.

42

Insurance Investigation Techniques: Casualty

Joseph P. Cicale

During the past 20 years, there have been more dramatic and significant changes in the casualty insurance business than in all its prior years of development. We have observed changes which have affected not only the solvency of major insurance companies but also the lives of every man, woman, and child in the United States. These changes, particularly in tort litigation, have altered the entire concept of investigation, claims handling, and adjusting.

In the early 1970s, the notorious Keeton-O'Connell proposition (no fault) blossomed into automobile reparation acts, which have since become law in most states. The reduction or elimination of the less severe fender-bender bodily injury claims has allowed the industry to concentrate on the more severe, potentially high-verdict, automobile accident claims. Claims managers, independent adjusters, and attorneys can concentrate on the investigation of more substantial claims, knowing that the smaller, lower court cases can be resolved with minimal investigation. In the late 1960s, the Liberty Mutual Insurance Company revolutionized the casualty claims investigation field through the use of inexperienced college graduate claim representatives as desk adjusters. No longer was it necessary to make expense allocation to private investigators or higher-salaried field representatives to investigate the lower-valued, less-exposure cases. Investigations took on a routine format, with desk adjusters handling close to 80 percent of the incoming claims. By and large, the industry has accepted the desk adjuster, realizing that through telephone investigation, recorded interviews, and the U.S. mail, a claims file could be and usually is better investigated than in prior years.

In addition to the modification in the *Automobile Tort Law,* even more significant developments have occurred with respect to products liability litigation. The enactment of the *Consumer Products Safety Act in 1972,* coupled with the movement toward strict liability in products liability lawsuits, has resulted in greater awareness arising from the analysis of these actions. Manufacturers became accountable for the risks arising out of the use of their products to the extent that they should have foreseen the danger to potential users. Of the products involved in this litigation, clearly the most controversial include highly flammable fabrics, automobiles as a whole (as well as their parts), building materials made of asbestos, and prescription as well as over-the-counter drugs. Over the past 20 years, bodily injury claims arising out of the use of the aforementioned products have resulted in not only high jury verdicts but also high defense costs, and in some cases punitive damages lodged against the manufacturer. All these factors have revolutionized the current scope of investigation, as we will bring out in this chapter.

The 1970s presented the industry with a whole new outlook in the area of extracontractual liability and the responsibilities of the insurance carrier toward its policyholder. Federal- and state-imposed privacy acts, as well as the *Model Unfair Claim Settlement Act,* have added to the difficulties faced by insurance investigators. Never before was it necessary that an insurance company worry about "bad faith" judgments, punitive damage awards, and the civil rights of third-party plaintiffs. The exchange of information between insurance companies has been limited, and fact gathering in general now requires careful probing for fear of violations of the civil rights of the people or the corporations being investigated. The next few pages will bring up to date the current practices and difficulties experienced by the insurance investigator within the various categories of casualty insurance.

AUTOMOBILE INSURANCE
CLAIM INVESTIGATION

The investigation of claims generated from the automobile insurance policy involves concern for not only adversary third-party but also insured first-party claims. The advent of *no-fault* statutes has forced the insurance investigator to spend considerably more time in accident investigation of the insured's own claim. For example, in New York State, with a no-fault personal injury protection limit of a minimum of $50,000 for injuries, adjusters are compelled to turn their attention toward an injured driver, as well as toward passengers, pedestrians, or occupants of other vehicles involved in that accident. In many instances, the injury suffered by the insured driver could result in greater payment through the applicable no-fault law than would have resulted from any litigation started by an injured third party.

Another area of concern with respect to automobile claim investigation arises out of *physical damage* coverages. First-party comprehensive theft, fire, and collision claims must be explored in many of the same ways used for the investigation of third-party claims. Despite the existence of the National Automobile Theft Bureau and other associations designed to thwart automobile theft schemes, the problem continues to increase immensely each year. An even greater resurgence in the frequency and severity of automobile thefts followed the gasoline crisis over the summer of 1979. Gas-guzzling luxury automobiles became victims to owners who could not afford or did not care to pay over $1 a gallon for these low-miles-per-gallon automobiles. Needless to say, this type of individual, nonorganized fraud is difficult to investigate or even prosecute unless the evidence is ironclad. To combat organized automobile theft rings, the automobile industry in 1964 adopted a standard numbering system to identify vehicles. All American-manufactured vehicles now have a vehicle identification number (VIN). It not only remains unique to that individual vehicle, but also identifies the manufacturer, the year of manufacture, and the model and body style.

These and similar automobile fraud schemes have contributed their share to the tremendous increase in the cost to the consumer of automobile physical damage insurance today, although much of the increase is also due to the spiraling cost of parts and labor. These high costs, however, themselves tend to foster more fraud by providing even higher profit potential for individuals or body shops. In the Northeast, automobile collision and theft coverages are so expensive that many motorists can no longer afford to carry such first-party protection.

Whether the automobile claim is classified as a third-party bodily injury, property damage, or as a physical damage claim, the basic elements of casualty investigation remain the same. All investigations of automobile casualty claims and suits take on the same format, and differ only in intensity, expense, and priority. They can be broken down into three distinct categories: (1) coverage, (2) liability, and (3) damages. We will treat each separately, as each requires specific exploratory techniques to come to a definitive conclusion.

Coverage

Whether a claim results in payment of a $50 towing bill or a $2 million bodily injury liability suit, the principles of coverage investigation remain the same. The investigator, claims supervisor, claims attorney, or claims manager must first establish the existence of the automobile policy, including such components as the policy number, effective dates, policy limits, and identification of the insured vehicle.

By far the majority of all claim first reports which come into a local insurance claims department entail no coverage problems whatsoever. However, for the small minority that do present problems, swift action must be taken in order to avoid unnecessary anxiety for the insurance carrier that may be estopped from denying coverage based on the coverage exclusion or breach of contract on the part of the policyholder. Such factors as proper identification of the vehicle, permissive use given to the driver, use of the vehicle excluded by the policy, and late reporting of the accident by the insured all require quick and decisive investigative decisions. Generally speaking, the technique at this stage would be a review of the policy contract, discussion with the broker, a statement from the policyholder or driver, and proper identification of the automobile involved in the accident. Having overcome the coverage problems, the claims investigator can now concentrate on investigating the liability or "fault" of the parties involved in the automobile accident.

Liability—Investigation Techniques

Without question, the investigation of the liability issues in automobile accident claims requires the most time, expense, and investigative experience. The scope of inquiry into automobile accidents that determines the liability of the parties involved depends greatly on the *motor vehicle law* of the particular state. Generally, case law involving automobile litigation is similar throughout the 50 states and District of Columbia. The variations are in the no-fault statutes, guest statutes, rights-of-pedestrian laws, and the difference between comparative and contributory negligence. Other than these distinctions, investigations of automobile accidents by casualty insurance investigators are uniform. Clearly, investigation of any casualty insurance matter demands the immediate gathering of critical evidence obtained through immediate and direct contact with not only the injured third party but also the policyholder.

Signed Statements. *A statement by the adverse driver is of primary importance,* taking precedence over all other contacts in gathering critical evidence. Clearly, on commencing this study of an automobile accident, the insurance investigator usually is already armed with an accident report, statement, or other information concerning the insured driver's interpretation of the accident facts. It is this account, whether recorded or handwritten, through a standardized form or deposition, that will become critical in evaluating the liability situation. The purpose of the signed statement (recorded interview) is to preserve the evidence. It is to be the exact account of the story told by this witness and it is to be signed by the supplier of the statement to attest to its authenticity. Its use varies, depending on the viewpoint of the person requiring the statement. For the insurance investigator, it is the easiest and quickest way to get accident facts from the driver of an automobile before the facts are forgotten or maybe "modified," due to the intervention of a lawyer or the insurance carrier of the adverse driver. Having the appearance of a "legal" document in that it is a sworn statement, it also serves the investigator as a psychological tool.

The importance of the signed statement to the trial attorney is even more dramatic. Since negligence trials take several years to emerge, the statement can be used by the witness prior to trail to refresh recollection of the distant past event. Should an adverse witness testify to a version different from that recorded on the statement, then clearly the sworn statement can be used to discredit that witness. Following closely the statement of the drivers in importance is the statement from the injured party or claimants who suffer injury or property damage as a result of this incident. Injured accident victims are protected in most states which have statutes that make it unlawful for either an investigator or the individual's own attorney to interrogate a victim who is confined to a hospital within a prescribed period (usually the first 15 days after admission). Typical of such a statute is the one contained in the penal law of New York State. Since it would be a crime for an investigator to violate that statute, he or she would have to obtain written consent of the in-patient in order for the interview to take place.

Clearly, a sworn statement from an injured claimant immediately after the accident will not only discourage overtreatment by a physician, but would also mitigate possible exaggeration of the extent of the total injury picture by the injured party's lawyer in litigation.

Since the statement is the story of the event as told by the injured claimant, it should, as would a newspaper account, answer the questions of who, what, when, where, and why. The preservation of this information at the early stages of the investigation will be the basis of further injury and probing for accident facts. When taking signed statements from witnesses, the interviewer must make it clear that only the facts within their knowledge are to be taken and that opinions, judgments, or conclusions are to be avoided. Since injured parties are usually adverse witnesses, their interests are usually in opposition to those of the insured and, naturally, their versions of occurrences would be favorable to themselves and unfavorable to the insured. Generally severely injured accident victims are represented by attorneys, which hampers the ability to take signed statements in the beginning stages of investigation.

Photographs. Of secondary importance as critical evidence in the primary stages of accident investigation, would be *photographs* of the locus of the accident or of the vehicles involved in the collision. Since the main purpose of taking photographs is to have a permanent record of the conditions as they existed at the time of the accident, they should, of course, be taken as soon as possible, before any transformation occurs in the scene or the vehicle. Commercial photographs can be important in the defense of a case, not only by showing the locus of the accident but also by illustrating the point of contact through pictures both of vehicles and of skid marks which may have remained on the road surface. For the photographs to be useful, it is vital that they be taken at the same time of year so that foliage or conditions of snow and ice will be similar, and also at the same time of day or night so that the shadow formations and lighting conditions will be analogous.

A few simple photographic rules apply to most automobile accidents: (1) All snapshots of the accident should be taken from both the eye level and the viewpoint of all drivers involved and all witnesses. (2) A permanent reference point should be included in all photographs, such as a fire hydrant, traffic light, manhole cover, or a specific tree. (3) All obstructions which may have blocked the driver's view of stop signs, road signs, traffic lights, or pedestrians should be included. It would be helpful for the investigator to take the photograph while accompanied by the driver or an eyewitness.

When photographing the claimant's automobile, investigators must remember the claimant's "right to privacy," as protected in the First, Fourth, and Fifth Amendments to the Constitution. They should not enter a claimant's garage or fenced-in driveway to photograph his or her automobile. Naturally, pictures of highways, and of automobiles on highways or in repair shops or even in a claimant's unfenced driveway are permissible.

Frequently, the police or detectives who have investigated the occurrence will take their own photographs. These shots are very important, since they have been taken by an impartial agency, and usually immediately after the accident. At the trial, these prints often can assure the success or failure of the defendant's case.

Witnesses. The investigation of liability continues with statements of interested or disinterested witnesses. A witness is defined as a person who testifies to what he or she has seen, heard, or otherwise came to know. This definition, therefore, includes not only the parties to the accident, but also all others who have acquired some knowledge of the facts. A potential witness may testify to facts acquired through the use of any of the senses. A witness can be classified as either friendly or unfriendly with regard to assistance given to the interviewer.

The friendly witness may not necessarily support the defense but makes the evidence readily accessible to the investigator and generally cooperates in giving all the information available. An unfriendly witness may choose not to get involved in the case or may be unfriendly merely because his interests favor the claimant.

The most difficult to deal with is the witness who is hostile and shows unfriendliness. It is that witness who exhibits definite bias or prejudice against the defendant which has no basis in fact. Whatever the motivation for the hostility, the witness usually is of little benefit to either side of the investigation. Therefore, it is important for the investigator to recognize this hostility and, if possible, get a signed statement which will clearly indicate it.

Before a statement can be taken, a witness must be identified and located. Insurance investigators generally use their own devices for identification and location of witnesses if it is not provided with the report by the insured to the insurance company. There are several official sources available for locating or identifying witnesses.

Official Reports. The police report (blotter) is readily obtainable and is generally the primary official report to consult when trying to locate the names and addresses of witnesses. Other available documents include state motor vehicle reports filed by both involved parties, fire department reports, and in some cases state motor vehicle inspection results.

Canvass. Last, but of equal prominence, would be the canvass of the neighborhood where the accident occurred. An investigator often visits all the homes or apartment houses in the vicinity of the accident, hoping to find a witness. Though slow and painstaking, it can produce remarkable results. It is important that the investigator, although aggressive, not be "unreasonably intrusive" by trespassing to gain entrance where a witness may have the expectation of privacy. This may constitute grounds for a civil damage action and may result in any evidence obtained being held inadmissible. An insurer and an investigator could be held liable for invasion of privacy for obtaining the name and address of a witness by deception. Deception may consist of *giving misinformation* about identity or purpose, but it may also consist of *failing to make proper disclosure*.

Damages

On completion of coverage and liability issues, the investigator should concentrate on the injury or damages sustained by the claimant. Securing medical information has been hindered in recent years by federal privacy legislation and numerous other regulations governing banking, insurance, and service industries. The prohibition of certain forms of discrimination has the effect of increasing privacy protection for the individual.

Injury Verification. The casualty insurance industry has the obligation to all policyholders and to the insurance buying public to pay suitable claims promptly but to resists exaggerated and fraudulent claims. That means verification of injuries and damages is essential in every bodily injury or property damage case. Since the doctor-patient privilege is generally recognized across the United States, most medical reports can be obtained only by means of a signed authorization by the patient to the hospital or physician. Most physicians will refuse to furnish medical reports without prior consent by the patient. Occasionally, claimants are reluctant to give an authorization, or their attorneys may refuse or at least delay in presenting the insurance company with a signed affidavit. A full analysis of the injury sustained by a claimant generally includes hospital records, attending physicians' reports and records, and medical reports covering preexisting injuries or diseases. However, even before procuring these official records, one must not overlook the information that can be obtained from the claimant and incorporated in his or her signed statement or recorded interview. Whether the knowledge is secured orally or in writing from the injured party, it should include:

1. A detailed account and description of all objective evidence of injury (for example, bleeding, lacerations, and open wounds).

2. A complete list of subjective complaints, including when they first developed and their duration.

3. Information on first aid or other assistance rendered at the scene of the accident, including the identity of the good samaritan.

4. Names and addresses of hospitals or doctors to whom the claimant was taken immediately after the accident.

5. Names and addresses of the family physician and/or specialist who subsequently treated the injured party.

6. Dates of all visits and admissions to hospitals, as well as visits to doctors and specialists.

7. Details concerning duration of treatment, confinement to bed, and length of disability from work.

8. A complete record of relevant previous medical history of the injured party.

After extraction of data given to the interviewer by the injured claimant, a follow-up investigation can be commenced to verify the allegations or attack the authenticity of the claimant's injury and medical bills. When dealing directly with an injured party who expresses nervousness about furnishing the investigator with a signed authorization, the injured party should be given a medical report form with instructions to have the physician complete the form and forward it to the insurance company. Naturally, this makes it unnecessary for the claimant to give an authorization to obtain medical information. While the law varies from state to state, it is proper for a claims investigator to ask for a medical report from a physician despite the fact that no authorization is available. However, the insurance company representative must never use any subterfuge or deceit in requesting medical information and must promptly report the truth if pressed to present a signed authorization.

Exaggerated Claims.　It is not unusual for medical expenses to be built up either by claimants who pretend to be more injured than they really are or by physicians who treat accident victims. The injuries are often of the soft-tissue type: strains, sprains, backaches, headaches, contusions, and so on, which create a great deal of pain and suffering with no objective findings. These types of injuries require closer scrutiny by the investigator and the carrier's medical consultant. In order to detect fraud or reduce the consequences of medical treatment, the investigator should be alert to certain factors that generally give evidence that the alleged injury warrants closer inspection: (1) The damage to the claimant's car is minor, but the medical bill resulting from bodily injury is large. (2) The Central Index Bureau check reveals that an injured claimant has had numerous other claims with insurance companies. (3) The injury bears no causal relationship to the accident itself. (4) The physician who issued the medical bill or estimate cannot be located or has no record of such a patient. A company named in a lost wage statement cannot be located or has no record of such an employee. (5) The claimant seems to know more about the settlement process than would be reasonable, considering his or her background and experience.

Since these minor injury claims are often quickly settled to protect the interests of policyholders, professional claimants can and do make tidy incomes on settlements that are often only a few hundred dollars each.

Hospital Records. In addition to the information obtained from physicians, the claims investigator may decide that a review of the patient's hospital record is needed. Hospital records are important for the following reasons: (1) to verify the history of the injury, (2) to discover prior medical conditions, (3) to verify that all the treatment that the insurance company is paying for relates to the injury, (4) to obtain expert information on the nature and the extent of the injury, and (5) to determine if the hospital is overcharging.

Nurses' notes might also provide important investigative material to verify the patient's pain and suffering or to develop more information on prior existing medical conditions. These hospital records and abstracts serve merely to clarify or attack a physician's opinion. Regrettably, the Institute of Medicine has issued a report on a study about the "Reliability of Hospital Discharge Abstracts," which disclosed that the diagnosis was inaccurate in more than one-third of the cases examined and that the description of procedures was inaccurate in more than 25 percent of the cases. In addition, it was found that the principal diagnosis on the medical records was inaccurately reflected in 26.8 percent of the cases, and in another 10.7 percent of the cases, it was impossible to identify the principal diagnosis on the medical record. This information is rather startling in light of the dependence the investigator often places on hospital discharge abstracts.

Activity Checks. As a final technique, the insurance investigator is often called on to conduct an activity check or surveillance of the injured party. This "eyeball" examination of the injured claimant is usually done when the investigator has received information from some informant that the injured claimant's activities are not consistent with the alleged injuries. A surveillance is usually reserved for a claimant suffering a severe injury, especially cases involving burns, spinal cord injuries, severe lacerations, and paralysis. The injured claimant should not just be checked with clothing on, but if possible, the actual site of the injury should be visually checked and pictures secured. Activity checks are used in cases involving extended disability, and these checks either verify or help the investigator reduce or eliminate the period of disability. Again, the primary sources are direct observation of the injured person and contact with neighbors and local businesses. The following should be done on an activity check: (1) Verify that the claimant is still living and is still at the same address. (2) Provide a brief physical description of the claimant, including comments on appearance, attitude, and activities. There should also be comments on whether the activities appear to be consistent with the complaints and medical reports on the injured claimant. (3) Determine if there are any obvious signs indicating that the claimant is working, such as a new car or home repairs. (4) Finally, interview neighbors, coworkers, and local business owners concerning their knowledge of the claimant's activities.

Activity checks and surveillances are investigative techniques used infrequently. On a public street or any other public place, a person has no legal right to be alone, and it is not an invasion of privacy to do no more than follow the injured party about and to observe him or her. Neither is it an invasion of privacy to take a person's photograph in public. If an insurance representative undertakes a surveillance of a supposedly malingering claimant, we need have no fear of invasion of privacy as long as the investigator's activities are reasonable. Definitely, the photographer cannot "set a claimant up"; for example, letting air out of a tire of his or her automobile in order to photograph the injured party in the physical activity of changing that tire.

At this juncture, the investigator has completed the investigation concerning coverage, liability, and damage factors in the automobile accident case and is now equipped to evaluate and dispose of the claim. Clearly, the results of the investigation in all three areas will give the investigator the necessary information for successful negotiation, settlement, or denial of the claim. We now turn toward other areas of casualty claims investigation.

PUBLIC LIABILITY CLAIM INVESTIGATION

The basic principles for the investigation of all casualty insurance claims are the same. Such matters as planning and preparation, medical investigation, physical facts (photographs and diagrams), and locating and interviewing witnesses have been adequately covered in the preceding section.

Public liability claims fall under a myriad of classifications. The types of claims run the gamut from objects falling on people to false arrest; they occur on floors, sidewalks, stairways, in public buildings, in private homes, and in every other imaginable place. Therefore, it is impossible to outline investigative techniques that would cover all types of claims classified as public or general liability injuries. In recent years, there has been greater concern, and therefore, more intense investigation in the areas of products liability and professional malpractice liability.

Looking for a Partner

In public liability investigation, more than in automobile liability investigation, we encounter situations that justify a cause of action against another wrongdoer. The claims representative is usually called on to gather evidence to show that someone else other than the insured is the primary negligent party. Armed with this knowledge, the investigator must then put that party and its carrier on notice concerning their responsibility and at the same time, if necessary, ask them to defend the claim or suit.

Premises open to the public usually carry general liability insurance to protect owners against suits by people injured on those premises; this category of public liability claim is most common. Such coverage for protection against claims by the public is carried by retail businesses, including stores, motels, restaurants, office buildings, and government buildings such as post offices and libraries.

Types of Accidents

Typical accidents include slipping on spilled oil on a supermarket floor, tripping over rugs or wires in public places, slipping on ice or snow on sidewalks, and accidents occurring at construction sites. The same priorities and format used in taking signed statements in automobile liability cases apply to the general liability signed statement. The statement itself differs, however, from the automobile statement because of the need to obtain a detailed, accurate description of the premises, the weather conditions, and the original destination of the injured party. The statement taken from the injured party should contain a complete account of the accident facts as well as a description of the place of the accident. Invariably, the investigator will find that the claimant's observation of the surroundings is not accurate and he or she probably will not recall essential facts about the area. If this is true, the injured party's lack of recollection should be incorporated in the statement. The place of accident must always be established with certainty within the claimant's signed statement. Very often, it will be found that portions of a premises are leased to others or that the store owner retains control of only main corridors, elevators, and stairways and a lessee is, in fact, in control of the accident location. The question of responsibility depends on who has control of the premises, including its maintenance and operation. Therefore, the investigation of these accidents should always include reference to leases, hold-harmless agreements, and any other written documents referring to the duty of maintenance and repair of the accident site.

Product Liability

Although similar to the investigation of premises liability claims, the investigation of product liability claims requires greater imagination, ingenuity, and experience. Products liability insurance covers bodily injuries and property damage arising out of defects in food, medicine, manufactured equipment, or any other products and also liability arising out of defects in construction work which may cause injury after work has been completed. The investigator may represent the manufacturer, wholesaler, jobber, retailer, distributor, or maintenance, repair, and service agency. It is important for the investigator to remember that the alleged defect complained of may have occurred anywhere along the line from the manufacturer down to and including the consumer.

For the most part, product liability claims do not involve serious injury, and very often the alleged defect is nothing more than something which is quite natural to the product. However, the deleterious effects of some products to life and the quality of life have increasingly become critical issues in such claims, e.g., cigarettes and female hygiene products.

Product liability claims are often unique, since they usually arise out of what are known as "blind" accidents, to which there are no witnesses other than the claimants or their relatives. This, along with the fact that we are dealing with a field that is exceedingly varied, makes it impossible to outline the investigation for every product which might be subject to a claim. Consequently, when investigating a products liability matter, one must consider the basis for recovery. Manufacturers can be liable for harm caused by the lawful use of the product in a manner and for a purpose that was intended if they failed to exercise reasonable care in manufacturing the product.

Manufacturers must recognize that if the product is not carefully made, it may involve an unreasonable risk of harm to those lawfully using it and to those who should be expected to be in the vicinity of its probable use.

With this in mind, the investigator must be concerned primarily with everything related to the identification, purpose, date of manufacture, and intended use of the product. In addition, the investigation must cover all advertising, printed material, including instructions, and testing results of the product causing the injury.

Safety Standards

Additionally, the investigation must include the review of safety standards and statutes. In most jurisdictions, the standards for manufacturers of a particular product are set out in a safety code or statute, and there are private organizations engaged in recognizing compliance with their standards. For example, there is an American Standard Safety Code for portable wood ladders and the Underwriters Laboratory for electrical products. Violation of a safety statute generally constitutes negligence per se. Finally, the investigator must recognize that the manufacturer's duty is not just to use reasonable care in the designing or manufacturing of the product but also to *warn*, even though the product is made perfectly. There exists a duty to warn the public if foreseeable and latent dangers attendant on proper and intended use of the product. These and other factors, such as implied warranty leading to strict liability, often tax the imagination and the ingenuity of the claims adjuster.

WORKER'S COMPENSATION CLAIMS INVESTIGATION

As stated, the basic principles of casualty claims investigation are the same whether the subject matter be automobile or public liability. This also holds true for employment-related claims. In the investigation of Worker's Compensation and Employer's Liability claims, the measure of an employer's responsibility is governed by state law, and the test of liability is not negligence but whether or not the accident arose out of and in the course of employment. In spite of this difference, statements taken from the injured claimant or witnesses follow the same format as other statements, with additional information being sought on items peculiar to work-related injuries. Of particular interest in the investigation of these claims is the medical treatment received by the claimant. It is obligatory for claims people to familiarize themselves with the law of their jurisdiction concerning medical treatment of the injured party. Medical reports and bills must be scrutinized and carefully reviewed for content and checked against available fee schedules. The primary goals is to see that the injured claimant obtains the best medical care at the most reasonable cost and is able to return to work as soon as possible.

Rehabilitation of Claimant

It is not unusual for a claims person to take a personal interest in the treatment and eventual rehabilitation of an injured claimant. Unlike the work in automobile and public liability investigation, the investigator's attempt is to return the injured party to gainful employment rather than preparing and gathering evidence for defense of each lawsuit. There are many instances in compensation where there is no absolute procedure to close a case. In some states, even a lump sum settlement agreed on by both parties with the approval of the Worker's Compensation Board does not prevent a claimant from reopening a case in the future. It is, therefore, good business and common sense for the insurance industry to do everything reasonably possible to rehabilitate injured employees and return them to work. It is often cheaper, in the long run, to make a greater initial expenditure toward proper medical care and rehabilitation services.

CONCLUSION

In each of the three areas of casualty investigation, prompt and thorough action is the foundation for a successful claim result. It allows the investigator to obtain the information while it is still fresh in the minds of all parties, so that the investigator and the insurance company can arrive at the truth more quickly and easily. Once the investigation is concluded, the decisions of the claims department of a casualty insurance company will follow through either by arranging for a settlement or by declining the claim courteously and firmly.

43

Property Insurance Loss Investigation

Harold S. Daynard

THE PROPERTY INSURANCE APPROACH

Because of the special relationship between an insurance company and its policyholder, procedures which may be appropriate for police, public defenders, or civil adversaries cannot be considered standard procedures for loss departments of property insurance underwriters.

The insured and the insurer are parties to a formal agreement—bound by the law of contract and subject to the traditional presumption that a contract is entered into in good faith and that its terms will be faithfully complied with on both sides. This is the basis for the guidelines of conduct for insurance representatives.

Should the facts of loss or the manner in which an insurance claim is presented suggests an attempts fraud and/or deceit as to the amount or character of claim, investigatory procedures are intensified and may coalesce with the usual procedures appropriate to any adversary proceeding. The approach to insurance investigation emphasizes open-mindedness, promptness, and fairness, without sacrificing the degree of thoroughness required by the size and importance of a particular claim.

Types of Insurance Adjusters

The claims representative of a property insurance underwriter is normally referred to as an "adjuster" rather than an "investigator." Insurance company personnel employed in this area are *staff adjusters* as opposed to the *independent adjuster*. The independent adjusting profession is comprised of experts trained in insurance and loss service procedures, who, in many states, are subject to licensing, bonding, and ethical practice laws.

Adjusters who represent the policyholder are known as *public adjusters*. These individuals assist the public (the policyholders) in the preparation and presentation of claims to underwriters and are licensed specially for this purpose. As policyholder agents, their functions and objective differ in many respects from those of the insurance company adjuster and are beyond the scope of this chapter.

The Property Insurance Policy

The course and character of claim service varies with the type of property insurance involved. A property insurance policy generally insures certain property described by (1) designation of class (textiles, metals, clothing, shoes, musical instruments, fine arts, and so on); (2) enumeration of specific objects (for example, individual items of jewelry, paintings, or other objects of art); or (3) description of a dwelling or other building structure, including its location.

Following identification of the property insured, the contract usually specifies the following:

- The perils insured against—that is, *all* risks or "stated" perils such as fire, lightning, windstorm, vandalism, theft, burglary, and flood. So-called all-risk coverage usually (but not necessarily) excludes extraordinary risks such as flood, earthquake, acts of war, and nuclear fission. Also excluded are such "maintenance-type" perils as wear and tear and bookkeeping losses, including inventory shortages.

- Conditions that require certain acts by the policyholder at the time of loss, including prompt notification of loss to insurers, timely filing of proper documents of claim, and specific procedures in damage claims.

- Limited period of insurance—from inception date to expiration date.

- Designation of encumbrances on insured property and third party to whom losses if any, may be payable.

- Time limits for filing proof of loss, instituting suit on the claim, and paying claims, requirements for settling claims, for examination of books, and for optional examination under oath of the policyholder. A Proof of Loss form, in which a sworn statement of loss including facts and figures is set forth, is required from the policyholder by the insurer.

Objectives of Property Insurance Investigation

Although the nature and scope of any investigation will depend on the type of claim and insurance coverage applicable, the objects of the investigation are generally to:

- Determine whether the assured has proved a loss (1) caused by an event insured against, (2) within the period of the policy, and (3) to property described in the policy.

- Verify that the assured has performed all obligations required under the terms and conditions of the insurance.

- Verify that the loss was not brought about by a cause or did not involve property which is excluded by the terms of the policy.

- Determine the amount of loss and/or damage and, if authorized by underwriters, agree on an adjustment.

- Familiarize the policyholder with the procedures necessary to conclude the claim and, frequently, to assist the assured in a manner not inconsistent with the adjuster's obligations to the underwriter.

INVESTIGATION PROCEDURES

To accomplish the foregoing objectives, the adjuster employs certain standard procedures, which follow.

Interview and Statements

In a meeting with the policyholder, the adjuster takes a statement where appropriate. The interview and statement may be narrative or question and answer in form and may be oral, written, or taped. Written statements are desirable in the following cases:

- The cause of loss is not apparent from a physical inspection; for example, theft, burglary, misappropriation of property, vandalism, and fire or windstorm damages, where facts peculiarly within the knowledge of the assured could help explain the origin or cause of the casualty.

- The loss is of suspicious origin.

- There are doubts relative to insurance coverages.

- There is a question of ownership or insurable interest in the property.

- The assured has committed an act to prejudice the rights of underwriters; for example, delayed notice of loss or issued releases to responsible third parties.

- The claim appears excessive or indicates possible fraud.

- The adjuster wishes to record facts to preserve evidence or statements of assured or witness.

- There are facts to warrant a claim against a third party.

    More detailed information relative to questioning the assured and written statements can be found in the list of references on page 43-15.
    In general, an interview includes:

- Identity of the assured, nature of assured's residence and occupancy thereof (on a Residence Loss Form).

- Date, description, and sequence of events leading up to and through the casualty.

- Time and results of any reports to police or fire officials.

- Itemization and description of property involved.

- Statement of facts pertinent to the acquisition and value of the property.

    In business losses, it is usual to interview a principal of the firm to obtain details relative to the firm's structure, a brief business history (including a description of its operations, locations, and previous losses, if any), a sequential narrative of the facts leading up to the casualty, reference to the property involved, and the records in evidence of its manufacture, acquisition, and value.

In all cases, the assured should be encouraged to state in logical sequence the events leading up to the casualty. Because policyholders may be inclined to ramble and become confused, reluctant, nervous, or upset, they should be assured that the matter will be handled on its merits. At all times patience, tact, and tolerance are required on the part of the insurance company representative.

In instances in which property is out of sight due to theft or fire, the assured may be asked to produce witnesses and verifiable documentary evidence of the existence, identity, and value of the property.

Examination Under Oath

When obtaining statements, the adjuster must consider a special standard provision in property insurance policies—the right to examine the policyholder under oath. This clause usually reads as follows:

> The insured, as often as may be reasonably required, shall exhibit to any person designated by this Company all that remains of any property herein described, and submit to examination under oath by any person named by this Company, and subscribe the same; and, as often as may be reasonably required, shall produce for examination all books of account, bills, invoices, and other vouchers, or certified copies thereof if originals be lost, at such reasonable time and place as may be designated by this Company or its representative, and shall permit extracts and copies thereof to be made.

Note that this allows examination "as often as may reasonably be required." While this is a typical clause, some do not afford the company as broad a privilege. Usually, examination under oath is reserved for cases in which special scrutiny of the facts is required—cases in which there exists questionable insurance coverage, suspicion of fraud, or inability to obtain the facts through routine adjuster investigation. Although there appears to be no reason why he or she cannot do so if experienced and qualified, ordinarily the adjuster does not conduct an examination under oath but leaves this task to company counsel.

Prior to the examination under oath, the insurer issues a formal written notice to the policyholder to appear at a specific time and place before a designated individual for the purpose of being examined, pursuant to stated policy provision. The time must be reasonable and the place convenient. The assured appears at the designated place, usually with counsel or some other representative (although not required), is sworn in before a notary (stenographer), and the interrogation is commenced by the insurer's representative.

The assured may be examined on all matters relative to the risk, the casualty, and the property involved. All pertinent questions must be answered, even questions which the assured contends may incriminate him or her. The fact that information given may be incriminating is not a justification for the assured's refusal to answer, since an examination under oath conducted pursuant to the terms of an insurance contract is not a criminal proceeding. Furthermore, inasmuch as an examination under oath usually takes place while no suit is pending, there is no judge available to settle procedural disputes.

Counsel for the assured has no right to object to any question but may advise the assured to answer or not to answer. The latter is done at the risk of providing the insurer with a defense based on assured's refusal to respond to a material question.

Although an examination under oath is frequently conducted in an atmosphere of friendliness, legally, it is regarded as an adversary procedure. Under such circumstances, counsel for the policyholder is no more entitled to aid the witness in giving answers than he or she would be in court. Nor is counsel entitled to cross-examine or reexamine, either during the interrogation or after the insurer's representative has completed interrogation.

Because of its broad and protected scope, the underwriter's examination of an assured under oath constitutes a vital fact-finding procedure. Although adjusters are not usually involved except to aid an underwriter's counsel, nonetheless, they should realize the significance of this proceeding and must eschew any conduct that would reasonably be construed to waive or prejudice the company's right to examine. For instance, the adjuster should not represent, suggest, or imply that the statement being taken from an insured must be sworn to or that it will suffice in lieu of an examination under oath. According to some attorneys, a written statement obtained by an adjuster must not be of such depth or detail that the assured may later claim that the company's right to examination has already been fulfilled and that therefore the policyholder need only swear to the statement already made.

Although an examination under oath is not a routine investigatory tool used by the insurance adjuster, the investigation is nevertheless performed with an awareness that the insurer may wish to exercise that right. If preliminary investigation suggests the advisability of an examination under oath, the adjuster's activity should thereafter be limited to unearthing the potential problems and implementing the facts about which the assured later may be questioned under oath. However, the adjuster who concludes that a loss claim is proper, routine, and unlikely to involve an examination under oath will usually go the full route and settle the loss, assuming, of course, he or she has such authority.

Inspections

Inspections of the insured property are required in all cases of damage; inspection of the location involved should be made in cases of burglary and theft.

Damage Losses. Inspection of the insured property should be made with these objectives in mind:

- To identify the property involved and ascertain whether it conforms with the description of the property insured under the policy; for example, number and address of the insured structure, the category or class of insured personal property, and the identity of a piece of property specifically scheduled.

- To confirm that the property is located at an insured location. (Some policies insure property "wherever located"; others insure only at specified locations.)

- To ascertain and appraise damage and to fix value, loss, and damage figures. To accomplish this, the adjuster is expected to possess expert knowledge concerning ordinary types of property; in the case of high-value types of property, the adjuster may need to enlist the aid of a specialist to fix a damage and/or a value.

- To take appropriate steps to help the assured minimize the loss by employing proper salvage, protection, and safekeeping procedures.

Under the terms of the Standard Fire Insurance policy, policyholders are required, at their own expense, to arrange for the separation of damaged and undamaged merchandise and to submit an inventory of the property involved. Following this, it becomes the insurance company adjuster's job to identify, inspect, and confirm the descriptions and values indicated on the inventory. When claim personnel cannot be at the loss scene, photographs will serve as graphic aids and can be used as evidentiary material in a suit to enforce a subrogation claim against a responsible third party. ("Subrogation" is discussed later in this chapter.)

Burglary and Theft Losses. Inspection of premises should be made in all cases of burglary and theft. A visual analysis is required to determine the point of break-in and entry; evidence of forcible entry is frequently required by insurance policies. The means of entrance to and exit from the premises should be checked to confirm accessibility. An analysis of the premises' physical nature often will prove that the merchandise allegedly removed was minimal, irrespective of the amount claimed, simply because of access or egress difficulties. Through inspections the adjuster can also report on the physical aspects of the risk. Such information may appropriately include:

- Whether an insured structure is fire-resistant, sprinklered, or adequately protected with safeguards to reduce exposure to burglary or theft.

- A description of "housekeeping" in premises—type of maintenance of commercial inventories, stowage, access to fire fighters, and use of skids; presence or absence of fire extinguishers at fire-exposed areas; types of packing, cartoning, boxing, crating, or plastic covering on products; security procedures; and so on.

- The type of neighborhood and adjoining areas, proximity to fire hydrants, fire stations, police stations, alarm boxes, road access, stability and viability of the area.

Audit

When loss involves property out of sight, that is stolen or destroyed in a fire, its existence, identity, and value must be determined from books, records, or documentary data supplied by the assured.

In commercial losses, an audit is required to establish a book statement of the loss, including a check of inventory records, purchases, sales, and other factors to determine quantity of inventory which presumably was on hand immediately prior to the casualty. A postloss inventory is then taken to determine inventory remaining after the casualty. The computed "on hand" inventory before the casualty less the postloss inventory equals the loss. Audits of this kind often require the assistance of a professional accountant.

THE FINAL ADJUSTING PROCESS—FIXING LOSS AND DAMAGE

Because the ultimate objective in handling a claim is to adjust it, logically this process follows completion of investigation, confirmation of insurance coverage, and verification of the policyholder's fulfillment of the contractual requisites.

The term "adjustment" encompasses two phases of agreement. First, a mutually acceptable loss and damage figure must be fixed. Second, there must exist agreement on a net collectible amount after application of the terms of insurance. The latter may be less than the agreed loss and damage because of either insurance limits or a "deductible" or coinsurance.

The following examples illustrate how the "net collectible" may reduce actual agreed loss and damage. Reduction by applying insurance limit:

Agreed loss—$10,000

Amount of insurance—$5000

Policyholder collects maximum of—$5000

Reduction by Deductible

Agreed loss—$10,000

Amount of insurance—$15,000

Deductible—$100

The policy may provide that from "each and every loss" the sum of $100 (or any agreed amount) shall be deducted. Such a provision reduces the policy premium by eliminating the risk of claims less than the deductible amount.

Loss as agreed—$10,000

Deductible—$100

Net Collectible—$9000

Reduction by Coinsurance.   In this case, the policyholder will collect only that portion of the agreed loss that the amount of insurance carried bears, in mathematical ratio, to the actual and total values at risk (or a percentage thereof). The intent is to benefit the policyholder who pays more premium for higher amounts of insurance consistent with the true values of the insured property. The term "coinsurance" derives from the fact that those who carry less insurance become coinsurers with the underwriter when a partial loss is sustained. For example:

Agreed loss—$10,000

Insurance carried—$15,000

Actual value of insured property—$30,000

Insurance Required

Under 80% coinsurance clause—80% of $30,000=$24,000

Under 90% coinsurance clause—90% of $30,000=$27,000

Under 100% coinsurance clause—100% of $30,000=$30,000

Net Collectible

Under 80% clause—$15,000/24,000 × 10,000=$6,250.00

Under 90% clause—$15,000/27,000 × 10,000=$5,555.56

Under 100% clause—$15,000/30,000 × 10,000=$5,000.00

Although it is usually found in dwelling, building, and inventory stock policies, not all policies of property insurance contain a coinsurance clause. The crucial factor in the application of coinsurance is the determination and agreement on total values at risk—a controversial, legal, and practical problem which complicates this aspect of property insurance adjusting.

Although the amount ultimately collectible on an insurance policy is determined by a formula applied mechanically according to the policy limit and deductible or coinsurance clauses where applicable, reaching a proper dollar amount on loss and damage entails a much more complex procedure and demands adjusting experience and expertise. Included in the process are:

- Determining the policyholder's or claimant's insurable interest.
- Minimizing the loss.
- Eliminating uninsured factors.
- Establishing a value basis.
- Agreeing on an adjusted loss.
- Dealing with salvage.

Determining "Insurable Interest"

Property insurance policies are available not only to owners but to others who have only a partial proprietary or only a custodial interest. Examples are real or chattel mortgagees, lienors, and bailees. Examples of the latter are museums (where property of others may be displayed); textile, fur, and other processors; and cleaners and launderers. The latter may insure the owner's goods for full value or agreed limited value or only their liability for the goods. They may insure their charges for work done. Thus "insurable interests" can and do vary in scope.

Thus one of the first steps in the loss and damage assessment procedure requires the adjuster to ascertain the nature and extent of the policyholder's interest in the property and to restrict loss and damage allowances to within the bounds of such interest and within the limits prescribed by policy terms.

Minimizing Loss

Legally, it is the claimant's duty to take all reasonable steps toward minimizing loss and damage for which contractual benefits from another party are sought. In insurance matters, one of the adjuster's primary functions is to ensure that this is done and to provide all necessary assistance to that end. Proof of the adjuster's experience and competence often emerges in this crucial loss-reducing process.

Some routine steps taken to protect exposed property from further damage are boarding up damaged structure to prevent access by thieves or vandals; placing interim guard services at sites of loss; hastening temporary repairs to fire- or wind-damaged roofs to protect interior property from exposure to the elements; shoring up hazardous damaged structural areas pending permanent repairs; prompt removal of damaged merchandise from unsafe areas; and cleaning, wiping down, deodorizing, or other processing to prevent mildew, rust, corrosion, contamination, or other further damage. Such procedures test the adjuster's efficiency in enlisting the aid of salvors and repair sources.

Expenses incurred by reasonable efforts to minimize loss normally are insured under property policies. A "Sue and Labor" clause permits the policyholder to take such action and to expend such labor as may be reasonable and necessary to avoid potential further damage after an insured loss has occurred.

Eliminating Uninsured Factors

Assessment of a loss under a property insurance policy presumes the elimination of loss factors which preexisted or otherwise have no relevance to the insured casualty. Included in this category are wear and tear, depreciation, obsolescence, prior damage, and shrinkage—loss-reducing elements which often provide the key to a proper and fair adjustment. The following examples illustrate the point.

A used article of clothing or piece of machinery loses value with age and/or wear and tear. Depending on the length and nature of its use, the property depreciates in value and an appropriate percentage should be applied against its replacement value.

An inventory of stock may have become devalued prior to loss due to style change, unavailability or improvement of a specific model, discontinuance of replacement parts, and so on. As a result, a percentage reduction of value due to obsolescence is proper.

Whether repaired or unrepaired, prior damages normally diminish the value of any piece of property. In fired buildings, there may exist unrepaired prior damages or repaired damages which have weakened or reduced the utility of the structure. Prior damage constitutes a vital factor in assessing value or loss to antiques. There is scarcely a single antique article which has not sustained prior damage and repairs. Such conditions often are not discernible except through laboratory analysis or the dismantling of the item—normally and wisely only done by underwriters' experts and common in the case of valuable violins or paintings. Proof of prior damage usually is the most cogent answer to a claim for loss in value alleged to be caused by insured casualty.

Shrinkage is an accounting term that refers to the decrease in inventory value by reason of employee theft, shoplifting, bookkeeping or production errors, waste, and other common occurrences in business which shrink inventories before sale. Experienced adjusters with sufficient accounting background can determine from inventory records a normal shrinkage percentage and thereby reduce values to a proper amount.

Establishing a Value Basis

The final prerequisite to agreement of loss and damage is that of establishing a basis for determining value, a basis which can be justified by the terms of the insurance policy. A usual provision stipulates that the property is insured for its "actual cash value not exceeding replacement value." Actual Cash Value (ACV) is not defined in the standard insurance contract. Pertinent facts used to establish ACV include: replacement value, depreciated value, market value, original cost, reproduction value, depreciation, and obsolescence. How these factors are applied can make an enormous difference in results. As a consequence, controversy about its meaning—in and outside the courts—has been ongoing.

Insurance policies may be endorsed or manuscript written to insure the property at selling price or selling price less unearned charges or selling price plus or minus a given percentage. Such clauses simplify value determination by designating an auditable basis of value.

Final Agreement on Loss and Damage

Once all preliminary investigative procedures and other requirements have been met, the adjuster prepares and proposes to the assured or the proper claimant, or public adjuster a loss and damage figure. Counterproposals may be received, and honest differences may be resolved by further analysis of figures, reinspections, or reasonable compromise. It is here that the experience, technical knowledge, competence, sense of fairness, and negotiating talents of the adjuster bear on the results—qualities on which the adjuster's principal, the underwriter, depends.

SPECIAL ADJUSTMENT CONSIDERATIONS

Salvage

In cases where loss involves damaged property, agreement on loss and damage may relate to salvage in either of two ways: (1) If the agreed amount includes the full value of the salvageable property, the adjuster (through a salvor) takes possession of the property to be sold for the account of the underwriter. (2) Should the assured agree to retain such property to dispose of at best possible advantage, the adjuster includes in the settlement figure a percentage allowance for the estimated reduction in the value of that property.

Retention of Experts

The breadth of the property insurance field exposes the adjuster to nearly every type of insurable object. Neophytes in the business may think of the property insurance adjuster as concentrating on roof damages, dwelling fires, and household effects—occasionally varied by a routine business loss. This, indeed may be the area of trainee concentration. The full scope of the property loss adjuster, however, includes claims involving such diverse properties as textiles (apparel; piece goods, including woolens, synthetics, soft goods, carpets, and rugs), plastics, rubber, electronics, metal, auto parts, paints, paper, leather, shoes, gloves, handbags, furs, jewelry, soaps, chemicals, foods, household utensils, furniture, machinery, lumber, antiques and objects of art, coins, stamps, and musical instruments. In addition to the infinite variety of personal property, real property includes private and multiple dwellings, cooperatives, condominiums, warehouses, factories, mills, office and loft buildings, oil wells, and every other type of structure.

While many property adjusters specialize in one or more of the foregoing areas, the best of them still has limitations and, therefore, the retention of experts in specific areas is common. For example, to pinpoint cause and place of origin of a suspicious fire, an arson expert may be required; complicated audits require certified public accountants; builders and engineering consultants may be needed to investigate complex structural damages; and experts specializing in merchandise or jewelry, fur, or fine arts may be required for controverted problems in those categories.

In all such instances, it is expected that the adjuster will brief the consultant and define the scope of the required work to avoid duplication of activity between the consultant and the adjuster—thereby avoiding needless expense.

Subrogation

Subrogation adds yet another facet to the handling of property insurance loss. Deriving from common law, it permits an insurer who has paid a claim to step into the shoes of a policyholder and assert any right the policyholder may have against a third party who may have been responsible for the loss. Adjusters are obligated to protect this right by extending their investigations into cause and origin of loss to establish a basis (supported by legally admissible evidence) for enforcement of the insurer's subrogation right against any responsible third party. The following examples illustrate how a property insurance adjuster should project his investigation beyond a verification of a policyholder's claim.

Fire Damages Premises and/or Contents. The fire did not have its origin on the assured's premises. To protect the principal's potential subrogation rights, the adjuster should establish where the fire started, the name and address of the occupant of premises of origin, and the cause of the fire. The adjuster should pinpoint the exact acts of carelessness which caused or contributed to the origin; identify defective conditions or maintenance involved; and identify the party responsible.

Loss or Damage by Bailee

If the assured's property is burned while in custody of another, the adjuster should develop fire origin, check evidence of carelessness, and ascertain custodian's insurance coverage. If property is stolen while in custody of a bailee, the facts must be ascertained. Was due care used to properly safeguard the goods? If the goods were in custody of a carrier, an analysis of the facts and the carrier's liability, including pertinent documentation, is required.

Loss of Stock. An insured manufacturer sustains loss of stock by employee theft. In addition to confirming loss and fixing an insured value, the adjuster is sometimes required to pursue rights against the guilty employees and to arrange for restitution, if possible, in a manner consistent with the police or public prosecutor's role in the case.

Burglary. The insured premises are burglarized and the alarm system fails to function properly, allowing the perpetrators more time to remove goods. The adjuster should obtain a copy of the alarm contract plus expert analysis of how the system failed. Such action may lay a foundation for an enforceable claim against the alarm company.

Although far from complete, the foregoing examples typify situations which call for special subrogation investigations.

Limitations on Adjuster Conduct

In following claim service procedures, property insurance adjusters should be constantly alert to the ramifications of the contractual relationship between their principals and policyholders. These impose certain limitations on the adjuster's conduct.

As a representative of the insurer, the adjuster must do nothing to waive the principal's rights under the insurance contact; must avoid misinforming or misleading the insured relative to the latter's rights; and must not preclude the insurer's assertion of any available defense to the claim.

When in doubt or without authority to make a commitment on behalf of the underwriters, the property insurance adjuster must avoid saying or doing anything which might mislead the policyholder into believing that an uninsured claim will be paid or that a policy violation will be excused. Further, the insurance contract implicitly obliges each party to deal with the other in good faith— an obligation bolstered by the *Uniform Unfair Claim Practice* laws recommended by the insurance commissioners of the various states and adopted almost universally in the United States.

If committed without just cause and performed with such frequency as to indicate a general business practice, any of the following acts by an insurer may be regarded as an unfair claim settlement practice:

- Knowingly misrepresenting to claimant pertinent facts or policy provisions relating to coverages at issue.

- Failing to acknowledge with reasonable promptness pertinent communications with respect to claims arising under its policies.

- Failing to adopt and implement reasonable standards for the prompt investigation of claims arising under its policies.

- Not attempting in good faith to effectuate prompt, fair, and equitable settlements of claims submitted in which liability has become reasonably clear.

- Compelling policyholders to institute suits to recover amounts due under its policies by offering substantially less than the amounts ultimately recovered in suits brought by them.

Usually these general provisions are implemented by special regulations of the state department of insurance, many of which frequently impose deadlines for answering communications or making contact with interested parties and in the investigation and settlement of claims.

Violations may be penalized by fines and, under some circumstances, may constitute grounds for a punitive damage suit.

In some states, additional responsibilities are placed on adjusters by the law of punitive damages. *Punitive damages* are damages awarded to a plaintiff in excess of due compensation for the loss under a property insurance contract as a penalty against the underwriter or the underwriter's agent because of unfair, oppressive, harassing, abusive, or deceitful conduct.

Inasmuch as punitive damages may far exceed the insured limits under a property insurance contract, adjusters should be especially careful to avoid "bad faith" conduct. For this reason, investigators who are too aggressive or overzealous or possess a repertory of "dirty tricks" have no place in the property insurance field. Rather, the exemplary property insurance adjuster is motivated solely by a sense of responsibility and fairness.

THE POLICYHOLDER AND THE IDEAL ADJUSTER

This review has emphasized the extraordinary responsibilities of the property insurance adjuster imposed by contractual relationship between the insurer and the parties subject to investigation—the potential beneficiaries of the insurance adjustment. Such is the framework within which the property adjuster meets with policyholder and witnesses; takes statements; assembles data in support of the claim; makes inspections; audits; participates in preservation and salvage procedures; and, finally, negotiates a settlement or initiates legal or quasi-legal procedures to resist the claim. These matters have been painted here with broad brush strokes; nonetheless, it should be clear that property insurance adjusting is a singularly complex profession, sufficiently broad to warrant specialization in its many different phases.

The written material on the subject of adjusting spans tens of thousands of pages and is included in numerous college and professional school courses which involve several years' study. Beyond this, insurance adjusters are usually regarded as trainees for their first few years in the profession.

Beginning adjusters usually confine their efforts to a single class of adjusting such as fire and its allied lines, burglary and theft, transportation and cargo, or general casualty and liability investigations. Master adjusters with broad experience in all lines are known as general adjusters, a designation requiring a special test in most states. The importance of experience, confidence, and professionalism cannot be overemphasized.

For any policyholder, a property insurance claim, regardless of its size, is a serious matter. Ordinarily, policyholders do not have many insurance claims during their lives, and when they suffer a casualty involving their own possessions, the occurrence involves some degree of trauma and sometimes anger, sharpened by an attitude of defiance. The consequent psychological factors with which the adjuster must deal are clear.

Insured victims normally presume that the underwriter is now bound to compensate them. After all they have been paying premiums for some time; therefore, up to the point of loss, the benefits of the insurance contract have been going one way—from them to the insurance company.

Now that a casualty has been suffered, the assured thinks, "I will now learn what I have been paying premiums for." In this mental state, the seriousness of the occurrence often becomes exaggerated. Adjusters have seen this reaction too often to ignore it. "My kitchen is smoked up from a frying pan fire. You must come at once," says the housewife. "The roof in my store is leaking, and my entire stock is about to be ruined. Why aren't you here to take care of it," demands the storekeeper.

Indeed, seriously destructive casualties can either threaten or disrupt the very existence of a household or business, and the urgency can be real. However, whether real or catastrophic merely in the mind and imagination of the policyholder, immediate attention and service is demanded and required of the adjuster. Moreover, the policyholder in the throes of a casualty expects that the insurance company representative will appear on the scene and instantly reverse the course of cruel fate which has brought about the calamity.

The wise adjuster will anticipate and must be prepared to deal with an understandably upset and demanding assured. Such considerations bring to mind the frequently posed question: What are the qualifications of an ideal adjuster? Although the answer is likely to make the bionic man look like a two-penny toy, attributes that have been ascribed to the ideal adjuster include:

- Pleasant, businesslike, neutral appearance.

- Intelligence and articulateness.

- Education; knowledge about property insurance contracts and loss procedures, simple and complex.

- At least a smattering of legal background, for understanding the basic rights of all concerned parties.

- Patience and courtesy.

- Comprehension of psychology and sociology—to help in dealing with all types of clients, showing empathy toward all ethnic groups, and controlling any situation in which unreasonable conduct of personality conflicts are encountered.

- Honesty; capability of resisting irregular overtures.

- Conversance, if not expertise, with almost every type of property, real or personal, household or business; does not appear ignorant or incompetent when discussing with a housewife a loss of expensive furnishings or talking shop with a jeweler, furrier, tanner, building owner, fine arts dealer, or manufacturer of toys, plastic, textiles, leather, machinery; and so on.

- Familiarity with and privileged "in's" to officialdom (police, fire marshalls, FBI, Bureau of Records, and so on); can cut through red tape to get necessary data.

- Proficiency in communications; reports and memos are readable—not too long or too short, to the point yet touching all bases.

- Good organization administratively; does not need to be badgered for reports or status memos; maintains a good diary system; avoids delays and mistakes in paperwork.

- Sound judgment in negotiating; neither "give the store away" nor "lowballs" a reasonable policyholder.

- Overall sense of balance, poise, and restraint when necessary, aggressiveness when called for; does not say too much or too little, avoids placing the company in a position of weakness yet does not come on too strong; by and large, generates a good impression with everyone.

Both underwriters and policyholders would like their property loss investigations to be handled by such a person—a biological phenomenon who is nonexistent and unsynthesizable, to be sure, but singularly representative of what both expect.

REFERENCES

Books

Baudreau, John F., et al. *Arson and Arson Investigation (Survey and Assessment)*. Washington D.C.: U.S. Government Printing Office, Stock No. 027-000-006001, 1977.
Reed, Thomas. *Adjustment of Property Losses*. 4th ed. New York: McGraw-Hill, Inc., 1977.
Rhodda, William H. *Property and Liability Insurance*. Englewood Cliffs, NJ: Prentice-Hall, Inc., 1966.

Articles

Daynard, Harold S. "Statement Taking." *Trends in Adjusting*. Newsletter 43, Daynard and Van Thunen Co., Inc., One World Trade Center, New York, N.Y.
[md3]. "Guideline to Evaluating Personal Property." *Trends in Adjusting*. Special Issue Newsletter, Daynard and Van Thunen Co., Inc. (October 1977).
Gwertzman, Max J. "Examination Under Oath." *Insurance Advocate*, 45 John St., New York, N.Y.
Pfeffer, Milton F. "Actual Cash Value." *Insurance Advocate*.

Reports

American Insurance Association. *Fire Arson Seminar*. New York, N.Y.

44

Arson Insurance Investigation

Property Claim Services, American Insurance Association

EXCLUSION OF ACCIDENTAL CAUSES

The first step in recognizing arson is the exclusion of all accidental causes. Possibly the best method is to cast out the obviously impossible causes and thus narrow the field of probability. The investigator should be familiar with the generally accepted causes of accidental fire and should inquire into the following:

The Electric system: Fuses, bridged with wire or foil or in which pennies have been inserted; broken or rotted insulation; overloading of circuits defective switches or fixtures; wiring not installed in accordance with the local code or the National Electric Code.

Electric equipment: Not of approved type; defective; fire originated close to equipment such as iron or other heating element; fire traceable to paper shades on electric bulbs.

Gas. Leaks in pipes or defective stoves or heating unit.

Pets. Presence of dog or cat and its possible contribution to cause of fire.

Painting equipment: Carelessness with paint, paint rags, linseed oil, turpentine, and so on.

Heating units: Overheated stoves; clothing dried too close to fireplaces or open flames; overheated steam pipes; faulty chimneys or flues; explosions resulting from kerosene stoves; stoves overturned in dark by pets, during flight, and so on.

SOURCE: Reprinted with permission from the American Insurance Association, Property Claims Services.

Sun: Concentration of sun's rays on bubbles in glass window panes, convex shaving mirrors, odd-shaped bottles, and so on.

Lightning: Check on duration of storm.

Children: Accidentally, while at play.

Smoking: Careless disposal of cigars, cigarettes, or pipe ashes; falling asleep while smoking in chair, auto, bed, and so on.

Storage of hay: Date stored and condition.

Other causes are less common, but any possibility should be thoroughly explored. Some of the less common causes are sparks from electric motors or friction caused by running machinery; rubbish and brush fires spreading to a nearby building; ignition of hot grease, tar, oil, or like substance; explosion of natural or artificial gases; fireworks; sparks from an outdoor fire or a passing locomotive; or improperly combining chemical solutions.

A good rule for an adjuster to remember is that no listing of possible accidental causes can be considered all-inclusive. Some fires are the result of odd and unusual accidental ignition, but in order for a fire to start, it is necessary to combine combustible material with a source of ignition. These ignition sources are fairly well established and include open flames, electric arcs, heating and cooking devices, moving machinery, chemical processes, and spontaneous ignition. If any of these sources can be located in a specific section of the building, it should be determined whether it was possible for the source to combine with a combustible material and result in a fire.

Firefighters can help in the discovery of suspicious fires. Seek their active cooperation, talk to them, and listen to their stories. After all, fire and fire prevention is their business. Every day they risk their lives to fight fire, and aiding the arson investigation is just another means of doing so.

One of the explanations for the great activity of the professional torches during the Depression of the 1930s was the commonly held belief that a fire could be set and in burning obliterate all evidence of incendiarism. The smart criminal today realizes that this is far from true. The development of laboratory facilities and techniques such as the spectograph, the gas chromatograph, the ultraviolet light, the infrared ray, and the vacuum distillation process; the high level of training among arson investigators; and the alertness of firefighters are all increasing the likelihood of detection.

Set fires leave telltale signs. These signs may be so obvious that the first firefighter on the scene will suspect arson, or they may be so well concealed that months of patient investigation will be required to show that the fire was set. However, the sign is always present. It may not scream out "This is arson!" but it may whisper "This is a suspicious fire."

The superior officer on the first fire truck to near the scene, on coming into view of the fire, will "size up" the fire and the building. If two or more separate fires are noted, this officer will immediately be aware of the probability of arson. So will the first firefighters to enter the building if they detect a strong odor of kerosene or other petroleum products—unless their presence is accounted for by the occupancy of the building. An unaccountably rapid spread or intensity of a fire is also suspicious.

There are many of these signs which are encountered again and again at fire scenes; some point directly to arson, while others serve to alert the firefighters and officers at the scene. From a study of the burned building to a search of the debris, the telltale signs most encountered are now discussed.

The Burned Building.   The type of building in which the fire occurs may indicate a set fire under some circumstances. A fire of considerable size at the time the first apparatus arrives on the scene is suspicious if it is in a modern fireproof building. Modern loft and warehouse construction has also eliminated many of the accidental causes of fire as well as provided means for preventing fire travel.

Separate Fires.   Perhaps the most conclusive sign of fire setting is a number of separate fires. When two or three separate fires break out within a building or group of buildings or even in one room or store, it is almost certain that accident or misfortune can be ruled out and arson definitely suspected.

Color of Smoke and Flames.   Some fires burn with little or no smoke, but they are the exception rather than the rule. Combustion of materials is usually incomplete and there is some smoke. The characteristics of smoke very often assist in identifying the substances that started or boosted the fire.

As H. Rethoret notes in his fine book *Fire Investigations*, the observation of smoke must be made at the start of a fire. Once a fire has assumed major proportions, the value of an observation of smoke is lost, for the fire is then consuming the building itself and the smoke will not indicate the materials used by the arsonist. It is therefore extremely important to locate and question the first person who saw the fire and the first firefighters at the scene.

When white smoke appears before the water from the fire hoses comes into contact with the fire, it indicates humid materials burning. Burning hay and vegetable matter in stable and barn fires give off a white or light gray smoke. Phosphorus, an incendiary agent, also gives off a heavy white smoke but with a distinct garlic odor and a noxious effect on those inhaling quantities of it. (Phosphorus is used in the preparation of wartime chemical agents.)

Biting smoke, irritating the nose and throat and causing lachrymation and coughing, indicates the presence of chlorine—another wartime chemical agent. The inhalation of smoke containing chlorine gas is also dangerous.

Black smoke indicates lack of air; but if accompanied by large flames, it generally indicates the burning of a material with a petroleum base. Unless petroleum, tar, coal, rubber, or like compounds are stored within the burning building, it is possible that some fire setter used a petroleum product to accelerate the blaze.

Reddish brown, thick yellow, or brownish yellow smoke is an indication that films, or substances containing nitrocellulose fiber, sulfur, or sulfuric, nitric, or hydrochloric acid are burning. If later investigation fails to reveal that any quantities of such substances are normally stored in the building, then incendiarism can be suspected.

To a great extent, the appearance of smoke is also governed by the supply of oxygen available to the fire. This also governs the flames. No flames or comparatively small flames indicate lack of air. More flames than smoke indicates the burning of dry substances. Large flames indicate a good supply of oxygen, while erratic flames shooting at odd and unusual intervals indicate the presence of an accumulation of some gases. When the flames swirl around in a sort of pattern and are accompanied by a cloud of dust and fine ash, it indicates better-than-average ventilation at the fire. Sparks in large quantities indicate powdery substances are burning in a well-ventilated fire.

The color of the flames is a good indication of the intensity of the fire, an important factor in determining incendiarism. A reddish glow indicates a heat of about 500°C, a real light red, about 1000°C. Red flames also indicate the presence of petroleum as does the appearance of tongues of flame on the water running off from the fire. A fire temperature of close to 1100°C is indicated by a yellow glow, and a blinding white fire usually reaches a temperature of 1500°C.

Though large quantities of alcohol will burn with an orange flame, a blue flame reveals the use of alcohol as a fire accelerant, and although not used frequently because the color of the flames readily identifies it, there is a possibility an investigator may encounter its use.

Size of Fire. This is important when correlated with the type of alarm, the time received, and the time of arrival of the first apparatus. Fires make what might be termed "normal progress." Such progress can be estimated after an examination of the materials burned, the building, and the normal ventilation offered to the fire. Thus, the time element and the degree of headway made by the flames become important factors to anyone probing into possible incendiarism.

Direction of Travel. While it is acknowledged that no two fires in buildings burn in identical fashion, it is also necessary to point out that fires can be expected to make normal progress through various types of buildings. Experienced firefighters can usually determine whether a fire has spread abnormally fast when they take into consideration the type of construction, the channels of ventilation, the combustibility of the contents of the building, and the circumstances surrounding the sending of the alarm.

It is known that hot gases rise and fire tends to sweep upwards until blocked by some obstacle. It then seeks holes, cracks, or outlets through which to escape. If none is present, the flames mushroom out horizontally until the fire can bend around the obstruction or find some break through which to continue its progress. Dumbwaiter shafts in tenement houses and elevator shafts in hotels and apartment houses have furnished tragic examples of the speedy progress of a fire and then the mushrooming of the smoke and flames horizontally into hallways when the fire meets the dead end at the top of the shaft.

A fire does not spread nearly so rapidly in a horizontal direction unless favorable ventilation is present, or possibly the wall surfaces have been treated with a flammable substance. When a fire has spread in a direction which normally would not be expected, it might be suspected to have been incendiary.

Another point to be borne in mind when seeking to determine the direction of the burning is the depth of the charring at various points on the studding or beams in a building and the pattern of burning as indicated by the charring, scorching, blistering, and soot deposits in a room or about a building.

Sometimes a fire setter will seek to better ventilate a building by cutting holes between rooms or floors, opening windows, tying back doors, or blocking up fire doors. Sprinkler systems have also been made inoperative to permit a fire to spread. In most cases, the means used to ventilate a building or damage a sprinkler system are readily visible if the fire is quickly extinguished. Unless the structure is burned to the ground, a close inspection may reveal the arsonist's techniques; and even when it is burned to the ground, the unusual speed of travel may cast suspicion on the fire.

Intensity. The degree of heat given off by a fire and the color of its flames often indicate that some accelerant has been added to the materials normally present in a building and alert the firefighters or investigators to look for further evidence of the use of flammable liquids or compounds. Possibly some difficulty in extinguishing the fire will lead firefighters to suspect the presence of such fluids as gasoline and kerosene. Fires react to a stream of water in various fashions. If a flame burns brighter when hit with a hose stream or if the flames change color when the water strikes them, any experienced firefighter is alerted to the probability of arson.

Odors. There is little question that the odor of such flammable substances as gasoline, kerosene, and alcohol has trapped more arsonists than any other telltale sign. Because arsonists seek a substance which will make the blaze certain and which will burn up any evidence of arson, kerosene, alcohol, and gasoline spring to their minds. All three will burn, but in burning up the evidence of arson, a readily identifiable odor is given off and this points to a fire setter.

An investigator can easily learn to recognize the odors of various flammable liquids. By placing small amounts in wide-mouthed glass jars, shutting the eyes, opening a jar, and guessing its contents, the investigator will soon be able to promptly identify the various odors.

Condition of Contents. Persons intending to touch off a fire frequently remove objects of value or items to which they are sentimentally attached. Clothing; personal papers—particularly bankbooks and insurance policies; and such articles as typewriters, television sets, and objects associated with the arsonist's hobby are likely to be removed before household fires are set. Pets are frequently left with relatives before the fire. Stores and other business establishments sometimes remove the major portion of their inventory or replace valuable merchandise with "distress" out-of-style articles.

Doors and Windows. Locked doors and obstructed entrances and passageways sometimes point to an effort to impede firefighters in their attempts to fight the fire. Doors or windows showing marks of forced entry may point to arson preceded by burglary or possibly arson by someone without a key to the premises.

Windows which are obstructed frequently point directly to a *touch-off*—a set fire. The arsonist does not want the fire detected by a chance passerby and therefore will pin down shades and cover windows with drapes, blankets, and even papers. In one case on the West Coast, an investigator found the inside of the glass in the hallway door of a recently burned tenement painted black. Not satisfied with the owner's attempt to blame it on children in the neighborhood, the investigator cited it as an attempt to obstruct the view of the hallway from the street. Since the fire originated in the rear of the hallway, it was promptly classified as suspicious. Children would have splashed the paint carelessly on the door, but examination of glass fragments revealed two coats of paint had been skillfully applied with all the brush marks running neatly in one direction, apparently the work of an expert painter.

Familiar Faces. Pyromaniacs—psychopathic fire setters—are marked by their tendency to remain at a fire scene "to watch the fun," as one of them remarked when questioned by a fire marshall. Numerous good arrests have been made because of an alert firefighter or police officer noting a familiar face in a crowd at a fire. Such recognition usually occurs when several fires take place within a few days or hours of each other.

Interested Bystanders. Persons in the crowd about a fire who strive to help when no help is needed or who seem unduly interested in the fire are prime suspects. This is particularly true in "vanity" fires because the fire setter's object is to appear as a hero. Other arsonists cannot refrain from questioning firefighters and police about the origin of the fire and whether there is anything to mark it as suspicious.

Other Suspicious Circumstances. What may alert a firefighter or an adjuster at a fire scene may be difficult to define. Many times there is just "something" about the fire that is not quite normal. It may be that a search of the debris revealed a trace of candle grease or some object which might be part of a mechanical fire-setting device. It may be something about the time of the alarm—shortly after the storeowner left for the night—or it may be failure to fully explain an attempt to fight the fire with inadequate equipment without sending an alarm. Or possibly the point of origin or the weather does not tie in with a householder's explanation of the cause of the fire. Whatever the sign that alerted those first on the scene, the investigator must exploit the first telltale sign, the sign that labels a fire "suspicious—worthy of further investigation."

SET FIRES

When a fire is classified as suspicious, it is then the task of the arson investigator to determine if it is in fact a *touch-off*. At this point, all plausible accidental causes have been excluded and observation at the fire scene has pointed to either the possible use of some fire accelerant or the setting of a fire without the use of a recognizable accelerant. It is now up to the arson investigator to determine the modus operandi of the fire setter.

Point of Origin

Initially, the important point to be established at any fire is at what point in the building it originated. This point of origin frequently may be established by an examination of witnesses, by an inspection of the debris at the fire scene, or both.

The first person to be questioned is the discoverer of the fire; the second is the person who turned in the alarm; and, last, any other witnesses who can be found. All should be interrogated about their identities, their business in the area of the fire, what attracted their attention to it, the time of observation, and their positions in relation to the fire at that time. When it has been ascertained that a witness was in a position to view the fire (time and place of observation), then the investigator seeks to learn the exact location of the blaze, its size, its intensity, and the speed of its spread. Witnesses will also be questioned about other persons in the vicinity. Did they observe one of the other witnesses? Did they observe anyone in or about the premises just before or immediately following the fire?

In many cases, there is only a single witness; one person discovered the fire and turned in the alarm, and diligent inquiry fails to uncover any other witnesses.

The person who turned in the alarm will also be questioned about whether a fire box, telephone, or other means was used. It is also important to try to learn the length of time that elapsed between the discovery of the fire and the time the alarm was dispatched.

All experienced arson investigators know that the identity of these witnesses, their business in the area at the time of the fire, and what attracted their attention to it are three vital questions in any investigation of fire setting. It is astonishing the number of times, year after year, that investigators have come across the fire setter among the small number of persons who "discovered" the fire, who turned in the alarm, or who were on hand before the fire apparatus and helped direct the firemen to the scene. Individuals who have come to the attention of police and fire departments as chronic "false-alarm ringers" have, in many instances, later blossomed out as thrill-seeking fire setters.

An inspection of the debris must always be made, first to determine the point of origin and, second, to uncover the arsonist's technique.

Charring of wood occurs as a fire burns, the "alligatoring" of the surface varying as the wood is consumed. When a fire is extinguished quickly, the charring is only slightly below the surface and the alligatoring shows large segments or squares. As the fire continues, the charring goes deeper into the wood and the segments of the alligatoring become smaller. The search for "alligatoring" will not only help locate the point of origin but may also reveal the existence of two or more separate fires.

Tracing liquid accelerants to the place of spillage aids in definitely locating the point of origin of any fire in which such fluids were used. Any fluid will flow downward to a lower level and in such movement will flow around any fixed object in its path. Therefore a fluid fire accelerant such as gasoline, kerosene, turpentine, or alcohol may be traceable from the point of spillage to its lowest point. Quite frequently, unburned quantities of such liquids are found in rooms below the fire, in cellars, or in portions of a foundation, as a considerable quantity of such fluid sometimes runs down to a low point out of range of the fire. These fluid accelerants will sometimes pool on a large, level floor and burn from the outside of the pool toward the center, leaving a distinctive mark on the floor. These accelerants also cause deep charring, which sometimes neatly charts the flow of the flammable fluid used by the fire setter. Cases have been encountered in which charring traced the path of the accelerant into cracks of the floor to the underside of the floorboards. In addition, these fluids will mar furniture and painted surfaces upon which they may have been splashed and which may be found untouched by the fire.

The point of origin itself points to many suspicious fires. Arsonists place their fire-setting devices where the flames will take hold, while many accidental fires occur in locations where they burn out instead of gaining headway. Thus, the location of the point of origin may be of great help in excluding accidental causes.

Fire-Setting Mechanisms

It is the duty of an arson investigator to search the debris of a suspicious fire, particularly around the point of origin, to gather evidence pointing to the mechanism used by the fire setter.

Any arsonist may use the simplest of methods—a match and some paper—or elaborate mechanical or chemical means to start and accelerate a fire.

An incendiary mechanism may be mechanical or chemical. It consists of an ignition device, possibly a timing mechanism, one or more "plants" to feed or accelerate the initial flame, and frequently "trailers" to spread the fire about the building, sometimes from plant to plant.

Ignition and Timing Mechanisms

An ignition device may be simple (a match, for instance) or it may be a complex mechanical or chemical device which can be timed to go off hours or even days after it is set. This latter type provides a time lag between the time of setting and the outbreak of the fire and gives the fire setter an opportunity to leave the scene and possibly establish an alibi for the time of the actual fire.

Matches. Frequently a match is struck by the arsonist, but only juvenile arsonists and pyromaniacs seem to favor this method. Other fire setters want some delay, so they adapt the ordinary match to some timing mechanism.

Several matches may be affixed to a lighted cigarette with a rubber band or scotch tape, with the heads of the matches about halfway down the cigarette from its glowing end. In some cases, the matches are just laid alongside the cigarette. Books of paper matches have also enjoyed popularity. Since cigarettes will continue to burn when laid on their sides, they are effective ignition devices; the slow-burning cigarette allows the fire setter a few minutes to get away from the scene before the fire makes any headway.

Matches are also used in conjunction with numerous mechanical devices. One misguided arsonist hooked them up with his telephone, strapping them to the ringing mechanism in a wall box and inserting a piece of abrasive board in place of the bell. This "brain" thought he could set a fire from miles away by calling his home. However, his estranged wife had a change of heart and came home unexpectedly. She settled down to await the amateur fire setter's return. It was not long before she noticed a wisp of smoke from a pile of old clothing on the floor of the living room. Frightened, she called the fire department. The ignition device had been activated but had fizzled out. The firefighters carefully preserved the rags (wet down with lighter fluid), the matches, and the abrasive board, and arranged a warm reception for the husband who had planned "the perfect crime."

Unburned or partially burned matches about the point of origin should be carefully preserved for examination and comparison. A suspect may be carrying similar matches or the book from which paper matches have been torn.

Candles. As a timed ignition device, candles have been in use by arsonists for over a century. A candle will burn at various rates, depending on its composition and size. Thick candles burn slowly, and long candles naturally burn for a longer period than short candles.

Some years ago, Dr. Richard Steinmetz established a table of the burning time of candles of various compositions and sizes in his fine text *Arson Investigator's Manual.* This table can be summed up as follows:

Composition	Diameter	Time to burn 1 in.
Tallow	$3/4''$	61 minutes
Wax	$7/8''$	57 minutes
Paraffin	$13/16''$	63 minutes

Arson investigators sometimes work on a rule of thumb of an hour's burning time for each inch of candle of above diameters. Of course, this is only guesswork, and the investigator must arrive at a more definite time when a little more information is secured about the candle used in the fire. The fire setter makes experiments before a fire so that the burning time will fit into the arson plans. Once the average burning time of the candle is known, the arsonist can adjust to a desired time lag merely by cutting the candle to the proper length. The candle is therefore not only an ignition unit, but also a device which can be adjusted within certain limits to set a fire hours after the arsonists has departed from the scene of the crime.

Candles are mostly used in conjunction with containers of easily combustible materials, which are sometimes set within or close to other containers of flammable liquids or in an area sprinkled with such accelerants. However, candles leave a deposit of wax as their telltale sign. It may have soaked into the wood of a floor or it may be found in a pool at the low point of a floor or table top. Another sign is the protection afforded the floor or table top by such wax— the spot upon which the candle rested will show less charring than the surrounding area. In many cases, a part of the candle and possibly the container in which the candle was placed may be found in a search of the fire scene.

Chemicals. Various chemical combinations have been used to set fires. Saboteurs have used such means for years. Units which provide for an acid to be released upon some combination of chemicals is a favorite device, with the acid releasing itself by eating its way through the cork or even the metal of its container. The time lag from setting to ignition can be estimated with some certainty by an arsonist with a little knowledge of chemistry.

Various rubber receptacles, such as hot water and ice bags or contraceptives, have been used for a phosphorus and water ignition device. A pinhole is made in the rubber container, allowing the water to seep out. Once it drains below the level of the phosphorus, ignition takes place. As this chemical ignites on contact with air, a time lag is secured by controlling the amount of water and the size of the hole in the container.

Even the ordinary fire setter sometimes utilizes a chemical which ignites on contact with water, setting up a device actuated by the next rainstorm. Holes in the roof or some connection to the gutter system have been used to trigger this device. Another device is the diversion of the sewage line in a building, set up at night but planned to trigger off the next morning when the toilet is flushed for the first time.

Most chemical ignition units leave some residue or have a distinctive odor, or both. Naturally, the debris must be analyzed at a laboratory when it is suspected that chemicals have been employed for ignition.

Fortunately, most arsonists are not equipped with the knowledge required for the use of chemical ignition or timing devices, nor are the machinery and tools necessary for the construction of some of these devices readily available. Unless prepared by a saboteur, the device will probably be fairly simple. The more complex units are encountered as a rule only in time of war, and usually in the possession of a frustrated enemy agent who has not had the opportunity to use them.

Gas. Although not commonly encountered, the combination of gas and the pilot light on the kitchen stoves of many residents is always a possibility. Illuminating gas rises to the ceiling, being lighter than air, and then slowly moves down to floor level as it continues to escape. When it reaches a combustion buildup, it is close to the pilot-light level and an explosion, usually followed by fire, takes place. A candle placed in a room adjoining the kitchen has also been utilized as a means of ignition. Therefore arson investigators must remember that while such explosions normally follow suicide attempts or stem from accidental causes, it is possible that an incendiary may use an ordinary gas range as an arson tool. In such cases, the investigator should get help from an engineer of the local public utility. The time lag between the initial release of the gas and the explosion can be estimated from the size of the room involved, number of openings, type of gas, and related data. For example, a normal kitchen of about 10 by 15 feet with a 9-foot ceiling equals a total volume of 1350 cubic feet. When 71 cubic feet of gas is introduced into the room, the lowest limit of explosive range will have been reached. In a well-ventilated room it is almost impossible to build up to this limit, but an arsonist will seal off the room or rooms concerned so that the gas volume will build up. In a fairly well-sealed room, a single burner left open on a kitchen gas stove will deliver sufficient gas to reach the explosive range in about 5 hours. The oven jets will build up the same volume of gas in 2 hours, and if the stove has an oven and four burners and all of them are left open, the lower explosive limit of gas volume can be reached in from 30 minutes to 1 hour.

What has prevented the widespread use of gas as an arson tool and thwarted some attempts to use it is its smell. Neighbors detect the gas odor and call police or firefighters, or break in themselves and thus ruin a carefully planned arson attempt.

Electrical Systems. Any wiring system, including doorbell and telephone circuits, can be used in fire setting. Ignition devices hooked to the wiring systems of buildings have been used throughout the country as arson tools. The time lag can be established by a study of the habits of the persons using the premises in which the fire is to be set. Possibly a security guard may switch on the light every hour while inspecting the various portions of the building on rounds of inspection; employees turn on the lights at the time of opening; and so on.

While a doorbell system can be used in the same manner to trigger an ignition device, the possibility of flaws in the timing precludes any widespread use. The bell may be rung by some chance visitor and upset the carefully laid plans of the fire setter.

Telephone timing devices have the same fault; a "wrong number" or an unexpected call and the fire is under way, possibly days ahead of schedule.

Electrical appliances have also been used to set off fires. An open heater is placed close to a flimsy set of curtains, and an apparently accidental fire results. An iron can be set in its usual position; overheating serves to ignite the ironing board cover; and, again, an apparently accidental fire results. Or perhaps an electrical circuit is deliberately overloaded with several appliances until some portion of it heats up. Sometimes an accelerant or "booster" such as kerosene is dropped into a switch box; and there have been a few cases in which a length of normal wiring was removed and a lighter wire substituted so that it would overheat and, without blowing the fuses, serve as an ignition device.

Investigators will generally find that some physical trace of an electrical ignition device can be discovered after a fire. Some portion will not be completely destroyed.

Mechanical. Alarm clocks were once a favored weapon of arsonists. A simple alarm clock, some wire, and a small battery—and a fire setter was "in business." But after a search of the fire debris disclosed the remains of an alarm clock, the arsonist was in trouble and usually on the way to prison. The arsonists utilized the lead hammer which normally hammers away at the alarm bell as a tool—to break a glass tube which will then feed flammable matter to a fixed flame; to push over a container of chemicals into a container of other chemicals; to close an open electrical circuit; or, by attaching matches to the hammer so that they will be pressed back and forth against an abrasive surface, to ignite a previously prepared "set" of flammable material. The clock is actuated by simply setting the alarm for a certain time, at which point the alarm "goes off" and the lead hammer starts to swing. The weights in a grandfather's clock have also been utilized in a similar manner.

Mechanical devices which the minds of fire setters have dreamed up beggar description. Some are childish, some are worthy of master craftsmen, and others are truly fiendish. Unfortunately for many of these ingenious incendiaries, their infernal machines will not burn and can later be hung like millstones around their necks.

Plants

Any preparation for the unlawful setting of fires is termed a *plant*. It is the material placed about the ignition device to feed the initial flame. Newspapers, wood shavings, excelsior, rags, clothing, curtains, blankets, and cotton waste are some of the materials used in plants. Newspapers and excelsior seem to be the most frequently used material, with cotton waste being used extensively in factory or industrial fires.

Accelerants or "boosters" to speed the progress of the fire are also part of the plant. Kerosene and gasoline are favored boosters, with alcohol, lighter fluid, paint thinners, and other solvents enjoying some popularity. However, any flammable fluid or compound may be used to accelerate the blaze.

Trailers

Trailers are used to spread the fire. A trailer is ignited as a result of the blaze kindled in the primary plant by the ignition device, and it carries the fire to other parts of a room or building. Sometimes the trailer will simply carry the fire to these other locations, the arsonist depending on the flames from the trailer to spread the fire; but usually a trailer will end in a secondary plant, that is, another pile of papers or excelsior sprinkled with gasoline, kerosene, or some other booster.

From the primary plant, a fire setter may lay four trailers to an equal number of secondary plants, thus securing four separate fires from the one ignition device.

Rope or toilet paper soaked in alcohol or like fluid, motion picture film, dynamite fuses, gunpowder, and other such substances have been used as trailers. Sometimes rags or newspapers are soaked in some fire accelerant and twisted into a rope. On other occasions, an arsonist will use a fluid fire accelerant such as kerosene as a trailer by pouring a liberal quantity on the floor in a desired path.

Incendiary Fires

When any fire-setting device, any components of the various ignition and timing units, or any of the materials used in plants or trailers as previously described are found in premises in which a suspicious fire has occurred, then the classification of the fire can be made. Unless the presence of materials used by fire setters bears some relation to the occupancy of the premises, the blaze should be classified as incendiary.

When kerosene, gasoline, excelsior, candles, and like substances are discovered about the point of origin of a suspicious fire, it is evidence of arson, and if the investigator can prove this material had no right to be in the premises, then the corpus delicti has been established; that is, the presumption of accident has been overcome as established by law and the body of the crime has been proved—that the fire occurred from some criminal agency.

EVIDENCE

Evidence is what tends to prove or disprove any matter in question or to influence the belief respecting it. It is all the means by which an alleged matter of fact, the truth of which is submitted to investigation, is established or disproved.

It is vital that arson investigators be familiar with the technical aspects of evidence in general and the handling and analysis of physical evidence in particular. Otherwise, valuable evidence may be overlooked or ruined by improper handling during an investigation.

Direct Evidence

Direct evidence is that evidence directly proving any matter, as opposed to circumstantial evidence. It is evidence of a fact in dispute, sworn to by those who have actual knowledge of it by means of their senses. Direct evidence has been held to exist when the thing to be proved is directly attested to by those who speak from their own actual and personal knowledge of its existence.

In an arson case, direct evidence of the burning by the defendant would be the testimony of a witness who saw the defendant bend down, strike a match, and apply it to the building for whose burning the defendant is on trial. However, direct evidence is the exception rather than the rule in an arson case. Very few people ever see someone set a fire.

Circumstantial (Indirect) Evidence

In no other crime does circumstantial evidence play such an important part as in arson. In fact, most cases are predicated on circumstantial rather than direct evidence.

Circumstantial, or indirect, evidence consists of facts which usually attend other facts sought to be proved. Richardson, in his "Law of Evidence," defines it as evidence that relates to facts other than those in issue, which by human experience have been found to be so associated with the fact in issue that the latter may be reasonably inferred therefrom.

This type of evidence must *establish* collateral facts from which the facts in issue will follow as a logical inference. Circumstantial evidence can be said to exist when the thing to be proved is to be inferred from other facts *satisfactorily proved* [*People v. Palmer*, N.Y.S. Rep. 817, 820 (1887)]. Circumstantial evidence consists of reasoning from facts which are known (proved) to establish a point in issue. The process would be fatally circular if the basic point from which the inference is to be made had not been satisfactorily established. Certainly, one inference cannot be the basis for another inference.

When circumstantial evidence is relied on for a conviction, the proved collateral facts, when taken together, must be of a conclusive nature and tendency, leading as a whole to a reasonable inference that the accused, and no one else, committed the offense as charged.

In a legal sense, circumstantial evidence is not regarded as inferior to direct evidence; and in many instances it is more reliable than direct evidence, especially since proof by circumstantial evidence usually requires a large number of witnesses, each testifying to some small portion of the overall picture, so that a number of perjured witnesses would be necessary to produce an unjust conviction, whereas one perjured witness giving direct testimony might accomplish such a wrongful act.

Physical Evidence

Physical evidence is any clue, trace, impression, or thing so connected with the case as to throw some light upon it. Usually such evidence is mute, requiring the facilities of a scientific laboratory, the techniques of laboratory technicians, and the testimony of such experts before it is of much value.

Arson investigators should secure qualified aid in any case in which expert testimony may be developed as a result of the analysis of physical evidence. Evidence of top value has been ruined by amateur technicians, by persons who, because of insufficient training or experience in the field concerned, could not qualify as experts to testify as to their findings upon trial.

All that is expected of the investigator is knowledge of what the technicians in a properly equipped laboratory can do and proper handling and forwarding of evidence so that its value is not lessened or destroyed entirely before arrival at the laboratory.

ALIBIS, MOTIVES, AND THE CORPUS DELICTI

The establishment of an alibi is the defense normally in the minds of the majority of fire setters: "I'll prove that I was somewhere else at the time of the fire. How could they suspect me?" Arsonists viewing their possible involvement in a planned fire in a more realistic light will add. "They'll probably suspect me, but if my alibi stands up, how can they prove I was involved?" Members of this second group realize that they may be numbered among the suspects because of the benefits or profits they stand to derive from the fire. These alluring prospects are what motivated them to scheme and plan and finally set the fire. Thus a close relationship between alibis and motives often is built up. Both breed in the mind of the fire setter during the period of planning. One can be broken down or overcome, and the other can usually be discovered.

Alibis

The purpose of timing devices, sometimes termed "long-range ignition units," is to give the fire setter a chance to establish an alibi. So, also, is the employment of accomplices. Both permit the establishing of an alibi, a claim of being at some other location at or about the time of the fire. It is one of the most frequently encountered defenses to suspicion of arson.

When an alibi defense is encountered, it is necessary to overcome it and place the suspect at the fire scene at or about the time of its outbreak unless (1) the use of a timing device can be shown, its time lag pinpointed, and the suspect placed at the scene at the time of the actual fire setting, or (2) the employment of an accomplice can be proved.

Motives

The question of the presence or lack of a motive deserves serious consideration in all fire inquiries; the guilt or innocence of a suspect may sometimes hinge on the discovery and proof of motive.

Fires are set by two types of fire setters, persons with a motive for setting a fire and those without any rational motive. In the first group are those individuals who desire fires either for profit, for revenge, to conceal evidence of other crimes, or for intimidation. In the second group we have the pathological fire setters and the pyromaniacs. They range from imbeciles to apparently well adjusted persons with a compulsive neurosis. This second group must also include the thrill-seekers, the "heroes," the vandals, and the juveniles. No rational motive activates any of these persons. It must be remembered, however, that a pyromaniac may also set a revenge fire. Being unduly interested in fire, such an individual naturally seizes upon it as a weapon of revenge. In fact, Lewis and Yarnell (*Pathological Fire Setting*) estimate that 25 percent of the more typical pyromaniacs set at least one direct hate fire in the course of their fire-setting activities. Motivation may also be of an odd and unusual nature, the result of twisted thinking.

In determining motive, an insurance representative concentrates on three major factors: the point of origin of the fire, the modus operandi of the arsonist, and the identity of persons who might benefit from the fire.

The first two factors aid in discovering whether the fire was set by an arsonist with a rational motive or by a pyromaniac. Pyromaniacs use those portions of buildings accessible to the public as the point of origin for their fires. Firebugs do not set fire to their own homes or places of business; they set fires in places where they can make ready entry and hurried exit. Hallways, easily accessible basements, roofs, spaces under porches or garages, and public toilets are the scenes of their efforts.

Nor is the preparation of a firebug's plant as extensive as that of an arsonist with a normal motive. The pathological fire setter uses a few twists of newspaper, rubbish, and possibly a baby carriage found in a hallway as the plant and a match as the ignition device. The arsonist with a rational motive employs more elaborate preparations, usually marked by accelerants or fire boosters.

Motive alone is not sufficient to classify a blaze as incendiary, but in fraud fire cases, a motive may be strong enough for it to be termed a telltale sign and permit classification of a fire as suspicious. Motive is not an essential element of the crime of arson, but evidence of strong motive helps to eliminate accident or misfortune as probable causes. Proof of motive also serves to bolster evidence tending to prove criminal intent on the part of the arsonist.

While it is not absolutely necessary to establish a positive motive on the part of the accused in the trial of an arson case, it is extremely helpful. Curtis in his *Law of Arson* admits that when the prosecution fails to show a motive which might lead the accused to set a fire, the evidence is more carefully scrutinized to determine its worth, and without proof of motive the courts often hold that the prosecution has not fulfilled its burden of proof.

Since arson is a crime of stealth, committed with great secrecy, it is not usually possible to produce witnesses who will be able to give direct evidence of a suspect's guilt. Most cases are based on circumstantial evidence; therefore the importance of discovering motive cannot be overemphasized.

After exploring the avenues of both opportunity and probability, the motivation can be brought into focus by asking several questions: Who had the opportunity to set the fire? Who would have a reason to set it? Would any of the possible reasons for desiring the fire be sufficient motivation for the persons under suspicion?

Quite a few suspects may be in the group of those having the opportunity to set the blaze, but the field will narrow when possible reasons are explored and it will be further reduced when the motivation is considered with respect to the background, personal characteristics, past activities, and financial status of each suspect. Ten individuals may have had an opportunity to set a fire, but only four or five had good reasons for wanting a blaze. And of this number, only one or two would risk possible disclosure as fire setters for the anticipated profit or satisfaction to be secured as a result of the fire.

When a profit motive exists, it is usually fairly simple to determine those with possible motives. It is a case of who will benefit from the damage wrought by the blaze.

Fires motivated by revenge, to conceal crime, or to intimate are more difficult to analyze. It is difficult to ascertain either the *who* or the *why*. The identity of the suspects, as well as their reasons for wanting the fire, are the major goals of a successful inquiry.

Intent

Intent is an essential element of the crime of arson. A person who intentionally sets a fire does so willfully; such an act implies knowledge and purpose. A willful burning is a malicious one, the malice of the fire setter being inferred from the intent. When a person intentionally performs a wrongful act, it is safe to term it malicious; and setting a fire under circumstances which permit it to be termed arson is certainly a wrongful act.

The intent may be inferred from the act itself if the inevitable consequence of the act is the burning of the building or if the particular purpose cannot be effected without such burning. All persons are held responsible for the necessary and natural consequences of their acts and are held to have intended to produce such consequences.

It has also been held that persons commit arson when they set fire to or burn a building in the commission of some felony such as burglary, even though there is no specific intent in the mind of the accused to set fire to or burn the building [*People v.Fanshawe*, 137 N.Y. 68, 32 N.E. 1102].

Quite frequently, a clever fire setter will set a fraud fire and claim carelessness to mask its incendiary nature. In cases of this type, arsonists often point out the obvious points of origin of the fires and bitterly blame themselves for their carelessness. The lack of appropriate laws in such cases handicaps insurance representatives, but, fortunately, many of these cases are resolved by a background investigation of the insured, a little delving into possible "needs" for the fire, and possibly an uncovering of some preplanning in anticipation of the fire.

Attempted Arson

After conceiving a plan to set a fire, a person may undergo a change of mind. However, to be free from guilt for "attempted arson," the plan must be abandoned voluntarily and not because it is frustrated by an unexpected obstacle or condition.

Unless the intent to set a fire progresses to an overt act of some kind, no crime is committed. An overt act is one done to carry out the intention and it must lead toward the consummation of the intent. It should be an act such as would normally effect the desired result—a fire. It does not have to be the final act of igniting the blaze, but should be one of a series of acts which would generally result in a fire. An attempt is complete with an opportunity occurs and the intending perpetrator has performed some act tending to accomplish this purpose.

When two or more persons conspire to commit an act of arson, the initiation of the conspiracy is complete at the time of their agreement, but the actual attempted arson requires opportunity and an overt act.

Essential ingredients of an attempted arson are:

1. An intent to set a fire under circumstances constituting arson if carried out.

2. An overt act in furtherance of such intent.

3. A failure to burn.

Corpus Delicti

It is a rule of law in regard to arson that every fire is presumed to be of accidental origin. This presumption has to be overcome before an arson charge can be established. Therefore, a prime fact to be established by competent evidence is that the building was burned by someone with a criminal design. It is necessary to prove that the burning was the willful act of some person and not the result of accidental or natural causes.

In proving the corpus delicti, it is essential that all accidental causes of fire be eliminated. Unless direct evidence of fire setting can be secured, it is a fundamental rule of all arson investigations that every possible cause except incendiarism be eliminated. The task then is to detail the suspicious circumstances surrounding the fire which indicate the work of an arsonist. Since direct evidence of fire setting by the defendant is not frequently encountered, this is the usual manner of establishing the corpus delicti.

A corpus delicti is established when the investigation has developed enough facts to prove upon presentation in court that the building in question burned and that such burning resulted from the intentional criminal act of some person.

FIRES FOR PROFIT

Arson for profit is the first motive to be considered. It accounts for more fires than the public or many police officers realize. However, there is usually sufficient time to investigate crimes of this type. Unless the aid of a professional torch has been secured, there is no need to apprehend the perpetrator before another blaze is set. Profit-motivated fire setters are not going to run away; they must stay in order to collect their insurance or otherwise profit from the fire. And no fire insurance firm is in a hurry to pay fraudulent claims resulting from profit-motivated fires.

Fraud Fires

Even otherwise honest persons have been known to set fires for the purpose of defrauding an insurance company. Someone who is at heart law-abiding, who would run from robbery or burglary, who becomes upset at a reprimand from a traffic officer, and whose children are carefully guarded from minor transgressions, may become an arsonist for profit.

It is indeed strange to burn and steal and then rationalize the arson and larceny. The fire itself is not to hurt anyone, just to conceal the evidence of fire setting and to make possible the fraudulent claim by damaging the stock or gutting the building.

A large number of businesses operate on little or no capital. Others are in debt or make little or no profit. It would appear obvious that an operator of any well-insured business that is operating at a loss would profit from an extensive fire. But, was that individual responsible for the fire setting? Was this the motivation? It is only by studying the circumstances of each case that one can safely arrive at any conclusion. Business difficulties mean nothing to some people, while others become extremely worried and sometimes conclude that, for them, the choice is either suicide or arson. Fortunately, the more desperate the need, the less the attempt to conceal the arson, and there is little likelihood of successfully concealing motive when a business enterprise is in real financial difficulty.

"Business" Fires.   Sometimes termed "commercial" fires, business fires result from the acts of business.

Prosperity sometimes bypasses a few enterprises. A ready market for some product may suddenly tighten up and result in a large inventory at the factory. Unexpected sales resistance may result in a failure to receive orders which had been counted on in stockpiling a supply of necessary raw materials. Possibly a seasonal business will face several "dead" months with a large inventory on hand and the probability that new styles will make their present models "trash" merchandise by the next season. In any event, great losses can be anticipated; the stock on hand cannot be moved through normal channels. The sale of such "distress" merchandise brings very little cash. Some shady merchants have a saying to fit such situations—"Sell it to the insurance company!"

Sometimes manufacturers are faced with the problem of retooling to produce new models; radical changes in manufacturing methods may require the scrapping of valuable machines in a normally busy plant. Or there may be some other urgent need for ready cash. Such situations breed arson.

Possibly an estate is tied up in some heavily insured business. Five or six heirs must await liquidation before they can realize their inheritance. The idea of converting the insurance into cash may occur to one or more of them, and a fire results.

Sometimes land is more valuable without the buildings; other times a business may outgrow its quarters. A few persons may seize upon such instances as golden opportunities for profit or to secure funds for larger quarters.

A building may be condemned for occupancy because of a building or fire code violation. Rather than laying out the money to rehabilitate it or paying for demolishing it, and unwilling to let it stand idle and become a tax burden, the owner may have it burned down and attempt to collect from the insurance companies. During the past few years, in several cities it was not unusual for schemers to buy up dilapidated, unoccupied buildings for a nominal sum, place insurance on them, leave the city, and arrange to have fires break out in the buildings during their absence at a safe "alibi" distance.

Many buildings in rural areas are erected on land that does not belong to the building owner. When notified by the landowner to remove the structure from the property for any one of a number of reasons, building owners have been known to set fire to the building and then submit a claim for an accidental fire loss.

Partnership. Partners disagree: one may think the firm can weather a financial crisis; the other may think only of bankruptcy. Possibly one partner would like to buy out the firm but does not have the cash or the other partner may refuse to sell. One partner may be satisfied with small profits, while the other may be unhappy at the limited success of the enterprise. It is a fertile ground for fraud fires based on complex motivations.

The Insured. The most logical suspect in such cases is the policyholder—the individual who will profit most from the fire. In some cases it is the occupant of rented premises, while at other times it is the building owner who expects to profit from damage to the structure rather than from damage to stock and fixtures. However, in recent years landlords have found rentals very profitable and unless an urgent need for cash exists will not burn a building bringing in a profit.

The initial inquiry concerning a policyholder suspected of setting a fire to defraud the insurer is a brief financial worth and personal background study. What is the policyholder's equity in the property? How much cash has this individual on hand? What is the value of other assets? An analysis of the person's debts is made and the nature of the debts is thoroughly explored. If a business enterprise is concerned, a like audit is made; if a partnership, each partner will be thoroughly checked. Income tax, sales tax, and other tax records are of particular value in such studies. In the course of such initial inquiry, it must be remembered that not everyone in debt or everyone whose personal habits may be open to criticism sets fraud fires. Many business firms are operated closed to bankruptcy for years and many persons never get out of debt, and such concerns or individuals sometimes suffer perfectly legitimate fires.

Civil Action as a Deterrent. The need for proof beyond a reasonable doubt upon a criminal charge of arson sometimes places the investigator of fraud fires in a strange position. The investigator may be certain that it is arson, but the utmost diligence may have failed to secure proof which will convict the accused under the law. Sometimes the rules of evidence handicap a prosecution. Other times a small link may be missing from a substantial chain of evidence; even though it is obviously arson, it cannot be proved to a moral certainty in court.

However, when an investigator can prove the allegation of deliberate fire setting by a fair preponderance of evidence, the case can be taken to the civil courts of most states. In a civil action, it is not necessary to prove a fact beyond a reasonable doubt but only to prove it by a fair preponderance of evidence. The simple method is for the insurance company concerned to refuse to honor the proof of loss submitted by the insured and examine the insured under oath, as provided on the policy, with a view of possibly entering into an affirmative defense of arson on a civil case or, when the facts will not support a civil defense of arson, a civil defense of fraud by the insured before or after the fire.

The best deterrent to fraud fires is arrest, conviction, and imprisonment. But failing that, anything that eliminates the profit from such fires will also serve as a deterrent. Perhaps we cannot put an arsonist-for-profit in jail, but at least we can withhold the profits by this technique of forcing a civil action.

Overinsurance. A strong inducement is present when policies are issued in amounts far in excess of the true value of the insured property, or when due care is not exercised at renewal periods. Possibly the value of the premises concerned may have depreciated during the life of the original policy, or perhaps some other circumstances which point to the insured as a poor risk may have developed. A poor risk who is determined to get insurance coverage can invariably "shop around" and obtain it, frequently through an agency located at some distance from the premises covered.

Fires for Indirect Profit

Fraud fires are not the only blazes motivated by profit. A fraud fire is an effort by a policyholder to swindle an insurance company. The basic motive pinpoints the prime suspect—the insured.

In fires for an indirect profit, the motive is more obscure and, naturally, so is the suspect. Possibly it was set by a competitor in business. A contractor may have ignited the fire in order to secure a lucrative rebuilding contract. Or perhaps some individual seeking a position as a security guard may have lighted the blaze to firmly establish the need for such services. Whatever the motive is in any single case, it can be safely assumed that because of its remoteness, it will be far from evident. The arson investigator must really "dig" into cases that are suspected of being fires for indirect profit.

In cases of indirect profit, the most likely motives are to stifle competition, to stimulate "new business," and to secure employment. And the most likely suspects are security guards, firefighters, police officers, and other "protectors."

CLAIM REPRESENTATIVE'S CONTACT WITH AUTHORITIES

When adjusters, for obvious and valid reasons, suspect that a fire was intentionally set for any purpose or motive but, more specifically, for fraud, they are encouraged to follow the standard operating procedure set out below, rather than proceed willy-nilly on their own independent inquiries, thus exposing their companies to unwarranted lawsuits.

The following should be promptly contacted:

Chief of the fire department. Firefighters who were at the scene may possess information to confirm or allay suspicions because of what they saw on arrival or during the firefighting. If necessary, those who were at the scene should be conferred with, especially those "first in" the premises.

Chief of the police department (if within the police department jurisdiction). The arson investigator or other assigned detective should be spoken with concerning the results of any preliminary investigation which may have been conducted.

Fire marshall, state police, or county sheriff (whichever agency has jurisdiction in rural or urban ares).

The purposes of making these contacts as soon as possible after the incident are to establish whether the fire may have been recognized as having been set and to determine if a criminal investigation has been started. If the information received is negative, the information that has aroused the adjuster's suspicion can be supplied and the feasibility of a criminal investigation discussed.

When an investigation is in progress, the adjuster should determine from the fire chief which of the fire personnel are cooperating or working with the criminal investigator and determine from the police chief, fire marshall, state police, county sheriff, or prosecutor the name of the investigator and the case number assigned. It may also be well to determine when and where the investigator may be contacted. Finally, adjusters should assure the investigating agency of their cooperation and advise where they may be contacted.

MOTIVES FOR FIRES

1. The insured is desperate for immediate funds due to:

    a. Gambling.
    b. Heavy doctor and hospital expenses.
    c. Threat of mortgage foreclosure on business or home.
    d. Extortion by criminal associates.
    e. Blackmail for any of hundreds of causes.

2. Obsolete or valueless merchandise or equipment:

    a. The business has not been successful enough to move inventory.
    b. Radical new process renders old equipment too costly to operate or not adaptable to new processing.
    c. The business has not made sufficient profit to permit regular replacement or upgrading of equipment.
    d. Purchasing agent bought materials based on an increased production; production decreased and better material came on market.

3. Property does not sell readily because:

    a. It is a large mansion, with 20 rooms and large grounds, that does not sell because of the high cost of upkeep.

b. The location of property reduces salability.
c. It is an obsolete factory building no longer suitable for modern assembly-line production.
d. It is an old-fashioned bank building (one story), not suited for other commercial purposes.

4. The insured structure is to be abandoned because:

   a. Maintenance costs make use of the structure uneconomical.
   b. Owner is moving to large or more modern quarters.
   c. Vandalism has reduced structure to untenantable condition.
   d. Crime conditions around structure force removal of work force.

5. The insured desires to liquidate a business quickly due to:

   a. Disagreement with partner(s).
   b. Marital problems.
   c. Health problems.
   d. Criminal pressures.
   e. Leaving the country.
   f. Emergence of competition.
   g. Labor problems.

6. The insured is unable to fill contracts due to:

   a. Labor problems.
   b. Materials unavailable.
   c. Equipment breakdown.
   d. Material cost increase.

7. A seasonal business is terminated due to:

   a. Its being a resort location.
   b. Unseasonable weather.
   c. Ordinance affecting future operation.
   d. New business opportunity.
   e. Labor problems.

8. High inventory due to:

   a. Purchases of too great a quantity.
   b. Recession; low turnover.
   c. Fashion change.
   d. Season change.

9. Poor general business conditions due to:

   a. Recession.
   b. Labor problems.
   c. Increased competition.
   d. "Buggy Whips."
   e. Rural area; crop failure.

10. The owner lacks business ability—

   a. a good technician but a poor salesperson.
   b. "Shoestring" start.

     c. Cannot supervise others.

     d. Cannot or will not negotiate with union representative.

11. Raw materials are not available because:

     a. The only supplier is bankrupt.

     b. Federal government curtails import.

     c. Labor costs curtail production.

12. There are legal problems with builder or seller due to:

     a. Failure to meet specifications.

     b. Disappointment with purchase; attempt to rescind agreement; withholding payment.

     c. Suit to rescind contract by seller.

13. New highway bypasses insured's business location, with:

     a. No access to quick-stop food store or business depending on stop-in auto traffic.

     b. A motel stuck between distant exits of thruway.

     c. Main traffic artery downgraded to local traffic only.

14. Condemnation proceedings in progress due to:

     a. Low value placed on property by government body.

     b. No adequate replacement structure available in market area.

ODORS

During the interior examination, the adjuster must be aware of the many indicators that could negate an apparent accidental cause. One of these indicators that may be observed, or reported by others, is any unusual odor that might point to a substance used in setting or sustaining a set fire.

Odors are retained in rags that can be removed from the debris and identified, even after they have been wet. Odors of woolen and cotton materials differ and are readily identified.

1. The odor of sulfur might indicate that a candle, such as is used to fumigate the premises against rodents and other pests, has been used to ignite the fire.

2. Film and toilet articles with a nitrocelluloid base have a pungent odor similar to camphor.

3. Burning phosphorous has an odor similar to wet match heads and produces the sensation of a coating on the tongue when the fumes are breathed or inhaled.

4. Carbon bisulphide has an odor similar to rotten garbage.

5. Manufactured gas carried with it a peculiar odor which is readily recognizable.

6. Natural gas is required by law to be odorized so that it may be readily distinguishable. When the odor of gas is identified, the gas cocks and pipes should be checked immediately.

7. Odors of various moth or insect sprays are generally "sweet" or perfumy. Manufacturers of insect and other types of sprays use different perfumes in their compounds to produce varying odors. Most of these products have a petroleum base and produce a gas which is heavier than air.

8. Ammonia has a very pungent odor which is readily recognized. It is generally used by the arsonist to keep firefighters out of the building or to kill the odor of gasoline. Ammonia is not explosive unless it is mixed with other materials or is impure; its employment by the arsonist may be termed a counterirritant.

9. The odor of gunpowder is similar to that of burned firecrackers; turpentine, paint thinners, lacquers, and linseed oil all have odors peculiar to themselves.

ADJUSTER'S CHECKLIST

1. Check and verify *all coverage.*
2. Proceed to fire scene as quickly as possible.
3. Inspect building with insured or ask permission to inspect it; advise insured to obtain detailed estimate of cost of repairs; advise insured to prepare inventory of damaged items; develop information on by whom, when, and how fire was discovered.
4. Walk through interior of building and make cursory inspection.
5. Begin inspection on exterior.
6. Continue inspection on interior.
7. Look for *origin.*
8. Look for *cause.*
9. Start interior inspection in area of origin.
10. Follow path of fire through the building.
11. Obtain statements from insured and witnesses, if warranted.
12. Talk to responding firefighters.
13. Call local police headquarters if warranted.
14. Contact agent.
15. Contact the fire marshall.
16. Contact the arson squad.
17. At your office prepare your estimate.
18. Review your file.
19. Clean your file.
20. Write preliminary report.
21. Discuss the loss with your supervisor.

QUESTIONS TO ASK THE RESPONDING FIRE DEPARTMENT

1. What time was the first alarm received? How? From whom?
2. What was the time of their arrival on the scene?
3. What were the general conditions of the fire scene on their arrival, such as the extent of the fire and its apparent center or centers?
4. Did anyone meet them or did they see anyone upon arrival at the scene?

5. What colors were the smoke and flames? From where were they coming? Did they appear unusual?

6. Which doors and windows were secured upon arrival and which were unsecured?
   If entry was forced, did they check to make sure it was secure before forcing entry and how did they force entry?

7. Where did the fire appear to be centered?

8. Were there any signs of separate fires?

9. Were there any unusual odors? Where were the odors apparently coming from? When, during the fire, did the odor become noticeable and where were the firefighters when they first smelled it? How strong was the odor?

10. Were any fires unusually difficult to extinguish or did any fires reignite? If so, where?

11. Were police on the scene and when did they arrive?

12. Did any spectators or neighbors make any comments regarding the fire? If so, identify and describe them.

All information in the foregoing article was used with the permission of Property Claim Services, American Insurance Association. According to The American Insurance Association, the information was obtained from sources believed to be reliable. However, the American Insurance Association, its companies and employees make no guarantee of results and assume no liability in connection with either the information given or the suggestions made. Further, the company states it cannot be assumed that every acceptable procedure is contained in the account, or that abnormal or unusual circumstances may not warrant or require further or additional procedure.

45

Undercover Investigations and Sting Operations in the Private Sector: User and Provider Views

David E. Zeldin

Kimberly A. Cordray

Undercover investigations and sting operations are sophisticated and effective private security strategies employed to ferret out wrongdoers, control dishonesty, and apprehend thieves. Since these services are usually provided by a loss control and prevention firm for a business, this chapter focuses on the client/firm partnership—its essential qualities and "chemistry." Criteria for client selection of an investigation agency and the management of its highly surreptitious operations are set forth.

PRELUDE

Much like the legal profession, private security is divided into many different areas of specialization. It is estimated that over four million people are employed in the many facets of it throughout the United States. Because of the growth of the burgeoning security industry, quite a few states have developed a myriad of new laws to govern the security industry. Many of these laws force the security industry to properly train and investigate its employees. Security personnel usually work in either a proprietary or contract security force.

Proprietary Security

Most corporations have their own security departments, which are usually specialized in the area of their discipline. Proprietary security is designed, by its very nature, to deal with everyday problems within the scope of a particular business environment. When situations occur beyond its expertise or personnel availability, proprietary security calls on the assistance of a specialized service provider (outside contractor).

Throughout the business world, almost every type of industry has its own proprietary security and its own reasons for using contract security. For example, most retail stores have security managers, assistants, supervisors, investigators to conduct internal and various fraud probes, store detectives to apprehend shoplifters, and security guards. However, when undercover investigations are required, an outside contractor is almost always called in. The thought of maintaining a crew of undercover investigators within the scope of a proprietary security department is practically unheard of. While an individual store or other type of business will almost certainly maintain its own guard force, it is ordinarily unable to cover its requirements for special events or emergencies. In those instances, it is usually necessary to use a contract agency. While larger chains may have their own alarm or locksmith personnel, their smaller counterparts most often seek outside assistance.

Contract Security

Security guard and investigation agencies top the list for contract security services. Equipment providers are generally contractual and not proprietary. That means that closed-circuit television and alarm installations are very rarely set up by proprietary security.

When a proprietary security force is faced with any type of situation beyond its control and expertise, it ordinarily turns to an outside agency. Furthermore, since it is often almost impossible for the proprietary department to recruit and retain enough personnel for the many functions of security, reaching outside the firm is commonplace. Thus, undercover investigations many times is just the area called on for its know-how and resources in contract security.

USERS OF UNDERCOVER INVESTIGATIONS AND STING OPERATIONS

American business has used undercover investigations and sting operations for more than a half century. These methods of attacking employee dishonesty, drug abuse, and other drains on corporate profits have become an aggressive part of the loss prevention and security industry during the past 20 years.

While the largest corporate users of undercover investigations and sting operations are America's retailers, probes of this type can be found throughout all aspects of business. Heavy industry might be most concerned with drug abuse, a computer manufacturer with theft of company secrets. An apparel or cosmetic firm may be equally concerned with the confidentiality of patterns of formulas as with the stealing of finished products. The retailer, however, is primarily oriented toward theft of money and inventory. Whatever the orientation and goals, the operations are the same.

All investigations start when a decision is made that there is a need and funding is allocated to pursue a course of action. An undercover investigator will be placed or a sting operation begun. First, we shall deal with the placement of an undercover investigator.

The user of the services, normally referred to as the client, has many specific goals and desires. For example, Company X has discovered a 1.5 percent shortage after an inventory at a warehouse facility. Another firm may be faced with any of the following types of situations, also known as *methods of employee dishonesty*, and makes the painful determination that it is the victim of internal larceny and other related problems. Of the following list of the methods used, some are specific to retailing, but variations are common to all businesses. Naturally, since the dishonest employees probably do not read a script, most of them pick their method and reshape it a little as circumstances dictate. It should be understood that each one of these procedures is modified enough by the employees to fit many different industries and situations. Interestingly, most dishonest employees, once apprehended, are flabbergasted to learn that their method was not unique to them.

Methods of Employee Dishonesty

The Dishonest General Office Employee.　These individuals often take substantial amounts of stationery supplies in small daily quantities.

The Receiving and Shipping Thief.　This employee works in either of these areas and can steal entire cases of goods, instead of merely single items. Moreover, such workers have been known to make many types of illegal deals with truck drivers.

The Warehouse Crook.　Like their counterparts in the receiving and shipping departments, warehouse workers have access to entire cartons of merchandise. Many documented cases exist of such persons simply leaving the facility, carrying boxes of goods, and stashing them outside the building to be retrieved by them later on.

The White-Collar Criminal.　As in so many other businesses, the opportunities for white-collar crime also exist in retail establishments. Buyers can take kickbacks; accountants and controllers may embezzle funds; selling floor supervisors and managers sometimes operate in collusion with lower-echelon employees, including cashiers and/or salespersons. Furthermore, padded expense accounts are commonplace among white-collar criminals.

The Security Bribe Taker. In exchange for favorable actions and releases, store detectives and guards have been known to request and/or receive bribes from shoplifters.

The Service Department Thief. Such thieves operate in departments where services are performed for customers, for example, the jewelry repair section or the auto repair shops. In such cases, "undercounter" deals are made with the customer for more service than is officially paid for. A garage mechanic, for instance, might officially charge a customer for much less than the actual work completed.

Cashier Void Game. In this method, a cashier either takes advantage of a supervisor or acts in concert with a dishonest one. The employee theft is perpetrated by the cashier who creates a bogus void transaction and then steals the exact amount of money from the register drawer.

Cashier Refund Game. As in the "void game," the cashier uses either a dishonest or an inefficient manager. In this case, the cashier uses the return policy of giving money to customers as the method of theft. For example, a cashier can fill out a refund voucher and simply replace the voucher for cash.

Simple Cashier Theft ("Till Tapping"). In the more widely practical type of cashier theft, the cashier simply removes a certain amount of cash from the register and pockets it.

The Cashier Shoplifter Helper. In this method, the cashier acts in concert with the shoplifter by either underringing the purchases made or adding several items to the "customer's" bag. There is a variation of this procedure, namely, the cashier prepares a bag of merchandise before the shoplifter arrives and merely hands the entire bag of merchandise to him/her.

The Salesperson Shoplifter Helper (Underringing Merchandise). Such thefts are accomplished in a manner similar to those involving the cashier. There is, however, a variation: To aid the shoplifter, the salesperson intentionally gives the cashier an incorrect price on the merchandise.

The Fitting-Room Thief. Hired to protect the company's merchandise that goes into fitting rooms, the dishonest employee can intentionally allow shoplifters to return less than they bring in. Such employees have been known to go so far as placing the items in the fitting room before the confederate arrives.

The Underwriting Salesperson. A blatant form of theft is a tactic that involves a salesperson who intentionally miswrites the items, quantities, or prices on invoice slips.

The Customer Pickup Thief. Employees who load customer merchandise into cars often find themselves in an easy position to steal. A typical case involves the customer who offers such an employee an extra large "tip" for either substituting merchandise or adding more to the pickup than the customer paid for.

The Mailroom Thief. Numerous theft cases have been uncovered in which employees responsible for sending merchandise to customers have instead sent it to friends, relatives, or even their own address.

The Garbage Thief. Security personnel find that one of the most prevalent retail thieves is the porter or garbage collector. This thief simply adds the items to be stolen to the regular garbage pickup and returns later to complete the theft.

The Cash Office Thief. Although similar to dishonest cashiers, crooked cash office employees can often deflect signs of their activity to cashiers or other employees for long periods. For instance, a cash office employee can extract a few dollars from the individual cash drawers of several cashiers, merely making it appear that minor errors were made by cashiers.

Blatant Security and Management Thieves. Because they possess security clearance, store managers and security personnel may return to the building after work hours to steal, whereupon they can be apprehended.

Techniques of Apprehending Dishonest Employees

The retail investigator uses a variety of techniques to apprehend dishonest employees. These include integrity shopping, surveillance, marking merchandise and money, "seeding" and "salting" cash drawers, observations by store detectives, and, of course, the method we shall discuss, namely, undercover investigations.

Selecting the Right Investigation Agency

After making the determination that the best course of action is the placement of an undercover investigator, the company must next decide whether to use proprietary personnel or an outside contractor. Since very few corporations opt for their own undercover force, Company X resolves to seek an outside private investigation firm.

Prior to actually initiating the undercover probe, if an ongoing relationship does not already exist with an investigation firm, the client must find the one it will employ. The search for the right company begins with the security/loss prevention team; it networks within its professional organizations (professional security organizations are covered later in this chapter) or seeks references from competitors. Usually, obtaining the names of three reputable firms is a good first step. Looking in the *Yellow Pages* or depending on advertising and direct mail campaigns is not advisable, since most true professionals do not advertise in this fashion.

Considerations Given in the Selection of the Agency. Management's first step is to call each firm and have its principal or branch manager personally appear for an interview. While interviewing these representatives of prospective agencies, it is of primary importance to ensure that the right "chemistry" exists between the agency and the client. It is equally important that the following considerations be given in the selection:

1. *Compliance with state statutes:* If your state requires that the firm be licensed, bonded, and insured, the potential client should verify that the firm under consideration is in full compliance.
2. *Insurance:* Obtain a certificate of insurance proving that the firm has at least $1 million coverage with a comprehensive general liability and errors and omissions policy. The policy must be specifically designed for the security and private investigation industry. It is usually considered best to have the client named as an "Additional Insured" on the policy.
3. *Experience:* Make sure the firm's principals have at least five years of experience in conducting undercover investigations in your type industry.
4. *Education:* What are the principal's education and background? What are the education and background of the firm's executives and undercover supervisors?
5. *Criminal history:* Have the firm and its principals ever been indicted, convicted, or sued in a matter related to its security business?
6. *Recruiting methods:* How does the firm recruit its undercover investigators?
7. *Minimum standards:* As a minimum, the following standards should be met for the investigators:
   a. High school graduate or GED.
   b. No history of alcohol or drug abuse, as *verified* by a drug screening program.
   c. Passing a comprehensive background investigation, including polygraph examination (when permitted by the *Employee Polygraph Protection Act*), that covers a personality profile, background history with no record of criminal convictions, personal and professional references, employment history, education and military verification, credit profile and motor vehicle report (where permissible by law).
   d. Make sure the firm allows the client to review the personnel and background investigation files of their undercover investigators.
   e. Make sure the firm allows the client to meet the undercover investigator prior to being placed on assignment.
   f. Make sure the agency fully trains and supervises every undercover investigator prior to being placed on an assignment.
   g. The firm must have a policy of daily contact with its undercover investigators.
   h. Request a copy of the firm's training manuals.
   i. Make sure the firm or its principals are members of enough professional organizations to ensure their standing in the security community. For example, the American Society for Industrial Security (ASIS), with over 26,000 worldwide members, is a must for professional security personnel. ASIS has a certification program based on a lengthy application and examination known as the Certified Protection Professional Program (CPP), which designates the professionals who pass the examination to be a CPP. Membership in the Academy of Security Educators and Trainers (ASET) is often a sign that the agency's employees are probably well trained. The agency should be a member of a state association of investigators for each state within which it operates, as well as the National Council of

Investigation and Security Services. Furthermore, when the agency specializes in an industry, it is normally a good idea for it to be associated with a related industry organization, such as the National Retail Federation. Finally, to ensure that the agency maintains close liaison with the law enforcement community, it is suggested that either the agency or its principals maintain membership in various law enforcement organizations, such as the National Association of Chiefs of Police, the International Narcotic Enforcement Officers Association, American Academy for Professional Law Enforcement, and the like.

Selecting the Right Undercover Investigator

Once the agency has been selected, the client and the agency should first determine the profile of the suspects, if possible. The selection of the proper undercover investigator is conditioned by the profile of the suspects that the undercover investigator will be expected to infiltrate.

A sincere effort must be made to ensure that the undercover investigator or agent is of the same or a compatible background as the suspects. For example, care should be taken that the investigator's ethnic, cultural, religious, age, and sociological likeness approximates the profile of the suspects.

The next decision is whether the position would be better suited for an experienced or a novice investigator. Contrary to popular opinion, newly trained agents are often more effective in the performance of a successful probe. The newly trained investigator usually has not yet developed prejudices, opinions, and habits that tend to hamper a fresh investigative outlook. Conversely, the chief advantage of an experienced agent is the knowledge of his/her proven ability and consistency of performance. The experienced investigator is less likely to become a dishonest employee or a "walk-off." The latter is one of the chief risks in using inexperienced personnel, since they may decide that they really do not like being an undercover investigator.

THE RELATIONSHIP BETWEEN THE CLIENT AND THE AGENCY

Once an agency has been selected, the "chemistry" must begin. That is, it is of paramount importance for a successful investigation that the client and agency establish a relationship of mutual respect, trust, and confidence.

Since an undercover investigation is so strongly rooted in the latter, lack of trust will almost certainly guarantee a failure.

MANAGING THE UNDERCOVER INVESTIGATION

The success of an undercover investigation program does not occur by accident or by itself. It is the client's responsibility to effectively manage and control the agency. Even though the client and the agency have an established relationship and trust, the client cannot abdicate his/her responsibility by allowing the agency to run the entire investigation by itself.

The client has personal knowledge of the operation, as well as of the personalities and politics of the organization. In addition, the client usually has some suspects and leads, and this input expedites the personality blending or infiltration of the agent into a specific group of suspects.

Furthermore, the client has first-hand knowledge of the company and its actual job requirements. That is, if the undercover investigator does not successfully perform the "cover" job, he or she will be terminated or disciplined. Naturally, if that should occur, the undercover investigation is prematurely concluded, without obtaining the successful results expected.

The overall success and legality of an undercover investigation assumes that the agency will not report on union business or information, unless the action is criminal in nature. When union members meet to lay plans to better their working conditions, they are not planning criminal actions. As long as they are not agitators, it is illegal for an agency to report on their activities. However, it is legal and required by most clients to report the existence of outside union organizers who are not company employees.

Importance of Properly Adapting to the Cover Job

When training an undercover investigator for a new assignment, it is most important to make sure that agents are taught to relax. They must get to know their "cover" and "cover story." They have to learn not to try to unearth theft or other serious malpractices in this critical period. Nothing is more unusual than a new employee asking a lot of questions. Instead, new investigators should get to know the people they are working with by listening to conversations and watching them perform on their jobs. During the breaking-in period, the new agent should also prepare a "cast of characters." This is accomplished by listing the names, titles, descriptions, and other information relating to all personnel. The ongoing list will eventually include the names of all the employees with whom the agent comes into contact.

It should be noted that client and agency participation at this stage of operation is essential in the preparation of the agent's cover job. As one might imagine, it would not be effective to have undercover investigators apply for a job using their true identity, address, education, and background. Often, undercover investigators must omit their education and experience from the cover job application in order to blend into the client's work force.

Tremendous care must be taken by case managers to ensure proper preparation of the operative's background and the type of approach he or she makes to the client company. There are two commonly used approaches. The first, known as a *cold approach*, is the best way to get an agent into a company; unfortunately, it is also the most expensive for the client and the most difficult for the agency. In this manner of hiring, the agent approaches the client company armed with only the false background, a good story, and the hope of being hired. Since no one at the client location is aware of the placement, the safety and security of the operation are guaranteed. Naturally, without inside help it is much more time-consuming and difficult for the agent to be hired. The second type of hiring is a *controlled placement.* In this method, someone within the client firm is made aware of the placement to assist in the hiring process. When there is a need for this to occur, a human resources or personnel executive is usually brought into the confidence of the partnership.

UNDERSTANDING MOTIVATION OF THE AGENCY

It would seem too simple to mention that a client should motivate the agency by just paying its fees and providing more placements of additional agents. Understanding the complex needs of motivation requires the client to sometimes treat the agency as one would treat an eager employee. Just as the employee is not motivated by merely receiving a paycheck, an agency needs more positive feedback to ensure its ability to motivate its undercover operatives. We must always remember the relationship between the agency and the client mirrors the performance of the agent. For an investigation to be successful, the client and agency must work together as one unit. The "partnership" that must exist will be discussed shortly.

COORDINATION OF THE INVESTIGATION

As already stated, if the client simply hires the agency and walks away without additional input or responsibility, the investigative outcome will be very one-sided. Furthermore, the results will probably not reach the goals established by the client at the outset. As "partners," the client and the agency usually establish guidelines and protocol for solving some of the daily problems and desires, such as what information the client would like to receive by telephone, in written reports, or in person. Usually, it is a combination of the three. For example, we suggest at least three telephone contacts per week between the client and the agency, coupled with personal meetings and written reports. At the minimum, written reports and personal meetings (debriefings) ought to occur monthly. The personal meetings should often include the undercover agent, client, and agency representative. This brings us to a common error made by clients and investigators alike, namely that these meetings should never occur in a public place, such as a restaurant. If at all possible they should take place in the agency's office.

Telephone Calls

Two different types of telephone calls are part of the reporting process. First, the agency, through its account executive or manager, will communicate with the undercover investigator at least once each day. Second, whenever available information dictates, the account manager is expected to call the client. At a minimum, the account manager should be calling the client three times each week.

Written Reports

The importance of the written report should never be overlooked. While there are probably as many report formats and styles of writing as there are agencies, there are two common formats. The simple approach to report writing is a chronological listing of all events throughout the course of the investigation. This format is the easiest and quickest to prepare. However, it is effective only for clients who use less than five agents at a time; otherwise, the client's responsibility for reading and keeping up with the progress is enormous.

The more efficient format is one designed and implemented between the joint efforts of the client and agency. That is, the "partnership" so often mentioned must be called upon to devise a written report format to complement both the needs of the client and the agency. In most situations, the points of interest most important to the specific needs of the client are highlighted in the report. For example, if a manufacturer is most interested in drug abuse, theft, and safety problems, those items will be concentrated on. All related areas will be covered as well, including employee misconduct, poor supervision, poor work performance, security issues, and operational concerns.

One of the issues often overlooked concerns the security of the written report. We believe that written reports should never be sent to any client office. Instead, they should be mailed to clients at their home addresses or at a secure post office box. Furthermore, clients must be vigilant in their efforts to always refrain from bringing an undercover report to the store, office, factory, or other work site. One of the most important parts of an agent's training concerns security and safety of written reports and notes.

Debriefings

Whenever possible, the client should bring all investigative information to the debriefings, including lists of suspects that may have been gathered from other sources, as well as photographs, if available. Since most companies have picture identification cards, extra photographs of employees (suspects) are usually available. As alluded to elsewhere in this chapter, the interaction between the agency, operative, and client is most important. While the agency should be debriefing the investigator at least once each week, it is generally recommended that the client join in the debriefing process on an average of once each month. Naturally, if specific situations occur that require more client participation, it is almost always suggested.

The Overanxious Client. A client who becomes overanxious and attempts to contact the agent directly for a verbal or written report risks placing the entire operation in jeopardy. Even if other employees do not realize that the operative is checking on them, they shy away from the agent because they realize he has some special relationship or friendship with the boss or security. The undercover investigator should make every effort to avoid the client who seems to be trying to make an approach, and at the first opportunity contact the agency to conduct a proper debriefing.

However, on occasion it is necessary for either the client or the agency to contact an undercover investigator immediately. Most agencies have established an emergency code, which requires the operative to call the agency supervisor or account executive at once.

AGENCY MANAGEMENT OF UNDERCOVER OPERATIVES

Methods of personnel motivation are often the subject of numerous seminars and college courses in human resources. It is important that undercover investigators be treated as though they are special and performing a vitally important function. We must always understand, if undercover investigators steal, reveal their identity, or become vindictive, then the overall undercover program suffers a major setback. The suspects will now be prepared and careful in the presence of new employees.

The properly motivated and praised agent will not look to outsiders to receive compliments and appreciation. In addition to paying the investigators a higher-than-average salary and benefit plan, the agency must be liberal with its dissemination of bonuses. This is often an area subject to abuses. Agents should never receive bonus pay for the apprehension of suspects, but rather for displaying such qualities as honesty, attendance, report writing, judgment, following direction, and overall work performance. Reward for these qualities tends to increase the employee's morale and level of professionalism in the industry as a whole.

COORDINATION AND DIRECTION WITHIN THE AGENCY

Accountability is the key to a successful undercover program. To ensure the value and integrity of the information being reported to the client, numerous safeguards must be practiced by the agency. These controls are part of the daily lives of the agency's principals and executives. Account supervisors and managers have to be thoroughly trained and geared toward their responsibility for accountability.

Agency Procedures

Agency procedures include several logs, records, and forms that ensure that account supervisors have daily telephone contact with each undercover investigator. Since this contact may occur more than once each day, proper procedures should be available to assist supervisors. Similarly, steps to ensure a minimum of weekly personal debriefings are necessary. Since supervisors are required to make detailed notes during every telephone and personal contact with the investigators, agency measures must be available that guarantee the needed accountability. These procedures should also demand that the supervisor fully question the validity and accuracy of all information. This is a most important task of an undercover account supervisor.

Control, supervision, and accountability cannot end with the account supervisor. There must be a way for highly qualified corporate executives to verify the data and to corroborate its validity. This requires that account supervisors report on the progress of each investigation to their superiors on a regular schedule. Very significant for the overall control of an undercover probe is individual agent security. In the next section, the rules that agents must follow are addressed; however, there are also agency rules. Let us talk about these first.

Agency Rules. The design of the agency offices should be conducive to a secure operation and help to counter the threat of compromising security or losing confidential data. For example, closed-circuit television cameras and video recorders should be used to keep a permanent record of all persons entering and leaving the investigation offices. Moreover, computer security within the agency is crucial. The agency design must also permit the safe passage of several agents without the probability of them inadvertently meeting each other. Remember, operation security of the investigation requires that individual agents do not meet each other.

Undercover Investigator's Rules. To safeguard their cover and personal security, as well as the successful investigation, it is very important that agents live by the following rules:

1. They must never reveal their cover to anyone.

2. They must be told never to play detective. Any employees quizzing people, acting suspiciously, or otherwise attracting attention to themselves become the subjects of public scrutiny.

3. Agents must be prohibited from violating any laws.

4. Daily calls and written reports are an absolute requirement.

5. Agents may not contact the client for any reason, unless given specific permission in advance.

6. Agents may not borrow money from the client company or from any employee on the job; nor should they lend money to anyone.

7. Agents should never bring employees from the client company home with them. The general idea must always be to meet at the other person's home. This also gives the agent a chance to see if stolen items may be there.

8. One of the most important rules of the undercover investigation is never to trap anyone into wrongdoing. As security professionals, we never want to be accused of having taken advantage of someone's weakness, that is, of tempting someone into doing something dishonest or wrong. Undercover investigators or managers do not want to teach people how to be dishonest or to force them to disobey regulations. Instead, they aim to discover what is actually going on, not to create what is going on. We must always live by the principle: *Never create a thief!*

9. Agents should never loaf on the job, become a behavior or discipline problem, make it necessary for a foreman or a supervisor to reprimand them for lateness, penalize them for idling or absenteeism, or fire them for insubordination.

10. The agents should be taught never to bring any agency reports to the job. No hiding place is safe—not a glove compartment, car trunk, handbag, or even a public locker off the client's premises. Numerous instances and stories of undercover investigators having their vehicles stolen with the reports inside have surfaced.

11. The agents must not interfere with any suspect, no matter what the violation might be, unless they are required to do so by the stipulations of the cover job, for example, if one is an undercover store detective or security guard.

12. It is important for agents not to participate in improprieties unnecessarily, especially at the beginning of an assignment.

Proof of Agent's Work. Most clients are very concerned with proof that the undercover investigator actually worked during the billing period. Moreover, if the agent has a problem with tardiness and absenteeism, the assignment could be prematurely terminated by a low-level supervisor, without personal knowledge that he or she just fired an undercover investigator. If the agency operates with a due diligence and in a professional manner, it will have preestablished controls to ensure that its investigators work as reported. It was found that the best way to ensure an agent's work at the required shifts and proper daily and weekly hours, as well as verifying their punctuality, is through use of the client's pay stubs. That is, since the agents are actually registered as employees of the client company and receive regular paychecks from it, the agency can simply demand timely receipts of these pay stubs. Careful inspection of them leads to weekly proof that the investigators report for work on time and work their entire scheduled shifts.

Importance of Proper Forms to Ensure Compliance; Computerization. Each of the procedures described previously can be easily enforced in a modern investigative office through the use of computerization. This means, keeping control of undercover or sting agents and assignments through the use of input screens or forms for each procedure. Furthermore, hard copies of the forms should be available for field work. One must be prepared for those late night and weekend calls when not sitting at the desk. Input screens and forms should be designed to effectively monitor the agent's daily calls and weekly debriefings. Additional forms control and monitor the validity of information and the progress of each case. Still other forms or screens enable effective supervision by corporate officers of the account supervisors.

One last input screen or form is a control sheet that can be used by clients to monitor the progress of individual agencies. This is useful when a large client uses multiple agencies and large numbers of investigators spread throughout multiple locations.

THE "PARTNERSHIP"

As alluded to previously, the successful conclusion of internal investigations—namely, the apprehension of dishonest employees—requires a partnership between the agency and the client. Just as the agency should never take actions or make apprehensions without client participation, the client should strenuously avoid actions that adversely affect the agency, without taking its "partner" into consideration.

Once an apprehension has occurred, the undercover investigator is out of the picture. The agent is replaced by a representative of the client or the agency, who will perform a highly professional interview or interrogation of the suspect. This interview is based on information developed as a result of the undercover investigation efforts. It is important for the interviewer to avoid compromising the identity of any undercover investigators while questioning the subject. All too often, the success of undercover or sting operations is jeopardized as a result of an inexperienced or improperly conducted interrogation. For a successful undercover program, all interviews are conducted by personnel experienced in undercover investigations. Since it is quite common for an agent to be the only person taken into the suspect's confidence, the interviewer must use special precautions to avoid revealing the identity of the agent or the fact that he or she betrayed the confidence of the suspect.

Note, that undercover-related interrogations are usually conducted by someone within the contract security agency. Therefore, the agency normally performs enough interrogations to maintain a staff of interviewers with specific know-how in this area. Generally, the only proprietary security departments able to maintain the required expertise and staff are those with large undercover programs, such as major retailers with multiple locations.

VARIOUS TYPES OF UNDERCOVER AND STING OPERATIONS

Theft Investigations

The most common type of internal investigation in American business deals with finding dishonest employees. To do so, the agent must ascertain the type of theft occurring. The simple facts that there is an inventory loss and that there was no mistake in the "paperwork" to account for it provide the basis to start the investigation. However, much more involved is the task of determining the exact nature and location of the thefts. Conversely, if we consider the case of a large office discovering the apparent theft of business equipment or expensive supplies, we can see the need for placing an undercover investigator in the work environment to determine the nature and scope of the losses. Obviously, if there is only one way in or out of the office, the simple installation of a covert camera might be more cost-effective. Usually, though, large offices do not lend themselves to such easy solutions. Besides, sometimes the theft of personal property is involved, such as handbags or even a mechanic's tools (from an automotive dealership). Thus, the placement of an undercover operative is necessary.

Note that these are only limited examples of client theft. Also, almost any business with more than five employees and some product or service to steal is a potential user of undercover services. Even if a company is only involved with raw materials, documented cases prove the need for undercover investigations there too.

Once the need for an undercover investigation has been established and the specific location for the agent decided, the case is ready to begin. The agent's background and cover story must be carefully prepared by the client and agency together.

Drug Abuse Investigations

While drug abuse in the workplace is a common problem and usually a significant part of undercover investigations, in some situations it is actually the primary reason. Specifically, drug abuse not only affects an employee's need for additional money and desire to steal, but it also creates a tremendous liability in areas of accident prevention, safety, and public image.

Operational Issues Requiring Investigations

Employee misconduct, work performance, supervision, poor morale, labor problems, and general operational issues all contribute to the need for undercover investigations. In some situations, these areas of concern are more prevalent than even thefts or drug abuse and thus are reasons for initiating an undercover operation.

Information Security Investigation

In today's high-tech world, information security and the protection of proprietary information has emerged as a concern mandating the need for undercover operations. Thefts of trade secrets, such as new product information, customer lists, financial data, training manuals, company policy manuals, recipes, formulas, clothing patterns, diagrams, structural plans, realty proposals, business expansion plans, and computer software are all potential targets for information thieves.

Sexual Harassment and Discrimination Investigations

Prior to October 1991, the mention of an undercover investigation dealing with sexual harassment and discrimination would have been the subject of ridicule. However, national attention resulting from the Thomas Confirmation Hearings in the United States Senate has elevated the need for this type of investigation. Corporations, never giving this subject a thought other than in the preparation of a company policy, have suddenly placed it high on the agenda. Human resource executives, previously aghast at the thought of such undercover investigations in corporate America, are now pleading for more budgetary funds aimed at undercover investigations to ferret out sexual harassment and discrimination.

THE UNDERCOVER STING OPERATION: HOW IT DIFFERS FROM OTHER UNDERCOVER INVESTIGATIONS

The sting operation is not an ordinary undercover investigation. It differs in that it moves quickly and is preplanned to be fast and effective. Normally, an undercover probe lasts anywhere from 12 weeks to a year. In contrast, the undercover sting operation is usually concluded in less than a week. The sting is a secondary investigation used to react to known intelligence, previously identified during the course of an ongoing undercover probe. It is often designed to protect the identity of an undercover investigator. Sometimes, it seeks to alleviate symptoms and cure problems on an immediate basis, as well as to protect and enforce the cover of the primary operative. The technique may be used to enhance the cover of long-term agents, in place for more than a year. In the event of a criminal prosecution or civil litigation resulting from an undercover operation, a sting will usually add a greater degree of credibility to the agent's testimony, as well as providing another witness in court. The surprise element is the key to the success. Moving quickly is effective in confusing people and diverting their attention from the primary agent. Highly experienced secondary and sting agents are often apprehended with the suspects as a method of protecting the security of the operation.

Sting operations are used by governmental agencies and private investigators on a regular basis to capture glamorous headlines for otherwise mundane investigations. When known suspects have to be convinced about the reliability of a cover story, a sting is often the proper course of action. In other words, when suspects question the truth of a cover story, a sting will help to confirm its validity in their minds. Remember, the bad guys have to believe that the undercover operative is one of them.

Types of Stings

In addition to apprehending perpetrators, sting operations often recoup property and merchandise. Quite frequently these scenarios are used to recover faux merchandise or "knock-offs." The more expensive the merchandise, the more likely it is that someone will try to copy it. For example, if an insurance company paid a large sum because of an art theft, a sting operation may be set up in an attempt to recover the original art. Automobile dealerships have been known to repurchase their own vehicles from thieves, since the asking price is usually less than their insurance deductible. Retailers and manufacturers have rebought truckloads of merchandise through the establishment of store front sting operations. All these situations have common factors: the flashing or promise of large sums of money, payment of only nominal sums, and an apprehension.

CONCLUSION

In most closely held corporations, the decision to conduct an undercover investigation or sting operation rests with the chief executive officer or president. In larger corporations, with a proprietary department, the same decision is usually made either by the corporate director of security and loss prevention or by the coordinator of undercover investigations, based on their ability to provide suitable budgetary justification to undertake the additional undercover probes.

The ability to provide budget justification to senior financial management is very difficult and often highly specialized within the corporate security structure. Uninformed executives and stockholders tend to view the proprietary security department as a pure expense item. Moreover, since undercover and sting operations are generally performed by a contract security agency and administered by the proprietary department, financial officers seek to reduce these budgets rather than increase them.

The budget justification process must include a statistical analysis to prove the actual return on investment (ROI), profitability, and cost-effectiveness of a major commitment to the undercover program. These statistics should include examples of the productivity gained by having one employee performing two functions, that is, one in the cover job and one as an investigator. While making this point, it is advantageous to present the savings of salary, an employee benefit package, and payroll taxes. Furthermore, in any sales-related organization where the undercover operative is actually employed in that capacity, the income derived from the agent's sales efforts should be considered too. It is also necessary to prove the value of the apprehensions made in terms of actual financial recovery, as well as the value from preventing future thefts by the now terminated dishonest employee. The improvement of the general operation and business environment resulting from information reported in the undercover program should also be included in the justification.

Although utilization of undercover operatives is designed to be an apprehension-related program and not of deterrent value, the long-term effect on employees witnessing apprehensions of coworkers leaves a monumental impression on the minds of the remaining employees.

46

Data Base Intelligence Investigations

Ben Jacobson

The changing climate of information gathering, from the index card files of the 1950s to today's speed search of computerized libraries, affords the investigator the opportunity for accurate, up-to-date, convenient research from a vast network of information centers. Certainly, the introduction of the microchip in the early 1970s and the resulting PC inundation of our homes and offices have made it possible for even ordinary citizens to access over 2000 data bases or mainframe infobanks in the United States. Through telephone linkage, personal computer, modem, and printer, the world of information gathering is available to any solicitor. Furthermore, information networks and data base services provide investigators, businesses, public agencies, and individuals with quick facts on any subject. Understanding data intelligence, along with its availability, accessibility, and usage, greatly enhances the investigative effort.

Orwellian philosophers would suggest that information networks have proven that Big Brother is indeed watching us all. The global ability to collect data and report events as they occur clearly defines the factors that benefit any information-gathering projects.

In the case histories provided throughout this examination, data research was utilized to collect accurate, on-the-spot, and detailed information. These case histories offer the specifics of the efforts and the speed with which data was retrieved and disseminated to clients.

COMPETITIVE INTELLIGENCE

The foundation of competitive intelligence is in the ability of library sciences, research technology, network data bases, telecommunications, and computers to interface with the speed of a telephone call. The quick search techniques enable the solicitor to recover data from various global sources.

Information gathering may be found in different forms, such as:

- Due diligence examinations.
- Employment background investigations.
- Intelligence concerning businesses or individuals.
- Financial data collection.
- Business profiling.
- Public identity searches.
- Civil litigation identifications.
- Corporate ownership.
- Corporate affiliations.
- Business credit.
- Executive identity.
- Business history.
- Corporate director affiliations.
- Personal profiling.
- Individual credit histories.
- Criminal conviction records.
- Property ownership.

Without breaching the restrictions of privacy, the gathering of data from public sources can create a clear portrayal of an individual or a business. The picture may either support initial information or offer contradictory facts not provided by the individual. This is illustrated in the following case:

Case 1.   Corporate owners of a Washington-D.C.-based restaurant chain were selling their business to investors, who represented that they had substantial assets and were associated with enterprises in Australia. At the request of the corporate owners, a data base investigation was conducted into the professional backgrounds of the investors. In addition, their business activities in Australia were investigated.

Results.   Within two hours from the time of the assignment from a New York City research center, a wealth of information surfaced from public records and an on-line newspaper morgue based in Sydney and Queensland, Australia. The newspaper publications were on line and linked to the New York research center via telephone communications. Articles previously written about these investors and their practices revealed that they were the subjects of a criminal fraud investigation by law enforcement authorities. In fact, the data base information pointed to a whole pattern of deception against business owners in Australia. Now they were using the same method in their efforts to gain control of a U.S. restaurant chain valued at $30 million. At the time of the research, the subjects were wanted for questioning. The authorities were looking for them in Spain, while they were actually in the United States. Naturally, the client immediately notified United States law enforcement agencies.

Not only was the information accurate and up-to-date, although it had traveled half-way around the globe, but data base networks revealed facts that in the past would have required weeks of research and communications.

Records in the Public Domain

In the public domain, an amazing amount of records is maintained on individuals and firms. These types of files are certainly adequate for a quick decision in today's business environment. The data can also be used to impeach a person's credibility, testimony, or even whether he or she is the person one wishes to marry. These records include:

- Personal credit history.
- Driving history.
- Property ownership.
- Professional licensing.
- Bankruptcy searches.
- Professional reputation.
- Criminal convictions.
- Address verification.
- Bank affiliations.
- Liens/judgments.
- Civil litigation.
- Motor vehicle ownership.
- Business affiliations.
- Education verification.
- Employment history.
- Secondary residence.
- Telephone verification.
- References/neighbors.

In the development of an individual profile, the data collected is a true representation of official public records maintained in county clerk administrative offices, public agencies and private institutions. These agencies act as clearinghouses for public domain and private files. The information may represent years of assembled data. Therefore, the inflated resumé or the indulgent letter from the qualified expert becomes obsolete. Besides, resumés and letters of professional accomplishments usually omit negative information. The examiner of public domain records can resolve open questions.

Case 2.   An expert witness resumé to the Supreme Court of New York State claimed that the subject expert had graduated from Harvard Business and Law Schools.

Facts.   The subject was an expert in his respected field and recognized by the industry as the consultative authority. Due diligence inquiry verified that the subject did not graduate from Harvard Law School. Official records of Harvard showed he did attend the first year of law school, but he never earned a degree there.

Results. The subject's credibility as an expert witness and status as an authority in the field were immediately questioned. Thus the plaintiff side, for which he was testifying, withdrew him as an expert from its strategy.

EXAMINING THE INFORMATION AVAILABLE

Data available to any on-line investigator provides a smorgasbord of facts from accessed libraries. To broaden the search and to clarify the situation for the reader, we shall examine the specifics of particular probes, resource origins, authority (where required), and relativity of information collected. International and domestic data will be put in proper perspectives.

Searches and Data Available

Credit Profiles. Research furnishes the applicant's credit profile. This report looks into a subject's payment history, public records that may include liens, judgments or bankruptcies, personal debt load, banking relations or affiliations, employment, and credit performance. In addition, this file verifies social security numbers and addresses to credit reporting companies. (That is, if a consumer credit application is submitted, the information from the application is transferred to the credit file of the reporting credit agency.)

Reporting Agencies. Accessing credit history files is provided through hundreds of credit-reporting corporations. However, each of these corporations reaches into three reporting companies for its information, namely, Trans Union, TRW, and Equifax (CBI). Reporting companies maintain credit dossiers on any person who ever received a bank loan, mortgage, credit card, or auto loan, or on anyone whoever applied for any other type of credit. Note that even applicants who were rejected for credit have had a credit file opened by these companies, which would have been negative. These files can be accessed via on-line computing. In most instances, the on-line assistance available to investigators is through third-party service agreements.

Legal Authority. Accessing personal credit information of a target is protected by the *Fair Credit Reporting Act* found under Title 15, U.S. Code Section 1681. All 50 states maintain compatible legislation. Under the statute, a person who willfully obtains information on a subject from a consumer reporting agency under false pretenses shall be fined not more than $5000 or imprisoned not more than one year or both. The subscriber shall be required to identify the purpose of any credit report issued.

The permissible purposes for obtaining consumer credit reports without specific written authorization of the individual on whom it is issued are:

1. In response to an order of the court of competent jurisdiction.

2. To extend credit or to review or collect a credit account.

3. For the underwriting of an insurance policy, but not for the investigation of claims involving the claim.

4. To assist in determining an individual's eligibility for a government-issued license or other government benefit.

5. Any other legitimate business need for information in connection with business transactions involving the consumer.

Driving History. Accessed through the state's motor vehicles departments, this information may provide important insights into the character of an individual, since it furnishes information on accidents, summonses issued and their disposition, suspensions, and convictions of motor vehicle violations (including driving while intoxicated or impaired). Such data may offer the solicitor a clear picture concerning the subject's level of responsibility and behavioral patterns. For the company considering the hiring of the individual as a school bus driver, truck driver, chauffeur, or vehicle operator, the motor vehicle history could reduce exposure to liability claims and even prevent its use by an opponent's defense in a court case (if the appointment of the person and litigation suggest reckless behavior).

Additional information supplies the subject's driver identification number. The information in most states has encoded into his ID number the date of birth, year of birth, or county reference number where the license was issued. The license also provides a residential address, date of birth, expiration date, and in most states the date when it was first issued. Furthermore, the data furnishes a brief description of the licensee: color of eyes, height, weight, and color of hair.

Investigators can use the information to locate individuals, verify addresses, identify vehicles driven, owned, or registered by the subject.

Case 3. Investigators were attempting to determine the locations of an individual's extortion activity of small businesses. Through the use of motor vehicle records, the target's car was identified. Moving violations and parking summonses were researched. The results revealed the vehicle received numerous summonses at locations near many small businesses. The investigators obtained the listing of the places and interviewed their owners, who confirmed that the individual was active in their area. This inquiry was conducted by private investigators on behalf of corporate clients.

Property Ownership. Property records are available though the files of county clerk's offices in various counties and municipalities throughout the United States. Ownership records include:

1. *Official deed:* The name of the actual owner and lien holder of the property.

2. *Record of mortgage:* The name and date of mortgage holders, addresses of holders and the borrowers, and persons responsible for payment of the mortgage (generally, the owners of the property). If a corporation is the mortgagee, the signature and name of an officer of the same or the name of a legal representative for the filings, liens, official notifications are included.

3. *Survey of property:* A complete official property description comprised of street location, town, city, county, state. Usually, it is found in ledgers (books) under a certain page number, such as Book 435, page 19.

As with other searches, this information is becoming available on line, but currently it is probed by contractors and input into data base service companies.

Professional Associations.   To profile individuals who have achieved in a particular field and are quoted and recognized in books, articles, interviews, and other published sources, the investigator accesses data base intelligence networks. After all, these offer reviews of articles about and by professionals, along with interviews concerning particular professions, such as legal, accounting, medical, engineering, banking, small business ownership, financial planning, and so on. They also keep track of professional associations newsletters, magazines, *The Wall Street Journal*, corporate directors' data bases, and news articles from the individual's hometown. Also available are listings of association members. While these lists may be protected from the basic flood of junk mailers, they are obtainable at annual conventions and may be even offered for sale by many associations.

Therefore, identifying the professional affiliations of an individual may be as easy as knowing which data base to tap, the key words to conduct the search, and the ability to scan for pertinent information. If John Doe is a member of the New York Bar Association, he is probably also a member of the American Bar Association; if he participates in corporate ventures, he may be the director of a corporation. Thus, a probe listing corporate directors may uncover his affiliations. Furthermore, if he is a partner in a law firm, the public filing of the partnership is on hand. A business credit profile may reveal him to be named "Partner in Charge" of the firm. The listings will show the year he graduated from law school, undergraduate courses at what university, degrees earned, year and date admitted to the bar, firms where employed, dates of employment, type of specialty practiced, and names of associates. Included would be the listing of the individual's memberships in professional associations.

This method can be used for searches in any profession, business, and licensed skilled trade. Hence, a fairly credible document may be developed based on data provided by the source—the professionals themselves.

Professional Licensing.   As with other public information, licensing by county, state, federal agencies, and by local municipalities is covered under the umbrella of the *Freedom of Information Act*. A request for verification of licensing information may include the date of license issuance, the applicant's professional qualifications, the address of his or her business, sponsors (if any), the purpose of license, any complaints, suspensions, hearings, or interruptions of license. Of course, personal data may not be part of the *Freedom of Information Act* request.

Bankruptcy Search.   The filing of bankruptcy is a public document kept in the local county clerk's office under the individual or corporate name. It can be probed through data base networks. These searches encompass business credit, personal credit, liens/judgments, and asset verification. Upon proof of a bankruptcy filing, a physical search of the bankruptcy court will furnish all the necessary additional information pertaining to a workout agreement or dissolution of the corporate assets through a court-ordered auction or sale. The petition or filing generally covers facts about the corporation and the principals, such as personal assets, property, location of residence, telephone contact, legal counsel, reason for the bankruptcy filing, and claims from creditors.

Address Verification. Often an individual may maintain several documents and records with various addresses. For the purpose of verifying the target's address, searches in data bases that maintain personal histories (such as motor vehicle records, consumer credit report, telephone verification directories and resident listings) will assist in providing identification and confirmation.

Through data base services, specially tailored programs allow for the immediate return of data pertaining to address and name checks. These data bases may be directly on line with state motor vehicle departments or credit reporting agencies and services, which supply telephone listing verification by name and address.

Note that some states are following California's example in limiting immediate information from motor vehicle records and other state agencies. California responded to the death of actress Rebecca Schaffer. Investigation revealed that she had been murdered after her killer had obtained the young star's address from the state motor vehicle records. California now permits only law enforcement officials access to such data. All other requests must be accompanied with an explanation for this information. Applications are considered, reviewed, and either complied with or rejected. Court-ordered access is available.

Social Security Verification. Social security information is considered confidential and protected by the Social Security Administration. Data base information services are marketing information, which produces the social security numbers of individuals. This data is obviously obtained through on-line searches of consumer credit reporting information, then matched with the subject's address and state of residence, and immediately turned around in the form of accessed social security number verification. The fraudulent use of a social security number (SS#) is a violation of federal statutes. Often the searches and verifications of a person's social security number has uncovered an individual using more than one number. However, before calling in the FBI, the investigator should remember that the accuracy of information in credit reporting agencies is often not very precise. Credit reporting agencies and data base networks can make mistakes in transposing numbers, in input, and in filing information. Confirmation that a person is utilizing more than one SS# can be found in applications for credit sent to various banks, mortgage companies, and credit agencies. If several applications have been filed and the signatures are one and the same as the target's, then there may be cause to issue an alert.

Private investigation agencies have reported that, at times, an employee has been found to access the SS#s of other individuals or the general public, and then use this information to develop personal credit profiles. These perpetrators have been prosecuted under a variety of state and/or federal statutes.

Bank Affiliations. Identifying the banking relations of a corporation or individual is done by accessing data base intelligence through the business credit profile or consumer credit report. In each search, bank affiliations are presented as a means of credit reporting and verification of business affiliations. In some instances, the banking data may include the account numbers of loan transactions, certificates of deposit, and savings accounts. All verbal verifications of accounts and other information may be conducted by telephone at the branch, at the bank's relations index, or at the consumer information center. This establishes a lead to banking records. However, if there is a need for certified, hard-copy (written) bank records, a subpoena is necessary.

Liens/Judgments. This intelligence is accessed directly on line through data base information networks, which provide tailored services. It includes the county, state, and file number of the lien or judgment. *Liens* may be found in the form of *Uniform Commercial Code (UCC)* filings for a business, or against autos, homes, and personal belongings by banks and mortgage holders. In addition, a "mechanics" lien is usually the filing of an individual claim against property for services rendered that have not been paid for.

Judgments are orders of the court against an individual or a corporation. The filing is based on an award of the court in an action against the subject and will furnish the date of the filing, amount of the judgment, and whether the filing is open or satisfied. This information can also be found in the county clerk's offices.

Criminal Convictions. Criminal court conviction records, including arrests, may be obtained by accessing information via the *Freedom of Information Act*. The data is available through research of the county court record system or in some states through the state or superior court clerk's offices.

By using certain on-line information services, the subscriber may request the data. Then it is researched by the contractor in a particular county, input into the mainframe, and accessed at the investigator's behest. General research time is 24 to 48 hours; however, in some jurisdictions probes may take 4 to 6 weeks. The turnaround time is based on the input of the service and their ability to have an individual available to research such information and input the data into the service company's computer system.

This individualized hand search allows room for misinformation and lack of data due to human input error, misrepresentations, or misinterpretations. As state agencies and county clerk offices computerize, more direct on-line services will become available.

Public access to police arrest and allegation information, such as criminal arrest records ("rap sheets"), of the accused (in contrast to the convict) are not within the parameters of the National Criminal Information Center (NCIC) in Washington, D.C., or other law enforcement indexes. While these searches are on tap for the law enforcement community as the official course of agency business and are accessed via official request, the private investigator or corporate security director cannot obtain such data. Despite occasional claims to the contrary, it is a violation of the law for the private investigator to acquire it; and if a private investigator (usually a former law enforcement officer), through the use of confidential contacts, gains such classified intelligence, he or she cannot disclose it for public or client use.

With regard to pending court cases, the index files of active cases may be probed at the court of records. In New York City, for a registered fee, the clerk of any county criminal court office will search the records of the court system to determine if a case is active, closed, or dismissed. The filing of the forms produces results within 24 hours.

Legal Authority. Criminal conviction records' releases are guaranteed under the *Freedom of Information Act*. In most instances, a court clerk will provide the information. Matters of sealed files, pending appeals, pending continued investigations, active grand jury investigations, or even the court-ordered expelling of court records may be the cause for not recovering the data requested. Limited facts of currently pending cases before the court are obtainable, and these comprise the initial complaint, identification of the plaintiff, identification of the defendant, as well as address and age, docket number (file #), charges pending, bail, and dates of arraignment or hearing.

Civil Litigation. *Litigation* is the process of law in which a civil action or accusation against an individual or corporation is filed and pursued in a court of law. Data base information is available through various sources, which may include legal publications and filing of the court docket. In the Lexis/Nexis Database even a synopsis of the case may be reviewed. On-line information can procure instant data on a variety of subjects from trademark infringement to medical malpractice, from auto accidents to professional liability actions.

Data base information normally reveals the court of records, the identification of the contestants, counsel of the plaintiff or the defendant, the docket number (court filing number), and the facts of the case. Review of civil litigation records may assist in the development of data in defense or complaint; it can be used to verify credibility of the individuals or counsel, and might be utilized as a source of information for other legal action.

Furthermore, civil litigation documentation may be found in business credit filings or consumer credit reports. To obtain the facts on current litigation still pending in a jurisdiction, often a physical search is necessary because this information is not directly on line. Data base services utilize researchers to obtain and input such facts into their networks. This is generally done upon specific request for the particular data.

Business Affiliations. Through the business credit report, Dun & Bradstreet business filings, professional affiliations indexes, corporate directors data base, and an individual's consumer credit report, business affiliations and associations can be developed. The information may be useful in profiling an individual or in making available the names of associates who can be contacted for further data. In addition, the search may provide facts that could impeach the individual, support the competitor's business development, and provide investors or financial institutions with a clear picture of the individual and his or her rival.

On-Line Research

Data base research can be obtained through contracting agencies that sell information as a service. The organizations provide data available on line from many sources around the world. Naturally, all the information is in the public domain. That means, it is on hand without restrictions and falls within the parameters of the *Freedom of Information Act*. Obviously, medical records, tax filings, military data, or social security information do not belong in this class. To acquire this material, authorized releases and written correspondence with a particular agency are necessary.

Some on-line information belongs to an area whose classification is gray. Since it is not covered by the *Privacy Act*, it is available for search. In fact, it is being offered by some data services through the use of contractors under the guise of public domain records. Employment history, credit data, and a criminal convict's arrest history are just three such categories.

It suffices to say that altogether a wealth of useful information is at your fingertips from airline schedules to generic names of your prescription drugs, from stock prices to genealogical research, from SEC filings to aerospace technology, from bank mergers to trade affiliations, and the ever growing data on John Doe.

Data Bases. Depending on the type of information required, the investigator may want to tap one of the following data bases:

Mead Data Central (NEXIS). Consisting of networks of business news information services, this presents the full text of contributions of more than 160 information sources. These include leading international newspapers, magazines, professional publications, trade journals, newsletters, and wire services, specifically, *The New York Times, Washington Post, Los Angeles Times, Financial Times of London, Business Week, Fortune, Forbes, The Associated Press, Reuters, Business Wire,* and *PR Newswire,* to name a few.

Mead Data Central (LEXIS). This is a comprehensive legal data base reporting on federal, state, and other court actions, which may include bankruptcy and military court cases and Securities Exchange Commission hearings. Furthermore, LEXIS offers legal references for the United Kingdom, New Zealand, Australia, and France. (In all instances, only decided cases are covered.) Within LEXIS one may access:

LEXPAT for patent information.

EXCHANGE for financial services.

NAARS for accounting data (from the American Institute of Certified Public Accountants).

Dialog. This network contains several hundred data bases, with every conceivable topic ranging from aerospace to zoology.

Case 4. A client requested information pertaining to accidents involving a particular vehicle.

Requirements. Search input required concentrated queued questions, such as:

Accidents involving Mazda RX7.

Recalls involving Mazda RX7.

National Safety Research, with respect to Mazda RX7.

The data bases providing such facts were accessed, and they include consumer reports, National Automobile Safety Testing Reports, newspaper files, *The Wall Street Journal,* and *The New York Times.* These publications deal with articles related to auto accidents and auto recalls.

Results. The collected information furnished the client with the necessary data to achieve his objective because it was available on line through public domain documents.

Dow Jones News/Retrieval Service. This supplies the full text of *The Wall Street Journal,* including the current day news, stock quotes, and other business and financial data bases.

Quicksearch. This service provides full company profiles on quoted firms and publicly traded corporations. In a matter of seconds, the subscriber reaches into articles from *Baron's, Forbes, Fortune, Money,* and the *Washington Post,* to name a few, and learns the corporate histories of 750,000 companies through Dun & Bradstreet. Competitor data is sorted by company, industry, product, analysts' earning forecasts, SEC filings, and current business news.

VU/TEXT Information Services. Information on people, companies, industries, and events reported in over 35 newspapers is found here. This data base covers the full text of the *Boston Globe, Chicago Tribune, Washington post, Los Angeles Times, The Philadelphia Inquirer,* and many others. It also reaches into 140 regional business journals, such as *Crains New York* and *Atlanta Business Chronicle.*

Datatek/Datatimes. On-line to over 70 data bases, this data base's information includes full text retrieval of data from newspapers throughout the United States, Canada, and Australia, such as *The Chicago Sun-Times, The Seattle Times, The Dallas Morning News,* and *The Minneapolis Star Tribune,* and newswire services from the United States, Canada, and Japan, plus business information from 15,000 publicly traded companies.

Dun & Bradstreet Credit Services. This is the largest supplier of business information.

Dun's Financial Profiles is a detailed spreadsheet presentation of a firm's financial statements and 14 key business ratios. This contains a line-by-line comparison to the industry for a period of three years. Actual financial statements are available on more than 850,000 private and public United States companies.

Duns Watch keeps track of all the significant changes within the past 12 months of the inquired company using a DUNSPRINT terminal or a personal computer.

Family Tree is a unique service that identifies the ultimate parent company and its subsidiaries, divisions, and branches. This allows for developing corporate locations, officers, and affiliations.

International Duns Print, an on-line information data base of Dun & Bradstreet, covers over one million businesses located throughout Europe, Australia, and Canada.

Duns Financial Records is a unique data base of Dun & Bradstreet Credit Services and Dun's Marketing Services. The information contains accurate and extensive financial data on more than 700,000 businesses.

Pergamon Infoline. This worldwide leader in on-line distribution of scientific, technical, patent, and business information has two important data bases available: *Who Owns Whom* and *The Reference Book of Corporate Management.*

Newsnet. This data base distributes specialized business newsletter information with over 300 on-line services. Most publications are exclusive to Newsnet, and they include *USA Today, TRW Business Profiles,* and numerous international journals.

Info Globe. The electronic publisher of Canada's national newspaper, *The Globe Mail,* this information network contains the *Globe* and *Mail* on-line, the Canadian Financial Database, *Who's Who in Canadian Business,* and *The Northern Miner On-Line,* Canada's mineral resources newspaper. *Info Globe* publishes the *Canadian Periodical Index* (CPI) from the Canadian Library Association. Newspapers on-line include the *Ottawa Citizen, The Gazette, The Sotham News, The Toronto Star,* and the *Windsor Star.*

Info Mart. This Canadian data base has French language newspapers on-line.

Canadian Systems Group. Being a corporate directory of Canadian companies, this data base has files on corporate names, addresses, ownership, federal corporations and directors, and an intercorporate ownership directory. Files of bankruptcy are also available.

Textline. A good source of data on British companies and directors, this has an abstract format and covers all British newspapers (both national and local), plus every major Western European national newspaper. It also maintains useful Middle Eastern files and Japanese data bases.

Data Star. As an on-line international service, it provides access to the world's leading information sources of business, pharmaceutical companies and products, science, and medicine. *Data Star* carries information on Dutch, German, and Austrian corporations.

Questel. This data base specializes in chemical, patent, and trademark information, including *EPAT,* the data base of European patent registry, *FPAT* dealing with French patent registry, and TMINT Trademarks International. *Questel* maintains on-line data on French corporations and legal information services.

Linkage.   Data base intelligence gathering is successful only if the researcher can develop linkage between the targeted subject and the various data bases researched and has the ability to incorporate the information into a meaningful document. This linkage ("data-link") enables the researcher to qualify the data, verify that the subject matter is one and the same, and access numerous data bases to formulate the hypothesis. In other words, if data base A contains information of professional identifiers, data base B uncovers facts for personal profiling, and data base C contains data regarding litigation of the subject matter, then the use of these three data bases leads to a meaningful report of the subject.

Linking the three is a separate issue of formatting the search elements configured from a specific computer designed report and its communication with the printer. This format can be designed in the outset or after downloading the research information onto a floppy disk. The design can be formatted upon leaving the on-line mode. (This is most cost-effective.)

One of the objectives of data-linking information is the ability to reduce the on-line research to a clearly written document. This is important because often investigators are confronted with fragmented data, which does not allow them to link the subject matter together. That happens when the identifiers are maintained separately, and the linkage from each data base does not use the common denominators. The result is that each piece of data may appear to be that of a separate subject. The reader would then formulate opinions based on singular facts rather than on multipliers, which should clearly define the subject's activities. This is analogous to an artist painting in one dimension on a monocolor, flat screen. The perspective of the viewer would be skewed.

Linkage is also important in the development of leads for the researcher. As the information unfolds onto the computer screen, data may offer new avenues of research. For example, if the on-line information identifies a particular corporation in the *Dun's Report*, the category of SIC NUMBER may also appear. This number represents a companions corporation that maintains a business relationship with the firm being searched. Hence, the data-link to the SIC NUMBER may furnish new facts about the corporation or its principals. In the case of individual linkage, a search of the KALEX data base may provide addresses of the subject target. Linking data base searches, the cross-index address directory can now confirm the current address, possibly the telephone number of the target, how long the individual has lived at the location, and the names and telephone numbers of neighbors.

New Dimensions in Data Base Research

The changing climate of personal computing has added a new dimension to researching information. Currently offered in the marketplace is an individual library of CD disks that contain massive bytes of information stored similar to that of a music compact disk. It is classified as CD-ROM information systems. The ability to arm the personal computer with volumes of data without having to utilize a telecommunications modem link will advance the researcher to a more independent information junky. This will push the data base information business into an accessible library of data without the expensive fees of initial sign-up costs and monthly billings of data base services, not to mention the saving of telephone costs.

CD-ROM research is as simple as inputting the CD disk into a drive, which is linked to the desktop computer. Through proper inputting of a phrase, word, or search request, the disk is scanned for the category, which appears within seconds on the screen of the computer for reading, saving, or printing. Just typing in the selected words instantly puts the viewer into the pages of the encyclopedia, law books, newspaper articles, professional listings, or any subject contained on the disk. The hundreds of disks that contain any information needed by investigators replace the floppy disk of computing and on-line services while maintaining accessibility to a personal library of newsletters, corporate profiles, newspapers, magazines, and lists, lists, lists. One of the most significant advances in personal computing since the creation of the hard disk drive, CD-ROM will introduce the researcher to a library of data that will alter the approach and methods used to recover information. This change is a time saver and allows the investigator to melt the data from the CD into a formatter report already stored on the hard drive of the computer. Instead of the researcher having to leave one data base, sign off, then sign on to another, CD-ROM provides the ability to change disks at your desk and continue the research.

CD-ROM disks contain 680 megabtyes of stored facts. This data can be accessed in 380 milliseconds—lightning quick! Through the use of interface cards compatible with your PC, the probe capabilities allow for research independence. Some of the available CD's are:

Microsoft 91 Bookshelf contains a dictionary, thesaurus, encyclopedia, almanac, and quotations.

Business Databank offers the latest on world population trends, precise income data per capita, and GNP information, plus the highest and lowest information rates throughout the world and population densities.

National Directory of Addresses and Telephone Numbers is a list of addresses and telephone numbers by states and cities.

Business contains the *Nation's Business, D & B Reports,* the *Financial Post, Success, Adweek's Marketing,* and other business publications.

Computers contains such sources as *PC Magazine, Computing, PC User, Home Office Computing,* and so on.

Magazines is a comprehensive periodical library covering business, arts, technology, health, politics, sports, and the like, plus over 100,000 abstracts for more than 340 magazines, newsletters, and trade journals. *U.S. News and World Report, The New Republic, Stereo Review,* and *Good Housekeeping* are just a few examples of those available.

Newsweek Interactive is the first general interest magazine on CD-ROM. Beginning January 1993, it will be offering annual subscriptions for quarterly CDs and is considering monthly publications.

Time-Warner, Inc. publishes its annual, *Time Magazine Compact Almanac* on CD-ROM and has published one-shot Time versions on the Berlin Wall and Desert Storm.

Other disks, such as Languages, Maps of the World, World History, Newspaper Publications, Business Profiles, represent some of the data on tap for CD-ROM users.

Interpretations: Understanding Business Credit Filings and Personal Credit Reports

The investigator who recovers data from business financial records or the personal credit report will find a maze of language and code interpretations totally foreign to everyday life. The following explanation should prepare investigators to interpret and understand the information provided when examining the UCC-1 filing system and consumer credit reports.

Uniform Commercial Code (UCC)—1 Filings. The UCC filing system is based on procedures that are supposed to ensure the protection of assets. That means, when lenders approve the secured loan application of a business, they are required to file a report that serves to notify other secured lenders of the transaction. In other words, it lets them know that the assets of a certain company have already been used as collateral and that therefore any further loan applications need to be considered with appropriate caution. Unfortunately, due to overload and errors, this warning does not always reach the intended parties.

Although on-line data base probes should reveal all UCC filings when a business credit is obtained, complications of overload at the Secretary of State's office may prevent the record from appearing immediately. Thus, an investigator may report a finding that a UCC search is clear, when in fact it is not, and the lender, litigation attorney, bankruptcy trustee all get an incorrect picture. What can researchers do? They should report that pending filings are possible, thereby clarifying the probe as complete to date with the clause, and that the overload of filings requires an additional check sometime soon in the future. Many lenders approve the loans and hope for their clearance from liens or presently unfound UCC filings.

This crisis in UCC reporting is a national dilemma. It has left the banking community, commercial lender, and business on their own (at least, to a great extent) and open to litigation. And the investigator may fear exposure if the final report is not clarified with the caveat that the UCC system is suffering from overload.

Nationally, UCC filings have increased dramatically, since secured lenders have become more aware of the need to act responsibly and to protect their interests by properly documented filings. This has caused a veritable tidal wave of filings in state offices, where they are processed manually, rather than through automation. Cabinets are filling each day with financing statements, continuation, and termination notices; and state employees complain about backlogs and understaffed departments.

Estimates that the secured lender will have a slight chance of getting correct information from the public recording officer adds to the paradox that the obligation of filing reports ensures protection of assets.

In many states, certificates of UCC searches are only available to private search companies, thus violating the *Freedom of Information Act* requirements. Most states are moving to allow probes to be conducted independent of filing officials, but offer little support to novice searchers, leaving them on their own.

Other than the overload, secured lenders may also occasionally contribute to errors on applications. These may be typographical. Examples:

Misspelling: Jones instead of Jonas.

Punctuation errors: ABC instead of A.B.C., Inc.

Incomplete names: Steve's Auto instead of Stephen's Automotive Repair Shop.

Abbreviations: Int'l instead of International.

Wrong names: CAD Aero, Inc. instead of DAC Aero Inc.

Missing designations: Inc., Corp., Co., Ltd.

These errors increase the probability that the documents will be misfiled and that a search will not uncover them because of an exact identification filing process. The same could happen if the probe is computerized. Programming mistakes can also add to the inability to find the material.

Consumer Credit. Our credit reporting system compiles consumer credit information and distributes it to clients and subscribers. This function is guaranteed by the *Fair Credit Protection Act*. There are three credit reporting bureaus and hundreds of small local centers and affiliations. The big three are:

1. TRW Credit Information Services.
2. Trans Union Credit Information.
3. CBI/Equifax.

Information Origination. The usual methods utilized by credit bureaus to obtain consumer records is through subscribers. Lending institutions provide the credit and payment history of a potential applicant. In return, the subscribers report their borrowers' payment histories, loan amounts, schedule, address, social security number, date of birth, and employment to the credit bureaus. The credit bureau is responsible to record or place in the individual's credit file whatever information the subscriber has reported.

Public Record Filings. Credit bureaus obtain data from public information filings. This may include judgments, tax liens, wage garnishments, notices of defaults, or litigation findings. As previously mentioned, the credit reporting is not always very precise. Errors and computerized mismatches occur. Misinformation, based on data reported by banks and lending agencies, creeps in, making a file inaccurate, incomplete, obsolete, or misleading. Besides, credit bureau input is often done manually, allowing for human blunders in misidentifying an individual, reporting the wrong docket number in a judgment filing, the wrong amount, or omitting the date and location even if it was satisfied.

This data can greatly affect the consumer's ability to obtain or extend credit. Moreover, in many instances, such information is used in background investigations for employment purposes. Inaccurate credit reporting has caused many from getting the job they had applied for. Yet they may not even be aware of the reason or know what to do about the problem.

Two statutes, the *Fair Credit Reporting Act* and *State Consumer Credit Reporting Act*, place the responsibility on consumers to correct the error, not on the credit bureaus, but the consumers may be totally ignorant of the mistake. Therefore, researchers who obtain a consumer credit report and use the findings may indeed by delivering misinformation. However, the right to dispute such errors and have the data removed may not be theirs. The following example shows how a mistake can greatly change the scope of the inquiry.

An investigator obtains a consumer credit report for the purpose of subject identification in a business transaction. The information stated on the credit report is the subject's address, social security number, and year of birth. But the subject has changed his address and, in addition, one digit of his social security number is different. Now the credit report reads like "Who is Who" in default judgments. Is this the same individual? Has the subject changed his identity? Has the credit agency reported inaccurate data? For the investigator, this is dangerous territory. Much may be at stake for the subject: his job, a loan, or a business transaction. The best preventative measure is *not to take* the credit report at face value, but rather to research the information further to confirm the data, that is, probe the county clerk's office filings, motor vehicle information, postal verification of address, and other sources, and utilize the credit report as an information advisory only. Furthermore, the investigator must remember that consumer reports are protected by the *Fair Credit Reporting Act*. Hence, privacy is guaranteed, unless the access is required for specific legitimate reasons, as mentioned earlier in this chapter.

47

Technological Advances and Investigations

Ben Jacobson

Lorin Jacobson

The rapid technological progress of the past two decades has produced great advances within the world of criminal and civil investigations. These changes can be ascribed to the development of microchip processing, computer-driven search methods, video transmission improvements, inventions of cellular and laser devices, and forensic research technology, to name a few. With new innovations and the imagination of the investigator, scientists and engineers have helped to define the applications and potential use of the latest equipment. The purpose of this article is to make the reader aware of the means and aids available in any probe, whether it be public or private. Specifically, today's investigators need to familiarize themselves with such modern resources as infrared particle sprays for crime scene searches, computer-generated information data, night vision cameras and scopes, motion detectors, microwave and other transmitters, cellular telephone systems, communications networking, parabolic listening devices, biometric security systems, retinal scanning, voice and signature biometrics, and nonbiometric systems, and much more.

USAGE FOR TODAY'S SECURITY AND LAW ENFORCEMENT AGENCIES
Biometric Systems

Finger/Palm Print Examination. Years of technology and the use of fingerprinting by law enforcement agencies have prepared the development of biomet-

47-1

ric systems—quick identification resources. Through the employment of digital finger and palm prints, scanning instantly recognizes a person. Upon identification, the individual is then cleared for admission to a secured area, such as a critical research or engineering facility. This system is currently being explored for immediate processing of prisoners in a correctional or law enforcement environment.

Finger Ridge Readers. These devices are used in securing facilities and computer terminals. The individual seeking access places any finger into a scanning slot. Within seconds, microprocessors read (that is, scan) and translate the fingerprint into digital codes, while the unit tries to find a match against a listing of codes within the computer's memory. The computerized memory then signals back to the processor and permits access to authorized and identified individuals to enter sensitive areas, blocking others.

In a similar system the unit requires the placing of fingers into four slots so that the configuration of the hand, including the curves, length, and webbing can be measured electronically.

Other systems scan fingerprints through glass plates and use pattern recognition to read the print. This technique is used by many high-tech corporations and government facilities as a method of screening access and entrance to an area. Adding a printer to the search capabilities, a permanent record is maintained for research at a future date.

Palm Imprints. This method offers identification through reading selected sections of the palm. The focus on the palm print is a 2-inch square, concentrated in the center of the palm. A xenon flash illuminates the area, which in turn sends an image to a camera that is read by an 8086 microprocessor. The unit also allows for keyboard input through digital numeric coding, which will match an identification number and display, thus allowing access.

Voice and Signature Biometrics. Voice and signature systems, considered less reliable than finger or palm reader systems, offer identification based on an individual's voice or signature.

Voice Pattern Identification Systems. In this arrangement an individual's speech pattern is measured. The identification process is based on algorithms searched through a complex method of predictive coding. Comparative speech patterns are referred to select words placed in the processor by the intended user.

Signature Identification. How is it accomplished? It is achieved through a comparison of the forces generated by the pressure and spacing of the writer. The signature processor is not being used in personality analysis, fortune telling, or the visual matching of handwritten notes. Instead, the memory processor compares the written passwords and determines the authenticity of the writer. In the signature identification system, an electronic coded pen, connected to a microchip gauge, provides the computer with the pitch, roll, raw data, and force information. The directions of the written letters of X, Y, and Z are engaged. Six signature samples are required for the level of comparison to be accomplished. There are 20 such levels in each signature.

COMPUTER SYSTEMS AND LAW ENFORCEMENT APPLICATIONS

Computerization has reached into the world of law enforcement and crime fighting. While in the past the public law enforcer often relied on a card filing system (index), a manual search of records (by hand), the memory of experienced investigators, and often luck, today only luck remains. The computer systems available to large and small police and sheriff's departments and federal agencies give investigators the opportunity to expand their knowledge of any subject, increase their comparative capability skills, and examine files not only within the single department, but also by accessing data and comparing information nationally. The following section presents the systems nationally available to the law enforcement community.

National Crime Information Center (NCIC). The NCIC is an information data base in Washington, D.C., which is monitored and controlled by the Federal Bureau of Investigation. It allows all authorized law enforcement agencies throughout the United States and federal law enforcement officers (even around the world) to access its massive computerized library of stored data. The retrieval process includes files of individuals' criminal histories, missing persons, arrest warrants, stolen property, pilfered securities, registered property (guns and vehicles), even people considered dangerous to the President of the United States. This data base can assist law enforcement officers in tracking patterns of crime, furnish profiles of serial killers, or report Canadian law enforcement arrest warrants. The collected information also includes forensic and crime laboratory data.

NCIC utilizes two IBM 3033 mainframe computers in a fail-safe configuration system. The data is stored in custom and commercial software. Over 17,000 computer terminals are linked to these data base terminals through telecommunications and modems, and the NCIC is accessed more than a half million times a day by local law enforcement authorities.

Treasury Enforcement Communications System (TECS). TECS was designed for the United States Treasury Department's fight against crime. It is operated by the U.S. Customs Service and used by other Treasury Department agencies established in a network of some 1600 terminals located throughout the United States at division officers. Transmissions are scrambled (encrypted) to meet National Security Agency standards. Users must log on by identification to the operations system and entry of the day's secret access code. Each agency within the Treasury Department uses the generic software and hardware, but maintains its own data base files; and each agency may shield data and request information from other agencies in the system. In addition, other federal agencies and Interpol utilize TECS indirectly through the submission of a written request to the appropriate group within the Treasury Department. Agency-appointed representatives determine and control the information provided in hardcopy form.

Organized Crime Information System (OCIS). OCIS is a computerized data base maintained and controlled by the Federal Bureau of Investigation. This system stores information on known and suspected organized crime figures and their activities.

New York State Police Identification Network (NYSPIN). This network offers a statewide law enforcement communications system, which includes research to provide criminal histories, firearms control, stolen vehicle identifications, wanted individuals, missing persons, stolen property identification, and so on. The information is accessed by local, state, and federal law enforcement agencies through a central computer located in Albany, New York. NYSPIN also offers digital communications networking between mobile terminals, transmitting data and requests through a keyboard and visual display monitor. Therefore, accessibility is available through communication links to mobile units in the field.

Automated and Fingerprint Identification System (AFIS). AFIS resources have brought the law enforcement community out of the dark ages into today's space age technology. The system scans fingerprints submitted by law enforcement agencies, thereby creating a unique pattern and library index of individual prints. The information is translated into binary codes, which allow the computer to conduct searches and access distinct prints that are compared and processed at the rate of approximately 500 per second. Furthermore, with the information of AFIS, it has become possible to probe submitted prints or latent prints from a crime scene with great accuracy. The program captures, stores, and reads data secured on an optic disc and displays it on a verification screen. The resolution of the print on the disk is transposed into an image for display on the screen. Document readers scan fingerprints to identify, research, digitize, and store for future reference.

To ensure and maximize the efforts of the law enforcement establishment and to increase the ability to interface with each agency's automation, the American National Standard for Information Exchange was developed. It permits data exchanged between different AFIS systems to be read. Each AFIS user is required to utilize similar software. Consequently, AFIS users are able to match fingerprints taken from crime scenes with known prints from other jurisdictions.

Automated Crime Profiling. The National Center for Analysis of Violent Crimes (NCAVC), managed by the Federal Bureau of Investigation, was set up to analyze crimes and profile the personality of the offender. Specifically, using artificial intelligence, it traces the philosophical activities related to violent crime to detect, predict, and prevent it. The model is divided into reactive and proactive strategies. Violent crimes are reported to NCAVC to assist in the development of patterns and classifications, which help in the recognition of trends and profiles of an incident.

Violent Crime Apprehension Program (VICAP). VICAP is a data base located at the headquarters of the Federal Bureau of Investigation. It maintains information on unsolved homicides reported by NCAVC. Records from NCAVC are entered on line using secured telecommunications. VICAP compares over 100 categories of new cases. Each case is stored in a data base for comparison. In a rank order, the program sorts and lists matching or similar patterns of the violent crimes from the information system. The data base offers the investigator the ability, known as "template pattern matching," to begin a profile of the offender.

Utilizing crime pattern recognition computer programs, the profiling and consultation program assists in the detection and prediction of violent criminal behavior. Arson Information Management System, another program of the Federal Bureau of Investigation, analyzes the crime patterns through computer-generated information profiles. This data management program has allowed the FBI to predict the time, date, and location of future incidents. It also permits for the tracking of persons suspected or known to the FBI as arsonists.

Artificial intelligence users have the ability to compute and project the activities of organized criminal enterprises, terrorist groups, and gangs. Computer-assisted linguistic analysis is also being developed to aid in the evaluation of the contents of written and oral communications in matters of extortion, bombings, and terror incidents. The purpose is to determine the author of the communication and profile the viability of the threat (threat assessment).

Telecommunications Advancement

In recent years there have been many advancements in the field of telecommunications. For one thing, the rotary dialer was replaced by the electronic telephone switching system, for another, computer management of telecommunication systems allows for the change from hardwired telephones to microprocessor systems. The investigator is faced with new dimensions in the protection of information. These elements include communications interference through eavesdropping or misdirected data via transmission alterations.

Eavesdropping and Wire-Tapping and Countermeasures (SWEEP). Information loss is always a concern to the investigator. This same problem exists for any corporation, partnership, or municipal agency. Eavesdropping, also known as bugging, has generally been thought of as the tool of government law enforcement agencies. However, in today's business climate, the availability of over-the-counter products and new inventions have fashioned a growing recourse to industrial espionage, armchair private investigators, do-it-yourselfers, and the professional eavesdropper. Naturally, modern innovations have also changed the face of bugs. They come in different forms, sizes, and power levels. Legally, only law enforcement agencies, under court orders, have the right to wire-tap and listen in on individuals. So why the explosion of engagement in such activities? The answer is technology and its availability. While it is against the law to purchase and own a transmitter (a bug), commercialism has allowed the conversion of bugs, transmitters, receivers, and telephone listening devices into common household appliances. Over-the-counter products, such as wireless microphones, remote telephone transmitters, cellular telephone systems, babysitting listening devices, and even FM radios permit amateurs as well as professionals to eavesdrop. Moreover, almost anybody can afford such commodities. Some of them cost less then $50. Often the item is being coupled with a portable tap recorder to capture the conversation. Many users are husbands or wives in a breakup (divorce). While an unsuspecting spouse lives in an environment marked by the suspicion of the other, he or she can easily be spied upon. All that is needed is a telephone recording control device from any electronics or telephone store to tape the conversations from remote phone lines and preserve them through a connection to a tape recorder.

It is not illegal within most states of our country to record our own conversations with someone else even without the other person's awareness of it. There are a few exceptions. Certainly, a furor was raised when President Nixon was caught with tapes. The media has stressed that this was deplorable and a violation of the law. In fact, the only violation that may have taken place was the recording of conversations between third parties in the Oval Office. But the President was not involved in those, and therefore the question of illegal eavesdropping became irrelevant.

In the Hollywood movie, *The Conversation*, an eavesdropper applied his trade on-site. Today he can be miles away or not present at all. Through the technology available, conversations can be remotely transmitted to distances as far as telephone communications can reach, that is, worldwide.

It should be noted that, if there is someone putting in bugs, then there will be someone else searching for and removing them. The law enforcement community, corporate America, and private citizens contract and employ technical surveillance countermeasures experts to SWEEP the residence, office, and telephone system clean of any interference. Like an exterminator, these specialists carefully examine the location, telephone closets, lines, and devices, watching for common indicators in a physical and electronic search. The uninformed expect them to look behind hanging pictures, under the bed and sofa, or in the air conditioning and heating vents. While this is done during the physical search, technological advances allow them to examine the airwaves and telephone lines to determine the existence of a listening device, transmitters, or wiretap, which may be monitoring at the time of the sweep operation. If technicians locate the gadget, it may be advantageous to leave it in place and not inform the listener of the discovery. Therefore, many clients of countermeasures talk from their corporate telephones or the suspected room of the requested search. This gives the victim the opportunity to feed the listener false information or even to identify the intruders before they get a chance to pack their bags and leave. It may also be wise to notify law enforcement at this point of the illegal penetration.

Listeners, for their part, can either elect to remove the tap (bug) before the specialist conducts the search or allow it to remain and walk away from the device (known as a "throw away"), only to be possibly replaced another day, as needed.

Not only are corporations, government agencies, and public figures concerned about eavesdropping, but also the criminal element employs countermeasure experts (often former law enforcement personnel) to sweep their homes, businesses, and telephones. This is brought out in the following case: A technician advised his client, an individual associated with organized crime, that his home was clean (free from bugging devices). While the specialist was leaving the house, he was stopped by members of an FBI task force. They asked for his identification and seized his equipment. He was lucky that he had not found the listening devices placed by the government. Had he uncovered and removed them, law enforcement could have charged him with numerous crimes, such as obstruction of justice, destroying government property, and the like. As it was, he had to testify before a federal grand jury to explain his actions.

The most commonly used devices in wire-tapping and eavesdropping operations are listed and described, followed by a similar enumeration of the equipment of the countermeasure expert.

Commonly Used Devices of the Eavesdropper

A/D converter: A circuit that converts information from analog to digital format.

Acoustic patch: The placement of a microphone near a loudspeaker or earphone.

Amplifier: An electrical circuit to convert small electrical signals, increasing the voltage and power levels.

Audio frequency: Frequencies the human ear can detect, 15,000 to 20,000 Hertz. Only 300 to 3000 Hertz are transmitted via telephone.

Blue box: An illegal device utilized to enter operator circuits from a subscriber line. The device emits a tone employed by the telephone company to activate a toll-free circuit for operator use.

Bug: A clandestine listening device, generally a small radio transmitter, or hidden microphone.

Bypass: Alteration of a telephone instrument so that it passes audio even with the handset on the telephone cradle.

Carbon microphone: A microphone that requires variations in resistance of carbon granules.

Central office: Telephone company switching equipment that provides local exchange telephone service, designated by the first three digits of the telephone number.

Cheese box: A device used to interconnect two telephone lines terminated at the same premises. The device allows the user of direct long distance dialing to receive expected calls at a specific time without being charged for a completed toll call and without letting the other party know his or her actual location.

Condensor microphone: A microphone that depends on the generation of electricity charged by the deformation of a crystal.

D/A converter: A circuit that converts information from digital to analog.

Dedicated line: A telephone line leased to a customer for specific communication use (also known as a leased line). It is often found in corporations and computer transmitted information network facilities.

Digital: Any information in discrete form using a binary number system.

Directional microphone: A microphone that is sensitive to audio frequencies coming from one direction, rejecting audio frequencies from other directions.

Drop-in: A series wire-tap built on the back of a telephone handset's carbon microphone.

Dynamic microphone: A common type of coil attached to a diaphragm and surrounded by a magnetic field from a permanent magnet.

Electric microphone: A permanently charged condensor microphone with a low-mass diaphragm, less responsive to clothing noise.

Hookswitch: Contacts inside a telephone that remove the telephone from the line circuit when the handset is on the hook. (Listening into a room is possible while the telephone is not in use.)

Infinity transmitter (harmonica bug): A transmitter designed for installation in a telephone instrument. It transmits audio received from the carbon telephone. It is activated before the ring or answer of the phone.

Intercept: The acquisition of the contents of any wire or oral communications through the use of electronic, mechanical, or other devices.

Magnetic microphone: Uses variations in the reluctance of a magnetic circuit.

Minitap: A single form of capacitively isolated tap.

Parallel radio tap: A radio frequency tap transmitter.

Parasitic device: A series radio frequency wire-tap, which uses the telephone line as an antenna.

Red box: An illegal device used to gain free time on payphones. Simulates tones that signal that money has been deposited.

Series radio tap: A radio transmitter that usually obtains power from the telephone line, installed in line with one wire.

Third-wire bypass: A telephone bypass method in which one wire in the instrument mounting cord is used to gain access to either the carbon microphone or the dynamic earpiece.

Transmitter: The microphone of the telephone instrument, or any device that radiates radio frequency (RF) energy.

Countermeasures Technical Equipment.   This list consists of alerting and nonalerting systems, designed to assist the technician in finding a listening device.

Frequency analyzer: An advanced receiver that examines the entire spectrum of radio frequency (RF) and demodulates at any megahertz. This instrument is used to locate room transmitters (bugs) or a wireless telephone tap that transmits over a radio frequency (parallel radio tap, series radio tap, parasitic device). It can be used in nonalerting and alerting sweeps.

Multimeter: An electrical analyzer that examines the unusual impedance of telephone electricity. With the proper equations, it is possible to read whether a parallel or serial tap is on the telephone line. Used for balanced line testing and ohms readings of telephone lines.

Feedback detector: Searches the airwaves for radio frequencies emanating from an RF transmitter. Only good for active transmitter discovery.

Time domain reflectors: Sends a pulsation through the telephone or electric lines; reads for splices, breaks and shorts; provides the technician with the ability to determine the distance from the search location to the break; and makes possible the location of in-line taps (serial or parallel).

Telephone system lineworkers instruments: These include handsets capable of listening and talking on line, and punch tools used to correct loose wire connections. Crimpers, soldering tools, and screwdrivers are all necessary equipment to repair wires and wall cords in cases of accidents or for separating in-line taps from the system. Fuses of varying sizes are needed because telephone systems often blow fuses when tests are conducted.

Nonlinear junction detector: Outdated, but used by many senior sweep techs. It finds nonlinear junctions in walls and will also show wires and nails in walls. Therefore, it is an exotic metal detector.

Surveillance by Electronics in Today's Investigations

360° Tracking System.   Tracking systems have been developed to increase the probability of maintaining continuity and observations of the targeted subject. Most tracking systems are operated by government law enforcement agencies. They are coupled with other technology, such as cellular communications, modem, base station search computing, and software designed to map communities. In one system on the market since 1987, the use of binary coding as focal points to a fixed community map calls the tracking device anywhere from every 30 seconds to one hour. Each call initiates a signal that transmits the binary-coded position of the vehicle, which is then translated into a mapping location and pinpointed on a monitor screen or laser printer. The time, date, and place of the vehicle's movement, its time at stops, and its continuation of progress are all recorded.

This system is not practical for the law enforcement community due to the size and requirements of the interfacing technology. It is being used by corporate America and government agencies to maintain a record of valued employees' movements, especially those who are in fear of becoming or who are kidnapping victims. It is also employed by trucking organizations for management of products' movement. In all cases the driver and/or executive are aware of the tracking system's function.

Other Tracking Systems. Other tracking systems utilize radio frequency transmissions pulsated in tone format and reporting to a directional receiver. Many of these devices are operated by law enforcement for trailing criminal elements. In one particular case, an RF transmitter was placed on the undercarriage of the vehicle of an extortionist. The individual had been in negotiations with an art dealer who had lost 11 valuable paintings, estimated at $500,000, in a burglary of his residence. The art dealer was approached by the extortionist (artnapper) to buy the works back for a specific price. Law enforcement agents working on the case were notified and began surveillance. Upon identification of the artnapper, a tracking device was placed on his personal vehicle. This permitted the trailing to continue with little chance of detection. Using the device allowed the surveillance team to set back a considerable distance, as long as the receiver continued to actively guide and signal to the receiver being monitored by the surveillance team.

After days of tracking and meetings with the artnapper, an agreement was reached to purchase back the paintings. The target accepted the money, promised that the artworks would be returned within 24 hours, and left with an attache case filled with the dealer's cash. His vehicle was kept under constant surveillance and, through the tracking device, the subject led the investigative team to a restaurant in midtown New York City. The car remained parked on the street, while he ate dinner with his associates. Upon leaving the restaurant, he was observed with others removing paintings from the restaurant and placing them in his vehicle. All subjects were arrested, and the valued art pieces were recovered.

Tracking devices have been converted into a system to locate stolen vehicles. Working in conjunction with law enforcement, the Lo-Jack system is activated through computerized microprocessing and coding. The silent transmitter signal is sent through a law enforcement tracking connection via cellular transmission. The receiver translates the information into a location, and the vehicle is found.

Video Surveillance. The great advances in the field of video technology and recording systems have not only opened up many new avenues for investigators, both public and private, to obtain their findings, but have also simplified their work in many instances and produced much better-quality evidence. For example, in the past 8-mm films were commonly used in photography. These required some elements of experience, plus the film had to be developed by others. In contrast, the video taping systems of today have eliminated the developing process and instantly replay an incident on television or a monitor.

The caliber of the pictures vary with size and the low light (LUX) capabilities. Often private investigators use over-the-counter 8-mm camcorder systems. Although the quality is less than professional, the video taping is generally adequate for the presentation needed. VHS and [fr3/4]-inch systems provide more professional-looking, clear pictures, but the taping device is larger than a camcorder.

Some systems offer 8-mm converters to be shown in VHS format. A cartridge accepting 8-mm tapes allows for the conversion to VHS.

Furthermore, the advent of wireless transmissions through airwaves and the technology of receivers, converters, recorders, and microwave linkage allow the transmission of video from many places to a surveillance van or plant location. The camera may be as small as a cigarette box and placed in a book on a shelf, coupled with a transmitter microphone and input into a receiver recording VCR system at a remote location. Yet the image becomes available on the monitor and is being recorded off-site from the incident.

With the advances of video technology, we are also seeing a surge of personal camcording and taping by private citizens. In one case, which gained national attention, parents suspected their babysitter of abusing their child. With the help of a hidden camcorder, the babysitter was captured on videotape striking the child several times with a wooden spoon.

Technical improvements have coupled the camcorder, minicamera, transmitters, and receivers to secure businesses, homes, vehicles, and the like. Remote-controlled power-driven motors and zoom lenses capture incidents even at distances from the camera location. In one instance, a zoom lens was used to obtain the license plate number of a private sanitation truck caught illegally dumping waste in a field. The lens zoomed to read and video tape the plate and then panned the scene to show the activity of the truckers.

Video taping instruments have the ability to date- and time-stamp pictures. Therefore, a recording of the particular date and time of an incident clearly furnishes the specifics for prosecution either in criminal or civil litigation.

Coming full circle, night vision scopes and lenses can be added to the camcorder or video camera during twilight and night hours. Developed for military purposes, this technology is now widely employed by law enforcement and private sector investigators in the surveillance of individuals and places.

Ultra low light imaging increases resolution and overall system versatility. These passive night vision viewers amplify the starlight or existing light up to 75,000 times. This light amplification produces sharp, high contrast, green images on the darkest nights—even in total blackness. The versatility of night scopes is proven by various uses: photography, closed-circuit television systems, camcorder video, secured lighting, telephotos, eyepieces, laser research applications, and weapon systems.

Closed-Circuit Television Systems (CCTV). CCTV has become the common technology for security systems of businesses and government institutions. Advanced technology has afforded a dramatic change in the components of CCTV. Usually it is hard-wired directly to the recording system by cabling through a wall, ceiling, or floor, which hides it from sight as well as from tampering or accidental damage. The cameras used today are microchip quality, not the old tube models. They vary in sizes, lenses, and capabilities. Some can provide mobility through motorized mounts and zoom up to actions closely. Creative security specialists and law enforcement personnel have masked and disguised CCTV cameras in mannequins, books, fire suppression sprinkler systems, and other places.

Split quad screen viewing is available through splitters and switching capabilities. The quad screen enables the monitor to project four locations on one screen at the same time. Thus, the viewer is able to watch over four places within one facility or wherever the cameras are placed. Recording is done through VCR taping. In a sweep conducted at a conference center planned for government meetings, the hotel rooms were found to have hidden cameras placed within the television speakers to record the sexual habits of attending guests.

Pinhole lens capability allows for a fully concealed instrument, while the lens is exposed to receive a 180° video spectrum.

Other Advances in Technology

Other important innovations that are useful in the field of investigation are now discussed.

X-Ray Spray. This unique aerosol spray enables the user to view the contents of an envelope without opening it. After approximately 30 to 60 seconds, the envelope returns to its original state without leaving a trace.

Voice Scramblers. The purpose of voice scramblers is to protect conversations via telephone lines. A digital LED display notifies users that the scramble mode is in operation. Eavesdroppers hear only gibberish tones.

Digital Voice Changer. This device alters the pitch and tone of speakers, making them sound like different persons on the telephone.

Mail Screening. The system analyzes bundles, packages, and letters. It is capable of detecting all known letter bomb detonating devices while ignoring harmless stationary items. Other systems utilize X-ray technology to look into packages and determine the contents. In the X-ray viewing, often the clarity and training of the technician create false impressions.

Fiber Optic Video Transmission. This type of transmission is immune to the effects of electrical interference, ground loops, high voltage, water, or hazardous environments. It is excellent in drop ceilings where other communications and transmissions may interfere with wired cabled systems.

Wireless Alarm Systems. Wireless transmitters utilize radio frequency transmission and digital encoding, and they can be useful during the course of certain investigations. Having the ability to contact a doorway or install a motion detector in the room, the transmitter can alert investigators to movements of the target. In one case, a wireless door contact was used to identify intruders of an office that had served as a storage area for company products. Previously, the room had not been secured because incidents of theft had not been common. Only the door was protected by a normal dead bolt lock. Through the use of wireless alarm and remote video recording, the suspects were caught in the act. The wireless transmitter alerted the base station to the penetration, and the remote hidden camera began recording upon activation of the alarm system.

Wireless transmitters, digital receivers and relays, or power-boosted sources permit communications among the units to go between floors, hallways, walls, and even buildings. Some receivers can be programmed to accept numerous locations of transmitters, with an encoded identification of a particular transmitter to define the location. Often these systems are employed in mobile protection of secured witnesses and/or in corporate executive protection. The security staff can secure a room, place the transmitter inside, put the subject to sleep, and be in another hotel room, confident in knowing that, should the target's room be penetrated, the alarm will alert the team to respond.

Wireless transmitters are also located in museums, art galleries, and department stores to protect displays. A break in the transmitter contacts generates an alarm to the base station. Other variations of transmitter security include transmitters in packages to prevent pilferage from a facility. As the package travels from the location with the offender, a signal is sent at a designated point of departure or department. The alarm transmits an immediate signal, which allows security personnel to stop and question the individual.

Teleconferencing and Satellite Communications. Cable and microwave transmission enables the law enforcement community to develop networking systems that may incorporate training or facilitate communications between command and headquarters. Interactive conferencing, using television monitoring and telephone calls, permits those in the field to talk to headquarters or other participants. Mobile communication commands can link headquarters to any incident they respond to, as well as televise and transmit conversations through microwave transmission. This makes it possible for the police chief or other designated officials to make command decisions without being physically present at the site of the occurrence.

CONCLUSION

Noting these technological innovations in the methods used to conduct investigations, our fast-paced age of ever new scientific discoveries offers fresh surprises constantly. Forensic medicine and its explosion into the world of DNA identification processing has afforded the victims of crimes and the law enforcement community a new vehicle to provide precise data concerning the identity of offenders from crime scene residue. Investigative knowledge and the utilization of computer-generated information systems, microprocessing and digital communications, tracking equipment or even night vision scopes for surveillance—all expand investigators' skills and increase their chances for success. While many researchers may think of these products as instruments not available to them or not functional in their operations, the creative investigator usually takes advantage of technology to benefit and advance a probe.

Note: legal restriction on the use of the equipment examined in this chapter may be covered by guarantees to the rights of privacy and secured by the Constitution of the United States for protection against unwarranted searches or seizures. Consult your local criminal procedural code and guidelines administered in your particular state or commonwealth.

48

Theft of Utility Services

Robert S. Charland

The crime category, "theft of services," involves tens of thousands of participants and results in billions of dollars of losses to the utilities and their ratepayers. This crime is not even acknowledged as being committed in many areas of the country, much less being categorized in the Uniform Crime Reports; however, it is growing at an alarming rate.

This chapter, in discussing utilities and their services, will generally refer to the gas and electric services provided by investor-owned or public-owned utilities. In 1980 there were 286 investor-owned utilities in the United States, and they accounted for nearly 80 percent of the energy sold to customers. There were nearly 3000 government-owned utilities which made up the remainder. Almost every person in the United States is a customer or user of energy supplied by a utility. Other kinds of utility companies also provide a variety of services to the public. Some of these are: telephone service companies, telegraph, water, steam, and pay television. The discussion in this chapter, however, is confined to the theft of services (TOS) violations which are directed against gas and electric utilities. The methods used in those thefts apply equally to the theft of the other services mentioned.

THE PROBLEM

In any sale of a commodity a transaction take place. When you purchase a pair of shoes, you take your purchase to the cash register and you exchange money for the goods. When you have a haircut, you pay the barber at the register. In the case of the delivery of gas and/or electricity to the customer, the commodity is the energy that will be consumed. The electric kilowatt hours or the cubic feet of gas consumed by the user of the service is the "thing" in transaction. Gas and/or electricity are not intangibles; they are commodities, and thus "things" subject to theft as determined by at least one court of law. The consumption of the service is metered, and bills are sent to the customer. The metering device can be thought of as the utility's cash register. Virtually all the schemes examined in the TOS problem will deal with the various methods used to beat the cash register (circumvent the meter). To keep the discussion manageable, utility customers are considered to be either residential or commercial users. Commercial customers normally enjoy a somewhat lower rate scale, based on consumption, since it is assumed that their consumption far exceeds that of the residential customer. It can therefore be assumed that if commercial customers consume more energy and if they decide to engage in stealing energy, their larceny will be a much greater loss to the utility. Is it not reasonable then to assume that they will be far more receptive to the overtures of the professional plumber or electrician who can install and conceal illegal bypass devices? In the trade these people are referred to as "fixers." Commercial customers are usually in a better financial position to afford the services of the fixers. Furthermore they are usually convinced, and rightly so in many cases, that the diversion methods used by fixers will be more sophisticated and difficult to detect, thus cutting down the chances of being arrested. The ordinary homeowner, on the other hand, most often engages in TOS in an amateurish fashion.

The point of the theft in most "steals" is usually near the metering equipment. Commonly, gas service is routed around the meter by some type of unauthorized plumbing device or bypass. Electric service is commonly diverted past the meter by the use of unauthorized conductors or jumpers. Either type of service may also be stolen by tampering directly with the operation of the meter.

Various methods will be described here which involve removing meters and/or tampering with utility equipment at the meter. In these cases the energy thief first has to remove or alter the sealing devices which have been installed by the utility at the meter to prevent tampering. The seals are placed on such equipment to aid in the detection of tampering with the meter.

METHODS USED

Electric Jumpers

The meter is removed from its socket and two metal strips or wires (conductors) are inserted into the jaws of the socket. The circuit is thereby completed, and this allows the electric current to flow through the conductor material (jumpers) and into the wiring of the customer. Figures 48.1 and 48.2 are photographs de-

Figure 48.1 Meter with missing seals. **Figure 48.2** Meter with jumper jaws.

picting this particular type of violation. Figure 48.1 shows the meter with the seals missing, as it would appear to the casual observer. Figure 48.2 shows the meter after removal by the investigator; the jumpers can be seen in the jaws of the meter socket. In the jumpered configuration the meter is frequently reinserted into the socket jaws along with the jumpers. In so doing, the jaws are thus spread apart and the meter sits rather loosely in the socket. In this situation it does, in fact, record a portion of the true consumption. However, depending on the type of conductive material used, a substantial portion of the energy is shunted past the meter and is not recorded. All types of jumpers have been used to complete the circuit. At other times, when a customer's service has been shut off by the utility for nonpayment of a bill, faulty or dangerous wiring, and so on, the meter is physically removed from the meter box and a blank shield is installed across the meter box. This is referred to as a "blanked-off" meter box. Frequently the customer who has been blanked off will remove the shield and insert jumpers into the jaws of the socket. Naturally, the entire consumption becomes a *direct steal*, since no metering device is present. In a recent case, depicted in Fig. 48.3, the jumpers used were ordinary eating utensils, knives and forks. As can be seen in Fig. 48.4, the current arced to the meter box and the entire meter box was thereby energized. The meter box was located on the outside of the house and was in such a location that neighborhood children had ready

Figure 48.3 Utensils used as jumpers.

Figure 48.4 Meter box energized.

access to it. They could have easily come in contact with the box. An added danger was that there was a permanent area of ground dampness just beneath the meter box. As can be seen in Fig. 48.3, the arcing of the current melted portions of the jumpers.

Riser and Pole Jumpers

While these are separate types of thefts, they are similar enough to be commented on jointly, in the interest of brevity. Although normal shutoff of the service usually takes place at the meter, there are instances when the service is cut off at the point where the utility wires are first attached to the building. This point is normally located near the roof peak or eaves, and is referred to as the *riser*. In other instances the service is cut off at the utility pole itself. These further cutoff actions are taken by the utility when the customer has once been shut off at the meter and has subsequently jumpered or restored service in some fashion. If the customer has a history of having jumpered, the utility cuts the customer "at the riser." This means that the *service drop* (wires strung from the utility pole to the building) is disconnected at the point of connection with the customer's riser. The next step would be to cut the customer's service at the pole. Here again, the customer will sometimes climb up the utility pole and reconnect the wires. The next action to be taken by the utility is to "drop the service," this being the complete removal of the entire set of service lines that had been strung between the utility pole and the customer's building. The thief may then decide to string his own line from the pole to the riser and into the building. Needless to say, this is extremely dangerous. The jumpers used could be any sort of conductive material. A most common practice in this type of steal is to attach ordinary booster cables of the type used to start motor vehicles with dead batteries. This same technique is used where the customer's service is supplied from a point on the utility wires between two poles. This is termed a "midspan jump." Figure 48.5 depicts this type of case.

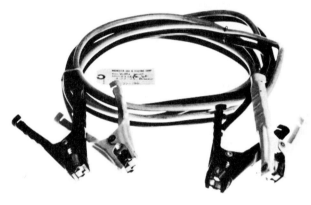

Figure 48.5 Midspan jump.

Inverted Electric Meter

One of the drawbacks of the attempts to standardize equipment for the utility industry is that manufacturers have designed meters as simply as possible. The four blades on the rear of the meter are perfectly aligned to fit into four jaws in the meter box. This symmetrical alignment unfortunately allows a meter to be installed either right side up or inverted. Any suggestions concerning design changes are usually thwarted, because of the tremendous costs involved in the replacement of the 96 million meters already in use in this country. This common TOS involves the customer who removes the meter from its socket and then reinserts it upside down. The current flows through the meter but causes the recording dials to operate in reverse. The customer thus actually reduces the registered consumption the more current is used. The greater the consumption, the lower the reading. The customer must remember what the scheduled meter reading date is and must conduct the steal between those dates, remembering also to correctly replace the meter and the seal sometime before the next scheduled reading. Furthermore, the customer must make certain that the consumption indicator is replaced at a higher reading than the last reading since a reading of less than the prior reading would be a clear indicator of an inverted meter steal. Often, the customer goes off on vacation and remembers to stop the milk, hold the mail, notify the paper boy, and so on, but forgets to reset the meter.

Drilled Meter Glass

In this type of steal the fixer drills a tiny hole in the glass face of the meter, usually in the side. Once the aperture is made, a foreign object such as a wire or nail is inserted to a point just underneath the meter disk. A small weight is hung on the outside end of the nail and the glass acts as a fulcrum. The disk is thus raised to a point where it is either slowed down or stopped by friction. The electric current flows through the meter unimpeded but the meter registers only a fraction of the customer's total use. In a case of this type, a customer may be operating a three-bay welding shop and receive an average bill of less than $30 a month. The customer, like the customer with the inverted meter, has to remember to remove the device at the proper time. Without a high-speed drill and a special drill bit, the customer will usually have a problem with this type of steal. The special glass used in the meter glass face shatters easily, spalls, or puckers when drilled. The pucker resembles a BB hole, and it never fails to amaze the utility employees how many customers claim to have children target practicing by shooting at the sides of their meters.

Tampered Meter

In a gas meter tamper the customer usually removes the glass face plate covering the meter dials and turns the dial hands backwards, remembering to keep the altered dial hands in their proper sequence and taking extreme care not to break the hands or to score the paint on the dial face. The hands are most fragile and the special paint used on the dial faces quickly indicates any scratches. It is more difficult to get at the dials in an electric meter tamper but the same caution must be observed. The glass of the electric meter can be screwed off but this breaks certain delicate tamper-indicator seals. Once the thief gains entry into the electric meter there are a number of methods that may be used to retard the recording of the consumption. The energy thief can tamper with the dials or worm gears, remove teeth from gears, slow down dials, and so on. In fact, there are approximately 38 different possible methods of tampering used in this type of steal. A tampered-with meter, when accomplished by a professional fixer, is most difficult to detect. This type of violation is more common to the commercial than the residential account. In most instances where the residential steal is a tampered meter, it is easily detected.

Magnets

When a large magnet is placed on the glass face of the electric meter, it may alter the electromagnetic field in which the disk turns and/or slow down the rotation of the disk. This may result in a higher indication of consumption; however, it is no longer commonly used.

Bypass Piping

In the common gas steal some sort of unauthorized plumbing is used to divert the gas around the metering equipment. Several types of bypasses are used. Rigid pipe fixtures are sometimes installed by professional plumbers who are acting as fixers, but the more common bypass piping is copper or aluminum tubing, flexible hose, rubber or garden hose, vacuum cleaner hose, and so on. In most of these situations the gaskets and thread seals are either nonexistent or not properly made up. This, of course, allows the gas to leak, and the accumulation of gas to an explosive saturation point is not uncommon.

Reversed Gas Meter

Similar to the inverted electric meter, the gas meter is disconnected from the gas line piping and is replaced in a reversed configuration. The gas flowing backwards through the meter will then "blow back" the indicator hands on the meter dial faces, and the recorded consumption is thereby reduced as the actual consumption increases. This practice is relatively common. Of course, the clear danger involved here is not only in the leaking gaskets, but the free flow of large amounts of gas, if not properly stoppered, as the meter is disconnected to be reversed. As previously noted, the thief must remember to correct the illegal situation before the meter is scheduled to be read.

Alligator Clips

These clips are attached to wiring, sometimes bared, and used in the same fashion as the electrical jumpers previously discussed, the advantage to the thief being that the jump need not be located close to the meter. By the use of alligator clips and an extension cord, the jump points can, in fact, be some distance from the meter.

Stolen Meters

Gas and electric meters are stolen frequently from abandoned buildings, construction sites, homes where the owner is away on vacation, and so on. These stolen meters are frequently used by the thief in the same fashion that an authorized meter is used. The authorized meter is removed by the miscreant in mid-read cycle. The stolen meter is inserted and is used until just before the next scheduled read. The advantage of this system, usually used on outside meters, is that to the casual observer nothing appears amiss, and unless the seal and the serial number of the meter are checked, the steal usually goes unnoticed even by utility personnel working in the area of the meter.

Sophisticated Thefts

Professional fixers, whether plumbers or electricians, usually install their diversions or tamper with the meter in a way extremely difficult to detect or observe. The installation of cable attached to underground electric service and shunted to the rear of the panel box is one method. The installation of permanent jumpers in the rear of the meter box mounts is another. The installation of tees or taps in the gas lines far ahead of the gas meter is commonly done by professional fixers. In many of the professional steals the bypass equipment is hidden behind false walls constructed expressly to conceal the diversion. Contractors, builders, electricians, and plumbers sometimes join forces to steal energy during construction of the building. Not only do they steal electric current to operate their equipment while constructing the building, they also steal gas to heat the building by running large heater units called salamanders. These salamanders are also used to dry plaster walls and ceilings and to cure concrete and terrazzo floors, cement block walls, and so on. Finally, these tradespeople install sophisticated steals hidden right in the basic building construction. For example, the general contractor, who specialized in electric work, can build his own corporate facility and include the capability for himself to engage in TOS at his convenience by use of hidden cutoff switches.

Lockouts

Finally there are the "meter butchers." This type of steal is done by the customer who is usually very unsophisticated and usually a resident of the inner city. This thief simply takes a wrench, twists off the locking devices which have been installed by the utility (usually after nonpayment), restores the service, and flagrantly steals until discovered—usually in a scheduled read that cycles out in two or four months.

There is another practice that is not uncommon but that is not often brought to the attention of investigators. Investigators should be familiar with it, however, since they may be notified about it and must know how to proceed. This is when the customer has a neighbor or a tenant who taps into the customer on the customer side of the meter. The utility company only has a legitimate interest in those steals which are put on the lines ahead of the metering equipment. Once the energy is past the meter and a steal is made, it is the concern of the person who has purchased the energy. This type of theft does not fall within the penal law as a TOS since it occurs on the other (customer) side of the meter. The energy has already been measured and "sold" to the customer. Once the customer's neighbor steals it, the crime becomes a larceny from the customer, who must institute the criminal complaint and may also proceed civilly against the neighbor. Although these types of incidents are not frequently reported, they seem to be on the increase, especially in multiple dwellings with common basements and metering areas.

The basic goal in most TOS cases is to obtain energy from the utility's gas and/or electric lines with the consumption unmetered or only partially metered.

THE PERPETRATORS

More and more utilities have found that their own employees are moonlighting as fixers. A large utility in New York State declared an amnesty period for any of its employees who were involved in TOS and who came forth with admissions. The result was that a large number of their trusted employees took advantage of the grace period. The number was so high that it amazed even the most cynical of the security staff personnel.

Not only are utility employees involved in TOS, there is a growing body of evidence that indicates that organized crime figures have recently entered the growing and lucrative field. A large Midwestern utility has estimated that organized crime losses cost them over $5 million per year in 1980. Another large utility near Chicago makes a conservative estimate of around $7 million. In the state of New Jersey, the art has been developed to the point where organized crime controls franchise areas, which it "leases" out to various fixers. The fixer charges the customer a set fee for the original installation, and the customer then pays a monthly fee prorated on the percentage of monthly savings from the reduced utility bills. The trend is for the fixer to collect half of the savings and to pass on half of that to the organized crime figures as their commission. The customer is solicited by the mob figure, the installation is by mob figures, and the payments are collected by mob members. A new wrinkle is that the job has started to offer tie-in sales to several of the high-energy consumers. As an example, they will offer to fix the meter of a pizza restaurant and will also sell stolen flour, olive oil, and so on, at reduced prices.

Another trend that is developing among many of the commercial customers with high energy requirements is the discussion of methods of TOS at the regional meeting. High-energy customers are laundromats, pizza restaurants, fast food chains, bakeries, welding shops, and so on. At business conferences the managers are exhorted to reduce their overhead, so they discuss ways that they can cut expenses. A good way for them to reduce their overhead is by TOS, so they compare notes, exchange names of fixers, and so on. Supermarkets with high-energy-use equipment, along with restaurants and taverns, are among the growing number of users of the fixers' services.

Not only is the mob involved but the traditional word of mouth between neighbors and relatives plays a significant role in the spread of TOS among residential customers. Where a residential steal is discovered, there is an excellent chance that neighbors and/or relatives have also been shown the techniques and have installed their own devices.

A major influence on the increasing number of persons involved in TOS has been the so-called underground press, which regularly publishes do-it-yourself instructions and diagrams on how to steal services. Added to this is the growing body of persons who are allied with environmental protest groups, hippies, antinuclear groups, and those customers who accept larcenous behavior as part of the new morality. These people tend to rationalize TOS as not being an illegal activity, feeling that theft from a large impersonal business institution simply is not criminal.

Experience indicates that the inner-city poor engage in TOS of an electric service more than of the gas service. Rough estimates show the ratio to be about 60 percent electric steals to 40 percent gas steals. In the more affluent suburbs, the opposite is true. This is probably because the services of a gas fixer cannot easily be afforded by the ghetto dweller. About 60 percent of the total steals are in the urban areas and 40 percent are in the suburbs and rural areas.

In some areas served by metropolitan utilities, prosecution is sought for only the most flagrant violations. The prosecutors in some areas refuse to even consider a case for court unless the utility can show that the thief has stolen service worth over a set amount, any less the utility is forced to write off as an uncollectible debt or to try to recover civilly. In a recent case, investigators uncovered gas thefts in five apartment buildings owned by one realty company. The estimated loss to the utility was over $50,000 per year in 1977. The thefts were hidden behind false walls and had been going on for almost 10 years.

In an attempt to determine the magnitude of the problem, a questionnaire was sent to a number of utilities in January 1977, requesting that they report the number of cases involving TOS that their respective companies had *verified* during 1976. In this selected group, by no means the entire industry, the responding utilities indicated that they had verified 44,475 TOS cases out of a reported 189,814 incidents. As the utility reporting methods become more refined and sophisticated, it is anticipated that these early efforts to determine the magnitude will prove to have been underestimates of the problem.

THE LEGAL PROBLEMS

In viewing the problem of TOS from the point of view of law enforcement, the four legal areas of most concern are (1) presumption, (2) *scienter*, (3) crime category, and (4) access.

Presumption

On September 1, 1976 in New York State, the amended Penal Law Section 165 took effect. This revision created the presumption that the person (usually the customer of record) who received the benefit of the diversion was presumed to have been the actor in the criminal offense.

165.15 Theft of Services

A person is guilty of theft of services when: He knowingly accepts or receive the use and benefit of service, including gas, steam or electricity service, which should pass through a meter but has been diverted therefrom, or which has been prevented from being correctly registered by a meter provided therefor, or which has been diverted from the pipes, wires, or conductors of the supplier thereof. In any prosecution under this subdivision proof that service has been intentionally diverted from passing through a meter, or has been intentionally prevented from being correctly registered by a meter provided therefor, or has been intentionally diverted from the pipes, wires, or conductors of the supplier thereof, shall be presumptive evidence that the person who accepts or receives the use and benefit of such service has done so with knowledge of the condition so existing; or

With intent to avoid payment by himself or another person for a prospective or already rendered service the charge or compensation for which is measured by a meter or other mechanical device, he tampers with such device or with other equipment related thereto, or in any manner attempts to prevent the meter or device from performing its measuring function, without the consent of the supplier of the service. In any prosecution under this subdivision, proof that a meter or related equipment has been tampered with or otherwise intentionally prevented from performing its measuring function without the consent of the supplier of the service shall be presumptive evidence that the person to whom the service which is at the time being furnished by or through such meter or related equipment has, with intent to avoid payment by himself or another person for a prospective or already rendered service, created or caused to be created with reference to such meter or related equipment, the condition so existing. A person who tampers with such a device or equipment without the consent of the supplier of the service is presumed to do so.

Acknowledgement of this presumption is crucial because, without it, preparation of an effective prosecution is almost impossible. Without it, the actor must either be observed committing the criminal act, or must make an admission coupled with strong circumstantial evidence. Even with the presumption, a number of magistrates have taken a position that the presumption is unconstitutional or that a simple denial by the actor sufficiently overcomes such presumption. Pointing up the difficulties involved in a criminal investigation in a jurisdiction without presumption is a recent case involving computer analysis, remote metering, camera and TV surveillance, surveillance by utility personnel accompanied by private detectives and public enforcement personnel, interview, and statements. The case was under active investigation for 2½ years, resulted in a 291-count indictment, and may never go to a trial jury.

On the other hand, Judge Herbert Shapiro sitting in the New York State Supreme Court in Bronx County in *People v. Castenada* [92 Misc.2d 687], took a more realistic position in his decision affirming the constitutionality of the presumption, saying, "Is it likely that there is some modern-day Robin Hood roaming our basements tampering with meters to the benefit of unknown consumers and to the detriment of the utility?…It would seem too illogical and contrary to experience to conclude that the meter tampering was done without the knowledge of the one benefited thereby…."

Scienter

Scienter (knowledge) is, in a practical sense, a matter of criminal intent. Since intent is not a matter of fact, it then becomes a question of proof which is discernible and eventually must be decided by the jury. The investigator must devote considerable time and effort to accomplish this.

Crime Category

Many investigators feel that the law must be changed. TOS cases are given low priority by law enforcement and prosecution personnel who simply do not feel they have the resources to cope with crimes that are not in a felony category. In those few jurisdictions that have classified the more serious TOS violations as felonies, the results have been most impressive in curtailing the problem.

Access

In any investigation of a TOS violation, access to the meter area is of the highest priority. Most thefts are occasioned at or near the meter. The utility representative or law enforcement officer may seek entry into the basement of the building but frequently is admitted only after the items used in the theft (jumpers/bypass piping) have been removed or disconnected. The perpetrators usually give some excuse while they or their confederates quickly disassemble the illegal devices. In many cases, the diverter simply plays possum and refuses to respond to repeated knocking on the door, doorbell ringing, and so on. Written notice to the customer can sometimes bring access, but this type of prior warning and entry by appointment only occasionally results in the discovery of a theft. Search warrants have been sought and obtained in a few jurisdictions; however, this method is the exception rather than the rule. Most magistrates are quite reluctant to issue search warrants and they demand somewhat more than the reasonable grounds which apply to other, more routine applications.

Subterfuge by police or utility investigators has been effectively used in the past. This is unfortunate, since the end never justifies this means. As an example, some investigators pretend that they have smelled the odor of escaping gas and have forced their entry into a basement under the cover of their official right to prevent an explosion. There have been cases where the investigators have covertly dispersed a gas odorant either from a can of the chemical or from a sniff/scratch card. This distinctive odor is mixed into the odorless natural gas to alert the customer to leaks.

Access to a premises by utility personnel is authorized under the *New York State Transportation Corporations Law*, Article 2, Section 14. When customers apply for service from a utility, they sign an application and agree to abide by the tariff which, in effect, states that they will allow the utility to inspect and examine its pipes, wires, and so on in the building at all reasonable times. Refusal to allow such entry and inspection on demand is deemed to be a hindering, and in theory the person is liable to forfeit a sum of $25 for each such refusal. This section is seldom, if ever, applied since the process for invoking it is so cumbersome (small claims court proceedings, judgment, collection, and so on). Some utilities have issued copies of the tariff, laminated in plastic, to their employees for display to the customer. This method has met with only limited success. According to the rules of the Public Service Commission, access may be demanded only once per year. In effect, this allows diversions to be continued for long periods while the customers submit bimonthly postcard reads of their own meters.

One of the other legal difficulties confronting those involved in the TOS investigations is that by requiring meters to be set outside the building rather than inside, the meter is made public. The vulnerability to public access is a built-in affirmative defense for the actor who then can claim no knowledge of who would do such a thing as to invert the meter, and so on. Since virtually all new construction now requires that the meters be set outside the building, the exposure of meters to ordinary acts of criminal mischief, theft, and tampering has increased.

In multiple dwelling cases, the service cannot be discontinued at the riser, pole, or curb, since to do so would cut off service to the other, legitimate customers.

Other Hindrances to Prosecution. While not associated with the access problem, another hindrance to prosecution is that, in most cases, one of the first questions the enforcement agency or prosecutor will pose is "How much energy was stolen?" In a prosecution-for-larceny approach, this question is germane; in TOS alone, it is not.

By using a threat of criminal action to force payment of back bills or as a collection device, the utility becomes liable to a charge of malicious prosecution even though a tort action may legally flow from the completed criminal action.

These and other caveats must be carefully considered prior to instituting criminal action.

SOLUTIONS

Detection

In order to effectively deal with the problem, it must first be detected. How do the utilities discover TOS violations? Several methods are used, the most successful and common being the training of meter readers (and other employees who have frequent entry/access) to observe and detect such thefts. In many utilities, the meter reader is an entry-level position. The readers receive little instruction other than basic meter reading since it is anticipated that they will soon move into other areas of the utility's operation such as linework or gas line construction. Also, with the high volume of meters to be read each day, the meter reader can spend only a few seconds at each location. However, as the utilities became more sensitive to the true amounts involved in the theft loss, meter readers are now being trained in how to observe and report such thefts. Incentives are paid for each *verified* report. These incentives are paid out to all utility personnel, but by far the greatest percentage of reports come from the meter readers. Nearly all utilities now have such incentive programs, and some have adopted a practice to provide for increased incentives for the discovery of a high-magnitude theft.

One most common indication of a possible theft is the cut seal on the meter. While many contractors have ready access to sealing devices, most average customers do not have such an advantage. The contractor is able to cut a seal, insert the jumpers, and reseal the box, thereby avoiding detection for a considerable length of time. The average customer is unable to do this, so must reseal with a defective unit. Considerable ingenuity in this area has been displayed. Seals are cut, crimped, and reinserted into the sealing loops, and they become almost impossible to detect visually. In other cases the seal wire is left intact and the sealing loops are cut. The object is to allow the meter to be removed and/or tampered with without giving the appearance of having tampered with the integrity of the seal.

Computers are now being used to detect thefts. The estimated consumption is programmed in, and if the account shows a significant variance, either high or low, the account is reviewed. Other indicators are comparisons with previous years' bills, taking into account averaging heating days, the addition of major energy-use appliances such as pool heaters, and so on.

The use of fraudulent accounts is common. When a customer is "shut-off nonpayment" (SONP), an account is often reopened in another family member's name, the wife's maiden name, or a totally fictitious name. In one franchise area, those persons who are SONP reapply for service in less than 20 percent of the cases. Most of these SONP accounts are either reopened under a pretext name or TOS is instituted.

Very infrequently, a theft is reported by an anonymous source, usually a disgruntled employee or a neighbor. Other reports come from firefighters called to a blaze, fire marshalls, building inspectors, and employees of sister utilities (telephone installers, water meter readers). But the large majority of cases are discovered either through the detection of a tampered seal or by trained meter readers.

Prevention

A current school of thought holds that prevention is the best possible solution. To accomplish this, a number of steps are being taken by the industry.

Outside Meters. Statistically the number of tampered-with meters installed outside the building is less than those inside. This also helps to solve the access problem. This area becomes an enforcement trade-off, as earlier noted. Since most people are basically honest, the advantage is to have the meters outside.

Remote Metering. Meters are installed either at the pole or at some central location far removed from the customer. The use of meters which transmit digital readouts electronically is also being examined.

Nonreversible Meters. Both gas and electric meters are to a great extent reversible at present. By using different-size fittings on the gas meter and irregularly spaced blades on the electric meter, this defect is overcome. The problem associated with replacing meters in an entire service area is one of cost. Even the least expensive meters fall in the $30 price range, plus the labor expense to change the meter, install new equipment, and so on. In a franchise area of one million customers, the cost prohibition is obvious.

Antitampering Devices. All sorts of such devices are now being developed. High-security locking rings on meters, self-destructing meter screws, meter alarms, distinctive paints, sealing tapes, and warning stickers are only a few of the recent technological improvements. The list is becoming almost endless as the industry begins to respond to the problem.

Better-Trained Utility Personnel. Not only are the meter readers being trained to detect thefts; many utilities are now requiring that *all* their employees receive some similar instruction.

Asset Protection Forces. Almost ever private utility now allocates some employee positions exclusively to the investigation of TOS cases.

SONP Follow-Up. An increasing amount of time is being devoted to the follow-up of shutoffs. In increasing numbers, customers simply turn their service back on after the SONP.

In addition to the steps outlined above, the author advocates better training of criminal justice personnel. The utility industry's TOS subcommittee will soon be making a proposal to the member utilities to fund a training film and a number of informational seminars. The industry is attempting to establish training outlines and other aides to be provided to police academies, district attorneys' seminars and judicial conferences. An ongoing program of training must be presented to the criminal justice community to make them aware of the magnitude of the problem. The utilities must additionally provide this information to criminal justice/police science students, grand jury associations, media groups, and so on. Police personnel must be trained to respond to TOS as to any other complaint and be able to effectively deal with the situation as it is presented to them (issue appearance ticket, obtain evidence and statements, testify). Average citizens must also be informed and educated about the problem, especially since it directly affects them. The physical dangers associated with tampering with utility equipment must be pointed out to the public. In a recent case the leaking gas tamper filled the entire house with explosive gas. In another, the diverter was knocked off the utility pole twice while trying to reconnect his own service after being SONP.

CONCLUSION

TOS is not a new problem; however, it certainly is one which is expanding at an alarming rate. The losses are staggering and affect all the honest ratepayers. Our society must recognize and acknowledge that our old attitudes toward this crime must be changed. Utility action to meet the challenge is being implemented. The public sector (criminal justice) must be informed and trained in ways to complement the efforts of the utility industry. Outmoded laws need to be reviewed and amended where required. Sophisticated preventive measures offer the best long-range solution. Strict and impartial criminal enforcement must be instituted where required, especially in areas where organized crime has gained access. Civil remedies must be streamlined for use against the lesser violators (treble damages, back-billing, use of arbitration panels, and so on). Unless these steps are taken, the utility industry will be forced to seek insufferable rate increases; or to surrender and become public power authorities; or finally, to face bankruptcy.

PART 8
Terrorism and Hostage Taking

49

Terrorism: An International Issue

Ben Jacobson

Joseph J. Grau

Johanna M. Grau

Terrorism in its raw form defies the typical, theoretical explanations, observations, and procedures of the seasoned investigator. It exists in opposition to the establishment and stability of society and thrives on fanatical commitment to a cause or ideology. Despite the fact that a growing number of individual governments have stepped up their efforts to curb it, it has remained a prominent international concern. With increasingly sophisticated technology, electronics, and arms available to terrorist organizations, the question arises, what can we expect next? Will these groups carry out a spectacular act, such as dropping a nuclear device on a heavily populated area or using bacterial weapons against their "enemies"? What will stop those who seem immune to favorable public opinion, who put little value on casualties, including those within their own ranks, whose objective has become everything, and who are often sponsored by their own governments? To protect us against such a calamity, federal, state, and local law enforcement authorities in the United States have developed programs to investigate, profile, monitor, and collect information concerning individuals, organizations, and countries engaging in rhetoric of terror and violence.

This chapter serves as an overview of the section on terrorism by defining it, examining the motives of terrorist groups (international, subnational, and domestic), identifying federal statutes used in prosecuting its members and pointing out some general preventive measures. The main body of data was supplied by the U.S. Department of Justice, Federal Bureau of Investigation, Terrorist

Research and Analytical Center, Counterterrorism Section, and Criminal Investigative Division. More specifically, information was gleaned from the reports of the *FBI Analysis of Terrorist Incidents and Terrorism in the United States,* 1985 through 1990.

DEFINITIONS OF TERRORISM AND COUNTERTERRORISM

The Federal Bureau of Investigations presents the following definitions to establish exactly what is meant by a certain term.

Terrorism

Terrorism is the unlawful use of force or violence against persons or property to intimidate or coerce a government, the civilian population, or any segment thereof, in furtherance of political or social objectives.[1]

The FBI distinguishes between two types of terrorism in the United States:

1. *Domestic:* This "involves groups or individuals whose terrorist activities are directed at elements of our Government or population without foreign direction."[2]
2. *International:* This "involves terrorist activity committed by groups and individuals who are foreign-based and/or directed by countries or groups outside the United States or whose activities transcend national boundaries."[3]

Terrorist Incident

A terrorist incident is a violent act, or an act dangerous to human life, in violation of the criminal laws of the United States or any state, to intimidate or coerce a government, the civilian population, or any segment thereof, in furtherance of political or social objectives.[4]

Suspected Terrorist Incident

This is a potential act of terrorism; however, responsibility for the act cannot be attributed to a known or suspected terrorist group. Assessment of the circumstances surrounding that act will determine its inclusion in this category. Also, additional information through investigation can cause a redesignation of a suspected terrorist incident to a terrorist incident status.[5]

Terrorism Prevention

A documented instance in which a violent act by a known or suspected terrorist group or individual with the means and a proven propensity for violence is successfully interdicted through investigative activity.[6]

Counterterrorism Investigative Guidelines and Statutory Authority

Domestic terrorism investigations are conducted in accordance with the "Attorney General Guidelines for General Crimes, Racketeering Enterprises and Domestic Security/Terrorism Investigations." International terrorism investigations are conducted in accordance with the "Attorney General Guidelines for FBI Foreign Intelligence Collection and Foreign Counterintelligence Investigations."

While the FBI has been charged with the lead Federal agency authority to investigate acts of terrorism in the United States, there is no all-encompassing Federal law concerning this issue. The FBI bases its investigative and prosecutive efforts on several existing Federal criminal statutes.

Also, due to terrorist attacks against American citizens abroad, Congress passed the *Comprehensive Crime Control Act of 1984*. Chapter XX of the Act deals with hostage taking. The *Omnibus Diplomatic Security and Antiterrorism Act of 1986* created a new section of the U.S. Code which expands Federal jurisdiction in matters of extraterritoriality to include homicide, conspiracy to commit homicide, or physical violence committed against a U.S. national abroad as part of a terrorist endeavor.

The following statutes also give the FBI extraterritorial authority to investigate terrorist crimes committed outside the United States:

- Aircraft Piracy and Related Offenses
- Crimes Against Internationally Protected Persons
- Crimes Against Select United States Officials
- Crimes Committed Within the Special Maritime Jurisdiction of the United States.
- Piracy

U.S. extraterritorial jurisdiction may be asserted in a foreign country provided there is approval from the host country and close procedural coordination with the U.S. Department of State.[7]

Note: For a fuller listing of the most frequently used federal statutes relating to terrorism see the appendix on page 49-15.

TERRORIST GROUP MOTIVATIONS

Any society can fall prey to terrorist activities—even the most stable—despite a government's increased attempt to curb them. Therefore, the solution to the problem must include motivational considerations.

According to the FBI reports, terrorism in all its forms contains certain recurring elements:

- A terrorist group is formed to change an existing political system or to right an alleged wrong which, in its view, cannot be accomplished by working within the system;
- A fanaticism or fervor develops within a political, social or revolutionary ideology, sufficient to justify acts of violence by the group and to focus public attention on its goals.
- Elements of secrecy and clandestine activity exist in the group's operation.
- The group procures and provides training, funding, weapons and other support for its members; and
- Participants in terrorist activity are generally members of a structured group with defined leadership.[8]

In addition, two practical concepts are present: (1) The commission of terrorist acts is less expensive than waging war, in terms of manpower and revenue, and (2) such acts normally receive extensive publicity through international media, thereby focusing attention on, and generating potential support or sympathy for the cause.[9]

When broad concepts are coupled with specific social and political desires, they make for a complete package of motivations and represent a means of legitimizing causes and violence in international as well as in domestic groups.

International Groups

The principal motivation behind most international terrorist organizations is political. Within this general concept fall two types of groups who espouse political rhetoric: state-sponsored and subnational groups.

State-Sponsored Groups. These groups "represent governments or governmental factions which support terrorism as an instrument of state policy." They aim to further the foreign policy goals of their regimes and keep tabs on antigovernment elements worldwide. This has been particularly true among certain Middle Eastern nations, such as Iran, Libya, and Syria, which have trained and used terrorists and utilized government intelligence and military services in support of terrorist operations. Their main objective is the "showcasing" of revolutionary ideology in other parts of the world; their political beliefs are often complemented by religious motivations and thoughts. In fact, interpretations of religious teachings may serve as justification for any act and spawn surrogate terrorists in other countries to carry out these deeds, allowing state sponsors an alibi and a measure of plausible deniability.

Subnational Groups. The members of this category work for political change. They are antigovernment elements that seek to overthrow their present regimes in order to create their own independent states within the boundaries of their nations (e.g., the Basques, Irish, Palestinians, or Sikhs). Groups that represent these interests are active not only in the area of dispute but generally worldwide. Thus, the victims of subnational terrorists are not limited to the country of the group's primary focus.

Domestic Groups

In this classification belong those terrorist groups who are indigenous to the United States. They operate in our nation, and their causes relate to the American social and political environment. In a nutshell, they seek to bring about change in our government and its policies by violent means. Some general subdivisions follow.

Leftwing Groups. These espouse a Marxist-Leninist doctrine and see themselves as the "protectors" and "liberators" of the American people in their fight against capitalism. They generally believe that their objectives can be realized through revolution. In the past, they were involved in a multitude of issues ranging from anti-United States stances to protest movements to anti-imperialist views.

Rightwing Groups. Rightwing groups typically are reminiscent of Nazi Germany, insofar as they profess the doctrine of superiority of the white race and are strongly antiblack and antisemitic. Although their main goal is white dominion over the United States, the focus and manifestation may vary along ethnic, religious, and cultural lines.

Puerto Rican Groups. These terrorist groups are inspired by strong nationalism—by their drive towards total independence from the United States. They seek to eliminate "U.S. imperialism" over the island, which means, particularly, the U.S. judicial and military presence there.

Jewish Terrorist Groups. Some Jewish terrorist elements operate in the United States. They include the Jewish Defenders, the United Jewish Underground, the Jewish Direct Action, and the Jewish Defense League (JDL). All take a strong pro-Israel stance and have sabotaged interests that they viewed as anti-Israel. Although everyone of these organizations has taken "credit" for terrorist incidents (especially in New York), the majority of these acts were claimed on behalf of the JDL.

Narcoterrorism

The marriage between narcotics trafficking organizations and insurgency/terrorist enterprises has become a topic of international concern. Such alliances threaten the stability of the nation in which they operate. They also imperil our government's policy objectives in those countries as well as the national security of the United States. The term "narcoterrorism" implies the combination of drug trafficking with the commission of violent acts, in other words, meaning drug trafficking by insurgent/terrorist groups to possibly influence government policy. The FBI has been aware for years that a cooperative relationship exists between terrorist organizations and narcotics traffickers in drug source countries, such as Colombia and Peru. Terrorist elements receive funding from drug lords through fees they collect for protecting growing areas, processing facilities, and distribution routes.

Special Interest Terrorism

This category principally relates to specific interests rather than political change. Through terrorist activities these groups attempt to force various segments of society and the general public to change attitudes about issues they consider important. Two such special interest groups exist in the United States. One is the animal-rights-oriented Animal Liberation Front (ALF) and the other the small, radical, environmentalist Evan Mecham Eco-Terrorist International Conspiracy (EMETIC). ALF maintains that humans are not the only important species on earth and opposes the use of animals in medical or scientific research. Therefore, its targets include medical and scientific laboratories, butcher shops, and stores that sell fur.

EMETIC contends that wilderness areas, wild plants, and animals ought to be protected from man, and that mankind should live in harmony with nature. While many people endorse similar views, they differ from these organizations in that they do not commit crimes to further their beliefs.

Although people often dismiss terrorist acts as senseless violence, actually, the perpetrators do have many objectives. The prime ones are to create fear and to intimidate, especially by committing dramatic, shocking deeds, that will guarantee them a wide degree of publicity. The crime scene becomes a theater in which the acts are aimed more at the people watching than the victims. Since most terrorist organizations are small, it becomes all the more critical that the feat be spectacular to give a distorted impression of the importance of their cause and the strength of their movement.

Apart from the propaganda value, other key motives are present:

1. *Obtaining concessions:* An example is the payment of ransom or the release of prisoners. An illustration is the hijacking of Kuwaiti Flight 422 in April of 1988 by Hezbollah terrorists seeking the freedom of 17 Shiite inmates of Kuwait prisons.

2. *Revenge:* According to the press, this had been the motivation for the bombing of Pan Am Flight 103 over Scotland on December 21, 1988, which killed 270 people. Specifically, it was committed in retribution for the accidental downing of an Iranian airliner by the U.S. cruiser *Vincennes* some six months earlier.

3. *Destroying state enemies:* This is a major aim of state-sponsored terrorists. For example, in February 1990 the FBI arrested an American citizen in California, who had been hired by a foreign diplomat to assassinate two foes of the diplomat's government. Another earlier instance (1983) involved a plot by Iranian students to chain the doors of a Seattle, Washington, theater

and set it afire, while several hundred opponents of Khomeini were watching a performance.

4. *The breakdown of social/political order:* This motive is typical of revolutionary or anarchistic terrorists. Two prime examples are Germany's Red Army Faction (RAF) and Italy's Brigate Rosse (BR), also known as Red Brigades. Both groups aim to destroy the existing forms of government in their countries through armed struggle and replace it with a revolutionary regime. The RAF successfully targeted and assassinated leading figures who symbolize imperialism and capitalism, such as the 1989 murder of Deutsche Bank Chairman Alfred Herrhausen. The BR's most notorious acts included the 1988 killing of Christian Democrat Senator Roberto Ruffili and the 1978 kidnap/murder of former Italian Prime Minister Aldo Moro, then president of Italy's Christian Democratic Party.

5. *Survival:* Terrorist groups need to perpetrate violent acts in order to retain credibility and reaffirm their purpose, in other words, to maintain their reason to exist. Furthermore, these activities reduce internal tensions and give the group cohesiveness.

TIMING OF INCIDENTS

As a general rule, highly skilled "professional" terrorist groups strike when the timing of acts is best for them. Therefore, they do not permit external events, such as the Gulf War, to dictate when to attack what targets, although they may use the Gulf War as a pretext or justification. Crucial operations require thorough logistical preparations, proper training, surveillance, and careful selection of targets (those that seem particularly vulnerable), and often gathering of additional intelligence. Moreover, the assault should pose a minimum of risk coupled with a maximum probability of success.

It has been observed that terrorists sometimes choose dates that are symbolically important for them. For example, Yu Kikumura, a member of the Japanese Red Army (JRA), was arrested in New Jersey transporting explosives in his car that he had intended to set off on the anniversary date of the U.S. bombing of Libya.

IMPACT OF THE GULF WAR

With the beginning of the Persian Gulf crisis in August 1990 and the threat of increased terrorist attacks (Saddam Hussein had called for a *jihad* or holy war against the United States and its allies), heightened security measures were taken throughout the United States, especially at airports, nuclear power plants, military installations across the country, Government buildings, and our borders with Canada and Mexico. From January 16, 1991 through March 15, 1991, over 200 terrorist acts were committed worldwide, and about half of them were directed against U.S. targets. Most of them resulted in property damage. According to State Department figures, none of the attacks against U.S. interests was performed by traditional Middle Eastern terrorist groups, but rather by indigenous organizations. This may have been due to our increased security and proactive measures, the speed of the coalition military success, and the "diplomatic" pressure on nations that had previously sponsored terrorism.

The Postwar Threat in Perspective

Since high-security alerts around the world cannot be kept up indefinitely without justification, sooner or later security may tend to return more or less to the levels that existed before the Gulf War. Nevertheless, this does not mean that the threat of terrorism has passed. The United States is a large country with long borders, an open society, and global political involvement. Therefore, it will remain vulnerable to terrorist activity. However, the threat needs to be put in proper perspective and should not cause us to panic or change our life. Intimidation and fear, especially fear of the unexpected and the elusive enemy, are the most effective weapons of terrorists. Our judgment must be based on the available facts concerning the probability of a terrorist attack. In 1991, there were relatively few incidents, most likely a benefit of our enhanced security. This, of course, is a strong argument against returning to previous security levels, especially with the ever-growing sophistication of the terrorist's tools.

HIGH-TECH TERRORISM

The great advances in technology, electronics, and weaponry have also been utilized by terrorist organizations in recent years. With the collapse of the Soviet Union, more sophisticated devices and arms will become available to them on the black market. Thus, the question is raised as to whether terrorists of the future will escalate violence into new dimensions. Are we going to see spectacular acts of mass destruction involving the use of nuclear, chemical, or biological arms? We know that some terrorist groups are so committed to the righteousness of their causes and ideologies, so disdainful of public opinion, and so unconcerned with destruction and casualties that they are quite capable of such a horrendous deed.

Moreover, our critical service networks—electric power, oil and natural gas, the telephone, interstate highways, air travel, telecommunications, the shipping industry, water supplies, financial transactions, and railroads are very vulnerable and could easily become a prime target of a terrorist group.

Hence, the potential certainly exists to create havoc, to damage highly populated industrial nations in various ways, especially through the destruction of critical services in their network infrastructure, and to kill large numbers of civilians by diverse means that will be briefly explored below.

The New Challenge of Nuclear, Biological, and Chemical Terrorism

The danger of nuclear, biological, and chemical terrorism continues to concern the FBI. In fact, many authorities believe that the eventual use of these deadly, volatile, and sometimes undetectable substances by terrorist groups is inevitable, particularly when revolutionary zeal is combined with fanatical religious fervor.

The Threat of Nuclear Terrorism.   Potential acts of nuclear terrorism include:

1. Acquisition of a nuclear device from a possibly friendly source, such as an Islamic former Soviet republic, and threatened or actual use of it.
2. Construction and threatened usage of an improvised nuclear bomb.
3. Capture of a nuclear weapon.
4. Assault on or sabotage of a nuclear arms production facility, an atomic power plant, or a nuclear waste storage site.
5. Attacking or stealing nuclear materials in transport.
6. Theft and utilization of radioactive substances as contaminants or in dispersion devices.

At the present moment, the FBI considers it more likely that a group will perpetrate a credible hoax involving any of these options as an act of extortion or garnering public attention than having and actually using a nuclear device. However, the agency recognizes its responsibility to collect as much timely intelligence as possible in order to prevent an attack or at least to respond to a crisis effectively through contingency planning.

The Threat of Biological/Chemical Terrorism.   The danger of biological/chemical terrorism presents a particular concern to the FBI because, compared to nuclear devices, biological/chemical agents are much more easily acquired, cheap to produce, and more difficult to detect. They can also be used against a variety of targets. The list of possible acts of biological/chemical terrorism includes:

1. A threat or real attempt to spread viruses and disease organisms among civilians, especially in densely populated areas, among livestock, agricultural products, water supplies, and natural resources.
2. The threat to explode or actually detonate an improvised or stolen chemical weapon.
3. The threat or the act of chemically contaminating municipal water supplies.
4. The threatened or ventured sabotage of a chemical production or storage facility.
5. A credible hoax of any of the preceding alternatives.

The likelihood that someone will commit an act of biological/chemical terrorism is considerably greater at the time of this writing than nuclear terrorism, particularly when we consider that (1) chemicals reportedly were used during the Iran/Iraq War; (2) chemical and biological agents had been readily available to terrorist groups and their state sponsors until the public furor during the Gulf War; and (3) for years the media had given increased attention to the potential uses of chemical/biological devices.

High-Tech Conventional Terrorism. The most likely means of future terrorist attacks involve high-tech conventional weapons and electronics. This may not sound as dramatic as nuclear or biological/chemical assaults. Nevertheless, it is a cause of considerable uneasiness. After all, terrorists today have access to advanced communication and surveillance devices, remote-controlled instruments for detonating bombs, high-order explosives, long-range rocket delivery systems, electromagnetic pulse generators (these can be employed to erase computer data bases of national security, banking, financial or other essential records), time-delay bombs with digital timers that may be set to detonate the device months later, and undetectable firearms and explosives.

Techno Terrorists and Computing. While we concentrate on the use of advanced technology and weapons as the tools of the techno terrorist, one particular aspect deserves special treatment: computer-generated disruption. The use of telecommunications, modems, and satellite transmissions has created a smaller, more accessible world. From the mountains of one country to the jungles of another, personal computers, linked by transmission, can enter corporations, military installations, governmental operations, and financial institutions and alter, erase, order, transfer, and obtain data that is believed secured. Terrorists utilizing these advances no longer need to travel and risk exposure, when the means at their disposal permit them to disrupt or even endanger the lives of the population upon instruction. It is feasible for terrorists to drain a financial institution of its resources (using the stolen funds to finance other terror activities) or to cancel telecommunication networks. Our protected communication networks and computer centers have concentrated on the physical aspects of security; yet story after story emerges in our news and law enforcement files describing how individuals bypass computer-protected passwords and are able to acquire highly sensitive corporate information and even to enter military databanks. While the usual response is that the information was not critical, maybe the definition of "critical" needs to be explored. The Gulf War gave computer hackers the opportunity to penetrate sensitive military data relating to troop movement. Employing hackers is obviously very beneficial to terrorist organizations, insofar as it advances their capabilities to dilute corporate finances, undermine the reliability of military confidential data, and disrupt the world's government information networks.

PREVENTION OF TERRORIST ACTIVITIES

While this chapter does not deal with actual investigative methods to stop or counteract terrorism, it will delineate some general preventive procedures.

Countering Techno Terrorists

Countering techno terrorists is a complicated, but not impossible chore. Intelligence networks of governmental services—such as covert operations, military surveillance, law enforcement informants, to name a few—can greatly reduce the opportunities for such violence. The two most important areas are maintaining an effective national technical ability to counter terrorism and improving the national response. Thus, the Nuclear Emergency Search Team (NEST) was established by President Gerald Ford to respond to possible nuclear incidents. Specifically, the organization's objectives are to find nuclear materials and weapons, even if planted in a large city, and disarm them. Much of NEST's technology is classified; however, it is known that their resources include radiation detectors and a whole range of other detection devices, lasers so sensitive that they can lift fingerprints from threatening and extortion messages, psychologists, psycholinguists, and, of course, the support of law enforcement and regulatory agencies. Their own personnel consist mainly of scientists and technicians, and their equipment can be placed in rented trucks, postal vans, attache cases, women's purses, and helicopters, thus guaranteeing a low profile. They are able to reach any scene in the United States within two hours.

Corporate Response to Acts of Techno Terrorism. What can the national corporate security manager do if a nuclear threat develops on the company's premises? He or she should notify the local FBI at once. This office will call the FBI's assistant director for criminal investigations, who manages the FBI's command post in Washington, D.C. NEST crews will be alerted, while the FBI and other experts try to establish whether the threat is real or not. If it turns out to be credible, the nearest regional NEST center will rush the appropriate specialists to the scene of the threat.

In general, it is a good idea if security managers of large corporations become familiar and interface with regional FBI offices. This ensures that the firm, as well as the federal teams who may respond to the facilities, is educated as to the concern's products, materials, storage areas, and security plans. These safety programs, which are formulated by the security director and other corporate representatives, may include not only the protection of the company's assets from disruption and terror attacks, but also the preparation for an emergency response to a potential incident. Encompassed in these should be a notification procedure to federal and local law enforcement agencies, political and emergency preparedness representatives. All ought to be brought into the process to train, educate, and counter any possible terrorist act. After all, planning and readiness are critical if an incident develops.

The Corporate Environment

Terrorist activities are often aimed at key individuals of a corporation. Therefore, preventive measures are specifically directed toward reducing the probability of becoming a victim and assuring safe business travel and marketing of products. Such an approach is "proactive," rather than "reactive" or after-the-fact.

Most terror attacks rely on the element of surprise to be successful because this allows the perpetrator(s) to control the situation while the countermeasures program is first getting into place. Preparing for a possible assault not only lessens confusion (and panic) by allowing for a regimented plan of action, it will also enable responding government agencies and law enforcement the opportunity to have immediate access to data that may be helpful in locating, identifying, and communicating for a victim's release. Moreover, it increases people's awareness of likely dangers and helps them make proper judgments in given circumstances, often before matters get out of hand.

Many international corporations plan for kidnappings or terrorist acts against employees and their family members living in foreign countries. They have devised designs that include a special fund for emergency expenses related to extortion, immediate travel, and extracting of individuals from threatened environments.

Establishing a Security Counterterror Program. Prior to the development and implementation of any counterterror program, a member of management must be designated as the responsible authority within the corporation to direct, plan, enforce, and follow through with such a procedure. This assignment is usually given to a professional from the law enforcement community or military.

Overall, the security program should cover personal safety planning, screening of potential employees, visitor identification, and, when necessary, escorting guests to secured areas. In addition, vendors, contractors, service personnel, and other nonemployees need to be identified or checked out.

The physical protection of any company facility—such as corporate officers, manufacturing plants, warehouses, and the like—is the first level of defense. A good plan, however, does not stop there and includes airplanes, trucks, boats, and shipments. It takes into account the training of security personnel and the teaching of employees; and it reinforces instructions with manuals. Besides, it considers a continuous review of guidelines, procedures, physical access, alarms, and notification policies. Certainly, some level of protection should be achieved through the use of security personnel, surveillance camera systems, and computerized card access.

Corporate management also has to allow for independent vulnerability tests, that is, conducting a security audit outside its own program.

High on the priority list needs to be personal safety planning. Unfortunately, many senior executives fail to reflect on the vulnerability of their position and activities as a potential target; nor do they always remember that even family members can become subjects of terrorist attacks. All too often bankers and other important individuals realize this only after a spouse or child has been seized and is held for ransom in an extortion scheme. Therefore, the importance of an executive's cooperation cannot be stressed enough.

Vulnerability assessments should be required of all management and senior executives. Their obligation to the shareholders and owners of the company necessitates their participation in such a program, which should comprise travel plan evaluations, hotel accommodations, and preparation for immediate removal from foreign countries, plus assessments of residences and family profiles, which would include family history, contacts, medical and banking references, telephone contacts, insurance policy information, passport data, countries frequently visited, photographs and fingerprints of all family members, vehicles used, auto rental and credit card information, listing of vacation homes or frequently used vacation locations, schools and colleges of children, and their telephone contact numbers.

Furthermore, it is recommended that a safe room be established if they live in a highly volatile country or community where anticorporate sentiment runs high. This room should allow for the safety of personnel and family members with communication capabilities, camera monitoring of the facility, food for a selected period (up to 90 days), fire extinguishers, gas masks, bullet-resistant suits, and water. First aid, candles, bomb blankets, portable radios, battery-powered electricity, electric stove, and other life support devices will greatly assist in the survival and safekeeping.

Special Events Management

The scene: Munich, Germany. The year: 1972. The event: the summer Olympics. The incident: the murder of Israeli athletes by Arab terrorists. Since this episode, elaborate security measures have become mandatory at special events, starting with the Pan American Games held in San Juan, Puerto Rico, in July 1979.

Exactly what is a special event? The FBI defines it as any event of such national or international significance occurring within the territory of the United States which makes it:

(1) an attractive target for terrorists and/or intelligence indicates a credible threat that a terrorist act will be committed at the event;

(2) of such a nature that the potential for collecting significant classified intelligence by hostile foreign governments exists; or

(3) an event of such national or international ramifications that FBI presence would logically be warranted to fulfill its investigative responsibilities.

Generally speaking, local, state, and federal law enforcement authorities—other than the FBI—are responsible for providing protection for special events taking place in the United Sates. The main input of the FBI on those occasions is to supply threat-related information in support of local police agencies.

In addition, the FBI, in coordination with the U.S. Department of State (USDS), has assisted foreign nations in their pre-Olympic planning upon request from their governments (e.g., the 1988 summer Olympics in Seoul, Korea, the 1992 Winter Olympic Games in Albertville, France, the 1992 summer Olympics in Barcelona, Spain, and the 1996 Summer Olympic Games).

APPENDIX. MOST FREQUENTLY USED FEDERAL STATUTES

In the absence of an all-encompassing federal law dealing with the issue of terrorism, the FBI depends on several different federal statues in its investigative and prosecutive efforts. The following are the most important:[10]

Title 18, United States Code

Chapter 7—Assault

Section 112: Protection of foreign officials, official guests, and internationally protected persons

Chapter 14—Civil Rights

Section 241: Conspiracy against rights of citizens

Section 242: Deprivation of rights under color of law

Section 245: Federally protected activities

Chapter 19—Conspiracy

Section 371: Conspiracy to commit offense or defraud United States

Section 373: Solicitation to commit a crime of violence

Chapter 25—Counterfeiting and Forgery

Section 472: Uttering counterfeit obligations or securities

Section 473: Dealing in counterfeit obligations or securities

Chapter 40—Importation, Manufacture, Distribution and Storage of Explosive Materials

Section 842: Unlawful acts

Section 844: Penalties

Chapter 41—Extortion and Threat

Section 873: Extortion by officers or employees of the United States

Section 875: Interstate communications

Section 876: Mailing threatening communications

Chapter 44—Firearms

Section 922: Unlawful acts

Section 924: Penalties

Chapter 47—Fraud and False Statements

Section 1001: Statements or entries generally

Section 1028: Fraud and related activity in connection with identification documents

Chapter 49—Fugitives from Justice

Section 1071: Concealing person from arrest

Section 1073: Flight to avoid prosecution or giving testimony

Section 1074: Flight to avoid prosecution for damaging or destroying any building or other real or personal property

Chapter 51—Homicide

Section 1114: Protection of officers and employees of the United States

Chapter 55—Kidnapping

Section 1203: Hostage taking

Chapter 95—Racketeering

Section 1951: Interference with commerce by threats of violence

Section 1952: Interstate and foreign travel or transportation in aid of racketeering activity

Section 1952b: Violent crime in aid of racketeering activity

Chapter 96—Racketeer-Influenced and Corrupt Organizations

Section 1961: Definitions

Section 1962: Prohibited activities

Chapter 103—Robbery and Burglary

Section 2113: Bank robbery and incidental crimes

Appendix II—Unlawful Possession or Receipt of Firearms

Section 1202: Receipt, possession, or transportation of firearms

Chapter 113—Stolen Property

Section 2314: Transportation of stolen goods, securities, moneys, fraudulent state tax stamps, or articles used in counterfeiting

Section 2315: Sale or receipt of stolen goods, securities, moneys, or fraudulent State tax stamps

Chapter 113A—Extraterritorial Jurisdiction Over Terrorist Acts Abroad Against United States Nationals

Section 2331: Terrorist acts abroad against United States nationals

Chapter 115—Treason, Sedition, and Subversive Activities

Section 2384: Seditious conspiracy

Section 2385: Advocating overthrow of Government

Title 26, United States Code

Chapter 53—Machine Guns, Destructive Devices, and Certain Other Firearms

Section 5861: Prohibited act

Section 5871: Penalties

Title 42, United States Code

Chapter 7—Social Security

Section 408: Penalties

NOTES

[1]*Terrorism in the United States* (Washington, D.C.: U.S. Department of Justice, Federal Bureau of Investigation, Terrorist Research and Analytical Center, Counterterrorism Section, Criminal Investigative Division, 1990, Appendix A, Definitions), p. 25.

[2]Ibid.

[3]Ibid.

[4]Ibid.

[5]Ibid.

[6]Ibid.

[7]Ibid. and *Terrorism in the United States*, 1988, p. 36.

[8]*Terrorism in the United States*, December 31, 1989, p. 15.

[9]Ibid.

[10]Ibid, pp. 44–46.

50
Terrorism: Assessment and Defensive Techniques

Isaac Yeffet

L. H. Coven

Thwarting the ever-present threat of terrorist activities depends on effective counterterrorist intelligence, both offensive and defensive. This chapter discusses both aspects and then focuses on the use of defensive intelligence in the "target-hardening" process. *Target hardening* is composed of three essential techniques: (1) threat assessment, (2) security survey, and (3) contingency planning. The chapter concludes with a case study appraisal of civil aviation and the contemporary terrorist threat.

Sound intelligence is the primary investigative weapon in the war against terrorism. The investigative function covers a wide variety of activities related to gathering and coordination of information, as well as the deployment of resources and actions to be taken.

OFFENSIVE INTELLIGENCE

Offensive intelligence is utilized in response to a specific threat received in relation to a terrorist group and a known target(s). Its principal objective is to prevent the actual act and secondarily to have a deterrent impact on the suspect group. It provides answers to the following questions:

1. Who is involved? What is the group identification?

2. How many are involved? What is the cell configuration?

3. What equipment and resources are available to the group members?
4. Where is the location of the operating base?
5. What are the structural aspects of the operating base? How thick are the walls? How many doors and windows are there? How many rooms are there? Are there plans available for the facility?
6. What kind of electronic equipment is present in the facility?
7. What are the differences between night and day? Physically? Population? Merchants? Traffic flow? Law enforcement?
8. Are there security personnel? Day? Night?
9. What are the communication systems in the site?
10. Where is the closest help available to the group?
11. Where is the headquarters of the group located?
12. What is the motivational aspect of the proposed act?

The gathering of this information involves support from agencies of other governments around the world. The knowledge gained should provide the basis for a preemptive strike to force a change in the group's plans and/or location. The possession of sensitive intelligence information and the strike damage promote a general feeling of uncertainty among terrorist leaders and concern over the location of other bases.

Procedurally, the role of intelligence develops in the following sequence:

1. Information is received regarding a possible threat.
2. The intelligence organization begins to test the information received:
    a. Military reconnaissance provides photographic data.
    b. Other friendly intelligence agencies are cross-referenced to verify and expand information. As many confirmations as possible are gathered to assess risk and credibility.
    c. Within legal constraints, Interpol may confirm the whereabouts and travel routes of connected parties.
3. The agent who supplied the information is tested.
    a. A polygraph examination is conducted.
    b. All character references for the individual are rechecked.
    c. The agent's status has been constantly updated. Loyalty quotient is reconfirmed.
    d. Information is compared to other information gained from agents in the area.
    e. The agent is asked to sketch and describe the location of group members in detail. This information is compared to the reconnaissance data.
4. A special unit is assigned to visit the area and clarify details through electronic and human surveillance.
5. Undercover personnel are utilized to gather more information and to help solve logistical problems. This requires considerable advance planning and the proper "cover" to ensure success. Documents, lodging, and vehicular requirements (land or sea) require coordination.
6. The strike initiative is planned.
    a. Determine and coordinate proper agencies to be involved, such as military specialists.
    b. Determine the time element, such as a night strike for cover.

 c. Determine a diversionary technique, like an air attack and special unit or land attack and special unit.

 d. For domestic targets, emphasize isolation, arrest, interrogation, and prosecution as opposed to military alternatives. Facility must be thoroughly searched for weapons, documents, and incriminating evidence.

DEFENSIVE INTELLIGENCE

Defensive intelligence is not utilized in response to a specific threat. Operationally, it has one (or a combination) of three objectives:

1. To retaliate after a incident has occurred.

2. To destabilize a group through preemptive action aimed at a specific target without connection to a known threat.

3. To evaluate and adjust the security system (target hardening).

Retaliation. When retaliation is necessary, the system has failed. In this instance the target is known, either due to the failure of the offensive program to act in a timely fashion or because the fundamentals of prevention have been unsuccessful. The same procedural elements apply as during the offensive condition with the exception of the agent needing to be tested. Confirmation of location, numbers, equipment, weapons, vulnerabilities, and motivations is essential.

 The primary purposes are:

- To reinforce the diminishing rate of return for the terrorist group, to show that retribution is highly probable and extremely costly.

- To diminish any reinforcement of purpose and/or achievement experienced by the group or its leaders.

- To heighten the very real and apparent penalty for taking credit for an event to further a cause. This produces a substantial dilemma and organizational strain. The cause must be made public, yet it is safer to remain anonymous.

- To create confusion over terrorist locations that may become the center of retaliation; to promote drain on terrorist resources necessary to protect a wider variety of positions.

Destabilization. The use of intelligence to immobilize and unsettle group members and leaders is an essential ingredient in the antiterrorist arsenal. Destabilization is fostered through the active selection of targets for specific purposes. It is target-specific, not threat-specific as in the case of offensive intelligence. Due to the seemingly random selection of targets, it acts as an indirect deterrent. In reality, offensive intelligence and this variety of defensive intelligence occur almost equally. Once again, all the preparation and procedural elements of offensive intelligence are operative.

Evaluation/Target Hardening. The constant need to evaluate and adjust security systems requires continual intelligence input. Gathering of intelligence for offensive or defensive purposes relative to preemptive action is difficult and can provide only limited protection. Its most advantageous use is in relationship to preventive measures.

Adjusting security systems in reaction to sound intelligence reduces vulnerabilities, diminishes damages in the event of an actual attack, and, most importantly, acts as a deterrent. All of these effects are commonly referred to as *target hardening*, which is aimed at developing an awareness of physical and operational threats in the use of force against a particular asset. The objectives of the target-hardening process are twofold: (1) to prevent or deny access to the target, and (2) to eliminate the opportunity to place or conceal a weapon or device that might cause damage, destroy property, or result in injury or death.

Components of the Evaluation Process

Three components of the evaluation process are: (1) threat assessment, (2) security survey, and (3) contingency planning.

Threat Assessment. This component enables the security professional to measure the possibility, probability, and predictability of the threat, and thereby to properly allocate security resources. It facilitates the review of the current status of information sources and helps delineate the accuracy of data. As part of the intelligence process, the threat assessment involves collection, evaluation, collation, analysis, and ultimately the correspondent conclusions and recommendations for action. Specifically, it requires:

- A systematic, logical, and orderly process that is adhered to and given priority. Assessment teams must be given deadlines and be monitored in this regard. Results must be presented in written form and be clear and concise.

- This process must be timely. Information may "turn" very quickly and result in wasted effort. Therefore, an assessment must be periodically updated in response to terrorist events and changes in tactics on the international scene.

- The information provided must be focused on the specific operational needs of the target. A variety of sources provide intelligence data. This data will be no more than informative if not refined and directed to specific facilities or areas. An effort should be made to develop sources that challenge preconceived ideas, that is, human contacts within the threat environment not normally associated with the intelligence community.

- Information must be usable, objective, and reliable. Input, if inaccurate or presented from an inappropriate perspective, can render the entire process ineffective. In this regard, those who prepare the threat assessment must have the suitable background experience for the specific target environment. They must be ready to accept a challenge to previously held concepts or prior assessments. The tendency to use this information to legitimize past decisions or procedures already in place is extremely dangerous. An effort must be made to focus on the current relevancy. Who or what is the immediate threat? Each piece of intelligence information must be evaluated for reliability and validity. This must be done before adjustments are made to the security system. Misinformation or "negative" intelligence is oftentimes used to confuse, mislead, or evaluate the security force.

- Dissemination and proper utilization of the information is the ultimate goal of the entire assessment process. Assuring the timeliness and accuracy of the assessment is only a prerequisite to the completion of the overall objective. Effective dissemination of the findings to those who have the authority, skills, and ability to use the knowledge is imperative. Proper procedures must be in place to guarantee circulation to the key decision makers. Only in this way will the entity at risk have the ability to respond to a potential incident.

The quality of the end user is as important as the threat assessment itself. To effectively utilize assessment content, end users must have the following qualifications: (1) a "need to know"; (2) the ability to make decisions and direct assets; (3) innovativeness and creativity; (4) analytical and critical skills; (5) open-mindedness and flexibility. Additionally, they must have strong communicative skills (oral and written) to be able to enlighten others. Finally, prior experience with threat information and familiarity with the specific threat environment is essential.

Benefits of the Threat Assessment Component. The incalculable benefits of threat assessment may be briefly summarized as follows:

- It is the most effective and valuable use of intelligence information.
- It provides a working guideline to evaluate risk and exposure levels.
- It provides continual feedback on terrorist methods and intentions.
- It updates terrorist group organizational strengths and weaknesses.
- It provides a framework to evaluate field experience.
- It promotes a comparison of current conditions to historical evidence.
- It tests the security system providing insight to vulnerabilities and encourages necessary adjustments.
- It breaks the security "routine," one of the greatest dangers to any security system.
- It enhances alertness on the part of security personnel, by providing contemporaneous evaluation techniques.
- It enables proper review of security personnel.
- It establishes the proper balance between the utilization of security equipment and the human element.
- It fosters evaluation of the dissemination process to ensure that those who need specific information get it.
- It enables the upgrading of security in the most cost-effective manner: (1) avoids the waste of "overkill" associated with the lack of information, (2) almost always results in better deployment of equipment and manpower, and (3) incorporates the time element factor in adjusting for special situations. All of this results in more effective contingency planning.

The Security Survey. An operational and physical audit of the target under consideration, the security survey is a natural follow-up to the threat assessment and coordinates with the assessment information. A thorough understanding of the threat analysis enables a more pragmatic approach to the survey/audit process and results in a fuller appreciation of the target's vulnerabilities. Those conducting the survey must have detailed knowledge of the target and all operational systems. Additionally, they should have a working knowledge of related subject matter, such as weapons technology, explosives security, terrorist activity, and historical precedents. Finally, as with those who must act on the threat assessment, they must be in a position of authority and possess the requisite skills to act on the survey input. When completed, the survey should become a part of the overall security program and be incorporated into contingency planning and operations, should that become necessary.

There are five phases in the security survey that clearly point to the need for considerable expertise:

Phase I: The anticipation of the threat and proper utilization of the threat assessment information to maintain a proper balance in the total spectrum of the security survey. Anticipation, kept in the proper perspective, is the key to organization of the task.

Phase II: The ability to recognize and interpret what is perceived to be a risk.

Phase III: The responsibility to organize, realize, and properly convey conclusions and recommendations.

Phase IV: The ability to weigh and analyze the cost to reduce the opportunity for terror or crime. The depth of protection and delay time, as deterrent factors in the elimination of opportunity, must be quantified in terms of cost. The implementation of a recommendation cannot exceed the cost of the item to be protected. In the terrorist arena, however, the cost of protecting human life makes this element the most difficult.

Phase V: Finally, the action taken based on the suggestions of the surveyor. The individual taking action must possess the commensurate responsibility and authority to act.

The survey and resulting report must be systematic and comprehensive. Nothing can be overlooked, no detail considered too trivial. The approach must be to consider the entire security envelope and all layers of protection. The physical status of the facility must be compared and contrasted to operations and to the procedural elements of the security program. At a minimum the survey should include:

Facility description:

Location/proximity to other facilities

Physical configuration

Function(s) performed

Staffing levels (types and numbers)

Visitor access (use and characteristics)

Law enforcement presence

Seasonal considerations that impact operations

External perimeter security:

Fences, gates, natural barriers

Zones of operation (safe distance to target)

Lighting conditions (natural and artificial)

Access controls

Areas of cover (equipment and human presence)

Intrusion-detection systems

Patrol procedures

Building(s) perimeter security:

Doors, windows, walls, roofs

Floors, basements, sub-basements

Building(s) internal security:

Connecting doors, walls

Ceilings, ductwork

Vaults, safes, storage areas, restrooms

Areas of cover (equipment and human presence)

Locks and hardware

Lighting

Intrusion-detection systems

Fire and safety systems

Operations/security procedures:

Security organization, staffing, supervision, training

Key controls

Hours of operation, opening and closing checklists

Employee controls, background, screening, identification

Visitor and patron controls, records, passes, restricted areas

High-value asset security

Communications (operations, emergency, security)

Incident reporting

Maintenance/housekeeping/vendor controls

Emergency/contingency plans

This list is by no means exhaustive but serves to identify the placement of the security survey within the defensive intelligence program. The surveyor is an educated and experienced investigative tool, who must possess a number of talents, including the ability to:

■ Analyze threats and vulnerabilities.

■ Make critical observations of physical and operational conditions.

- Break operations down into separate parts to uncover motives, causes, and effects.

- Use pretexts when necessary to elicit honest and accurate information.

- Verify the accuracy, genuineness, and validity of the subject matter under inquiry. Remove doubt by remaining independent throughout the audit.

- Isolate improprieties and segregate them from the survey task.

- Establish the truth through diligent investigation.

- Draw appropriate conclusions from accumulated facts.

Contingency Planning.   The third component takes into consideration the data provided by the threat assessment, along with the security status provided by the survey/audit analysis, and establishes procedures to deal with changing threat levels. It is a structured process that measures the potential for disruption by terrorist organizations, and culminates in a state of preparedness with the following objectives:

- The promotion of security through the emphasis of prevention and deterrence measures.

- Clarification and designation of duties and responsibilities for the various organizational units in the security plan.

- Enabling of the adjustment and enhancement of security on a timely basis.

- Establishment of minimum security standards and procedures.

- Establishment of a concise security plan that coordinates the responsibilities and relationships of the involved authorities.

Contingency planning requires a preplanned formalized organization, and implementation guidelines that include the physical and operational security plans and the emergency plan. The emergency plan covers incident response for fire, explosion, natural disaster, and the like.

The threat assessment information is constantly updated and compared to new entries. Data is collated on methodology, tactics, types of weapons and devices, individual profiles, and the form of demands. The intelligence is centralized to facilitate expedient review should a threat change or an incident occur. The bank of information provided by the threat assessment allows for contingency planning that sets levels of response for varying conditions.

The primary elements of the contingency plan include:

Definition of the rules and guidelines of engagement:

Establish appropriate response and tactics.

Identify elements and objectives to verify threat.

Set requisites for security forces and emergency support groups.

Maintain a controlled environment.

Identification of resources and definition of tasks:

Specify tasks and assign to operational elements.

Review operational and support responsibilities, and coordinate with overall objective.

Identify resources based on definition of tasks.

Assignment of responsibilities to organizational and operational elements:

Assignments are based on task requirements and functional areas of responsibility.

Ensure that the assigned responsibility will be performed.

Determine primary responsibility if more than one group or agency is involved.

Establishing a training program to test and evaluate the plan:

Identify training personnel.

Utilize exercises and incident "role playing."

Establish positive feedback to ensure that exercises and testing produce the necessary changes in the plan.

Revise the response organization, tasks, and assignments where appropriate.

Identify functional support as required.

Contingency planning allows for effective response in the face of changing threats. It evaluates the means, opportunity, and capability of the terrorist organization by tracking activity and continuously updating the information base. It provides a cost-effective approach for the protection of assets and human life.

These basic tenets of good security, including the effective use of intelligence mechanisms, are universally applicable in both the public and private sectors. The public sector and certain segments of the private sector (notably, the nuclear energy field) have been more diligent and therefore more successful in implementing these principles.

TARGET HARDENING AND CIVIL AVIATION

Civil aviation is by no means the only attractive target to the terrorist mentality. Any facility, installation, or human target that will provide easy access, cause excessive hardship, attract media attention, and impact on a large audience is subject to consideration. A list of physical targets might include power plants, natural sources of fuel, toxic chemical producers, the electronic media, water supplies, communications facilities, data centers, automated factories, military and diplomatic installations. Human targets include military personnel, governmental officials, diplomatic employees, business leaders, and media personalities.

Yet civil aviation has increasingly become a favorite target, suffering devastating terrorist attacks, because it has failed to respond to the most important aspect of the defensive intelligence function, that is, evaluation and, more specifically, target hardening.

The Lockerbie Disaster

In December 1988, a Pan American jumbo jet (Flight 103) departed Heathrow airport in London, en route to the United States. As it reached cruising altitude, over Lockerbie, Scotland, it was blown out of the sky, killing 259 on board and 11 on the ground. It was quickly ascertained the tragedy was most likely the result of a terrorist's bomb. This incident, more than any other in recent history, has revived public concern about terrorism. A Presidential Commission, investigating the circumstances, delivered a lengthy report to the President on May 15, 1990. It severely criticized the Federal Aviation Administration (FAA) for laxity and a reactive posture. Air carriers were, and still are, being scrutinized and pressured to increase the quality of security. The Air Transport Association (ATA), the industry association, and Pan Am management rejected allegations of negligence by pointing out that Pan Am was only an innocent victim, the real target being the United States government. The ATA went on to state that the civil aviation industry required the government to take a greater role in providing proper security, either through financial assistance or by taking over the security function altogether. The debate over responsibility for the security of civil aviation continues in the face of the terrorist threat.

Factors Contributing to the Vulnerability of Civil Aviation

Pan Am and the entire civil aviation community have been affected by a number of factors, both internal and external, contributing to their very vulnerable contemporary position.

First, the technological revolution (of which the jet age is a part) has created an atmosphere of limitless expansion. Virtually every industrial, governmental, and military function has been affected. This so-called globalization effect has created great centers of exposure and an abundance of targets whose destruction can bring catastrophic results. Moreover, the terrorists have profited from technological advances in weaponry, communication, and transportation. The speed, scope, and range of contacts among terrorist groups have been significantly magnified, resulting in greater coordination and enhanced striking power. Targets are no longer localized; ease of movement can quickly and efficiently transport terrorists to a site anywhere in the world, and just as efficiently remove them to safety. Conversely (and quite conveniently), if they choose to be patient and plan carefully, this ease of movement can bring the target to the terrorist's own territory (Pan Am 103). Finally, and of extreme importance, is the role of the media. The primary goal of terrorists is to reach the largest audience possible. Computer technology, satellite communications, and, once again, speed of transportation expedite media coverage and almost instantaneously capture the attention of the international community. Civil aviation is, at once, a tool and a target.

Second, American foreign policy in relation to acts of terrorism has grown steadily hard line since the Nixon presidency. As a result of attacks on Americans by international terrorist groups throughout the 1960s and particularly after the Munich Olympic massacre in 1972, the United States began a "no concession, no ransom" policy. Attacks on U.S. embassies and military sites in the late 1970s and early 1980s inspired more tangible efforts to protect foreign installations. Security at these locations has been strengthened considerably through the use of electronic surveillance, upgraded alarm and access systems, physical barriers, and Marine security guards. In essence, the government has responded by implementing policies and security mechanism that make its assets considerably harder to attack. Terrorists are not interested in military victories of the kind that produce "heroes." They seek to disrupt, to coerce, to make a cause known. Opportunities are restricted by long-term planning and financial considerations. Personnel must be chosen, trained, and assigned to tasks very carefully. Therefore, targets are also selected very carefully so as to provide the highest probability of success and connected publicity. Hard targets will be avoided for those more readily accessible. The result of the governmental initiatives has been to shift the burden of prevention to the private sector including civil aviation.

Third, the deregulation of the airline industry has had a dramatic financial impact. As summarized by Moore:

> In the past few years, the carriers who have disappeared from the scene are too numerous to mention; others are now barely hanging on. Of 150 airlines started after 1978, the first year of deregulation, 118 have failed or merged with other carriers. Even the venerable Civil Aeronautics Board disappeared from the domestic scene with deregulation. After deregulation, carriers no longer filed for just one or two new destinations a year; their expansion was dramatic—too dramatic in some instances. Some carriers bit off more than they could chew.[1]

All of this has had the effect of placing security far lower on the priority list than can be described as prudent. The pressures of the competitive marketplace divert the attentions and funds of airlines management to performance matters and revenue considerations; daily economic survival has become the overriding issue.

Fourth, the present security program mandated by the FAA is outdated. It stems from a spate of aircraft hijackings that occurred during the late 1960s and early 1970s, both domestic and international. The establishment of 100-percent predeparture screening of passengers and their carry-on items, and the implementation of the Air Carrier Standard Security Program (ACSSP) proved to be effective in the deterrence of the skyjacking threat. Although the ACSSP has been continually amended to attempt modernization, it has not kept pace with the adaptations of the terrorist enemy. Passenger screening relies on X-ray interpretation for carry-on items and metal detectors for the passengers. The system is concentrating on a threat that is more than 20 years old. Even the test devices used by the FAA to monitor carrier performance, such as a large dynamite bomb, pipe bomb, hand grenade, and toy pistols, have limited application in today's threat environment. The weapon of choice of the modern-day terrorist is an improvised explosive device (IED) utilizing sophisticated timing mechanisms and plastic explosives. Metal detectors and X-ray machines are not engineered to readily identify this type of device. The explosive used to destroy Pan Am 103 was discovered to be semtex, manufactured in Czechoslovakia and possibly the most potent ever to be produced (less than two pounds was used). "Czechoslovakian President Vaclav Havel said recently that his country, under the previous regime, exported to Libya 1000 tons of semtex, an amount Havel said is sufficient for the world terrorist community to make bombs for 150 years."[2] Simply stated, the equipment used today is not capable of reliably and consistently detecting the contemporary threat.

Coupled to the reliance on questionable equipment is the lack of attention to human input. Airlines routinely use contract guard companies to perform screening functions. These contracts are very often awarded to the lowest bidder, thereby ensuring that personnel will be poorly paid and not career-oriented. Not surprisingly, the cost to train these employees must be kept to a minimum and the results can be less than impressive. Recently the ATA established upgraded standards of employment and training guidelines for security screeners, and the FAA amended the ACSSP to coordinate with this effort. Unfortunately, although these standards and guidelines are a step in the right direction, they represent "catch-up" for years of neglect and only superficially correct some deficiencies. ATA has also developed a profile on the attributes of a superior screener (psychological testing) to help evaluate potential employees. Although this concept certainly has merit, it is a sad footnote that the representative for the company responsible for developing the test indicated at an annual ATA Security Seminar "the reading comprehension level had been geared to the fourth grade."

Fifth, the security function is not adequately defined and assigned to appropriate parties. It is not uncommon for the airline security department to be totally disassociated from passenger and baggage screening. Generally, this function is left to the airline's local operations manager (referred to as the station manager) who deals with the contract company's security representative. In some instances, the responsibility may rest with the airline controller or local financial manager. These individuals have many other pressing matters to attend to and are not professional security personnel. The security budget inevitably ends up intermingled with other operations and maintenance department budgets, allowing more flexibility in maneuvering for limited resources. Many times the result is an inflated security budget improperly representing expenditures. Additionally, this arrangement produces a conflict of interests for the operations manager, having to measure security concerns against performance and revenue production. Meanwhile the trained security professionals attend to more specific cost-related issues, such as ticket fraud and employee theft. These issues are more quantifiable against the bottom line and require the immediate attention of security experts. One general manager of security for a large international airline was overheard stating vociferously that his job was to control ticket fraud, not to screen passengers. This same person, while testifying before a Congressional Committee evaluating airline security, was aware neither of the number of personnel used to perform the screening function at the airline's station, nor of the amount of their hourly pay. Isolating the security department from the screening apparatus and placing it in the hands of operations managers are counterproductive measures that weaken the entire program.

Sixth, airports are difficult to protect. An abundance of valuable assets within the airport structure are sensitive targets. In addition, airports are transient in nature; people, cargo, and other materials and goods are constantly moving into and out of the protected area. A list of targets might include passenger terminals, fuel tank farms, public parking areas, unattended baggage areas, air operations areas, law enforcement facilities, public transportation areas, and others. The security professional must be aware of all these potential targets and also take into consideration the traffic flow during and after normal operational time frames. Passenger terminals present an especially difficult security problem. Most terminals were built with passenger convenience in mind, not security. They have an abundance of corridors and access points, many of which eventually lead out to the air operations area. Many taxiways pass within short distances of the terminal buildings and roofs, providing easy access for a would-be terrorist. Many airports have insufficient perimeter security and rely on distance and open area to act as a deterrent. Most land-side operations allow vehicles to pick up and drop off passengers within close proximity to the terminals. All these factors make the airport an attractive and soft target for terrorist groups.

Seventh, aircraft conveniently place persons from many different countries in a compact and movable "container" (Pan Am 103 carried passengers from 21 different countries). An airliner carrying passengers of many nationalities may be hijacked or destroyed, in order to exert pressure on the governments representing these individuals, to impel yet another government (the target) to accede to the demands of the terrorists.

CONCLUSION

1. Sound intelligence is the key to combatting terrorism, which is a unique form of criminal violence. The motives and methods of the terrorists present great obstacles to containment and deterrence of their activities. Postincident investigations in pursuit of justice become hopelessly bogged down in the unmanageable complications of international negotiations and political arrangements. Jurisdictional restrictions hamper law enforcement action, and lengthy, frustrating legal proceedings produce very limited results. The emphasis must be on preventive measures, not reactive solutions.

2. Defensive intelligence, utilizing the techniques of threat assessment, security survey, and contingency planning, is the primary weapon in the antiterrorist arsenal. When properly and diligently applied, these techniques provide for healthy, preventive security systems and promote target hardening. Terrorists seek wide recognition and attack where there is the highest probability of success. They will always measure their target carefully; hard targets will be avoided.

3. Civil aviation has become an increasingly attractive terrorist target. Subjected to a number of external market and economic pressures, the industry has failed to adjust to a changing threat. Security has fallen into a dangerous routine, and previously held concepts or assessments have not been adequately challenged. The security function has been assigned to those who have neither the required expertise nor the familiarity with the contemporary threat to act appropriately. There is an unhealthy reliance on outmoded technology and equipment to supplant the human surveillance function.

4. The FAA has maintained a reactive posture. Reporting on the Lockerbie tragedy, the President's Commission made 64 different recommendations for improvement in civil aviation security, noting "the destruction of Pan Am 103 may well have been preventable."[3] They found many flaws in the security system (human and technological), in FAA procedures and monitoring efforts, and in the proper dissemination of intelligence information to parties in "need-to-know" positions with the proper ability and authority to act. Throughout the report they emphasized the need for well-trained, highly motivated security personnel.

5. The United States has been fortunate not to have had to endure the volume of terrorist events experienced in other parts of the world. However, this may be coming to an end. The primary reason we have avoided the wrath of international terrorism at home is the logistical complications faced by terrorists as they plan, implement, and retreat from an operation. Much of their support for training bases, instructors, safe houses, weapons, explosives, forged documents, and finances has been willingly supplied by Eastern block countries. It simply has not been practical to strike in the West. However, we must recognize

the political transformation that has occurred in Eastern Europe and the Soviet Union. The democratization of these parts of the world will have significant impact on terrorist activities. As communist support withers, and security becomes tighter overseas (we have already seen signs of this happening), the shift to softer targets will inevitably occur. We must anticipate this possibility and prepare for its eventuality. As the President's Commission stated:

> It would be totally unacceptable to this Commission to rest on any conclusion that there is no domestic threat of terrorist violence against civil aviation until a plane is blown out of the U.S. skies.[4]

In conclusion, reacting to disaster is no longer tolerable. Proactive mechanisms based on accurate and timely intelligence that produce resistant targets is our strongest weapon against terrorism. We must start immediately to prevent another Pan Am 103.

NOTES

[1]K. C. Moore, *Airport, Aircraft, and Airline Security*, 2d ed. (Boston: Butterworth-Heinemann, 1991), p. xiii.

[2]President's Commission on Aviation Security and Terrorism, *Report to the President*, GPO Publication No. 0-226-884 (Washington, D.C.: U.S. Government Printing Office, 1990), p. 114.

[3]Ibid., p. i.

[4]Ibid., p. 80.

51

Hostage Taking: The Psychology of the Captor

Moorhead Kennedy

While I was held hostage by militant Iranian students and had little to do but read, I came across a passage in Gibbon's *Decline and Fall of the Roman Empire*. A city had handed over some of its citizens as hostages to a Roman general as surety for its compliance with a treaty. The city did not comply, which gave the Roman general every reason to execute them.

Instead, he spared their lives. Gibbon describes the hostages weeping with relief at the general's magnanimity. Since we, Iran's hostages, were not "out of the woods" ourselves, I identified strongly with the story.

The point is that the term *hostage* used to be a *legitimate* status. Today, the term most commonly refers to the *unlawful* taking and holding of innocent persons against their will in order to achieve a desired end.

This chapter identifies for the investigator key psychological factors to be exploited in dealing with a hostage taking. They could help to identify and forestall potential hostage situations. They could affect the personality of the negotiator selected, the style and timing of the negotiation, the decision whether or not to intervene (make a "rescue attempt"), whether or when to offer concessions, and what they should or should not be, and many other considerations.

The hope is that these insights will prove useful in postcaptivity interrogation of the captor and in the debriefing of the hostage.

HOSTAGE TAKING AND CRIME

We generally categorize hostage takers as criminals or terrorists. In February 1986, the Vice President's Task Force on Terrorism defined terrorism as:

the unlawful use or threat of violence against persons or property to further political or social objectives. It is generally intended to intimidate or coerce a government, individuals or groups to modify their behavior or policies. The terrorist's methods may include hostage-taking...

Criminal hostage taking lacks the political or social agenda that characterizes the terrorist. The line between criminals and terrorists, however, is easily blurred, especially in the case of terrorists who have been in the business for so long that the aspirations and/or grievances that originally brought them into terrorism, if not entirely forgotten, are no longer controlling. The means can corrupt the ends.

HOSTAGE TAKING AND GOVERNMENTS

Although hostage taking is normally regarded as an act of a subnational terrorist or criminal group, governments also kidnap civilians and hold them hostage. Hostage taking by governments is to be distinguished from a government's taking political prisoners, as in Central and South America, in the West Bank and Gaza, and, until recently, in the Soviet Union and South Africa. While such holding also violates the human rights of the victim, it is not considered hostage taking unless it embodies, or is expected to embody, some condition for their release.

Among other examples of the role of hostage taking by governments, my own taking by a political action group, the "Students in the Path of the Imam," was later ratified by the Revolutionary Government of Iran. Iran and Syria supported hostage-holding Lebanese Muslim Shiite groups in the 1980s. External political and economic factors caused both governments to withdraw that support in the 1990s. This helped to make possible the negotiated release of the Western hostages in 1991.

One spectacular example has been the taking and holding by the Israeli Government of Sheikh Obeid, a Shiite Muslim clergyman. The "snatch" was accomplished through a helicopter raid into Lebanese territory.

MOTIVES FOR TAKING AND HOLDING HOSTAGES

While some motives for taking and holding hostages are common to criminals and terrorists alike, others are more appropriate to the goals and grievances that are the mark of the terrorist. Whatever the purpose of the hostage taking, like any human activity it will be inspired by a mixture of motives. These include inner drives, necessities of life, and professional objectives.

Violence

For captors predisposed to violence, and seeking outlets for it, hostage taking offers many and varied distinct opportunities. The predisposition to violence can be exacerbated not only by drugs, but also by the captors' fear for their own safety. Particularly in the early hours following the hostage taking, before the hostage takers have settled into their new roles as captors, or if something goes wrong with their plan, they can panic and turn violent, striking out at hostages who refuse to cooperate.

Some of the violence, of course, is used to frighten hostages into submission or to gain more attention for their cause. Many captors have been diagnosed as "pseudo-psychopaths," putting on violent behaviors not because they are strongly of that disposition, but because the role they have adopted calls for it.

Money and Greed

Financial incentives are of more than one kind and reflect more than one motive. They include:

1. *Primary:* The ransom itself is the principal objective of the taking. This is more typical of criminal than terrorist behavior, although, as noted, the line is easily blurred.

2. *Ancillary:* Taking hostages becomes one means among many for raising funds for other terrorist activities. Whether from private donors, subsidies from governments, side businesses, or ransom, terrorist organizations must support themselves financially in some manner.

3. *Incidental:* Hostage taking generates opportunities for captors in their individual capacities to earn income. For example, two of our guards, "Mailman" and Hassan, went into business for themselves. Having appropriated plastic garbage bags from the Embassy commissary, they sought ways to market them for Iranian housewives.

Employment

Like crime, terrorism offers meaning and excitement to rootless, unemployed, and unskilled young people without hope of opportunity in legitimate occupations. Not limited to the Middle East or the Third World, some root causes of terrorism, as well as of crime, are latent in the American scene. Consider an educational system that does not adequately prepare young people for employment, coupled with a faltering economy that may disappoint the hopes, especially of minority groups. Highly labor-intensive, hostage holding provides jobs for the unskilled.

Sense of Importance, Prestige

Through the taking and holding of hostages, particularly prominent ones, captors can acquire prestige and a sense of importance not otherwise available to them. As one example, a group of Iranian hostages was moved to Isfahan for three months. At the end, as we were led away to be returned to Tehran, one of the locally hired guards began to cry. Guarding us had clearly been the biggest moment of his life, never again to be repeated.

Similarly, in Lebanon, Shiite captors, who otherwise would be unknown outside their community, have found themselves world figures, negotiating with the United Nations and sovereign governments.

Power

Brian Jenkins, a terrorism expert from the Rand Corporation, has written that "terrorism is about being in control, about having power." Like leaders in organized crime, terrorist leaders have strong power drives. If frustrated by existing political, social, and economic circumstances, they hope to gain power by irregular means.

It has been argued that many captors in fact suffer from feelings of inadequacy and low self-esteem. Especially when combined with prestige and publicity, power bolsters self-esteem. Some of our guards clearly relished the power that they were able to exercise over their hostages.

Security

A major drive of hostage takers, in part, security reflects feelings of inadequacy. More importantly, prolonged hostage holding increases the risk factor in their operation. At the same time, holding hostages can in itself be a form of insurance against armed liberation and subsequent retaliation.

Security, combined with prestige and investment, have been suggested as among the reasons why Lebanese Shiite groups held onto their Western hostages years after the reasons alleged for the taking had ceased to be relevant.

Bonding

Among the motives that draw young people into terrorism is a need to belong. Terrorists attach importance to deeds that bond their group. Hostage taking and holding, unlike a short-term activity such as a raid or demolition, is a continuing assertion of group purpose and identity.

Relationships with Hostages

Throughout a prolonged captivity, relationships develop between captor and captive. My fellow hostage, Col. Charles Scott, kept in touch with his guard long after his release. My guard, Abbas, used to listen to my wife, Louisa, on Voice of America. "Your wife," he told me, "is doing so much to effect your release."

Such normal human relationships should be distinguished from the so-called "Stockholm syndrome," in which the hostage becomes dependent on and identifies with the captor, to the point of taking the captor's side as against that of possible liberators. Hostages suffering from this identification often turn strongly against their captors after a period of time.

Assertion of Sense of Identity

Hostage taking is a way of reminding the world that a nation or group exists, with aspirations and values to be taken seriously. A familiar parallel is that of adolescents, who in an effort to establish their own identity distinct from their parents, and in search of recognition of that identity, engage in attention-getting acts.

On the fifth anniversary of the embassy takeover, on "ABC Nightline," I asked Hossein Sheikholeslam, my former senior captor, what they had hoped to gain from taking and holding the staff of the U.S. Embassy. He replied that, before the takeover, many Americans did not know where Iran was. Since the takeover, Americans understand, "What Iran says, what Iran stands for."

Intimidation and Political Leverage

Hostages can be taken and held in order to induce others to pursue a course of action desired by the captors, or to forestall action they wish to prevent. For example, Western hostages in Beirut were taken on the pretext of forestalling the execution and to force the release of the "ad-Da'wa 17." These were Muslim Shiite terrorists arrested, tried, and convicted by the government of Kuwait for murder and arson.

Even when two members of its ruling family were taken hostage on a hijacked airliner in order to force the same release, the Kuwaiti Government held firm. The "ad-Da'wa 17" were liberated by the invading Iraqi Army in 1991. They returned to Lebanon, where some reportedly participated in the negotiation to release the Western hostages.

Retaliation/Revenge/Punishment

Hostage taking offers opportunities to pay back an individual, nation, or society for real and fancied grievances. American hostages from TWA 847 in Beirut, in June 1985, were shown mutilated survivors of villages earlier bombarded by the U.S. Navy. One hostage, a Navy diver, had already been murdered.

Distinctions among these motives are not easy to draw. For example, our captors used to tell us, "We're not punishing *you*. We have nothing against you personally. We are punishing *America* for its great crimes." At the same time, they threatened to "turn us over to the courts" to be tried individually for "espionage."

On the domestic scene, hostages are sometimes held in punishment for alleged personal wrongs to the holder, such as marital infidelity or loss of employment, or because they are in some way deemed symbolic of injuries the holder claims to have suffered at the hands of society (perhaps from the class of people represented by the hostages).

Retaliation equates with reprisal and often embodies an element of intimidation (already discussed). For example, the German occupation authorities in France during World War II took and executed hostages in reprisal for armed action against them by the French Resistance, to discourage such activities in the future.

Publicity

As our senior captor in Iran pointed out, through hostage holding, his small radical group found itself "on prime time." Complete with agonizing families, hostage holding lends itself to TV, which in turn makes the cause of the captors known worldwide.

Investment

Once hostages are taken, they become costly in terms of time, energy, financial expense, and other forms of support. Captors are reluctant to let go of their investment without some benefit gained.

Indoctrination and Propaganda

Hostage holding offers captors a captive audience, one that cannot get up and leave if bored by the presentation. For example, in the early days of my own captivity our captors showed us films of the Jaleh Square Massacre of September 1978, in which the former Shah of Iran's Imperial Guard fired on unarmed students. Then they reminded us how President Carter, committed to human rights, had reiterated his support for the Shah even after the massacre.

In showing us these films, our captors expressed the hope that we would, upon our release, "tell the truth" to the American public. Similarly, the captors of TWA 847, who displayed mutilated villagers to their hostages, expressed the same hope. Our captors could not, however, make up their minds whether they wanted to "convert" us or, through our mistreatment, "punish America for its great crimes."

On the night before our release, they returned to the theme that we might go home to tell their version of events. By their conduct toward us, however, they had largely forfeited that possibility.

Efforts to indoctrinate hostages can be turned around against the captor. For example, we had a guard called Hassan who, among his other duties, escorted us to the showers in another building of the Embassy compound. This privilege was accorded us once every 10 days.

One evening, Hassan took it upon himself to indoctrinate us. We were told about the evils of the former Shah, and the support he had enjoyed from the United States government. America was clearly responsible for all that had gone wrong in Iran. Finally, I spoke out: "All right, Hassan, what did the Shah do? He locked you up, cut you off from contact with your families, and *gave you showers once every 10 days!* If, Hassan, what the Shah did was wrong, what are you doing to us?" Taken aback, Hassan said something about punishing America, not us, and left our cell, never to attempt our indoctrination again.

Quite independent of efforts to indoctrinate them, hostages emerge with varying viewpoints toward their captors' causes, but all shaped by their experience. Some of us in Iran, like some of the passengers on TWA 847, emerged feeling that we had gained a deeper understanding of the causes of Third World antipathy towards the United States.

But others, in both hostage groups as well as among individual "Beirut hostages" not released until much later, emerged more hostile to their captors and their causes than they otherwise might have. Generally, this difference depended not on the captor or the cause, but on the personality of the hostage and on the coping devices relied on by the hostage to get through captivity. The Stockholm syndrome has been mentioned. Some Beirut hostages reported that they had been sustained by a high level of anger. Some, like myself, chose acceptance of our situation and of our captors.

JUSTIFICATIONS FOR TAKING AND HOLDING HOSTAGES

Terrorists justify hostage taking in terms of higher goals or grievances. These can be political and national, religious and ideological, or economic and social in nature. A homeland is to be recovered, an oppressor overthrown, an ethnic or cultural minority given fairer treatment or political autonomy, a God-given or secular belief system and accompanying way of life advanced or defended, or a more equitable distribution of the world's goods and opportunities made possible.

A more complex series of justifications may be classified under maintaining ethnicity and culture. This category was brought to the world's attention on November 8, 1991, when terrorist elements blew up the main building of the American University of Beirut (AUB) on the occasion of the University's 125th anniversary. AUB is emblematic of Western influences that many Muslim fundamentalists consider antithetical to their beliefs, cultural patterns, or vision of the kind of Middle East they want. They want the influence of the West ended, because, as they argue:

- Its personal values, epitomized by recreational as opposed to family-centered sex, are decadent.

- Its social and economic values are wasteful and greedy, favoring the rich instead of the poor.

- The gap between self-proclaimed American political values and its foreign policy is hypocritical.

- Superficially appealing secular Western values will undermine their own Muslim values, which they consider superior.

- The acceptance of Western values and ideas impedes the development of their own sense of identity (already discussed).

Almost all the American hostages held by Shiite Muslim groups in Beirut were similarly emblematic. They are communicators of Western culture: Christian missionaries, media correspondents, or, in the vast majority, faculty and staff of American educational institutions in Lebanon. Taking and holding them reflected their rejection of the West.

In the United States, as evidenced in the 1991 gubernatorial elections in Louisiana, some groups define their identities through rejection of other races and cultures. Some see their traditions and values threatened by these groups. For example, *The Covenant, the Sword, and the Arm of the Lord* believe that God's chosen people do not include Jews or blacks. Many such groups further their objectives through terrorism.

AMBIVALENCES OF THE HOSTAGE TAKER

Cultural

Hostage takers can entertain very mixed feelings about the dominant cultural forces they are trying to resist. Much as they may reject our values and resent our relative success, they envy it, and would like to achieve what we have achieved. To many who feel threatened by our dynamic culture, we Americans nevertheless remain role models.

Such mixed feelings often take the form of love/hatred or admiration/low self-esteem. The violence displayed towards hostages, as well as criticisms of the United States—hitting out at that which makes them feel inferior—is a reflection of these mixed feelings.

Other hostage takers handle these conflicts without apparent stress. One evening, our room guard received a visitor, clearly a member of our captor group. Unlike our guards, however, who pridefully wore their captured Marine fatigues, this young man was a vision of preppiness—wearing a sports jacket, button-down shirt, tie, gray flannels. I asked him where he was going. He replied, "I'm returning to Georgetown."

Moral and Ethical

Hostage takers often display absolute certainty that their cause is "right." Because they are in the minority as well, this combination, in their eyes, justifies criminal acts such as hostage holding. This paradox was well expressed by Alexander Ulianov, a terrorist (and older brother of Lenin), who in 1887 was executed by the Tsar's government. In his farewell letter to his mother, he wrote:

> Terror is the only form of defense to which a minority strong only in terms of its spiritual strength, and knowledge of the rightness of its cause, can resort, against the physical strength of the majority.

Hostage takers often start out as idealists, with a concern for justice and a rankling sense of injustice. Yet hostage taking is itself a denial of justice to its victims. This generates an ambivalence that can be a source of strain to captors. One of our more idealistic guards, finally accepting that our captivity was unlikely to spark a world revolution, resigned. Over the longer term, hostage holding can corrupt a seemingly laudable larger purpose.

As we have also noted, captors may engage in violent behavior in order to intimidate their hostages. This can arouse in them feelings of guilt. Sometimes they will attempt to make amends through gentle or even caring behavior. Hostages never know which behavior they are likely to encounter.

For example, during the "mock execution" of the Iran hostages in February 1980, designed only to frighten us, our captors wore masks. Afterwards, talking to us, Hassan tried to pretend that the mock execution had been carried on by a different group. (Thanks to his height, I had easily recognized him in the moments before we were blindfolded). Later, some of our captors apologized for their unnecessarily brutal behavior.

On November 18, 1991, Terry Waite and Thomas Sutherland were released after years of captivity, which they spent chained to a wall. Their Lebanese Shiite captors reportedly said to them: "We apologize for having captured you. We recognize now that this was a wrong thing to do, that holding hostages serves no useful constructive purpose."

MAILMAN: PORTRAIT OF A HOSTAGE TAKER

The personality of Mailman, our senior guard for four months, illustrates the intertwining of motives, justifications, and ambivalences.

Mailman had an almost parental interest in his charges. When a Mullah (Muslim clergyman) came to visit, Mailman, who found out that I spoke some Arabic, got me to say something in that language. As the Mullah and I conversed in Arabic, Mailman stood by proudly, like a parent basking in a child's accomplishments.

Mailman liked to give us things—such as candies and cookies—and he expected us to be grateful. His most important gift, mail from home, was censored and not always delivered. This occasioned strains. One day, convinced that Mail man was holding back on me, I lost my temper.

Mailman was furious. "You will not curse me," he said, and stomped out of the room. The next day, after I had apologized, Mailman reappeared with some color photographs of my parent's home on the Maine Coast, taken from a letter I was obviously not destined to receive. "I thought," he said, "that these would look nice on your wall."

Mailman hoped for the favorable regard of his charges. With those who had advanced degrees, like myself, and more sophisticated than he, he could not feel entirely comfortable. We knew that he spent a great deal of time with the younger Marines, whom he thought he could impress more easily. The Marines despised him, however, referred to him as "Eel."

This hurt Mailman's feelings. "Some of the hostages," he said to us with a baffled look on his face, "are very severe."

Mailman's desire to please, combined with a flair for administration, brought us such benefits as a library and an exercise room. He was particularly proud of his video tape theatre, situated in a former Embassy office.

Mailman liked the most sentimental Walt Disney films and, most objectionable to me, *Gilligan's Island*. Since this was *his* video tape theatre, and since he saw himself as an authority figure, it was not up to us to question his taste.

The walls of the video tape theatre were decorated with posters intended to indoctrinate us. One featured the Chicago Police beating up student demonstrators at the Democratic Convention of 1968. "You see," Mailman would say, pointing to the poster, *"human rights."* On another wall, a poster exhorted America to "Stay out of our country, stay out of our region." One day, I could stand it no longer.

"Mailman," I said, "Suppose the Russians invade your country as they are now invading Afghanistan. What will you do?"

"Oh," Mailman replied, in no way embarrassed, "You will have to come to our defense. We're too important to you."

One day, an International Red Cross representative was brought in to see us. He told us that some of the hostages had been interrogated extensively about their alleged intelligence activities before the takeover, to the point where some were suffering from depression. Had this happened to any of us?

No one replied, because no one dared. Mailman was keeping his eyes fixed on my roommate, Rick Kupke. Shortly before, in the library, after the rest of us had been led back to our room, Mailman had held Kupke back. He then cross-examined him on why, on the day of the takeover of the Embassy, Kupke had helped to destroy the central files.

Kupke had already paid for doing his duty. The students who broke into the code room, in interrogating Kupke, had threatened to cut his eyes out. Mailman knew that there was nothing further to be learned from Kupke. Interrogating him anew had only provided an outlet for Mailman's cruel streak.

"Don't ever forget," Mailman once reminded us, "we can keep you tied to a chair for the rest of your time with us, or we can kill you."

CONCLUSIONS

Hostage takers are not faceless Indians like those portrayed in early westerns. They are people. We may not agree with their ideals, and certainly not with their definitions of what is morally permissible to do in order to pursue them.

Disapproval by itself, however, is never enough. The first step in dealing with a hostage taking is to try to understand the complex personality and drives of the captor. The hostage negotiator needs to communicate an understanding of the captors' goals and needs.

Underestimating the role of the ideological or other "higher" motivations would be as great a mistake as romanticizing the captors or overrating the extent to which their "better side" in fact determines their behavior.

52

Hostage Negotiation: Guidelines for a Team Approach

Anne R. Sowinski

Hostage negotiation is a very complex process of moves and countermoves by a law enforcement hostage team to save lives and to resolve a volatile conflict situation. Since there are always two parties to a conflict, the process also involves actions by one or more hostage takers with goals diametrically opposed to those of the negotiators.

The complexity of the situation is exacerbated by the heightened emotions of the hostage takers' mood swings and a breakdown of their coping mechanisms. When such a crisis situation develops, cool-headed police intervention must be taken. The hostage negotiation team and guidelines for implementing its rationale are discussed in this chapter. Most people would agree that it has been proven to be the most effective approach by law enforcement in achieving a peaceful, life-saving resolution of hostage-taking situations.

The negotiating police response requires harmonious team action. Specialized police units, at times from different law enforcement jurisdictions, must work cohesively and uniformly towards the common goal of the safe release of the hostage. To achieve this ultimate goal, as much time as necessary is allotted for negotiations. The primary concern is the safety of all persons. Deadly physical force should be used only as a last resort to protect lives.

EMERGENCE OF THE NEGOTIATED APPROACH

Hostage negotiation has achieved tremendous technological advances since its inception immediately after the Attica State Prison riot in 1971 and the Munich

Massacre in 1972. On September 9, 1971, in the maximum security prison at Attica, New York, 1200 prisoners seized "D Yard," taking dozens of hostages. The demands were numerous and extreme. In the four violent ensuing days, a guard and three inmates would die at the hands of prisoners; 10 hostages and 29 inmates were killed by correction officers, and state troopers and 89 more would be left seriously wounded. This would become the deadliest prison uprising ever in American history. Over 20 years have passed, and civil and class-action lawsuits are still being settled with damages totaling in the millions.

One year later, on September 5, 1972, eight Palestinians would enter the Israeli dormitory at the Olympic Village in Munich, Germany, taking nine athletes hostage. Twenty hours later, four hostages and one German police officer would be killed by gunfire, and four additional hostages would be killed by a hand grenade, all at the hands of the terrorists.

Prior to 1972, the standard police practice in dealing with hostage takers had been to offer two choices: surrender or face a full police assault. Immense political and personal ramifications, suffering, and death had been encountered in both Attica and Munich. The resulting tragedies begged for a better solution. Law enforcement had to find an alternative to a full police assault. In the ensuing years, hostage negotiation has proved to be a viable life-saving option.

INTELLIGENCE GATHERING

In the negotiated approach, every member is involved in the team effort; each has a vital role to play. When time permits, the hostage negotiator has many resources available to attain the ultimate goal of safe hostage release.

Modern technology has provided sophisticated information-gathering devices. The state-of-the-art electronics available to the hostage negotiator include contact microphones and under-door sound-enhanced microphones. Essential for the hostage negotiation team is video equipment such as camcorders, pole cameras, pinhole camera lenses, long-range telephoto cameras, hand-held monitors, and audio equipment such as body transmitters and tape recorders. Additional technical equipment, such as infrared light goggles, fiber optics, and night vision scopes, greatly enhance the intelligence gathering necessary for the extended hostage situation. Telephones adapted for negotiations, mobile cellular telephones, and portable fax machines enhance communication capabilities. The robot, previously used for bomb disposal, has been adapted for hostage situations. It has the capability of intelligence gathering utilizing audio and video viewing and recording. The need for various equipment depends on the situation. Personnel should be dedicated specifically for this technical response and support.

Contacts should be available for assistance on a 24-hour basis within various utility companies such as gas, electric, telephone, and water. Control of utilities has proven to be invaluable for hostage negotiators. For example, the telephone could be disconnected preventing incoming and outgoing calls, both of which can seriously hinder negotiations. During a recent hostage situation in New York City, media personnel called the hostage taker and began interviewing him in the midst of police negotiations. Turning off the water supply and controlling the heating or air conditioning can create a very uncomfortable environment for the subject. If the subject has a television or radio, disconnecting the electricity prevents information regarding the police operations from being revealed. This can be very critical to negotiations. Water and electricity could later become bargaining tools.

The information age has also brought with it the art of criminal investigative analysis. While not a new concept, it has become much more sophisticated. Using psychology in evaluating a hostage situation is another tool for acquiring the safe release of the hostage. (It is employed in criminal investigative analysis as explained in Chap. 28. This approach can be utilized in conjunction with other investigative tools and negotiation techniques.

TEAM ROLE RESPONSIBILITY

The hostage negotiation team consists of several roles: the primary negotiator, the coach or backup negotiator, the scribe, the floating negotiator, the investigative team, and the hostage supervisor/team leader.

The Primary Negotiator

The primary negotiator is selected on the ability to communicate and establish rapport with the hostage taker. The race, age, sex, vernacular, and phraseology of the primary negotiator should be similar to those of the subject. Having common personal traits can be beneficial, although their absence is not critical.

A premise in early negotiation theory was that the female negotiator could only be used in the limited capacity of negotiating with a female hostage taker. Experience has shown that the female negotiator is just as effective as the male negotiator regardless of the hostage taker's sex. Depending on the situation, the female negotiator can come across as less threatening and create a calmer atmosphere conducive to a peaceful resolution.

A fundamental principle for the primary negotiator is to avoid lying. Tricks and deceit only harm whatever progress may have been attained. Once a negotiator is caught in a lie, regaining credibility becomes extremely difficult, if possible at all. When a lie does occur, the only option may be to replace the primary negotiator. The lie just creates one more obstacle with which the replacing negotiator must contend. It also presents problems for the negotiation team in the event this individual is confronted at a later date.

Avoid making unrealistic promises to the hostage taker. This compromises the credibility of the primary negotiator.

Personalizing the hostage can create a more humanistic environment, thereby decreasing the incidence of violence. Avoid buzz words such as "hostage," "kill," "shoot," and "prison." For example, a male may be holding his wife hostage in a domestic situation. Reference should be made to her by first name. The hostage taker may be less likely to inflict harm on "Mary"—a specific person, than on the "hostage"—a vague general category.

Remain nonjudgmental and keep the subject in a problem-solving mode. This aids in the venting process, which diffuses emotions leading to a nonviolent resolution.

All demands, as well as requests made by the hostage taker, are communicated directly from the primary negotiator to the backup negotiator. The backup negotiator also prevents interruptions while negotiations are in progress.

Suggestions or communications will pass solely through this route and must not be violated by any person regardless of rank or position.

The primary negotiator can encourage what is known as the Stockholm syndrome, which was first identified on August 23, 1973 in a bank robbery in Stockholm, Sweden. In that incident, a prison escapee, brandishing a submachine gun, held four employees hostage for six days. Surprisingly, the hostages feared the police more than their captor. At the culmination of the incident, the hostages felt no animosity towards their captor. The positive feelings manifested by the hostages toward the hostage taker, accompanied by negative feelings toward the police, are indicative of the Stockholm syndrome. Furthermore, the hostage taker can develop positive feelings toward the hostages. Feelings of hostility toward the police can continue even after the situation has ended. The police will be viewed by the hostages as perpetuating the hostage situation.

Evidence of positive feelings are created when the hostages become protective of the hostage taker. It is believed that the subject "took away" their life and then gave it back. This may also extend beyond the incident. One of the hostages from the Stockholm siege became so emotionally involved that she later became engaged to the hostage taker.

The Stockholm syndrome is believed to be an automatic, unconscious, emotional response experienced by the traumatized victim and the subject. It requires that the hostage have an extremely high stress level while being in a life-threatening situation. A positive emotional bond can be created and nurtured by the hostage, the hostage taker, and the police. The hostage interprets the absence of negative experiences such as beatings, tortures, and sexual assaults as positive actions. Although not always evident, this syndrome frequently occurs as a coping mechanism. As long as no overt abuse is inflicted on the hostage, time will assist the hostage negotiator in encouraging the Stockholm syndrome. If the hostages are isolated, the negotiator can attempt to encourage interaction. Discussing the hostages' health and family matters personalizes the situation. Humane qualities should be emphasized by the hostage negotiator. The stronger the Stockholm syndrome develops, the less likely the hostage taker will harm the hostages.

Backup Negotiator

The backup negotiator monitors negotiations. Coaching and supporting the primary negotiator is very important. If the primary negotiator requires rest or even replacement, the backup is the likely candidate to continue negotiations. The stress levels must also be monitored. The primary negotiator cannot get so deeply involved with the subject that objectivity is lost.

Scribe

The scribe is responsible for documenting critical information necessary for the negotiation process. This data includes identifications, descriptions, weapons involved, demands, deadlines, time and number of firearm rounds discharged, in addition to supervisors and other personnel present at the scene. This is documented for visual observation by writing on a large easel pad or butcher block type of paper. The paper is then taped to a prominent wall where negotiations are taking place. The scribe could become another candidate for replacement of the primary negotiator, if necessary.

Floating Negotiator

The floating negotiator moves freely between the inner and outer perimeters. The *inner perimeter* is a frozen area, strictly consisting of the incident location. Ballistic protection is required appropriate to the level of threat present. Entrance into the inner perimeter should be restricted to the minimum amount of police personnel necessary. The *outer perimeter*, an area sufficiently removed from the actual scene of the incident, is for members of the media, civilians, and additional police. Transporting needed equipment, reliefs, and other necessary tasks is the responsibility of the floating negotiator.

Reliefs are critical in an extended hostage situation. A rotation process is recommended for reliefs. Arriving negotiators need to be updated prior to becoming involved in the negotiation process. The scribe relieves the backup negotiator; the backup negotiator relieves the primary negotiator, thus optimizing all resources.

Investigative Team

The investigative team consists of negotiators as well as detective investigators who conduct canvasses and interviews, gathering as much intelligence as possible relative to both the subject and the hostage. Past criminal records, along with medical and psychiatric histories, are necessary for profiling the hostage taker. Occupations, military experience, gang or terrorist affiliations, marital status, religion, and drug/alcohol use are all important factors that need to be exposed. This information can assist in the decision-making process necessary for the safety of all persons.

Hostage Supervisor/Team Leader

The hostage negotiation supervisor/team leader is responsible for providing adequate negotiators and supervising them accordingly, in addition to conferring with and assisting the tactical team supervisor and the on-scene commander. Sufficient expense funds must be made available for any purchases that may facilitate negotiations.

While the hostage supervisor/team leader is the buffer between the primary negotiator and ranking officers, caution must be exercised so that negotiation and command duties are kept separate. Commanders and other high-ranking officers need to understand that negotiators don't command and commanders don't negotiate. If the hostage taker believes that the negotiator is a high-ranking official, a quick resolution may be expected. Avoid creating the belief that the negotiator is the final decision maker. This may have serious negative repercussions. The on-scene commander and other high-ranking officials must make objective assessments and command decisions without being influenced by personal dealings with the hostage taker. Therefore, maintain role distinctions within the hostage team so that all aspects of a hostage situation can be addressed and resolved.

Every position on the hostage negotiation team is important for securing the safe release of the hostage(s). The coordination and team effort instrumental in attaining this goal involve supervisors, negotiators, the investigative team, the technical assistance response team, the tactical team, and various jurisdictional agencies.

COMMUNICATION

A universal tactic utilized by hostage negotiators is the effective use of time. The negotiator must be cognizant of the "creeping up" effect that can occur as time passes. As rapport is established, the negotiator seeks to gain the confidence of the hostage taker. A false sense of security can develop and the negotiator may get physically closer (creep up), thereby creating a dangerous situation. If the subject possesses a weapon other than a firearm, a zone of safety is to be established that is greater than the effective range of that weapon. Approximately 20 feet should be the minimum distance between the negotiator and the hostage taker. If the subject does not remain stationary, the zone of safety must still be maintained. All members of the team must observe the zone of safety. The passage of time can cause the police to act precipitously. Mental, physical, and emotional fatigue affect not only the hostage taker but also the negotiator.

One of many benefits realized through the effective use of time is that it allows the negotiator to communicate with the hostage taker. The means of communication can vary depending on the situation. A verbal dialogue can be safely initiated by using the bullhorn. Because is it utilized at a distance, it is a very impersonal method of communications. The bullhorn distorts the negotiator's voice and masks emotions that may need to be communicated. Wearing ballistic protection can fatigue the negotiator. While the bullhorn may be an effective tool to initiate dialogue, its effectiveness can diminish during extended negotiations.

Face-to-face negotiation is another means of communication. In early negotiation theory, it was considered the most effective method even with an armed subject. Although effective, it is unpredictable and extremely dangerous, and the loss of just one life is too costly. Face-to-face negotiations with an armed subject must be avoided. If the subject is suicidal, the police could be set up for a "suicide by cop." In other words, the individual could deliberately provoke the police into taking his or her life. Maintaining eye contact with two or more subjects is extremely difficult, if not impossible. Furthermore, it creates additional risks. The negotiator would not be able to observe the movements of all the hostage takers, increasing the possibility of injuries. The primary negotiator cannot be coached in full view of the hostage taker; therefore the possibility of a backup negotiator is sacrificed. Cover and concealment remain two very significant factors, which should never be overlooked. The hostage negotiator must remain aware of the zone of safety as well as alternate escape routes in the event of a tactical maneuver. Therefore, face-to-face negotiations with the hostage takers must be avoided.

If it has been confirmed that the hostage taker is not armed, face-to-face negotiations may occur only after a good rapport has been maintained and approval has been received from supervisors present. The tactical team must be aware that this will occur for the possible redeployment of resources.

Modern technological advances have had a great impact on hostage negotiations. One significant development is the crisis telephone. This telephone, modified with the capability of tape recording negotiations, has proven to be an ideal method of communications in most situations. The tapes can be played back for intelligence as well as for future training use. It is personal and private, and the negotiator can be totally removed from the immediate area to a more suitable environment. The ballistic protection can be removed, further putting the negotiator at ease. This reduces stress and anxiety that can affect both the hostage negotiator and the subject. With the capability of additional head phones, additional negotiators can monitor the dialogue. The monitoring negotiator could relieve or replace the primary negotiator, if necessary. The crisis telephone also prevents outsiders, such as family members or the media, from disrupting any progress that may have been achieved.

The contents of what is said during negotiations, known as *talk tactics*, is crucial in attaining a successful resolution. The concepts and skills of active listening are invaluable for crisis intervention. The negotiator must remain objective and nonjudgmental. Being sympathetic creates pity; overinvolvement defeats the negotiator's goals. Feelings are cornerstones in crisis intervention. Circumstances create different feelings in each individual. The negotiator can empathize with those feelings even though never experiencing them. For example, every person experiences happiness and sadness at one time or another, in varying degrees, throughout life. While the circumstances causing these emotions may differ, the feelings remain similar. The negotiator must be understanding while remaining objective and nonjudgmental.

The negotiator must actively listen for the subject's repressed emotions. Once revealed, the contents of what is said and how it is said may influence consequent behavior. Emotion labeling can be a very effective tool. For example, the negotiator may say, "You are angry," "It sounds like you feel depressed," and "I'm hearing sadness in your voice." This skill also elicits feedback that encourages dialogue. If emotion labeling is not effective, paraphrasing the hostages' statements and reflecting key words could elicit further conversation. All this allows for the passage of time, the defusing of emotions and the development of rapport.

Values also influence behavior. The value placed on any demand or request by the hostage taker (such as cigarettes, soda, food) must never be taken lightly. What is important to the subject must be just as important to the negotiator.

Additional listening skills include effective pauses and minimal encouragers. The best negotiator is a good listener. Silence very often facilitates dialogue. Minimal words and phrases, often used in "shrink talk," are clues that the subject is being heard. Examples are, "I see," "yes," "Okay," and even "uh-huh."

Open-ended questions also encourage conversation. Asking how, what, when, and where questions allow the venting process to continue and can also reveal important intelligence. Refrain from asking "why" questions as they typically force the hostage taker to defend and justify actions, which may create adverse reactions.

Many cultures exist in this diverse society. Members of the hostage negotiation team should reflect the various ethnic cultures. For example, it is desirable to have bilingual hostage negotiators to avoid the use of interpreters. However, caution must be exercised when negotiating in a language other than English. Adequate interpreters may not be available for the benefit of the backup, scribe, and other members of the team. Dialects within a language can further create communication barriers. One advantage of negotiating in English is that the hostage takers must slow down their thought process, which in turn will slow down the dialogue. This deescalates the emotions of the hostage taker, thereby facilitating the negotiation process.

MEASURING NEGOTIATION EFFECTIVENESS

Evidence that negotiations are progressing can be judged by several signs. Indications from the hostage taker are diffused emotions evident by a slower rate of speech and a lower tone of voice. The subject will speak for longer periods of time and about more personal concerns. The frequency in threats of violence will decrease. Deadlines will be overlooked. Injuries to hostages will cease, and some or all hostages may be released. When any or all of these signs are evident, the passage of time and continued negotiations will be advantageous. Most often, the longer a hostage situation continues, the more likely it will be successfully resolved.

TRAINING/CROSS TRAINING

Law enforcement consist of dedicated men and women with special talents and abilities that can be further enhanced through continued training. Joint training sessions, conducted periodically between the tactical team and hostage negotiators, afford the opportunity to exchange ideas and debrief past incidents. This medium can also be used to cultivate liaisons with other city, state, and federal law enforcement agencies. Guest lecturers in specialized areas, such as alcohol/drug abuse, AIDS awareness, suicide, and mental health, can serve to enhance the knowledge and ability to render the safe resolution of a hostage situation. Practical training with role playing is beneficial for supervisors, negotiators, and tactical team members. Through role reversal, they gain a better understanding of the distinct responsibilities and functions required by each team member.

CONCLUSION

Hostage negotiation has made great strides since the long dark days of Attica and Munich. Modern technology, experience, skilled communications, and training have greatly benefited present-day negotiation techniques and strategies. Law enforcement is entering the twenty-first century with the knowledge that hostage negotiation is no longer an unproven theory. Evidence clearly indicates that the ultimate goal is not only safe hostage release, but also the safety of all persons involved. Hostage negotiation plays a vital role in the accomplishment of this objective.

53

The Investigator at the Hostage Scene

Wayne T. Seay

THE THREE MAJOR ROLES

On the surface, police emergency response seems to deny the routine methodology of the detective. A prime example of a situation where the investigator's role is not readily apparent to the casual observer is at the hostage scene. In the excitement of the initial confrontation and in the ensuing drama of life-and-death negotiations, little thought is given to the mundane tasks of canvassing, interviewing, record checking, evidence gathering, statement taking, and testifying. Yet all these and many more investigative functions are vital to the hostage scene, not only for an adequate prosecution after the fact, but also for a successful conclusion to the crisis itself.

Depending on the size of the police agency and the relative strength of its detective division, investigators may perform any of three major roles:

First, detectives are prime candidates to be negotiators. In departments large enough to maintain a hostage negotiating team, members with investigative experience are favored for the task. In smaller departments investigators are often called upon to perform the negotiating function on an individual basis.

Second, whether called upon to negotiate or not, detectives are charged with certain investigative chores at hostage scenes. Among the most important of these is the securing of intelligence information for the negotiators.

Third, when the emergency is over the investigative phase of the incident takes precedence. The detective must be prepared to perform the traditional investigative function that follows every serious criminal act.

INVESTIGATOR AS NEGOTIATOR

In such large Eastern police departments as New York City and Nassau County, detectives form the nucleus of hostage negotiating teams. Most experts recommend the use of investigators as negotiators, either as members of a team or as individuals. The reason generally expressed for this preference is that investigators are usually experienced police officers who have dealt with a great number of people under varying circumstances.

While most police officers can be trained to negotiate, detectives are considered top prospects because they practice the skills of good negotiating in their daily duties. Detectives do more canvassing, more interviewing, and more interrogating than uniformed police officers. Their success as investigators depends in large measure on their ability to deal with people.

This ability, natural or job-developed, cannot be relied on to save lives in hostage situations. Negotiators, regardless of their skill, must know the guidelines that have been developed through hundreds of successful hostage incidents. Whether the negotiators adhere to the guidelines or not depends on their judgment of the subject and the situation, but they must be aware of what has succeeded in the past in order to make a knowledgeable decision.

The distinction between guidelines and rules is an important one. Rules imply hard and fast regulations that must be followed. Guidelines are suggested courses of action that have succeeded in prior instances. No rules exist for hostage negotiations.

The unpredictable nature of hostage situations demands that negotiators be granted a great deal of latitude in approach and response. Guidelines provide recommendations based on experience. Negotiators should know that they can choose to disregard the guidelines but should do so only with good reason.

Departmental policy must be established before guidelines can be adopted. The administration must decide in advance whether to permit negotiations for drugs or alcohol, whether to allow for a change of location during the negotiations, whether access to transportation will be considered, and so on. Once these determinations have been made, the suggested guidelines will help negotiators plot their course through the negotiating labyrinth.

Negotiating theory can be thought of as twofold: general and specific. General guidelines deal with the reasoning behind negotiating attempts and with the attitudes of negotiators. Understanding the objectives and knowing the priorities of hostage negotiations are prerequisites to success.

Once the general concepts are clear, the negotiator must become familiar with specific guidelines. Specifics provide pathways that others have found safe. While no method can be considered foolproof, past successes can suggest approaches that are supported by logic and experience.

General Guidelines

The negotiator must have a satisfactory answer to the commonly asked question: Why negotiate? The answer to the question lies in the primary objective of hostage negotiating—to save lives. If the primary objective were to effect arrests, then negotiations could be considered a monumental waste of time and money and effort. Apprehensions could be made most expeditiously by direct assault, as is done in many foreign nations.

It is important to note the distinction between nations undergoing military guerrilla attacks and the isolated problems facing American police agencies. True terrorist attacks are a genuine rarity in the United States, where most hostage incidents result from the actions of mentally disturbed persons or criminals inadvertently pressured into seizing hostages to further their escapes.

Even if terrorist attacks were behind local hostage-taking incidents, police administrators would find military tactics difficult to justify when used at the expense of hostages. So long as the priority in hostage situations is to preserve life, some form of negotiating effort must be expended.

Time has proved negotiating to be effective in saving the lives of hostages, police, and even hostage takers. If this fact is accepted, then the question posed should really be, why *not* negotiate?

Nothing is to be lost by trying to negotiate, because assault tactics can remain an alternative if negotiations fail. Many experts have noted that easily escalated emotions are difficult to deescalate. For this reason alone, negotiating should be tried first. After an assault is attempted and fails, it will be difficult to establish a basis for dispassionate discussion.

A recurring objective to negotiating is the notion that a humanistic approach coddles criminals. Everyone wants the police to teach hostage takers a lesson that will deter other potential offenders. The deterrence value of any unyielding attitude towards hostage takers is highly questionable. Mentally disturbed persons seldom consider the consequences of their acts; criminals trapped by swift police response take hostages as a reflex action, not as the result of cold calculation; and terrorists are fanatics who have resolved to die for their cause.

Police are duty bound to accomplish their primary goal—saving life. Critics who complain the loudest about pampering criminals have not placed themselves or their loved ones in the place of the hostages. With that very personal viewpoint held before the coldly objective remedy of storming the hostage site, most demands for lesson teaching would dissolve into pleas for more restraint.

If negotiating is to be the police alternative, how should it be handled? The determination of method may be made in part by the type of hostage holder faced.

Types of Hostage Takers

Care must be exercised in trying to categorize hostage takers. Human beings are too widely divergent to be easily labeled as one type or another. Frequently the types converge, as when a mentally ill or emotionally deranged person holds up a store or bank. With this caution in mind, negotiators should remember that attempts have been made to identify the three most likely types of hostage takers and to provide some guidelines for dealing with each.

Criminal. This category is typified by the stickup robbers caught in the act by swift police response who take hostages to guarantee their escape. It is clear from the outset that their original intent had nothing to do with the taking of hostages. It is also clear that their goal is to escape.

The first confrontation with a trapped robber is extremely volatile. His instinctive, panic-stricken reaction is dangerously unpredictable. After time to cool down has been granted, criminals-turned-hostage-takers are the most rational of all subjects. Their motives and intent are known and they will usually listen to reason.

Mentally Disturbed.   A category such as this necessarily covers a wide range of disorders, from depression to paranoid schizophrenia. The important thing about mentally disturbed subjects is their complete unpredictability, not just in the beginning as with some other types, but throughout the negotiations, no matter how long they go on. The utmost caution must be exercised in these, the most frustrating of negotiations.

Terrorist.   Little in the way of meaningful negotiations can be accomplished when one side is demanding concessions which the other side is powerless to grant. Frequently terrorists demand, as they did in Munich, that a government of some *other* country free political prisoners in exchange for their hostages. Negotiators have nothing to offer unless the affected country agrees to cooperate, and so must do what they can to keep the hostages alive. Sometimes the terrorist demands are mere rhetoric, designed to attract attention to their cause, publicize their plight, and punctuate their dramatic demise, hostages and all. Police negotiators have little hope for sincere bargaining if the terrorists are truly dedicated fanatics.

If tactical solutions are required, the negotiator still provides a valuable service—buying time for plans to be made and presenting the hostage holders with a distracting focal point. In either case, the negotiator should proceed with a sincere effort to bargain for the release of the hostages. This effort should be designed around the specific guidelines that have succeeded so well in the past.

Specific Guidelines

Slow Everything Down.   This, the number one guideline on practically everyone's list, is the closest thing to a rule in negotiating theory. Stalling for time works to the benefit of negotiators in several ways:

1. Containment and negotiation decrease stress and anxiety through the passage of time.

2. When emotion subsides, rational thinking returns, as the subject calms down enough to consider his position and his alternatives.

3. The hostages' lives become more secure as time passes, and the subject realizes the value of their safety.

4. The passage of time also aids hostages by increasing the subject's awareness of them as persons, thereby diminishing his or her willingness to harm them.

5. A long-range benefit of slowing everything down is that eventually fatigue will set in, alertness will fade, and the will to resist will falter.

(Police must guard against the same symptoms by establishing regular relief periods for personnel.)

Weapons Are Not Negotiable.   This guideline comes across sounding like a hard and fast rule, because of the obvious dangers attached. While the final decision to bargain for a weapon rests with the agency's policy, the person who violates this guideline does so at great peril. In a hostage incident the police weapon may be the only loaded, properly functioning weapon available to the hostage taker. If traded it may be used to kill hostages as well as police. The message to all police, and to negotiators in particular, is that the officer who surrenders a weapon will probably be killed with it.

Hostages Should Not Be Substituted. Substitute hostages and weapons are referred to as the nonnegotiable items of hostage negotiations. In both cases the negotiators should ask themselves why the subject is asking for the item demanded. In the case of the substitute hostage, subjects may be seeking to replace a hostage they are becoming fond of, with one they will feel free to kill if need be. Or they may want a hostage to kill without qualms because they have decided to end the situation that way. In either case the substitute hostage is in more acute danger than the original hostage. If the substitute hostage is a police officer, the danger becomes immediate.

Try to Get Something in Return for Each Demand. This is the whole point of negotiating. If police allow the subject to take charge, the bargaining will turn into a giveaway that produces nothing. Conversely, if police get too hard-nosed, the subject's frustrations could have deadly consequences. The objective should be to seek a give-and-take relationship that will set the tone for a future trade to free the hostages. Of course, it is not always possible to get something back for every demand, but that is the goal of the negotiator and it should at least be attempted. The favored attitude is one that is firm but not overpowering.

Avoid Unnecessary Lies. This guideline raises the question of what is a necessary lie. Quite a bit of controversy has raged over this point. Some academic commentators have insisted that negotiators should never lie under any circumstances, lest they destroy the future credibility of all negotiations. These idealists would allow a hostage to die before compromising a principle.

Some police officers consider the entire negotiation to be nothing more or less than a great con job. To them, the end justifies the means and any lie is acceptable so long as the negotiator does not get caught telling it.

Moderation is probably the most acceptable guideline about lying. Negotiations should be handled as sincere attempts to bargain, with lies told only when absolutely necessary. Saving a life is a necessity.

Be Careful About Using Friends or Relatives to Negotiate. Before any decision is made to try negotiating with nonpolice personnel, including clergy and doctors, a full investigation should be made to determine the relationship existing between the subject and the proposed negotiator. The hostage taker may be found to have a profound fear, dislike, contempt, or distrust of the proposed negotiator, which could cause an opposite reaction to the one sought. In no single area is intelligence gathering more vital.

Face-to-Face Negotiation Is the Most Effective and the Most Dangerous Form. Negotiator and subject can best relate to each other when they can see each other. This obvious statement of fact is true of all human relations but takes on special significance in the context of hostage negotiations. The negotiator can calm the subject and put him or her at ease better when they can see each other than when speaking through a bullhorn or telephone or around a corner. The sought-after transference of empathy can best take place between two people facing each other.

Unfortunately, in a hostage situation the negotiator who can be seen can also be shot. Before a face-to-face meeting is granted to a gun-wielding hostage taker, the relationship should have stabilized between negotiator and subject and every precaution must be taken. Face-to-face negotiation with an armed subject is not a step to be taken lightly.

Nourish Hopes of Subject.   Persons without hope are desperate and inclined to take chances or to martyr themselves and their hostages.

Avoid Deadlines.   This is part of the admonition to slow down. Deadlines should not be given by negotiators, and every effort should be made to discourage the subject from issuing deadlines.

Avoid Extremes.   Do not promise to grant any wildly outrageous demands that are obviously impossible. If the subject is testing the negotiator, a hasty promise will prove something to him. On the other hand, do not automatically reject a demand that seems unreasonable, but may be negotiated into something acceptable. Use both extremes as everything else is used—to stall for time.

Do Not Talk to Hostages.   Grant hostage holders the center stage they are demanding by their actions. Any attempts by the negotiator to allay the fear of hostages will probably be resented by the subject. They want to be recognized as the sole holders of power over the hostages.

Do Not Offer Suggestions.   Let hostage takers wrestle with the problems of their situation. Their mental efforts will tire them while they keep their minds occupied.

Command of the Hostage Scene.   Command of the scene should go to the senior officer present, but *not* to the leader of the negotiating team or to the leader of the assault team. This recommendation is based on the need for each of these specialized functions to have the full attention of their leaders, without regard for such details as traffic routing, perimeter control, media liaison, relief assignments, food and coffee, and so on. This system also provides the agency with an ultimate decision maker who is neutral to both the negotiating and assault functions but dependent on the opinions and expertise of both. Properly handled, this procedure provides checks and balances for crisis decisions.

If a Hostage Is Executed.   Originally, the guidelines for this situation called for an immediate cessation of the negotiations and a forthwith assault. The theory was that hostage holders who had demonstrated a willingness to kill captives would continue to kill them unless prevented by the police. This concept has become questionable in the light of recent developments. The totality of the circumstances will indicate whether or not further negotiations will be productive. In any event, assaultive actions must be carefully assessed in terms of need, practicality, and chances of success.

From this brief summary of theory, it is clear that hostage negotiating involves no mystique but does require a knowledge of the guidelines and an ability to communicate. Negotiators should be intelligent and able to think clearly under stress. Negotiators must be slow to anger and virtually immune to personal and ethnic attacks. They must have a high tolerance for uncertainty and frustration.

Finally, an effective negotiator needs the common sense, experience, and courage to violate the guidelines when circumstances indicate an unusual approach may succeed. Negotiators have succeeded for the most part by adhering to recommended procedures, but rare occasions have proved the value of individual assessment and innovative action.

INVESTIGATOR AS INTELLIGENCE GATHERER

Investigators may or may not be involved in the actual negotiations, but they will certainly be expected to gather the intelligence needed by the negotiators. No one, no matter how skilled, can perform at peak without information. In addition to general and specific guidelines, the negotiator needs to know as much as possible about the subject in the shortest possible time and also needs to know as much as possible about the hostages and the premises involved.

The negotiator must have information about the person being dealt with in order to strike a responsive chord in the subject. The negotiator must know the identity of and information about the hostages in order to bargain for their safety. The negotiator and the assault team members must know the layout of the premises in case a tactical resolution becomes necessary.

Hostage Taker Information

Who are the hostage takers? Are they stickup artists who panicked at police arrival and reacted by seizing hostages? Are they professional robbers who want only to escape, or are they mentally disturbed individuals? Are they terrorists seeking publicity for a cause or criminals trying to rationalize their unlawful conduct? Only good intelligence gathering can answer these questions for the negotiator.

Initial impressions of the hostage situation will alter with the passage of time. If reliable intelligence is gathered promptly, police can set the tone for a successful negotiation. The longer a negotiator must operate in the dark or with sketchy information the more hazardous the negotiations will be.

Intelligence gathering makes the difference. The energetic investigator will find many sources of information, among them the following:

Premises.   If the hostages are being held in a private residence, every effort must be made to identify the owner and occupants of the building. In cases involving mentally disturbed hostage takers, the incident frequently occurs in the subject's home. If a commercial building is involved, the ownership and occupancy may reveal much about the identity of persons inside and motivations of the subjects. Investigators can seek this information from neighbors, postal officials, telephone directories, utility company records, autos parked nearby, and police emergency business files.

Vehicles. The area should be canvassed for parked vehicles that may belong to the hostage taker or hostages. Motor vehicle record checks will often supply names, addresses, dates of birth, and other information about the persons in the hostage site. Even stolen cars at the scene can supply the investigator with details through fingerprint examinations and inventories of personal items found inside. The location from which the car was stolen may be pertinent.

Neighbors. A routine canvass of the neighborhood can turn up valuable intelligence about people, cars, and nearby locations.

Witnesses. Persons who saw the crime or any of the people involved in the incident should be interviewed in detail for names, descriptions, numbers of persons involved, and details about location and/or cars.

Family and Friends. As soon as subjects have been identified, the investigator should begin locating anyone who knows them to obtain in-depth information. Wives, husbands, lovers, children, parents, siblings, relatives, and friends are excellent sources of personal data. Negotiators need to know the subject's likes and dislikes, strengths and weaknesses, occupations and hobbies, personal history, and recent stresses in order to establish rapport and gain motivational insights. Investigators should caution the negotiator about the sources of this information, because the viewpoints of such persons are frequently colored by emotions. It is not unusual for investigators to extract contrasting opinions from persons close to the subject.

Employees, Employers, Fellow Workers. Great insights can be obtained from these sources regarding the subject's recent activities, moods, statements, threats, and state of mind. Again, the investigator must be wary of the possibility of slanted perspectives.

Mail Carriers, Delivery People, and so on. Efforts to locate regular visitors of a casual nature (repair people, installers, and so on) can be repaid by leads to relatives, friends, employers, physicians.

Doctors and Psychiatrists. The patient-doctor relationship hurdle can often be cleared if the physician is convinced that lives are at stake. Professional opinions and recommendations can be invaluable aids to the negotiator. Investigators and negotiators must acknowledge the confidentiality of any such information and should abide by any commitment given to physicians in return for assistance.

Records. Standard record checks cannot be left out of any investigation. Names should be checked for previous arrest record, ownership, driver's license information, outstanding warrants, and so on. Frequently, a positive "hit" on a subject's name will lead to photographs of suspects. Photos can then be obtained for viewing by witnesses for confirmation or elimination.

Miscellaneous. No detail is too insignificant for the consideration of negotiators in learning the nature of a subject. They will want to know if the hostage holder has a criminal record and if so, what kinds of violations, when, and how many. Was the subject ever imprisoned?

The negotiators will be interested in the health record of the subject, particularly in regard to any mental problems. They will want to know if the subject has any specialized skills: Can the person drive a car? Fly a plane? Has he or she expert knowledge of weapons or explosives? Does the subject have any unusual habits? Is he or she homosexual? Addicted? Does the subject gamble or drink? Belong to any religious sect, special group, or gang? Is the hostage taker married? Are there children? If so, what are their names and ages?

Personal problems of the subject are of prime interest. Has the hostage holder recently been divorced or jilted? Is he on parole or probation? Being sued by anyone? Does he or she have any particular business or legal problems?

The present condition of the hostage holder is important: hungry? tired? drunk? high? angry?

Hostage Information

Many of the same sources listed in regard to hostage takers can be relied on to provide intelligence about the hostages. Negotiators should know how many hostages are being held, their sex, age, and health and their potential for additional problems.

In the early stages of negotiations, not much is known about the hostages or their captors. Negotiators are in a weak bargaining position so long as they know so little about the people they are dealing with and for.

The number of hostages is vital because it is the basis for determining when all have been freed. Sex and age are important factors in figuring the emotional climate of the scene and the logistical problems of the hostage holders. The very young, the very old, and the sick or infirm may be a liability to the subject because of the care they require. These victims can sometimes be negotiated to freedom early in the incident, if the subject can be convinced that the liability they represent to him is an unnecessary problem.

Investigators must be particularly attuned to the value of debriefing released hostages. No better source of intelligence exists for determining the number of remaining hostages, the identity and condition of each, the number and identity of hostage holders, and the prevailing mood of all concerned. From released hostages, investigators can learn about the people still inside and about the premises itself. Investigators must explore the possibility that released hostages may not be truthful because of promises to their captors or threats of reprisal against them or other hostages.

Hostage Scene Information

Negotiators and assault teams need to know the physical layout of the premises wherein the hostages are detained. Investigators should determine the size of the building, whether or not it adjoins another building, and the location of all doors and windows. Type and condition of locks should be ascertained.

Partitions, walls, closets, and rooms on each floor should be diagramed, with particular emphasis given to locations of kitchens and bathrooms.

Whenever possible, investigators should pinpoint any telephone installations. Areas where hostages are known to be held or rooms favored by the hostage holders should be indicated to negotiators and assault teams. Fuse boxes and circuit breaker panels should be located and exterior connections for utilities isolated, if possible.

Availability of food and water, alcoholic beverages, first aid supplies, electrical appliances, medicine, drugs, weapons, ammunition, and so on in the premises should be determined by the investigators.

The sources of all this information are many and varied. Owners of the property, former owners or occupants, escaped or released hostages, neighbors, employees, maintenance workers, maids, delivery people, utility company employees, movers, installers of telephones or air conditioners or washing machines or dryers or carpets, or anyone who may have been inside the premises are all potential sources of this type of intelligence. Investigators should not ignore the possibility of examining nearby homes with the same floor plan as the subject location. Local police who may have been called to the premises at some time in the past should also be quizzed. A less likely source, but not to be overlooked if needed, is the architect or builder of the structure. Nothing that can be of help should be ignored.

Investigators can help locate vantage points where observers can be stationed, perimeter patrols established, or antisniper personnel positioned. Assault planning should be done with the aid of the investigators who gathered the intelligence.

INVESTIGATOR AS EVIDENCE GATHERER

Throughout the hostage incident, police attention must be focused on the emergency situation involving a threat to human life. When the emergency is over, the traditional investigative phase of the incident will take charge.

While the uniformed officers return to patrol duties and the negotiators resume their respective duties, the investigator is expected to follow up and complete the case. At this point in most hostage situations, the hostages will have been saved, released, or killed. The hostage takers will be under arrest or undergoing psychiatric examination. Whatever the outcome, investigators must proceed as if a prosecution will ensue.

Negotiators should not be expected to take part in the arrest or processing of prisoners unless such arrangement was part of the negotiated settlement. The credibility of negotiators depends, in part, on their ability to maintain a position of trust with the subjects in case they are called on to negotiate with the same parties again in the future.

Investigators will make certain that the crime scene is preserved and that photos are taken and evidence collected, safeguarded, and forwarded for laboratory examination as required. Photographs, fingerprints, blood, ballistics, diagrams, and any other physical evidence will be the responsibility of the investigator.

Witnesses' statements must be taken as well as those of released hostages. It should be noted that newly freed hostages may display intense sympathy for their captors and an equally intense disapproval of police and police actions. These seemingly extraordinary reactions are common to hostages who have been held prisoner for a lengthy period. Investigators must be familiar with this attitude and must handle such witnesses with patience and tact. Often, the early reactions of hostages will change as the reality of the situation replaces their artificial obligation to the hostage taker who "saved their lives" by not killing them.

Sometimes released hostages continue in efforts to support their former captors and refuse to cooperate with prosecution efforts. These persons will have to be treated as hostile witnesses before the grand jury and any trial jury.

Investigators will be responsible for careful preparation of the case, filing of charges, and court presentation. Vocal recordings of negotiations, if made, should be preserved for trial. At this point negotiators will have to relinquish their neutrality and testify against the defendants. The criminal prosecution, once begun, must receive maximum police effort.

CONCLUSION

Investigators are key personnel in the conduct of any hostage situation. They may act as negotiators, in which case they must learn the general and specific guidelines to effective negotiating; or they may act as intelligence gatherers, in which event they must make every effort to obtain all possible information that may aid negotiations. Finally, investigators will be responsible for investigating and helping prosecute any crimes committed. For this traditional investigative function, detectives will find that a knowledge of negotiating goals and procedures assists them in their duties.

PART 9

Selected Areas of Investigation

54

Purloining the World's Art

Donald L. Mason

The soaring sales prices of the world's great art—paintings, sculptures, bronzes, archaeological artifacts, etc.—have made art theft an exorbitantly lucrative offense. Not only is it the second largest international crime (after narcotic trafficking), but drug lords are compounding the problem by laundering their dirty money through art deals.

This chapter identifies precautionary measures and loss prevention programs to counter the purloining and criminal disposal operations involved. The techniques and technical aspects of art theft investigations, the use of informants, liaison programs, rewards, and the handling of recovered art are explained, as well as training programs for specialists in art theft investigation. Reference sources and the names of those who should be informed of art thefts are provided.

SPIRALING ART PRICES TRIGGER RECORD ART THEFTS WORLDWIDE

During the past 30 years the underworld has been observing the changes taking place in the realm of art with obvious intrigue, where record sales prices in almost every category have more than kept pace with our economy. When did this tremendous interest in art sales begin? I like to use the Metropolitan Museum of Art's purchase of Rembrandt's oil painting, *Aristotle Contemplating the Bust of Homer*, for $2 million in 1961 as a landmark. It was the first painting sold publicly for over a million dollars and resulted in enormous publicity throughout the world. Skyrocketing sales followed. Here are a few examples: In 1970 the Metropolitan Museum of Art purchased Diego Velázquez's *Juan de Pareja* for $5.5 million and Titian's painting, *Death of Actaeon* fetched a cool $4 million in 1971. An American painting by Frederick E. Church called *Icebergs* was sold for a record $2.5 million in October 1979 by Sotheby's in New York.

The upward spiral continued throughout the 1980s. Van Gogh's *Irises* went for an unbelievable $53.9 million in 1987. In 1989 alone paintings by Paul

Gauguin were bought for $22 million, Willem de Koonig for $18 million, two paintings by Pablo Picasso for $37 million and $43.5 million, respectively, and a Frederick Remington painting for $4.3 million.

Though auction sales went through a severe decline in 1990, reflecting a weakened economy, there were also some indicators that the value of art would be maintained. An illustration of this upbeat outlook was John Constable's painting, *The Lock*, which Sotheby's sold in London and the Thyssen Foundation bought for $21 million. In addition, a Pierre Auguste Renoir painting, *Au Moulin de la Galette*, made history on May 17, 1990, when it was auctioned for an incredible $78.1 million at Sotheby's in New York.

The fantastic growth in value of art in only three decades has triggered the nefarious mind of the criminal and provided a feast! The art theft problem has been compounded by the fact that the world's repositories of art: churches, castles, libraries, galleries, museums, private homes, and archaeological sites have had little or, in a vast number of cases, no security to protect their treasurers from the thief.

Italy, with its great collections of art and low priorities for security to protect its cultural heritage, has suffered staggering numbers of art thefts. Churches and castles are the most popular targets for art thieves in Italy, as they are in France and other European nations. In North America, private collectors, art galleries, and museums, in that order, are the most frequently victimized targets for art thefts.

During the March 1977, CINOA (an international confederation of art dealers) International Conference on the Theft of Art, held in Paris, Commissioner Bernard Warren of New Scotland Yard announced that as of the end of 1976, some 6800 art objects were listed as stolen on their computerized system of indexing stolen art objects. He was encouraged by the overall results of the computer system.

At the same conference Italy's Colonel Pio Alferano, Chef du Nacleo Tutèla del Patrimonio Artistico, reported some 75,000 recoveries of stolen art objects and 3000 arrests during the previous five years. He advised the author that he hoped Italy would be able to computerize art thefts in the near future.

Gilbert B. Raguideau, Director, French Central Officer for the Repression of Art Thefts (COR-ART), presented his nation's art theft statistics at the international Symposium on Art Security, held at the University of Delaware in February 1979 (an event chaired by the author). He said France began a serious effort to record the national statistics on art thefts in 1970. In 1970, 1261 paintings were stolen in France. In 1978, the figure was 2807. In 1970, there were burglaries at 227 churches, 112 castles, 37 museums, and 69 art galleries. In 1978, the figures were: 174 churches, 178 castles, 64 museums, and 115 art galleries. In 1977, 3507 private individuals in France were victims of art thefts; in 1978, there were nearly 4000 victims.

M. Raguideau said all works of art attract thieves but paintings were the most popular: 2721 paintings were stolen in 1977, 2807 in 1978. Next in popularity were statues: 326 stolen in 1977, 2754 in 1978. He also said that 283 tapestries were stolen in 1977, 205 in 1978; and that 239 lithographs, prints, engravings, and drawings were stolen in 1977, 400 in 1978.

Austria, Belgium, Germany, The Netherlands, Sweden, Switzerland, Greece, Turkey, India, Egypt, Mexico, Canada, and the United States are other nations where art thefts have become a significant problem.

Unfortunately, it is not possible to cite such accurate figures for the United States. American police departments do not specify types of stolen property when submitting theft reports to their record centers. Therefore, the crime statistics submitted to the FBI's annual publication, "Crime in the United States—Uniform Crime Reports" do not reflect art theft figures, just the fact that a burglary, robbery, or larceny has taken place. The publication's 1976 report revealed that the total number of offenses occurring in the three categories of burglary, robbery, and larceny was 9,780,810. Total dollar loss to victims for these crimes was $2,742,000,000. An average of 21 percent of all the reported cases from these three categories was cleared. The 1976 report also revealed a 33-percent overall average increase in the same three categories for the years 1972 to 1976. The year 1976 was selected arbitrarily by the author for the purpose of the study.

While we have no idea exactly what the statistics are for art thefts in the United States, we do know they would be culled from these classifications. In a conservative approach to these figures, let us say that they amounted to 5 percent of the total property losses of $2,742 million. That would mean that the value of art thefts in the United States for 1976 comes to more than $137.1 million. However, with the steady and dramatic increase in the worth of art year after year, this figure immediately becomes meaningless. Just consider that art objects valued at around $200 million were taken in a single robbery from the Gardner Museum in 1990!

The seriousness of America's art theft problem was ruthlessly demonstrated in December 1978, when a Rembrandt painting called *Portrait of a Rabbi* (Fig. 54.1), estimated at $1 million, and three lower-priced Dutch paintings were stolen from the M. H. de Young Museum in San Francisco. There have been no recoveries in that case. The San Francisco robbery was followed a few days later by the theft of three Cézanne paintings valued at more than $3 million from the Art Institute of Chicago. Fortunately, the three Cézannes were regained. Two months later, in February 1979, while a conference on art thefts at the University of Delaware was in session, a Greek marble head, worth $150,000, was ripped off its pedestal and stolen from the Metropolitan Museum of Art in New York City, while guards were being rotated. (It has since been recovered.)

In the 1980s, the looting of art works has continued to be a major problem in America. In 1982 a young doctor in Philadelphia was arrested after police found approximately $2 million worth of art in his apartment, much of which was stolen. Then in 1988 an Edouard Manet painting, valued at more than $1 million, was taken from a Long Island museum. In another theft, also in 1988, two very precious paintings by the fifteenth-century Italian master, Fra Angelico, were purloined from a New York City gallery. A year later thieves took two Grandma Moses paintings, estimated at $200,000, from a Boston art gallery. In 1990 the FBI located the eighteenth-century painting, *Our Lady of Sorrows*, in a thief's home near San Gabriel, California, which had been stolen 14 years previously from the altar of a Roman Catholic mission in San Gabriel.

There is also a paucity of information available concerning the value of all stolen art. A billion dollars is a sum often heard, and an article in the Toronto (Canada) *Weekend Magazine* described the theft of Picasso's painting, *Woman in a Hat Holding the Head of a Sheep*, worth $450,000, from the Mira Godara Gallery in Toronto on February 17, 1979.[1] The article said, the painting "joined the swelling ranks of stolen and unrecovered works of art which now number in the hundreds of thousands and whose collective value is measured in billions of dollars."

The worldwide picture of purloining art is doubly disturbing, since thefts have increased consistently, and only about 5 percent of the objects are recovered.[2]

Figure 54.1 *Portrait of a Rabbi*, by Rembrandt (oil painting) was stolen from M. H. de Young Museum, San Francisco, December 1978 and has not been recovered.

International Transportation of Stolen Art

There is considerable evidence that stolen art is often transported from one country to another. National borders apparently offer little resistance to the purloiner of art. For example, in 1936, during a battle in the Spanish Civil War, an El Greco painting, *The Immaculate Conception*, was taken from an apartment in a little town outside Madrid, Spain. Subsequently, the stolen painting was transported to Mexico, then to Los Angeles, California, and was ultimately recovered by the writer in New York City in June 1971. Rubens' *Assumption of the Virgin*, missing since 1976 from the Strasbourg (France) Museum of Fine Arts, was found in Germany in January 1977. A Wassily Kandinsky painting, *Soft Interpretations*, was robbed in 1975 from Otto Preminger's New York office, and it was regained in Basel, Switzerland in July 1976 after traveling from New York to Philadelphia, back to New York, and finally to Basel. The Serra Brothers' altar painting, *Gozos de la Virgen*, taken in 1972 from a church in Abella de Conca, Spain, was recouped in New York in November 1977. A Rembrandt painting, stolen in 1971 from the Bonnat Museum in Bayonne, France, was recovered in Buffalo, New York in July 1977, as a result of a combined local police and an FBI sting operation. A painting by Goya, the object of a heist in 1987 from a museum at Rosario, Argentina, was found in Miami, Florida. A Rembrandt drawing, taken in the Netherlands in 1979 was retrieved in New York in 1989. A large collection of art in Ireland has fallen twice to thieves. In 1974 the Irish Republican Army stole the collection and asked for a ransom without success. The paintings were recouped several days later. In 1986 the same collection was purloined again. One of the pieces was found in Turkey, but the main part is still missing. And an Irish citizen was arrested by the FBI for smuggling Irish gravestones and other "stolen artifacts from St. Dermot's sixth century monastic site on Inchcleraum Island (Quaker Island)."[3] In January, 1991, the smuggler arrived in Miami with his loot in a sailboat. He was subsequently arrested in an FBI sting operation when he attempted to sell the purloined artifacts to Boston College's John J. Burns Library of Rare Books and Special Collections, which houses one of the nation's most comprehensive collections of Irish historical and cultural materials.

VIOLENCE IN COMMITTING ART THEFTS

While some writers and even some law enforcement authorities believe art crimes are committed only by art-oriented, well-dressed, well-spoken individuals, evidence suggests that for the most part art thieves are much like any other thieves. They shoot museum guards and murder private collectors; they steal from their employers; they swindle the greedy collector or dealer; they are "art-nappers" instead of kidnappers, or they shoplift paintings or small bronze sculptures instead of suits, groceries, or fine wines.

Samples of violence used while committing art crimes would have to include the shooting of a guard while taking four paintings from the Worcester, Massachusetts, Art Museum, in May 1972.

In September 1972, three masked individuals, armed with sawed-off shotguns, gained entrance to the Montreal Museum of Fine Arts through one of the skylights and slid down a rope to the floor below. They ambushed, bound, and gaged three security guards and stole 18 paintings, valued then at more than $2 million, which have never been recovered. Of the 18 missing paintings, three are Rembrandt's *Landscape with Cottages*, Gainsborough's *Portrait of Brigadier General Sir Robert Fletcher*, and Corot's *Jeunc Fille Accoudée sur le Bras Gauche*.

In February 1976, three armed men overpowered guards at the Papal Palace in Avignon, France and stole 119 Picasso paintings (since recovered).

In April 1975, a Rembrandt painting was stolen from the Boston Museum of Fine Arts by two armed men (the painting has since been recovered).

In January 1974, a Coral Gables, Florida, woman was bound and then suffocated by robbers who entered her home and stole four paintings. In March 1974, two well-dressed men gained entrance to a young woman's New York City apartment by posing as florists making a delivery. One of the men pulled a revolver on the woman and the other tied her hands and feet with electrical cord. They then robbed the woman of furs, jewelry, and a $30,000 Picasso pastel drawing called *La Toilette*. A *New York Times* article, dated August 8, 1974, reported that "a stolen Picasso drawing was recovered yesterday in the apartment of an East Side resident by an undercover agent who posed as an appraiser....The police said that a Federal Bureau of Investigation art recovery specialist, posing as an appraiser, had recovered the drawing."[4]

In 1985 the Marmottan Museum in Paris (France) was entered by gunmen who proceeded to steal nine impressionist paintings valued at over $12 million.

In 1989 two men used subterfuge and violence to commit a theft of art worth $4 million. The robbers, dressed as police officers, asked a New York City art restorer to authenticate a painting. When the restorer started to examine it, the robbers beat and handcuffed him.

Similar methods were used during the biggest art theft ever recorded in America. During the early morning hours of March 18, 1990, two men in police uniforms persuaded two young guards to let them into the elegant Isabella Stewart Gardner Museum in Boston. After gaining admission, the robbers bound and gagged the two guards, neutralized the security system,

Figure 54.2 *Chez Tortoni,* by Edouard Manet (oil painting), was stolen from the Isabella Gardner Museum, Boston, March 18, 1980.

and proceeded to successfully purloin art estimated at $200 million. The missing pieces include:

1. Jan Vermeer, *The Concert*, oil on canvas, 72.5 × 64.7 centimeters.

2. Edouard Manet, *Chez Tortoni*, oil on canvas, 26 × 34 centimeters (Fig. 54.2).

3. Rembrandt, *Lady and Gentleman in Black*, oil on canvas, 131 × 109 centimeters.

4. Rembrandt, *Storm on the Sea of Galilee*, oil on canvas, 161.7 × 129.8 centimeters.

5. Rembrandt, *Self Portrait*, etching, ca. 1634, $1\frac{3}{4}$ × 2 inches.

6. Govaert Flinck, *Landscape with an Obelisk*, oil on oak panel, 54.5 × 71 centimeters.

7. A Chinese bronze beaker from the Shang dynasty, height $10\frac{1}{2}$ inches, diameter $6\frac{1}{8}$ inches, weight 2 pounds 7 ounces.

8–11. Four works by Degas, including two of mounted jockeys, a wall scene outside a city, and a sketch depicting numerous topics, such as ballet dancers, musicians, two smoking chimneys, and a water scene with sail boats.

12. An American gilded wooden eagle.

Please notify your local FBI office if you believe you have pertinent information concerning the Gardner Museum robbery or any other art theft mentioned in this article.

HOW CRIMINALS DISPOSE OF STOLEN ART

Where does all the stolen art go? The art thief often gets rid of hot art by leaving it with a "fence," or middleman. Either the fence will buy the stolen art outright, usually for about 10 percent of its known value, or an agreement will be reached whereby he or she will find a client for the stolen art for a specified sum. The clients of the fence vary in occupation but often are other criminals or members of the public at large who do not care from whom they buy an object as long as they feel they are buying it at bargain prices. One criminal told the author he looked forward to coming home each evening to enjoy the stolen paintings he had hung on his living room wall.

Art thieves also try to sell their stolen wares to galleries, antique shops, or restorers or try to slip them through auction house sales. Another thief known to the author operated successfully for about two years by stealing small paintings, porcelains, or statues from one gallery and selling them to a nearby gallery a short time later—without ever being asked any questions about their ownership.

The involvement of some tradespeople in buying or selling stolen artworks is not a new development but was officially declared a factor in the overall picture of art crimes in a survey conducted by Interpol (International Criminal Police Organization). Thirty-seven countries responded to the survey, and certain conclusions were discussed during the November 1973 UNESCO Conference on Art Theft and Other Forms of Illicit Transfer of Ownership, in Belgium:

> (a) The great majority of thefts occur in public or private places where there is no system of technical protection or where the system of protection is insufficient;

(b) Cultural property of great artistic and commercial value is recovered more easily than items of lesser value which are more easily negotiated;

(c) In the great majority of cases of cultural property which has been recovered, professionals in the art trade (secondhand dealers, retailers, antique dealers, etc.) have, at one time or another, been concerned.[5]

PLANNING A SECURITY PROGRAM

Referring once more to the 1973 Interpol 37-country survey on art thefts, we note that one of the reasons for art purloining was the failure of the responsible parties to take protective measures against it. However, as thefts have escalated, an awareness has finally developed that certain security measures are mandatory for the protection of our cultural heritage. Crime, particularly robberies, has caused a boom in the security business, both in the manufacture of security devices and in the growth of guard service companies.

The average person has little knowledge of the security field and is as vulnerable to the unprincipled vendor of security instruments, as is the new collector of art objects to the con man who occasionally may be found in the art community.

The investigator may be asked to advise the collector, gallery owner, or institution on security matters. An investigator not trained in this field may suggest that advice from a professional security consultant should be sought. The security consultant will be able to help design a security program for the individual needs of a client. There is a security program available for every budget. Remember to ask the vendor for references and seek the advice of colleagues regarding the reliability of the security company involved!

During the past 15 years museums, galleries, and private collectors have taken steps to secure their collections. In spite of these precautions, art theft remains too attractive for thieves to ignore, particularly when they read how the value of art continues to soar. Though many museums spend millions of dollars annually on security programs, it is difficult to prepare against the vandal, theft from within, subterfuge in gaining admission to closed museums and human shortcomings. The art thief will continue to steal, but we all should do as much as we possible can to hinder his success rate.[6]

TRAINING THE ART THEFT INVESTIGATOR

Law enforcement in the United States continues to virtually ignore the urgent need for specialized training in art theft investigations. This is particularly frustrating and confusing, since we constantly hear and read about the low recovery rate for stolen art works and the fact that art theft is the second biggest international crime (second only to narcotics).

Police Specialists by Country

The FBI realized the significance of the art theft crisis and became the first U.S. law enforcement agency to appoint specialists to this field. The author was assigned to investigate art crimes in 1965, worked this specialty exclusively for eight years, then developed a squad of four agents to assist in contending with an ever-increasing case load, until retiring in 1976. As of 1991, the FBI had no investigator commissioned full-time to art crimes. The New York City Police Department, the largest department in the United Sates, followed suit in 1971 and historically has assigned one officer to investigate art thefts. The U.S. Customs Department has had someone appointed to this specialty in New York on a part-time basis. For the past several years the Los Angeles Police Department has had an Art Theft Detail (one man) assigned to their burglary squad. That means three people are handling art theft cases (and one is part-time) in all of the United States. No other U.S. police agency—local, county, state, or federal—is known to have trained personnel involved in the investigation of purloined art.

Canada has come aboard by working out a program between the Royal Canadian Mounted Police at Ottawa and Interpol in listing art crimes. Austria, Germany, Mexico, Spain, Sweden, and Switzerland have long had investigators engaged in this specialty. The English refer to their unit as the Arts and Antiques Squad at New Scotland Yard; the French national Police call their art squad the French Central Office for the Repression of Art Thefts (COR-ART), and the Italians have the Carabineri Tutela Patrimonio Artistico, which employs about 80 persons.

One argument advanced against assigning specialists to this type of investigation is that there is not sufficient activity in this field to warrant such action. The author certainly did not find this line of reasoning to be valid. I believe every major police department in the United States should have trained personnel designated to fight the art crime crisis.

A Training Program for Specialists

Once an officer or a group of officers is assigned to conduct art theft investigations, a training program should be developed. Investigative techniques, art history, the art market, developing abilities to recognize fraudulent art, police liaison with the art community, developing art informants in the underworld and in the art community, security problems in protecting art, modern record-keeping procedures, and undercover operations are some of the logical curriculum considerations for the training program. The police department may wish to turn to the art community for assistance in gathering competent instructors in specialized areas. Museums, universities, auction houses, and art associations are all potential resources for this type of assistance.

However, it is in the field of liaison with the art community and in the development of art informants, that professional investigators should concentrate their efforts. Maximum attention to these two areas should result in a successful program.

Informant and Liaison Program

When representatives of the New York City Police Department contacted the author for suggestions concerning the development of an art squad, they wanted to know why the FBI's program had become successful in New York and their own initial attempts had fallen short of their expectations. A superior informant and liaison program with the art community was the answer.

In this case, liaison means continuous communication with artists, galleries, museums, auction houses, appraisers, art libraries, and restorers. Liaison means always being available to the art community when problems or questions arise regarding theft, security, or art fraud matters. Once the art world realizes the sincerity of the program, caseload, arrests, and recoveries of stolen artworks will increase notably.

A good liaison program will also result in noteworthy informant coverage, and it is axiomatic that the police department with outstanding informants will consistently solve cases and the department with poor-quality informants will have a poor case-solution rate.

Informants are people who inform the authorities about activities they believe are illegal. Some inform for money, some for revenge, some for love-hate reasons, some because they have a detective complex, some because they truly feel a moral obligation to do so, some because they are police "buffs," and some because they want a favor from law enforcement authorities.

Informants may be developed within the art community. They often are sincere, honest people who demand anonymity. The request should always be honored.

Competent police officers also develop informants in the underworld. They must handle these people with great care, as carelessness may lead to exposure of the informants and even to an informant's murder.

The national police agency has tremendous advantages over most local police departments concerning informants. Probably one of the most important advantages is that the national agency has more money available to spend on informants. It also has informants available in every state to help solve crimes. The author recalls several out-of-state informants furnishing information on New York art cases which led to arrests and recovery of stolen art objects. The FBI's criminal informant program is vast and successful. The information derived from informants is continuously shared with local authorities, but the informants' identities are protected. Many thousands of local criminal cases are solved each year through the efforts of FBI informants. Good informants, the telephone, an automobile, and capable undercover operators are law enforcement's most valuable tools.

Police departments should encourage personnel who show an ability and interest in undercover operations. I do not want to dwell on undercover techniques, but the ability of a law enforcement agency to put a man or woman into an underworld art fencing operation, or the ability of an officer to pose as an art appraiser, insurance adjuster, or buyer or seller of art is a tremendously effective weapon for exposing criminals and recovering stolen art objects.

PRECAUTIONS FOR COLLECTORS, DEALERS, AND MUSEUM ADMINISTRATORS

Collectors, dealers, and museum administrators can take certain precautions to protect themselves from purchasing false or stolen art.

Experience should have taught us by now that people lose their powers of reason when confronted with a bargain. Everyone seems to have been guilty, at one time or another, of rushing into a purchase, especially if the seller presents it as a super deal. We fail to ask ourselves why we should be offered a painting or print at such a fantastic discount. But buyer beware! The object may very well be fraudulent or stolen.

If there are doubts about the authenticity of an art work, an established art consultant, a museum, or an art association should be contacted for advice. The Art Dealers Association of America, Inc. (ADAA) (575 Madison Avenue, New York, NY 10022) and The International Foundation for Art Research, Inc. (46 East 70th Street, New York, NY 10021) will provide professional assistance regarding authenticity.

THE NEED FOR NATIONAL AND INTERNATIONAL COMPUTERIZED INDEXES OF STOLEN ART

The art crimes investigator faces similar problems to those of other property crime investigators. Often, after an arrest has occurred and a sought piece of art has been recovered, additional art may be found during the arrest. Then another problem frequently presents itself: identification of the art and its owner. This is a recurrent puzzle for all investigators of property crime. For example, the New York Police Department in the past has tried to resolve this difficulty by holding exhibitions of recovered jewelry, open to the public, hoping to identify its owners so that the property could be returned. However, in spite of the fact that the press gave excellent coverage to the events, only a few people were able to identify and recoup their property. For the art investigator this problem was compounded by the fact that there was no central index to which the investigator could refer, either for leads or to enter art theft reports.

While serving as a special agent in the FBI, the author in 1972 twice made official suggestions to have art thefts entered into the computerized records of the National Crimes Information Center (NCIC). The NCIC is a computerized FBI data base in Washington, D.C., which is constantly receiving and recording messages from law enforcement agencies throughout the United States. The messages concern such items as fugitives, stolen property identifiable by numbers, such as guns, cameras, securities, automobiles, boats, stereos—but not art. The author's suggestions were denied, but the FBI had the recommendations under consideration and started a manual index of stolen art. And in January 1980 the Bureau commenced a limited program in the computerization of art theft, entering approximately 1000 stolen art reports. The FBI computer is not tied into the NCIC, but is assigned to the Document Section of the FBI Laboratory in Washington, D.C. The index is called the National Stolen Art File (NSAF) and as of 1991 had over 6000 entries. Before accepting a stolen art report, the Bureau requires that the request be made by a police agency conducting a criminal inquiry. Another prerequisite is that the art submitted consist only of paintings, sculpture, or prints and be valued at $2000 or more per object. Once the details of the theft are received, the data is entered into the computer, where it is reviewed to see if the objects have been previously recorded. If no match-up is realized, the computer retains the details for future inquiries which presumably will lead to recoveries of stolen art and arrests.

England's New Scotland Yard and the French National Police computerize their art theft reports, and the Italians by 1987 had their computer system for tracking stolen art well established. On October 6, 1992, Constance Lowenthal, Executive Director, International Foundation for Art Research (IFAR), 46 E 70th Street, NY advised the writer that her organization is in frequent contact with Colonel E. Conforti, Carbineri, Piazza Saint Ignatius, Rome, Italy, whose stolen art inventory is now completely computerized. Some 80 persons are assigned to investigate Italy's massive art crimes problem. Italy has also published photographs and descriptions of pilfered art annually in a book titled, *Servizio Perle Ricerche Delle Opere D'Arte Rubate.*

Others have called for an art theft index. "A usable international register of art thefts should be established," said William A. Bostick, administrator and secretary of the Detroit Institute of Arts.[7] The value of an index was confirmed by Pranay Gupte, who said:

> Because there is no system of instant communication among the various national and international law enforcement agencies involved in the control of art theft, there is virtually no way these authorities can alert legitimate dealers with sufficient speed to what has been stolen before it comes up for sale.[8]

The urgency for an international art theft index becomes more apparent each year. A likely location for such a computer terminal might be Interpol Headquarters in Lyons, France. The system could be organized as follows: When an art theft is reported to the FBI's National Stolen Art File, the Bureau would record the data and simultaneously alert pertinent American sources and Interpol with the same details. Interpol would then notify their worldwide contacts. All of the other participating countries would utilize the same method in reporting their art crimes.

Since the National Stolen Art File is not available to the public, the need for a similar index in the private sector, available for review by anyone, becomes evident. In 1976 (with input from the author as a consultant in 1976 to 1977), the International Foundation for Art Research (IFAR) started its art theft index in New York City, and as of 1991 had recorded over 30,000 stolen art reports.

However, long before IFAR existed, the Art Dealers Association of America (ADAA) led the way in gathering records of stolen art and issuing notices of the thefts to its membership, museums, galleries, insurance companies, and law enforcement agencies without charge. The ADAA has recently transferred most of its stolen art records to IFAR, but still keeps its members advised of the art theft crisis.

TECHNIQUES AND TECHNICAL ASPECTS OF ART CRIMES INVESTIGATIONS

The art crimes investigator should devise a form for recording art thefts. The form should include such details as:

■ The name, address, and telephone number of the victim of the theft.

- The name of the artist, title of the work stolen, medium (such as oil on canvas, oil on wood panel, watercolor, pastel, and so on).
- Size (vertical measurement first).
- Signature and where it is located on art object.
- Any other information that would help identify the object.
- The identity, address, and telephone number of the police agency advised.
- The date of theft.
- The date when theft was reported to police.
- Information concerning the insurance company involved.
- A photograph of the object.

The sample form in Fig. 54.3 was devised to record art thefts reported to the International Guide to Missing Treasures.

Name: _____

Address: _____

Telephone number (with area code): _____

Name of artist or school: _____

Title: _____

Medium: _____

Date: _____

Size: _____

Signature as it appears on work: _____

Where it appears: _____

If work is a multiple, numbering as it appears: _____

Where numbering appears: _____

Any books, catalogues, etc. where work is illustrated: _____

Any other identifying information: _____

Police agency to which theft was reported: _____

Address: _____

Telephone number (with area code): _____

Name of law enforcement official to contact: _____

Date of theft: _____

Date of theft report to police: _____

Insurance company: _____

Address: _____

Telephone number (with area code): _____

Agent's name: _____

Reward (if offered): _____

Please attach photograph.

Figure 54.3 International Guide to Missing Treasures theft report form.

Investigators should determine and record the names, addresses, and telephone numbers of experts in various schools of art in their localities, so that these persons can be called on for expertise in their given field—abstract, American, impressionism, pointillism, Egyptology, and so on. Appraisers, academicians, museums, auction houses, galleries, and art associations are likely sources for these experts.

Investigators should also devise a list of informants and people in the art community to notify by telephone when an art theft occurs. These same people and others should be furnished photographs and full descriptions of the stolen art as soon as they are available. The telephone technique is used frequently in Europe, and the English and French police find it especially effective during the first 48 hours after a theft, the period during which many thieves attempt to sell their stolen art to tradespeople.

Investigators' chances of recovering an art object without a photograph of it are minimal. How can they look for something they have not seen? There is no more pertinent piece of advice the investigator can offer to a collector than to be certain that the entire inventory of art is photographed. Motion picture film and video tape are excellent methods of recording a collection, as is still photography. The use of a camcorder is highly recommended, for it allows the photographer to record an entire collection quickly and accurately. It is suggested the collectors be taped, making remarks about each object, including its measurement. A review of the tape on the VCR will quickly determine if any additional information should be included or if all the objects have been photographed successfully.

Insurance remains one of our great protections against theft. But insurance companies should refuse to cover property that has not been photographed. The pictures and descriptions of the collector's inventory should be maintained by the insurance company, by an appropriate attorney, or in the collector's safe deposit box.

Handling Recovered Art

Very little has been written about the unusual circumstances generally associated with art theft recoveries. Yet the investigator, upon recovering stolen art, often is faced with unique and multiple responsibilities. How should the recovered art be treated? To be facetious—very carefully; the investigator may well be protecting a national treasure.

When a painting is recovered, the investigator should initial it for evidentiary purposes. A small gummed label affixed to the reverse side of the canvas or stretcher usually will suffice. A felt-tip pen may also be used to initial the stretcher, which is the small wood frame beneath the main frame to which the canvas is attached.

Photographs should be taken of the recovered art immediately. Black and white film is adequate for identification, but colored film may also be used. The photographs should be made a part of the investigative report, with copies being forwarded to the prosecuting attorney. The importance of the photograph is that it will later serve as an indication of the exact condition of the work at the time of recovery and will counter any subsequent claims to the contrary. Paintings should be photographed on both the front and reverse sides of the canvas, and sculptures should be photographed from several angles, including the bottom of the base.

Law enforcement agencies rarely plan their facilities to accommodate recovered artworks, which require carefully controlled temperature and humidity for optimum preservation. For this reason, it is recommended that the prosecutor immediately be advised of the unusual and fragile nature of the recovered property. Prosecutors generally welcome this type of information and will often agree to storing the art in a bonded warehouse. It is recommended that a professional packer be retained if the art is to be stored or shipped. Some prosecutors may prefer to release the artwork to the institution or person from whom it was stolen, on the condition that it will not be shown or sold before the case has been resolved in court.

Careless handling of an object of art can result in the loss of that creation to humanity forever. The author recalls one case in which a painting was in such horrendous condition at the time of recovery that most of the paint crumbled and fell from the canvas. Thieves had secreted the painting, covered with burlap and leaves, in a forest for several weeks, and foul weather had destroyed it. Upon examination, a museum conservator sadly related that the canvas could not be restored.

Since the required chemicals could damage the canvas and depreciate the value of the painting, fingerprint examination of the painting should not be attempted. The frame, however, can be removed and examined for fingerprints. Though an ornately carved frame seldom lends itself to a meaningful fingerprint examination, the reverse side of the frame is flat and is a logical site for dusting.

There is another examination the investigator should not overlook. A thief stealing a painting often will use a sharp instrument, such as a razor, to cut the canvas away from the frame. The investigator should retain and preserve as evidence the strips of canvas left in the frame. The author remembers recovering a stolen painting and noting that a bottom strip of the canvas was missing. Further investigation disclosed that the police department that had originally investigated the theft had kept the empty frame in which remained a strip of canvas from the bottom of the painting. An examination of the recovered painting and the strip of canvas determined they fit like two pieces of a jigsaw puzzle, thus providing concrete evidence that the recovered painting was indeed identical to the one reported stolen.

Rewards

Some insurance adjustors and law enforcement authorities have expressed great concern over the growing trend of offering rewards for the return of valuable stolen art objects, especially those objects that are well insured. A typical reward for a $500,000 painting might bring $50,000 or 10 percent of the value.

Yet the practice of recovering stolen art through a reward presents some interesting questions that must be addressed. Doesn't the prospect of offering a reward tend to promote the business of crime?

What if a valuable art collection is stolen and the collection is not insured? These were the facts reported when art valued at $200 million was taken from the Isabella Stewart Gardner Museum in Boston in March 1990. Many eyebrows were raised after the Gardner Museum theft when Sotheby's and Christie's auction houses, at the request of the Federal Bureau of Investigation, agreed to put up a $1 million reward for the return of the Gardner Museum pieces. In March 1990, Anne Hawley, the museum's director, said the offer was made possible by a highly unusual agreement between

Sotheby's and Christie's art auction houses, which will underwrite the reward.[9] Ms. Hawley stated that the museum had decided to offer the reward at the urging of the FBI, which thought it would be very helpful in the investigation, especially because $1 million was a "magical" number.

For law enforcement officers participating in reward cases, great care must be taken to assure that their activities do not violate the law. Contact should be maintained with the officer's legal department throughout the reward procedure. This is an important suggestion because so many of the United States have different laws pertaining to rewards.

Various Operandi of the Art Thief

For many years art thieves, some quite sophisticated, have specialized in the theft of art from archaeological diggings, museums, castles, galleries, libraries, cathedrals, schools, and the private residences of the collectors. The purloiners bypass or neutralize alarm systems, gain access through skylights or through a wall or floor of a neighboring gallery or apartment. Other robbers gain admission to their "target" building by subterfuge and violence, as was the case in the Gardner Museum incident. The "smash and grab" technique has been utilized a great deal. This method involves smashing a plate glass window on a store front, grabbing an art object, and making a successful escape. In 1991 "smash and grab" thieves used automobiles to shatter gallery windows in England in order to carry out art thefts. Burglars planning this type of robbery often set off window alarms and time the police response before carrying out such a theft.

A technique currently in vogue is to have a man enter an art gallery during business hours, grab a painting off a wall near the front entrance, while a lone employee is on duty at the far end of the gallery. The thief then dashes outside with the painting, joins his partner in an automobile, and escapes. A very successful robber would strike when the weather is bad. He would enter a gallery during the day, take a small painting off the wall, remove it from the frame, replace the empty frame on the wall, place the painting in a large inside pocket of his raincoat, and escape casually walking away from the scene.

Many art thefts are inside jobs, and they can be substantial. A handyman of the Detroit Institute of Arts was arrested for purloining over $400,000 worth of art objects from the Institute. The Art Institute of Chicago had three Cézanne paintings valued at over $1 million stolen by an employee. A guard at the Walters Gallery in Baltimore, Maryland, pled guilty of stealing hundreds of thousands of dollars worth of oriental art from his place of employment. And then there was the Chicago art thief who used public transportation (CTA) during his theft escapades and became distraught when the CTA went on strike. Finally, we have learned of a 20-year-old art thief in Paris who found it very easy to steal art from museums. He said it was like shopping in a supermarket. He may have found it effortless, but he was arrested, and a judge sentenced him to three years in jail.

IRON CURTAIN VANISHES AND CRIME BURGEONS

An alarming development has unfolded as the European bloc of Communist nations raised the Iron Curtain and welcomed democracy. All areas of crime immediately increased, as gangs found travel easier and police control greatly reduced. This development has already resulted in some significant thefts of art. In December 1990 a painting by Lucas Cranach, valued at over $200,000, was stolen from the Czechoslovakia National Gallery in Prague. The same gallery was the victim of another robbery when four Picasso paintings worth $30 million were purloined in May 1991. Fortunately the four Picasso paintings were recovered in Bayreuth, Germany, in June 1991. Cathedrals, churches, and museums have been early victims of this surge in crime, and unless security measures are quickly put in place, the pillage will continue.

DRUGS AND STOLEN ART

During the past several years there have been rumors that stolen art was being used as collateral for the purchase of illegal drugs, or that drug lords have been able to buy art from sales of drugs. These rumors have been verified as several cases have emerged indicating art thieves are dealing in narcotics. One example is that of a notorious art thief who was arrested in Illinois for trafficking in drugs and interstate transportation of stolen property (art). He received a prison sentence of 20 years.

WHO SHOULD BE INFORMED ABOUT ART THEFTS

The investigator should consider alerting the following individuals or organizations about art theft cases. In so doing, they should include complete descriptions and available photographs of the missing objects.

1. National Stolen Art File, Laboratory Division, Document Section, FBIHQ, Washington, D.C. 20535, (202) 324-4434.

2. F.B.I., Interstate Transportation of Stolen Property Squad, 26 Federal Plaza, New York, NY 10278, (212) 335-2700.

3. Donald L. Mason (former senior art crimes investigator for the FBI), Security and Fine Arts Consultant, P.O. Box 102, Haworth, NJ 07641.

4. Robert E. Spiel Associates, Inc. (former art theft investigator for the FBI), 155 North Michigan Avenue, Suite 500, Chicago, IL 60601, (312) 861-1313.

5. Commanding Officer, Property Recovery Squad, New York City Police Department, 1 Police Plaza, New York, NY 10038, (212) 374-3823.

6. U.S. Treasury Department, Customs Service, Room 410K, Team 203, 6 World Trade Center, New York, NY 10048, (212) 466-5500, ext. 5709.

7. The International Foundation for Art Research, Inc., 46 East 70th Street, New York, NY 10021, (212) 879-1780.

8. The Art Dealers Association of America, 575 Madison Avenue, New York, NY 10022, (212) 940-8590.

9. Art Theft Detail, Burglary Squad, Los Angeles Police Department, Room 319, 150 N. Los Angeles Street, Los Angeles, CA 90012, (213) 485-2524.

10. National Central Interpol, Cultural Property Unit, 1200 Alta Vista Drive, Ottawa, Ontario, Canada K1AOR2, 0101-613-993-3232.

11. Auction houses in your area should be notified. Three of the largest ones in the United States are Sotheby's, 1334 York Avenue, New York, NY 10021,

(212) 606-7000; Christie's, 502 Park Avenue, New York, NY 10022, (212) 546-1000; Phillips, 406 East 79th Street, New York, NY 10021, (212) 570-4830.

12. *TRACE*, monthly magazine for retrieving stolen works of art and antiques, Head Office, 163 Citadel Rd., The Hoe, Plymouth, Devon PL12HU, England, 0752-228727.

13. Interpol, c/o U.S. Department of Justice, Washington, D.C. 20530, (202) 739-2876.

NOTES

[1] "Taking Pictures," *Weekend Magazine* (October 13, 1979).

[2] *Art Gallery* (November 1976).

[3] *The New York Times* (September 1, 1991).

[4] "Stolen Picasso Found by FBI Appraiser," *The New York Times* (August 8, 1974).

[5] "Theft of Cultural Property: A report by the Interpol General Secretariat to the Organization's Forty-Second General Assembly," *Museum* (quarterly review published by UNESCO) XXVI, no. 1 (1974):61.

[6] Many of these facts are developed by Donald L. Mason in his book, *The Fine Art of Art Security*, (Van Nostrand Reinhold, New York, 1979).

[7] William A. Bostick, "The Ethics of Museum Acquisitions," *Museum*, XXVI, no. 1 (1974).

[8] Pranay Gupte, "The Big Business of Art Theft," *Portfolio Magazine* (April 1979).

[9] Anne Hawley, *The New York Times* (March 21, 1990).

55

Campus Security

James R. Sutton

Investigative activity that takes place on college campuses shares the same basic principles as any other civil or criminal probe. While the specific procedures might vary from one institution or jurisdiction to another, the rules remain the same. The need to follow proper legal procedures in collecting evidence, interviewing suspects, and obtaining information from victims and witnesses is essential; otherwise successful prosecution or litigation will be highly improbable. However, the similarities end there. Efficacious probes in this context require the investigator to keep in mind the unique institutional nature of college campuses and the demographic characteristics of student bodies, faculty, and staff. More important, it demands knowledge of laws that have specific applicability to institutions of higher education and a familiarity with standard procedures used to ensure the safety and security of students and employees.

BACKGROUND

Security on college campuses reflects the same issues and concerns that are important to the great majority of our nation's citizens. Violent crime has increased in most institutions of higher education in the past three decades, reflecting a similar tendency in the rest of the country. This trend has raised considerable concern among students and their parents, many of whom make considerable personal sacrifices to put their children through college.

Historically, security in colleges and universities was a marginal concern to law enforcement agencies. In the first half of the century, institutions of higher education were relatively small and their populations highly homogeneous. Some were located in rural enclaves, while others existed on the fringes of urban areas. However, the influx of World War II veterans and the subsequent baby boom altered the generally tranquil mood of college campuses. By the 1950s a number of colleges developed security programs and hired personnel to implement them. These programs were mostly staffed by poorly trained security guards with limited responsibilities and legal power.

The turmoil of the 1960s and 1970s demanded increasing police resources to deal with campus security. At that time, law enforcement's preoccupation with colleges involved student activism. Confrontations most often revolved around such issues as the antiwar movement, civil rights, and the recreational use of narcotics. To meet the challenge and ease the demand on municipal resources, a number of the large private colleges and most of the state universities formed their own police departments and staffed them with sworn officers.

However, in the last decade the concerns of law enforcement and college administrators changed from controlling student activism (although that remains a marginal problem) to protecting all students from crime and preventing some students from engaging in criminal activity against their peers. In an examination conducted by the Center for the Study and Prevention of Campus Violence in 1990, it was determined that at least 80 percent of campus crime was committed by students.

Student Right-to-Know and Campus Security Act

The shifting focus of campus security resulted from the increasing number of violent crimes against students and the ensuing law suits and demands by parents that some action be taken. Several highly publicized incidents served to heighten the concern of students, parents, employees, and legislative bodies. The *Student Right-to-Know and Campus Security Act*[1] emerged out of this preoccupation. Previous to the enactment of this law, the absence of standardized reporting requirements concerning crime complicated the development of a clear picture of the problem. The following statistics, compiled by a variety of agencies, highlighted the confusion of often conflicting numbers. During the Senate hearings on Public Law 101-542, Senator Arlen Specter (R-Pa) cited a 1988 campus crime survey that found 31 students killed, 653 rapes, and 1800 armed robberies. The 1988 figures collected by the Center for the Study and Prevention of Campus Violence (CSPCV) at Towson State University (TSU) in Maryland indicated there were 639 sexual assaults, 2598 physical assaults, and 6 homicides in a sample of 368 colleges. In 1989, the 10 percent of American colleges and universities that chose to report campus crimes to the Federal Bureau of Investigation's Uniform Crime Report (UCR) recorded a total of 2 murders, 241 forcible rapes, 1683 cases of aggravated assault, and 417 cases of arson. Nationally, the *Chronicle of Higher Education* reported in 1990 that there were 8,175,008 students enrolled at 2127 four-year colleges. A survey conducted by *USA Today* in December 1990 disclosed campus crime occurred at a rate of 26 per 1000 students, approximately half of the 57 per 1000 rate for the nation. David Merkowitz of the American Council on Education noted that colleges are generally safer than the communities around them; however, the statistics also revealed a large number of crimes involving students did not occur on campus. Prior to PL 101-405, many schools reported data through local police agencies, yet the campus statistics were not itemized in the final summaries of these agencies. The number of disparate and often conflicting statistics exacerbated the frustration of students and their parents, particularly those who had been victims of crime.

The driving force behind the *Student Right-to-Know and Campus Security Act* was provided by the parents of a 19-year-old freshman who was raped, tortured, and murdered in her dorm at Lehigh University in Pennsylvania in April 1986. The 1990 slaying of five college students in Gainesville, Florida served to focus renewed attention on a legal effort to compel schools to disclose campus crime statistics. The Act represented a legislative solution to the perceived problem that some colleges and universities were less than candid about the crime risks existing on their campuses. In fact, there is evidence that some colleges paid lip service to security concerns, while placing a low priority on developing truly effective security programs. A 1989 survey for the Carnegie Foundation for the Advancement of Teaching found that only 20 percent of college presidents said that increasing the quality of campus security was "very important." This was the lowest percentage of 20 possible changes in their schools they were asked to rate.

Public attitudes concerning crime on campus have resulted in an increasing number of law suits against colleges and universities. Courts in various states have held academic institutions liable for failing to protect students and employees from foreseeable criminal activity. Publication of crime statistics, as required by PL 101-405, will make it easier to establish liability and will facilitate gathering the information required for a civil action. At least two dozen cases involving campus crime are currently working their way through appellate courts in various states. Security on Campus, Inc., a nonprofit corporation, maintains a data base concerning college crime and tracks the number of legal actions against universities. (See "Sources & Resources Section" later in this chapter for additional information.)

Perception Versus Reality

Among the major problems facing college administrators responsible for security and campus police is not only the issue of actual crime trends—which might include sporadic high-visibility incidents—but also the perception of security by students, parents, and employees, in other words, their subjective opinion regarding their own safety. It is not surprising that in most institutions of higher education there is a significant discrepancy between actual crimes disclosed to the police and the number of self-reported incidents, that is, students and employees who identify themselves as having been victims of crime in surveys. There are a variety of reasons for underreporting crime; one of the most common is the desire by many students and employees to avoid the hassle of dealing with law enforcement authorities. While minor property thefts, vandalism against property, assaults, and batteries are understandably underreported, there is the matter of serious crimes, particularly those of a sexual nature or those involving ethnic minorities, that are not divulged because victims believe the system is not responsive.

National surveys indicate that 25 percent of female undergraduates have been victims of rape or attempted rape, and that 84 percent were acquainted with their assailants. Rape is far more common on campus than statistics show. Reliable studies reveal that only 1 in 10 college victims report rape, making it the most underpublicized campus crime. For many victims, the burden of reporting the incident and enduring the adversarial nature of investigation and prosecution is too much to bear. Furthermore, male students involved in rapes are rarely disciplined. An estimated 1 percent of all male students known to have taken part in an incident of this nature are prosecuted according to Gail Abarbanel, director of the Rape Treatment Center at Santa Monica Hospital in Southern California. Beth Baldinger, a Princeton, New Jersey attorney who has represented over 15 students—all rape victims—disclosed that many colleges discourage reporting and prosecution. Sandy Silverman of the Onondaga County District Attorney's office in Syracuse, New York noted that people are afraid to damage their reputation or, worse yet, to be ostracized for the negative publicity they bring upon the institution.

Even the *Student Right-to-Know and Campus Security Act* appears to be flawed in this respect. The law requires reporting rape but not sexual assault. Many schools classify as sexual assault incidents that in other institutions fit the legal definition of rape. Such downgrading can make many schools appear safer than they really are. In many states rape is a felony, wile sexual assault or battery is a misdemeanor. Few schools have advocates to help victims prosecute, and when they do their use seems to be declining. Furthermore, many of the colleges that had advocates have eliminated the position in an effort to reduce spending in "nonessential" programs.

Students, parents, and employees are uneasy about the occurrence of crime on campus, but their fears are generally based on anecdotal and often ambiguous information. Concern rises sharply when a notorious incident of campus violence takes place, but is soon forgotten, especially by those not directly affected. Current research indicates that without independent, legitimate statistics, most individuals will not rely on their perception of the frequency of crime in an area or the seriousness of the crime problem in forming judgments about their own personal safety or fear of becoming a crime victim. Indeed, much research shows that individuals generally see themselves as less vulnerable than other people, except their close friends. Other inquiries also point out that people believe that victims of violent crime are usually "loners," physically weaker and in some respect, wittingly or unwittingly, responsible by having placed themselves in harm's way.

In the past, campus security was not a burning issue at most schools, and law enforcement intervention was seen as intrusive and confrontational. Students wanted to come and go and have guests as they pleased. Any interference with this freedom was resented and resisted. Robert Hill, former president of the National Association of Independent Colleges and vice president for university relations at Syracuse University, noted that "colleges and universities responded to the kind of freedom students make clear they want. Now there is a desire for tighter security." David Stormer, assistant vice president for safety and environmental health at Penn State University and former president of the International Association of Campus Law Enforcement Administrators agrees. He said: "The students of the late 80's and early 90's want retribution and action much quicker than the system at most schools is capable of delivering."

If the school's institutions fail to respond fast enough, some students are all too willing to go outside the system. An example of this trend is what is referred to as "guerilla tactics," which have been used at several colleges. They consist of informal organizations of female students who publicize the names of male students alleged to have been involved in incidents of date rape or sexual assault. This is accomplished by notes on student bulletin boards, "zines" (informal newsletters and magazines), word-of-mouth, and even graffiti in women's bathrooms. While the seriousness of the rape problem is acknowledged, there are well founded concerns that wrongfully accused male students will be unable to challenge the claims or clear their names.

The willingness of students to take matters into their own hands also accounts for the increasing number of confrontations among student groups. The most common issue in these conflicts is race. Like rape, race-related hate crimes are grossly underreported at most colleges. Nonetheless, many institutions are struggling to issue appropriate policy to deal with hate crimes without infringing on First Amendment rights or standards of academic freedom. Incidents involving sex and race offer the most serious investigative challenges. Investigators must be scrupulously impartial and objective: otherwise they will lose credibility. Claims and counterclaims made by the adversaries have to be carefully and methodically corroborated. Incidents involving deaths, aggravated assaults, rapes, and other serious crimes will continue to be investigated by law enforcement authorities and prosecuted, and ensuing litigation will involve many of these grave offenses. However, the trend indicates that an increasing number of civil actions will result from hate crimes and harassment incidents, as victims, parents, employees, and survivors seek compensatory and punitive damages.

Nationwide research disclosed that two demographic characteristics, gender and minority status, were consistently related to:

- A fear of victimization.

- General judgments about the seriousness and prevalence of crime on campus.

- Impressions of the efficiency of campus police.

Females and ethnic or life-style minorities (such as gay students) reported more-than-average personal fear of becoming a victim of a violent crime while on campus and were less satisfied with the performance of law enforcement, security, and school authorities to protect them against wrongdoing. Most institutions of higher education are attempting to develop programs to address real concerns and explore ways in which the campus community can be made more aware of actual crime problems, while at the same time dispelling rumors and misperceptions that tend to create a climate of fear. Research has shown that professionalism, politeness, and an honest consideration of student safety were the most salient dimensions that influenced students' evaluations of campus police.

Student groups formed along ethnic lines insist that racist attitudes have left many minority students feeling discouraged and isolated, and have contributed to a high dropout rate among them. The disparity of views underscores a widening gap on campuses across the country between the perceptions of whites and minorities in evaluating the educational and economic opportunities afforded to each group. Robert Purvis, legal director for the national Institute Against Prejudice and Violence (NIAPV) in Baltimore, Maryland, pointed out that there is a startling difference between the way minority and white students view each other's situations. The report, based on case studies at 12 colleges across the country, indicates that there is an increase in ethnic tensions on campuses and in the expression of those tensions in a violent manner. Presently, there is no comprehensive nationwide research on how many racially motivated crimes occur on campus, largely because the majority of such incidents go unreported. In a 1990 study, NIAPV estimated that 20 to 25 percent of minority (college) students were victimized, a figure reckoned at somewhere between 800,000 to 1 million students a year.

What Is a Campus?

One of the most important considerations in conducting civil or criminal investigations involving incidents on or about colleges or universities is the determination of jurisdiction. In many cases it is difficult to differentiate campus boundaries. Many students are victims of crime while near, or while travelling to and from, the campus. Although off-campus crime is not the responsibility of the campus police, in most cases close cooperation exists between the campus police and other law enforcement agencies in the area. Collaborative efforts are frequent. This highlights the importance of developing a productive and cooperative relationship with police agencies that have some jurisdictional responsibility for crimes involving students off campus. The 1990 slaying of five college students in Gainesville, Florida emphasized the importance of cooperation. The killings served as an illustration of how off-campus crimes can have a paralyzing effect on the entire university community, even though campus police have no jurisdictional control over these kind of situations. Ironically, in 1989 Florida enacted the campus security information bill. But under the law the Gainesville slayings will not be included in the crime statistics report for the University of Florida or Santa Fe Community College, where the victims were students because the killings occurred in off-campus apartments. Under the *Student Right-to-Know and Campus Security Act,* educational institutions will be required to report crimes committed against students regardless of whether they take place on or off campus.

Although the *Student Right-to-Know and Campus Security Act* ensures that collecting and reporting mechanisms will be consistent from state to state, precision will still be troublesome. Many of the nation's major colleges are located in densely populated urban areas, such as Atlanta, Boston, Chicago, Detroit, Los Angeles, and New York. Conditions beyond the school's control might distinctly affect the security climate and crime rate. For example, rates may vary widely depending on such conditions. The most significant factor is the location of the campus. Is it an inner-city neighborhood or a rural hamlet, primarily a commuter campus or does it have many students in dormitories? Are its stadiums and pavilions used frequently for outside sport events or rock concerts? Even such seemingly minor circumstances as whether the school has night classes can have an impact on its crime statistics. The case of Illinois is typical for the rest of the country. Northern Illinois University in De Kalb with 24,680 students reported 465 violent and property crimes in 1988. That is almost half as many as disclosed by the University of Illinois at Chicago, with a similar enrollment and 823 crimes. The difference is that UI-Chicago is located in the inner city while De Kalb is not.

The effectiveness of campus law enforcement also tends to create the appearance of a higher crime rate. For instance, students are more willing to divulge crime incidents when they perceive the police as responsive and effective. A proactive aggressive crime control strategy will also result in a higher number of arrests. Most officials who are concerned about campus security realize that statistics provide, at best, a partial view of campus security. Their significance is more realistic when the context in which these occur is placed in a proper perspective.

For the purpose of public Law 101-542, the term *campus* includes not only buildings and property owned or controlled by the institution (within the same reasonably contiguous geographic area and used in support of or related to its educational purposes), but also any buildings or property owned or controlled by recognized student organizations. The fact that these properties may lie outside the jurisdiction of the campus police is acknowledged in the law. It requires the monitoring and recording through local police agencies of criminal activity at these locations. The policy statement indicates institutions should make "reasonable efforts" to gather such data, but does not impose on local law enforcement any obligation that they cooperate. In most cases, fraternity, sorority, and other organizational housing units will be considered part of the campus, regardless of the location and ownership. Technically, other areas that may be included within the definition of "campus" are recreation/camp sites, research facilities, and teaching hospitals. Branch campuses, schools, or divisions that are not within a reasonably contiguous geographic area are considered separate campuses.

CRIME AWARENESS AND CAMPUS SECURITY ACT OF 1990

The sections of Public Law 101-542, *Crime Awareness and Campus Security Act of 1990* that are most relevant to the duties of investigators will be discussed. However, there is a caveat. The law as presently constituted has many ambiguities that need to be resolved by the issuance of regulations by the Department of Education (due to be finalized in 1992). Until these ambiguities are resolved, the advice of legal counsel should be sought when there is conflict with established university procedures or the activities contravene the letter and intent of Public Law 101-542. An example of such conflict involves a 1974 privacy protection law known as the *Buckley Amendment*, which bars colleges from releasing information about individual students without their consent. The Education Department has in the past indicated that colleges would violate the law if they released the names of students arrested by campus police officers. The Department threatened to cut off federal funds to institutions that violated the *Buckley Amendment*. In July 1991, Senator Tim Wirth of Colorado introduced an amendment that would allow colleges to release crime reports; however, to date the issue remains unresolved. Nonetheless, the Education Department announced in mid-1991 that it would propose free-standing legislation to allow colleges to release crime reports.

The Conference Report

The Conference Report (Report 101-883), issued by the House of Representatives on October 16, 1990, made the following observations that are relevant not only to students, parents, and employees of institutions of higher education, but to persons conducting criminal or civil investigations on campuses.

Section 202—Findings

(1) The reported incidence of crime, particularly violent crime on some college campuses has steadily risen in recent years.
(2) Although annual "National Campus Violence Surveys" indicate that roughly 80 percent of campus crimes are committed by a student upon another student and that approximately 95 percent of the campus crimes that are violent are alcohol or drug related, there is currently no comprehensive data on campus crimes.
(3) Out of 8,000 postsecondary institutions participating in federal student aid programs only 352 colleges and universities voluntarily provide crime statistics directly through the Uniform Crime Report of the Federal Bureau of Investigation; and other institutions report data indirectly through local police agencies or states in a manner that does not permit campus statistics to be separated.
(4) Several state legislatures have adopted or are considering legislation to require the reporting of campus crime statistics and dissemination of security practices and procedures, but the bills are not uniform in their requirements and standards.

(5) Students and employees of institutions of higher education should be aware of the incidents of crime on campus and policies and procedures to prevent or to report occurrences of crime.

(6) Applicants for enrollment at a college or university and their parents should have access to information about the crime statistics of that institution and its security policies and procedures.

(7) While many institutions have established crime preventive measures to increase the safety of campuses, there is a clear need

   a. to encourage the development on all campuses of security policies and procedures;

   b. for uniformity and consistency in the reporting of crimes on campuses; and

   c. to encourage the development of policies and procedures to address sexual assaults and racial violence on college campuses.

Section 203—Disclosure of Disciplinary Proceeding Outcomes to Crime Victims

Section 438(b) of the General Education Provision Act (20 United States Code U.S.C.) 1232q (b) is amended by adding at the end thereof the following new paragraph:

"(6) Nothing in this section shall be construed to prohibit an institution of postsecondary education from disclosing, to an alleged victim of any crime of violence (as that term is defined in section 16 of Title 18 U.S.C.) the results of any disciplinary proceeding conducted by such institution against the alleged perpetrator of such crime with respect to such crime."

Section 204—Disclosure of Campus Security Policy and Campus Crime Statistics

(*a*) Disclosure requirements—Section 485 of the Act (20 U.S.C. 11092) (as amended by section 102 and 104) is further amended by adding at the end thereof the following new subsection:

"(*f*) Disclosure of Campus Security policy and Campus Crime Statistics—

"(1) Each eligible institution participating in any program under this title shall on August 1, 1991, begin to collect the following information with respect to campus crime statistics and campus security policies of that institution, and beginning August 1, 1992, and each year thereafter, prepare, publish and distribute, through appropriate publications or mailings, to all current students and employees, and to any applicant for enrollment or employment upon request, an annual security report containing at least the following information with respect to the campus security policies and campus crime statistics of that institution:

"(*A*) A statement of current campus policies regarding procedures and facilities for students and others to report criminal actions or other emergencies occurring on campus and policies concerning the institution's response to such reports.

"(*B*) A statement of current policies concerning security and access to campus facilities, including campus residences and security considerations used in the maintenance of campus facilities.

"(C) A statement of current policies concerning campus law enforcement, including:

"(i) the enforcement authority of security personnel, including their working relationship with state and local police agencies; and

"(ii) policies which encourage accurate and prompt reporting of all crimes to the campus police and the appropriate police agencies.

"(D) A description of the type and frequency of the programs designed to inform students and employees about campus security procedures and practices and to encourage students and employees to be responsible for their own security and the security of others.

"(E) A description of programs designed to inform students and employees about the prevention of crimes.

"(F) Statistics concerning the occurrence on campus, during the most recent school year, and during the preceding school years for which data are available, of the following criminal offenses reported to the campus security authorities or local police agencies

"(i) murder;

"(ii) rape;

"(iii) robbery;

"(iv) aggravated assault;

"(v) burglary; and

"(vi) motor vehicle theft.

"(G) A statement of policy concerning the monitoring and recording through local police agencies of criminal activity at off-campus student organizations which are recognized by the institution and that are engaged in by students attending the institution, including those student organizations with off-campus housing facilities.

"(H) Statistics concerning the number of arrests for the following crime occurring on campus:

"(i) liquor law violations;

"(ii) drug abuse violations; and

"(iii) weapons possessions.

"(I) A statement of policy regarding the possession, use, and sale of alcoholic beverages and enforcement of state underage drinking laws and a statement of policy regarding the possession, use, and sale of illegal drugs and enforcement of Federal and State drug laws and a description of any drug or alcohol abuse education program as required under section 1213 of this act.

(2) (Paragraph omitted)

(3) (Paragraph omitted)

(4) (Paragraph omitted)

(A) (Paragraph omitted)

"(B) in coordination with representatives of institutions of higher education, (the Secretary of the Department of Education shall) identify exemplary campus security policies, procedures, and practices and disseminate information concerning those policies and procedures, and practices that have proven effective in the reduction of campus crime.

"(5) (A) For purposes of this subsection, the term `campus' includes—

"(i) any building or property owned or controlled by the institution of higher education within the same reasonably contiguous geographic area and used by the institution in direct support of, or related to its educational purposes; or

"(ii) any building or property owned or controlled by student organizations recognized by the institution.

(B) (Paragraph omitted)

"(6) The statistics described in paragraphs (1) (F) and (1) (H) shall be compiled in accordance with the definitions used in the uniform crime reporting system of the Department of Justice, Federal Bureau of Investigation, and the modifications in such definitions as implemented pursuant to the Hate Crime Statistics Act."

In addition to the federal legislation, several states have enacted crime disclosure statutes, and other state legislatures are planning similar measures. Regardless of the state requirements, the provisions of the *Crime Awareness and Campus Security Act of 1990* compel all institutions of higher learning, even those located in states with no disclosure requirements, to submit the necessary information for inclusion in the Federal Bureau of Investigation's Uniform Crime Report (UCR).

States that presently have campus crime disclosure statutes include Connecticut, Delaware, Florida, Louisiana, New York, Tennessee, Virginia, Washington, and Wisconsin. A brief description of each follows:

Connecticut

HB 5921 (Public Act No. 90-259) applies to all institutions of higher education and requires them to provide annual statistics of UCR Part I crimes to students, applicants and employees upon request. The school must also notify at the beginning of the year—in writing—all concerned of the availability of these reports.

Delaware

Chapter 89, Title 14, Delaware Code (HB 606) applies to all institutions with on-campus residence halls. It requires submission of monthly crime statistic reports to the institution's Chief Executive Officer (CEO), which contains at least all UCR Part I offenses and are part of the public record. An annual crime statistic report is to be published in a campus newspaper or other suitable way prescribed by the CEO. This report is also provided to any person upon request. The law further requires the institution to publish security policy information in the college or university catalog.

Florida

Act 89-142 applies to all institutions of higher education and requires an annual assessment of physical plant safety; the audit report is forwarded to the state legislature. The institutions must also give notice that a statistical report regarding campus crime is available upon request.

Louisiana

Act 543 (HB 223) applies to all institutions of higher education and requires monthly statistical reports to the campus management board of all UCR Part I offenses. Such reports are part of the public record. The law also mandates the institution to publish security policy information in the college or university catalog.

New York

S 7170/A 9624 applies to all institutions and deals primarily with sexual assault. The bill requires colleges and universities to provide information to incoming students about the applicable laws, penalties, and procedures for handling sex offenses, as well as the methods the college employs to advise students about security procedures.

Tennessee

Public Acts, Chapter 317 (Senate Bill 1406) applies to all institutions and requires that a statistical report regarding campus crime be provided upon request to applicants for admission and new employees. The availability of this information must be made known to all formal applicants for admission.

The law also requires security policy information to be provided upon request to applicants for admission and/or employment and to current students and employees. The contents of the policy also needs to be disseminated through the posting of public notices, which state that the information is available and explain how it may be obtained.

Virginia

Section 23-9.1:1 of the Virginia Code applies only to public institutions and requires these colleges to make copies of their most recent State UCR report available to any interested party upon request.

Washington

SB 6626 applies only to four-year public institutions who are required, upon request, to provide three-year summaries of their State UCR reports to all applicants and new employees, both of whom must be notified of the availability of this information. These statistics must also be furnished annually to all students and employees in a brochure format.

Wisconsin

Assembly Bill 431 applies only to public institutions and deals with sexual assault and harassment. The bill requires institutions to annually supply to all students "printed material" containing information on sexual assault by acquaintances and sexual harassment. It should also include the legal definitions of, and penalties for, sexual assault, sexual exploitation, and harassment. The dean of students is required to compile the statistics. Campus employees who witness a sexual assault on the campus or receive a report of such an incident from a student are required by this statute to notify the dean of students. Persons who have responsibility for conducting investigations on universities or college campuses should familiarize themselves with proposed, pending, or recently enacted legislation similar to the statutes noted herein. Investigators should also be cognizant of existing criminal or penal code statutes that are applicable to colleges and universities or that pertain specifically to students and employees of these institutions.

STANDARD SECURITY PROCEDURES

There is a noticeable degree of conflict between an ideal academic environment, with its tradition of free movement and access, and the requirements to make a campus a reasonably secure place for all members of the institution. The concept of reasonable security and administrative responsibility provides direction in achieving this balance.

What Is Reasonable Security?

Almost all institutions of higher education periodically review their efforts to make their respective campuses reasonably secure places for students and employees. While these efforts may vary from one jurisdiction or institution to another or may even be referred to by different names, such as Campus Security or Campus Police, their activities invariably fall within the public safety service concept. This concept is basically one in which those functions of the university or college that are intended to eliminate campus environmental hazards or are related to the protection and preservation of life and property are incorporated in one professionally staffed, service-oriented organization. To be credible in the academic community, these services must be comparable to the professional academic services offered in other areas of the campus.

The public safety service concept involves administrative implementation through the establishment of three main functional areas that are of concern to all segments of the institution: (1) protective services, (2) safety services, and (3) traffic safety and control services. These three elementary support functions are geared towards providing a unique service to students, academic staff, employees, and visitors. Although law enforcement is a significant segment of public safety service, it is not necessarily its sole focus. The public safety role is directed at supporting, preserving, and fostering the academic and institutional strategy of the college or university. If this role is effectively accomplished, the individual student, faculty member, researcher, employee, and visitor will develop a clear understanding of the legitimacy and importance of the public safety function in maintaining a suitable, viable climate for teaching, studying, researching, and providing community service.

Public safety services in the context of an institution of higher education are normally provided on a 24-hour basis by professionally trained law enforcement officers. These public safety officers generally have nothing to do with student discipline. Law enforcement authority in the case of public institutions usually comes directly from the state, so that there is no question of legal capability or responsibility. Private colleges and public universities are best served by ensuring that their campus police officers are properly deputized by state or local authorities with regard to the enforcement of laws (not student conduct regulations) on campus.

The concept of "reasonable security," as used by most administrators, chancellors, and directors of institutions of higher education, recognizes the need to maintain a balance between an open campus and a secure campus. It also acknowledges that the risk of becoming a victim of violent crime will often vary by factors over which the institution has little control, such as crime in the surrounding community or broader social issues that might create conflict within the campus. Nevertheless, school administrators have a clear responsibility to maintain a reasonably secure campus and to take initiatives to minimize or eliminate foreseeable dangers. Failure to do so results in substantial legal liability for the institution.

Administrative Responsibility

Administrative responsibility for campus security is normally assigned to a specific individual, who might be the campus chief of police or director of security. Whatever the name of the position, this person will frequently report to one of the institution's senior administrators, such as a dean or vice chancellor. Additionally, each institution will generally designate another individual with the duty to respond to safety and/or security emergencies. Depending on the specific procedures for each college, this person might be assigned to administration, physical plant, or the campus police.

Responsibility for the campus security systems should at a minimum ensure that:

1. Security needs are taken into account in the design, maintenance, and operation of the institution's buildings, grounds, and equipment.

2. Students and other members of the institutional community are adequately informed about security risks and procedures.

3. Security personnel are adequately screened, trained, equipped, and supervised by the institution or its contractor.

4. The number of security personnel utilized is adequate to perform the functions assigned to the department. If no security personnel are used, the campus should be made reasonably secure by other appropriate means.

5. Data regarding security incidents is collected and analyzed, and the results of the review are used to undertake preventive action or improve operations.

Some of the more progressive institutions have established campus-wide committees to periodically review their security policies and emergency response procedures in reaction to emerging trends or legislative requirements. These committees will normally be headed by a senior administrator, and the team will include representatives from a wide range of campus agencies. For example, many campuses may take in representatives from campus safety and security, student affairs, admissions, legal counsel, university relations and public information, personnel, academic/faculty affairs, and student government. In some instances, smaller subcommittees are formed to deal with problem areas or address specific issues.

Common Practices to Minimize the Likelihood of Violent Crime on Campus

Normally each institution develops a set of policies and procedures that reflect its own unique concerns, conditions, and priorities. The practices identified in this section are representative of what is found at most colleges and universities; however, actual operations may vary widely. Investigators conducting inquiries in this context are strongly urged to familiarize themselves and document, where possible, the specific policies and procedures used by the institutions with which they are concerned.

Crime Prevention Programs

1. *Personal safety talks:* These are one-on-one conversations or briefings with specific students, employees, or parents regarding individual threats or unique conditions that merit this type of approach. Related activities include Walk & Talk Crime Prevention programs, Informational Ride-Along with Campus Police, and the like.

2. *Crime awareness seminars:* These can be provided to all students/employees or to a certain category, such as females. The presentations can address a host of security concerns or be specifically focused on a particular problem. The most effective seminars are those that address actual concerns, provide factual information, and make low-key realistic recommendations. Related activities include orientation of the new employees and students, parents' night security information booth, and the like. If the college has a large number of foreign students, audio visual crime awareness prevention presentations would be made in the students' language.

3. *Handout crime prevention material:* This may be pamphlets and leaflets addressing specific areas of concern, such as dorm security, rape prevention, and related subjects. Material that is mass produced by crime prevention organizations is the least effective, while material produced in-house and pertaining to specific issues or areas of concern is well received. With the advent of computerized desk-top publishing systems, these types of pamphlets/leaflets are used with increasing frequency.

4. *Public affairs:* Campus police and other security officials will normally provide information on major crimes to the institution's office of public affairs. Exceptions to the process will include cases that are in progress or where dissemination of the information would constitute a violation of law or be contrary to the institution's rules. Information properly disseminated can be used to answer questions from the news media and be employed to control rumors. The material can also be furnished to in-campus publications, such as a student newspaper and other publications.

5. *Security surveys:* They can be used to evaluate the entire security program of the institution on an annual basis, or they can focus on a specific facility or problem area. They can be conducted by external consultants or by appropriate employees, generally senior security administrators. One of the primary advantages of these surveys is that they provide comprehensive documentation of the institution's efforts to improve security and are excellent instruments to develop effective long-term plans.

6. *Communications equipment:* A number of colleges and universities employ a variety of equipment to allow employees and students to communicate with public safety in case of an emergency. Some systems consist of network emergency call boxes installed at strategic locations. They provide instantaneous, hand-free, two-way communication with campus police. A system of this type has been installed at the University of Illinois campus in Chicago. It is connected to a computer that furnishes a detailed description of the location. Eventually, these call boxes will be integrated with video monitors, situated in the immediate area, and will supply visual data to supplement voice communication. Other institutions are experimenting with personal transmitters that are carried by students/employees and that can be activated in an emergency to identify the user's location. This "star wars" type of equipment is in a prototypical stage and is not expected to be widely available in the near future.

Ground Security and Access. At the majority of institutions, entry into most buildings is restricted after normal hours, usually at the conclusion of evening classes. In other facilities access might be continuously controlled for security or safety reasons. Some buildings might be managed by Pass-Desk Check Points with security guards or police officers; and other sections might be monitored by card readers or CCTV, while sensitive sectors, offices, or buildings will be equipped with intrusion alarms.

Grounds personnel and other physical plant employees are normally considered part of a Campus Watch Program and are directed to transmit safety and security hazards. Campus police and security committees or even student groups are encouraged to report any environmental condition that creates a risk of crime, such as excessive growth of bushes, inadequate lighting, malfunctioning alarms, and the like.

Escort Services. Most institutions provide some type of shuttle, transportation, or personal escort service on a 24-hour basis. Depending on the circumstances, police officers, security guards, or members of the student patrol can be used as escorts. Shuttle services normally include transportation between the college's main areas and the dormitories or housing units. Frequently, they also furnish transferal to main centers for public conveyance, such as train stations and bus depots. These services have proven to be an important component of campus crime prevention programs, and their availability is advertised and promoted.

Campus Law Enforcement. Campus law enforcement is multifaceted.

Police/Security Officers. In almost all instances, persons serving in a law enforcement capacity in an institution of higher education are required to successfully complete a basic law enforcement training course and comply with all other requisites mandated by the state legislature for all bona fide peace officers. The instruction is regulated, supervised, and often provided by a state-designated law enforcement training board. Included in basic training courses is knowledge of state laws, arrest procedures, constitutional rights, and at least 40 hours of mandatory firearms instruction. Upon completion of basic training, all officers must pass some form of certification examination given by the board. Officers are then given provisional probationary status and assigned to a field training program. Further education is usually furnished through a variety of police/criminal-justice-related programs supplied by regional law enforcement or academic institutions. Additionally, almost all campus police departments have policy manuals, general orders, special orders, as well as written rules and regulations applying to the department's personnel.

Although security guards and members of student patrol programs have no police powers and are discouraged from intervening in police matters, they are thoroughly familiarized with the training and responsibilities of peace officers.

Cooperation with Other Law Enforcement Agencies.   Most campus police departments or security operations have a long, mutually beneficial relationship with the municipal and state police agencies in their jurisdiction. Command, patrol, and special units normally meet on a regular basis. Their memorandums of understanding (portions of which might be regulated by state law) include such items as multijurisdictional task forces or hot-pursuit policies, and they might also involve circumstances under which jurisdictional lines can be crossed, as well as mutual aid agreements. In most instances, the campus public safety communications system has direct links with adjacent agencies and can be immediately activated as needed.

Use of Force/Firearms Policies.   The use of force, particularly of firearms by campus police, is a contentious issue fraught with considerable danger. The training of campus police officers in the proper use of firearms takes on a high priority due to the nature of the officers' responsibilities. In most institutions campus police officers carry weapons only after they meet all the requirements mandated by the respective state for peace officer certification. The application of force is clearly spelled out in the department's general orders and is normally far more restrictive than what state laws mandate.

Student Patrol and Nondeputized Security Personnel.   Most colleges and universities assign some limited security responsibilities to unarmed security guards and student employees. These are civilian personnel with no arrest authority, although they frequently receive special training and are uniformed and equipped with two-way communications. They carry no firearms. Their main function is to serve as a physical presence and enhance the security program as highly visible "eyes and ears" for the campus police. Their utilization is cost-effective in that they also contribute a variety of services not normally provided by sworn officers, such as escort and after-hours building access control, thus freeing police officers for more critical duties.

Special Events.   Those institutions whose stadiums and auditoriums are used for nonacademic functions open to the public, such as rock concerts or sports, will frequently hire off-duty city, county, and state officers on a part-time basis. These officers are experienced, trained traffic and crowd control experts, normally directed by an on-duty campus police supervisor. The responsibilities of such part-timers are spelled out in the department's general orders. Frequently, their authority is limited to that of an "in-house security officer" with no peace officer status. In other words, efforts are made to restrict their authority to comply with campus regulations. However, this varies widely from one jurisdiction to another, and therefore the specific regulation should be documented if relevant to a given situation.

Campus Demonstrations.   The specific policies vary from one institution to another and range from very lenient to restrictive; however, the majority of them contain some or all of the following requirements, which generally come after a review of state and federal law. Great policy changes in the recent past relate to student unions and residence halls where demonstrations are prohibited to ensure safety and minimize disruption of university business. Peaceful dissent and the opportunity to present differing points of view are an important aspect of democracy and the academic experience. But protest must be balanced against the rights of others to carry out programs, conduct university business, and be free from undue harassment. Campus procedures related to protests and/or demonstrations generally prohibit disruptions within campus facilities, particularly where safety, the free-flow of pedestrians, or campus order is involved. When a demonstration is anticipated (planned, spontaneous, or otherwise), a site consistent with legal requirements will normally be designated by the campus police in consultation with appropriate university officials.

A demonstration organized by one or more identifiable organizations, either campus or external, is usually deemed to be a "campus event." As such it is subjected to the same constraints and procedural rules governing other campus events. Organizations that plan to use campus facilities are generally required to follow specific procedures in requesting appropriate space. The overall intention of these regulations and policies is to clearly spell out the rights and responsibilities of individuals and students on campus. They are designed to protect our rights to express opinions in an environment conducive to free speech and the rule of law.

SOURCES AND RESOURCES

This section contains the names, addresses, and telephone numbers of organizations active in the field of campus security and represent a potential source of information and expertise for civil and criminal investigators. It is by no means exhaustive, but rather intended to serve as a preliminary avenue for additional research (names and addresses verified as of December 1991):

1. American Council on Education (ACE), One Dupont Circle, Washington, D.C. 20036, (202) 939-9300. Among the varied activities of ACE is its legal council monitoring of litigation and legislation involving issues pertaining to campus security.

2. Campus Security Resources, Inc., 2300 Clarendon Boulevard, Suite 204, Arlington, VA 22201, (703) 351-5610. Codirector is William D'Urso, a private consulting company specializing in campus security.

3. Campus Violence Prevention Center (CVPC), Towson State University, Towson, MD 21204, (410) 830-2178. The CVPC has conducted extensive research into the problem of campus violence and has compiled a significant volume of data on the topic. The Center's violence prevention resource guide, a comprehensive annotated bibliography of the collected information and a copy of *Safe House*, a quarterly publication, is provided free with membership enrollment. The Center's director is Robert Cave.

4. International Association of Campus Law Enforcement Administrators (IACLA), 638 Prospect Avenue, Hartford, CT 06105, (203) 233-4531. IACLA publishes the highly regarded *Journal*, which focuses primarily on campus law enforcement trends and issues. The Association's director is Peter J. Berry.

5. National Association of College and University Business Officers (NACUBO), One Dupont Circle, Suite 500, Washington, D.C. 20036-1178, (202) 861-2500. NACUBO has conducted an extensive analysis of the *Crime Awareness and Campus Security Act* and has collected data from member institutions. This information includes descriptions of institutional policies

and procedures, which can be shared with others, as well as copies of procedures employed to meet the "timely reports" requirement for warning the campus community about crimes considered to be a threat to students and employees.

6. Security on Campus, Inc., 618 Shoemaker Road, Gulph Mills, PA 19406. This nonprofit corporation was founded by the parents of Joanne Clery, a 19-year-old freshman who was killed in her dorm at Lehigh University in Pennsylvania. It provides support services for victims and their parents.

7. Victim Assistance Legal Organization, Frank Carrington, Esq., 4530 Oceanfront, Virginia Beach, VA 23451, (804) 422-2692. Frank Carrington served as legal counsel for Security on Campus, Inc., and is presently on the Board of Directors. Recently, he formed VALOR, a nonprofit corporation that maintains a data base of lawsuits filed against institutions of higher education regarding security issues. Frank Carrington served as legal counsel for the parents of Joanne Clery.

NOTE

[1]Public Law 101-542, enacted by the House of Representatives, 101st Congress, on October 16, 1990.

56
Investigation of Sexual Assault Crimes

Fortunato J. De Luca

PUBLIC AWARENESS

During the past few years, statistics have shown an increase in the reported crimes of sexual assault. This increase indicates either an increase in the actual incidence of sexual assault or increased reporting due to the public's confidence in its police.

Public awareness concerning the reality of the crimes of sexual assault has increased for several reasons. In addition to several television dramatizations dealing with rape and sexual abuse of children, there have been several movies dealing with rape. Furthermore, a judge in the Midwest was censured for his judicial conduct while presiding at a rape case, and this received wide media coverage.

Unfortunately, not all the recent attention by the media has presented the criminal justice system in a favorable light; however, more and more attention is being given to the sexual assault problem by those in policy-making positions. For example, in some places during the past few years, units have been set up outside the police department to work in conjunction with the police in rape investigation. Furthermore, municipal task forces on rape have been formed— agencies designed to serve in cooperation with the police and departments of hospitals and social services.

SEXUAL ASSAULT DEFINED

Rape, sodomy, and sexual abuse by forcible compulsion comprise the basic offenses included in most local criminal law statutes. To have carnal knowledge of a person by force (against that person's will) would constitute a sex crime.

The concept is fairly simple, but the investigation of sex crimes is more complex. An investigator attending a sex crimes seminar will undoubtedly be informed of the current psychological interpretation which states that rape is not a sex crime but a serious physical assault in which the offender uses sexual means to denigrate or otherwise act out violently toward the victim. In such a case, the assailant is not motivated by sexual gratification but, rather, by other psychological stimuli such as scapegoating, proving masculinity, or degrading the victim for self-aggrandizement.

Some sex crime statutes, however, are written to include sexual gratification as a necessary element of the crime. For example, sexual contact is defined as the touching of the sexual parts of a person for the purpose of gratifying sexual desire of either party.

Will the question of whether or not there is sexual gratification on the part of the assailant affect the successful prosecution of a sex case? Can the defense be made that since there was no gratification on the part of the assailant, as substantiated by some current psychologists, there then exist grounds for the dismissal of a sex crime? I doubt it.

Many experienced investigators admit that the investigation of sex crimes is not always a preferred assignment; however, these same individuals show no hesitation concerning homicide, robbery, or assault investigative assignments. Why the hesitation and reluctance when facing a sex crimes investigation? Most investigators with ability and some understanding of the unique aspects of the crime would function as well in investigating sexual assaults as in any other investigative assignment, especially if the investigator realizes that sexual assault is not merely a sexual immoral act but an act of severe aggression and hostility that can, and often does, debilitate its victim.

CONCEPTS OF INVESTIGATIVE ASSIGNMENTS

Invariably, whenever the subject of rape is discussed, a guess is ventured as to the number of rapes which occur yet go unreported. The number of unreported rapes is said to be 10 times that of those reported; and the reasons for these unreported cases vary. Psychologists cite shame, guilt, and the victim's embarrassment—to name but a few; and, unfortunately, police officers have little influence on such reasoning. When, however, the reason given stems from lack of confidence in the police force, then police officers may be in a position to influence the public's image of them and the subsequent handling of sexual assault cases.

In the investigation of the crime of sexual assault, the police administrator must first determine whether the case should be assigned to a "specialty squad" which investigates sexual assault cases exclusively or to an investigative unit designed to investigate all types of crimes. There are advantages to each type of case assignment.

Designed to investigate first-degree sexual assaults, sexual assault specialty squads are now functioning in numerous police departments; and there are several valid reasons for this.

First and most important, expertise is developed through the repeated handling of one type of investigation. Technical expertise is developed in the areas of forensic, laboratory, and hospital procedures. Also, the sex crimes investigator develops a certain expertise in the areas of victimology and in investigative techniques.

Another advantage offered by the specialty squad concept is the facility with which a centralized unit can handle a pattern, or repetitive, type of crime. Such squads more readily identify the pattern which crosses precinct boundaries and are more likely to communicate with other area specialty squads regarding those which cross area boundaries. This type of squad set-up does, however, pose a potential problem, namely, that of possibly losing the interest which is generated at a local level. Nonetheless, this can be overcome by frequent and meaningful communications between the specialty squad and the local unit.

Regardless of the concept chosen—specialty squad or more general investigative unit—some training is essential regarding the types of cases, the victimology, and the investigative techniques which emphasize the aspects unique to sexual assaults.

TYPES OF CASES

Most investigators recognize the existence of difficulties inherent in the various types of police investigation. Psychopathic killers are often the most difficult to identify and apprehend, because they kill without apparent motive. The terrorist bomber may leave a trail of death and destruction but not enough evidence to lead to a successful apprehension. In cases of purse snatching or street robbery, which involve a one-time encounter between the offender and the victim, identification of the subject by the victim may be difficult.

Sexual assault investigations also have specific characteristics which may present problems to the investigator, including such elements as force and age.

Force as an Element

In the majority of sex crime investigations, the severity of the crime is based on two main criteria: (1) the use of force and (2) the age of the parties involved.

The issue of forcible compulsion is sometimes obvious and at other times more subtle. Therefore, the investigator must first analyze all the data surrounding the act and then classify the crime. Weapons are not essential to establish the element of force. For example, a victim who is threatened and alone on a rooftop may give in to a rapist's demands; this is properly classified as a forcible rape. On the other hand, if a potential victim is out with a date and told she will have to walk home from a location if she does not give in, the investigator may not be able to establish force as an element.

Age as an Element

The ages of both the victim and the offender usually enable the investigator to classify a sex crime more readily. Usually the investigator simply takes the ages of the victim and the offender, consults the penal code, and classifies the crime accordingly. For example, the ages used to classify the various sex crimes by degree in the state of New York are as follows:

1. *First-degree crimes:* Victim is less than 11 and legally unable to give consent.

2. *Second-degree crimes:* Victim is less than 14 and offender more than 18 years.

3. *Third-degree crimes:* Victim is less than 17 and offender is more than 21 years.

It can be noted that the older the "consenting victim" and the younger the offender the less serious the offense.

BASIC TYPES OF SEX CRIMES INVESTIGATIONS

Sex crimes investigations usually involve four basic types of cases: (1) the pattern case involving hard-core rapists, (2) the known-offender case involving some type of opportunist rapist, (3) the unfounded case, and (4) the referred case.

The Pattern Case

According to most literature in the field, the recidivist rate for the sex offender is very high. Additionally, the offender is defined as an individual for whom normal sexual outlets are either unavailable or unacceptable and who may be compelled to act out violence in a sexual assault. Bearing these concepts in mind, it is small wonder that approximately 40 percent of the assigned sex crimes investigations involve cases in which the assailant has either struck before or will strike again. Therefore, investigative effort must be directed accordingly.

These concepts are very important to the success of apprehending the pattern rapist. Since in this type of investigation the subject will usually strike repeatedly before being apprehended, all data must be recorded meticulously, including the correct identification of MOs and complete descriptions.

Some patterns are readily identified. For example, the age of the victims may be unique, as in a case involving elderly women (over 70 years old) who were the victims of a pattern rapist. Other telltale elements may involve: (1) unique MOs—burglar using fire escape entry, assailant accosting victims in elevators and proceeding to rooftop; (2) a unique physical characteristic of assailant—missing fingers, scars on face; or (3) unique demands of assailant—may require victim to perform certain acts.

Other cases involving the same assailant may not be so readily identified as patterns. In an area that investigates many cases each year with a large number involving unknown assailants, it may not be readily apparent which comprise clusters involving the same pattern rapists. For this reason, meticulous interviews must be conducted and facts included in reports. A standard routine format should include: time of assault; date; day of week; place of occurrence; victim's sex, age, and address; activity prior to incident; assailant's MO, weapons, language; peculiar acts demanded or performed; and details of assault.

Once the reports are complete, they should be reviewed by an analyst; then, it is hoped, trends will become apparent. Remember, not all of these "same assailant" cases will be obvious and a proper review and analysis by a member of the unit specifically assigned to that task is essential.

Some departments have relied on computer systems to aid in pattern analysis and detection. However, in larger departments, this system has not proved functional for a variety of reasons, including the large volume of cases, insufficient information submitted by investigators, and personnel shortages at the computer base. In my opinion, the bottom line is that it is very difficult to translate the intimate subjective details of an incident into computer language, which is inherently objective.

New York City had a four-page categorized data analysis form, which included 48 forced-choice checkoff categories for perpetrator information. For example, the form offered 20 choices to describe the relationship (if any) between the victim and the offender. The form was very complete, but the information supplied by the victim was too subjective—not surprisingly, since the victim was relating data observed while in a highly emotional state.

Given that we are talking of an assailant with a moustache; however, victims' recollections will vary. Some will remember more than others. One victim may not recall facial hair while another might, and a computer may not allow for this discrepancy. The analyst, on the other hand, would be able to compensate for some deviations, considering the traumatized state of the victim. Even basic descriptions of the same subject are sometimes very distorted. For example, as related by several victims the same assailant's height often varies greatly. Thus, it is evident that there are many variables that are potentially subjective, including weight, hair color, clothing, hair style, and so on. The larger the volume of cases submitted to a computer, the more specific the breakdowns will be and hence the less likely it becomes that the computer will recognize the less obvious pattern cases.

The computer may identify the obvious cases, but the more subtle pattern cases will be identified faster at the local squad or district office, depending on the accuracy of the reports and the competent evaluation of similar incidents by the in-house squad-level analyst. At the local level discrepancies can be more readily addressed by direct conferral of the analyst and the investigator and resolved on the spot.

As incidents are identified as similar and a pattern is suspected, a small investigative team should be assigned to work specifically on these pattern cases. Often, similar cases that are assigned to different investigators go unresolved because there is a lack of communication and coordination. Therefore, once a pattern is discerned and a team assigned, all similar cases are reviewed and reevaluated by that team.

The following example will illustrate the above concept. Over the past three years, I have worked on assignments involving 12 to 15 identified pattern investigations. These pattern cases consisted of anywhere from 2 to 10 cases per pattern before the assailants were apprehended. The total complement of the squad has been from 15 to 18 investigators. In each of these pattern investigations, one or two investigators have been assigned as pattern investigators as the need arose—one or two out of 18 to coordinate the pattern investigation.

Once the team is assigned, it proceeds to review and conduct an in-depth analysis of each case. It will reinterview each victim, witness, and even the investigator who was initially assigned to the case. The need for this procedure cannot be emphasized strongly enough, for only through an intimate knowledge of each case can the team begin to assimilate data and coordinate any additional resources it may receive.

Team coordination must include the dissemination of information to field or uniformed personnel, since these units must be familiar with pattern-type investigations in their areas. Obviously, once armed with a description and MO, such units will be on the lookout for and will apprehend the subject going to or coming from an incident.

In most pattern investigations, arrests of the subjects are made directly by an alerted uniformed patrol officer or indirectly by information supplied by a patrol officer. In one pattern investigation, which involved a subject who accosted the victim on the street at knifepoint and then proceeded to a darkened street area to commit the sexual assault, apprehension was made in a routine street robbery of a female at knifepoint. In the incident for which the subject was arrested, no sexual advances were made; however, the uniformed officer had recognized the similarity in the MO. Although no sex was involved, a knife was used and the victim was on the street between the hours that the subject was known to strike. The point is this: The officer had been informed; he was aware of this particular pattern investigation; and he notified the investigating squad of the similarities. The squad's follow-up investigation included a line-up in which five of the five rape victims identified the subject.

The awareness of particular pattern information by uniformed and field personnel is also important in determining what peculiar or specific information to look for at crime scenes so that certain items of potential value may be properly safeguarded.

For example, one subject of a pattern investigation was known to bleed profusely from the penis during forced fellatio. Responding to a sexual assault scene, uniformed officers were advised of this fact and could act accordingly to safeguard this type of evidence were it observed. Since they were aware of what the investigator deemed important, they were also in a better position to ask the victim specific questions at the scene. In sum, the investigator who spends some time in personally addressing an outgoing uniformed platoon not only adds a sense of importance to the investigation, but also may be ensuring its successful conclusion.

The crime scene units responsible for the locations in which the crime occurs should also be thoroughly familiar with ongoing pattern investigations. Specific and detailed information concerning prior crime scenes involving the same subject would give added directions to processing a crime scene.

Street crime units (plainclothes) and decoy units should also be considered for use when appropriate. Pattern investigations can be very successful when the information about the pattern has been disseminated and resources within the police department have been coordinated. In this type of investigation, the traditional gap between investigator and patrol officer must be bridged; and the impetus to cultivate a cooperative effort must come from the investigator.

Information that is kept "close to the chest" does not always produce a successful investigation. The subject in a sex crimes investigation involving patterns is usually a hard-core, solo assailant. Unlike the narcotics investigation, there are usually no paid informants; unlike the homicide investigation, there are seldom witnesses who will come forward. In the sex crimes investigation, unless an atmosphere of cooperation is established and police resources are utilized to the fullest by the investigator, the information that is obtained from the witness may be the only information that is forthcoming.

The Known-Offender Case

This type of sexual assault case involves parties who are known to each other and includes an assailant who is usually an "opportunist" rapist. Such cases represent approximately 37 percent of an investigator's caseload and also have a high percentage of clearance since the victim can usually identify the assailant. Known-offender cases include a wide variety of situations such as:

1. The case in which a child is assaulted by a known party—family member, family friend, babysitter, boyfriend of family member, grocer, and so on.

2. The case in which a prior sexual relationship existed; for example, assault by an ex-boyfriend.

3. The case in which a victim is assaulted by a known person but with whom there has been no prior sexual or social relationship—landlord, rental agent, doctor, teacher, police officer, minister, and so on.

4. The case in which a victim is assaulted by someone with whom there has been a social relationship; for example, a rape during a date or a rape in which the victim is "offered a ride home" at the end of a social event.

Ordinarily such cases do not involve the hard-core rapist, per se, but experience has shown that forcible sexual assaults have been committed by such "opportunist" rapists. They differ from the pattern rapist in the sense that if a particular set of specific circumstances had not existed, the assailant probably would not have gone out and prowled the streets searching for a victim.

That is not to say that these individuals do not repeat this particular MO in which they assault people known to them, for some of them do. For example, two cases were reported in which the same named assailant had raped two different victims, three nights apart. At the end of an evening of socializing at a local tavern, he had offered to drive the victims (whom he knew) home, then proceeded to rape them. During an interview with one of the victims, we were told she had learned that he had done this several times before and that victims had not reported the incidents. This was his MO; this was his pattern.

In such cases, it is often difficult to establish the element of force. It is my opinion that many known-offender cases go unreported because the victim holds herself responsible when, in fact, she has been forcibly assaulted. While force may be difficult to establish, it is not impossible. Torn clothing and physical trauma, as well as noted emotional trauma, may fortify an investigator's case. Such traditional evidence as semen slides may not aid a prosecution since the defense would probably claim sex by mutual consent.

In these situations, the experience and intuition of the sex crimes investigator will be put to task, for evidence must be presented which shows that an illegal rather than an immoral or unethical act has, in fact, been committed. In some cases, the court's position has been that a victim's demeanor was a precipitating fact to a rape. Although in a particular case the jurist who took that position was censured and removed from the bench, such attitudes may still be prevalent and, if so, must be dealt with effectively through a thorough and convincing investigation.

The Unfounded Case

Although approximately 77 percent of the cases investigated represent valid sexual assaults, experience has shown that a significant portion of a sex crimes investigator's time is also spend investigating false allegations of sexual assaults. In fact, after investigation approximately 19 percent of reported cases are classified as unfounded—that is, false or baseless complaints.

This fact is meaningful for two reasons. First, the sex crimes investigator must keep in mind that one out of every five cases will be a false report. Not only is this high percentage of false reporting unique to sex crimes investigations, but also it accounts for a considerable amount of an investigator's time. Such cases often require as much in-depth investigation as do bona fide complaints and thus may require many investigative hours before they can be closed.

Second, the investigator is placed in a precarious position. Once having become suspicious of a false report, his or her focus takes a different direction, and often the alleged victim will notice the change. The investigator must remain objective, nonjudgmental, and aware of the various reasons for the false reporting. By remaining sensitive and understanding, the investigator does not solidify the alleged victim into a position of being less likely to disclose the truth. The prime objective is for the victims themselves to understand. This may be accomplished by pointing out obvious flaws or improbabilities and the futility of pursuing the false report. Most "victims" who are shown a sympathetic and objective attitude will recant. On the other hand, experience has shown that an accusatory, recriminating, hard-line approach may give the "victim" no alternative but to stick to the story, even when it is apparent that the incident could not have occurred as stated. In cases that are not so readily disproved but are, in fact, false incidents, the "victim" may be the only one who can clear the case. If the "victim" does not recant, the investigation ends in an unresolved case.

With respect to motives for false reports, most investigators are aware of the incidence of falsely reported crimes and of the reasons people have given for them, such as insurance fraud in cases of arson, robbery, or burglary; and revenge in narcotics cases. Following are reasons commonly given for alleged sexual assaults.

Cover-up Stories.   This category includes allegations fabricated by the "victim" to cover up a forbidden activity, for example, overstaying a curfew. It has been used by runaways, truants, wives, and girlfriends to avoid accusations or unpleasant questioning by concerned family or friends. One such case was reported by a teen-age girl who had stayed out all night with her boyfriend while her grandmother babysat. She feared her grandmother would chastise her, so she made up the story of a kidnapping and rape.

Desire to Change Residence.   Welfare recipients have been known to claim they were victims of serious crimes, because they wished to change their residence at the expense of their welfare department.

False Allegations by Prostitutes.   Known prostitutes have been known to file reports for several reasons, including: (1) a "John's" failure to pay the agreed-on price for a sex act; and (2) the desire to receive a free abortion, claiming the pregnancy resulted from a rape. Often such "victims" give false names and addresses and are not heard from again.

The sex crimes investigator must realize the importance of unfounded cases to both the image and the credibility of the squad and to the sense of security in the community. In fact, nothing could be more damaging to an investigative unit than the accusation of improper or insensitive handling of a sex crimes victim. Often, from the onset unfounded cases gain media attention, and the only way of maintaining community confidence is through properly conducted inquiry into unfounded cases. The importance of documenting the specific reasons for such cases cannot be overemphasized.

The Referred Case

Although relatively few in number, some crimes assigned to the sex crimes investigator are not sex crimes cases. Even those investigative units that handle sex crimes exclusively find that about 4 percent of the total caseload is comprised of these misclassified cases. After an initial interview of the victim, such cases are referred to other investigative units.

Experience has shown that cases are misclassified for a number of reasons, among which are the following:

1. *Incomplete preliminary interview by the reporting officer.* This can occur when the reporting officer does not fully establish what has taken place at a crime scene. For example, a victim of a robbery in an elevator may report that she was almost raped, and the responding officer may classify it as "attempted rape." A subsequent interview may reveal that the victim "did not like the way the suspect looked at me"; that "it was as if he wanted to rape me." the point is that once a sexual assault is alleged some officers are reluctant to proceed further into an interview.

2. *A "second-party" report of an incident.* This can occur when an uninformed party reports a crime at the unsolicited request of a "victim." For example, the parent may report some "unnatural behavior" toward a child. The child, who may have been unresponsive to the parent, may respond to the investigator who, in turn, learns that while a physical assault occurred, no sexual assault was involved.

3. *An erroneous classification.* This can occur through a simple misinterpretation of the law. For example, in New York State a person is deemed incapable of consent when he or she is less than 17 years of age. It is a crime for a male to have intercourse with a female who is less than 17 years old; however, it is a felony if he is over 21 years old and a misdemeanor if he is less than 21 years old. The seriousness of the crime, felony, or misdemeanor may determine which unit investigates a case. If wrongly classified, it will be referred to the proper unit.

While the referred case usually does not cause any insurmountable hardship, its investigation can result in an unnecessary delay in the proper investigation of a case and sometimes results in duplication of effort. Although I doubt that these misclassifications can be eliminated, they can certainly be reduced through some training of those involved in the preliminary procedures. Perhaps it would be in a sex crimes investigator's best interest to present an informative lecture to an in-service training class or an outgoing platoon. Such time spent on the training end could result in less unnecessary time spent on the investigative end.

VICTIMOLOGY

Frequently the police officer's role includes dealing with persons who are in highly emotional or crisis states. In fact, rare indeed is the police investigator who has not dealt with individuals involved in a crisis situation. Comforting victims of accidents and their families are situations in which police officers are usually experienced. Among the most difficult are situations that involve informing a parent that his or her child has been killed. These experiences, however, better prepare the police investigator for dealing with crime victims constructively and productively and in an understanding and empathetic way.

Although simple, the reasons for understanding some aspects of victimology are important. Aside from the humanitarian aspect, a cooperative victim can constitute a key element in the investigator's successful completion of a case, thus directly influencing the investigator's effectiveness.

The Sexual Assault Victim

Current psychological literature is replete with studies that deal with crime victims, and the concepts explored are not complex. They deal with how people react to the stress of a sudden and arbitrary event and how this reaction affects the individual's coping and functioning stability.

Through consideration of these few concepts, sex crimes investigators can better understand the behavior of sexual assault victims with whom they will deal. For instance, they will better understand the fear and terror that could cause a rape victim to jump out a four-story window to her death when, as her apartment was being burglarized, she feared she would be sexually assaulted again. They will be able to better understand the confusion and conflict a rape victim displays in relating her traumatic experience. They may be able to better understand the feelings of shame, guilt, or embarrassment which seem inherent in sex crimes victims. They may even gain insight into why a prostitute, to whom sex is not strictly a personal and intimate matter, may exhibit symptoms of crisis reaction ranging from childlike behavior to shock to anger after a sexual assault. Finally, they may come to realize that the most unique aspect of a sex crimes investigation is the effects such crimes have on their victims. These effects range from subtle to devastating, from short-term to long-term. In fact, in more than most other criminal acts against a person, the crimes of sexual assault can influence the complete life-style of its victims.

To explain the effects of crisis and trauma on crime victims, several variables must be considered in the context of different types of crimes. These crime victimization variables include intrusion, violation of self, loss of control and autonomy, violence, and physical and psychological injury. The formula is simply that the greater the number of variables present, the more stressful will be the victimization and the stronger will be its potential effects.

In the majority of cases involving burglary, the victim is not usually confronted by the offender. Therefore, the related victimization variables usually do not include a loss of control or autonomy, nor is there violence and physical injury. As a result of the feeling of intrusion and violation of self, there may be some psychological injury.

On the other hand, the victim of an armed robbery is usually confronted by the offender and suffers a loss of control or autonomy. Although there may be no violence resulting in physical injury, the psychological injury is present due to intrusion and violation of self.

Finally, these two victims may be contrasted with the sexual assault victim who not only is confronted by the offender but suffers a total loss of control and autonomy as well. Almost always, violence or the threat of violence is used and often physical injury results. Usually the psychological injury is immense and sometimes overpowering. Short of homicide, this offense has been described as the ultimate intrusion or violation.

In addition to the somewhat defined variables and their influence on the victim's behavior and adjustment, there exist the more difficult and ambiguous concepts of shame, guilt, and embarrassment that affect sex crimes victims.

Besides being unique to sex crimes, these feelings also are almost universally felt by the victims.

Typical of victims' sentiments are that they "contributed to the assault" or gave in to a "fate worse than death." These sentiments are not realistic, and the investigator should make this known to the victim. Such attitudes reflect past as well as present cultural influence; the sex crimes investigator who is aware of the potential for these feelings can aid the victim in dealing with them. They are counterproductive to the victim's prognosis and to the investigation as well.

For sexual assault victims, the potential for behavioral disruption is severe, and the development of fears and phobias among them is common. Their view of the world as a now hostile environment will certainly influence their daily lives. Whether or not victims become emotionally debilitated may depend on a variety of factors. In addition to recommending various social agencies which may be available to victims in their time of crisis, investigators must realize the full importance of their potential influence on the victims. Aside from apprehending and prosecuting offenders, they must strive to understand the victims' present fragile state and how an investigator's attitude and demeanor can affect a victim's recovery from this trauma and continuance of life in a productive way.

The Child Victim

Approximately 30 percent—3 out of 10—of the cases assigned to an investigator will involve child victims, male and female, under the age of 15 years. In general, children as crime victims present unique variables to the scope of an investigation; and when a child is the victim of a sexual assault, those variables may become more complex.

In the first place, the child victim may not be able to express himself or herself in adult terms. Therefore, eliciting the factual elements of a crime first requires the establishment of a vocabulary level which the child can understand.

Second, dealing with the parents of the child victim may prove more difficult than dealing with the child. For example, if the child was not terrorized or otherwise physically assaulted, he or she may not suffer greatly from the sexual assault. However, if the parent's reaction is that of great emotion, the child will pick up on this reaction. During the interview, the investigator must also remain as unemotional as possible. Otherwise, the child may interpret an adverse reaction as being to something he or she has done wrong or something for which he or she is responsible.

In dealing with any witness, the investigator should control the interview, but this is especially true with children. The investigator must take particular care to avoid becoming suggestive about what transpired, for the child victim is quick to realize that something out of the ordinary is taking place, and the attention of the police, hospital room personnel, and other interested parties may cause varied reactions ranging from total silence to complete fabrication of an incident.

Statistics have shown that 15 percent of the cases involving child victims have been unfounded. Although this figure is slightly lower than the 20 percent listed for unfounded cases in the general population, the reasons, as disclosed through follow-up investigations, are infinite—ranging from attempting to avoid parental disapproval, to avoiding school, to telling a detective what the child thought he wanted to hear.

In one incident, an 8-year-old male reported that he had been taken to an abandoned building and anally sodomized, and he provided a detailed description of his assailant. Questioning by the investigator disclosed some minor discrepancies, and the youth was gently confronted with these inconsistencies. At this time, he told of how he had taken a shortcut through an abandoned building, which he was strictly forbidden to do by his parents. In so doing, he had fallen into some rubbish and had spilled paint on his clothing. He then went home and told his mother the story of the sexual assault. He kept to the story through the hospital examination, the initial report to uniformed personnel, and the initial report to the assigned investigator.

Another incident involved four children: two females, one 11 years old and one 12; and two males, one 9 years old and one 7. It was reported that the girls had been gang-raped in their hallway on their way to school. The male children stated they had witnessed the entire incident. The assigned detectives immediately responded to the hospital. The two girls recounted the assault; showed torn garments; and even displayed patches of hair cut from their heads, which they claimed their assailants had done. Meanwhile, the media had responded to the emergency room and requested an interview with the assigned detectives. Having become doubtful about the story by this time, the detectives asked that the interview be delayed. The reporter, however, had a deadline to meet and interviewed the mother of one of the victims. By the time the interview was aired that evening, the detectives were almost certain that the children had fabricated the story. Nonetheless, the story received wide media coverage and had the potential of building widespread community interest and anxiety as well. The next morning, however, the children were confronted with various discrepancies including the fact that the hospital report showed no sexual activity and intact hymens in both girls. The girls then casually told of how they had wanted to miss school and that one of the boys had wanted to ride in a police car. So they made up the story. It was quite complex and took several hours of investigative time to disprove.

Another unique aspect pertaining to child victims of sexual assaults is that in almost 50 percent of the cases investigated, the children knew their assailants. (The figure for the general population sampled is around 37 percent; that is, 37 percent of all sexual assault victims have had prior acquaintance with their assailants.) The significance of this statistic is that in one of two cases the child was victimized by someone he or she knew. The assailants include natural parents, boyfriends of relatives, common-law husbands of relatives, babysitters, grocery store operators, doctors, and dentists. The list is endless.

Another significant factor in those assaults in which the offender is known is that it is often an ongoing situation which has been taking place over a period of time. The reasons for the victim's reluctance to report such assaults are as varied as the list of assailants: fear of assailant; fear of an adverse reaction from parent, in the case where a daughter is assaulted by a mother's boyfriend; fear of being implicated as a willing participant; parental neglect; and a child's feeling that the wishes of parent or relative assailants must be complied with—to name only a few.

Volumes of investigative and psychological literature have been written dealing with children who are crime victims, and the techniques suggested for interviewing children vary in their scope; the bottom line, however, is that the investigator feel comfortable and competent with the investigative technique chosen. Dealing with child victims of sexual assaults can certainly be distressing, but the investigator should consider that children may be protected to some extent by various psychological defense mechanisms.

Furthermore, because the child's life-style and coping mechanisms are not yet so well established, the investigator's chances for having a positive influence on the child's future ability to cope with the experience are greater than when working with the adult victim.

FIRST OFFICER ON THE SCENE OF THE SEXUAL ASSAULT

Although the administrative procedure for the actual investigative case assignment may vary from one police agency to another, certain procedural steps are universal: Usually the victim of the crime reports the crime and a field or uniformed officer responds and makes the initial report. The first officer on the scene in a sexual assault investigation plays a crucial role. In addition to the routine aspects of safeguarding the crime scene, this officer should have some basic knowledge of the unique elements of the sexual assault investigation, for instance that the confidence of the victim and the victim's family may have to be gained so that the elements of the crime can be established; the first officer also may have to transport the victim for hospital treatment and instruct the victim and the hospital room personnel as to certain evidentiary procedures. A discussion of the first officer's responsibilities follows.

Gaining Confidence

Reactions to victimization are as varied as personalities, and I have seen such reactions range from complete hysteria to total silence. It is therefore the responsibility of the first officer to arrive to minimize the trauma of the victim and to get sufficient information for establishing certain elements of a crime. In obtaining this information, the officer must show compassion, understanding, and patience, for this may very well set the tone for all future contact the police will have with this victim.

Although probably in an unnatural emotional state, the victim will be forming an opinion of the "first authority figure's" attitude. If this opinion is favorable, future communication with the victim will be greatly enhanced. On the other hand, a victim who senses a lack of support or callousness may not cooperate, and this will have a direct bearing on the investigator's work, which is greatly influenced by the victim's behavior. Investigators must realize that their success depends on the victim's favorable and persistent attitude to pursue the investigation.

The Victim's Family

Often the victim's family is also under severe emotional stress and must be treated accordingly by the first officer. Reactions are very unpredictable and may range from terror to outrage to aggression. The officer must bear this in mind, offering as much understanding to the victim's family as to the victim.

Safeguarding the Crime Scene

Experienced investigators realize that the importance of safeguarding a crime scene cannot be overestimated. Inexperienced officers, however, may not become believers until they see the results of a thorough crime scene search.

Except for the "blood-stained" or "bullet-riddled" crime scene, in which the clues or evidence to be gathered are obvious, a crime scene search may be tedious, routine, or seemingly not worth the effort. Many investigators, however, can point to *the* case that made them believers in crime scene searches. Even the "impossible" crime scene is dealt with thoroughly by the competent investigator; for example, the site of a bombing or arson, an abandoned building cluttered with debris.

The case that made me a believer involved a particularly long and difficult investigation that covered a period of several months in which seven young males were sexually molested. Due to the ages of the victims, the vital information was conflicting. For example, several descriptions were given for the offender, while the MO (in which the offender offered the victim money to help him move some objects from abandoned buildings) remained somewhat constant.

Community pressure was building, uniformed patrols were beefed up, and suspects were questioned with little result. The break in the case came when the offender attacked his eighth victim in a garbage-strewn abandoned building. Unknowingly, he dropped from his pocket a court docket slip with his name and docket number on it. The slip was recovered by the forensic unit on the scene, turned over to the investigating officers for follow-up investigation, and the offender was apprehended and convicted. The point of the thorough crime scene search was made—even against improbable odds.

Instructing and Transporting the Victim

In some police departments, policy requires the reporting or first officer to transport the victim to the hospital. In these cases, the officer should be familiar with basic hospital emergency room treatment in order to allay some of the anxiety the victim is sure to feel and also to explain certain evidence-gathering procedures that are necessary. Since timing is crucial, the first officer usually instructs the victim to follow a few simple but basic directions, including the following:

1. Do not wash or douche.
2. Safeguard items of clothing or bedding so they can be taken to the police laboratory for semen and blood analysis.
3. Safeguard any torn clothing for evidentiary value.

In addition, the first officer may have to instruct hospital personnel concerning the importance of certain information required by the police, namely:

1. Results of an internal and external examination, including semen slides from the vagina or anus; notation of any bruises or injuries internally or externally.
2. If the hospital is equipped, an analysis of semen for motility (moving sperm cells).
3. A set of slides taken for processing in the police laboratory.

INVESTIGATIVE FUNCTION

To properly carry out the investigative function in any given situation, investigative skills must be acquired in two areas. One area involves a knowledge of general investigative skills which can be applied universally to most investigative efforts and includes skills in the areas of interviewing and interrogation; crime scene; and resources; for example, motor vehicle records and criminal records. The other area involves a knowledge of investigative skills which are applicable to specific criminal acts. The following section focuses on, but is not limited to, the investigative techniques which are applicable to sexual assault investigations.

Evidence Gathering

A crucial function of the investigator is that of obtaining evidence which will fortify the case and sustain a conviction. As most investigators know, evidence, as a category, is unlimited and can defy the imagination in any attempt to present the all-inclusive list. To the sex crimes investigator, however, there are several routine procedures to be considered in attempting to gather supporting evidence. Included are the following:

Semen.   The presence of semen can be confirmed in several ways. It can be gathered through taking cervical, vaginal, rectal, or oral smears, or it can be found in clothing, furniture, bedding, or tissues or clothing used as wipes. Suspected items of clothing such as panties or pants should be submitted for lab analysis. Also, semen has certain properties that are apparent under a fluorescent light. Microscopic tests can determine the presence of spermatozoa.

In addition to submitting a victim's clothing, a suspect's clothing may also be submitted for testing, provided the individual is apprehended within a reasonable time following the incident.

Additionally, semen has properties which enable it to be typed. Certain considerations, however, may render this test fruitless: The assailant may be a "nonsecreter," meaning his semen cannot be typed; there may not be enough fluid to type; the sample may be contaminated by other body fluids; for example, a semen stain on a victim's panties may also contain vaginal fluid, sweat, or urine.

Microscopic tests for motility (moving spermatozoa) can be conducted by hospital personnel. A positive test indicates that spermatozoa are probably of recent deposit. Opinions vary concerning the time during which this test can be conducted, the consensus ranging between 6 and 72 hours.

When evaluating test results for semen or spermatozoa, the investigator must consider two important concepts. A positive test indicates sexual activity and serves to corroborate the investigation of the forced sexual assault. However, the investigator should establish if and when the victim was recently involved in consensual sexual activity. If the victim was involved in consensual sexual activity within hours before the sexual assault, then a positive test result in itself would not necessarily be conclusive.

On the other hand, a negative test result does not mean there was no sexual activity, for many sexual offenders are unable to obtain or sustain an erection during the sexual assault. Furthermore, often they do not climax or ejaculate during the assault, for many reasons, both psychological and physiological. The investigator who is aware of this phenomenon will not depend heavily on such evidence or the lack of it, to the exclusion of other evidence. In addition, the investigator may be called upon to testify concerning negative test results and should be qualified to answer pertinent questions effectively.

Bite Marks.   Occasionally, sexual assault victims are bitten during the assault. When a bite is inflicted on a victim, the teeth leave distinct pattern characteristics. These characteristics can be matched to a suspect's bite mark pattern.

Dental experts in the field have been successful in establishing enough similarity between bit marks on victims and dental impressions taken from suspects to sustain a conclusive finding.

Bite marks should be photographed from the victim's body as soon as possible, for they dissipate with time. These photos are maintained in police custody along with all other evidence.

Serological evidence in the form of saliva washings can also be taken from the area of the bite. If a bite was inflicted through clothing, clothing washings can be obtained. A genetic analysis of the saliva may enable a determination of certain genetic characteristics in addition to blood type information.

Pubic Hair.   As a result of violent sexual contact during an assault, sometimes trace evidence in the form of pubic hair of the suspect can be recovered. As a part of "emergency room" evidence, several municipal hospitals submit pubic hair combings in addition to other tests and reports of victim treatment.

Through technological development in the field of hair analysis, findings are becoming more and more specific. Such an analysis can establish conclusively whether the hair is human, what part of the body it came from, whether it is of recent deposit, if it is dyed or of natural color, and the race of the donor. Although not conclusive, genetic analysis can also establish with fair certainty several serological characteristics, including blood type and other blood characteristics, when follicle samples are intact. Although it may not be admissible in court because it is not conclusive, this type of test can aid the investigator in the elimination of a suspect. For example, a hair specimen analysis may indicate that the assailant had blood type B. A suspect with blood type B could not be convicted on this evidence alone, but the investigator could eliminate a suspect who did not have type B blood.

Bruises.   Physical injuries that result during a sexual assault should be fully documented. Those injuries that are not on intimate parts of a victim's body should be recorded in the investigator's notes. Photos of these injuries can also have great impact in a court presentation. Such injuries, as well as injuries sustained on intimate parts of a victim's body, should be fully documented by hospital personnel as part of the victim's hospital records or chart.

Torn Clothing.   In a sexual assault, frequently clothing is forcibly removed from the victim and is damaged in the process. This type of corroborative evidence should be safeguarded and vouchered for court presentation. In a crime where force is a key element, all indications of it are essential.

Other Evidence.   The foregoing list is by no means all-inclusive, but it does represent some of the types of evidence which are almost always present at the crime scene. Other evidence might include the suspect's fingerprints, trace evidence left by the suspect, or ropes or bindings used by the assailant—the list is endless but no evidence should be overlooked.

Investigative Techniques

Experienced investigators usually will follow certain procedures in conducting their investigations. Although this section deals with several procedures with which most investigators are familiar, it emphasizes their use in the sexual assault investigation.

Male or Female Investigator. One of the first issues to be addressed in assigning an investigation is, "Will the sex crimes victim be likely to prefer a male or a female investigator." Although I have reviewed and assigned over 3000 sexual assault cases, it has been rare that a victim has indicated an investigator preference based on sex. Of the 17 investigators who staff my office, almost half are women. However, we have received only about five preferential requests. In one instance, a female teen-age victim requested a male investigator. In other instances, usually it has been the family of the victim which has requested a female investigator. In still another instance, the mother of a 10-year-old male sodomy victim requested a female officer.

From past experience, it seems safe to conclude that the sex of the investigator is not a significant factor. If the victim indicates a preference, by all means it should be honored. Otherwise, ability and sensitivity should be the determinants in case assignment.

When to Interview. In my opinion, the victim should be interviewed as soon as possible. And if the victim can handle it, the questioning about the facts and the description of the offender should be detailed. If the initial interview is handled competently, quite often the victim will relate most of the facts regarding the incident and rapport will be established between the victim and the investigator.

Within a short period, a day or two, the investigator should conduct a second interview, for experience has shown that victims tend to recall details omitted during the initial interview.

With the concurrence of the victim, the victim's family should also be contacted as soon as possible. Often the family is thrown into a traumatic state and the sooner they can be made aware of the situation, the better they will be able to cope with it. Many hospitals in New York City maintain family crisis units which are specifically designed to deal with sexual assault situations.

Who Is Present at Interview. During the interview of an 18-year-old female who had been raped, the mother insisted on being present. After several minutes, it became apparent that the victim was too shy to speak in front of her mother, and she asked her mother to leave the room. Once the mother was gone, the victim had no trouble relating the incident.

Generally speaking, the interview should involve the victim and the interviewer; and family members, hospital staff, and other police personnel should not be present. Family members, especially, can be a disruptive or intimidating force during an interview.

The setting for the interview should be as private as possible and one which the victim does not find distracting. A room in the victim's home, a small conference or interview room at the hospital or police station—all provide the privacy that is preferred.

If the victim wants a family member present and if the interview can be conducted without disruption under these circumstances, the request should be honored.

The Canvass. Canvassing is essential in most serious criminal investigations. Usually conducted in the crime scene vicinity, it is a door-to-door questioning of people, with the hope of uncovering a witness. In addition to fulfilling its primary role of locating a witness, the sex crimes investigator may find that the canvass brings forth the unreported crime victim. Because many sex crimes, both completed and attempted, go unreported, this would not be unusual. Furthermore, the newly located victim may be the one who can provide some key data to the investigation.

Photo Files.   Several factors contribute to the effective use of photo files and computer-activated photo array systems. First, it is fairly well established that sexual assault involves violence or the threat of violence. Second, it is usually not a first-offender crime. Third, it can be fairly assumed that the crime is recidivistic and that most assailants are familiar with the area in which they strike; that is, for the most part they are locals.

In conducting this procedure, the investigator should bear in mind that it is both tedious and time-consuming; however, if the array is voluminous, the victim need not complete it at one sitting. Even more vital, the investigator must take a positive approach in instructing the witness. A witness who becomes overwhelmed by a sense of futility at being placed in a room full of photo drawers, may just go through the motions and quickly become discouraged. In this type of crime, chances favor discovering the assailant in the photo drawers, and the witness should be encouraged to feel the likelihood of success.

Polygraph.   The results of the polygraph or lie detector are not allowable in a court presentation as incriminating evidence nor are they conclusive; nevertheless, the results can be of value, particularly to the sex crimes investigator. Since approximately 20 percent of all reported sex crimes are false reports and since some of these reports are highly improbable, the adamant "victim" may be asked and agree to take a polygraph test. Those individuals who feel it is fruitless to continue with a false report will recant before taking the test. Those who feel they can "beat the machine" will go ahead—usually failing the test.

On occasion, a sexual assault victim has misidentified an innocent person as the assailant. Such a mistake is usually the result of a chance street encounter in which the "suspect" resembles the assailant. Because of the great stress and trauma inherent in a sexual assault, it stands to reason that a victim's ability to identify an assailant may be impaired.

In this situation, the "suspect" may be unable to provide an alibi, even though all other investigative indicators seem to suggest that the "suspect" is a very improbable assailant. Here the polygraph could be an aid in eliminating the individual as a suspect.

As an investigative tool, the polygraph should be used with discretion—its strengths and weaknesses kept in mind by the investigator. If the investigator is objective and sincere in pointing out apparent discrepancies or improbabilities, a real victim will realize that polygraph results can fortify the investigation's direction and outcome.

Hypnosis.   Employing hypnosis in the sexual assault case has proved quite successful. An inherent characteristic of the sexual assault is that it inflicts psychological injuries on its victims in varying degrees. Such injuries may trigger certain psychological defense mechanisms that impair the victim's ability to recall certain details. Hypnosis may enable the victim to recall and relate some vital bits of information regarding the incident. In conjunction with an artist, it may even be used to compose a sketch of the assailant.

Prior Investigative Experience. The "catch-all" technique draws from investigative experience gained from other assignments. When unique situations arise for which there are no established guidelines, the sex crimes investigator can use this technique effectively. For example, surveillance is a routine investigative technique for the narcotics investigator, but the sex crimes investigator rarely employs it. In one case, however, it was successfully employed in the apprehension of a rapist. Six weeks after he had assaulted her, the assailant embarked on a two-day attempt to cajole the victim into meeting him for a date.

Over this two-day period, the victim received a series of instructions from the assailant. She was directed to go to various phone booths throughout the city for instructions, and she was also told what means of transportation to use, including buses and subways. In an effort to assist in the investigation and end a terror-filled ordeal, the victim was willing to comply with the assailant's wishes. Meanwhile, the investigators continuously instructed the victim concerning negotiations with the assailant. The effective surveillance of the victim, recorded telephone conversations between the victim and assailant, and the patience and tenacity of the investigators—all these factors were vital and ultimately resulted in the successful apprehension and conviction of the assailant.

Regarding the use of investigative techniques and procedures, the bottom line is that the individual case and circumstances will dictate which methods are best suited to the investigation. The investigator's knowledge of these techniques, coupled with experience, imagination, and resourcefulness, greatly enhance the chances for success.

To modern-day investigators of sexual assault crimes, the challenge is real. Faced with limited financial and personnel resources and an increased demand for their services, their methods must be precisely and efficiently developed and geared to the unique aspects and problems inherent in the sex crimes investigation.

57

Child Abuse Investigation

James F. Haran

Henry Ilian

Tula Hawkins-Lacy

This chapter covers the problem of child abuse and/or neglect, as well as the efforts of states to engage the problem through the establishment of a central registry with free hot lines. The authors list certain mandated reporters of child abuse and describe the follow-up investigative procedure by child protective service workers. Finally, they present a detailed account of investigative phases from developing the complaint, through field investigation by child protective workers to the case's conclusion in one of two ways: (1) closing it as unfounded or (2) initiating social service remedial steps or criminal prosecution, if deemed necessary or in the best interest of the child.

THE SCOPE OF THE PROBLEM OF CHILD ABUSE

In 1990 there were over 2.5 million reports of child abuse or neglect nationwide. The New York State Child Abuse and Maltreatment Register alone (Child Abuse Hotline: 1-800-342-3720) received some 129,709 reports of this nature involving 212,767 children. Child abuse hotline numbers are usually listed in telephone directories. This register gets 356 complaints on an average day, and its function is to coordinate and track them. Subsequent investigation has established that approximately 42 percent are substantiated, but nevertheless the numbers are appalling. Of course, the facts of a case are unknown at the time of the charge. In 1990 in New York State 201 children's deaths, up 2 percent from 1989, were alleged to have resulted from child abuse or neglect. Nationally the number of fatalities was 1211, up 1 percent from 1989. Accusations of child sexual abuse in New York State totaled 9814. These figures denote reported incidents, and, judging from studies of unreported crimes in general, probably greatly underrepresent the extent of actual abuse and maltreatment.

COPING WITH THE PROBLEM

The first step in coping with this reprehensible activity is to have a central clearinghouse where complaints of this nature can be gathered and steps taken to investigate and either substantiate or dismiss the allegations as unfounded. No interview can begin if a report is not made. Federal legislation in 1974 made child abuse prevention, as well as the related treatment funds, available to the states contingent on the adoption of a number of provisions. One of these was the creation of a statewide reporting system for abuse and neglect. As a result of this legislation, all states, the District of Columbia, Puerto Rico, and the Virgin Islands enacted similar laws. Consequently, child abuse and neglect allegations are handled comparably throughout the United States. Many states establish central registers with toll-free hotline numbers for this purpose. The New York State Department of Social Services operates a statewide register that accepts and screens calls from people who have a reasonable cause to suspect that a minor has been abused or neglected. The Register accepts phone calls 24 hours a day, seven days a week. Although, for all intents and purposes, a phone call to the Register begins the process of a child protective investigation, all persons who make an oral report must submit a written statement of their allegations within 48 hours. At the Register, trained operators obtain as much information as possible concerning the abuse, perpetrator, victim, and other details. This data forms the basis of a subsequent field probe. Then the Register forwards the complaint to the local office of Child Protective Services, usually a division of the County Department of Social Services, which promptly initiates a field investigation and undertakes the necessary follow-up steps.

Although anyone can file a complaint with the Register, New York State, for example, has mandated by statute that certain professionals and officials who regularly deal with adults and children must report suspect cases as soon as possible to avoid further abuse or potential harm. Mandated reporters are assigned a specific number by which they may reach the Register. These persons include doctors, nurses, school officials, foster care workers, police officers, peace officers, district attorneys, and a wide complement of social service workers.

The intervention of Child Protective Services can be triggered only by such disclosures. Mandated reporters, whenever they have reasonable cause to suspect that a child coming before them in their professional or official capacity is abused or maltreated, are obliged to reveal such a condition. However, a reporter, whether an official or a private citizen, is not expected to conduct an investigation and draw a conclusion, but only to report on personal knowledge that he or she may have good reason to suspect maltreatment.

Reporters are afforded certain legal protections from liability when acting in good faith and within the scope of their official duties. The only exception would be willful misconduct or gross negligence on their part. Their confidentiality is also protected, but their identities are generally accessible to the child protection worker/investigator. Reporting a case means only that a probe will occur, not that a determination of abuse or neglect is going to be made or that a child will be removed from the family.

The State Register screens all calls, and these must meet certain criteria in order to be recorded: (1) There must be a child under 18 years involved; (2) the alleged act should fit into the legal definition of abuse or neglect, as defined by the *Family Court Act* and/or *Social Service Law*, Section 371; and (3) the deed has to be committed by either a parent or other person legally responsible for the child. Paramours, who act as a parent or care for a child, although they are not legally responsible for it, are also subject to a child protective investigation.

Once a report is accepted by the state Register, it is telexed or faxed to the local district with the responsibility to conduct the probe. In New York State the county is the local district; whereas in New York City, which comprises five counties or boroughs, the child protective system is managed by one agency, the Child Welfare Administration, an arm of the city's Human Resources Administration. The report, however, is sent directly to the appropriate local office within each of the five boroughs.

ABUSE AND NEGLECT UNDER THE LAW

One cannot verify if abuse or neglect has occurred, unless one has a framework that clearly states what is meant by abuse, neglect, sexual abuse, and/or emotional maltreatment. The legal definition of abuse or neglect, promulgated by a state's legislative body, is the major framework that gives structure and form to the determination of abuse and/or neglect for the child protective worker. In New York State, the definitions of abuse and neglect are found in both the *Social Service Law*, which governs the State Department of Social Services which, in turn, supervises and monitors the municipal localities, and the *Family Court Act*, which governs the operations of the family court. *Social Service Law* states the parameters of the child protective investigation. Its definitions are used by the worker to make a determination whether, in fact, abuse or neglect has occurred. Both the *Social Service Law* and the *Family Court Act* promulgate the roles and responsibilities of the child protective system and, in turn, the child protective worker.

All the states have some form of similar legislation. The specific legal definitions can vary from state to state. In New York, Article 10 of the *Family Court Act* and Section 371 of the *Social Services Law* contain the legal definitions of abuse and neglect. These definitions set the parameters and are the tools that the child protective worker must use to determine legally if abuse or neglect has occurred.

Definitions of the Three Principal Types of Abuse

In New York there are three principal types of abuse or maltreatment: physical abuse, maltreatment or neglect, and sexual abuse. The law defines each type.

Physical Abuse. An *abused* child is one who is under 18 years of age whose parent or other person legally responsible for his or her care inflicts or allows to be inflicted upon the child, or creates or allows to be created, a physical injury or a substantial risk thereof by other than accidental means, which causes or creates a substantial risk of death, serious or protracted disfigurement, or protracted impairment of physical or emotional health, or protracted loss of impairment of the functions of a bodily organ.

Maltreatment or Neglect.   A *maltreated or neglected* child is one who is under 18 years of age and whose physical, mental, or emotional condition has been impaired or is in imminent danger of becoming impaired as a result of failure of the parent or other person legally responsible for his or her care to exercise a minimum degree of care in:

1. Supplying the child with food, clothing, shelter, or compulsory education, or medical, dental, optometrical, or surgical care though financially able to do so or offered financial or other reasonable means to do so.

2. Providing the child with proper supervision or guardianship, or by unreasonably inflicting or allowing to be inflicted harm or a substantial risk thereof, including the use of excessive corporal punishment, or by misusing drugs or alcohol to the extent that the parent loses self-control of his or her actions or by abandoning the child.

Sexual Abuse.   A *sexually abused* child is one whose parents or other persons responsible for his care commit or allow to be committed a sex offense as defined in Article 130 of the *Penal Law*, commit incest, allow or permit or encourage such a child to engage in prostitution, or allow such a child to engage in acts of conduct constituting a sexual performance.

In addition, *Social Services Law* specifically defines abuse and maltreatment as it relates to a child who is living away from the home in a residential care program. A staff member of a medical or other public or private institution, school, facility, or agency who suspects child abuse or maltreatment must immediately notify the person in charge of such institution, school, facility, or agency or the designee. That person then also becomes responsible for reporting or causing report to be made to the State Central Register of Child Abuse and Maltreatment.

For example, the law is very clear that the parent or other person legally responsible must not cause injury to the child. By adding the provision of "creating or allowing to be created," the law protects the child from situations and circumstances that may not immediately injure the child, but have the potential to do so. An illustration of the parent inflicting harm would be the parent taking a baseball bat to punish a 6-year-old and hitting the child, causing the child's leg to be broken. If a second parent watches the injury being inflicted and does nothing to protect the child, that parent is also guilty of being abusive by permitting the injury to occur. The phrase "creating or allowing to be created a substantial risk of physical injury," would be illustrated if the parent in the preceding example swung the bat at the child, but the child ducked, so that the bat missed and there was no injury. That parent would nevertheless be considered abusive under the legal definition, even though the child was not injured. Likewise, the parent who witnesses the first parent swinging the bat and does nothing to protect the child would be guilty of abuse on the grounds that he or she allowed a dangerous situation to be created.

Physical abuse is both physically and psychologically harmful to the children involved. However, abuse of this type is relatively easily determined through investigative observation and findings, coupled with medical documentation, examination results, X-rays, color photographs, and other means. This is not to say that thorough investigative work must not still be done and credible evidence gathered to prove the abuse and be acceptable for court presentation, if necessary.

By far the largest number of child abuse complaints involve maltreatment and/or neglect. (Both terms are used, but mean essentially the same thing.) Physical neglect can usually be documented by a competent investigator—if not immediately, then over time. Emotional neglect, while just as real and damaging in some cases as physical abuse, is generally more subtle and difficult to establish. More often than not, neglect is due to the omission of care and responsible action rather than direct abuse of a child. Nevertheless, the provision of minimally adequate and responsible care in given circumstances is often a difficult judgment call on the part of the child protective investigator. The issues surrounding emotional maltreatment are very gray and very difficult to prove. Emotional maltreatment under the legal definition of neglect includes "a state of substantially diminished psychological or intellectual functioning in the child related to such factors as failure to thrive, control of aggressive or self-destructive impulses, ability to think and reason, or acting out or misbehavior." However, such impairment must be clearly attributable to the unwillingness or inability of the parent to exercise a minimum degree of care toward the child.

Proving emotional maltreatment is very difficult for the child protective worker. Usually, it is easier to substantiate other more tangible allegations than this particular charge. Thus, although stated in law, the reality is that there is rarely a finding or a determination of such maltreatment solely on its own merit. Most times it is easier to prove abuse or neglect than to establish emotional maltreatment. It involves not only the observable facts of the case, but also the value judgments of the worker and those of the individuals responsible for the care of the children. Needless to say, in our pluralistic society there can be different levels of value judgments. Ultimately, child protective workers are expected to use their own value sets to determine what a minimally acceptable degree of care is. Even when acting in good faith and drawing on field experience, child protective workers may find their decisions not supported by family court judges who use their own value judgment and experience to determine neglect or the seriousness of neglect. This is, of course, very troubling to the protective worker.

Establishing that a parent or other person reasonably responsible has inflicted harm on the child is another gray area for the child protective worker and the court to decide. For example, many ethical and cultural issues come into play when considering if excessive corporal punishment occurred. In New York State parents are permitted to use corporal punishment on their children. Because the parent is allowed to spank the child, it is the degree of the spanking that will determine if excessive force was used. What one child protective worker or one family court judge decides about the guilt or innocence of an accused parent might be entirely different if the same case was investigated by a second child protective worker and a finding made by a second family court judge. These differences can reflect the values, mores, and culture of the individuals making the decision.

Another point of importance is that parents cannot be judged neglectful by failing to provide a child with a minimum degree of care if they are financially unable to do so. A parent with no source of income cannot be found neglectful in failing to provide the child with food, clothing, medical care, and the like, if that parent has no money to do so. It is only when resources are made available to parents, and they still fail to provide the minimum degree of care, that the worker or court can decide that neglect is present.

The last category, sexual abuse, is defined in accordance with the *Penal Code* of the State of New York. There is a broad range of definitions of sexual abuse in the Code. This means that a parent who touches the child in a sexual manner is as guilty of sexual abuse as the parent who has been found to have raped or penetrated the child with his penis. Medical documentation is necessary and, as in all cases, evidence is essential to prove the court case. Documented sexual cases involving violation of the *Penal Code* become criminal matters, and are usually carried to completion jointly with the police while the protective workers assist the victims as necessary.

Making a determination of abuse or neglect by itself does not automatically mean that the child will be removed or placed in protective custody. The test for placing the child in protective custody against the wishes of the parent is the child protective worker's belief and proof that the child would be in "imminent danger" of harm if he or she remained in the care and custody of the parent. Once removal has occurred, the case comes under the jurisdiction of the family court. The court has the sole authority to "remand" or place the child on a more permanent status to the Commissioner of Social Services. The child protective worker has the ability to put the child in protective custody only on a temporary basis. The law clearly states that the worker must bring the case before a judge in the family court "forthwith," which usually means within 24 hours. The *Family Court Act* is "designed to provide due process of law for determining when the state, through its family court, may intervene against the wishes of a parent on behalf of a child so that the child's needs are properly met."[1] This ensures that, if a child must be removed from the parent because that child is in imminent danger of harm or in imminent danger of being harmed in the future, then due process is afforded the parents or other persons legally responsible for the child's care.

THE ROLE OF CHILD PROTECTIVE SERVICES

Because child protection exists in two very different and often conflicting worlds of social work and law, the investigation of child abuse and neglect is different in its goals from other types of criminal or civil probes. Its aim is not merely to uncover the facts so that a perpetrator can be brought to justice, but concomitantly to balance two apparently conflicting objectives. The first is to determine if assuring a child's safety warrants involuntarily separating that child from a parent. The second is to conduct the investigation in such a way that, whether the situation requires removal, groundwork is laid for possible future efforts to reconstitute family life. The role of a child protective investigator is to be both friend and foe to the family at the same time.

The problems that modern society faces regarding child abuse and neglect are not easy ones to handle. The challenge is on both the personal and professional level. On the personal level, crimes against children awaken a rage against those who commit such hideous assaults. But, as professionals, child protective workers must not allow their emotions to prejudice or cloud their attempt to develop a relationship of trust with the parents subject to investigation. They must gain information from parents who often cannot communicate, or are too fearful to trust, as well as provide clarity in an often murky area of accusations and allegations. They must make a distinction between parents too overwhelmed or too immature to function effectively without assistance and those pathological individuals who enjoy inflicting pain and attempt to hide their tracks in a mirage of lies and false appearances.

Today the challenge is to supply quality case work and investigation services with a shrinking public dollar. When properly provided, these services can enhance the likelihood of constructive results—assisting a family to keep a child at home or, when this is not possible, finding appropriate substitute arrangements for the child while helping the parents to improve their ability to function. If possible, keeping the child at home or shortening a stay in foster care, is ultimately more cost-effective to the taxpayers and is most often in the best interests of the child.

SOCIAL WORK AND THE LAW

The tension between social work and the law is a conflict endemic to the child protective investigation. Rooted in both domains, child protective work requires the person carrying out the investigation to reconcile the demands. There must be order for society to exist. This need for order and social control is reflected in the case worker's ability to protect abused or neglected children by removing them from a negligent parent and providing an alternative living arrangement. Society also exercises its commitment to the protection of children by stipulating that a child protective service worker can remove a child who has not actually been abused or neglected by a parent, but who in the judgment of the caseworker is in imminent danger of being harmed or is in danger of being harmed in the foreseeable future. This calls for judgments to be based on both facts and opinions interpreted by the case worker.

The authority to protect children originates in the common law tradition of *parens patriae.* This concept, which emerged over several centuries, refers to the power of the state to assume the role of a parent and to intervene by means of a court or public agency to protect a child or other dependent person. The objective of *parens patriae* today is similar—to help children grow up as responsible citizens and prevent antisocial behavior. Today the concept of *parens patriae* is still interpreted as providing for the "best interest of the child," usually through the judicial role of the family court judge.

Kadushin and Martin,[2] speaking from the perspective of the social worker, describe the obligation of the state in more explicit terms. The state is ultimately a parent to all children. When birth parents neglect, abuse, or exploit the child, the state has the legal right and responsibility to intervene to protect the child. The state delegates this authority to the protective service agency, so that, in effect, the agency functions as an arm of the state and operates with legal sanctions. In such situations, not only does the protective service agency have the right to intervene, it has the duty to do so.

Although our society has undertaken a commitment to protect children from abusive and neglectful parents, tension has historically existed—and exists today—between the need to do this and the right of parents to raise their children as they see fit. The law is replete with conflicts surrounding our society's dual commitment to guard children and to allow parents to raise them without governmental intervention. Due process protections are in place at every step of the child protective investigation, and parents must be informed of the nature of the process and of their right to challenge their accusers in open court. Federal and state laws guard the confidentiality of those who file reports of abuse and neglect, as well as protecting them from the risk of law suits for making such reports. Permanency planning, a concept originating in the child development literature and now enshrined in both federal and state legislations, is intended both to ensure that children are not removed from their parents unnecessarily, and that public and private agencies, charged with the protection and care of children, exert diligent efforts to return them home. The concept of permanency planning is a recognition of the fact that, to develop appropriately, a child requires the sense of emotional stability that comes from having permanent ties with a person or persons who constitute the child's biological parents. In terms of child welfare law, this translates to children's right either to be quickly returned to their parents, once the situation causing the risk is alleviated (through the provision of Social Services), or to find permanency in another home with permanent adoptive parents.

In the law, the tension between protecting the child and protecting the parents from unnecessary interventions is glaring. For example, in New York State a child protective worker is obligated to remove a child in a situation of imminent danger, but the same worker must concurrently exercise diligent effort to keep the child at home.

The conflict between the best interests of the child and the right of parents to raise their children is sealed within the adversarial system, in which two parties with different stories challenge each other until the truth is determined by an impartial third party who decides the verdict. Legal thinking aims for precision. Facts must be presented according to rules of evidence, and investigations have to follow acceptable legal guidelines.

Although several fields within social work require practitioners to make assessments bearing on such substantive matters as individuals' freedom or child custody, the profession has never been entirely at home in this role. While social workers frequently work with involuntary clients, such as those under court order to receive counseling, the typical model of social work practice was developed primarily for work with a client who asks for help. This is reflected in the code of ethics established by the National Association of Social Workers, which calls for client self-determination.[3] In this more typical situation, concrete circumstances do not depend on a social worker's report, and the social worker's assessment is not likely to feature in a court proceeding.

The purpose of information gathering for social workers is, as Kadushin observes, to "understand the client in relation to the social problem situation."[4] Although in social work practice, it is usually necessary to arrive at a determination, diagnosis, or service plan, the information gained is seen as provisional and subject to revision as the helping relationship develops.

Therefore, the child protective worker must learn to gather information within two conflicting frameworks and for two purposes. To serve as evidence in court, facts must be precise and fixed. They must derive from something seen, heard, touched, or tasted to be admissible as evidence. As the basis for an assessment of social functioning, facts are provisional and subject to later revision or elaboration. Likewise, the service plan resulting from the assessment is also provisional and subject to later revision as new information emerges or as the situation changes. As a further complication, the process of data gathering must be undertaken within the context of developing a helping relationship. The child protective service worker must not only act to determine if abuse or neglect has occurred, protect children from further harm by removing them against parental wishes, but also make a social work assessment in order to provide services to the parents.

All of these requirements are made in a system with various cultural and religious values and norms. The child protective service worker must communicate with families of different cultures, norms, and mores. Although child abuse and neglect can cut across all cultural, racial, and economic lines, the typical client is often a person who is poor and a member of a minority group. The court can become the stage for the various conflicts played out through child abuse investigations between mainstream value systems and religious and cultural groups with different designs of values and norms.

ASSESSMENT IN CHILD PROTECTIVE SERVICES

The core of the child protective investigation is the process of assessment. Three types of assessments are necessary: (1) risk of harm to the child or children; (2) whether the allegation can be substantiated; and (3) what types of services might be appropriate to achieve a home environment in which it is safe for the child or children to remain with the parents.

The American Humane Association has taken a leading role in standard-setting and training in child protection. The Association's handbook *Helping in Child Protective Services* describes the initial assessment by the case worker as "probably the most difficult and discomforting part of the process...." They go on to say that it should be conducted "with an open mind, a humanistic orientation and no desire to establish guilt...." Its aim should be "recognizing abuse and neglect, protecting children, and offering help to families...." As such, it is "an integral and positive part of the helping process."[5] The child protective investigation must be seen in the context of a system to provide services to families at risk.

Authors Kadushin and Martin identify eight situations in which child protective services are appropriate, although, as they note, statutory definitions differ among states.[6] These are:

1. Physical abuse.

2. Malnourishment, poor clothing, lack of proper shelter, sleeping arrangements, attendance, or supervision. Included is also a "failure to thrive" syndrome, which describes infants who fail to grow and develop at a normal rate.

3. Denial of essential medial care.

4. Failure to ensure that the child attends school regularly.

5. Exploitation, overwork.

6. Exposure to unwholesome or demoralizing circumstances.

7. Sexual abuse.

8. Emotional abuse and neglect involving denial of the normal experiences that permit a child to feel loved, wanted, secure, and worthy.[7]

BEGINNING A CHILD PROTECTIVE INVESTIGATION

There are three general phases in the investigation of suspected child abuse and neglect: the prefield stage, the field stage, and termination stage.

Prefield Stage

In the prefield phase, analysis of the report received from the Central Register of suspected child abuse and neglect is done and the source of the report is contacted. Various other checks are made before the case is assigned to a worker. These include looking into past child protective records to determine if there has been a previous substantiated case or if there is currently an active case in the local district or any other district in the City. The State Central Register is also responsible to check for previous indicated cases before the allegation is sent to the field location. Knowing the prior history is essential in making a determination of current risk to the child or children. In addition, there is a computer check to identify the possible whereabouts of children named in the report, if applicable, and an income maintenance check is performed to probe if welfare benefits are being received by any of the family members. The income maintenance check is helpful in locating families and verifying family composition, and the case history is essential when assessing the family and understanding its dynamics. These checks, along with the report, help to determine risk to the child and are fundamental parts of the prefield evaluation. This information is gathered before the case is assigned to the case worker.

At this stage of the investigation the child protective worker must determine the factors that may indicate imminent risk or danger in each individual case. According to *Social Service Law*, the child protective case workers must begin their investigation within 24 hours of receiving the report. They have to make a home visit within 48 hours. Because some 50 percent of the cases that are investigated are unfounded, the worker and supervisor must make some decisions as to which cases have to be visited immediately, not waiting the 24 hours. The timeliness of the child protective worker making a home probe can be the key to protecting a child. After the case worker and first-line supervisor review the reports, looking for conditions that constitute risk factors, the case worker contacts the source of the report for additional information. The report that the worker receives contains the name, address, and phone number of the source of the report. Contacting the source of the report is essential because this person, especially if it is a mandated reporter, usually has a wealth of data not contained in the report that can help the worker make an assessment, determining the location of the family and imminent risk to the children. All child protective workers must begin their investigation by contacting the source of the report. This individual can tell them where the children are, describe the injury or the allegation in detail, correct any false information contained in the report, and give interpretations of the children and the family.

High-risk factors increase the possibility that the child is in imminent danger. These high-risk indicators alert the case worker and the line supervisor that there is possibly an immediate problem, and that they must respond rapidly to the situation and immediately visit the home to assess the state of affairs. High-risk indicators include:

1. *The severity of the allegation:* The more severe the injury, the greater the risk of further harm to that child or to other children in the family who have not been hurt yet. Broken bones, fractures, burns, lacerations, eye injuries, sexual abuse traumas, such as torn hymens, genital bleeding, and/or rectal lacerations are typical injuries that would be considered severe.

2. *Children left alone:* Children, especially a child under 6, left alone is indicative of severe neglect. Children left alone are in an extremely dangerous situa-

tion. They can set fires, fall out of windows, and likewise harm and/or maim themselves or their siblings.

3. *The age of the child/children:* The younger the children, the higher the risk that they cannot protect themselves, even temporarily, from the parent. Developmental issues also impact on risk to the child. Certain ages and stages of development, such as the "terrible twos," when it is normal for the child to say no to the parent, increase immediate danger to the child. Also important is the number of children in a family and collectively the ages and stages of their development. With multiple children the parent has less control, and the chances increase that one or more may be harmed in the immediate future.

4. *Suicidal or homicidal threats of the parent:* Homicidal and suicidal threats by a parent must be taken seriously by the worker. In suicide attempts the parent, in personal pain and loneliness, can unfortunately decide to kill the child as well.

5. *The whereabouts of the child/children:* Determining the actual whereabouts of children is crucial to estimating risk. If the children are currently in a safe environment, a hospital for example, this may decrease the immediate risk to their health and safety. On the other hand, if their whereabouts are unknown or if they are at home, and the locality or the identity of the perpetrator are undetermined, the risk of additional harm increases.

6. *Psychiatrically impaired parent:* If the parent or the alleged perpetrator is known to be psychotic or has a history of mental illness, there is increased danger to the child. Also, if the parent or alleged perpetrator has a record of violence, this adds to the risk of the children.

7. *Prior history:* Serious injury can result from isolated or one-time incidents of abuse and neglect. Therefore, analysis of a person's background is not always an indicator of danger. Nevertheless, the case worker must be alert at all times to certain patterns that a prior history might reveal. If there has been an escalation of the severity of the allegation or the number of children involved in the report or if there is a shorter time span between incidents, there is heightened risk.

The beginning or prefield analysis of the case is a very important part of a successful child protective investigation. Asking questions about the report and of the source and evaluating the data received are essential components of the probe even before the case worker makes a home visit and engages the family. The goal of the child protective worker in all stages of the investigation is to decide if imminent danger exists, determine if abuse or neglect is present, and choose the appropriate services for the family as a whole.

The Field Stage of the Investigation

Having reviewed all the available information, case workers are now ready to start the field phase by approaching the alleged victim, the family members, and other relevant sources of information in the community. As in all probes, case workers' primary tools are their interviews and observations. While case workers have dual job functions—the social service and the investigative duties—the latter now take precedence. The facts of the case complaint must be established, corroborated where possible, and evidence accumulated to the point where reliable conclusions can be drawn. Although child abuse of any kind may be personally repugnant to investigator case workers, they must maintain an open mind in order to reach the facts.

Interviewing is a delicate skill, which at all costs has to avoid confrontational episodes that close down all communication. The attitude of the interviewer is expressed in many ways—tone of voice, impatience, refusal to listen, body language, facial expression, and dress. Every individual has an innate dignity as a human being. If this is appreciated, the respect will be reciprocated and, at minimum, a civil and polite relationship between case worker and victim or abuser will be nurtured and grow. This does not mean the worker has to agree with all or any of the actions of the interviewee. However, people are very sensitive to hostile attitudes, and they will not be cooperative to strangers, talking to them about serious personal matters, especially when they display a confrontational approach, either overtly or implicitly. Complainants, neighbors, school officials, teachers, and relatives are generally helpful in matters of child abuse questioning. There are always exceptions, but a correct, professional, nonthreatening attitude most often succeeds in literally opening doors and gaining relevant information. It is also most likely to be fruitful in dealing with an alleged perpetrator of abuse or neglect.

Case workers, however, must remain alert and concerned about personal safety issues at all times. If they think that the situation is likely to be dangerous, they can bring in the police.

Next to establishing and creating a basis for a rapport with the interviewees, it is important to state the purpose of the dialogue. This immediately sets the parameters of the planned discussion and alleviates any suspicions as to why the worker-investigator desires to talk. Even children should be advised why they are being interviewed. The confidentiality of the informant must be discussed and honestly related. It is advisable to make notations for accuracy and later recall. Since these are considered by some to be inhibiting to the flow of talk, they should be kept to a minimum and mostly be concerned with identifying data.

Furthermore, notes should be made of relevant conversations as soon as possible after the interview. Modern pocket-sized cassette recorders, which can easily be carried in the field are invaluable for this purpose. However, they should be utilized rarely, if ever, during a meeting and particularly not without the consent of the person interviewed. The notes are invaluable in the subsequent completion of the case report to assist in reaching a case conclusion, sharing the data with a supervisor and/or follow-up worker, and, if necessary, presenting a case in court. The ability of an investigator to relate findings in a clear, concise, and concrete manner is important and is developed by most investigative workers with direction and supervisory review over time.

After interviewing skills, the next important tool of the child protective worker is personal observation, a verification technique often concomitant with the interview. Remember that at the field phase of the probe the child protective worker's role is that of an investigator and trained observer. For example, the neglect complaint may state that the children are undernourished, always hungry, and poorly clothed. The parent may say this is untrue. The investigator asks to see the children and observes they do appear thin, they are dirty, dressed inappropriately for the winter weather, and the older ones are not at school. Their meals can be discussed with the parent, and it is reasonable to ask to see what food staples are in the home. Simultaneously the physical condition of the home is observed, sleeping arrangements viewed, and the degree of control and discipline or lack of it exhibited by the parent. All these factors are to be duly noted and evaluated, perhaps further in future follow-up visits. Table 57.1 lists typical abuse indicators, which constitute an excellent overview of factors to be observed in child abuse cases.[8]

Interviewing children is a particularly delicate skill, especially so with those who have been abused sexually. Some children (ages 1 to 3) may be too young to be questioned, but others, despite their chronological age, may be quite talkative although ostensibly shy and withdrawn at first. Each case is unique. Again the worker must establish a friendly relationship with the child to elicit information about the abuse. Engaging the child is paramount to successfully drawing out the facts you need. It is helpful for the interviewers to get in touch with the child themselves before the dialogue begins. Children see adults as caretakers and providers, and they may shy away from an interviewer who has traits or characteristics similar to the alleged perpetrator or parent who has harmed them.

Case workers must be relaxed, get at the child's eye level, and be prepared to use nonverbal tools, such as crayons and paper to engage the child. Although it may appear that an older child will be able to communicate with the interviewer, children who have been abused or neglected may express their trauma by regressing to a younger stage of development. Case workers have to be mindful that they are strangers to the child and must establish the reason for their presence. The beginning discussion should include matters in the child's life that are more positive than the abuse, for example, school, friends, games, favorite television shows, and the like. This safe beginning serves a twofold purpose: first, to engage the child and assess his or her ability to communicate and second, to determine the child's accuracy in disclosing the more stressful events centering around the abuse or neglect. If children are unable to accurately talk about their school, birthday, grade level, teacher, and so on, they may be considered less credible than children who are capable of correctly describing these important factors in their lives.

Explaining the purpose of the interview in terms the child can grasp is also essential. Moreover, the worker must establish a common language with the child, who cannot be expected to have the vocabulary and sophistication level of the adult. Open-ended questions ought to be asked first, followed by more direct questions for clarification. Leading queries should be avoided completely. With older children confidentiality has to be discussed openly. In all cases, effort should be directed toward eliciting as detailed a description of the abuse as possible. This can be followed by questions as to the feelings of the child about the abusive conduct.

After workers obtain what information they can get about the incident(s) from the child, a closing discussion less stressful to the child ought to occur. This conversation may include congratulating children on how well they have done and a brief consultation as to what they can expect next. The case worker should be reassuring to the child without making false promises. It is always important to acknowledge how difficult it may have been for the child and that the role of the case worker is to try to make things better for the child and the family. Caution must be used when deciding how to utilize the information that has been drawn out from children. Using a minor's direct statements against a parent may have a long-lasting detrimental effect on the family unit. Data gathered from children should be used with much discretion. Some children may feel relieved to have the opportunity to recount their trauma; others may be very upset psychologically. This can be particularly true in sexual abuse cases, which involve distinct *Penal Code* violations, and the victim may be subject to multiple interviews by parents, police, district attorneys, psychologist, medical personnel, and others.

Table 57.1 Physical and Behavioral Indicators of Child Abuse and Neglect

Type of child abuse or neglect	Physical indicators	Behavioral indicators
Physical Abuse	Unexplained bruises and welts: - on face, lips, mouth - on torso, back, buttocks, thighs - in various stages of healing - clustered, forming regular patterns - reflecting shape of article used to inflict (electrical cord, belt buckle) - on several different surface areas - regularly appear after absence, weekend or vacation Unexplained burns: - cigar, cigarette burns, especially on soles, palms, back or buttocks - immersion burns (sock-like, glove-like, doughnut shaped on buttocks or genitalia) - patterned like electric burner, iron, etc. - rope burns on arms, legs, neck or torso Unexplained fractures: - to skull, nose, facial structure - in various stages of healing - multiple or spiral fractures Unexplained lacerations or abrasions: - to mouth, lips, gums, eyes - to external genitalia	Wary of adult contacts Apprehensive when other children cry Behavioral extremes: - aggressiveness or withdrawal Frightened of parents Afraid to go home Reports injury by parents
Physical Neglect	Consistent hunger, poor hygiene, inappropriate dress Consistent lack of supervision, especially in dangerous activities or for long periods Unattended physical problems or medical needs Abandonment	Begging, stealing food Extended stays at school early arrival and late (departure) Constant fatigue, listlessness or falling asleep in class Alcohol or drug abuse Delinquency (e.g., thefts) States there is no caretaker
Sexual Abuse	Difficulty in walking or sitting Torn, stained, or bloody underclothing Pain or itching in genital area bruises or bleeding in external genitalia or vaginal or anal areas Venereal disease, especially in pre-teens Pregnancy	Unwilling to change for gym or participate in physical education class Withdrawal, fantasy or infantile behavior Bizarre, sophisticated or unusual sexual behavior or knowledge

Table 57.1 (*Continued*) Physical and Behavioral Indicators of Child Abuse and Neglect

Type of child abuse or neglect	Physical indicators	Behavioral indicators
Sexual Abuse (Continued)		Poor peer relationships
		Delinquent or runaway
		Reports sexual assault by caretaker
Emotional Maltreatment	Speech disorders	Habit disorders (sucking, biting, rocking, etc.)
	Lags in physical development	Conduct disorders (antisocial, destructive, etc.)
	Failure to thrive	
		Neurotic traits (sleep disorders, inhibition of play)
		Psychoneurotic reactions (hysteria, obsession, compulsion, phobias, hypochondria)
		Behavior extremes: - compliant, passive - aggressive, demanding
		Overly adaptive behavior: - inappropriately adult - inappropriately infant
		Developmental lags (mental, emotional)
		Attempted suicide

SOURCE: U.S. Department of Health and Human Services, National Center on Child Abuse and Neglect, *The User Manual Series* (U.S. Government Printing Office, Washington, DC 1980).

The Final Phase

The final or termination phase of the investigation is built on and flows from the prefield and field phases. This stage consists basically of evaluating all the gathered information and making a decision as to whether the allegations are founded or not. If the imputed abuse has not been established, the case will be closed. On the other hand, if the assertions are substantiated with credible facts and evidence, then any number of events might occur. If the child has not been in imminent danger, extensive social service provisions would be implemented to alleviate the family deficiencies and provide the needed services and/or other necessities for parent and child. In addition, ongoing supervision by the child protective worker would probably occur. If the child had been removed from the home due to imminent danger of physical or psychological harm, the court would make a legal finding of abuse and neglect against the perpetrators. At the same time, the court could decide if it would be safe for the child to return home with extensive services and ongoing supervision, or if further temporary or even permanent removal is warranted. Some cases of abuse and neglect can conclude with the criminal prosecution of the abuser.

CONCLUSION

Child abuse is a complex problem and can become a very volatile issue in any specific case. Most attention is placed on the abuse of young children because they are considered defenseless and unable to reach those who could protect them. However, the adolescent is equally prone to abuse of all sorts. A government study estimated that half of the 650,000 abused and neglected children annually are 12 years of age or older. Furthermore, three-quarters of these adolescents are never reported or referred to child protection agencies. What can the average citizen do to impact on these problems? The interested person should not try to be an investigator or a therapist. These functions are best left to the professional child protective workers. They have the experience and access to the resources to manage such complex cases. As a citizen they can listen to troubled children, believe them, respect their privacy, be supportive, be their advocates, be knowledgeable about community resources, and by all means notify the proper authorities immediately for the sake of the child. There are countless books and articles available about all aspects of child abuse. Your local librarian can be of assistance in seeking them out. There are too many to cite here, but the following few are recommended, and each source leads to others.

SOURCES

Hoorwitz, Aaron, *The Clinical Detective, Techniques in the Evaluation of Sexual Abuse*. New York: W. W. Norton & Co., 1992.

Besharov, Douglas, *Combating Child Abuse*. Washington, D.C.: AEI Press, 1990.

The Federation on Child Abuse and Neglect, 134 South Swan Street, Albany, NY 12210 (call 1-800-342-PIRC).

Guide to New York Child Protective Services System, rev. ed., NY: New York State Assembly Subcommittee in Child Abuse, Albany.

Mandated Reporter Manual, New York State Child Protective Services.

Wolerton, Lorraine, *What's a Teacher to Do*, Escape Project, Department of Human Development and Family Studies, College of Human Ecology Cornell University, Ithaca, NY, 1987.

NOTES

[1] *Family Court Act of 1990.*

[2] A. Kadushin, *The Social Worker Interview: A Guide for Human Service Professionals*, 3d ed. New York: Columbia University Press, 1990), p. 225.

[3] National Association of Social Workers, "Social Work Code of Ethics," *Encyclopedia of Social Work*, 18th ed. (Silver Springs, MD: NASW Press, 1987).

[4] Kadushin, p. 12.

[5] American Humane Association, *Helping in Child Protective Services*, edited by W. M. Holder and C. Mohr (Englewood, CO: American Humane Association, 1980), p. 108.

[6] A. Kadushin and J. Martin, *Child Welfare Services*, 4th ed. (New York: Macmillan, 1988), p. 226.

[7] Kadushin and Martin (1988), p. 226.

[8] U.S. Department of Health and Human Services, National Center on Child Abuse and

Neglect, *The User Manual Series* (Washington, D.C.: U.S. Government Printing Office, 1980).

BIBLIOGRAPHY

American Humane Association, *Helping in Child Protective Services*, W. M. Holder and C. Mohr. Englewood, CO: American Humane Association, 1980.

Giovannoni, J. M., "Child Abuse and Neglect: An Overview," in J. Laird and A. Hartman (eds.), *A Handbook of Child Welfare: Context, Knowledge and Practice.* New York: The Free Press, 1985.

HRA/Child Welfare Administration, *Foster Care Overview, Fiscal Year 1991.* New York: HRA/Child Welfare Administration, 1991.

Janchill, Sr. M. P., *Guidelines for Decision-Making in Child Welfare.* New York: Human Service Workshops, 1981.

Kadushin, A. and Martin, J., *Child Welfare Services*, 4th ed. New York: Macmillan, 1988.

Kadushin, A., *The Social Work Interview: A Guide for Human Service Professionals*, 3d ed. New York: Columbia University Press, 1990.

Magazino, C. J., "Services to Families and Children at Risk of Separation," in B. McGowan and W. Meenan (eds.), *Child Welfare: Current Dilemmas, Future Directions.* Itasca, IL: F. E. Peacock, 1983, pp. 479–502.

National Association of Social Workers, "Social Work Code of Ethics," in *Encyclopedia of Social Work*, 18th ed. Silver Springs, MD: NASW Press, 1987.

New York State Bureau of Service Information System, *Reporting Highlights. Reports (1989).* Albany, NY: New York State Bureau of Service Information System.

Videka-Sherman, L., "Child Abuse and Neglect," in A. Gitterman (ed.), *Handbook of Social Work Practice with Vulnerable Populations.* New York: Columbia University Press, 1991.

58

Investigation of Environmental Crimes

John F. Haskins

Recent environmental disasters have aroused public reaction. First-hand community experiences, as well as state and national calamities, have led to the enactment of new environmental legislation, the creation of regulatory agencies, and the initiation of criminal and civil investigations. This chapter discusses the extremely complex "system," addresses the meaning of hazardous waste, and identifies some signals, pitfalls, and problems involved in gathering evidence for the prosecution of environmental wrongdoing.

HISTORICAL PERSPECTIVE

Environmental Disasters Stir Public Reaction

The public became acutely aware of environmental issues following the publicity surrounding the now infamous Love Canal episode during the early 1970s. This environmental disaster served not only as an eye opener for the people directly affected—the population of the Buffalo and Niagara Falls area near the Hooker Chemical Company's disposal site at Love Canal—but also for the rank and file living anywhere in New York State and the nation.

In Elizabeth, New Jersey an even more spectacular event took place in the early 1980s. An accident in a storage area filled with tens of thousands of hazardous waste drums caused a huge explosion and fire.

In Times Beach, Missouri, oil spread on dirt roads to control dust was found to be contaminated with dioxin, a chemical so dangerous that its concentrations are measured in parts per billion.

And the list could go on and on.

In each of these cases, an appreciation of the horrors of exposure to improperly disposed hazardous wastes started in the disturbed community and rapidly spread to the whole state and the nation. Under pressure of public outrage, state legislatures and the federal government began to take action, passing statutes that created criminal sanctions for mishandling and improperly discarding such materials.

Environmental Statute Development

The history of environmental criminal law spans a little over 20 years. Compared to the total body of law, this is very recent. At the national level, the *Rivers and Harbors Act of 1899* was one of the first to try to establish control over water pollution. But it was not until the 1960s and through the 1970s and '80s that Congress set more serious environmental standards with the *Clean Air Act, Clean Waters Act, Toxic Substances Control Act (TSCA), Resource Conservation and Recovery Act (RCRA), Comprehensive Environmental Response Compensation and Recovery Act (CERCLA),* and finally the *Superfund Amendments Reauthorization Act (SARA).*

At the New York State level, 1972 became a landmark period for the creation of environmental legislation with the passage of its *Air Pollution Control Act, Water Pollution Control Act, Stream Protection Act,* and the *Environmental Quality Bond Act.* The state *Solid and Hazardous Waste Act in 1980* was an adoption of the federal *RCRA.* The state *Environmental Superfund* legislation passed in 1982, and the *Hazardous Substances Bulk Storage Act* followed in 1986. Recent state actions include the bottle return legislation, low-level radioactive waste bill, and medical waste statutes.

One of the most significant regional environmental initiatives took place in 1980. Following a meeting of the Northeastern states' attorneys general, environmental agencies, and the federal Environmental Protection Agency, the Northeast Hazardous Waste Project was formed. This project was established as an association to conduct training and exchange information in the hazardous waste field for environmental prosecutors and regulators seeking to combat illegal activities. Subsequently, environmental criminal investigators were added to this group, as the need became more obvious and state programs expanded.

DEFINING ENVIRONMENTAL WRONGDOING

This section addresses the two key questions: What is hazardous waste, and what is environmental crime?

Hazardous Waste. The general term *waste* in New York State environmental conservation law covers "any garbage, refuse, sludge...and other discarded material, including solid, liquid, semi-solid or contained gaseous material resulting from industrial, commercial, mining and agricultural operations and from community activities...."

Hazardous waste means a waste or combination of wastes that, because of its quantity, concentration, or physical, chemical, or infectious characteristics, may:

- Cause or significantly contribute to an increase in mortality or an increase in serious, irreversible, or incapacitating reversible illness.

- Or pose a substantial present or potential hazard to human health or the environment when improperly treated, stored, transported, disposed, or otherwise managed.

Understanding these and hundreds of other definitions is very important for the investigation of environmental crimes.

Environmental Crime. Before discussing environmental crime, let us first look at the arrangement that is intended to safeguard our ecosystem!

The plan that protects individuals and their habitats is a combination of regulation of industry through the creation of rules to be observed, self-reporting by the companies involved, and monitoring of a firm's activities by the government. This regulatory approach establishes standards for the generators, transporters, and disposers of waste. It covers treatment, storage, and disposal facilities (TSDFs), with oversight and inspection by a government agency.

It should be noted that refuse generated by private individuals and other noncommercial waste is exempt by definition and therefore not regulated under this arrangement.

The system includes rules and regulations to specify how waste is to be handled and provides for tracking it from "cradle to grave," or from the industrial generator through the transporter to the ultimate disposal or treatment.

Industry must:

- Report activity.

- Obtain permits from the regulating agency.

- Catalog and test chemicals used and waste produced.

- Pay taxes based on the volumes of waste.

- Keep accurate records.

- Train employees.

- Reduce waste and exposure to a harmful environment.

- Prevent and immediately report spills, leaks, or releases.

- Provide proper technology, treatment, and on-site storage prior to disposal.

It becomes apparent that these requirements reflect a tremendous cost for protecting the environment and citizens from unnecessary exposure to pollution. One of the main ingredients of the success of these types of programs is reliance on industry to notify the government of its activities and to comply with the complex rules and regulations that implement control programs. Government oversight, for its part, primarily depends on infrequent inspections of facilities and remote monitoring through required reports and permits issued to limit the type of activities that may be undertaken. Administrative control to enforce the regulations is normally authorized by legislation, in addition to criminal sanctions imposed for noncompliance.

The types of criminal activity and motivations involved in environmental crime are basically the same as other illegal pursuits, with financial gain and greed the most prevalent.

Some general types of environmental crime are:

- Pollution in various forms, without authorization or permit, that involves releases of hazardous substances into the air, water, or ground.

- Endangering the public health or safety of noninvolved citizens by releases of hazardous substances into the environment.
- Fraud, conspiracy, or financial crimes.
- Bribery, false reporting, forgery, and falsifying business records.
- Failure to obey regulatory requirements of permits and reporting.
- Causing injury to wildlife or the environment.

Early in the environmental pollution era, the crimes were commonly referred to as "midnight dumpers," or the blatant pouring and unloading of waste in remote areas. Today's criminals are often much more sophisticated, using the "system" and methodically creating false records and reports while disposing of waste in less obvious ways.

As an example, a company obtains the proper permits and files the proper records with a regulatory agency, but falsifies the information on the reports. Instead of shipping the waste as the manifest form suggests, it may be mixed with the company's normal sewer discharge, a little at a time over an extended period.

Such companies and individuals are often on the border of profitability. They cheat and cut corners to get an edge on the competition at the expense of both the environment and their own employees' safety. Frequently, their crimes are reported by citizens or employees who are aware of their activities and recognize the deleterious environmental consequences.

CRIMINAL AND CIVIL ENVIRONMENTAL INVESTIGATIONS IN NEW YORK

Cooperating Agencies and Functions

The New York State Department of Environmental Conservation (DEC) is the primary agency responsible for most environmental programs in the state. DEC issues permits, conducts inspections, and is charged with monitoring all activities involving hazardous substances, wastes, and the environment.

Authority and duties are assigned by the state legislature for such items as the collection and reporting of data on hazardous substances and industry involvement. DEC is the responsible link to federal programs and the liaison with the Environmental Protection Agency, providing the required information and reporting for New York to the federal government. The Department of Environmental Conservation writes and implements rules and regulations to administer the hazardous waste program, and monitors the environment in addition to investigating and ensuring clean-up of contaminated sites. Furthermore, it works closely with the New York State Department of health on all issues regarding human exposure to pollutants. DEC is primarily responsible for investigating, coordinating, and enforcing environmental laws and regulations. It utilizes a variety of administrative, civil, and criminal authorities to carry out the provisions of the *Environmental Conservation Law* (*ECL*) and Title 6 of the New York Codes, Rules and Regulations. *ECL* is the body of statutes enacted by the New York State legislature. Title 6 is that section of the Codes, Rules and Regulations promulgated by DEC.

Authority for the enforcement of the *Environmental Conservation Law* is assigned to the Division of Law Enforcement within the DEC. This authority includes the criminal investigation of all aspects of environmental law. The division is organized into two groups: uniformed environmental conservation officers (ECOs) and plainclothed environmental conservation investigators (ECIs). The latter group comprises the Bureau of Environmental Conservation Investigation (BECI). The organization and responsibilities of each group are very similar to those of traditional police, with uniform and detective categories and functions.

The ECO's duties are: patrol, complaint response, summary arrest, and initial investigation of environmental offenses. In New York ECOs are unique, insofar as their tasks range from game-wardenlike coverage of hunting, fishing, and trapping laws to responsibility for enforcement of all environmental statutes pertaining to water, air, and solid waste.

ECOs serve a critical series of functions in cooperation with the Environmental Conservation Investigators (ECIs), such as first response, securing the crime scene, communicating to the office, gathering initial information and witnesses, and getting an investigation started. Then the ECIs continue with the long-term probes. They have the responsibility of bringing an environmental felon to the point of prosecution.

Interaction and cooperation between these functional groups within DEC continue throughout the various stages of the investigation. For example, in the execution of a search warrant, each plays a role. Uniformed officers provide initial site entry and security, while the plainclothed investigators conduct interviews and gather evidence, such as records and files.

There is one difference with respect to assignment, namely, that ECOs patrol sectors within the county where they reside and are part of that community. They are therefore of considerable assistance in providing local information for the investigation. Investigators, on the other hand, are assigned to a district and may conduct probes hundreds of miles apart or even routinely in another state.

The New York State Attorney General's office is the chief prosecutor for civil and criminal environmental offenses referred by the DEC. This office has an environmental section, complete with criminal investigators. It also defends the state, its employees or programs in suits brought against them.

The New York State Department of Health is responsible for monitoring the health of the citizens of New York. In relation to environmental programs, the Health Department operates an extensive laboratory for the scientific analysis of samples for certain types of contaminants. It writes and implements rules and regulations for the health care industry, including inspecting and checking health care facilities. Finally, it samples and keeps tabs on water supplies for public drinking and recreational uses, such as swimming.

Other agencies involved in New York on the state or local level include:

- The state Organized Crime Task Force (OCTF), which enters a case when an element of public corruption or organized crime is present.

- The New York State Police, which join in a situation when the death of a person has occurred or when illicit drug manufacturing chemicals are discovered, or for highway inspections of the trucking industry.

- County-level agencies, such as the district attorney's offices, that often prosecute environmental cases. Some have dedicated environmental components as, for example, in Suffolk County and Brooklyn, which are complete with specialized attorneys and investigators.

■ In addition, many county-level health departments are involved through their normal activities.

On the federal level, the U.S. Environmental Protection Agency (EPA) occupies the most important place. For policy and federal regulations, EPA is the link to implementation of congressional programs for environmental safety by providing funding, oversight, and assistance to state programs for clean-ups and responses to major environmental disasters; its capabilities exceed those of most states.

Other agencies include the U.S. Department of Justice and the U.S. Attorney's office for prosecutions at the federal level, the EPA's criminal investigations unit, the Federal Bureau of Investigation, the U.S. Coast Guard for marine enforcement, U.S. Customs for any international movement, and lastly the Department of Defense when waste or employees from federal defense facilities or defense contractors are involved.

It is obvious from this listing of local, state, and federal agencies and their responsibilities, that there is considerable overlapping of jurisdictions and joint accountability. Given the scope of the operational framework, it can be seen that full cooperation and intensive, constant communication are the keys to any successful prosecution.

Policies and Procedures of Environmental Investigations

The top-level management of environmental investigations begins in the state legislature and governor's office. Program initiatives start with the passage of statutes and the creation of ideas for new programs. If there is extensive public pressure as, for example, after the wash-up of needles and medical waste on the beaches of Long Island and New Jersey during the summer of 1989, new legislation with felony provisions for improper disposal of regulated materials is enacted.

Priorities are communicated to specific agencies for the establishment and implementation of a program that addresses the problems, investigates the responsible parties, and brings the results to public attention.

As in most organizations, policy decisions are made by top management, but middle-management leaders also bear heavy responsibility. This principle is applicable in the Department of Environmental Conservation too. The director of the Division of Law Enforcement and the assistant director in charge of the Bureau of Environmental Conservation Investigations (BECI) set the goals and objectives for investigative initiatives. Time frames for the completion and reassignment of equipment and the manpower to accomplish the objectives are often necessary for any major push. In the case of the wash-up of medical waste and needles on public beaches, many reassignments of duties were necessary to successfully complete the investigation of these incidents.

At the next management level, an individual captain in charge of a BECI district office is accountable for the execution of the policy and objectives of each project. The captain, through lieutenants, makes staff and equipment assignments, and monitors the progress of individual investigations. The captain and the lieutenants coordinate with other staff members, programs, technical support, uniformed officers, regulatory personnel, other agencies and prosecutors. It is the captain's duty to report up along the chain of command on progress, on all administrative matters, and on budgeting. The lieutenants are essential for supervising and coordinating the various facets of the operation so that the investigation comes together. They bring in technicians, other program members, agencies, and prosecutors. This involvement allows the investigator to continue working in the field, conducting interviews, and gathering the evidence. The lieutenant is in charge of putting out the occasional brush fires that flare up over "turf issues" and personality clashes, while providing the needed assistance and logistics to get the job done. This is an essential component of any major environmental crime investigation.

SIGNALS AND EVIDENCE OF ENVIRONMENTAL CRIME

Types and Examples of Crimes

Environmental crimes can be found in a wide variety of industries, starting with the manufacturer or facility. They take place where hazardous and other industrial wastes are created. Traditionally, the primary motives are financial gain and expediency. As already mentioned, the costs for the proper management and disposal of wastes can be substantial. Criminal short-cuts may increase profits. For example, the price of lawfully discarding a single 55-gallon drum of hazardous pollutants varies anywhere from a few hundred to several thousand dollars for transportation to a licensed disposal facility, treatment, incineration, or burying. The cost relates to the distance the material must be shipped, the type of waste, its availability, and the difficulty of treatment and/or disposal required. Generally, the more dangerous or potent the material, the more expensive it is to handle and discard it.

Crimes at manufacturing facilities are usually from older, less efficient operations and are caused by poor maintenance, indifferent corporate officials, and a company's economic woes. They can be very short-sighted. For example, a national firm that makes and distributes a liquid product for consumption purchased an additional local factory for the same commodity. In the newly acquired plant the officials engaged repeatedly in falsifying the discharge monitoring reports, which are required to be filed in conjunction with water discharge permits. They broke the law because management did not want to spend the money to properly maintain their water treatment system; they were trying to save in order to look good to their new corporate bosses. The national headquarters of the firm cooperated fully with the investigation and, of course, ended up paying a substantial fine for the pollution and other violations created by the local employees. The individuals involved were convicted on various counts, fined, and had their employment terminated.

The transportation function remains an important aspect of environmental crime. Waste haulers, too, are required to obtain permits, file reports, and maintain records. Generally, their criminal motive is also profit-related, involving the cost of legal versus unlawful disposal of wastes, the availability of dump locations and the shipping distances.

A classic example of transporter crime arose several years ago, when an enterprising individual in the New York City area contracted with several large hospitals to remove their regulated infectious or so-called "red bag" waste. This material included needles, operating room refuse, bloody gauze and bandages, and even body parts. The contractor was transporting the waste to a Pennsylvania incinerator for disposal when the state closed down the site because of numerous operating violations, leaving the hauler without a dumping location. The individual kept quiet about his problems and continued to pick up the medical wastes as before, collecting tens of thousands of dollars from his clients. Then he rented an empty warehouse in a semiresidential area and stockpiled tons of hospital waste there in the middle of summer. Switching the waste from red to green bags, he took it to the Freshkills landfill on Staten Island, where it was illegally disposed of without any treatment. Finally, the quantity of refuse became more than he could handle. Neighbors of the warehouse started to complain about the smell and insects. Eventually, the transporter was arrested at the warehouse with about 14 tons of hazardous waste. Unfortunately, this case preceded the current felony provisions in New York statutes. Therefore, the contractor got off fairly easily. He was primarily prosecuted for financial fraud and falsified record-keeping.

The final type of environmental crime comprises the actual criminal dumping by individuals and manufacturers. They can be divided into two major groups: those within and those outside the "system." *Within* are companies that have notified the regulatory agency of their waste stream and have obtained the necessary permits and authorization. *Outside* the "system" are firms that produce waste, but have never notified the regulatory agency or procured the necessary permits. Each can be an environmental offender by mismanaging or improperly discarding their refuse. Some companies acquire the proper permits and partially comply, such as the liquid product manufacturer. Although he had discharge permits for the waste water, he did not observe the limitations of the discharges; he filed the required reports, but falsified the information in them.

Other companies have no permits at all. They simply pour the waste down a drain or "out back" on the ground. An example of this case involved a manufacturer who took his waste paints and solvents, mixed them with sawdust, and on his own property dug a hole with a backhoe and buried them "out back." The firm had not notified DEC of its waste; it never legally disposed of it with a licensed transporter and the proper manifest designed to track it. A former employee was the key to discovering the unlawful activity.

Another illustration of environmental crime relates to an employee who was soon to retire and stole drums of hazardous waste from a film manufacturer because of the silver it contained. He rented a backhoe, intending to bury them on a remote property to save them as a retirement bonus, dig them up later and sell the silver. A hunter discovered his backhoe, a large hole in the ground and the drums; he filed a complaint, which led to the employee's eventual arrest and prosecution. The employee was convicted and fired by his company without any retirement benefits.

Information and Evidence Gathering

The investigation of environmental crimes is not unlike any other criminal probe. All the typical, standard police procedures apply: use of informants, interviewing of witnesses and suspects, surveillance and electronic equipment, video, photography, recorded conversations and wire-tapped phone communications with eavesdropping warrants. The primary differences are not technique, but the subject of the investigation, the body of law, and the complicated rules and regulations involved.

In environmental crime there is great reliance on such components as regulatory personnel to explain permits and reports, technicians to obtain samples of hazardous wastes without contaminating themselves, and the understanding of complex regulations and laws with numerous exemptions, exclusions, and concepts that make the difference between a crime and a legal activity. Another important factor is that an environmental offender can be a major corporation with millions of dollars at stake and the best defense lawyers available at unlimited cost.

Definitely, the use of intuitive senses, experienced police hunches, and tedious reviews of reports, files, computer printouts, numerous interviews, and long hours of boredom at surveillance sites are the same as in any criminal investigation. The same frustrations exist, along with the mountains of paperwork, reports, telephone calls, and changes in planning.

Differences are evident in the number of specialized team members, such as technicians, regulators, uniformed officers, and others required in nearly all environmental crimes; they are manifest in the absolute need to clean up and remedy the pollution caused. Sometimes this necessitates actually giving up a criminal case in order to protect the environment and to proceed instead with only civil prosecutions to remedy the contamination. Yet preserving a crime scene is hardly an issue when a hazardous waste is about to enter a water supply or a sewer that may cause an explosion in a city.

Pitfalls and Problems

Hazardous waste can be very dangerous and insidious by, for example, causing cancer years after exposure. Very expensive equipment may be ruined and a municipal water supply or an individual citizen's well water contaminated. Under certain circumstances safety equipment is necessary, such as upon entering an enclosed area to obtain a sample or to record label information on containers. Handling of hazardous samples for evidence or seizing an entire tank truck to arrest the driver for illegally transporting or disposing dangerous waste can create major problems. Because of differences in evidentiary rules, conflicts arise from a parallel proceeding to prosecute criminally and civilly to procure remedies.

In addition, the media and the public usually react sharply to environmental incidents. Often the crime scene is trampled by local police, fire, health, other officials, or bystanders. One of the worst problems arises when a major factory or other facility, with hundreds of employees, has its normal operations disrupted by the execution of a search warrant to obtain evidence from a portion of the facility. The logistics and manpower for such a warrant can be a source of major concern.

An extremely important aspect of a trial is explaining the complicated regulations and overcoming the sympathy for the "overregulated" local industry that employs half the local community. Environmental crime is sometimes viewed as a victimless crime, without any obvious assault on the people or harmful result—especially when a gradual degradation or pollution is only beginning to occur.

Other difficulties revolve around the constitutional issues of access, with differing criminal search and seizure warrant powers and regulatory statute authority concerning the inspection and review of permits and records. A graphic example involved the loss of a major pesticides criminal case, partially due to this regulatory-versus-criminal search warrant authority issue.

Keys to Success for Investigators

Remember that the primary purpose of criminal prosecution is not to punish, but to discover the truth by presenting impartial evidence to a jury or judge. However, all laws bear sanctions for violations, and wrongdoers must receive some penalties and punishments.

Preparation for trial is a critical stage for the investigator. In that role one may not prejudge the person, company, or facts. Making assumptions and working on the basis of these can be a sure formula for failure. Avoiding an ego trip and listening to other ideas and interpretations of the evidence may lead the investigator toward a totally different target from the one at the outset. Impartiality is an important aspect of evidence review. One should let the evidence lead the way instead of picking the target or working toward a presumption of guilt. It is the key for an investigator in presenting the case to the prosecutor. One must always be accurate and truthful. The time to discover mistakes is during this phase of review, not in front of a jury.

Organization of the sometimes voluminous file material and evidence is of great importance. Two suggestions for standard procedure are a file table of contents and a chronological tabulation of data. A separate section for "Rosario" materials, which contains all the investigator's notes taken during the probe, may save time and stress later.

It cannot be emphasized too strongly that the three basic elements in case preparation are accuracy, completeness, and honesty. There are, of course, other important keys, such as:

- Training to remain current on case law, new statute modifications, and changes in the state codes, rules, and regulations. This is especially vital in the constantly changing field of environmental law.

- The use of modern techniques and tools, such as the computer, for recording evidence at a crime scene. This can save many hours of manual work. Programs for laptop or portable computers can list all evidence seized at a search warrant site and even print a receipt for seizure and chain of custody records. The expense for certain electronic equipment, such as time-lapse video recorders or microwave video transmitters to a remote receiving location from slave cameras, will save many thousands of dollars in hours that might otherwise be required to maintain an extended surveillance.

Nevertheless, the fundamental skills of a police investigator remain essential and applicable in environmental crime probes. A continual sense of inquiry and the aggressive pursuit of information to explain "why" and "how" are still the most important qualities.

The Need for Public Support

Environmental laws and environmental criminal investigations, to a large extent, grew from an outraged public demanding action and solutions to industrial pollution and hazardous chemical disposal without close governmental regulation.

It is ironic today that the same public, following widespread government regulation and remedial action to oversee industry and clean up pollution, is often loudly opposed to any local solutions to help overcome the problems.

The solutions of expensive, modern regional landfills, incineration, and individualized reduction of waste and recycling are seemingly unwelcome wherever they are proposed. There appears to be a gradual erosion of public support for some solutions, and the siting of disposal facilities and incinerators is extremely difficult. The creation of wastes continues while the issues and options are being debated.

The current efforts of public hearings, cooperation among government, the public, and private industry sectors, and the continued debate about the best solutions appear to be the basis for real future success in meeting the environmental challenges.

59

Scientific Fraud

Linda Little

Just as computer-related crimes tried the expertise of white-collar crime investigators in the 1970s and '80s, crimes involving scientific fraud are a new law enforcement challenge for the 1990s.

It's not that scientific fraud is new. The snake oil and traveling medicine shows were early versions of scientific fraud. They were also easily proven frauds. And Charles Dawson's "Piltdown Man" in the early 1900s was a more difficult case. It took 38 years to determine that the skull found in a gravel bed in England was not a prehistoric species but instead a forgery.[1] Although scientific fraud is not a new phenomenon, the fact that federal law enforcement has begun an organized effort to face the challenge is both new and exciting.

WHAT IS SCIENTIFIC FRAUD?

There is a distinction between scientific fraud and scientific misconduct. Criminal fraud in science, like other criminal fraud, requires a misrepresentation of a material fact. This kind of fraud can manifest itself in a false statement to the Food and Drug Administration (FDA) in clinical drug trials to support new drug applications. It can be a misrepresentation in progress reports on research to a grant-funding agency like the National Institute of health (NIH) to continue receiving grant funds. A misrepresentation of material research facts to a funding or licensing authority like the National Science Foundation or the Environmental Protection Agency could also be scientific fraud.

Scientific misconduct, on the other hand, can involve fraud, but it more often involves unethical conduct: plagiarism, theft of research ideas, and sloppy science. By its nature, scientific misconduct is not a matter for criminal investiga-

SOURCE: *Federal Investigator*, Vol. 9, No. 1 (Fall 1991), pp. 27, 48–49, with permission of the author.

tion or prosecution. Scientific fraud, on the other hand, should be aggressively pursued and prosecuted criminally.

THE PROBLEM

Scientific fraud might not be considered a significant problem if its impact is not weighed. At the Department of Health and Human Services (HHS), over the last couple of years, we have been shaken by the impact of scientific fraud.

One scientific fraud case grew out of a health care fraud investigation of a scientist who falsified research submitted to a drug company in support of a new drug application to the Food and Drug Administration.[2] We investigated a doctor who was treating Medicare patients as part of a clinical drug study. The doctor was not providing the services for which he was billing Medicare, and he was not administering the required protocol for the drug tests. Hence, his research data was flawed. The impact of this case was mild compared to some other cases that followed. A number of patients were harmed by a lack of good medical care, but the situation could have been much worse if we hadn't pursued the investigation.

Next we were confronted by a situation in which a researcher falsified progress reports to lead the NIH to continue his grants. He was not, in fact, conducting the research he claimed. In this case, the impact was even greater. This researcher's work was used by subsequent researchers as a foundation for their own research, and therefore subsequent research was tainted. Since then, we've become involved in numerous criminal fraud cases like this one.

Perhaps the greatest impact of scientific fraud emerged from the generic drug scandal. When we discovered that a handful of FDA officials in the generic drug approval process were taking payoffs, we suspected that scientific fraud was also involved. Investigations began to disclose that indeed it was, and criminal charges were filed in the investigation. Consider for a moment, though, the impact that this corruption has had on public confidence in the integrity of generic drugs. The damage is incalculable. Regardless of what the agency does to convince the public that integrity has been restored, a cloud of doubt will probably remain for some people.

In addition to drugs, the FDA grants approval for medical devices and food supplements. It is responsible for protecting the blood supply and ensuring that the public is safe from radiation. All of these tasks hinge on scientific findings. As government protection measures, they have a tremendous impact on all Americans. Scientific fraud in these programs could have devastating consequences on public health and safety.

Recently, we have come to recognize yet another area of scientific fraud with tremendous impact—intramural research. Aside from corruption, scientific fraud by HHS researchers must be the direst form of employee misconduct! Consider for a moment the impact on HHS if it is found that some of our own research is tainted by fraud or even by scientific misconduct! Such findings could destroy public confidence in the integrity of government research. For this reason, we encourage our programs to ensure their own integrity and vigorously pursue audits and inspections of these programs to protect the process and to detect problems before they occur.

Fortunately, we are not flooded with cases of scientific fraud. But when they arise, they have great impact. Other federal programs may find scientific fraud in their programs. Scientifically oriented agencies like the Environmental Protection Agency, the National Science Foundation, and the Department of Energy, to name a few, all may be vulnerable.

THE CHALLENGE

Scientific investigations are not typical fraud cases. The investigator looking for a simple false statement or a false document will be frustrated early. These are scientifically based investigations, and they require more ingenuity.

Unusual investigations call for unique investigative methods. Whoever heard of conducting an investigation using a panel of experts? Whoever heard of giving the subject of the investigation a copy of the report before being charged and accepting his or her response in writing or orally before a panel? These methods are heretical to investigators. But they are necessary, and they work.

At HHS, when we are dealing with a potential scientific fraud relating to a research grant, we work with an office at NIH established to conduct scientific fraud and scientific misconduct investigations. The office assembles panels of experts to examine the research, laboratory notebooks, slides, essays, and all the scientific aspects of the research. At the early stages, the investigator, while providing expertise in terms of evidence gathering, interviewing, and the like, is not an active player at this stage.

When the investigation gets to the point that it appears a crime has occurred, the investigator takes over to prepare the case for referral for prosecution. This description may oversimplify the tedious drudgery of this approach to putting a case like this together, but the system works. That's not to say, however, that the system is not without its problems.

One problem that can, and often does, arise is dissension among the panel members. Different opinions and orientations sometimes set the scientific panel members off on different tracks, causing them to bicker and become inflexible, and bogging down the whole investigation. It's up to the investigator to keep the panel on track and objective.

Another problem with these panels is that members are not trained investigators. Their different orientations sometime create difficulties in their questioning of witnesses and the subject. It's the investigator's responsibility to ensure that panel activities produce meaningful results.

Scientific fraud investigations can take an inordinate amount of time to complete. Sometimes investigators end up in a race against the statute of limitations expiration. Panel members dealing with scientific issues cannot be rushed. For this reason, it is important for the investigator to become familiar with the subject matter and for the panel members to ensure that they are moving as fast as possible toward a resolution.

Finally, since not many of these cases have been prosecuted, there may not be a great deal of interest on the part of U.S. attorneys. It's another responsibility of the investigator to meet the challenge by selling the case to the prosecutor by showing impact. The fact that a researcher said he made a slide of a virus when he did not may be a false statement, but how many prosecutors can get excited about prosecuting a case like that? However, no one would dispute the merits of a case if the nonexistent slide was used to make untrue medical claims that proved harmful to the public in the end.

CONCLUSION

The potential for harm by those who engage in acts of scientific fraud demands law enforcement's commitment to meeting this new challenge. Establishing methods to deal with scientific fraud allegations is an easy first step. Devoting the resources and energy to investigate these cases is more difficult. However, the law enforcement community cannot afford to overlook or shortchange scientific fraud investigations. Our society may be too sophisticated to fall for the snake oil pitch, but there will be other Piltdown Man and similar scandals we can't ignore.

NOTES

[1] *American Heritage Dictionary* (New York: Houghton Miffin Co., 1978), p. 944.

[2] Bruno Varano, "When Fraud is Dangerous," *The Investigators Journal* (Fall 1989), pp. 34–35.

60
Extortion

Michael S. Emanuelo

The act of extortion, as any police investigator will verify, is one of the most difficult crimes to investigate. Robbery, with essentially the same elements as extortion, can easily be termed an "open-and-shut case" when compared to extortion. In robbery offenses the victims are approached and forced through fear to give up their property. In many instances the offender is not known by the victim. Therefore, the injured party registers a complaint with little fear of retaliation. Extortion, on the other hand, is an ongoing crime in which the extortioner usually is known by the victim, who is led to believe that at any given moment injury threatened will become actual. This belief is the insurance extortioners have against victims registering complaints with law enforcement agencies. In general, the only time victims go to the police is when they can no longer pay the extortioners. Even when victims "go public," investigators experience difficulty extracting from them information necessary to ensure a conviction. This usually results from the victim's belief that the extortioner will eventually get even.

A majority of cases involving extortion are planned in advance to provide the least amount of risk to the extortioner while obtaining the maximum of funds from the victims.

IDENTIFYING THE CRIME

One of the first important steps in investigating extortion is identifying the act. The investigator must understand all elements of the crime to consider the act a criminal violation. In extortion two elements must be known and understood. First, is it the extortioner's intent to gain property from the victim? The law in most states provides a very broad definition of property. It ranges from personal property, that is, money or jewelry, to intangible property, that is, a business enterprise in which the victim has an interest. A business enterprise could be a major corporation or a one-person operation such as a candy store or even a milk route.

For the second element to exist, the victim's property must be obtained by use of fear or force. It is the use of this coercive activity that separates extortion from simple larceny.

The law, once again, provides the officer with a broad definition of what constitutes force or fear in this criminal act. Fear is instilled in victims when they are led to reasonably believe they are in danger of being harmed. The injury does not necessarily have to lead to hospitalization, disfigurement, or even death. Rather, it can be a simple verbal warning carrying a threat of punishment. For example, the extortioner threatens a vague physical penalty if property is not given up. Loan sharks, as it will be shown later, often employ threats to collect the illegal and excessive interest which they impose on their victims.

Many extortioners, blackmailers, or kidnappers resort to written messages to induce fear by pointing to the harm that may come to the victim or to a third party. It should be kept in mind that written and verbal threats employed by the extortioners do not have to come directly but can be relayed through a confederate.

The force used in extortion is a physical act, such as the burning of the victim's skin with a lit cigarette, an arson attempt on the victim's home or business, or the delivery of a written document intended to intimidate.

TARGETING THE EXTORTIONER

Identifying the target in an extortion investigation is the most difficult phase of the case. The difficulty usually arises when investigators are not familiar with the tools of their trade and the available data. Good investigators are able to reach out to various agencies to gather any and all information available. This data will eventually aid the inquiry.

Some investigators have difficulty when they become satisfied with identifying the target for arrest only. The successful conclusion of an extortion case is not the arrest. It is the conviction in a court of law that yields the rewards. To assist in the goal of obtaining a conviction in any extortion case, it is important that the investigator know everything possible about the target.

Profile Folder

To assist in gathering and documenting information, in addition to maintaining a case folder, a profile folder should be established. The profile folder should be formulated so that a law enforcement agent detached from the investigation will be able to locate the target and carry on the investigation with the information supplied.

The profile folder should contain basic information such as name, address, and date of birth; an up-to-date photograph; locations frequented; vehicles owned or operated; and most important, comrades or confederates associated with the target. Figure 60.1, known as a "modus operandi sheet," is a suggested format to be placed in the folder.

It is strongly suggested that, in addition to the "MO Sheet," the profile folder contain any and all documents that will support as much information on the sheet as possible. For example, any arrest records, any surveillance photos of the target and/or associates, or a computer printout of the target's driver's license and registration. The information on the MO Sheet should be only facts, not hearsay.

Case No. 301/80

Page 1 of 2

Date: 20 July 80

Name: Shark, Joseph E.   D.O.B. 2-23-42

Address: 1608 Main Street
Victimville, N.Y.

Alias or nickname: "Joey teeth"

Tel. No. (home) 212-492-0145   (bus) 201-685-0144

Crininal No.'s:

   State Criminal No. 3906386R

   F.B.I. No.   475-160C

   Other Criminal No. 31261 - N.J.

Description:

   Sex M Hair Brn Eyes Brn Height 6'4" Weight 280

   Other 2" Scar right Lower Jaw.

Criminal Record:

Date arrested	Charge	Disposition
2/28/64	Extortion	1 YR Probation
6/25/71	Assault 2°	Dismissed

Non-Criminal No's:

   Social Security No. 083-32-0117

   Drivers License No. 514530-66014-66312-42 State N.Y.

   Others (permits,etc) Pistol Permit 31206 State N.J.

Vehicle Information; (owned or operated)
   684 TBV. (NY) 1979 Blue Lincoln Sdn.

Figure 60.1 Modus operandi sheet.

The profile folder also becomes handy when and if the target decides at time of trial to take the witness stand. Instead of the investigator running around at the last minute gathering information, the completed profile folder will support any questions. Many prosecuting attorneys find this folder useful when it is necessary to attempt to discredit the witness.

Case No. 301/80

Page 2 of 2

Business: Acme Floor Covering (owner)

Address: 69-76 North B'way
Suckersburg N.J.

Previous address and/or summer home.

1. 60 1ST Ave N.Y.C.   from 1965   to 1971

2. 108 Simpson Ave, Nutley N.J. from 1971   to 1976

Associates:

Name	Criminal No.
John Doe	376-419A (FBI)
Richard Roe	4196453Q
Alex Silver	(None)

Activities:

(A) Known: Extortion

(B) Suspected: Gambling, extortion, Loansharking

Remarks:

1964 Arrest — Extortion— used baseball bat,
complainant is still victim

will drive own car but is driven around by

Alex silver

Det. Goodfriend 13166
Investigator   Badge #

Figure 60.1 (*Continued*) Modus operandi sheet.

Gathering Data for the Profile Folder.   The starting point in gathering facts for the folder usually is the interviewing of complainants. It is important to patiently "dig out" all information from the complainant concerning the target such as full name (if known); areas frequented; a detailed description; and, most important, whether the target operates a vehicle.

A driver's license can provide various sources of facts. It gives the target's current address and any vehicles owned. However, most important, it gives the date of birth. There are two methods used to obtain the target's driver's license. The first method is through the motor vehicle bureau's computer. Most states have computer centers for such information. A search will usually turn up the target's license. However, there are times when the target has a common name and there may be literally hundreds of persons with the same name. Incorrect spelling of the last name might make it impossible to locate in a computer search.

Therefore, the second method of obtaining information from a driver's license is suggested. Frequented locations identified by the complainant offer the opportunity for a vehicle spot-check to obtain personal data. The spot-check procedure should be used by uniformed personnel. When the target is stopped, driver's license information should be written down. If, by chance, driving without a license, the target must be properly identified. There may be a secondary advantage of a vehicle spot-check: If the target is chauffeured by an associate, the identification of another target may aid the inquiry. If your target has other persons in the vehicle, they too can be identified by requesting proper identification; thus other associates may be revealed.

Once the target's date of birth is obtained, identification can be completed. The next step should be to determine if any prior criminal record exists. The investigator must check local law enforcement records usually found in units identified as bureaus of criminal identification. These units compile data on persons arrested and processed through the local criminal justice system. Other agencies that maintain such facts are the state bureaus of criminal identification and the FBI. Within FBI headquarters in Washington, D.C., printable crimes nationwide are forwarded for statistics and for identifying offenders. A central repository assists local law enforcement in identifying targets of investigators.

If the target was ever arrested, a copy of the arrest record or report should be obtained. From the arrest report associates may be identified. It may also be necessary to interview the complainant or witnesses involved in previous arrests. This will also give past addresses of the target.

The last important phase in completing the profile folder is to verify the target's address. This is usually done through the local gas, electric, and telephone companies which cover the target's residence. When official law enforcement need is identified, the companies cooperate if they can. Another information agency, that sometimes is overlooked, is the post office, which maintains a change-of-address file for at least one year. It may also be advantageous to interview the mail carrier who services the target's residence and usually knows most people on the route. However, caution should be used when exposing an active inquiry.

THE EXTORTION VICTIM

By far the most important piece of evidence besides physical evidence in any extortion case is the victim. It is usually the victim's testimony that will lead to either a conviction or an acquittal in court. When interviewing the victim, extreme care should be taken. A few important facts should be kept in mind. First, the only reason victims complain is that they are in trouble—short on payments and fearful of physical harm. Second, they feel in jeopardy by talking to the police, much more so by making a formal complaint. Last, they may not trust the police. It is extremely important that victims be made comfortable during interviews. The investigator must gain the victims' confidence if they are expected not to distort their involvement with the extortioners.

Victims uncovered during ongoing investigations present problems to many investigators. They have not made complaints; in fact, they are generally annoyed when discovered by police. Extreme caution should be taken when interviewing this type of victim, who will attempt by lies to get out of involvement in any case.

Knowing the difficulty involved with extortion victims and their tendency to lie or exaggerate, it is important that the investigator corroborate the victim's story. If possible, have the victim meet with the extortioner, perhaps wired or with an undercover officer. This tactic not only verifies the victim's story but adds to the evidence gathering which is essential to the prosecution of the case.

It is suggested that a profile folder on each victim be created. It is just as important to know the victim as to know the target. It could be a disaster for the prosecution if the defense attorney comes up with an arrest record or other damaging data that would discredit the victim on the witness stand. The investigator must be prepared to protect the credibility of witnesses. This can be done only by knowing the victim. However, extreme caution should be used when preparing these folders. It is imperative that the victims remain unaware of their existence. If they should find out, their confidence could be lost. A case could come to a sudden halt as the result of lack of cooperation.

It should be remembered that the testimony of a complainant may not be sufficient to ensure a conviction. However, testimony along with gathered physical evidence such as taped conversations, photo surveillance, or undercover operations will offer corroboration and support a prosecutorial presentation of facts.

THE EXTORTION RACKETS

Extortion is generally associated with persons participating in organized criminal activity. Due to the low risk and high profit potential, it has been embraced by syndicated criminals as a means of amassing money and power. Extortion has produced a large and steady income, providing funds that have been used to finance illegal activities such as gambling and narcotics traffic. However, more frequently it is employed to collect payments from gambling or loan-sharking victims reluctant to repay debts.

The Protection Racket

The protection racket is a popular extortion method used by organized-crime and other offenders. It provides for a steady income and the creation of a treasury. Aside from the profit incentive, it produces something more important than money—a reputation. To have a successful operation, the extortioner must be capable of inducing a long and lasting fear in the victim, and must be able to ward off any competitors. This ability earns one a "rep," which is important among key crime figures and lesser criminals.

The protection racket is extortion in its purest form and is basically very simple. For example, a merchant (the usual target) is forced to pay a fee for protection—not necessarily from some unknown vandal but, rather, from the extortioner.

Organizing a Neighborhood for a Protection Racket. This profitable activity can be easily accomplished. The extortioner introduces himself to the merchants he wishes to organize by explaining a "problem" in the neighborhood and asking if they would like to take advantage of his "umbrella protection." Preceding his visit, there are often acts of vandalism on some property, such as painted obscenities on a plate glass window. He offers his services for a percentage of business profits or a fixed price. If, by chance, a merchant chooses to test the extortioner's reputation, the latter has an opportunity to flex his muscle.

It is not necessary for the extortioner to attack each merchant he wishes to "score." Rather, he can select the weakest; that is, one whom he feels will not complain to the police. This merchant becomes his target of attack. For instance, he might strike first by breaking windows, followed by an arson attempt, and if there still are no results, a burglary is arranged in which property is taken or damaged. After each incident the extortioner allows the merchants' grapevine to do the rest. These subtle hints will usually move other merchants to fall in line.

The same tactic can be used even after the extortioner has an operational protection racket. Problems such as late or no payments or even the hint that a complaint to the police is forthcoming provoke acts of coercion that can whip everyone back in line.

The overt protection racket exists despite concentrated effort by various law enforcement agencies to suppress it. However, because of police pressure, organized crime has changed its tactics by becoming more selective in determining extortion targets.

In the process of target selection, organized crime has found a particular business area that can be easily developed for protection racket penetration. A retail bar is dependent on a liquor license for profit. In most states a liquor license is governed by stringent rules and regulations. The slightest violation could result in suspension or even revocation. For example, numerous brawls and disorderly complaints over a given period, or arrests for criminal violations (for example, prostitution, gambling, or narcotics) within the premises can jeopardize a license.

Using the law for his purpose, the extortioner is ready to attack the bar. The scheme could take effect with the first incident or it might take numerous "hints" before the owner is ready to meet the demanding terms. The extortioner usually approaches the bar owner by explaining the rules and regulations governing the license, by offering protection against any violations that may occur, by noting connections with the liquor license agency, and by indicating that no one would cause trouble when the word is spread that the bar is under *his* protection. If the owner refuses, the extortioner must then begin to use muscle.

The first part of the attack frequently involves two men entering the premises and seating themselves at opposite ends of the bar. After a few drinks, profanity is exchanged. With these degrading remarks, a physical altercation develops. While not many punches are thrown, extensive damage is caused.

The following day the extortioner returns and offers his sympathy about the damage. If the owner does not catch the hint, a few more damaging fights are called for, involving different participants. This pressure should bring the bar owner into the payment process.

Extortion through Services. A recent scheme developed to extort money from merchants is taking hold in the business community just as the simple protection racket did many years ago. The extortioner, instead of offering protection, now offers businesses a legitimate service. For example, to a bar owner he will offer to sell mixers for drinks—club soda, ginger ale, orange juice, and so on. To a restaurant owner, he will supply a laundry service for waiters' uniforms, tablecloths, and napkins. For a fruit or fish market, he offers a delivery service from the market so the owner does not have to transport the goods. To the local butcher shop he provides a knife-sharpening service.

The extortioner represents himself as a legitimate sales representative. However, investigation reveals that businesses have little or no choice of service and supply. They pay the extortioner any amount of money for such services.

The extortioner can use two tactics to score these merchants. The first works similarly to the methods used in the simple protection racket. He lets the merchant know he is going to supply a service, and there is no choice but to accept. The second is usually used when the merchant refuses to buy his services. In this approach, the extortioner cuts off the legitimate supplier from the merchant, removing competition for essential services. Pressure and coercion on the legitimate supplier, such as beating workers or destruction of property, will bring the necessary effect.

This type of extortion scheme seldom comes to the attention of the police. Businesses are usually vulnerable and approachable because the money extorted does not come from their profits but from the pockets of the consumer. The prices of products or services are simply raised to cover the losses suffered from the extortion scheme.

Investigating the Protection Racket

The protection racket is difficult to investigate, because it involves emotions, the strongest being fear. Seldom is a victim caught up in a protection racket willing to give information. This type of investigation is usually a long-term investigation, not an open-and-shut case.

Physical evidence must be gathered to provide corroboration of any data. Fear may inhibit input from victims. The testimony of one victim may weaken the case if the story is not corroborated by physical evidence. Testimony in open court by a victim may change when face-to-face contact is made. Fear of the extortioner may alter testimony.

In setting up an extortion case, the main goal, aside from gathering extensive physical evidence documentation, is to locate many victims to present as witnesses. Victims are essential to display for the court the overall scheme. Another advantage of bringing as many victims as possible to court is to aid in building the confidence of each. The old saying, "There is safety in numbers," applies, as each victim gains confidence in knowing that others are also testifying against the extortioner.

Locating Other Victims.   This is usually a difficult aspect in the investigation. However, two basic tricks of the trade can assist: (1) If the target uses a telephone to contact his victims, an ex parte order (wire-tap) should be obtained. This would yield not only physical evidence but also a list of victims who can be identified and interviewed. However, it is unusual for any extortioner in a protection racket to use a telephone. He is usually a street person who goes from one victim to another. Therefore the investigator should be a street person also. (2) Covert surveillance operations will reveal the extortioner. Surveillance will disclose the target's pattern of movement, which is always helpful in uncovering and interviewing victims. Presenting them with the facts that are known will lead the victims to believe that more knowledge about them exists. They will have a tendency to answer questions with more honesty. A lot depends on whom the victims fear more, law enforcement or the extortioner; this will govern their answers. Therefore the investigator should know as much as possible about the victim.

The ideal situation would be to set up an undercover operation in the area of the protection racket. From the legal wire-taps and the surveillance reports, the ideal situation can be formulated to establish contact with the extortioner. A cooperative victim may also introduce the extortioner. The rewards of a covert operation are numerous: Not only is there a law enforcement witness, the undercover officer, but the best physical evidence available for corroboration.

CRIMINAL USURY

Criminal usury, often known as "loan sharking," is the lending of money or property and charging an interest rate in excess of the legal rate.

The loan sharking racket is a lucrative enterprise for those wishing to invest money in an illegal business. However, to become successful, would-be loan sharks must possess three important capabilities. They must be individuals who (1) have access to money for investment, (2) know enough people willing to pay the excessive rate of interest, and (3) last and most important, have a reputation for exacting repayment at the exorbitant rate.

Extortion has always been associated with criminal usury. It is extortion or the threat of extortion that gives the loan shark the insurance policy he needs to collect his rate of interest as well as the loan itself. Over the years loan sharks have used a variety of techniques to collect their "vig" (interest). When examined closely, these methods can be classified into two separate but similar types: (1) physical extortion and (2) implied extortion.

Physical extortion is simply causing injury to victims who do not pay the vig. Beating victims, burning their businesses or homes, and beating or kidnapping their family members are all visible methods used. The law recognizes other types of physical extortion, such as "verbal threat" and "implied injury."

Although a *verbal threat* does not cause a physical injury to the victim or his property or family, it can cause injurious mental stress. Such threats as "I'll break your legs if you don't pay" or "I'll burn your home and kill your kids" are common examples of the verbal threat.

Another extortion method is the *implied injury*. The shark might light a cigar and put it dangerously close to the victim's eyes or face. Just far enough away *not* to cause an injury, but close enough for the heat to be felt. A Molotov cocktail (a bottle filled with gasoline and a piece of rag for a wick) lit and thrown at the victim's residence is an effective message.

The loan shark, taking a lesson from his counterpart, the extortioner in the protection racket, does not have to apply the physical extortion method to each victim. It is safer and profitable to apply extortion techniques in phases to the weakest victims, allowing the "grapevine" to do the rest.

Phase one is the verbal threat against the victim and, depending on the mental state of the victim, could yield the results the shark desires. Many victims caught up in a loan shark scheme realize that the loan shark's threats will be carried out, if necessary, in accordance with his reputation. A verbal threat can be used only once on a victim. If it does not produce the desired results, the loan shark must quickly and swiftly move to phase two or lose face among his victims and, consequently, his control over them.

In phase two, the loan shark applies the implied injury method. The enforcement of the verbal threat *almost* becomes reality, increasing the victim's fear of the loan shark. Victims are made to realize that by the charity of the loan shark, they have escaped severe physical injury. If both phases fail, phase three is then implemented, which will surely yield the desired effect. Here, the loan shark actually causes a physical injury to the victim, his family, or his personal property. It should be kept in mind that the loan shark does not have to personally perform this act. He can hire a third party to do the dirty work.

Loan sharks generally are reluctant to use physical extortion techniques to secure their weekly payment of interest from victims. They know the court's view on usury and extortion. The law sees criminal usury as a nonviolent crime; however, when physical pressures are applied to collect, it takes a longer and harder look at the usury and the offender.

Loan sharks also create a dilemma when they use physical methods of extortion. If the physical injury is severe, the victim may go into hiding and avoid payment. All a loan shark wants is to get paid. If he pushes his victim too far, the possibility increases that law enforcement assistance may be requested. Nevertheless, it is important for a loan shark to establish his "rep" with victims, or they will not pay the usurious rates. In order to placate the mood of the court and still maintain a "rep" with his "clients," the shark often attempts to apply the implied injury technique.

There are several ways of applying this "soft-soap" extortion technique. Usually, it starts at the first meeting between the shark and his victim, when the terms and conditions of the usurious loan have been explained. The "conversation" might run this way: "I know you and I are going to get along real well as long as you meet your obligations. I'm sure I won't have to call your house and ask you to please make your payments. You know family should be excluded from business deals." In this conversation the userer's tone is that of a friend and adviser. He explains to the victim that family should not get involved in business transactions. It is difficult in a court to make an extortion threat out of that piece of conversation, although the victim is getting the message intended—that the victim's family is also involved if payment is not made.

Organized crime, with its reputation for successfully employing extortionary methods, has been the major force behind the criminal usury racket for many years. However, a large group of userers are not necessarily affiliated with organized crime. These individuals are known by organized crime figures and in law enforcement agencies as "independents."

For example, independent loan sharks operate in the military service. A platoon sergeant or company commander can always be counted on to lend personal friends some money between paydays for a slight service charge. Independent loan sharks do not have to depend on extortionary methods to ensure payment. They simply work on supply and demand. If a victim fails to pay the required vig, which is now up to $1000 for every $5000 lent (in actuality, known as a "6-for-5" loan), the independent simply will never extend this person any more money and will "blackball" him as a bad risk. It is this blackball list that is feared—not overt extortion. The independent can survive because his loans usually are very small and a couple of "stiffs" will not put him out of business, nor will they complain to law enforcement authorities.

Investigating Criminal Usury

Before initiating an investigation into a loan shark extortion case involving criminal usury, the investigator should know something about this type of victim. First of all, such an individual has the same fears as the protection racket victim. This person, however, will cooperate by providing more than enough information and even other help, if needed, whereas the protection racket victim often will hide as much information as possible. When the loan shark victim comes with an extortion complaint, he or she seeks protection because the loan shark has more than likely already exhausted phases one, two, and possibly three.

The investigator should quickly take advantage of the victim's fear. The first step is to have the victim contact the loan shark. Any conversation should be taped or witness corroboration obtained, because possession of the extortion conversation is essential for the case. Note that the extortion communication should be in phase one; if it occurs in any other phase, it is a summary arrest.

Provided that the extortion act is only in phase one, the second step can be moved to. Here it is advisable to make the weekly vig payments, because evidence is needed that the target is actually a loan shark. If the decision is made to "buy and bust," the money should be marked; thus it will become evidence when the target is arrested with it on his person. If a "buy and bust" is not involved, the following procedure is acceptable. First, the complainant victim is searched immediately prior to meeting with the loan shark and all the victim's property, including the money that will be given to the loan shark, is carefully listed. Second, the complainant meeting occurs in a public place—a location where the investigator can watch the ongoing happenings. It is ideal (but not required) to have obtained a video taped recording of the before-search, the identification of property, the "meet," the after-search, and the second property identification. Such a record provides a picture of the flow of events and is ideal for court presentation. It is advisable that the victim be searched immediately after leaving the loan shark. At this time, all the victim's property should be carefully listed. Only one item should be missing—the payoff money. The procedure, with all the details should be incorporated in the case folder.

The third and final step consists of an attempt to infiltrate the loan shark operation by introducing an operative who will become the next victim. This can be accomplished quite easily, because the loan shark depends on a victim to provide other victims. (He doesn't advertise in *The Wall Street Journal*.) This dependency can be used by having the complainant act as a "steerer," who introduces the undercover operative to the loan shark. This new "victim" will prove an ideal witness, not only for the loan shark case but also for the extortion aspect.

Although it may not be advisable to have everyone introduced to court immediately, it is wise to uncover as many victims as possible. The procedures described previously should be used to identify extortion racket victims. In addition, the loan shark himself can become the investigator's greatest aide, and for several reasons. He maintains uncoded master records in a secret place; for example, in a safety deposit box or buried in the ground. More accessible is the daily coded notebook that he usually carries on his person. This source may identify coded names and telephone numbers of his victims and associates.

CONCLUSION

Whether it is loan sharking or a protection operation, extortion is difficult to prove. The investigator must gather extensive physical evidence and provide corroboration to substantiate complaints from victims. Efforts to maintain a close relationship with victims provide such individuals with a protective emotional blanket of security—a highly important investigative aspect, since vic-

Master Record		
Alex Wonderman (o) 212-134-6700		3 points $1000
1/1/92	30 vig	1000
1/7/92	30	1000
1/14/92	30	1000
1/21/92	30	1000
1/27/92	1,030 Total	—
Joe from Mike's restaurant 337-8800		$500 @ $60 fr. 10 wks
1/1/92	60	540
1/7/92	60	480
1/24/92	120	360
1/27/92	60	300
2/3/92	60	240
2/10/92	60	180
2/17/92	60	120
2/24/92	60	60
3/2/92	60	—

Daily Record
Monday 3/3/92
Wonderman 30V Joey fr. Paul's 60V Mary Shape 100V

tims' emotional stability is vital to the favorable outcome of the inquiry and prosecution.

In deciding investigative direction, determinations of covert or information gathering to support complaints must provide the necessary answers to suppress the aggressive *blackmailer*. Methods for gathering physical evidence should include photo surveillance, electronic overhears, and personal contacts (which are the best for this type of investigation).

In addition, the extortion investigator's efforts should be directed toward recovering personal records pertaining to the victims. While these may be encoded and difficult to recover, such data will prove vital in identifying unknown victims. Moreover, it can provide the investigator with a picture of the income from this illicit business. Once determined, a cooperative effort can be initiated with IRS agents who, in turn, can explore a civil action relative to tax evasion. This effort may provide an additional method of curtailing hidden crime against business and society.

Finally, although this chapter has treated extortion as investigated on the state level, the same techniques can be applied at the federal level. Certainly, an exploration of federal codes should be pursued if particular events do not meet the criteria of local statutes in seeking to obtain a conviction.

61

Managing Investigations into Public Corruption

Richard J. Condon

CORRUPTION INVESTIGATIONS

This operational guide on managing a corruption investigation is written to assist investigators and prosecutors in conducting a major corruption investigation.* The following assumptions are made in the writing of this guide:

1. The scope of the investigation is such that it will involve the full-time efforts of attorneys, investigators, auditors, and support personnel.

2. The nature of the investigation is such that there is a probability that attempts will be made to compromise the investigation.

3. The crime under investigation is ongoing rather than completed. While many of the investigative steps taken would be the same for both completed

*This project was supported by Grant Number 77-TA-99-0008 awarded to the Battelle Memorial Institute Law and Justice Study Center by the Law Enforcement Assistance Administration, U.S. Department of Justice, under the *Omnibus Crime Control and Safe Streets Act of 1968*, as amended. Points of view or opinions stated in this document are those of the author and do not necessarily represent the official position or policies of the U.S. Department of Justice.

and ongoing crimes, there are additional options open to the investigative team when investigating an ongoing conspiracy. They may be able to "influence the environment" to affect the direction of the investigation. For example, an undercover officer may be able to prevent, delay, or change the location of a meeting to further an investigative end. This proactive method of investigating is less likely to be possible when the crime under investigation has already been completed.

4. The jurisdiction is one in which court-authorized eavesdropping is not provided for in the law, but one-party consensual recordings are permitted. The focus of investigative effort might differ substantially in jurisdictions which permit electronic surveillance.

SECURITY OF INVESTIGATION

Any major corruption investigation is subject to being compromised either from without or from within. Attention must be paid to both the physical security of the investigative headquarters and to the integrity of the investigative team. Consideration should be given to the following:

Location of Operation Headquarters.   Is the facility in a secure building? Is it alarmed? What provisions have been made for response by a member of the investigative staff in the event of a fire or burglar alarm activation? What provisions have been made for supervision of cleaning personnel and other outside people in the building? Has provision been made for periodic checks of telephone lines and for bugging devices?

Assignment of Personnel.   Have investigators, attorneys, and any support personnel been screened? Is the investigative staff as small as possible consistent with accomplishing its mission? Is it necessary to assign everyone to the unit, or is it possible to provide some of the staff with cover assignments, thus disguising the magnitude of the undertaking?

Other Considerations.   (1) What provisions have been made regarding radio communications? Is the frequency used relatively safe? Is it possible to employ a code in transmitting? Have investigators been briefed on radio security, for example, to make license plate check requests by phone rather than over the air? (2) What provisions have been made regarding records checks? Is it possible to have your own computer terminal at operational headquarters? Is it possible to limit responsibility for records checks to one investigator; for example, the intelligence officer? Can provisions be made for this investigator to have direct access to as many agency and outside files as possible, thus limiting exposure of area of inquiry to others?

MAINTENANCE OF RECORDS

Records should be maintained readily available to the investigative personnel and attorneys assigned to the investigation. They should not be readily available to anyone else.

Original records should not be taken from the records area. Information such as license plates, addresses, and photographs should be duplicated, if necessary, for use by field personnel.

Arrangement of files will depend on the complexity of the investigation. Basic files will include:

- Name cards, including aliases or nicknames.

- Address cards, including locations frequented by subjects.

- License plate cards, including information on persons who use the vehicle as well as the registered owner.

- Telephone number cards, containing information on the subscriber and other subjects who may be contacted at the number (See Fig. 61.1 for facsimiles of each of these cards.)

Information should be duplicated on each type of card: A name card should also note locations frequented by the named subject, automobiles used, a physical description of the subject, and a photo of the subject if one is available. The address cards should contain the names of subjects who reside at or frequent the address and automobiles registered to people who live at the address. This information will provide a quick reference for field personnel following a known subject to an unfamiliar location or who observe an unknown subject arriving in an automobile at a suspect location.

Among other records useful during a long-term investigation are: (1) a brief chronology of events kept as a running account of meetings and payoffs which take place over the life of the investigation; (2) a breakdown by "subjects" as to their involvement, for example, meetings attended by them; and (3) an alias file, with reference to true names.

Intelligence officers should familiarize themselves with unusual sources of information both within and outside law enforcement agencies.

For example, the Office of the Special Prosecutor to Investigate Corruption in the Criminal Justice System in New York City maintains files that are primarily concerned with bribery involving organized crime figures and public officials—especially in the criminal justice system. There is also a special nursing home prosecutor who maintains records relating to bribery and frauds in the health services area.

EXAMINATION OF REPORTS

Investigative reports should be examined daily by the supervising investigator, the intelligence officer, and the case attorney. Each of these examinations serves a different purpose.

The supervising investigator will be primarily concerned with the information contained in the reports to help in keeping abreast of the investigation and briefing other investigative teams. The supervisor will also be concerned with the completeness and accuracy of the reports.

The intelligence officer should dissect the reports, culling from them names, addresses, and license plate numbers and extracting descriptions of unknown subjects to check against descriptions of unknown subjects from prior reports by other investigators. A file of these descriptions should be maintained, noting on which report(s) they appear, so that if subsequent identifications are made,

```
        EXCHANGE              NUMBER           AREA CODE              DATE

Pub? _____  Non-Pub? _____  Installation Date: _____
                                                                    ┌──────────────┐
Subscriber _____      │              │
                                                                    │              │
Address: _____       │              │
                 NUMBER                    STREET                   └──────────────┘
                                                                        Boro. #


        BOROUGH OR CITY AND STATE              SPECIFIC LOCATION


REMARKS: _____

_____

_____

_____


TELEPHONE CARD                    Cross Reference on Name and Address Card
Form 2 (3-73)                     OFFICE OF SPECIAL PROSECUTOR
```

```
            Plate                      Year & Make              Date
                                                            ┌──────────────┐
            State                      Type & Color         │              │
                                                            │              │
Owner: _____    │              │
                                                            └──────────────┘
Address: _____        Boro. #
                  Number·              Street

        Borough or City and State              Specific Location
Bus. Address: _____

REMARKS: _____

_____

_____


PLATE CARD – Cross-reference on Name & Address Card
Form 5 (3-73)      OFFICE OF SPECIAL PROSECUTOR
```

Figure 61.1 Facsimiles of various cards.

the earlier reports may be updated and the information disseminated to the investigative teams.

The case attorney should be concerned with the reports as providing a framework for a grand jury presentation and, eventually, a trial. They are documents that will be at issue as prior statements of witnesses available to the defense at

Name _____

Date

Address _____

Number   Street

_____

Borough or City and State

DESCRIPTION: _____

_____ B # _____ KG # _____

Boro. #

Auto Reg.: _____ Phone # _____

REMARKS: _____

_____

_____

_____

NAME CARD   Cross Reference on Address and Plate or Phone Card
Form 3 (3-73)   OFFICE OF SPECIAL PROSECUTOR

Number   Street   Date

Borough or City and State   Specific Location   Pct.

Name: _____

B # _____ KG # _____ E # _____

Boro. #

Auto Reg.: _____ Phone # _____

REMARKS: _____

_____

_____

_____

ADDRESS CARD   Cross Reference on Name, Plate or Phone Card
Form 4 (3-73)   OFFICE OF SPECIAL PROSECUTOR

Figure 61.1 (*Continued*)

hearings and trial. The case attorney should be satisfied that the reports are clear and unambiguous. When two or more investigators are on the same surveillance, the reports should accurately reflect what each saw and will be able to testify to.

The supervising investigator, the intelligence officer, and the case attorney should periodically reread earlier reports in order to discover patterns that may be developing. Such rereading can help to better understand prior reports in the light of subsequent information obtained, such as identifications of previously unknown subjects or the type of activity taking place at an observed location.

STORAGE OF TAPES AND OTHER EVIDENCE

The chain of custody of tapes used in consent recordings and in connection with court-ordered eavesdropping, where allowed, must be carefully maintained. Tapes should be sequentially numbered and only virgin tapes should be used.

Whenever possible, one investigator should be responsible for signing out the tape, putting the heading on it (Fig. 61.2 contains a sample tape heading for a concealable recorder and a telephone call), placing it on the subject, retrieving it from the subject, and signing it back into the "tech" room for duplication and storage.

Tapes and other evidence with identifying information should be logged into an evidence book and stored in a secure, limited-access area. The use of a safe is strongly suggested, with knowledge of the combination limited to as few persons as possible.

SAMPLE TAPE HEADING FOR A CONCEALABLE RECORDER AND A TELEPHONE CALL

If equipment is used by a tech unit, the technical unit should record the following information on tape:

1. Title and name.
2. Date and time.
3. Description of equipment, including serial number.

USE OF INFORMANTS

The two most important rules to be followed in dealing with an informant are (1) you must control the informant, and (2) you must keep your word. These rules may seem obvious, but any investigator or attorney who has dealt with a number of informants will recognize how costly it can be to violate either of these tenets.

Informants should be registered with the agency and their identities closely guarded. Whenever possible, at least two investigators should have a working relationship with each informant.

Compensation for paid informants should come from a special fund, not from the pockets of the investigators. This fund should be set up with controls that allow accounting for disbursements, but without unnecessarily revealing the informant's identity. One way to accomplish this is for the investigator to submit vouchers which state that the check drawn is to be used for confidential infor-

---

Test for Concealable Recorder (Nagra, etc.)

Investigator:

The time is_____. The date is_____. This is (Inv.)_____testing (*describe equipment*). Present with me is (are)_____. This device has been placed on the person of (Mr./Mrs.)_____ to record an upcoming conversation with_____. For the purpose of voice identification will you please state your name and address?_____. Did you give permission to place this recording device on your person?_____. Do you want the conversation with_____ to be recorded?_____. The time is now_____and the recorder is being turned to the off position pending the upcoming conversation. This is_____. The time is_____. The date is_____. Present with me is (Mr.)_____. (Mr.)_____ is about to dial telephone number_____ to speak with_____. (Mr.)_____ do you give permission to record this telephone conservation? (answer) _____. Please state your name and address for the record_____.

Figure 61.2 Sample tape heading for concealable recorder on a telephone call.

mation from informant No.—. The check should then be cashed by the investigator and the money given to the informant, who executes a receipt for it. These receipts should be numbered and maintained in the informant's confidential file.

Informants who are providing information in return for consideration in cases in which they are defendants should be told just what the agency is prepared to do to help them. Any such negotiations should be handled by the case attorney, not the investigator. No promise should be made that cannot be kept. If an informant's testimony is going to be needed, this should be made clear to the informant at the outset.

In dealing with informants, it is important to utilize their knowledge of the participants in the conspiracy and their opinions on various tactics under consideration. Their opinions, however, should *not* be the controlling factor in deciding how to proceed. Informants will often suggest or insist on a course of action that the investigator feels would not work or would not accomplish the investigative end. Informants may suggest a particular course of action because it is safer or easier for them, because it prolongs the period of time that they are being compensated, or because it avoids jeopardizing participants in the conspiracy they wish to protect. The investigator must be willing to overrule informants, even if it means that they will no longer cooperate and the investigation will be hampered. All too often, inexperienced investigators and/or attorneys allow informants to dictate the direction an investigation will take, only to find in the end that the only benefit obtained was to the informant.

USE OF "TURNED" SUSPECTS

The two crucial decisions to be made in attempting to have persons who are part of the conspiracy become agents or to "turn" them are (1) whom to approach, and (2) if and when to make the approach.

Ideally, the person approached will be the least culpable of the conspirators and also be in the best position to further the investigation. Realistically, a decision will have to be made between someone who is in a good position to help but is a main participant, and someone who is in a position less advantageous to the investigation but who is also less culpable.

However, investigators probably would not be looking to turn someone if there were other investigative avenues open. Therefore, having to offer someone a deal in return for cooperation must be viewed as the alternative to not making a case against any of the parties to the conspiracy. So it is decided who is (1) most apt to cooperate, (2) in a position to further the investigation by cooperating, and (3) not the main subject of the investigation.

Deciding if and when to attempt to turn someone is an equally crucial decision. If the attempt fails, the fact that a particular crime is being investigated will more than likely be exposed. This can sometimes be avoided if the person to be turned is engaged in more than one form of criminal activity. This individual should be approached on the crime of less interest, so that a failure will not expose the investigation of the crime which is of primary importance.

As important as the decision to attempt to turn someone is, equally important is at what time the attempt is made. Time is needed to persuade the subject to cooperate. If the approach is made at a time when his or her presence will be missed somewhere else, the purpose may be defeated. If the subject cannot accompany the investigator because of having to be somewhere else, it is likely that the approach will be reported to coconspirators. Prior surveillance should be conducted to assure that there will be time to convince the subject to cooperate.

If the attempt succeeds, the investigator should be aware that a turned subject will not necessarily stay turned and may at any time expose the investigation. No more information than is absolutely necessary should be revealed. A "turned" subject must be controlled even more than an informant.

USE OF UNDERCOVER INVESTIGATORS

The use of undercover investigators offers obvious advantages over the use of either informants or turned criminals. Undercovers are trained investigators who will be more objective in reporting on a situation than either the informant or the turned criminal and can be trusted more. They are also more reputable on the witness stand.

The cover provided for an undercover should be as complete as is necessary to the investigation being conducted. It should be assumed that at some point an undercover's background and/or identity will be questioned; therefore the necessary documentation must be provided to stand up to such a check. Social security cards, credit cards, and a driver's license are a few of the more basic documents the undercover should possess.

Contact with an undercover should be limited to as few investigators as practical. When meetings are necessary, they should take place away from police facilities. Arrangements should be made for someone to take care of unusual personal obligations that cannot be met by the undercover because of the assignment.

A well-placed undercover investigator will not only be in a position to provide intelligence but may also be able to delay or prevent actions that would do irreparable harm. Of less significance but perhaps more important to the investigation, the undercover may be able to provide direction to the rest of the investigative team, especially to the auditors. There have been instances of undercover investigators penetrating sufficiently high in an organization to be able to accept the service of subpoenas and assure they were complied with fully.

CONSENT RECORDINGS

Electronic eavesdropping as an investigative tool is not treated in this guide because many jurisdictions do not have the statutory authority to intercept telephone conversations or mechanically overhear conversations without the consent of one of the parties. However, most jurisdictions do permit the recording of conversations when one party consents to the overhearing.

The use of consent recordings is important when informants and turned criminals are being relied on. Their unsupported testimony is likely to be suspect, as both classes of witnesses have something to gain from cooperating. The informant may have been promised a financial reward or a consideration in sentencing if a defendant in a case. A turned participant in the conspiracy under investigation is obviously seeking consideration. It is important to be able to support their testimony with additional or corroborative evidence. The use of consent recordings is one way to accomplish this.

Consent recordings may be made of telephone calls, by concealing a recorder or transmitter on the person of the agent, or by wiring an automobile, room, or other place where a meeting is to take place. One caution to be noted when wiring a room or car to overhear the agent's conversation is that if the agent leaves the vehicle or room and two or more people remain and continue the conversation, unaware that it is being recorded, an illegal eavesdropping situation exists.

The two most common methods of wiring the person of an agent are to use either a transmitter or a body recorder. Each has advantages and disadvantages.

The transmitter is more easily concealable, consisting of only a microphone and a power source. The conversation is broadcast by the transmitter to listening agents nearby and is recorded on a tape recorder in their possession. The use of the transmitter allows the monitoring agents to overhear the conversation and helps ensure the safety of the agent by putting the investigator in a position to take action if the need arises.

The range of the transmitter is limited and can be affected by the decibel level in the air, the density of buildings, and soundproofing. Therefore, it is not recommended that a transmitter be used alone unless conditions are ideal.

The body recorder is larger than the transmitter and thus is less easily concealable. It does not broadcast the conversation, but rather records it on a self-contained tape recorder. The body recorder will be far less affected by the decibel level in the air and not at all by the surroundings. The conversation cannot, however, be monitored by backup agents.

Wherever possible, it is recommended that both a body recorder and a transmitter be used to record the conversation.

USE OF AUDITOR-INVESTIGATORS

Auditors are essential to the investigation of white-collar crime. Money or something else of value is the common thread that runs through every type of fraud and every act of corruption. The areas where auditors will be of most value are (1) uncovering the source of bribe payments, (2) tracing and following the trail of bribe payments, (3) uncovering the nature of the fraud under investigation, and (4) determining the income engendered by illegal activities.

The traditional sources of bribe payments from organized crime to public officials are monies received from gambling, loan sharking, and narcotics. It is when the attempt is being made to establish the source of a commercial bribe or a bribe from a so-called legitimate business to a public official or organized crime figure that the skills of the auditors are needed. Some of the methods of diverting assets to pay bribes that have been uncovered in recent years include the following activities:

1. Banks receive large deposits from organized-crime-controlled unions, then make loans to borrowers recommended by the unions. These loans are never paid back.

2. Selected people are employed as salespersons, troubleshooters, and consultants at a salary and with an expense account. Of course, little work is expected in return for the monies paid.

3. A line of credit is established at a Las Vegas casino, which allows the recipient to gamble and lose, with the markers made good by the briber.

4. Tables are purchased or ads taken in journals in connection with political dinners in order to obtain contracts.

5. The use of company automobiles, boats, apartments, suites in resorts, and tickets to shows or sporting events are bestowed as payment for favors.

6. Property or other assets of considerable value are purchased for far less than the true market value.

It is important that the auditors be thoroughly familiar with all aspects of an investigation. In one investigation into the pornographic movie business, auditors were able to determine the volume of income from peep shows, based on the life of the bulb used in the projectors and the number of bulbs purchased over a period of time.

In a medicaid investigation, auditors were able to establish the fee being charged by a laboratory for tests. This fee minus the kickbacks being paid to the medicaid mill was not enough to cover the cost of the testing. Investigators then discovered that the tests were not being performed and the laboratory was merely sending back every result as normal.

As business becomes more complex and as schemes are uncovered, the methods of diverting assets and perpetrating frauds will become more complex too, requiring an even greater use of auditors in corruption investigations.

ISSUANCE OF PROCESS

At some stage of the investigation, it becomes necessary to issue process. If the investigation has been covert up to this point, the subjects will now become aware of it. Even the issuance of subpoenae duces tecum to banks and other noninvolved parties will most likely result in notification to the subject(s).

The first decision then is at what point should process be issued. It must be considered whether "going public" will help or hinder the investigation. Will the issuance of process interfere with any undercover aspects of the investigation, or will it help by stimulating activity on the part of the conspirators?

If the decision is made to issue process, the next decision is in what form the process should be issued. Do the records sought constitute evidence of a crime? Would they be destroyed if subpoenaed? Are they personal records, the subpoenaing of which may confer immunity on the subject? Is there probable cause for issuing a search warrant?

The answers to these questions may well determine the outcome of the investigation. Therefore, there should be a full discussion between the attorneys and supervising investigators before any decision is made.

INVESTIGATIVE GRAND JURY

The use of a grand jury in an investigation is usually the last step taken. At this point, most other investigative steps will have been exhausted or are dependent on the existence of the grand jury to be completed. For example, in New York State, subpoenas cannot generally be issued except to compel the appearance of persons before or the surrendering of records to the grand jury.

The investigative grand jury is a powerful weapon, if used intelligently. A grand jury may confer immunity on a witness and thereby compel truthful testimony. The immunized witness is faced with the choice of testifying truthfully and, it is hoped, aiding the investigation, or committing contempt or perjury and being indicted for those crimes.

The success or failure of the investigation may very well depend on the decisions made on how the grand jury is used. The sequence of witnesses called is crucial. Each question asked of a witness imparts information to the subjects of the investigation. If witness A is questioned about a meeting with subject B, it must be assumed that B will learn that investigators know the meeting took place. The questions put to A may reveal to B that there was electronic surveillance of the meeting or that C, who also attended the meeting, was a government agent. On the other hand, questions may be asked in such a way as to leave the impression that electronic surveillance was used when in fact it was not.

When B is questioned in the grand jury, he is aware of the questions asked of A and may be in a position to conform his testimony to that of witness A. In addition, an unsuspecting witness, not aware of the parameters of the investigation, may have risked waiving immunity, but, based on the questions asked of prior witnesses, may now decide to testify only with immunity from prosecution.

The length of time allowed to pass between the calling of witnesses may also be crucial: Evidence may be destroyed or altered, potential witnesses may leave the jurisdiction before they are subpoenaed, and agreements may be entered into as to who will "take the rap."

Prosecutors should be aware that the use of the investigative grand jury has come under increased scrutiny. On the federal level, a congressional committee is examining the role of the grand jury with a view toward changing unfair procedures.

In New York, attorneys in the grand jury are allowed by law to accompany witnesses who have waived immunity. Often the focus of defense attacks seems to be centered more on the conduct of the prosecutor and less on the conduct of the investigators in the field. In a number of prosecutions in the New York area, the conduct of the prosecutor has become enough of an issue to result in dismissals or reversals based on prosecutorial mistakes or at least in the requirement that a prosecutor other than the one who conducted the investigation be assigned to try the case.

COOPERATION BETWEEN INVESTIGATORS AND PROSECUTORS

In any joint investigation where the investigators and prosecutors are working together as a team, as opposed to investigations in which the prosecutor is not consulted until the case is made, certain ground rules should be established at the outset. Someone must be in overall control of the effort. Normally, this should be the prosecutor who in the end will have to present the evidence to secure an indictment and eventually try the case.

This is not to say that prosecutors should attempt to direct field operations. They should not. Experienced investigators should be in charge of the day-to-day investigative effort. The prosecutor should serve as a legal guide and, more important, provide overall direction in the investigation.

The prosecutor plays a difficult role in a joint investigation, having to be at one and the same time an active, enthusiastic member of the team and an objective, cautious judge as to whether the evidence gathered is enough to justify the impaneling of a grand jury, the issuance of search warrants, or the application for electronic eavesdropping. It is very easy for the prosecutor to get caught up in the chase and make mistakes that in the courtroom can prove fatal. The prosecutor must always keep in mind that somewhere down the road, motions to suppress and controvert and dismiss must be contended with.

There must be full and open communication between the investigators and the prosecutors. Investigative mistakes should not be concealed from the prosecutor. Nothing makes a prosecutor more unhappy than to have the defense uncover an investigative mistake that has been kept from the prosecutor.

Prosecutors have to overcome the professional barrier often existing between them and the investigators. It is not unusual for investigators to be reluctant to be completely frank and open with the prosecutor on a case. Investigators are aware that today's prosecutor is likely to be next year's defense attorney and feel that the less the prosecutor knows, the better off the investigators are.

Prosecutors should take pains to inform the investigators of not only their legal decisions, —for example, not to apply for a warrant—but also the reasoning behind the decisions. This will not only make for a smoother relationship, but also help to make investigators more knowledgeable.

Prosecutors should not assume that because someone has been an investigator for a number of years, he or she is an experienced witness requiring little or no preparation before taking the witness stand. One of the by-products of expanded plea bargaining is that many investigators may not testify in an adversary proceeding for a period of years. This is especially true of investigators who work on complex, long-term investigations.

The prosecutor should take pains to thoroughly prepare the investigator as to both direct testimony and the likely lines of cross-examination. This will help to prevent the bitterness often evidenced between a prosecutor who feels the investigative witness ruined the case and an investigator who feels not only left at the mercy of the defense attorney by the prosecutor, but that the prosecutor also asked questions the investigator could not answer.

There should be a clear understanding between the investigators and prosecutors on how contact with the media will be maintained. There should be no leaking of information by either attorneys or investigators. Besides jeopardizing the investigation, the premature release of information can damage the working relationship between the investigators and attorneys.

In any joint investigation, and especially in complex, long-term investigations, friction will develop between investigators and prosecutors. Nothing positive will be accomplished by letting these situations go unresolved; indeed, much harm may be done to the investigation if misunderstandings and disagreements are not cleared up. There must be a climate that allows for free and open discussion when differences arise, in order that they may be resolved and the efforts of the entire investigative team be directed toward the successful conclusion of the investigation.

62

Decoding Illicit Activity Records

Leonard H. Miller

CODES AND CIPHERS

That operators in the illegal numbers racket employ codes or ciphers is evidenced by the frequency with which these items are seized or come into police possession through arrests.

Why do people involved in the numbers racket take the time to encrypt their records of illegal gambling activity? A large percentage do not, but more and more are now doing so. They do it for the same reason that other criminals encode messages: They have information that they do not want known if they are arrested or their records are seized. The majority of people who use enciphered messages or codes feel secure in their concealment of dates, bettors, names, bets or wagers, payouts, summary accounts, and so on, and in the feeling that law enforcement will not be able to decipher them and consequently may be forced to drop prosecution.

The most prolific use of encrypted intelligence in the criminal justice field during recent years has involved gambling. Notes in some form of code or cipher are made by policy operators in recording illegal betting activities associated with the numbers racket.

Codes are elements such as letters, numbers, or symbols which are used to represent a whole word, phrase, sentence, and so on; for example, #39 might be a policy runner named John Smith. *R&H* might be interpreted to mean "using the race and handle method." *P/C* can be read as "percentage cut."

While the terms "ciphers" and "codes" are frequently used interchangeably, they have a fundamental difference, demonstrated by the following examples.

Substitution Ciphers

The letters of the plain text are replaced by other letters, figures, or symbols but do not change their relative positions.

Tic-Tac-Toe

9	8	7
6	5	4
3	2	1

(C)   (O)

Writers using this type of cipher could record their bets by using the numbered sections; for example, a bet on the number 260 and a wager of $1 with a $0.60 combination would be written as follows:

A bet on the number 391 and a wager of $0.30 would be written as follows:

⌐⌐⌐ ⌐⌐

A similar type of tic-tac-toe is written in the following manner:

STU	VWX	YZ
JKL	MNO	PQR
GHI	DEF	ABC

This cipher uses the first letter in the three-letter group that is represented by the portion of the box immediately next to or around it; therefore

S = ⌐   V = ⊔   Y = ⌐   J = ⌐   M = ☐

When the plain-text or alphabet letter occupies the second position in the three-letter group, a dot • is inserted within the aforementioned symbol; therefore

T = •⌐   E = ⌐•⌐   H = •⌐   Q = ⌐•   B = ⌐•

When the plain text letter occupies the third position in the group, two dots (••) are placed within the symbols; therefore

O = [••]   R = [••]   L = [••]   U = •• | X = ⌊•• |

This process follows through for the entire plain text alphabet. As a further example, if a person were to send a "coded" message such as, "The cops are coming—Move" to the bank or office, it would be written like this

This would not be easily understood if by chance it fell into the wrong hands.

In another simple substitution cipher, the letters of the plain text are changed or replaced by numbers; for example,

C	U	M	B	E	R	L	A	N	D
0	9	8	7	6	5	4	3	2	1

A writer using this type of cipher could record wagers in the following manner: The number 139 for $1 bet would be written D A U D C C - L M (LM being the bettor). The number 467 for $3.50 bet would be written L E B A R C - L M (LM being the bettor). Bets or wagers or records like the above are easily recorded but difficult to understand. To make it more difficult, the selection process in this case would be done at random. See the following example:

X	P	E	T	H	D	L	Q	F	Y
7	0	6	1	9	4	3	5	2	8

Using this random selection process, the number 148 for $1 bet would be written T D Y T P P.

Another type of cipher which has been used for recording telephone numbers in a policy operation is blank music sheets on which telephone numbers are placed; for example, as follows:

Telephone number 535-4344   Telephone number 516 988-5567

Several other types of telephone ciphering have been observed. These include but are not limited to switching numbers around, dropping one number, subtracting or adding numbers as in the "10 code." With this one, 10 is subtracted from or added to the first or last part of the telephone number; for example,

535-4344 (real number)	988-5567 (written number)
− 10	+ 10
535-4334 (written number)	988-6567 (real number)

Anyone viewing a telephone book with ciphered numbers would have all the wrong phone numbers. The person who wrote them would simply dial the number, adding or subtracting 10. The different ways telephone numbers can be coded are limitless.

In ciphers, for each letter of the alphabet or plain text, there is a related element in the cipher text; for example,

Plain Text

A B C D E F G H I J K L M N O P Q R S T U V W X Y Z

Cipher Alphabet

Z Y H B Q R S T O I P A C E L U M D F G J K X N V W

In this example, the letters in the ciphered text have been chosen at random. Thus the message "MOVE-THE-MONEY" would be written as follows:

CLKQG-TQCLE-QVXXX

Note that the ciphered text has been arranged in groups of five letters, using Xs to fill in the open spaces. Setting out groups of five letters is a traditional way of ciphering.

Plain Text

A B C D E F G H I J K L M N O P Q R S T U R W X Y Z

Cipher Text

1 2 3 4 5 6 7 8 9 10 11 12 13 14 15 16 17 18 19 20 21 22 23 24 25 26

Thus "race method," or R, would be written as 18; "handle method," or H, could be written as 8; "combination," or C, would be written as 3.

In the following cipher, a group of two or three letters can stand for the same number:

1	2	3	4	5	6	7	8	9	0
A	B	C	D	E	F	G	H I		J

K L M N O P Q R S T
U V W X Y Z – – – –

Thus, 1 = A, K, or U; 4 = D, N, or X; 6 = F, P, or Z. For example, the number 470 for $1 bet would be written as follows:

470 for $1 = D G J A J J
or
N Q T K T T
or
X Q T U T T

Transportation Ciphers

In a cipher, the letters stay the same as in the plain text, that is, A B C D E[ell], but they are moved around or their order is changed. This, of course, must be done so that both parties are aware of the arrangement. The individual letters in the plain text remain exactly as normal when used in the enciphered message but are arranged in a different order. For example:

C Y O L P - L G I O B - T

Reading every other letter from left to right, this message reads "COP GOT-"; then reading from right to left and reading every other letter, "BILLY"; the total message: "COP GOT BILLY."

For a last example of transportation ciphers: "Do not move the bank money today" may be enciphered to read

D O N O T M O V E
T H E B A N K M O
N E Y T O D A Y

The message is then written from the vertical columns of three, into groups of five written horizontally. Xs are used to round out the empty spaces.

D T N O H - E N E Y O - B T T A O - M N D O K - A V M Y E - O X X X X

Wagering and Financial Records

People involved in the illegal numbers racket are acutely aware of the problems they face if apprehended by the police with regard to wager records, financial records, and paraphernalia used in their operation. Wager records are important to the investigative process. Wager records probably, in most cases, do not contain bettors' names. The identities found on the records will be those of the writers. At an organizational level above the writer, investigation frequently encounters charts of bets above a certain amount arranged numerically on a chart so that layoff decisions can be made in another operation. Financial records typ-

ically list writers and their balances and include adding machine tapes, also referred to as ribbons, showing the writer's gross action and computations used
to determine the net amount due the bank.

63
Narcotics Buy Operations

Vernon J. Geberth

Thursday, August 20, 1745 hours (5:45 P.M.). The location is the southeast corner of 81st Street and Amsterdam Avenue on Manhattan's Upper West Side.

A narcotics dealer named Irv has been busily selling his "product," sometimes in open view, for the last two hours. Among the many persons standing on the corner are an anxious "clientele" who are being "served" by Irv. They eagerly hand over their ill-gotten cash for the small glassine packets that Irv calls his "product."

As the junkies and "locals" mill about and the dealer named Irv does his thing, a police surveillance team, using a 35-mm camera equipped with a 300-mm telescopic lens records the action.

In fact, all the police really have to do at this point, is to pick up one of Irv's "customers," seize the evidence, and go back and lock up Irv for "sale." However, that is not the plan. The information supplied to the police is that Irv is only one of many street dealers working for a dude named Sly. Arresting Irv is not going to affect Sly's operation, and as soon as Irv gets busted another dealer will take his place. The trick is to get to Sly through Irv. The method is called the *narcotics buy operation.*

As the narcotics investigators make their observations, Irv is seen in conversation with two more customers. Irv starts to walk off the "set" with the customers, and the photographer begins to snap away with the camera. While he serves these two "white cats" with his product, a police photographer catches the entire transaction on film. As Irv heads back to the set, another apparent customer is observed approaching the corner. He looks like the other persons in the area, and he "raps" the language of the street as well as anyone else in the crowd. He walks up to Irv, says all the right words, and asks if he can buy a "spoon" (approximately 1/8th ounce). They haggle over the price a little, and then the agreed amount is $350. The new customer shows Irv his bankroll and assures him his money is good. Now, since Irv does not go around the street

SOURCE: Reprinted by permission of the author: From *Law and Order*, Vol. 27, No. 1, Jan. 1979.

with 1/8th ounce of dope in his pocket, he is forced to go to his supplier, Sly. About 15 minutes later he returns with the "goods." Since a deal of this nature cannot "go down" in the street they agree to go into a local bar, which of course is a front for Sly. Once inside, they go into the lavatory, lock the door, and complete the deal. While this is going on, members of the backup team of narco investigators have been making observations on all of Irv's movements. After the deal has been completed, the new customer tells Irv that if his product is as good as claimed, he will be back regularly. Maybe Irv could make a little extra if he does the right thing, assuring Irv that even if Irv takes him to his man (Sly) the customer will still take care of him (Irv).

Just another narcotics buy? No. The last customer was "The Man," an undercover police officer, who has just made a narcotics buy, gathering a valuable piece of evidence against Irv and his supplier Sly for future prosecution. In addition the field team has not only pinpointed Sly's pad, but has remained in the area long enough to watch Irv dutifully turn over the cash to a person they believe to be Sly. The new customer soon becomes a regular, and eventually meets not only Irv and his counterparts, but starts to deal with Sly "direct."

Two months later, Sly and four of his street dealers are arrested under supreme court warrants charging them with sales of narcotics. Another narcotics buy operation has successfully been completed.

The narcotics buy operation is probably the most effective investigative technique used so far by the police in their war against narcotics. Basically, a narcotics buy operation involves an agent, either an undercover police officer or an informant, who makes the buy or purchase of narcotics from the dealer.

This may sound quite simple, but it is not. The narcotics buy operation is the most potentially dangerous, tricky, and unpredictable investigative technique.

It might be basic enough in theory or procedure, but in actuality involves some of the most intricate negotiations, ingenuity, or police maneuvers imaginable. Many variables present themselves during the delicate and dangerous interplay between police agent and dealer.

Some of the possible variables that may confront the narcotics investigator and/or undercover agent are as follows:

1. The human behavior and personalities of both the agent and dealer are unpredictable.
2. The conditions of the *set* (the location where the sales are taking place) are unpredictable.
3. The required movements of the police backup team trying to maintain surveillance and react to actions of the dealer and/or undercover cannot be planned.
4. Traffic, vehicular and pedestrian, affects both observation and movement.
5. Weather: rainy or clear, night or day, changing conditions such as storm or snow.
6. Conditions given by the dealer to the undercover, under which he will complete the deal. Although negotiable, these situations are never controllable. The undercover has to have options available to him that he can employ, and these options have to be realistic.
7. Mechanical breakdown, and/or equipment failure: Backup autos may malfunction or break down, transmitting difficulty may occur, or batteries used on the undercover or in backup units may go dead. In addition certain areas are "radio-dead zones," where transmissions are impossible.
8. Erratic actions by the dealer and/or evasive methods taken by the subject to avoid surveillance make the "tail" or effective observations impossible.

9. Third-party situations:
   a. The dealer's connection or "supply" runs out.
   b. Someone fouls up on the proposed meet time.
   c. Some unexpected police action by other police officers unaware of the buy operation. This can occur against the subject, the undercover, or both.
10. The rip-off—when the dealer or his people rob the undercover officer. This is without a doubt the most dangerous situation that can occur during a buy operation, and only the undercover can determine what action he or she will take or how to handle the situation. Even with a predetermined signal of trouble, those first few seconds of the crisis lie heavily upon the undercover. Another situation under this category, although not as dangerous, is the "beat" package whereby the undercover is sold a phony or "dummy" bag. Short of examining the contents, which is nearly impossible to do effectively in front of the subject, there is not much the undercover can do. However, immediately upon discovering the "beat," the undercover with a backup team should make it his business to get back to that dealer and put in his complaint, or make his "beef." The same goes for a "short" package, one that weighs less than the agreed-on purchase. This is what a dope dealer would do; so the undercover does the same.

These, of course, are not the only variables; however, they are the most common problems encountered by the narcotics investigator. Experienced supervisors and investigators of this type of case must realize the possibility of these situations. Although they will not be able to control all the situations in all circumstances, they should be able to perceive potential problems in their planning and be prepared for appropriate alternative action. They will then ensure the safety of the undercover officers, and also preserve the integrity and provide for the successful termination of the operations.

SETTING UP THE NARCOTICS BUY OPERATION

The narcotics buy operation requires a well-planned and systematic approach and appraisal of conditions. Just as in any successful sales campaign or business venture, the input of the parties involved in the operation or process is the most valuable tool in determining what plan of action will be taken. If the democratic process in decision making exists anywhere in the police function, it certainly is evident and should be a requirement in the implementation and planning of the narcotics buy operation.

To be effective, the narcotics buy operation must be as inconspicuous as the subculture it hopes to penetrate. The actions of each of the officers involved in the case must be invisible to the point that people in the area are not aware of their presence.

Hence a *tactical plan* is a necessity. Any format may be implemented; however, I have found through my experience that there are 10 basic subjects and procedures one should consider in any such tactical plan in the narcotics buy operation. Following are examples.

1. An initial survey of the area where the buy is to take place should be conducted to alert the surveillant to the type of dress worn by persons in the area and types of vehicles, such as taxis, trucks, or work crew vehicles. The preliminary survey is important so that appropriate vantage points and good observa-

tion locations can be determined beforehand and proper assignments made. I implemented a technique whereby a tactical plan sketch of the area was employed, which gave the officers a visible portrait of the area, with streets and buildings identified.

2. The team meeting should take place the day of the proposed buy, allowing ample time to discuss the purposes and objectives of the operation and obtain from the participants any information about the subject or location where the buy is to go down. (The names of members who are present should be noted for future court presentation, which may require their presence.)

3. The subject to be "bought" should be identified by name and/or pictures which can be distributed to the *field team* or by a description if no pictures are available. In addition any autos and/or license plate numbers should be made known as well as any distinctive mannerisms on the part of the subject, including his or her dress and style, especially if they stand out.

4. The undercover officer, as well as the informant if one is to be used, should be known to the entire field team. It is very important that every team member be aware of each other's presence and assignments. The undercover officer should personally discuss his or her plan of action with the team. This point cannot be overstressed. During this phase of the planning, the team and the undercover officer become fully aware of each other's conception of the operation. In addition, the options available to the undercover officer will be discussed as well as the corresponding alternative actions. An example of some options are: fronting the money, leaving the set in an auto, entering a building, leaving the set, or buying only half the package. Also during this exchange, a *predetermined signal* should be agreed on whereby the field team will be advised by the undercover of a dangerous situation requiring immediate response or indication that the buy went down; or a signal for the backup team to move in and effect an arrest, as in cases of *buy and bust* operations, where the arrest is made immediately after the undercover's buy.

An example of some signals that have been used are as follows: removing one's hat; scratching one's head or nose; removing one's glasses; or, if in an auto, using the four-way flashers, hitting the brake lights, blowing the horn, or opening the trunk or hood. Any number of actions may be employed, as long as the undercover officer feels comfortable with a particular signal and the field team can readily observe this signal from their vantage point.

5. Details of the time and place of the buy and a description of the area should be gone over as well as a description of possible hazards and vantage points, including a description of any premises that the undercover will be entering. This phase is closely related to the points in the tactical plan sketch done either on a blackboard or by a diagram, and is very important should the backup team have to enter the building or should forced entry become necessary.

6. A listing of equipment used by the officers indicating which officer is assigned is of the utmost importance to later prosecution. Many a case has been lost because of investigating officers failing to take note of their locations during the observations or to note the make, model, or type of equipment they were using. As an example, if photos are to be used in the investigation, not only must the camera used be identified, but the number of frames shot, the officer taking the photos, and the film type (35 mm) and lens type used must be recorded.

Likewise, the power of a pair of binoculars should be noted and the type of autos used; and a record should be made of any mechanical devices, such as tape recorders, "Kel" transmitters and receivers, and portable radios, listed by name and/or serial number.

7. A written description of assignments should be noted on the tactical plan, so that each member knows his or her assignment and responsibility. Likewise, it should be required that written reports be submitted by each backup team, so as to corroborate the actions of the undercover or informant.

8. If moving surveillance is to be employed, proper nondescript autos should be used, such as taxis and commercial vehicles. These autos should be operated by one person as opposed to the police "giveaway" team pattern. Female officers are an added asset to this type of surveillance. Another very good technique that can be used in certain urban areas is the "marked radio car" manned by two uniformed narcotics investigators. This can be an invaluable tool in moving close to the subjects, as long as the investigators do not assume a position which gives the appearance that they are watching the subject. Or, these marked cars can be used with the ruse of a "routine stop" if the subject is in a vehicle, requiring the subject's identification. (Uniformed marked radio cars are often completely disregarded as a threat of arrest by certain dealers in urban areas because their presence is considered a normal routine of city life.)

9. A proposed meet location after the buy should be established, so that the undercover can meet with a member of the field team and a supervisor in order to secure the evidence and give immediate information about the subject. Many times this information can be relayed by radio to the backup teams remaining in the area in order to follow up on the buy; thus in some cases they are actually able to follow the "bought" subject back to the supplier.

10. At the conclusion of the buy operation and after the evidence has been secured and all the participating officers are back at their base of operations, a critique or discussion by these officers and the undercover officer usually proves advantageous to all parties. Many times during the buy operation, things may happen on the set that the backup team was not aware of, or the undercover officer may inadvertently do something that makes the backup team nervous or takes them by surprise. This is the time to go over the whole sequence of events. It is amazing to observe how among even the most experienced and seasoned officers certain things have slipped by them or how the most common or innocent occurrence can upset an entire operation. The purpose of this critique should not be to fix blame but to serve as an investigative aid for the participating officers in the preparation of their case.

Prior to leaving for the set location, all members should be instructed to synchronize their watches.

DOCUMENTING THE NARCOTICS BUY

To effectively prosecute a person for the offense of criminally selling a dangerous drug, the undercover officer and/or police agent must have documented evidence of the purchase of narcotics from the defendant. This documentation is accomplished not only by the purchase itself but by the entire strategic and careful planning process discussed in this chapter. If all the members participating in the operation are aware of their specific assignments and duties, their written reports should act as corroborative documentation of the buy.

The best documentation, of course, is the taped recording of the transaction. The undercover or agent who is wearing a recording device or transmitter should attempt to mention the type of package being purchased, such as quarter or nickel bag, and the amount of money being paid. This conversation can relate to the purity of the product if the agent is engaged in a high-level buy where such conversation would be not only logical but expected. On many occasions it may be impractical or dangerous to wear a wire, or recorder. In this case the best alternative action might be to call the subject by phone later, with a recording device attached to the phone, and engage in conversation that obviously refers to the prior sale. Or the undercover may arrange to meet the subject at a later time or date and, while wearing a recorder, confirm the original sale. Again, I must state that this type of documentation is the ultimate degree of proof of sale, and if the slightest chance of an officer's safety is involved, *forget it.*

Finally, the undercover's report should be as inclusive as possible, referring to the subject by name if known, describing in detail any pertinent conversation, and relating in narrative form exactly what transpired between undercover and subject.

This should be preceded by a brief paragraph by the undercover giving a concise account of the buy, such as:

> On the above date, time, and place, the undersigned did purchase from the above named subject(s) (AMOUNT), containing a white substance of alleged (HEROIN or COCAINE) in return for (AMOUNT) in U.S. currency.

An added caption should be included to show the custody of evidence.

> The evidence was signed, recorded, and vouchered by the undersigned and (NAMES OF WITNESSING OFFICERS). (In New York City Police Department there is a sign and seal procedure.) The above evidence was delivered to_____ by _____ (GIVE DEPOSITION).

Reports from the Field Team

Immediately upon completion of the buy and after the critique, the backup officers should prepare their official reports for the supervisor. These reports should indicate:

1. The times of their observations and what they observed.
2. Any descriptions of vehicles, persons, and so on.
3. Whether or not they can identify the seller.
4. Times of meets with undercover and/or informant.

In addition, the field team is responsible for:

1. Recording the "buy money" prior to the buy (this can be done by xeroxing) for inclusion in case folder.

2. Safeguarding any tapes used in the buy operation, including cassette tapes, Nagra (body recorder) tapes, and Kel tapes (transmitter tapes).

3. Any photo negatives taken; to be recorded as previously mentioned.

4. Safeguarding and vouchering any papers given the undercover or informant by the subject, to be handled as evidence.

The Case Folder

The supervisor should designate a *case officer*, whose responsibility will be to maintain and update the official *case folder*. This case folder will be a chronological record of the entire investigation, encompassing all official reports prepared in connection with the narcotics buy operation.

The use of forms as an investigative aid is a highly recommended technique, and the tactical plan, which can be reduced to an official form, is without doubt a necessary ingredient to the success of the operation. However, I caution the reader not to let the tactical plan form, or any other form for that matter, become an end in itself. The tactical plan is only a tool or guide to be used in the planning process. It should not become a biblical or administrative panacea for "paper-tiger" commanders, who are neither street-wise nor adaptable to split-second change and are usually more concerned with form and with control of personnel than with the specific objectives of the investigation. This type of supervisor has been known to use such forms only as a cover in the event that something goes wrong during the investigation, and should not be assigned to operational commands.

A more realistic approach would be to appreciate the variables presented in this chapter, choose among alternative actions, develop a game plan, and then remember: *The only thing that you can be sure about in a narcotics buy operation is that you cannot be sure about anything.*

THE TACTICAL PLAN AND SKETCH

A drawing of the location where the buy is supposed to go down, indicating the street locations and traffic flow, is a valuable visual aid in explaining and clarifying the assignments of the personnel who will be taking part in the operation.

The set is the southeast corner of 81st Street and Amsterdam Avenue. This location can be very effectively covered from the *roof observation point*. The officers at this location can advise the other units of any pertinent information. (Never assign only one person to a rooftop surveillance. Always assign at least two; one to make observations and one to watch the other's back.)

Unit 1, by locating in the westbound block of West 81st Street, can make some observations in the rearview mirror. Also Unit 2 located two blocks south of the location may be able to spot some activity. Units 3 and 4 are in the area in case a moving surveillance should occur. If this should happen, there are now four mobile units to conduct a tail. However, if there is no movement by the subject into an auto or taxi, the mobile units should remain in their positions and allow the observation units to report and make their observations. The observation truck unit should have been parked some time prior to the actual buy in order not to arouse any suspicion. The personnel assigned to this unit not only can watch the set but also can make any pertinent observations on the stash location. This unit is the first to arrive and the last to leave, and usually makes the most valuable observations and gets the best photos. Also this unit can supply important information to the backup units and the undercover before they arrive on the set.

Subject Index

Case Citation Index

State v. Mitchell 491 S.W. 2d 292 (MO. 1973), 10-9
State v. Saunders 102 Ariz. 565 (1969), 10-4, 10-5, 10-6
Steagald v. United States 451 U.S. 204 (1981), 9-7
Steere Tank Lines, Inc. v. United States 149 F. Supp. 814 (D. Md. 1957), 14-27n
Stone v. California 376 U.S. 483 (1964), 8-22
Suffolk County Water Auth. v. Union Carbide Corp. No. 90-14163 (N.Y. Sup. Ct., May 2, 1991), 14-20n

Taylor v. Alabama 457 U.S. 687 (1982), 9-3
Tennessee v. Garner 471 U.S. 1 (1985), 9-12, 16-2 to 16-3
Terry v. Ohio 392 U.S. 1 (1968), 7-4, 7-6, 7-11, 7-16, 7-17, 9-1 to 9-2, 9-8
Texas-Oklahoma Express, Inc. v. United States 429 F. 2d 100 (10th Cir., 1970), 14-27n
Thompson v. Louisiana 469 U.S. 17, 21 (1984), 8-17
Thompson v. Wainwright 601 F. 2d 768 (5th Cir., 1979), 10-27
Towne v. Dugger 899 F. 2d 1104 (11th Cir., 1990), 10-27

Ullmann v. United States 350 U.S. 422, 76 S. Ct. 497, 100 L. Ed. 2d 511, reh. denied, 351 U.S. 928, 76 S. Ct. 777, 100 L. Ed. 2d 1415 (1956), 11-8, 11-9
United States ex rel Argo v. Platt 6684 F. Supp. 1459D1452 (N.D. Illinois, 1988), 10-23
United States ex rel Caserino v. Dnno 259 F. Supp. 784 (S.D. N.Y., 1966), 10-21
United States ex rel Eulenmuller v. Fay 240 F. Supp. 591 (D.C. N.Y., 1965), cert. denied, 384 U.S. 964 (1966), 9-12
United States v. ABOW-SADIA 785 F. 2d, 1, 10 (1st Cir., 1986), 10-16
United States v. Aceto Agricultural Chems. Corp. 872 F. 2d 1373 (8th Cir., 1989), 14-4
United States v. AGY 394 F. 2d 94 (6th Cir., 1967), 10-4, 10-5
United States v. Akin 562 F. 2d 459, 464 (7th Cir., 1977), cert. denied, 435 U.S. 933 (1978), 8-22
United States v. Alba 732 F. Supp. 306, 309-310 (D. Conn., 1990), 10-16
United States v. American Radiator & Standard Sanitary Corp. 433 F. 2d 174 (3rd Cir., 1970), 14-16
United States v. Amrep Corp. 560 F. 2d 539 (2nd Cir., 1977), 14-26n

United States v. Anderson 752 F. Supp. 565, (E.D. N.Y., 1990), 10-15
United States v. Anderson 752 F. Supp. 565, 568 (E.D. N.Y., 1990) affd. 929 F. 2d 96 (2nd Cir., 1991), 8-20
United States v. Antonelli 434 F. 2d 335 (2nd Cir., 1970), 10-8
United States v. Argent Corp. No. CIV-83-0523BB, 21 ERC 1345 (D. N.M. May 4, 1984), 14-21n
United States v. Armour 168 F. 2d 342, 344 (3rd Cir., 1948), 14-16
United States v. Averell 296 F. Supp. 1064 (S.D. N.Y., 1969), 8-5, 10-4, 10-6
United States v. Bailey 468 F. 2d 652, 660 (5th Cir., 1972), 10-16
United States v. Barone 330 F. 2d 543, 545 (2nd Cir., 1964), 8-16
United States v. Beale 921 F. 2d 1412, 1415 (11th Cir., 1991), 10-21
United States v. Bekowies 432 F. 2d 8, 13 (9th Cir., 1970), 10-4
United States v. Beraun-Panez 812 F. 2d 578, 580 (9th Cir., 1987), 10-3, 10-6, 10-7
United States v. Bily 406 F. Supp. 726, 728-729 (DC Pa., 1975), 8-21
United States v. Bland 908 F. 2d 471 (9th Cir., 1990), 10-15, 10-18
United States v. Block 590 F. 2d 535 (4th Cir., 1978), 8-22
United States v. Boston 508 F. 2d 1171 (2nd Cir., 1974), 10-12
United States v. Briley 726 F. 2d 1301 (8th Cir., 1984), 9-6
United States v. Buettner-Janusch 646 F. 2d 759, 764 (2nd Cir., 1981), cert. denied, 454 U.S. 830 (1981), 8-19
United States v. Burke 700 F. 2d 70 (2nd Cir., 1983), 10-4
United States v. Calvente 722 F. 2d 1019, 1023-1024 (2nd Cir., 1983), cert. denied, 471 U.S. 1021 (1985), 8-20
United States v. Castellano 488 F. 2d 65 (5th Cir., 1974), 10-7
United States v. Chadwell 427 F. Supp. 692 (D. Del., 1977), 8-13
United States v. Cohen 317 F. Supp. 1049, 1050-1051 (D. Neb., 1970), 10-6
United States v. Crews 445 U.S. 463 (1980), 9-14n
United States v. D'Antoni 856 F. 2d 975, 980 (7th Cir., 1988), 10-22, 10-24
United States v. Darby 744 F. 2d 1508 (11th Cir.) cert. denied, 471 U.S. 1100 (1985), 9-5
United States v. De Parias 805 F. 2d 1447 (11th Cir., 1986) cert. denied, 482 U.S. 916 (1987), 8-21

About the Editor

Joseph J. Grau, Ph.D., is the Director of the Security Administration Program in the Department of Criminal Justice and Security Administration., College of Management, Long Island University, C. W. Post Campus, Brookville, New York. For 28 years he has been responsible for reviewing dissertations, manuals, and projects of inservice field personnel from various areas of criminal justice and private security. He is vice president for Academic Affairs, the Academy of Security Educators and Trainers, a charter member of the Federal Investigators Association, and a member of many leading professional criminal justice organizations. His article "Managing Trade Secrets" recently appeared in a special issue of the *Legal Studies Forum*, which focused on the increasingly significant topic of intellectual property rights.